"The writers seem to have experienced every rooster-packed bus and lunar-surfaced mattress about which they write."

— *The New York Times*

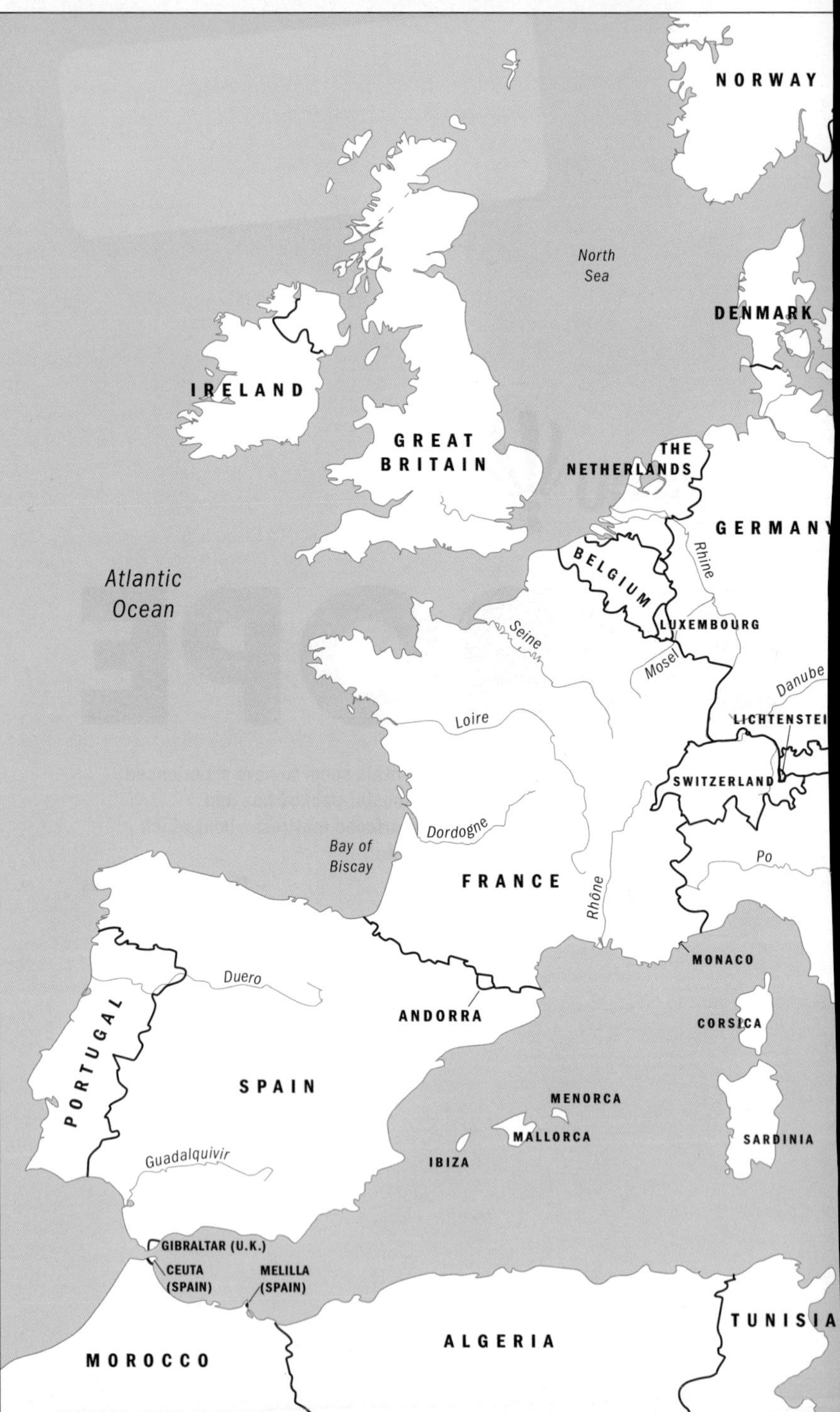
NORWAY
North Sea
DENMARK
IRELAND
GREAT BRITAIN
THE NETHERLANDS
GERMANY
BELGIUM
Rhine
Atlantic Ocean
LUXEMBOURG
Seine
Mosel
Danube
Loire
LICHTENSTEI
SWITZERLAND
Dordogne
Bay of Biscay
Po
FRANCE
Rhône
MONACO
Duero
ANDORRA
PORTUGAL
CORSICA
SPAIN
MENORCA
MALLORCA
SARDINIA
Guadalquivir
IBIZA
GIBRALTAR (U.K.)
CEUTA (SPAIN)
MELILLA (SPAIN)
TUNISIA
ALGERIA
MOROCCO

FINLAND
SWEDEN
ESTONIA
RUSSIA
LATVIA
Baltic Sea
LITHUANIA
RUSSIA
BELARUS
Vistula
POLAND
Elbe
Oder
UKRAINE
CZECH REPUBLIC
SLOVAKIA
MOLDOVA
AUSTRIA
HUNGARY
ROMANIA
SLOVENIA
CROATIA
Danube
Black Sea
BOSNIA & HERZ.
SERBIA
SAN MARINO
BULGARIA
MONT.
KOS.
Adriatic Sea
ALBANIA
MACEDONIA
ITALY
TURKEY
Aegean Sea
GREECE
Tyrrhenian Sea
Ionian Sea
SICILY
RHODES
N
LG
CRETE
Mediterranean Sea
MALTA
0
200 kilometers
0
200 miles

CONTENTS

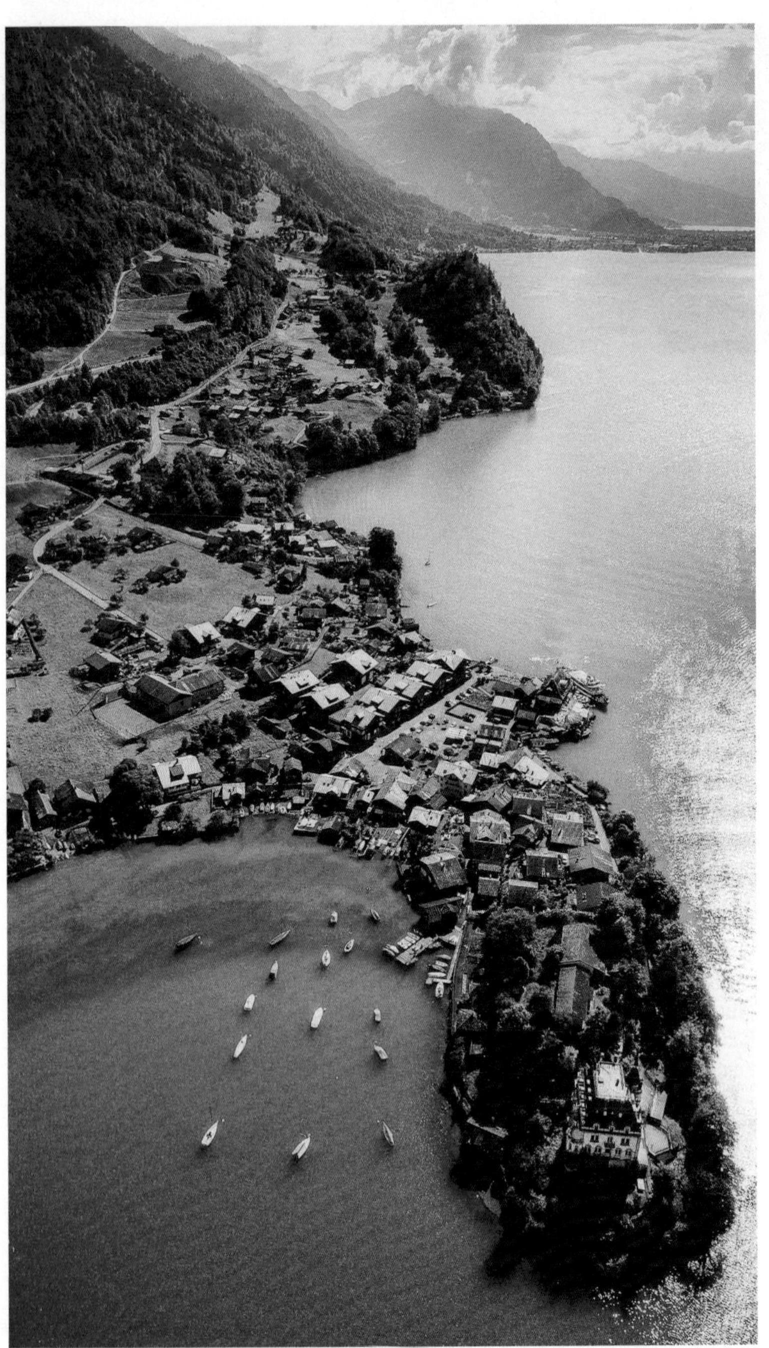

MEET THE TEAM

MASTHEAD

Jessica Luo
Publishing Director

Jessica is a junior concentrating in Neuroscience fascinated in all things brains yet finds herself stumbling into jobs that require wordy skills. Being from the Silicon Valley, she is consistently and unfailingly amazed by the ever-changing Cambridge weather. Find her swinging some sticks with the Harvard varsity women's golf team, eating copious amounts of peanut butter, or using Google Maps (for someone who works for a travel guide, she has an oddly terrible sense of direction). Her hobbies include hunting for new R&B artists, wearing workout clothes as regular clothes (it's athleisure), and falling asleep in wildly inappropriate situations.

Francesca Malatesta
Editor-in-Chief

Francesca is a junior living in the coveted Pforzheimer House and studying History and Literature. Born and raised in Nahant, Massachusetts, she feels most at home by the ocean. Outside of *Let's Go,* Francesca can be found reading outside, binge-watching reality TV with her roommate, enjoying a cup of coffee (read: multiple), or starting yet another new hobby. A sucker for spontaneity, Francesca has been known to suddenly appear in random destinations across the globe with her Instagram as the only indicator that she had even left Boston. She is happiest when she is hiking, swimming, or spending quality time with friends and family whom she values above all else.

Michelle Borbon
Associate Editor

A 2019 Harvard graduate, Michelle concentrated in Social Studies and has a post-grad job with the American Civil Liberties Union. At *Let's Go,* Michelle performed the crucial task of gate-keeping the worst puns and pencilling in cringe jokes of her own. When she's not putting together equally embarrassing mood boards, Michelle can be found in midwestern states coaching the Harvard Debate Council, keeping up with the #discourse on Twitter, or watercolor painting on cute lil' postcards. She loves bright colors even when they don't go well together, unironically watching weird Vice documentaries, and the jungalow trend in interior design.

RESEARCHER-WRITERS

Margaret Canady
This summer, Margaret found herself in Greece and the region of Tuscany, Italy, quite far from her tried and true Texas roots. Armed only with a terrible sense of direction and a half-empty travel sized bottle of suntan lotion, she braved the difficulties of Mediterranean traveling, which included having too many sunsets to watch and too much good art to review. When not pretending she knows how to pronounce Greek words, she studies psychology and dance, which have nothing (or everything) to do with world traveling, depending on your perspective.

Eric Chin
Warm Mediterranean sun on the back of his neck, the feeling of sand between his toes on an Italian beach, champagne on a tiled French portico… Wait—Eric's going where? Iceland and Scandinavia? *Shit.* He may have to trade in sandals for hiking boots and survive on a diet of sheep's head and "putrescent" shark meat (seriously, look it up), but at least he'll get to take advantage of the free education, right? He'll just have to settle for climbing behind waterfalls, kayaking through fjords, and fulfilling his mission of finding as much IKEA furniture as he possibly can.

Austin Eder
Austin spent her sophomore summer city-hopping in Spain after trading her desk chair for a 40-liter backpack. She felt right at home on the cobblestone streets of Granada's Albaicín, where the scents of tanned leather and the clicks of castanets mingle in the air. When not putting her navigational skills to good use and reviewing museums, restaurants, bars, and the like, Austin spends her extra time discussing politics, economics, and social justice at Harvard's Institute of Politics, writing freelance for campus publications, and producing short films.

Megan Galbreath
Healthy base tan, courtesy of the unyielding sun in Megan's hometown in southwest Florida? Check. An insistence that gallivanting through Germany and Austria all summer does, in fact, count as exercise–after all, those cathedral steps aren't going to climb themselves! While neuroscience and chemistry may be this coffee-loving, fashion-adoring springboard diver's forte, Megan is hoping to expand her appreciation for the finer things in life (beer, currywurst, schnitzel…) before returning to the reality that all good things must come to an end.

Lucy Golub
Navigationally challenged to a fault, Lucy has no idea what she's doing. But she's an expert at faking-it-til-you-make-it. Follow along as she discovers hidden gems throughout Great Britain and Ireland, often truly by accident. Getting lost (sometimes on purpose) results in discovering hole-in-the-wall restaurants and colorful murals off the beaten path. In the classroom, she studies Social Studies, which means she's got the being-social-in-a-hostel thing down. A New York City native, Lucy's an expert on making the most of a city and its neighborhoods.

Kristine Guillaume
Kristine traded her editor's desk at Let's Go HQ for an even more unglamorous life: a pack stuffed to the brim with extra underwear, much-needed shower shoes for grimy hostel bathrooms, and ridiculously rationed quantities of body lotion and hair product to tame the frizz. Once packed, she took her set of extra fine pens and trusty Moleskine to the south of France. When Kristine isn't consuming ungodly amounts of *beurre, pain, et vin,* she enjoys drinking English Breakfast Tea and serving as the Preseident of *The Harvard Crimson.*

Adrian Horton
Hailing from Cincinnati, Ohio, Adrian will be honing her bakery-finding skills in Greece and southern Italy this summer. Prior work experience: ranch-hand, gardener, fruit bat cage cleaner, one-time contributor to her hometown's Wikipedia page. Her current interests include distance running, 90s music, and convincing people she has seen all of *Game of Thrones* (she hasn't, but oh my god wasn't the Red Wedding BANANAS?!). When she isn't watching YouTube videos, she studies History and Literature at Harvard and sometimes writes about pop culture.

Sam Lincoln
Sam is a sophomore who usually needs a haircut. He leads trips for the First-Year Outdoor Program and Outing Club and manages the alpine ski team. This love for the mountains is reflected in his destinations for this summer: Denmark, Belgium, and the Netherlands…wait. While he might not be straying too far from sea level, Sam's still looking forward to the many high points of his trip—eating chocolate in Antwerp, eating chocolate in Bruges, eating chocolate in Brussels, and making friends with the deer that live in that one deer sanctuary north of Copenhagen.

Jessica Moore
This summer, Jessica roamed through many winding French streets in search of three things: white wine, red wine, and rose. With just a single phone power bank and absolutely no understanding of the French language, she found just what she was looking for along with many, many croissants. Her adventures ranged from trying to get a French SIM card from a man who spoke no English to lugging her 40L Osprey pack up a 3 mile mountain hike to get to her AirBnB. On her trip, she found a profound new love of lavender, macaroons, and waking up early.

Will Rhatigan
Kristine traded her editor's desk at Let's Go HQ for an even more unglamorous life: a pack stuffed to the brim with extra underwear, much-needed shower shoes for grimy hostel bathrooms, and ridiculously rationed quantities of body lotion and hair product to tame the frizz. Once packed, she took her set of extra fine pens and trusty Moleskine to the south of France. When Kristine isn't consuming ungodly amounts of *beurre, pain, et vin,* she spends most of her time in her office as Preseident of *The Harvard Crimson.*

Marissa Saenger
To take full advantage of the Northern summer's endless daylight, Marissa will squeeze every last minute of hiking, running, splashing, and climbing into itinerary through Iceland and Scandinavia. Bananas and coffee are all she needs to fuel up for marathon-treks through rugged mountains, thundering waterfalls, jagged cliffs, and rocky fjords, though trying to keep her two sets of clothing clean in the process might be one of the greatest challenges this world has ever known. Marissa studied engineering and environmental policy.

Lydia Tahraoui
Lydia packed two pairs of shoes for her travels in Slovenia, Croatia, and Montenegro. She is counting on her well-worn, well-loved sneakers to carry her through coastal markets along the Adriatic, majestic ruins of ancient cities, and Balkan national parks. She also packed a pair of festive sandals, intended for long walks on the beach and questionable hostel showers alike. When she isn't carefully curating the most austere of packing lists, Lydia enjoys crafting incredibly niche Spotify playlists and reminding people that she is from California.

Luke Williams

Any reasonable person would say bringing six books on a seven week backpacking trip through Hungary, Poland, and Czechia is just asking for a heavier backpack. Fortunately, Luke is a not-very-reasonable person. *clears throat pretentiously* He'd like you to know that six books on hand are the minimum necessary for literary inspiration. Luke will return to Harvard in the fall as a much more tan (read: sunburnt) sophomore concentrating in Social Studies and Philosophy while still overcommitting himself to theater, journalism, and debate.

Jospeh Winters

Meet Joseph: senior, Earth and Planetary Science concentrator, vagrant vacationer. He spent eight weeks in search of the Iberian Peninsula's best veggie burger, but en route discovered a bunch of famous monuments, museums, and cultural landmarks—coincidentally, enough to cover a whole section of *Let's Go 2020!* When he's not investigating tapas restaurants, Joseph enjoys distance running, playing piano, cooking, specialty coffee shops, and occasionally finishing a Thursday NYT crossword puzzle.

We've had our adventure,
now it's time to have yours.
- The Let's Go Team

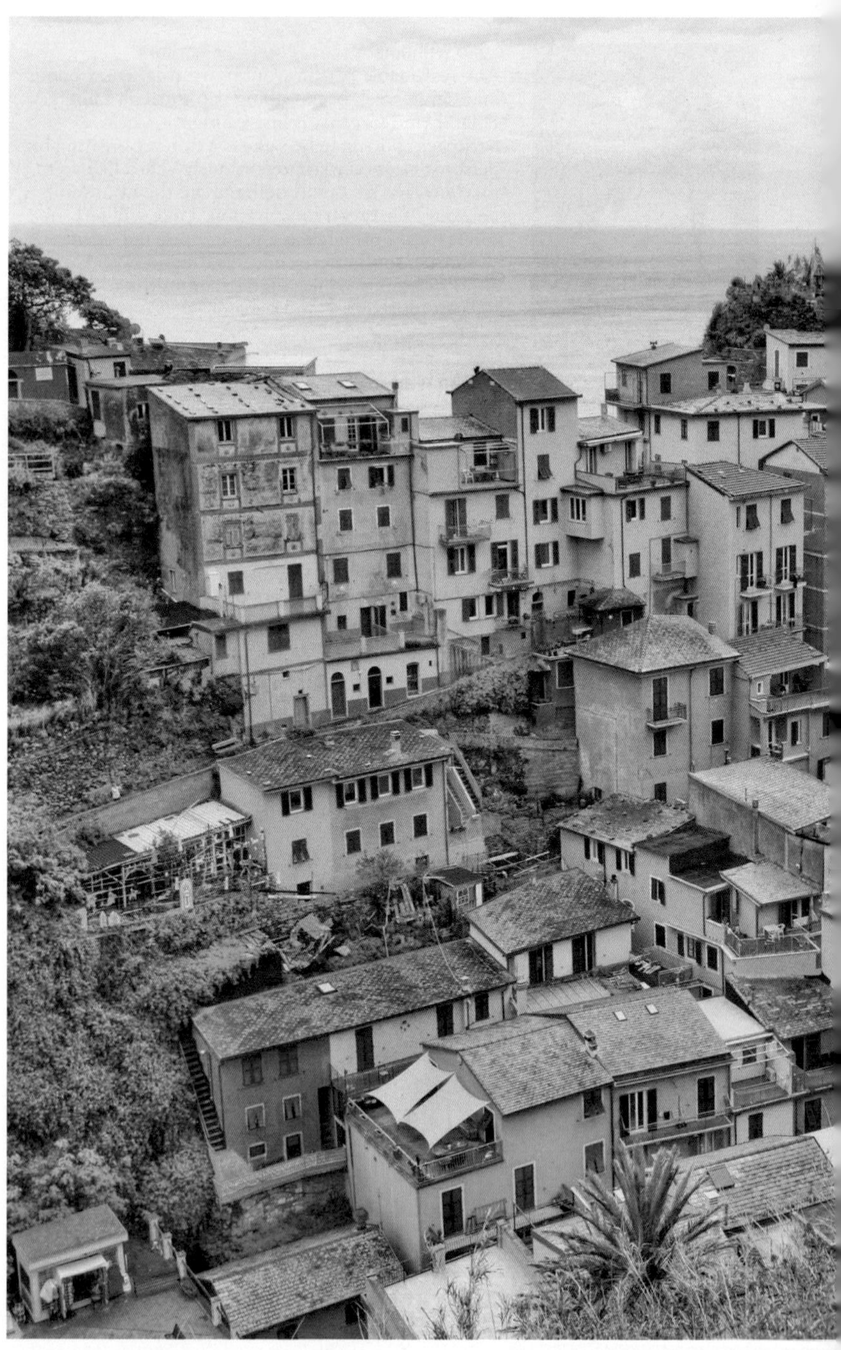

DISCOVER EUROPE

So, you want to go to Europe? But how could you not? There's something awfully romantic about spending midnight in Paris, watching the lights glisten on the famed La Seine. There's something special about hearing the growls and grunts of cars on and around the *vias* and *piazzas* of Rome. There's something magical about walking on the streets of London in front of Buckingham Palace as the roads close down for the iconic Changing of the Guard.

Europe—rich with history, culture, art, and adventure—is the ultimate destination for any backpacker from any background. For all the hullabaloo around this small continent, the fairytale-like legends that you hear from old men in parks, friends, and parents are, for the most part, true stories. Well, maybe all except Uncle Marty's story claiming he found an old manuscript of *Ulysses* on a Dublin bar crawl..

Pub crawls and pretentious reading material aside, Europe awaits you. Paraglide above the Swiss Alps, shimmy your way into Berlin's most exclusive clubs, or scuba dive between two tectonic plates in Iceland. When in Dubrovnik, find love on Lokrum Island and, in Athens, find your Adonis or Aphrodite. Get blown away by the beat of Pamplona's Running of the Bulls and cheer on European sports teams in Munich's beer gardens. Europe has been, and will likely continue to be, the starting point for the adventures of students all around the world. Join the company of your fellow wanderlust-stricken adventure seekers and set your trip apart from the rest.

Ready, set, *Let's Go*!

WHEN TO GO

Summer is the most popular time to travel to Europe, meaning that if you take a trip during high season, thousands of backpackers will be right there with you. It's the perfect opportunity to meet students from around the world in various hostels, restaurants with communal tables, and in the long lines for incredible churches and monuments (small talk is a real thing, especially if you're alone). While it is very possible to complete a budget trip in the summertime, it's important to note that the season's many festivals can jack up prices for accommodations, restaurants, and general sightseeing. Keep an eye out for huge summertime events such as Pamplona's Running of the Bulls, Dublin's Bloomsday, Lisbon's Festas de Lisboa, and Edinburgh's Fringe. You'll need to plan ahead—like way ahead—if you intend to travel while these world-renowned events take place. They're definitely worth the extra effort (and perhaps even the extra cash).

If you're not into the summer backpacking experience, late spring and early autumn attract fewer tourists, meaning that you can save a bit on airfare and bookings, but it can be difficult to take time off during these seasons. Unfortunately, spring break isn't quite long enough to do a full tour.

For those looking to celebrate the holidays in Venice or shred the slopes of the Italian Alps, winter travel is also a viable option. However, this isn't the best time to hit the clubs of Ibiza or take a walking tour of Prague. You'll also find that some hotels, restaurants, and sights have reduced hours or are on vacation…from you.

SUGGESTED ITINERARIES

THE GRAND TOUR (40 DAYS)

For the travel-hungry soul who wants to see the most famous highlights of Europe—buckle up, you're in for a wild ride. We highly recommend tackling this bad boy with the trusty help of budget airlines or a rail pass.

- **LONDON** (4 days)—God save the Queen. Your first stop on your full-fledged adventure begins in an English-speaking country (baby steps). Make London your cup of tea by delving into its music culture and royal history. Here's hoping you'll catch a glimpse of the Queen (no, no, no not Elizabeth, J.K. Rowling). **(see p. 270)**
- **COPENHAGEN** (2 days)—It's time to venture north, as in Nordic. Blond people, Viking history, a whole soap opera of feuds with Sweden, and, of course, insane taxes await you in Denmark. Time to immerse yourself in Copenhagen's *hygge*. **(see p. 137)**
- **AMSTERDAM** (3 days)—Amsterdam has it all: imperial history, artistic pedigree, and killer music. Burn some calories in one of the most bike-friendly cities in the world and see some classic Dutch windmills. Let's not forget crossing over to the dark side either; if you so choose, the coffeeshop scene is out there—just keep this part of the trip to yourself (Mom doesn't want to know). **(see p. 458)**
- **PARIS** (4 days)—Go ahead, be romantic. This is the quintessential European destination for artists, lovers, tourists, foodies, and romantics alike. If you don't go here on your Grand Tour, you didn't go to Europe. Paris, *enchanté*. **(see p. 189)**
- **BARCELONA** (3 days)—Get your Gaudí on in one of the hottest (and we mean searing hot) parts of Europe. Architecture geeks will be awestruck by the beauty of La Sagrada Familia, foodies will triumph in the exquisite Catalan cuisine, and soccer fans will rejoice in the buzz of one of the world's most beloved teams at the Camp Nou. Let's get Messi. **(see p.558)**
- **LISBON** (2 days)—Part of the beauty of Lisbon is that it's largely undiscovered. This hidden gem is bound to blow your mind with its seafood delights and geographic wonders. It's time for leg day, so gear up to hike as you soak up the sun and culture in Lisboa. **(see p. 528)**
- **MADRID** (2 days)—The Spanish capital reigns with the promise of pitchers of sangria, one of the most poppin' nightlife scenes on the globe, and countless opportunities to explore Spanish history from the Age of Exploration to present day. Madrid loves you already and you will fall for it even harder. **(see p. 584)**
- **ROME** (4 days)—Hop on that vespa, baby. It's time to talk fast, move your hands fast, and drive even faster. Get the best of the old Roman Empire and the new Roman paradise in the Eternal City. Gelato will cool you down as you climb Palatine Hill and pretend to be a gladiator in The Roman Colosseum. **(see p. 412)**
- **FLORENCE** (3 days)—Travel back in time to the Renaissance and get #cultured in this epicenter of art. This is Michelangelo's hometown, but today it is a modern hotspot for art, music, shopping, and gelato-mongering. **(see p. 393)**

- **PRAGUE** (3 days)—Prague's Old Town looks like a fairytale and it's time to make your dreams come true. This often-overlooked gem boasts must-sees like the Charles Bridge and castle, but the young and grungy bars, beer gardens, and galleries are more eager to see you. **(see p. 117)**
- **MUNICH** (2 days)—Munich is the quintessential German city, layered in tradition. It's a little quiter than other cities, but you can still appreciate its Bavarian roots as you tour its high-quality beer gardens. **(see p. 243)**
- **BERLIN** (3 days)—Pick up the pace and head to a city that never sleeps. Riddled with the history of a war-torn city and trendy, exclusive club, Berlin is a true cosmopolitan center. Make sure you say, "Hallo!" to Merkel for us. **(see p. 214)**
- **ATHENS** (3 days)—Make your way back down south and turn up the temperature. Climb Mount Olympus, walk around the ruins of the Acropolis, and find your Adonis or Aphrodite under the sweet, Greek sun. Apollo, is that you? **(see p. 304)**
- **SPLIT** (2 days)—Top it all off in the Balkans. Split is the place to cool down, relax, and enjoy the beach as you dance the night away. **(see p. 91)**

ISLAND HOPPING (14 DAYS)

Does Europe even have any islands, you ask? That's preposterous. Tons of lively ones eagerly await you on your European adventure. We're talking palm trees, sand, pebbly beaches, bumping party beats, and master DJs. Tell Corona we've found our beach.

- **IBIZA** (2 days)—Kick it off with superstar DJs like David Guetta and show Mike Posner you can handle a rager better than he can in the nightclubs of this iconic Spanish island. **(see p. 577)**
- **MYKONOS** (3 days)—Party animals all around the world hear the word "Mykonos" and know it's the holy grail of fun. Skip the architectural wonders of Ancient Greece and head straight here for nights to remember. **(see p. 318)**
- **HVAR** (3 days)—Hvar are you doing today? Not good? Swing by this Croatian island on the iconic Riva of Hvar. You've got nothing but clubbing, beach parties, and cheap alcohol ahead of you. **(see p. 83)**
- **VENICE** (3 days)—Okay, well Venice isn't exactly one island. Think more along the lines of 118. Venice is connected by a series of foot bridges that cross over the city's 170 boat canals. Close out your trip with a little culture on the glass-making island of Murano and with the lace-specialists in Burano. **(see p. 434)**

STOP AND SMELL THE ROSES (23 DAYS)

If you've got a green thumb, then you'll be glad to know Europe has much for you to see in the form of extravagance. The Romans, for example, were fixated with controlling nature and, as a result, created beautiful gardens with immaculately manicured plants in the strangest of shapes. We're not quite sure of the origins of the other gardens around the continent, but these are feats of man and nature that would make even the most talented gardener jealous. What do *you* have? Tomato vines? Growing upside down? Amateur.

- **FLORENCE** (3 days)—The Boboli Gardens at Florence's Palazzo Pitti are truly a sight to behold. Climb lots (and we mean lots) of stairs as you walk through what feels like the gardens of Sleeping Beauty's castle—without Maleficent trying to keep the prince out. **(see p. 393)**
- **VIENNA** (4 days)—The gardens of Schönnbrunn Palace await your royal highness. And, if that doesn't entertain you, the Hapsburgs also have gardens at the Belvedere for your pleasure. **(see p. 42)**
- **PARIS** (5 days)—The Jardin des Plantes lies in the fifth arrondissement and is the main botanical garden in France. **(see p. 189)**
- **BARCELONA** (4 days)—Parc Guëll. Garden? Outdoor space? Architectural wonder of Antoni Gaudí? All of the above. (**see p. 558**)
- **MALMÖ** (2 days)—*Aah* Slottsträdgården, complete with orderly, manicured hedges, and multiple plots including a Steppe Garden and Japanese Garden that will make your jaw drop. **(see p. 616)**
- **LONDON** (5 days)—The Royal Parks are undoubtedly majestic. Hyde Park and Regent's Park are full of green spaces in an urban setting while the famed Kensington Gardens serves as the front yard for a king, situated right in front of the stunning Kensington Palace. **(see p. 270)**

CALL OF THE WILD (12 DAYS)

We get it—you're Wilderness First-Aid Certified, you've spent every summer as a camp counselor in the middle of the forest, and you've hiked 111 miles solo. You're coming to Europe for the outdoor adventures—to get in touch with nature, if you will. In that case, we've got you covered. Lace up your hiking boots.

- **REYKJAVIK** (3 days)—Reykjavik is an excellent place to set up camp to do outdoorsy day trips in Iceland. Some of our favorites include the Blue Lagoon and Golden Circle. **(see p. 354)**
- **OSLO** (2 days)—Oslo Sommerpark is guaranteed to put the overeager kid spirit back in you, featuring a wicked obstacle course that allows you to climb 20 meters into the trees. Tarzan who? **(see p. 486)**
- **GIMMELWALD** (3 days)—This secluded mountain town in the Alps is a hidden gem: paraglide in the mountains, watch glaciers collide, and hike difficult, pristine trails. **(see p. 639)**
- **SPLIT** (2 days)—Get a drink on the rocks and then cliff jump off the rocks (into the Mediterranean). Note: *Let's Go* does not endorse drinking and jumping. **(see p. 91)**
- **LAGOS** (2 days)—If outdoor adventures at the beach are what you seek, opt for a change of pace in southern Portugal, kayaking off the coast in the Iberian Peninsula. **(see p. 523)**

HOW TO USE THIS BOOK

CHAPTERS

Let's Go Europe 2020 covers 23 countries in its 22 chapters. Each chapter contains comprehensive content that is designed to make your trip easy to plan. Chapters are organized in alphabetical order by country, so the book kicks off with Austria and culminates with Switzerland. The countries covered in this book are Austria, Belgium, Croatia, Czechia, Denmark, France, Germany, Great Britain, Greece, Hungary, Iceland, Ireland, Italy, Montenegro, The Netherlands, Norway, Poland, Portugal, Slovakia, Slovenia, Spain, Sweden, and Switzerland.

Each chapter has been written by at least one *Let's Go* **Researcher-Writer.** Researcher-Writers (RWs) are students at Harvard College who spend a maximum of eight weeks of their summer covering a pre-planned route of cities for publication in *Let's Go Europe.* Credits are given after the name of each city.

Within a chapter, cities are arranged in alphabetical order, so don't be alarmed when you see the France chapter begins with Avignon instead of Paris. We promise we did not forget Paris; we did our due diligence.

Structure of a Chapter

Each chapter begins with a country introduction and, from there, it is divided into city sections. The first section in a city always consists of an **introduction** followed by an **orientation** and **city essentials,** which includes all of the important information you should know—the location of tourist offices, police stations, hospitals, a list of BGLTQ+ resources, and numbers to call in the event of an emergency—before traveling to a given place. Although Google Maps is a fantastic resource that can be downloaded on your phone and accessed offline, it is important to pick up a paper map from a tourist office in case of emergency.

On to the fun stuff: city chapters include several sections, each of which will help you plan your days. These sections are also in alphabetical order, with our *Let's Go* Thumbpicked™ establishments listed first and followed by all of the other wonderful things we've covered:

Sights: Our "Sights" section is further broken down into four categories—Culture, Landmarks, Museums, and Outdoors.

Culture: These listings cover everything from churches to theaters to markets to interesting bookstores.

Landmarks: These are your Eiffel Towers, Colosseums, and Buckingham Palaces. All of the biggest sights and attractions are listed here.

Museums: Fairly self-explanatory, but here's where you'll find Prague's Dox, Paris' Louvre, and Madrid's Prado.

Outdoors: Here's where you'll find listings of a city's green spaces, beaches, and outdoor activities.

Food: You need to eat when you're abroad, right? For your convenience, we have included restaurants that cater to a backpacker's budget with a few splurge options interspersed. Treat yo' self.

Nightlife: Sleep all day, party all night, sightsee all day, party all night—whatever your travel lifestyle is, we've got the right bars, clubs, and cafés to ensure your evenings are well spent.

Listings—a.k.a. reviews of individual establishments—constitute the majority of *Let's Go's* content, and consist of essential information (address, phone number, website, and hours), a review of a given establishment, followed by any miscellaneous information that may be useful.

ESTABLISHMENT NAME ($-$$$)
Address; phone number; website; hours
Review goes here.
Miscellaneous information such as prices, cash/card, dietary restrictions, whether or not an establishment is certified BGLTQ+ friendly, wheelchair accessibility, etc.

Every piece of content in *Let's Go Europe 2020*—the introductions, the orientations, the essentials, the listings, and the features—was researched and updated during the summers of 2018 and 2019.

The end of each country chapter contains a **country essentials** page in which we detail information that is applicable to the entire country. This includes the country code, regulations and laws surrounding drug and alcohol use, and country-wide safety and health information. This also contains information about attitudes toward BGLTQ+ travelers and minorities.

The *Let's Go* Thumbpick™

is an icon you will see a lot in this book. Whenever a listing has a Thumbpick™ next to the establishment name, it indicates that it was a favorite of the Researcher-Writer who visited that city. These are, in other words, our top-choice accommodations, sights, and food and nightlife establishments.

Price Diversity

Another set of icons in the book corresponds to what we call our "price diversity" scale, which approximates how much money you can expect to spend at a given establishment. We have noted price diversity in our Food listings only. In this section, we estimate the average amount one traveler will spend in one sitting. Keep in mind that no scale can allow for the quirks of all individual establishments.

BEFORE YOU GO

Planning a good trip takes a lot more effort than you think it will. The worst thing you can do is get off the plane in Warsaw, for example, and not know what you want to do or what resources are available to you. Each chapter of this book includes a list of country-specific resources that will help you out in a pinch, but this chapter contains overarching information for all of Europe. We've condensed the knowledge we've acquired over 60 years of travel to ensure you have a safe, enjoyable experience in Europe. Planning your trip? Check. How to get around? Check. Safety and health resources? Check. There is also a phrasebook at the back of the book for your convenience.

PLANNING YOUR TRIP

DOCUMENTS AND FORMALITIES

There's a lot of country-specific information when it comes to visas and work permits, but don't forget the most important piece of documentation: your passport.

Passport

You cannot board a plane to another country without a passport. If you do not have a passport, you should apply for one several months in advance, as the process can take a long time. US citizens can apply for a passport online at www.travel.state.gov or at a local United States Post Office. Adult passports are valid for 10 years while children's passports are valid for five. If you already have a passport, check the expiration date of your document before booking any flights or accommodations. **Your passport must be valid for at least six months after you return from your trip in order to travel to Europe. Your passport should also have at least two blank pages, depending on your destination.**

Visas

Those lucky enough to be EU citizens will not need a visa to travel throughout the continent. Being an EU citizen has other perks too, such as shorter security lines. Citizens of Australia, Canada, New Zealand, United States, and various other non-EU countries, however, do not need a visa for a stay of up to 90 days. This three-month period begins upon entry to any of the EU's **freedom-of-movement zones.** Those staying longer than 90 days may apply for a longer-term visa; consult an embassy or consulate for more information.

Double check entry requirements at the nearest embassy or consulate for up-to-date information, as political situations can make it easier or more difficult to move between countries. US citizens can also consult www.travel.state.gov. Keep in mind that admittance to a country as a traveler does not include the right to work, which is authorized only by a work permit. You should check online for the process of obtaining a work permit for the country in which you are planning to work.

THE EUROPEAN UNION: HOW IT WORKS

The European Union is a union of 28 countries within the continent of Europe based in Brussels, Belgium. This number still includes the United Kingdom. The countries covered in this book that are not part of the European Union are Iceland, Norway, Montenegro, and Switzerland.

The European Union's policy of freedom of movement means that most border controls have been abolished and visa policies harmonized. This treaty, formerly known as the Schengen Agreement, means you still have to carry a passport (or government-issued ID card for EU citizens) when crossing an internal border, but, once you've been admitted to one country, you're free to travel to other participating states. Iceland and Norway are members of the Schengen Agreement, meaning that the rule extends to those countries as well.

It is important, however, to note that recent fears over immigration have led to calls for suspension of this freedom-of-movement and strengthening of borders. One of the most covered situations is **Brexit,** the vote by the citizens of the United Kingdom to leave the European Union. Lawmakers from the United Kingdom and the European Union, as of August 2018, are still in conversation about the new border restrictions and rules between the United Kingdom and European Union, so it is important to inform yourself about the situation before planning travel to the UK.

TIME DIFFERENCES

Most of Europe is on Central European Time, which is 1hr ahead of Greenwich Mean Time (GMT) and observes Daylight Savings Time in the summer. This means that, in summer, it is 6hr ahead of New York City, 9hr ahead of Los Angeles, 1hr. ahead of the British Isles, 8hr behind Sydney, and 10hr behind New Zealand. In winter, it is 10hr behind Sydney and 12hr behind New Zealand. However, the UK, Ireland, and Portugal are on GMT, also known as Western European Time, which means they are 1hr behind the Central European Time countries. In addition, Greece and some parts of Eastern Europe are on Eastern European Time, which means they are 1hr ahead of Central European Time countries.

MONEY MATTERS

BEFORE YOU GO

Call your bank. The first thing you should do is alert your bank that you will be abroad for a period of time. You should be prepared to give the bank representative the exact dates of your travel and where you will be if you plan to use your debit card in that country. Keep in mind that there may be a foreign transaction charge from your bank whenever you use your card. If your bank is a local US bank that does not have branches outside of a given city, you may want to consider changing your bank or opening a new account to one that is more widespread so that you can access customer service lines with larger networks in case of emergency.

Before you go, you should decide which credit cards to use before packing. It is advisable to pack credit cards that are widely accepted in Europe to avoid being caught in a pinch where you do not have any form of payment. Call your credit card company before going to alert them you will be abroad. As with banks, be prepared to give the representative the exact dates of your travel. Some credit card companies have online systems in which you can input the dates of your travel to skip the step of calling ahead.

CURRENCY BREAKDOWN

Nineteen countries in Europe use the euro, which is the currency of the European Union, meaning you will not have to worry about changing currencies when you hop from country to country. If you are traveling outside of the eurozone, however, you should be aware that you will need to convert once you leave. Countries outside the eurozone in the European Union are Croatia, Czechia, Denmark, Hungary, Sweden, and the United Kingdom. For an up-to-date list, check a currency converter (such as www.xe.com).

GETTING MONEY FROM HOME

Things happen and, if they do, you might need money. The easiest and cheapest solution to get you out of a pinch is to have someone back home make a deposit to your bank account directly. If this isn't possible, consider one of the following options:

Wiring Money

Arranging a **bank money transfer** means asking a bank back home to wire money to a bank wherever you are. This is the cheapest way to transfer cash, but it's also a slow process, taking several days. Note that some banks may only release your funds in local currency, potentially sticking you with a poor exchange rate; you should inquire about this in advance.

Money transfer services like **Western Union** are faster and more convenient than bank transfers—but also much pricier. Western Union has many locations worldwide. To find one, visit www.westernunion.com or call the appropriate number:

- Australia: 1800 173 833
- Canada: 800 235 0000
- UK: 0808 234 9168
- US: 800 325 6000
- France: 08 00 90 01 91

Money transfer services are also available to American Express cardholders and at selected Thomas Cook offices.

US State Department (US Citizens Only)

In serious emergencies only, the US State Department will help your family or friends forward money within hours to the nearest consular office, which will then disburse it according to instructions for a $30 fee. If you wish to use this service, you must contact the Overseas Citizens Services division of the US State Department (+1 202 501 444 or, from the US, 888 407 4747)

WITHDRAWING MONEY WHILE ABROAD

ATMs are readily available throughout Europe, excluding some rural areas, so you should also check ahead of time if you will be able to withdraw money in a given country. To use a debit or credit card to withdraw money from a cash machine (ATM) in Europe, you must have a four-digit Personal Identification Number (PIN). If your PIN is longer than four digits, ask your bank whether you can just use the first four digits or whether you'll need a new one. If your PIN includes a 0, you may need to make a new PIN, as some ATM machines in Europe do not have that key.

Travelers with alphabetical rather than numerical PINs may also be thrown off by the absence of letters on European cash machines. Here are the corresponding numbers to use:

- QZ = 1
- ABC = 2
- DEF = 3
- GHI = 4
- JKL = 5
- MNO = 6
- PRS = 7
- TUV = 8
- WXY = 9

It is also important to note that if you mistakenly punch the wrong code into the machine multiple (often three) times, it can swallow up your card for good.

Credit cards do not usually come with PINs, so if you intend to use ATMs in Europe with a credit card to get cash advances, call your credit card company before leaving to request one.

DEBIT AND CREDIT CARD FRAUD

If you check your account and notice that money has been stolen or is missing, you should call your bank immediately to remedy the situation and file a claim for the missing money. Many credit card companies have similar help lines and some online applications will allow you to automatically freeze your account. For this reason, we recommend that you always have some form of hard cash on you at all times.

TIPPING

Unlike in the United States, Europe does not have some unwritten universal tipping code of conduct. No one in the world tips like Americans, so tipping might just be a giveaway that you are a tourist. Although you are not required to tip, you can still leave one; even just 10% will seem quite generous.

TAXES

Members of the EU have a value-added tax (VAT) of varying percentages. It is most often between 19-21%. Non-EU citizens have the opportunity to be refunded this tax if you are taking these goods home. When shopping, make sure to ask for a VAT refund form that you can present with the goods and receipts at customs upon departure. Note: you must have the goods with you in order to be refunded.

GETTING AROUND

BY PLANE

Commercial Airlines

For small-scale travel on the continent, *Let's Go* suggests budget airlines for budget travelers, but more traditional carriers have begun to offer competitive deals. We recommend searching on www.cheapflights.com for the most affordable flights to Europe. You should look to book flights months in advance.

Budget Airlines

No-frills airlines make hopscotching around Europe by air remarkably affordable, as long as you avoid their rip-off fees. The following airlines will be useful for traveling across the pond and hopping from country to country:

- EasyJet: www.easyjet.com
- Eurowings: www.eurowings.com
- Iceland Air: www.icelandair.com
- Norwegian: www.norwegian.com
- Ryanair: www.ryanair.com
- Pegasus: www.flypgs.com
- Transavia: www.transavia.com
- Wizz Air: www.wizzair.com

BY TRAIN

European trains are generally comfortable, convenient, and reasonably swift. You should always make sure you are in the correct car, **as sometimes trains split midway through route to dock at different destinations.** Towns in parentheses on European train schedules require a train switch at the town listed immediately before the parentheses.

You can either buy a **railpass,** which, for a high price, allows you unlimited, flexible travel within a particular region for a given period of time, or buy individual **point-to-point** tickets as you go. Almost all countries give students or youths (under 26, usually) direct discounts on regular domestic rail tickets and many also sell a student or youth card that provides 20-50% off all fares for up to a year. Tickets can be bought at stations, but most Western European countries offer big discounts to travelers booking online in advance.

Check out the following sites to get discounts on train tickets and book trips in advance:

- www.raileurope.com
- www.railsaver.com
- www.rome2rio.com

BY BUS

Although train travel is much more comfortable, it may be cheaper to travel via bus from city to city. There are numerous operators across the continent, but Eurolines is the largest company running international coach services (www.eurolines.com). Inquire about 15- or 30-day passes when you book. For a higher price tag, Busabout offers numerous hop-on-hop-off bus circuits covering 29 of Europe's best bus hubs (www.busabout.com).

With that in mind, it is highly advised that you avoid travel at night via bus at all costs. It is much safer to book an early morning trip than it is to leave in the dead of the night, as drivers can be exhausted and many roads are narrow and unsafe to navigate in the dark. *Let's Go* has a policy with our Researcher-Writers in which we do not allow them to travel via bus at night.

PLACES TO STAY

For the budget traveler, accommodations options are limited, as expensive hotels are out of price range. That means hostels will be your best friend. You should, at least for the first few nights of your stay, book a hostel before departing, that way you do not land without a place to stay. We recommend using HostelWorld (www.hostelworld.com), Homestay (www.homestay.com), or Booking.com (www.booking.com) to make reservations.

There are a few red flags to look out for before deciding to stay at a hostel, even if you have already made a reservation online. We advise looking at the area or neighborhood surrounding the hostel to see if it feels and looks safe. If it does not, we recommend finding another hostel in a more suitable area. Many a time there are hostels with little lighting in front of the establishment, which is a signal that it is not completely safe. Many hostels have 24hr security and lockout times, which can be reassuring. In addition, you should avoid hostels where you see pests, bedbugs, or signs of rampant uncleanliness. If you feel uncomfortable talking to staff members or if staff members make sexual advances, this is also a concern and you should find another place to spend the night.

SAFETY AND HEALTH

In any crisis, the most important thing to do is **keep calm.** In every chapter, we have included the address of the nearest US embassy or consulate so that you can seek help in an emergency; your country's embassy is your best resource in precarious situations. The following government offices can also provide travel information and advisories.

- Australia: Department of Foreign Affairs and Trade (+61 2 6261 3305; www.smartraveller.gov.au)

- Canada: Global Affairs of Canada (+1 800 267 8376; www.international.gc.ca)
- New Zealand: Ministry of Foreign Affairs and Trade (+64 4 439 8000; www.safetravel.govt.nz)
- UK: Foreign and Commonwealth Office (+44 20 7008 1500; www.fco.gov.uk)
- US: Department of State (+1 888 407 4747 from the US, +1 202 501 4444 from abroad; www.travel.state.gov)

PRE-DEPARTURE HEALTH

Matching a prescription to a foreign drug equivalent is not always safe, easy, or even possible. Remember to take **prescription drugs** with you and carry up-to-date prescriptions or a statement from your doctor stating the medication's trade names, manufacturers, chemical names, and dosages. Be sure to keep all your medication in your carry-on luggage.

Immunizations and Precautions

Travelers over two years of age should make sure that the following vaccinations are up to date:

- MMR (for measles, mumps, and rubella)
- DTaP or Td (for diphtheria, tetanus, and pertussis)
- IPV (for polio)
- Hib (for Hemophilus influenzae B)
- HepB (for Hepatitis B)

For recommendations on other immunizations and prophylaxis, check with a doctor and consult the **Centers for Disease Control and Prevention (CDC)** in the US (800 232 4636; www.cdc.gov/travel) or the equivalent in your home country.

KEEPING IN TOUCH

BY EMAIL AND INTERNET

Wireless hot spots (Wi-Fi) make internet access possible in public and remote places. Unfortunately, they can also pose security risks. Hot spots are public, open networks that use unencrypted, unsecured connections. They are susceptible to hacks and "packet sniffing"—the theft of passwords and other private information. To prevent problems, disable "ad hoc" mode, turn off file sharing and network discover, encrypt your email, turn on your firewall, beware of phony networks, and watch for over-the-shoulder creeps. **Data roaming** lets you use mobile data abroad, but it can be pricey. If you refuse to "later 'gram" and hyperventilate at the idea of losing access to Google, first consider that you are many hours ahead of the United States and can post when you return to your hostel and remember that Google Maps is available offline. If that doesn't placate you, though, you should get an international travel plan with your carrier or consider getting a local phone.

BY TELEPHONE

If you have internet access, your best (i.e. cheapest, most convenient, and most tech-savvy) means of calling home are probably Skype, FaceTime, or whatever calling app you prefer. **Prepaid phone cards** are common and a relatively inexpensive means of calling abroad. Each one comes with a Personal Identification Number (PIN) and a toll-free access number. Call the access number and follow the subsequent directions for dialing your PIN. To purchase prepaid phone cards, check online for the best rates (www.callingcard.com).

Another option is a **calling card,** linked to a major national telecommunications service in your home country. Calls are billed collect or to your account. Cards generally come with instructions for dialing both domestically and internationally. Placing a collect call through an international operator can be expensive but may be necessary in case of an emergency. You can frequently call collect without even possessing a company's calling card just by calling its access number and following the instructions.

How to Make a Call

1. Dial the international dialing prefix,
   - Australia: 0011
   - Canada or the US: 011
   - Ireland, New Zealand, and most of Europe: 00
2. Then the country code of the country you want to call,
   - Australia: 61
   - Austria: 43
   - Belgium: 32
   - Canada: 1
   - Croatia: 385
   - Czech Republic: 420
   - Denmark: 45
   - France: 33
   - Germany: 49
   - Greece: 30
   - Hungary: 36
   - Ireland: 353
   - Italy: 39
   - The Netherlands: 31
   - Norway: 47
   - New Zealand: 64
   - Poland: 48
   - Portugal: 351
   - Slovakia: 421
   - Slovenia: 386
   - Spain: 34
   - Sweden: 46
   - Switzerland: 41
   - UK: 44
   - US: 1
3. Followed by the city/area code,
4. And finally the local number.

Cellular Phones

The international standard for cellular phones is the **Global System for Mobile Communication (GSM).** To make and receive calls in Europe, you will need a GSM-compatible phone and a **SIM (Subscriber Identity Module) card,** a country-specific, thumbnail-sized chip that gives you a local phone number and plugs you into the local network. Most SIM cards will work in any country, but the charges for this can vary wildly, so check with your carrier and decide whether it might be cheaper to get a new SIM at your destination. Many European SIM cards are prepaid, and incoming calls are frequently free. You can buy additional cards or vouchers (usually available at convenience stores) to "top up" your phone. For more information on GSM phones, check out www.telestial.com. Companies like Cellular Abroad (www.cellularabroad.com) and **OneSimCard** (www.onesimcard.com) rent cell phones and SIM cards that work in a variety of destinations around the world.

AUSTRIA

In a cheesy movie, Germany would be the high school's star quarterback and Austria would be the beautiful, rich, somewhat aloof theater girl that he's always chasing after. Think Sharpay Evans, but with less pink, much less glitter, and more refinement. The Central European country has given birth to some of Europe's greatest minds, including Mozart and Strauss.

Even if you stumble into Austria with nothing more than a tolerance for classical music, you'll soon find yourself twirling through Salzburg's green hills, arms spread wide and face to the sky, belting "The Hills are Alive," with a full orchestra to back you up. Okay, maybe all you can afford on that somewhat-limited budget is a jazz quartet. But either way, you'll be frolicking through the blooming meadows, surrounded by staggering mountains, imposing fortresses, and gorgeous castles.

Soon enough, all that marching and singing will have you hankering for a coffee break. That's where the world-famous Viennese café culture comes in. Vienna is the epitome of sophistication and grandeur, with its renowned ballets, intricate architecture, and relaxed pace. When the high society elegance of Sunday Mass at St. Stephen's Cathedral or black-tie evenings at the Vienna State Opera gets to be overwhelming, escape to the quaint Austrian countryside. In small, quiet lake towns like Hallstatt, you'll find glistening, deep blue lakes and rustic charm nestled amongst salt mines and snow-capped mountains. So, what are you doing sitting here wasting your time reading this? Your dream girl is out there, now go get her!

HALLSTATT

Coverage by **Megan Galbreath**

She could hear those church bells ringing, ringing. And up in the mountains, that whole town singing, singing. Hallstatt is an idyllic lakeside village touted as one of the most romantic destinations in all of Austria. Don't worry though, even you single songbirds can enjoy the history and beauty of the region. After all, humans have been reveling in the glory of the Hallstatt Lake for nearly 9,000 years—there had to have been some unattached fellows over time. Speaking of time, if you were to travel back to Hallstatt circa 2500 BCE, you would catch a glimpse of the world's first salt miners in action. That's right, this UNESCO World Heritage Site is home to the oldest salt mines in the whole damn world. Even through the chaos of the last few millennia—forging for "white gold" with prehistoric tools, rejoicing in the invention of iron, being conquered by the Romans, avoiding the Nazis during WWII—Hallstatt has stayed true to its roots, maintaining an active mine to this day. When you arrive, you'll find not just a cultural and historical wonder, but also a dazzling, picturesque, "pinch-me-I-must-be-dreaming" place that proves that sometimes the best things in life *do* come in tiny packages.

ORIENTATION

You're more likely to get lost in the mall than lose your way in Hallstatt. The town is only 1.5km long and has just one main road. Sure, you might turn a corner to get to the salt mines or sneak down a side street for lunch, but you'll always be able to find your way home to Hallstatt Lake by walking east. The charming village lies on the lake's western bank, directly across from **Obertraun.** Chances are high that one of the first things you'll do after you arrive is dash off in search of the perfect snapshot of the enchanting villas. We reccomend starting at the northernmost edge of Hallstatt with the **"Postcard Angle Viewpoint."** As you mosy south, you'll pass the **Charnel House,** cross **Marktplatz,** and spot the **Hallstatt Museum** to the west. At this point, **Seestraße** becomes the name of the game. The historic street takes you on a riverfront promenade past traditional Austrian restaurants and darling trinket shops to the southern edge of town, where you'll find the tourist office, bus station, and supermarket. Just west of the tourist office lies the entrance to the salt mines and hiking trails.

ESSENTIALS

GETTING THERE

We recommend taking the scenic drive through Austria's mountains and lake towns from Salzburg (1.5hr), Munich (2.5hr), or Vienna (3.5hr) to Hallstatt. As an aside, travel by car is the only direct route to Hallstatt from any nearby major cities. Once here, parking is available at your accommodation or the city's parking area, which is located south of the tourist office (€12/day). Before you depart for Hallstatt, make sure to purchase a Motorway Toll Sticker at the post office, gas station, or Austrian Automobile Club and affix it to your windshield, as clearly-visible stickers are required for all vehicles on Austria's motorways. Visitors arriving by train should download the ÖBB Scotty app or visit www.oebb.at/en to purchase tickets for the best route to Hallstatt. Once you arrive at the train station, you will have to take a 10min ferry ride (€6 round-trip) across Lake Hallstatt to reach the city on the western banks. Finally, travel by bus operates through the Postbus line and requires multiple connections from everywhere but other lakeside towns in the Dachstein Salzkammergut region.

GETTING AROUND

If you want to escape Hallstatt, you'll have to do it Von Trapp family-style: by foot over the Austrian mountains. We're only joking. Sort of. Once you arrive, you'll be hoofing it through the pedestrianized town. On the bright side, the entire lakeside village is only 1.5km long and can be crossed at a leisurely pace in 30min—that is, unless you meander into all the eye-catching souvenir and trinket shops along the way. Other nearby towns in the Dachstein Salzkammergut region such as Obertraun, Gosau, and Bad Ischl can be reached by the Postbus line (20-30min ride). For all you intrepid explorers, the Navia wooden Zille, or "Fuhre" chugs across Lake Hallstatt to Obertraun (30min) and back (€10 round-trip) on a breathtaking scenic route.

PRACTICAL INFORMATION

Tourist Offices: The Hallstatt Tourist Office is one of the few locations in the city with free Wi-Fi and public toilets (€1). Make sure to download the Hallstatt App, which features a real-time GPS map and more useful information. Ferienregion Dachstein Salzkammergut (Seestraße 99; 5 9509530; www.dachstein-salzkammergut.at/en; open Apr-Aug M-F 8:30am-6pm, Sa-Su 9am-3pm, Sep-Oct M-F 8am-5pm, Sa-Su 9am-3pm, Nov-Mar M-F 8:30am-5pm, Sa 9am-2pm)

Banks/ATMs/Currency Exchange: Expect to pay cash most places, only larger restaurants associated with hotels accept credit cards. There are three ATMs in Hallstatt. One is located in the Hallstatt city center, outside the post office (open daily 24hr). The second is located at the bank next to the tourist office (Sparkasse Salzkammergut AG; Seestraße 99; 05 0100 49505; open M 8am-noon, 2-4:30pm, T-F 8am-noon). An ATM is also located outside the supermarket (open daily 24hr).

Post Offices: There is one post office in Hallstatt, located just south of Marktplatz. Post (Seestraße 169; 6134 8201; open M-Tu 8am-1pm, W 8am-1pm, 2pm-5pm, Th-F 8am-1pm).

Public Restrooms: There are public toilets located in Marktplatz, next to the tourist office, at the entrance to the salt mines, and at Badestrand (the public park located at the southernmost edge of the town). Use of the toilets requires a €1 fee, though the restrooms at the public park are free.

Internet: Wi-Fi is sparse in Hallstatt. Free Wi-Fi is found at the tourist office, Marktplatz, and the salt mines. Of note are Die Gemischtwarenhandlung am See (café), Gasthof Simony (restaurant), and Bacht's Polreich (café), three of the only dining establishments that offer Wi-Fi to customers.

BGLTQ+ Resources: Due to its small size, there are few BGLTQ+ resources in Hallstatt. Check out the resources available in Salzburg (www.salzburg.info/en/salzburg/gays-and-friends).

EMERGENCY INFORMATION

Emergency Number: 133.

Police: Hallstatt's police station is located south of the tourist office (Seelände 30). There is also a larger police department headquartered in Gosau, which is 20min by car or 30min by public transport from Hallstatt (Vordertalstraße 9; 43 6136 8821).

US Embassy: The nearest US Embassy is located in Vienna, which is roughly a 3.5hr drive or 4.5hr train ride from Hallstatt (Boltzmanngasse 16; 43 1313390; at.usembassy.gov).

Rape Crisis Center: A rape crisis center is located roughly 40 miles from Hallstatt. Frauennotruf Salzburg (Paracelsusstraße 12, 5020 Salzburg; 1.5hr by car, 2.5hr by train). They also offer a 24/7 emergency hotline (662 881100) and more resources on their website at www.frauennotruf-salzburg.at/en.

Hospitals: The nearest hospital is located in Bad Aussee, which is roughly 25min from Hallstatt by car. Salzkammergut Klinikum Bad Ischl is also located about 25min from Hallstatt by car.

- LKH Rottenmann (Sommerberg-seetraße 396, 8990 Bad Aussee; 3622 525550; www.lkh-rottenmann.at; open daily 24hr).

- Salzkammergut Klinikum Bad Ischl (Doktor-Mayer-Straße 8-10, 4820 Bad Ischl; 50 554720; www.ooeg.at; open daily 24hr).

Pharmacies: There is one pharmacy located in Hallstatt, at the doctor's office.

- Dr. med.univ. Sonja Gapp (Salzbergstraße 224; 6134 8401; www.ordination-gapp.at; open M-Tu 8am-noon, W 5pm-7pm, F 8am-noon).

SIGHTS

CULTURE

CHARNEL HOUSE IN ST. MICHAEL'S CHAPEL

Kirchenweg 40; 6134 8279; www.kath.hallstatt.net/gr-gott; open daily May-Oct 10am-6pm

The Charnel House is cooler than the Catacombs of Paris. Yeah, we went there. If anything, you have to admit that it scored way better real estate. After all, the house of bones is wedged on the side of a mountain that overlooks a gorgeous lakeside town, while the Catacombs are, well, in the dark, decaying underworld of a dingy, dirty city. Like its famed French counterpart, the creation of the Charnel House was the city's response to an overcrowded graveyard. Beginning in 1720, graves were opened and the skulls and large bones were removed, cleaned, and bleached by the sun. Skulls were decorated with the family name, date of death, and floral motifs.

i Admission to Charnel House €1.50, entry to the chapel and church free; no wheelchair accessibility

KALVARIENBERG CHURCH (CALVARY CHURCH)

Kalvarienberg 3; 6134 8279; www.kath.hallstatt.net; open daily 9am-5pm

Are you even an explorer if you haven't hiked up an overgrown, mossy, slippery path past an abandoned hotel to a creepy, pale-pink church at the base of a mountain? Between the hotel's broken window panes and the unnerving sacrificial Jesus scene at the entrance to Kalvarienberg Church, you'll have to tip toe up to the wrought-iron gate of the chapel while half-expecting some lost miner's ghost to jump out at you with a "Boo!" Despite ample qualitative evidence, the small baroque church is touted as an idyllic and romantic honeymoon stop. The beautifully-carved crucifixion figures and weapon-wielding cherubs look almost as entrancing as the view over Hallstatt itself.

i Free; no wheelchair accessibility

LANDMARKS

LUTHERAN PROTESTANT CHURCH OF CHRIST

Landungspl. 101; hours vary

Hallstatt's Protestants used to have some serious beef with the Catholic Church. In the 1600s, the Archbishop of Salzburg burned the homes of the city's Protestant preachers before condemning them to death. Some 200 years later, the town's Protestant population finally got what they wanted: some long-deserved respect and a stunning church. Today, its clock tower spire defines the Hallstatt skyline—a particularly impressive feat, considering it's competing with towering mountains and charming rustic cottages. Visitors who happen by **Marktplatz** have no choice but to wander through the parish's open doors into the understated, yet entrancing foyer. There, you'll find a welcoming note of encouragement from the pastor inviting you to sign the guestbook and wishing you a pleasant day. Heck, he may even tug at your heartstrings enough to convince you to donate to the historical church's upkeep.

i Free; limited wheelchair accessibility

JANU SPORT SHOP

Seestraße 50; 6134 8298; www.dachstein-sport.at; open daily 9am-6pm

Now, before you get all riled up, wondering why in the world we would send you to a sport shop when you're in one of the most historical villages of all of Europe, let us explain. That history you're all concerned about? It lies beneath Janu's sales-racks and souvenirs. During the widening of the cellar in the early 1990s, workers stumbled across some of the oldest and most well-preserved artifacts ever discovered in Hallstatt. Yep. Somehow, the sport shop was once the site of an ancient Roman bathhouse, a Middle-Aged timber storage yard, a royal Habsburg court, and a modern salt mine forge. Now that the excavation site has graduated to the status of "tourist attraction," feel free to don your hard hat and clamber on down to Hallstatt's hidden gem.

i Free; no wheelchair accessibility

MUSEUMS

HALLSTATT MUSEUM

Seestraße 56; 6134 828015; www.museum-hallstatt.at; open May-Sept daily 10am-6pm, Oct daily 10am-4pm, Nov-Mar W-Su 11am-3pm, Apr daily 10am-4pm

Ahh, museums. The perfect warm, dry space to hide out from the rain on a cold, dreary day, and add a bit of knowledge to that noggin—unless you're in Hallstatt, apparently. While chances are pretty high that you won't see another soul on your 45-minute jaunt through 7,000 years of history, it's all the king's horses and men that are really missing out. The Hallstatt Museum celebrates the journey of this **UNESCO World Heritage Site** by displaying everything from fossils to 3,000-year-old leather shoe fragments to well-preserved ancient butterbur toilet paper. Museum curators were even thoughtful enough to provide you with the recipe for a barley and pork stew commonly eaten by Hallstatt's early salt miners—a recipe that archaeologists reverse-engineered from the salt miner's preserved, used toilet paper.

i Admission €10, €8 reduced; last entry 1hr before close; no wheelchair accessibility

OUTDOORS

HALLSTÄTTER SEE (LAKE HALLSTATT)

Open daily 24hr

They say that a trip to the lake should be at the top of your bucket list and considering that arrival by ferry is one of the few ways to get to Hallstatt, it'll be pretty easy to check that off. Thank u, next. Whoa there, not so fast! You're not escaping the dazzling, crystal-clear blue-green waters that easily. Mostly because the stunning 8.6 sq. km beauty is visible from almost every cobblestone and corner in the petite, picturesque village. Paul Revere, light two lanterns because the best way to enjoy Hallstatt Lake's entrancing sparkle is not by land, but rather by sea. Kayak, swan boat, motorboat, paddle boat, wooden boat, excursion boat. If it floats, you can probably rent it. Just make sure to keep your steady land legs under you at all times—the glacial waters never top chilly 70° F. Did someone say polar plunge?

i Motorboat, paddle boat, and kayak rentals from €10; ferry tours from €12; Novia fuhre round-trip to Obertraun (1hr) €10

WALDBACHSTRUB WATERFALL

Klausalm 4830, Hallstatt; open daily 24hr

We say wasserfall, you say waterfall. Potato, potahto. If you just follow the trail signs, you'll eventually get there. And if not, you'll likely end up reveling in the wonder of the 12,000-year-old **Glacier Garden.** Its intricate tide pools and jaw-dropping clarity will make you swear that movies were filmed. If you do wind up lost, just traipse on down the rocky path back to the beginner-level gravel trail, which will deposit you in front of the roaring Waldbachstrub Waterfall in less than 20 minutes. If you're thinking "But...this is vacation. Physical exercise is not on the itinerary," you'll just have to make an exception. Enjoy a jaunt through the shaded woods as you listen to chirping birds and the babbling stream before arriving at a majestic waterfall; you'll barely break a sweat.

i Free; easy hike on gravel path, 2hr round-trip; no wheelchair accessibility

FOOD

BACHT'S POLREICH

Seestraße 89; 676 6515594; open 10am-7pm, kitchen open 11am-6pm

Bacht's Polreich is great if you're looking to break out of that traditional Austrian fare funk. The waterfront café offers a small selection of soups, salads, and pasta—like Olive Garden, but without the unlimited piping-hot breadsticks, cheese-smothered house greens, and endless minestrone. Okay, so it's nothing like Olive Garden (thank God). At least you'll sit down to a hot meal at one of Hallstatt's more modern dining establishments and be able to eat your meal in peaceful, moderately-priced tranquility at the base of the mountains. Alright, and for you folks that can't seem to get enough of the sea bass, schnitzel, and spätzle that overtake every menu in Hallstatt, you'll be pleased to find that the easy-going bartender will pour you a cold one to pair with them every time.

i Appetizers from €5, meals from €9; cash only; vegetarian options available; limited wheelchair accessibility; outdoor seating available

DIE GEMISCHTWARENHANDLUNG AM SEE ($$)

Gosaumühlstraße 62; 664 6362216; open daily 9am-6pm

You've marched up and down Hallstatt for hours, wandered into all three cafés hunting for Wi-Fi, and just about torn your hair out looking for a place to kick back, charge your phone, and relax with a decent cappuccino... when there, appearing like a drop of rain in the great California drought, you spot the tiny neon pink letters on the chalkboard out front: "Free Wi-Fi." You stumble through the door, plop onto the worn couch against the back wall, and ask for a double espresso and the Wi-Fi password (which is, ironically, "nopassword"). Die Gemischtwarenhandlung am See becomes the saving grace of your trip. To be clear—NOT the money-saving grace. The charming little café will run you dry if you try to order anything except a coffee.

i Coffee, soda, beer, and wine from €3.5, snacks and dessert from €4; vegetarian options available; wheelchair accessible; outdoor seating available; free Wi-Fi

MUK'S SCHMANKERL ($)

Seestraße 139; 664 1225530; open daily 10am, closing time varies from 5-7pm

Muk's is the lakeside café of your childhood dreams. Pizza, grilled cheese, tomato soup, and ice cream are all that it has to offer—in other words, you're set for life. The small nook is more of a dash-then-dine kind of place. Good luck snagging a coveted seat on the couch next to the power outlet or claiming rights to a white tea chair overlooking the sparkling waters of **Lake Hallstatt.** You know what else looks mighty fine, other than the café's matching blue and white tiled walls and the charming "love" sign above the door frame? Your pocketbook after your purchase. In fact, you might just be able to afford two toasties and two scoops of mint chocolate chip.

i Coffee from €2.30, sandwiches from €4, pizza €9; cash only; vegetarian options available; limited wheelchair accessibility; outdoor seating available

NIGHTLIFE

MARKTBEISL ZUR RUTH ($)

Marktplatz 59; 6134 20017; www.marktbeisl.at; open daily 11am-2am, closed on W in winter

This is the only bar in all of Hallstatt, take it or leave it. Its bar? Pretty darn simple, too. Visitors have their pick between two types of wine (white or red) and three kinds of beer, all on tap.

If you really want to go crazy, you could order a mixed drink or spritzer, though we're not sure this quiet vacation spot is quite ready for that. All joking aside, Martbeisl Zur Ruth does the job just fine. Escape your suffocating hotel bar, see **Marktplatz** lit up against the starry night sky, fight tooth and nail for one of the two seats at the counter, and toast the half-clothed woman on the old-timey advert for Willi's Wine Bar. Who knows, maybe you'll even get the bartender to offer you a cigarette.

i No cover, beer from €3.10, wine €3.60; snacks served until 10pm; credit card minimum of €15; partial wheelchair accessibility; outdoor seating available

SALZBURG

Coverage by **Megan Galbreath**

Most believe that Salzburg got its humble beginnings in the salt trade—hence its namesake, "Mountain of Salt." Though it is true that the mountain of "white gold" made the Prince Archbishops that ruled here a mountain of money, Salzburg's modest roots actually date back to the eighth century, when St. Rupert established St. Peter's Abbey and Monastery. The quiet, relaxed mountain town proved to be perfectly suited to the monks' lives of solitude...that is, until the Archbishops of the sixteenth century decided to transform the quaint settlement into one of the world's grandest baroque cities. For the next 200 years, Salzburg's rulers used the wealth from the salt trade to construct grand palaces, towering cathedrals, and gorgeous gardens. Beginning in the early 1800s, Salzburg became something of a master at the game of Hot Potato. The prospering town was transferred from Bavaria to Austria, integrated into Austria-Hungary, dissolved into the First Republic of German Austria, and was finally annexed by the German Third Reich, all within a span of 130 years. Thanks to its flourishing classical music scene and *The Sound of Music*'s timeless beauty, the popular town has only grown more desirable in recent decades. Today, over 6.5 million visitors flock to Austria's fourth-largest city, hoping to catch a glimpse of Mozart's birthplace, Archbishop Markus' elegant baroque architecture, Red Bull's dynasty, and Julie Andrews' kingdom.

ORIENTATION

Salzburg = simple. When navigating themselves, most visitors only need to be concerned with one question: are you north or south of the **River Salzach?** Those who find themselves in the south are likely wandering the pedestrianized **Old Town,** prized for its key landmarks, historic plazas, and bountiful museums. Visitors will find no shortage of Austrian café culture, tantalizing bakeries, and traditional restaurants along the cobblestone streets of **Getreidegasse** and **Mozartplatz.** Also of note is the mountain **Mönschberg,** the **Hohensalzburg Fortress,** and **St. Peter's Cemetery,** which lie just south of the bustling city center. If you responded north, then you'll likely find yourself in **New Town,** also known as **Right Bank.** The area is home to the pedestrianized, charming **Linzergasse Street,** which features lively bars and relaxed restaurants. A few blocks northwest of Linzergasse are the famed **Mirabell Palace** and **Mirabell Gardens.** The latter is a gorgeous place to spend the evening overlooking the river and mountains with a bottle of wine and freshly prepared snack from one of the area's bakeries. Finally, the **Hauptbahnhof** borders the northernmost edge of Salzburg, and will likely serve as the "kumbaya, come full circle," landmark for most travelers, as travel by train and bus are the most popular ways to arrive and depart from the historic city.

ESSENTIALS

GETTING THERE

Salzburg Airport W.A. Mozart is located about 2.5 miles southwest of the city center. Travelers flying into Austria's second-largest airport can then take a 10-15min taxi ride (€20) to their final destination. The airport is also connected to the Hauptbahnhof (central train station) by Obus line 2 and to the city center by Obus line 10 (both are 20min rides, €2.90). All arriving trains and buses disembark at the Hauptbahnhof, which is located a bit north of the city center. From there, visitors can take a taxi to their final destination, ride Obus lines 1, 3, 5, or 6 (15min ride, €2.90) to downtown, or walk the remaining 15-20min to their accommodation.

GETTING AROUND

Despite being the fourth-largest Austrian city, Salzburg is rather small and easy to get around. Unless you are traveling to the airport or outer-lying nightclubs, bars, or cultural attractions, we recommend walking. In fact, many areas of Salzburg are pedestrianized, including Old Town, where many major historic landmarks, museums, and cafés are located. Salzubrg's city center can be crossed in about 20min by foot. As with most major cities, public transportation is also an option. Salzburg is serviced by a bus and bus-trolley (Obus) system that offers single-ride, 24hr, or week passes for purchase. Finally, taxis are readily accessible. The starting fare is €3.80, plus €0.80/km.

PRACTICAL INFORMATION

Tourist Offices: Salzburg has two tourist offices, housed at the Salzburg Main Station (Hauptbahnhof) and Mozartplatz Square. Here is the info for the Mozartplatz location (Mozartplatz 5; 6628 898 73 30; open Jan-Mar M-Sa 9am-6pm, Apr-June daily 9am-6pm, Jul daily 9am-6:30pm, Aug daily 9am-7pm, Sept-Oct 16 daily 9am-6pm, Oct 17-Nov M-Sa 9am-6pm, Dec daily 9am-6pm).

Banks/ATMs/Currency Exchange: Expect to pay cash at most establishments in Salzburg, particularly those outside the city center. ATMs (*geldautomats*) are found around the city, and usually offer the best exchange rates. We have listed one bank located in the city center just west of Mozart's Birthplace: Volksbank Salzburg (Münzgasse 1; 66 284 32 33; www.volksbanksalzburg.at; open M-F 9:30am-12:30pm, 2:30pm-4:30pm).

Post Offices: There are a couple post offices located in Salzburg. We have listed one located near Mirabell Palace, next to Bawag PSK (an Austrian bank). Postfiliale (Schrannengasse 10C; 081 001 01 00; www.post.at; open M-F 8am-6pm).

Public Restrooms: Most toilets are only available to paying customers inside cafés, restaurants, and museums. That said, there are several public toilets within Salzburg, including four in the city center and two at Mirabell Palace. There is a €0.50 fee to use public toilets in Salzburg. Map the one nearest you at www.salzburg.info/en/travel-info/interactive-map.

Internet: Salzburg offers free Wi-Fi hotspots between 5am-midnight at several locations, including Mirabell Gardens, Rathaus (city hall), Getreidegasse, Mozartplatz, Kapitelplatz, Kajetanerplatz, and Makartsteg bridge.

BGLTQ+ Resources: The Salzburg Tourist Office publishes the GayGuide Salzburg, which contains information on the best nightlife, meetups, and tourism attractions in the city for members of the BGLTQ+ community. Visit their website www.salzburg.info/en/salzburg/gays-and-friends for more information and additional weblinks, or swing by the tourist office in person to pick up a brochure.

EMERGENCY INFORMATION

Emergency Number: 112.

Police: 133. Polizeiinspektion Rathaus (Rudolfskai 2; 4359 133 55 88; www.polizei.at; open daily 24hr) is located downtown across from city hall.

There is also a police station near the central train station (Polizeiinspektion Bahnhof; Südtiroler Platz 3; 4359 133 55 82; open daily 24hr).

US Embassy: The only US Embassy in Austria is located in Vienna, which is roughly a 3hr drive or 2.5hr train ride from Salzburg (Boltzmanngasse 16; 43 131 33 90; at.usembassy.gov). In case of emergencies, the US Consulate in Munich may be more accessible (Königinstraße 5; 89 28880; de.usembassy.gov/embassy-consulates/munich).

Rape Crisis Center: Frauennotruf Salzburg offers a emergency hotline (open daily 24hr) and in-person services for women who have been sexually harassed or assaulted (Paracelsusstraße 12; 66 288 11 00; www.frauenberatung-freiraum.at; open Tu and Th 10am-noon, 1pm-3pm).

Hospitals: Salzburg offers emergency services at several public and private hospitals, including:

- Unfallkrankenhaus Hospital (Dr. Franz-Rehrl-Platz 5; 593 934 40 00; open daily 24hr).

Pharmacies: In general, pharmacies (*apotheke*) in Salzburg are open M-F 8am-6pm and Sa 8am-noon. We have listed one pharmacy located just north of Mirabell Palace, though pharmacies are scattered throughout the city.

- Salvator Apotheke (Mirabellplatz 5; 66 287 14 11; open M-F 8am-6pm, Sa 8am-noon).

SIGHTS

CULTURE

AUGUSTINER BRÄU

Lindhofstraße 7; 66 243 12 46; www.augustinerbier.at; open M-F 3pm-11pm, Sa-Su 2:30pm-11pm

Monks began this brewery in 1621, and it's still living in the Stone Ages. At Augustiner Brau, the beer is served in stone steins, complete with the clasped lid that was originally designed to protect kings from being poisoned in the **Middle Ages**. Austria's largest beer garden lies under the shade of a grove of chestnut trees, just around the corner

from the **River Salzach**. On any given night, you'll find a crowd of 3,000, who come for the experience of washing their own mug in the stone basin and stay for the cheap traditional Austrian snacks. What better way to end a hike up Mönchsberg than with a frothy cold one at base camp?

i Beer from €5, snacks from €4, meals from €9; cash only; wheelchair accessible

ST. PETER'S CEMETERY AND CATACOMBS

Kapitelpl. 8; 66 284 78 98; www.stift-st-peter.at/en; cemetery open Apr-Sep daily 6:30am-7:45pm, Oct-Mar daily 6:30am-6pm; catacombs open daily May-Oct 10am-12:30pm and 1pm-6pm, Nov-Apr daily 10am-12:30pm and 1pm-5pm

Hide and seek? In the cemetery? The Von Trapp family couldn't have chosen a location a bit less...macabre? St. Peter's was made famous by the *Sound of Music*'s great escape scene, though monks have been escaping to the cemetery and its catacombs for centuries. According to legend, hermit monks started hiding out in the mountain's natural caves as early as the sixth century. Talk about a life of solitude. Today, visitors can climb 48 rocky steps to visit the resting site of Mozart's sister, **Nannerl.** Apparently being related to the child prodigy destined you to eternity in the boonies. To be fair, these boonies sit at the base of **Mönschberg,** surrounded by beautiful mountains, luscious flowers, and the grand **Hohensalzburg Fortress**...so, maybe Nannerl lucked out in the afterlife, after all.

i Cemetery admission free, catacombs admission €2, €1.50 reduced; cemetery wheelchair accessible, catacombs not wheelchair accessible

SALZBURG CATHEDRAL

Domplatz 1a; 6628 047 79 50; www.salzburger-dom.at; open Jan-Feb M-Sa 8am-5pm, Su 1pm-5pm, Mar-Apr M-Sa 8am-6pm, Su 1pm-6pm, May-Sep M-Sa 8am-7pm, Su 1pm-7pm, Oct M-Sa 8am-6pm, Su 1pm-6pm, Nov M-Sa 8am-5pm, Su 1pm-5pm, Dec M-Sa 8am-6pm, Su 1pm-6pm

"If at first you don't succeed, try, try again" seems to be the motto of this nearly 1300-year old cathedral. The relatively modern structure has been the shining star of Salzburg's skyline since it was first completed by bishop Virgil in 774. Over the years, multiple fires—and eventually, bombs during WWII—destroyed the church, so that the newest version of the intricate, baroque building dates only to 1959. See the remains of earlier versions in the cathedral's crypt, which is pretty cool (literally and figuratively...after all, you did just descend into an underground, dark stone chamber). As if windowless rooms dedicated to the dead weren't spooky enough, Salzburg church officials decided to surprise visitors with a mini grim reaper that flies around the room. Lord, help us all.

i Admission free; guided tours €5, wheelchair accessible; crypt open daily M-Sa 10am-5pm, Su 1pm-5pm

LANDMARKS

FORTRESS HOHENSALZBURG

Mönchsberg 34; 6628 424 30 11; www.salzburg-burgen.at/en/hohensalzburg-castle; open May-Sept daily 9am-7pm, Oct-Apr daily 9:30am-5pm

For an accurate mental image of Hohensalzburg Fortress, just picture a knight in shining armor beating his fists on his chest and erupting with a roar before going into battle. That kind of barbarian brute strength is one of the few ways to accurately portray the fortitude of a fortress that has never been overtaken. Oh, people have tried—for weeks, the town's peasants attempted to oust **Prince Archbishop Matthäus Lang** in 1525—but the impenetrable stone walls and soldiers' wit always won. That said, apparently the museum's curators suspect that Salzburg's easily fooled peasants would have outsmarted today's generation, seeing as every information card is written on a "Dick sees Jane and Spot run" level. Good thing even the scarecrow from The Wizard of Oz could enjoy this outing. All you need is a pair of eyes to fangirl over the glorious view.

i Basic ticket (round-trip funicular, audio guide, museum entry) €12.90; last entry 1hr before close; limited wheelchair accessibility, must be arranged in advance

MIRABELL GARDENS

Mirabellplatz; 6 628 07 20; www.salzburg.info/en/sights/top10/mirabell-palace-gardens; gardens open daily 6am-dusk, palace open daily 8am-6pm

"When you know the notes to sing, you can sing most anything. Together!" **Johann Ernst von Thun** is probably pretty ticked that he straggles in at second place to **Julie Andrews** and the Von Trapp children when it comes to reasons why the Mirabell Gardens are so famous. The Prince Archbishop redesigned the landscape in 1690, integrating the baroque, geometric patterns into the Salzburg landscape. Today, the real reason for the Gardens' appeal lies with the famed *Sound of Music* scene, where the children dance around the Pegasus Fountain. We dare you to don your own hand-sewn, drape-derived play clothes and sing "Do-Re-Mi" under the trellis before scampering off toward the Dwarf Garden for more shenanigans.

i Free; wheelchair accessible; public toilets €0.50

RESIDENZPLATZ

Residenzplatz 4; open daily 24hr

It seems like Residenzplatz got the memo. The grand square is the perfect example of the age-old advice to always surround yourself with people who are better than you, so that you, too, may one day achieve greatness. In Residenzplatz's case, it chose the **Salzburg Museum, DomQuartier, the Salzburg Cathedral,** and **Mozartplatz.** That's not to say that the historic plaza doesn't pull its own weight. At its center lies a regal baroque fountain featuring four snorting horses, three dancing dolphins, two scalloped basins, and a triton in the airy breeze. Today, the area regularly hosts sporting events, football watch parties, live concerts, and music festivals. It also functions as a home base for Salzburg's horse and carriage scheme, where for just €98 (50-minute ride), you can add the classically romantic ride around the city to the list of your favorite things.

i Free; wheelchair accessible

MUSEUMS

DOMQUARTIER MUSEUM

Residenzplatz 1; 6628 042 21 09; www.domquartier.at/en; open W-M Sep-Jun 10am-5pm, Jul-Aug 10am-6pm

Don't you try to put DomQuartier into a box. Gosh darn it, it's more than a museum. In fact, the touchy historical complex includes two museums, the **Salzburg Cathedral,** the **Salzburg Prince Archbishops' former residence**...and perhaps a perfumery? Though not marketed as such, DomQuartier smells like a heavenly mixture of incense, Hawaiian Tropic sunscreen, blooming flowers, and for some inexplicable reason, fresh coffee grounds. Now bottle some of that up and sell it at the museum gift shop. Salzburg sorcery aside, the impressive complex houses elaborate, gem-crusted chalices, detailed ivory carvings, a dope state sleigh from the 1800s, and a gorgeous viewing platform overlooking nearby **Residenzplatz.** Not to be missed is the Residenzgalerie's sixteenth-nineteenth century European painting exhibit, which features raw, vibrant pigments of the most commonly-used colors of the era.

i Admission €13, €10 reduced includes audio guide; last entry 1hr before close; wheelchair accessible

MOZART'S GEBURTHAUS (MOZART'S BIRTHPLACE)

Getreidegasse 9; 66 284 43 13; www.mozarteum.at/en/museums/mozarts-birthplace; open Sept-June daily 9am-5:30pm, Jul-Aug daily 8:30am-7pm

If you ever feel like getting upstaged by a five-year old, just head over to Mozart's Birthplace. The child prodigy had already learned to play the violin and piano by the time most kids were in the glue-tasting stage of life. It doesn't help that the museum really plays up the entire family, dedicating a room to each member and bestowing them with lavish praises. To be fair, it's not like you and your sister traveled the European courts as child musical prodigies like Mozart and Maria Anna "Nannerl" did in the 1760s. In addition to getting schooled on the influential composer's accomplishments, visitors have the chance to view original compositions, early music books, pictures, memorabilia...and 4 locks of hair, 3 of which are confirmed by DNA analysis to come from the same person.

i Admission €11, €9 reduced; guided tour by prior arrangement; last entry 30min before closing; no wheelchair accessibility

OUTDOORS

MÖNCHSBERG

Lift entrance at Gstättengasse 13; 6628 884 97 50; open daily 24hr; lift operates Oct-Jun M 8am-7pm, Tu-Su 8am-9pm, Jul-Aug daily 8am-11pm

Mönschberg is the exact opposite of the tip of the iceberg. When you start your hike, you know exactly what you're getting yourself into: a tiring, sweaty, and exhilarating climb. The 308m peak lies just west of **Old Town** and is one of five mountains in Salzburg. So, how do you pick the tall and mighty lookout point out of a lineup? Just look for the **Museum der Moderne**—a relatively simple building built into the mountain that ironically resembles an old stone castle. After all, is it even contemporary art if it doesn't make you squint, tilt your head, and think "But..."? Ponderings aside, if the trek through the meadows and woodlands doesn't take your breath away, don't get too cocky. The breathtaking panoramic view from the top of Mönschberg will have you reaching for your emergency inhaler soon enough. Happy climbing.

i Free; round-trip lift ticket €3.80, single trip lift ticket €2.50; lift wheelchair accessible

FOOD

BÄRENWIRT ($$)

Müllner Hauptstraße 8; 66 242 24 04; www.baerenwirt-salzburg.at; open daily 11am-11pm, kitchen open 11:30am-2pm and 5:30pm-9:30pm with snacks served 2pm-5:30pm

An Austrian restaurant is famous for its...fried chicken? You betcha. KFC move outta the way, there's a new finger-lickin' good fella in town. Or maybe an old-but-new-to-you fella? Bärenwirt was one of the first inns to be established in Salzburg, with hospitality dating back to 1663. Given that the historic restaurant has had over 350 years to perfect their recipes, it's no wonder their goulash soup, smoked char, wiener schnitzel, egg dumplings, and, of course, fried chicken, have diners making reservations weeks in advance. The warm, inviting establishment has a homely cottage feel, complete with fire logs stacked by the door and embroidered pincushions on each hand carved seat. We recommend dining on the traditional fare before dashing across the street to **Augustiner Brau,** whose monk-ly ties rival the holiness of your Bärenwirt fried half-chicken. Hallelujah.

i Drinks from €3, meals from €10; limited wheelchair accessibility; outdoor seating available; reservations recommended

BOSNA GRILL ($)

Getreidegasse 33; 66 284 14 83; open M-Sa 11am-7pm, Su 2pm-7pm

Overhead costs at the Balkan Grill must be cheap. Maybe that's how they've managed to stay in business since 1950, despite charging dirt-cheap prices in the heart of **Old Town.** Hell, for €3.80/dog, they could roll each brat in the dirt and coat it with a fine layer of gravel before serving them up and people would still dutifully hand their coins over the counter. Some say God gave us five fingers for manual dexterity, but after chowing down on a simple, juicy hotdog, you might start to think it was just a master plan leading up to holding a Balkan Grill delicacy. After all, how else are you supposed to tick off each of the five ways you can order your dog, if you don't have five fingers? We recommend the classic: two grilled pork bratwursts smothered in onions and parsley, squished between two toasted slices of white bread. Avoid on a first date.

i Drinks from €2, hot dogs €3.80; cash only; wheelchair accessible; no seating available

COFFEE HOUSE SALZBURG ($$)

Linzergasse 39; 66 287 43 00; www.coffeehouse.at; open Su-Th 9am-8pm, F-Sa 9am-10pm

Though simple, its name is pretty fitting. Walking through the doors of Coffee House feels like coming home. Worn brown leather couches fill the floor, stately trunks serve as tables, and warm lighting casts a comforting glow over the space. Across the back wall lies an expansive bookshelf, lined with thick volumes, shiny new novellas, and quirky knick-knacks. After passing all the ice cream shops lining the upscale, boutique Linzergasse avenue, you might be tempted to deny your sweet tooth yet another indulgence...chances are though that you'll eventually cave to Coffee House's decadent banana bread or fluffy meringue pie. For the true homebody experience, snag a spot on the coveted recliner, crack open the spine of that book you've been carrying around for three weeks, and try to avoid scattering crumbs from your lunchtime panini all over the furniture.

i Coffee and pastries from €3, food from €6; cash only; vegetarian options available; wheelchair accessible; outdoor seating available; free Wi-Fi

PANINOTECA ($)

Waaglplatz 5; 664 392 81 80; open daily 9am-6pm

Do you ever wander around Europe wishing for a sandwich with more substance than half of a hard boiled egg stuffed between two slices of stale bread? The continent has the whole pastry thing down, but sandwiches? Put some meat on 'em! Paninoteca luckily caters to a more sensible sandwich mentality. Layered between two warm, crunchy focaccia slices lies tender roast beef and ~gasp~ veggies! Yes folks, colorful, fresh produce does exist outside of farmers' markets. The modern Italian joint serves up a variety of carnivorous and vegetarian paninis, pastas, and salads. Once you spot the thick subs lined up before the minuscule grill (seriously, we've seen marble kitchen islands larger than Paninoteca's cooking space), it'll be all you can do to keep from piling those suckers onto the motorbike jutting out of the wall and making for the hills.

i Drinks from €3, paninis from €6, lunch specials from €11; wheelchair accessible; outdoor seating available

NIGHTLIFE

AFRO CAFÉ ($$)

Bürgerspitalplatz 5; 662 844 88 80; www.afrocafé.at/en; open M-Th 9am-11pm, F-Sa 9am-midnight

Boogie woogie woogie. Knocking back drinks at this hot pink, sequined, eclectic bar is quite the experience. The African-inspired atmosphere is funky, fun, and totally unlike the traditional Austrian cafés scattered around Salzburg. Here on the African plains, a glitzy snake mural slithers across the ceiling, colored beads clank against the windows, and hodge-podge multimedia sculptures made to look like steer heads are mounted to the walls. You'll have to arrive early in the evening if you want to snag a neon yellow seat on the terrace—though in this case, maybe second is the best because then you can lounge on the comfy, springy couches that line the walls. After all, when was the last time you bounced on the couch in tune to the jazz hit "So What" before signaling to the bartender for a second round. Peace signs only.

i No cover, drinks from €4, food from €9; BGLTQ+ friendly; outdoor seating available

FLIP ($)

Gstättengasse 17; 66 284 36 43; open Su-W 3pm-4am, Th-Sa 3pm-5am

What came first: Flip Bar or flip cup? Though the rowdy college drinking game fails to make an appearance (sadly, all good things must come to an end, and apparently flip cup has no place in the real world), the rambunctious crowd that usually accompanies it staggers out in full force on weekend nights. Thanks to Flip's prime location on the corner of **Gstättengasse** and **Oftättengaffe,** the bar is the shining star of Salzburg's nightlife scene. Flanked by **Soda Club** to its right and **Motto Bar** to its left, Flip has no choice but to listen to the devilish musings of the party masters whispering in both of its ears. For your own devilish time, put on that devilish grin and waltz in between 7-9pm to find the Holy Trinity: a buy-one, get-two-free deal that'll have you praying for just a mild hangover the next morning.

i No cover, drinks from €3, cocktails from €7; limited wheelchair accessibility; outdoor seating available; happy hour buy 1 get 2 daily 7pm-9pm

MONKEYS ($$)

Imbergstraße 2A; open Su-Th 11:30am-1am, F-Sa 11:30am-2am

Monkey see, monkey do, monkey drinks and so do you. The riverfront bar offers unparalleled views of the raging **River Salzach,** set against the picturesque backdrop of Salzburg's lush, green mountains and imposing stone fortress. By day, Monkeys functions as a relaxed café, a spot for locals to retire on the terrace with a spritzer and not a care in the world. Come evening, the jungle springs alive. College students flock from the caves and young adults swing down from the canopy to gather at the lively watering hole. The crowd's cacophony gives the call of the wild a run for its mon(k)ey, though you'll probably find their German rendition of "Summer of '69" a bit more harmonious than parrot squeals and baboon screeches.

i No cover, beer from €3.50, wine and spritzers from €5, cocktails from €8; BGLTQ+ friendly; wheelchair accessible; majority outdoor seating

VIENNA

Coverage by **Megan Galbreath**

Close your eyes, take a deep breath, and let the City of Dreams whisk you away on a magical journey. Are you looking for decadent chocolate cake or a sweet apple strudel? How about a traditional veal wiener schnitzel or hearty goulash? Mélange and cappuccinos, maybe? Or perhaps you need to work up an appetite first, moseying around cobblestoned streets and wandering through grand gardens and peaceful palaces (yes, palaces, plural: as in, multiple Baroque beauties within the city limits)? Now, don't be surprised if you pass an opera house, concert hall, and dance theater—or all three on your way to lunch. Hoping to get your arts and classical music fix? Splurge for tickets to the Vienna Opera Ball and see one of the most graceful and elegant performances in the world at the famous Vienna State Opera House. Or did you blow through all your hard-earned cash on a spring break trip to Cabo, meaning you're on a tight budget until that good ol' j-o-b starts? No worries! Just hit up Naschmarkt for one of the best kebabs you'll ever taste in your life, then hustle over to the Opera House to snag a standing-room ticket to the ballet, all for under €8. If you forgot to pack your ball gown, or at least a respectable, unstained t-shirt, then it's a good thing you're in one of the fashion capitals of the world. Scrumptious food, unmatched art, revered museums, traditional café culture, world-famous classical music, royal history—what more could you want in a city? Get yourself a gal who can do it all. Or just head to Vienna. The short-term commitment is probably cheaper anyways.

ORIENTATION

Much like the famed arrondissements of Paris, the twenty-three districts of Vienna spiral out from the historic city center: a rich cultural district. Here, visitors will find important monuments such as **St. Stephen's Cathedral,** as well as the **Goldenes Quartier,** revered for its luxury shopping and glamorous jewelry stores. Encircling the historic city center is **Ringstraße (Ring Boulevard)**—the most useful way to orient yourself in Vienna. The boulevard was once the location of the old city wall, but was torn down around 1900 to make room for the grand and notable landmarks that line it today: **Naschmarkt, the Vienna State Opera House, MuseumsQuartier, Hofburg Palace, Volksgarten,** and **Rathaus** line the southern and western edges, making for a directionally-challenged traveler's dream. For some of the best boutique shopping, hipster café culture, and classy nightlife in the city, visit the trendy, boho neighborhoods of **Neubau** and **Mariahilf,** which lie to the west of Ringstraße. Not to be missed is the impressive **Schönbrunn Palace,** which lies about 45 minutes southwest of the city center. Finally, jumping northwest of the first district will have travelers crossing the **Danube Canal** into **Prater,** an open and refreshing neighborhood best known for its amusement park.

ESSENTIALS

GETTING THERE

The Vienna Airport (Flughafen Wien) connects visitors from 71 countries to the City of Dreams. Since the airport is located about 9mi. southeast of the city center, travelers who arrive by plane must complete their journey with public transportation or a short taxi ride (about €40). The City Airport Train (CAT) reaches Wien Mitte (the Vienna city center) in about 16min. (single trip €12, round-trip €21), while the ÖBB-run S7 train takes about 25min. (€4.20). If you are traveling to Vienna from nearby European countries, we recommend traveling by train, as Austrian trains are comfortable, fast, and relatively inexpensive. All ÖBB long-distance trains stop at Vienna Central Station (Wien Hauptbahnhof) and Wien-Meidling Station. The most economical way to reach Vienna is by bus. Travelers arriving at the International Bus Terminal can then take public transportation to downtown Vienna (10min.) or to their final destination.

GETTING AROUND

Vienna is rather spread out, so we recommend using public transportation if you plan to travel outside the historic city center. The buses, trams, trains, and underground lines that make up the public transport network are easily accessible and navigable (single ride €2.40). During the week, night buses replace the underground lines from 12:30am-5am, though the U runs around the clock on the weekends. Make sure to validate your ticket after purchase, as being caught without a ticket or with an unvalidated ticket incurs a fine. For those who want the chance to work off the famous Viennese sachertorte, apple strudel, and mélange you're bound to indulge in, you're in luck! Bicycling is fairly common, and Citybike Wien offers an extremely inexpensive option for all our budget travelers (one-time registration fee €1, first hour of each ride free, second hour €1, third hour €2). Of course, walking is always an option. In fact, exploring the historic landmarks, museums, cultural events, and cafés of the inner city is best done by foot, as seeing the stunning architecture is half the experience.

PRACTICAL INFORMATION

Tourist Offices: Vienna has three tourist offices, found in the city center (Albertinaplatz, corner of Maysedergasse; open daily 9am-7pm), main train station (Am Hauptbahnhof 1; open daily 9am-7pm), and the airport (1300 Schwechat; open daily 7am-10pm). The city also offers an extremely comprehensive and user-friendly website at www.wien.info/en for information related to travel, events, and residential life.

Banks/ATMs/Currency Exchange: Many establishments in Vienna accept credit cards, particularly within the city center. That said, you should always have some cash on hand, especially if you plan to dine at more traditional restaurants and cafés. We have listed one bank located across from St. Stephen's Cathedral.

- Bank Austria (Stephansplatz 2; 50 50532120; www.bankaustria.at; atm open daily 24hr)

Post Offices: There are many post offices in Vienna. They tend to be open M-F 8am-6pm. To find the one nearest you, visit www.post.at. The post office we have listed is located in the city center, and it is one of two post offices open throughout the day and over the weekend in Vienna.

- Post Office (Fleishmarkt 19; open M-F 7am-10pm, Sa-Su 9am-10pm).

Public Restrooms: Expect most toilets to only be available to paying customers inside cafés, restaurants, and museums. Public toilets (WC) are found in the inner city and many parks, though usage incurs a €0.50 fee. Find the one closest to you using the interactive city map at www.wien.info/en/citymap#map.

Internet: Vienna offers a broad network of over 400 Wi-Fi hotspots, designated as "Freewave" or "Austrian Free Wifi." Most plazas in the inner district, as well as many train stations, are hotspot hubs, though connections can be spotty. It is fairly common for cafés and restaurants to offer internet to their guests, as well. Visit www.wien.info/en/travel-info/faqs/wlan to find the free Wi-Fi nearest you.

BGLTQ+ Resources: The Tourist Office offers a comprehensive website with information on the best nightlife, dining establishments, cultural events, sports groups, and even historic city tours for BGLTQ+ travelers. Visit www.wien.info/en/vienna-for/gay-lesbian to plan your trip.

EMERGENCY INFORMATION

Emergency Number: 112

Police: 113. Police officers are present throughout Vienna, partly derived from the fact that police stations are available all over the city. The following is located near Hofburg Palace (Minoritenplatz 9; www.polizei.gv.at).

US Embassy: Vienna contains the only U.S. Embassy in all of Austria (Boltzmanngasse 16; 43 1313390; at.usembassy.gov).

Rape Crisis Center: Helpful information for victims of sexual harassment and assault can be found at www.infovictims.at/at_en/006_servicos/paginas/006_001. Verein Notruf is a Vienna-based counseling service that offers advice for rape victims (Rötzergasse 13; 43 1 523 22 22; www.frauenberatung.at; open M noon-5pm, Tu-Th 9am-2pm). Additionally, a hotline open daily 24hr is available at 71719.

Hospitals: Vienna is serviced by a range of hospitals. We have listed the two largest.

- Allgemeines Krankenhaus (AKH) typically treats sickness and disease, but can handle a range of medical issues in the case of life-threatening emergencies (Währinger Gürtel 18-20; 1 40400 0; open daily 24hr).
- Unfallkrankenhaus (UKH) tends to treat traumatic injuries, but is equipped to deal with other medical issues in the case of life-threatening emergencies (Kundratstraße 37; 5 93 934 50 00; open daily 24hr).

Pharmacies: In general, pharmacies (*apotheke*) are open M-F 8am-6pm and Sa 8am-noon. They are scattered throughout the city. For information about Vienna's 24-hour standby drugstore service, call 1455.

- Zum Goldenen Hirschen (Kohlmarkt 11; www.zumgoldenen-hirschen.wien.at; open M-F 8am-6pm, Sa 8am-noon).

SIGHTS

CULTURE

NASCHMARKT

Naschmarkt; www.naschmarkt-vienna.com; open M-F 6am-7:30pm, Sa 6am-5pm

Naschmarkt is no run-of-the-mill European market. What started as a dairy market in the 1780s has moo-ved onto bigger and better things. The eastern end near **MuseumsQuartier** is particularly popular for its semi-permanent restaurants, which serve up mouthwatering fare from all corners of the world. If the steep prices have you reaching for your opera spectacles to double check that your eyesight hasn't failed you, continue chugging along another half-kilometer to the frenzied-yet-friendly fast-food stalls, where you'll find enough sausage, falafel, and kebabs to feed your extended family for a month. With meals starting at just €3, proprietors practically give away food (actually, they do give away food... make sure to snag a fudge sample or handful of roasted pecans for dessert). To see Naschmarkt in its full glory, swing by on Saturday and watch locals haggle goods down to the penny at the weekly flea market.

i Free, food and drink prices vary; wheelchair accessible; flea market Sa 6:30am-6pm

SPANISH RIDING SCHOOL

Michaelerplatz 1; 43 1 5339031; www.srs.at/en; open Mar-Dec daily 9am-4pm, Jan-Feb Tu-Su 9am-4pm, shows and guided tours daily, times vary

Walking into the Spanish Riding School feels a bit like marching into the Colosseum. If the Colosseum, ya know, hosted royal horse shows rather than brutal fights to the death. On second thought, do real live horses actually prance around the stadium and perform a choreographed pas de deux? Because the open-aired Stephansplatz down the road smells more of eau de manure than this oversized beach volleyball court. If someone could get the **Head Rider** on the phone, we'd like the number for whatever cleaning crew they use. Or maybe that's just the magic of the world-famous Lipizzaner breed, which, together with its riders, has stunned the crowd with elegant and classic **Haute École** performances since the 1730s. Better giddy on up, cowboy and get there early for tickets, unless you want to be on pooper-scooper duty for the duration of the show.

i Shows from €13; guided tours €18, €14 reduced; wheelchair accessible, but call in advance for arrangements

VIENNA STATE OPERA

Opernring 2; 43 1 514442250; www.wiener-staatsoper.at; performance and show times vary

Boom went the dynamite. Or, in the case of the Vienna State Opera House, bang went the bomb that hit the main stage and burned down 2/3 of the original structure two weeks before the end of WWII. Still, the show went on, just as it had from the late 1860s until early 1944. Following the war, the city rebuilt the world-famous theater and prized city landmark. Gone was the dazzling, hanging crystal chandelier that dripped in gemstones and the outdated, run-down stage system. In their places now stands a three-ton extravagant ball of brilliance that lights up the entire theater, and a 17-story open space behind the curtain at center stage. The best part? A slice of apple strudel puts a bigger dent in your wallet than the €3 ticket you scored to revel in the harmonious glory of the Vienna Philharmonic or State Ballet.

i Tours €7.50, €3.50 reduced; standing room at performances from €3; tour times vary by season; wheelchair accessible

LANDMARKS

AUSTRIAN NATIONAL LIBRARY

Josefsplatz 1; 4 315 34 10; www.onb.ac.at/en; open Jun-Sep F-W 10am-6pm, Th 10am-9pm, Oct-May Tu-W 10am-6pm, Th 10am-9pm, F-Su 10am-6pm

If Disneyland Paris didn't make your itinerary, have no fear. **The State Hall** at the Austrian National Library will have you twirling around the room in awe just like Belle when she stumbled into the Beast's library. In the eighteenth century, **Emperor Karl VI** wished the stunning Baroque library into existence as a private wing in the **Hofburg Palace.** Nowadays, some 200,000 old volumes and two rare Venetian globes call this grand room home. When you're not sliding across the dark-paneled bookshelves on a rolling ladder or leafing through a leather-bound manuscript, try looking up at the exquisite frescoes on the ceiling, which could honestly be their own attraction.

i Admission to State Hall €8, €6 reduced; call 15 341 04 64 in advance to arrange English guided tours; wheelchair accessible

BELVEDERE PALACE

Prinz Eugen-Straße 27; 17 955 71 34; www.belvedere.at/palaces; Upper Belvedere open Sa-Th 9am-6pm, F 9am-9pm, entrance time slot required; Lower Belvedere open Sa-Th 10am-6pm, F 10am-9pm; Belvedere 21 open W 11am-9pm, Th 11am-6pm, F 11am-9pm, Sa-Su 11am-6pm

If this were a fairy tale from the 1600s, Belvedere Palace would be the prettier, younger, more demure stepchild that Queen Schönbrunn tries to hide away in the woods. While Belvedere's paparazzi coverage doesn't quite rival that of the expansive **Schönbrunn** or central **Hofburg Palaces,** the (slightly) more relaxed atmosphere offers visitors the chance to stop and smell the roses, without fear of being stampeded to death in the royal stables. In fact, you'll feel almost like Prince Eugene himself, summertime strolling through the privy garden and gallivanting around the colorful corridors. Either that, or a lowly commoner, lining up to see the **Gustav Klimt** exhibit and fighting with the other tourists for a snapshot of "The Kiss" like it's the Mona Lisa. At least the lovers' eyes don't follow you upstairs to the captivating Impressionism exhibit.

i Upper Belvedere €16, €13.50 reduced, audio guide €5; Lower Belvedere €14, reduced €11, audio guide €4; Belvedere 21 €8, reduced €6; combination tickets €25, reduced €21, audio guide €7; wheelchair accessible

KAISERGRUFT (HABSBURG CRYPT)

Neuer Markt; 43 1 512685388; www.kapuzinergruft.com/en; open F-W 10am-6pm, Th 9am-6pm

It's a strange feeling when you realize that there are nearly 150 very famous, very rich dead people entombed around you. Things get even more unsettling when you shuffle into one of the final rooms and find that the low, stone arches and gray pebbled walls make it feel like you're the one in the sarcophagus. To be fair, the house rules posted at the entrance to the Imperial Crypt make it pretty clear that you're about to waltz into a sacred underground space. The Habsburg Crypt was founded in 1618 by **Empress Anna von Tirol** and has been racking up the royals ever since. Kaisergruft manages to confer a refreshing and humbling change of pace from the typical royal residences of the city—not to mention, a blessed escape from the Viennese summer heat.

i Admission €7.50, €6.50 reduced; English guided tours W-Sa 3:30pm; last entry 20min. before close; wheelchair accessible

SCHÖNBRUNN PALACE

Schloß Schönbrunn; 181 1130; www.schoenbrunn.at/en; open daily Apr-Jun 8am-5:30pm, Jul-Aug 8am-6:30pm, Sep-Oct 8am-5:30pm, Nov-Mar 8am-5pm; main park open daily 6:30am, closing time varies by season; garden opening hours vary

It was a soldier with a dagger in the Billiards Room. Just kidding. While you will see the room where the royal court once racked 'em up, no murders here. Just some tiny royal beds where two beloved Habsburg emperors passed away from natural causes. Guess people weren't quite life-sized back

in the 1800s. Either that, or the royal incestuous practices kept folks smaller than the average commoner. Honestly, you might not be surprised if the answer is the latter after viewing all the portraits in the royal state rooms. Every single one of Maria Theresa's sixteen children look exactly the same. You'd think a 600-year old royal line would have been able to afford an artist with more versatility. At least they splurged for the mood lighting and rare oak paneling in the Rich Room.
i Admission €16, €14.50 reduced; combination tickets available; main park free, other gardens from €4.50, reduced €3.50; wheelchair accessible

MUSEUMS

ALBERTINA

Albertinaplatz 1; 43 1 534830; www.albertina.at/en; open Sa-Tu 10am-6pm, W 10am-9pm, Th 10am-6pm, F 10am-9pm

Like most Viennese museums, the Albertina Museum is half art collection, half Imperial Palace. Unlike the rest, it features the world's largest and most valuable graphical art collection. We're not talking thousands, or even hundreds of thousands. No, my lady, the print and drawing number tallies up to a staggering 1.06 million pieces. If only you had a dollar for every print housed under Albertina's roof—you might actually be able to afford that **Picasso** you've been eyeing since cabinet three. Yet, somehow the stunning works from **Dürer** and **Cézanne** manage to be upstaged by **Monet's** breathtaking water lilies and **Degas'** delicate dancers. In addition to fascinating prints, Albertina also features a wonderful **Impressionism, Pointillism,** and **Fauvism collection,** sure to leave visitors wondering if they've died and gone to museum heaven.
i Admission €16, €11 reduced, guided tours and audio tours €4

HAUS DER MUSIK (HOUSE OF MUSIC)

Seilerstätte 30; 43 1 513 4850; www.hdm.com/en; open daily 10am-10pm

You know you're in for a good time when the only way to get to the first exhibit is to hop up a piano key staircase and craft your own tune. Haus der Musik is an interactive sound museum, with a focus on Vienna's greatest hits: the **Philharmonic, Beethoven, Haydn,** and more await you. Get a laugh out of the pocket violins (who knew there was such a thing!) or a physics lesson from the sonisphere science display. Between the virtual reality dice games that let you make your own melody and the electronic remakes of Mozart, you'll be waltzing through this magical museum of music. The only non-magical part? Waiting in line for a chance to play with nearly every toy. Fingers crossed that the schoolkids who overrun Haus der Musik have learned to share.
i Admission €13, €9 reduced; last entry 9:30pm; wheelchair accessible

MUMOK

MuseumsQuartier, Museumsplatz 1; 1 52 5000; www.mumok.at; open M 2pm-7pm, Tu-W 10am-7pm, Th 10am-9pm, F-Su 10am-7pm

Mumok is everything you look for in a partner: suave, modern, and cultured, with more to it than meets the eye. While the other eligible bachelors in **MuseumsQuartier** may have a more regal, old-school charm, Mumok stands out from the crowd with collections based on pop art and realism. Think "mysterious brooding artist" with a flair for the dramatic and just a touch

of cynicism. The contemporary art museum houses permanent pieces from the likes of **Andy Warhol** and **Yoko Ono,** as well as extensive rotating collections and installations. For those of you lucky enough to be around on Thursday night, grab a drink at **Café Hansi,** the only bar in the world where you become the art.

i Admission €12, €9 reduced; wheelchair accessible; Café Hansi open Th 6pm-9pm

WIEN MUSEUM MUSA

Felderstraße 6-8; 43 1 400085169; www.wienmuseum.at/en; open Tu-Su 10am-6pm

Now presenting: Me! A story written, produced, and directed by Vienna. Acting and instrumental credits to the City of Music. Set design by the City of Dreams. At least, that's how you might imagine the conversation went when the board of the Wien Museum sat around the table and decided the city needed not one, but two, museums on its history and art, as well as eighteen specialized residences and excavations. In their defense, Vienna has been around for ages and cultivated some of the greatest minds to ever exist. While the Wien Museum on Karlsplatz is undergoing extensive renovations, MUSA will be home to both the Viennese contemporary art collection and its cultural history exhibition. Trippy "brain pictures" intermingle with Neolithic artifacts and large-scale city models in an experience that bends the space-time continuum and leaves you slightly confused, but mostly in awe.

i Admission €7, €5 reduced, first Su of month free; wheelchair accessible; will exhibit pieces from Wien Museum on Karlsplatz during expansion and renovation

OUTDOORS

KRAPFENWALDLBAD

Krapfenwaldgasse 65-73; 1 320 15 01; open May-Aug M-F 9am-8pm, Sa-Su 8am-8pm

This peaceful pool has the best view over Vienna, by far. Sorry, not sorry **Danube Tower**. Ladies, grab those floppy hats and gents, fetch those sunnies because you're in for a lazy day soaking up some good ol' Vitamin D on the lawn. Get there before noon to snag a coveted recliner, which may be the only pool chair in the whole world where you can fall asleep and wake up without needing a visit to the chiropractor after your supposed "relaxation day." Sure, it may be a hike to reach the mini mountain, but at least the bumping bus ride takes you through the wine country in Grinzing. It also means you have to return through the wine country. What a shame it would be to waste a trip to the vineyards. Maybe while you're up splashing around Krapfenwaldlbad's infinity pool, you should put in a phone call to your folks and tell them you'll be late for dinner.

i Admission €5.60; wheelchair accessible

PRATER

Prater; 1 729 20 00; www.praterwien.com/en; park open daily 10am-midnight, rides open mid-May-Oct, ride hours vary

This sprawling theme park is like your county fair on steroids. Easily queasy folks can enjoy the view over northern Vienna from the **Giant Ferris Wheel** or test their navigation skills in the **Labyrinth,** while more adventurous adrenaline-junkies can reach new heights on the **Death Drop.** Soon enough, you'll be eating fried food and sickening sweets 'til they're coming out of your (chocolate) eyeballs. We're talking cotton candy, soft serve, bosna, and langos (Hungarian deep-fried dough). Just a word of warning—while spinning, twirling, and waltzing around at 120 kilometers an hour on **Extasy** may be pure joy, it only lasts for five minutes. The humiliation you feel after barfing up those crazy carnival concoctions? Yeah, that lingers a tad longer.

i Free entry, ride prices from €2; wheelchair accessible; credit cards accepted at most rides

THE CANAL

Open daily 24hr

Visiting Vienna without a trip to the Danube Canal is like flaunting through Paris without lounging by the Seine: practically impossible and definitely a shame. During the summer months, the winding paths near **Schwedenplatz** offer a wonderful place for an afternoon rollerblade session or a relaxed evening stroll. Grab a Radler (or two) and a friend (or three). The more the merrier—who wants to be drinking alone on the water with only an oversized crow flapping overhead for company? For those who'd rather kick back and relax with a pool day, visit **Badeschiff Wien,** where the sun deck lets you tan your beach-bum bum. After, make your way to one of the artificial beach bars that dot the canal for your Margaritaville fill.

i Free; limited wheelchair accessibility

FOOD

1500 FOODMAKERS ($$$)

25hours Hotel, Lerchenfelder Straße 1-3; 15 215 18 45; www.1500foodmakers.at/en; open M-Th noon-midnight, F noon-1am, Sa 12:30pm-1am, Su 12:30pm-midnight; kitchen open M-F noon-3pm and 6pm-11pm, Sa-Su 12:30pm-3pm and 6pm-11pm

Though the cosmopolitan restaurant features modern Italian fare, it somehow manages to give off a retro vibe, making for a quirky—and tasty—dining delight. Between feasting under the cavernous industrial lights and doing a double take at the old amber medicine bottles lining the entrance, you'll be thanking the Viennese gods for sending you this break from the city's traditional hoity-toity cafés. Our only suggestion for the suave bistro: add a classic mustache pop-art logo to match the jazzy vibe.

i Entrées from €8, drinks from €4; vegetarian options available; wheelchair accessible; outdoor seating available

CAFÉ IN DER BURGGASSE24 ($$)

Burggasse 24; 43 677 63076341; open daily 10am-10pm

Dropping in for a coffee break at the hipster café is like flipping through the pages of *Vogue*'s "Who Wore It Better?" This week's rivalry: the vintage clothing store itself versus the charming little café nestled inside. Do you splurge on a classic Burberry plaid scarf, or treat yourself to a trendy açai bowl and Mama Rose's Lemonade? Answer: you're on vacation, so obviously both. (If only.) Luckily, the trendy **Neubau** café offers up crowd favorites (did someone say all-day breakfast?) at consignment store prices. Try a bowl of berry-topped, honey-drizzled porridge, or indulge in a thick slice of key lime cheesecake paired with a frothy cappuccino. Pro tip: snag a cushy spot on the couch next to the roaring fire for the best view of the intense chess tournaments that take place in the back room. Checkmate.

i Drinks from €3, food from €5; cash only; vegetarian options available; wheelchair accessible; outdoor seating available

MOZART'S RESTAURANT ($$)

Haidmannsgasse 8; 43 1 8920878; www.mozartsvienna.com; open Su-Th 5pm-1am, F-Sa 5pm-2am

Yes, it's called Mozart's, and yes, it serves traditional Austrian food, but Americans can still have a soft spot for the famed classical composer. After all, the rustic restaurant certainly has a passion for delivering up some first-class good ol' US-of-A style burgers. And the sweet potato fries? Those mouth-watering crispers will make you wonder what kind of voodoo magical water Austrian farmers use on their crops. Whatever it is, you can't get that in Idaho. The best part isn't even slurping up a hearty goulash soup under the antler-fashioned lamp or gorging yourself on schnitzel and a spritz next to hand-carved wooden murals. Nope. It's that Mozart's gets how the world works.

i Entrées from €8; vegetarian options available; limited wheelchair accessibility; outdoor seating available

PHIL ($)

Gumpendorfer Straße 10-12; 43 1 5810489; www.phil.business.site; open M 5pm-1am, Tu-Sa 9am-1am, Su 9am-midnight

Phil sounds like the name of a khaki-wearing insurance salesman, not a vintage, hipster, and somewhat melodramatic café/bar/bookstore/

BRATISLAVA

You think you've had it rough until you visit a city that has been broken up and re-united, had war waged against it, and seen the crown passed between feuding neighbors time and time again. Though the capital city of Slovakia is young on paper, it's been a rather long and rocky ride. Bratislava's key location on the Danube River has made it appealing since Neolithic times, when man first settled the area—if only that guy knew what a can of worms he was about to open. For the next 2000 years or so, the Celts, Mongols, Germans, Hungarians, Habsburgs, and a half-dozen other groups fought for and defended the important port city. Things finally calmed down in 1993, when modern-day Slovakia emerged from the Velvet Revolution. Today, visitors will find a town teeming with similar impromptu open-air performances, historic landmarks, stylish architecture, and a lively nightlife scene, which together give rise to the vibrant and rich culture of modern Bratislava.

The main central train station, **Bratislava Hlavná Stanica (hl. st.),** lies north of the city center while the smaller station, **Bratislava-Petržalka,** lies south. Everything else with which visitors need to be concerned can be found between. It is also helpful to note that the **Danube River** borders the southern edge of the historical district, and the only attraction south of the river is the **UFO Observation Deck** and its futuristic design is easily recognizable. As for the city center itself: the northern edge is marked by **Michael's Gate,** the eastern by **Nedbalka Gallery,** and the western by **St. Martin's Cathedral.** Most palaces, museums, landmarks, shops, and cafés of note lie within their borders.

GETTING THERE

Bratislava is located just 1hr from Vienna Central Station (Wien Hauptbahnhof), making it easy to get there, explore some castles and palaces, and be back to your hostel bed in time to catch the latest episode of *Stranger Things*. Best of all? Round-trip tickets through the ÖBB are only €16 and they're valid all day for public transport within Bratislava.

GETTING AROUND

Whether it's good or bad news, one thing is for certain: once you reach downtown, you'll be hoofing it old-style through the historical city center. Most shops and restaurants in the area line cobblestone streets that are accessible only to pedestrians, meaning that to see any of the major landmarks or relax at any of the cafés, you'll have to get there on foot. Luckily, the central district contains all the palaces, museums, and cathedrals.

Swing by...

BLUE CHURCH

Bezručova 2; 25 273 35 72; www.modrykostol.fara.sk; open M-Sa 7am-7:30am and 5:30pm-7pm, Su 7am-noon and 5:30pm-7pm

You've seen countless Gothic cathedrals, dozens of ornate churches, and even a handful of extravagant synagogues since you embarked on your European excursion. Trust us when we say that none of them compare to the whimsical Bratislava Blue Church. Constructed at the turn of the twentieth century, the Blue Church is a new popular destination for fairy-tale weddings and adorable baptisms. Not surprising, considering the **Art Nouveau** building looks like the play set version of Cinderella's Castle. Heck, with all its soft edges and rounded spires, it looks like the architects even thought to baby-proof it, too.

i Free; wheelchair accessible; Mass M-Sa 7am and 6pm, Su 8am, 9:30am, 11am, and 6pm

Check out...

NEBALKA GALLERY

Nedbalova 17; 25 441 02 87; www.nedbalka.sk/en; open Tu-Su 1pm-7pm

Nedbalka is like the dashing new director of a luxury fashion brand who decides to waltz in, completely override the system, and steal the show. The chic, contemporary exhibition is technically a museum, though in reality it functions as a rather impressive and captivating art gallery. Circling each floor feels more like perusing for the newest addition to your home study, rather than wandering around a stiff educational institution. While the fresh-faced collection of over 600 Slovak artworks focuses mainly on oil and multimedia paintings, you'll also find a fair number of dramatic and risqué statues to imitate and send back to the fam for a good laugh (or new blackmail content).

i Admission €5, €3 reduced; wheelchair accessible; English guided tour available €20 if requested in advance

Don't miss...

MICHAEL'S GATE

Michalská 22; 25 443 30 44; plaza open daily 24hr, tower and museum open Tu-F 10am-5pm, Sa-Su 11am-6pm

Either times have changed or our eyes have gotten really bad because we certainly didn't see a grand wrought-iron gate or flashing neon "Welcome to Bratislava" sign here. Then again, the only preserved gate of the city's fortification system dates to the fourteenth century, so maybe we should cut it some slack. While Michael's Gate(way) to fame goes back hundreds of years, it certainly knows how to maintain its status in the public eye. Each day, the shops and restaurants in the bustling cobblestone streets below overflow with eager travelers, who are wined, dined, and serenaded by some of the best that Bratislava has to offer. We recommend ascending the tower for an enchanting view of **Bratislava Castle** and **Old Town,** before retiring to the plaza to people-watch and soak in the local culture.

i Museum admission €5, €3 reduced; no wheelchair accessibility

Grab a bite at...

URBAN HOUSE ($)

Laurinska 14; 90 400 10 21; www.urbanhouse.sk/en; open M-F 9am-midnight, Sa 9am-2am, Su 9am-11pm

Pizza for breakfast? Piping hot with crunchy crust and ooey-gooey layers of cheese? A slice that wasn't pulled from the back of the fridge in a hungover, half-hearted attempt at nutrition after a rough night out on the town? Yes, please. Though the rest of the tasty lunchtime treats at Urban House aren't available until 1pm on the weekends, the hipster bistro understands that there are some insatiable needs on a schedule of their own. After all, you can't have a sign suggesting that pizza is like sex (even when it's bad, it's good) if you can't deliver. Luckily, artisan pizza isn't the only crowd-favorite that the artsy café serves up. Early risers can sink into an oversized leather chair with a simple filter coffee and scrumptious chia pudding, while #Instafamous wannabe influencers can display their avocado toast in front of a book-lined wall.

i Breakfast from €5, lunch from €7, drinks from €2.50; vegetarian options available; limited wheelchair accessibility; outdoor seating available record shop. Despite wearing about five different hats (it's also a kino), it works. In fact, Phil just wouldn't be Phil if it didn't have an eclectic and antique yet somehow chic vibe. Here, visitors are invited to grab any ol' cookbook, graphic novel, memoir, romance, or fairy tale off the shelves and crack open the spine while enjoying a rich double espresso macchiato or a refreshing mint tea lemonade. If you like it (or stain it or tear it), you buy it. If not, back on the shelf it goes, eager to find a new home, and off you go to find solace in a deep bowl of muesli or a giant, delicious slice of apple pie.

i Breakfast from €7.50 (served daily until 4pm), snacks from €4, drinks from €3; vegetarian options available; limited wheelchair accessibility; outdoor seating available

NIGHTLIFE

KRYPT

Berggasse/Wasagasse; www.krypt.bar; open Th-Sa 8pm-close

Glamorous cocktail bar? Clandestine underground location? Architectural masterpiece? Check, check, and check. Once a semi-legal jazz club during the 1950s and 1960s, today the chic space serves exquisite cocktails in a jaw-dropping vault cellar. Unlike the unsettling **Habsburg Crypt** up the street, this Krypt is notably void of dead, decaying royal bodies. In fact, the exotic, refined bar is nothing short of lively and soulful, especially late on Friday nights. Join the mix of young professionals and stylish Viennese at the flawless marble-and-walnut bar counter or cozy up to your new neighbor at an intimate booth in the alcove. Here, smart fashion is a must, and mood lighting is a given. After all, how else is the contemporary, classy cavern supposed to live up to its mysterious and refined origins?

i No cover, drinks from €10; press white doorbell for entry

TRAVEL SHACK VIENNA

Mariahilfer Gürtel 21; 43 1 9610131; www.travelshackvienna.com; open daily 5pm-4am

The backpack-wearing dog with antlers logo outside the entrance should have been the first indication that nights at the raunchy dive bar are a tad unusual. The second hint? Two words: meat pies. You probably shouldn't trust the empanada-shaped brown lumps in the case near the door. No matter how enticing they look after your third "Tequila Suicide," nothing is worth the risk of accidental food poisoning. As it is, the happy hour drink deals and game-day-level college scene already have you on your way to alcohol poisoning. At the risk of sounding like your (very wise) mother, we'll echo Travel Shack Vienna's constant reminders to drink responsibly. Though the traveling, young crowd is constantly changing, the eclectic bar's disco balls and specialty "Cum Shots" show up to the party daily. Keep 'em coming.

i No cover, drinks and specialty shots from €3

CLUB U

Otto Wagner Pavillon Karlsplatz; 43 1 5059904; www.club-u.at; open daily 9pm-4am

Club who? Club U. As in, club you above the head with techno music, then nurse you back to health with soulful tunes. Good thing the intimate club serves up some strong (and cheap) cocktails to take off that edge. While there are a lot of things that the U could stand for—upbeat, unequivocal, unexpected, underpants—a quick look around Karlsplatz will have you realizing that Club U's name refers to Vienna's underground trains, which connect directly to the basement via a small, hidden passage. Even without the crowded dance floor, double bar, and petite garden, a visit to the eclectic club would be worth it just to see the Art Nouveau architecture of the Otto Wagner Pavillon in which it's housed. En garde to the avant-garde!

i No cover, wine from €2, beer from €4, cocktails from €5; cocktail happy hour 9pm-11pm

AUSTRIA ESSENTIALS

MONEY

Tipping: It is common for service charges (10-12.5%) to be included in the bill at restaurants, so check whether the tip has already been added. In cases where tips have not been included, it is customary to leave 5-10%. If you receive exceptional service at establishments that have already included the service charge, you can add an extra small tip (generally no more than 5%). Patrons typically round to the nearest full euro amount. For example, if the waiter states that the price of the bill is €8, respond with €9 and they will include the tip. It is standard to tip a taxi driver roughly 10% and public toilet attendants around €0.50.

Taxes: Most Austrian goods include a 20% VAT in their listed price. A reduced tax of 10% is applied to food, drinks, hotel accommodations, books, and newspapers, while a reduced tax of 13% is applied to agricultural products, transportation, and admission to cultural events like theaters. Non-EU visitors can claim VAT refunds within three months of purchase. To do so, request a Tax Free Shopping Check (export papers) from the retailer, and make sure to keep the original receipt. Present both, along with the goods, at the airport Customs Service to have the invoice stamped and approved. Mail the stamped invoice back to the original store upon return to your home country.

HEALTH AND SAFETY

Local Laws and Police: Austrian police are reliable and generally have a visible presence throughout cities, especially downtown and in major transportation hubs. Be sure to have your passport with you when interacting with police officers, as they may ask to see it. Under Austrian law, if you do not have your passport on you, you must be able to produce it within one hour. Local laws vary.

Drugs and Alcohol: The legal drinking age is 16 for beer and wine, and 18 for spirits. Of note is that open containers are legal on the streets in Austria, though not on public transportation. That said, drinking in public in Vienna is largely frowned upon. Public drunkenness is very uncommon and can not only carry hefty fines but also jeopardize your safety. Use or possession of illegal drugs in Austria carry harsh prison sentences and exorbitant fines. Tobacco products can be purchased in grocery stores or tobacco stores (marked with a sign of a cigarette), though sales to those under the age of 18 are illegal.

Prescription Drugs: Common pain-relieving drugs such as aspirin, ibuprofen (Advil), acetaminophen (Tylenol) and antihistamines are available at Austrian pharmacies (*apotheken*). Most drugs, including antibiotics, require a prescription, so plan accordingly and travel with them in their original packaging.

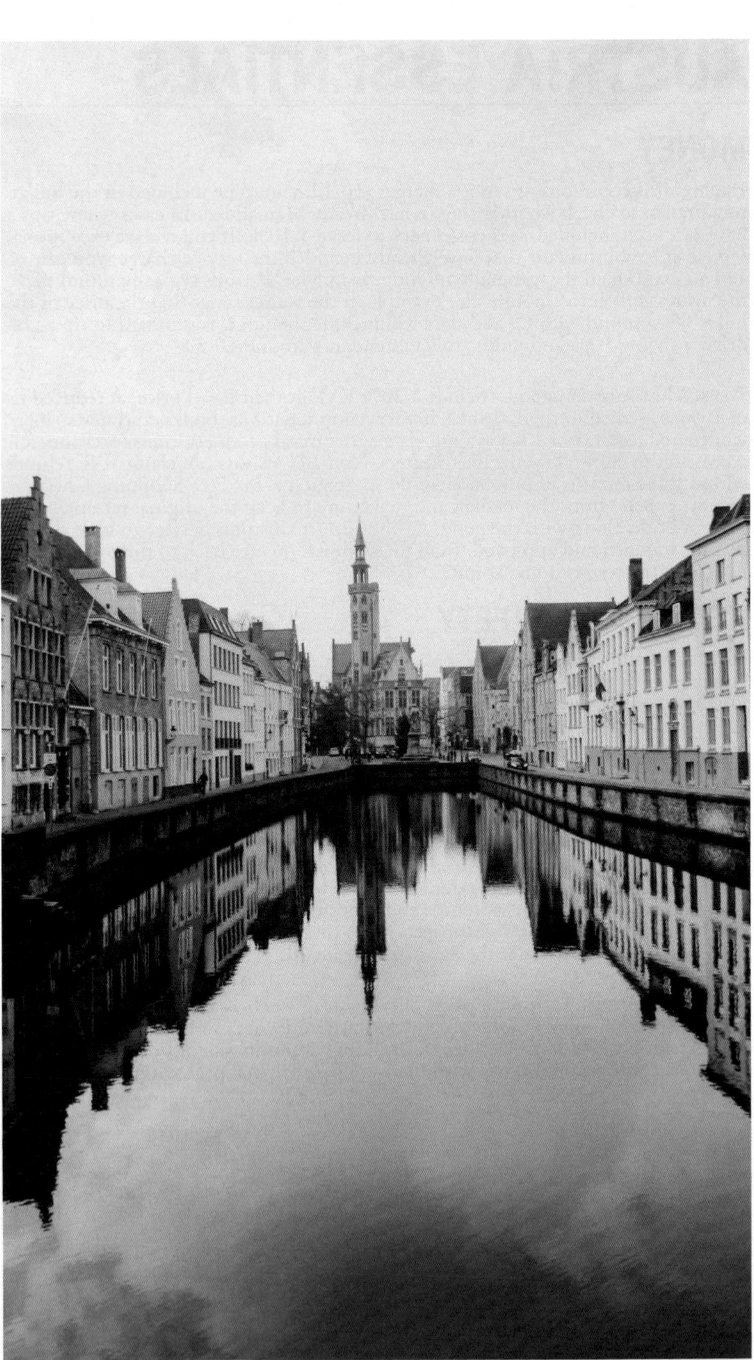

BELGIUM

Belgium is a country that tends to be misunderstood. Questions like "They speak French and Dutch?", "Why would you go to Brussels?", and "But I thought (insert invention here) was from France?" might get thrown around a lot, but Belgium is worth a visit and, at the very least, an attempt to understand its vibrant, multifaceted culture. Its northern Flemish and southern Wallonian halves cause some linguistic and political tension, but the people of Belgium primarily, and proudly, see themselves as Belgian.

While the countryside is studded with small, idyllic Medieval towns and the natural beauty of the Ardennes provides for a stunning rural backdrop, Belgium's urban centers explode with art, architecture, and food. Brussels, the capital, also serves as the seat of the European Union and NATO, which guarantees a continuous stream of young, international professionals looking to help change the world (and to blow off steam after a long day).

As far as Belgian specialties go, it's not all chocolate, beer, waffles, and Belgian (not French) fries. Moules-frites, jenever, carbonade flamande, and waterzooi are all local delicacies that provide even more fodder for a hungry traveler's stomach. In the art world, Belgium knocks it out of the park with legendary Flemish Primitives like Jan van Eyck, Baroque painters like Peter Paul Rubens, and surrealists like René Magritte. Though it's sometimes overlooked as a destination in the typical Eurotrip itinerary, the country is stuffed with undiscovered gems that are hipper, cheaper, and less touristy than those you'd find on the beaten path.

BRUSSELS

Coverage by **Sam Lincoln**

Everything in Brussels has two names—one Dutch and the other French. Even the city itself has two different names—the Dutch Brussel and the French Bruxelles. This linguistic mélange reflects its melting pot status and aptitude for letting otherwise distinct cultures flourish alongside one another. Bruxellois tend to be laid-back and welcoming, especially as Brussels is less of a tourist madhouse than many other European cities. Thanks to "Brusselization," the term for the city's late-20th century habit of tearing down historic buildings and slapping modern high-rises in the middle of otherwise sleepy neighborhoods, even the tourist hotspots have their gold-covered guild houses sitting right next to looming glass and steel banks and corporate offices. The result? Brussels feels like a real, living city, unlike some of its painstakingly preserved counterparts throughout Europe. Students, businesspeople, and tourists intermingle in downtown cafés and restaurants, and the streets are awash with Dutch, English, and French conversation. Brussels is a high-energy spot full of wonderful food—it's got some of the most Michelin star restaurants of any city in the world, but delicious budget dining options also abound—spacious parks full of middle-aged joggers, and vibrant nightlife.

ORIENTATION

The beautiful squares full of historic architecture and ensuing mobs of tourists mostly lie in the city center, with **The Grand Place** being by far the busiest and most photogenic one. To the southeast rises the **Mont des Arts**, a hilltop neighborhood full of museums, concert halls, and the royal palace. On the southern side of the hill is the trendy **Sablon** neighborhood, home to lots of art galleries and trendy chocolate shops, while down the hill to the east lies the **European Quarter**. Here you'll find quite a few young professionals, the headquarters of the **European Union**, and eventually the stately **Parc du Cinquantenaire.** Just northwest of the Grand Place sits the increasingly hip Dansaert neighborhood, which boasts both eclectic shopping and amazing restaurants. North of the city proper is the Laeken neighborhood, home to the **Atomium** statue, the spacious **Parc du Laeken**, and the royal family's full-time residence. South of the city center is the upscale **Ixelles** neighborhood, through the middle of which runs the uber-chic Avenue Louise straight to the lovely **Bois de la Cambre** park.

ESSENTIALS

GETTING THERE

Brussels Airport lies northeast of the city center. The easiest way to get into the city is by train, which you can catch right from the airport for €8.90. Much farther away from the city sits the Charleroi airport, where budget airline (think Ryanair) flights to Brussels land. You save around 40 minutes by taking a taxi into the city center from there, but the taking the A bus to Charleroi Sud and then the train to Brussels proper also works. The most centrally located train station is, of course, Brussels Central, but the Brussels North (Bruxelles-Nord/Brussels-Noord) and Brussels Middle (Bruxelles-Midi/ Brussels-Zuid) stations may be more convenient depending on where you're staying.

GETTING AROUND

Bus, tram, and metro lines run across the city and are fairly easy to use. It's possible to use the same type of ticket for all three. Tickets cost €2.10 if purchased ahead of time, but €2.50 if bought onboard. To navigate the city center, it's easier to walk, rent a bike from the Villo! Service (€1.60 for a day, or €8.20 for a week), or rent an electric scooter from a service like Lime (prices vary, starting at €1 to unlock your ride and €0.15 per minute of riding).

PRACTICAL INFORMATION

Tourist Offices: The website visit.brussels has two office locations: one up on the Mont des Arts and one right in the town hall. Mont des Arts (Rue Royale 2-4, 02 513 89 40; visit.brussels/en; open M-F 9am-6pm, Sa-Su 10am-6pm).

Banks/ATMs/Currency Exchange: There are banks located throughout the city and ATMs are easy to find close to any of the shopping centers. An ING bank location (with an ATM) is just a few steps from the Grand-Place (Rue du Marché Aux Herbes 9; 02 506 42 90; open M 8:30am-1pm, 2pm-5pm, T 8:30am-1pm, W 8:30am-1pm, 2pm-5pm, Th 8:30am-1pm, F 8:30am-1pm, 2pm-5pm).

Post Offices: There's a post office a few blocks north of the Grand-Place (Anspachlaan 1/5, 02 201 23 46; open M-F 8:30am-6pm, Sa 10am-4pm).

Public Restrooms: Restrooms are easy to find around Brussels and most cafés will let you use their restroom.

Internet: Wi-Fi is easy to find in Brussels. You can find free Wi-Fi at cafés and the wifi.brussels service has placed free hotspots around the city in main public areas.

BGLTQ+ Resources: Brussels is a very progressive city, and its Rainbowhouse is home to many BGLTQ+ organizations that serve the Brussels area. Their website is a great place to start looking for community spaces and events, or visit their office for more information (Rue du Marché au Charbon 42; 02 503 59 90; open M-F 10am-6pm).

EMERGENCY INFORMATION

Emergency Number: 112.

Police: The Bruxelles Capitale Ixelles police force has a number of stations throughout the city, but one that serves the city center is on the Rue du Marché au Charbon (Rue de Marché au Charbon 30; 02 279 77 11; open daily 24hr).

US Embassy: The US Embassy in Brussels is located on embassy row just across from the Parc de Bruxelles (Boulevard du Régent 27; 02 811 40 00; be.usembassy.gov; open M-F 7:30am-5:30pm).

Rape Crisis Center: The Centre de Prise en charge des Violences Sexuelles of CHU Hospital welcomes all victims of sexual violence (320 Rue Haute; 02 535 45 42; open daily 24hr).

Hospitals: The hospital that serves the city proper is CHU Saint-Pierre. It has a special International Patients Service for travelers in need of medical attention.

- CHU Saint-Pierre (13 Rue des Alexiens, emergency department at 290 Rue Haute; stpierre-bru.be/en/international-services; the international patients service may be reached at 02 506 71 41).

Pharmacies: Pharmacies in Brussels are not open 24/7, but instead pharmacies will rotate through holding the "night shift." To find out which pharmacies are open when, head to upb-avb.be/pharmacies-de-garde. The website is in French, but has an interactive list of the city's pharmacies and a chart displaying which ones are open during the night.

- Universal Pharmacy (Rue Antoine Dansaert 1; 25 11 89 66; open M-Sa 9am-7pm)

SIGHTS

CULTURE

THE GRAND-PLACE

Grand Place; open daily 24hr

The Grand-Place reigns supreme as the indisputable cherry on top of Brussels' pile of beautiful and dramatic architecture. Located dead-center in the city proper, the square is the beating heart and is fittingly featured on a great many of its tourism-focused publications. Its history stretches back well into the **Middle Ages,** but thanks to a particularly ruthless cannon barrage from the French during the **9 Years' War,** almost all of the Grand-Place's gilded guild halls (ha) were built in the mid-1690s. Because of its beauty and prominence, expect to find it full of people throughout the day. That is, unless you happen to visit in mid-August on an even-numbered year, when more than 500,000 flowers carpet the center of the square.

i Free, wheelchair accessible

BOZAR CENTER FOR FINE ARTS

Rue Ravensteinstraat 23; 02 507 84 30; bozar.be/en; exhibitions open T-W 10am-6pm, Th 10am-9pm, F-Su 10am-6pm, concert/performance/spectacle times vary

The Bozar Center for Fine Arts supports and provides a platform for the arts. During the day, it hosts expositions and exhibitions in fine art, literature, cinema, architecture, theater, dance...the list goes on. It's a space for both rising stars and established artists to present their crafts, and as a complement lectures and debates are also held to help promote dialogue and critical thinking amongst locals and visitors alike. On evenings throughout the year, musicians from many genres (with an emphasis on jazz and classical) also put on concerts. With its constant support of both Belgian and international artists, Bozar shines like a star in Brussels's rich art scene as a standout venue for seeing, listening to, and celebrating some outstanding tastemakers and their creativity.

i Show and exhibit prices vary, expositions are €2 on Wednesdays for anyone under 26; wheelchair accessible

LANDMARKS

ATOMIUM

Square de l'Atomium; 02 475 47 75; atomium.be; open daily 10am-6pm

Brussels has some big balls, and the Atomium is here to prove it. Built in preparation for the Brussels World's Fair in 1958, this set of 9 massive steel spheres arranged to resemble the structure of an iron crystal (enlarged 165 billion times) dominates the skyline of northern Brussels and has become something of an emblem for the city. Nowadays, the Atomium opens to visitors throughout the year. Head straight to the uppermost ball to get a bird's-eye view of the city; or take a set of escalators and stairs to the lower spheres, which host an annually rotating set of exhibitions that take advantage of the sculpture's unique architecture and historic setting.

i Admission €15, €8 students, last admission 30 minutes before closing; the highest sphere (the view!) is wheelchair accessible, but the lower spheres are not

CINQUANTENAIRE ARCH

Cinquantenaire Park/Rue des Ménapiens 18; T-Su 9am-5pm

Nestled at the back of the beautiful **Cinquantenaire Park** is the Cinquantenaire Arch, a monumentally triumphal arch originally planned for the 50th anniversary of Belgian independence and expanded gradually throughout the early twentieth century. Though the arch looks beautiful from the ground, climb to the top for the real treat: a view of the surrounding city. Unlike many urban vantage points, it's free to access (and worth every penny). Unfortunately, however, you must go through the **Royal Museum of the Armed Forces and Military History,** which isn't free. On the brightside, the museum is packed with military gear, vehicles, and weaponry from Belgium's history.

i Admission to museum €10, €8 reduced; no wheelchair accessibility to arch

SAINT MICHAEL AND SAINT GUDULA CATHEDRAL

Place Sainte-Gudule; 02 217 83 45; cathedralisbruxellensis.be/en; open M-F 7am-6pm, Sa 8am-5pm, Su 1-6pm

Brussels's imposing cathedral sits on a hillside above the rest of the city. Inside, it's got everything you know and love about European cathedrals: sky-high vaulted ceilings, ornate gilding on the statuary, and lots of marble. However, two things set this cathedral apart from the competition. One is the pulpit, an exquisite wooden structure sculpted to depict the garden of Eden, complete with Adam and Eve's expulsion from said garden. The second is the cathedral

under the cathedral—excavations related to a renovation in the 80s revealed an old Romanesque church lying in the footprint of the current cathedral, and those ruins are preserved in an exhibit underneath the cathedral.
i Free admission to the cathedral proper, church treasures exhibit €2, old church archeological site €1; limited wheelchair accessibility

SAINT NICHOLAS CHURCH

Rue au Beurre; 02 513 80 22; upbxlcentre.be/eglises/saint-nicolas; open M-F 10am-5:30, Sa-Su 9am-6pm

It's all too fitting that the patron saint of this church, situated right by one of Brussels's best shopping areas, is **Saint Nicholas,** also the patron saint of merchants. In fact, the exterior of the church is actually lined with storefronts. Typical Chrisitan iconography fills the interior, though. A few things that make Saint Nicholas stand out: the striking, vibrant stained glass window at the back of the church (best seen on a day with plenty of sun) and the show-stealing altar in the **Chapel of Our Lady of Peace** at the front of the church.
i Free; limited wheelchair accessibility

MUSEUMS

MUSÉE HORTA

Rue Américaine 25; 02 543 04 90; hortamuseum.be/en; open T-F 2pm-5:30pm, Sa-Su 11am-5:30pm

In Brussels, Victor Horta is synonymous with the **Art Nouveau** movement that swept through the city around the turn of the twentieth century. In fact, he introduced it to the city for the first time in the early 1890s with his **Hôtel Tassel**. Between 1898 and 1901, the prominent architect and designer designed and built his own exquisite house, and since the late 1960s it's been open to the public as a testament to his vision and to the beauty of the movement he crusaded. A residence originally meant to house three people and now subject to tens of thousands of visitors annually, phones, cameras, and other electronic devices are not permitted within the premises. But trust us—you'll be so enraptured by the architecture around you that you won't notice the lapse in your 'gram.
i Admission €10, €5 reduced; last entry 30 minutes before closing; no wheelchair accessibility

AUTOWORLD

Parc du Cinquantenaire 11; 02 736 41 65; autoworld.be; open Apr 1-Sep 30 daily 10am-6pm, Oct 1-Mar 31 M-F 10am-5pm, Sa-Su 10am-6pm

Occupying one of the large exhibition halls built into the Cinquantenaire Arch complex in **Cinquantenaire Park**, Autoworld is a museum dedicated to the automobile. Based around the car collection of the Mahy family, the main floor of the museum is organized into several showcases of the different eras and competing automotive companies. Upstairs, the focus shifts to the world of automotive design and racing. You'll see a fair share of Ferraris, Lamborghinis, and Porsches, but the highlights of the museum are the hidden gems of the automobile world—cars like an amphibious sedan and a nonsensical three-wheeler designed by an aircraft manufacturer.
i Admission €12, €9 reduced, audio guide included; wheelchair accessible

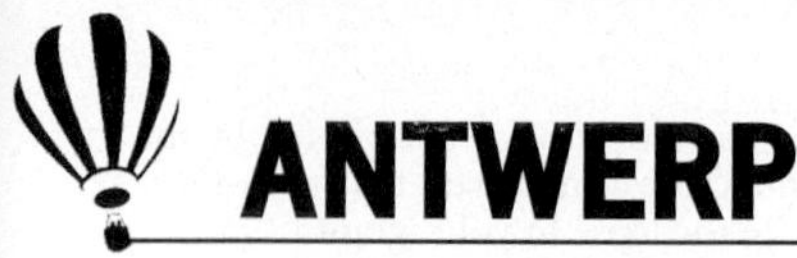

ANTWERP

From a castle on the river to a main square sprinkled with gold-plated guildhalls, Antwerp talks a big game and manages to deliver. The city is dripping in elegance: its marble-lined train station is considered one of the world's most beautiful, and more than 80 percent of the world's rough diamonds pass through its legendary diamond district. Firmly on the Dutch side of things, Antwerp still boasts a strong international community and a worldly vibe—you'd be surprised by how much BBQ you can find here. Whether you're strolling along the Scheldt River, exploring its historic Oude Stad district and its Flemish Renaissance architecture, or just hopping from museum to museum to museum (there are a lot of museums), a day in Antwerp will be a welcome change of pace and scenery from the hustle and bustle of Brussels.

Arrive at the gorgeous **Antwerpen-Centraal** train station, which, despite the name, sits to the east of much of the historic city center and famous sights. The station is right next to the **Antwerp Zoo** at the northeastern corner of the **diamond district.** Due west stretches the main shopping street of **De Keyserlei,** which runs through the city and changes names to **Meir, Schoenmarkt, Reyndersstraat,** and, further west, to **Vlasmarkt.** Plenty of museums and restaurants are scattered around the street as it makes its way towards the river and through the **Oude Stad,** or "Old City." Just to the north lives the magnificent cathedral and the iconic guild-hall-lined **Grote Markt** square, while to the south lie some of the city's most prominent museums and the theater district, **Theaterbuurt.**

GETTING THERE

Trains, both international and national, arrive at Antwerpen-Centraal, the city's main train station on the eastern side of the city with easy connections to the bus and metro. Trains stopping in Antwerp depart from Brussels' Central Station about every 10min. throughout the day—for an exact schedule and to purchase tickets, visit the SNCB website or download their app. There's also a small international airport serving Antwerp, to which the Antwerpen-Berchem train station (Antwerp's southernmost train station) provides national connections. Buses 51, 52, and 53 depart every 15 min. from the airport and take you to Antwerpen-Berchem in less than 10 min.

GETTING AROUND

Antwerp has a bus and tram system, for which tickets can be purchased at machines located at many of the stops and some newsstands or supermarkets. An individual ticket costs €3, while a day ticket costs €7. In addition, you can rent bikes from Antwerp's public bike rental service or rent scooters from a service like Lime or Bird. Bikes are free for the first 30 minutes, €0.50 for the second, €1 for the third, and €5/hr for every hr thereafter. Scooter prices vary, but Lime tends to be on the cheaper side starting at €1 to rent and €0.15 per min. of riding.

Check out...

DIAMOND LAND

Appelmansstraat 33A; 03 369 07 80; diamondland.be; tour times vary

How could you visit the diamond capital of the world and not see some diamonds? At DiamondLand, get a guided tour of a diamond showroom and see expert goldsmiths and diamond polishers at work making beautiful jewelry. The tour introduces you to how diamonds are cut and prepared for sale while teaching you about the quality assessments that give diamonds their sky-high prices. Your guide also shows you dozens of different diamonds, lets you get a closer look at the intricacies of well-cut stones, and pulls out countless examples of diamond jewelry. If you get lucky, they might even let you slap some of that ice—tens of thousands of euros of it—on your wrist for a quick photo. Then, in typical industry fashion, they try to sell it to you.

i Free tours (reserve through their website); no wheelchair accessibility

Swing by...

ANTWERP CATHEDRAL

Handschoenmarkt; 03 213 99 51; mkaweb.be/site/english/050.html; open M-F 10am-5pm, Sa 10am-3pm, Su 1pm-5pm

Europe's great cathedrals once housed dozens of exquisite oil paintings from some of the world's most celebrated painters, crafted specifically for religious use. Though many of the cathedrals have since relinquished their collections to various prominent art museums, Antwerp's cathedral managed to win back its paintings. Thus, instead of massive bare stone walls and pillars, lavish triptychs and altarpieces painted by various Flemish masters, including the famous Peter Paul Rubens, fill the cathedral. The front of the cathedral also exhibits a few contemporary art installations; most striking is a life-size migrant camp cast in bronze and painted blue, white, and gold. Should you grow hungry during your visit, there's also an in-house bistro—we'd like to see the Vatican top that.

i Admission €6, €4 reduced; wheelchair accessible

Grab a bite at...

AMADEUS ANTWERPEN 1 ($$)

Sint Paulusplaats 20; 493 09 33 29; madeus-resto.be/en/amadeus-antwerpen-1-aan-de-kaaien; open M-Th 6pm-11pm, F-Sa 6pm-24pm, Su 5pm-11pm

Walking into the first Antwerp Amadeus location (there are now two) feels like stepping into a 50s diner that's been cross-bred with a gilded-age barber shop. A waiter quickly ushers you to a table topped with a red-and-white checkered tablecloth and a jug of merlot. Once you sit down, you face a simple choice: do you want all-you-can-eat ribs, or do you want all-you-can-eat ribs? Answer correctly and you'll soon be served a rack of ribs longer than your forearm, a baked potato with a very garlic-y house mustard, and a gravy boat full of the house barbecue sauce. They've certainly got a clever business model—you'll be lucky if you can finish your first serving of ribs.

i All-you-can-eat ribs €17.95; vegetarian and gluten-free options available; limited wheelchair accessibility

CENTRE BELGE DE LA BANDE DESSINÉE (BELGIAN COMIC STRIP CENTER)

Rue des Sables 20; 02 219 19 80; cbbd.be; open daily 10am-6pm

Bandes dessinées, or comic strips, hold an important place in Belgian culture. Humorous characters like **Tintin** and **Asterix** are household names, and we can see why. The medium casts a wide net, including everything from serious and intricately painted dramas to wordless collections of humorous short scenes. The Centre Belge de la Bande Dessinée, housed in a beautiful former department store designed by Art-Nouveau legend Victor Horta, is a tribute to Belgium's contributions to(and obsession with) this iconic art form. The museum breaks down the comic strip creation process into the drawing, script-writing, and production processes, and culminates with numerous displays of the finished works of Belgian artists and authors. After exploring the museum, visitors can flip through hundreds of comic books in the library and bookstore.

i Admission €10, €7 reduced; wheelchair accessible

MUSEUM OF MUSICAL INSTRUMENTS

Montagne de la Cour 2; 2 545 01 30; mim.be/en; open M-F 9:30am-5pm, Sa-Su 10am-5pm

It's hard to say what's cooler—the museum itself, or the beautiful Art Nouveau building in which it resides. Step past the famous steel facade to be greeted by several floors packed with every instrument imaginable. And by that we really mean every. instrument. imaginable. There are dozens of different types of pianos, dozens of variations of the violin, and an endless amont of drums. At some points, the line between instrument and sculpture blurs wonderfully, but the audio guide always sets the record straight by offering you an example of what the strange, curved thing in front of you actually sounds like.

i Admission €10, €4 reduced; audio guide €2; wheelchair accessible

MUSÉES ROYAUX DES BEAUX-ARTS DE BELGIQUE (ROYAL MUSEUMS OF FINE ARTS OF BELGIUM)

Mont des Arts; 02 508 32 11; fine-arts-museum.be/en; Old Masters & Fin-de-Siècle Museum open T-F 10am-5pm, Sa-Su 11am-6pm, Magritte Museum open M-F 10am-5pm, Sa-Su 11am-6pm, Weirtz & Meunier Museums open T-F 10am-noon and 12:45-5pm

This consortium of museums is perched on top of the aptly named **Mont des Arts** (hill of the arts), and collectively they showcase the best of Beligan art in five distinct institutions. There's the **Old Masters Museum,** the **Fin-de-Siècle** (end of the nineteenth century) **Museum,** and then the **Meunier, Wiertz,** and **Magritte** museums. Those last three are named for some of the Belgium art world's heaviest hitters—make sure you don't miss **René Magritte's** wackadoodle surrealism and drawings of a pipe. Plus, it's not like any other museums are open on Mondays.

i Admission for all museums €15, €5 reduced, admission to Old Masters &Fin-deSiècle museums €10, €3 reduced, admission to Magritte museum €10, €3 reduced, admission to Wiertz & Meunier museums free; wheelchair accessible

OUTDOORS

PARC DE BRUXELLES

Place de Palais; open daily 24hr

The Parc de Bruxelles, also called the Parc de Royal, is the oldest public park in Brussels. It's a lovely expanse of trees and paths that sits right on top of the **Mont des Arts** in front of the **Royal Palace.** Home to a huge fountain and numerous little cafés that offer shady outdoor seating, the park is a beautiful place for a walk—or, if you want to pretend to be a local, a vigorous jog—and also hosts concerts throughout the warmer months. In the opposite corner from the Royal Palace sits the **Théâtre Royal Du Parc,** which offers a classy opportunity to catch a show at the end of a long day of exploring the city.

i Free; wheelchair accessible

PARC DU LAEKEN

Open daily 24hr

Parc du Laeken, a grassy tree-studded expanse outside of the city proper right next to the **Atomium** sculpture, is a wonderful alternative to the stately but still urban parks that dot downtown Brussels. Laeken sits in a slightly less urban area and is landscaped with an emphasis on wide open lawns and tree-lined paths, not fountains and mini-cafés. In other words, it's probably the best place in Brussels to throw a frisbee with some friends. As an added bonus, there's a beautiful gothic monument to **King Leopold (I or II or III maybe IVIVIVI?)** towards the middle of the park with a view straight to the stately royal residence, **Chateau du Laeken**, across the street.

i Free; wheelchair accessible

FOOD

NOORDZEE ($)

Sint-Katelijnestraat 45; 02 513 11 92; noordzeemerdunord.be; open Tu-Sa 11am-6pm, Su 11am-8pm

Let us paint you a picture: it's a lazy Saturday morning, and the fishmonger's shop is packed with people. This isn't just any fishmonger's, however. This is Noordzee, and the object of the crowd's fixation is the stainless steel counter that runs around the exterior of the corner shop. On one side of the counter, people line up (sort of) to order some of the freshest seafood around. On the other side of the counter, a singing group of young line cooks prepare food at lightning speed. Open-faced fried tuna sandwiches and sizzling swordfish steaks accompany bottles of Argentinian white in the ice buckets and are passed along to waiting customers, who must bring their feast over to the only available dining area: a stretch of high-top tables across the street.

i Entrées from €5; wheelchair accessible

9 ET VOISINS ($$)

Arteveldestraat 1; 02 512 90 49; 9-et-voisins.be/en; open M-F 4pm-1am, Sa-Su noon-1am

For traditional, reasonably priced Belgian fare, why not head to a traditional, reasonably priced Belgian restaurant? Enter 9 et Voisins, which started serving Brussels almost a century ago and probably hasn't changed its menu since. Situated in a high-ceiled building with a cozy brick interior, this great spot serves generous portions of hearty Belgian goodness. We highly recommend the sausages with stoemp, a typical Flemish dish. As should be expected, there's plenty of sidewalk seating available in the warmer months. The only non-traditional thing about the place is that it stays open on Mondays.

i Entrées from €12.69, beer from €2.47; vegetarian and gluten free options available; limited wheelchair accessibility

CAFÉ GEORGETTE ($)

Rue de la Fourche 37/39; 02 512 18 12; cafegeorgette.be/en/cafe-restaurant-chip-shop-chez-georgette; open M-Th noon-10pm, F-Sa noon-11pm, Su noon-10pm

Café Georgette seems like a typical street-side restaurant just a few blocks up from the **Grand-Place**. Its distinguishing feature is its Belgian

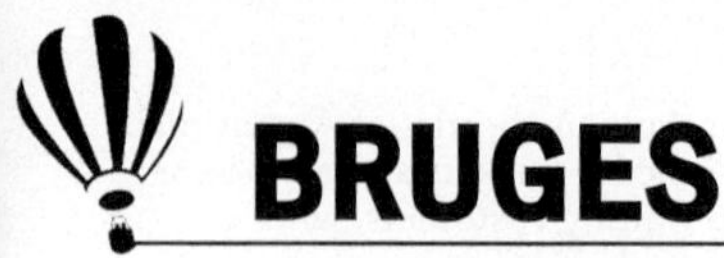

BRUGES

Bruges may be tiny, but it packs a lot of Medieval punch into its small package. The towers of the Church of Our Lady, St. Salvator Cathedral, and the Belfry define the city's historic skyline, while the tourist action centers around the beautiful Place du Marché and its gorgeous Flemish storefronts. If you leave the city center and meander down its small cobblestone streets, you'll find some lesser known gems that go largely unnoticed by the masses. These highlights include a canal-side park filled with swans, numerous tiny local cafés, and some very beautiful architecture.

Navigating Bruges is pretty darn easy—it's about the size of a Walmart parking lot, and most of its tourist hotspots stay close to the central **Place du Marché.** On one side of the square lies the famous **Belfry,** and just south of the square are the **St. Salvator Cathedral** and the **Church of Our Lady.** Heading into town from the train station, you'll probably make your way towards these landmarks along some of Bruges' beautiful shopping streets: **Steenstraat** approaches the Place du Marché from the southwest, while **Vlamingstraat** leads north away from the hubbub and towards a quieter, less touristy area of town.

GETTING THERE

Trains run from Brussels Central Station to Bruges very frequently—it's about an hour-long ride, with departures every 15-20 minutes. Because of Bruges' size, there's only one station and it's within walking distance of the town center.

GETTING AROUND

No need to worry about navigating Flemish public transport in Bruges—it's a supremely walkable city. There are bike rentals available should you wish to get around the outskirts of the city faster.

Check out...

BEER MUSEUM

Breidelstraat 3; 50 69 92 29; mybeerexperience.com; open daily 10am-6pm

Hey, you're in Belgium. Time to bone up on your beer knowledge. Luckily, the Beer Museum—just a few steps off the Place du Marché—is here to help. Step into the museum and explore the beer-brewing process from start to finish through interactive tours. You can even taste raw barley (yum?) and run your hands through buckets of hops. The journey ends at the museum's in-house bar, where you can sample a wide selection of Belgian beer and put your newfound knowledge to work by deconstructing flavor profiles. If you're not careful, you might feel compelled to grow a beard and spend the rest of your travel budget on flannels.

i Admission €16 with beer tasting, €10 without; iPad guide included; no wheelchair accessibility

Don't miss...

THE BELFRY

Markt 7; 05 044 87 43; visitbruges.be/en/belfort-belfry; open daily 9:30am-6pm

Belfries, common in Flanders and Northern France, were celebrated as symbols of municipal autonomy in the Middle Ages. The one in Bruges is stunning—even if getting to the top of this tall tower means €8, a potentially long wait, and 366 steps. The climb pays off when you reach the top and see that Bruges is every bit as photogenic from above as it is from the ground. As an extra treat, every 15 minutes the belfry's elaborate system of bells play a melodic tune. It's only mildly deafening when you're standing two feet away from the bells, but don't worry, you've got a long walk down to recover.

i Admission €12, €10 reduced; no wheelchair accessibility

Swing by...

MUSEUM-GALLERY XPO: SALVADOR DALÍ

Markt 7; dali-interart.be/engl_collecties.htm; open daily 10am-6pm

Bruges might not be the place you expect to find a permanent exhibition dedicated to the works of one of Spain's greatest surrealists, but here we are. From the man who brought you melting clocks, inside the exhibition hall just below the Belfry is a rotating exhibit pulled from one of the world's larger private collections of Dalí's works (its owner happens to be a local). The works look just as wild, explicit, and occasionally disturbing as you'd expect from someone who once said "I am in a permanent state of intellectual erection." The interior of the hall feels like it might have been hastily put together by the maestro himself: there's a disorienting array of mirrors, oddly colored wallpaper, and a number of stuffed peacocks keeping visitors company.

i Admission €10, €8 reduced; wheelchair accessible

Grab a bite at...

@TATTIE'S ($)

Jan Van Eyckplein 3; 05 069 29 54; tattiesbrugge.com; open M-F 8am-5pm, Sa 9am-5pm

For the price of an appetizer at one of the city's more centrally located restaurants, you could get two huge ciabatta paninis filled with tuna, pastrami, chicken—you name it. We're pretty sure we even met Tattie—or who we like to call the abstract idea of the ideal sandwich shop given human form—but either way it's a wonder this place cuts a profit. If you're in need of refreshment, try one of their fresh fruit smoothies and make sure to ask if they have any seasonal varieties available; their rotating specials aren't listed on the menu.

i Sandwiches from €3.40, paninis from €4.20; limited wheelchair accessibility fries, ordered right at a window into their open-air kitchen and served piping hot in a paper cone. These are fries are brought, glowing, from the gods themselves—twice fried in beef fat, accompanied by a house curry-mustard, and just absolutely delicious. Ignore the rest of the menu; €3.50 gets you a veritable mountain of crispy potato goodness. Heading to Georgette for a snack is decidedly one of the better decisions you could make while visiting Brussels.

i Fries from €3.50, wheelchair accessible

FANNY THAI ($)

Jules Van Praet 36; 02 502 64 22; fannythai.com/en; open M-F noon-2:45pm, 6pm-11:15pm, Sa-Su noon-11:15pm

Of the many different Thai restaurants in Brussels (and there are a surprising amount), Fanny Thai stands out not just with its great food but with its wonderful prices. The best quantity to price ratio can be found on the lunch menu, which offers a two-course meal for the price of an appetizer at most of the other nearby restaurants. If you peruse the menu and want more variety, not to worry! **Rue Jules Van Praet** is lined with a remarkable spread of world cuisine, from a cantonese restaurant to a pita shop.

i Lunch from €9.50; vegetarian, vegan, and gluten-free options available; limited wheelchair accessibility; outdoor seating available

KIPKOT ($$)

Place Sainte-Catherine 8; 02 513 06 01; kipkot.be; open T-F noon-2pm, 6:30pm-10pm, Sa noon-10:30pm, Su noon-10pm

Forget chocolate, fries, or beer—sometimes, all you need is some good chicken. That's the specialty of Kipkot, whose two locations in Brussels dole out some of the most scrumptious rotisserie chicken in the city. The restaurants are casual, efficient, and hell-bent on getting you that bird whichever way you want it. Their rotisseries come with a wide variety of sides, from the standard heap of Belgian fries to a delicious apple compote. If rotisserie isn't your thing, the chicken cheeseburger is a filling, yummy, and less expensive option that shouldn't be overlooked.

i 1/4 chicken from €15.50, chicken cheeseburger from €12; vegetarian, vegan, and gluten free options available; limited wheelchair accessibility

LE PAIN QUOTIDIEN ($$)

Rue Antoine Dansaert 16; 02 502 23 61; lepainquotidien.com; open daily 7am-7pm

Though Le Pain Quotidien (meaning "daily bread") now has locations in more than 20 countries, it all started right here in Brussels. Enter the original location close to the center of town and the vibe feels more "local bakery," than "global chain." While locals pop in and out throughout the day to pick up their day's loaf of bread, the best way to experience Le Pain is to stay and sit down for a quick meal. The ol' PQ serves a delicious assortment of breakfast and brunch-y eats on its menu, some of which are mainstays and some of which change seasonally. Tartines, their speciality, are open faced sandwiches served on their signature sourdough bread.

i Tartines from €9.95, coffee from €2.95; vegan, vegetarian, and gluten-free options available; no wheelchair accessibility

NIGHTLIFE

LA PHARMACIE ANGLAISE

Coudenberg 66; 489 56 07 36; lapharmacieanglaise.com; open T-Th 5:30pm-1am, F-Sa 5:30pm-2am

It may surprise you that La Pharmacie Anglaise is not, in fact, an English pharmacy. It is a bar housed inside an old pharmacy. And, this pharma—I mean, bar makes for a stately but extremely unusual cocktail experience. Ring a doorbell and be greeted by a doorman (think steampunk hat and thick beard) who will lead you to armchairs in the book, bottle, and foliage-lined main room. If you want to score a seat, we highly recommend a reservation. Inside find a relatively spacious outdoor patio and a very much not spacious second floor seating arrangement. Once settled, prepare to sort through a menu of sophisticated cocktails and equally sophisticated mocktails prepared with seasonal ingredients. We warn you: the cocktails come at prices that could buy you a full meal elsewhere in the city.

i Cocktails from €14, mocktails from €10; no wheelchair accessibility

DELIRIUM

Impasse de la Fidélité 4; 02 514 44 34; deliriumvillage.com; open M-Th 10am-4am, F-Sa 10am-6am, Sunday 10am-3am

"How can y—how can you come to Brussels and not go to Delirium?" So said a 20-something Belgian, who stumbled past us on a street one evening. Delirium is something of a powerhouse in the Brussels nightlife scene. This so-called "Village" occupies an entire alley just a few steps away from the Grand-Place, and its central location draws mobs of travelers and locals alike throughout the week. The party really starts late on weekend nights, when the village's bars overflow with people looking to have one or two or several dozen of Delirium's record-holding list of over 2000 beers. If you get 2000 beers in and haven't felt a buzz, there's also an absinthe bar (but you have a problem).

i Beer prices vary; no wheelchair accessibility

PLACE DU LUXEMBOURG

European Quarter; hours vary by venue

This stately square in the **European Quarter** completely transforms on Thursday nights. Hundreds of young professionals from the surrounding European institutions, including the **European Parliament,** spill into it right after work to blow off steam—some even come still donning their work suits. If you really want to live like a local, buy some cheap beers from the closest convenience store and claim a place in the grass in the middle of the square. You'll find plenty of English-speaking friends, as much of the European Quarter's international crowd uses English at work.

i Venue prices vary; limited wheelchair accessibility

GHENT

Coverage by **Sam Lincoln**

Quite a bit has happened since people first settled at the confluence of the Lys and Scheldt Rivers in the seventh century. Ghent was a center for the cloth trade during the Middle Ages, was home of some iconic Flemish masters and big dogs in the early northern Renaissance, and even played a hand in ending the War of 1812 between England and the US (see: the Treaty of Ghent). There's a lot of historical appeal, but Ghent also has a sophisticated modern edge thanks to a lively street art scene and institutions like the Design Museum and Public Library. Now a mid-sized city and the capital of the East Flanders province, it boasts scenic inland waterways, old guild halls with stately Flemish gables, and a skyline dominated by the towering spires of a church, a cathedral, and the famous Belfry. It's a charming place to visit, but it's seemingly an even better place to live or study. Unlike some of its painstakingly preserved neighbors, Ghent isn't afraid to throw some bold glass-and-steel architecture here and there and get a little experimental with some of its housing developments. The result is a set of niche bars, photogenic squares, and fascinating museums that make this city the whole package.

ORIENTATION

The waterways that attracted Ghent's first inhabitants still curve through the city, acting as reference points and drawing you to many of the city's cafés and restaurants. On the northern side of the city center, you'll find the famous castle of **Gravensteen**, right on the water. Just south of Gravensteen are the three dominating buildings of Ghent's skyline located in the heart of the city and arranged in a line from west to east: **St. Nicholas's Church**, the **Belfry**, and **St. Bavo's Cathedral.** Just north from there is the historic restaurant and café-lined **Vrijdagmarkt Square**, while outside the city center to the south is **Citadelpark** and two of the city's major art museums, the **Museum voor Schone Kunsten (SMK)** and the **SMAK Contemporary Art Museum.**

ESSENTIALS

GETTING THERE

Ghent is accessible by train from any of Brussels' major train stations, as well as from the Brussels Airport (BRU). Trains will mostly likely run to the Gent-Sint-Pieters Station. For access to Ghent via a private bus service like Flixbus, services might use the Dampoort station. From Sint-Pieters, the #1 tram will take you right to the center of town. From Dampoort, a number of municipal buses will also take you to the center of town but you'd probably be able to walk there just as fast.

GETTING AROUND

While buses and trams criss-cross Ghent, most of the prominent sights and experiences are available within walking distance. Should you want to explore a little further, you can purchase tickets for public transportation through Linjwinkels at some stations and supermarkets—you can also purchase them on the bus or tram, but it'll cost up to 50% more. If you plan on using public transportation frequently, your best bet would be to buy a 1, 3, or 5 day ticket (for €7, €14, or €20, respectively). You can also rent a bike from Fietsambassade—they have locations at Dampoort, Sint-Pieters, and under the Stadshal in the center of town. The prices start at €9 for 4 hours, €12 for a day, and €34 for a week. For guaranteed bike access, you may have to reserve a bike in advance.

PRACTICAL INFORMATION

Tourist Offices: Tourist Information Center (Sint-Veerleplein 5; 9 266 56 60; visit.gent.be/en/see-do/inquiry-desk-visit-gent; open daily 10am-6pm).

Banks/ATMs/Currency Exchange: ATMs are located throughout the city. ING has a branch with an ATM right down the street from the Belfry (Belfortstraat 18; 09 266 19 50; open M-F 9am-12:30pm, ATM open daily 5am-11:30pm).

Post Offices: There's a Belgian Post (bpost) office right down the street from the Cathedral. Added bonus: it has an ATM. Postkantoor Gent Centrum (Lange Kruisstraat 55; open M-F 9:30am-6pm, Sa 9:30am-3pm).

Internet: There is Wi-Fi available in many coffee shops throughout Ghent, as well as at the Ghent Public Library (Miriam Makebaplein 1; 9 210 10 10; open M-Sa 10am-7pm).

BGLTQ+ Resources: Ghent is a progressive city with a large student population, and they actively work to make their city more inclusive to people of all identities. For information on Ghent's progress, visit www.rainbowcities.com/node/82. For BGLTQ+-oriented travel tips focused on Ghent, consider using websites such as Ellgeebe (www.ellgeebe.com/en/destinations/europe/belgium/ghent) or TravelGay (www.travelgay.com/destination/gay-belgium/gay-ghent/). The Belgian LGBTQ hotline is 800 99 533.

EMERGENCY INFORMATION

Emergency Number: 112; for a non-emergency call the police general information line at 09 266 61 11.

Police: The central police station for Ghent is located right by the Belfry, but the main station open 24hr is further away.

- Central location (Belfortstraat 4; 09 266 61 30; open M-Sa 8am-4:30pm, Su 10am-4:30pm).
- General location (Antonius Triest-laan 12; 09 266 61 11; open daily 24hr).

Rape Crisis Center: RAINN hotline (1-800-656-4673) or SOS Viol, a

Belgian hotline for victims of sexual assault (2 534 36 36; open M-Th 9am-5pm, F 1pm-5pm).

Hospitals: Ghent University Hospital is one of the largest hospitals in Belgium.

- Ghent University Hospital (Corneel Heymanslaan 10; 09 332 21 11, call 112 in case of emergency).

Pharmacies: Small Green crosses mark pharmacies, which are located throughout the city. In case of a closed pharmacy during the night or on weekends, some pharmacies have a list of pharmacists available on display. Extra fees may apply.

- Apotheek Cattebeke (Sint-Michielsstraat 15; 09 225 29 65; M-F 8:30am-12:45pm and 1:30pm-6:30pm).

SIGHTS

CULTURE

KLIEN BEGIJNHOF GHENT

Lange Violettestraat 235; kleinbegijnhof-gent.wixsite.com/home; open daily 6:30am-10pm

Our-Lady Ter Hooyen was originally a "beguinage," a residence for women who wished to cohabit in a religious setting without needing to take the formal vows that would be required in a monastery. Today, the homes are no longer used for religious purposes and the place has been converted into a quiet little residential neighborhood. The cobblestone streets are deserted and the sounds of the city are replaced with chirping birds and rustling trees. Its idyllic brick townhouses have been immaculately preserved, and a few otherwise abandoned buildings have been reclaimed and converted into artists' studios making it a marvelous place for a quiet picnic or stroll.

i Free; wheelchair accessible

VRIJDAGMARKT

Vrijdagmarkt; open F 7:30am-1pm, Sa 11am-6:30pm

The Vrijdagmarkt is a square surrounded by eighteenth-century guildhalls that house cafés, bars, and restaurants. However, it's also the site of one of Ghent's oldest traditions. Since 1199, the square transforms into a market on Fridays (hence the name: Vrijdag=Friday, Markt=market). There's also a Saturday market, but "vrijdagenzaterdagmarkt" would be a mouthful even for the Flemish. Once you've explored the market stalls and seen the vendors peddling everything from fresh fish to pantyhose, check out the statue of the statesman **Jacob van Artevelde** (who was murdered here in 1345) and try a selection of the **Dulle Griet** tavern's 500-strong beer list.

i Prices vary; wheelchair accessible

LANDMARKS

BELFRY OF GHENT

Sint-Baafsplein; 9 233 39 54; belfortgent.be/en/information; open daily 10am-6pm

The construction of Ghent's belfry began around 1313. A visit to the bell tower today will take you through the cloth halls (relics from Ghent's textile-trading glory days) and the hidden "secrecy room," where a German command center was concealed with a false floor during World War II. Taking the stairs or elevator up into the tower will reveal the enormous drum and elaborate system of bells. For a special treat, time your visit so that you are in the tower when they chime on the

hour. It's like sitting inside a building-sized music box! This **UNESCO World Heritage** site also displays various dragon vanes in honor of the mascot of the city.

i Admission €8, €2.70 reduced; last ticket sold 30 minutes before closing; no wheelchair accessibility

ST. BAVO'S CATHEDRAL

Sint-Baafsplein; 09 225 16 26; www.sintbaafskathedraal.be/en/index.html; open Apr 1-Oct 31 M-Sa 8:30am-6:00pm, Su 1pm-6pm, Nov 1-Mar 31 8:30am-5pm, Su 1pm-5pm

As one of Ghent's **three major towers**, St. Bavo's Cathedral is an understandable tourist hotspot. In addition to having plenty of typical cathedral things, St. Bavo is also home to the legendary **Ghent Altarpiece**. Also known as the Adoration of the Mystic Lamb, this fifteenth-century 24-panel polyptych was painted by the legendary **Jan van Eyck** and his brother. It's currently undergoing restoration at the **MSK** museum but as panels are completed, they are brought back to their rightful place in the cathedral. Once a day, from noon-1pm, the polyptych is closed so that the equally exquisite exterior may be enjoyed. It's a must-see for anyone passionate about European art.

i Free, altarpiece exhibit €4; cash only

MUSEUMS

DESIGN MUSEUM

Jan Breydelstraat 5; 9 267 99 99; www.designmuseumgent.be/en; open M-T 9:30am-5:30pm, Th-F 9am-5:30pm, Sa-Su 10am-6pm

Tucked inside a grand mansion of a textile magnate, Ghent's Design Museum is a celebration of Belgian design culture in all its shapes and sizes. The exhibits are set up to highlight juxtapositions between the old and the new—you'll find ultramodern, high-concept course on display in wood paneled drawing rooms with hand-painted wallpaper, or a minimalist armchair sitting beside a marble fireplace with woven silk hangings. The museum is also host to a rotating selection of special exhibits that highlight different components of the design process from the use of animal products to the consideration of sustainability.

i Admission €8, €2 reduced; limited wheelchair accessibility

MUSEUM VOOR SCHONE KUNSTEN

Fernand Scribedreef 1; 02 323 67 00; www.mskgent.be/en; open T-F 9:30am-5:30pm, Sa-Su 10am-6pm

The "MSK," a stately museum, sits in the corner of the scenic **Citadel Park**. As one of Ghent's flagship art museums, most of the MSK is dedicated to the exhibition of prominent Dutch artists such as **Panamerenko**. His famous piece Aeromodeller, a large airship, designed to be kept afloat with a large balloon, is among the most memorable artworks displayed at the museum. The MSK is also the site of the ongoing restoration of the **Ghent Altarpiece**, the altarpiece belonging to **St. Bavo's Cathedral** and one of Europe's oldest oil paintings. Because the restoration will take more than a decade to complete, the museum has set up a fascinating exhibit dedicated to exploring the extremely complicated and painstaking process of returning a celebrated painting to its former glory.

Admission €8, €2 reduced; admission to temporary exhibition €12/€2; wheelchair accessible

OUTDOORS

CITADELPARK

Citadelpark; open daily 24hr

The Citadel Park, named after a fortress that used to sit on its grounds in the 1800s, is one of the larger natural spaces in the city. It's got all the trappings of a successful urban park: some beautiful water features (including a waterfall), lots of lawn, and plenty of strategically-placed benches. An old bandstand in the northern half of the park has become a center for comedy, concerts, and the occasional yoga class. The artsiness doesn't stop there, however: right in the middle of the park is Ghent's formidable contemporary arts museum, **Stedelijk Museum voor Actuele Kunst (SMAK),** and right across the street is the city's fine arts museum, **Museum voor Schone Kunsten (MSK).**

Free; limited wheelchair accessibility

FOOD

SOUP'R ($)

Sint Niklaasstraat 9; open T-Sa 11:30am-4pm

There are few food combinations more desirable than the ol' soup and sandwich. Luckily for us, Soup'r has honed their skills in that department down to a science. You can pick from a wide variety of soups and sandwiches from a range of culinary traditions—a brothy Jewish soup here, a Thai noodle soup there. Their drink options are pretty standard, but they've got a killer house elderflower lemonade that's not to be missed. Portion sizes vary, but you'll want at least a small soup to go with a sandwich. A large soup, on the other hand, could be a meal unto itself.

Soup from €4.50, sandwiches from €4; no wheelchair accessibility

BIJ FILIP ($)

Pensmarkt 8; open M-T 11:30am-8:30pm, Th-F 11:30am-8:30pm, Sa-Su 11am-9pm

This tiny little fry stand improbably built into the side of Ghent's historic Grand Butchery might just have the cheapest food in the city. For 2 euros, Filip will serve you up a basket of fries and a sauce of your choice. And, for an additional 1-2 euros you can add a "side" of meats like fried chicken or beef stew. There are a few high top tables scattered outside the stand, but the pro move is to take your fries on an afternoon stroll around the city's gorgeous medieval center. If you're still hungry, you can always order a second round of fries and sides—or a third, or a fourth—and still wind up paying less than you would at any of the nearby restaurants.

Fries from €2, sides from €1.50; wheelchair accessible

FRITUUR TARTAAR ($)

Heilige Geeststraat 3; 499 22 19 07; open T-Su 11:30am-10:30pm

Frituur Tartaar has taken the liberty of putting together a special meal to show off some of Flanders' classic fare. For just 9 euros, you can get a full meal at this hip little restaurant tucked into a side street just across from Ghent's towering **Belfry.** You'll be treated to a hearty beef stew, an extremely generous heap of fries, and your choice of drink. The cashier told us the deal was put together to "educate" tourists, but then he got scolded by his boss. The verdict: it's cheap, authentic Flemish cuisine, but it wasn't *not* designed with tourists in mind.

Stew combo €9; no wheelchair accessibility

VOORUIT ($$)

Sint-Pietersnieuwstraat 23; 09 267 28 20; vooruit.be/en/cafe/Vooruit_Cafe_Terrace; open M noon-8pm, Tu-Sa noon-9:30pm, Su noon-8:30pm

Vooruit is housed in one of Ghent's architectural gems, an old festival center that has since been converted to a concert hall. Besides being one of the city's leading cultural spaces, it also has a beautiful restaurant and terrace perfect for soaking up some sun. Vooruit has the unlikely distinction of being known for its delicious, hearty bowls of spaghetti—a nice break from all those fries you've been eating. Because it's right next to Ghent's major university, Vooruit becomes a major congregating spot for students throughout the school year. Even in summertime, you'll find plenty of young and hip locals hanging out, getting some work done, and sipping on rosé sangria made with Vooruit's secret house recipe.

i Spaghetti €11.70, rosé sangria €8.50; vegan, vegetarian, and gluten-free options available; wheelchair accessible

NIGHTLIFE

'T VELOOTJE

Kalversteeg 4-2; 486 83 86 48; open daily noon-3am

Trying to describe the strange and wonderful experience of having a beer at 't Velootje is like Alice trying to describe Wonderland to your average Joe. You'll be greeted on the tiny street by Lieven, the owner, identifiable by his short shorts and fuzzy beard. An eccentric man with a welcoming spirit, he'll show you his bar-cum-house-cum-storage unit, where bicycles cover just about every vertical and horizontal surface. He even claims to have a bike from Napoleon III. Patrons are encouraged to chat, get to know each other, and sign the thick guest book—people from all over the world have come here for the conversation and the beer. There's even a brewery in Maine that makes a beer named after Lieven.

i Beer from €6; cash only; BGTLQ+ friendly; limited wheelchair accessibility

HOT CLUB

Schuddevisstraatje 2; www.hotclub.gent/index.php; open daily 3pm-3am

At a place with a name like Hot Club, you might expect a dark, sweaty nightclub where the only thing keeping you there is the cover you already forked over. In fact, Hot Club is not a nightclub at all. It's a classy affair—a small jazz bar with live music five nights a week named after **Hot Club de France**, a Parisian jazz club that opened in the 30s. If you duck down a narrow alley, you'll find a charming courtyard and a small bar with a stage and piano at the ready. Hot Club is no party palace (there's a sign hanging on stage reminding guests to be quiet during concerts), but everyone's got a little jazz cat in them.

i Cocktails from €6.50, beer from €2.40; no wheelchair accessibility

'T DREUPELKOT

Groentenmarkt 12; 09 224 21 20; www.dreupelkot.be/t-dreupelkot; open M-Th 11am-1:30am, F 11am-2am, Sa-Su 2pm-2am

Not everybody is a fan of gin, but that may be because not everybody has been to 'T Dreupelkot. This quiet little bar tucked into a picturesque, canal-side building right by Ghent's historic center serves one thing, and one thing only: *genever*, a traditional Dutch liquor and predecessor to gin. Whatever you do, don't ask for mixer. They don't do cocktails. Instead, you should explain what your favorite flavors are and the bartender will guide you through the more than 110 varieties of gin—many of them either made in house or in Ghent—that Dreupelkot has to offer. You can find everything from fruity ginger, blood orange, and pineapple varieties to more unusual ones with flavor descriptions like "tiramisu" or "gingerbread."

i Shots from €2.50; no wheelchair accessibility

BELGIUM ESSENTIALS

VISAS

As an EU member state and a member of the Schengen Zone, you can visit Belgium as a U.S. citizen with no visa for up to 90 days for business and tourist purposes.

MONEY

Tipping: In Belgium, service charges are included in the bill at restaurants, so there is no need to leave a tip; waiters are paid fully for their service. If you receive excellent service, feel free to round up the bill or leave a 5-10% tip. Tips in bars are uncommon.

Taxes: The marked price of goods in Belgium includes a value-added tax (VAT). This tax is generally levied at 21%, although some goods are subjected to higher rates. Non-EU citizens who are taking these goods home unused may be refunded this tax. When making these purchases, make sure to keep your receipts and ask to fill out a VAT Refund Form. Go to the customs office (located at most airports or other border locations) with said goods to have your refund forms stamped before leaving the EU. Refunds must be claimed within three months.

SAFETY AND HEALTH

Local Laws and Police: Police in Belgium are reliable and almost always kind to tourists. If you need assistance, do not hesitate to reach out or ask a patrolling officer.

Drugs and Alcohol: In Belgium, you must be 16 years old to purchase beverages containing less than 1.2% of distilled alcohol and 18 years for buying beverages containing more than 1.2% distilled alcohol. The minimum age requirement for consuming alcoholic beverages is the same as the minimum age requirement for purchasing. Drinking in public is a cultural norm, but public drunkenness is frowned upon. Belgium's attitude towards drugs is traditional and conservative; marijuana is illegal.

BGLTQ+ Travelers: Belgium is quite progressive and has many resources for members of the BGLTQ+ community. There are no legal restrictions on same-sex sexual relations or the organization of BGLTQ+ events.

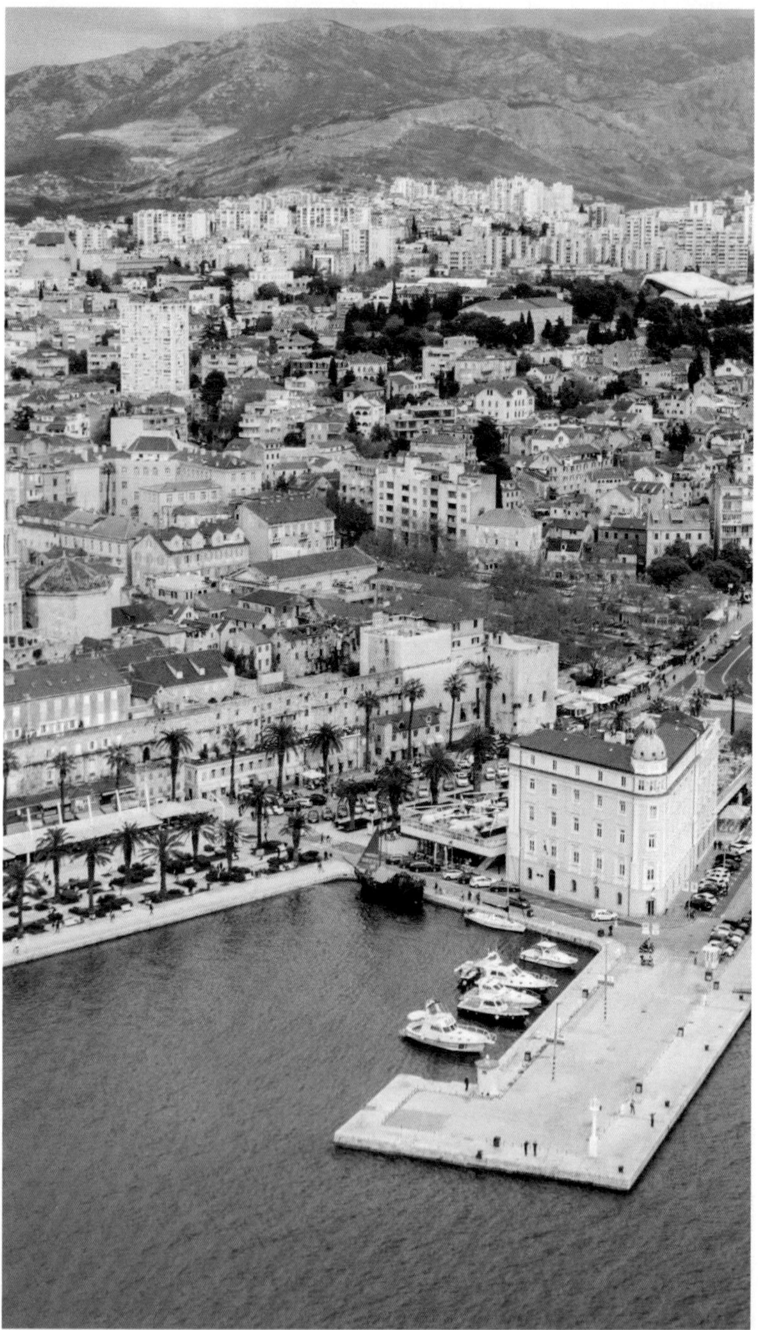

CROATIA

This is the country that gave the world both the necktie and the parachute, so unsurprisingly it's a bit like James Bond—sexy, elegant, but not afraid to down *rakija* shots at 2am before going hiking, sailing, and cliff jumping the next morning. Plus, a location smack dab in the middle of Europe means that Croatia combines everything we like about the western and eastern halves of the continent, not to mention easy access to major European cities. It's a place where you can go out with friends for pizza before belting out Croatian pop hits at a locals-only club or lounge on one of its many islands like you're ballin' at St. Tropez, but on a Balkan budget.

Don't be fooled by the country's communist past: while less than 30 years ago Croatia was a key part of Yugoslavia, the scars of communism and the subsequent wars of independence seem to be almost repaired. Traveling across Croatia you'll see that the country's L-shape creates two distinct sides: the coast and the hinterland. Zagreb falls in the latter category, showing strong influence from Austria in both its architecture and cuisine.

Here you'll see churches with onion domes and try gastronomic specialties such as *štrukli,* a savory version of baked strudel with cheese. The coast, however, historically had stronger connections with Italy, so brace yourself for Roman ruins, seafood, and risotto galore. And the best part: though Croatia is well-established as a tourist destination, its location in the Balkans translates to ideal prices. Oh, and did we mention the islands? Croatia's got over 1000 of 'em. So take your pick: Hvar-ever you like it, there's an island for that. Welcome to budget-traveler heaven. Cliff jump in Split, appreciate the art of Ivan Meštrović in galleries across the country, and sip ridiculously good coffee in one of Zagreb's ubiquitous cafés. *Živjeli,* my friends.

DUBROVNIK

Coverage by **Lydia Tahraoui**

Your grandma loves Dubrovnik, your second cousin twice-removed won't shut up about his trip here, and your ex-girlfriend's uncle's stepfather's in-laws are still posting photos on Facebook from their time in the city. What's with all the hype? Well, for starters, Dubrovnik looks drop-dead gorgeous. After just one day, you'll find yourself looking up study-abroad options, figuring out how to get a work visa, and researching dual-citizenship options.There are beaches, bars, and baroque architecture—and that's just the B's. Prices in the city are expensive, but cheap supermarkets, takeaway restaurants, and bakeries make budget life bearable. Outside of the Old Town, tourists can enjoy plenty of outdoor activities: climbing Mt. Srđ is a definite favorite and so is cruising over to Lokrum Island. But, let's be real: you came here for the coast, so grab your suntan lotion, because it's Croatian Riviera time.

ORIENTATION

Most of the sites you really care about are located in the **Old Town,** which is surrounded by massive medieval walls. The only entrances to the Old Town are through the city gates—the main ones are the **Pile** to the west, and the **Ploce** to the east. The bus station is a 20-minute bus ride to the west of the city, and the airport is located 30 minutes to the south. The Old Town's main street is the **Stradun,** but the rest of the city is dominated by narrow alleyways and stairs, punctuated with the occasional piazza. The city center is walkable, and public transit is really only needed for day trips or rides to the airport. If you plan on island hopping from Dubrovnik, you'll need to head to **Dubrovnik Port,** a 15-minute drive westwards from the Old Town. The airport shuttle stop is next to the cable car station, and tickets are 30-40kn.

ESSENTIALS

GETTING THERE

Both international and domestic airlines land at Dubrovnik Airport, which is sometimes also referred to as Čilipi Airport. For budget deals, look at carriers such as Norwegian, Croatian Airlines, and Easyjet. The airport is located about 10 miles outside of the city center, so take a bus or a cab into town. Alternatively, take a ferry to Dubrovnik from Bari, Italy, or neighboring Croatian islands. And, if you don't quite have your sealegs, there are overland bus routes that connect Dubrovnik to most major Croatian cities, including Split and Zagreb. Just know, overland routes may end up taking longer than ferry rides because of visa checkpoints.

GETTING AROUND

Dubrovnik's Old Town is pretty compact, which means you can easily get around by foot. You will most likely not be staying in the Old Town (because hello, expensive accommodations) but 99% of what's interesting in Dubrovnik is located there. Don't worry though, because buses regularly connect the various parts of Dubrovnik to the Old Town. Just be sure to exit at the Pile Gate stop, a major hub that connects many different bus lines. Pro tip: if you're staying outside the city, walk to the Old Town and take a bus home (otherwise, you'll be walking uphill). If you're looking to take day trips to nearby islands, you'll want to catch boats and ferries from Dubrovnik's Port, which is just a 15-minute drive from the Old Town.

PRACTICAL INFORMATION

Tourist Offices: Pile Gate Tourist Information Center (Brsalje 5; 20 312 015; tzdubrovnik.hr; open daily 8am-9pm).

Banks/ATMs/Currency Exchange: ATMs and banks are located throughout the town. Look for Splitsha Banks. If you need to take out money, here's an ATM near the Old Town, Zagrebačka banka (Stradun 4; 800 00 24; open 24hr).

Post Offices: Here's Dubrovnik's Central Post Office, Hrvatska pošta (Vukovarska 16; 20 362 068; open M-F 7am-8pm, Sa 8am-2pm).

Public Restrooms: There are two public restrooms at Pile Gate, right in Dubrovnik's Old Town (Vrata od Pila; entry for 5kn; open daily from 7am-11pm).

Internet: As in most cities, almost all the cafés and restaurants in Dubrovnik offer free Wi-Fi. Unfortunately, however, most public areas don't have free Wi-Fi connections.

BGLTQ+ Resources: A good resource for members of the BGLTQ+ community is gaywelcome.com/gay-dubrovnik.php. Here, you can find recommendations for gay-friendly travel in Dubrovnik.

EMERGENCY INFORMATION

Emergency Number: 112.

Police: You can call the police line at 192. We have listed a centrally located station.

- Dubrovnik Police Station (Dr. Ante Starcevica 13; 20 443 777).

US Embassy: The closest US Embassy is located in Zagreb.

- U.S. Embassy Zagreb (Ul. Thomasa Jeffersona 2; 16 612 200; hr.usembassy.gov; open M-F 8am-4:30pm).

Rape Crisis Center: There is a Rape Crisis Center based in Zagreb.

- Center for Women War Victims–ROSA (14 551 128; czzzr.hr; open daily 10am-6pm).

Hospitals: Dubrovnik's main hospital:

- General Hospital Dubrovnik: (Roka Mišetića 2; 20 431 777; www.bolnica-du.hr; open 24hr).

Pharmacies: There are several pharmacies throughout Dubrovnik; we've listed one centrally located in the downtown area.

- Pharmacy Dubrovnik, Bell Tower (Stradun 4; 20 418 990; open M-F 7am-8pm).

SIGHTS

CULTURE

RECTOR'S PALACE DUBROVNIK

Pred Dvorom 3; 20 321 422; open daily 9am-6pm

Croatia is a very straightforward country: the landmarks are named with great frankness. So, as you can probably surmise, Rector's Palace Dubrovnik is a palace that used to serve as the seat of the Roman Rector in, well, Dubrovnik. For those of you who need a quick refresher in Roman politics, recall that the Rector served as a Roman governor. When Rome ruled Dubrovnik, the Rector acted as the leader of the whole political operation. Obviously, someone with that kind of power needs an opulent palace to match, but before the palace, there was a defense building in the same location. This less-gaudy building burned in a rapturous fire in 1435, upon which the town said hey, let's build a palace which subsequently suffered damage in a gunpowder explosion. You could say a bit of bad luck haunts the site but don't worry—that luck ended up turning right around. The palace was reconstructed in the Renaissance style with just a touch of Gothic flair, and today, you can check out the palace in all its architectural beauty. Be sure to duck into its many ornate rooms and its adjoining museum to learn more about Dubrovnik's ultra-glamorous past as the center seat of the **Republic of Ragusa.**

i Admission 130kn, 50kn reduced; wheelchair accessible

DUBROVNIK CABLE CAR

Kralja Petra Krešimira IV; 20 325 393; dubrovnikcablecar.com; open daily Jan 9am-4pm, Feb-Mar 9am-5pm, Apr 9am-8pm, May 9am-9pm, June-Aug 9am-midnight, Sept 9am-10pm, Oct daily 9am-8pm, Nov daily 9am-5pm, Dec 9am-4pm

Sometimes you have to earn sweeping views by enduring strenuous hikes up challenging peaks. Other times, you can get all the perks of high elevation minus the typical exertion. It's times like this when that beloved innovation, the cable car, comes in handy. Head into the Dubrovnik Cable Car Station just outside of the **Old Town** to take a three-minute ride up **Srđ Mountain,** a popular viewpoint that's part of Croatia's **Dinaric Alps.** The ride itself is pretty worthwhile in its own right, and—just so you're aware—super conducive to producing an excellent time lapse video. But you're really ascending those 1300 feet for the payoff of the breathtaking vantage points at the top of this mountain. Sneak peeks of the **Adriatic Sea, Lokrum Island,** the **Elaphiti Islands,** and **Old Town Dubrovnik.** Insider tip: find the path behind the concrete fort, located just west of the top cable car station, if you want to avoid paying for the trip down.

i Adult round-trip tickets from 170kn, adult one-way tickets from 90kn; wheelchair accessible

STRADUN

Stradun; open 24hr

This is the place to see and be seen in Dubrovnik. Although Dubrovnik weaves together narrow streets and winding alleyways, Stradun is the **Old Town**'s main walkway. Get ready to strut your stuff on this expensive, tourist-infested stretch of stone-paved glory that crosses town to connect the **Ploce** and **Pile** gates. **Onofrio's Fountain,** one of the city's most important landmarks (with potable water!), lies on the Pile side while the **City Hall Bell Tower,** home to two sculpted copper boys who strike the bells every hour, flanks the street at the other end. The limestone that paves Stradun's streets may look pretty but is incredibly slippery. A fair number of tourists lose their footing here, which makes for its own special brand of entertainment—don't forget your good walking shoes!

i Free; wheelchair accessible

LANDMARKS

CITY WALLS

Gundulićeva Poljana, 20 638 801, wallsofdubrovnik.com, open daily Apr-May 8am-6:30pm, June-Jul 8am-7:30pm, Aug 8am-7pm, Sept 1-14 8am-6:30pm, Sept 14-30 8am-6pm, Oct 8am-5:30pm, Nov-Mar 9am-3pm

From the window to the two-kilometer walls, you won't be getting low, but you will be climbing up to considerable heights on Dubrovnik's City Walls. The City Walls are an incredible example of top-tier fortification construction, so kudos to those Middle Age architects. Forget swashbuckling pirates or armies though; these days, the walls only protect Dubrovnik against thousands of cruise-ship tourists. We promise you: there's really nowhere else in Europe like this. The city walls still stand almost entirely intact and completely encircle the city. Real *Game of Thrones* fans (and to be honest, probably even the fakest of fans, too) will recognize the City Walls as the real-life equivalent to King's Landing. If you want to get the full Seven Kingdoms experience, make sure you check out **Bokar's Fortress** and **Minčeta Tower,** which the show featured prominently.

Admission 200kn, student admission with valid Croatia Student Card, International Student Card, or European Youth Card 50kn; no wheelchair accessibility

CHURCH OF ST. IGNATIUS

Poljana Rudera Boškovića 7; 20 323 500; open daily 8am-7pm

If you start to feel like you're in Rome whilst trekking up to the Church St. Ignatius, then take a second to remind yourself that no, you're in Croatia, duh. But don't be too hard on yourself, your brief moment of geographical confusion is more than understandable. Italian architect **Pietro Passalacqua,** who designed the steps leading up to the church, modelled them on Rome's **Spanish Steps.** Once you've climbed this internationally appealing set of stairs, you'll find yourself at the base of a baroque Catholic church. The Jesuits partially financed its construction, and as any Georgetown student will tell you, the Jesuits don't mess around. So, it's not really a surprise that their church occupies one of the most prominent vantage points in the **Old Town.** Even if you've seen other Jesuit churches before, pay special attention to this one because of its exceptionally innovative **Lourdes Grotto.** What's a Lourdes Grotto, you ask? To us heathens, that basically means there's a man-made cave with a statue of the **Virgin Mary** that was built in the late seventeenth century.

Free; limited wheelchair accessibility

FORT LOVRIJENAC

Tabakarije 29; open Apr-May 8am-6:30pm, June-Jul 8am-7:30pm, Aug 8am-7pm, Sept 1-14 8am-6:30pm, Sept 14-30 8am-6pm, Oct 8am-5:30pm, Nov-Mar 9am-3pm

This is the sans-CGI Red Keep from *Game of Thrones*, and it looks far less impressive than it does on the show. For starters, no dragons have even encircled Fort Lovrijenac and you definitely won't find the King (or Queen—hey Cersei) of the Seven Kingdoms here, but you can explore a small internal courtyard with three stories worth of steps, cannons, and ramparts. Beware that visitors who stay past closing time get locked inside. And even though that's an experience in its own right, recall that fortresses were built to keep people out, not in.

Admission free with City Walls tickets; separate admission 50kn; no wheelchair accessibility

MUSEUMS

MUSEUM OF CROATIAN WAR OF INDEPENDENCE

Srd 2; 21 340 800; mestrovic.hr; open May 2-Sep 30 Tu-Su 9am-7pm, Oct-Apr Tu-Sa 9am-4pm, Su 10am-3pm

To add to the list of things school didn't teach us (but probably should have), let's chat about the **Yugoslav Wars.** This series of conflicts swept the Balkan region at the beginning of the 1990s, as the **Socialist Federal Republic of Yugoslavia** began to crumble apart piece by piece. Croatia broke away from Yugoslavia in 1991, and soon became embroiled in conflict with its neighbors. The Museum of Croatian War of Independence, or the Homeland War Museum, memorializes the 1991-1995 conflict, which involved Croatia, Serbia, and Montenegro. Through its sixteen themed exhibitions, the museum uses primary documents, photographs, videos, and war memorabilia to present a study of what Croats call the **Homeland War.** The museum offers an important perspective on a conflict we all could stand to learn a little more about, but just keep in mind that the narrative presented is firmly from the Croatian perspective.

Admission 30kn, 15kn reduced; cash only; no wheelchair accessibility

FRANCISCAN MONASTERY AND PHARMACY

Šetalište Ivana Meštrovića 46; 21 340 800; mestrovic.hr; open daily Apr-Oct 9am-6pm, Nov-Mar 9am-6pm

This is the seventeenth-century version of CVS, located conveniently close to **Pile Gate.** Forget endless aisles and industrial fluorescent lighting, this isn't your average old pharmacy. If that's what you're looking for, you can stop next door at the functioning pharmacy that the Franciscans continue to run (it's all in the family). This pharmacy was founded back in 1317 as an in-house Franciscan friars' one-stop drug shop, because even friars care about efficiency. Later opened up for public use, today it houses a quirkily specific exhibit on the art of pharmacy. The main attraction of the complex, however, remains the cloister. Columns topped with Gothic quatrefoils stand in the picturesque setting and rooms leading off the cloister feature religious art from the history of the complex.

i Admission 30kn; limited wheelchair accessibility

MARITIME MUSEUM

Tvrdava Sv. Ivana; 20 323 904; dumus.hr; open daily 9am-6pm

You're in the middle of one of Croatia's most famous seaside cities, so it makes sense to learn a little more about Croatian seafaring history whilst here. On this (sea)front, the Maritime Museum of Dubrovnik's got you covered. Since its early days, Dubrovnik's prime seaside location has played quite a role in shaping the city's history. The museum's exhibits track the evolution of maritime trade, shipbuilding, and seagoing in Dubrovnik and beyond. Through its displays of maps, written documents, ship instruments, and other artifacts, the museum covers a lot of historical ground. Trace the **Dalmatian Coast's** nautical evolution from its **Republic of Ragusa** days all the way up to the present. On the chance that the museum's well-organized displays ignite a burning passion for maritime history deep in your soul, you can further research your newfound niche interest at the museum's extensive library.

i Admission 80kn, 25kn reduced; no wheelchair accessibility

MUSEUM OF MODERN ART DUBROVNIK

Frana Supila 23; 20 426 590; ugdubrovnik.hr; open Tu-Su 9am-8pm

This museum bursts at the seams with the works of Croatia's most famous artists...which means you probably can't recognize any of the names featured here. They're still super talented, we swear. Situated in an old palace, the museum dedicates itself to twentieth-century and contemporary art from the Dubrovnik area. Jury's still out on whether English language descriptions would help with the understanding of the abstract Dalmatian art. We can't say for certain, because multilingual translations of exhibits are seriously lacking. Hey, at least this gives you an opportunity to brush up on your niche, art-related Croatian vocabulary words, and that's definitely going to come in handy. If anything, though, appreciate the courtyard for its stunning views of the **Old Town** and a few sculptures by our guy **Ivan Meitrovic.**

i Admission 20kn; no wheelchair accessibility

OUTDOORS

LOKRUM ISLAND

Setalista Petra Preradovica

Welcome to Lokrum Island, a coastal paradise within a coastal paradise. Located just a short ferry ride outside of Dubrovnik, Lokrum Island seems like an ideal romantic getaway with its heart shaped botanical gardens and azure waters. That is, until middle-aged tourists start mimicking the peacocks that roam freely on the island. If you can overcome those terrifying, soul-crushing sounds, trek over from the small harbor to the old **Benedictine Monastery.** Legend has it that when the monks were kicked off the island, they left a curse on all those who come to Lokrum to seek pleasure. So instead, come as a *Game of Thrones* pilgrim to see an exact copy of the Iron Throne located in the visitors' center. Just try not to derive any pleasure from the experience on account of, you know, the curse (easier said than done, we admit).

i Round-trip ferry 120kn, island entrance 90kn; limited wheelchair accessibility; last ferry departs at 7pm daily

UVALA LAPAD BEACH

Masarykov put

We've got nothing against the pebbles that line the shores of most of Croatia's beaches. They're responsible for keeping that Adriatic water so clear, and for this, we sincerely thank them. But let's be honest: sometimes, all a traveler wants is a little bit of sand under their feet. So if you've got sandy shores on your mind, then look no further than Uvala Lapad Beach. Located on the Lapad peninsula, Uvala Lapad is about a 10-minute drive from **Old Town.** It's also situated right on the bay's main boulevard, a strip lined with plenty of shops, restaurants, dessert parlors, and bars—meaning you'll have no trouble fulfilling whatever intensely specific craving you developed while gleefully splashing around in Uvala Lapad's bright blue waves.

i Free; wheelchair accessible

FOOD

BARBA ($$)

Boškovićeva 5; 91 205 3488; open daily 11am-midnight

See food, sea food, grab food, go with food: this basically summarizes Barba's whole philosophy to coastal cuisine. Allow us to provide some context. Barba's an on-the-go seafood spot tucked into an **Old Town** alleyway and they're all about serving up gourmet, fish-based dishes with great efficiency. The menu is simple yet satisfying, and incorporates some seafood-inspired twists on staple dishes. We're especially big fans of their burgers, which come in four fishy variations: sardine, octopus, tuna, and shrimp. Stick around and enjoy your meal inside the restaurant, or you can see what you like, grab it, and go with it. Barba's a quick and tasty option for the busy traveler, and it's also a pretty stand out for the budget traveler as Barba prices the entrees relatively affordably—by Dubrovnik standards, of course.

i Burgers from 63kn; no wheelchair accessibility

BABIĆ BAKERY ($)

Frana Supila 2; open daily 6:30am-10pm

Your wallet's been drained, but somehow, your traitor of a digestive system refuses to remain content with your daily diet of salami-and-cheese. You need some variety, but you also need to save up your remaining kuna to ensure that you have a bed to sleep in tonight. In such a pinch, do as the locals do and head directly over to one of Dubrovnik's many bakeries. We like Babić because the prices stay cheap and the breads, boreks, and beverages are genuinely tasty. You're more likely to find oodles of carbs than nutritionally square snacks here, but any one of Babić's bakery treats add that bit of variety desperately missing in your diet—without breaking the bank.

i Croissants from 6kn, coffee from 6kn; wheelchair accessible

GOSSIP ($)

Boškovićeva ul. 1; 20 321 745; open daily 9am-3am

If you're trying to cool down on a warm Dubrovnik day, but the cost of the cocktails at beachy bars break your heart, then we have some uplifting news for you. You don't have to venture much further than **Stradun Street** for the powerful combination of creamy ice cream and refreshingly strong mojitos. Gossip daylights (and moonlights too, for that matter—thank you, generous opening hours) as a godsend of a mojito bar. Grab a scoop of ice cream inside the store itself and from a little stand towards the front, pick up a freshly made mojito for half the price of what most beach bars charge. Best of all, you can take either treat with you for the road. We don't know why, but somehow mojitos taste even better when you're sipping on 'em from the top of a medieval fortress.

i One scoop of ice cream from 14kn, mojitos from 35kn; cash only; wheelchair accessible

NISHTA CAFÉ ($$)

Prijeko bb; 20 322 088; nishtarestaurant.com; open M-Sa 11:30am-10pm

Nishta Café puts in the work to make vegan food exciting. Some people say that vegan cuisine, with its soy protein approach to cheese and its agave nectar approach to honey, is inherently creative—but for everyone who still has their doubts about this, let's talk about Nishta Café. The menu is chock full of vegan, vegetarian, and raw food options, but this isn't your grandma's (or your second-cousin-who's-been-vegan-for-a-year-and-claims-she-can-make-any-dish-vegan) vegan food. Oh no, Nishta plays in the big leagues. We're talking a daily changing menu, with dishes like beluga lentil rice crêpes topped with an apple mint sauce, or arame algae salad with dried fruits and avocado-lime ice cream. Nishta's entire list of dishes overflows with terms we don't fully understand, but sincerely want to taste.

i Entrees from 45kn; wheelchair accessible; vegetarian and vegan options

TAJ MAHAL ($$$)

Nikole Gučetića 2; tajmahal-dubrovnik.com; open daily 10am-midnight

Forget India and instead take a (culinary) trip to neighboring Bosnia, the kind of cuisine that Dubrovnik's Taj Mahal actually specializes in (despite its strangely misleading name). After eating all of the fish options typical of the Croatian coast, these massive meat platters provide welcome relief for carnivorous backpackers. While the prices are average, the portion sizes are explosively not. Bowls of fresh-out-of-the-oven bread accompany dishes with plenty of hearty sides such as kumpir, a traditional stuffed potato dish. Other options include shish kebabs and pljeskavica—essentially a hamburger with a bun that's large enough to satisfy any and all homesickness you may feel for the U.S. of A. But if you want a truly Bosnian culinary experience, try the *cevapi.*

i Entrees from 90kn; wheelchair accessible

NIGHTLIFE

CAFÉ BUŽA

Crijevićeva 9; 95 883 1750; open daily 8am-10pm

It can be a little tricky to find Café Buža, tucked away against a beachside cliff. But once you see a sign that reads "cold drinks with the most beautiful view", you can relax and know that you're heading in the right direction. This sign is true to its word, in that Café Buža actually delivers on this promise. There's your favorite cold beverages being served up at the bar for reasonable (Dubrovnik) prices, and you get to enjoy them while sitting on a cliff that's just isolated enough to feel genuinely special. Plenty of Café Buža's patrons take advantage of this ideal location by jumping off the cliff and plunging into the cool blue waters below.

i Beer from 41kn, wine from 46kn; no wheelchair accessibility

CULTURE CLUB REVELIN

Trg Gaje Bulata 4; centralclub.hr; 91 3323 234; open 12:30am-6am

Never judge a book by its cover, and definitely never judge a club by its medieval exterior. When walking up to Culture Club Revelin, you'll likely think to yourself: hey, this looks like your average cool and cultured tower from the Middle Ages. When you walk into that smoky interior, you'll come face to face with glowing balls hanging from the ceiling, dancers in neon costume, and strippers in cages. Did they twerk to electronica in the Middle Ages? In spite of it all—or perhaps, indeed, because of it—Culture Club Revelin is basically where every party-minded traveler between the age of 18 to I'm-still-young-at-heart ends up. The music alternates between electronic dance music and U.S. Top 40 Charts, with bass-oriented remixes of pop songs to bridge the gap in between.

i Cover charge 100kn for women, 130kn for men, entry free before midnight; beer from 35kn; limited wheelchair accessibility

SKYBAR NIGHTCLUB

Šetalište Petra Preradovića 2; 95 510 2271; open daily 11pm-4:30am

Walking down the stairs into Skybar Nightclub feels a bit like descending through Dante's levels of Hell. The levels gradually shift up in intensity, starting at a semi-chill hang-out space and ending at the final floor, where the bass speaker five feet over your head sends pulsing shock waves throughout your body. The songs tend to border on obscure (at least to American club-goers), and the soundtrack never really incorporates much variety beyond what can only be described as Balkan electronica. Drinks cost a pretty penny, but its location outside the **Pile Gate** makes Skybar Nightclub easily accessible. Best to drink before coming to this place.

i Cover 30kn; no wheelchair accessibility

HVAR

Coverage by **Lydia Tahraoui**

Okay, so your YouTube channel didn't take off like you'd hoped it would. Your rapping career hit its high point upon securing 7 streams on SoundCloud. You've tagged your Insta posts with all the hashtags you can think of, but your #likes are still #lackluster. Fame keeps eluding you, but no matter: you can still party like a celebrity in Hvar. It's the island of choice for your fave movie stars, rappers, singers, and social elites. It's also a hot spot for bohemian backpackers and college kids looking to let loose, all united by mutual appreciation of beautiful beaches and raging parties. Hvar has the wildest nightlife of anywhere on the Adriatic, with clubs that party on until the wee hours of the morn—or until your tipsy self accidentally falls into the surrounding sea, whichever happens first. For those rare moments when you're sober, there's plenty of other stuff to do, too, with all of Hvar's beaches and sea caves. And even if you're not the adventurous type, the Venetian architecture and year-round sun makes this a nice place to just relax. Sure, it's pricey, but hey—maybe a pic against the shimmering backdrop of Hvar's bright blue seawater is just what you need to spark your influencer career.

ORIENTATION

Hvar Town is the largest tourist destination on the island, which also consists of other cities like **Stari Grad** and **Jelsa.** The central point of Hvar Town is the **Pjaca,** the town's main square. The square marks the location of the eighteenth-century **St. Stephen's Cathedral of Hvar.** The cathedral is pretty hard to miss, so if you're don't see it, you're really not looking. The **Riva** area, which acts as homebase for much of the nightlife in Hvar, lies to the west of the Pjaca. If you're wanting to do some more sightseeing, the **Franciscan Monastery** sits south of the Pjaca and the **Fortica Spanjola** is north.

ESSENTIALS

GETTING THERE

If traveling internationally, the closest international airports are in Split and Dubrovnik. From there, you'll need to take additional transportation to Hvar via ferry. Take a ferry directly from Split, or a cross-island ferry from Korcula, Vis, or Brac. An international ferry line also runs from Italy and stops in Hvar. Most ferries dock at Stari Grad, from which you take a 20-minute bus ride Hvar Town.

GETTING AROUND

Hvar Town is pretty small and easily walkable, so don't worry about using public transportation or taxis. To get to other cities on the island, grab a bus from the Hvar Town bus station—conveniently located right in the city center. It connects visitors to Stari Grad, Jelsa, or Sucuraj, the three other towns on the island. The buses make several stops along the way. Stari Grad attracts many day-trippers from Hvar, and the bus there takes about 20 minutes.

PRACTICAL INFORMATION

Tourist Offices: Hvar Tourist Board (Stjepana 42; 02 174 10 59; visithvar.hr; open daily 8am-8pm).

Banks/ATMs/Currency Exchange: There aren't a whole lot of banks on the island, but you'll find a couple near St. Stephen's Cathedral. Here's one: OTP Bank (Obala riva 10; 07 220 63 54; otpbanka.hu; open M-F 8am-2pm, Sa 8am-12pm).

Post Offices: There are a couple post offices scattered throughout the island. Here's one in Hvar Town: Hrvatska pošta (Obala Riva 19; open Jun 15-Sep 15 M-Sa 7am-9pm, Sep 16-Jun 14 M-F 7am-7pm, Sa 8am-12pm).

Public Restrooms: There aren't a ton of public toilets on the island, but you can find one located at Ulica Uvala Vira 7. Otherwise, your best bet is to duck into a restaurant or café.

Internet: You can get free Wi-Fi at the Tourist Board's office, which is located at Stjepana 42. Most of the cafés and restaurants here have the Wi-Fi hookup, so duck in for some connectivity.

BGLTQ+ Resources: There isn't a designated BGLTQ+ Resource Center on Hvar Island, but you can reach out to the LGBT Center in nearby Split (Ul. kralja Tomislava 8, 91 620 8990).

EMERGENCY INFORMATION

Emergency Number: 112.

Police: Here's a police office located in Hvar Town:

- Policija Hvar (Ive Milicica 5; 02 150 4239).

US Embassy: Come on, you didn't really think Hvar had their own US Embassy on the island, did you? Regardless, you can reach out to the Embassy in Zagreb for all of your American needs.

- US Embassy Zagreb (Ul. Thomasa Jeffersona 2; 16 612 200; hr.usembassy.gov; open M-F 8am-4:30pm).

Rape Crisis Center: There is a Rape Crisis Center based in Zagreb. Here's the info:

- Center for Women War Victims - ROSA (014 551 128; czzzr.hr; open daily 10am-6pm).

Hospitals: Here's the main health center in Hvar Town:

- Health Center Hvar (Biskupa Jurja Dubokovića 3; main number 021 778 046; emergency room number 021 717 099; emergency room open 24hr).

Pharmacies: The main pharmacy in Hvar is conveniently located right next to the health center:

- Ljekarna Lakoš-Marušić (Sv. Stjepana 18; 0 21 741 002; open M-F 7am-8pm, Sa 7:30am-3pm).

SIGHTS

CULTURE

VRBOSKA

Vrboska 21463

When people plan a visit to Hvar, they tend to focus their itinerary on, well, Hvar itself. But this 42-mile long island has much to offer beyond Hvar Town. Case in point: allow us to introduce Vrboska, the cutest little fishing village you've never heard of. Located 30 minutes to the east of Hvar, Vrboska is Hvar's smallest—and, dare we say, quaintest—settlement. The village cozily hugs a bright blue bay, and its (relatively) remote location means that Vrboska tends to be much less crowded than Hvar Town, making the settlement an ideal getaway from the touristy hubbub downtown. Locals sometimes call the village Little Venice thanks to its intricate canal system and narrow stone alleyways; basically, it's got all the perks of Venice, minus the hordes of tourists. While in Vrboska, make sure to check out the **Church of St. Marija** and the oodles of stone bridges. If you're feeling outdoorsy, take a hike in Vrboska's pine forest, which we would be so bold as to argue is the most tranquil spot on the whole damn island.

i Free; wheelchair accessible

DOMINICAN MONASTERY & CHURCH OF ST. MARK

Sv. Stjepana

Once upon a time, a Dominican monastery-slash-church-combo stood at this site. Notable Croatians used the monastery for big-name speeches (ugh, we would've killed to hear Dominican monk **Vinko Pribojević's** "On the Origin and Glory of the Slavs") and important municipal meetings that brought together Hvar's hottest political leaders. The church stands totally in ruins now, but those ruins still look quite picturesque and definitely merit a visit. Although it's apparently too dangerous to enter the church itself, the guardian may be kind enough to let you into the courtyard outside the church, which houses old graves. Not your typical graveyard, the space feels ethereal with palm trees, marble tombstones, and old stone pavement. If you don't catch such a stroke of luck and nothing is open, hop on up the steps to the concrete walkway and enjoy its stellar views of the church bell tower and Hvar Town.

i Free; no wheelchair accessibility

SVETA NEDELJA

Sveta Nedjelja

The real trailblazers out there should prepare to explore of one Hvar's hottest hidden gems. This sleepy, sunny village is tucked away beneath Hvar's highest peak, Sveti Nikola. Just 7 miles to the southeast of Hvar Town, Sveta Nedelja is chock full of adventurous activities to suit the most venturesome of sensibilities. If you're not averse to deep, dark spaces, hike up to the Sveta Nedelja cave and catch a glimpse of the tiny church hidden inside the echo-y caverns. The village also attracts daredevil free climbers, thanks to its scraggy cliffs and awe-inspiring views, so if you're comfortable with your ability to ascend steep topographies then ready your gear. And if you're not feeling quite so audacious, worry not: Sveta Nedelja also rose to fame because of its role as the most famous producer of Hvar red wine, *plavac*. Feel free to sit back and sip on a glass of rich plavac wine as you watch other people scramble up and down rocky cliffs. We won't judge.

i Free; limited wheelchair accessibility

LANDMARKS

ST. STEPHEN'S CATHEDRAL OF HVAR

Sv. Stjepana; 0 99 576 3019; open 9am-noon, 4pm-6pm

All roads lead to St. Stephen Square, so visitors inevitably stumble upon St. Stephen's Cathedral whether or not they plan to. Don't worry, it's easy on the eyes. The cathedral lies right on the main piazza and dominates the city's skyline. It's basically the most iconic architectural landmark on the island, and it's white stone façade typifies Dalmatian churches. The church dedicates itself to St. Stephen—the patron saint of Hvar. Inside, expect to see well-preserved artwork by the Venetian artists who worked on the cathedral when Hvar was part of the Republic. Keep a special eye out for the **Madonna and Child** rendition on the altar, a proto-Venetian piece that dates back to the thirteenth century, making it one of the oldest works of its kind in all of Dalmatia.

i Admission 10kn; wheelchair accessible

FORTICA SPANJOLA

Biskupa Jurja Dubokovica; 021 742 608; open daily 8am-9pm

Forget romantic sunset pictures on the beach: Fortica Spanjola is the place to go for those golden hour photoshoots. This fortress protected Hvar over centuries of rule by the Byzantines, Venetians, and French, just to name a few. While it's a bit of a hike to get up here (read: stairs galore), the views make it all worth it and your legs will thank you for the unintended workout later. If you don't feel like paying for the fortress itself, walk around below the fort, where the views still stun visitors and light up Instagram feeds. We recommend visiting the fortress right at sunset, when pink rays hit Hvar's tan stone.

i Admission 40kn; no wheelchair accessibility

VENETIAN LOGGIA

The Palace Hvar Hotel, Svetog Stjepana; 021 742 977; open daily 24hr

In case you need a reminder that the Venetians used rule over Hvar, look no further than Hvar's *loggia*. First of all, the word "Venetian" is literally right in the name. But beyond that, few architectural features look more Venetian than a good old-fashioned *loggia*. We forgive you if you struggle a bit with southern European architectural terms: a *loggia* is basically an exterior gallery with one or more open sides. Simple enough, right? Theoretically, Hvar's *loggia* dates back to the thirteenth century, but its early days are shrouded in mystery. No one really knows what it looked like back then, but we do know that the Turks burned the whole *loggia* to the ground in the sixteenth century. Subsequently, some iconic late-Renaissance architects rebuilt it, and now it remains one of the best examples of Renaissance architecture on the island. The *loggia* belongs to **The Palace Hvar Hotel,** which trendily repurposed the *loggia* to serve as a café and spa for hotel guests.

i Free; limited wheelchair accessibility

MUSEUMS

FISHERMAN'S MUSEUM

Sabotova kola, Vrboska; 0 21 741 009; open M-T 9:30am-noon, 6pm-9pm; Th-Su 9:30am-noon, 6pm-9pm

This tiny museum is hidden away in the middle of Hvar's fishing village, **Vrboska.** What this museum lacks in space (and in English translations!), it more than makes up for with its collection of local fishing equipment, tools, marine specimens, and models—including a scaled recreation of a fisherman's house. The museum weaves together intricate tales of how Croatian fisherman lived way back in yesteryear, providing charming insights on Adriatic island life. The guides are incredibly helpful, so feel free to ask all of your burning fish-related questions. We're sure you've got a few.

i Admission 10kn

OUTDOORS

DUBOVICA BEACH

Dubovica 21450, Zaraće

Welcome to the promised land, AKA the setting for your most envy-inducing Instagram post to date. Dubovica feels a bit out of the way, but it's so stunningly beautiful that tourists from across the island gladly embrace the moderately strenuous hike down to it shores on the reg. First things first, let's talk logistics. The beach lies about 5 miles to the east of Hvar Town and hides away in a secluded, shimmering, pine tree-lined bay. Swoon. Arrive at the entry point to the trail down by water taxi or, you know, regular taxi from Hvar Town. From this entry point, it's a 10 minute hike down to the pebble-lined shores. In return for your valiant efforts, you'll be rewarded with the most pristine, picturesque slice of paradise you've ever seen in your life. And no, that's not hyperbole: breathtaking bright blue skies, brighter blue waters, and craggy coasts await.

i Free; no wheelchair accessibility

FOOD

ALVIŽ ($$)

Dolac 2; 0 21 742 797; hvar-alviz.com; open 6pm-midnight

Is the secret to Alviž's pizzas in the tomato garden on the terrace? Years of experience? The local water? We'll never know, but we do know that they quickly churn out fresh pies straight from the oven. Plus, with its low prices, Alviž offers much-needed relief from the higher priced seafood and meat that most Hvar Town digs serve. The cheese melts onto the plate, the smooth sauce balances out the crunchy crust, and the toppings sit perfectly proportioned above it all. Basically, this checks off all our boxes on the Great Pizza Checklist (oh, you better believe we carry a physical checklist). If you're not feeling pizza tonight, try plenty of savory entrées at similar prices, such as vegetable risotto and mussels alla Buzana. There's always a good mix of both locals and tourists dining here on any given night—a testament to that universal truth: nothing brings people together like pizza.

i Pizza from 50kn, entrees from 70kn; wheelchair accessible

DALMATINO ($$$)

Sveti Marak 1; dalmatino-hvar.com; open M-Sa 11am-midnight

We're not sure people ever really have bad days in Hvar (I mean, it's a wild island getaway, what's not to like?), but if they did, a dinner at Dalmatino would turn that right around. Sure, diners here smile at artisanally arranged plates of thick, creamy pastas and delicately seasoned, ocean-fresh fish. But more importantly, they beam at the incredibly attentive service. The waitstaff and owners at Dalmatino go out of their way to ensure that diners remember their experiences, with generous hospitality and a penchant for great conversation. And if all this isn't enough, the laid-back, romantic atmosphere flips even the deepest of frowns upside down. By the end of your meal, even your pretty substantial bill won't be enough to damper the mood. Listen, you deserve this indulgence, okay?

i Pasta from 90n, fish from 140kn; wheelchair accessible

FIG HVAR

Ivana Frane Biundovica 3; 021 717 203; figrestaurants.com; open daily 10am-11pm

After too many consecutive nights of binge drinking, your organs are seriously begging for some—anything—healthy. Appease your digestive system by heading over to Fig, our happily healthy Hvar dig of choice. Fig waits for you just off of the main square, in a charmingly (or claustrophobically, depending on your tastes) tiny alleyway filled with cute tables that are topped with photogenic turquoise dishware. The food tastes just as good as it looks, which is saying something since basically everything on this menu looks ridiculously photogenic. The perfectly green lettuce crunches in your mouth, the goat cheese is cloudlike in its fluffiness, and the flatbreads are striped with sauces scrumptious enough to make you forget that this food is actually supposed to be healthy.

i Flatbreads from 55kn; limited wheelchair accessibility

KONOBA MENEGO ($$)

Kroz Grodu 26; 021 717 411; menego.hr; open M-F noon-2:30pm and 6pm-11pm, Sa-Su 6pm-11pm

If you'd like a (literal) taste of what it'd be like to have a Croatian grandmother, look no further than Konoba Menego. Inside this cozy restaurant, stand right in the kitchen of the Dalmatia matriarch you never had; the charming decor and welcoming environment only add to this homey ambiance. The menu serves up some good old-fashioned Croatian comfort food, cooked with fresh ingredients and, we're sure, lots of love. Konoba Menego cooks

STARI GRAD

If your World War II history is a little mixed up, let us set the record straight for you. Stari Grad is not Stalingrad. The only battles waged here are between wealthy French tourists competing over the bill at a restaurant. In Stari Grad, waiters serve wine by the liter over dinners that last long into the night. It's where the lowkey yachters and upper-middle-class Western European tourists come to get away from the hubbub of their real lives. Like moths buzzing to a light, tourists gravitate to Stari Grad for the historic architecture, relaxed nightlife, and plentiful vineyards, but in numbers much less than neighboring Hvar. So don your striped sailor shirt and do as the yachters do: visit the many breathtaking churches, bike through Ancient Greek vineyards, and stroll along the stone cornice.

Stari Grad hugs a protected bay on the northern side of **Hvar Island.** To the north of the town are the **Kabal Hills,** and to the south lie the peaks of Hvar. If arriving by boat, you'll dock at **Stari Grad Port,** which sits on the western side of the town. Directly to the east of the port, you'll find **Stari Grad Plain** and **Tvrdalj Castle.** If you continue east from there, you'll end up at the bus station.

GETTING THERE

Stari Grad is on the island of Hvar, which is most often reached by waterborne vehicles, AKA boats, boats, boats. The Port of Stari Grad, the largest island port on Hvar, sits a hop and a skip away from the town itself. Conveniently, it receives frequent ferries from Split. If you're traveling to Stari Grad from Hvar, you can also take a 20 min bus that'll get you right to the town center.

GETTING AROUND

Stari Grad is best explored by foot: you can easily visit all of the town's sites by walking. The town surrounds the rounded interior of an inlet and has characteristically narrow streets, so it wouldn't make much sense to try driving around. If walking the streets of Stari Grad bores you a bit too much, try a bike rental service called Hvar Life right in town. Just be warned that tourists normally crowd the streets, so make sure to sharpen your reflexes and quicken your response times in order to avoid potential crashes.

Don't miss...

TVRDALJ CASTLE

Riva Stari Grad; 021 765 068; open daily 10am-1pm and 5:30pm-8:30pm

We think that the socialist impulse to Eat the Rich is worth intellectual consideration, but even the most Marxist among us may find a soft spot for Certifiable Rich Guy Petar Hektorovic, founder of this very castle. The castle started out as the opulent (potentially excessive?) summer residence of Hektorovic, a local nobleman and accomplished poet. But it eventually opened its doors to the proles during the sixteenth century, when the Ottomans attacked Hvar. The benevolent Hektorovic fortified his home so that it could shelter his fellow citizens from attack, giving new meaning to the concept of communal welfare. Perhaps not all members of the bourgeoisie are so bad. Political musings aside, today Tvrdalj remains a well-preserved Renaissance castle with practical fortification, sunny terraces, a luxe interior courtyard, and an ethereal fish pond to boot. There's also a lush garden filled with medicinal plants and aromatic herbs, which serves as a perfect spot for relaxing, reflecting, and considering the intricacies of sociopolitical theory.

i Admission 15kn; no wheelchair accessibility

Check out...

DOMINICAN MONASTERY OF ST. PETER THE MARTYR

Kod Sv Petra 3; 0 21 765 442; 8am-6pm

Art history nerds should know two things about Tintoretto: he was Venetian and he's still famous. Points for longevity. How did one of his paintings end up in this obscure Dominican monastery? Well, a few centuries back this part of the world used to be controlled by Venice under the rule of the Doge (who was basically a duke, and definitely not the cringey c. 2013 meme). Beyond Tintoretto's Pieta, the church and courtyard of the monastery look beautiful, complete with flower-covered columns and arches. The museum, included with admission, doesn't provide significant English descriptions, but does display important Greek and Roman artifacts from the nearby UNESCO World Heritage Site, Stari Grad Plain.

i Admission to church and museum 20kn

Stop by...

STARI GRAD PLAIN

Stari Grad Plain; open daily 24hr

A plain by any other name would be as sweet, and Stari Grad Plain is a real life testament to this. It's been called a lot of different things over the years; to the Greeks, it was Chora Pharu, to the Romans, it was Ager Pharensis, but to us, it's now very plainly and very simply Stari Grad Plain—a UNESCO World Heritage Site. After creating the first settlement at Stari Grad, the Greeks divided up the nearby fields into small family plots that have been used continuously for 24 centuries. Within the fields, there is a grid system of roads and dirt trails that connect chapels and ancient ruins—making hiking or biking easy. Alternatively, you could check out the village of Doland and the Church of St. Michael Archangel for a view of the entire plain. Bike rentals start at 70kn for half a day. A detailed guide to the ruins and sights of the plain is available from the tourist office.

i Free; 70kn bike rental; limited wheelchair accessibility

Grab a bite at...

EREMITAZ ($$)

Obala hrvatskih branitelja 1P; 915 428 395; open daily noon-3pm and 6pm-midnight

With the best waterfront views in town and a location in a sixteenth-century hermitage, we're unsure how Eremitaz stays in business with entrees starting at 80kn. But when something's good, don't question it. Eremitaz is across from the main part of town and a relaxing walk (or dare we suggest, Vespa ride) gets you there in 10 minutes (or less…we didn't actually take a Vespa). The same family has owned this restaurant for years, and the dishes have that hearty richness that can only come from generations of dedication to the art of Dalmatian cuisine. With its laid-back atmosphere and scenic outdoor seating, this is the perfect place to camp out at for a nice long meal.

i Starters from 25kn, entrées from 60kn; no wheelchair accessibility strictly local dishes, which means that the selection feels somewhat limited. Nonetheless, Konoba Menego has got the coastal cuisine down pat, so be sure to sample local red wines and *prsut*, a Dalmatian-style prosciutto dish.

i Appetizers from 35kn, plates from 60kn; limited wheelchair accessibility

MIZAROLA ($$)

Vinka Pribojevića 2; 98 799 978; open daily noon-midnight

Eating on a budget in Hvar feels hard. Eating good food on a budget is damn near impossible. Fortunately, Mizarola makes the impossible possible with their 55kn pizza and 80kn pastas, which satisfy your wallet as much as your stomach. But don't get us wrong: we'd come here even if the prices compared to the rest of Hvar—well, probably, if we had any money left after the previous night's clubbing misadventures. The terrace stands next to the red-tiled roof of an old chapel and the food tastes blissfully well-seasoned. Plus, the servers are genuinely nice human beings—always an added bonus. Although, let's be honest: as long as Mizarola prices pizzas at 55kn, the waitstaff could probably get away with very lightly kicking us and we still wouldn't complain.

i Pizza from 55kn, pasta from 80kn; no wheelchair accessibility

NIGHTLIFE

CARPE DIEM

Riva 32; 993 776 776; carpe-diem-beach-hvar.com; open daily mid-May-end of Sep 9am-2am

Before you even arrive to the shores of Hvar, you'll hear tales of the mystical Carpe Diem. At this point, Hvar's top nightclub soars to unchartable levels of celebrity—a pretty fitting status, as it's hosted some of Hollywood's hottest throughout its storied history (hi, Tom Cruise, and hello, Prince Harry). The luxe yachters who come to Carpe Diem walk on the literal red carpet and pretend that Hvar is the French Riviera. Carpe Diem prices drinks accordingly, so may we suggest a pregame with grocery store drinks? After all, we can't all afford to party like Jay-Z (yet another high-profile Hvar visitor, for the record). In high season, the club goes until late in the morning. Outside, a warm lounge with ridiculously comfy wicker sofas welcomes those looking for a more relaxed party.

i No cover; drinks from 50kn; limited wheelchair accessibility

KIVA BAR

Fabrika 26; 97 609 6113; open daily 9pm-2:30am

We're pretty sure Croatia is in the EU, and even more sure that the EU bans smoking inside buildings, but Kiva Bar does not give a shit. Wild stuff happens here. People pack into small spaces where strangers grind on strangers—not out of attraction, but due to sheer necessity—and ordering a drink from the bar requires a sometimes uncomfortable level of intimacy. Don't be surprised to see fiery sparklers, girls dancing on the bar, and spilled alcohol. At least there's a decent, consistently roaring soundtrack to accompany the night's shenanigans. If you're looking for an experience akin to fighting your way through a mosh pit, though, look no further than Bar Kiva.

i No cover; beer from 45kn, cocktails from 50kn; limited wheelchair accessibility

KONOBA KATARINA

Kroz Grodu 22; 955 475 438 ; open M-Sa 10am-1pm and 6pm-midnight, Su 6pm-midnight

This is the Croatian family wine cellar you never knew you needed. We're talking stone floors and ceilings, demijohns, and homemade wooden seating. Konoba Katarina even proudly displays family photos, so how's that for authenticity? The place emits some serious old-world vibes, which conveniently happen to be our favorite type of vibes. Though the appetizers are limited and expensive, the glasses of wine are some of the cheapest in Hvar. Hey, if you're eating less, you're drinking more, and isn't that why you're here? Enjoy a glass on the steps or inside as you turn back time and savor a quiet, laid-back night on the island. Believe us, these can be hard to come by.

i Wine from 8kn, appetizers from 50kn; no wheelchair accessibility

LOLA BAR

Sveti Marak; 92 233 1410; open daily 6pm-2am

Some bars make tasty cocktails. Some bars curate a hip atmosphere. Some bars serve ridiculously good food. And then there's Lola Bar, which boasts all this and more. How's that for well-roundedness? Lola Bar draws a crowd mostly comprised of chill, friendly foreigners who've got that effortlessly cool look down pat. Whether they stop by for the intoxicatingly indie soundtrack, the sweetly refreshing mojitos, or the smoky spare ribs is anyone's guess. Either way, Lola Bar successfully manages to strike that enviable balance between bustling party hub and chill hangout spot, and for this, we thank them.

i No cover, drinks from 60kn; wheelchair accessible

SPLIT

Coverage by **Lydia Tahraoui**

Split is a city of superlatives. There's a ton of prestigious, important titles this city can claim: Home to the World's Most Complete Remains of a Roman Palace (hello, Diocletian's Palace), Home to the World's Oldest Catholic Cathedral That's Still Used in its Original Structure Without Needing Complete Renovation (we're looking at you, St. Domnius' Cathedral), and The Best Place to Party While Still Feeling Cultured Because You're Totally Exploring Split's Roman Ruins Too. Okay, so that last one is highly subjective, but we would still argue that it's fundamentally representative. Balkan cities don't typically conjure images of palm trees, but then again, Split falls far from your average Balkan city. With plenty of Roman monuments to gawk at, cliffs to jump off, and works of art to admire, Split splits off from the rest of its Balkan buddies. In reality, though, you don't need to make much of an effort to enjoy Split. If your idea of a good time happens to be dancing at the Ultra music festival or partying on the beach until 6am, Split welcomes you with open arms.

ORIENTATION

Humans first settled in Split centuries ago, and we're not sure they really cared about strategic, organized city planning back then. Because of that, Split's not easily divisible into separate regions. If we were to "Split" it, though, we'd say there are two main parts: **Old Town** and the waterfront **Riva**. To be frank, though, the entire city could fit inside **Diocletian's Palace,** which sits front and center in Old Town. Weave through the tiny, compact streets of Old Town Split to uncover all its nooks and crannies, including, but not limited to shops, restaurants, and museums. Just south of Old Town lies the renowned Riva, best known for its breathtaking views of the **Dalmatian coast** and lively nightlife scene. If you're looking to escape, the neighborhoods flanking Old Town, **Veli Varos** and **Manus**, offer a quaint reprieve.

ESSENTIALS

GETTING THERE

For those traveling by air, Split is serviced by Split Airport, also called Resnik Airport. The internationally connected airport offers mostly seasonal flights, so be sure to double check available options if you're planning an out-of-season trip. The airport lies about 12 miles outside of the Split city center, and you can grab a bus or a taxi into the city from there. If you're staying on an island, or further down the coast in Dubrovnik, grab a ferry to Split. Water routes are quicker and more efficient than overland routes, and ticket prices are reasonable. Just keep in mind that while the ferries are great for transportation within Croatia, the only available international connection is to Italy.

GETTING AROUND

If you're sticking to Split's Old Town, walking is not only your easiest option but also your only option. The tiny streets and alleyways are as narrow as high school hallways at points, so you literally don't have the option to travel by car, rail, or bus. If you're heading outside of the Old Town, however, the local bus service runs reliably and consistently. Public buses connect the Split city center with the city suburbs, as well as neighboring cities like Omis (Bus #60) and Trogir (Bus #37). Purchase tickets at Tisak kiosks or on the bus. If you choose to take a taxi, just make sure you confirm that your driver's got the meter on; like in most places, overcharging tourists is (surprise, surprise) not unprecedented here, so it's better safe than sorry.

PRACTICAL INFORMATION

Tourist Offices: Tourist Information Center Riva (Obala Hrvatskog Narodnog Preporoda 9; 021 360 066; visitsplit.com; open daily 8am-9pm).

Banks/ATMs/Currency Exchange: ATMs are located throughout the town. There are plenty located on the Riva, such as Splitsha Bank ATMs. ATMs in Croatia typically dispense cash in 100 and 200kn bills, which can get annoying.

Post Offices: There are a number of post offices around Split. Here's one for reference: Pošta (Hercegovačka 1; open M-Sa 7am-8pm).

Public Restrooms: There's a clean, centrally located public restroom over at Kralja Tomislava street, close to the post office.

Internet: Almost all the cafés and restaurants in Split offer free Wi-Fi. There are also public hotspots over at the Riva Promenade and Fish Market.

BGLTQ+ Resources: LGBT Center Split (Ul. kralja Tomislava 8; 916 208 990).

EMERGENCY INFORMATION

Emergency Number: 112.

Police: You can call the police line at 192 or visit the following station

- Split Police Station (Mike Tripala br. 6; 021 504 510).

US Embassy: The closest US Embassy is located in Zagreb. Here's the address:

- US Embassy Zagreb (Ul. Thomasa Jeffersona 2; 01 661 2200; hr.usembassy.gov; open M-F 8am-4:30pm).

Rape Crisis Center: There is a Rape Crisis Center based in Zagreb. Here's the info:

- Center for Women War Victims–ROSA (01 455 11 28; czzzr.hr; open daily 10am-6pm).

Hospitals: Here's Split's main hospital:

- Hospital Firule (Spinčićeva 1; 021 556 111; kbsplit.hr; open daily 24hr).

Pharmacies: There are several pharmacies throughout Split, but here's a 24hr one:

- Lučac (Pupačićeva 4; 021 533 188; open 24hr).

SIGHTS

CULTURE

CROATIAN NATIONAL THEATRE

Trg Gaje Bulata 1; 021 344 999; hnk-split.hr; box office open M-F 9am-8pm, Sa 9am-1pm

The performances at the Croatian National Theater are truly straight out of *Amadeus* (it's a period film, people). The 1893 theater was constructed in Neoclassical style and its interior will remind you of the great opera houses of Europe (because obviously, you know the great opera houses of Europe). Like any self-respecting opera house, it's got the red velvet chairs and gilded box seating. Throughout the year, the theater puts on operas,

ballets, and concerts—all at dirt cheap prices. Who said cultured revelry had to be expensive? So don your cleanest, least wrinkled shirt and try not to be intimidated by the elegantly dressed, music-loving locals as you take a break from the sun and soak up some culture.
i Tickets from 25kn; wheelchair accessible; semi-formal dress recommended

LANDMARKS

DIOCLETIAN'S PALACE

Dioklecijanova ul. 1; 977 790 719; open daily 24hr

Gather around for a quick history lesson, folks. Here's the lowdown: the Greeks first founded Split as a Greek colony in the third (or second, no one can really say for sure) century B.C. Split's neighbor Salona eventually became the capital of the Roman Province of Dalmatia. Flash forward a couple centuries and Split itself is on the come up. Because of its proximity (it's all about location, location, location), Roman Emperor Diocletian chose Split as a new retirement palace. That palace is, rather intuitively, Diocletian's Palace. Back in the day, Romans lauded the palace for its opulence, and these gaudy features remain remarkably intact. Ruins everywhere are extremely jealous of Diocletian's pristine condition. But if that's not impressive enough for you, maybe this will be: Diocletian's Palace was a key filming location for the fourth season of *Game of Thrones*. Winter is coming, but only figuratively. Split boasts a truly temperate climate, thank you very much.
i Free; wheelchair accessible

ST. DOMNIUS CATHEDRAL

Kraj Svetog Duje 5; 021 342 589; zg-nadbi-skupija.hr; open daily June-Sept 8am-8pm, May-Oct 7am-noon, 5pm-7pm, Nov-Apr 7am-noon

Something you'll quickly learn about Split: this city is really good at preserving its super old buildings. St. Domnius Cathedral is no exception to this rule. Emperor Diocletian first commissioned St. Domnius way back in 305 A.D. as a personal mausoleum. Consecrated in the seventh century, it's since acquired some new fangled architectural additions—just to keep up with the times. Most notable is the Cathedral's bell tower, which was added around 1100 A.D. in the Romanesque style, and then rebuilt in 1908, minus the Romanesque inspo. Located within walking distance of **Diocletian's Palace** and the **Temple of Jupiter**, St. Domnius Cathedral is easy to reach and convenient to enter. If you're into a bargain, you can buy combo cathedral and temple tickets for a decent deal.
i Cathedral admission from 20kn; cathedral and temple admission from 25kn; limited wheelchair accessibility (inquire ahead of time for accomodations)

TEMPLE OF JUPITER

Kraj Svetog Ivana 2; 021 345 602; open daily June-Sept 8am-8pm, Oct-May 12:30pm-6:30pm, Nov-Apr 8am-5pm

The Romans started building this temple at the end of the third century in honor of the Emperor Diocletian's divine father: the supreme god, Jupiter. Construction came to a halt, however, when Diocletian threw the Romans for a loop with his abdication in 305 A.D. As a result, parts of the temple linger, still incomplete. Finished or not, the temple makes for a pretty cool place to visit. Inside, find depictions of several gods and heroes decorating its walls: there's **Hercules, Apollo,** and, of course, **Jupiter** himself. Outside, find a sphinx standing guard just before the temple's entrance. Fun fact: this sphinx is one of twelve brought from Egypt by Emperor Diocletian. The Temple is located within the **Diocletian's Palace** complex, so it's within walking distance of most of Split's most iconic cultural spots. You can buy combo tickets that'll get you into both the Temple of Jupiter and **St. Domnius Cathedral.**
i Tickets must be bought in conjunction with cathedral admission; cathedral and temple admission from 25kn; limited wheel-chair accessibility

MUSEUMS

MUZEJ GRADE SPLITA (CITY MUSEUM OF SPLIT)

Papalićeva 1; 021 360 171; mgst.net; open daily 8:30am-9pm

While walking through Split, you may find yourself wondering: what role did this city play in the Roman Empire? What happened once the Romans were out of the picture? What did the people really think of the twelve sculptured sphinxes that found a home here? For answers to all these questions and more, look no further than Split City Museum. The museum functions as a giant guide to all the history visitors experience but frequently fail to fully understand in downtown Split. Something we learned, for example: locals used to fear the Egyptian sphinxes brought in by our guy Emperor Diocletian, because they thought sphinxes brought bad luck. Fair enough. The museum's collection covers Split's history from start to present and the building is an attraction in its own right. The second floor's Gothic ceiling is one of the few remaining pieces of Gothic architecture in the city. And man, do we love an iconic ceiling.

i Admission 20kn, 10kn reduced; limited wheelchair accessibility

GALERIJA MEŠTROVIĆ

Šetalište Ivana Meštrovića 46; 021 340 800; mestrovic.hr; open May 2-Sept 30 Tu-Su 9am-7pm, Oct 1-Apr 30 Tu-Sa 9am-4pm, Su 10am-3pm

Ivan Meštrović is that Croatian artist you've never heard of, but really should have. He's essentially Rodin, minus most of the fame. The little celebrity status that Meštrović enjoyed, however, gave him enough to afford a giant villa and, once you're that rich, does fame truly matter? Ponder this philosophical question while gazing at Meštrović's mesmerizing secessionist sculptures located inside the villa, out the surrounding garden, and in a chapel 200 meters down the street. The artist's works were influenced heavily by religious and classical themes. The museum's a bit of a walk from the **Old Town,** but when else can you learn about a delightfully niche Croatian artist by strolling through a stunning seaside gallery?

i Admission 15kn; limited wheelchair accessibility

OUTDOORS

BACVICE BEACH

Setalista Petra Preradovica; open daily 24hr

Bacvice Beach earns the coveted title of "Split's hottest beach" for three reasons. Reason number one: Bacvive's prime location—the beach stretches out into the ocean just a fifteen minute walk from the city center, so head in the direction of the bus station and keep walking. Reason number two: the 20-plus feet of clear, knee-deep water—perfect for doggy paddling to your heart's content. And finally, reason number three: Bacvice is the home of picigin, a game of group hacky sack played with a racquetball that puts your family beach volleyball tournaments to shame. Players' falls here are more dramatic than a Croatian soccer player trying to get his opponent a red card (Siri, how do you say "flop" in Croatian?). Stick around Bacvice in the evening if you're looking for raucous nightlife, because the beach comes to life in the high summer and goes hard until the early hours of the morn. Plus, legend has it that drunk picigin is even more fun than sober picigin.

i Free; wheelchair accessible

MARJAN FOREST PARK

Obala Hrvatskog Narodnog Preporoda 25; open daily 24hr

Let's be honest: you've let your exercise routine fall by the wayside since you've been abroad, and we can't blame you. It's seriously hard to find a good gym while traveling, okay, and that's when a visit to Park Marjan comes in handy. So, fine, they don't necessarily have exercise equipment, but they do have stairs upon stairs upon stairs. Overlooking Split, Park Marjan is the giant mountain (okay, maybe not giant, but large enough to substitute for leg day) topped with a cross and the Croatian flag. Once you get to the top, you'll receive adequate compensation in the form of pretty breathtaking views (if your breath hasn't already been taken, that is) and lots of shade. Word to the wise: bring water and food as after the **Teraca Vidilica,** Marjan has only one water pump and nowhere to purchase sustenance. The stairs to the park are located on the western side of Split, so just keep going uphill and you'll eventually get there, we promise. And when the going gets tough, remember: you could be burning those *strukli* calories on a treadmill but instead you're burning them whilst climbing a beautiful hill in Split, Croatia. Move over, Barry's Boot Camp.

i Free; no wheelchair accessibility

FOOD

ARTIČOK ($$)

Bana Josipa Jelačića 19; 021 819 324; articoksplit.eatbu.hr; open M-Sa 9am-midnight

Artičok puts the art in artichoke, and we mean that quite literally. Allow us to break down this restaurant's name: the art refers to, well, art—just as it appears on a plate or on display. The čok (it's a ch sound, guys!) is taken from a Croatian word that means "a nibble." And to you astute readers who wonder about the remaining i, we suspect that this stands for "I very much enjoyed my meal here," because that's what you'll be saying. Murals fit for a modern art museum cover the interior walls of this restaurant. Jazz music that's as smooth as the tomato sauce garnishing the oh-so-good homemade gnocchi booms throughout the restaurant, adding to Artičok's cultured vibes. Prices are slightly lower compared to the bland tourist trap places near **Diocletian's Palace,** but an authentic gastronomic experience that also includes dishes outside of traditional Dalmatian cuisine truly makes Artičok a gem.

i Entrees from 60kn; wheelchair accessible

MAKA MAKA ($$)

Pistura ul. 1; open daily 9am-11pm

In a city filled with Roman ruins and temples of the gods, Maka Maka caters to the city's health gods and goddesses. Maka Maka dishes out a bunch of variations one two key dishes: açai bowls and poke bowls. Apart from being bowls, the two dishes don't have much in common except for the fact that they are both delicious—and that Maka Maka does both of them incredibly well. The prices are pretty on par with the rest of Split's restaurant, plus you get the bonus ego boost of knowing that finally, for the first time on your trip, you are eating healthily. Your organs will be thanking you, we're sure. The raw fish is certifiably fresh, and the açai bowls both fill and refresh. Plus, strings of fairy lights decorate Maka Maka's outdoor seating area, which means the space photographs just as well as the food.

i Açai bowls from 55kn, poke bowls from 70kn; wheelchair accessible

STARI PLAC ($$)

Street Zrinsko-Frankopanska 6; 021 785 290; stari-plac.hr; open Su-Th 8am-11pm, Fri-Sa 8am-midnight

We're pretty sure every Split-based Instagram influencer snags a pic of the crêpes over at Stari Plac, and this joint's got the well-established online rep to show for it. We're serious: if you want to get hyped for your meal, check out

Stari Plac's location tag for droolworthy (and artistic!) pictures of remarkably diverse crêpes. This restaurant serves up the sweet, they serve up the savory, they serve up the Twix-flavored crêpes with caramel drizzle, chocolate filling, and mascarpone to boot. It's a bit of a trek from Split city center, and it's more popular among tourists than locals but we think the walk's worth it for the satisfaction of knowing you've eaten crêpes just as Croatians do.

i Crêpes from 25kn; cash only; wheelchair accessible

NIGHTLIFE

ACADEMIA GHETTO CLUB

Dosud 10; 1 091 197 7790; open Tu-Th 4pm-midnight, F-Sa 5pm-1am, Su 4pm-midnight

People come here to rage, but not in the all-you-can-drink-pub-crawl kind of way. It's more like the "let's have a stimulating intellectual conversation" kind of way. Thus, it's not surprising that Academia Ghetto Club is one of the few places in Split well stocked with absinthe. Never fear: should absinthe not suit your taste, but another niche alcohol does, go for the specials on Armenian brandy and then head outside to Academia's spacious courtyard to talk like Hemingway. Locals especially like spending time at Academia, so if you're looking to check out some authentically Splićanin nightlife spots then start here. They host plenty of live entertainment and regularly schedule events to keep things interesting, though to be honest, it doesn't take much effort for this place to stay interesting. Thanks to its artsy underground aesthetic and eclectically bizarre decor, Academia serves up some genuinely indie vibes.

i Beer from 20kn, cocktails from 50kn; limited wheelchair accessibility

CAFFE-CLUB BAČVICE

Šetalište Petra Preradovića 2; 955 102 271; open daily 11pm-4:30am

If you're looking to party by the beach, then look no further than Bačvice. When all else fails and the bars shut down, Bačvice faithfully waits for you with its dance floors popping, its alcohol flowing, and its raging going late into the morning. Come here to meet tons tourists at varying degrees of sobriety. If nothing else, night revelers at Bačvice look forward to memorable (or not so memorable?) nights, because Split beach parties go hard. Yes, Bačvice is a bit of a walk from downtown. Yes, the club could be a little bit nicer. And yes, it's easy to fall into the water because (fair warning) the sidewalks don't have guardrails. But that might not be the worst thing, because after a long night of drunken debauchery, there's nothing like a sunrise swim to cure a hangover.

i Beer from 20kn, cocktails from 30kn; limited wheelchair accessibility

ZAGREB

Coverage by **Lydia Tahraoui**

When people think of Croatia, they usually don't think of cityscapes. Well, they're thinking wrong. Zagreb's got all the culture of a typical European capital, minus the congestion. In true Croatian fashion, Zagreb is chill. It's laid back. And it's full of surprises. It's the kind of place where craft coffee is artisanally brewed—with a kick of rum. Your favorite restaurant is tucked away into the back of a secret tunnel. Oh, and Zagreb's thirteenth century Gothic Cathedral? Yeah, the three chandeliers you see hanging in its halls were sourced from a Vegas casino. Listen, Zagreb's nothing if not nuanced. Peel back the layers of history that have shaped the city: it's been Austro-Hungarian, it's been under Nazi control, it's been part of communist Yugoslavia. Throughout it all, however, Zagreb remains the kind of place where people come together over a hot plate of melted cheesy goodness. Because if you're not talking *štrukli*, Zagreb doesn't want to talk.

ORIENTATION

Zagreb is Croatia's biggest city, but by most measures, it's still pretty small. That's good for us because it means Zagreb is easy to navigate. There's a **Lower Town** and an **Upper Town. Lower Town** is comparatively newer and really took off during Zagreb's communist days. It's home to lots of residences, urban spaces, and office buildings. If that doesn't sound all too enticing, don't worry. The really exciting spots are all concentrated in **Upper Town**, which is Zagreb's historical center. At the heart of **Upper Town** is **Ban Josip Jelačić Square,** the main meeting spot for locals and tourists alike. All tram lines run through **Ban Jelačić Square,** meaning it's a convenient starting point for your Upper Town escapades. There's plenty of Austro-Hungarian architectural hotspots to discover, like the **Cathedral of Zagreb** which lies to the northeast of Jelačić Square, and **St. Mark's Church** which you'll find towards the northwest. Near **St. Mark's Church,** you'll find several museums including the quirky **Museum of Naïve Art** and the buzzworthy **Museum of Broken Relationships.**

ESSENTIALS

GETTING THERE

If you're arriving from outside Europe, fly into Zagreb Airport, Croatia's largest air hub. The airport serves tons of international and domestic airlines. The airport is about six miles southeast of Zagreb Central Station, and from there, you can either take an Uber or a bus into town. If you're already in Europe, you can get to Zagreb by train or bus. It's well connected on continental train and bus lines. The train will get you the Central Station (Trg kralja Tomislava 12), which is a major railway hub with connections to tons of different destinations both in and out of Croatia. The cheaper option—the bus—takes you Zagreb Bus Station (Avenija Marina Držića 4), which is about a thirty minute walk from the city center.

GETTING AROUND

Zagreb operates a well-connected tram system with major hubs at Ban Jelačić Square and Zagreb Central Station. Day passes cost 30kn and are valid for 24 hours. At the city's outskirts, you'll have to make the switch from tram to bus lines. Zagreb's Upper Town is also very walkable, as most tourist spots are in close proximity to one another. If you don't feel like making the walk to Upper Town, though, you can catch a ride on the funicular. A one way ticket will set you back 4kn.

PRACTICAL INFORMATION

Tourist Offices: Tourist Information Center (Trg bana J. Jelačića 11; 14 814 051; infozagreb.hr; open M-F 8:30am-9pm, Sa-Su 9am-6pm).

Banks/ATMs/Currency Exchange: There are tons of banks and ATMs throughout Zagreb. Here's one near city center: Addiko Bank (Trg bana Josipa Jelačića 3,16 030 000, addiko.hr, open M-F 8am-7pm, Sa 8am-noon).

Post Offices: There are a number of post offices around Zagreb. Here's one for reference: Hrvatska pošta (Jurišićeva ul. 13, open M-F 7am-8pm, Sa 7am-2pm).

Public Restrooms: There are public bathrooms at Grič Tunnel. Here's the address: Grič Tunnel (Mesnička ul. 19).

Internet: There's free Wi-Fi available throughout the city center under the network name Grad Zagreb. It's actually pretty speedy, and (bonus!) you don't need to sign up in order to gain connectivity. You can also find Wi-Fi at most restaurants and cafés.

BGLTQ+ Resources: Iskorak (Petrinjska ul. 27; 91 244 46 66; www.iskorak.hr; open M, W, F 4:30pm-6:30pm).

EMERGENCY INFORMATION

Emergency Number: 112. The American Embassy also has an emergency number for US Citizens, which you can reach at 16 612 400.

Police: Call the police line at 192 or visit the police station at Zagreb Police Department (Petrinjska ul. 30; 1 4563 111; zagrebacka-policija.gov.hr; open M-Th 7:30am-5PM).

US Embassy: Embassy of the United States (Ul. Thomasa Jeffersona 2; 16 612 200; hr.usembassy.gov; open M-F 8am-4:30pm).

Rape Crisis Center: Center for Women War Victims-ROSA (14 551 128; czzzr.hr; open daily 10am-6pm).

Hospitals: Here's Zagreb's main hospital:

- Clinical Hospital Center Zagreb: (Salata 2; 14 920 019; open daily 24hr).

Pharmacies: There are several pharmacies throughout Zagreb, but here's one close to the city center

- Gradska ljekarna Zagreb: (Trg bana Josipa Jelačića 3; 14 816 159; open 24hr).

SIGHTS

CULTURE

ST. MARK'S CHURCH

Trg Sv. Marka 5; 14 851 611; open daily 7:15am-7pm

The bright tiles on the roof of St. Mark's Church depict Zagreb and Croatia's coat of arms, which makes for the perfect photo op to show everyone back home that you are, indeed, in Croatia. St. Mark's is a late Gothic, Romanesque parish church that was first built in the thirteenth century. Since then, it's gotten a couple of major makeovers to keep it fresh. On top of its main entrance lie statues of **Joseph, St. Mark, the Twelve Apostles,** and... half of **Mary.** Yeah, so unfortunately, part of the Mary statue is missing, but apart from that the church stands in remarkably good condition. The front doors are usually closed, but the side entrance is sometimes unlocked. Try using the door closest to the Croatian parliament building to get a peek of the interior.

i Free; wheelchair accessible

DOLAC MARKET

Dolac 9; open M-Sa 7am-3pm, Su 7am-1pm

All the locals go to Dolac Market to do their grocery shopping, which means you should probably head on over, too. Not only is a trip to this open air farmer's market an authentic experience, but it's also budget friendly. You can find tons of fruits, vegetables, cheeses, flowers, and souvenirs for competitive prices. Vendors come from all different regions of Croatia, meaning that there's a remarkably diverse inventory of goods you can browse. Plus, the market bustles just steps away from Ribnjak Park, so grab a basket full of good eats at Dolac Market before stopping by the park for your quaint Croatian picnic.

i Free entrance, stand prices vary; limited wheelchair accessibility

FUNICULAR

Uspinjača; 14 833 912; zet.hr; open daily 6:30am-10pm

Welcome to Europe's shortest, safest, and quickest funicular ride. If you don't know what a funicular is, think of it as a tram with amazing thigh strength (because it climbs up steep inclines regularly). Zagreb's funicular can boast that since its inception in 1890, it's been accident free. To be fair, the funicular is about 217 feet long and the ride from top to bottom takes less than a minute, so there's not really much room for catastrophe to strike. Still, we're going to give credit where credit is due. The funicular was built over a century ago to connect Zagreb's **Upper** and **Lower Towns,** but we're guessing that over the years, Zagreb's locals have stopped minding the climb. Today, the funicular is now more of a tourist novelty than anything else, but it makes for a fun ride and brief reprieve from the heavy, heavy burden of walking.

i Tickets from 4kn; limited wheelchair accessibility (for a map of accessible stations, check out www.total-croatia-news.com/zagreb-blog/16747-zagreb-for-people-with-disabilities-a-guide)

LANDMARKS

TUNEL GRIČ

Ilica 8; open daily 9am-9pm

Need to update your Instagram with James Bond-style dramatic photos of yourself? Tunel Grič is Zagreb's very own air-raid-shelter-turned-subterranean-pedestrian-passageway. Translation: a long tunnel with surprisingly good lighting and dramatic cavernous spaces. Zagreb built the tunnel during World War II to protect civilians from bombings, but ended up completing it right as the war finished up. No points for good timing here. You can still make out wartime instructions painted onto the sides of the tunnel, such as commands to remain seated until air raid alarms have gone off. It's chilling, eerie, and surprisingly very temperate. If we haven't convinced you yet, listen: where else can you go and walk in a tunnel just for kicks? (Put your hand down, Montreal, we're talking about Europe).

i Free; wheelchair accessible

ZAGREB CATHEDRAL

Kaptol 31; 14 814 727; zg-nadbiskupija.hr; open M-Sa 10am-5pm, Su 2pm-5pm

Zagreb Cathedral boasts Gothic spires, plenty of gargoyles, a bell tower, and three chandeliers from a Vegas casino. Yes, one of these things is not like the other, but we think that this diverse mix is part of what distinguishes the cathedral from others. It's not pretentious or austere like some other architectural monuments you'll stumble upon throughout Europe (we're not going to name names!). In fact, the Cathedral is much like Zagreb itself: open, accessible, and eclectic. Zagreb began construction on the cathedral way back in the eleventh century and first declared it complete in 1217. History hasn't always been kind to Zagreb Cathedral, though: the Mongols destroyed it in 1242, Zagreb rebuilt it, only to have an earthquake in 1880 seriously damage it again. Zagreb once again rebuilt the cathedral shortly thereafter, after which weather conditions subjected the structure to major wear and tear. The cathedral has been under renovation for the past fifteen years, but it's still fully functional and open to the public. Make sure to wear appropriate attire on your visit to this historic location.

i Free; no wheelchair accessibility

ZAKMARDIJEVE STUBE (ZAKMARDIJEVE STAIRS)

Zakmardijeve Stube; open daily 24hr

There's something about falling in love that makes you want to secure a lock onto a foreign structure, as a symbolic testament to the unbreakability of your romantic connection. It's just human instinct, we think. In service of this innate desire, Paris has the Pont des Arts, Rome has the Ponte Milvio, and Zagreb has the Zakmardijeve Stairs. At the top of the stairs peep some of the most breathtaking—and most romantic—views of the city. You'll also find tons of lovelocks, adorned with lovers' initials and Sharpie-drawn hearts in accordance with that time-honored tradition. For the most skeptical among us, keep in mind that the **Museum of Broken Relationships** is minutes away from the Stairs. Hey, we warned you that Zagreb is nothing if not dualistic.

i Free; no wheelchair accessibility

MUSEUMS

MUSEUM OF BROKEN RELATIONSHIPS

Ćirilometodska ul. 2; 14 851 021; brokenships.com; open daily June-Sept 9am-10:30pm, Oct-May 9am-8pm

We all have different ways of dealing with the material memories of an ex. Some of us will maturely deliver a former lover's belongings back to them, undamaged and respectfully packed. Some of us will follow the lead of every breakup movie ever, and burn their things in destructive, yet cleansing, ritual. Still others will collect their ex's stuff, write up a poignant reflection on the demise of their relationship, and ship the package off to Zagreb. These are the people we have to thank for the Museum of Broken Relationships, which is home to a curated collection of personal objects from previous paramours. The museum is housed in a former Baroque palace, and the beauty of its building reflects the tragically beautiful nature of the stories contained within its walls. The narratives that accompany each object tug at your heartstrings, leaving you to reflect on the universality of heartbreak. It's one of those rare museums that is able to turn objects into experiences, and even though the subject matter can feel heavy, there's something so reassuringly human about the narratives the museum weaves together.

i Adults 40kn, 30kn reduced; wheelchair accessible

MUSEUM OF CONTEMPORARY ART

Avenija Dubrovnik 17; 16 052 700; msu.hr; open T-F 11am-6pm, Sa 11am-8pm, Su 11am-6pm

Maybe it's the violins hanging from the ceiling or the museum's Brutalist concrete architecture, but the Museum of Contemporary Art feels like a scene from a dystopian nightmare. The wacky exhibits waiting inside only augment this totally freaky ambiance. We're talking naked women laying on trees, optical illusions, and giant piles of coconuts. But the real reason to take the 15-minute tram ride out here is the three-story slide, which does not disappoint in the slightest. Who said art can't be fun? Some more serious works in the museum's collection engage with contemporary sociopolitical developments in what used to be Yugoslavia. Don't miss a powerful installation by prominent Croatian artist **Sanja Iveković,** which grapples with violence against women in the Balkans. This museum's trippy, but no one can say it isn't multifaceted.

i Admission 30kn; 15kn reduced; wheelchair accessible

MUSEUM OF NAÏVE ART

Ćirilometodska ul. 3; 14 851 911; hmnu.hr; open M-Sa 10am-6pm, Su 10am-1pm

The Museum of Naïve Art showcases the work of, well, naïve artists. Before you get a bee in your bonnet, rest assured that the use of "naïve" here is not a dig. Naive art is also sometimes described as the art of the modern primitives...wait, sorry, that also sounds like a slight. Okay, so the best way to describe the naïve art is like this: have you ever looked at an artwork and thought "I could totally paint that?" That's the whole concept between Croatia's most important twentieth-century art movement. The museum's collections contain works from painters and sculptors who have no art training whatsoever, and many of the pieces are remarkable for their childlike simplicity. Look, we're not saying that your little cousin could've probably made half the paintings here, but if you're thinking about submitting their doodles...

i Admission 25 kn, 15kn reduced; no wheelchair accessibility

OUTDOORS

ZRINJEVAC PARK

Trg Nikole Šubića Zrinskog; open daily 24hr

Back in the nineteenth century, Zagreb's locals would strut down this park's promenade to see and to be seen. On their good bonnet days, they'd show up and flex their latest fits, doing laps around the park's fountains and posing seductively against the charmingly quaint **Meteorological Post.** Or, you know, something like that. Zrinjevac

Park is still a pretty popular local spot—it's not hard to see why. The park is located on Zagreb's **Green Horseshoe,** a U-shaped expanse that contains numerous public parks and greeneries, and Zrinjevac is probably the crown jewel of them all. There's a promenade that feels more like a runway, an ornate music pavilion that looks straight out of a historical romance novel, and plenty of wide open spaces where you can lay out and soak up that southern European sun. Plus, it's close to a ton of historical buildings, like the **Supreme Court of Croatia** and the **Archaeological Museum,** making it the perfect place to stop and take a quick break from all that sightseeing.

i Free; wheelchair accessible

ART PARK

Strossmayerovo šetalište 99; open daily 24hr

Make sure to look appropriately stylish when you show up to Art Park, or else you run the risk of being outdressed by the trees. Talk about embarrassing. This park boasts graffiti, murals, and fancily dressed foliage adorned with bright colors and intricate patterns. Art Park constitutes a fairly new addition to the Zagreb itineraries, but it's definitely one worth seeing. For years, this little park had been abandoned and totally off the radar, until a street art collective called "Pimp My Pump" brought a group of local artists together to give it a total makeover back in 2016. It's now a popular destination for picnics, festivals, concerts, and graffiti jams.

i Free; limited wheelchair accessibility

BOTANICAL GARDENS

Marulićev trg 9a; 14 898 066; botanickivrt.biol.pmf.hr; open March M-Tu 9am-2:30pm, W-Su 9am-5pm, Apr-Sept M-Tu 9am-2:30pm, W-Su 9am-7pm, Oct M-Tu 9am-2:30pm, W-Su 9am-6pm, Nov M-Tu 9am-2:30pm, W-Su 9am-4pm

Zagreb's no concrete jungle, but even so, sometimes you just need a great escape from the (relative) hustle and bustle of (relative) big city life. Enter: the Botanical Gardens. Welcome to 5 hectares of ponds, plants, trees, and leaves. They exhibit all your botanical garden must-haves: there's scenic walkways, shady benches, and some photogenic bridges thrown in for good measure. It's the perfect place to take a leisurely stroll and reflect upon life, love, and the importance of addressing climate change in order to preserve such heavenly green oases (seriously, Save. The. Bees.).

i Free; wheelchair accessible

FOOD

LA ŠTRUK ($)

Skalinska ul. 5; 14 837 701; open M-Sa 11am-10pm, Su 11:30am-11pm

We're totally lovestruck with La Štruk and here's why: their speciality is bubbling dish of melted doughy and cheesy goodness that's a traditional staple of Croatian cuisine. We're talking, of course, about *štrukli*: the devil incarnate for every lactose intolerant person ever. But if you can handle your lactose, then prepared to be wooed. La Štruk only serves *štrukli,* and the good folks at La Štruk really know how to do it right. The most typical version is baked in a casserole dish, but you can also get it cooked, boiled, or soup'ed. La Štruk also gets major bonus points for the picturesque garden terrace hidden around the corner, where you can dine under the warm Croatian sun.

i Štrukli from 30kn; limited wheelchair accessibility

OTTO & FRANK ($$)

Ivana Tkalčića 20; 14 824 288; open M-Th 8am-12am, F-Sa 8am-1am, Su 9am-10pm

There are a couple things all people have in common: we all have hopes, we all have dreams, and we all have a shared appreciation for a really good brunch. And, if your hopes and dreams can be described as finding a really good brunch spot in Zagreb, then we are here to deliver. Otto & Frank is the early afternoon eatery of your fantasies, complete with some monochromatic hipster decor, an upbeat soundtrack and a ton of sweet and savory brunch options. Plus, there's a selection of speciality boozy beverages, like a frozen popsicle cocktail that is dangerously refreshing. Try to head over before noon, because in true Cinderella fashion, some of the sweeter breakfast staples expire by then.

i Plates from 32kn; wheelchair accessible

STARI FIJAKER ($$)

Mesnička ul. 6; 14 833 829; starifijaker.hr; open M-Sa 11am-11pm, Su 11am-10pm

If Zagreb were Pawnee and restaurants were people, Stari Fijaker would be Ron Swanson: unapologetically traditional, meat-loving, and a little over the top—but hey, we aren't complaining. Stari Fijaker cares for your physical, emotional, and spiritual (yes, spiritual) needs, with its large portions of hearty Balkan food, comfortable chairs, and large crucifix (because of course). Who doesn't need a bit more Jesus in their life after a week of partying on the Croatian coast? The menu, with English translations, consists of traditional dishes such as shepherd's stew: think goulash with gnocchi, a pretty on-the-dot culinary representation of the Hungarian and Italian cultural influences throughout Croatia.

i Plates from 50kn; wheelchair accessible

NIGHTLIFE

A MOST UNUSUAL GARDEN

Horvaćanska cesta 3; 91 464 69 00; open daily 8am-midnight

A sculpture of an octopus with a giant cucumber in a bathtub greets you the second you walk into A Most Unusual Garden. That's not even the strangest thing about this bar, and for that, we are grateful. Part gin bar, part treehouse, part wall murals, but all quirky weirdness, this garden makes bargoers feel like characters in *Alice in Wonderland.* Aside from the steampunk decor, there's a large outdoor seating with steps, tables, and—the coup de grace!—a treehouse. All of this lies underneath fairy lights and empty bottles of gin lit with candles, contributing to a bizarre but kind of romantic ambiance.

i No cover, drinks from 20kn; limited wheel chair accessibility

RAKHIA BAR

Tkalčića 45; 98 964 05 87; open daily 10am-2am

So here's a little language lesson: the first Croatian word you need to learn is *rakija.* Found throughout the Balkans, this fruit brandy is the national drink of Croatia. And Rakhia Bar serves up every type of *rakija* you can imagine. The plum favor hits the strongest, but we're partial to the fruity pangs of the pear. With over fifty options, why not find your personal pick? Just be careful not to pick too many, or else the bar's steampunk interior might make your stomach turn. Oh, and grab a bite to eat before you head on over: it doesn't matter how high you think your tolerance is, you've never really experienced a hangover until you've experienced a Balkan hangover.

i No cover, shots from 11kn; wheelchair accessible

TOLKEIN'S HOUSE

Opatovina ul. 49; 14 852 050; open M-F 7am-midnight, Sa 8am-12am, Su 9am-11pm

A pub with walls covered in swords, maps of Middle Earth, and maces? Now that's what we're Tolkien about. Just be careful not to confuse Tolkien's House with a hobbit house, because that's in New Zealand, people. But if a small pub with lots of *Lord of the Rings* paraphernalia and a solid selection of craft beers sounds up your alley, head over to this little pub that's a local favorite. This is also one of the few places in Zagreb that offers draught ciders, so if you're partial to some fruity flavors then look no further. We think Bilbo would approve.

i No cover, beers from 20kn; cash only; limited wheelchair accessibility

CROATIA ESSENTIALS

VISAS

Croatia is a member of the European Union. Citizens from Australia, Canada, New Zealand, the US, and many other non-EU countries do not require a visa for stays up to 90 days. Citizens of other EU countries may enter Croatia using only their national identity cards. Passports are required for everyone else. Despite being part of the EU, Croatia is not in the Schengen Area. However, holders of a Schengen visa are allowed to visit Croatia for up to 90 days without the need of an additional visa.

MONEY

Currency: Despite being a member of the EU, Croatia is not in the Eurozone and uses the Croatia kuna (HRK or kn) as its currency. ATMs offer the most competitive exchange rates, and it's helpful to have some cash on you, as most budget accommodations and some restaurants are cash-only. Larger establishments are usually happy to take card.

Tipping: Tipping is not usually expected, but is often appreciate in Croatia. For bars and cafes, tips are not expected, but it is common to round up the bill. So, if the bill comes to 18kn, leave 20kn. Tipping in restaurants is much more common, and you should tip your server about 10% for good service. Cab drivers won't expect tips, but it is courteous to round up.

SAFETY AND HEALTH

Local Laws and Police: Croatia is generally a very safe place for tourists, but petty crime is not unheard of. The police tend to be helpful and responsive, but you're unlikely to pass by officers whilst just walking around. If you need assistance, stop by a local station.

BGLTQ+ Travel: Homosexuality has been legal in Croatia since 1977. It is also illegal to discriminate on the basis of sexuality and production of homophobic material can result in up to one year of imprisonment. There is still controversy, however, and homosexuality is still not widely accepted in some regions of Croatia. Public displays of affection between same-sex couples may be met with hostility.

Drugs and Alcohol: The minimum age to purchase alcohol in Croatia is 18, though technically there is no minimum drinking age (cheers!) Remember to drink responsibly and to never drink and drive. The legal blood alcohol content for driving in Croatia is under 0.05%, significantly lower than the US limit of 0.08%. The possession of small amounts of illicit drugs intended for personal use was decriminalized in 2013, and is now punishable by fines ranging between 650 to 2600.

Travelers with Disabilities: Croatia is largely not wheelchair accessible, as many of the sights require climbing stairs to reach the main attraction, and elevators are not often provided. Streets themselves in Croatia often do not lend themselves to wheelchair travel, as they are evely paved and many are cobbled.

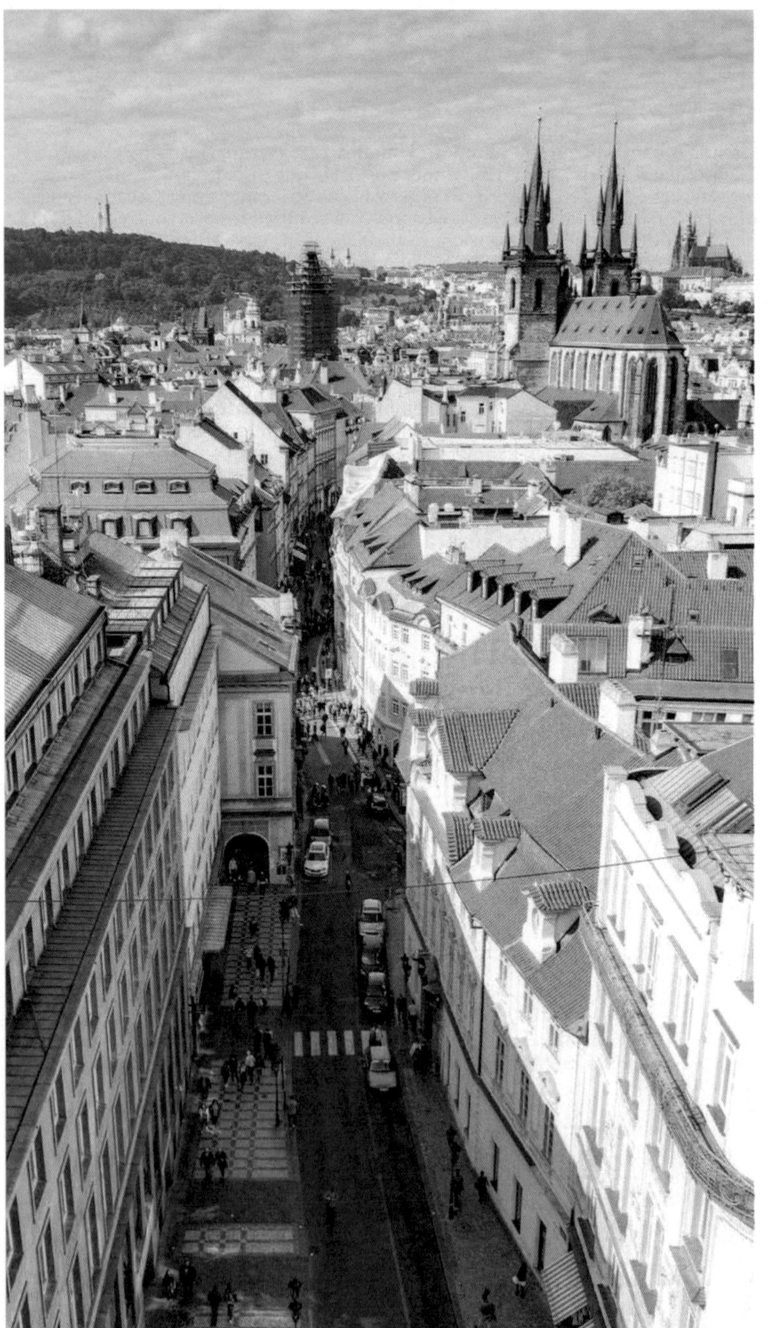

CZECHIA

In more ways than one, Czechia is the country version of a Jackson Pollock painting. You can see clear physical similarities in any old plane ride: mountains, hills, forests, fields, and valleys dot the Czech landscape like splatters of paint, creating a country that could be right out of J.R.R. Tolkien's imagination. Rivered medieval towns like Pilsen and Cesky Krumlov reveal themselves perfectly preserved in hidden valleys and basins. The kaleidoscopic splendor of spa towns like Karlovy Vary dominate the western border of Czechia, lending color to this state-scale Pollock-flavored masterpiece. If you look a little closer, the Pollock similarities become even clearer.

Anyone who sees a Pollock painting sees something different, and any traveler of Czechia walks away loving a different aspect of the country. The grizzled backpacker explores the northern mountains and forests of Bohemian Switzerland. The history aficionado makes camp in towns like Brno and Olomouc and refuses to leave. And the culture junky, they follow Austro-Hungarian Queen Maria Theresa's advice that without the Czech lands, the empire would be empty fields, and without Prague, the Czech lands would be empty fields.

Prague is the spiritual, economic, cultural, and de facto capital of central Europe. Exploring Prague's long and winding roads reveals countless relics of Czechia's medieval, Austro-Hungarian, and Nazi/Soviet occupied past. But at every turn, you realize the presentation's different. That Czechia isn't your average everyday Warsaw Pact country. No, Czechia is Central Europe's golden child—home of the bloodless Velvet Revolution that removed communist sovereignty in a mere ten days. In Czechia you're sure to find an indomitable national spirit, a wealth of natural beauty, and a totally underrated country.

KARLOVY VARY

Coverage by **Luke Williams**

Karlovy Vary is pretty much the *Stranger Things* of Central European tourist destinations: It's beloved by everybody and has absolutely no right to be as good as it is. Located in a valley between three overconfident hills, Karlovy Vary has always been a picturesque "mountain" town founded on a wealth of hot springs and geysers that erupt throughout the city. While the town always enjoyed domestic fame for its "healing waters," by the nineteenth century the Ruskies flooded KV every summer following the healing of their gout-ridden tzar, and everyone else soon followed. Alongside the who's who of France and England came artists like Goethe and Beethoven looking for inspiration in the bubbling waters, and by the twentieth century the town's rainbow pseudo-Renaissance main road was graced with one of Europe's largest film festivals: Karlovy Vary International Film Festival, which still attracts stars like Jude Law, John Travolta, and Uma Thurman every year. More than a few big-budget Hollywood movies film in Karlovy Vary on the regular. While the majority of tourists today are geyser-chasing geezers with thicc wallets hailing from Florida, Frankfurt, and the former Soviet Union, do this town right since it's not only cheap for students, but also incredibly welcoming. So honor the home of 007's *Casino Royale* and suit up in your tuxedo (read: t-shirt and jorts), lounge back in that Astin Martin (read: that one affordable spa's bathtub), and spend your days relaxing in this Czech edition of Colorado Ski Town, USA.

ORIENTATION

Karlovy Vary is dramatically split between the residential area north of the **Ohře River** and the tourist-fueled mountainside spa town south of the Ohře. On the "unlikely" chance that you're visiting Karlovy Vary for, you know, spas, hiking, fantastical settings, and magical geothermal hot springs, you will only be interested in the southern region which is split into a **Riverwalk** and **Downtown.** During the day, the Riverwalk boasts all the action, divided by the **Tepla River** into eastern and western halves. On the east side of the river you won't find much besides the **Municipal Theater** and **Kaiserbad Spa.** Looking west, you'll find landmarks like the **Mill Colonnade, Vřídelní Colonnade,** and all of the high-end restaurants, art galleries, and shopping you could ask for. At the southern end of the Riverwalk lies the home of the Film Festival: the **Grandhotel Pupp.** Meanwhile, the northern end of the Riverwalk begins at **Elizabeth's Spa-Lazne V** on the west side and the monolithic **Hotel Thermal** on the east side. Come nightfall, the Riverwalk all but shuts down, and the town's action transitions to what we're going to call downtown, the small modernized region northwest of the Riverwalk filled with great cheap hotels, a movie theater and mall, and a few clubs, bars, and restaurants. Furthermore, the downtown is home to **Becherplatz,** the historic home of the **Jan Becher Distillery.** Moving outside of Riverwalk area, the **Moser Glassworks Factory and Museum** is located a 15-minute drive northwest of the Riverwalk accessible by bus, and many a hiking path and secret stairway lead into the hills along the west side's edge, giving you access to such landmarks as the **Diana Observation Tower** and **Bristol Palace.**

ESSENTIALS

GETTING THERE

The most convenient way to get to Karlovy Vary from Prague is via bus, which will disembark at either the Tržnice bus terminal or Dolní nádraží, the main bus station, which is a 5min. walk from the city center. A map of the bus stops in Karlovy Vary can be found online. Alternatively, if you're arriving via train, you will arrive at Horni Nadrazi, located north of the city center across the Ohře River. It's a 10min. walk from the station to the city center, but it's much more convenient to wait for bus #1 or #13, both of which are one stop away from Tržnice terminal.

GETTING AROUND

Karlovy Vary is very walkable, and it takes around 25min. to walk along the Tepla from the northernmost landmark, Elizabeth's Spa-Lazne V, to the southernmost landmark, Grandhotel Pupp. A bus system (a map of the stops can be found at www.dpkv.cz/cz/mapa-zastavek-mhd) can take you around the main town as well as to places in the greater Karlovy Vary region (buses #1, #16, #22, and #23). Single trip tickets start at 18Kč. Two night bus lines run from 10:30pm into the early hours of the morning. Intercity buses that run across Czechia can be taken to the Loket Castle, a 30min. journey.

PRACTICAL INFORMATION

Tourist Offices: The primary tourist information center is located in the district north of the riverwalk. Information center of Karlovy Vary (T. G. Masaryka 883/53; 355 321 171; www.karlovyvary.cz; open daily 9am-5pm).

Banks/ATMs/Currency Exchange: Many ATMs are found on or nearby T.G. Msasaryka St. South of Dvořákovy Sady (Dvořák Park), ATMs can be found along the east bank of the Tepla River. We recommend withdrawing cash from ATMs instead of nearby banks or currency exchanges, as sometimes rates can be higher in the downtown Karlovy Vary area. One ATM is housed within the Becherplatz building (T. G. Masaryka 282/57; 800 521 521; www.kb.cz; open daily 9am-7pm).

Post Offices: A post office is located just across the river from Hotel Thermal. Czech Post (T. G. Masaryka 559/1; 954 330 304; www.ceskaposta.cz; open M-F 7:30am-7pm, Sa 8am-1pm, Su 8am-noon).

Public Restrooms: Public restrooms are along the riverwalk, with a central location in Dvořákovy Sady (360 01 Karlovy Vary; open daily 9am-6pm).

Internet: Free Wi-Fi is available in most cafés, restaurants, and spas.

BGLTQ+ Resources: Czechia is generally considered one of the most liberal central European nations in terms of BGLTQ+ rights, having legalized same-sex partnerships in 2006. While Czech society is accepting and tolerant, however, BGLTQ+ individuals do not yet have full legal equality. Czechia-wide BGLTQ+ online counseling service Sbarvouven is listed here (www.sbarvouven.cz; open daily 24hr).

EMERGENCY INFORMATION

Emergency Number: 112

Police: The closest police headquarters to the downtown area is located west of the northern end of the riverwalk area. City Police (Moskevská 913/34; 353 118 911; www.mpkv.cz; open daily 24hr).

US Embassy: The nearest US Embassy is in Prague (Tržiště 365/15; 257 022 000; open M-F 9am-4:30pm).

Rape Crisis Center: While there is no rape crisis center in Karlovy Vary, Centrum Elektra is located in Prague and provides a support hotline for women suffering from sexual abuse or violence (Chomutovická 1444/2; 739 441 879; www.centrumelektra.cz; open W 3pm-6pm).

Hospitals: The general emergency number is 353 114 640. The nearest hospitals are located northwest of the northern end of the riverwalk.

- Karlovy Vary Regional Hospital (Bezručova 1190/19; 354 225 111; www.nemkv.cz; open daily 24hr).

SIGHTS

CULTURE

BRISTOL PALACE AND KAISERBAD SPA

Kaiserbad Spa Mariánskolázeňská 2, Bristol Palace Zámecký vrch 918/34; Bristol Palace 353 341 906; www.bristolgroup.cz; Kaiserbad Spa open daily 10am-6pm, Bristol Palace open daily 24hr

If you haven't seen Wes Anderson's *The Grand Budapest Hotel,* now is the time.You're in Karlovy Vary, and that pink hotel is too, baby! Our working theory is that Our Lord and Savior Wes graced the KV film festival with his presence when writing *Grand Budapest,* and suddenly he happened upon the Bristol Palace: a massive pink Victorian-esque hotel sitting on a cliff overlooking all of western KV. After you've kissed the ground Wes walked on, go visit **Kaiserbad Spa-Lazne I**—aka Mr. Bond's Casino Royale. Besides being one of KV's original modern spa complexes, the Renaissance-style Kaiserbad Spa served as the exterior for the eponymous casino in 2006's *Casino Royale.* Nowadays, the spa is classified a national landmark (due to its age, not Mr. Bond) and is open for anyone to explore and get a feel for old Karlovy Vary.

i Free; limited wheelchair accessibility

KARLOVY VARY CITY GALLERY

Stará Louka 26; 353 223 641; www.mgkv.cz; open daily 10am-6pm

Seeing as most Karlovy Vary patrons treat 30,000Kč like a good day's roll of toilet paper, you'd think the local art gallery would put so many 0's on the price tags they'd look like bowls of spaghetti-O's. Instead, Karlovy Vary City Gallery is a sweet, completely unmerited surprise—we have never, ever been to a "mountain town" art gallery selling local art this fairly priced. Given that all the art is created by residents whose bios you can read alongside their art, the works displayed and sold often change dramatically. That said, the local specialties seems to be pop-art, sculptures, and artistic renditions of Karlovy Vary's spa cups. That's right, if you're looking for a high-quality souvenir and, like us, think the spa-cups are fun, you can grab beautiful ceramic renditions of the characteristic cupolas for as little as 400Kč, all the while doing your public duty to support local art.

i Art from 400Kč; wheelchair accessible

LANDMARKS

MILL COLONNADE

Mlýnské nábř.; 721 763 890; open daily 24hr

Fret not if the concept of a "colonnade" doesn't conjure a clear image in your head. A proper colonnade is not understood, but experienced. Opened in 1881, this 132-meter long, 123 column'ed open-air temple looks like an angry Zeus plucked the Pantheon off the Acropolis, stretched it out like silly putty, then dropped it into Karlovy Vary's open arms. Besides being very proud of its columns, the Mill Colonnade takes pride in housing five of Karlovy Vary's 13 drinkable springs. And while it's the third colonnade to call the **Riverwalk's** center square home, the wealth of springs has kept it the emcee of the Karlovy Vary daydream: the largest crowds of tourists and countless Beatles cover-bands with very big dreams.

i Free; limited wheelchair accessibility

MUNICIPAL THEATRE

Divadelní nám. 21; 351 170 011; www.karlovarske-divadlo.cz; open M-F 9am-5pm, Sa-Su 10am-5pm

If there's one place in Karlovy Vary that we can't stand, it's the Municipal Theatre. This is partly because it's full of seats, but also because its stunning Neo-Baroque beauty is (almost) too much to bear. Built in 1884 along the **Vltava River,** the Theater is considered one of the country's most magnificent interiors, notably painted by a couple of goofy Austrian twenty-somethings named **Gustav and Ernst Klimt.** Their greatest contribution is the incredibly intricate, hand-painted curtain that hangs in front of the stage. As far as we can tell, the theater doesn't put on any English-language productions, but it often hosts orchestras, ballet, jazz nights, and operas.

i Entrance free, performance tickets from 50Kč; limited wheelchair accessibility

VŘÍDELNÍ COLONNADE (SPRING COLONNADE)

Divadelní nám. 2036/2; open M-F 9am-5pm, Sa-Su 10am-5pm

Karlovy Vary's second-largest and only modern Colonnade complex features three hot springs, a second story art gallery, a basement tour of the underground springs, and an outside bar and artificial beach setting. But our theory on why Vřídelní Colonnade is so popular goes beyond these surface-level features. We think Karlovy Vary probably attracts so many senior citizens because they think the natural geyser fountain at the steps of the Vřídelní Colonnade's front door is actually the famous Fountain of Youth—shooting near-boiling water 12 feet into the air and giving off vape-god quantities of anti-aging vapor. Or maybe it's all the hot spring water we drank inside just going to our heads.

i Free; wheelchair accessible

MUSEUMS

JAN BECHER MUSEUM

T. G. Masaryka 282/57; 359 578 142; www.becherovka.com; open Tu-Su 9am-5pm

We've concluded that it's a requirement for every small Central European country to have a national herbal liqueur. Hungary has *Unicum* and Czechia has *Becherovka*—both are herb-based liqueurs made in the nineteenth century to be drank alone or in tea, coffee, or citrus mixers. And while our allegiance lies with *Unicum,* Karlovy Vary is the home of *Becherovka,* and boy, will you hear about that from every local and sign post you see. The Jan Becher Museum offers visitors a chance to explore the history of *Becherovka* inside the original distillery building. You'll examine *Becherovka*-related artifacts, learn about how it became the national Czech drink, and get to smell the drink's secret herbal mixtures. The tour ends with a tasting session where you can put that college degree to good use and effortlessly down four shots of *Becherovka's* different iterations.

i Tour 180Kč, 120Kč reduced; English tour times vary; wheelchair accessible

MOSER GLASS FACTORY AND MUSEUM

Kpt. Jaroše 46/19; 353 416 132; www.moser.com; museum open daily 9am-5pm, factory open daily 9am-2:30pm

Moser makes glassware like Mercedes Benz makes cars. Yes, in a factory—but also to an insanely high and damn-near artful standard. Founded in 1857, this factory has produced Europe's most celebrated luxury glassware since WWI, toted for street cred by everyone from Whoopi Goldberg to the Austrian royal family. While the museum can get a little dry and basically follows the formula "Moser did 'x' collection in 'y' year which was cool because [insert boring-ass reason] and owned by 'z' dynasty," we highly recommend a 30-minute tour of the glassworks factory, during which you'll see 1200-degree (Celsius!) furnaces and sweat drenched men blowing long, thick pipes. . .because that's how glass is made, you filthy animal. When your foray into voyeurism has finished, we also suggest hitting the gift shop—while you won't be able to afford a measly shot glass in this store unless you're coming from Buckingham Palace, this is the largest collection of glassware and glass-art on the factory's site, and it's definitely worth seeing.

i Museum and Glassworks tour 180Kč, 100Kč reduced; wheelchair accessible

OUTDOORS

DEER JUMP LOOKOUT AND DIANA OBSERVATION TOWER

Deer Jump Pod Jelením skokem 395/26, Diana Vrch přátelství 360 01; Diana 353 222 872; www.dianakv.cz; Deer Jump and hiking paths open daily 24hr, tower open daily 9am-6:45pm

We assure you, no one left the nursing home's door open—all the grandparents constantly wandering Karlovy Vary's extensive hiking paths have the right idea. Per the doctor's orders, hiking is usually included as part of a spa-patient's well-balanced diet, so Karlovy Vary has naturally become chock-full of everything from glorified walking paths to challenging backwoods hiking. Deer Jump Lookout and Diana Observation Tower are undoubtedly the most popular trails, with the former being a 15-minute hike from the Riverwalk and the latter being 45 minutes from Deer Jump Lookout. While the trails are very basic, the scenery is the best we've experienced in Central Europe. Upon making it to Diana Tower, you can grab lunch at the hilltop restaurant, check out the peacock-filled mini-zoo, and then head down the hill via funicular or continue hiking, as many of KV's hiking paths begin at Diana Tower.

i Hiking and tower admission free, funicular 60Kč; no wheelchair accessibility; ground access to Deer Jump Lookout through an alleyway north of Karlovy Vary City Gallery

FOOD

BAGEL LOUNGE ($)

T. G. Masaryka 825/45; 720 022 123; www.bagellounge.cz; open M-Th 8am-8pm, F-Sa 8am-10pm, Su 8am-7pm

There's nothing like Bagel Lounge to demonstrate that the Cold War is well and truly over: this is a modern millennial bagel café paradise most commonly frequented by young American and Russian travelers. Probably the only restaurant in town where you won't hear someone rasp, "Back in my day," Bagel Lounge blasts American pop music across its cool couch-and-table setup. While the menu features a decent breakfast selection and few non-bagel side options, all the greatest hits are among the 20-plus bagel-sandwich options. While we won't argue the bagels themselves are anything special, it's what the Lounge does with the bagels—they love combining cold meat, cream cheese, and jelly, for instance—that makes this place noteworthy. Maybe they'd throw in some hot peppers for experimental fidelity. Whatever the combo, these Frankenstein bagels sure do make us feel alive.

i Entreés from 119Kč; vegetarian options available; wheelchair accessible

NHÂ'T BÁO RESTAURANT ($)

Bělehradská 1094/4; 774 555 588; open M-Sa 11am-10pm

Let's be real: Karlovy Vary is no culinary paradise, especially for travelers on a budget. It's remarkably difficult to find any exceptional food in this town that comes in under 400Kč. That said, Nhâ't Báo Restaurant took a look at this trend and decided to revolutionize the Karlovy Vary culinary scene. Staffed by Vietnamese cooks—a rare sighting in Central Europe—this restaurant offers up incredible wok, pho, and curry based options, for meat-lovers and vegans alike. In fact, this is the only restaurant we ate at in Karlovy Vary that attracted just as much local attention as tourist attention. Nhâ't Báo Restaurant is very new player in the Karlovy foodie game, so if you can't find it on Google Maps or online anywhere, don't fret. That's to be expected. Just search "Foggy Shisha Bar," a Karlovy Vary mainstay, and Nhâ't Báo Restaurant will be adjacent to the west.

i Entreés from 109Kč, beer from 28Kč; vegan and vegetarian options available; wheelchair accessible

REPUBLIKA COFFEE ($)

T. G. Masaryka 894/28; open M-F 7am-7pm, Sa-Su 8am-7pm

The walls may not be plastered with gold, but they're papered with drawings that travelers leave behind. The tables are filled with scrambled eggs, toast, wacky eggs Benedict combos, and pastries as far as the eye can see. The wooden chairs absorb the constant chatter between traveler and server.

Suffice to say, Republika Coffee is the budget traveler's no-brainer. Located right in the middle of downtown, which tends to be where students and budget travelers stay, Republika's intimate little shop fills with hungry breakfast goers throughout the day. And with a coffee menu this good, cheap, and extensive, the baristas are revered shamans that guide the caffeine-starved wanderer through a dark-roasted vision of enlightenment. The conversation, coffee, and crazy eggs Benedict are all incredible. If you eat at one breakfast joint in Karlovy Vary, make it Republika.

i Entreés from 79Kč, coffee from 60Kč; vegetarian options available; wheelchair accessible

NIGHTLIFE

MOLLY CLUB, LOUNGE, AND SHISHA BAR

Jaltská 5; www.clubmolly.cz; open M-Th 2pm-midnight, F-Sa 2pm-5am, Su 3pm-midnight

Molly Club is a newcomer to the Karlovy Vary nightclub scene and is poised to change the whole game. This large club has a full bar, a lounge and hookah space, and a small dance floor complete with lavish light setups and a live DJ every Friday and Saturday. The drink menu is basic, but well-performed, and it's really the size and aesthetic of Molly that shine through. Compared to other clubs in town, Molly Club not only attracts a much younger, more lively crowd, but it's also noticeably cleaner and the staff are much more attentive to customer's needs. Furthermore, the inside looks like an interior decorator designed it while LSD—and that's not a bad thing. Giant pop-art portraits of rock stars span entire walls, chandeliers hang from the ceiling, candelabras jut from the walls at odd angles, lighting spans from orange to purple, and there's a massive white fireplace next to the front door. For a town with virtually no club scene, Molly Club goes above-and-beyond to fill a much needed void.

i Beer from 25Kč, cocktails from 95Kč; no wheelchair accessibility

GRANDHOTEL PUPP CASINO

Mírové nám. 6; 724 892 444; www.casinopupp.cz; open daily 7pm-4am

Hotels in Karlovy Vary lead advertising campaigns to convince travelers that Karlovy Vary lives up to its James Bond in *Casino Royale* status as a foremost high-stakes gambling town. Spoiler alert: it doesn't. That said, there's really not much in the way of good bars or clubs in the town, so we figured why not follow those fancy Floridian examples and hit the slots? Grandhotel Pupp Casino is a large, two-roomed casino featuring American roulette, Russian Poker, blackjack, and plenty of slot machines. Provided you know a little bit about gambling, this is a very friendly casino, and honestly playing Russian Poker with old Russian people who speak broken English is one of the most fun things we've done in Europe.

i Free, table antes start at 100Kč, increase to 200Kč later in the night; casual dress, pants/jeans and passport required; wheelchair accessible

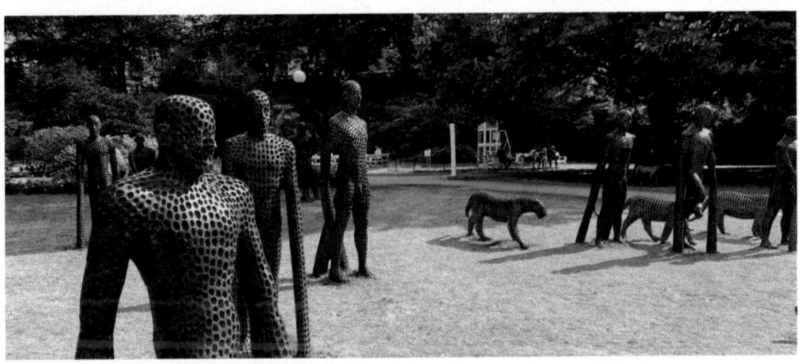

OLOMOUC

Coverage by **Luke Williams**

Visiting Olomouc, we couldn't help but come to the conclusion that Olomouc is Czechia's Santa Fe. Both are quaint region-defining cities that evolved from religious beginnings and now go hard on café and art gallery culture. However, a few revisions are necessary. Take Santa Fe, place it in the middle of a Czech basin created by surrounding hillsides, tack on 800 years of history, and convert the architecture to rainbow-colored Gothic and Renaissance masterworks. Then delete the pervasive smell of weed and hippie subculture and replace it with an unshakable Christian faith and a massive student population. And if that doesn't sound like the most charming little historical hiccup, then what more do you want? Olomouc is relentless in everything it does—its Old Town is dense and unapologetic. You want 1000 years of Catholic church history? How about 15 churches in a one mile radius? Old fortresses leftover from the Napoleonic wars? Cafés? Microbreweries? Universities? A castle? You got it. All of this is no more than a five minute walk from the main square. For most of its history, Olomouc was the most important city in Moravia—what is now eastern Czechia and used to be a key territory for the Hapsburg empire. Kings were crowned and killed here, stinky cheese ripened and sold, Gothic high-art rose like weeds and churches adorned the medieval streets like flowers. Yet, in Olomouc there's never a single tourist in sight. Not only is this little city the perfect one or two day trip from Prague, but it unfolds at your whim, always feeling like an authentic slice of provincial Czech life laid out just for you.

ORIENTATION

While Olomouc is a large-ish city, most areas outside of the twisty-turvy **Old Town** are relentlessly suburban, and you'll really only be interested in exploring the center of it all. So, get acquainted with the **Upper Square** and **Lower Square** first. No matter how lost are, you can always walk in the general direction of these adjacent squares and arrive at one or the other, as Olomouc's Old Town is a square-centric universe. Once you've gotten the two major squares down, take a walk down **Pekařská nám.** and **Sovobody tř.** Pekařská is the Old Town's primary east-west street, and you'll be visiting it often if you have any interest in seeing the best architecture Olomouc has to offer as well as the **Olomouc Museum of Art**, **Republic Square**, and **St. Wenceslas Cathedral** at the far eastern end. On the other hand, Sovobody runs north-south along the western edge of town. At the southern end is Olomouc's major shopping center **Galerie Šantovka** and at the north, Olomouc's **Hussite Church**. Sovobody also happens to be where most of Olomouc's more serious late night restaurants, bars, and clubs set up camp on Saturday nights. Godspeed, Padawan.

ESSENTIALS

GETTING THERE

Trains and buses regularly run from Budapest, Vienna, Bratislava, Kraków, and Prague to Olomouc. It is centrally located between Ostrava and Brno, and most trips to and from Prague will take you through Olomouc. All trains and buses arrive at Olomouc hl.n. (Olomouc Main Station), which lies a mile east from the heart of the Old Town. Upon exiting the station, there is a smaller tram station directly in front of the train station. You can purchase a single ride ticket at any yellow station near the tram tracks for 14Kč. Tram numbers 3, 4, and 6, go west from Olomouc hl.n. into the heart of Old Town, where most hostels and hotels are located.

GETTING AROUND

Olomouc's Old Town is very walkable. Every point of interest in the city lies no more than a 20 minute walk from the Upper Square. That said, if you prefer not to walk, Olomouc services an extensive tram system within the Old Town area. Tram stops are plentiful and marked with yellow ticket stations and signs that show tram arrival times. Tickets may be purchased at the tram stops, and must be validated onboard or you risk being fined by a plainclothes police officer. Single ride tickets cost 14Kč and full-day tickets 46Kč. Tram numbers 3, 4, and 6 are the primary Old Town trams, running a constant east-west route along Pekařská nám. For traveling north and south, tram numbers 3 and 7 run along Sovobody tř., a north-south street on the western edge of Old Town.

PRACTICAL INFORMATION

Tourist Offices: The central Olomouc Tourist Information Center is located in the northern end of City Hall in Upper Square. Olomouc Information Center (Horní nám. 583; 585 513 385; www.tourism.olomouc.eu; open daily 9am-7pm).

Banks/ATMs/Currency Exchange: ATM's and currency exchange centers are plentiful in the Upper Square area. Here's a convenient location Moneta ATM (Sovobody tř. 31; 224 443 636; www.moneta.cz; open daily 24hr).

Post Offices: There are three government-run Česká Pošta (Czech Post) centers within Old Town. The most accessible is listed here: Česká Pošta (Křížkovského 844/3; 585 203 542; www.ceskaposta.cz; open M-F 8am-6pm).

Public Restrooms: While there are almost no public restrooms outside of the Upper Square's City Hall, most cafés and restaurants have restrooms available to customers.

Internet: Most restaurants and cafés throughout the Old Town offer free Wi-Fi.

BGLTQ+ Resources: Czechia is generally considered one of the most liberal central European nations in terms of BGLTQ+ rights, legalizing same-sex partnerships in 2006. However, while Czech society is accepting and tolerant, BGLTQ+ individuals do not yet have full legal equality. Czechia-wide BGLTQ+ online counseling service Sbarvouven is listed here (www.sbarvouven.cz; open daily 24hr).

EMERGENCY INFORMATION

Emergency Number: 112.

Police: The Olomouc Old Town is very well policed both during the day and at night. The police headquarters is located at the southern edge of Old Town and its information is listed here (Kateřinská 779/23; 585 209 511; www.mp-olomouc.cz; open daily 24hr).

US Embassy: The nearest US Embassy is in Prague and its information is listed here (Tržiště 365/15; cz.usembassy.gov/embassy/prague, 257 022 000; open M-F 9am-4:30pm).

Rape Crisis Center: While there is no rape crisis center in Olomouc, Centrum Elektra is located in Prague and provides a support hotline for those suffering from sexual abuse or violence. Centrum Elektra (Chomutovická 1444/2; 739 441 879; www.centrumelektra.cz; open W 3pm-6pm).

Hospitals: Unfortunately for tourists, all of Olomouc's hospitals are located well outside of Old Town. The two primary care hospitals are listed below. We recommend going to the University Hospital if possible, but the Military Hospital should serve civilians in an emergency.

- University Hospital Olomouc (I.P. Pavlova 185/6; 585 851 111; www.fnol.cz; open daily 24hr).
- Military Hospital Olomouc (Sušilovo nám. 5; 973 407 150; www.vnol.cz; open M-Th 7am-3:45pm, F 7am-2:30pm).

Pharmacies: Pharmacies in Czechia are called *Lékárnas*.

- Pharmacy U Pöttingea (Palackého 626/3; 585 223 782; open M-F 7:30am-6pm).

SIGHTS

CULTURE

THE SEVEN FOUNTAINS OF OLOMOUC

Horní nám, Dolní nám, and Republicky nám; open daily 24hr

Olomouc has daddy issues, okay? And since no reality TV show host ever broke the news to Olomouc that Julius Caesar and Neptune are not, in fact, its fathers, Olomouc went through both the seventeenth and eighteenth centuries employing Olomouc-born artists to build gothic fountains commemorating all the city's mythological daddies. Of course, the fountains also brought much-needed drinking water to all the thirsty commoners, finally proving to Olomouc's religious elite that Jesus' water of life isn't exactly hydrating. The Lower Square shows off fountains one and three: Neptune and Jupiter, Olomouc's self-chosen protector gods. Republic Square features fountain number four: the mysterious Triton Fountain, brought to you by an unknown early eighteenth-century artist who produced abstract art way before their time. The final four fountains all reside in the Upper Square, from the Mercury, Hercules, and Julius Caesar fountains to the final 2002 Arion Fountain—a triumph of Olomouc artistry depicting the mythological Greek poet Arion capturing a dolphin and celebrating Olomouc's rebirth following the fall of Soviet occupation.

i Free; wheelchair accessible

CHURCH OF ST. MICHAEL

Na Hradě; 603 282 975; www.svatymichal.cz; open M-Tu 9am-4pm, W 9am-10am and noon-5pm, Th-F 9am-4pm, Sa 10am-5pm, Su 10am-5pm

Olomouc's **Old Town** features 15 churches spanning over 1000 years of history, five Christian denominations, and countless architectural styles. While the **Church of Our Lady of the Snows** and **Church of St. Gorazd** make for really stunning visits, if you're looking for a more local-frequented church, look no farther than Church of St. Michael. This thirteenth-century hilltop church isn't much to look at on the outside, but one step inside brings you right into the fold of local life. This is the hidden, three-domed, Gothic and Baroque masterwork of a building where locals find midday refuge from the summer heat.

i Free; no wheelchair accessibility

LOMENÁ GALERIE

Denisova 284/30; 587 207 111; www.lomena.gallery; open daily 24hr

The Lomená Galerie may be the only art gallery in Czechia where you can find such student-inspired masterpieces as graffiti reading, "What do we say to the God of Fucks? Not today." A short tunnel carved into a former Jesuit University Building, the Lomená Galerie is a protected public space where anyone can get approval from the **Olomouc Museum of Natural History** to add their own artwork to the tunnel's white walls. And once the walls fill up with everything from caffeine-fueled poetry and cubist portraits to irreverent graffiti, they get painted over with white and a whole new cycle of Olomouc artistry begins again. And being close to Olomouc's flagship **Palacký University,** the Lomená Galerie is also surrounded by student-oriented murals and wall-art, like a larger-than-life depiction of Marie Curie and an ancient Czech king taking a selfie together in the spirit of quintessentially Czechian fanfiction.

i Free; wheelchair accessible

LANDMARKS

UPPER SQUARE AND LOWER SQUARE

Horní nám. and Dolní nám.; open daily 24hr

Upper Square and Lower Square would definitely be tracks one and two if Olomouc had a greatest hits album. The Upper Square boasts Olomouc's spiritual icon: the locally-built eighteenth-century **Holy Trinity Column** erected to commemorate the end of a particularly nasty plague and now the largest gothic column in Europe. Beside the column stands the 600-year-old Renaissance-style **City Hall** housing the **Olomouc Astronomical Clock**—an astronomical clock larger and grander than Prague's and one of the few Olomouci architectural victims of WWII. After retreating Nazis destroyed the clock, the Soviets later rebuilt it, turning the original Czech noblemen paintings into depictions of proletariat workers. Majestic in its own right, the southern Lower Square features the Trinity Column's predecessor: the 1713 **Marian Column,** also built to commemorate the end of a plague. Besides tributes to some really bad luck with plagues, one more Olomouci hallmark in the squares is the countless number of animal sculptures carved into buildings above doors—rather than create addresses and street names, the medieval residents of Olomouc would just refer to buildings as the "dragon" building or the "unicorn" building.

i Free; wheelchair accessible

MUSEUMS

ARCHDIOCESAN MUSEUM

Václavské nám. 811/4; 585 514 190; www.muo.cz; open Tu-Su 10am-6pm

Don't be fooled by the boring name. Not only is this museum housed in the historic **Olomouc Castle,** but it will constantly force you to wonder if it's a history museum, a church tour, or some Czech Renaissance art gallery. Or maybe, it's a collection of Czech national treasures mixed with a modern art gallery. In the end, the Archdiocesan Museum does it all. One minute, you're walking through the terrace where **King Wenceslas III** was assassinated and into a royal chapel. Next thing you know, a whirlwind carries you into a room decorated with all the medieval Moravian noble family's coat of arms, then you're staring baby Jesus in the face—both in paint and wooden form—and riding in a monumental golden eighteenth-century archbishop's carriage wondering how in the hell you found your way into such an incredible museum.

i Admission 100Kč, 50Kč reduced, Sunday admission free; last entry 30min. before closing; wheelchair accessible

OLOMOUC MUSEUM OF ART

Denisova 824/47; 585 514 111; www.olmuart.cz; open Tu-Su 10am-6pm

Furrowing its eyebrows at the phrase "You can't have your cake and eat it too," the Olomouc Museum of Art said "Of course I can. That's how cake works," and decided to be both a traditional art museum and modern art gallery. And oh boy, does it pull off this identity crisis with poise. Your first stop is floor one: two temporary modern art exhibitions focusing on contemporary Czech artists and featuring everything from modern sculpting, photography, and painting to exhibitions on the history of modern Czechian art. Then, head up to floor four: the **Panorama Room.** Take a good look on Olomouc from above and get to feeling reflective, because floors three and two present you with Czechian art from 1900-2000, as it goes from confronting the experimental techniques of cubism and surrealism to grappling with the startling realities of Soviet occupation.

i Admission 100Kč, 50Kč reduced, Sunday admission free; last entry 30min. before closing; no wheelchair accessibility

OUTDOORS

BEZRUČOVY SADY AND KRONENFESTUNG FORTRESS (BEZRUČOVY PARK AND KRONENFESTUNG FORTRESS)

Bezručovy Sady and 17. Listopadu 7; 585 726 111 and 603 553 933; www.flora-ol.cz and www.pevnostolomouc.cz; Park open daily 24hr, Fortress open Tu-Su 9am-5pm

Like Woody and Buzz, Batman and Robin, a 20-year-old and Netflix, every city needs a reliable companion to keep it happy. Perhaps the superhero and sidekick duo we didn't know we needed but the one we definitely deserve, Bezručovy Park fits into the **Olomouc Old Town** like the perfect curled up little spoon (we're not kidding, check a map). Featuring a cliffside river walk past romantic old gazebos and fortress ruins, Bezručovy Park is no sight to be missed. And when you've walked the walk and talked the talk, cross the crosswalk over the river and visit Kronenfestung Fortress at the heart of Bezručovy Park. A relic from

Olomouc's nineteenth century days as a key Austro-Hungarian military bastion, Kronenfestung Fortress is now no more than a meager community center. So, while going inside isn't all that jazz, take a walk around the walls and the courtyard and you'll definitely be left razzle-dazzled.

i Free; wheelchair accessible; enter fortress from the south

BOTANICKÁ ZAHRADA UNIVERZITY PALACKÉHO (PALACKÝ UNIVERSITY BOTANICAL GARDEN)

U botanické Zahrady 920; 585 634 832; www.garden.upol.cz; open Apr M-F 8am-4pm, May-Sept M-F 8am-6pm, Oct M-F 8am-4pm

The Palacký University Botanical Garden is basically the antithesis to that sorry excuse for a garden you had in middle school that looked more like a burial ground for strawberry plants than a garden. This botanical garden has its roots sunk deep into the Olomouc fabric—the original botanical garden was founded in 1787, and after a century or two of shifting location and ownership, the current rendition of the Olomouc botanical garden surfaced in 1956 under the purview of Palacký University. Count on seeing students tending to the garden during your visit—the plant variety is vast and the small botanical garden takes a lot of upkeep to maintain such distinct areas as a creek, a flower garden, and a romantic forest sitting area. And when you're done soaking up the #nature, visit nearby **Smetanovy Park** and grab some mini-donuts from the numerous stands.

i Free; wheelchair accessible

FOOD

CODO VIETNAMESE DELI ($$)

Palackého 642/13; 797 852 616; open daily 10:30am-10pm

As absurd as it sounds, Codo Vietnamese Deli crafts some of the best Thai and Vietnamese food we've had inside and outside of Europe. For those of you who face existential dread when Thai food isn't available to you at regular intervals, here's your sweet, sweet relief. Codo does great honor to the surprisingly sizable Olomouc Vientamese population—offering every dish from traditional Vietnamese pho and Thai curry to experimental stir fry with some Czechian twists. The restaurant's setting is refreshingly modern and dedicates itself to Olomouc's student population with pizzazz. And if you're in the mood for some solid Japanese craft beer, Codo's got you covered there too. Really, there just isn't a better place to eat in all of Olomouc, so settle in and saddle up your sriracha bottle because you're in for one serious ride.

i Entreés from 129Kč, beer from 25Kč; vegetarian and vegan options available; wheelchair accessible

THE BUNS AND FAENCY FRIES ($)

174/2, Panská and Ztracená 317/15; 605 700 811 and 733 123 456; www.faency-fries.cz; Buns open Tu-Th 11am-10pm, F 11am-midnight, Sa 2pm-midnight, Faency Fries open M-F 11am-8pm, Sa 1pm-7pm

While "buns" and "fries" may constitute enough Freudian imagery to be sexually suggestive, we promise that visiting these two square-side food stands will satisfy nothing but your tastebuds. Let's make short shrift: The Buns is a greasy-spoon burger joint on the eastern side of **Lower Square** offering signature patties like the "pulled-beef-BBQ burger" and even a solid vegan burger option. And once you take a bite of the artwork that is a burger from The Buns, calories will become no more than a nasty conspiracy theory as you go on the prowl for freshly-fried French relief. Lucky for you, Faency Fries is only a five minute walk north off of **Upper Square**—providing just enough time to inhale your burger before you order some chili mayo, vegan dip, or chili cheese canola-oil masterpieces.

i Burgers from 130Kč, fries from 38Kč; vegetarian and vegan options available; wheelchair accessible

NIGHTLIFE

THE BLACK STUFF IRISH PUB & WHISKEY BAR

1. máje 807/19; 774 697 909; www.blackstuff.cz; open M-Th 5pm-2am, F-Sa 5pm-3am, Su 5pm-midnight

Olomouc having The Black Stuff reminds you a lot of that one kid who never studied for tests or read any of the required readings but always got 100's, had a steady partner, and will probably cure cancer. How can a small town like Olomouc justify housing one of the best bars Central Europe has to offer? We don't know, but this isn't hyperbole or opinion—The Black Stuff has been listed as **one of the world's 30 best whiskey bars,** the three dedicated bartenders have won numerous awards in European mixology competitions, and the bar itself is decorated with over 1,400 bottles of liquor in glass cases lining every wall. With a menu over 50 pages long covering beers and cocktails from every corner of the globe and brought to you in an authentic wood-and-brick, Irish-pub setting, The Black Stuff is really a gem of an experience.

i Beer from 30Kč, cocktails from 89Kč; cash only; wheelchair accessible

VERTIGO

Univerzitní 227/6; 777 059 150; www.klubvertigo.cz; open M-Th 1pm-2am, F-Sa 4pm-2am, Su 4pm-midnight

Looking for a visit to The Pleasure Garden? Participating in The Prude's Fall? Well, forget you were ever The Farmer's Wife and rename yourself The Mountain Eagle because a night at Alfred Hitchcock themed student bar Vertigo will bring out the Psycho in you. No matter if you're Rich and Strange, on a tight Rope, or frozen by Stage Fright, say goodbye to your hostel's Rear Window and get ready for a night full of cheap drinks, raucous tabletop dancing, and regrettable conversations with The Wrong Man. Whether you met your dance partner as Strangers on a Train or you go by Mr. & Mrs. Smith, Vertigo's two floors, small dance floor, and walls covered in pictures of James Stewart, Grace Kelly, Cary Grant, and the Hitch himself will ensure that you have a night that never goes Downhill.

i Beer from 30Kč; limited wheelchair accessibility

PRAGUE

Coverage by **Luke Williams**

If, like every person in our hostel, you fall into the trap of exploring only the Old Town and Prague Castle, you'll rightly end up calling Prague "suffocating," "narrow," and "claustrophobic." Yes, Prague is beautiful and steeped in history, but that also means there's more tourists to tickle, tackle, and thwart in Old Town Square than in Times Square itself. Spend more than a day in Old Town and you're going to lose your mind. So here's the best advice we can give you for Prague: **Get the hell out of Old Town.** So long as you remember to GTHOOT, Prague will be your favorite European gem, no contest. This is the city of a million faces—its size unfolds for miles, revealing residential district after residential district, brought to you by Renaissance-fueled technicolor and stereo dynamic locals. Prague is the city you've been waiting for, as long as you're willing to get lost. So go. Get lost in the rough-and-tumble Nusle neighborhood, the high-falutin' Podolí District, the arts-oriented Prague 7 and Maniny Districts, and the confident and quiet, student-oriented Florenc and Žižkov Districts. Prague has more to offer than any city you've ever been to: Grotesque faces peer out from the Dripstone Wall, John Lennon is in immortal combat with communism in Mala Strana, the Holešovice District hosts too many international fairs to count, clubs like Lucerna and Vzorkovna take you underground to remember the 80's, and the distant 1000-year-old Vyšehrad fortress watches over everything—begging you to get the **hell** out of Old Town.

ORIENTATION

During your obligatory day in tourist-occupied **Old Town,** you'll want to check out **Josefov,** home of the Jewish Quarter, to the north of **Old Town Square.** If you're still interested in living out your zombie flick fantasies, fight off more hordes of tourists in the arguably more interesting **Mala Strana (Lesser Town)** and **Hradcany (Castle District).** Now it's time to get experimental. Using the **Vltava River** that splits Prague into a **West Bank** and **East Bank** and your position relative to the city's center at Old Town Square as your guide, it's hard to get lost. Much like Budapest, this city invites the eager walker into its fold, begging you to unleash the sunblock, fanny packs, and travel guides to go granola. If you're looking to experience the local side of things, you should keep a few main districts in mind. To the north of Old Town Square across the Vltava lies the grungy but artsy **Prague 7, Holešovice,** and **Maniny Districts.** Northeast of OTS lies the quiet, student-oriented **Florenc District.** Southeast of OTS lies the young-minded, beer-café-filled, and vegan-restaurant-lined **Žižkov, Vinohrady,** and **Staré Vršovice Districts.** If you're feeling adventurous, take the time to visit our favorite sites in the city 20 minutes south of OTS across the **Nusle Bridge:** the **Vyšehrad Fortress, Podolí,** and **Pankrác Districts.**

ESSENTIALS

GETTING THERE

No direct train or bus lines run from the airport to the city center, but there are buses that connect to metro lines which will take you into the city. Bus #119 runs from the airport to Veleslavin metro station on the green Line A. Bus #100 runs from the airport to Zličín metro station on the yellow Line B. Both these lines will take you into the city center. The total journey is approximately 40 minutes. Purchase tickets from public transport counters in Terminals 1 and 2 from 7am-10pm. Alternatively, use the coin-operated vending machines at the bus stop. Note that drivers usually only accept small bills and change. You may need to purchase a half-price ticket (10Kč) for larger pieces of luggage. Remember to validate tickets in the yellow machines before boarding any public transportation. If you're arriving by train, you'll most likely disembark at Praha hl.n. (Prague Main Station), located at the southeast corner of New Town. The railway station is connected to the metro system (red Line C). One stop north will connect you to the yellow Line B, and one stop south to the green Line C; both will take you to the city center. Most international buses disembark at Florenc Bus Station, which is just east of Old Town.

GETTING AROUND

The public transport system is convenient and consists of three metro lines (green Line A, yellow Line B, red Line C), trams, and buses. The same ticket is used for all forms of public transportation. Ticket options start at 24Kč for 30min. on a tram or five stops on a metro train. Be sure to validate your ticket in the yellow machines on buses and trams or at the base of escalators in metro stations. Plainclothes police officers will often inspect tickets. They are notoriously strict and will fine you up to 1000Kč if you haven't validated your ticket. The metro runs from 5am-midnight and buses and trams operate from 4:30am-12:15am. Night buses and trams operate less frequently after that time. The central point of nighttime transfers is Lazarska in Nove Mesto. Be wary of potential pickpockets on crowded trains, trams, buses, and in crowded public areas. Particular hotspots are Old Town Square, the Charles Bridge, and trams #22 and #23. In case you need quick and more convenient transportation than public transport, Uber and Bolt both work in Prague. We recommend using Bolt, as the drivers are usually certified taxi drivers and the rates are more consistent.

PRACTICAL INFORMATION

Tourist Offices: This office is note very busy and conveniently located: Old Town Hall Tourist and Information Center (Staroměstské nám. 1; 221 714 714; open daily 9am-7pm).

Banks/ATMs/Currency Exchange: ATMs can be found in the city center and tourist areas, belonging to local and international banks. We've listed a centrally located ATM here: Travelex ATM (Ánenská 203; 221 105 336; www.travelex.cz).

Post Offices: A centrally located office is listed here: Česká pošta (Kaprova 40/12; 954 211 001; www.ceskaposta.cz; open M-F 8am-7pm).

Public Restrooms: There aren't many public restrooms throughout the city; most public buildings and restaurants have accessible restrooms. There's an quiet restroom in Old Town Square—located in the Kinsky Palace courtyard (Týn; 603 444 165; open daily 9am-8pm).

Internet: Free Wi-Fi can be accessed at nearly every café, hostel, and most restaurants.

BGLTQ+ Resources: Czechia is generally considered one of the most liberal central European nations in terms of BGLTQ+ rights, legalizing same-sex partnerships in 2006. While Czech society is accepting and tolerant, BGLTQ+ individuals do not yet have full legal equality. Czechia-wide BGLTQ+ online counseling service Sbarvouven is listed here. (www.sbarvouven.cz; open daily 24hr).

EMERGENCY INFORMATION

Emergency Number: 112

Police: Police maintain a reliable presence throughout Old Town and New Town. (Jungmannovo nám. 771/9; 974 851 750; open daily 24hr).

US Embassy: The US Embassy is located in Mala Strana near Malostranské nám (Tržiště 365/15; 257 022 000; open M-F 9am-4:30pm).

Rape Crisis Center: Centrum Elektra provides a support hotline for victims suffering from sexual abuse or violence. (Chomutovická 1444/2; 739 441 879; www.centrumelektra.cz; open W 3pm-6pm).

Hospitals: Most of Prague's hospitals are located west, north, and south of the city center in the more residential areas of Prague. Two close, reliable options are listed here.

- University Hospital in Motol (V Úvalu 84; 224 431 111; www.fnmotoal.cz; open daily 24hr).
- General University Hospital in Prague (U Nemocnice 499/2; 224 961 111; www.vfn.cz; open daily 24hr).

Pharmacies: Pharmacies in Prague are known as "Lékárna's" and are generally advertised with green crosses.

- Black Rose Pharmacy (Panská 894/4; 221 014 712; open M-F 8am-7pm).
- Dr. Max Lékárna (Vodičkova 40; 224 235 847; www.drmax.cz; open M-F 8am-8pm, Sa 9am-6pm).

SIGHTS

CULTURE

NUSLE AND PODOLÍ DISTRICTS

Nusle and Podolí; open daily 24hr

Tucked between the hills of **Old Town** and **Pankrác,** Nusle is Prague's most accessible workingman's district. Under the **Nusle Bridge** you'll find a valley full of intimate, rainbow-colored streets where pubs spring up like weeds, lines of schoolchildren walk the streets, and independent cafés pioneer bold new coffee blends to fit the rough-and-tumble feel. Only a 20-minute walk south of Old Town and the perfect stop on your way to Vyšehrad, Nusle is an absolute must for any traveler who finds herself wondering "Where the hell are all the locals?" After giving Nusle its due, head 15 minutes southwest to the riverside Podolí neighborhood—one of Prague's up-and-coming higher-class districts centered around the Prague Waterworks Museum. Experienced together, Nusle and Podolí provide one of the most satisfying glimpses into the real Prague that any traveler is likely to get.

i Free; wheelchair accessible

ŽIŽKOV AND STARÉ VRŠOVICE DISTRICTS

Žižkov (center at Žižkov TV Tower, Mahlerovy Sady 1), Staré Vršovice (center at Heroldovy Sady); open daily 24hr

It may be just a rumor, but we've heard more than once that Žižkov has more bars per capita than any other major city district in Europe. Perhaps the most easily accessible local-oriented district of Prague, Žižkov houses some seriously unappreciated wonders like the **Žižkov TV Tower,** the 1930s *Blade Runner*-esque **Church of the Most Sacred Heart,** and some of the best food festivals in the city. What was once a blue-collar district is quickly taking notes from Florenc and becoming a student-oriented space, alongside its southern neighbor **Staré Vršovice**—Prague's unapologetic café and vegan restaurant capital district. While other hotspots in the area include the popular **Riegrovy Park** and historic hillside **Bezručovy Garden,** these technically are part of the monolithic **Vinohrady District**...but really we can just act like they're part of the Žižkov-Staré Vršovice partnership and you can experience some rose-tinted local life without worrying about the details.

i Free; wheelchair accessible

BIO OKO CINEMA

Františka Křížka 460/15; 233 382 606; www.biooko.net; open M-F 10am-1pm, Sa-Su 11am-1pm

Bio Oko is one of Prague's many cult landmarks that a discerning tourist would be lucky to ever even find. The 1960s neon-light-ridden façade invokes Soviet-era socialist realism even as the movie posters plastered on the outside advertise the crunchiest Cannes darlings you're likely to find at an art house movie theater. Every screening at Bio Oko is basically a public event—do yourself a favor and buy yourself a ticket to one of the "English friendly" showings on their website. Don't be afraid to treat yourself: as soon as you arrive you'll be greeted with hordes of young locals celebrating Jim Jarmusch and David Lynch with near-constant toasts at the in-house bar and lounge area. After the libations have been raised, clinked, and consumed, head on into the massive two-story vintage cinema for a film experience like you've never imagined. Unless, of course, you read *The Perks of Being a Wallflower* in high school and decided to devote your life to *Rocky Horror Picture Show* screenings. In that case, you'll be right at home.

i Tickets from 140Kč; movie times vary, check website; wheelchair accessible

LENNON WALL

Velkopřevorské náměstí; open daily 24hr

As long as you didn't read *The Catcher in the Rye* and get any wild ideas about taking a grand stand against all the phonies, you're bound to enjoy this living relic of Czechia's communist past. This unlikely wall hidden in the dense maze of **Mala Strana** became one of the most potent sites of 1980s student protests against communism in Czechia, as students would frequently gather to graffiti the wall with countless depictions of Lennon's face and the now-infamous phrase: "We want Lennonism, not Leninism." Take the long and winding road to one of Prague's most colorful sites that's bound to make you twist and shout. Street musicians crowd the place like it's American Idol circa 2010, and if their renditions of *Yellow Submarine* aren't enough to give you nostalgia for yesterday, then you need to buy a ticket to ride right back home. After you've plastered your own Lennon-centric graffiti on the wall, hop on over to the adjacent **Kampa Island** to visit Czech sculptor David Cerny's "Giant Barcode Babies" and lounge back in one of Prague's great outdoor paradises.

i Free; wheelchair accessible

STRAHOV MONASTERY

Strahovské nádvoří 1/132; 233 107 704; www.strahovskyklaster.cz; open daily 9am-5pm, ticket booth closed daily noon-1pm

The Strahov Monastery is one of Prague's most underrated tourist attractions—but that also means it provides a well-needed break from the tourist-filled streets of **Mala Strana.** The perfect stop before climbing **Petrin Hill,** visit the Strahov Monastery to see two of Europe's most beautiful interiors: the twin monastery libraries lovingly coined the **Theological Hall** and **Philosophical Hall.** A ticket to the monastery's gallery also earns you free rein to explore the twelfth-century meeting halls, courtyards, and reception rooms of one of Prague's most fascinating buildings. As if that weren't enough, a visit to the pastel pink-and-white monastery **Basilica** is free and the hillside restaurants just east of the monastery serve freshly brewed beer alongside some of the best views of Prague you're going to get.

i Library admission 120Kč, 60Kč reduced, library and gallery 200Kč, 100Kč reduced; wheelchair accessible

LANDMARKS

NUSLE BRIDGE

Bridge begins just south of B. Němcové 1881/5; open daily 24hr

For all we care, leave the Charles Bridge and its hyperinflated self-image to the likes of Rick Steves readers and Regina George groupies. What the Nusle Bridge lacks in history it makes up for in sheer grandeur. This monumental land bridge spans the entire Nusle valley to connect the two hills of Prague's downtown: **Old Town** to the north and residential **Pankrác** to the south. Walking across the Nusle could very well be the first time you realize Holy shit! There's so much more to Prague than a very disappointing astronomical clock and crowds of tourists! This is the definitive way to get a feel for the "Second City," as we've come to call it in our overactive imagination. Not only does crossing the Nusle deliver you to the tourist-free and infinitely more interesting storied side of Prague, but it offers the opportunity to experience locally-sourced nirvana.

i Free; wheelchair accessible

REPUBLIC SQUARE

Náměstí Republiky; open daily 24hr

If Old Town's three squares were each a *Star Wars* trilogy, Republic Square would undoubtedly be the prequels. Criminally underappreciated, appealing in the most unexpected ways, and fostering a cult following, Republic Square is the only area in all of Old Town that you're likely to find any locals. Not only does Republic Square contain some of Prague's most remarkable architecture, from the unforgettable **Municipal House** to the **Hybernia Theatre** and **Powder Tower,** it's also home to food festivals, street magicians, and two of Prague's grandest shopping centers. Whether you're a high-browed eurotrash supporter who exclusively shops at the **Katva Mall** or a believer in the Americanized pink pastel palace that is the **Prague Palladium Mall,** we guarantee Republic Square will keep you occupied for a few hours with ease. Soak in the modern art that decorates the square, talk shop with wise locals on the newest Prague fashions, or visit the **Museum of Communism** to truly bask in the glory of the Republic.

i Free; wheelchair accessible

SS. CYRIL AND METHODIUS CATHEDRAL

Resslova 9a; 224 920 686; www.pravoslavnacirkev.cz; open Tu-Sa 9am-5pm

Three and a half years into Nazi occupation, a small group of Czech and Slovack men successfully assasinated a high-ranking Nazi official: Reinhard Heydrich, the "Butcher of Prague." Immediately after, Nazi officials cracked down on the rest of the country, completely erasing two towns and their populace from the face of Czechia and putting hundreds of young men from Prague on trial. As chaos reigned outside, the assassins hid for a month in the crypt of Ss. Cyril and Methodius Cathedral—a prominent Orthodox church located in the heart of Prague. Eventually, the men were betrayed and Nazis stormed the crypt, killing every one of the assassins. Today, the crypt has been turned into Prague's most moving monument and museum, and you can still see much of the carnage from the gunfight that ensued when the Nazis stormed the crypt.

i Free; no wheelchair accessibility

WENCESLAS SQUARE

Václavské nám.; open daily 24hr

Wenceslas Square is the geographic and cultural opposite of **Old Town Square.** Where Old Town Square is a relic of medieval and Renaissance Prague, Wenceslas Square is a still-changing remnant of early twentieth-century Prague. This massive square hosts some of Prague's highest-end shopping alongside century-old department

stores that made their way into Kafka's stories. While walking around Wenceslas Square is certainly worthwhile, our favorite feature of the Square is **Academia Bookstore and Café.** Not only does Academia have one of the best collections of English works in the city, but if you grab something to eat or drink at the second story café you can sit outside on the store's balcony—directly above hundreds of tourists' heads. So if you read *1984* and thought to yourself, "I want to be like Big Brother when I grow up," Academia could not be more doubleplusgood.

i Free; wheelchair accessible

MUSEUMS

DOX CENTRE FOR CONTEMPORARY ART

Poupětova 1; 295 568 123; www.dox.cz; open M 10am-6pm, W 11am-7pm, Th 11am-9pm, F 11am-7pm, Sa-Su 10am-6pm

Few museums have as much balls as the DOX Centre—from its purposeful maze layout to signs that tell you you're simultaneously going the "Right Way," "Wrong Way," and "Only Way," the DOX Centre downright wants you to get lost. Taking inspiration from museum motto "You first need to get lost to find yourself," this five-story modern-art Mecca not only houses up to five exhibitions throughout its maze, but also a giant wooden zeppelin hanging off the roof of the building. We've never been to an art museum as engaging and rewarding as DOX. Nothing is out of the question: A sculpture, film, and VR exhibition on Heavy Metal-inspired art? Check. A gallery filled with irreverent modern pop art? You betcha. A retrospective on Czech architecture? Only if we can display full-sized replicas doused in glorious mood lighting.

i Admission 180Kč, 90Kč reduced; last entry 30min. before closing; wheelchair accessible

KAFKA MUSEUM

Cihelná 635/2b; 257 535 373; www.kafkamuseum.cz; open daily 10am-6pm

By the time you see Prague's three Kafka monuments in as many days, you'll probably begin to understand just how proud Prague is of its foremost native son. Born and raised in Old Town, Kafka's novels and short stories are usually credited with founding modern literature, giving crucial life support to the surrealists and absurdists in anticipation of postmodernism. Mala Strana's Kafka Museum takes you on a darkly fantastic and disorienting journey through Kafka's personal and professional life, filled with countless artifacts, haunting overhead classical music, and cerebral settings. Whether you're a complete Kafka head or have never heard of *The Metamorphosis*, this museum tells an accessible story and focuses on the author's most universal themes—"lighthearted" topics like alienation, self-loathing, and disorientation—to draw everyone in on equally vulnerable footing.

i Admission 260Kč, 180Kč reduced; last entry 1hr. before closing; no wheelchair accessibility

MUSEUM OF MINIATURES

Strahovské nádvoří 11; 233 352 371; www.muzeumminiatur.cz; open daily 9am-5pm

If you're like us, upon hearing the phrase "miniature art" you probably rolled your eyes and immediately decided to pass. Think again. What if we told you that when you look through the museum's microscopes you'll see some of the most inventive and amusing art you've ever laid eyes on? Here's a taste: Christ's face carved into a poppy seed, a boat on stormy seas carved into a mosquito's wing, and gold leaf cars driving down a human hair highway. What about a full-length novel condensed into less than a square inch? A perfect recreation of the *Mona Lisa* smaller than your fingernail? Forget all your snobby friends who decided the Louvre is lyfe—the Museum of Miniatures is the fantastical sum of one man's life, work, and his pioneering avant-garde artistic techniques.

i Admission 130Kč, 70Kč reduced; wheelchair accessible

MUSEUM OF COMMUNISM

V Celnici 1031/4; 224 212 966; www.museumofcommunism.com; open daily 9am-9pm

While Marx and our college professors may argue that "Sharing is caring, and caring is communism," Prague's Museum of Communism is out to set that argument straight. Making no claims concerning telling an unbiased story, the MoC uses immersive environments and carefully-crafted personal and historical narratives to give visitors a bird's eye view of communism in Czechia, as it progressed from Marx's dream to the gulag's nightmare. The curators of the MoC are here to present you with just how the history of Marx's utopia went so wrong. You'll explore the early days of blue-collar support fowr proletariat paradises throughout the Eastern Bloc, and then be slammed with grim facts and figures arguing that while communism looks good on paper, the Czech people are here to tell you that humans + utopian ideals = real-life toilet-paper-starved dystopias featuring too many oppressive regimes and gruesome deaths to count.

i Admission 290Kč, 250Kč reduced; last entry 1hr. before closing; no wheelchair accessibility

OUTDOORS

PALACE GARDENS BELOW PRAGUE CASTLE AND WALLENSTEIN GARDEN

Palace Gardens, Valdštejnská 158/14, 257 214 817, www.palacove-zahrady.cz, open daily 10am-6pm; Wallenstein Garden, Letenská 123/4, 257 075 707, www.senat.cz, open M-F 7:30am-6pm, Sa-Su 10am-6pm

The Palace Gardens are set up on a hill right below the castle, full of no-expenses-spared statues, hedge mazes, and grottos. Luckily, the gardens are relatively unknown to tourists and a ticket purchase practically promises you'll feel like Odysseus wandering through the lavish lotus eater's island. When you're done indulging your King's Landing fantasies, head on down to **Wallenstein Garden**—the former privately-owned garden is crowded with everything from massive koi ponds, a classical Italian theater, and wild peacocks—to the haunting seventeenth-century Dripstone Wall. The Dripstone was built as part of the original garden to give it a "fantastic" quality, but we think the Wallensteins were really time traveling *Game of Thrones* fans who loved Arya's trip to the Faceless Men, because this wall is full of grimacing human faces.

i Palace Gardens 80Kč, 60Kč reduced, Wallenstein Garden free; Palace Garden limited wheelchair accessibility

VYŠEHRAD FORTRESS

V Pevnosti 159/5b; 241 410 348; www.praha-vysehrad.cz; open daily 9:30am-5pm

The Tom Holland to the Prague Castle's Andrew Garfield, the Vyšehrad Fortress is your friendly, neighborhood tenth-century castle that proves unexpected alternatives are incredibly satisfying. Practically devoid of crowds, the fortress complex is home to Prague's oldest buildings (see **St. Martin's Rotunda),** most unapologetic royal relics (see the **Brick Gate and Saints Peter and Paul Cathedral),** and some of the city's most famous departed in the equal parts beautiful and somber **Vyšehrad Cemetery.** Here you'll get the best views of Prague in the city, as the Vyšehrad is one of the few landmarks that allows you to look down on **Old Town, Mala Strana,** and southern Prague all at once. The two hours you spend here will be some of your best memories of Prague, and we're just left grateful that 10,000 years ago a really foolish king designated this castle as the city's foremost future tourist attraction.

i Vyšehrad admission free; Church of St. Peter and St. Paul 50Kč, 30Kč reduced; limited wheelchair accessibility

BOHEMIAN SWITZERLAND

Bohemian Switzerland National Park is Czechia's foremost nature reserve and recipient of the "National Park With The Coolest Name Award" for the last nineteen years and counting. Welcome to a sprawling collection of canyons, sandstone mountains, and fields speckled with medieval castles, monasteries, and natural wonders. Two hours from Prague, the park doesn't attract many international tourists: it's actually considered a favorite local destination for native Germans and Czechs alike. And following in the footsteps of all inseparable duos, what would Bohemian Switzerland be without its northern counterpart Saxon Switzerland? Much less interesting, for one. Part of Bohemian Switzerland's allure is due to the fact that you can cross the border into Germany with ease—and some of the park's best sites are actually in Germany. Not that anyone's keeping score, but if we're interested in only the main attractions, the Czechs have the largest sandstone arch in Europe and riverboat rides through two gorges—while Germany can only brag about the Bastei, a medieval bridge carved into the top of a mountain. And if you're planning on getting a little bit more Bohemian than one day allows, make sure to head over to Tisá southwest of the park and explore the Tisá Rock Labyrinth.

For anyone coming from Prague and staying for one day, Bohemian Switzerland begins in the town of **Hřensko,** situated at the southwestern corner of the larger park. You can access the first two major trailheads by walking east down Hřensko's main street. The south side of the street brings you to **Edmund Gorge** and keeping on the north side of the street for 30 minutes due east brings you to the **Pravčická Arch** trailhead. We recommend starting with the Pravčická Arch trail, then tackling **Gabriela's Trail** which leads you farther east and into the small **Mezní Louka** mountain resort. From Mezní Louka, you can head farther east up the **Schauenstein** trail if you're looking to summit a medieval thirteenth-century castle ruin. Either way, the Schaunstein trail brings you right back to Mezní Louka, from which you can head south down an undriven road full of backpackers toward the small town of **Mezná.** Finally, from Mezná you will be able to head farther south until you're walking alongside the **Elbe River.** Head west as soon as you reach the river to take a boat through Edmund Gorge.

GETTING THERE

This can get complicated, so we're going to keep it as simple as possible. Trains run from Praha hl.n. to the town of Děčín almost every hour, arriving at Děčín hl.n. with tickets starting at 150Kč. Upon arriving in Děčín, you have two options. The first is to take a 25-45min. bus ride from the train station to Hřensko. Bus tickets start at 20Kč. The other option is to take a 15-minute taxi, starting from 300Kč. Next, you have two more options: exit the bus/taxi early and walk through Hřensko for 30min. before reaching the first trail, or you can go directly to the trailhead for Pravčická Brana. If the extended option sounds like your style, ask to be dropped off at "Obecní urad-Rathaus," and if the shorter trip is your choice, get off at "Tri prameny."

GETTING AROUND

Buses run throughout the entire park and bus stops are clearly marked on every map you come across—and maps won't be in short supply. If you're fed up with walking and need some sweet AC, hop on a bus and ride it to your next trailhead or all the way home. Just know that sometimes bus wait times can be as long as 45min. When leaving the park from the entrance to Hřensko, no taxis will be present and both Uber and Bolt are unavailable in the area. You must go back to Děčín via bus, using the bus stop on the western side of the street and buying a 29Kč ticket onboard. Important: Since buses can sometimes take 45min. to arrive, plan accordingly. You should try to be at the bus stop at least an hour before your train back to Prague, just to be safe.

Don't miss...

SCHAUENSTEIN CASTLE RUINS AND THE LITTLE ARCH

Šaunštejn, Jetřichovice; open daily 24hr

Only in Central Europe could you just hike to the ruins of a medieval castle—but don't expect the journey to be easy. While the rest of the trails listed are little more than glorified walking paths crammed with tourists, the trail to Schauenstein's ruins is both challenging and extremely rewarding. After roughly an hour of summiting a sandstone giant and walking through Middle Earthian forests, you'll come to an asphalt crossroads. Consult the trail markers and take a quick five minute detour to see the **Little Arch**—basically a mini version of the Pravčická Arch you'll be able to stand inside for some Insta gold. We're not kidding, these views are worthy of royalty. **Important:** We recommend consulting an info stand in Mezní Louka before heading to the trailhead to make sure you're going up the right way. To return, either go back the way you came or take the asphalt road at the crossroads back down to Mezní Louka for a faster descent.

i No wheelchair accessibility; trailhead located just east of Restaurace U Forta; from Mezní Louka estimated 85min., return trip estimated 70min., Little Arch located just before descent toward Schauenstein Castle

Check out...

BOAT RIDE THROUGH EDMUND GORGE

Edmundova Soutěska; boat rides open daily 9am-6pm

After a descent from **Mezná** or a short walk from the **Hřensko** downtown, you'll arrive upon an offshoot of the **Elbe River** that runs between two massive cliffs, collectively considered the Edmund Gorge—just one of Bohemian Switzerland's two canyons and the one most easily accessible within a daytrip. And as luck would have it, you can get down and dirty in the river by hopping into a 30-person rowboat captained by an eccentric Czech or German native who not only shouts "Ahoy!" at the top of his lungs constantly but also thinks that his tour guiding is the beginning of his stand-up comedy career. It doesn't matter that the tours are only given in Czech and German—you'll catch all the major sights like the **King Kong rock** and **Moby Dick rock** as well as have a blast watching the locals lose their shit at what to you is only incoherent mumbling.

i Admission 80Kč; no wheelchair accessibility; boat ride only way to cross gorge, ride lasts 20min., estimated 30min. from downtown Hřensko, 70min. from Mezní Louka

Grab a bite at...

RESTAURACE U FORTA ($$)

Mezná 37; 412 554 090; www.uforta.cz; open M-Th noon-9pm

If we told you that one of the best restaurants in America was right next to Yellowstone's Ol' Faithful, you'd look at us like we'd lost our mind. But we're not going to tell you that. We're going to tell you that one of our favorite traditional Czech restaurants is in the middle of Bohemian Switzerland, situated in a basin surrounded by mountains and fields, with close access to almost every trailhead you could ever want. If you find yourself finishing Gabriela's Trail with the need for duck and dumplings, salmon fillet, boar steak, or, our favorite, dill soup, U Forta is the place to stop for both a beer and the will to continue.

i Entrées from 155Kč, beer from 35Kč; wheelchair accessible from adjacent bus stop

HAVLICEK GARDENS

Havlíčkovy sady; 236 044 111; open daily 6am-10pm

Prague is to city parks as New York City is to hot dog stands: They're everywhere, they all look the same, and no one has any clue which ones will make you regret visiting and which will be worth a second, third, or forty-fifth visit. We've come to the grand conclusion that Havlicek is the only official city park worth making the walk to. A historic and still-operating vineyard is planted squarely on the sloped hill the gardens call home, flourishing with fresh grapes you may or may not be allowed to harvest and eat fresh. To the west of the vineyard lies the most romantic spot in all of Prague: the **Havlicek pond and grotto,** a Baroque masterpiece fountain with a cave-like backdrop and pastel-colored houses decorating the distance. A trip east of the vineyard will reveal remaining Renaissance buildings, and traveling both north and south will justify the gardens' remote location with vegan and beer cafés galore.

i Free; wheelchair accessible

PETRIN HILL AND KINSKY GARDEN

Petrin Tower (Petřínské sady 633), Kinsky Garden west of Petrin beyond Hunger Wall; 257 320 112; Petrin Hill and Kinsky Garden open daily 24hr, Petrin Tower open daily 10am-10pm

Petrin Hill is Prague's outdoor destination, but with its convenient and iconic location, how could you resist climbing to the top and admiring Prague's take on the Eiffel Tower? While funiculars shuttle people from the hill's eastern base to the top, at the risk of sounding like an angry grandpa, we think that's just taking all the fun(icular) out of climbing the hill. The greatest hits on the Kinsky side of things are the art gallery turned *Lord of the Rings* cottage **Prague's Magical Cavern** and the **Carpathian Ruthenian Orthodox Church** that's moved across countries three times in its long history.

i Parks free, Petrin Tower 150Kč, reduced 80Kč; wheelchair accessible

FOOD

CAFÉ LOUVRE ($)

Národní 22; 224 930 949; www.cafelouvre.cz; open M-F 8am-11:30pm, Sa-Su 9am-11:30pm

Oui, oui, mon ami: Praha and Paris can be friends sometimes. And what happens when they work together? For one, a century-old Parisan café serving traditional Czech food right off one of downtown's main streets. A touch of Paris is evident from the pink and white walls in the restaurant, the golden espresso machine, and the mahogany billiards room. And much to everyone's surprise, this legendary café—a frequent haunt of Einstein *and* Kafka—is really, really cheap. For some of the best quality pancakes in the city and a few of the most creative egg preparations in Czechia you'll pay no more than 250Kč. The coffee is as strong as the breakfast menu is long, and while we highly recommend catching the Louvre in the morning, they also have full lunch and dinner menus that we're certain will make you wish they made a Lunch and Dinner at Tiffany's.

i Entreés from 89Kč, coffee from 47Kč; reservation recommended; vegetarian options available; no wheelchair accessibility

GARUDA RESTAURANT ($$)

M. Horákové 686/12; 730 890 424; www.garudarestaurant.cz; open daily 10:30am-10pm

Garuda is a special place. If you ever find yourself exploring **Prague 7**, perhaps to go to **Letna Park**, **Bio Oko**, or the **Trade Fair Palace**, Garuda Restaurant is the place to eat. Squarely in the middle of Prague 7 lies this Budda, Ganesha, and Shiva-covered Indonesian culinary wonderland. Thanks to coffee and smoothie selections that will have you buying your plane ticket to southeast Asia, Garuda does Asian food better than anywhere else in Prague. Not only do the meat- or tofu-based curry, noodles, and salad dishes come cheap, but if you're a fan of Thai or Vietnamese cuisine this is the next step toward enlightenment.

i Entreés from 195Kč; gluten-free, vegan, and vegetarian options available; wheelchair accessible

MOMENT KAVARNA ($)

Slezská 62; 775 431 430; open M-F 10am-9pm, Sa-Su 9am-9pm

Once upon a time, in a land far, far away (20min.) from Old Town called **Žižkov,** there's a little café that is Prague's quintessential coffee and breakfast dive. The manager struts and frets about the place, dressed in neon from his toes to his face. He declares "Madonna Hour" from the front door, while weary customers eat vegan cuisine and shout "More!" From tofu scramble, pancakes, and sausage assortments to curries, cakes, and bagel burgers, everything at Moment is made with love (and entirely vegan ingredients, to be sure). Expect sweet addiction, local attention, and almond-milk cappuccino benedictions. And let it be known that not only veggie-heads honor these hallowed halls—many of Moment's frequent patrons are breakfast lovers who know Moment is as good as it gets.

i Entreés from 95Kč, baked goods from 75Kč, coffee from 42Kč; vegan food only, gluten free-options available; wheelchair accessible

RESTAURACE U BANSETHŮ ($)

Táborská 389/49; 724 582 721; www.ubansethu.cz; open daily 11am-midnight

Czech food normally makes us Czech out. We just can't get into menus that exclusively feature meat and potatoes and actively shun flavor. That said, nestled nicely in the **Nusle** district lies a legendary local pub called Restaurace U Bansethů, and it's not hyperbole to say this is the place that made us fall in love with Czech cuisine. A hidden homey bar and brewery, U Bansethů goes for the rugged "cabin in the woods" look, employing only masterchef Czech grandmothers who carry silver pots and pans around a wooden-walled restaurant adorned with animal heads and vintage portraits. If you're able to negotiate a seat, you'll face the classic Czech assortment of duck liver/paté/heart/goulash/burger/meatloaf and grilled/boiled/pickled sausages with steak, schnitzel, and ham thrown in for "variety." But we promise, **you will never have Czech food this good**. We're betting it's all the grandma-grown magic at work in the kitchens, ensuring your duck, dumplings, and sauerkraut will be a near-religious experience.

i Entreés from 69Kč, beer from 27Kč; wheelchair accessible

NAŠE MASO ($)

Dlouhá 727/39; 222 311 378; www.nase-maso.cz; open M-Sa 8:30am-10pm

On an idyllic street just northeast of **Old Town Square,** Naše Maso sits between a bakery and dessert shop, presenting the perfect lunchtime triple-threat. If you manage to brute-force your way past all of the locals cramming into Naše Maso to procure tonight's fresh duck liver, you'll find a small, no-frills menu offering classic Czech sausage preparations, a cheeseburger, and a wagyu beef cheeseburger. You may hear from your hostel proprietor that Naše Maso has the best burger in the city, and we can confirm. Assembled right beside hanging cow carcasses, your burger will feature the best combo of beef, onions, cheese, and mustard you're going to grab in Europe.

i Entreés from 95Kč; limited wheelchair accessibility

SATSANG ($)

Krymská 24; 267 314 903; open M-F 5pm-11pm, Sa-Su brunch 1am-4pm and dinner 5pm-11pm

Satsang's got it all: It's right in the middle of **Staré Vršovice** square laden with cafés and restaurants, it offers plenty of vegan and meat-heavy fare, and it's housed in an old brick and mortar cellar-style restaurant with an open kitchen. On one hand, this is the place vegan tofu-scramble lovers go when they die—Satsang has an entire two pages of their menu dedicated to a "Build your own tofu-scramble." On the other hand, the locals dive into the pancakes, eggs benedict, curry, wok, and bottomless mimosas like it's their last day on earth. A hodge-podge mixture of a modern vegan café, ancient beer hall, and innovative asian restaurant, Satsang is definitely not a joint you should pass on.

i Entreés from 115Kč; mostly vegan and vegetarian; wheelchair accessible

SUPER TRAMP COFFEE $

Opatovická 160/18; 777 446 022; open M-F 8am-8pm, Su 10am-5pm

While the name recalls a glorified one-hit wonder 70s rock band, we think the better reference is from the 80s: Super Tramp Coffee is for all those Super Freaks who are pretty kinky for hidden, locals-only coffee shops with incredibly diverse menus, breakfast fare, and pastries to boot. Here lies the hallowed site of Prague's best **espresso tonic**—our favorite coffee drink of all time and a Czech specialty—and the most cathartic little café in the city. Seated in the courtyard of an apartment complex not far from **Old Town,** most of Super Tramp's seating is outside and occupied by students who fill the massive, communal wooden tables with perfect academic flair. If you have work to do or just want to get an inimitable taste of the local life not far from Old Town, you can't do any more super than Super Tramp.

i Coffee from 45Kč, baked goods from 60Kč; vegetarian options available; no wheelchair accessibility

NIGHTLIFE

CLUB VZORKOVNA

Národní 339/11; open daily 7pm-4am

In both the below street-level sense and the shabby and cool sense, Vzorkovna is an underground playground. After a steep descent, you'll meet a circle of swings suspended from the ceiling, walk through a brightly-lit room with three foosball tables and a neon soaked blacklight bar, pass leather seats nailed to the wall, and eventually stumble on rooms ranging from 80s music videos screening parties to a two-story redlight live music lounge with a dance floor. You'll encounter every shade of local, from shirtless punks to 20-something hipsters, bachelorette parties and two dogs so large you'll think they're wolfkin. The drinks aren't half bad either—our favorite bar (there are three) specializes in tea-based cocktails, offering matcha vodka and green tea mojitos.

i No cover, beer from 20Kč, cocktails from 50Kč; cash only; no wheelchair accessibility

KASÁRNA KARLÍN (KARLÍN BARRACKS)

Prvního pluku 20/2; www.kasarnakarlin.cz; open M-F 1pm-midnight, Sa-Su 10am-midnight

Revitalized military barracks, art gallery, café, and community space by day, raucous outdoor and indoor club by night, Kasárna Karlín harnesses the former frenetic military setting and puts its old garages to good use—filling the night with techno music, cheap drinks, and a local-fueled dance floor fervor. With a garden of towering trees and statues of everything from unicorns to floating spacemen, there's no place more fun than Kasárna Karlín to start your night. And even if you can't make your way to **Florenc** come sundown, a daytime excursion to the barracks reveals one of Prague's most rewarding local watering-holes and the site of many local artists' prized works.

i Check website for show times

LUCERNA MUSIC BAR

Štěpánská 61; 224 224 537; www.lucerna.cz; generally open F-Sa 10pm-5am

The dream of the 80s is alive—almost every Friday and Saturday night, classic club mainstay of inner-city Prague Lucerna Music Bar hosts an 80s and 90s themed dance party in a two-story, mega-dance floor crammed with everyone from dude bros to French food critics. Housed in a historic theater complex just off of **Wenceslas Square,** Lucerna manages to wed high and low culture without breaking a sweat, using minimal lighting and focusing on the movie theater sized screen above the dance floor that runs like a Czech-American throwback MTV channel. There is just no atmosphere this fun in the city—the club is packed every night it's open. Make sure to check the website before going. When not holding music video dance parties, Lucerna hosts some of Prague's most high-profile concerts.

i Cover 100Kč, beer from 43Kč; hours vary, check website; BGLTQ+ friendly; no wheelchair accessibility

CZECHIA ESSENTIALS

VISAS

Czechia is a member of the EU and the Schengen Area. Citizens from Australia, Canada, New Zealand, the US, and many other non-EU countries do not require a visa for stays up to 90 days. However, if you plan to spend time in other Schengen countries, note that the 90-day period applies cumulatively to all of them.

MONEY

Currency: Although Czechia is a member of the EU, it is not in the Eurozone and uses the Czech Koruna, denoted by Kč and CZK, as its currency. ATMs can be found in shopping malls, banks, and most public spaces. Avoid currency exchanges at airports and use ATMs instead. The best currency exchanges are those that advertise the "buy" and "sell" rates, which allow you to calculate exactly how much you will receive and don't charge a commission fee. To find out what out-of-network or international fees your credit card or debit card may be subjected to, contact your bank.

Tipping: In restaurants, tips are usually not included in the bill, so it's customary to tip 10-15% for good service. Another way to tip is to round your bill to the nearest 10Kč and then add 10% of the total. When you pay the bill, include the tip. A 10% tip for taxis is acceptable. It is not customary to leave tips on the table before you leave.

SAFETY AND HEALTH

Local Laws and Police: Czech police have a reliable reputation and you should not hesitate to contact them if needed. Be sure to carry your passport with you, as police have the right to ask for identification. However, police can sometimes be unhelpful if you're the victim of a currency exchange scam, in which case it's best to seek advice from your embassy or consulate.

Drugs and Alcohol: If you carry insulin, syringes, or any prescription drugs on your person, you must also carry a copy of the prescription and a doctor's note. The drinking age is 18. There is a zero-tolerance policy for people who drive under the influence, meaning the legal blood alcohol content (BAC) is zero. Specifically within Prague: Don't fall for the "Buy Weed Here" scam run by nearly every market within Old Town. The retail of marijuana is illegal in the Czech republic, and anything being advertised as a marijuana-related product either contains ineffective trace elements or CBD.

Petty Crime and Scams: A common scam in bars and nightclubs involves a local woman inviting a traveler in to buy her drinks, which end up costing exorbitant prices. The proprietors may then use force to ensure the bill is paid. In bars, never open a tab and instead pay for each drink as you order it, as the tab bill may include drinks you never ordered, and once again, the proprietors may force you to pay. Check the prices of drinks before ordering

Credit Card Fraud: Credit card fraud is also common. If you think you've been a victim of this, contact your credit card company immediately.

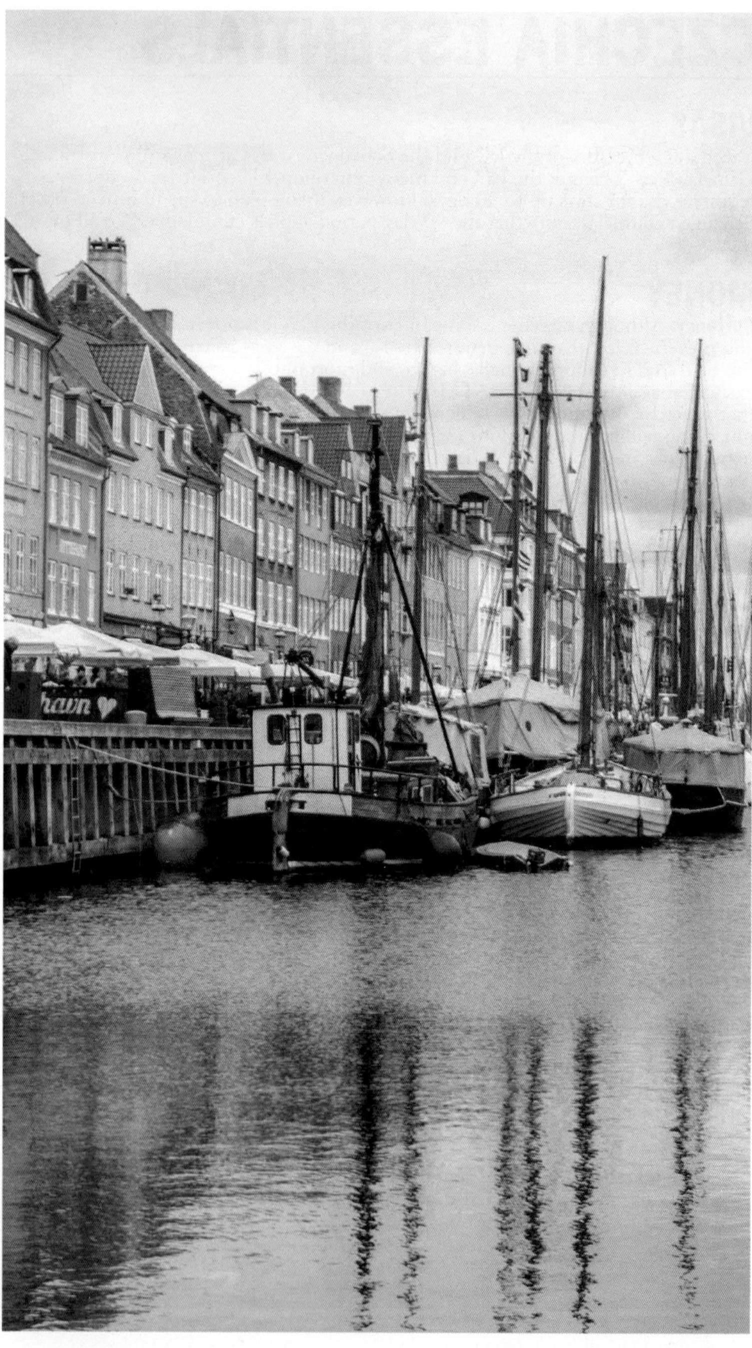
havn

DENMARK

The Scandinavian countries are Mitch McConnell's worst nightmare. They're the ultimate "nanny states"—overly taxing their people and ruthlessly ensuring them an exceptionally high quality of life and a safety net the size and shape of a king-sized bed. Compared to Sweden and Norway, however, Denmark plays things fast and loose. Unlike its two uptight siblings, Denmark doesn't have a ridiculous government monopoly on alcohol—thank goodness, because the Danes love to drink all day (and all night). The lifestyle works, because the Danes are routinely ranked in the top three happiest countries in the world. A lot of that could probably be attributed to a cultural mindset that's impossible to define (see: *hygge*) that prioritizes fun, coziness, and contentment. How lucky we are that we get to travel there and share a little bit of that joy?

Like its northern neighbors, Denmark hasn't quite forgotten about its Viking past, but those axe-wielding ancestors are far from their only cultural fixation. Lately, they seem determined to take some of the country's retired and crumbling industrial infrastructure and convert it into hipster-friendly spaces: coffee shops, niche art galleries, microbreweries, and concert venues have all sprung up—and continue to spring up—in the nation's old shipyards, manufacturing centers, and meatpacking districts. Fear not, however—the great experiences that await in Denmark don't exclusively occur in metal-clad buildings with concrete floors and sliding doors. This is still Europe, after all, and Denmark has its fair share of Renaissance castles, picturesque canals, and bicycle lanes. And lest you be lulled into thinking you're in Amsterdam, Paris, or Berlin, the Scandanavian cost of living is always there to snap you back to reality.

Though you may not be able to get as far on a dollar, that high quality of life means the quality of everything else is pretty darn good, too—from sleek, luxurious "hostels" to "street food" markets that would make a Michelin-starred establishment do a double take. They say money can't buy happiness, but give half your income to the government and it turns out things will end up going well.

AARHUS

Coverage by **Sam Lincoln**

Aarhus has come a long way since it was founded in the eighth century as a Viking settlement. Over the centuries, buildings rose, buildings burned, Christianity and the plague arrived with mixed results, and people poured in—so many people that Aarhus is now Denmark's second largest city. Today, Aarhus still constantly changes its look. The old industrial harbor now houses apartment buildings designed to look like icebergs and library/playground hybrids that remind us of spaceships, but the city hasn't forgotten its origins. The oldest part of town, Latinerkvarteret, remains a cultural center for shops and restaurants, and despite several new high-rise buildings, the towering spire of Aarhus Cathedral remains the tallest point in the city. Thanks to a large student population, Aarhus is Denmark's youngest city demographically and boasts the nightlife and hip cafés to match. Combine those with a bustling tourism industry, and the result is everything from budget hostels to luxury hotels, burgers and Vietnamese street food to Michelin-starred restaurants, and Irish pubs to Bond-style cocktail bars. Copenhagen may traditionally be the city to visit in Denmark, but you'd be remiss not to give Aarhus a shot.

ORIENTATION

Aarhus doesn't have neighborhoods that are as distinct as, say, Copenhagen's, but there are certainly areas with distinct vibes and character. The area known as **Midtbyen** stretches north from **Aarhus H** to several streets past **Aarhus Cathedral**. Here you'll find almost all the major sights in the city, including restaurants, museums, and the busy nightlife streets of **Åboulevarden, Skolegade,** and **Frederiksgade.** Just south of Midtbyen and across the railway tracks of Aarhus Central Station is **Frederiksbjerg,** home to Aarhus' one concerted urban planning efforts and a picturesque residential neighborhood. On the opposite side of the city, just north of Midtbyen between Aarhus Cathedral and the Ring 1 Road to the north, is **Latinerkvarteret** (the Latin Quarter), the oldest part of the city. To the west of Latinerkvarteret is **Vesterbro,** a largely-residential neighborhood that includes the beautiful **Botanical Garden** and the cultural attraction of **Den Gamle By.**

ESSENTIALS

GETTING THERE

Aarhus Airport (AAR) is a tiny airport located about 35mi. northeast of the city. Departures mostly go to Copenhagen. There is an airport bus between Aarhus Central Station and Aarhus Airport scheduled for each flight. Tickets can be purchased on the bus for DKK 115. The easiest way to get to Aarhus is by train via Copenhagen, which usually takes about 4 hours. Aarhus's main train station is Aarhus Central Station (Aarhus H), and there are many trains between Aarhus H and Copenhagen Central Station (København H) each day. DSB operates train service in Denmark. Purchase tickets (DKK 399) can at either station, or through the DSB app.

GETTING AROUND

Most attractions are within walking distance. To go beyond the city center (to the Moesgaard Museum, for example), Aarhus has a system of buses run by Midttrafik with several ticket options. Single tickets can be purchased with cash on the bus for DKK 22 for two zones, which covers the city center and immediate suburbs. Tickets can also be purchased for 24hr (DKK 80), 48hr (DKK 120) or 72hr (DKK 160) at the Aarhus bus station (Aarhus Rutebilstation, Fredensgade 45). Of course, the Danes love their bicycles, and Aarhus is no exception. Donkey Republic, the bike rental service, has bikes throughout the city that can be unlocked through their app. Prices vary, but typically start at DKK 12-15 for a 15min. bike ride. As always, make sure to read up on Danish rules and regulations behind bicycle use. For a more expensive but undeniably fun option, scooter rental services like Voi have moved in recently—you can take a scooter off the street and unlock it in-app, then leave it in any public space when you're done.

PRACTICAL INFORMATION

Tourist Offices: Dokk1 (Hack Kampmanns Plads 2; 87 31 50 10; visitaarhus.com; open M-W 10am-4pm, Th 10am-6pm, F 10am-4pm).

Banks/ATMs/Currency Exchange: Credit and debit cards are widely accepted in Aarhus, though you may have to pay a small fee to use an international card. Currency exchange and ATMs (sometimes called "pengeautomat") can be found at Aarhus Central Station or by the main shopping streets of Sønder Allé and Store Torv.

Post Offices: The Danish postal service is run by PostNord (Posthus Superbrugsen; Vesterbro Torv 1; 70 70 70 30; open M-Sa 11am-7pm).

Internet: Free internet is widely available in Aarhus, and can be found in hostels, museums, and most cafés and coffee shops. Many shops and restaurants will advertise free Wi-Fi with window stickers.

BGLTQ+ Resources: LGBT Aarhus may be found on Facebook @ LGBTAarhus, or reached at 86 13 19 48. LGBT Denmark is an available resource at lgbt.dk/english-2.

EMERGENCY INFORMATION

Emergency Number: 112. The police can be reached at 114 for non-emergency situations.

Police: The Police Headquarters in Aarhus can be found near Dokk1 (Ridderstræde, 87 31 14 48; open daily 9am-9:30pm and 24hr for emergencies).

Rape Crisis Center: The Center for Rape Victims is a a part of the emergency department of Aarhus University Hospital (Palle Juul-Jensens Boulevard 161, Entrance J3; 78 46 35 43; open daily 24hr).

Hospitals: The main hospital in Aarhus is Aarhus University Hospital. In an emergency, call 112. In urgent, non-emergency situations, call the emergency doctor service at 70 11 31 31.

- Emergency Department (Palle Juul-Jensens Boulevard 161; open daily 24hr).

Pharmacies: Pharmacies (called *apotek* in Danish) can be found on main streets. This one is located right by Aarhus Cathedral.

- Løve Apotek (Store Torv 5; 86 12 00 22; open daily 6am-midnight).

SIGHTS

CULTURE

DEN GAMLE BY

Viborgvej 2; 86 12 31 88; dengamleby.dk; open daily 10am-3pm, Feb 9-Mar 31 10am-4pm, Apr 1-June 28 10am-5pm, June 29-Sep 8 10am-6pm, Sep 9-Dec 31 10am-5pm

Just a few feet off a pretty standard, modern-looking Aarhus street sits a small town made up of a number of historic buildings collected from around Denmark, assembled in one place, and restored. The result is a crash course in Danish life through the centuries. Each building has been furnished with the appropriate trappings of a Danish residence, or pastry shop, or auto mechanic—you name it, Den Gamle By has got it. As you progress through the town, the interiors and exteriors morph and progress through time, meaning you might exit a Baroque middle class drawing room and find yourself in a mid-twentieth century laundry room with all the appropriate appliances. The level of attention to detail, the

clustering of several hundred years of history into relatively small area, *and* the fact that almost every building is open to exploration make Den Gamle By immersive to the point of being slightly disorienting—it's like traveling in a time machine operated by the world's most impatient mad scientist.

i Admission Jan 1-Mar 31 DKK 110, DKK 55 reduced; admission Apr 1-Dec 31 DKK 135, DKK 70 reduced; limited wheelchair accessibility

GODSBANEN

Skovgaardsgade 3; 25 22 12 10; godsbanen.dk/english; hours vary

Any Danish city with even a shred of hipness has some extremely large industrial space that's been converted into a cultural center. Aarhus steps up to the plate with Godsbanen, a former freight train station that has been overhauled and outfitted with pretty much every arts-related facility you can think of. For the performance-inclined, Godsbanen is home to a theater that provides residencies for up-and-coming playwrights, a cinema that screens indie films, several spaces for showcasing local art, the studios of various local professional artists, ample music space, a very chic and very expensive all-you-can-eat gourmet buffet…the list goes on. You could live here and never run out of things to do.

i Prices vary, wheelchair accessible

MUSIKHUSET

Thomas Jensens Allé; 89 40 90 00; musikhusetaarhus.dk/en; foyer open daily 11am-6pm, box office open M-Sa noon-5pm and 1hr before show starts

Musikhuset is Scandinavia's largest concert hall, and the star power it brings to town proves it. That includes not only big names in pop music present and past, but it also includes some serious talent in the world of classical music—for which Musikhuset has its own, dedicated venue. The Royal Academy of Music Aarhus also has a lasting residency with the concert hall, granting up-and-coming students and musicians the opportunity to perform under Denmark's biggest spotlight. Whether you're looking for an opera, a symphony, a comedy show, or rock and roll—or even if you're looking for some eclectic combination of all of the above—Musikhuset's got you covered.

i Show prices vary, wheelchair accessible

LANDMARKS

AARHUS CATHEDRAL

Store Torv; 86 20 54 00; aarhusdomkirke.dk/english; open May 1-Sept 30 M-Sa 9:30am-4pm, Oct 1-Apr 30 daily 10am-3pm, closed for renovation Sept 1 2019-Apr 12 2020

Aarhus Cathedral has changed its look more often than Miley Cyrus over the years. Since construction began in the twelfth century, the cathedral has been built up, burned down, expanded, rand restyled multiple times. The vast interior is packed with everything you've come to expect out of an old cathedral: paintings, statues, gravestones, gold leaf, and pipe organs (yes, plural—the small one sits right by the altar, the larger one is being renovated by the entrance to the nave). Tall windows illuminate the vaulted Gothic arches, decorated with murals that feel minimalist (how Scandinavian!) when compared with the lavish adorments found in the other great cathedrals of Europe.

i Free admission; wheelchair accessible

DOME OF VISIONS

Pier 2; domeofvisions.dk/dome-of-visions; open M-F noon-6pm, Sa-Su 10am-6pm

If you walk along the Aarhus harbor, you'll notice that a few massive, modern constructions have sprung up right on the water where the old industrial harbor used to be. Among those, you may also notice a small and strange semi-sphere. From afar, it looks like the top half of a glass bubble. This is the Dome of Visions, a building owned by the municipality of Aarhus and used for a wide variety of activities: raves, dance classes, meetings, yoga—you name it. In the center of the dome is a small café run by a branch of ActionAid, an NGO that fights poverty around the world. As you might be able to tell, it's an enclave for all that is hip and progressive. Because so much light gets in the through the dome, trees and an assortment of other plants dot the space. A delightful amount of comfy couches, chairs, and tables make the Dome an amazing place to relax.

i Free admission; limited wheelchair accessibility

MUSEUMS

AROS AARHUS KUNSTMUSEUM

Aros Allé 2; 87 30 66 00; en.aros.dk; open M-F 10am-9pm, Sa-Su 10am-5pm

Aarhus, like any Danish city worth its *smørrebrød,* is no stranger to a vibrant and occasionally wacko contemporary art scene. Here, it centers around ARoS, a large museum in Midtbyen and home to a significant permanent collection. The most memorable might be Ron Mueck's *Boy* sculpture, a 15 foot, 1100 pound sculpture of, you guessed it, a boy—as well as a constantly rotating selection of special exhibitions that make full use of the considerable space available. Installations range in size from small portraits to sprawling, multi-room, interactive engagements. The whole museum is topped off by Y***our Rainbow Panorama,*** a walkway lined with multicolored glass that runs in a circle around the top of the building and lets you see Aarhus laid out below through rose-colored (and violet-colored, blue-colored, green-colored, yellow-colored, orange colored…) glasses.

i Admission DKK 140, DKK 110 reduced; wheelchair accessible

MOESGAARD MUSEUM

Moesgård Allé 15; 87 39 40 00; moesgaardmuseum.dk/en; open Tu 10am-5pm, Wed 10am-9pm, Th-Su 10am-5pm

If you want to look at dead people but don't have the time to become a coroner, consider paying the Moesgaard Museum a visit—it takes an archeological and ethnographical approach to human history, and, historically-speaking, a lot of people have died. As you would expect, Moesgaard displays plenty of skulls, bodies, and corresponding artifacts. One highlight is a corpse incredibly preserved for over 2000 years in a peat bog—all things considered, he looks great. Architects carved the building that houses the museum out of a small hill, and its grass-covered roof slopes up from right from the ground. Climbing up the roof (a Danish hike!) offers a beautiful view of the surrounding countryside and the sea.

i Admission DKK 140, DKK 110 reduced; wheelchair accessible

OUTDOORS

BOTANICAL GARDENS

Peter Holms Vej; 87 15 54 15; sciencemuseerne.dk/en; open daily 24hr, Tropical Houses open May 1-Sep 30 M-F 9am-4pm, Sa-Su 10am-5pm, Oct 1-Apr 30 M-F 9am-5pm, Sa-Su 10am-5pm

The Botanical Gardens maintain a beautiful swath of flowers and trees in the middle of Aarhus. A cursory exploration reveals that it's more park than garden, and it also includes a most un-Danish amount of topographical variation. Because of the slight hills that give the park its diverse topography, there are many spots where it's impossible to view anything other than what is within the garden—nature obscures the city. The gardens are an oasis in which you can relax on the grass, attend a concert at the natural hillside auditorium in the corner of the park or, if you're feeling the need for some more flower power, head into the Tropical Houses in the Botanical Garden and take a look at plants brought from all over the world.

i Free; wheelchair accessible

MOESGAARD STRAND

Strandskovvej 2; open daily 24hr

South of Aarhus—just a hop, skip, and a jump via bus #31—stands Moesgaard Strand, a large stretch of beach looking out onto the **Bay of Aarhus.** Its waters have earned **Blue Flag** status, indicating exceptional cleanliness and safety. As a bonus, the **Marselisborg Forest** runs right up to the beach and contains nearly a dozen kilometers of trail that run through more than 500 acres of forests and fields. From Moesgaard Museum there are some Donkey Republic bikes you can rent to get you to the beach.

i Free; wheelchair accessible

FOOD

AARHUS STREET FOOD ($$)

Ny Banegaardsgade 4; aarhusstreetfood.com; open M-Th 11:30am-9pm, F-Sa 11:30am-10pm (bar closes later), Su 11:30-9pm

If you've ever been indecisive about where to eat, Aarhus Street Food is your dream destination. Food stands are designed to look like anything from corrugated metal shipping containers to plywood-clad, cartoon-lemonade-stand-style shops. You'll find everything from Afro-Carribean jerk chicken and fries cooked in duck fat to Danish classics like *rugbrød* and *flæskesteg.* Entrée prices and portions vary so pay attention—pairing a crêpe amuse-bouche with a traditional Ugandan main course and polishing off your meal with a dessert sandwich of Nutella, peanut butter, and marshmallow will rack up quite the bill.

i Prices vary; some stalls cash-only; gluten-free, vegan, and vegetarian options available; wheelchair accessible

HANTWERK ($$)

Fiskerivej 2D; 91 25 62 57; havnefronten.dk/?page_id=610; open W-Th 4pm-10pm, F 2pm-midnight, Sa noon-midnight

If you ask them, the waiters say Hantewerk is not a restaurant. It's not a "gastropub" or "bistro" either. "Hantwerk… is Hantwerk." Thanks for the help, guys! Though it sits right by the heart of the old industrial port, Hantewerk refuses to move into new digs. It occupies an old engineering hall with massive sliding garage doors, and on a nice day they'll be fully raised, effectively removing one of the restaurant's four walls and welcoming in a gentle sea breeze. The place emphasizes the beer, though the food is well thought out and crafted with care. It's made in-house by a brewery called Humleland, whose vessels bubble behind the bar. The beer won't cost you more than what you'd expect from a small-scale Danish brewery, but the food might sting your wallet.

i Bar menu from DKK 25, small plates from DKK 118, beer from DKK 40, wine from DKK 55; vegetarian, vegan, and gluten-free options available; wheelchair accessible

PHO C&P ($)

Sønder Allé 14; 86 16 16 42; pho-cp.dk; open M-Th noon-8:30pm, F-Su noon-9:30pm

Pho C&P brings delicious, street-food-inspired Vietnamese cuisine straight to your table in healthy portion sizes and extremely reasonable (for Denmark) prices. Aarhus is lucky to have it around, and boy don't the locals know it—show up during peak dining hours and every table will be locked down with a reservation. Fear not! They offer takeout, and if you show up outside of the main mealtimes you'll often be able to snag a table that's been reserved for later on. Their specialties include traditional pho soup, banh hoi rice vermicelli dish, and my quang noodles.

i Main dishes from DKK 79, beer from DKK 35; vegetarian and vegan options available; no wheelchair accessibility

NIGHTLIFE

SHEN MAO

Sankt Clemens Torv 17; shenmao.dk; open Th-Sa 9:30pm-5am

Have you ever been struck with a sudden urge to play ping pong while dancing your ass off in a nightclub? Neither have we, but Shen Mao manages to pull quite a crowd for that very reason. Walk in the door and it looks just like any other club—there's a DJ spinning a standard set of top 40 hits and there's a bar in the corner doling out copious amounts of cheap beer and cocktails. Nestled in its own room just off the dance floor, a ping pong table is surrounded by a crowd of young locals playing game after game of "around the world"—a line rotates around the table, and each person hits the ball once before passing off the paddle to the next person.

i No cover, shots from DKK 25, beer from DKK 25, mixed drinks from DKK 45; wheelchair accessible

FATTER ESKIL

Skolegade 25; 21 35 44 11; Fattereskil.dk; open W 8pm-midnight, Th 8pm-2am, F 4pm-5am, Sa 8pm-5am

Fatter Eskil is one of Aarhus's top live music venues with concerts most Wednesday through Saturday nights. Performances range from rock and metal to R&B and dance music, and even after the concert ends, a DJ often comes on to keep the party going. Admission to Thursday Jam Nights is free and it's a great opportunity to hop on stage for a song or two or just sit back and enjoy the show. If you're not feeling the vibe, or if the place dies down after the show ends, Fatter Eskil is located on **Skolegade,** which is also home to a number of hip bars and nightclubs.

i Cover varies, shots from DKK 20, beer from DKK 35, cocktails from DKK 75; BGLTQ+ friendly; limited wheelchair accessibility

COPENHAGEN

Coverage by **Sam Lincoln**

There are a few things that generally hold true of Scandinavian cities: they're small (Stockholm, Scandinavia's largest, tops the list with just under one million people), they're expensive, and they're obsessed with Vikings. In short, they're great places to travel, but get a bit sleepy after a few days. Copenhagen is different. It's not just the capital city of Denmark, it feels like the cultural capital of all of Scandinavia. Between the city itself and the many towns within reach via commuter rail, Copenhagen boasts truly impressive Renaissance castles, Baroque gardens that would make Louis XIV raise an eyebrow, and one of the best food and microbrewery scenes in the north. There's something for everyone here, from the casual nightclubs of the Meatpacking District and the smoky bars of Nørrebro, to the bohemian paradise of Christiania with its alternative architecture and open marijuana trade. The discerning diner will love Copenhagen's massive food halls and local delicacies. Don't miss the *smørrebrød* or the greasy, crunchy goodness of *flæskesteg*. The casual cyclist will be amazed both by the sophistication of the city's bike lanes, and by how uncharacteristically aggressive a Dane on a bicycle can be. It won't be cheap (nothing in the Nordics ever is), but Copenhagen is one of the only Scandinavian cities where you could spend a week and still not have scratched the surface. It's small but busy, modern but timeless, and of course, it's very, very *hygge*.

ORIENTATION

The city center of **Copenhagen** (also known as **Indre By** or **København K**), extends from **Copenhagen Central Station** all the way to the northern end of the city. Like city centers everywhere, it's touristy, crowded, and expensive. It's also where you'll find many of Copenhagen's main attractions, including **Strøget** (one of Europe's longest pedestrianized shopping streets), a number of museums and palaces, and the people-watching meccas of **Kongens Nytorv** and **Nyhavn.** Just to the east is **Christianshavn,** a network of islands and canals constructed by **Christian IV .** Within Christianshavn is the offbeat community (and favorite of twenty-somethings from all over the world) of **Christiania,** famous for its open marijuana trade. North of the city center is **Østerbro,** an upscale residential neighborhood with plentiful parks and high prices. Just west is a funkier alternative: **Nørrebro,** a classic example of a once-heavily-immigrant neighborhood overtaken by broke hipsters and art students. Directly west of the city center is **Frederiksberg,** another wealthy neighborhood filled with parks and baby strollers. South of **Frederiksberg** is **Vesterbro,** home to the **Meatpacking District** and old **Carlsberg Brewery.** Copenhagen is also a great hub for exploring other cities on the island of **Zealand,** Denmark's largest (except Greenland). To the west is **Roskilde,** one of Denmark's foremost Viking cities, and to the north are **Helsingør** and **Hillerød,** home to famous Renaissance castles.

ESSENTIALS

GETTING THERE

Copenhagen Airport, Kastrup (CPH), known as Københavns Lufthavn in Danish, is Scandinavia's busiest. The metro is the easiest way to get to and from the airport; Copenhagen's main train station is Copenhagen Central Station (København H), which connects to the rest of Scandinavia and other major European cities.

GETTING AROUND

Copenhagen's public transportation system includes buses, a metro, and trains, which are all covered under the same ticket. The capital region is divided into zones, with ticket prices varying accordingly. The minimum ticket distance is a Zone 2 ticket, for DKK 24, which will get you to most places within Copenhagen proper. Tickets can be purchased at metro stations or through the DOT Mobilbilletter app on your phone, but you can also buy them on buses with cash. Passes are available that allow unlimited public transportation: a 24 hr pass is DKK 80 and a 72hr pass is DKK 200. Copenhagen is also easily navigable by bike. Bikes can be rented through a company like Donkey Republic, which has an app and will get you on the road in no time. If you plan on cycling, take some time to familiarize yourself with the Danish laws and expectations for cyclists.

PRACTICAL INFORMATION

Tourist Offices: Copenhagen Visitor Service (Vesterbrogade 4; 70 22 24 42; check www.visitcopenhagen.com for monthly hours, but generally open 9am-5pm or later during peak seasons).

Banks/ATMs/Currency Exchange: Credit and debit cards are widely accepted in Copenhagen. ATMs can be found on the street and outside most banks. A branch of Forex Bank can be found inside Copenhagen Central Station (Hovedbanegården, Bernstorffsgade 16; 33 11 22 20; open daily 8am-8pm).

Post Offices: There is a centrally located post office on Landemærket (Landemærket 21; 70 70 70 30; open M-F 8am-7pm, Sa 10am-4pm).

Internet: Internet is widely available in Copenhagen. Most cafés and many museums provide free Wi-Fi, as do Copenhagen Central Station and the visitor center.

BGLTQ+ Resources: Denmark is one of the most gay-friendly cities in Scandinavia and in the world, and that's saying a lot. It's home to Denmark's oldest gay bar, Centralhjørnet, and there's even an app (Copenhagen Gay Guide) dedicated to identifying BGLTQ+ establishments for travellers across the city. LGBT Denmark is the national organization for BGLTQ+ advocacy (Nygade 7, 33 13 19 48).

EMERGENCY INFORMATION

Emergency Number: 112.

Police: the Copenhagen Police Headquarters is located near Copenhagen Central Station (non-emergency number is 114; open M-F 8am-9pm, Sa-Su 10am-5pm).

US Embassy: There is a US Embassy in Copenhagen (Dag Hammarskjölds Allé 24; 33 41 71 00; office open M-F 8:30am-4pm, appointments M-Th 9am-noon).

Rape Crisis Center: The Centre for Victims of Sexual Assault at Rigshospitalet has a 24hr crisis center and hotline; it's recommended you call before visiting the center (Blegdamsvej 9; 35 45 50 32).

Hospitals: Always call 1813 before going to the emergency room or you may not be admitted. The doctor or nurse with whom you speak will be able to refer you to a hospital emergency department or urgent care center (Bispebjerg Hospital, Bispebjerg Bakke 23; 38 63 50 00).

Pharmacies: Pharmacies (called *apotek* in Danish) are prolific. Here is a centrally located one:

- Steno Apotek (Vesterbrogade 6C; 33 14 82 66, open daily 24hr).

SIGHTS

CULTURE

KULTURTÅRNET

Knippelsbro 2; 28 71 28 15; kulturtaarnet.dk/english; open W-F 3pm-9pm, Sa noon-8pm, Su noon-8pm

There are two constants in Copenhagen: bridges and cafés. Culture Tower combines the two in one very manageable package. Situated on the heavily-trafficked **Knippel's Bridge** in one of two famous copper-clad

control towers, the Culture Tower is an incredible non-profit operation that breathes life into a building that's been closed to the public for decades. Head on in during regular hours to grab a coffee (or beer) and snack, then head up the spiraling center staircase toward the top-floor wraparound lookout. Given that it's the only bridge-slash-situated building you access, this also might be the only time you'll get 360-degree views of Copenhagen's harbor. Check online for the Culture Tower calendar to find out about special events, which include concerts, poetry readings, and gastronomy. Make sure to book tickets well in advance; it's one of the lowest-capacity spaces around.

i Admission DKK 20, coffee DKK 15; no wheelchair accessibility

DYRHAVSBAKKEN

Dyrehavevej 62; 39 63 35 44; bakken.dk/english; open M-Th noon-10pm, F-Sa noon-midnight, Su noon-10pm

Dyrehavsbakken, or simply Bakken, has the honor of being the oldest operating amusement park in the world. Just north of Copenhagen, only twenty minutes away by metro, is a world of fun that's been cranking out thrills since 1583 and thus predates the much more famous **Tivoli Gardens** by about two and a half centuries. Don't expect the pomp and circumstance of Tivoli here—Bakken has free entry,

roller coasters from the 1930s, and the singular goal of providing you a classic no-frills amusement park experience.
i Admission free, rides from DKK 15; limited wheelchair accessibility

NYHAVN

Indre By; Open daily 24hr

Can you say you've been to Copenhagen if you don't have any photos of Nyhavn? Probably, but your friends won't believe you. This canal-side stretch of city is only a few blocks long, but its brightly painted restaurants and cafés have wormed their way onto just about every brochure, postcard, and tour bus in Copenhagen. Its present day-time popularity belies its past as the city's rough-and-tumble red light district—just one "gentleman's club" remains, and the remaining buildings are now all devoted to fleecing ignorant tourists of their pocket change. To keep your pockets full, bring food and drink from a cheaper part of the city and enjoy the beautiful buildings and majestic wooden ships.
i Prices vary; wheelchair accessible

ROSENBORG CASTLE

Øster Voldgade 4A; 33 15 32 86; kongernessamling.dk/en/rosenborg; open Jan 2-Feb 7 T-Su 10am-3pm, Feb 8-23 daily 10am-3pm, Feb 24-Apr 3 T-Su 10am-3pm, Apr 4-13 daily 10am-4pm, Apr 14-15 daily 10am-3pm, Apr 16-May 31 daily 10am-4pm, June 1-Aug 31 daily 9am-5pm, Sep 1-Oct 31 daily 10am-4pm, Nov 1-Dec 22 T-Su 10am-3pm, Dec 26-30 daily 10am-4pm, Dec 31 daily 10am-3pm

In case you were wondering about the historic wealth of the Danish royal family, or about what it would look like if the kings of Denmark loaded up a relatively small castle (as castles go, at least) with as many absurd treasures as could feasibly fit in its many rooms, then wonder no more! Enter a summer home less than three kilometers away from the royal family's main residence. Delightful! Don't miss the narwhal horn throne, the Danish crown jewels in the basement treasury, or the bottles of wine from 1615—still served at the Queen's New Year's dinner—that apparently tastes like dry sherry.
i Admission DKK 115, DKK 75 reduced; last entry 20min. before closing; no wheelchair accessibility

LANDMARKS

COPENHAGEN CITY HALL

Rådhuspladsen 1; 33 66 33 66; international.kk.dk; open M-F 9am-4pm, Sa 9:30am-1pm

Despite Copenhagen's city hall being a somewhat-popular tourist destination, it's a working building. Visit it during the work week to see a healthy mix of tourists and bureaucrats hustling from one room to the next. Much of the building is open to exploration, with a fair amount of side rooms worth poking your head into—two highlights are the stately two-story reading room and the room containing watchmaker Jen Olsen's hyper-accurate 1955 World Clock. If you're itching for some altitude, you can also visit the clocktower twice a day during the week and once on Saturday. Brave the 300 steps from the ground level up to the open air lookout just below the famous clock face and you'll be rewarded with a 360-degree view of Copenhagen.
i Free, tower admission DKK 40; limited wheelchair accessibility

GRUNDVIG'S CHURCH

På Bjerget 14B; 35 81 54 42; grundtvigskirke.dk/m/page/5125/about-church; open T-W 9am-4pm, Th 9am-6pm, F-Sa 9am-4pm, Su noon-4pm (summertime) or Su noon-3pm (wintertime)

Grundtvig's Church sits on the northern edge of the Copenhagen municipality. It's a little bit out of the way, but well worth the schlep—though it may be lesser known than many of its more centrally located counterparts, Grundtvig's Church is one of the most striking buildings in Copenhagen. The sinister exterior may look like a monument to Darth Vader's helmet, but the interior is bathed in an unusually warm glow thanks to the massive windows and light sandy brick. Don't expect any gilded sculpture, Christian iconography, or intricate stained glass, however. The nave is almost entirely devoid of the detailing present in your typical European church; instead you'll find bare brick from floor to ceiling. The stand-out minimalism of the interior makes the architecture of the columns and ceiling mesmerizingly repetitive. If you had to wait in a lobby before getting into heaven, it would look a lot like this.

i Free; no wheelchair accessibility

KRONBORG CASTLE

Helsingør; 49 21 30 78; www.kongeligeslotte.dk/en; open Jan-Mar Tu-Su 11am-4pm, Apr-May daily 11am-4pm, June-Sept daily 10am-5:30pm, Oct daily 11am-4pm, Nov-Dec Tu-Su 11am-4pm

Kronborg Castle is one of northern Europe's finest Renaissance castles, and it's yours to explore. The grounds, the courtyard, and the castle are worth a long, slow stroll. If you want a view, climb one of the towers and enjoy a rooftop with a panoramic vista of surrounding Helsingør and neighboring Sweden. The real fun to be had isn't up at the top of the castle, though—it's far below it. The crypts are a pitch black network of tunnels that run underneath Kronborg and are mostly pitch black. They're open to exploration, at your own peril.

i Jan-May and Sept-Dec admission DKK 95, DKK 85 reduced; June-Aug admission DKK 145, DDK 135 reduced; last entry 30 minutes before closing; limited wheelchair accessibility

THE ROUND TOWER

Købmagergade 52A; 33 73 03 73; rundetaarn.dk/en; open daily 10am-8pm, observatory open Su June 30-Aug 11 1pm-4pm

You can't go to Europe without climbing a few sets of spiral stairs. They're practically unavoidable in the churches, fortresses, and palaces that make up the backbone of European tourist fodder. The Round Tower seeks to shake things up a bit: instead of steps, a wide ramp wraps around a center pillar seven and a half times. This is significant for two historical reasons: first, the ride ramp allowed nobility to reach the top on horseback. More importantly, however, there are unicycle races up to the top—the current fastest ascent took a mere one minute and forty-eight seconds. Perched on the roof of the round tower sits Europe's oldest functioning astronomical observatory, which is open to the public on some summer afternoons.

i Admission DKK 25; no wheelchair accessibility

MUSEUMS

COPENHAGEN CONTEMPORARY ART CENTER

Refshalevej 173A; 29 89 72 88; www.cphco.org/en; open T-W 11am-6pm; Th 11am-9pm; Fri-Su 11am-6pm

Copenhagen is no stranger to the warehouse-turned-into-something-artsy movement, and the Copenhagen Contemporary art center proves it. Tucked inside the ground floor of a former welding hall in the former shipyard Burmeister & Wain on Refshaleøen Island, the art center divides 75,000 square feet of concrete and steel into just three rooms that accommodate large-scale sculpture and painting projects. The art is often interactive, and the space hosts regular performances and events tailored to the exhibition on display. Late summer 2019 brings the opening of the second floor of the welding hall, more than doubling the gallery space and allowing for even more ambitious presentations.

i Admission DKK 90, DKK 65 reduced; wheelchair accessible

LOUISIANA MUSEUM OF MODERN ART

Gammel Strandvej 13; 49 19 07 19; www.louisiana.dk/en; open T-F 11am-10pm, Sa-Su 11am-6pm

Situated in an old, ivy-covered country house that's grown a number of modern, zig-zagging gallery space additions, the Louisiana Museum of Modern Art is one of the world's finest modern art museums. Wander through the halls and discover the massive collection, including a standard fare of big names—Picasso, Warhol, etc.—as well as some artists both local and international you may have never heard of. As you head from exhibit to exhibit, you'll wind up spending a fair amount of time outdoors—the grounds are covered with paths connecting the different wings of the museum, and they lead you right through an outdoor sculpture garden that covers most of the grounds.

i Admission DKK 125, DKK 110 reduced; wheelchair accessible

NATURAL HISTORY MUSEUM OF DENMARK

Gothersgade 130; 35 32 22 22; geologi.snm.ku.dk/english; Zoological Museum open Tu-Su 10am-4pm, Geological Museum open Tu-Su 10am-5pm, Botanical Garden open daily Oct 1-Mar 31 8:30am-4pm, Apr 1-Sep 30 8:30am-6pm

The Natural History Museum of Denmark is divided into three distinct spaces: the Zoological Museum, the Geological Museum, and the Botanical Garden. The first two offer more or less what you'd expect—lots and lots of stuffed animals (the formerly-living kind, not the toy kind), fancy rock collections, and some exceptional special exhibitions. The Botanical Garden ranks as one of Copenhagen's more remarkable outdoor spaces, presenting the largest collection of plants in the city. An added bonus: in the opposite corner of the garden from the Geological Museum stands a marvelous Butterfly House, home to a beautiful collection of brightly-colored butterflies and their flight-challenged caterpillar counterparts.

i Admission DKK 105, DKK 50 reduced; tickets include access to all three components of the museum, free admission to the Botanical Garden (but not the Butterfly House); limited wheelchair accessibility

THE CISTERNS

Søndermarken; 30 73 80 32; cisternerne.dk/en; open T-W 11am-6pm, Th 11-8pm, Su 11am-6pm

In the aftermath of Copenhagen's cholera outbreak in the nineteenth century, the city got its act together on clean water and created the cisterns, a massive underground reservoir beneath Søndermarken park. City planners drained the reservoir in the 1980s, and now the cavernous space hosts rotating exhibitions of contemporary art. Booming, moaning, sweeping beautiful ambient music plays in the background coming in and out, complementing a striking visual display that features what appears to be floating blue letters. Groundwater still permeates the floor of the space, parts are even partially flooded. In the event of especially deep water, complimentary rubber boots are available.

i Admission DKK 70, DKK 50 reduced; no wheelchair accessibility

OUTDOORS

JÆGERSBORG DYREHAVE

Klampenborg; open daily 24hr

If you take the C train 20 minutes north to Klampenborg from Copenhagen Central Station, you'll find yourself at the gates to 1000 acres of beautifully-spaced forest and wide open meadow. This is Dyrehaven, a deer sanctuary, former royal hunting ground, and one of the nicest parks in the greater Copenhagen area. Rent a bike at the Klampenborg station and you'll be ready to set off through the mellow, rolling hills of the park.

You won't have to look hard for the deer—they're everywhere. To get the best vantage point, head to the entrance closest to the station, continue straight until you reach Peter Lieps Hus (the park's restaurant, nestled within a thatched roof cottage) and then take a right. Before you will stand around three kilometers of open path, at the end, which sits a sea-side royal hunting "lodge" (palace).

i Free admission; wheelchair accessible

HARBOUR CIRCLE

Nyhavn; open daily 24hr

You can't say you've been to Copenhagen if you haven't biked around Harbour Circle. And while it's true that cyclists can occasionally overwhelm the streets, the waterfront remains pretty empty, especially during the evening. Harbour Circle is a 13 km loop of bike path that surrounds the central chunk of Copenhagen's harbor (or "extra-wide canal," if you'd prefer). The loop starts in Nyhavn and heads across the water into Christianshavn. As you bike along, you'll find four different bridges that allow you to cut back across the harbor and make your trip as long or as short as you want. The path runs past expansive waterfront parks, shopping centers, and several sleepy residential neighborhoods. If you're game and looking for a bike to rent, we recommend the bike-sharing app Donkey Republic.

i Bikes available starting at DKK 15 for the first 15 minutes of riding, DKK 18 for the first 30 minutes, and DKK 30 for the first hour; expect to spend at least an hour on the path

FOOD

ABSALON ($)

Sønder Blvd. 73; 38 03 02 21; absaloncph.dk/?lang=en; open daily 7am-midnight

From the outside, Absalon looks like an old brick church in Vesterbro. The inside has been emptied out, painted in bright colors, and transformed into a community event space. Every day at 6pm, the space becomes a banquet hall where a chef—hired for the evening from a local restaurant—prepares a veritable feast. Reserve a ticket online and the staff will seat you with up to eight total strangers at one of the long tables. It's up to you to decide who goes into the kitchen and grabs the food for the group, who distributes the plates, and who pours the beer. Most people who eat at Absalon live in Copenhagen, so it's a fantastic way to meet some locals and get a feel for the community.

i Meals from DKK 50; vegetarian options available; wheelchair accessible; show up by 5:45pm for dinner

AAMANNS DELI & TAKEAWAY ($$$)

Øster Farimagsgade 10; 20 90 52 01; aamanns.dk/deli/?lang=en; open M-Su 11am-8pm

Literally meaning "butter and bread" in Danish, the *smørrebrød* is an open-faced sandwich topped with meat or fish, cheese, and garnishes. Though it's by default a pretty unpretentious dish, that doesn't mean that there isn't any room for a little culinary—and price—elevation. Enter Adam Aamann, who has transformed the *smørrebrød* into an art form in not one but *five* restaurants in Copenhagen—two of which are included in the 2019 Michelin Guide. Aamanns Deli & Takeaway is not one of those two, but it has the advantage of slightly lower prices, pre-prepared picnic baskets. With the King's Garden right around the corner, why not treat

yourself to an amazing take on a Danish staple and eat it while sitting on some of Denmark's finest grass? And if it's *that* kind of picnic, Aamanns also offers homemade *snaps*—a traditional Scandinavian adult beverage—to liven things up.

i Individual cold smørrebrød from DKK 65, warm from DKK 95, snaps from DKK 55; vegetarian options available; no wheelchair accessibility; last order taken at 7pm

FAETTER FAETTER TOAST BAR ($$)

Griffenfeldsgade 17; 88 13 21 20; faetter-faetter.dk; open Th-Sa 11am-midnight, Su 11am-5pm; kitchen open Th-Sa 11am-10pm, Su 11am-4:30pm

Faetter Faetter is not a restaurant. Rather, it's a "toast bar," meaning their entrées are some variation on a grilled sandwich, or a "toast." Particularly notable is the croque monsieur, a big kid take on the ol' ham and cheese that would make even a viking weep tears of joy. Find seating both indoors and outdoors but in fairly limited supply—if you're headed over during peak hours make sure to book a table in advance.

i Toasts from DKK 75; vegetarian options available; limited wheelchair accessibility

FRESH BAGEL ($)

Vestergade 12; 38 33 30 00; fresh-bagel.business.site; open M-Sa 10am-7pm

Eating at Fresh Bagel is a good idea for two reasons: bagel sandwiches taste delicious *and* they're dirt cheap. Even better, they're waiting just a block away from Strøget, Copenhagen's main pedestrian shopping street. Choose a type of bagel, choose a cream cheese flavor, choose a meat—it's all chicken, but with different seasonings—and then choose some toppings. In less than three minutes flat, you'll have a bespoke grilled bagel sandwich in your hand. You're welcome to eat there or take it with you to go. We recommend the latter. Find a cobblestone square with some benches and boom—you've got yourself a picnic!

i Bagel sandwich from DKK 58, salads from DKK 49, 10% student discount; no wheelchair accessibility

GRØD ($)

Jægersborggade 50; 50 58 55 79; groed.com/en; open M-F 7:30am-9pm, Sa-Su 9am-9pm

If you've ever dreamed about eating porridge three meals a day, Grød is a match made in heaven. For those of us who haven't even started to think about thinking that, it's a testament to Grød's good grub that it's still a match made in heaven. Who would think that a porridge-only restaurant could still pack so much variety? If you want to try some yummy local fare, go for the "Grøddeller" from the lunch/dinner menu (served until 9pm): cabbage salad, apples, potatoes, and almonds with a risotto pattie and mustard vinaigrette served on bread from **Brødflov,** a local bakery. If you want to play it safe, the açai blueberry bowl will make you feel like you're back home at your open-concept loft in Brooklyn.

i Morning bowls from DKK 45, lunch/dinner bowls from DKK 70; gluten-free, vegetarian, and vegan options available; no wheelchair accessibility

KØDBYENS HØKER ($)

Slagtehusgade 7A; 25 12 72 02; open M-W 9am-3pm, Th 9am-8pm, F 9am-10pm, Sa 11am-8pm, Su 11am-3pm

Kødbyens Høker comes pretty close to being a literal hole in the wall—you walk up to a window in the side of an old building in the meatpacking district to order, and a lone cashier-turned-chef-turned-waiter handles most of the customer experience. There's no real brick and mortar "restaurant" experience here; seating is all outdoors on a series of picnic tables, with only an extendable awning to protect from inclement weather. In Danish, "Kødbyens Høker" roughly means "Meat Town Vendor," which is both a helpful reminder that you're eating at an old slaughterhouse and an indication of a culinary theme. They specialize in the *flæskestegs*-sandwich, a traditional Danish pork sandwich on homemade brioche.

i Flæskestegs-sandwich from DKK 55; vegetarian options available; wheelchair accessible

NEXT DOOR CAFÉ ($)

Larsbjørnsstræde 23; 27 12 08 18; nextdoorcafe.dk; open M-F 7am-6pm, Sa-Su 9am-6pm

Next Door Café is so hip it almost isn't hip because of how well it fits the stereotype of the hip neighborhood café. Step down into their little basement oasis and be greeted by smooth 90's grooves and very purple walls. Lest you think the funky vibe is artificial, years of built up memorabilia left by customers cover each of the café's tables, frozen in time underneath a glass tabletop. Try their breakfast specialty, homemade *müsli* (Swiss granola) with *skyr* (fancy Icelandic yogurt) and fresh fruit, or go in for a sizable lunch salad plate or sandwich. Oh! And don't sleep on the house-made juice!

i Breakfast from 40, sandwiches from DKK 50, salads from DKK 55, juices from DKK 45; vegetarian and gluten free options available; no wheelchair accessibility

PALUDAN BOG & CAFÉ ($$)

Fiolestræde 10-12; 33 15 06 75; www.paludan-cafe.dk/home-eng; café open M-Th 9am-10pm, F 9am-11pm, Sa 10am-11pm, Su 10am-10pm; bookstore open M-F 10am-6pm, Sa 10am-3pm

Paludan Bogcafé is the Hotel California of Copenhagen's cafés—you can come any time you like (as long as it's during operating hours, of course), but you might not want to leave. Ever. Sink into one of the couches in the book-lined rear room or sit at a table underneath the second floor balcony library, wait for brunch to arrive, and prepare to have a seriously pleasant time. Next Door Café is located on a University of Copenhagen campus, so you'll find yourself surrounded by students, writers, and young professionals buckled down on assignments, chatting away over coffee, scribbling away on their next masterpiece, or reading a book curled up in the corner.

i Coffee and espresso drinks from DKK 15, entrées from DKK 65; gluten-free, vegan, and vegetarian options available; limited wheelchair accessibility

NIGHTLIFE

JOLENE

Flæsketorvet 81-85; jolene.dk; open Th 10pm-4am, F-Sa 8pm-4:30am

The only light on Jolene's dance floor comes from a number of slowly turning disco balls suspended from the ceiling. If you're wondering where to find the party in Copenhagen, it's probably already here. When Jolene first opened back in 2007, they shut down within four months because of the sheer amount of noise complaints they received. Rather than quiet down, they just moved to the meatpacking district, and found a spot where no one would break up the party. With no cover and an aggressively unpretentious attitude, ("This is Not a Fucking Cocktail Bar" is written in chalk on the wall behind the bar), Jolene is a sweaty, breakneck shortcut to a night in the fast lane.

i No cover, wine from DKK 50, beer from DKK 37, shots from DKK 20; BGLTQ+ friendly; wheelchair accessible

BAKKEN

Flæsketorvet 19-21; bakkenkbh.dk; open Th 10pm-5am, F-Sa 8pm-5am

Bakken exists to bring the party, and to bring it to as many people as can fit on the dance floor. Fiercely inclusive and dedicated to the love of ground-shaking dance music, Bakken starts off a weekend night pretending to be a pleasant industrial bar with outdoor seating, and then transforms into a raucous free-for-all by the early hours of the morning. Once the nightclub butterfly emerges from its bar-with-a-patio cocoon, as it were, expect a sizable line outside of the door. It might not be the swankiest way to go out on the town in Copenhagen, but it could be the sweatiest.

i No cover, beer from DKK 30, mixed drinks from DKK 60, shots from DKK 25; wheelchair accessible; DJs start spinning at 11pm

LA FONTAINE

Kompagnistræde 11; 33 11 60 98; lafonatine.dk; open daily 8pm-5am

La Fontaine is a place best known for the jam sessions that break out on stage when the Copenhagen Jazz Festival takes the city by storm, in the absence of live music, this candlelit jazz bar becomes a mellow spot to sit and have a hushed conversation. Whether you're beginning the night with a 8pm beer at La Fontaine or you're ending the night with a 4am beer at La Fontaine, expect largely the same experience—but the beer will be cheaper at 4am.

i Beer from DKK 35; no wheelchair accessibility

LIDKOEB

Vesterbrogade 72B; 33 11 20 10; lidkoeb.dk; open Tu-Sa 4pm-2am, Su 6pm-2am

It's the end of a long day on the road, you never want to see another castle again, and if you have to cut through one more town square with a bronze statue of a guy on a horse you're going to have a breakdown. We've all been there—you need a drink, but not just any drink. Something special. Enter: Lidkoeb. Filled to the brim with the trendiest denizens of Copenhagen, this cocktail joint is tucked in a nondescript back alley between Frederiksberg and Vesterbro. Take a seat and explain the drink of your dreams to one of the expert mixologists; in no time you'll have it sitting in front of you. They even offer numerous non-alcoholic cocktails made with the same care. Your wallet will tell you no, but your body will tell you yes.

i Cocktails from DKK 80; limited wheelchair accessibility

MIKKELLER BAR

Viktoriagade 8B; 33 31 04 15; www.mikkeller.dk; open M-W 1pm-1am, Th-F 1pm-2am, Sa noon-2am, Su 1pm-1am

Mikkeller Bar does one thing, and one thing very well. That thing is beer. Walk downstairs into this hip basement bar and be confronted by 20 ever-changing beer options, and not much else. There's technically a selection of actual food available, but it's not exactly a gourmet menu: we're talking beef jerky, nuts, chips, and maybe some cheese. Don't come to eat, come to drink some of the city's best brewed beverages. Mikkeller draws both 20-something students unwinding from a day of class and businessmen and women unwinding from a day of work. This is a place to enjoy delicious, if pricey, drinks with a side of mellow conversation.

i Beer from DKK 55; BGLTQ+ friendly; no wheelchair accessibility

DENMARK ESSENTIALS

VISAS

Denmark is a member of the European Union and is part of the Schengen Area, so US citizens can stay in Denmark for up to 90 days without a visa.

MONEY

Currency: Denmark's currency is the Danish krone, officially abbreviated DKK and locally used interchangeably with kr.

Credit/Debit Cards: Cards are accepted at the vast majority of establishments, and some have even gone cash free. However, there may be a small fee for using an international card. It's worth noting that you could be charged a similar fee for withdrawing from a foreign ATM, so check with your bank about foreign fees or consider getting a traveller's credit or debit card without foreign ATM fees.

Tipping: Tipping in Denmark is neither expected nor required; in fact, a service charge is normally included in the bill at most restaurants. As always, a tip is appreciated, so if you feel you received exceptional service, feel free to round up the bill or toss in an additional 5-10%.

Taxes: Like other Scandinavian countries, Denmark has a sky-high VAT rate of 25%—it's included in all prices, though, so you won't have to worry about on-the-fly mental math. If you're doing a bit of shopping and worried about this price bump, you should know that foreign citizens (outside Scandinavia and the EU) purchasing goods in Denmark are eligible for a VAT refund provided the minimum purchase per shop exceeds DKK 300. Two refund companies offer this service: Global Blue and Tax Free Worldwide. Be sure to consult their websites for more information on how to validate and claim your refund. Save your receipts!

SAFETY AND HEALTH

Drugs and Alcohol: Though there is technically no drinking age in Denmark, there are purchasing ages: you must be at least 16 years old to purchase any beverage with an alcohol content between 1.2% and 16.5%, and over 18 years old to purchase any beverage with an alcohol content higher than 16.5%. To be served in restaurants, bars, or clubs, you must also be over 18.

BGLTQ+ Travelers: Denmark (and especially Copenhagen) is very progressive in terms of its BGLTQ+ rights. Hostels, restaurants, and nightlife establishments tend to be very welcoming, and big cities like Aarhus and Copenhagen have extensive BGLTQ+ nightlife scenes. LGBT Denmark is a useful resource for more information: lgbt.dk/english-2.

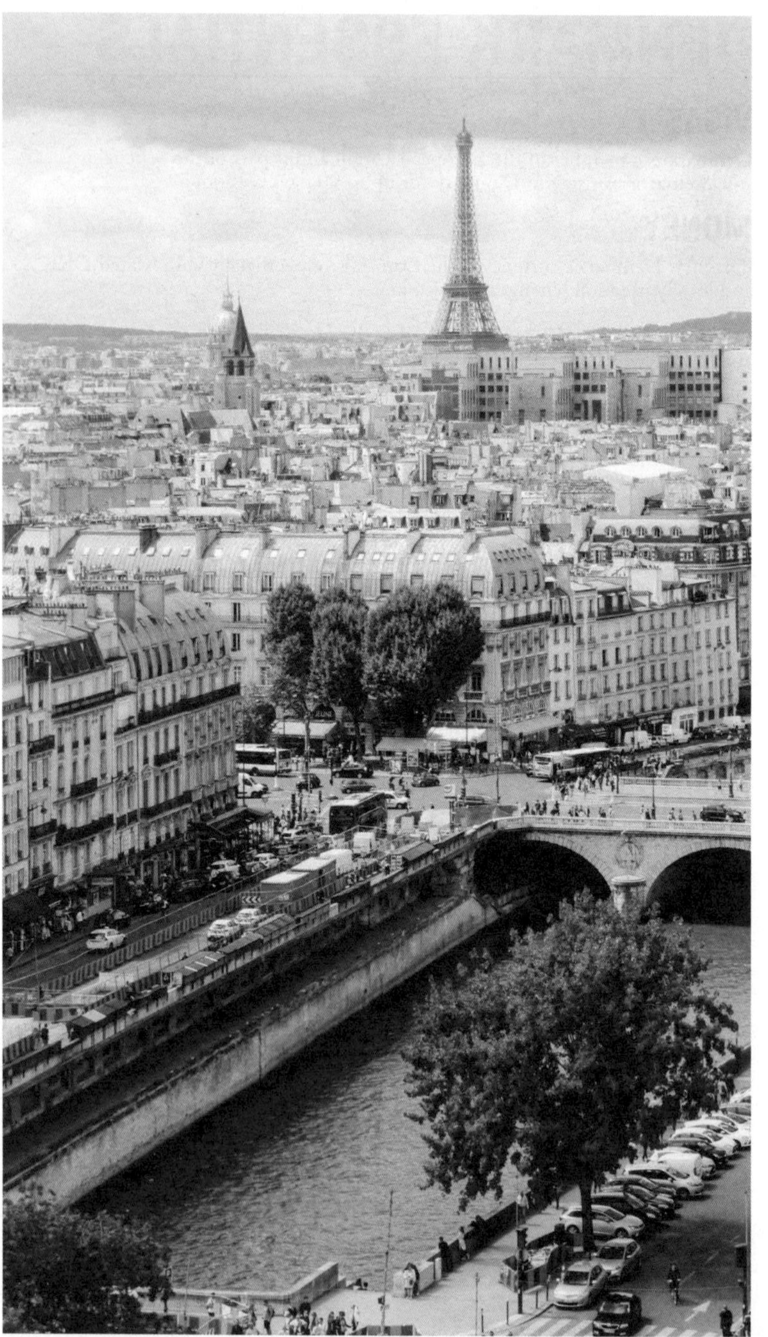

FRANCE

If France were a person, it would have been named the Sexiest Alive for the past twenty centuries. If you don't believe us, just close your eyes and picture a night in France. Did you imagine twinkling lights? A waterfront view? Soft guitar music playing in the background? A half empty bottle of wine? Damn, that's sexy. Paris, the well-known capital of the country, oozes hot confidence. When the world yearns for great fashion and food, it turns to Paris and Paris delivers. Switzerland may boast soaring mountains, Berlin bumping clubs, Spain gorgeous beaches, Italy fashionable shopping streets, and Britain idyllic rural life, but France has it all. Yet within the endless, lush green countryside that seems to constitute all of France when viewed out of a train window, every major attraction that might bring you to another country in Europe is hidden, often all within those sleepy villages.

A vast territory situated at the crossroads of Western Europe, France has been at the center of almost every major event in Western history, from the Crusades to Imperialism to the World Wars. This centrality, often the source of great suffering for the French people, has also built the nation's incredible richness of culture. Behind the marauding armies that have traversed France for thousands of years, and the armies of its own that the nation has deployed all over the globe, remain a signature of every development that transformed life in the Western World, all of which have been processed through the intricacies of French tradition and have emerged from the other side more elegant and refined. In recent years, the transformation has continued, as the nation struggles to reconcile itself with a new wave of migration that adds a challenging new richness to the concept of French culture.

A journey through the nation will take you past ancient villages that seem frozen in time, sprawling concrete housing complexes, an overwhelming number of horrifyingly opulent chateaus, and wide open countryside that makes it hard to believe that sixty-six million people are hiding between the hills and dales. France's resilience can only be explained by the tremendous *joie de vivre* of the nation's inhabitants, who never seem to put aside the love for family, friends, food, and the other simple pleasures that make life worth living.

AVIGNON

Coverage by **Jessica Moore**

If you took a very concentrated amount of lavender and turned it into a city, you would get Avignon. A relaxing and tranquil escape from the more bustling cities in France, this Provence town oozes aromatherapy from its pores. A trip here guarantees rest and relaxation. The city has deep ties to Catholicism and remained under Papal rule during the fourteenth century. Over the years, the city passed hands from conqueror to conqueror, and its fortified walls today stand as the last remnants of Avignon's daunting past. The Roman cathedrals and other Gothic relics that draw in visitors from around the world may seem few enough in number to explore in just a day, or even an afternoon, but an extended visit to Avignon promises to reveal the city's wilder side. Here, backpackers looking for a reprieve bunk up with those looking for some of the smaller and more intimate pubs and nightclubs France has to offer, and both spend their nights dreaming of medieval battles and tranquil lavender fields.

ORIENTATION

The medieval, walled city of Avignon is dense and easily walkable. **La Gare Avignon Centre,** the main train station, sits right outside the massive gates to the city. The main street in the city, **Rue de la République,** runs north-south through the town and is lined with shops and cafés. This street stretches out south from **Place de l'Horloge,** the largest square in the city. From here, bypass the carousel on your way to the **Palais des Papes.** Behind the Palais de Papes grows a beautiful garden, **Les Rocher des Domes.** At the far end of the garden, catch panoramic views of Avignon and walk down a steep staircase that leads to the ground level where you can access the **River Rhône** and **le Pont d'Avignon.**

ESSENTIALS

GETTING THERE

There is a small international airport in Avignon (AVN), but the nearby Marseille (MRS) or Montpellier (MPL) airports may offer cheaper options at only a short train or bus ride away. Trains to Avignon arrive at Gare d'Avignon-Centre, just across the street from Avignon's old city gates. The TGV high-speed trains service the city from Gare d'Avignon TGV, which is a five minute train ride from Gare Centre, at €1.30.

GETTING AROUND

Avignon's local buses service the outskirts of the city walls, but once inside the city, everything is easily accessible on foot. The furthest attraction in the city, **Fort Saint-André,** can be reached by taking the Blue Line #5, which costs €1.50 for a single journey.

PRACTICAL INFORMATION

Tourist Offices: Find the main tour office here (41 Cours Jean Jaurés; 04 32 74 32 74; www.avignon-tourisme.com; open M-F 9am-6pm and Su 10am-5pm).

Banks/ATMs/Currency Exchange: A good bank to exchange and withdraw money from is BNP Paribas (3 Rue de la Balance; 04 90 14 41 00; open M-F 8:30am-noon and 1:30pm-5pm).

Post Offices: Those looking to send mail can check out La Poste (Cours Président Kennedy; open M-F 8:30am-12:30pm, 1:30pm-6pm, and Sa 9:15am-noon).

Internet: The tourist office, cafés, and most restaurants offer free Wi-Fi.

BGLTQ+ Resources: Visit www.gay-provence.org for tips on accomodations, restaurants, events, and nightlife in the region.

EMERGENCY INFORMATION

Emergency Number: 112.
Police: Local police can be reached at 04 90 16 81 00.
US Embassy: The closest US consulate is in Marseille (12 Bd. Paul Peytral; 04 91 55 09 47; open M-F 9am-noon and 2pm-5pm).
Rape Crisis Center: While there is no crisis center in Avignon specifically, you can contact this European-wide organization: Rape Crisis Network Europe (www.inavem.org; 01 45 88 19 00).
Hospitals: For a reliable hospital, check out the following.

- Avignon Central Hospital (Centre Hospitalier Général; 305 Rue Raoul Follereau; 04 32 75 33 33; open daily 24hr).

Pharmacies: Pharmacies have somewhat variable hours compared to the US. Below is a pharmacy that is centrally located.

- Pharmacie Des Halles (52 Rue de la Bonneterie; 04 90 82 54 27; open M-Sa 8:30am-12:30pm and 2pm-7:30pm).

SIGHTS

CULTURE

CATHÉDRALE NOTRE-DAME DES DOMS D'AVIGNON

Pl. du Palais; 04 90 82 12 21; www.cathedrale-avignon.fr; open M-Sa 7:30am-8:30pm, winter M-Sa 8am-8:30pm

Hey, even churches get a little work done from time to time, and after a face-lift in 2013, this cathedral is in tip-top shape for its close up. The cathedral underwent a 30-month long restoration lasting until 2016, the first since its original debut in the year 1838. Inside, you'll find beautiful frescos, and a Romanesque nave decorated in the classic Gothic style of Southern France. High above the city, this chapel offers a beautiful view of the nearby **Palais des Papes** and historic heart of the city.

i Free; last entry 20min. before closing; wheelchair accessible

ÉGLISE SAINT-AGRICOL

23 Rue Saint-Agricol; 04 90 82 17 87; www.saintagricol.paroisse84.fr; open M-F 5:30pm-6:30pm

The Church of Saint Agricol looks like a nine year old with a massive lego kit designed it. Three rectangular buildings comprise the church, and the towering red doors only add to the boxy design of the building. Built in the seventh century by the Bishop Saint Agricol himself, this church is considered a historic monument in Avignon. Its square design hides its obviously gothic interior, and the intricate details on the façade of the church's entrance are, alone, worth the trip.

i Free; no wheelchair accessibility

LANDMARKS

PALAIS DES PAPES

Place du Palais; 04 32 74 32 74; www.palais-des-papes.com; open daily 9am-7pm

Let's be honest here: the Palais des Papes is probably the only reason you're in Avignon. And sure, you've probably seen 15 other Gothic buildings. And yes, it is one of the most expensive places you've visited in days. But you'll be damned if you aren't going to strap on the interactive guided iPad and email yourself a selfie with a Pope from its app. A visit to the Palais des Papes is simply non-negotiable while in Avignon. This **UNESCO World Heritage Site** was built in 1335 and is the largest Gothic palace in all of Europe. With over 25 rooms decorated with wall murals and frescoes, this place packs in nearly 650,000 visitors a year. The audio-visual guide that comes with your entrance ticket shows you a revamped version of the faded decor and tells the dramatic history of this site.

i Reduced admission €10; last entry 30min. before closing; no wheelchair accessibility

AVIGNON CITY WALL

39 Rue Notre Dame des 7 Douleurs; open daily 24hr

Sure, this wall doesn't feature a massive moat and drawbridge but it remains a sight to behold. The city of Avignon is fully enclosed by miles of stone, and we're unsure if that's a local move to keep tourists out or to keep all of the incredible city sights in. Built in the fourteenth century, the wall highlights the importance of fortifications in early French architecture. Some hypothesize that the Romans first constructed a wall here in the first century, but archaeologists have yet to confirm the rumors. Regardless, what makes this wall truly striking is the contrast between the muted stone and vibrant lavender surrounding it.

i Free, wheelchair accessible

HÔTEL DE VILLE

Place de l'Horloge; 04 90 80 80 00; open M-F 8:00am-4:30pm

The City Hall of Avignon flies the highest density of French flags from its roof of the entire country. Okay, that might be a bit of an exaggeration, but the classic French flags that line the exterior and central building offer a beautiful contrast to the high, white marble pillars that fill the interior of the hall. While inside, keep an eye out for Hôtel de Ville's adorable clock tower, which will charm your pants off every hour on the hour with a Pixar-like display of cheer and frivolity.

i Free, wheelchair accessible

PONT D'AVIGNON

Pont d'Avignon; 04 32 74 32 74; www.avignon-pont.com; summer open daily 9am-7pm, winter open daily 9:30am-7pm

The classic saying, "we'll cross that bridge when we get to it," only applies to roughly half of the Pont D'Avignon. This bridge is about as useful as a raft—massive flooding destroyed nearly half of it hundreds of years ago. It's hard to take in views of the bridge from atop the bridge itself, but the free audio guide makes a visit to the brick ruins well worth it. In the guide, you'll hear the edge-of-your-seat story of the shepard Benezet, who at the age of 12 received a divine image of building the Pont D'Avignon. In super-hero like fashion, Benzet developed super strength to build the bridge that (unfortunately) could not stand the test of time.

i Reduced admission €3; no wheelchair accessibility

MUSEUMS

MUSÉE ANGLADON

5 Rue Laboureur; 04 90 82 29 03; www.angladon.com; open T-Su 1pm-6pm

Steering France into the twentieth and twenty-first centuries, the Musée Angladon features works by Picasso and Van Gogh, among other renowned modern artists. The exhibits line the walls of an exquisite and elaborate home, and the art and house furniture will have you daydreaming of your own personal in-home museum. Visit Musée Angladon to escape the unrelenting Renaissance paintings featured in exhibits around the country, or simply to enjoy its unique ambiance. Either way, your trip is sure to be worth it.

i Reduced admission €6.50; wheelchair accessible; last entry 30min. before close

MUSÉE CALVET

65 Rue Joseph Vernet; 04 90 86 33 84; www.musee-calvet.org; open W-M 10am-1pm, 2pm-6pm

The Musée Calvet is sort of like a buffet for art. The museum features works that span across centuries, styles, and even continents. At times, this results in continents or eras that are less robustly presented than others, but not every buffet has a perfect spread between food groups. The museum features paintings, sculptures, and antiquities for a whopping viewing price tag of "free"—making it a haven for backpackers and students alike.

i Free; no wheelchair accessibility

MUSÉE DU PETIT PALAIS

Palais des archevêques; 04 90 86 44 58; www.petit-palais.org; open W-M 10am-1pm and 2pm-6pm

So you're an Art History Major and you think you know the Medieval period, huh? Well, until you've visited this museum, you haven't even scratched the surface of Medieval art. A **UNESCO Heritage Museum,** the Musée du Petit Palais features over 300 pieces of Italian religious art from the pre-renaissance era. Here you'll find captivating works from **Boticelli, Carpaccio,** and **Giovanni di Paulo.** Despite its small exterior in contrast to the looming Palais des Popes across the street, the towering inside corridors flaunt massive statues sure to make even the tallest of visitors feel small. These statues sit alongside antiquities and frescos that give the museum a truly elegant feel.

i Reduced admission €3; wheelchair accessible; guided tours available upon request; last entry 30min. before close

OUTDOORS

JARDIN DES DOMS

2 Montée des Moulins; 04 32 74 32 74; open M-F 9am-6pm and Sa 9am-5pm

Learn the origin of the game "Duck, duck, goose!" at the Jardin des Doms. With enough ducks and geese to make your head spin, this garden is known for its massive pond. If you're lucky, you'll arrive to find a very full pond in front of you, the perfect place to enjoy an ice cream from the café that overlooks the water. And, well, if you're unlucky, that pond will look sort of like an unfilled swimming pool with a little green mold. Either way, the back of the Jardin des Doms features incredible panoramic views of Avignon, the **Pont D'Avignon**, and the **Rhône River.** From here, trails lead to the waterfront and the entrance to the Pont D'Avignon.

i Free; wheelchair accessible

WALKING PATH BY PROMENADE DU CANAL

31 Avenue Gabriel Péri; opn daily 24hr

This 6km long, flat path is perfect for the cardio-freaks among you that are missing their treadmills most right now. Also accepting of bikers and walkers, this path starts at the Promenade du Canal, right beside the **Tour Phillipe le Bel** in **Villeneuve-lès-Avignon.** If you're not incredibly interested in the full loop, a bridge to the other side of the canal marks the halfway point in the walk (and potential turnaround point for those looking for a quicker journey). Summer visitors be warned: few trees provide shade near Promenade du Canal, so wear sunscreen or bring a hat.

i Free; wheelchair accessible

FOOD

E.A.T ESTAMINET ARÔMES ET TENTATIONS ($$)

8 Rue Mazan; 04 90 83 46 74; www.restaurant-eat.com; open Th-Tu noon-1:45pm and 7pm-9:30pm

With a farm-to-table menu at grocery store-to-hostel prices, you can fill your stomach with delectable vegetables and mouth watering meaty meals here. Your grandma's house with a modern twist, this white-walled restaurant features a splash of colorful decor sure to put a smile on your face. Plus, if you're looking for dinner and entertainment, simply ask your waitress for crayons to color over the brown paper place-stations. Make sure to save room for dessert, though—their array of cakes and chocolates taste far too good to resist.

i Entrées from €10, dessert from €6; vegetarian options available; wheelchair accessible

GINETTE ET MARCEL ($)

25-27 Place des Corps Saints; 04 90 85 58 70; open daily 10:30am-11:30pm

A first look at Ginette et Marcel, with its yarn-covered bike sitting out front, has patrons wondering whether they really stumbled upon a restaurant or craft store. Some might argue that the tartines waiting inside Ginette et Marcel are themselves works of craftsmanship,

and we support that claim. With an incredible array of tartines, or open-faced sandwiches, Ginette et Marcel has given the sandwich a fancy new look. These treats are hearty and delicious, and the old, 1920s vibe of the restaurant gives the place a feel that's worth returning to again and again.

i Tartines from €4.60; vegetarian options available; wheelchair accessible

L'AMISTA ($)

23 Rue de la Bonneterie; 06 19 24 15 47; open Tu-Th noon-3pm and 6:30pm-10pm, F-Sa noon-10pm

If you find yourself craving a blast back to your childhood, look no further than L'Amista. This restaurant looks like it doubles as an elementary school classroom, decorated with primary colors, a full chalkboard wall, and photos and excerpts from the French children's book "Martine." Their tapas selection seems almost endless, and the most intense of their selections, the cassette de tapas, is a huge box of appetizers that can be wonderfully shared by two people or more. If tapas aren't your thing, then this place also features a wide array of face-sized salads.

i Tapas from €4, large salads from €14, sangria €3; happy hour Th-Sa 6:30pm-8pm; vegetarian and vegan options available; wheelchair accessible

LA SOU'PAPE ($)

51 Rue de la Grande Fusterie; 09 81 46 23 34; open M-F 8:30am-6pm

Don't let the tragic interior design of La Sou'pape deter you from entering. Tucked away on a quiet street, La Sou'pape is where locals come to hide. Despite it's neon green walls and horrendously mismatched purple chairs, this place knows how to design something far more important: good food. As far off the beaten track as you can get in Avignon (and trust us, it isn't far), this small café serves up incredible lunches and breakfasts sure to fill any weary traveler's stomach—without emptying their wallet.

i Sandwiches from €5; vegetarian options available; wheelchair accessible

LE VINTAGE ($$$)

10 Rue Galante; 04 86 65 48 54; open daily noon-3pm and 7pm-11pm

Get ready to experience the finest dining Avignon offers budget travelers. We reccomend opting for their pre-set lunch menu, which offers hefty portion sizes for a minimal cost. Even if you come for dinner, the small dent in your budget will still be worth it, as this restaurant offers only the highest quality modern and regional French cuisine. Made solely from in-season ingredients, the food comes out so fresh it's kicking.

i Meals from €18; reservations recommended; vegetarian options available; wheelchair accessible

NIGHTLIFE

H036 BAR

17 Rue de la République, first floor; 04 32 40 50 60; open daily 24hr

Lively, international, and English speaking crowds fill this bar nightly. If you're in search of friends, look no further than H036: the beer, sangria, and tapas keep churning out all night long, and the bar games provide ample opportunities to chat up strangers. Challenge your new mates to a heated game of pool, or invest in a late-night game of Monopoly from the bar's expansive board game collection. With balconies overlooking the city, an open-sky outdoor area, and a homey indoor feel, you might just decide to move into HO36.

i Beer from €4, wine from €3, tapas from €4; wheelchair accessible

LALOGÈNE

1 Place Pie; 04 86 81 60 76; open M-Sa 7:30am-1am, Su 8:30am-1am

Lalogène is like your friend who's a senior in college but somehow still can't stick to their major. It truly can't decide whether it's a bar or a raging nightclub. With a relaxed environment on its outdoor patio and cheap selection of beers and wines, you'll want to sit back and take in an evening of lightly sipping on rosé outside. Inside, however, Lalogène's wild side stirs chaotically—electro pop oozes from its speakers, sparkling walls glitter in your face, and tequila shots circulate consistently.

i Beer and wine from €3; wheelchair accessible

LA PLACE

3 Place Pie; 06 11 56 17 18; open daily 7:30am-1am

What is *the* place to go out in Avignon? Oh, La Place. Yes, what is the place? La Place! Avoid an awkward, albeit funny, interaction like this when you visit Avignon, and just head straight to La Place, which truly is the place for nightlife in the city. The bar itself features a great terrace but inside the bar is where the magic happens. With white walls and a ring-shaped lighting fixture that looks like it should be hanging on the inside of a futuristic space ship, this place is churning out bass-filled tunes perfect to dance the night away to. As expected, parties are bigger on the weekends than the weekdays.

i Beer from €4; wheelchair accessible

BIARRITZ

Coverage by **Jessica Moore**

One does not simply vacation in Biarritz; one *summers* in Biarritz. The city's rich roots can be traced back to when Napoléon III and his wife, Empress Eugénie, began summering here way back in the mid-nineteenth century. But don't let its royal status deter you—Biarritz also boasts France's highest density of laid-back surfers. The city is fit for both travelers seeking to experience the ritzy side of France and those looking to drop their backpack in a hostel, dig their feet into a sandy beach, and enjoy the free beauty all around.

ORIENTATION

The downtown area of Biarritz, and most active area in the city, can be found along its beaches. There are four main beaches in Biarritz that stretch from **La Plage de Milady** to **Pointe Saint Martin Lighthouse.** The seaside trail **Le Circuit Bord de Mer** will lead you right from the lighthouse to the most popular and largest of these beaches, **La Grande Plage**. Along the same coast you'll find the **Port du Pecheûr,** or fisherman's port, and past that lies the **Pointe Atalaye,** where the Virgin Rock stands. To the southern end of the Virgin Rock lies the **Aquarium, Port Vieux, Plage de la Côte de Basques,** then the **Plage de la Marbella,** and finally, the **Plage de Milady.** Past these beaches, you'll find the ocean-themed interactive museum, **La Cité de l'Ocean.** Inland from the coast lies **Rue Gambetta,** featuring Biarritz's best shops and restaurants, which eventually leads to **Les Halles,** the town market.

ESSENTIALS

GETTING THERE

Biarritz has an airport with daily incoming flights from other cities in the European Union. Additionally, the city features a train station with a direct connection to Paris, as well as other French cities, making travel to Biarritz easy by bus, plane, or train.

GETTING AROUND

Biarritz is easily walkable, but should you want to take a bus, keep your eyes peeled for the Chronoplus system. Each €1 euro ride is valid for one hour, including connections. Tickets can be purchased on the bus with cash or in tobacco shops. Day passes cost at €2. The C Line Bus connects the airport to the train station as well.

PRACTICAL INFORMATION

Tourist Offices: Biarritz Tourisme (Square d'Ixelles; 05 59 22 37 10; www.tourisme.biarritz.fr; open M-F 9am-6pm, Sa 10am-12pm and 2pm-5pm, Su 10am-1pm).

Banks/ATMs/Currency Exchange: ATMs can be found on most street corners in Biarritz. A local bank and ATM can be found at Point Nickel (108 Avenue de Verdun; open M-Sa 6:30am-8pm).

Post Offices: La Poste (17 Rue de la Poste; open M-F 9am-5:30pm, Sa 9am-noon).
Public Restrooms: A small service charge of €0.20 may be required (31 Boulevard du Général de Gaulle).
BGLTQ+ Resources: Les Bascos (10 Rue Jacques Laffitte - 64100 Bayonne; 06 69 64 36 27 and 05 59 20 04 01).

EMERGENCY INFORMATION

Emergency Number: 112.
Police: Commissariat de Police (1 Avenue Joseph Petit; 05 59 01 22 22).
Rape Crisis Center: Listed here is a helpline available for victims of physical, sexual, or pyschological abuse. Rape Crisis Network Europe (01 45 88 19 00; www.inavem.org; helpline open daily 9am-9pm).
Hospitals: Here is Biarritz's main hospital:

- Emergency Main Sud Aquitaine (21 Rue de l'Estagnas; 05 59 22 46 00; open daily 24hr).

Pharmacies: Pharmacies are easy to find around the city of Biarritz.

- Pharmacy South Station (20 Avenue du Maréchal Foch; 05 59 24 12 82; open M-Sa 9am-7:30pm).

SIGHTS

CULTURE

COLORAMA

50 Avenue de l'Impératrice; tourisme.biarritz.fr/fr/actualites/colorama-festival; open daily Jul 10-Aug 1 10:30am-1pm and 3pm-9pm

Is street art really street art if it isn't on an actual street? Call up your philosophy major friends to get Kant's perspective on these questions, because we're still stumped. COLORAMA challenges the classic perspective on what counts as street art (or art at all), as its galleries display floor-to-ceiling paintings by the most unconventional artists. This establishment, whose exterior looks straight off Route 66, is a wonder to the eyes and may give you the distinct urge to go buy spray paint.

i Admission €5; wheelchair accessible

ÉGLISE SAINT MARTIN DE BIARRITZ (SAINT MARTIN CHURCH OF BIARRITZ)

4 Rue Saint-Martin; 05 59 23 08 36; www.paroisse-biarritz.fr/eglises/saint-martin.php; open daily 2pm-6pm

When you see the Church of Saint Martin, your first thought will be "Wow, it's a little bland on the outside for a church in Europe," and your second thought will be "Thank God it isn't Gothic." Okay, maybe this is your first stop in Europe so you aren't quite over Gothic architecture yet. Either way, this church is an aesthetic saving grace. Its understated approach to worship contrasts the overwhelming elegance of Biarritz, making the Church of Saint-Martin stand out with poise and sophistication.

i Free; wheelchair accessible

CHAPELLE IMPERIALE (PARISH OF NOTRE DAME DU ROCHER)

Avenue Reine Victoria; 05 59 22 37 10; open Tu-W 4pm-6pm, hours subject to change

They say purple is the color of sexual frustration. If that's true, then we have some questions for Napoleon III, who built this deep-purple chapel in 1864. Whether Napoleon III had a—er—sexually fulfilling life or not, today the chapel stands as the "Jewel of Biarritz," so clearly its purple hue has taken on a different meaning. Locals work hard to keep this jewel well hidden—navigating the open hours of this site can be tricky, and tours are given by appointment only.

i Admission €3; guided tours by appointment only; wheelchair accessible

CRYPT SAINTE EUGÉNIE

Place Sainte-Eugénie; 05 59 24 07 43; www.paroisse-biarritz.fr/eglises/sainte-eugenie.php; open Tu-Sa 2pm-7pm

When modern day explorers finally unearthed the Crypt of Saint Eugénie, the French faced the relatable conundrum of keeping the crypt as is or turning it into a contemporary art museum. They went with option #2. Today, the crypt holds an interesting collection of abstract art. If you're searching for dead bodies and a cool, underground crypt vibe, this is not the place for you.

i Free; no wheelchair accessibility

LANDMARKS

PHARE DE BIARRITZ (BIARRITZ LIGHTHOUSE)

60 B Esp, Espl. Elisabeth II; 05 59 22 37 10; open daily 2pm-6:30pm

The lighthouse of Biarritz looms over the city's beaches like a professional basketball player looms over a six-year-old. Standing 73 meters above sea level, this place has been shining light on the Côte d'Azur since 1834. Navigate up its spiral staircases for astonishing panoramas of the mountain peppered coast and the Atlantic Ocean or enjoy views from the outside where hydrangeas and tamarisk trees line cobbled paths.

i Admission €3; no wheelchair accessibility

PORT DES PÊCHEURS (FISHERS' PORT)

Allée Port des Pêcheurs; open daily 24hr

While you won't find any skipper captains clad in bright yellow fishing suits or holding giant fishing nets in this fisherman's port, you will find a collection of picturesque houses. These beautiful houses with brightly painted wooden doors and shutters have been renovated and now hold some of Biarritz's best seaside restaurants. The small block bustles with people, many coming to and from Port des Pêcheurs' small beach.

i Free; limited wheelchair accessibility

ROCHER DE LA VIERGE (THE VIRGIN ROCK)

Espl. de la Vierge; 05 59 22 37 10; open daily 24hr

The Virgin Rock is to Biarritz as the Statue of Liberty is to New York. She stands on an island, tourists flock from all over to see her, and she could not be more covered in bird poop. Birds or not, the Virgin Rock is a beautiful landmark and must-see for any visitor to the region. The bridge connecting it to the mainland was built in 1865 and, despite years of being worn down by the Atlantic, the monument still stands strong today. Visit this spot to take in the ocean around you, the statue above you, and the city behind you.

i Free; limited wheelchair accessibility

MUSEUMS

AQUARIUM DE BIARRITZ

Esplanade du Rocher de la Vierge; 05 59 22 75 40; www.aquariumbiarritz.com; open daily 9:30am-7pm

This aquarium contains two key things we're sure you won't find anywhere else in France, the largest sea turtles and sea lions you may ever see. We have no idea what they're feeding these babies, but boy, are they *hefty*. Additionally, the aquarium possesses an array of tanks filled with almost every possible underwater creature you can imagine, including a 15-foot long, bright green eel. Catch the sea lions snoring on rocks outside, wave hello to the turtles, and hope all three of you have eaten enough today to avoid starvation.

i Admission €15, €13 reduced; wheelchair accessible

BIARRITZ HISTORY MUSEUM

Eglise St Andrews, Rue Broquedis; 05 59 24 86 28; www.tourisme.biarritz.fr/en/discover/sites-and-museums-biarritz/historical-museum; open Tu-Sa 10am-12:30pm and 2pm-6:30pm

This quirky museum puts Biarritz's bizarre history into full view. Built into a church and situated off a narrow road in the center of town, this hidden time capsule will transport you through the development of one of France's most popular destinations. If the Biarritz History Museum were to ever compete in Project Runway, you can be sure that design critic Tim Gunn would be yelling at her to "Edit down! Keep it simple and crisp!" An extremely uncrisp museum, the Biarritz History Museum clashes patterns, packs on the detail, and would have killed the 2019 Met Gala with its campiness. Odd exhibits greet visitors from every corner, including a stuffed white bear (truly a complete monstrosity) and surf boards.

i Admission €4; wheelchair accessible

OUTDOORS

BIARRITZ BEACHES

Allée Winston Churchill; 05 59 22 37 10; open daily 24hr

If you need any convincing that you should check out Biarritz's beaches

while you're in France, we took at least five million pictures, suffered from an extreme sunburn, and trudged through Biarritz with sore swimming muscles and still want to go back. With four main beaches, you have some prime options to choose from during your time in the city. As its name suggests, **Le Grande Plage** is the largest and most accessible of all the beaches and a favorite for sunbathers, small dogs, and surfers alike. Its nearby neighbor, the **Plage Port Vieux,** is a protected area without waves or wind and popular with families. You will find **Plage Miramar** right below the **Phare de Biarritz**—a great spot for surfers looking for a thrill. First time surfers will find a home at the **Côte de Basque,** a beach with perfect beginner waves.
i Free; limited wheelchair accessibility

CÔTE DE BASQUE

Avenue Beau Rivage

Before heading to the Côte de Basque, you'll need to learn a few key phrases, namely, "Hang 10," "Surf's Up," and "Awesome, bro." The ultimate surfer's beach, there isn't much "beach" to be found here when the tide is high. Not fit for lounging or sunbathing, this beach sits below high cliffs with ample graffiti to view while you shred the gnar below. Whether it's your first time surfing or you're a professional looking to scope out the competition waters, the Côte de Basque welcomes you.
i Free; free shuttle for wheelchair access

FOOD

3 SALSAS ($$)

5 Rue Harispe; 05 59 23 04 53; www.3salsas.fr; open M noon-2pm and 7pm-2am, Tu-Sa 7pm-2am

If you consider guacamole to be a 'salsa' then you are exactly the kind of person that 3 Salsas caters to. We're sorry, but as good as it may be, guacamole is not salsa. We'll let 3 Salsas' oversight slide because they make up for it with incredible Spanish dishes. As possibly the only place in France that doesn't believe in small portion sizes, you'll leave 3 Salsas full and happy. Don't skip the margaritas either, they pair extremely well with the food and the bartender doesn't skimp on the tequila.
i Entrées from €12; vegetarian options available; wheelchair accessible

DODIN ($$)

Quai de la Grande Plage; 05 59 22 10 43; www.dodin-biarritz.fr; open daily 9am-7pm

Even if Dodin had the worst pastries in all of France, we'd still recommend it to you simply for its floor-to-ceiling windows and prime seafront property smack in front of **Le Grande Plage.** Thankfully though, Dodin features great eats and a menu that will make you wonder how bread could possibly taste so good. In fact, their breakfast was so good that it kept bringing us back again and again. There's no better way to start your day than sipping a cappuccino by the ocean.
i Meals from €9; vegetarian options available; wheelchair accessible

BEACH GARDEN ($)

31 Boulevard du Général de Gaulle; 09 72 84 73 46; open daily 10am-4pm

In a saddening twist, Beach Garden does not feature a garden at all. This small shop is more of a place to grab a quick bite to-go than to stay in for a sit-down lunch, as the beach itself really acts as Beach Garden's prime seating and eating location. Grab anything from a simple salad to a gourmet bagel. We suggest coming here for lunch with a beach towel, ordering a salad and a bagel (gotta carbo load for le surf), pairing your meal with a bottle of wine, and heading straight to Biarritz's sandy shores.

Lunch entreées from €11; vegetarian and vegan options available; wheelchair accessible

BLÉ NOIR ($)

1 Boulevard du Général de Gaulle; 05 59 24 31 77; open daily noon-10pm

When you say the name "Blé Noir" outloud, it may sound like a dissatisfied exclamation, but this place will leave you anything but. You'll be overlooking the ocean in this small restaurant that slings crêpes out by the plateful. With large open windows, an airy feel, and more crêpe topping combinations than you could imagine, Blé Noir keeps the French food tradition alive. If you're feeling extra hungry, we recommend going with one of the heartier options, and steering away from the all-too-good sweet crêpes, even if Nutella sounds irresistible.

Crêpes from €5; vegetarian options available; wheelchair accessible

MILWAUKEE CAFÉ ($$)

2 Rue du Helder; 05 59 54 17 04; open Tu-Su 9am-5pm

Milwaukee Café is probably the closest you'll ever get to being in Milwaukee, except for, you know, being in Milwaukee itself. Built from the ground up by a Milwaukee expat, this charming spot serves excellent American cuisine and the pour-over coffee you've been searching for. A modern shop infused with a mom-and-pop feel, Milwaukee café features a gorgeous patio and enough twinkle lights to rival any college dorm room.

Sandwiches from €5, meals from €12; vegetarian options available; wheelchair accessible

LE PIM'PI ($$$)

14 Avenue de Verdun; 05 59 24 12 62; open Tu-Sa noon-2pm and 7:30-10pm

Le Pim'pi is the closest you, budget traveler, will get to a Michelin-level dining experience while in Biarritz. The smell of fresh caught seafood paired with locally grown vegetables wafts through the air while the waitstaff recommends dishes, each with the perfect wine pairing to boot. No matter how full you are after your entrée, don't skip dessert—Le Pim'pi's are delectable, indulgent, to die for.

Meals from €21; vegetarian options available; wheelchair accessible

NIGHTLIFE

NEWQUAY BAR ($)

20 Place Georges Clemenceau; 05 59 22 19 90; open Tu-Su 9am-2pm

If Newquay Bar was meant to be a hidden gem for students in Biarritz, the owners did a very poor job of hiding it. Kick back in a La-Z-Boy-style leather chair and sip on a reasonably-priced beer as you watch a sports game or, for you intellectual types, whatever random documentary Newquay has decided to put on. Here, locals and tourists bond over cheap shots and pop music—a surefire combination.

Beer from €3, shots from €2; limited wheelchair accessibility

LE CAVEAU ($$)

4 Rue Gambetta; 05 59 24 16 17; open daily midnight-5am

Pride in a bottle. This BGLTQ+ nightclub features a large bar, a long drink menu, and a dance floor that's always pumping. The place warms up around 1am, when well-dressed twenty-something flood through its doors ready for a party. Be warned: the bouncers will turn you away if you're not lookin' sharp and over 25.

Cover €12, drinks from €8; 25+ only; BGLTQ+ friendly; wheelchair accessible

DUPLEX ($$)

24 Avenue Edouard VII; 05 59 24 65 39; www.nightclub-biarritz.com; open W midnight-6am, Th-Sa 11pm-6am, Su 11pm-midnight

With questionable dance floor names like "The Cotton Club" and "Pulp," it's hard to tell what vibe Duplex is going for until you're inside. Its above 25 floor, the "Cotton Club" feels as lush and extravagant as its name suggests. The "Pulp" attracts younger crowds and what it lacks in VIP exclusivity, arched ceilings, and extravagant glowing bars, it makes up for in party. Here, house

SAINT-JEAN-DE-LUZ

When Ernest Hemingway wrote about little French villages by the seaside where old men become existential, he was writing about Saint-Jean-de-Luz. This small but luxurious town is everything you would imagine a fishing town in France would be. Shops and restaurants line narrow, winding streets with cute souvenirs and an impeccable range of food fare. The humble city rose to its current glory as an elegant destination when King Louis XIV and his wife Maria Theresa wed here in 1660. A summer spot fit for kings and queens, Saint-Jean-de-Luz sits right outside of Basque Country, a mere 10km from the Spanish border. With a beach to dig your toes into, shops to explore, and great food to fill you with, Saint-Jean-de-Luz has everything the avid explorer could need and more.

Saint-Jean-de-Luz is a smaller city with a center at **Place Louis XIV,** a lively square. On the northwest end, the city is flanked by **Le Grande Plage.** It's main street, **Rue Léon Gambetta** runs parallel to this beach and is lined with shops and restaurants. Another wonderful street to stroll down is **Promenade Jacques,** which runs from the lighthouse to the beach below.

GETTING THERE

Saint-Jean-de-Luz shares a train station with the city of Ciboure, and recieves trains incoming from surrounding towns including Bayonne and Biarritz. Buses also run from the nearby cities of Biarritz, Bayonne, and Hendaye through Ouibus, TCRB, and Basque Bondissant. The city is located off of highway A-63, a 20min. drive from Biarritz, and a 30min. drive from San Sebastian.

GETTING AROUND

Since Saint-Jean-de-Luz is such a small town, your walking shoes are all you need. Trust us, you could traverse the entire city in less than 20 minutes on foot! If you drive in though, a free shuttle bus runs in the summer connecting the parking lots of Chantaco and Parc des Sports to the town center.

Check out...

L'ÉGLISE SAINT JEAN BAPTISTE

Rue Léon Gambetta; 05 59 26 08 81; www.saint-jean-de-luz.com/fr/18303-/; open daily 8am-noon and 3pm-7pm

Charlie may have gotten a golden ticket, but Saint-Jean-de-Luz has a golden cathedral. While it may seem like one of many Gothic, Catholic churches in France, this church is almost overbearingly covered in gold and filled with precious statues that were the backdrop to Louis XIV and Maria Theresa's imperial wedding. You can thank the Spanish for that because they go all-out on their churches. Even amongst all of this opulence, the church still holds onto its Basque influences, with a sailboat hanging from the ceiling and rich dark wood adorning the rafters.

i Free, limited wheelchair accessibility

Swing by...

MAISON LOUIS XIV

6 Place Louis XIV; 05 59 26 27 58; www.maison-louis-xiv.fr; open daily 9am-8pm

Louis XIV was a very normal man who always slept sitting up out of fear of suffocating under his sheets. Despite his complete twooby-ness, he somehow married a Spanish Empress (something or other to do with ending a war). See, an absolutely normal man in every way. This museum, in the home where Louis XIV signed the **Treaty of Pyrenees** in 1659, puts this very normal man's life and odd quirks on full display. Take in his incredibly short bed and wonder how his wife slept with him all those years or contemplate how many mannequins they can fit into one museum. Despite the weird vibes Louis XIV will give you from beyond the grave, you're sure to have fun during your visit.

i Full ticket €6.50, €4 reduced; guided visits only; tours every 40min July-Aug, last tour is 30min before close; no wheelchair accessible

Don't miss...

LA GRANDE PLAGE

64500 Saint-Jean-de-Luz

This is not your average beach. With golden sand and a flat topography, this beach's waves are more like pancakes than the roaring ones of its nearby neighbor, Biarritz. For this reason, the coast packs on the people (none of whom seem to have packed on the pounds) in its summer months. A local favorite, Saint-Jean-de-Luzians (did someone say Deleuze?) come to La Grande Plage to sunbathe, paddle board, or swim in a much more laid-back setting. Don't be surprised to find women here topless, men in speedos, and the occasional dog with swim shoes on.

i Free; limited wheelchair accessibility

Grab a bite at...

LA TAVERNE BASQUE

5 Rue de la République; 05 59 23 12 40; open daily noon-2:30pm and 7pm-10:30pm

In Basque Country, they do many things well, but the thing they do best is food. In this restaurant, you can savor the best of Basque cuisine by sampling incredible hams, toro soup, and of course, one of their many duck options. The pan-seared fish meal will have you feeling ritzy while the delicious selection of white wines (most of which pair well with seafood!) will have you feeling a bit ditzy. With large windows and wooden walls that give the place an almost modern feel, this is the perfect spot to sit back and indulge in regional cuisine.

i Three course meal from €21; vegetarian options available; limited wheelchair accessibility music blasts all night long, and you're sure to find drinks as sugary as the daddies in the Cotton Club.

i Cover €15; drinks from €4; wheelchair accessible

EDEN ROCK CAFÉ ($$$)

2-4 Espl. du Port Vieux; 06 59 68 18 24; open daily 11am-2am

Eden Rock Café is truly a little slice of the biblical garden come to life in Biarritz. Sitting right over the Plage de Miramar, this café's name comes from not only its rocky cliffs, but also the rock music it blasts deep into the night. Get here early enough and you'll be able to secure a spot right on the edges of the bar, which offers one of the best views of sunset in all of Biarritz. If you're hungry, Eden Rock Café also features an extensive menu with great seafood bites, making this the perfect night out in Biarritz.

i Beers from €6, cocktails from €9; no wheelchair accessibility

BORDEAUX

Coverage by **Kristine Guillaume**

Welcome to Wine Country. No, not Napa Valley, you uncultured swine. Bordeaux is ten times better. A city loaded with culture and, obviously, wine, Bordeaux has truly earned its place as the epicenter of beauty and sophistication in southwestern France. Years ago, when the city rose to fame for its bustling Chartons district, where wine merchants perfected blends of reds and whites, merchants and owners of the renowned *châteaus* wrote about the port, calling it the Port of the Moon, for its stunning, ornate architecture along the Garonne River. Today, the glistening reflections of landmarks such as Place de la Bourse in the water make it impossible to question the Bordeaux's status as a UNESCO World Heritage Site. Yet, even with its ancient Roman and French history, the city has transformed from the *Belle au Bois Dormant* (Sleeping Beauty) to a bustling, cosmopolitan center with a trendy student nightlife scene and outdoor concert venues on the river. Not too far from the main city are Atlantic beach towns just a bus ride away if you're looking to enjoy the surf and sun.

ORIENTATION

The Garonne River divides Bordeaux in two parts, with its center on the western bank. **Les Quais,** the riverfront boardwalk, stretches between the two main bridges, **Pont de Pierre** and **Pont Jacques Chaban Delmas.** Along Les Quais, you'll find everything from skate parks to green spaces to restaurants. The main attraction along the boardwalk, however, is the city center at **Place de la Bourse,** in front of which is **Miroir d'Eau.** The city center, also called **Vieille Ville** (Old City) opens up to **Promenade Sainte-Catherine,** the longest pedestrian street in Europe lined with cafés, restaurants, and boutiques. To the north of Vielle Ville is the **Triangle D'Or** neighborhood, the wealthiest area in all of Bordeaux, where you'll find three main boulevards at have vertices at **Le Grande Théâtre, Place Gambetta,** and **Place Tourny.** North of Vielle Ville is the famous **Chartrons district,** known for its former status as a port city and even farther north is an industrial area, which is home to **Base Sous Marine** and the decanter-shaped **Cité du Vin.** South of Vielle Ville is the **Saint Michel** neighborhood, known for having the highest concentration of ethnic food in Bordeaux. On the eastern bank of the Garonne is the **Bastide** area, where you can find outdoor spaces like **Darwin Ecosystème.**

ESSENTIALS

GETTING THERE

If flying, you'll land at Bordeaux-Mérignac Airport, which is 9km from the city center. The Jetbus (€7) runs directly between the airport and the main train station, Gare Saint Jean, every 30min. The ride itself is 30min. To save money, you can take the Line 1 bus (€1.40) to Gare Saint-Jean. If arriving by train, you'll dock at Gare Saint-Jean, which is a 15min. tram ride away from the city center. Take tram line C to Place de la Bourse (€1.60).

GETTING AROUND

The tramway is the most convenient mode of public transportation in the city. Trams depart roughly every 5min. from street-side stops (single ride €1.60). The most essential tram lines are Line C, which runs to the city center (Place de la Bourse) and Line B, which runs to Cité du Vin and Cathédrale Saint-Andre. Another option is to use Bordeaux's city bikes, VCub, which has docking stations throughout the city (24hr pass €1.60). If you venture across the river, take the ferry (€2), which runs from the Stalingrad station on the eastern bank to Quinconces on the eastern. Also, the Transports Bordeaux Métropole (TBM) operates over 80 bus lines that serve the greater urban Bordeaux area.

PRACTICAL INFORMATION

Tourist Offices: 12 Cours du 30 Juillet; 5 56 00 66 00; www.bordeaux-tourisme.com; open M-Sa 9:30am-1pm and 2pm-7pm.
Banks/ATMs/Currency Exchange: There are BNP branches located near the Opéra and in the Chartrons district (BNP Paribas Bordeaux: 40 Cours du Chapeau-Rouge; 820 82 00 01; open M-F 9am-5:30pm).
Post Offices: La Poste Bordeaux (29 Allée de Tourny; open M 9am-6pm, Tu 10am-6pm, W-F 9am-6pm, Sa 9am-noon)
Public Restrooms: You can easily find public restrooms, labeled "Toilettes," along the banks of the Garonne River. There is one located just in front of Place de la Bourse.
Internet: Bordeaux is covered with public Wi-Fi spots. Simply click "Wifi Bordeaux" on your phone network. Free Wi-Fi is also offered in all municipal buildings, including the tourist office.
BGLTQ+ Resources: LGBT Association of Aquitaine; www.le-girofard.org

EMERGENCY INFORMATION

Emergency Number: 112.
Police: Hôtel de Police, Commissariat Central (23 Rue François de Sourdis; 05 57 85 77 77; open daily 24hr).
US Embassy: There is a US consulate in Bordeaux (89 Quai des Chartrons; 01 43 12 48 65).
Rape Crisis Center: Rape Crisis Network Europe (www.inavem.org; 01 45 88 19 00).
Hospitals:

- Hôpital Saint André (1 Rue Jean Burguet; 05 56 79 56 79; open daily 24hr).

Pharmacies:

- Pharmacie (30 Pl. des Capucins; 05 56 91 62 66; open daily 24hr).

SIGHTS

CULTURE

LA CITÉ DU VIN

134 Quai de Bacalan; 05 56 16 20 20; www.laciteduvin.com/fr; open daily 9:30am-7:30pm

La Cité du Vin is an impressive architectural feat: the structure itself is modeled after a decanter, so you already know that this glitzy, brand-spanking-new sight isn't going to disappoint. Established in 2016, Cité du Vin quickly overshadowed its younger sister, **Musée du Vin et du Négoce,** with its extensive exhibits about wine, modern features, and wine tastings. At the end of the day, we appreciated the smaller sibling a little bit more. Call us old-fashioned, but we'd rather have the three wine tastings in the **Chartrons district** than the two Cité du Vin offers (more is better, especially when it comes to wine). Plus, the entrance to La Cité du Vin is steep at €20. Yeah, you heard us. €20.

i Admission €20, €14 reduced; limited wheelchair accessibility

PALAIS GALLIEN

Rue du Docteur Albert Barraud; 33 5 56 00 66 00; open daily 24hr

Bordeaux is just under 1000 miles from Rome, but, even with that distance, you're bound to find a piece of Roman history in wine country. Located just a few blocks away from the **Jardin des Plantes,** Palais Gallien is a Gallo-Roman amphitheatre that holds the very prestigious title of the oldest Roman ruin in Bordeaux. Although it serves today as a shelter for French pigeons, it has managed to keep its majesty throughout the centuries of wear and tear by even the most unsuspecting of guests (rumor has it that Palais Gallien was a hang-out spot for prostitutes and witches in the seventeenth century). Walk by at night to see the structure lit up courtesy of the bright lights implanted in the ground.

i Free; daily tours €3 June 1-Sept 30 10:30am-3:30 pm, evening visits €5 Sa 9:30pm in July-Aug; wheelchair accessible

LANDMARKS

BASILIQUE SAINT-MICHEL

Pl. Meynard; 05 56 94 30 50; open daily 8am-noon and 1pm-6pm

The city of Bordeaux may be a **UNESCO World Heritage Site,** but the Basilique Saint-Michel is one all on its own. This fourteenth-century basilica, although a bit of a walk from the city center, is well worth a trip. The interior is typical of a Gothic European cathedral, bearing some similarity to the nearby **Cathédrale Saint-André,** but it has an older, more lived-in feel. Take a walk around the basilica and then climb its bell tower, the **Fleche de St. Michel,** for a leg workout and fantastic view of the city below. On Fridays and Sundays, you'll find an outdoor market of the antique and produce varieties in the adjacent square.

i Free; tower and crypt €5, €3.50 reduced; last entry 30min. before closing; limited wheelchair accessibility

CATHÉDRALE SAINT-ANDRÉ

Pl. Pey Berland; 05 56 52 68 10; open daily June-Sept 10am-1pm and 3pm-7:30pm (until 7 pm on Su in July and Aug); daily Oct-May 10am-noon and 2 pm-6 pm (until 7 pm on M, W, Sa); closed on M mornings year-round

Take a deep breath because you're about to have it taken away. The Cathédrale Saint-André, also known as the Bordeaux Cathedral, stands tall in the middle of Place Pey-Berland with its magnificent Gothic architecture of the Aquitaine region. Over many years, the Bordelaise have made improvements to the structure, elevating the nave with pointed arches, restoring the giant organ, and opening the royal portal. The cathedral, apart from serving as a religious center, was formerly an animal feed store during the French Revolution (which is kind of gross when you think about it) and was destroyed during WWI. Since then, it has been restored to its former glory with intricately decorated chapels dedicated to various saints and stunning biblically-inspired works of art.

i Free; last entry 30min. before closing; wheelchair accessible

TOUR PEY-BERLAND

Pl. Pey-Berland; 05 56 81 26 25; www.pey-berland.fr; open daily Jan-May 10am-12:30pm and 2pm-5pm, daily June-Sept 10am-1:15pm and 2pm-6pm, daily Oct-Dec 10am-12:30pm and 2pm-5:30pm

Forget the StairMaster; the Tour Pey-Berland has your leg workout covered. The 233-step Gothic structure is the bell tower of the **Cathédrale Saint-Andre** and offers the most incredible panoramic 360-degree view of Bordeaux. Built in the fifteenth century, the tower lacked bells until 1853 and just served as a towering structure for a few hundred years. Now, though, you can climb up the tower and read about the history of every neighborhood of Bordeaux, including the **Saint-Michel** and **Chartrons** districts, on the descriptive plaques on the first landing. Pro-tip: bring water on your trek up the bell tower, as the climb is remarkably dizzying.

i Admission €6, free for EU residents and EU students 18-25 years old; last entry 30min. before closing; no wheelchair accessibility

MUSEUMS

MUSÉE DU VIN ET DU NÉGOCE

Cellier des Chartrons; 41 Rue Borie; 05 56 90 19 13; www.museeduvinbordeaux.com; open daily 10am-6pm

Do not overlook the Musée du Vin et de Négoce for the comparatively glitzy **La Cité du Vin.** This small museum, located in the **Chartrons district,** is designed like the wine cellars the merchants of the district used to produce the highly prized Bordeaux wines. The first hallway of the museum is an in-depth look into the history of the Port of the Moon. The second hall explains how the wine was made, with the actual barrels and machines used to age the wine to perfection. After you walk through the museum, you'll enjoy tasting two wines as a museum guide gives you a comprehensive introduction to the specific wine regions of Bordeaux.

i Admission €10, €5 reduced, fee includes two wine tastings; limited wheelchair accessibility

CAPC MUSÉE D'ART CONTEMPORAIN DE BORDEAUX

7 rue Ferrère; 05 56 00 81 50; www.capc-bordeaux.fr; open Tu 11am-6pm, W 11am-8pm, Th-Su 11am-6pm

Contemporary art is weird. And the CAPC is no exception. This museum takes weird to the max, exhibiting videos of a naked man desperately trying to straighten his sheets, a female doll lying face down on the ground, and abstract rows of rocks. There's an interesting room on the upper level with seaweed-like strings hanging from the ceiling spelling out the words displaisir and plaisir, complemented by an eerie blue light spelling out fragments of caveat-like sentences. It's safe to say this is the stuff of nightmares and yes, after visiting, we had quite a few. When we visited, the ground floor displayed the work of Columbian artist **Beatriz González,** whose profound and sad exhibition with a lot to say about the political state of Colombia we appreciated very much.

i Admission €7, €4 reduced; wheelchair accessible

MUSÉE DES BEAUX ARTS

20 Cours d'Albret; 05 56 10 20 56; www.musba-bordeaux.fr; open M, W-Su 11am-6pm

Bordeaux's Musée des Beaux Arts is what you'd expect: rows of art with pictures of Jesus and Jesus' mom. The museum is separated into two wings: fifteenth to seventeenth century and eighteenth to twentieth century. While the first contains mostly the aforementioned variety of paintings, the second contains works by many Bordelaise artists. The museum boasts a fair amount of works by renowned artists, including masterpieces by **Matisse, Monet,** and **Renoir** in its high-ceilinged exhibits.

i Admission €4, €2 reduced; wheelchair accessible

OUTDOORS

DARWIN ECO-SYSTÈME

87 Quai des Queyries; 05 56 77 52 06; open M-F 8:30am-6pm

The Rive Droite of Bordeaux seems to always live in the shadow of its left-leaning sibling. But to ignore this side of the **Garonne** would be a huge mistake, especially when Darwin Eco-système dwells just across from the **Chartrons District.** Darwin, a repurposed military barrack, is part of

Bordeaux's rejuvenation as a modern city. Come here to enjoy drinks on the banks of the river, complemented with a filling meal surrounded by vintage décor. This is the hub of urban culture in Bordeaux, complete with co-working spaces, an art gallery, and a skate park called the Hangar (we swear it was inspired by Avril Lavigne's 2002 hit "Sk8ter Boi," but that's just our opinion. Who knew the French were into angsty teen pop?).

i Free, hangar €5; limited wheelchair accessibility

BASE SOUS-MARINE

Bd. Alfred Daney; 05 56 11 11 50; open T-Su 1:30pm-7pm

If World War II history is your thing, then you came to the right place. Venture to the outskirts of Bordeaux to a submarine base tucked away just steps from the **Cité du Vin** tram stop. Base Sous-Marine was one of five bases built on the Atlantic coast for fleets of German and Italian U-boats during the German occupation. The 42,000-meter structure, which was built between 1941 and 1943, looks like a huge hunk of rock from afar, but portions of it are open to the public. When we last visited, the submarine base was undergoing renovations and therefore closed to visitors, but will be open in 2019.

i Admission €5, €3 reduced, free first Su of the month when open to the public; tours €3 with ticket, tours on W 5pm-6pm, Sa 4pm-5pm; limited wheelchair accessibility

FOOD

L'AGNEAU À LA BRAISE ($$$)

13 Rue du Pas-Saint Georges; 05 56 52 24 89; www.lagneaualabraise.com; open M-Sa 7pm-11pm

Don't get us wrong: we're all for solo travel and solo eating. After all, taking yourself out for a meal is on every single one of those "Ten Steps to Your 'Eat, Pray, Love' Experience" Buzzfeed lists. But L'Agneau à la Braise probably isn't the place to do it. It is, however, the place to treat yourself to a nice dinner. Serving typical French fare, this restaurant in the **Saint Pierre** neighborhood of Bordeaux provides an intimate setting for you and your backpacker friends. We recommend trying their rib-eye steak or their leg of lamb, both cooked perfectly to make your dinner delicious and flavorful (and you'll get to watch the chefs cook your meat from the dining room). Pair your meat with wine straight from the famous Bordelaise chateaus you've been hearing about to round out a meal you'll reminisce about forever.

i Entrées from €20, wine from €10; vegetarian options available; wheelchair accessible

FUFU BORDEAUX ($$)

37 Rue Saint-Rémi; 5 56 52 10 29; www.restaurantfufu.com; open M-F 11:30am-3pm and 6:30pm-11pm

Locals and tourists alike have heard of FuFu, and the crowds lining up at its door are living proof that this small, Japanese noodle bar has a cult following. With a wide selection of everything from ramen to stir fry to dumplings, FuFu's specialty is delicious noodles with perfectly salted broth and eggs. Choose from a basic ramen with pork or spice it up with a miso flavor. If noodles aren't your cup of tea, go for a spicy, flavorful wok dish and watch the skilled chefs prepare them right before your eyes. FuFu has a second location not too far from the first, where you can stop by for your second noodle dish (trust us, you'll want it).

i Entrées from €9, side dishes from €4, sake from €4, soft drinks from €3; vegetarian options available; wheelchair accessible

CAFÉ NAPOLEON ($)

6 bis Cours du 30 Juillet; 05 56 81 52 26; open daily 7am-9pm

Located just steps away from the grand opera, Café Napoleon is the ideal place to stop for your morning or midday coffee. The seats of the café spill out onto the sidewalk where you can watch eager tourists stroll onto the bustling boutique-lined streets of the city center. The café's interior, however, is a grand, mint-green wallpapered space featuring life-sized mirrors with ornate frames—perhaps a testament to its namesake: Napoleon (although we're pretty sure the mirrors are much much taller than he was). Like all its counterparts, this café boasts a delicious, flavorful espresso (paired with a biscuit) for just €2, but you'll find yourself coughing up at least €5 for a cup of tea (along with some coughs thanks to the lady chain-smoking next to you).

Espresso from €2, other drinks from €3; vegetarian options available; wheelchair accessible

NOM D'UNE CRÊPE ($)

32 rue Saint Remi; 05 56 06 46 81; open daily noon-2:30pm and 7pm-10:30pm

Just a few blocks away from **Place de la Bourse** lies the perfect destination to satisfy your craving for a French crêpe. Nom d'Une Crêpe offers a series of deals on both savory and sweet crêpes, ranging from your classic *fraise* to *oeufs avec jambon*. That's strawberries and eggs with ham, respectively, for those of you who haven't picked up French yet. The interior of the restaurant resembles that of a wine cellar, which seems to be a common theme in Bordeaux. Order a cup of tea for a midday refresher and leave enough room in your stomach for at least two delectable crêpes: you won't want to miss out.

Menu classique €11.90, crêpes from €9, coffee and tea from €2

NIGHTLIFE

BAD MOTHER FUCKER ($)

16 Cours de l'Argonne; 09 86 50 94 68; open daily 5pm-2am

If you're looking to meet some strange characters that won't have their nose stuck in a glass of wine that smells "oaky," swing by this bar to say enchanté to some bad motherfuckers. We're not quite sure what word to use to encapsulate the atmosphere of this pub: Grungy? Alternative? Punk? Whatever it is, you're bound to enjoy a wild night consisting of Rolling Stones' hits, a wide selection of beers, billiards, and—if you're lucky—live music. So drop your wine glass and pick up a pint. Embrace the intensely red walls of this joint and grow a mullet: it's time to be a bad motherfucker (but even better to be one during happy hour from 5pm-8pm).

Beer and wine from €5, shots from €3; wheelchair accessible

THE STARFISH PUB ($)

24 Rue Sainte Colombe; 05 56 52 88 61; open M-F 4pm-2am, Sa 2pm-2am, Su 2pm-midnight

For the love of all that is good in the world, you can finally put away your wine connoisseur alter-ego and let loose at this popping underground club and warm red and yellow-walled bar. This hotspot is a big draw for young backpackers, Erasmus students, and locals from all walks of life. If you're lucky, you'll be able to belt out a classic French song on karaoke night or listen to local musicians during Starfish's jam sessions. Pro tip: come during happy hour (5:30pm-8:30pm) before the bar gets really crowded for sweet deals on all your favorite drinks (wine included).

Drinks from €3; wheelchair accessible

SYMBIOSE ($$)

4 Quai des Chartrons; 05 56 23 67 15; open M noon-2:30pm, Tu-F noon-2:30pm and 7pm-2pm, Sa 7pm-2am

At first blush, Symbiose looks like a hippie café joint that probably serves from the organic-only, grass-fed variety. Wrong. Located in the **Chartrons** district, Symbiose features a lovely fusion of tapas cuisine using meats such as chicken and duck in flavorful combinations only Ratatouille's Remy could have come up with. But the surprise about a Symbiose and its welcoming wood-paneled interior doesn't end there. Behind the grandfather clock at the back of the restaurant is a secret door, transforming this unassuming joint into a speakeasy right in the historical wine district.

Lunch entrées from €13, dinner entrées from €20, plates from €8, drinks from €5; reservations recommended; wheelchair accessible

CANNES

Coverage by **Jessica Moore**

Dig your best dress and finest button-down out of the bottom of your backpack and hope they aren't too wrinkled for wear—you've just made it to Cannes, the land of the elite. This household name is synonymous with affluence, extravagance, and class, and unlike the backpacker-friendly nearby cities of Nice and Marseille, Cannes caters almost exclusively to the most exclusive class out there. One walk down the yacht-filled port or the designer-filled La Croisette explains what we mean. The host of the annual Cannes Film Festival, this city is your number-one shot at running into your celebrity crush. Regardless of whether they're A or B-list celebrities, Cannes bursts at the seams with designer-wearing, small-dog totting Kim Kardashian look-alikes. But don't let its high style fool you, with the right planning and the tricks in our guide in tow, Cannes can become a backpacker's dream full of sandy beaches, fine dining, and happy wallets.

ORIENTATION

Just a 30-minute train ride away from Nice, the beautiful city of Cannes is a perfect day trip for those looking to get away without breaking the bank on accommodations. The city of Cannes lies right along the Mediterranean, and the closer to the shores you get, the more shops, restaurants, and nightclubs you're bound to find. The true center of the city lies in **Vieux Port,** or the Old Port. Here, you will find the **Palais des Festivals et des Congrès,** the center where the annual **Cannes Film Festival** takes place. To the east of this center you'll find another yacht-filled port as well as the famous nightclub district. Just west of the Vieux Port sits the **Old Town,** called **Le Suquet. Boulevard de la Croisette,** an upscale street lined with flashy stores from top-brand designers, connects the entirety of the city. As you go further inland, the **Rue d'Antibes** mirrors La Croisette in connecting the city east to west.

ESSENTIALS

GETTING THERE

The Côte d'Azur airport in Nice is the closest airport to Cannes, located about 20km away. Only private planes visit Cannes' own airport, the smaller Cannes-Mandelieu. From the Côte d'Azur airport, you can take a 20min. train ride into Cannes for €6. The city also receives TGV (high speed) and TER (regional) trains from all over the country at its two train stations. Cannes is the primary station in the city center, and Cannes la Bocca is situated in the more suburban part of the city.

GETTING AROUND

A compact but packed city, the best way to get around Cannes is on foot. Walking the entirety of the city from start to finish only takes about 40min., but if walking around in the summer heat isn't your thing, the city also has the Palm Bus service. The Palm Bus consists of five lines, all passing through the main Hôtel de Ville stop, right across from the Vieux Port. You can purchase tickets on the bus, at tabac shops, or at the tourist office on Boulevard de la Croisette. Buses run daily from 6am-9pm, and a singular night line takes over from 9pm-2am. Tickets range from €1.50 for a single ride to €12 for ten trips.

PRACTICAL INFORMATION

Tourist Offices: Cannes' main tourist office is located near the Palais des Festivals et des Congrès (1 Blvd de la Croisette; 04 92 99 82 22; www.cannes-destination.com; open daily Mar-Oct 9am-7pm, Nov-Feb 10am-7pm, July-Aug 9am-8pm).

Banks/ATMs/Currency Exchange: Banks, ATMs, and exchange centers are found all over the city, with most surrounding the Palais des Festivals et des Congrès (61 Boulevard de la Croisette; 04 93 94 22 14; open M-F

8:30am-12:30pm and 1:30pm-5:30pm and Sa 8:30am-12:30pm).

Post Offices: The main post office can be found at (22 Rue Bivouac Napoléon; 04 93 25 84 14; open M-F 9am-1pm, 2pm-6pm, Sa 9am-12:30pm).

Public Restrooms: Public restrooms line the beach area in Cannes (06400 Cannes; open daily 9:30am-8pm).

Internet: There is free Wi-Fi at the train station and the central tourist office.

BGLTQ+ Resources: Centre BGLTQ Côte d'Azur (123 Rue de Roquebillière; www.centrelgbt06.fr; 09 81 93 14 82; open M 9:30am-8pm, Tu 9:30am-5:30pm, W 9:30am-8pm, Th 9:30am-5:30pm, F 9:30am-8pm, and Sa 4pm-8pm).

EMERGENCY INFORMATION

Emergency Number: 112.

Police: Police Municipale (2 Quai Saint-Pierre; 08 00 1171 18; open daily 24hr).

US Embassy: The nearest US Embassy is located in Marseille:

- Marseille US Embassy (12 Bd. Paul Peytral; 04 91 55 09 47; fr.usembassy.gov/embassy-consulates/marseille; M-F 9am-noon and 2pm-5pm).

Rape Crisis Center: Find assistance at the follow Cannes location:

- Institut National d'Aide aux Victimes et de Médiation (14 Rue Ferrus; 01 45 88 19 00; open daily 9am-9pm).

Hospitals: The primary hospital is in the center of town:

- Hospital Centre Cannes (15 Avenue des Broussailles; 04 93 69 70 00; open daily 24hr).

Pharmacies: Pharmacies are denoted with a green cross. When the cross is lit, the stores are most likely open.

- Pharmacie Monge Cannes Riviera (36 Rue d'Antibes; 04 93 39 01 29; open daily 8:30am-8pm).

SIGHTS

CULTURE

BOULEVARD DE LA CROISETTE

Bd de la Croisette; open daily 24hr

What do Ariana Grande, Justin Timberlake, and Beyoncé all have in common? They've all definitely strolled down the Boulevard de la Croisette, shopping bags in tow. This designer-store-lined strip rose to fame in its role as the closest thing to a mall that celebrities ever experience, and is a home to top brand names like Dolce & Gabbana and Armani. La Croisette is perhaps one of the only places in the world where department stores staff their own bouncers, and where it feels like just window shopping should come at a price. The road to fame is lined with palm trees, chic restaurants, and only the best brand stores, making La Croisette your best chance at running into the rich and famous while in Cannes.

i Shop prices vary; street free; wheelchair accessible

MARCHE FORVILLE

6 Rue du Marché Forville; open Tu-Su 7:30am-1pm

Like a young starlet that rose to fame from humble beginnings, Cannes still remembers its humble roots as a fishing village. The Marche Forville pays homage to a bygone era in Cannes, one where fishermen and farmers sold local produce daily at open air markets just like this one, and people haggled over the price of blueberries. The market features wide lanes, and is split into areas based on the produce sold. Here, local cheesemakers churn out the wheels, wine sellers bring their best bottles, and genius chefs dish out ready-made foods like paella from one giant pot in the center of the mart.

i Market prices vary; cash only; wheelchair accessible

LANDMARKS

FORT ROYAL & MUSÉE DE LA MER

Ile Sainte Marguerite, 1 Place Bernard Cornut-Gentille; 04 93 43 18 17; open daily Oct-Mar 10:30am-1:15pm and 2:15-4:45pm, Apr-May 10:30am-1:15pm and 2:15pm-5:45pm, June-Sept 10am-5:45pm

The ferry ride to Fort Royal is perhaps the cheapest boat ride in all of Cannes, and Fort Royal itself offers some of the cheapest entertainment in the city as well. On the beautiful island of **Saint Marguerite,** take in panoramic views of the French coast and the mediteranean, or explore the many landmarks on the island. Take to the **Fort Royal** and experience the Spanish influence on Cannes, as Spain built the fort in 1635 during its control of the region. Afterwards, adventure to the **State Prison,** which held infamous criminals like the Man in the Iron Mask. From there, walk to the **Musée de la Mer,** which exhibits ruins uncovered in the Mediterranean Sea and dives into the island's history as a Roman trading port.

i Admission €6, students under 26 free; limited wheelchair accessibility; guided tours available upon advance request (call to organize)

PALAIS DES FESTIVALS ET DES CONGRÈS

1 bd. De la Croisette; 04 92 99 84 00; opening hours vary based on performances

The Cannes Film Festival. Oh, you've heard of it? In May, this glass-faced building glows with the flash of cameras and bright lights as movie projectors and red carpets transform the building for the annual film festival. Here, A-list artists present their newest works and receive criticism from the best names in the business. Designed by architect and visionary **Sir Hubert Bennet,** this venue hosts the **Cannes Lions International Festival of Creativity.** During the months between this event and the film festival, visitors can book tours of the site, but must do so in advance online or at the tourist office.

i Admission €6; wheelchair accessible; reservation recommended

MUSEUMS

CENTRE D'ART LA MALMAISON

47 Boulevard de la Croisette; 04 97 06 44 90; open daily Oct-Mar 10am-1pm, 2pm-6pm, Apr-Sept 11am-8pm

No, you weren't drugged upon entering the Centre d'Art La Malmaison, you've simply stepped into a psychedelic visual experience like no other. This modern museum prides itself on offering exhibits from solely twentieth and twenty-first-century artists, and likes to track down the most intense, boggling designers out there. Recently, they've shown works by the late **Niki de Saint Phalle** and even **Picasso.** Having no permanent collection, the museum shows solely rotating selections by prestigious artists from around the globe. But fear not, there's never a chance that you'll end up here with boring exhibits; the Centre d'Art La Malmaison always searches for the wackiest, most questionable works in the art world.

i Ticket price varies based on the current exposition; no wheelchair accessibility

GALERIE VIACELI

5 Rue du Pas de la Mule; 01 42 74 80 54; www.galerievieceli.com; open Tu-Sa 11am-1pm, 3pm-7pm

Ah, darling, it is now time to learn the important difference between a gallery and a museum. The lower class goes to museums to view and experience art, and we, the elite, go to galleries to purchase art. The Galerie Viaceli is much more of a gallery than it is a museum, and upon entering, the staff quickly size ups whether you're there to view the art or to buy it. But, have no fear, once this initial glance-over ends, you're free to view the incredible paintings and sculptures that line the walls of this modern art gallery. Because works are meant to fit nearly anyone's fancy, the place lacks a bit of cohesion, but that just means you're sure to find something you'll love.

i Free entry; limited wheelchair accessibility

OUTDOORS

PLAGE DU MIDI

Bd. Jean Hubert; open daily 9am-6pm

If the idea of seeing one more yacht makes your stomach churn, or you can't stand the thought of walking into another store where even breathing costs €20, then the Plage du Midi welcomes you. This lovely beach lies right across from the center of town, and features tan, sandy shores, a long dock, and countless stands serving up crêpes and icecream. A family beach, the place usually swells with sandcastles, dogs, and little kids learning to swim for the first time, giving the entire place a nostalgic feel. With buoys out in the water for you to sunbathe on after a long swim, and a dock to jump off of, Plague du Midi offers endless options for fun and relaxation.

i Free; limited wheelchair access

FOOD

LE TROQUET A SOUPES ($$)

64 Rue Meynadier; 09 83 71 92 92; open Tu-Sa 11:30am-8:30pm

In this world, few things are incredibly simple and yet so wonderful; soup is one of them. One amazing, well-traveled woman named Sylvia, owns and almost entirely runs this small restaurant. Enter her shop and hear about how her travels to Peru influenced her *ceviche*—or how her days in Mexico taught her the best way to stew up *chili con carne*. Whatever dish you try here, you're sure to walk away with a happy belly and a pretty happy wallet. If that's not enough, you may even walk away with a friend in Sylvia herself, who is more than enough of a reason to visit the shop.

i Plate of the day from €13, soups and salads from €7; vegetarian options available; limited wheelchair access

L'EPICURIEUX ($$$)

6 Rue des Frères Casanova; 06 64 50 11 82; open M-Th noon-3pm, 6:30pm-10pm, Fr-Sa noon-3pm, 6:30pm-10:30pm

In Cannes, it seems that fine dining comes at a price tag that starts at expensive and goes up from there. Thankfully, that is not the case at L'Epicurieux. This small restaurant in the heart of Cannes serves up incredible dishes, from homemade pasta with truffle sauce to French classics like *foie gras*. With chic interior design and a wine list longer than the actual menu, this place oozes with a sophisticated, high-class dining feel. But, a true friend of the saying 'champagne taste, beer budget,' you can safely walk away here with a meal for less than €20, unless, of course, you decide to splurge on a dessert, which we highly recommend.

i Dinner from €15; vegetarian and vegan options available; limited wheelchair access

PHILCAT ($)

Prom. de la Pantiero; 04 93 38 43 42; open daily 9am-7:30pm

Philcat is about as confusing as its name. To start, the place scored prime property right along the coast and across from the center of town but manages to stay incredibly affordable. Second, cats are nowhere to be found here, nor a single man named Phil. Regardless, the place holds steady to its values of offering low-cost food in a prime Cannes location. Happily sit back in one of their chairs by the sea and chow down on a filling sandwich, sip a beer, and leave for less than the price of entering a single store on **La Croisette**. This blue-and-white restaurant cooks up a backpacker's dream on the Mediterranean, all with a friendly smile and incredible views.

i Sandwiches from €5; card minimum €15; vegetarian options available; wheelchair accessible

NIGHTLIFE

QUAY'S IRISH PUB

17 Quai Saint-Pierre; 04 93 39 27 84; open daily noon-2am

Quay's Irish Pub is something of a shock upon entering. With its fully wooden floors and ceilings, to its American-dollar-bill-lined walls, to the cacophony of English being spoken inside, you may feel like you stepped away from France entirely and into a British sports bar. At this bar, they serve up well-priced drinks that make it a perfect stop before heading onto the exuberantly-priced nightclubs in Cannes. If you're lucky, you may even visit on a night where they pull out the karaoke machine and spend your evening singing along to "Don't Stop Believing" and "Piano Man."

i Beer from €4, shots from €5; minimum card charge €8; happy hour 5pm-8pm; wheelchair accessible

GOTHA CLUB

Place Franklin Roosevelt; 04 28 70 20 20; www.gotha-club.com; open daily midnight-7am

The Sperry and salmon-colored-shirt-wearing Hamptons crowd recognizes Gotha Club as one of the best nightclubs in the world. They might not be mistaken, since Gotha Club feels like no other experience. We recommend showing up before 12:30pm. Arrive any later and the bouncers will scrutinize every rag on your body, letting only the finest clad and most sober enter. Once inside though, experience the high life, as VIP lounges line the dance floor and drinks start at €15. Drinking here puts you back a pretty penny, so we recommend imbibing a bit before you get to Gotha Club if you plan on being tipsy. Don't go too hard though, or you risk being coaxed into splitting a €600 bottle of champagne with the son of a French billionaire.

i Cover €15; beer from €16, alcohol from €18; dressy attire required; limited wheelchair accessibility

LYON

Coverage by **Kristine Guillaume**

It's all too easy to overlook Lyon as a random city smack in between Paris and the French Riviera. Skipping over it may seem, at first blush, like a small sacrifice for the beaches of Nice or the mélange of culture in Marseille. But to do so would be a grave mistake. Lyon, the gastronomic capital of France, has much to offer in the form of delectable *bouchons,* hearty meat-centric dishes paired with all your French favorites: bread, cheese, and wine. Here, you can spend each night trying a different edible part of a pig or cow after a day of climbing Roman ruins, admiring masterpieces in the city's many museums, or roaming the cobblestone streets of Vieux Lyon—a UNESCO World Heritage Site in itself. Gear up for *bouchon* after *bouchon,* and get ready to immerse yourself in the vibrant culture of Lyon—influenced by its importance in the Roman Empire, its deep ties to Catholicism, and its status as an epicenter of intellectual development throughout the years.

ORIENTATION

Lyon is a city in the southeastern part of France, located just two hours south of Paris. The city itself contains two rivers: the **Rhône** and the **Saône.** The two rivers converge at the southern tip of the city, creating the famous peninsula **Presqu'île.** In the northern part of Presqu'île are many famous landmarks including **Hôtel de Ville** and **Place Bellecour.** In addition to the rivers, the city of Lyon is bounded by two hills: **Fourvière,** the site of **Vieux Lyon** (Old Town) and **La Basilique de Notre Dame,** and **Croix-Rousse,** the part of town where the silk workers resided during Lyon's economic prime. There are nine arrondissements in the city; the first and second arrondissements, the site of **Place des Terreaux** and **Place Bellecour,** contains the most attractions. **Vieux Lyon** makes up the fifth arrondissement while **Parc de la Tête D'Or,** on the eastern side of the Rhône, makes up the sixth. The **Part-Dieu** train station is located in the third arrondissement, along with **Les Halles de Lyon—Paul Bocuse.**

ESSENTIALS

GETTING THERE

If flying, Lyon St-Exupéry airport is the closest to the city center. From the airport, there is a 30min. express tram called Rhône express to Lyon Part-Dieu train station (€15, students €13). The tram runs daily from 4:25pm to midnight every 15-30min. We recommend purchasing your ticket ahead of time (www.rhoneexpress.fr), but there are ticket machines for purchase upon arrival at the airport. If traveling by train, there are two main train stations: Part-Dieu, located in the third arrondissement, and Perrache, located on the southern tip of Presqu'île. Both stations are located about 20min. away via metro from the city center. The cheapest way to get into Lyon is via bus. Most arrive in Part-Dieu station.

GETTING AROUND

The best way to get around Lyon is to walk. If you'd like to bike, you can rent one with Velo'v service. The first 30min. of each ride are free and every additional 30min. costs €1 for a maximum of 24hr. A day-long ticket is €1.50 (which makes 10 times more sense). For the city's public transit (metro, bus, and tram), 1hr tickets are €1.80. There is also a ticket called Soirée that allows for unlimited travel from 7pm until the end of that day's service for just €3. The metro runs from 4am-12:30am and the buses from 5am-midnight. To get up to Fourvière and the Musée Gallo-Romain, there is a funicular at the Vieux Lyon Metro Station (round-trip €2.80).

PRACTICAL INFORMATION

Tourist Offices: Office du Tourisme et des Congrès du Grand Lyon (Pl. Bellecour; 04 72 77 69 69; open daily 9am-6pm).

Banks/ATMs/Currency Exchange: BNP Paribas (5 Rue de la République; 08 20 82 00 01; bank open Tu-Sa 8:30am-12:30pm and 1:45pm-6pm; ATMs open daily 24hr).

Post Offices: The main post office is located by Place Bellecour (10 Pl. Antonin Poncet; 08 99 23 24 62; open M-F 9am-7pm, Sa 9am-noon).

Public Restrooms: Most of Lyon's tourist offices have public toilets.

Internet: You can rent out a pocket Wi-Fi from the Tourist Information Office for €4 with Lyon City Card (regular price €8).

BGLTQ+ Resources: Ligne Azur is an organization that provides information and support to BGLTQ+ individuals (08 10 20 30 40; daily 8am-11pm).

EMERGENCY INFORMATION

Emergency Number: 112.

Police: Commissariat de police, second arrondissement (47 R. de la Charité; 04 78 42 26 56; open daily 24hr).

US Embassy: US Consulate of Lyon (1 Quai Jules Courmont; 01 43 12 48 60; open M-F 9:30am-5:30pm).

Rape Crisis Center: National Federation Women Solidarity (3919), not an emergency number. In case of emergency, call the police.

Hospitals:

- Hôpital Edouard Herriot (5 Pl. d'Arsonval; 08 25 08 25 69; open daily 24hr).

Pharmacies: Look for the green cross to find a pharmacy. There are plenty throughout the city.

- Great Pharmacie Lyonnaise (22 R. de la République; 04 72 56 44 00; open M-Sa 8am-11pm, Su 7pm-11pm).

SIGHTS

CULTURE

LES HALLES DE PAUL BOCUSE

102 Cours la Fayette; 04 78 60 32 82; www.halles-de-lyon-paulbocuse.com; open Tu-Sa 7am-10:30pm, most restaurants close around 6-7pm

Here lies the answer to all your food cravings. The holy grail of all things food, wine, and spirits, Les Halles de Paul Bocuse has everything you could imagine: *boulangers, fromagers, charcutiers, pâtissiers,* and so on. Walk through stall after stall of delicious and delectable aromas and pick up some of your favorite French staples. Although there are several restaurants for you to choose from, they might be a little out of your backpacker budget. Instead, stop by in the mid-afternoon and pick up a personalized assortment of fine wines, mouthwatering cheeses, and flavorful sausages to go.

i Stall prices vary; wheelchair accessible

OPÉRA NATIONAL DE LYON

Pl. de la Comédie ; 04 69 85 54 54; www.opera-lyon.com; ticket office open Tu-Sa noon-7pm; opera runs Sept-July

Situated right behind the grand **Hôtel de Ville** is the (arguably) grander Opéra National de Lyon, a massive glass-topped building. Throughout the year, the opera hosts dance performances, concerts, plays, special events, and, oh yeah, operas. Tickets don't come cheap

for a place as fancy as this, but, if you're lucky, you can snag one for €5 right before the show. Even if you're not seeing a performance, though, you can sit on the steps and listen to musicians perform or watch young teenagers practice dance performances on the opera's steps.

Tickets from €16, €5 tickets on sale 1hr before a show (if available); minimum age 5 years old; wheelchair accessible

VIEUX LYON

69005 Lyon 5ème; 04 72 10 30 30; hours vary by store

Yeah, you're not in Paris, but that doesn't mean you can't have your perfect Les Mis moment. On the **Fourvière** side of the **Saône** lies **Vieux Lyon,** the Old Town. Walk through its cobblestone streets, which strongly resemble the set of *Les Miserables,* or, perhaps more accurately, eighteenth-century France. There's even a little dip in the middle of the sidewalk that looks like a "drainage system" for sewage thrown out the window. It's kind of gross when you think about it…or even if you don't. Flat walking shoes are highly recommended for your stroll through the winding streets lined with *bouches authentiques* and local boutiques. In the center of Vieux Lyon is the metro station, which gives you full access to funiculars going up **Fourvière.**

Free; last funicular back to Vieux Lyon from Fourvière 10pm; no wheelchair accessibility

LANDMARKS

LA BASILIQUE NOTRE-DAME DE FOURVIÈRE

8 Pl. de Fourvière; 04 78 25 86 19; www.fourviere.org; basilica open daily 8am-6pm, Mass daily 7:30am, 9:30am, 11am, 5pm, museum daily 10am-12:30pm and 2pm-5:30pm

This nineteenth-century church stands tall atop **Fourvière Hill.** Decked out in gold and ornate patterns in greens, pinks, and teal blues, the basilica's magnificence commands respect. Check out the detailed paintings of scenes from the Bible, but don't stop there: head down to the **crypt,** a space just as ornately decorated as the basilica itself. Once you've finished, walk to the back of the building, where you'll find a perch from which you can view the entire city of Lyon and the **Saône River.** Apart from the views, the basilica bears historical significance, as it is dedicated to the Virgin Mary, who is said to have protected Lyon during the Franco-Prussian wars.

Free; wheelchair accessible

CATHÉDRALE SAINT JEAN DE BAPTISTE

Place St Jean; 06 60 83 53 97; www.cathedrale-lyon.cef.fr; open M-F 8:15am-7:45pm, Sa 8:15am-7pm, Su 8am-7pm

In the middle of **Vieux Lyon** stands the Cathédrale Saint Jean de Baptiste, the seat of the archdiocese in Lyon, considered by some to be the seat of the French church, making it a pretty big deal. The cathedral is a beautiful sandstone color with distinctive red doors, high ceilings, and intricately decorated stained-glass windows. Inside the left nave of the church, check out the *horloge astronomique,* a clock that mirrors the movement of the stars. The **treasury** of the church holds artifacts from the Byzantine Empire for your crash course in Lyonnais history. Behind the church is **Palais St. Jean,** which has a library just in case you're looking for more books about Lyon's ties to Catholicism.

Free; wheelchair accessible

PASSAGE THIAFFAIT

Between Rue René Leynaud and Rue Burdeau; store hours vary

Passage Thiaffait used to be a crime-infested alley, but, today, you need not fear anything so much as a stray cat. Named after **Monsieur Thiaffait,** the alley, which connects Rue René Leynaud and Rue Burdeau via two white staircases, is lined with chic boutiques, cafés, and artist workshops. Peruse the shops' offerings on your way to lunch in the **Croix-Rousse** district, but don't budget more than 20-30 minutes for this significant, yet small sight. The surrounding pastel-colored buildings do make for a good Instagram post, though.

Free; no wheelchair accessibility

PLACE BELLECOUR

Place Bellecour; 04 72 77 69 69; open daily 24hr

Place Bellecour holds the title of the largest square in Lyon and the largest pedestrian square in all of Europe. Today, it doesn't seem like much, except for an expanse of Mars-red pavement, a statue of Louis XIV in the middle, a tourist office, and a Ferris wheel for kids and adults who haven't quite grown up. Back in the day, however, the square itself held much more significance: it was the sight of royal parades for the king and executions via the guillotine during the French Revolution. Although the square isn't too spectacular in the daytime, give it another try in the evening when the Ferris wheel lights up in a display of vibrant colors.

i Free; wheelchair accessible

MUSEUMS

MUSÉE DES BEAUX ARTS

20 Pl. des Terreaux; 04 72 10 17 40; www.mba-lyon.fr; open M, W-Th 10am-6pm, F 10:30am-6pm, Sa-Su 10am-6pm

At last, the chance to hang with our artistically inclined pals: **Monet, Picasso,** and **Gauguin.** It feels like centuries since we've last gotten together! Probably because their art is from hundreds of years ago. Man, walking through all these carefully curated wings with art from Impressionists, Modernists, and Renaissance Art really takes us back to Monet's fascination with landscapes, that time Pablo discovered Cubism, and Paul's trip to Tahiti that he won't stop painting about! When we're finished with our *rendez-vous,* we're going to the extensive sculpture hall featuring works by **Rodin,** as well as the antiquities wing with **Ancient Egyptian, Greco-Roman, Muslim,** and **Ottoman relics.** The museum also puts on outstanding temporary exhibits, such as the one featuring Mexican artists like **Frida Kahlo** and **Diego Rivera.**

i Permanent collection admission €8, €4 reduced; temporary exhibition admission €12, €7 reduced; last entry 5:30pm; audio guide €1 in French, English, Italian, free downloadable app; wheelchair accessible

LUGDUNUM: MUSÉES GALLO-ROMAIN DE FOURVIÈRE

17 Rue Cleberg; 04 72 38 49 30; www.museegalloromain.grandlyon.com; museum open Tu-F 11am-6pm, Sa-Su 10am-6pm; archaeological site open daily Apr 15-Sept 15 7am-9pm, daily Sept 16-Apr 14 7am-7pm

If we had to name one thing Lyon is proud of, it would have to be its importance during its time as **Lugdunum,** a city of the Roman Empire founded in 43 BCE. Now, we agree, it's kind of weird to look back fondly on practically being colonized and ruled by an outside power (Stockholm Syndrome, anyone?), but Lugdunum was a powerhouse that laid the groundwork for the city Lyon became. The museum, which details everything about the ancient city—from its religious practices to palace structures to stunning mosaics—is expansive, spanning four descending floors. As cool as all this is, walking between artifact after artifact can get a little dusty and dry. Thankfully, you can actually climb the steps of the Gallo-Roman theatre outside. Just don't fall—it's steep!

i Permanent collection admission €4, €2.50 reduced, free under 18; temporary exhibitions admission €7, €4.50 reduced; last entry 5:30pm; wheelchair accessible

OUTDOORS

PARC DES HAUTEURS

Montée Nicolas de Lange; 04 72 69 47 60; open daily 24hr

Directly meaning "park of heights," the Parc des Hauteurs is more a hiking trail than anything else. The park, or trail, rather, connects the top of **Fourvière Hill** to the **cemetery of Loyasse.** There's a gold rose petal path that you can follow towards the **La Basilique Notre-Dame de Fourvière** or explore the rosary garden within the park. We recommend packing a lunch before coming up so that you can enjoy the views of Lyon's orange-tiled rooftops and the **Sâone River.**

i Free; last tram to Fourvière at 10pm; no wheelchair accessibility

PARC DE LA TÊTE D'OR

69006 Lyon; 04 72 69 47 60; www.loisirs-parcdelatetedor.com; mid-Apr-mid-Oct 6:30am-10:30pm, mid-Oct-mid-Apr 6:30am-8:30pm

On the east side of the **Rhône** lies a massive green space in the middle of Lyon's urban landscape: Parc de la Tête D'Or. Comparable to New York City's Central Park (although perhaps not as grand or expansive), the 117-hectare plot has everything you could want in a day outdoors: a lake filled with geese, a rose garden, and a zoo. For those of us that prefer the wonders of the great outdoors, the northern side of the park houses the **Musée d'Art Contemporain.** But, honestly, why wouldn't you appreciate a leisurely stroll in the greenery for a respite from the chaos of the otherwise bustling city?

Free; wheelchair accessible

FOOD

ATHINA ($)

3 Rue Romarin; 04 78 72 86 61; open Tu-Su noon-2pm and 7pm-10pm

There's a certain charm about small places, and Athina definitely has it. With only about six or seven tables, Athina boasts fast service and not-to-miss deals on Greek staples, including flavorful pork and chicken pitas with a side of scrumptious fries. Pair your meal with Greek beer and sit back as you enjoy your meal in the airy space, complete with inviting teal walls that make you feel like you're by the Mediterranean.

Entrées from €6; cash only; vegetarian options available; wheelchair accessible

L'AUBERGE DES CANUTS ($$)

8B Pl. Saint Jean; 09 86 50 89 66; www.auberge-des-canuts.com; open daily 8am-midnight

If you're looking for a taste of *bouchons Lyonnais* on a budget, you've hit the spot. Located just steps away from the **Cathédrale Saint-Jean de Baptiste** with walls reminiscent of the cobblestone streets of **Vieux Lyon,** L'Auberge des Canuts serves traditional dishes such as pork sausages in a red wine sauce on its convienent *prix-fixe* menu (€15.90). The staff only begins to prepare your next course once you've finished the one in front of you, so take your time. They're in no rush and you shouldn't be either. When you finally make it to dessert after savoring pork sausages in red wine sauce, and your server asks you if you want your *fromage blanc* with fruit sauce, say *oui* without hesitation. It's truly a treat.

Entrées from €14, prix-fixe menu from €16; card minimum €20; vegetarian options available; wheelchair accessible

CAFÉ 203 ($$)

9 Rue de Garet; 04 78 28 65 66; www.moncafé203.com; open noon-1am daily

If you're looking for a place for the perfect *rendez-vous,* look no further than Café 203. This bustling restaurant, although not an official *bouchon,* serves up traditional Lyonnaise dishes and then some. If you've had one too many sausages on your trip thus far, don't shy away from ordering one of Café 203's burgers or risottos for a good dose of familiarity. While you munch on your meal, in either the non-smoking or smoking area of the restaurant, look around at the tavern-like décor and listen to the friendly conversations of the locals and fellow tourists dining around you.

Entrées from €13, burgers from €12, beer and wine from €2.50; vegetarian options available; wheelchair accessible

A CHACUN SA TASSE ($)

2 Rue du Griffon; open M-Sa 8am-7pm

For a quick bite or *petit déjeuner*, swing by this tea shop, located a few blocks away from **Place des Terreaux.** Decorated in a warm orange with framed paintings hung on the walls, this café offers a wide array of teas, including green teas, black teas, and rooibos. The teas are steeped to perfection before being served. While you wait for your flavorful brew, pick up a French magazine on the café's bookshelves to brush up on your language skills or look smart as you attempt to read a piece on the EU's economic policy. For just €5.50, we were able to get a pot of delectable rose black tea and a plain croissant to start our day off on the right note.

i Pots of tea from €3.50, pastries from €2; vegetarian options available; wheelchair accessible

DIPLOID ($)

18 Rue de la Platière; 04 69 67 58 93; open M-F 9am-7pm, Sa 10am-7pm, Su 11am-7pm

An open space just a few blocks away from **Place des Terreaux,** Diploid is the perfect place to catch your breath with a cup of perfectly roasted coffee or freshly brewed tea. Diploid boasts a bright and welcoming atmosphere complete with calming teal blue walls, lights hanging from the ceiling, and wooden floors. Take your cappuccino with the locals as they work on their laptops using the café's free Wi-Fi, or converse with friends as upbeat English indie tunes play in the background. Diploid also offers a lunch menu that changes every now and then. Choose from a sandwich, entrée, or salad of the day and take a seat in the back room to enjoy your meal.

i Lunch from €10.50, coffee and tea from €3; vegetarian options available; wheelchair accessible

NIGHTLIFE

THE MONKEY CLUB

19 Pl. Tolozan; 04 78 27 99 29; www.themonkeyclub.fr; open M noon-2pm, Tu-W noon-2pm and 6:30pm-1am, Th-F noon-2pm and 6:30pm-3am, Sa 6:30pm-3am, Su 11am-4pm

This is the kind of place Don Draper would go for after-work drinks on a particularly stressful day. Or perhaps any day he can find an excuse for a drink, which means every day. Straight out of the set of *Mad Men,* The Monkey Club features a deep red interior with armchairs and dim lighting to set the mood for recovering from a long day of work. The bar is mostly frequented by locals, who order quality wines or shots that the bar aptly names prescriptions. Sadly, the drinks are relatively pricey, so save this venue for a planned splurge on the town or if you somehow find yourself a job to wine—we mean whine—about.

i Cocktails from €11, shots from €5, beers from €5; BGLTQ+ friendly; wheelchair accessible

BOMP!

1 Pl. Croix-Paquet; 09 73 18 78 43; open M-W 10am-1am, Th-F 10am-3am, Sa 4pm-3am

Café by day, restaurant in the afternoon, and bar by night, you could probably spend the whole day at Bomp! and never leave. Like most French shops and restaurants, the kitchen does close in the middle of the day though, so that's probably not the best idea. Bomp! has a space for every occasion: tables that spill onto the narrow sidewalk, an open, well-lit café area with round tables to chill with old friends and new, and an upstairs bar area complete with foosball tables. With happy hour deals selling drinks for just three or four euros, swing by for a lively night to meet locals (who are probably smoking outside) late into the night.

i Entrées from €10, beer and wine from €3, mixed drinks from €5; limited wheelchair accessibility

GROOM

6 Rue Roger Violi; www.groomlyon.com; open Tu-W 7:30pm-1am, Th 7:30pm-2am, F-Sa 7:30pm-4am

Tucked away under **Away Hostel and Coffee Shop** lies the new, hip kid on the block: Groom. With a dark interior and bright, popping lights—mostly the pink and white variety—Groom boasts a menu full of out-of-the-box cocktails intended to spice up your night. The cocktails, which start at around €12, are pricey, so if you're looking for something more budget-friendly, choose from their selection of beer and wine. Groom also has mocktails for those who want to stay sober, making it a perfect place for all kinds of party animals. And to ensure you party safe, there are empanadas on the menu to make sure those cocktails don't go down alone. Check out their online schedule of events before selecting a night to go—the club frequently hosts lively concerts, often with no cover.

i Beer and wine from €5, cocktails from €12, empanadas from €4; vegetarian options available; wheelchair accessible

MARSEILLE

Coverage by **Jessica Moore**

If Marseille was in your high school yearbook, it would have as prime real estate on the front pages the quarterback. Now, don't get us wrong, Marseille still ranks second to Paris when it comes to size and annual visitors, so it's more like the quarterback on the junior varsity team. However, Marseille has a few things Paris doesn't. For one, this mass of shops, cafés, and late-night clubs sits right on the Côte d'Azur, giving travelers the prime waterfront property that Paris only offers along the Seine. Plus, its nearby cliff- and beach-filled parks at the Calanques, mountainside views, and busy shopping center all work to make Marseille a perfect city for all types of travelers. With a history that dates all the way back to the Greeks, Marseille teems with charm and culture. In fact, in 2013, it was named the European Capital of Culture, and today the city brims with high-tech museums that put Marseille's culture proudly on display for all to see.

ORIENTATION

Marseille takes the concept of winding French roads to heart. Here, you won't find much of a direct layout, but landmarks help orient you to the city. The center of town is just east of the **Old Port**, which lies to the west of the city center at the inlet to the **Côte d'Azur**. **Cours Saint-Louis** marks the center of the city, and splits the city along its shores with the **Quai du Port** to the north and the **Quai de Rive Neuve** to the south along the port. North along the Quai du Port you'll find the **MuCEM,** the **Cathédrale La Major,** leading all the way up to the northern edge of the city at **L'Estaque.** To the south along the Quai de Rie Neuve you can find the highest point of the city at **Notre-Dame de la Garde.** Along this path you will also come across the **Palais du Pharo,** and the **Corniche J.F. Kennedy.** This leads to the southern edge of the city at **Les Plages,** and even further out of Marseille to the **Calanques.**

ESSENTIALS

GETTING THERE

One of the easiest ways to access Marseille is by train. The SNCF train station in Marseille is the Gare de Marseille St. Charles, located on the eastern side of the city. Local and regional trains offer access to Marseille from all over the country. Alternatively, you could fly into Marseille Provence Airport, which sits northwest of the city and receives flights from all over Europe. The Navette Marseille Aeroport Bus connects to the Gare de Marseille St. Charles for €13.40, it leaves every 15 minutes and takes about 25 minutes to reach the city center.

GETTING AROUND

Marseille expands across the French coast line. Although getting around by foot is pretty easy once in the Old Port, it may be helpful to use the local metro and bus system to go longer distances. Marseille services two underground subway lines, the blue M1, and the red M2. The blue line runs roughly east to west, and the M2 runs north to south. Both intersect at the Gare de Marseille St. Charles, and at the stop Castellane. The buses run until 1am daily. La Régie des transports de Marseille (RTM), connects almost all of the city and even provides rides to neighboring towns. Tickets can be bought on board for €2.

PRACTICAL INFORMATION

Tourist Offices: Office de Tourisme (11La Canebière; 08 26 50 05 00; www.marseille-tourisme.com; open M-Su 9am-6pm).

Banks/ATMs/Currency Exchange: Find banks and ATMs on nearly every street corner in Marseille. Here is one at Société Générale (15 La Canebière; 04 91 13 57 00; open M-F 8:30am-noon and 1:30pm-5:30pm, Sa 8:15am-12:45pm).

Post Offices: The primary post office in Marseille is La Poste (50 Rue de Rome; open M-Tu 8:30am-6pm, W 9am-6pm, Th-F 8:30am-6pm, and Sa 8:30am-12:30pm).

Internet: The tourist office features free Wi-Fi, as do other cafés and restaurants throughout the city.

BGLTQ+ Resources: www.gayprovence.org has tips on accomodations, restaurants, events, and nightlife in the region.

EMERGENCY INFORMATION

Emergency Number: 112.

Police: The local police phone number for emergencies is 17. Police station (2 Rue Antoine Becker; 4 91 39 80 00).

US Embassy: The closest US Embassy is in the Old Port of Marseille at (12 Bd. Paul Peytral; 04 91 55 09 47; M-F 9am-noon and 2pm-5pm).

Rape Crisis Center: Although there is no dedicated Rape Crisis Center in Marseille, the Rape Crisis Network Europe is available to all travelers (www.inavem.org; 01 45 88 19 00).

Hospitals: In the center of town you'll find the European Hospital Marseille (6 Rue Désirée Clary; 04 13 42 70 00; open daily 24hr).

- Hospital Timone is a bit further away from the city center (278 Rue Saint-Pierre; 04 91 38 00 00; open daily 24hr).

Pharmacies: The most central pharmacy in Marseille Pharmacie de la République, pharmacies line many of the streets in the city, and are demarcated by green crosses.

- Pharmacie de la République is at (7 Rue de la République; 04 91 90 32 27; open M-F 9am-7:30pm Sa 9:30am -7pm, Su 8am-8pm).
- Pharmacie des Cardinales (29 Rue César Aleman; 04 91 52 71 50; www.pharmaciedescardinales.fr; M-F 8:30am-7:30pm, Sa 9am-7pm).

SIGHTS

CULTURE

CATHÉDRALE LA MAJOR

Place de la Major; 04 91 90 52 87; opens daily 10am, Apr 1-Sept 30 closes 6:30pm, Oct 1-Mar 31 closes 5:30pm

The Cathédrale La Major makes no mistake in calling itself La Major. This place is *huge*. Now a national monument and home to the Archdiocese of Marseille, La Major and the nearby **Notre Dame Basilica** have been in a heated battle since the church first opened in 1893 over which Catholic establishment looks the most Gothic of all the Gothic churches in the city. La Major currently holds the winning title; just a few moments inside will tell you why. Gregorian chants echo through the halls of this cathedral, and long, marble-clad floors and ceilings spread out along expansive, narrow corridors. As an added, the ceilings and domes boast incredible art with whimsical geometric patterns that will have you staring up enough to cramp your neck muscles.

i Free; no wheelchair accessibility

LE COURS JULIEN

Cours Julien; open daily 24hr

Ayy mahn, don't worry, be happy! This is the mantra of Le Cours Julien, a street famous for the vibrant art that brings life into the square and restaurants surrounding it. Here, musicians sit outside throughout the day, spewing reggae hits and jamming in the afternoon sun. Vendors sell food from little tables in an almost family-style way, and at night, twinkling lights are turned on over the square's central pond. The art that lines these streets follows the first rule of graffiti: if you can't paint something better over it, don't paint anything at all. After decades of following this rule of thumb, it's clear to see why Cours Julien is such an impressive sight, holding the best of the best of Marseille's street art for decades.

i Free; limited wheelchair accessibility

LANDMARKS

CHATEAU D'IF

Embarcadère Frioul If, 1 Quai de la Fraternité; 06 03 06 25 26; www.chateau-if.fr; open daily 9:30am-6pm

The stuff of legends, the Chateau d'If is the prison that everyone's favorite protagonist, Edmond Dantés, was incarcerated in in Alexandre Dumas' *The Count of Monte Cristo.* This infamous fortress, and later, well-known prison, looms on a nearby island. As far as fortresses go, it does what every good island fortress does: protects the city from invasion, stands as an ominous warning to potential invaders, and runs an all-too expensive ferry ride for tourists. The steep price pales in comparison to the journey itself and the chance to explore this notorious and historic fort, all with a captivating ocean backdrop surround you.

i Reduced student price €5 to enter island; round trip ferry ride from Vieux Port €10.80; last entry 30 minutes before close; ferry tickets must be bought online one day in advance or at the dock the day of; remember to hold onto the ticket for the entirety of the journey

MAIRIE DE MARSEILLE (CITY HALL)

2 Place de la Major; 04 91 14 57 80; open M-F 8:30am-11:45am and 12:45pm-4:30pm, and Sa 9am-noon

Most city halls conjure images of courtrooms and jurors, boring big-wigs, and rooms with a claustrophobic shortage of windows. But the Mairie de Marseille is no ordinary city hall. Here, explore an archaic-looking building standing tall amongst the other, more modern buildings and storefronts in the Old Port. Mairie de Marseille's impressive stature hints at its long, French history, and just taking in its outdoor steps and patio make it well worth the visit. This building sits right on the waterfront across from the **Old Port**, meaning that visiting theater buffs experience serious *Les Miserables* flashbacks as they look at it's haunting stance over the Old Port. This extravagant town hall is now considered a historic monument, and hides a surprising secret. Its front doors are somewhat of a scam: you have to enter one building from a set of back doors, then cross a bridge connecting the two buildings if you want to see anything higher than the ground floor.

i Free; last entry 30 minutes before close; wheelchair accessible

VIEUX-PORT (OLD PORT)

Quai du Port; open daily 24hr

The Vieux-Port, or Old Port of Marseille, has undergone quite the makeover in the past few years. Disguising its true age better than Dolly Parton, this place buzzes with activity. At night, this vibrant part of town comes to life as people sit by the water or under terraces sipping wine and taking in the views. By day, places to eat and shop line the port, and the port itself offers access to boat rides, ferries to nearby islands, and kayak and canoe rentals. A modern site with an old name, the Old Port overflows with historic landmarks, but also features new and exciting installments like their endless-sky mirror pavilion, where a reflective roof above you offers the perfect spot for a mirror selfie.

i Free; wheelchair accessible

MUSEUMS

MUSÉE DES CIVILISATIONS DE L'EUROPE ET DE LA MÉDITERRANÉE (MUCEM)

1 Espl. J4; www.musem.org; 04 84 35 13 13; open W-M 11am-7pm

The Musée des Civilisations de l'Europe et de la Méditerranée has a name that's almost as big as its collections. Locals refer to it as the MuCEM, and even Google Maps refuses to acknowledge its long winded title. This massive museum could take an entire day to fully explore. But don't worry about getting bored: the modern exhibits offer interactive and engaging looks at the past and the museum itself sits on a beautiful monument. Built into a fortress right along Marseille's coastline, the MuCEM offers stunning views and an incredible landscape to explore without even buying a ticket. Chill in one of the seaside cafés, listen to the live music playing, or take a nap (yes, you really can) in one of the lounge chairs overlooking the ocean.

i Full price €9.50, €5 reduced; tours available to book in advance online; wheelchair accessible

OUTDOORS

PLAGE DES CATALANS

Plage des Catalans; open daily 24hr

Much like your best friend's relationship with their ex, things at this beach are rocky! Though its sandy shores may deceive you, we recommend packing some water shoes for this stop. The beach can become incredibly crowded in the summer months, and features bright, multi-colored towels, happy dogs, and vendors selling everything from ice cold beers to steaming crêpes. Pack up your sunscreen, because there aren't any trees to hide from the sun under at this beach, and it seems some locals like to take advantage of that. Don't be surprised if you find a semi-nude woman or speedo-clad man walking around these shores, as the French here have an intense fear of tan lines.

i Free; limited wheelchair access

FOOD

BURGER KILLER ($)

5 Quai de Rive Neuve; 04 91 06 58 29; open daily 11am-11:30pm

Burger Killer is essentially Burger King's brother—if that brother was French and enjoyed murdering people with food rather than ruling over hungry people with a smile. A hidden backpacker's gem located in the heart of the Old Port, this place is a haven for those finding Marseille's fine-dining a bit too heavy on the fines. Burger Killer offers an array of burgers and sides, perfect to fill the hearts and stomachs of every American that is crazily craving something fried and juicy. Have no fear regarding its name, as the only person killing burgers here will be you.

i Burgers from €4.90; vegetarian options available; wheelchair accessible

LE COMPTOIR DUGOMMIER ($)

14 Bvd Dugommier; 06 51 66 90 90; www.comptoirdugommier.fr; open M-F 7:30am-5pm

With its 1940's classic style, large indoor mirrors, and hanging green lights, we're pretty sure Le Comptoir Dugommier belongs on a TV set, and not on a French street. The place is just a little too perfect, with incredible breakfast meals (read: eggs instead of bread) and great French lunches, all at incredibly reasonable prices. The place almost always packs in a huge crowd. The best time of day to visit is in the early morning, when the bread is fresh and the waiters won't look at you the wrong way for attempting to order breakfast for lunch. In this restaurant, see people pouring over newspapers and sipping coffees with friends. A great escape from the norm in France, Le Comptoir Dugommier is a must-visit restaurant in the city.

i Breakfast from €5, lunch from €9; vegetarian options available; wheelchair accessible

RISTORANTE DEL ARTE ($$$)

31 Quai des Belges; 04 96 11 10 02; www.delarte.fr; open daily noon-10pm

Ristorante Del Arte exhibits the best kind of art there is: food art. A lavish restaurant on the shores of the Old Port, you may want to avoid any part of the menu that doesn't land under the header 'Pizza.' But, if you're looking to dip your toes in some fantastic French cuisine with a beautiful view, this place invites you to splurge. With an incredible and extensive menu featuring everything from seafood to seared steaks, Ristorante Del Arte dishes out meals that prove you get what you pay for.

i Pizzas from €10; vegetarian and vegan options available; wheelchair accessible

WOOD ($$)

8 Rue de la Guirlande; 04 91 91 93 42; open M-F 7:30am-4pm

From the looks of it, the restaurant WOOD gets its classic name from absolutely nothing other than a hidden fascination with trees. The inside of this restaurant doesn't even feature wood floors, but it does offer up some pretty incredible cuisine at great prices. The expansive patio right outside the storefront is the perfect place to sit and take in a *café creme,* or indulge in a larger lunch of beef and ravioli. It's canopied patios, white tiled floors, and baby-blue chairs lift you away to the land of lavish living, where fresh and healthy foods impatiently wait to cuddle up in your stomach. And, we concede, the wooden tables add a nice touch that just might be enough to warrant the restaurant's name.

i Breakfast from €4; lunch from €12; vegetarian and vegan options available; wheelchair accessible

NIGHTLIFE

CARRY NATION

Secret Address; 09 50 26 01 66; www.carrynation.fr; open Tu-Th 7pm-2am, F-Sa 6pm-2am, Su 7pm-2am

Alright buddy, what's the secret passcode? This ultra-elusive, prohibition-themed bar is so secretive you won't even find their address online, or even in this book for that matter. Hidden inside a wardrobe inside a locked souvenir shop somewhere in the heart of Marseille, this bar holds true to prohibition-era wonder. As you crawl through jackets and a dimly-lit tunnel to finally reach the bar, you may worry you're about to walk straight into a death trap, but have no fear, the open arms and liquor cabinets at Carry Nation await your arrival. To get the location and entry instructions, make a reservation online before you go (feel free to book the day of).

i Cocktails from €12; no wheelchair access

EXIT CAFÉ

12 Quai Rive Neuve; 04 91 54 29 43; open M-Th 11am-2am, F-Sa 11am-4am,Su 11am-2pm

While at Exit Café, the last thing to look for is an exit sign. This bar and nightclub packs crowds of people looking for great drinks with a waterfront view almost every night. A favorite stop for young people, Exit Café provides ample opportunities to meet fellow travelers while sitting on the terrace outside, watching the latest football game (sorry, not the American kind) on the giant screen on the first floor, or dancing the night away on their top-floor lounge. This place also serves up mega-drinks to share—or not to, if it's one of those nights. You can grab a 5-liter mojito or rum and coke here, and if you do, the hostel friends you met just a few hours ago are sure to become friends for life just a few sips in.

i 1 liter cocktails from €10, beer and wine from €3; BGLTQ+ friendly; limited wheelchair access

LES BERTHOM

31 Cours Honoré d'Estienne d'Orves; 09 67 73 07 22; www.lesberthom.com; open Su-M 5pm-midnight, Tu-W 5pm-1am, Th-Sa 5pm-2am

There are two types of people in the world: those that like beer, and those that don't. Les Berthom caters to the people that really, really like beer. With over 30 different types of beer to choose from, you'll be amazed by the concoctions this place can come up with. From peach to coffee-flavored beer, you could spend an entire night working your way through their elaborate menu. Their outdoor patio stays packed throughout happy hour, but indoors a great industrial-brewery vibe awaits you, with high ceilings and long wooden tables just asking for you to place pitchers on.

i Beers from €3.80; happy hour Su-Th 7pm to 9pm; wheelchair accessible

NICE

Coverage by **Kristine Guillaume**

Let's be honest. You came to Nice for the sunny beach days on the unfathomably blue waters of the French Riviera. And that's not such a bad idea. Nice is one of the most affordable cities along the Côte d'Azur, which may sound strange because it's hard on the budget-conscious backpacker wallet. But compare the city to its more bougie neighbors like Cannes and Monaco and you'll see what we mean. Nice boasts the picturesque Promenade des Anglais lined with many public beaches for you to perfect your tan. It's also centrally located among the other cities in the area, making it the ideal home base for daytrips to places such as the aforementioned Cannes and Monaco as well as Antibes, Menton, and Eze. Some backpackers even claim that those cities are nicer than Nice itself. But let's not make the mistake of thinking Nice is just for the coast and sun. The city has boatloads of culture for you to discover, including the works of Henri Matisse, Marc Chagall, and Russian Orthodox aristocrats. When you've had enough sun, take a moment to discover the more artsy side of the city. It's nice, we promise.

ORIENTATION

Nice is one of many cities on the renowned **Côte d'Azur,** otherwise known as the French Riviera. The city center is located on the **Bay of Angels,** a long stretch of beach that starts at the airport and culminates in **Colline du Château (Castle Hill),** which is obviously a hill just in front of **Vieux Nice,** the old part of the city located southeast of the city center. To get to the city center from **Gare Nice Ville,** you'll most likely walk down the boutique-lined **Avenue Jean-Médicin**, which ends in the city's largest pedestrian center: **Place Masséna.** From Place Masséna, you can walk straight onto the **Promenade des Anglais** for an incredible view of the Bay of Angels. **The Port,** located east of Castle Hill, is less touristy than Vieux Nice, but still has some of the best cheap restaurants in town. Slightly north of the city center is **Cimiez,** site of the former Roman city, Cemenelum, which is now filled with villas, including the **Matisse Museum.**

ESSENTIALS

GETTING THERE

If flying into Nice, you will land at Aéroport de Nice-Côte D'Azur, from which you can take express buses #98 and 99 into the city center (€6). The buses run every half hour from 6am-midnight. Alternatively, you can walk 10min. to a train station, Saint-Augustin, and take it one stop to Gare Nice Ville, Nice's main train station. The train ticket costs €1.60 and it is the same train that runs to Monaco and the Italian city of Ventimiglia. If traveling via train, you will dock at Gare Nice Ville, which connects to multiple cities along Côte D'Azur, Lyon, and Paris. Train tickets are usually expensive (€70 from Lyon, €100 from Paris), so it might be better to take a bus. We recommend Ouibus.

GETTING AROUND

Nice is easily walkable. The main train station is a 10min. walk from the city center and Vieux Nice (Old Nice). The city does have an extensive public transport system called the Ligne d'Azur consisting of over 130 bus routes that extend to villages in the Maritime Alps and a tram line that makes a U-shape through the city center and Vieux Nice running from 4:35am-1:35am. A solo-ticket for one journey costs €1.50 and a 24hr pass costs €5. Be sure to validate your ticket each time you board a bus or tram to avoid paying hefty fines. In the summer, it's a great idea to bike along the Promenade des Anglais. For that, use Velo Blue, which costs €1.50 with the first 30min. of travel free.

PRACTICAL INFORMATION

Tourist Offices: Promenade des Anglais Office du Tourisme (2, Promenade des Anglais; 08 92 70 74 07; www.nicetourisme.com).

Banks/ATMs/Currency Exchange: Banks and ATMs are ubiquitous throughout the city, but this branch of BNP Paribas is not too far from Place Masséna (2 Bd. Victor Hugo; 820 82 00 01; open M-F 9am-12:30pm and 2pm-7pm).

Post Offices: The main post office, called La Poste, is located across from the main train station (21 Av. Thiers; open M-F 8am-7pm, Sa 8am-12:30pm).

Public Restrooms: There are public restrooms on the Promenade des Anglais. One of them is located right outside Plage Beau Rivage (107 Quai États-Unis).

Internet: The city offers free Wi-Fi at certain tourist offices and parks. If you need to use a computer, there are various cybercafés around the city. You can also rent out a Wi-Fi hotspot at the Tourist Office for €7.90 per day.

BGLTQ+ Resources: Centre BGLTQ+ Côte d'Azur (123 Rue de Roquebillière; 09 81 93 14 82; www.centrelgbt06.fr; open M, W, F 9:30am-8pm, Sa 2pm-8pm).

EMERGENCY INFORMATION

Emergency Number: 112

Police: Central Police Station (1 Av. Maréchal Foch; 04 92 17 22 22; open daily 24hr, foreign visitor reception desk open daily 9am-5pm) For lost and found, go to Police Municipal (42 Rue Dabray 3906; open M-Th 8:30am-5pm, F 8:30am-3:45pm).

US Embassy: The nearest US consulate is in Marseille (Pl. Varian Fry; 01 43 12 48 85).

Rape Crisis Center: In case of all social issues or problems, call 115.

Hospitals: Many of the medical centers are located on the outskirts of the city. The Tourist Office recommends heading to Hôpital Pasteur in case of an emergency, although children would be better served at Lenval Hospital.

- Hôpital Pasteur (30 Voie Romaine; 04 92 03 77 77; open M-F 8am-6pm, Sa 9am-5:45pm).
- Lenval Hospital (57 Av. De la Californie; 04 92 03 03 03; open M-F 8am-6pm, Sa 8am-3:30pm).

Pharmacies:

- Pharmacie Masséna (7 Rue Masséna; 04 93 87 78 94; open daily 24hr).
- Pharmacie Riviera (66 Av. Jean Médecin; 04 93 62 54 44).

SIGHTS

CULTURE

CATHÉDRALE SAINT-NICOLAS DE NICE (RUSSIAN ORTHODOX CATHEDRAL OF NICE)

Av. Nicholas II; 09 81 09 53 45; www.sobor.fr; open daily 9am-6pm, access restricted from noon-2pm for celebrations

One of the few remaining structures from Byzantine times, the Cathédrale Saint-Nicolas is a marvel of Russian architecture. Candy-style cupolas that could've been uprooted from Saint Petersburg adorn the cathedral, and bells ring every half hour. Do a full 360-degree walk around the grounds to fully examine the building's blends of red, teal, white, and gold before heading inside to admire the arguably more gorgeous interior. Russian icons and motifs gold decorate the interior. Be sure to cover your knees and shoulders before heading in—even if it is one of those hot summer days. Women should bring some sort of scarf as a head covering if they plan to walk inside the cathedral.

i Free; wheelchair accessible

MARCHÉ AUX FLEURS COURS SALEYA (COURS SALEYA FLOWER MARKET)

Cours Saleya; 04 92 14 46 14; open Tu-Sa 6am-5:30pm, Su 6am-1pm

Make sure to pack those OTCs in your backpack, although we're not sure if any dose of Claritin, Allegra, or Zyrtec can save you from the pollen-fest of the Marché aux Fleurs in **Vieux Nice,** the city's old quarter. Just steps away from the waterfront, the market is filled with refreshing aromas of every flower imaginable. Besides flowers, the stands offer everything from scented soaps to fresh vegetables to ripe fruits, so you can solve your backpacker BO and get your daily dose of vitamins in one shot.

i Prices vary by stand; wheelchair accessible

PALAIS LASCARIS

15 Rue Droite; 04 93 62 72 40; Jan 2-June 22 M, W-Su 11am-6pm, June 23-Oct 15 M, W-Su 10am-6pm, Oct 16-Dec 31 M, W-Su 11am-6pm (closed Jan 1, Easter Sunday, May 1, Dec 25)

In the middle of the winding paths of **Vieux Nice** (Old Nice) lies Palais Lascaris, a seventeenth-century aristocratic building that serves as a musical instrument museum. The unassuming exterior opens up into a lavish and ornate interior, complete with beautifully decorated ceilings and gold-painted walls. Palais Lascaris is home to the second-largest collection of musical instruments in all of France, including cigar box guitars, harps with intricately painted flowers, and more oboes and clarinets than Squidward could ever imagine. Built in the sixteenth century by the family of Jean-Paul Lascaris, the house still has much of the furniture (including paintings of fat men) you'd expect of a French aristocratic family. Word to the wise: don't budget too much time for this museum, as your visit will be under an hour.

i Admission €6, students and under 18 free, part of Municipal museums day ticket €10; last entry 5:30pm; guided tours F at 3pm €6; no wheelchair accessibility

LANDMARKS

PLACE MASSÉNA

15 Pl. Masséna; 06 29 64 10 12; open daily 24hr

What makes Place Masséna so unmistakable? Is it the red Pompeiian buildings on all its sides? The brightly lit Ferris wheel that can be seen from a mile away? The perhaps overly massive fountain of the Greek god Apollo on the checked black and white patterned pavement? Or maybe it's just the fact that it's smack in the middle of Nice and you'll, without a doubt, walk through it on your way to the waterfront every day. Just after sundown, statues of seven naked men light up on raised poles in every color of the rainbow. It's kind of like a PG Burlesque show that kids can watch, but only adults really understand. Cher and Christina, where you at?

i Free; wheelchair accessible

COLLINE DU CHÂTEAU (CASTLE HILL)

Montee du Chateau; open daily Oct 1-Mar 31 8:30am-6pm, Apr 1-Sept 30 8:30am-8pm

Get in some cardio by climbing this 300-foot hill for an aerial view of the coastline you won't get anywhere else. The site of the former **Château de Nice,** the Castle Hill today is, for lack of a better word, crumbling, but there is a certain charm in its age that you'll discover as you navigate through the maze of paths, many (many) stairs, and stunning array of greenery. Before making your way to the summit, stop by **Bellana Tower** for the view of the **Bay of Angels** and you'll forget all about how your thighs hurt from the countless flights of stairs. If cardio isn't your thing, there is an elevator that will take you up to the top, where you'll find a playground, a man-made waterfall, and views of the port.

i Free; limited wheelchair accessibility

MUSEUMS

MUSÉE MATISSE

164 Av. des Arènes de Cimiez; 04 93 81 08 08; open daily Jan 2-June 22 11am-6pm, June 23-Oct 15 10am-6pm, Oct 16-Dec 31 11am-6pm

It'll take you a bus ride to get here, but once you arrive at this gorgeous red Genoese villa, you won't think twice about the commute. This small museum houses many of **Matisse's** earliest works, including paintings, sculptures, and cutouts. Although the museum doesn't house his most famous works (you'll find those throughout the rest of France and the world), it does offer an in-depth look into Matisse's life and the time he spent in the French Riviera, most significantly in Nice. When you've finished with your daily dose of artist trivia, take a walk around the surrounding **Arènes de Cimiez,** the ruins of a Roman amphitheatre.

i Municipal museums day ticket €10, 7-day ticket €20, day group ticket €8 per person; last entry 5:30pm; tours upon request; wheelchair accessible

MUSÉE MARC CHAGALL

6 Av. Dr Ménard; 04 93 53 87 20; www.muse-chagall.fr; open Nov 1-May 1 M, W-F 10am-5pm, May 2-Oct 31 M, W-F 10am-6pm (closed Jan 1, May 1, Dec 25)

Even if you know absolutely nothing about art (and would rather be at the beach), you should take some time to swing by the Musée Marc Chagall during your visit to Nice. There's something perfectly soothing about the Modernist's collection, which is housed in an expansive, open space with natural light. Fun fact: Chagall claimed that the "universe of light" is necessary to truly appreciate his artwork, which we don't exactly understand, but, whatever it is, it's working. When you've finished examining the stained glass windows and 17 biblically inspired paintings, check out the olive garden in which the museum is situated and yeah, sure, then you can make your way back to the beach.

i Admission €10, €8 reduced, under 18 free, free admission first Su of month; last entry 5:30pm; audio guide available; wheelchair accessible

MUSÉE D'ART MODERNE ET D'ART CONTEMPORAIN DE NICE (MAMAC)

Pl. Yves Klein; 04 97 13 42 01; www.mamac-org; open Jan 2-June 22 Tu-Su 11am-6pm, June 23-Oct 15 Tu-Su 10am-6pm, Oct 16-Dec 31 Tu-Su 11am-6pm

So abstract. So confused. Those are perhaps the two thoughts running through our minds as we climbed the many lit-up stairs of MAMAC. The building has magnificently airy galleries featuring everything from American pop art to the work of **Yves Klein,** painter and performance art pioneer, including his monochrome collection of works solely in the color blue. Some of our favorite pieces include a pile of trash, a pile of rocks, and a pile of boxes—all reminders of why our parents are terrified of us suddenly deciding to drop everything and become artists. The museum's true highlight is, however, the top floor, where you can walk around the terrace and admire views of Nice, including the **Tete Carée.**

i Admission €10, groups €8, students free; wheelchair accessible

OUTDOORS

PLAGE PUBLIQUE DE PONCHETTES (PONCHETTES BEACH)

70 Quai des États Unis; lifeguards on duty; open daily June 1-Sept 3 9am-6pm

You'll have the perfect beach day at any beach along **Promenade des Anglais,** but we recommend Ponchettes. This beach boasts a prime location just next to **Castle Hill,** a military citadel, and in front of **Vieux Nice,** the city's old quarter. Be warned that the beaches in Nice aren't exactly the sandy seafronts you might have imagined. Instead, you'll be walking through smooth pebbles, which is a surprising relief, since you won't get sand stuck in places sand should never be. Join the sunbathers, beach volleyball players, and swimmers by the shore to enjoy the ever-present sun on the Côte d'Azur.

i Free; no wheelchair accessibility

PROMENADE DES ANGLAIS

Promenade des Anglais; 07 12 34 56 78; open daily 24hr

Usually, Tinder bios that mention long walks on the beach are a red flag. But walks along the Promenade des Anglais are a different story. This expansive stretch of seafront sidewalk, complete with chairs and benches to admire the unbelievably blue water and pebble beaches of the French Riviera, is filled with beach-goers, annoyingly over-eager children, topless women, joggers, and everyone in between. You could easily spend an entire day hopping from beach to beach with sporadic walks on the Promenade des Anglais, but we also recommend renting a bike and using the cyclists' lanes for some exercise down by the sea.

i Free; wheelchair accessible

FOOD

SOCCA D'OR ($)

45 Rue Bonaparte; 04 93 56 52 93; www.restaurant-soccador-nice.fr; open M-Tu 11am-2pm and 6pm-10pm, Th-Sa 11am-2pm and 6pm-10pm

An authentic local hang, Socca D'Or is just steps away from the pier and offers a chance to try the Niçoise specialty: *socca* (duh). *Socca,* a chickpea pancake from Genoa, can be ordered in a variety of different portions, but we recommend getting a demi-plate along with one of Socca D'Or's large pizzas or salads. This is the kind of spot locals come and order without looking at the menu, so, when in doubt, just order what the person next to you is having. You'll be in luck if it happens to be one of the restaurant's scrumptious desserts, like a caramel crêpe. On particularly hot days, sit inside and admire paintings of the port, or brave the heat and sit on the restaurant's sidewalk terrace for a true Nice experience.

i Socca from €3, pizzas and salads from €8, beer and wine from €3; cash only; vegetarian options available; wheelchair accessible

MALONGO ($)

39 Av. Jean Médicin; 04 93 85 95 01; www.malongo.com; open daily 7:30am-7pm

The stereotypes are true: the French begin their day with an espresso, a croissant, and a cigarette (or four). Malongo is the perfect place to see these stereotypes in action. A decently sized café with bright orange walls on **Avenue Jean Médecin,** Malongo is a necessary stop on your way to the city center. Grab a carefully prepared warm drink and a pastry to kickstart your day. If espresso isn't your thing, the café offers a selection of green and black loose teas, cappuccinos, and lattes. Join the locals quickly ordering their petit dejeuner and watch the fast-moving barista prepare everything from coffee to croissants with cheerfulness and ease. Whoever said the French had to be grumpy?

i Coffee and tea from €4, pastries from €2; wheelchair accessible

PORTOVENERE ($$)

12 Rue Halévy; 04 93 88 24 92; www.portovenererestaurant.fr; open daily noon-3pm and 7pm-11pm

Nice is just 18 miles from the French-Italian border, which explains why there are so many Italian places. Portovenere, located just a few blocks from the **Promenade des Anglais,** is perfect for traditional Italian dishes. The restaurant's head chef walks around in colorful, patterned hats and chef pants, making sure all his customers are stuffed and satisfied. Choose your favorite pasta, whether that is spaghetti or tagliatelle, drown it in sauce, and you're home free. If you're feeling something a little heavier, go for a seafood or meat dish—we highly recommend the mussels.

i Entrées from €14; vegetarian options available; wheelchair accessible

LA STORIA ($)

1 Cours Saleya; 04 93 80 95 07; open daily 9am-11pm

The restaurants along **Marché aux Fleurs Cours Saleya** are tourist traps to be avoided. If you walk to the end of the marketplace, however, you'll stumble upon more reasonably priced restaurants just steps away from the **Promenade des Anglais,** like La Storia.

Serving up Niçoise specialties like socca with parmesan and tomatoes (€8.50), the restaurant has both an indoor and outdoor area with chairs spilling onto the sidewalk. La Storia also offers a large selection of pizzas (€9.50) that can feed two—split with a fellow beach bum to get bang for your buck. Pro-tip: sit outside, but specify if you'd like to be seated away from smoking patrons, as the staff do make an effort to make you comfortable.

i Pizzas from €9, pastas from €12, other entrées from €9, beer and wine €7, during happy hour €5; wheelchair accessible

NIGHTLIFE

HIGH CLUB ($$)

45 Promenade des Anglais; 07 81 88 42 04; www.highclub.fr; open Th-Su 11:45pm-5:30am

It's no secret that you came to Southern France to party and everyone knows the clubs are exclusive. High Club is no different. With themed nights such as "We Are High" Saturdays, High Club boasts an energetic club atmosphere with crowds of the young and restless dancing and bumping to the beats pounding through the speakers. Our caveat is that a poorly planned night will result in a high bill. There's a €10 cover, and, once inside, you'll have a Ted and Marshall moment where you realize the drinks cost more than the experience is worth. Stop at pubs before coming to High Club so you only need to worry about the cover.

i Cover €10, beer and wine from €12, cocktails from €16; limited wheelchair accessibility

MA NOLANS IRISH PUB ($)

5 Quai des Deux Emmanuel; 04 92 27 07 88; www.ma-nolans.com; open daily 11am-2am

Ma Nolans Irish Pub has a cult following and three locations in the Côte d'Azur area: one in **Vieux Nice** (Old Nice), one near the port, and one in the nearby ritzy city of **Cannes.** Open practically all day, Ma Nolans is a lovely place to stop midday for a Guinness before walking through the pollen attack that is the **Marché aux Fleurs Cours Saleya** or a relaxing setting after a day on the seafront. Take a seat inside or on the bar's sidewalk terrace to enjoy a drink or participate in one of many themed events, like live music nights, quiz nights, and game watch parties. If you're not the biggest sports fan, we recommend picking the team of the person next to you and making a friend over a pint.

i Beer from €4, cocktails from €8, shots from €5

WAKA BAR ($)

57 Quai des États-Unis; 04 93 87 94 61; open daily 9:30am-2am

Situated right on the **Promenade des Anglais,** Waka Bar is the ideal place to come after a long, restful day on the beach if you're looking to liven up your evening. The bar boasts a great menu, complete with a wide selection of cocktails and delicious pub grub choices, and a balcony that overlooks the **Bay of Angels.** Arrive just before the sun sets and join the crowd bumping to the reggae tunes as you enjoy the unparalleled view of the Côte d'Azur.

i Cocktails from €6, food from €10; wheelchair accessible

WAYNE'S BAR ($)

15 Rue de la Préfecture; 04 93 13 46 99; wwwlwaynes.fr/fr/accueil; open daily 10am-2am

We know you didn't come to Nice to go to an English-speaking bar, but Wayne's is an exception to the rule. Arguably the most popular bar in the area, Wayne's has a crowd at all hours for its busy dance floor filled with beach-goers galore. There's no escaping their enthusiastic head-bopping and swaying to live music from British bands and local DJs as you kick back another pint or shot (€6). Perhaps the liveliest part about Wayne's is the irresistible allure of and eventual obligation to dance on top of the sturdy wooden tables after a long day of lying on the pebble beach.

i Shots from €6, cocktails from €8, beers from €3; BGLTQ+ friendly

PARIS

Coverage by **Will Rhatigan**

Paris. Pa-ree. The type of word that makes you want to purse your lips together after saying it and make a loud kissing noise. *Mwa.* A tourist's week in Paris typically follows a predictable parabolic trajectory: you arrive in the city, discount the strange array of cheap wedding shops that surround Gare du Nord, and joyfully prepare yourself to bathe in the light of its giant golden monuments. Then, during your first two days, you find yourself entranced by the majesty and romance of its vast public squares, and develop an overwhelming desire to kiss random strangers on the street. On the third day, you become disgusted by the ridiculous amount of selfies being taken and begin to question how many people had to die in the construction of the innumerable lavish palaces. As time goes on, that wave of skepticism gradually fades as you discover that the city is so much more than a long row of Big Tan Buildings, and you venture away from the River Seine to discover a mind-blowing cultural diversity that offers much more than selfie opportunities and croissants.

ORIENTATION

They say that Paris is laid out like one of its famous escargots: unlike New York's rigid grids, Paris's meandering *rues* are divided into blob-shaped **arrondissements**, starting in the center and spiraling out like a snail shell. You'll always be able to tell which arrondissement an address comes from by looking at the last two digits of its zip code (750 are the first three, followed by the number of the neighborhood). The River Seine divides the city in two, symbolically separating the city into the northern **Rive Gauche** and southern **Rive Droite.** Generally speaking, the farther you travel from the river, the less touristy and less expensive the city becomes. The 1st arrondissement begins in the center of the city, just north of the river. It's home to the oldest and most tourist-packed spots: the **Louvre,** the **Tuileries Garden,** and the **Place de la Concorde.** Just north is the 2nd, a small and trendy neighborhood defined by **Rue Montorgueil,** a street lined with cafés, cheese shops, produce stands, clothing stores—you name it. To the immediate east, the 3rd and 4th arrondisments make up **Le Marais**, whose history as the Jewish and Gay neighborhood creates a lively cultural mix that can always be counted on for unique restaurants and bars.

Before crossing the river to the 5th, you'll encounter the Ile de la Cité and Ile St. Louis, two islands in the middle of the Seine that hold **Notre Dame** and form the Medieval core of the city. University students from schools like the famous **Sorbonne** crowd into the 5th arrondissement, or the **Latin Quarter** (so titled because all the students used to speak latin), while the 6th, **Saint-Germain-des-Prés**, hosts the old haunts of celebrated writers and intellectuals, making it a fashionable and expensive area with famous cafés and abundant bookstores. The 7th is the stuff of cliché postcards: clean, quiet, picturesque Paris streets mixed with views of the iconic **Eiffel Tower.**

Breaking up the order for the sake of simplicity, the Northern side of the river to the east holds the 8th and 16th arrondissements, expensive (read: lame) neighborhoods that are defined by the wide avenues surrounding the **Champs-Élysées,** where stereotypes of impossibly sleek, high-heeled Parisians come to life. To the North, the 17th offers a quieter area, where artists can find pretty cafés, and to the east you'll find the lively **Grands Boulevards** neighborhood of the 9th, where nightlife thrives every day of the week. On the northern edge of the city sits the diverse 18th, which holds the sex-shop rows in **Pigalle**, the splendid highest point in the city at **Montmartre,** and the lively West African neighborhood of **Chateau Rouge.** Continuing east on the spiral, the 10th and 19th are home to many hostels, and host the lively **Canal St. Martin** neighborhood as well as more affordable residential areas near the gorgeous **Parc des Buttes Chaumont.**

On the east side of the city, crowded bars, hidden gems, and lively side streets define the 11th and 12th, while the 20th is one of the quietest areas in Paris, home to the iconic **Père LaChaise** cemetery. Back on the outer ring of the Rive Gauche, the 13th, 14th, and 15th are more residential neighborhoods, each with their own character. The 13th reflects significant Asian influences along with the ancient-feeling **Buttes aux Cailles** neighborhood, the 14th has both sleepy streets and lively energy near Montparnasse, and the 15th holds hidden charm behind 1970's highrises. In case you think you've got it all figured out, you'll soon discover that there's as much complexity within each arrondissement's dense streets as there is in the artful layout of the city itself.

ESSENTIALS

GETTING THERE

Fly into either Charles de Gaulle or Orly airports. From Charles de Gaulle, take the RER B line directly into the city center. From Orly, take the T7 train line to Villejuif-Louis Aragon, where the 7 metro line can connect you to the rest of the city. Most international trains arrive at Gare du Nord, Gare de L'Est, or Gare de Lyon, all of which connect to several metro lines for transportation within Paris.

GETTING AROUND

The metro, SNCF, is the simplest way to get around Paris. Single tickets can be purchased at machines in all stations for €1.80, or weekly passes can be bought from station information counters for €27.80 that also include use of buses and larger commuter trains. Bike-sharing services are available around the city, with dockless smartphone-operated bikes such as MoBike generally being more convenient than the city-run Vélib bike-sharing stations. The hot new development in Paris transportation has been electric-scooter sharing, with companies such as Bird and Lime providing smartphone-operated rental scooters on streets all around the city. But Paris is small, and most streets tend to be beautiful and unique, so walking can often be your best bet.

PRACTICAL INFORMATION

Tourist Offices: The main tourist office is the Office du Tourisme et des Congrès de Paris - Bureau Hôtel de Ville. Located within the famous Hotel de Ville, this office provides comprehensive tourist information, free maps and guidebooks, and ticket sales for some of the major attractions such as the Louvre, Versailles, and cruises on the Seine (Hôtel de Ville, 29 rue de Rivoli, 4e; 01 49 52 42 63; www.parisinfo.com; open daily May 1-Aug 31 9am-7pm, Nov-Apr 10am-7pm).

Banks/ATMs/Currency Exchange: Major French banks include BNP Paribas, Banque Populaire, Société Générale, Crédit Mutuel, and more. Banque Populare (33 Rue de Rivoli, 08 20 33 61 77; open T-W 9am-6pm, Th 10am-6pm, F 9am-6pm, Sa 9am-5pm).

Post Offices: The main postal service in France is called La Poste, and has locations all over Paris. The central location near the Louvre has the longest hours (16 Rude Étienne Marcel, 2e; www.laposte.fr).

Public Restrooms: Public restrooms are located all around Paris, often in parks or near major tourist attractions.

Internet: Many cafés in Paris don't offer free Wi-Fi, so McDonald's may be your best friend in a pinch. Free internet access is also provided at nearly all of the city's major museums and international train stations.

BGLTQ+ Resources: The Centre LGBT Paris-Île-de-France offers free consultations, free health supplies, and social and cultural events for BGLTQ+ people (63 Rue Beaubourg, 3e; 01 43 57 21 47; open M-F 3:30pm-8pm, Sa 1pm-7pm, hours vary for different consulting services).

EMERGENCY INFORMATION

Emergency Number: 112.

Police: Each Paris Arrondissement has its own local police force, with locations listed at en.parisinfo.com/practical-paris/useful-info/staying-safe-in-paris/police-stations-in-paris. Dialing 3430 anywhere in France will connect you to the local police station. The most central location is Commissariat de Police du 1er arrondissement (45 place du Marché Saint-Honoré, 1e).

US Embassy: Embassy of the United States, Paris (2 Avenue Gabriel, 8e; 01 43 12 22 22; open M-F 9am-6pm).

Rape Crisis Center: Institut National d'Aide aux Victimes et de Médiation (14 Rue Ferrus, 14e ; 01 45 88 19 00; www.rcne.com/contact/countries/france).

Hospitals: The main hospital in Paris is Hôpital-Dieu de Paris. In an emergency, call 112.

- Hôpital-Dieu de Paris (1 Pl. du Parvis de Notre Dame, 4e; 01 42 34 82 34 ; open M-F 9am-4pm, emergency department open daily 24hr).
- Hopital St. Louis (1 Av. Claude Vellefaux, 10e; 01 42 65 88 29; open daily 24hr).

Pharmacies: Pharmacies, marked with a green cross, can be found on almost any street.

- Pharmacie Lafayette des Halles (10 Bl. De Sébastopol, 4e; 01 42 72 03 23 ; open daily 8:30am-9pm).
- Pharmacie St. Lazare (87 Rue Saint-Lazare, 9e; 01 48 74 11 11; open M-F 8:30am-9pm, Sa noon-1pm).

SIGHTS

CULTURE

AVENUE DES CHAMPS ÉLYSÉES

8e; open daily 24hr

This quintessential Parisian avenue began as an extension of the **Tuileries Garden,** but since the eighteenth century, it has been the fashionable street for strolling, seeing, and being seen. Stretching in a majestic line between the **Place de la Concorde** and the **Arc de Triomphe,** this long row of fashion boutiques, upscale restaurants, and famous bakeries has become the international symbol of French high culture, immortalized musically by Joe Dassin's "Les Champs-Élysée," a song we found ourselves humming for our entire time in Paris. Events such as the annual Bastille Day parade and the final stage of the Tour de France draw massive crowds to the wide sidewalks, but thousands of people can be found perusing the shops every day of the week.

i Free; wheelchair accessible

BUTTES AUX CAILLES

Rue de la Butte aux Cailles, 13e; open daily 24hr

Stepping out of the métro at Place d'Italie, you're acutely aware that you're in the center of modern France. A huge, glass-walled shopping center sits at your right, and cars whizz around the wide rotary. But walk 10 minutes south and up the winding cobblestone streets of the **Butte aux Cailles district,** and you'll find yourself in an ancient neighborhood that feels more like a tiny village in the Alps than the heart of Paris. With many buzzing cafés, bars, and restaurants lining its main street of low, old buildings, the neighborhood is energetic at all hours of the day, many of the patrons calling bartenders by name like they've been drinking there for years. But to remind you that you're in a culturally-diverse city, the neighborhood also boasts one of the most eclectic street art scenes in Paris.

i Free; wheelchair accessible

GALERIES LAFAYETTE

40 Bd. Haussman, 9e; 01 42 82 34 56; www.galerieslafayette.com; open M-Sa 9:30am-8:30pm, Su 11am-7pm

Do you ever get frustrated that your mink scarf is no longer in season? Do you hate it when your Prada boots get a little scuffed? Do you have a deep, overwhelming desire to sink your teeth into and suck the blood from the bodies of the working class? No? Well, then, you won't have much in common with many of the shoppers lurking in the designer racks at Galeries Lafayette, Paris's most famous department store. Visitors flock by the busload to throw euros at shoes, bags, suits, perfumes, and just about anything that will scream, "My parents own a boat." But there's lots to see even if you're not being crushed by the weight of your expendable income. It's a sort of cool to find out just which long-existing fashions designers will decide to make hip, or just how much one can charge a fool for a plain gray sweat-suit.

i Prices vary (over 1,000 for the sweatsuit); wheelchair accessible

MARCHÉ AUX PUCES DE SAINT-OUEN (FLEA MARKET OF SAINT OUEN)

124 Rue des Rosier, Saint-Ouen; www.marcheauxpuces-saintouen.com; open M 11am-5pm, Sa-Su 10am-5:30pm

When we travel, certain needs arise. We forget a toothbrush, a map, or sometimes, our third pair of Gucci flip flops. In Paris, the best place to pick up all those little things that slipped your mind is the Marché Aux Puces. Sitting just outside the city limits in neighboring Saint-Ouen, the vast outdoor marketplace is touted as the largest antiques market in the world—but that description really undersells the bric-a-brac you can buy in its over 1,700 stalls. 1813 original marble busts? Check. Garden gnomes giving you the finger? Check. One thousand varieties of handmade Supreme shirt fabrications? Check. Mostly the last one. Although most of what you'll walk through is remarkably creative takes on fake designer clothing, don't be surprised to find a boy in a newsboy cap and suspenders around the next corner yelling "R2D2 coffee tables! Get your R2D2 coffee tables here!" In the bizarre variety show you'll find in its endless maze of stalls, the Marché aux Puces de Saint-Ouen is the perfect place to escape the energy of the city to an even greater madness.

i Free; wheelchair accessible

PLACE DE LA BASTILLE

Pl. de la Bastille, 11e; open daily 24hr

While the storming of the Bastille prison by French revolutionaries in 1789 was a rather grim and violent affair, the area has really lightened its tone since the destruction of the dungeon that made it famous. Adjacent to the enormous column marking the space of the former jail, the Bastille neighborhood boasts the rowdiest, loudest, most eclectic row of bars in Paris. With a heart at the almost all-nightlife **Rue de Lappe**, this quarter stretches out north from the main square toward the **Canal St. Martin.** If you can't see the bars on a cloudy night don't worry—you'll be able to hear no problem. And if you're looking to foment another revolution this is the place to start; history is on your side and the masses are hot and ready.

i Bar prices vary; wheelchair accessible

PLACE DU TERTRE (ARTIST'S SQUARE)

Place de Tertre, 18e; open daily 24hr

In the heart of the neighborhood where iconic artists like Pablo Picasso, Vincent Van Gogh, Pierre-Auguste Renoir and many others once worked, this cobblestone square in **Montmartre** now houses a collection of artists vending their work to the public. While many of the works on sale don't match the innovation of the local art scene's founders—most include Paris landmarks or caricatures of tourists—the square is a great spot to hang out and observe the act of creation in progress all the same. You might not pick up a Van Gogh, but who knows, maybe one of a caricaturists' portraits will end up in the **Pompidou** next year.

i Stand prices vary; wheelchair accessible

LANDMARKS

L'ARC DE TRIOMPHE

Pl. Charles-de-Gaulle, 8e ; 01 55 37 73 77; monuments-nationaux.fr; open daily 10am-11pm

Assuming you played Little League, you are probably familiar with the concept that when you win something, you get a trophy. Usually it's a plastic statue in some sort of athletic stance, but when it's Napoleon building a trophy for himself, you get a 50-meter high tribute to military domination. L'Arc de Triomphe celebrates the conquests of Napoleon's Grande Armée, and has been the site of victorious military processions ever since, marched around by both the German and French during World War II. Underneath the Arch, the tomb of the unknown soldier reminds us of the price of militarism and massive celebrations of national pride. But the top of the arch has one of the best views in Paris, so enjoy a beautiful sunset while you reflect on centuries of violence.

i Admission €12; wheelchair accessible

BIBLIOTHÈQUE NATIONALE DE FRANCE (NATIONAL LIBRARY OF FRANCE)

Quai François Mauriac, 13e ; www.bnf.fr/en; open Tu-Sa 9am-8pm

While most of us think of libraries as old, dusty, and full of creaky wooden armchairs and octogenarians, the Bibliothèque Nationale de France (BnF) is a glistening, futuristic complex that looks like it was built to be Elon Musk's personal lair. Opened in 1996 as a library for the twenty-first century, the BnF is comprised of four identical towers framing a massive pavilion with an unearthly garden sunken in the middle of it all. The inside of the library boasts 15 million books and a series of exhibitions, the most impressive of which is a display of the enormous 1681 *Globes of Coronelli.* But outside of the academic library, the endless pavilion overlooking the **Seine** is buzzing with teenagers practicing dance and makes one of the most unique places to hang out in Paris.

i Free; library card needed to access reading rooms; wheelchair accessible

LES CATACOMBES

1 Ave du Colonel Henri Rol-Tanguy, 14e; 01 43 22 47 63; www.catacombes.paris.fr; open Tu-Su 10am-8:30pm

After waiting in line until you're almost ready to join the ranks of the skeletons yourself, you'll be welcomed into the chilly labyrinthine tunnels of the Paris Catacombes. Beginning in the late eighteenth century, when many graveyards were closed for public health reasons, the remains of thousands of decaying Parisians were transplanted deep into the underground. Millions of skulls and bones are stacked in neat arrangements that are surprisingly aesthetically pleasing, until you remember that they were once living, breathing human beings. It begs the questions: how does one get into the bone-arranging field? Do you start with an internship? Or are you simply promoted from being one of those kids that burns ants with a magnifying glass? In any case, the Paris underground is not for the faint of heart.

i Admission €13, skip-the-line available online for €19, under 17 free; last entry 7:30pm; no wheelchair accessibility

ÉGLISE SAINT-AUGUSTIN

8 Avenue César Caire, 8e; 01 45 22 01 35; open for visits M-F 10am-4:30pm, Sa 10am-noon

The Église St. Augustin is without a doubt one of the most impressive churches in Paris, yet somehow, no one seems to care. With massive arched ceilings, a tower dome, and stunning stained-glass windows, St. Augustin has the chops to compete with every other hotshot Catholic edifice in the city. Yet walk in on a weekday afternoon and you'll find yourself alone with five adorable old French women attending a prayer service commemorating the 140th anniversary of the death of a prince who perished in an obscure South African battle. For a taste of what the culture that created Paris's omnipresent monstrous cathedrals is actually like, St. Augustine is the unknown place to go.

i Free; wheelchair accessible

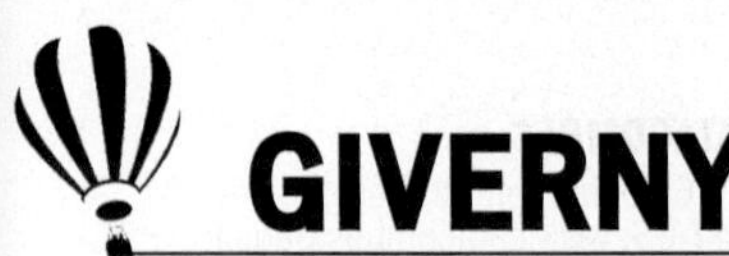

GIVERNY

In the introduction to *Democracy in America,* famed Frenchman Alexis de Tocqueville describes the Mississippi valley as "the finest habitation ever created for man." We're not sure where he got the idea to leave home from, because the valley stretching from Giverny to Vernon on the River Seine is surely one of the most fine and fertile landscapes on this fair earth. Giverny is only an hour's train ride from Paris, but it feels like a one-hundred-year journey back in time. Vines slither down Medieval buildings, lazy green streams meander through fields of cattle, and everything feels just a bit more innocent. If one of Snow White's seven dwarves popped up behind a small, red roofed house, you'd only be surprised that the other dwarves weren't with him. The small village, about 5 kilometers up the River Seine from the larger but still sleepy town of Vernon, is famous for hosting the beautiful house and gardens of the pathbreaking impressionist painter Claude Monet. At his home near the banks of the Seine, Monet spent the last forty years of his life tending to his garden and painting pastoral scenes and pictures of his coveted water lilies over and over again. Walking around the small village and the surrounding valley, it's easy to see he became so obsessed.

The train station in Vernon is minutes from the center of town, and following the clearly marked signs will lead you to the main square, where every storefront seems to end in "erie" (*Boulangerie, Patisserie, Boucherie, Fromagerie, Épicerie* etc.). Towards the Seine is a beautiful riverfront park, facing the looming row of cliffs across the valley. A 5-kilometer journey on a bike trail on the side of the Seine will lead to Giverny, where small shops and houses line the main road, and **Monet's House** and the **Museum of Impressionism** sit beyond a few Medieval walls next to a rotary. Here completes the path through Vernon-Giverny, although endless further explorations are possible.

GETTING THERE

The train station in Vernon is minutes from the center of town, and following the clearly marked signs will lead you to the main square. Towards the Seine is a beautiful riverfront park, facing the looming row of cliffs across the valley. A 5-kilometer journey on a bike trail on the side of the Seine will lead to Giverny, where small shops and houses line the main road, and Monet's House and the Museum of Impressionism sit beyond a few Medieval walls next to a rotary.

GETTING AROUND

€8 round-trip shuttles depart from the station in Vernon shortly after each train arrives. But since the river valley connecting the two towns might be the most beautiful part of the whole area, the journey is truly more important than the destination here, and you're better off renting a bike or walking. Rent bikes from L'Arrivée de Giverny, a shop directly across from the station, for €10, or walk along the beautiful path on the opposite side of the river all five miles to Giverny.

Check out...

MONET'S HOUSE AND GARDENS

84 Rue Claude Monet, Giverny; 02 32 51 28; Giverny.org; open daily 9:30am-6pm

While looking at the countless Monet paintings of flower fields and water lilies scattered around the museums of Paris often begs the question of how the artist didn't get bored, taking a tour around his personal paradise goes a long way toward providing an answer. Walking around his quaint house you see bright yellow rooms, a refurbished edition of his original studio, and sunlit kitchen where he made his breakfasts. Outside in the garden, flourishing flowers seem to cover every square inch, and the Japanese bridges over his waterlily pond is so damn picturesque that you might want to sit down and paint it four-hundred times yourself.

i Admission €9.50 for adults, €5.50 reduced; wheelchair accessible

Don't miss...

CLIFFS OF VERNON

Route de Magny en Vexin, Vernon

On the opposite bank from Vernon, at the tip of one of the long ridges that frames the River Seine, juts a tall white cliff that is impossible to miss from anywhere in the small town. Like any imposing mountain, as soon as you see it, there's nothing you'll want to do but climb. Follow Route de Magny en Vexin up the ridge until you see a small dirt path on your right, then climb that until you reach a sharp left turn. Just off the road at that point, you'll find yourself at the top of the cliff. Off the edge you receive a stunning few of the red-roofed town, and can look down the wide Seine for miles. It's then that you know for sure that this valley is the finest habitation ever made for man.

i Free; no wheelchair accessibility

Swing by...

MUSÉE DES IMPRESSIONNISMES GIVERNY

99 Rue Claude Monet, Giverny; 02 32 51 94 65; mdig.fr; open daily 10am-6pm

Just down the street from where the founding father of impressionism once worked, the small Musée des Impressionnismes Giverny houses a captivating collection of the artists' work, describing the influences that affected him at various points in his career, and showing his paintings side by side with his contemporaries. Although the gallery is small, the light crowds and pastoral landscape surrounding the museum allow you to feel a touch of the peace Monet must have felt while blissfully sketching his ten-thousandth flower in Giverny

i Admission €7.50 adults, €5 reduced; wheelchair accessible

Grab a bite at...

LE CAPUCHINE GIVERNY ($)

80 Rue Claude Monet, 02 32 51 76 67; open daily 10am-6pm

Walking out of Monet's gardens, it's hard to imagine going inside of a building while the scent of flowers is still fresh in your lungs. Luckily, Le Capuchine Giverny keeps the ambiance rolling straight through dinner, serving up fresh sandwiches and drinks on relaxed lawn tables while an electric piano softly plays in the background. Although the restaurant closes early, everything else is closed by 6pm as well—the term sleepy village exists for a reason, after all.

i Sandwiches from €6.50, Beer from €5.50; wheelchair accessible

EIFFEL TOWER

Champ de Mars, 5 Av. Anatole, 7e; 08 92 70 12 39; www.toureiffelparis/en; open daily mid-June–Sept 9:30 am-11:45pm, Oct-May 9am-12:45pm

The Eiffel tower was supposed to be destroyed after its use in the **1889 World's Fair**, but a vote by Parisian citizens to keep it determined its fate as a setting for wedding photos, the site of the highest concentration of selfie sticks per capital in the world, and a source of inspiration for the more creative sex shops around the **Moulin Rouge**. Enjoy a picnic in the surrounding park or sit wistfully gazing from the adjacent **Pont d'Iéna** bridge if you're not willing to wait up to one hour amongst the engaged couples, selfie-takers, and sex toy designers to actually get into the tower and see its incredible panoramic views. Just watch out for dangerously high wind levels caused by thousands of moon-eyed romantics collectively sighing.

i Age 18-24: €12.70 to top, €9.70 to middle. Adults: €25.40 to top, €19.40 to middle (cheaper by stairs); wheelchair accessible

LE PANTHÉON

Pl. du Panthéon, 5e; 01 44 32 18 00; paris-pantheon.fr/en; open daily Apr-Sept 10am-6:30pm, Oct-Mar 10am-6pm

Originally intended by Louis XV as a dedication to Geneviève, the patron saint of Paris, this enormous domed monolith became the secular temple of the nation. It pays homage to those killed during the World Wars and holds the tombs of figures considered fundamental to French culture in its underground crypt, including Victor Hugo, Marie Curie, Jacques Rousseau, and Voltaire. The inside of the structure is intimidating and empty, a massive cavern covered with paintings celebrating the glory of France, and a few still featuring dear St. Geneviève, ensuring she remains on Paris's side. In the center of the massive dome hangs **Foucault's pendulum,** which he used to prove the world rotates around itself. Walking out, it'll be up to you to decide if the empty cavern is glorious, or, like Albert Camus's family did when they refused to allow him to be buried there, a giant nationalist waste of space.

i Admission €9, under 26 €7; wheelchair accessible; tours of upper levels available

PÈRE LACHAISE CEMETERY

16 Rue du Repos, 20e; 01 55 25 82 10; open M-F 8am-6pm, Sa 8:30am-6pm, Su 9am-6pm

In contrast to the concealment of death in the **Catacombes**, Père Lachaise Cemetery is an enormous monument to the corpses lying beneath its gargantuan tombstones. In this coveted island of deathly serenity in the middle of the bustling city, long rows of small cathedrals built as the mausoleums of prominent Parisian families stretch out over a tranquil hillside. Housing the graves of **Oscar Wilde, Frédéric Chopin, Jim Morrison, Edith Piaf,** and many others, the cemetery displays a seemingly endless array of tributes to the dead that represent each family's prestige with the size and intricacy of the tombstone. Beautiful as many are, the long, black wall on the edge of the cemetery listing the names of Parisians who were killed during the First World War serves as a grim reminder of the negative consequences that accompany death's glorification.

i Free; wheelchair accessible

SACRÉ-COEUR (BASILICA OF THE SACRED HEART OF PARIS)

35 Rue de Chevalier de la Barre, 18e; 01 53 41 89 00; www.sacre-coeur-montmartre.com; basilica open daily 6am-10:30pm; dome open May-Sept 8:30am-8pm, Oct-Apr 9am-5pm

Gorgeous, enormous, omnipresent in every Parisian panorama, and swarmed by pickpockets and men hawking tiny eiffel towers, the Sacré-Coeur boasts the most overwhelmingly beautiful view over Paris. The Eiffel Tower? Non, you unoriginal Américain, C'est Sacré-Coeur. Looming atop the towering hill of **Montmartre** in the Northern corner of the city, Sacré-Coeur looks down over an endless ocean of glistening tan streets and church spires. Walk inside to feel oppressively miniscule beneath the cavernous dome and witness pilgrims from across the world bow their heads in displays of commitment to inspire even the most atheistic of us. For a lighter time, grab a baguette at any of the small boulangeries in the area, sit on the grass in front of the Basilique, and enjoy your aerial introduction to the City of Love.

i Basilica admission free, dome admission varies by day; no wheelchair accessibility; must cover shoulders to enter

SAINTE-CHAPELLE

8 Bd. Du Palais, 1e; 01 53 40 60 80; www.saint-chapelle.fr/en; open daily 9am-7pm

Most stains require the tough, grease-fighting, cleansing power of a Tide pen. But in the thirteenth century, King Louis IX threw caution to the wind and hired some folks to stain the living hell out of some glass, Gothic style. A reliquary and place of worship, this two-story chapel is home to a stunning collection of stained glass windows, each telling its own story. The mammoth windows, including an impressive rose one, flood the sanctuary with luminescence, which glints of chandeliers and golden ornamentation inside. The chapel often holds cultural events such as concerts in the summer months, so be sure to check the schedule before you go.

i Admission €10, €8 reduced; guided tours daily 11am-3pm; last entry 30min before closing, wheelchair accessible

SHAKESPEARE AND CO.

37 Rue de la Bucherie, 5e; 01 43 25 40 93; www.shakespeareandcompany.com; open M-Sa 10am-10pm, Su 12:30pm-8pm

While Paris's **Left Bank** may be most famous for French intellectual titans like **Jean-Paul Sartre, Albert Camus,** and **Simone de Beauvoir,** its cafés and bookshops have been the training grounds for some of the United States' most iconic writers. In two iterations, the first of which closed after the German occupation of Paris, bookstore and café Shakespeare and Co. has been the home base of the American intellectual diaspora, housing writers like **Ernest Hemingway, Gertrude Stein, Allen Ginsberg,** and **William Burroughs** at its cozy tables and, at times, in beds tucked between the narrow shelves. The store is still in full operation, and walking between its oddly arranged shelves and aisles feels like a journey into the mind of a brilliantly disorganized intellectual. Although its alumni list has made it a bit of a tourist hotspot in recent years, Shakespeare and Co. offers the best opportunity around to experience the literary environment that revolutionized the culture of the twentieth century.

i Admission free, books vary in price; limited wheelchair accessibility

MUSEUMS

ATELIER DES LUMIÈRES

38 Rue Saint-Maur, 11e; www.atelier-lumieres.com; open M 10am-6pm, W 10am-10pm, Th 10am-6pm, F-Sa 10am-10pm, Su 10am-7pm

Much of the most powerful still art seems to suggest movement. Brushstrokes glide like water, the bent arms of statues swing to their target, colors push back and forth against each other in a vivid tug of war. Atelier des Lumières takes the movement that dynamic art strives for very literally, adapting the work of famous painters to flow and dance in vivid projections across all four walls of a massive former iron smelter studio. Putting on a rotation of three light shows that play all day, the studio brings painting into physical motion, rotating portraits, waving trees in the wind, and giving speech to frozen faces. This year's adaptations of Van Gogh and traditional Japanese art beautifully capture the motion that the painters suggest, mesmerizing you as you sit at attention on the concrete floor of the renovated foundry.

i Admission from €14.50, €13.50 reduced; online purchase only; recommended to reserve a spot at least three days in advance; free bag check; wheelchair accessible

CENTRE GEORGES POMPIDOU

Pl. Georges-Pompidou, 4e ; 01 44 78 12 33; www.centrepompidou.fr/en; open M, W-Su 11am-9pm, level 6 special exhibitions open Th 11am-11pm

Your first indication that the Pompidou is going to get weird and wild is the fact that you enter the building through a giant translucent tube, and the next is that the art is bananas. We mean that in a figurative sense, but, after an hour at the Pompidou, you'd no longer be skeptical if you saw a bunch of bananas wearing little jackets and a sign that read something like "Costumed Fruit, 2011. Reinterpretation of light, fabric, and organic energy. Medium: tropical fruit, polyester." At the largest collection of modern and contemporary art in Europe, works by **Matisse** and **Cézanne** are displayed alongside photos of dogs straddling tables in creative positions, and a long video of a man slicing vegetables and placing them on his exposed *derrière*. Ahh, art.

i Admission €14, €11 reduced; tours Sa at noon; last entry 8pm; wheelchair accessible

FONDATION LOUIS VUITTON

8 av. du Mahatma Gandhi, 16e; 01 40 69 96 00; www.fondationlouisvuitton.fr; open M 11am-8pm, W-Th 11am-8pm, F 11am-9pm, Sa-Su 10am-8pm

The name Louis Vuitton immediately evokes extravagance, and, from the moment you walk within sight of the building, your expectations are confirmed. Housed in an enormous, bizarre piece of architecture nicknamed "the iceberg," the museum thinks big from top to bottom. Within the massive wings of the complex are 11 galleries, each of which shoots for size as well, most displaying only a few iconic modern paintings on the expansive walls. While the majesty of the whole affair seems a bit wasteful, the space given to each work compels us to linger and soak in our impressions. Don't miss the temporary exhibitions either—this year's show on impressionism includes some of the most famous works in the genre, all in a setting that invites you to be overpowered by creativity.

i Admission €16, €10 reduced; wheelchair accessible

MUNDOLINGUA: MUSÉE DES LANGUES (MUSEUM OF LANGUAGES)

10 Rue Servandoni, 6e; 01 56 81 65 79; www.mundolingua.org; open daily 10am-7pm

Paris is an endless labyrinth where every street corner, steep staircase, and alleyway holds a new surprise. Usually that surprise is a weird restaurant, an ancient store, or yet another Really Big Church™. Yet in this alley in the Latin Quarter, that surprise is a museum. Mundolingua feels like the inside of eccentric uncle's Brooklyn apartment, with a wild array of artifacts and information related to language packed tightly into three floors of dense material that somehow makes perfect sense. Within the collection is a scale replica of the Rosetta Stone, an enormous array of language-related DVD's you can watch in-museum, and an original enigma machine. Although the museum has a specific subject, roving around the homey space, talking to the friendly proprietor, and learning a ton about the development of language is one of the most magical journeys of discovery in Paris.

i Admission €7, €5 reduced; no wheelchair accessibility

MUSÉE DE PICASSO

5 Rue de Thorigny, 3e; 01 85 56 00 36; www.museepicassoparis.fr; open Tu-F 10:30am-6pm, Sa-Su 9:30am-6pm

Almost universally recognized as the most famous figure in modern art, Pablo Picasso has people studying almost every aspect of his life, from his evolution into the "blue period," to the underwear he wore while painting (photo evidence on the museum walls). The **Musée de Picasso** crafts a narrative of the artist's entire life, focusing as much on his artistic influences and personal affairs as it does on his work itself. With this personal focus, it's disappointing to see no mention of his status as one of the most notoriously domineering misogynists of the twentieth century. With this abusive history in mind, his grotesque, deconstructed representations of women begin to look a lot more ominous. All the same, viewing his groundbreaking works in their historical context is a fascinating exploration of how creativity mixes with power.

i Admission €15; wheelchair accessible; free bag check

MUSÉE DU LOUVRE

Rue de Rivoli, 1e; 01 40 20 50 50; www.louvre.fr; open M 9am-6pm, W 9am-9:45pm, Th 9am-6pm, F 9am-9:45pm, Sa-Su 9am-6pm

The Louvre. Oh, you've heard of it? Big glass pyramids, that one lady that doesn't smile with her teeth, tens of thousands of wide-eyed, easily confused tourists? We're guessing you have the basic info down, so here are some insider tips. Go in the morning or buy a Paris museum pass ahead of time to escape the lines. When observing the famous sculpture *Winged Liberty*, stand on the stairs from a three quarters angle on the left, the vantage point from which the artist originally intended it to be viewed. Avoid the *Mona Lisa* and the Italian Painters section like the plague if you don't like crowds. Plan ahead: the largest museum in the world can be overwhelming if you don't do your research. Unless, of course, you're just there to see our pal Mona.

i Admission €15; tours €12; wheelchair accessible

MUSÉE DU QUAI BRANLY- JACQUES CHIRAC

37 Quai Branly, 7e; 01 56 61 70 00; www.quaibranly.fr/en/; open T-W 11am-7pm, Th-Sa 11am-9pm, Su 11am-7pm

What do Yemeni feast dresses, Polynesian canoes, and West African ritual masks have in common? They were all snatched from other cultures by French colonizers and placed in the Musée du Quai Branly. In all fairness, the museum has made a reasonable effort to return objects of religious or cultural significance to their countries of origin in the past few years, and the extensive galleries of cultural artifacts now have the stated purpose of recognizing the role of indigenous art in our universal heritage. A tour through the museum is a thrilling exploration of international and historic art. Be sure to check out the special exhibition that takes up almost half of the museum—this year's exhibit on Oceania includes a fascinating examination of how indigenous culture influenced and reacted to modern art.

i Admission €10, access to temporary exhibitions €10; wheelchair accessible; free bag check

MUSÉE D'ORSAY

1 Rue de la Légion d'Honneur, 7e; 01 40 49 48 14; www.museeorsay.fr/en; open T-W 9:30am-6pm, Th 9:30am-9:45pm, Sa-Su 9:30am-6pm

Housed in a former train station, the Musée d'Orsay takes advantage of a cavernous main hall to showcase groundbreaking nineteenth century works of art in all the majesty they deserve. The enormous former platform of the station features the central sculpture gallery, where works by **Rodin, Pompon,** and others are highlighted as centerpieces of the enormous space. On its upper floors, the museum holds the largest collection of impressionist masterpieces in the world, bombarding you with so much **Degas, Monet, Manet, Renoir, Van Gogh** etc. etc. that you begin seeing the world in blurry, flowing brushstrokes. With all the clout of the **Louvre** but infinitely more manageable crowds, the Musée d'Orsay, might be the best all-encompassing art experience you can find in the city.

i Admission €14; tours €6 from 9:30am onward; last entry 5pm, Th 9pm; wheelchair accessible

OUTDOORS

PARC DES BUTTES CHAUMONT

1 Rue Botzaris, 19e ; 01 48 03 83 10; open daily summer 7am-10pm, winter 7am-8pm

Much of the 19th arrondissement feels like the most modern part of Paris—the buildings are tall, concrete, and brutalesque, and there is hardly a classic French façade in sight. But walk through the gates of the Parc des Buttes Chaumont and you'll find yourself instantly transported from industrial Paris to the heart of middle earth. The flat landscape turns into steep, rolling hills, tiny paths are hidden in the woods leading to caves and waterfalls, and a clifftop castle overlooks a picturesque lake in the middle of it all. On a weekend night, thousands of Parisians flock to picnic on the park, dispensing with the prudishness of the city's manicured gardens to play soccer on the grass, drink wine, and make out on sprawling picnic blankets. At sunset the hills promise hundreds of contrasting stunning views of the city. There's truly no better place in the city to while away a summer afternoon.

i Free; wheelchair accessible

BOIS DE BOULOGNE

16e; 01 53 92 82 82; en.parisinfo.com/paris-museum-monument/71494/Bois-de-Boulogne; open daily 24hr, not recommended after dark

Just a 15 minute walk from the **Avenue des Champs Élysées,** the Bois de Boulogne is a sprawling forest neighboring the heart of the city, containing beautiful lakes, winding forest paths, wide meadows, the **Roland Garros** tennis stadium (home of the French open), a zoo, and even a horse racing arena. At two and a half times the size of Central Park, the Bois de Boulogne would take weeks to understand fully, and even then you might be surprised to find what's hidden down a narrow path. Certain areas are hotspots for, um, solicitors, and you should be prepared to encounter every profession while out for a stroll. Just be sure to get out of the park before dark; while, like the rest of the Paris, the forest is fairly safe, it can be a center of illegal activity at night, and you'll want to hightail it out of there lest you wish to participate yourself.

i Free, can be accessed from points all alongside the Western edge of the city, wheelchair accessible

BOIS DE VINCENNES

46 Route de la Pyramide, 12e ; 01 49 57 15 15; vincennes-tourisme.fr; open daily 24hr, not recommended at night

In an area that the French kings once carefully guarded as their personal hunting grounds, the Bois de Vincennes is now a vast forest and public park, providing a seemingly endless area for exploration just on the outskirts of Paris. Along with the **Bois de Boulogne**, the park is one of the city's two "green lungs"—enormous natural areas that provide an outlet for rest and relaxation in the high-energy city. With manicured gardens, a near infinite amount of hiking trails, the old **Chateau de Vincennes,** and a horse racing track, among many other pockets of beauty, you could visit the Bois de Vincennes every day for years without discovering everything.

i Free; wheelchair accessible

JARDIN DU LUXEMBOURG

Rue de Médicis, Rue de Vaugirard, 6e ; open daily 7:30am-9:30pm

The Luxembourg Gardens stretch out in front of the Luxembourg Palace, once the home of King Henry IV's widow Marie de' Medici, but now the home of the French Senate. Hundreds of statues are scattered throughout the gardens along with tennis courts, greenhouses, cafés, ponds, and plenty of painters and writers. The greenery ranges from perfectly manicured in some areas to more natural in others, and there seems to be an unwritten code of conduct for when you can and cannot walk on the grass. A good rule of thumb: if it looks like that golf course your stepdad took you to once, you should probably find somewhere else to picnic.

i Free; wheelchair accessible; hours subject to change by season

TUILERIES GARDEN

113 Rue de Rivoli, 1e; open daily 7am-9pm

When the **Louvre** was still the royal palace, long before that large glass pyramid became the sight of countless gimmicky photos, the Tuileries were the gardens of kings, queens, courtiers, and the ever-present ducks. The gardens form the first section of the majestic runway stretching from the courtyard of the Louvre, down the **Champs-Élysée**, through the **Arc de Triomphe,** all the way to the skyscrapers of **La Défense.** While this main pathway can be packed, groves of perfectly shaped square trees on the side provide some seclusion and respite from the heat, dust, and tired tourists. Relax on the side of one of the many fountains or ogle at the countless valiant nude statues while you reflect on how preposterous it was that one family once made this manicured park their personal domain.

i Free; wheelchair accessible

FOOD

LE TEMPS DES CERISES ($$)

18-20 Rue de la Buttes aux Cailles, 13e; 01 45 89 69 48; open M-Sa 11:45am-2:30pm, 7pm-11:45 pm

Is ethical consumption possible under capitalism? Probably not. But Le Temps des Cerises might be as close as you can get at a Parisian restaurant. Founded in 1976 by a group of anarchist friends, this casual spot is run as a Société Cooperative Ouvrière [MIR1] de Production (SCOP), in which all decisions are made cooperatively and profits and ownership are equitably divided amongst the staff. Drawing inspiration from the Paris Commune of 1871, in which workers seized control of the city, the restaurant displays the official newspaper of the French Communist Party and relics from heavy industry on the wall. Keeping with the community spirit, the service is some of the friendliest in Paris and the traditional French fare is delicious and comfortable. Nestled in the old, artistic Buttes aux Cailles neighborhood, Le Temps des Cerises throws you joyfully into Paris's vibrant political history.

i Entrees from €12.50; outdoor seating available; wheelchair accessible

LA VIEILLE PIE ($$)

24 Rue Pajol, 18e; 09 83 39 04 39; lavielllepie.com; open M-F 8am-midnight, Sa-Su 9am-midnight

Missing home after a long day of taking selfies, buying cigarettes, trying to smoke them at cafés, and coughing? La Vieille Pie is the best spot in the city to devour timeless American fare—except the food makes a joke of anything you'd find in the States. With cozy wooden tables inside and pleasant outdoor dining, the restaurant is relaxing from the moment you sit down, and only becomes more so as the food arrives. Gargantuan portions of burgers, chicken sandwiches, and brunch specials all fill you up to the brim so pleasantly that you'll never want to bother with a puny escargot again. And although every dish is familiar, somehow each flavor is a scrumptious adventure. We must admit, France, you do American better.

i Burgers from €14; outdoor seating available; wheelchair accessible

BOLLYNAN ($)

12 Rue des Petits Carreaux Montorgueil, 2e; 01 45 08 40 51; open M-Sa 11am-11:30pm

Bollynan has all the charm of a common Parisian café: small outdoor tables spilling onto a lively pedestrian street, chic people smoking, a relaxed atmosphere. But unlike your typical spot, this restaurant features more flavors than "bread" and "slightly sweeter bread." It's known for its variety of a savory and sweet naan, as well as other flavorful staples of Indian cuisine. With each naan coming with a selection of four unique and delicious sauces, Bollynan might provide the most sumptuous array for €2 in the city. Add a juicy "naanwhich" onto that and you'll have an incredible, filling meal for €10. It's hard to imagine any cliché Parisian café doing better than that.

i Naan from €2, other dishes from €8; vegetarian options available; organic food available; wheelchair accessible

DES CRÊPES ET DES CAILLES ($)

13 Rue de la Butte aux Cailles, 13e; 01 45 81 68 69; open M-F noon-2pm and 7:30pm-11:30pm, Sa-Su 12:30pm-2:30pm and 7:30pm-11:30pm

Paris can be so diverse, eclectic, and international that sometimes you forget you're even in France. If you're missing some classic French charm, travel a few miles from the city center to the lively Buttes aux Cailles neighborhood and dig into some scrumptious traditional Breton crêpes. Themed after the original home of the delicious thin pancakes, the restaurant is decorated with marine artifacts from the region of Brittany, with ship portholes mounted on the walls and old nets and buoys hanging in a corner. A single cook fries up crepes on a griddle next to a take-out window, while a friendly server runs back and forth for table service. Sitting next to the cobbled street outside, it's hard to tell if you're in Paris or a tiny seaside village.

i Sweet crepes from €4, savory crepes from €8; wheelchair accessible

EL NOPAL ($)

3 Rue Eugene Varlin, 10e; 07 86 39 63 46; open Tu-Th noon-3pm and 7pm-10pm, F noon-3pm and 1-11pm, Sa 1-11pm, Su 1-9pm

El Nopal is literally a hole in the wall—you have to reach through a window to grab your burrito. Hidden amongst the Thai food joints, hip bars, and fashionable shopping of the Canal St. Martin neighborhood, El Nopal

VERSAILLES

In Versailles, the Chateau is everything. When King Louis XIV moved the royal court there in 1682, the small town had been nothing but the site of his father's small (relatively!) hunting lodge. Ok, his very large hunting lodge. Within a few years, the younger Louis built himself a staggeringly enormous palace at the site, constructing a town from scratch around his new home to house the thousands of lackeys he required to scrub the peasant off his boots. Built to follow the personal vision of one man and his close advisors, there's not a whole lot of spontaneity bursting out along Versailles' grand boulevards. Despite this lack of diversity in the town's streets, the many palaces boast a great diversity of different objects coated in gold. After escaping destruction during the French revolution, in which the cottage's owners were politely beheaded, the estates are now popular tourist attractions, ideal for spending a day away from the Paris. With the main chateau, Grand Trianon, Petit Trianon, stables, and gardens, it's near impossible to see everything at Versailles in a day. But if you keep your wits about you and avoid being squashed by a tour bus or trampled by the crowd rushing out of it, Versailles is the perfect place to gaze upon immense wealth and experience your politics drifting radically to the left.

The **Versailles Rive-Gauche train station** is just east of the **palace** itself and only a 10 minute walk from the palace gates. Inside the palace, the main attractions of the **royal apartments** and the **king's chambers,** are immediately to the right, although they should be even easier to find by following the vast herds of tourists. Enormous gardens stretch out to the west of the palace, bounded to the north by the two **Trianon estates.** Traveling east from the palace, you will reach the small town center where restaurants and souvenir shops abound, all revolving around the **Notre Dame de Versailles.**

GETTING THERE

From Paris, buy tickets at any automatic kiosk in the métro to Versailles-Château Rive Gauche. There are a number of lines that can be taken to get there, but the simplest is the RER line C. If leaving from other stations in Paris, you can shoot for stations in Versailles that are slightly further away like Versailles-Chantiers, or Versailles Rive-Droite.

GETTING AROUND

Versailles is small enough to traverse on foot, but there's also a mini train going between the main palace and the Trianon estate for €4.

Don't miss...

CHATEAU DE VERSAILLES

Place d'Armes, Versailles; en.chateauversailles.fr; open Tu-Su 9am-6:30pm

The château has played an important role in the history of both the French Monarchy and the rise of the Republic. Louis XVI and Marie-Antoinette were married here in 1770, just twenty-three years before their heads famously rolled off the guillotine during the French Revolution. After the palace was seized by revolutionaries in 1789, it lay empty for many years before being converted to a museum celebrating the glory of France. Today, visitors can walk through the chambers of Louis XIV, the State Apartments, the Gallery of Battles, and the Mesdames' Apartments. Once you see the blatant extravagance of the gold façades and chandeliers in the Hall of Mirrors, you will have no trouble imagining why the revolutionaries were so excited to decapitate their rulers.

i Admission €18, admission to Palace and full estate €20; recommended to buy online to avoid lines; limited wheelchair accessibility

Check out...

THE GALLERY OF GREAT BATTLES

Palace of Versailles; en.chateauversailles.fr; open Tu-Su 9am-6:30pm

As you wade through crowds in the State Apartments, you'll barely be able to make out the next room past the sea of selfie sticks. Push onward, brave one, for there is light and air on the other side of that army. The Gallery of Great Battles tends to be relatively less frequented than the surrounding rooms, and is without a doubt one of the most fascinating parts of the palace. Built by King Louis-Philippe as part of the museum to the glory of France, the gallery displays 33 enormous paintings of the most famous battles in French history, stretching all the way back to King Clovis's victory over the Alemanni in 496. It's fascinating to walk through the giant hall and watch how the armor and weapons changed over time. You'll come out thankful that you will (hopefully) never have to fight in any medieval battles.

i Get there by walking through the State Apartment; included in museum admission; wheelchair accessible

Grab a bite at...

APARTHÉ ($$)

1 bis Rue Sainte-Geneviève, Versailles; 01 30 21 26 57; open daily noon-2:30pm, 7pm-10:30pm

Although a long day poking around a château can be lots of fun, sometimes you become disgusted by the pretentiousness of it all and just want some good, hearty home cooking. Aparthé, located in the actual town of Versailles, far out of view of the palace itself, is the place to go. Serving traditional Brasserie fare like duck leg and steak frites, with a few innovations like a Tandoori chicken and a range of fish options, Aparthé reminds you why it doesn't take that much money to be happy. All the same, you're in the home of kings, so you'll have to pay a bit—there's just no need to bring your council of financial advisors.

i Entrees from €14.50; no wheelchair accessibility

or...

CREPARIE LA PLACE ($)

17 Rue Colbert, Versailles; 01 39 49 09 52; open M-F 10am-3pm and 7pm-11pm, Sa-Su 11am-11pm

Versailles is so huge that it can swallow you up, hold you for hours, and then finally spit you out once you've had the time to see 146 gold statues and made circles around the same fountain 16 times. It can be easy to get sucked into the expensive cafés and pondside restaurants, but getting a meal outside the chateau will not only save you money but also remind you that real people live in this town. Yeah, the one right next to that enormous castle. La Place is still within sight of the Chateau, so you can sit outside with a savory or sweet crêpe and continue to imagine yourself as Marie-Antoinette. Let them eat crêpes!

i Savory crepes from €8.50, sweet crepes from €4; salads from €14; outdoor seating available; no wheelchair accessibility

promises a hot and spicy respite from the refined elegance of Paris. Serving burritos (burrons), quesadillas, tacos, and other Mexican staples from its tiny take-out window, El Nopal is a welcome return to an American fast-food favorite. Don't expect a California Taco Truck though—the burritos will set you back ten euros—but grabbing one with a drink and picnicking on the nearby banks of the serene Canal St. Martin is well worth the Parisian price.
i Burritos from €10, 3 tacos from €9; take-out only; wheelchair accessible

HANOI ($$)

61 Rue Monsieur le Prince, 6e; 09 83 82 28 79; open daily 11am-2:30pm and 6pm-10:30pm

Pho anyone? Just because French cuisine is so hyped up doesn't mean you have to limit yourself to *confit au canard* and *steak frites* while you're in Paris. As the former imperial overlords of Vietnam, France attracts a significant number of its formerly oppressed subjects back, who have brought their delicious cooking with them. At Hanoi, grab some of the best Vietnamese food in the city, in a dark setting that highlights the whirlpool of flavors that spins in your mouth as you dig in.
i Meals from €10.80; limited wheelchair accessibility

LA CERISE SUR LA PIZZA ($$)

14 Rue Froissart, 3e ; 01 56 06 90 80; lacerisesurlapizza.fr; open daily noon-3:30pm, 7-11pm

Oh, pizza is Italian, you say? You want to focus your time in Paris on *lapin* and *escargot*? You won't deign to dip into a greasy pizza parlor in the world capital of *haute cuinise*? Soft ye, o dear friend, for your condescension is unwarranted—you can have your fresh, creative use of strange meats and dripping, cheesy delights all at once. At La Cerise sur Pizza, a huge menu of original pies invites you to marry your love of grease and cheese with your newfound tourist's appreciation of culinary innovation through rare topping options such as Merguez and Bresaola (traditional French sausages), and Scamorza (Italian cheese). But while the extravagant ingredients can be enticing, we'd recommend staying simple and ordering "Le Tomate Cerise," a simple cheese and pesto pizza with fresh, raw cherry tomatoes on top—probably the freshest thing you could put inside your body that includes the word "pizza" in the name.
i Pizzas from €10; take-out available; wheelchair accessible

LES CAVES DE BOURGOGNE ($$)

144 Rue Mouffetard, 5e ; 01 47 07 82 80; open daily 7am-2am

There's no better place for traditional French staples (*croque monsieur, confit de canard, charcuterie*). Mountains of delicious salads (especially the warm goat cheese and honey one) are surprisingly a bargain. Aside from the top-notch food, the ambiance is très français as well. Tables spill onto the lovely **Place Georges Moustaki**, overlooking a fountain hidden among tall flowers. In the summer, Cave La Bourgogne is packed with locals meeting for a drink or traditional French fare.
i Entrees €11, glass of wine from €4.50; outdoor seating available; limited wheelchair accessible

MIZNON ($)

22 Rue des Ecouffes, 4e; 01 4274 83 58; open M-Th noon-11pm, F noon-4pm, Su noon-11pm

This Israeli restaurant in the heart of **Le Marais** serves the best pita sandwiches around. Heck, they even have custom pita sandwich holders on the tables. But forget your average mystery-meat kebab—everything at Miznon screams fresh. Piles of raw vegetables decorate nearly every surface (unclear how this perishable interior design works), and you can watch the cooks slice up cucumbers, sprinkle cilantro, and grill lamb from your seat at the counter. Along with your sandwich, grab a whole ear of corn, a garlicky artichoke, or a giant head of charred cauliflower on the side. Miznon is the perfect spot for a quick lunch.
i Pita sandwiches from €8, vegetables from €3; vegan and vegetarian options available; no wheelchair accessibility

NIGHTLIFE

ROSA BONHEUR

Parc des Buttes Chaumont, 2 Allée de la Cascade, 19e; 01 42 00 00 45; rosabonheur.fr; open W-F noon-midnight, Sa-Su 10am-midnight

Pizza, beer, picnic tables, foosball, your mom's friends dancing, and a steamy summer evening: the timeless recipe for a good time. While you might remember these features from your elementary school's Parent-Teacher Organization "Spring Fling Beach Bash End-of-Year Cookout," Rosa Bonheur serves up all these classic ingredients on a gorgeous **Parc des Buttes Chaumont** hillside in a flavor that is wildly popular with Parisians of all ages. Sitting near the entrance of the city's most romantic park, the bar and restaurant plays classic music five nights a week on a casual dance floor and outdoor terrace draws about half the city on warm summer nights. On weekends you'll have to que up to squeeze into the tightly packed bar, but come on a weekday and enjoy some casual dancing, pizza, and foosball in a vibe you haven't felt since your dad's birthday cookout in 2009.

i Beer from €6, pizza from €12; foosball €1; no wheelchair accessibility

AMAZONAS RHUMERIE ÉSOTÉRIQUE

43 Rue de Lappe, 11e; 06 21 62 03 17; open Tu-Sa 6pm-2am

Pushing through the plastic vines and leaves hanging over the low entryway to Amazonas, you'll think you've stepped into the Brazilian rainforest. After stooping under the low ceilings and hanging creepers and reaching the tropically decorated bar, you might think you've come out in a Caribbean resort island. Turning around to see the plastic skulls, voodoo dolls, and menacing mannequins staring into the back of your head, you'll think you're in...we're not sure exactly. In a truly bizarre mixture of *Tarzan* and one of those unreasonably spooky cartoon movies, Amazonas creates probably the most unique atmosphere in Paris, all while serving eccentric rum cocktails that are the strongest thing you could try this side of Jack Sparrow's ship.

i Rum cocktails from €8.50; limited wheelchair accessibility

CANDELARIA

52 Rue de Saintonge, 3e ; 01 4274 41 28; open daily 6pm-2am

Upon first glance, Candelaria has the same basic features as any tiny taco place: greasy meat, fluorescent light, people covered in hot sauce. But walk past the row of taco toppings to an unmarked white door in the back, and you'll find yourself in a bumping bar full of Paris's "bobos" (read: hipsters). Once you get to the bar (it might take a while), a pick from one of Paris's most creative cocktail menus will be well worth the wait. Then you'll have everything you need for a fun night out: the lighting is dim, the people are buzzing, the aura is conspiratorial, and the Medieval stone walls are decorated with unidentifiable animal wool. So, while you're welcome to scarf down a few beef tongue tacos on your way in, let's just say there's more to try than what *meats* the eye.

i Cocktails from €12; tacos from €3.80; no wheelchair accessibility

LA MARINE

55Bis Quai de Valmy, 10e ; 01 42 39 69 81; lamarinecanalsaintmartin.com; open M-F 7:30am-2am, Sa-Su 8:30am-2am

After a few days strolling around Paris's narrow streets, even the harshest, most practical people will want to cast off their cufflinks and establish themselves as existentialist poets. There's no better place to try the role on than La Marine, where aspiring philosophers can nurse an espresso until the bar opens, then think over a glass of wine for the rest of the night, all while bathing in thought-inducing *Parisien* cigarette smoke.

With a wide outdoor terrace leaning towards the idyllic Canal St. Martin, **La Marine** is perhaps the most picturesque of the countless bar-restaurant-cafés scattered around Paris. Although the restaurant offers full service from noon to midnight, the beautiful atmosphere is perhaps best enjoyed over a glass of wine with friends, vigorously debating the implications of Camus's *The Myth of Sisyphus*.

***i** Glasses of wine from €4, cocktails from €9, mains €15; wheelchair accessible*

LITTLE RED DOOR

60 Rue Charlot, 3e; 01 42 71 19 32; www.lrdparis.com; open M-W 6pm-2am, Th-Sa 6pm-3am, Su 6pm-2am; last entry one hour before closing

Beer? Never heard of it. Wine? Nope. Vodka Red Bull? Well sure, but that's beside the point. At Little Red Door, nothing else flies. Your only choices are between their 11 extremely unique cocktails. On this year's menu, each is inspired by an untranslatable word from a different language and is presented with a beautiful full-page visual representation of its flavor. Pick whichever feeling speaks to you the most. You can check the description of each cocktail, but that doesn't exactly clear things up when the ingredients are innovations like fermented banana, panama wood, and green coffee. The entrance can be a bit tough to find at first because it's unmarked, but just look for the little red door, Sherlock.

***i** Cocktails from €13; no wheelchair accessible*

NIKI CLUB

10 Rue de Lappe, 11e; 01 48 06 52 67; open M 8pm-midnight,Tu-Su 8pm-5am

Do you know all the words to "I Love It" by Kanye West? Do you fancy yourself a "playa?" Do you have the international Fuccboi haircut? Are you in Paris for some reason? If the answer to any of the above questions is "Ye, Ye, Ye, [machine gun sounds]," then Niki Club is the place for you. In the heart of **La Bastille**'s row of rowdy bars, Niki Club imitates American Hip-Hop culture with a zest that few clubs in New York could match. Walk in to blasting Lil Yachty, "MTV Hits" playing on a TV, pulsing neon lights, and drunken Frenchmen waving their hands around over a bottle of Champagne with a firework sparkling above it. Bring twerking skills, readiness for a wild good time, and, if you're American, a sense of humor.

***i** Shots from €4, cocktails from €8, happy hour 8pm-10pm; limited wheelchair accessibility*

TOULON

Coverage by **Jessica Moore**

Toulon houses the infamous prison where Jean Valjean from *Les Miserables* spent 15 years as 24601. And although he may have not had the absolute best time in the city, his experience shouldn't deter you from visiting this historic and humble town. This famous city sits on the Mediterranean coast, and visitors from around the world come here annually by boat and train to see the sites the city offers, which often go overlooked by the average traveler through France. From mountainside views, to beach getaways, Toulon provides a fun reprieve for every traveler out there. Slip off your backpack in one of its home-style bed and breakfasts, and get ready to experience fishing, sailing, and the Mediterranean like never before. The arsenal here is to blame for the city's focus on the French Navy and the sea, and built in 1482 by Henry IV, this port city has been sinking ships and dropping anchors ever since.

ORIENTATION

Toulon is a smaller city in France marked by the **Mont Faron** to the northern end, and the **Port of Toulon** marking its southern edge. To the eastern most side of the city lies the **Plage du Mourillon** and the **Jardin d'Acclimatation.** The center of town is found along **Avenue du Général Leclerc** and **Boulevard de Strasbourg.** Here, you will find the historic **Old Port,** as well as important sites like the **Opéra House** and **Saint-Louis Cathedral.** Before the northern edge of the city at Mont Faron lies the **Gare de Toulon,** the city's train station, and before the port you will find great restaurants along the southern strip of **Quai Cronstadt,** as well as the nearby **Museum of the French Navy.**

ESSENTIALS

GETTING THERE

The local airport of Toulon, Toulon-Hyères International Airport, services daily flights from Paris, and offers limited and seasonal flights to other European Union countries. Located 18km outside of the city, you'll have to taxi into town, which costs anywhere from €20-€35. For this reason, we recommend flying into the nearby Marseille-Provence airport, and taking an hour and a half long train ride into the heart of the city. Toulon's train station, Centre-Ville Toulon, accepts tregional (TER) and high-speed (TGV) trains, and connects to stations all over the country. The train station is also right in the heart of town, making it the best way to get to the city. You can also access Toulon by ferry boats from Marseille and Nice, though you'll want to book in advance to avoid overcrowded and costly rides.

GETTING AROUND

The historic center and central square in Toulon are compact and easily traversed on foot. However, getting to top sights like Mont Faron and the nearby beaches requires other forms of transportation, as the walks cause blisters and sore feet. For this, taxis are the best way to get around, as they offer decently priced rides to the nearby attractions. Taxis Toulon are available daily 24hr, and can be reached at 04 94 93 51 51. A local bus service operates as part of a larger network that stretches outside of Toulon. This system, called Réseau Mistral, offers packages of 10 rides for €6.90, and can take you to top attractions throughout the city and nearby.

PRACTICAL INFORMATION

Tourist Offices: Office de Tourisme Provence Méditerranée-Bureau de Toulon (12 Place Louis Blanc; 04 94 18 53 00; www.toulontourisme.com; open M 9am-6pm, Tu 10am-6pm, W-Sa 9am-6pm, Su 9am-1pm).

Banks/ATMs/Currency Exchange: Find plenty of banks and ATMs in downtown Toulon. Here's one: CIC Banque Privée Toulon (48 Boulevard de Strasbourg; 04 94 11 59 10; www.cicbanqueprivee.com; open M-Th 8:30am-12:15pm and 1:45pm-5:45pm, F 8:30am-12:15pm and 1:45pm-5pm).

Post Offices: Here is a conveniently located post office: La Poste (Rue Prosper Ferrero; www.laposte.fr; open M-Tu 8:30am-6pm, W 8:30am-12:30pm and 1:30pm-5:30pm, Th 8:30am-12:30pm and 1:30pm-6pm, F 8:30am-6pm, Sa 8:30am-12pm).

Internet: The tourist office features free Wi-Fi, as well as other cafés and restaurants throughout the city.

BGLTQ+ Resources: www.gay-provence.org has tips on accomodations, restaurants, events and nightlife in the region.

EMERGENCY INFORMATION

Emergency Number: 112.

Police: You can contact the Toulon police for emergency and non-emergency situations (239 Rue Henri Poincaré; 04 98 03 24 00; open daily 24hr).

US Embassy: The closest US Embassy is in the nearby city of Marseille, a 1.5hr train ride away (12 Bd. Paul Peytral; 04 91 55 09 47; fr.usembassy.gov/embassy-consulates/marseille; open M-F 9am-noon and 2pm-5pm).

Rape Crisis Center: Although there is no official Rape Crisis Center in Toulon, the Rape Crisis Network in Europe is available to help travelers all over Europe (01 45 88 19 00; www.inavem.org).

Hospitals: There is one primary hospital in Toulon:

- Hospital Instruction Of Armées Sainte-Anne (2 Boulevard Sainte-Anne; 04 83 16 20 10; open daily 24hr).

Pharmacies: Pharmacies can be found throughout the city and are denoted with a green cross outside their door. If the cross is lit up, the store is most likely open.

- Pharmacy Lafayette du Théâtre (502 Rue Jean Jaurès; 04 94 92 21 43; open M-F 8:30am-7:30pm and Sa 8:30am-7pm).
- Pharmacy Champs De Mars (51 Avenue Colonel Fabien; 04 94 41 57 88; open M-F 8am-6pm).

SIGHTS

CULTURE

OLD TOWN

Vieux Ville; open daily 24hr

No, Old Town is not the name for a retirement home in Toulon where many old grandmothers sit around knitting and gossiping about the pool boy. Perhaps even more excitingly, Old Town is the historic center of the city. Here you'll find incredible eateries, shopping centers, and historic landmarks. The cobbled streets all lead to an incredible statue and fountain in the Old Town Square. While those relentless summer days have you daydreaming of jumping in for a quick splash, we advise against fountain floundering (it's embarrassing, pull yourself together!). You'll find the Old Town doesn't seem too old upon visiting—the result of some horrific bombings in Toulon during WWII. But that doesn't stop this city center from feeling historic and rich in cultural value, much like a real retirement home.

i Free; wheelchair accessible

OPÉRA DE TOULON

Bvd. de Strasbourg; 04 94 92 70 78; www.operadetoulon.fr; open M-F 10am-12:30pm and 2pm-5:30pm

The amount of drama you'll find at the Opera is enough to make any entrepreneuring traveler consider pitching a new reality TV series called "The Real Housewives of the Opera." This place features so much red tiling and ceiling drapes you'll think you walked into a color-blind person's nightmares. With high ceilings, beautiful archways, and marble stairs, you must see this building during your visit to Toulon. Built in 1862, the Toulon opera house holds the title as the second-largest opera house in all of France. Today, the building stands as a national historic monument, showing a limited series of operatic productions each year.

i Free to visit; limited wheelchair access

LANDMARKS

MONT FARON

Bld. Amiral Vence; 04 94 18 53 00; open daily 24hr

This giant mountain stands nearly 580m high, and looms over the city of Toulon below it. At its highest peak, you'll find a wide array of activities, from a zoo to a café, to a memorial dedicated to the 1944 Allied landings in Provence. An old-timey cable car saves visitors from another excruciatingly steep mountain hike, and operates daily to lift visitors up and down this giant beast of a natural wonder. Spend a few perfect hours at Mont Faron, or a languorous, revitalizing day. A natural escape from the bustling city below it, Mount Faron offers a unique experience on the Mediterranean that is often only marked by beaches.

i Cable car €7.30 each way; limited wheelchair accessibility

TOULON HARBOR

924 Corniche Bonaparte; 04 94 94 84 72; open Tu-Su 10am-noon and 2pm-6pm

Boats, cruise ships, and yachts, oh my! The Toulon Harbor teems with money and lavishness. This boat yard houses some of the largest ships docked in the Mediterraanean, short of those in

Cannes. Here, you'll truly see what makes Toulon a port city, as a sea of ships span out on the actual sealine in front of you. The streets lining the harbor brim full of shops, restaurants, and even museums, attracting tourists from all over Europe. Spend an afternoon here sitting by the docks, sipping a Spritz, and fantasizing about riding your own boat to Toulon and parking it in the luxurious port in front of you.

i Free; wheelchair accessible

MUSEUMS

HOTEL DES ARTS (MEDITERRANEAN CENTER OF ART)

236 Bld. Général Leclerc; 04 83 95 18 40; www.hda.var.fr; open Tu-Su 10am-6pm

One thing is certain, a trip to the Mediterranean Center of Art will trap even the closest of friend groups into heated arguments about whether or not photography is just as intense an art form as the works of Da Vinci or Picasso. This art museum in the center of Toulon's **Old Town** features extremely contemporary art (read: a bit weird). In this white-walled, entirely marble museum, you can explore high-contrast, bright exhibits. On our visit, the display was incredibly nostalgia-inducing, presenting America in the 1980s. But, along with their rotating exhibits, the Mediterranean Center of Arts curates education-based rooms with plenty of books to read and comfy chairs to lounge in, along with one totally blacked-out theater viewing room. Just be careful not to bump into anything too expensive!

i Free; last entry 30min. before closing; limited wheelchair accessibility

MUSEUM OF THE FRENCH NAVY

Place Monsenergue; 04 22 42 02 01; www.musee-marine.fr/toulon; open W-M 10am-6pm

Aye, Aye Captain! Sure, working for the French Navy doesn't seem nearly as fun at this museum as our mornings chowing down on Captain Crunch and watching Spongebob Squarepants. But, this museum offers a real and exciting insight into the history of the **French Navy.** The museum sits right on the **Port of Toulon,** and right outside you can see French Navy Seamen (and women!) doing the exact jobs the museum depicts from the earliest centuries of seamanship.

i Free; audio guides in five languages available; last entry is at 5:15pm; wheelchair accessible

OUTDOORS

JARDIN D'ACCLIMATATION DU MOURILLON

Littoral Frédéric Mistral; open daily 9am-7pm

Unfortunately, Leslie Knope would be ashamed by what seems to pass as a garden here in Toulon. This 'garden' is much less of a place to stop and smell the roses, and much more of one to take in palm trees and an expanse of green grass. Now, don't get us wrong, even though flowers don't teem in this garden, it's still the perfect place to take a picnic, do some morning yoga, or even to sunbathe. After weeks and weeks in massive French cities without green spaces, the Jardin d'Acclimatation du Mourillon proves that grass can, indeed, grow in France, and definitely sprouts greener than the city that sits on the other side of it.

i Free; wheelchair accessible

PLAGES DU MOURILLON

Plage du Mourillon; open daily 24hr

Remember that waterpark from your childhood that kept a little protected 'beach' for the kiddos? This is that beach. This small, protected cove offers a beach perfect for swimming, with few waves and a rock-less shore. The sandy, tan beach spreads out for a few kilometers, and on it you'll find brightly colored umbrellas, large beach towels, and little shops selling everything from crêpes and icecream to paddle board rentals. A relaxing, family-oriented beach, this place is perfect for stretching out to build your summer tan, opening up that book that's been sitting in the bottom of your backpack, or just watching the world go by as dogs and small kids run around you.

i Free; limited wheelchair access

FOOD

MAMAN ($$)

2 bis Rue Baudin; 07 62 32 39 65; open M-F noon-3pm

Oh, there's a reason why the name for Maman sounds suspiciously like "My Man!" This food truly tastes like the kind that'd make you want to pat your friend on the back and congratulate them for picking such a good spot to eat. A hidden gem, Maman feels like stumbling into someone's home, but once inside, its super chic style will prove you're in a very hip spot for lunch. This place serves up healthy food choices, catering to everyone from the gluten-free to the vegan among you. With a backdrop of blue tiles, clean, white walls, and a modern touch, Maman will draw you back again and again during your stay in Toulon.

i Three course meal €12; vegetarian, vegan, and gluten-free options available; wheelchair accessible

FEEL FOOD TOULON ($$)

8 Rue du Bon Pasteur; 06 43 55 71 86; open Tu-Sa 10am-midnight

Visitors to Toulon really feel the food at Feel Food Toulon. This place puts the 'hidden' in hidden gem, as it sits on a small, narrow alley that pedestrians frequently miss during their time in Toulon. Serving up feel-good foods that both satiate taste buds and keep waistlines happy, Feel Food Toulon prides itself on churning out tasty, healthy options, sure to fill the daily fruits and veggies requirement for any weary traveler. If you're unsure of what to try here, give their freshly-squeezed grapefruit juice and yogurt parfaits a spin. And, while you're at it, take some of these delicious eats back to the hostel with their to-go option!

i Plates from €12; vegetarian and vegan options available; wheelchair accessible

LE TERMINUS ($$)

7 Boulevard de Tessé; 04 94 92 21 04; open daily 7am-midnight

There's a time machine on the corner of **Boulevard de Tessé**. Be prepared to travel back to 1940's New York City at Le Terminus, which seems to be open nearly 24/7. Centered right outside the train station, Le Terminus welcomes visitors with a menu that shows no belief in the idea that breakfast or lunch can only be served during a certain time of day. With full, floor-to-ceiling windows, red and white checkered tablecloths, and a full red bar complete with neon signage, you're sure to be a little surprised by what may very well be the only true diner in France.

i Breakfast from €5, lunch from €10; vegetarian options available; wheelchair accessible

NIGHTLIFE

CICADA GIN DE PROVENCE

4 Place Gambetta; 09 86 70 47 88; www.cicadagin.com; open Tu-Sa 10am-12:30pm and 3pm-6:30pm

Cicada Gin de Provence lets you know two things right when you walk in the door: they love cicadas, and they serve a hell of a lot of gin. At this luxury bar, explore the gin-making process and experience the artistry that goes into crafting a bottle of this well-known alcohol. Surprisingly, gin isn't as simple as it seems. This opulent, grandiose bar also serves incredible cocktails, all of which feature gin in one way or another and prove that the gin and tonic is so last season. If that's not enough, you can come to Cicada just to consume enough gin to defeat an entire Russian army.

i Cocktails from €10; wheelchair accessible

FRANCE ESSENTIALS

VISAS

As a member of the European Union, France allows US Citizens to stay in the country for up to 90 days without requiring a visa.

MONEY

As with most European Union countries, France uses the euro.

Credit/Debit Cards: Travelers using American Express or Discover should be wary, as many French vendors do not accept these cards, though all other card carriers are generally accepted. In addition, most vendors require a minimum purchase of €15-€20 in order to pay by card. Thus, you'll most likely want to carry at least a small amount of cash with you at all times. To do so, there are many ATMs around the country, however, you will likely face withdrawal fees on top of international charges based on your specific card for taking cash out.

Tipping: Across the country, a service charge, known as a "service compris" is added to your bill in all bars and restaurants. However, some do choose to leave an additional tip on top of this to note exceptional service (around €1-€3). In upscale restaurants, it is not uncommon to leave a 5% tip, and for taxi service, it is a good gesture to tip up to 10%.

SAFETY AND HEALTH

Drugs and Alcohol: The drinking age for wine and beer in France is 16, with all alcohol appropriate for those 18 and up. To be able to buy alcohol in stores, you must be 18. There are no laws restricting open containers, however, leaving trash in the streets or engaging in disorderly conduct is generally frowned upon and may get you arrested. For driving, the legal blood-alcohol level is 0.05%, which is lower than that of the US, the UK, and Australia. Drugs of all kinds (other than prescription and over-the-counter) are strictly prohibited in France. Possession of marijuana, for example, can lead to substantial jail time or a hefty fine. All other prescription or over-the-counter drugs are bought in pharmacies.

Local Laws and Police: The French have two national police brigades, the first operate mostly in urban areas, including Paris, and is referred to as the Police Nationale. The second national group is the Gendarmerie, and they operate in rural cities with populations less than 23,000. Police municipale are the local police in France, and they are overseen by the mayor of their respective cities. Thus, they may or may not be armed based on the desires of the city's mayor.

Terrorism: The US Embassy has ranked France as a Level 2 country when it comes to terroristic threat, being one where you should exercise increased caution upon travelling. Recent attacks in the past few years across Paris and in other cities like Strasbourg show that France is susceptible to terroristic threats. Expect thorough luggage checks at airports and avoid packing items that may be deemed threatening, such as sharp objects.

GERMANY

If any country could pull off a one-man show, it's Germany. It already has experience being front and center on some of the world's grandest stages, having achieved childhood fame during its time as the Holy Roman Empire. Fast forward a few hundred years and it decided to try its hand in a new role as the nexus of the Prussian Empire. During this time, Germany learned to use some of its success to enjoy the finer things in life by fostering its intellectual side. Poetry, literature, and philosophy became some of Germany's favorite pastimes, and it picked up a side gig producing great thinkers and composers such as Immanuel Kant and Beethoven.

In 1871, Germany officially became a nation and settled into tranquility for a number of decades before donning its war-torn soldier cap. Unfortunately, Germany didn't play to its audience. The atrocious events of World War I and World War II—for which Germany was largely responsible—weren't received well by the rest of the world, hence ending Germany's career as Europe's golden child for the time being. After the wars, having lived in the limelight for so long, the Germans took a step back to appreciate some of the simpler things in life: beer, sausage, football, and fast cars. Today, you'll find Germany to be a young, vibrant, and multicultural country, with its own rising stars. The diverse personalities of Berlin, Hamburg, Cologne, Frankfurt, Potsdam, and Munich draw millions each year.

BERLIN

Coverage by **Megan Galbreath**

Berlin is the cool mom. You know, the one who tells you that your purple hair looks good and buys you all of Nirvana's old albums. She doesn't set a curfew, but always waits up with a late-night snack, and often a story or two from her own glory days. Trust us, she's been around the block. A city that was once literally divided in half, Berlin's tumultuous history gives rise to a culture with a "live in the moment" mentality. The people here party hard, eat cheap, delicious food, then party harder. But don't let that tough exterior fool you. Berlin is really a softie at heart with a sweet spot for history and the (street) arts. Fancy visiting a palace or a WWII museum? You might be able to find one or two or five on Museum Island alone. Looking for a street food or music festival? Sorry, those only happen a couple times a week. Can't decide between a power day of sightseeing or a leisurely day in the park? Good news: the city center offers both. If you're looking for a place that knows how to pull off that "sophisticated and cultured by day, hardcore punk by night" aesthetic, Berlin is it.

ORIENTATION

With such a long history, Berlin sports an impressive array of neighborhoods, each with their own story to share. In the southeast corner of Berlin lies the punk, artsy neighborhood of **Friedrichshain**, home to the gritty, industrial, and rebellious clubbing scene for which Berlin is infamous. Head west from Friedrichshain and cross the **Spree River** to encounter **Kreuzeberg**, Berlin's boho golden child, whose trendy bars and elite food scene dominate the south. Out west, find **Charlottenburg:** clean cut and tame, with shops, theaters, and cafés that cater to a more relaxed pace of life. Once the outcast, the up-and-coming **Wedding** district in the northwest is gaining popularity for its diverse, hipster culture and cheap eats. And finally, at the center of it all lies **Mitte**—our popular, rich, cultured friend who boasts many of the city's landmarks and museums. There's more to each neighborhood than meets the eye, and with enough time, you'll see the quirks and flairs that make them unforgettable.

ESSENTIALS

GETTING THERE

Berlin is serviced by two international airports: Tegel Airport, located in northwest Berlin is the larger and busier of the two, while Schönefeld Airport in the south is a common destination for smaller, budget airlines. International and domestic trains run through Central Station (Hauptbanhof). Prices vary based on booking date. National and international buses typically serve as the most economical option, and are handled at the Central Bus Station (ZOB) in Charlottenburg, or Ostbahnhof Bus Station, located east of Alexanderplatz.

GETTING AROUND

The public transportation network (BVG) is efficient, affordable, and extensive, involving the U-bahn (underground trains), S-bahn (above-ground trains), trams, metrotrams, and buses. An AB ticket services central Berlin to the city boundary, while an ABC ticket provides access to the surrounding areas and Potsdam. One-way tickets are good for two hours after purchase (AB €2.80, ABC €3.40), while daily and weekly tickets provide unlimited access. All tickets must be validated before use. The BVG is often patrolled by plainclothes policemen, and being caught with an expired ticket or without a validated ticket carries a penalty fee of €60. Berlin is also walker and biker-friendly.

PRACTICAL INFORMATION

Tourist Offices: Tourist offices are located at both Tegel Airport and Schönefeld Airport, as well as throughout the city.

- Brandenburg Gate (Pariser Platz; 030 250025; open daily Apr-Oct 9:30am-7pm, Nov-Mar 9:30am-6pm).
- Alexanderplatz (Hotel Park Inn Lobby, Alexanderplatz 7; 030 250025; open M-Sa 7am-9pm, Su 8am-6pm).

Banks/ATMs/Currency Exchange: Expect to use cash at most bars, clubs, and smaller shops and cafés, particularly those located outside of the city center. The best exchange rates are typically found by withdrawing funds from an ATM, rather than at currency exchange centers. Bank of America cardholders can avoid international ATM access fees by withdrawing funds at Deutsche Bank, since both banks are members of the Global ATM Alliance.

- Deutsche Bank (Friedrichstraße 181; 30 4606110; open M-F 10am-7pm, Sa 10am-6pm).

Post Offices: Post offices can be throughout the city. To find one, visit www.deutschepost.de/en.

- Deutsche Post (Frankfurter Allee 1; 228 4333112; open M-F 9am-1pm, 2-6pm, Sa 9am-1pm).

Public Restrooms: Public restrooms (marked as Toilette or WC) are not common. In some places, including train stations, expect to see an attendant or coin-operated turnstile collecting fees. In the few cases where an attendant is present but a fee is not required, it is customary to tip the attendant (around €0.50).

Internet: Free Wi-Fi is available at many cafés and museums, in addition to airports, train stations, and libraries. In 2016, the "Free Wifi Berlin" project was launched, offering 650 Wi-Fi hotspots throughout the city. Visit www.berlin.de/en/wifi to find the one nearest you.

BGLTQ+ Resources: Berlin is a colorful and tolerant city, celebrating Pride Week and other queer events and festivals throughout the year. Take advantage of the rich nightlife, embrace the queer districts, and retire for the night at one of the pink pillow Berlin Collection hotels, which actively support the Berlin LGBTQ+ community. Visit a Berlin Tourist Office for a flyer, map, and magazine outlining all queer neighborhoods and upcoming events.

EMERGENCY INFORMATION

Emergency Number: 112.

Police: 110; Der Polizeipräsident in Berlin (Platz der Luftbrücke 6; 030 46640; open daily 7am-7pm).

US Embassy: The only US Embassy in Germany is located in Berlin (Pariser Platz 2; 30 83050; e.usembassy.gov; open M-F 8:30am-5:30pm).

Rape Crisis Center: LARA offers anonymous counseling for women, girls, and transgender people over the age of 14 (Fuggerstr. 19; 030 2168888; www.lara-berlin.de; open M-F 9am-6pm). The Violence Against Women hotline also provides daily 24hr confidential support (00498000 116016).

Hospitals: DRK Klinken Berlin Mitte (Drontheimer Str. 39-40; 30 30356000; open daily 24hr).

Pharmacies: As a general rule, pharmacies (or apotheken) are open M-Sa from 9am-6pm. That said, each Berlin neighborhood is serviced by one pharmacy that is open daily 24hr in case of emergencies. The website www.movingto-berlin.com/pharmacies-in-Berlin provides a useful map to find them. We have listed one of many locations.

- Rossmann (Leipziger Str. 44; 30 20214721; rossmann.de; open M-Sa 8am-8pm).

SIGHTS

CULTURE

VABALI SPA

Seydlitzstr. 6; 30 9114860; www.vabali.de; open daily 9am-midnight

A morning at Vabali Spa can be summed up by two simple words: pure bliss. Looking for a calming and rejuvenating respite from endless sightseeing and non-stop museum hopping? Or maybe a spot to stop and rest those weary traveling feet? Vabali Spa has you covered (well, not covered, technically). Here, you can relax sans stress, sans electronics, sans

textiles...cleansing the toxins from your body at up to 200° F. The sheer silence of the resort means that it's just you and your thoughts for the next few hours—thoughts like, "This is the human equivalent of slowly roasting a Thanksgiving turkey." Maybe it's the water loss, maybe it's the experience of truly living, but you'll walk out of Vabali Spa feeling lighter than ever.
i Tickets 2hr €21.50, 4hr €28.50

HACKESCHEN HÖFE

Rosenthaler Str. 40-41; 30 28098010; hackeschehoefe.com; courtyard open daily 24hr, shop and café hours vary

Berlin has its very own secret garden? Actually, it has eight secret gardens. The network of hidden grottos is located in Mitte, just a stone's throw from **Museum Island** (disclaimer: throwing stones in downtown Berlin is not advised). Once the site of the historical **Scheunenviertel** (Barn Quarter), the art nouveau complex is now most revered as a symbol for the vibrant urban renewal of post-unification Berlin. Wandering through the maze of trinket shops, candy stores, art galleries, and boutiques feels a bit like a fairy tale. What doesn't feel like a fairy tale: arriving at 10am ready to shop 'til we drop, only to discover that most stores don't open until 11:30am.
i Free; wheelchair accessible

KINO BABYLON

Rosa-Luxemburg-Str. 30; 30 2425969; babylonberlin.eu; visit website for showtimes

Kino Babylon is one of Berlin's premier film houses, having survived a few trips through the ringer. The cinema opened in 1929 and escaped WWII largely unscathed. It later became a center of cultural events for East Berliners during the DDR regime. Today, moviegoers can continue to enjoy screenings in the original fashion: free silent film viewings are accompanied by a live organ at midnight on Saturdays. Cult classics, foreign language films, shorts, and documentaries that all often feature guest appearances from the filmmakers themselves. Keep a lookout for their legendary film festivals and series, like the Berlin International Film Festival in February.
i Tickets from €7; wheelchair accessible

MAUERPARK

Entrance at the corner of Bernauer Str. & Eberswalder Str.; park open daily 24hr, flea market open Sun 9am-6pm

If you didn't participate in the Sunday afternoon karaoke session at Mauerpark, did you even go to Berlin? Every Sunday, the venue transforms from a rundown neighborhood park into a vibrant flea market, riddled with sunbathers, family barbecues, makeshift dance parties, and of course, the amphitheater's famed karaokeville. Wandering through the stalls, you're bound to come across the traditional apparel, jewelry, old record, and household goods common to other flea markets. Mauerpark's true flavor comes from stands that offer things like sunglass tinting lessons, "edible wine," and "Mr. Pink's famous chocolate balls." Visitors are advised to come hungry so that they can take advantage of cheap eats like currywurst, pitas, roasted corn-on-the-cob, crepes, and ice-cream smothered waffles. Do not miss the Berlin Wall remnants, where graffiti artists are constantly retagging over previous street art pieces in the true Berliner fashion.
i Free; restrooms €0.50; first aid station available; karaoke begins at 3pm

LANDMARKS

EAST SIDE GALLERY

Mühlenstraße 47-80; 030 467986623; www.eastsidegalleryberlin.de; open daily 24hr

It's impressive, inspirational, and innovative. In the spring of 1990, over 100 artists redecorated this portion of the **Berlin Wall** with vibrant colors and brilliant images, preserving it from further destruction. The 1.3km stretch along the **Spree River** is probably the most tourist-heavy spot in East Berlin, but for good reason. Each mural carries a subtle–or often, not-so-subtle–political statement or view on humanity, reminding us that the world is bends at our fingertips. Depending on your camera's battery life (and the number of people attempting to recreate Dmitri Vrubel's Fraternal Kiss), the walk along the wall can take anywhere from 30 minutes to several hours.

i Free; guided history (1hr) and art tours (1.5hr) offered Sa at 10:30am and 11am (€3.50, reduced €2.50, students free), reservations required; wheelchair accessible

BERLINER DOM

Am Lustgarten; 30 20269136; www.berlinerdom.de/en; open Apr-Sept M-Sa 9am-8pm, Su noon-8pm, Oct-Mar M-Sa 9am-7pm, Su noon-7pm

265, 266, 267...made it! Climbing to the viewing deck for the Berliner Dom may have you wishing you had skipped that fourth cookie, but boy is it worth it. Back on sturdy ground, the main nave rivals the panoramic beauty with a sparkling marble and onyx altar, grandiose mosaics, and elaborate carvings. Of note are the ornate golden sarcophagi for Sophie Charlotte and King Friedrich I, tributes certainly fitting of a queen and king. Memorials to the rest of the Hohenzollern dynasty can be found in the crypt below. Architecture aficionados shouldn't leave without first visiting the **Berliner Dom Museum,** which features a small exhibit of replicas, floor plans, and statues from the cathedral's younger years.

i Admission €7, reduced €5, audio guide €4; last entry 1hr before closing; limited wheelchair accessibilty

BRANDENBURG GATE

Pariser Pl.; open daily 24hr

Paris may have the Arc de Triomphe, but Berlin has the Brandenburg Gate. Constructed in the late 1700s, this landmark has seen it all, from Napoleon's conquest of Berlin to the construction and subsequent fall of the Berlin Wall. Today, it serves as a symbol for the reunification of Germany, where one can stand at its base and regally survey **Pariser Platz,** just like the famed Quadriga sculpture that crowns the gate. It also acts as a "gateway" to notable landmarks and museums found in central Berlin: the **Reichstag** lies north and **Tiergarten Park** begins to the west. Visiting in the early morning or late evening helps avoid the crowds—sounds like a double win since you'll catch the gate during golden hour. Bonus points to any traveler who finds an "Instagram Boyfriend™" to snap their picture, like we did.

i Free; wheelchair accessible; private tours can be booked

CHARLOTTENBURG PALACE

Spandauer Damm 20-24; 033 19694200; www.spsg.de/en/palaces-gardens/object/charlottenburg-palace-old-palace; open Apr-Oct Tu-Su 10am-5:30pm, Nov-Mar Tu-Su 10am-4:30pm

Sophie Charlotte must have been a great hostess. The Prussian queen loved art and music; the delicate details found throughout her palace—including intricate SC monograms engraved in the ceiling corners and brightly-colored gilded flowers in the crown molding—hint at the beauty and wealth of the Hohenzollern rulers. Although WWII bombing damaged the palace, much of its former grace has been restored. This is particularly evident in the magnificent **Porcelain Cabinet,** where hundreds of flawless blue and white china pieces line the walls, matching the blue and white-tiled fireplaces present in the queen's chambers. Do not miss the adjoining **Charlottenburg Palace Gardens,** which combine baroque and English landscaping to create a serene spot amongst the towering trees and placid ponds.

i Palace admission €12, reduced €8; free audio guide; last entry 30min before closing; wheelchair accessible with assistance

MUSEUMS

ALTES MUSEUM

Am Lustgarten, Museum Island; 030 266424242; www.smb.museum/en/museums-institutions/altes-museum; Tu-W 10am-6pm, Th 10am-8pm, F-Su 10am-6pm

We thought our grandmother housed an impressive art collection, until we saw the Apulian luxury vase cabinet at The Altes Museum. Sorry Grandma, but there is no way that the clay pot we made in first grade can compete with intricate vases that date to 340 BCE. We should have guessed that the ancient sculptures, remarkable mummy portraits, and flawless bronze statuettes would upstage our young art career, given that the building's gorgeous Neoclassical architecture also attempts to outshine the nearby **Berliner Dom.** It seems impossible that the Greek, Etruscan, and Roman antiquities found inside exist in almost pristine condition—we can only hope to look that good when we are 6,000 years old! Yet, despite the age of the treasures inside, The Altes Museum knows how to stay young and hip—just check out the phallic exhibit in the Garden of Delights to know what we mean.

i Admission €10, reduced €5; last entry 30min. before closing; wheelchair accessible

BERLINISCHE GALERIE

Alte Jakobstraße 124-128; 30 78902600; www.berlinischegalerie.de; open W-M 10am-6pm

The immersive experience makes the Berlinische Galerie feel almost like a children's museum—a really sophisticated, innovative, high-end children's museum. The gallery exclusively exhibits modern art, photography, and architecture from Berlin-based artists. Yet, somehow curators find ways to push the bounds of this narrow perspective. In one room, we had stepped into an artificial but stormy downpour. In another, venture into a sculptural representation of Berlin's raw clubbing character. The Berlinische Galerie isn't your stereotypical, cut and dry, white-walled, long-halled art museum. Our favorite feature? An entire collection accessible to the blind and vision impaired. Here, visitors are encouraged to have tactile interaction with 3D representations of the museum's most famous works. Finally, a museum where you can touch the artwork!

i Admission €10, reduced €7; wheelchair accessible

HAMBURGER BAHNHOF

Invalidenstr. 50-51; 30 266424242; www.smb.museum/en/museums-institutions/hamburger-bahnhof; open Tu-W 10am-6pm, Th 10am-8pm, F 10am-6pm, Sa-Su 11am-6pm

Hamburger Bahnhof is one of the first modern art museums we visit where we don't think: "Did we just walk into a kindergarten classroom?" The museum's white walls and exposed concrete floor fit the artwork's minimalist aesthetic, allowing vibrant colors and neon lights to pop—especially the black light in the corner that we accidentally mistook for the lone soul leftover from Saturday night's rave. It takes time to wander through the hangar-sized showcase rooms, so visit in the evenings to avoid the large crowds. Installations border from mesmerizing (infinity mirror hallways) to unsettling (chainsaw sounds coming from a dark room in the corner), and it helps to arrive with your thinking cap on so you can fully absorb the meaning of felt draped over a steel pole.

i Admission €14, reduced €7; guided tours in English Sa-Su at noon; limited wheelchair accessibility

MEMORIAL TO THE MURDERED JEWS OF EUROPE

Cora-Berliner-Str. 1; 030 26394336; www.stiftung-denkmal.de/en/memorials/the-memorial-to-the-murdered-jews-of-europe; memorial open daily 24hr; information center open Apr-Sept Tu-Su 10am-8pm, Oct-Mar Tu-Su 10am-7pm

Berlin intentionally constructed this monument with visibility in mind and we agree that this humbling memorial cannot be missed. Over 2,700 concrete blocks rise almost poetically toward the sky in the aboveground field, bordered by **Pariser Platz** to the north and **Potsdamer Platz** to the south. Meandering through row after row of imposing, smooth pillars can bring about a somber air—first time you understand what it truly means to hear silence. The underground information center, which contains a permanent exhibition to commemorate the six million Jewish victims of the Holocaust, completes the journey. A focus on personal stories and documents allows for a poetic and quiet moment of reflection, providing a change of pace from the typical dynamic and vibrant nature of the city.

i Free but donations accepted; audio guide €3; free guided tour in English Sa 3pm; last museum entry 45 minutes before closing; wheelchair accessible

OUTDOORS

BADESCHIFF

Eichenstr. 4; 30 5332030; www.arena.berlin/en/location/badeschiff/; pool open daily 8am-10pm, beach open 8am-11pm in good weather

Waves from passing boats intermittently rock the floating pier. Adventurous sunbathers take paddle boards out on the river. Children shriek over the sound of Bobby McFerrin's "Don't Worry Be Happy." We have to wonder—is it even possible to feel something besides pure joy as you dive into the refreshing waters of the shockingly blue pool or grab a cocktail from the bar at this makeshift riverside beach? On the weekends, Badeschiff fills to capacity with beachgoers looking to escape city life, and there is often a wait to get in by noon. For a more relaxing tanning session, visit during the week.

i Admission €6.50, reduced €3.50; towel and blanket rental ea. €5 deposit, €2 fee; locker rental €5 key deposit, €1 fee; beer from €3.5, mixed drinks from €6, food from €4; vegan and vegetarian options available; cash only

TIERGARTEN PARK

Straße des 17. Juni; open daily 24hr

These former royal hunting grounds boast nearly 519 acres of greenery in the heart of Berlin, meaning that you literally cannot miss them. On the weekends, locals gather from all over the city for friendly competitions of spikeball, relaxing picnics in the shade, and even nude yoga—yes, you read that correctly. Those more inclined to remain clothed can rent a rowboat on the **Neuer See,** take a leisurely bike ride down one of the graveled paths, or start a soccer game in the **English Garden.** For the young at heart, relive your childhood at the **Berlin Zoo,** located at the southwest end of the park. Once you're through with a little R&R, feel free to grab a coffee at one of the park's cafés before re-embarking on your sightseeing quests.

i Free; limited wheelchair accessibility

FOOD

MUSTAFA'S GEMÜSE KEBAP ($)

Mehringdamm 32; open M-Th 10am-3am, F-Sa 10am-5am, Su 10am-3am

OMG? More like OMD! Oh. My. Döner. After one bite of Mustafa's, we realized that if we're praising any high power, it's the döner kebab gods. How is it that we, mere mortal humans, could be blessed with such a delicacy? Taste succulent, rich meat accentuated with crisp vegetables, melt-in-your-mouth feta salad, and delightfully tangy sauce, all enveloped in perfectly toasted bread like a warm hug. The gods placed this tantalizing treat amidst the garden of other cheap, late-night eats to tempt us—and give in to temptation we did, along with a hundred other young club-goers who decided to keep the party going around the lively Mehringdamm U-bahn stop. Now if only they could bless us with a shorter wait.

i Kebabs from €3.50; cash only; vegetarian options available

BURGERMEISTER ($)

Oberbaumstr. 8; burger-meister.de/en; open M-Th 11am-3am, F 11am-4am, Sa noon-4am, Su noon-3am

Burgermeister is your mother's worst nightmare. We're encouraging you to eat food that was prepared in the toilet? A public toilet, no less? Ma, relax. The former toilet house was converted into a fast food burger joint in 2006 and has been attracting tourists and locals alike ever since. Located at the intersection under the **Schlesisches Tor** U-bahn station, it receives its own fair share of traffic. Like every other public (women's) toilet, there's always a wait. Is that sesame seed-covered brioche bun and thin beef patty worth it? Maybe if you have extra time on your hands

POTSDAM

So, you want to see what it's like to live as a royal for the day? Just head over to Potsdam. With 16 palaces spread across three parks and the city center, it appears that Prussia's kings set their bars pretty high. Frederick the Great built the first, Sanssouci Palace, back in 1745. Since then, Potsdam has added not just royal summer residences, but also a Russian Colony (Alexandrovka), a Mansion Colony, and a Dutch Quarter to its repertoire. The wide range of elaborate architectural styles and cultural mixings has attracted everyone from nature lovers to filmmakers to Churchill, Truman, and Stalin: the allies held the Potsdam Conference at Cecilienhof Palace and signed the contract that led to the construction of the Berlin Wall. With all that history and culture, the city was granted status as a UNESCO World Heritage Site, one of the largest in Germany. Maybe the Prussian royalty knew what they were doing after all?

In its infancy, Prussian royalty intended to make Potsdam a picturesque summer retreat. For this reason, landmarks around the city are spread out and tend to take up their fair share of space. As a rule of thumb, nearly all the palaces lie west of the **Havel River. Sanssouci Park** contains 11 palaces spread across western Potsdam, and **New Garden** contains three palaces in the north. The city center, including the **Old Dutch Quarter,** is concentrated in a small area between them. **Babelsberg Park** borders the eastern banks of the Havel River, as does the **Potsdam Hauptbahnhof**. Joining the crowd in the east is the notable landmark **Alexandovka,** a former Russian Colony, as well as **Studio Babelsberg,** the oldest large-scale film studio in the world and the biggest film studio in Europe.

GETTING THERE

Potsdam is included in Tariff Zone C of Berlin's public transportation network (BVG), meaning a valid ABC ticket is all you need to get there. An ABC day ticket (€7.70) provides unlimited travel on any of the BVG's trains, trams, or buses until midnight, while a single journey (€3.40) ticket is good for two hours after purchase. There are two types of trains with service to Potsdam: the S-Bahn S7 line and the Regional Express 1 (RE1) train towards Brandenburg/Magdeburg. Travel from Berlin Hauptbahnhof to Potsdam Hauptbahnhof takes about 40 minutes on the S7 (trains every 10-30min), or about 25 minutes on the RE1 (trains every 30min from all major train stations).

GETTING AROUND

If you bought that ABC day ticket, kudos to you! As long as it's validated, you're free to use any public transportation in Potsdam. Bikes can also be rented for as little as €5 a day, and can come in handy since the city's palaces and parks are far from each other. Of course, walking is always an option for those who want to get their daily step count up. Streets in downtown and the historical districts are car-free.

Check out...

SANSSOUCI PALACE

Maulbeerallee; 331 9694200; www.spsg.de/en/palaces-gardens/object/sanssouci-palace; open Apr-Oct 10am-5:30pm, Nov-Mar 10am-4:30pm

Going to Potsdam without seeing Sanssouci Palace is like going to Paris without seeing the Eiffel Tower. You just don't. Except Sanssouci actually lives up to the hype. Inside the charming yellow abode is room after room after—you guessed it—room of coy cherubs, stenciled satin wallpaper, and gilded gold ceilings. In typical royal fashion, the palace goes out with a bang. The tour ends in the Voltaire Room, a jaw-dropping nook in floor-to-ceiling marigold. Man, if anyone knows how to pull off yellow, it's Sanssouci. Fair warning though—a visit is like trying to get a sitting with the king himself. Tickets are for set admission times, so we recommend buying them online to secure one of the limited slots. Afterwards, check out Sanssouci Park, which boasts 10 other palaces, including New Palace, Charlottenhof Palace, and Orangery Palace.

i *Admission €12, reduced €8, audio guides included; last entry 30min before closing; wheelchair accessible with assistance*

Don't miss...

NEW GARDEN

Am Neuen Garten; 331 9694200; open Tu-Su 8am-dusk

What are your summer plans? Oh, just vacationing at your grandparents' cottage in Cape Cod? Sorry, Chad, but looks like King Friedrich I has you beat. His summer residence, the Marble Palace, lies on the grounds of New Garden, a 102 hectare park that borders Holy Lake. Together, the serene spot attracts locals who love to jog, bike, and picnic to nature's melody: chirping birds and the faint rustle of leaves in the wind. In the lake, schools of minnows jump and dart amongst the frolicking swimmers and those brave enough to doggy paddle from bank to bank. As if that weren't enough, New Garden also houses Cecilienhof Palace, the final home erected by the Hohenzollern dynasty. Is it safe to say that Martha's Vineyard is out, and New Garden is in?

i *Free; limited wheelchair accessibility*

Grab a bite at...

LINDNER ($$)

Jägerstr. 16; 331 73042562; open M-F 9:30am-7pm, Sa 8:30am-7pm

"It's Lind-ner, not Lin-dor." If you didn't read that in Hermione Granger's voice, you should set your DVR to record Freeform's next Harry Potter movie marathon. Witches and wizards aside, this neighborhood deli is the real deal. Really, a place like that really exists in the tourist-heavy Potsdam city center? Yep, and Frau at the cured meats counter can confirm it. She usually sells to the local clientele, who come for Lindner's extensive selection of meats, cheeses, tortes, and traditional prepared German foods. Knowing full well that we were about as far from local as we could get (4,984 miles, to be exact), we just smiled and asked nicely. Turns out, that works. We walked out with potato salad, pork schnitzel, and a friendly conversation for under €10.

i *Prices for prepared foods based on weight, dessert from €3; wheelchair accessible* to pay homage to the cultural icon. When you're stumbling around at 2am on a Saturday morning after enjoying **Kreuzberg**'s nightlife scene, perhaps find a venue located more than two feet from the street.

i Burgers from €5, beer and soda from €2; cash only; vegetarian options available; wheelchair accessible

DISTRIKT COFFEE ($$)

Bergstr. 68; 176 32842953 open M-F 8:30am-5pm, Sa-Su 9:30am-5pm

Exposed brick walls and minimal industrial lighting? Açai superfood bowls and latte art? Worn, camel-colored leather couch and patrons curled up with a good book? The incessant screech of espresso machines, accentuated by a background hum of upbeat jazz music? Did someone say third-wave coffee? The high quality coffee movement burst onto the scene several years ago, gifting Berlin with yet another way to treat yourself. Distrikt Coffee sets itself apart by staying true to its neighborhood's culture, fitting in perfectly with the flower shop on the corner and the bookstore down the street. In other words, it's not just another poser. A popular brunch destination for the locals, get there early on the weekends to snag a coveted table—there's usually a wait within an hour of opening.

i Breakfast and lunch from €9, coffee from €3; outdoor seating available; limited wheelchair accessibility

MOGG ($$)

Auguststraße 11-13; 30 330060770; www.moggmogg.com; open M-F 11am-10pm, Sa 10am-10pm, Su 10am-8pm

If you rearrange Mogg, you get OMGG: oh my goodness gracious. As in, oh my goodness gracious, that was the best pastrami we've ever had. Mogg takes Jewish dining to a new level. The kitchen is built into the single room, deli-style, giving the space a familial, intimate feel. The fact that there's only three decorations in the entire place means that the food is front and center stage. It makes sense—why bother? The heaping mounds of tender, smoked meat and homemade whole grain mustard will steal the show every time. We recommend waiting until at least the second visit to feast upon the pan-seared salmon or shakshuka. Your first time should be special, and you won't regret going for Mogg's pastrami.

i Meals from €10, beer from €4, wine from €4; cash only

STEEL VINTAGE BIKES CAFÉ ($$)

Wilhelmstr. 91; 030 20623877; www.steel-vintage.com; open daily 8am-7pm

Steel Vintage Bikes Café has that "best all-around" kind of vibe that makes you wonder why all dining establishments in the tourist-heavy, museum-rich Berlin city center do not exude the same friendly, trendy air. In a land of tourist traps waiting to prey upon the next hangry and sweaty traveller, this chic café exists as a haven, where the birds chirp, the dogs play catch, and the locals relax. Take advantage of its proximity to **Potsdamer Platz** and **Pariser Platz,** and swing by for a homemade lemonade, fresh pastry, or other artfully-displayed Mediterranean-inspired dish. While our mom always taught us not to judge a book by the cover, this café shows us that we can—just take the hipster façade, outdoor oasis, and vintage bike shop in the back as proof.

i Breakfast from €5, lunch specials from €5, beer and wine from €4; vegetarian options available; wheelchair accessible

QUY NGUYEN VEGAN LIVING ($$)

Oranienburger Str. 7; 30 2828995; open M-Sa noon-11:30pm, Su 1pm-11:30pm

Take a break from all the currywurst and cleanse your palate with a refreshing, vegan take on a vermicelli bowl. Packed full of fresh veggies, tofu, and the hidden gem of bundled noodles, Quy Nguyen's lunch special leaves no customer dissatisfied. Chow down guilt free on this healthy, cheap option and watch travelers swarm past you to **Hackesche Hofe,** where pricier food options and tourist hotspots reside. Despite the café's lack of typical Berlin punch and character, you won't be sorry one bit.

i Lunch specials from €8; vegetarian and vegan options available; limited wheelchair accessibility; outdoor seating available

ZEIT FÜR BROT ($)

Alte Schönhauser Str. 4; 30 28046780; www.zeitfuerbrot.de; open M-F 7am-8pm, Sa 8am-8pm, Su 8am-6pm

Hansel and Gretel left a trail of breadcrumbs to find their way home. All you have to do is follow the alluring smell of chocolate croissants and artisanal bread from down the street and through the open doors of this neighborhood bakery. If you get there early enough, snag a müsli or Stulle (meats, cheese, and arugula on sourdough) just like German children do on their way to school. However, the real shining star that put Zeit on the map (and kept it in our hearts) is their famous butter-drenched cinnamon roll. Flavors like peanut butter & jam or chocolate & rhubarb may catch your eye, but it's a proven fact that nothing tastes sweeter than the classic. All we have to say is that the Pillsbury Doughboy has nothing on these cinnamon rolls, made fresh in house throughout the day.

i Breakfast from €6, sandwiches, pastries, and coffee from €3; vegan options available

NIGHTLIFE

KLUNKERKRANICH

Rooftop of Neuköllln Arcaden at Karl-Marx-Straße 66; www.klunkerkranich.org; open Mar 1-Apr 14 W-F 4pm-2am, Sa-Su noon-2am, Apr 15-Oct 15 daily noon-2am, Oct 16-Dec 31 W-F 4pm-2am, Sa-Su noon-2am

Easy, breezy, beautiful, Klunkerkranich. If you're not starting your night off watching the picturesque sunset from the giant sandbox in the middle of this rooftop bar, then you're doing something wrong. The locals flock to this hidden gem, only found by catching the parking garage elevator to the top floor. From there, follow the incessant laughter and techno beats—and if you happen to be unlucky, the smell of fresh urine—to the relaxed and lively bar. Or, better yet, hit the ground running at the "Vodka Water" booth, where you'll find a flower-crown-wearing drunkard pouring shots down an ice luge.

i Cover after 4pm varies; beer and wine from €3, cocktails from €9, shots from €2, bottle deposit €1; cash only; BGLTQ+ friendly

BERGHAIN

Am Wriezener Bahnhof; 30 29360210; www.berghain.de; open Th 10pm-6am, F midnight-9am, Sa midnight-6am, Su 24hr

Wilder than Coachella. More exclusive than a Grammy's after-party. Rivaled only by DC10 in Ibiza. The former power plant is now a hedonistic techno club, challenging locals and tourists alike to see if they have enough punk, flair, and soul to get past the club's notoriously discerning bouncers. Tips for getting in: 1) Dress in your most grungy, daring pieces. Platform army boots are a plus. 2) Arrive between 6am-8am or 12pm-3pm on Sunday, and you may just avoid the infamous three-hour line. 3) Act aloof and uninterested when you finally reach the door. 4) Send a silent prayer of thanks because by now you've gotten the subtle nod and a story for your future kids, proving that you were once indeed as cool and hip as you claim to be.

i Cover from €10, drinks from €3; cash only; BGLTQ+ friendly; closed-toed shoes, dark clothes recommended; stamp valid for re-entry all day

CLUB DER VISIONAERE

Am Flutgraben; 30 69518942; clubdervisionaere.com; open M-F 2pm-late, Sa-Su noon-late

Hindsight's 2020, but we shouldn't have had that fourth drink. Or the fifth. In all fairness, it was hard to see the harm in befriending yet another person at the Club der Visionaere's massive Sunday afternoon dance party. Find yourself adding some artwork to the graffitied walls of the upstairs pizza lounge alongside your six newest acquaintances, or sitting back and watching the sunset paint the sky with the colors of the wind. During the week, the club offers a more laid-back vibe, while still staying true to its techno, tatted-up core.

i Cover from €5, beer from €3, cocktails from €7, €0.50 bottle deposit, pizza from €7; cash only; BGLTQ+ friendly; casual dress; limited indoor seating

ELSE

An den Treptowers 10; 30 25 04 14 26; www.else.tv; open Apr-Oct Th-F 4pm-2am, Sa noon-late

Else is what happens when Mario Kart's Rainbow Road and Pixar's Wreck It Ralph give birth to a club. Is it a beer garden? A techno bar? A retro 1980s arcade? If the neon rainbow tunnel at the entrance didn't tip you off that you were in for a wild ride, maybe you'll get the hint when you stumble upon row after row of bus seats. Yes, bus seats, yes, inside neon purple and yellow shipping containers, with hot pink curtains that can be drawn back for total and complete privacy. All we have to say is what happens at the back of the bus, stays at the back of the bus. When you're done, uh, exploring, you can join the **Salami Social Club:** 26cm of pure pleasure (re: pizza) for "you + your mom," according to the sign at the door. All we know is that we'll be hitting up its indoor sister club, **Zur Wilden Renate,** come winter or bad weather. Good vibes only.

i Cover from €5, beer from €2.50, cocktails from €7, bottle deposit €1; cash only; BGLTQ+ friendly; casual dress; limited indoor seating

OHM

Köpenicker Str. 70; 17 78279352; ohm-berlin.com; open F-Sa midnight-late

You can't say that OHM didn't give you a fair warning. Depending on your luck, the "danger" signs left over from its power plant days could mean one of two things: turn around, there's no chance of getting into the club for at least two hours, or watch out, you're in for the time of your life. The small nightclub sports an intimate, avant-garde feel, magnified by the fact that it's housed in the same abandoned building as **Tresor.** Until recently, OHM was one of Berlin's best-kept secrets. Its experimental, electronic focus has started to put it on the map, so don't be surprised if there's already a line of 80+ people vying to get into "Baby Berghain" just minutes after it opens.

i Cover from €5, drinks from €2; cash only; closed toe-shoes only

COLOGNE

Coverage by **Megan Galbreath**

As the fourth-largest German city, Cologne has a lot of history—about 2000 years' worth, in fact. The Romans founded Colonia village in 50 AD. Its strategic location on the Rhine River eventually enabled it to become a key player in trade and commerce, leading to its establishment as a large and prosperous city during the Middle Ages. However, the discovery of America derailed its importance as a key link between Eastern and Western Europe, so the city switched to a more industrial focus following the Industrial Revolution. A couple hundred years came and went, and with them, nearly 90 percent of the inner city. WWII decimated Cologne, forcing it to rebuild from the rubble. It turns out that rock bottom was just what the city needed. In recent decades, Cologne regained its prosperous status within Germany, serving as a key shipping and trade port city once again. Today, visitors will find an energetic and welcoming town, filled with bustling cafés and pubs and the largest BGLTQ+ community in the country.

ORIENTATION

The **Rhine River** runs north to south in Cologne, splitting the city in two. Travelers will primarily explore areas to the west of the Rhine River, the area with the most landmarks, museums, parks, historical districts, and food scenes. The second major delineating marker in Cologne is the **Ring Boulevard,** which encircles central Cologne and separates it from the city's parks and outlying neighborhoods. At the heart of downtown lie the **Cologne Hauptbahnhof** and **Cologne Cathedral,** which border the western banks of the Rhine River. South of these landmarks, travelers will find **Old Town,** a tourist-heavy but lively neighborhood populated with many pubs and museums. West of Old Town lies **Neumarkt Quarter,**, an area known for its high-end shopping. Not to be missed are the **Belgian Quarter** and **Latin Quarter,** both of which sit just west of the Ring Boulevard. The two neighborhoods are popular with young crowds for their cheap eats and trendy, dynamic bar and clubbing scenes.

ESSENTIALS

GETTING THERE

The Köln Bonn Airport is a smaller international airport located southeast of Cologne. It is connected to central Cologne by a short ride on the Intercity-Express (ICE) network, which drops travelers off at the Cologne Hauptbahnhof (central train station). If you are traveling to Cologne from Europe, we recommend taking the train, as the central train station is located downtown. The Cologne Hauptbahnhof is the busiest railway station in Germany, servicing some 1,200 trains per day. From there, travelers can conveniently walk or take public transportation to their final destination. Travel by bus is also an option, but will require another 30 minute train ride to reach downtown because the Busbahnhof is located at the Köln Bonn Airport.

GETTING AROUND

Most major landmarks and museums are found in Cologne's condensed downtown, making walking the best option for getting around. Many areas within the popular Old Town are closed to traffic, so it is only possible to visit the sights and shopping districts located in central Cologne by foot. Public transportation (U-Bahn, S-Bahn, tram, and bus services) offers a highly accessible way to reach some of the outer-lying parks, including the Cologne Zoo, the Botanical Gardens, Hiroshima-Nagasaki Park, and Lindenthaler Tierpark (single ticket €3, day ticket €8.80). Popular food and bar districts such as the Latin Quarter and Belgian Quarter are about a 40 minute walk or a 15 minute train ride from the city center. Tram service ends at 1am on weekdays, but runs through the night on weekends. Biking is always an option, though not as popular in Cologne as in other major German cities.

PRACTICAL INFORMATION

Tourist Offices: The Cologne Tourism Service Center is conveniently located at the base of the Cologne Cathedral, across from the Cologne Hauptbahnhof.

- Köln Tourism Service Centre (Kardinal-Höffner-Platz 1; 221 346430; www.cologne-tourism.com; open M-Sa 9am-8pm, Su 10am-5pm).

Banks/ATMs/Currency Exchange: Many places in Cologne only accept cash, even within the city center. ATMs and banks are found throughout the city, and usually offer better exchange rates than currency exchange shops. Bank of America cardholders can avoid international ATM access fees by withdrawing cash from Deutsche Bank, since both banks are members of the Global ATM Alliance. The following is a convenient location near the Cologne Cathedral and Cologne Hauptbahnhof.

- Deutsche Bank (An den Dominikanern 11; 22 11420; deutsche-bank.de; open M 9am-1pm, 2pm-6pm, Tu-W 9am-1pm, 2pm-4pm, Th 9am-1pm, 2pm-6pm, F 9am-1pm, 2pm-3:30pm).

Post Offices: Nearly all post offices lie outside Ring Boulevard. We have listed the one convenient location within the city center.

- Deutsche Post (Hohe Pforte 4-6; deutschepost.de; open M-F 9am-6pm, Sa 9am-2pm).

Public Restrooms: Public restrooms (toilette or WC) are typically only available to paying customers inside cafés, restaurants, and museums. Public restrooms can be found in the Cologne Hauptbahnhof and Cologne Cathedral, but require a fee.

Internet: Cologne has a wonderful motto: "Free Wi-Fi for All." All of downtown is basically one giant free Wi-Fi hotspot (Hotspot.Koeln), meaning that Wi-Fi is available in the Cologne Hauptbahnhof, Cologne Cathedral, Old Town district, and Belgian Quarter. Some cafés also offer free Wi-Fi, which is convenient towards the outskirts of the city where city-sponsored hotspots are more rare.

BGLTQ+ Resources: The Cologne Tourism Service Center has an online guide called "Queer Cologne" that details the most popular BGLTQ+ neighborhoods, nightlife scenes, festivals, and events. Cologne's Christopher Street Day (Pride Day) is a particularly popular event, drawing over 1 million visitors from across Europe.

EMERGENCY INFORMATION

Emergency Number: 112.

Police: The Polizeiwache Stolkgasse police station is located near the Cologne Hauptbahnhof (Stollgasse 47; 221 229 4130).

US Embassy: The closest US Consulate is located in Dusseldorf (Willi-Becker-Allee 10, 40227 Dusseldorf; 211 788 8927). Contact or visit the US Embassy in Berlin for passport requests, special consular services, or visa information (Pariser Platz 2; 30 83050; de.usembassy.gov; open M-F 8:30am-5:30pm).

Rape Crisis Center: Violence Against Women offers free and confidential support daily 24hr to victims of assault or harassment (08000 116016).

Hospitals: Cologne offers health services through several hospitals and clinics. We have listed one.

- St. Marien Hospital (Kunibertskloster 11-13; 22 116290; open daily 24hr).

Pharmacies: There are several pharmacies in downtown Cologne, including three near the Cologne Hauptbahnhof. We have listed one convenient location.

- Dom-Apotheke (Bahnhofsvorplatz 1; 221 20050500; dom-apotheke-koeln.de; open M-F 8am-6:30pm, Sa 9am-6:30pm).

SIGHTS

CULTURE

OLD TOWN

Altstadt Neighborhood; open daily 24hr, shop and café openings vary

Saying that Cologne's Old Town is touristy is like saying that ice cream is the only acceptable way to end a long and hot beach day. Duh. Just like that mint chocolate chip double scoop, a venture into Old Town is inevitable, and for good reason. Bordered by the **Cologne Cathedral** to the north and by the **Rhine River** to the east, the neighborhood makes for gorgeous views and a lively atmosphere. Every evening, the masses spill out from brewhouses, cafés, and (of course) ice cream shops onto the cobblestone streets. There, they mingle with everyone from street performers to wedding parties, courtesy of **Old Town Hall**. Be sure to work up an appetite by browsing the area's funky art galleries and candy factories before retiring to the plaza for some evening refreshments and entertaining people-watching.

i Free; limited wheelchair accessibility

COLOGNE PHILHARMONIC

Bischofsgartenstraße 1; 221 280280; koelner-philharmonie.de; show times vary

The Cologne Philharmonic isn't your typical hoity-toity rich folks playground. Since 1986, the venue has catered to a variety of genres and shows, including jazz, folk, pop, and, of course, symphonic and chamber music. Unusual offerings include comedies and French dramas, set against a backdrop of Cologne's seasoned full orchestra and an additional vocal ensemble. Concert-goers will be pleasantly surprised to find amphitheater-style seating and large, plush chairs. In addition to the obvious practical, acoustic, and visual benefits, the architectural choices promote the idea of the symphony as a production, rather than merely the melody to which you might fall asleep. We'd recommend checking the website for available tickets in advance, especially because admission is free to a select number of afternoon shows.

i Tickets from €7, occasional free shows; wheelchair accessible

LANDMARKS

COLOGNE CATHEDRAL

Domkloster 4; www.koelner-dom.de; open May-Oct M-Sa 6am-9pm, Su 1pm-4:30pm, open Nov-Apr M-Sa 6am-7:30pm, Su 1pm-4:30pm

So, you spent two hours crafting last winter's gingerbread house masterpiece? Cologne spent nearly 600 years finishing their baby. Construction on the Cologne Cathedral began in 1248, but was delayed several times due to a lack of funds and resources. Today, the fully finished structure is the shining star of Cologne's skyline. Rising an imposing 157 meters above the **Rhine River,** the gothic-style landmark welcomes millions of visitors each year. For those of you looking to be another one in a million, remember to dress in your Sunday best. Modesty is the motto, and shoulders must be covered for entry. To fully appreciate the cathedral in its full glory, we recommend a Rhine River cruise, which provides the best vantage point for seeing Cologne's waterfront landmarks.

i Free; register in advance for English guided tours €8, reduced €6 M-Sa at 10:30am and 2:30pm, Su at 2:30pm; tower climb €5, reduced €2, check website for tower opening hours; wheelchair accessible

HOHENZOLLERN BRIDGE

Hohenzollern Bridge, near Cologne Hauptbahnhof; open daily 24hr

Just like the dynasty with which it shares its namesake, the Hohenzollern Bridge has a few notches on its belt. Though the bridge may not look like anything special from afar, it actually acted as one of Germany's most important defense points during WWII, before Allied airstrikes destroyed it in early 1945. Hohenzollern was repaired soon after, and today serves as the most heavily used bridge in Germany. But, we're not here to give you a brush up on your eighth-grade history. No, we're here to talk about that special little four letter word. No, the other four letter word. Looooove. In recent years, thousands of couples declare their commitment to each other by locking love padlocks—and in some kinky cases, handcuffs—to the bridge. Add your love story to the collection during a sunset stroll across Hohenzollern, then grab a romantic dinner at one of the nearby pubs in **Old Town.**

i Free, wheelchair accessible

MUSEUMS

FARINA FRAGRANCE MUSEUM

Obenmarspforten 21; 221 399 8994; www.farina.org; open M-Sa 10am-6pm, Su 11am-5pm

Thank Johann Maria Farina for the reason your date smells like birchwood and rain. Though in all fairness, we doubt that Farina expected his luxurious **Eau de Cologne** would go on to serve as the teenage male's favorite alternative to showering some 300 years after the creation of his first essence. At Farina Fragrance Museum, visitors learn about the history and art of modern perfume making, right in its homeland. Literally. The tour begins with a viewing of Farina's family home and office, before continuing to the long-awaited essence room. In case you were wondering, scents like "Moonlight Path" and "Sun-Ripened Raspberry" are not hidden in the cupboards. What can be found: elegant and subtle aromas crafted for each astrological sign. Looks like you've just found the perfect Mother's Day gift. You're welcome.

i Standard tour (45min) €5, includes perfume sample; historical tour (45min) €9, includes perfume sample; check website for english tour times; last tour 1hr before close; recommended to buy tickets online

MUSEUM LUDWIG

Heinrich-Böll-Platz; 22 122126165; www.museum-ludwig.de; open Tu-Su 10am-6pm, 1st Th of month 10am-10pm

A foreign city without a contemporary art museum?! *Gasp!* No need to get your knickers in a twist, we're just messing with you. In case you haven't tired of brightly colored paint-splattered canvases and photographs of ordinary people doing ordinary things, Museum Ludwig is here to save the day. The museum boasts a large collection of modern and contemporary pieces, with a focus on the mid-twentieth century pop-art movement. Visitors can spend a leisurely morning wandering through **Andy Warhol's** works and mistaking wax figures for museum-goers with an ungodly ability to not blink. Once you tire of analyzing abstract statements on consumerism in a post-war society, finish your tour by puzzling over Museum Ludwig's extensive **Pablo Picasso** painting collection.

i Admission €11, reduced €7.5, free under 18, first Th of month €7 from 5pm; audio guides downloadable online; wheelchair accessible

OUTDOORS

LINDENTHALER TIERPARK

Marcel-Proust-Promenade 1; 15 254548851; www.lindenthaler-tierpark.de; open Jan-Feb daily 9am-5pm, Mar M-Sa 8am-6pm, Su 9am-6pm, Apr M-Sa 8am-7pm, Su 9am-7pm, May-Aug M-Sa 8am-8pm, Su 9am-8pm, Sept M-Sa 8am-7pm, Su 9am-7pm, Oct M-Sa 8am-6pm, Su 9am-6pm, Nov daily 9am-5pm, Dec daily 9am-4pm

Why in God's name should you travel thirty minutes west from the hustle and bustle of downtown Cologne, just to visit a park? A park, for crying out loud! If you wanted to do that, you could just travel nine minutes down the street from your apartment, instead of nine hours to a different continent! Okay, but does that rinky-dinky little neighborhood park maintain a giant free petting zoo? That's right, at Lindenthaler Tierpark, visitors ride their horses through the trails right up to a wildlife park. Families love the zoo, probably because hand-feeding the donkeys, chickens, rams, and cows keeps the kids entertained for hours. A word of warning: don't be surprised when you stop for a picture, only to find out that the deer photograph better than you.

i Free entry; wheelchair accessible

FOOD

BAGATELLE ($)

Teutoburger Straße 17; 224 106 014; www.bagatelle.koeln; open M-Sa 5pm-1am, Su noon-midnight

Just a heads up that Bagatelle is not a bagel shop. The chic restaurant serves up something even better than everyone's favorite doughy, carbo-loaded breakfast food: French-style tapas at un-French-like prices. For just €3-5, you can buy yourself an expertly toasted croque monsieur or a satisfyingly rich zucchini soup. Salads, vegetarian plates, and pizzas round out the menu, offering a delightfully healthy cheap-eat amidst a land of döner kebabs, currywurst, and ice cream. A pessimist sees its distance from downtown as a downside, but all optimists would see the trek as an opportunity to treat themselves to another dish or dessert. Bagatelle oozes that classic French charm, from the postcard-style menus, to the colorful fleur-de-lis wallpaper, to the giant "Merci" sign above the door. No, Bagatelle, merci to you.

i Tapas from €3; cash only; wheelchair accessible; outdoor seating available

CAFÉ EXTRABLATT ($$)

Alter Markt 28-32; 221 257 2107; www.café-extrablatt.de; open M-Sa 8am-late, Su 9am-late

Extra, extra, read all about it! The newspaper-style menu's headline says it all: Breaking News! Breakfast Buffet! Under €11! The American-style café certainly lives up to its name. Café Extrablatt is, well, extra. When it's not busy stuffing patrons with French toast, eggs, bacon, tortes, cinnamon rolls, and more, the restaurant serves up all the classics your heart could desire. Cheeseburgers, salads, wraps, and soups draw crowds daily, filling the outdoor patio and two-floor interior with everyone from rowdy college students to cultured Philharmonic season ticket holders. Try snagging a seat in the plaza, where you'll revel in the constant action of **Old Town** and head bop along to the jazzy, upbeat ambience.

i Breakfast from €4, lunch from €9; vegetarian options available; wheelchair accessible

LUCCA ($)

Obenmarspforten 14; 127 095674; open M-Th 11am-10:30pm, F-Sa 11am-11pm, Su noon-9pm

The menu here is pretty simple: pizza, pasta, or salad, take it or leave it. Sometimes simple is good though, and Lucca just goes to show that a restaurant doesn't need to pull out all the stops to offer a warm, satisfying meal to hungry travelers. Despite its location in **Old Town,** the restaurant is a bit off the beaten path, which might explain why the prices stay in the more budget-travel range. It's simple motto, "Come as a guest, leave as a friend," means that waiters serve meals at a more relaxed pace, distinguishing Lucca from the energy and hustle of nearby larger pub plazas. For a quiet escape that won't break the bank, Lucca sings, "You've got a friend in me."

i Meals from €8; vegetarian options available; wheelchair accessible; outdoor seating available

MISS PÄPKI ($$)

Brüsseler Pl. 18; 116 834 971; www.miss-päpki.de; open M 9:30am-7pm, W-F 9:30am-7pm, Sa-Su 10:30am-7pm

Close your eyes and picture the most stereotypical, charming European café that you can. Does it have white metal tea chairs and fresh flowers on every table? How about jars of colored candies on the gelato counter? Certainly it includes a glass case containing piles of precariously-stacked mismatched teacups and saucers? Don't forget the blush pink walls and girl-power paintings that hang upon them. Is it nestled in the shade of a church, with grand brass bells that ring hourly? Now if you open your eyes, you'll find Miss Päpki. The warm, welcoming café offers a wonderful lunch selection of quiches, sandwiches, and salads, as well as an extensive coffee and wine list. Next time you find yourself lost in Cologne's **Belgian Quarter,** head on home to Miss Päpki's for a warm spot on the couch, a tasty latte, and a good book.

i Coffee from €2, cake from €3, lunch from €8; cash only; vegetarian options available; outdoor seating available

NIGHTLIFE

HERR PIMOCK ($$)

Aachener Str. 52; 221 511866; www.herr-pimock.de; open M-Th 10am-1am, F 10am-3am, Sa 9am-3am, Su 9am-1am

It must'a been the luck o' the Irish that scored us that free drink. Considering the shamrock-themed logo and bright green decor, perhaps a better name for the hip, lively bar would have been "Herr Shamrock." We wouldn't be surprised if the sign guy made a typo and the restaurant just went with it. That go-with-the-flow mentality seems to be fitting for a place that snagged prime real estate in the popping Ring bar scene. Its signature cocktail list draws a young crowd on the weekends, making it the perfect place to meet friends, both new and old. And the best part? Gone are the days of making that dreaded trek to search for late-night cheap eats after a night out on the town. Herr Pimock's kitchen stays open past midnight, allowing you to gorge yourself on pizza before promptly curling up in bed, while visions of leprechauns dance in your head.

i No cover, cocktails from €7, food from €8; outdoor seating available; take out available

LITTLE NONNA ($$)

Brabanter Str. 1; 159 496 610; littlenonna.de; open M-F 11:30am-1am, Sa-Su 11:30am-3am

What's better than your Nonna's house? It's comfortable, cozy, and always smells

of fresh baked cookies, just like this sweet bar. Little Nonna's bourgeoisie vibe offers a refreshing change of pace from the typical pubs and dive bars populated by younger weekend crowds. Though the royal blue-and-gold cocktail lounge is more popular for date night or a leisurely drink than for crazy clubbing thrill seekers, at least you can sleep well knowing that the high-quality tequila will be kind to you in the morning. If anything, the only headache you'll wind up with will be an inevitable sugar-induced hangover after overindulging in one-too-many slices of chocolate Nutella pizza. Fresh out of the oven, just like Nonna used to make.

i Cocktails from €7, beer from €2, wine from €6, food from €8; wheelchair accessible; outdoor seating available

FRANKFURT

Coverage by **Megan Galbreath**

When you arrive to Frankfurt, you won't be surprised to find that your new friends lovingly refer to it as "Mainhatten." The skyline of this financial powerhouse is adorned with modern skyscrapers, courtesy of its bustling business scene, giving this Main River city a rather un-German like look. Frankfurt's youth population adheres more to the "work hard, play hard," American mentality than most European cities—the whole city rocks a "business suit by day, little black dress by night" vibe. To write Frankfurt off as a "finance bro" stereotype, though, would be to ignore its centuries of history. Classical architecture stands tall next to staggering glass buildings, and the financial district flows seamlessly into its Old Town. Universities, theaters, opera houses, festivals, and at one point, the famed poet Goethe, have called Frankfurt home. Trendy bars, upscale shops, and exclusive restaurants intermingle with notable landmarks such as the grand Frankfurt Cathedral and the lovely, picturesque Römerberg. Large green gardens sprawl in the north, while museum after museum line the river in the south. Throughout it all, you'll find a friendly and dynamic crowd, filled with people looking to share the intricacies, quirks, and flairs of the multicultural and vivacious economic empire that is Frankfurt.

ORIENTATION

When in doubt, orient yourself using the **Main River,** which runs roughly east to west through the city. Since most arriving travelers pass through the **Hauptbahnhof** (central rail station), let's start there. The Hauptbahnhof lies on the northern bank of the Main River and conveniently serves as the western edge of the city. **Bahnhof Quarter** lies just east of the railway station, making it the perfect neighborhood for famished travelers looking to treat themselves to diverse dining options. A 30-minute jaunt north of Bahnhof Quarter will bring travelers to **Bockenheim,** a young, funky, and diverse neighborhood home to artsy cafés, boutique shopping, large parks, and **Goethe University.** If you were to journey east from Bahnhof Quarter instead, you would hit **Old Town:** a historical and dynamic neighborhood filled with major landmarks, serious shopping, and record-level restaurant real estate. Rounding out the neighborhoods north of the Main is the **Frankfurt Zoo** in the northeast, yet another young and upscale neighborhood popular for its worldly food options and trendy nightlife. South of the Main River are the more quiet, cultured residential neighborhoods like **Sachsenhausen**, as well as the notable **Museumsurfer stretch.** The collection of 12 museums borders the river's southern bank and is centrally located, meaning that all you have to do to end up in Old Town is pop back over the bridge.

ESSENTIALS

GETTING THERE

Frankfurt's prominent role in the business world makes it easily accessible. The Frankfurt Airport is Germany's busiest airport, serving airlines with flights from over 100 countries. Once you and your new suit-clad friends arrive, just hop on one of the airport's S-bahn (light-rail) trains, and take it the remaining 7 miles into central Frankfurt to the Hauptbahnhof (main railway station). Visitors arriving from other cities in the region will likely use the Deutsche Bahn (DB) railway network, as the train is a fast, cheap, and convenient way to get around Germany. Travelers arriving by rail will get in at the Hauptbahnhof. Those who made the journey using one of Germany's budget bus options will get in at the Busbahnhof, which is conveniently located across the street from the Hauptbahnhof. From the main station, the RMV's network of U-bahn (fast-rail), S-bahn, tram, and bus routes can get you to your final destination.

GETTING AROUND

Considering half the visitors are suitcase-wheeling businessmen and women, Frankfurt is very pedestrian-friendly. Downtown is condensed and the financial district borders the historic and cultural districts. Walking is the best option for getting around, and most places can be reached in less than 30min. by foot. For those hoping to give their walking shoes a break, biking is a great way to reach outlying destinations such as the botanical gardens in the northwest and the Zoo in the northeast. Call-a-Bike is a popular bike-sharing system, and rentals start at just €15 per day. Finally, like most German cities, public transportation is extensive, efficient, and effective. A network of trains, trams, and buses cross the city, and single-ride tickets are only €2.75 (day ticket €5.35). For travelers looking to keep the party going early into the morning, night buses replace train and tram service from 1am-5am.

PRACTICAL INFORMATION

Tourist Offices: Frankfurt has two main tourist offices, located at the Hauptbahnhof and Römer. Extensive information can also be found on their website at www.frankfurt-tourismus.de/en.

- Hauptbahnhof (Am Hauptbahnhof, open M-F 8am-9pm, Sa-Su 9am-6pm).
- Römer (Römerberg 27; 69 212 38800 open M-F 9:30am-5:30pm, Sa-Su 9:30am-4pm).

Banks/ATMs/Currency Exchange: Many places in Frankfurt are cash only, even within the city center. ATMs are found in banks around the city, and usually offer the best exchange rates. We have listed one convenient location outside the Hauptbahnhof.

- Deutsche Bank (Am Hauptbahnhof 12; 69 2385110; open M-Tu 9am-1pm, 2pm-4pm, W 9am-1p, Th 9am-1pm, Th 2pm-6pm, F 9am-1pm).

Post Offices: There are several post offices scattered throughout Frankfurt. We have listed one in Innerstadt.

- Deutsche Post (Zeil 90; 69 929050; www.deutschepost.de; open M-F 9:30am-8pm, Sa 9:30am-9pm).

Public Restrooms: Public toilettes (WC) are a rare find in Frankfurt, and do not exist on the banks of the Main River. Some public transportation hubs, such as the Hauptbahnhof, have toilets available to travelers for a €0.50 fee. Expect that most WCs are only available to paying customers inside cafés, restaurants, and museums. Even some Starbucks locations require a €0.50 toilet fee.

Internet: Despite its heavy business traffic, Frankfurt is slow to the free Wi-Fi scene. Hotspots exist at the MyZeil shopping mall and Kleinmarkthalle, both of which are located in the city center. Travel centers such as the airport and Hauptbahnhof also offer free Wi-Fi. Internet in outlying neighborhoods, and even many centrally-located cafés, is much more sparse, so try to download any directions or important information before leaving your accommodation for the day. When in doubt, find the nearest Starbucks, which is usually no more than 15min away.

BGLTQ+ Resources: Frankfurt Tourismus publishes an online LGBT+ Community guide featuring relevant information on events, festivals, shopping, nightlife, and meeting places for BGLTQ+ travelers. Check it out at www.frankfurt-tourismus.de/en/Frankfurt-for/LGBT-community2.

EMERGENCY INFORMATION

Emergency Number: 112

Police: There are several police stations located within the Frankfurt city lines. Polizeistation is found downtown, near the Innerstadt neighborhood (Zeil 33; 69 75510100; www.polizei.hessen.de; open daily 24hr).

US Embassy: Frankfurt features a US Consulate (Gießener Str. 30; 69 75350). For passport requests or visa information, contact or visit the US Embassy in Berlin.

Rape Crisis Center: LARA is a Berlin-based center and hotline for girls and transgender people over the age of 14 that have been abused or harrassed. They offer anonymous counseling daily 24hr at 030 2168888.

Hospitals: There are many hospitals in Frankfurt. Hospital of the Holy Spirit is located on the northern bank of the Main, just west of Old Town (Lange Str. 4-6; 69 21960; www.hospital-zum-heiligen-geist.de; open daily 24hr).

Pharmacies: Pharmacies (denoted by a large red A, or apotheke) are plentiful throughout the city. We have listed one convenient location near Old Town.

- Rossmann (Roßmarkt 5; 69 13886716; www.rossmann.de; open M-W 8:30am-8pm, Th-Sa 8:30am-9pm).

SIGHTS

CULTURE

FRANKFURT CATHEDRAL

Dom,platz 14; 69 2970320; www.dom-frankfurt.de; open Sa-Th 9am-8pm, F 1pm-8pm

If you decided to put away Google Maps, thinking to yourself, "Pfff, I don't need directions, there's no way that I can miss a giant cathedral,"... think again. Unlike most Gothic cathedrals, the Frankfurt Cathedral is not a defining figure on the city skyline. It should be—the 600-year-old structure escaped WWII with only minor damage, making it one of the oldest and most impressive architectural feats around—but the rise of Frankfurt as a modern financial empire has created some tough competition. Nevertheless, the regal landmark wears burnt orange well, a refreshing splash of color against the surrounding imposing glass buildings of the Innerstadt neighborhood. Interestingly, the main nave of the church features geometric stained glass patterns, rather than the typical religious images found in European cathedrals.

i Free; wheelchair accessible; observation tower admission €3, reduced €1.50, open daily 9am-6pm

KLEINMARKTHALLE

Hasengasse 5-7; 69 21233696; www.kleinmarkthalle.de; open M-F 8am-6pm, Sa 8am-4pm

This little piggy went to Kleinmarkt. This little piggy went home. This little piggy feasted on a roast beef sandwich...and a quiche Lorraine...and a chocolate bonbon...okay, you get the picture. Kleinmarkethalle is a delightful cultural experience nestled in the heart of historic downtown Frankfurt. The indoor market is relatively small by European standards, but still manages to offer all the delicacies you could wish for. Mornings at the market are a quiet affair, usually populated with locals doing some light shopping so if you're looking for a piece of the real action, arrive around lunchtime. Between the businessmen dashing in for a quick lunch, the children flitting about the stalls, and the neighboring shopkeepers cheerfully hustling each other, you'll have to squeeze your way in to order that delectable fruit fantasia crepe.

i Food and drink prices vary; wheelchair accessible

LANDMARKS

RÖMERBERG

Römerberg 23; plaza open daily 24hr

This district makes you feel as if you stumbled upon an antique, genuine gem, but it's actually another recent reconstruction. Blame WWII. Römerberg is one of Frankfurt's many historic districts that was decimated by Allied bombing, meaning that the picturesque fifteenth-century style half-timbered houses in the square are in fact younger than your grandmother. Don't worry though, a darling little lady in the square named Justitia makes granny look good. Justitia, better known as the **Statue of Justice,** has stood outside the **Römer** (city hall) since 1543. Home to Frankfurt's administration since the 1500s, the Römer is attractive in its own right, making Römerberg the perfect backdrop for your latest insta.

i Free; wheelchair accessible

GOETHE HOUSE

Großer Hirschgraben 23-25; 69 138800; www.goethehaus-frankfurt.de; open M-Sa 10am-6pm, Su 10am-5:30pm

Before you go to Goethe House… you might want to brush up on your eighteenth century German poets, specifically Goethe. If you skip this, we can assure you that this place will leave you bored and wondering why the heck anyone would want to see this dusty old house. Well, that's because Goethe himself was born, raised, and became famous in this not-so-humble abode. The home was sold to another family in 1795 when the final Goethe child married, but was later acquired for the public and set up as a memorial in 1863. One of the house's most impressive features is its astronomical clock from 1746 featuring a bear that falls onto his back when it is time to wind the clock up again. To that we say, another one bites the dust(y rooms), ah.

i Admission €7, reduced €3; partial wheelchair accessibility; Goethe European art museum entry included with ticket

RIVERFRONT PROMENADE

Untermainkai; open daily 24hr

Like scrambling an egg, this one's pretty self-explanatory. There's a river. There's a park along the river. There's a path down which you promenade in the park along the river. Put it all together and you get a riverfront promenade! This glorious stretch of nature on the northwest bank of the Main is a perfect place to run, bike, snog…wait, what? Yep, lots of PDA-loving romantics take their dates there for the killer views, so you'll find the Riverfront Promenade to be a popular place for lovebirds and songbirds to mix. Our recommendation? Grab a picnic blanket and an ice cream cone from the nearby **Bahnhof Quarter,** then make your own nest for the afternoon and watch the boats cruise by while reclining in the shade.

i Free; wheelchair accessible

MUSEUMS

LIEBIEGHAUS

Schaumainkai 71; 69 605098200; www.liebieghaus.de; open Tu-W 10am-6pm, Th 10am-9pm, F-Su 10am-6pm

They got your nose. And your nose. And your nose! And yoooouuur nose. Apparently, nobody in ancient Rome had noses. Luckily, it seems that humanity has evolved a bit since then, and those pointy little features started appearing on religious sculptures by the Middle Ages. At Liebieghaus, visitors can walk through "no nose Roman row" on their way to explore ancient Greek sculptures and carvings. Liebieghaus is a former villa containing figurines and statues dating from ancient Egypt to the Neoclassical period—for our non-math whizzes, that's nearly 5000 years of history. Not to be missed is the museum's extensive collection of baroque ivory sculptures, including pieces by the infamous **"Master of the Furies."** Although we're not quite sure what the dude was so angry about, his jaw-droppingly intricate pieces are flawless.

i Admission €7, reduced €5; wheelchair accessible

DEUTSCHES FILMINSTITUT & FILMMUSEUM (GERMAN FILM MUSEUM)

Schaumainkai 41; 961 220220; www.dff.film/en; open Tu-Th 10am-6pm, F 10am-8pm, Sa-Su 10am-6pm

Lights, camera, action. No, no, no, you're doing it all wrong. You start at the bottom floor and work your way up. Take two. Action. There you go. To all our go-getters, know that the DFF is one of the few museums where it actually hurts you to start on the top floor, all the way in the hectic twenty-first century world of video games and filmmaking. Rather, the proper way to visit the DFF is "Back to the Future" style as in starting on the first floor with a peep show from the past. Zoom past those panoramas and flip books, on to the second floor where you'll encounter information on the film production process, including costume design and storyboarding. Finish on the trippy third floor, where the special effects and throwback arcade music will make you feel like you've stepped into a Super Mario Bros. video game.

i Admission €6, reduced €3; wheelchair accessible; visit website for individual guided tour inquiries

OUTDOORS

PALMENGARTEN

Siesmayerstraße 61; 69 21239111; www.palmengarten.de; open daily Feb-Oct 9am-6pm; Nov-Jan 9am-4pm

If you're looking for a place to beat the heat, it's not Palmengarten. Unless you're camped out on a recliner under the shade of an oak tree. Surrounded by dancing butterflies, listening to the sound of chirping birds and breathing in the aroma of the rose garden in full bloom...yeah, that's a pretty nice way to spend the afternoon. This historical botanical garden lies northwest of the city center, near **Goethe University** and **Gruneberg Park.** For those who love nature, try falling in love in nature. The **Rose Garden House** gets rented out for weddings every spring and summer, meaning that you could take the term "wedding crashers" to a whole new level.

i Admission €7, reduced €3; wheelchair accessible

FOOD

DER FETTE BULLE ($$)

Kaiserstraße 73; 69 90757004; www.der-fettebulle.de; open M-Th 5pm-11pm, F-Sa noon-11pm, Su 10am-11pm

The wheel with the ale goes round and round, round and round, round and round...despite the nursery rhyme, Der Fette Bulle doesn't play games. The rowdy restaurant gets an A+ for two of the finer Bs in life: burgers and beer. Oh, and a big red F, for rosemary-seasoned fries dipped in homemade ketchup. While anxiously awaiting those letter grades, the sizzle of the grill and the sounds of summertime will have you on the edge of your seat (that and the fact that there's no AC, so you'll be competing with your date to have as little of your body touch the seat as humanly possible). When the time finally comes to chomp down on that juicy burger, the flavors in your mouth start doing a little tango, waltzing right along to the Latin music blasting through the speakers.

i Burgers from €8; vegetarian options available; wheelchair accessible; outdoor seating available

PICKNICK ($)

Weißadlergasse 7; 69 92884922; www.picknick-frankfurt.com; open M-Th 10am-10pm, F-Sa 10am-11pm, Su 10am-6pm

If you could only pick one, may we suggest that you pick Picknick? The Moroccan-style café is located in **Old Town** but comes across as anything but musty and outdated. The funky décor puts traditional café culture to shame, trading white doilies and flowered china for colorful tiled floors and floating lanterns. The walls are tastefully adorned with Moroccan movie posters, so you can dine with the stars by day and under the stars by night. Any endorsements for a Picknick hummus scrub body care line? For a Mo-rockin' good time, roll by and pair that mouthwatering meal with a glass of Frankfurt's famous *apfelwein* (apple wine).

i Breakfast from €5, lunch and dinner from €6, drinks from €3; cash only; vegan and vegetarian options available; wheelchair accessible; outdoor seating available

BRÜHMARKT ($)

Leipziger Str. 1; 69 71918122; www.bruehmarkt.de; open M-F 8am-6pm, Sa-Su 10am-6pm

Walking up to Brühmarkt will have you wondering if Halloween came early this yea or if the café just found a super sale on spooky decorations and bought out the whole stock. The modern coffeehouse is decked out completely in orange and black but not in a tacky way. Trick or treat? More like trick and treat at Brühmarkt. Rather than ghouls, monsters, and witches, you'll find hard working university students from nearby **Goethe University** inside… although if you wander in around finals period, you might just spot a few zombies searching for (their own) brains and reaching for another cappuccino. As for the treat? Indulge in a full German breakfast spread, then polish it off with a little lemon meringue pie or crispy apple tart.

i Meals from €6, coffee from €3; cash only; vegetarian options available; wheelchair accessible; outdoor seating available

GÓC PHO ($$)

Schärfengäßchen 6; 69 29723641; www.gocpho.de; open M-Th 11am-10pm, F-Sa 11am-11pm, Su noon-10pm

As our Vietnamese aunt always says, it's a good sign when you walk up to a pho shop and find it packed with others of Vietnamese descent. Góc Pho gets a big fat check mark here. The bustling street food kitchen always seems to have a wait, no matter the meal, no matter the day. With family-sized portions, decent prices, and a prime location in **Old Town,** the small restaurant draws foodies looking for a refreshing goi cuon or remedying vat of pho. The café is tucked into a street corner near the **Galeria Kaufhof** shopping plaza, but have no fear! To find it, just follow the rich aroma of peanut noodles and the sound of clinking beer bottles from **Römerburg,** past **Kleinmarthalle**, and into a low seat at one of Góc Pho's dark mahogany tables. Slurpy soup time starts now!

i Meals from €9; vegetarian options available

HUCKS LIEBLINGSPLATZ ($)

Schweizer Str. 30; 69 60607886; www.huckgmbh.de; open M-F 6:30am-8pm, Sa-Su 7:30am-8pm

Hucks is here to say goodbye to Frankfurt's pricey food scene. The corner café likes to spread the love, from the giant yellow heart above its doorway to its generous slices of chocolate cake to its wallet-friendly drinks menu. In a display case teeming with pastries and pretzels, pies and paninis, it's the family-sized focaccias that are the stars of the show. Piled high with breakfast goodies, those babies turn heads like Leonardo DiCaprio at the Oscars. Speaking of Oscars...Hucks is the perfect place for a rumbly tummy afterparty following your viewing of the golden man himself at the nearby **German Filmmuseum** in **Museumsufer.**

i Breakfast and lunch from €4, coffee from €2, drinks from €2.50; vegetarian options available; cash only; wheelchair accessible; outdoor seating available

SUPERKATO ($$)

Kornmarkt 3; 69 281006; open 10am-6:30pm

What kind of person in their right mind goes to a hole-in-the-wall sushi place? Answer: us! Superkato doesn't look like much on the outside—or on the inside, to be quite honest. Its most exciting feature is probably its refreshing AC and ice-cold (free!) water. That said, they also serve up some damn good sushi. A couple rolls of fresh fish and a pinch of eye-watering wasabi later, you'll be stuffed to the gills for the afternoon. The no-frills sushi joint and Japanese market is a favorite for locals looking for a quick bite, and Superkato starts swimming with businessmen on their lunch breaks around noon. Maybe it's the fact that they get to break up the monotony of sitting at a desk all day—Superkato offers standing-room-only countertops and tables.

i Sushi pieces from €1.50, boxes from €5; standing room only; no wheelchair accessibility

NIGHTLIFE

THE PARLOUR ($$$)

Zwingergasse 6; 69 90025808; open M-F 8pm-1am, Sa-Su 8pm-late

When you've had a tough day and a large glass of wine is simply calling my name, head over to the Parlour and unwind. Its speakeasy vibe and intimate setting sets the tone for intimate conversation. With drink prices quite high, only come here if you want to indulge in a bougie night out. Between the luscious black leather couches and the warmth of fine gin, it's all you can do not to curl up and fall asleep under the dim, soft lights...unless it's 3am on Saturday night and the roaring crowd keeps the exclusive cocktail bar going past close, just like Gatsby did in the roaring twenties.

i No cover, drinks from €14; cash only; BGLTQ+ friendly; 21+

BOCKENHEIMER WEINKONTOR ($)

Zwingergasse 6; 69 90025808; open Su-Th 5:30pm-midnight, F-Sa 5:30pm-1am

Talk about a hidden gem. You think you've made it to Bockenheimer Weinkontor when you see the giant brass gates, but oh no. You have to turn around in circles in the yard, peer into random windows, retrace your steps to make sure your eyes did not deceive you, walk back into the yard…and you thought the fatigue and confusion were supposed to hit after the wine! When you finally realize to take the stairs in the back-right corner, you'll be greeted by a comedic mask laughing at the tragedy that was your arrival. Luckily, you'll learn that you've traded your troubles for a wine bar sprung from the romantic Tuscan southern vineyards. Let your troubles fade away under the shade of the vine-covered terrace and indulge in a tapas or two because goodness knows you're here to stay.

i Wine from €5, tapas from €2; cash only; BGLTQ+ friendly; outdoor seating available

PLANK ($)

Elbestr. 15; 69 269 586 66; www.barplank.de; pen M-Th 10am-1am, F-Sa 10am-2pm

With a name like Plank, you'd think there'd be a pirate theme. No such luck. Unless you count the bar's bathroom graffiti, where the occasional former potty breaker decided to start cursing like a sailor. In that case, welcome aboard, mateys. By day, the café doubles as an art studio, drawing busy bee workers in with the sweet scent of free Wi-Fi. By night, the crowd turns into a rowdier bunch, swarming for the cheap drinks and central location in **Bahnhof Quarter.** Between the black walls, black bar stools, and black lights, you'll be wishing you could trade your beer goggles for night goggles. Though with the knowledgeable bartenders serving as your first mate, it's not like you'll need to order for yourself anyways.

i No cover, drinks from €3; cash only; wheelchair accessibility; outdoor seating available

HAMBURG

Coverage by **Megan Galbreath**

The second largest city in Germany has the first best museum in the country: the Chocolate Museum. Before you dash off to buy your plane ticket, you should know that it's not all fun and games at the Chocoversum (okay, it's mostly fun and games). Hachez throws in quite the history lesson, which makes sense considering that during its tenure as a long-standing port dynasty, Hamburg was a hub for cacao, coffee, and spice trading. The city holds a key position along the Elbe River, and serves as a "gateway to the world" for Germany. Once a member of the medieval Hanseatic Trading League, Hamburg later went on to be a leader in free trade during the reign of the Holy Roman Empire. Then came the 1800s, and with them, annexation by Napoleon (1810) and The Great Fire of 1842. Together, the two ravaged nearly one-third of the flourishing city. Skipping to the 1900s means that inevitable destruction of the city by WWI and WWII, both physically and as a leader in maritime trade. Given its long history, visitors may be initially surprised by Hamburg's contemporary architecture and chic city vibe, but with time will come to love its hidden history and idyllic charm.

ORIENTATION

Where's a big, red "easy" button when you need one? Hamburg is a compact, walkable city, whose extensive waterfront properties help to orient visitors in the right direction. Dozens of canals form the South Border and split off the **Elbe River,** giving rise to the modern maritime neighborhood of **HafenCity**. HafenCity includes the historical **Speicherstadt,** a small island on Hamburg's southernmost edge that contains nearly a dozen museums and cultural exhibition centers, including the newly constructed **Elbphilharmonie.** Just north of HafenCity lies the prestigious **Altstadt** district, home to many of the city's museums, as well as landmarks such as the **Rathaus**. Northeast of Altstadt, travelers will find **St. Georg,** a multicultural neighborhood celebrated as Hamburg's hub for BGLTQ+ life. Having reached the northern regions of the city, head west and cross the idyllic **Alster Lakes** into **Schanze,** a quirky and hipster neighborhood known for its boutique shopping by day, and its alternative bar culture by night. South of Schanze is **St. Pauli,** whose red-light district and famed sinful **Reeperbahn** are framed by an artistic residential neighborhood. Finally, heading east again brings you full circle to the glamorous **Neustadt,** a luxurious neighborhood known for its high-end shopping and café culture.

ESSENTIALS

GETTING THERE

Hamburg Airport is one of Germany's largest international airports. It is located about 7 miles north of the city center. Travelers arriving at the airport can complete their journey with a 25min. trip on the S1 S-Bahn to the Hauptbahnhof (central railway station). The Hauptbahnhof is where domestic train travelers will likely arrive, as it is the city's hub for local and national trains. Hamburg is also easily accessible by long-distance buses. The central bus station, Hamburg ZOB, is located right next to the Hauptbahnhof, making public transportation easily accessible upon arrival.

GETTING AROUND

Hamburg is a condensed city, so walking is the best option for most travelers. Major landmarks and attractions tend to be located within a 30min. walk of each other, and public transportation often does not directly connect Hamburg's sights. That said, the HVV provides underground trains, a light-rail network, buses, and ferries for those planning to travel extensively outside the city center (single ticket €2.30, daily ticket €7.80). Hamburg is also very biker-friendly, and even offers a local city bike program called StadtRAD Hamburg. Bikes can be rented from the program for €12/day and are available at 120 service points around the city.

PRACTICAL INFORMATION

Tourist Offices: Hamburg has three tourist offices located at the Hamburg Airport, Central Station, and the harbor (Landungsbrücken). Their Sales & Service Center can be reached at 040 30051701, M-Sa 9am-7pm. Central Station North (Hachmannplatz 16; open M-Sa 9am-7pm).

Banks/ATMs/Currency Exchange: Many establishments in Hamburg are cash only, especially outside the city center. ATMs are found in banks around the city, and usually offer the best exchange rates. Deutsche Bank (Spitalerstr. 16; 40 3095160; open M-W 9:30am-4pm, Th 9:30am-6pm, F 9:30am-4pm).

Post Offices: Several post offices are located throughout Hamburg, including in the city center. Deutsche Post (Mönckebergstr. 16; deutschepost.de; open M-Sa 10am-8pm).

Public Restrooms: Public restrooms are a rare find in Hamburg. Expect that most toilets are only available to paying customers inside cafés, restaurants, and museums. Visitors who are shopping or dining in the Neustadt district may be pleasantly surprised to find that are free toilets in the Hanseviertel Passage.

Internet: Hamburg is slowly coming around to the free Wi-Fi scene, and many hotspots have popped up around the city center in recent years.

BGLTQ+ Resources: The Hamburg official city website has a page geared towards residents to offer information about BGLTQ+ events, accommodation, nightlife, and more at www.hamburg.com/residents/lgbtqi.

EMERGENCY INFORMATION

Emergency Number: 112.

Police: 110; Polizeiwache Rathaus is located in the city center (Große Johannistraße 1; 40 428650).

US Embassy: There is a US Consulate in Hamburg (Alsterufer 27/28; 040 41171100). For passport requests, special consular services, or visa information, contact or visit the US Embassy in Berlin.

Rape Crisis Center: Violence Against Women offers an anonymous 24/7 support hotline for all forms of abuse (08000 116016). The Victim Support Centre Hamburg also offers services to victims of abuse, regardless of gender (040 381993; M 10am-1pm, Tu 10am-5pm, W 1pm-5pm, Th 10am-5pm, F 9am-noon).

Hospitals: To find the hospital nearest you, visit www.hamburg.de/krankenhausportal. The largest and most convenient is listed here.

- University Medical Center Hamburg-Eppendorf (Martinistr. 52; 040 74100; open daily 24hr).

Pharmacies: There are many pharmacies throughout Hamburg, denoted by a large red A (apotheke).

- Europa Apotheke (Bergstr. 14; 40 32527689; www.europa-apotheke-hamburg.de; open M-F 8am-8pm, Sa 9:30am-8pm).

SIGHTS

CULTURE

ELBPHILHARMONIE

Platz der Deutschen Einheit 1; 35 766666; www.elbphilharmonie.de; plaza open daily 9am-midnight

Try saying Elbphilharmonie five times fast. Luckily, its popular nickname is Elphi, so we'll just stick with that. The concert hall brings young blood to **HafenCity,** which is home to the historical **Speicherstadt.** Inaugurated in January 2017, you can recognize Elphi on the Hamburg skyline by its unusual roof, which resembles the crests of waves on the nearby **Elbe River.** The venue successfully mixed neo-gothic architecture with a modern glassy exterior, summing the city up in one building: classy, refined, and chic. Inside lies three concert theaters, meaning that you, too, could be cultured like Elphi if you choose to see a performance. Otherwise, feel free to check out its plaza, where you can gaze up at the sparkling exterior, or as we like to call it, the largest mirror in the world.

i *Plaza entrance free; purchase concert tickets online or by phone, prices vary; wheelchair accessible*

GÄNGEVIERTEL

Gängeviertel, Neustadt; open daily 24hr

Quirky, cultured, and colorful, the spunky Gängeviertel quarter knows how to put up a good fight. In the 1800s, the hipster art scene had a different name: home. Many of the city's workers lived in timber houses compacted into the winding alleyways, until a cholera outbreak forced an evacuation in the 1900s. Put on your time traveler's cap and fast forward another century to 2009, when investors attempted to knock down the remaining squatters' flats. In true German fashion, Hamburg's activists and artists fought back to preserve the small remaining piece of history in the now-high-end **Neustadt** neighborhood. Today, visitors peruse art galleries, gawk at street art, chat at the bike shop, or grab a coffee at one of the area's eclectic cafés.

i *Free*

ST. MICHAEL'S CHURCH

Englische Plank 1; 040 376780; www.st-michaelis.de; open May-Sep daily 9am-7:30pm, Oct daily 9am-6:30pm, Nov-Mar daily 10am-5:30pm, Apr daily 9am-6:30pm

Something borrowed, something blue. Hamburg's largest church was first constructed in 1606. Two fires and a world war later, St. Michael's iconic copper tower was reconstructed to shine upon the city in its full glory. Though the tower survived multiple restorations, both the baptism font and offering box survived all that chaos. Visitors can see the two timely pieces on display inside, "borrowed" from the second large-scale construction of the church in 1763.

Also inside: something blue. Decked out in white and "Tiffany blue" with gold accents, the main nave feels like being inside a cross between a grand piano and a wedding cake. For the full celebratory experience, we recommend visiting St. Michael's viewing tower, where the 360° vantage point gives you a glimpse into what life as a wedding cake topper.

i Tower admission €5, reduced €4, crypt admission €4, reduced €3, combination ticket €7, reduced €6; last admission 30min before closing; wheelchair accessible

LANDMARKS

DEICHSTRASSE

Deichstraße; open daily 24hr

Just a skip, hop, and a jump from **Speicherstadt** (okay, a *really* big jump), Deichstraße is the oldest remaining street in Hamburg. The 700-year old beauty has had a few facelifts thanks to the Great Fire of 1832, but the restored houses that line the cobblestoned streets still give visitors the feeling of passing through time. We recommend starting at the north end of the street, and slowly meandering south. Not only will you head in the direction of **HafenCity's** 11 museums and exhibitions, but you'll also see the modern, wavy glass exterior of the **Elbphilharmonie** in the skyline. The juxtaposition between old and new on Deichstraße is one of the most prominent examples of Hamburg's contrasting identities, and certainly something for the picture books.

i Free; limited wheelchair accessibility

PLANTEN UN BLOMEN

Planten un Blomen, St. Petersburger Str.; 40 428544723; www.plantenunblomen.hamburg.de; open Apr daily 7am-10pm, May-Sep daily 7am-11pm, Oct-Mar daily 7am-8pm

Planten un Blomen knows how to get hot and heavy, especially on a steamy summer day. The 116-acre park rose to fame for its greenhouse, whose free admission will tempt any budget-conscious traveler. While it may resemble a fogged-up old station wagon from afar, the most scandalous thing inside is the "Danger: poisonous" sign in the Royal Palm room. If you somehow miss the giant red letters and get too close, have no fear! The park's **Apothekergarten** (pharmacist's garden) offers an array of medicinal plants, where you can finally put that year of high school biology to good use. If all else fails, swing by the glorious rose garden to find the perfect blooms for your next "I'm so artsy" insta.

i Free; wheelchair accessible; covered area

SPEICHERSTADT

Speicherstadt; www.speicherstadtmuseum.de; open daily 24hr

The **UNESCO World Heritage Site** also happens to be the world's largest warehouse complex. Constructed in the 1880s, Speicherstadt stands not on, but in the **Elbe River.** Talk about a waterfront property. The canal-riddled complex initially opened as a free port, and at one point served as a hub for the trade of coffee, cocoa, and spices. Today, it houses a series of museums, cafés, and monuments that together create the **HafenCity District.** Built on oak logs, the neo-gothic brick buildings offer a sharp contrast to the surrounding modern glass architecture. For the best photo opportunities, head to **Block W,** where you can get a glimpse of the famed **Wasserschloss** and wonder what happened to Blocks Y and Z (hint: WWI halted their construction).

i Free; wheelchair accessible

MUSEUMS

CHOCOVERSUM BY HACHEZ

Meßberg 1; 40 41912300; www.chocoversum.de; open daily 10:15am-6:15pm with 90min guided tours

Chocoholics, unite! To any chocolate haters out there: we're so sorry for your loss. The Chocoversum is 90 minutes of pure joy. You'll feel like a kid in a candy shop as you dash between exhibits, learning about the history and ethics of chocolate making. The most important tip: come hungry. Visitors get to sample milk and dark chocolate at every stage of the chocolate-making process, from the cacao bean, to the little nibs, to the finished product. And the best part—even better than gorging yourself on chocolate waterfalls—souvenirs are included! Make a giant customizable chocolate bar at the chocolate factory, filled with all the goodies your heart

could ever desire. What are the odds that it even makes it out the door?

Tickets €12, reduced €11; check website for English tour times; wheelchair accessible

DEICHTORHALLEN HAMBURG

Deichtorstraße 1-2; 40 321030; www.deichtorhallen.de/en; open Tu-Su 11am-6pm

Famed for its rotating international exhibitions, Deichtorhallen exhibits contemporary art and photography. Dynamic and eye-catching, the photography house's ever-changing landscape reflects its early days. Originally constructed as the Hamburg Bahnhof, the museum transitioned into a wholesale flower market from the 1960s-1980s. Since the late 1980s, it has promoted twentieth and twenty first-century art amidst a backdrop of stunning architectural and historical landmarks: the **Speicherstadt**, **Elphilharmonie**, and **St. Catherine's Church** lie just across the canal to the west. When visiting Deichtorhallen, Lauren Greenfield's "Generation of Wealth: I Shop, Therefore I Am," photography exhibit, just might make you reconsider adding that 30th pair of shoes to our collection, maybe.

Admission €12, reduce €7, after 4pm on Tu €6; free guided tour Sa-Su at 4pm; wheelchair accessible

KUNSTHALLE HAMBURG

Glockengießerwall 5; 40 428131200; www.hamburger-kunsthalle.de; open Tu-W 10am-6pm, Th 10am-9pm, F-Su 10am-6pm

Kunsthalle is one of the largest museums in the country. Guess it kind of needs to be if it's going to fit seven centuries worth of European art inside. Pieces range from the Medieval Ages to contemporary time and in true Hamburg fashion, curators mix the young and the old. On your visit, admire the Da Vinci exhibit which flows into the modern art hall. To avoid the crowds, visit early in the morning. An added bonus, you'll be done in time for lunch so that you can take advantage of all the cheap, delicious eats around the **Hamburg Hauptbahnhof**.

Admission €14, reduced €8, Th 5:30-9pm €8, reduced €5; audio guide €4; wheelchair accessible

OUTDOORS

ALSTER LAKES

Alster Lakes, Jungfernstieg; open daily 24hr

Row, row, row your boat, all the way to the shops at **Neustadt.** The Alster Lakes are a man-made two-lake system, with the inner lake bordering the posh shopping area in central Hamburg. On a sunny summer day, the water is flooded with sailors, paddlers, and rowers, while the surrounding parks are overrun with joggers, cyclists, and sunbathers. Dozens of stark white sails stand out against the dazzling blue water, as much a normal part of the Hamburg landscape as the city's old church clock towers or city hall's spires. In the winter, the lake freezes over to create a large, natural ice-skating rink for thousands of locals and visitors. After taking a whirl (or several tumbles), treat yourself to a delectable hot chocolate from the **Godiva Café** on the nearby **Alsterfleet Canal.** You've earned it.

Free; wheelchair accessible; boat rentals available, price varies

FOOD

EDEL CURRY ($)

Große Bleichen 68; 40 35716262; www.edelcurry.de; open M-Sa 11am-10pm, Su noon-8pm

The US has gourmet burgers. The Germans? Gourmet currywurst. Located near the high-end **Neustadt** shopping district, Edel Curry puts a classy spin on Germany's favorite fast food. Decked out in black and yellow, the restaurant gives off a California Pizza Kitchen-esque vibe, right down to the brick wall framing the kitchen. With fashion empires like BVLGARIA, Louis Vuitton, and Chanel around the corner, your wallet will be thanking you for the lunchtime reprieve. On a nice day, try snagging a seat outside and a drink from the bar so you can refuel before (window) shopping the day away. As the saying goes, eat all the curry at Edel Curry.

i Currywurst from €4, beer from €3; limited wheelchair accessibility

MAMALICIOUS ($$)

Max-Brauer-Allee 277; 40 37026944; open M-Tu 9am-6pm, W-F 9am-7pm, Sa-Su 10am-7pm

"Let them eat cake!" Pancakes, that is. Mamalicious serves up tall stacks of light, fluffy pancakes, topped with mounds of fresh fruit or stuffed with succulent chocolate chips. The Canadian-style café offers traditional breakfast foods, with an untraditional twist: all dishes are 100 percent vegan and vegetarian, right down to the butter you're bound to layer onto your pancakes. And the real hidden gem? Unlimited hot coffee, a rarity in Europe. Served in an eclectic mug, it gives the breakfast joint the homely feeling that's usually reserved for curling up on the couch in the morning with a fresh cup of piping hot joe. Mamalicious? More like Mama-lick-the-plate clean.

i Breakfast from €7; cash only; vegan and vegetarian options only; limited wheelchair accessibility; outdoor seating available

NASCH ($)

Caffamacherreihe 49; 40 35581185; open M-F 9:30am-6pm, Sa 11am-6pm, Su noon-6pm

We swear that Germany has some kind of secret agenda to turn all tourists vegan. Nasch, yet another café whose cushion-lined window seats and counter-culture vibe draws you in, makes you stay with its steaming lattes and tantalizing tortes make you stay. Turns out that the vegan and vegetarian salads, paninis, and quiches must be more than okay as well, if the lunchtime line out the door gives any indication. Just like its **Gängviertel** neighborhood, Nasch is dripping with character and flair. From the sign in the window of a bear eating cake, to the eclectic mismatched antique sofas and chairs, to the bike-bench outside the front door, the café is one for the books—which all coincidentally happen to be stacked on the piano in the corner.

i Coffee from €2, lunch from €4, dessert from €3; cash only; outdoor seating available out back; free Wi-Fi

QUÁN ĐO ($)

Georgspl. 16; 40 32901737; www.quan-do.com; open M-Th 11:30am-9:30pm, F 11:30am-10pm, Sa noon-10pm, Su noon-9pm

Can do, Quán Đo! The Vietnamese street food kitchen knows how to serve up a mean vermicelli. And the pho! Diners leave feeling jubilant and content—exactly what the owners intended. Quán Đo (translation: red store) mimics the chaotic, yet comforting Vietnamese kitchen experience. In case you miss the blazing golden warrior statue atop the building, its fire-engine red façade will certainly catch your eye. To get a piece of the authentic street food action, visit during peak dining times, a.k.a. any time, since there's nearly always a wait.

i Meals from €7.50; cash only; vegetarian options available; wheelchair accessible; outdoor seating available

RINDERMARKTHALLE ($)

Neuer Kamp 31; 040 87976390; www.rindermarkthalle-stpauli.de; open M-Sa 10am-8pm

Steaks and shakes are all a gal needs in life. Or, at least all we need to power walk our way through **St. Pauli's** sights. So, how does one fuel up, you wonder? First, imagine a supermarket. Now, imagine three supermarkets, all under a mega supermarket roof, like one happy family. They go in for a big family hug, smothering little cousin Jimmy in the middle. Except cousin Jimmy is actually a food court, featuring everything from kumpir and currywurst to crepes and croissants. Welcome to Rindermarkthalle, aka the indecisive (or famished) traveler's paradise. Here, you can satisfy your every need, whether you're in your "health-kick" phase, or your "post-breakup, ice cream as every meal" phase. Or, better yet, wash down a salad with an Oreo shake from the butcher's station. Compromise at its finest.

i Meals from €4; wheelchair accessible; vegetarian and vegan options available

ZUM SPÄTZLE ($$)

Wexstr. 31; 040 35739516; zumspaetzle.de; M-Su noon-10pm, last seating at 9:30pm

Spätzle means "small sparrow," which fits this quaint restaurant well. Tucked into a nook near Hamburg's **Gängviertel** neighborhood, Zum Spätzle packs all the punch that you'd expect from the petite, plump bird. Speaking of plump...that's where you'll be headed if you, too, overindulge in owner Elizabeth Wehrle's rich, homestyle cooking. Spätzle virgins should know that they will soon be under the spell of a soft Swabian pasta, made with eggs and cheese that are handpicked by the owner. What you'll love about Zum Spätzle isn't its filling portions or friendly faces. Rather, it's the restaurant's genuine and rustic character. Just what the doctor ordered for any homesick travelers looking to feel like they've just sat down to dinner at grandma's house.

i Spätzle from €10; not wheelchair accessible

NIGHTLIFE

BERMUDA

Hamburger Burg 6; 40 38040937; bermuda-stpauli.de; open M-Sa 5pm-late, Su 2pm-late

Legend says that things that go into the Bermuda Triangle, never return. Luckily, all we lost was a few euros on our Tequila Sunrise and Sweet Malibu. At Bermuda, the beachy vibes buzz even stronger than the drinks. The sunset-esque hot pink and burnt orange hues of the building's exterior let you know that the night is just getting started, and the tiger mural hints that you're in for a wild time. Take a joy ride on the random dolphin that's strayed from its merry-go-round pod, then enjoy the live DJs on both of the club's dance floors. The next time the weather tries to ruin your Sunday beach trip, pop on over to Bermuda. It's sure to cure those rainy-day blues with its cocktail of the day, starting at 2pm.

i No cover, beer from €3, cocktails from €6; student night Tu-Th, beer €2, wine €2.50; cash only; BGLTQ+ friendly

KYTI VOO CAFÉ

Lange Reihe 82; 40 28055565; www.kytivoo.com; open M-Sa 5pm-late, Su 2pm-10pm

Yoo hoo, Kyti Voo! While you unfortunately cannot find your favorite childhood drink here, your adult taste buds are in luck. Kyti Voo is a large bar in **St. Georg** that specializes in craft beer and cocktails. Feeling adventurous on a Tuesday night? Try one of their beer, whisky, or gin tasting boards, starting at €8. The chic bar offers a low-key café culture vibe during the week, but like every millennial, knows how to turn up on the weekends. Expect the crowd to turn younger and more lively on Friday and Saturday nights. Now if only they had a bowtie-wearing Cheshire cat serving up drinks like their logo indicates.

i No cover, beer from €3, wine from €7, cocktails from €9; cocktail happy hour 5pm-8pm; cash only; BGLTQ+ friendly

SOMMERSALON

Spielbudenpl. 22; 40 38949837; www.sommersalon.de; open Su-Th 5pm-late, F-Sa 6pm-late

Toto, we're not in Kansas anymore. Located in the heart of the infamous **Reeperbahn,** Sommersalon serves up cocktails and beers at a relatively laid-back pace. With socks and bathing suits hanging over the bar to line dry and dozens of shoes strung through the tree on the patio, it may look like every day is laundry day...but hey, at least you know it's clean. Fancy a classic mojito or a bright blue vodka coconut milkshake? How about a lime green Mogli, garnished with a giant cherry gummy? The correct answer: all three! No need to make those tough calls at Sommersalon, where happy hour lasts until midnight, and the hangover until noon.

i No cover, beer from €3, wine from €4, cocktails from €8; happy hour until midnight; cash only; BGLTQ+ friendly; wheelchair accessible

MUNICH

Coverage by **Megan Galbreath**

Close your eyes and think of Germany. You're probably picturing lederhosen-clad men dancing through the cobblestoned streets, frothy beer over-spilling from liter-sized mugs at rambunctious beer gardens, bratwurst and wiener schnitzel on every corner...in other words, Munich. The city is your stereotypical Germany, but also so much more than that. Germans from other areas of the country might frown upon Bavarian tradition and scoff at the notion that the lively city is a fair characterization of the entire country, but who knows? Maybe they're just jealous that they aren't living in the Oktoberfest capital of the world where each day they could wander through food markets, revel in some of the country's most picturesque architecture, and shop at luxurious boutiques. The "Texas of Germany" is the country's third most populous city and a global center of art, culture, innovation and education. Today, residents of Munich enjoy a high standard of living and rich social life, though the town got its beginnings as a meager and humble small monk settlement in the mid-1100s. Across the ages, the area persevered through the bubonic plague, both World Wars, and the 1972 Olympic Massacre to become a thriving and multicultural city, steeped in conservative tradition, yet open to modern changes and trends.

ORIENTATION

Go big or go home, right? That's why we're going to start with **Old Town (Aldstadt),** a historic and bustling district at the heart of Munich. The area is famous for its landmarks, shopping, and tourist attractions, including **Marienplatz, Victualienmarkt,** and the **Munich Residence.** If you head north from Old Town's cobblestoned streets and medieval squares, you'll hit the gorgeous and expansive **English Garden**—an area popular with the young crowd thanks to the universities that lie just to the west in the neighborhood of **Maxvorstadt.** A cultural hotspot for Munich, Maxvorstadt houses many museums, boutique shops, and charming restaurants. Not to be outshined by the young, hip Maxvorstadt, the regal neighborhood of **Schwabing** borders the English Garden to the north. Once an artistic, bohemian quarter, the area is now the most stylish, expensive neighborhood in the city, filled with vibrant stores, classy restaurants, and trendy bars. Switching gears to neighborhoods south of Old Town, you're sure to encounter **Glockenbach,** a hotbed of activity with lively bistros, picturesque architecture, and some of the best BGLTQ+ nightlife in the city. Finally, we would be remiss if we left out **Isarvorstadt,** a neighborhood to the southwest of Old Town that hosts everyone's favorite October holiday: **Oktoberfest.**

ESSENTIALS

GETTING THERE

Munich is serviced by a large international airport (Flughafen München) located about 24 miles northeast of the city. Travelers arriving by plane will then have to take about a 45min. ride on the S-bahn (lines S1 or S8) to complete their journey into Munich. If you are traveling to Munich from within Germany or continental Europe, you will likely arrive by train at the Munich Hauptbahnhof (central train station), which is located just west of the city center. Travel by bus is also an economical and convenient option for those arriving from a nearby city. Often, travel by bus from Austria is a practical option, given Munich's proximity to the Austrian border. The ZOB (central bus station) is located just west of the Hauptbahnhof. From there, an extensive public transportation can take you to your final destination.

GETTING AROUND

Like most German cities, Munich has an excellent public transportation system. Travelers can take advantage of the MVV's U-bahn, S-bahn, tram, and bus services to reach outlying neighborhoods and the surrounding region, including Dachau. The price of single ride tickets, day tickets, 3-day tickets, and weekly tickets depends on the transport zone, but nearly every major sight or destination is located within zones 1, 2, or 3. Make sure to validate tickets after purchase, or risk paying the €60 fine if caught without a ticket, or with an expired or unvalidated ticket. Downtown (Old Town) contains many of Munich's most prominent landmarks, restaurants, and shopping districts, and can be crossed by foot in about 30 minutes. In fact, some of the more tourist-heavy areas of Old Town are restricted to pedestrians. Bike-sharing apps are also making their way onto the scene in Munich, and those who are comfortable cycling in cities may prefer this common mode of transportation.

PRACTICAL INFORMATION

Tourist Offices: The Munich Tourist Office is located downtown in City Hall (Rathaus) at Marienplatz (Marienplatz 2; 89 23396500; www.muenchen.de; open M-Sa 9:30am-7:30pm, Su 10am-6pm).

Banks/ATMs/Currency Exchange: Many bars and cafés in Munich only accept cash, especially outside the city center. ATMs are easily accessible, and typically offer the best exchange rates. Withdrawing funds from Deutsche Bank is a reliable option for all travelers, and Bank of America cardholders are able to avoid international ATM access fees here since both banks are members of the Global ATM Alliance. We have listed one located at Marienplatz in Old Town, across from the tourist office.

- Deutsche Bank (Marienplatz 21; 89 2311340; www.deutsche-bank.de; open M-Th 9:30am-5pm, F 9:30am-3pm).

Post Offices: No post offices are located within the inner city center, though most can be found around the "Ring" encircling the area. We have listed one location close to the Hauptbahnhof.

- Deutsche Post (Bahnhofplatz 1; 22 84333113; www.deutschepost.de; open M-F 8am-7pm, Sa 9am-3pm).

Public Restrooms: Expect that most public restrooms (toilette or WC) are available only to paying customers inside restaurants, cafés, and museums. Some major public transportation stations do offer toilets for a small fee (usually €0.50). Larger shopping malls such as the Galeria Kaufhof in Marienplatz offer free services, though it is standard to tip the attendant.

Internet: Free Wi-Fi is offered in Marienplatz and Odeonsplatz, as well as major public transportation stations. Many shops and malls in the downtown area also have their own public hotspots. There are nine Starbucks located within the city limits (five within the inner city center alone), so when in doubt, head to the one nearest you.

BGLTQ+ Resources: There are many online resources with tips for the best nightlife, associations, and community events for members of the BGLTQ+ community. Visitors should also visit the tourist office in Marienplatz for more information.

EMERGENCY INFORMATION

Emergency Number: 112.
Police: Polizeiinspektion München is located in Old Town (Hochbrückenstr. 7; 89 290800; open daily 24hr).
US Embassy: The US Consulate General Munich is located at (Königinstr. 5; 89 28880). For passport requests, special consular services, or visa information, it is necessary to contact or visit the US Embassy in Berlin.
Rape Crisis Center: The Protection Against Sexual Abuse and Discrimination Advice Service offers services through an office based in the Munich Olympic Park (Helene-Mayer-Ring 9; 89 357 135-40; open M-F 9am-noon). Frauennotruf München also offers a hotline for those who have suffered sexual assault or abuse (89 763737; www.frauennotruf-muenchen.de; hotline available M-F 10am-midnight, Sa-Su 6pm-midnight).
Hospitals: Several hospitals offer daily 24hr emergency services. Here is a centrally located one:

- Schwabing Hospital (Kölner Platz 1; 89 33040302; www.klinikum-muenchen.de).

Pharmacies: Pharmacies (denoted by a large red A, or apotheke) are plentiful in the city center, though most are closed on Sundays. We have listed one location in City Hall at Marienplatz.

- Rathaus-Apotheke (Marienplatz 8; 89 553520; www.rathausapotheke-muenchen.de; open M-Sa 9am-8pm).

SIGHTS

CULTURE

VIKTUALIENMARKT

Viktualienmarkt 3; 89 89068205; www.viktualienmarkt-muenchen.de; open M-Sa 8am-8pm

Come hungry, leave happy—and about 20 pounds heavier. We hope you packed your stretchy jeans because Viktualienmarkt is basically a culinary heaven on earth. Sweet or savory? Dirt cheap or high end? Juice diet or beer belly? At Munich's grand, historic food market, you can have it all. Pro tip: when you arrive, grab a small snack. Preferably something bread-based. Did someone say traditional Bavarian pretzel?? Your snack (pretzel) will 1) keep the hunger pains at bay while you peruse around and 2) serve as a handy dipping base for all the free samples you're about to encounter. Yes, free samples. So extensive and delicious, this place makes Costco look like child's play. After a tasting plate of cheese, olives, tapenades, wursts, and fruit, you might have just enough room to (muffin) top it off with some soft serve or a warm pastry. Bon appetit!

i Free, food and drink prices vary; wheelchair accessible; individual stall hours vary

BAYERISCHE STAATSOPER (NATIONAL THEATER)

Max-Joseph-Platz 2; www.staatsoper.de/en; show times vary

Honey, where is my opera suit? A last-minute trip to the Munich National Theater may have you feeling a bit like Frozone: anxious, overwhelmed, and utterly underdressed. You'll be scrambling to pair that wrinkled, definitely-been-worn-three-times-already skirt with your final semi-clean shirt. If you're lucky, you'll remember to dust the debris off your worn flats before strolling up to the historic opera house sans gown, sans wrap, and sans a care in the world. In fact, you may be laughing with glee because you arrived at the evening box office one hour before showtime and scored an incredibly cheap ticket to see the state ballet perform at the world's third largest opera house. Standing room only, schmanding room only, you made it to the big leagues. Someone, pop the champagne cork.

i Ticket prices vary; wheelchair accessible

DACHAU CONCENTRATION CAMP MEMORIAL

Alte Römerstraße 75; 81 31669970; www.kz-gedenkstaette-dachau.de; open daily 9am-5pm

If you have time for the four-five hour Dachau outing, do it. If you don't have the time, make it. The concentration camp memorial is humbling, heart wrenching, and will be the most unforgettable experience that you will have on your trip. The Germans constructed Dachau in 1933 before WWII began, and it was the only camp to exist throughout the length of the entire war. Visitors have access to an extensive museum, as well as most of the camp's original grounds. The makeshift barracks bring to life the reality of being forced to call this barren land home, while the crematorium sends shivers down your spine. Perhaps the most startling moment is when you realize that you have the chance to walk back out of the wrought-iron gates engraved with the camp's motto "Work Brings Freedom," while thousands who walked before you did not.

i Admission free, audio guide €4, reduced €3; English guided tours available, €3.50 (2.5hrs); wheelchair accessible

LANDMARKS

MARIENPLATZ

Marienplatz 1; plaza open daily 24hr

It's 5 o'clock somewhere rings true for Marienplatz not once, not twice, but three times a day. Happy hour strikes at 11am, noon, and 5pm, after the famed **Rathaus Glockenspiel** show commences. For ten blissful minutes, the hectic pace of Marienplatz slows. Heads cranes upwards, oohs and ahhs erupt, and the masses gather to gaze in wonder at the dancing men and galloping horses that spin around the famous clock tower. Those with enough foresight (or expendable cash) will grab a table at a nearby café for an unobstructed view of the chim cher-ee charade. After bearing witness to city hall's ten minutes of fame, the world is your oyster. In fact, brunch on some oysters at **Viktualienmarkt** or go see the seashell masterpiece at the **Munich Residence,** both just five minutes away.

i Free; wheelchair accessible; Glockenspiel show daily at 11am, noon, and 5pm

MUNICH RESIDENCE

Residenzstr. 1; 89 7908444; www.residenz-muenchen.de; museum and treasury open daily Apr-mid Oct 9am-6pm, mid-Oct-Mar 10am-5pm

Munich Residence is what happens when you can't seem to tell your partner "no." You've agreed on the budget and floor plans, you might have put aside a bit of extra cash for a jacuzzi...and by the time the darn thing is move-in ready, you've added a home theater, swimming pool, receiving room, garden, and mini golf course. Or in the case of the Munich Residence, it's courtyards, multiple wings, exquisite art, golden gilding, sacred relic rooms, porcelain cabinets, multiple chapels, and more. From 1508-1918, the palace served not just as the Bavarian seat of government, but also as the lavish home for the region's dukes, electors, and kings. Today, visitors can get marathon-ready by wandering through the 130 rooms on display, then pop over to nearby **Odeonplatz** for a little luxurious home-decor shopping themselves.

i Museum admission €7, reduced €6; combination museum and treasury admission €11, reduced €9; last entry 1hr before closing; partial wheelchair accessibility

BAVARIA STATUE

Theresienhöhe 16; open daily 24hr

It's **Lady Bavaria's** world, and we're all just living in it. Or at least that's how it seems when you arrive at the base of the statue and crane your neck up and up and up to gaze at the imposing bronze casting. The monumental figure was erected in 1850, and today has the proud honor of watching over Munich's annual **Oktoberfest.** The city considers the woman and her pet lion to be the epitome of Munich personification, and even granted her a Hall of Fame containing busts of Bavaria's most famous personalities. We just want to know why this so-called "personification" is holding a crown of oak leaves, rather than a frosted mug. Do better, Munich. In any case, cheers to Lady Bavaria!

i Free; wheelchair accessible

MUSEUMS

DEUTSCHES MUSEUM

Museumsinsel 1; 89 21791; www.deutsches-museum.de; open daily 9am-5pm

Alright, you mad scientist. Time to get your groove on at the largest science museum in the world. Come one, come all, and step right up to the Deutsches Museum, where the laboratory is your playground and the adventure is just beginning. This one goes out to all our future astronauts, physicists, engineers, and maritime explorers. All you dreamers would appreciate this little test drive along the various paths one could take in life. At Deutsches Museum, you can spend the day exploring over 25 different careers and maybe, just maybe, feel like a carefree kid once again.

i Admission €14, reduced €8, students €4.50; general tour available €3; last admission 4:30pm; wheelchair accessible; Deutsches Museum app available

BMW MUSEUM

Am Olympiapark 2; 89 125016001; www.bmw-welt.com/en/locations/museum; open T-Su 10am-6pm

Vroom vroom. At the BMW Museum, where the world of racing and sleek elitism is a family affair, your mum won't be telling you to get out her car. The futuristic museum is like a luxurious new version of hybrid cars: 50 percent history exhibit, 50 percent display room, and 100 percent pompous through and through. The sporty, dynamic design of the building will make you want to hop in one of those shiny, spotless motor bikes and take it for a spin, pretending to be a suave spy like 007. Coincidentally, you kind of can. After ogling the sweet ride made famous by James Bond, break open the piggy bank—or, more true to character, rob a bank—and take an elegant BMW for a test drive. Maybe your engine will even be displayed on the BMW Wall of Fame one day, you Formula 1 racer, you.

i Admission €10, reduced €7; last entry 30min before close; wheelchair accessible

PINAKOTHEK DER MODERNE

Barer Str. 40; 89 23805360; www.pinakothek-der-moderne.de/en; open Tu-W 10am-6pm, Th 10am-8pm, F-Su 10am-6pm

Out with the old, in with the new. In case the additional "e" in "Moderne" had you wishing you had actually paid attention in your ninth grade beginner foreign language class, we'll toss you a bone. The Pinakothek der Moderne is the most contemporary of the four museums in the **Pinakothek Museum Complex.** This famed house focuses on architecture, design, and fine art from across the twentieth and twenty-first centuries. More prominent permanent exhibits include surrealism, futurism, and the bauhaus movement. Though some of the more disturbing pieces give off a "the world is ending" apocalyptic vibe, we'd put a dollar on it (okay, two dollars) that you won't end up like the skeletal sculpture in the George Baselitz exhibit.

i Admission Tu-Sa €10, reduced €7, admission on Su €1; audio-guide available for €4.50; wheelchair accessible

OUTDOORS

ENGLISH GARDEN

Englischer Garten 80805; 89 38666390; www.muenchen.de/int/en/sights/parks/english-garden; open daily 24hr

Sunrise, sunburn, sunset, repeat. Lakeside, all night, refreshing, yeah baby. Nothing will ever be easy as paddling on **Kleinhesseloher See**, liquored up with nowhere to be. Munich's English Garden is one of the world's largest urban parks, and a popular spot for biking, barbecuing, tanning, and surfing. That's right, folks, surfing. Despite the lack of beachfront property, the park is famous for an artificial stream that allows riders to catch some waves. We hope your surfboard made the packing cut. If you happened to be hampered by an infuriating little thing called a luggage limit, just hang loose, dude. All you need are board shorts and sunscreen to wade through the streams or relax on the lawn. Pro tip: cool off with a beer at the park's famous Chinese Tower beer garden. Shirt and shoes required.

i Free; wheelchair accessible

OLYMPIAPARK

Spiridon-Louis-Ring 21; 89 30670; www.olympiapark.de/en/olympiapark-munich, open daily 9am, closing hours vary so check website

Munich's Olympic motto may have been "The Cheerful Games," but today Olympiapark subscribes to the more coy words of Nelly: "It's getting hot in here, so take off all your clothes." Shirtless dudes and swimsuit-clad women are a common sight at the 280-hectare park. After all, who can blame them? The nearest proper beach is over 300 miles away, so beach volleyball under the blazing sun in the middle of Olympiapark it is. Following the 1972 Olympics, Munich opened the park and many of its grand amenities to the community. Festivals and concerts are weekly occurrences, so check the park's website for a full list of events.

i Admission €9; admission €3.50; wheelchair accessible

FOOD

WAGNERS ($$)

Fraunhoferstraße 43; www.wagnersjuicery.com; open M 8am-6:30pm, W-F 8am-6:30pm, Sa-Su 10am-5pm

At Wagners, the only thing more gorgeous than the people is the food. Seriously, it's like the superfood café shone the bat signal one morning, and all the beautiful people in Munich flocked to put out the fire. Somehow though, the smoking hot under-30 crowd falls to the background at this lively, vibrant joint. Maybe it has something to do with the abundance of refreshing smoothie bowls, detox juices, scrumptious salads, and filling warm grain bowls that fill the menu boards at this trendy hangout. That, or the peanut butter berry bowl, a one-of-a-kind sight in the nut butter bare-forsaken land of Europe. For a jamming good time and the chance to watch your Instagram follower-count soar through the roof, join the spirited weekend crowd at your homeboy Wagners.

i Smoothies from €5, salads and bowls from €6; vegetarian and vegan options available; wheelchair accessible; outdoor seating available

ALOHA POKE ($$)

Türkenstraße 80; 89 85634893; www.aloha-poke.com; open M-Sa 11am-10pm, Su noon-10pm

You're three weeks into your trip. It's been nothing but currywurst, kebap, potato salad, and apple strudel for days. Your body is begging you for a fresh vegetable, a lean protein, a light and refreshing meal to detox from the cheap and heavy Asian fare that's been oh-so-kind to your wallet. You flock to **Maxvorstadt,** certain that the university neighborhood must have a health-conscious, college-student-budget-friendly dining option. There in the distance, line out the door, you spot the rainbow sign advertising Aloha Poke. Ever the millennial, you join the crowd, heels clicking in glee, head bobbing to the Hawaiian beach tunes. You gaze around and are transported to the Laguna Bay Boardwalk. Vibrant colors, Polaroid snapshots, and flip-flop clad students surround you. You spot the trendy Facebook "like" tracker on the counter and turn on your hotspot so you can bump them up to 4,087.

i Regular bowl €9.40; vegetarian options available; wheelchair accessible

CRÊPEFRUIT ($)

Marienplatz 8; www.crepefruit.com; open M-Sa 11:30am-10pm

Over 130 food stalls and not one fruity ice pop! Not one! Viktualienmarkt has ice cream, smoothies, and fresh fruit galore, but where do you go when you're looking to put them all together? You jaunt across the street to Crêpefruit, a little crêperie and popsicle stand nestled into the side of Munich's **Rathaus.** Black Plague hypochondriacs, have no fear. Not a single rat had been spotted at the sparkling and merry counter. In fact, there hadn't been much more than a cast-iron crêpe maker and no-waste pasta straws behind the glass. Environmentally-friendly AND deliciously refreshing? Can it get any better than this? No? Would you change your mind if you found out that it is as light on your wallet as it is on your stomach? Crêpefruit: 1, Viktualienmarkt: 0.

i Crepes and juices from €3; cash only; vegetarian options available; no seating; wheelchair accessible

GRENZSTEIN ($)

Elisabethmarkt Stand 10, Schwabing; 28 806357; open M-F 8:30am-6pm

You've just been to the lively, crowded, and fast-paced **Viktualienmarkt**. You show up to **Elisabethmarkt** and are greeted with...a few stalls selling fruits and vegetables. Some teens loitering on the edges, sipping coffee or a smoothie. And Grenzstein, rising like a phoenix out of the ashes in the middle of the plaza. The small, unsuspecting stall serves just four daily lunch specials. Given the delicious flavors, we'd suggest you try them all...but alas that luxury is only reserved for cows, whose four stomachs let them go tit-for-tat with Grenzstein. Instead, you'll have to settle for a rich, warm ratatouille, fluffy quiche, or gooey slice of lasagna. We just hope that you have room for a slice of crisp apple tart when you're done.

i *Lunch specials from €7, pastries from €3; cash only; vegetarian options available; not wheelchair accessible; outdoor seating available*

ITXASO ($$$)

Pestalozzistraße 7; 89 23708048; www.itxaso.de; open M-Th 5:30pm-midnight, F-Sa 5:30pm-1:30am

Time to whip out the pistols, bang bang. You're in for a Wild Wild West dual to the death. Or at the very least, a good old-fashioned brawl for the last table at the ever-popular Tex-Mex inspired tapas joint in **Sendlinger Tor.** Alright, smoking guns away, boys. The only thing that you'll be firing off is your order, in the hopes of snagging coveted dishes, like Itxaso's fresh seafood plates, before supplies run out for the night. At this point, your tummy's a'rumbling, your mouth's a'watering, and your brain's a'thinking that the best part about tiny plates means you don't need a partner to go "halfsies." 100 percent of those rich, wonderful flavors go straight to you—the only downside, so does the bill. What's life though if you don't live a little? So go forth and prosper on a cool, starry Saturday night in the midst of the boisterous Sendlinger nightlife scene.

i *Tapas from €6, beer and wine from €4; vegetarian options available; limited wheelchair accessibility; outdoor seating available*

MARAIS ($$)

Parkstraße 2; 89 50094552; www.café-marais.de; open Tu-Sa 8am-8pm, Su 10am-6pm

Ah yes, the lovely café Marais. The charming space shares not just the name, but also the ambience and prices to match the quirky, high-end **French quarter.** You've got to give it to them because the eclectic café definitely wins Munich's superlative for "Most On-Theme." From the worn jewelry, to the rustic chairs, to the warped mirrors, everything screams "antique flea market," only with collector's item prices. Even a trip to the WC will make you think you've traveled back to the golden age when you realize the flush capacity is operated by a hanging crystal string. Nevertheless, its vintage atmosphere makes it worth the trip (to the café, not the WC), if only to pick up a souvenir for grandma.

i *Paninis from €6.20, entrees from €12.50; vegetarian options available; limited wheelchair accessibility; outdoor seating available*

TRAM CAFÉ ($)

Müllerstraße 46; 89 45249483; www.tramcafé.de; open daily 11am-11pm

Why are we sending you to another crêpe place? We'll answer your sassy exasperation with a sassy hot take: savory crêpes & sweet crêpes. Tram Café offers warm, delicious, filling French favorites at smile-inducing prices. Walk up to the tram and call your order from the set menu, or get those creative juices flowing and make your own concoction. Then, watch in wonder as the grill master operates six crêpe stations at once, twirling, spinning, spreading, and folding each wonder into a mess-free, stringy cheese delight. Those who are so inclined can pop a squat onto a copper chair and munch along to the tram's edgy tunes, though we'd recommend taking your meal on the road toward nearby **Odeonsplatz.**

i *Savory crepes from €5, sweet crepes from €4; credit card minimum of €10; vegetarian options available; limited wheelchair accessibility; outdoor seating available*

NIGHTLIFE

CHINESISCHER TURM (CHINESE TOWER)

Englischer Garten 3; 89 38387327; www.chinaturm.de; open daily 10am-10pm

We're pretty sure there's a picture of Chineserturm next to the word "Biergarten" in the dictionary. Their signature green park benches hold thousands who travel from far and wide to guzzle their beer by the gallons. Alright, maybe that was a tad hyperbolic. Germans are impressive, but even they tap out after a liter or two of distilled wheat. What's more impressive than German tolerance levels and Chineserturm's cavernous mugs is the garden's extravagant Chinese Tower itself. Somehow, the jubilant melodies from the live brass band stationed inside are perfectly fitting for the space. After all, where else can you drink a German beer and eat a Bavarian pretzel sitting next to a Chinese tower and across from an Ethiopian exchange student in the middle of an English Garden?

i No cover, half-liter from €4.50, liter from €8.50; cash preferred; wheelchair accessible

COUCH CLUB

Klenzestraße 89; 8912 555778; www.couch-club.org; open Tu-Th 7pm-1am, F-Sa 7pm-3am

Couch potato, meet hot potato. The Couch Club features a constantly rotating crowd of young locals looking for a relaxed bar hangout. Like a lounge on the couch, put your feet up, and play a game of foosball kind of relaxed. So, how do you get back to your true couch potato roots? Step one: sow the seed. Plant that little tush into a nice, warm, worn spot in the corner. Soft lighting advised. Step two: liquid hydration. The more gin, the better. After all, you wouldn't want that gorgeous blossom to start wilting now, would you? Step three: tend to that baby with love and care. The happiest potatoes are those surrounded by other couch potatoes, so don't be afraid to make new friends and cultivate your own little community. Step four: harvest by 1am for best outcome.

i No cover, beer from €4, cocktails from €7; happy hour 7pm-9pm and midnight to close, many drinks €6.50; cash only

DIVE BAR

Reichenbachstraße 19; 89 45245877; www.divebar-munich.de; open Tu-Sa 7pm-2am

The number one rule of Dive Bar is you don't stay at Dive Bar. Then why, you wonder, would you ever visit the dark, somewhat dingy hole-in-the-wall? Would it be for the upside down red cowboy hat pinned to the ceiling? Or maybe to get a stereotypical leather-clad biker "mom" tattoo to match the stenciled skull and bones stickers that litter the wall. Perhaps to pat the head of the fake stuffed "Fluffy" when you realize how much you've missed your own dog? Or maybe just to grab a beer and to-go cocktail so that you can join the young, lively crowd hanging out down the street in the fountain at **Gartnerplatz.** The cheap Dive Bar is more of a halfway house for the under-30s that populate the rambunctious Gartnerplatz bar scene than a place to dance the night away. FYI, the "halfway" in "halfway house"? Yeah, that stands for halfway between the neighborhood's rocking ice cream shop and its rolling party.

i No cover, beer from €3, mixed drinks from €8; cash only

MILLA

Holzstraße 28; 89 18923101; www.milla-club.de; check website for event schedule

Mainstream? Milla? Anyone who describes the intimate, indie club venue as simply ordinary is off their rocker. If anything, its fresh, young talent is extraordinary. The eclectic space hosts everything from jazz jam sessions to hip-hop hype shows with artists from all over the world. You may start to wonder what kind of alternative tangle you've gotten yourself into when you spot the welcome sign suggesting what happens "the harder you look naked," but rest assured, Milla is a sexy club, not a sex club @KitKatBerlin. Classy and vintage is the name of the game, though hot and sweaty is the feel of the deal. The small room fills up and sells out fast, so be sure to buy concert tickets in advance.

i Cover from €5 on concert nights, drinks from €4; cash only; recommended to book concert tickets in advance

GERMANY ESSENTIALS

MONEY

Tipping: The value-added tax (VAT) and service charge are included in an item's listed price. All service staff are paid at least minimum wage, but as a general rule, it is polite and customary to tip an extra 5-10% for any sit-down service. To do so, mention the total you want to pay when they state the price of the bill. Patrons typically round to the nearest full euro amount. For example, if the waiter states that the price of the bill is €8, respond with €9 and they will include the tip. It is standard to tip a taxi driver at least €1, and public toilet attendants around €0.50.

Taxes: Most German goods include a 19% VAT in their listed price, although a reduced tax of 7% is applied to books, food, agricultural products, hotel accommodations, and public transport. Non-EU visitors can claim VAT refunds within three months of purchase. To do so, request a Tax Free Shopping Check (export papers) from the retailer, and make sure to keep the original receipt. Present both, along with the goods, at the airport Customs Service to have the invoice stamped and approved. Mail the stamped invoice back to the original store upon return to your home country.

SAFETY AND HEALTH

Local Laws and Police: The police force has a strong and comforting presence throughout Germany, especially in city centers and major transportation hubs. Local laws vary. Of note is that drinking in public is acceptable, while jaywalking is not. The German local saying is "red man, dead man," so wait for the green man at each street crossing, or risk paying the €5 fine.

Drugs and Alcohol: The legal drinking age is 16 for beer and wine, and 18 for spirits. Drinking in public is legal, but public drunkenness is frowned upon and can jeopardize your safety. German drug law is currently in flux, so while all drugs are technically illegal, prosecutors can (and usually do) choose to drop charges if you are caught with possession of small quantities of cannabis for personal use (typically less than 7.5g THC).

Prescription Drugs: Common pain-relieving drugs such as aspirin, ibuprofen (Advil), acetaminophen (Tylenol, or Paracetamol) and antihistamines are available at German pharmacies (apotheken), denoted by a large red A. Most drugs, including antibiotics, require a prescription, so plan accordingly. Pharmacies should not be confused with drugstores (drogeries), where you can buy toiletries.

GREAT BRITAIN

Stop whatever you're doing and make a list of Great Britain-related things. Keep going. Okay, stop. Were Liverpool's heartthrobs (aka the Beatles) on the list? What about football? No, not the kind that involves huge pads and smashing into other people, the kind that features lean athletes playing out a unique form of theatrical drama and graceful penalty kicks. Did you write down fish and chips, the heartiest of culinary creations and quite possibly your only source of sustenance as you visit the British isles? Plaid? Kilts? Blood sausage? Look it up. Sherlock Holmes, Ivanhoe, *Middlemarch, Pride and Prejudice?* Britain is a treasure trove for literature lovers. And, of course, we can't forget haggis.

Great Britain is indeed all of these things, but is far more than the sum of its parts. Its long history means that you can walk through a museum to discover it, or walk through the streets of London or a small village to find the remnants of a time long past. Its political system is complicated enough that you have to do a lot of reading. Its cuisine is out-there yet comforting enough to appeal to many. And though its role in the world has changed over the course of hundreds of years, Great Britain somehow always makes itself known.

From Elizabeth I's reign to the English Civil War and the execution of Charles I, to World War II, to today (Brexit, anyone?), the region has its own story to tell. Even now, it continues to evolve, as its place in the European Union appears precarious—yet one thing is certain: just like it always has, the world will continue watching every move it makes.

EDINBURGH

Coverage by **Lucy Golub**

A modern day city surrounding a twelfth-century castle built on an extinct volcano: Edinburgh sounds basically like an enchanting fairy tale. Edinburgh feels like a cross-hatching of time. Each stone is steeped in history. Home to thinkers like Adam Smith and David Hume who changed the way we live today, as well as countless other artists and figures, Edinburgh has the street cred to support the cultural name it's forged for itself. Combining stunning nature, history, and significant contributions to modern theatre (a month-long festival every year!), Edinburgh is a city that offers more to do the more you explore. Old-fashioned pubs offer pints while bagpipers in kilts busk on the street. Are we in 2019 or 1819? Edinburgh's beauty comes from the way it harkens to both. So climb those stairs, take your 10,000 steps, have a sip of whiskey, perhaps a bite of haggis (or not), and get ready to discover a time capsule of European history.

ORIENTATION

The **Edinburgh Castle** provides an almost-always visible guide to where you are. If you're close to the castle and the buildings around you look old, you're likely in the **Old Town,** the center of the city. **The Royal Mile** leads you past a bunch of souvenir shops to the castle. Almost parallel to the Royal Mile, **Grassmarket** and **Cowgate** house relaxed yet hip nightlife and restaurants. Between the old town and the new town, **Waverley Station** is a hub of train activity that can take you west towards **Haymarket** or east towards the airport. Nearby, **Princes Street** begins the **New Town,** home to more upscale shops, restaurants, and nightlife.

ESSENTIALS

GETTING THERE

The Edinburgh Airport offers an easy tram service to multiple locations around the city for only £4.50 one way or £7.50 round trip. It runs 24hr and comes every 15min. You can buy tickets with cash or card when you board. There are also two central train stations connected to the Scotrail system: Edinburgh Waverley and Haymarket. Waverley is closer to New Town and Old Town, and Haymarket is best for trips outside the city center.

GETTING AROUND

Good news! Edinburgh has Uber. Even better news! You won't need it. The city is easy to walk when it's not too cold, and there's cheap public transportation. A tram runs through Princes Street, and 24hr bus services can take you anywhere you need to go. The Transport for Edinburgh app lets you buy tickets for the tram or bus on your phone—otherwise, they take exact cash for their £1.70 fare. An app named MyTaxi or old-fashioned hailing a cab in the street are both alternatives for evening travel after a night out. Day tickets for public transport are your best best if you plan on taking the bus or tram more than once.

PRACTICAL INFORMATION

Tourist Offices: Most information can be found online, but a few offices exist if you have any in-person questions. (Edinburgh and Scotland Information Centre, Visitscotland, 3 Princes Street, 131 473 3868; www.visitscotland.com; Apr 1-June 2 open M-Sa 9am-5pm, Su 10am-5pm; June 3-30 open M-Sa 9am-6pm, Su 10am-6pm; July 1-Sept 8 open M-Sa 9am-7pm, Su 10am-7pm; Sept 9-March 31 open M-Sa 9am-5pm, Su 10am-5pm).

Banks/ATMs/Currency Exchange: Bank of Scotland has branches in multiple locations, and so do HSBC, BNY Mellon, and Barclays (Bank of Scotland; 300 Lawnmarket; 131 470 2007; bankofscotland.co.uk; open M-Tu 9am-5pm, W 9:30am-5pm, Th-F 9am-5pm).

Post Offices: There are post offices in every neighborhood. (3 Princes Street;

034 5611 2970; open M 9am-5pm, Tu 9:30am-5:30pm, W-Sa 9am-5:30pm).
Public Restrooms: The city offers 61 public toilets spread throughout. (Castlehill Public Toilet; 131 608 1100; open daily 10am-6pm, summer open daily 8am-6pm).
Internet: Most of the city center has free public Wi-Fi, as do the buses. It is also widely available in cafés and other public spaces.
BGLTQ+ Resources: LGBT Health and Wellbeing (9 Howe Street; www.lgbthealth.org.uk; 131 523 1100; open M-F 9am-5pm).

EMERGENCY INFORMATION

Emergency Number: 999.
Police: Police Scotland (14 St. Leonard's Street; 178 628 9070; open M-F 9am-12:30pm and 1:30-5pm).
US Embassy: Consulate General of the United States (3 Regent Terrace; 131 556 8315; open M-F 8:30am-5pm).
Rape Crisis Center: A hotline can be found at 08088 01 003 02, and you can go to Edinburgh Rape Crisis Center (17 Claremont Crescent; 131 556 9437; open M-F 9am-7pm).
Hospitals:

- Royal Infirmary of Edinburgh (51 Little France Crescent; 131 536 1000; open daily 24hr).
- St John's Hospital (Howden West, Livingston, West Lothian; 150 653 2000; open daily 24hr).

Pharmacies: These can be found scattered throughout the city.

- Boots (101-103 Princes Street; 013 1225 8331; boots.com; open M-W 8am-7pm, Th 8am-8pm, F-Sa 8am-7pm, Su 10am-6pm).

SIGHTS
CULTURE

DEAN VILLAGE AND WALK OF LEITH

Leith, open daily 24hr

After a busy day in the city, there's no better way to spend an hour on a sunny afternoon than a walk along the port on Leith's walkway and take a trip to Dean Village. A residential area outside of the city center, Dean Village comprises enchanting homes from the nineteenth century. The precious homes look like they're taken out of a storybook, making it hard to believe that people get to live there. Nearby **Mews** present picturesque homes to snap pictures of, but be sure to be respectful of the residents. Expect a leisurely walk to take about an hour. You can walk to the village from the **Royal Mile** (about 20min.), or take the bus (24, 29, or 42) to **Stockbridge,** and you can walk from the bridge of the Water of Leith to the **Modern Art Gallery** to embrace the full views.

i Free

GRASSMARKET

www.greatergrassmarket.co.uk; store and restaurant hours vary

Lively and bustling, Grassmarket provides an unparalleled view of the castle between the street's independent shops and restaurants. Some gems include **Oink** and **Mary's Milk Bar.** Next to Grassmarket, **Victoria Street**—the inspiration for J.K. Rowling's Diagon Alley—curves down from the hill. If you're trying to find a souvenir different from the kilts, shortbread, and whiskey at every tourist shop, Grassmarket's stores will answer your query. In the middle of the road, buskers play music on a central median, entertaining those eating at the restaurants outside. Steep staircases lead into the area from the castle, creating an air of centrality and reminding tourists that people used to be hanged right where they're currently enjoying lunch. Heartwarming.

i Free; store and restaurant prices; limited wheelchair accessibility

GREYFRIARS KIRKYARD

26A Candlemaker Row; greyfriarskirk.com/visit-us/kirkyard; open daily 24hr

Harry Potter fans rejoice—here you'll find the graves of a William McGonagall and Thomas Riddell, while some even claim the neighboring school **George Heriot** to be the inspiration for Hogwarts. For those not Harry Potter-inclined, the cemetery is still worth a visit. Estimations project over 100,000 bodies are buried in the hill of the cemetery, so you might occasionally find a bone. Yet as you walk through immaculately kept trees and flowers and families picnicking, you'll almost forget that the park is a graveyard. The cemetery is home to the legend of

Greyfriar's Bobby, the most loyal dog there ever was, and his memorial can be found right outside the graveyard. Seemingly sacrilegious, high school-aged students have been heard to frequent the cemetery after dark with new friends made at the pub.

i Free; limited wheelchair accessibility

LANDMARKS

EDINBURGH CASTLE

Castlehill; 131 225 9846; www.edinburgh-castle.scot; open daily Mar 26-Sept 30 9:30am-6pm, Oct 1-Mar 31 9:30am-5pm

You can't come to Edinburgh without seeing the city's castle; after all, Edinburgh is practically in its shadow. To really experience its majesty, though, you've got to go inside. Cough up the fee and allot two hours to walk around and explore. The torture demonstration might curdle your blood a little bit, and the war memorials have caused visitors to shed tears. The real treasure lies with the crown jewels—but not the diamonds. No, the real treasure is found with the Stone of Destiny, which is basically a giant rock. It's said that wherever the stone lies, the Scots shall rule. Hundreds of years of history pack themselves into the castle, and stepping in feels like stepping back in time.

i Admission from £17, student from £10.20; last entry 1hr before closing; limited wheelchair accessibility

CALTON HILL

2 Regent Rd.; open daily 24hr

Hands down the best place to watch the sunset in Edinburgh. Overlooking the whole city with a view of Arthur's seat, golden hour makes the hills glimmer. The hill itself contains landmarks within it, like the **National Monument,** a half finished acropolis-like structure that looms over the skyline. In fact, the monument itself at the top of the hill provides the best vantage point of the glow reflected on the yellow Gorse flowers and the glinting snowy hills in Holyrood park, or even of the slowly sinking sun. Couples and families picnic to enjoy the view of the setting sun over the dreamlike city. No, our eyes aren't tearing up at the beauty—it's just the wind.

i Free; no wheelchair accessibility

ST. GILES

High St.; 131 226 0674; www.stgilescathedral.org.uk; open April-Oct M-F 9am-7pm, Sa 9am-5pm, Su 1pm-5pm; Nov-Mar M-Sa 9am-5pm, Su 1pm-5pm

Stained-glass windows light up the room, and a hushed silence that comes from centuries of worship falls over the tourists who step inside. Each window tells a story, just like every name on benches and inscribed into walls. A cathedral of secret histories. A £2 photo doesn't really do the cathedral justice, but standing in the middle of the church under the flags of Scotland and the high arched ceiling creates tranquility. Services and concerts ring out on certain days of the week. A moment inside the church lets you forget the aggressive musicians outside on **the Royal Mile** and focus on Edinburgh's real draw: its history.

i Free, photo permit £2; main cathedral wheelchair accessible

MUSEUMS

NATIONAL MUSEUM

Chambers St.; 300 123 6789; www.nms.ac.uk/national-museum-of-scotland; open daily 10am-5pm

You could spend days in this museum and not see everything, so it's probably best not to try. But the highlights you shouldn't miss include **the Millennial clock** that animates every hour from 11am to 4pm, the Scottish history and archaeology galleries, the interactive screens, and machines (read: toys) in the science and technology galleries. If you're interested in literally anything in the world, this museum probably has information on it. Scottish pop music? Check. Festivals in Vietnam? Check. A giant stuffed alpaca next to a polar bear? Also check. And if you're unsure where to begin or tired of a paper map, check the museum's app.

i Free; wheelchair accessible; tours at 11am, 1pm, and 3pm

NATIONAL GALLERY OF MODERN ART

75 Belford Rd.; 131 624 6200; www.nationalgalleries.org/visit/scottish-national-gallery-modern-art; open daily 10am-5pm

Two majestic buildings provide hundreds of pieces of art for perusal, picturesque cafés, and outdoor areas for relaxation. Connecting the spaces is an outdoor sculpture gallery. Exhibits change every few months, but make sure to check out the reconstruction of sculptor Eduardo Paolozzi's studio in the Modern Two building, so you can drink up all the bright colors and learn about how the Edinburgh native (his parents were Italian immigrants, if you're confused) pioneered the pop art movement. Bus #13 offers an easy connection from Princes Street, but for the best route you should walk through **Dean Village.** Some exhibits charge, but most are free, and we recommend just skipping anything you have to pay for, because there's so much to see already between the two buildings.

i Free; lockers £1; wheelchair accessible

SCOTTISH NATIONAL GALLERY

The Mound; 131 624 6200; www.nationalgalleries.org; open M-W 10am-5pm, Th 10am-7pm, F-Su 10am-5pm

The National Gallery hosts Scotland's greatest works on permanent display for free. On Scotland's cloudy days, this centrally located museum provides a crimson-walled spot for an afternoon at the museum. The first rooms hold the Bridgewater loan—some of the most prized art on the continent. (Island?) While art aficionados may flock to the **Rembrandt** and **Titian** pieces, those looking for interesting and funny works shouldn't miss Henry Raeburn's *The Skating Minister.* Even those with no interest in art can enjoy a stroll through the museum with rooms that are easy to navigate. The museum also hosts classes and other special events like tours, talks, live music and BSL interpretations, most of which are free to attend. Beware of the noisy bagpipers on the street walking in, though.

i Free; wheelchair accessible

OUTDOORS

ARTHUR'S SEAT

Queen's Dr.; open daily 24hr

Don't think you can hike? Try anyway. Reaching the summit of Arthur's Seat feels like the making it to the top of the world. All of Edinburgh sprawls below your feet. There are multiple routes, and our recommendation is the path that begins from **Queen Street** next to the **Holyrood Palace.** From there, follow the left path to the top. Various stopping points along the way encourage you to take in the juxtaposition of the extinct volcano's natural beauty and the city. If you go at sunrise or sunset, it's especially picturesque. But if the weather is good, you'll have to brave the crowds no matter the time. And hey, if that couple with gray hair can make it up to the very top, you can, too.

i Free; no wheelchair accessibility

FOOD

BRUNCH AND SUPPER ($$)

37-39 George IV Bridge; 131 225 6690; brunchandsupper.co.uk; brunch M-Sa 8am-4pm, Su 10am-4pm; dinner Tu-Sa 6pm-10:30pm

Once known as simply "Brunch," this restaurant has expanded to serve two meals. You can probably guess what they are. But it's not just a gimmick—

the food is excellent. I mean, the brunch menu contains both sweet AND savory pancakes: what more could you want? Those looking for something healthy can get the veggie burrito or porridge, but why not just order a scone and live a little? They don't take reservations for brunch and get busy on the weekends, but the menu options provide something for everyone. And the portions are huge.

i Entrées from £7; vegan and vegetarian options available; reservation recomended for dinner

OINK ($)

34 Victoria St.; 077 7196 8233; www.oink-hogroast.co.uk; open M-Su 11am-5pm

If you don't like seeing a giant dead pig, this isn't the place for you. But if you're looking for cheap and delicious hog roast, Oink is a must. Once you step in the door, the smell of perfectly cooked pig will overwhelm you. Sizes range from a snack to a full meal. They go through a full pig everyday (plus a few extra "bums"), and when it's out, it's out. Choose your bread and you'll receive a heaping portion of pork. With four locations around the city, meat eaters can't miss Oink.

i Piglet from £3.10; limited wheelchair accessibility

THE PIEMAKER ($)

38 South Bridge; 131 558 1728; www.thepiemaker.co.uk; open M-W 9am-8:15 pm, Th-F 9am- 10:45pm, Sa 10am-10:45pm, Su 10:30am-7:45pm

Perfect for a late night snack or a quick lunch, this no frills eatery serves a collection of—you guessed it—pies. Located right off **the Royal Mile,** they serve more traditional Scottish fare like a haggis pie and a "Steak&Ale" special to a more creative mac and cheese pie. Seating along the window lets you people watch while enjoying your carb-filled meal. The Piemaker has been around since 1995, so it's practically a mainstay of Scottish culture by now.

TING THAI ($)

8-9 Teviot Pl.; 131 225 9801; www.tingthai-caravan.com; open Su-Th 11:30am-10pm, F-Sa 11:30am-11pm

There's a buzz about this restaurant—as you walk by Ting Thai, the quick-moving lines leading out the door and the wafting scent of pad thai will make you do a double take. Food served in a box has never tasted so gourmet. The restaurant is usually packed with students and adults alike, so expect to wait for a table during lunch and dinner. Big portions of hearty food with expertly prepared spices offer a hungry traveler a welcome, filling meal.

i Entreés from £6; cash only; gluten-free, vegan, vegetarian options available; limited wheelchair accessibility

NIGHTLIFE

LUCKY LIQUOR CO.

39A Queen St.; 131 226 3976; www.luckyliquorco.com; open daily 4pm-1am

Thirteen is the lucky number here. Thirteen homemade liqueurs complete 13 specialty cocktails that have a home on the menu for only 13 weeks. Way tinier than a typical bar, Lucky Liquor Co. feels intimate, with small drinks on small circular tables. Along the back wall, this season's colorful liquors glow. Because of their focus on limited liquors, the bartenders make every garnish and ingredient by hand, so you know the stone fruit shrub and dill-infused Akvavit cocktail you're getting is top notch. We don't know what those words mean either, but we do know the drinks are delicious and worth the price. With craft cocktails and a tiny space, you might assume that you'll be served by pretentious hipsters, but luckily that's not the case—the staff is down-to-earth and knowledgeable about their ingredients, adding the finishing touch to a pretty great bar.

i Drinks from £4, cocktails from £7; BGLTQ+ friendly; limited wheelchair accessibility

ST. ANDREWS BREWERY COMPANY

32-34 Potterrow; 131 662 9788; www.standrewsbrewingcompany.com; open daily noon-1am

Walking into St. Andrews Brewing Company feels like getting home after a long day. Musicians strum guitars and croon slow pop-punk songs on Thursdays, Fridays, and Saturdays. You'll find yourself surrounded by garden-themed decorations, but somehow it doesn't feel tacky. Big terracotta pots holding plants hang from the ceiling, and you can spot small buckets and shovels along the wooden walls and small booths as you sip on a £2.50 gin and tonic or a 2 for £8 house special cocktails or one of their many craft beers. Located near the **University of Edinburgh,** students chat, sing along, and enjoy their food, all the while lit by candlelight.

i No cover, drinks from £2.50, entrées from £13; BGLTQ+ friendly; wheelchair accessible; open mic on Th; live local musicians F-Sa

KENILWORTH'S PUB

152 Rose St.; 131 226 1773; www.nicholsonspubs.co.uk/restaurants/scotlandandnorthernireland/thekenilworthrosestreetedinburgh; open M-Th noon-11pm, F noon-midnight, Sa 11am-midnight, Sun noon-11pm

Think of a pub. You're probably picturing a dim and sticky bar, with people sloshing beer around. Kenilworth's isn't like that. It's more like a glamorous older cousin, complete with teal walls and gilded accents. Thanks to an extensive list of cask ales (fancy beer) and gins (you know this one), and outdoor seating on **Rose Street,** Kenilworth's oozes class without any pretension. Drinks are still pretty cheap, but the crowd skews a little older and local. If you're looking for a traditional Scottish pub, here's your answer. If you get the fish and chips or haggis with a pint you're basically British already, aye? The pub deceives with its size—more seats fit on the inside than you'd think, so even if it looks full, stop in.

i Beer from £4; BGLTQ+ friendly; limited wheelchair accessibility

GLASGOW

Coverage by **Lucy Golub**

Glasgow's city motto can be read from the center square, where you'll find a bright pink sign emblazoned with the words "People Make Glasgow." And it's true. While often overlooked in favor of charming Edinburgh, Glasgow's thriving music scene, art venues, museums and shopping leave little to be desired. It takes a local to make you fall in love with the city, so when a friendly Glaswegian chats with you at a pub, listen. When they talk about what life is like for them, you'll hear about their version of the city, learn about the film festival of the week, and discover the latest gig in this UNESCO World Heritage music city. While the early twentieth-century Charles Rennie Mackintosh architecture in the city center creates a grand outer body for the city, the real bloodline comes from the people, who open your eyes to the creativity bubbling around every corner. Glasgow is real. The city isn't made for tourists, but since you're here anyway, let the people show you around. After all, the life inside is what makes it worth experiencing.

ORIENTATION

This large city is split up into different areas, each with a distinct personality. The north part of the city above **The River Clyde** is home to the city center with **Buchanan Street, Merchant City,** and **St. Enochs Square.** Further north lies **Sauchiehall Street,** which contains much of the nightlife scene. To the west, **Kelvingrove Park** and the **West End** are home to greenery and cute cafés. Between the West End and the center, **Finnieston** is home to new trendy restaurants, the neighborhood a victim of recent gentrification. Finally, to the east, the **Glasgow Cathedral** and other attractions are only a 25-minute walk from the center.

ESSENTIALS

GETTING THERE

Glasgow is easily accessible by bus (Citylink or Megabus) as well as train on the Scotrail, which stops at Glasgow Central and Glasgow Queen Street. The airport is about 15min. from the city, and buses can be caught from Buchanan Street. The Airport Express departs about every 10min. and is £7.50.

GETTING AROUND

Buses or walking are the easiest ways to get around the city. You can also hail taxis on the street, though students usually use Uber. Another option is Glasgow Taxis, a large taxi company. The subway is small and runs in a circle, and day tickets are available for £4.10 for an all-day pass. Bus passes can be purchased for £4.50 for all-day, otherwise they accept contactless credit cards or exact change.

PRACTICAL INFORMATION

Tourist Offices: VisitScotland Glasgow iCentre (156a/158 Buchanan Street; www.visitscotland.com/info/services/glasgow-icentre-p332751; Nov-Apr open M-Sa 9am-5pm, Su 10am-4pm; May-Oct open M-W 9am-6pm, Th 9:30am-6pm, F-Sa 9am-6pm, Su 10am-4pm; July-Aug open M-W 9am-6pm, Th 9:30am-6pm, F-Sa 9am-6pm).

Banks/ATMs/Currency Exchange: There are many banks and ATMs on the streets. Barclays ATM (5 George Square; 343 734 9354; open daily 24hr).

Post Offices: Post offices are limited in the city. (136 West Nile St.; 354 611 2970; open M-Sa 9am-5:30pm).

Public Restrooms: Public restrooms are rare, but most restaurants and cafés have them (43 St Vincent Pl.; 141 287 9700; open daily 24hr).

Internet: Public Wi-Fi is available around the city, and many cafés and restaurants offer it as well.

BGLTQ+ Resources: LGBT Youth Scotland (30 Bell St (3/2); 141 552 7425; www.lgbtyouth.org.uk).

EMERGENCY INFORMATION

Emergency Number: 9990. The non-emergency medical number is 111.

Police: Baird Street Police (6 Baird St.; www.scotland.police.uk/police-stations/greater-glasgow/153070; open daily 8am-6pm, closed 12:30pm-1:30pm).

US Embassy: There is no US Embassy in Glasgow, but there is a Consulate General of the US in Edinburgh (3 Regent Terr.; 131 556 8315; open M-F 8:30am-5pm).

Rape Crisis Center: Rape Crisis Centre (30 Bell St.; 141 552 3201; www.glasgowclyderapecrisis.org.uk).

Hospitals:

- Glasgow Royal Infirmary (84 Castle St.; 141 211 4000; emergency room open 24hr) .
- Queen Elizabeth Hospital (1345 Govan Rd.; 121 627 2000; open daily 24hr).

Pharmacies:

- High Street Pharmacy (128 High St.; 141 552 5929; M-F 9am-6pm, Sa 9am-5:30pm).
- Abbey Chemist (83 Trongate; 141 552 2528; M-Sa 9am-5:30pm).

SIGHTS

CULTURE

ASHTON LANE

Ashton Ln.; establishment hours vary

The cosmopolitan **West End** is filled with bars and restaurants that surround the cobbled streets, with vines hanging overhead. Ashton Lane brings a quaint air to an industrial city, briefly allowing you to forget the bustle only a few minutes' walk away. A small cinema connects to a bright and rustic themed restaurant called **The Gardener,** where you can order brunch and bring some of the menu items inside, or go for a bite then a show. (Trust us: the gnocchi bites are a must.) On Sundays, market stalls fill the street selling food and crafts. Although the street is small, it's lively and picturesque, and a perfect spot to have lunch before checking out the nearby **Hunterian Museum** or **Kelvingrove Park.**

i Prices vary; wheelchair accessibility varies

BUCHANAN STREET

Buchanan St.; establishment hours vary

A mile-long shopping street begins at **Sauchiehall Street** and spans the remaining length down to **St. Enoch Square.** If you're looking for a brand-name store, you'll find it here. From international powerhouses like H&M to random tacky tourist shops, if you're in a purchasing mood, Buchanan Street has your answer. You'll also find two Starbucks locations across the street from each other and a busker or magician every few steps. Busy businesspeople push past meandering tourists as they gawk at the architecture, and parents chase children keen on running away. If not to shop, Buchanan Street is the place to people-watch, reminding you that Glasgow is a living, breathing, thriving city.

i Prices vary; wheelchair accessibility varies

GLASGOW FILM THEATER

12 Rose St.; 141 332 6535; www.glasgowfilm.org; box office open Su-F noon-15min. after start of final film, Sa 11am-15min. after start of final film

Glasgow Film Theater isn't a regular movie theater; it's a cool movie theater. They feature different flicks ranging from big-budget classics to to National Theater Live screenings to niche productions that the manager found at film festivals. Best of all, a bar upstairs serves Scottish snacks and drinks that guests are encouraged to bring into the theater. This is no AMC. Elegant stairs and walls made from dark wood highlight the upscale nature of the venue. If you're lucky, come for one of the film festivals hosted here and experience the true Glasgow artsy film scene. Or come to the Moana sing-along…who are we to judge?

i Adults £10.50, £7.50 reduced, shows on Tu and F £6.50; wheelchair accessible; captioned; autism-friendly, and dementia-friendly showings available

LANDMARKS

CATHEDRAL AND THE NECROPOLIS

Castle St.; www.glasgowcathedral.org; open Oct-Mar M-Sa 10am-4pm, Su 1pm-3:30pm, lower church closes 3:15pm; April-Sept M-Sa 9:30am-5:30pm, Su 1pm-4:30pm, lower church closes at 4:45pm

Thousands of visitors have walked through and prayed in this stained-glass-filled stone church. The cathedral still hosts services, as well as recitals, amplified by the echo from the vast arches above. Nearby, 50,000 bodies lay to rest in the Necropolis, including a memorial to John Knox, even though he isn't buried here. The tombstones loom over the horizon, themselves works of art, and some of which were designed by **Charles Rennie Mackintosh.** It's a little creepy perusing the graves, but the expansiveness and intricacy of each makes the Necropolis worth a wander.

i Free; tours available; last entry 30min. before closing; limited wheelchair accessibility

GLASGOW CITY CHAMBERS

George Sq.; 141 287 4018; https://www.glasgow.gov.uk/index.aspx?articleid=19136; open M-F 8:30am-5pm

You might want to consider running for Glasgow city government just to enter this building. Alternatively, you can take one of their guided tours to explore the inside of this massive icon, right in **George Square.** The definition of "City Chambers" remains unclear after the visit, but what we do know is that the building is stunning. Tall ceilings with aligning arches evoke images of castles, while long staircases complete with marble and detailed tile mosaics makes you wonder just how much money the government of Glasgow really has. The building hosts events and awards ceremonies, but is there an award for how stunning the building itself is? There should be.

i Free; free 45min. tours at 10:30am, 2:30pm; wheelchair accessible

LIGHTHOUSE

11 Mitchell Ln.; 141 276 5365; www.thelighthouse.co.uk; open M-Sa 10:30am-5pm, Sun noon-5pm

The Lighthouse stands above much of Glasgow's (admittedly short) skyline. As Scotland's center for Design and Architecture, the building is home to galleries, studios, and a **Charles Rennie Mackintosh** exhibit, because, of course. But more importantly, the Lighthouse's tower has a beautiful panoramic vantage point of the city. 135 steps stand between you and the best views, so you can get that Insta caption that's worth the exercise and actually lives up to #views. For those not looking to visit the rotating exhibitions, you won't need too much time in this building; a half-hour should do the trick. Upstairs and outside, various significant people's favorite places in Glasgow are denoted on plaques that point your eye in their direction of choice.

i Free; limited wheelchair accessibility

THE WILLOW TEA ROOMS

97 Buchanan St.; 141 204 5242; www.willowtearooms.co.uk; open M-Sa 9am-6:30pm, Su 10:30am-5pm

Glasgow's original afternoon tea, tailored to the no-BS nature of a Glaswegian: big portions and a good deal. Although tea can sometimes feel stuffy, the vibe is just refined enough here. An afternoon tea includes four mini sandwiches, a scone, a pastry, and, of course, your choice of tea. The food is good, but the experience is the real draw. The servers, dressed a in classic black and white uniform, charm locals and tourists alike. Upstairs, in the China Tea Room, geometric turquoise walls and dividers brighten the room. Luckily, you can order afternoon tea in the morning, or breakfast at 5pm, so the Tea Rooms are perfect for a meal or snack and immersion in a **Charles Rennie Mackintosh**-designed room.

i Entrées from £5; no wheelchair accessibility; same-day reservations accepted

MUSEUMS

CENTRE FOR CONTEMPORARY ARTS

350 Sauchiehall St.; 141 352 4900; www.cca-glasgow.com; open M-Th 10am-midnight, F-Sa 10am-1am, Su noon-midnight; galleries open Tu-Sa 11am-6pm, Su noon-6pm

This place is basically arts central. The Centre comprises a cinema, theater, offices, and galleries, as well as two late-night bars and a vegan restaurant. Two privately run shops greet you in the main lobby, but the most interesting part of the building is just standing there and taking it all in. Peeking out from the main lobby, an open skylit courtyard hosts comfy couches and dark tables, softly illuminated from the glow of string lights. It seems like Glasgow's most creative people gather here for a drink at the end of the day. At night, the Centre has shows whose titles range from "Pity Party Film Club: Assholes" to "Freedom to Run." We recommend checking out the resident artists in the galleries before they close, then hanging around to see who you meet.

i Tickets from £5; wheelchair accessible; BGLTQ+ friendly

HUNTERIAN MUSEUM AND HUNTERIAN ART GALLERY

University Ave.; 141 330 4221; https://www.gla.ac.uk/hunterian/; open Tu-Sa 10am-5pm, Su 11am-4pm

What do the world's smallest dinosaur footprint and paintings by Raphael have in common (other than the fact that they're priceless)? Answer: you can find them both in the Hunterian Museum and Art Gallery. Enter the **University of Glasgow** campus and follow the signs for the Hunterian Museum, and you can find five floors of displays on surgical tools, archaeology, fossils, and the life of William Hunter, the museum's namesake. A few minute's walk across the street lies the Art Gallery. Home to a sculpture garden and several rooms of masterpieces contrasting the light teal and deep red walls, the Art Gallery also offers entry (£5 fee) to an exhibit on Glasgow's own **Charles Rennie Mackintosh.**

i Free, some exhibits charge; free tours at 11am, noon, 2pm, 3pm; last entry to art gallery 4:15pm (Su 3:15pm); wheelchair accessible

KELVINGROVE ART GALLERY AND MUSEUM

Argyle St.; 141 276 9599; https://www.glasgowlife.org.uk/museums/venues/kelvingrove-art-gallery-and-museum; open M-Sa 10am-5pm, Su 11am-5pm

The foreboding brick walls of this massive museum can be seen from all over **Kelvingrove Park,** inviting tourists and locals alike to come in for a wander of the three floors and many exhibits. With displays ranging from the history of tartan cloth to rainforest biodiversity, you can spend an afternoon in the free museum and not get bored. We recommend the Glasgow-specific exhibits that detail the city's rebirth in the 90s, rising from an old industrial hub to the art and music center it is today. Of course, there's an exhibit on **Charles Rennie Mackintosh** that you can't miss. Some exhibits charge, but even without them, the museum holds more than you can see through the naturally lit and decorated center areas—make sure to look up to see the floating heads—through the wings. The art gallery and museum take up separate sides of the same building, so it's easy to check out both.

i Free, some exhibits charge; free tours on weekends; wheelchair accessible

FOOD

BREAD MEATS BREAD ($$)

104 St Vincent St.; 141 249 9898; www.breadmeatsbread.com; open M-Su 11am-10pm

Late night last night? Bread Meats Bread welcomes the hungover with its elaborate menu of delicious carb, meat, cheese, and fried combos. This place doesn't serve your average greasy hamburger. The name describes a burger, technically, and that's what you'll get at this restaurant. But what the name doesn't tell you is that here, you'll eat one of the best fried chicken burgers or grilled cheese sandwiches found in Scotland. Bread Meats Bread won multiple well-deserved "Best Burger in Glasgow" awards. Order a side to receive heaping piles of french fries, or try the vegan poutine. With chipper staff and large windows looking out onto the street and letting in sunlight, Bread Meats Bread is the carb-filled wonder you didn't know you needed. Around noon, people pack in, so try and get there earlier to avoid a wait.

i Entrées from £8; vegan and vegetarian options available; wheelchair accessible

'BABS ($$)

49 West Nile St.; 141 465 1882; babs.co.uk; open daily noon-10pm

This place is a little fancier than your typical side-of-the-street late-night joint. Be prepared to eat kebabs with a fork and knife. And we're so thankful. Customers who step in the door are immediately greeted by fragrant cooking, mosaic tiles, and a plethora of plants at this Mediterranean eatery. A small fountain bubbles in the corner, transporting guests away from Scotland. Founded by the same team as **Bread Meats Bread,** 'Babs offers kickass dishes with fresh and high quality ingredients. Don't let the fork and knife intimidate you—come in for a killer lamb or halloumi plated kebab, and enjoy.

i Entrées from £9; vegan and vegetarian options available; limited wheelchair accessibility

MONO ($$)

12 King St.; 141 553 2400; www.monocafebar.com; open daily noon-9pm; bar open Su-Th 11am-11pm, F-Sa 11am-1am

When you enter, you'll spot their in house microbrewery to your right—that's where they make their own lemonade. *Shakes head* Classic hipster vegans. Don't let the intimidatingly cool staff deter you from this hip vegan bar and restaurant. With food options from mac n' cheese to pear, chickpea, and blue cheese dressing pizza, their menu provides something for the pickiest meat-eater and a well-versed vegan ordering seitan. In the corner, a live DJ spins records or a musician strums a guitar to provide live music ambiance. Outside, young Glaswegians sip their beer at wood tables, completing the casual hip, young, and welcoming aesthetic found throughout the place.

i Entrées from £7; vegan options available; wheelchair accessible; reservation recommended

PAESANO PIZZA ($-$$)

94 Miller St.; 141 258 5565; paesanopizza.co.uk; open Su-Th noon-10:30pm, F-Sa noon-midnight

Paesano Pizza brands itself Glasgow's first traditional wood-fired pizza place. You can watch the magic happen in the industrial yet homey building, where pizza chefs toss the dough right in front of you. A perfectly plump, legitimately light and amazingly airy crust meets high quality ingredients from Italy to create a culinary masterpiece. In case you forget where you are, a large light up sign hangs from the wall sporting the name of the restaurant. They don't take reservations, but the pizza is worth the wait.

i Pizzas from £5; vegetarian options available; wheelchair accessible

NIGHTLIFE

SPEAKEASY ($)

10 John Street; 845 166 6063; speakeasy-glasgow.co.uk; open W-Sa 5pm-3am

One of the least sneaky speakeasies we've ever seen, Speakeasy lets everybody in and prides itself on it. A gay bar in the center of **Merchant City,** Speakeasy welcomes guests with dark lights and red plush walls. On Saturdays, the upstairs level—called The Trophy Room—opens up for dancing to classic 80s cheesy music and super ballads. Thursdays host karaoke night, and if you're there on a Friday, you may be able to catch a drag show parade around the bar, ensuring that everyone has a good time. Grab a cocktail jug and open your heart for a rowdy night.

i Cover £3 on Sa, food from £8, drinks from £4; cash only; BGLTQ+ friendly; wheelchair accessible

SUPER BARIO ($$)

7 King St.; open daily noon-midnight

Customers can let out their inner child while feeding their outer adult—you can sip a beer while playing pinball or Super Monkey Ball. Small enough that you might just miss it, this arcade-themed bar aptly titled Super Bario sits on a small street, identifiable by the bells and clicks of arcade games and yells of success (or defeat) that emanate into the street. Locals frequent the games, especially the free ones. Some of the games are even two player, giving you the perfect opportunity to meet a new friend. Go for the novelty; stay for the nostalgia.

i No cover, drinks from £7, games up to £1; BGLTQ+ friendly; limited wheelchair accessibility

WAXY O'CONNORS ($)

44 West George St.; 141 354 5154; www.waxyoconnors.co.uk/index.php/welcome-to-waxys-glasgow; open M-Th noon-11pm, F noon-midnight, Sa 10am-midnight, Su 11am-11pm

Waxy O'Connors is is the beating heart of a giant tree. Three floors containing nine bars leave guests with endless opportunities throughout the maze of activity. Wood is everywhere. Flags hang from staircases adorned with stained glass, while massive tree branches stretch from the walls to the ceilings. Waxy O'Connors isn't just a bar; it's an experience. You can often find live music or locals and tourists yelling at the TV blaring the latest football match.

i Food from £8, drinks from £4; cash only; BGLTQ+ friendly; limited wheelchair accessibility

LIVERPOOL

Coverage by **Lucy Golub**

A city best known for its musical contributions to the world—namely the Beatles—Liverpool is also famous for its football. Yet, with the exception of a few streets, the city doesn't actually feel like a tourist hub. It feels like a living, breathing remnant of an industrial hub, a port that connects England to the world. But the city isn't just a vestige of the past; lively streets of restaurants shops and bars are home to a flourishing culture. People come from all over the world to visit and live in Liverpool, as seen by the different types of food dotting the sidewalks of Bold Street. The carnival-like Albert Docks and museums embody the different features of the city. Often overlooked in favor of bigger cities like London and Manchester, those who skip this gem are missing out. Although Brits may not be known for their friendliness, Scousers might just change your mind. Come for the music and the sports. Stay for the city itself.

ORIENTATION

Liverpool is on the water, and the west of the city comprises **Albert Docks** and the **Baltic Triangle.** To the east lies the picturesque **Georgian Quarter,** the **Liverpool Cathedral** and the University, as well as surrounding stores and nightlife on **Hope Street.** In the center of the city, you'll find more museums and nightlife encompassing **Bold Street** and **Ropewalks.** Nearby, **Chinatown** and the **Chinese Arch** welcome visitors. Further inland and slightly south, Liverpool's **South End** are the Beatles' childhood homes, including the now-famous **Penny Lane** and **Sefton Park.** To the north of the center, the football field draws crowds on game days.

ESSENTIALS

GETTING THERE

If you fly, you'll likely end up in the city's closest airport, John Lennon Airport. From the airport, the 80A and 86A buses run to the city centre with plenty of stops. The 86A runs 24hr, so no matter what time your flight gets in, you'll be able to leave the airport without a problem. You can use the Merseyside Travel Planner (www.jp.merseytravel.gov.uk) to plan your route if you come by train or bus. There's a bus stop right at Liverpool ONE in the city center, and a train station at Lime Street as well.

GETTING AROUND

Like other small cities in England, Liverpool is relatively walkable. To get to tourist attractions further from the city center, like the football fields or Penny Lane, Liverpool is well served by bus. You can read specifics online at www.merseytravel.gov.uk, but the buses take cash on board (around £2, less for students), and daily tickets are available for £4.80.

PRACTICAL INFORMATION

Tourist Offices: Tourist Information Centre (Anchor Courtyard Albert Dock; 151 707 0729; www.visitliverpool.com; open daily Oct-Mar 10am-4:30pm, Apr-Sept 10am-5:30pm).

Banks/ATMs/Currency Exchange: Banks and ATMs are common in busy areas. Here's one: NatWest Liverpool ONE (2-8 Church St.; 345 788 8444; open M-Tu 9am-6pm, W 10am-6pm, Th-F 9am-6pm, Sa 9am-5pm).

Post Offices: Liverpool Post Office (1-3 South John St.; 151 707 6606; open M-Sa 9am-5:30pm, Su 11am-3pm).

Public Restrooms: Public restrooms at Liverpool Lime Street Station (Lime St.; open M-F 3:15am-12:40am, Sa 3:15am-12:35am, Su 7am-12:30am).

Internet: Most cafés, bars, museums, and hotels have free Wi-Fi.

BGLTQ+ Resources: The Armistead Project offers confidential support and information (Hanover St.; 0151 247 6560; www.merseycare.nhs.uk/our-services/physical-health-services/armistead; open M-F 10am-6pm).

EMERGENCY INFORMATION

Emergency Number: 999
Police: Merseyside Police have locations all around the city. Headquarters at (Canning Pl.; non-emergency number 101; www.merseysidepolice.uk).
US Embassy: The closest U.S. embassy is in London (33 Nine Elms Ln., London; 20 7499 9000).
Rape Crisis Center: RASA Merseyside provides support for survivors of sexual assault. (2 and 3 Stella Nova, Washington Parade, Bootle; www.rasamerseyside.org; helpline staffed Tu 6pm-8pm, Th 6pm-8pm, F noon-2pm).
Hospitals:

- Royal Liverpool University Hospital (Prescot St.; 151 706 2000; open daily 24hr)
- Broadgreen Hospital (Thomas Dr.; 151 282 6000; open daily 24hr).

Pharmacies: Pharmacies are very easy to locate.

- Boots (18 Great Charlotte St., Clayton Sq.; 151 709 4711; open M-Sa 8:15am-7pm).

SIGHTS

CULTURE

BOLD STREET

Bold St., store hours vary

Vintage stores. Buzzing bars. Vibrant cuisine. And it's all at your fingertips. Here, Liverpool's cultures converge—so much so that almost all visitors can find what they're searching for. If you're on the hunt for a hipster café full of green juice and vegan pancakes, look no further than **Love Thy Neighbor.** Craving something a little less Instagram-edgy? **Kabsah Café Bazaar** serves piping hot Moroccan food, fez hats included. Or if you're looking for some new threads, thrift shops line the streets—check out **Cow Vintage** or **Take 2.** Whoever said Liverpool wasn't trendy clearly never stepped foot onto this street. You could easily spend a day here alternating between eating and shopping—don't say we didn't warn you.

i Prices vary; wheelchair accessible

THE BLUE COAT

School Ln.; 151 702 5324; www.thebluecoat.org.uk; open M-Sa 9am-6pm, Su 11am-6pm

The Blue Coat—an art gallery with a community center attached—has it all. You can browse galleries and watch performances, eat at a café and sit in an outdoor garden, visit a tailor (if you bought a suit at one of the vintage shops only to realize it doesn't actually fit you) and get a new do at the hairdresser. Exhibits in the galleries change often—check the website for the most up-to-date information. Upstairs in the galleries, a large room offers couches, books, and an area to relax. Programming at night includes shows, workshops, and talks. The bulletin boards are covered in flyers advertising other performances and vintage sales. If you don't like food or getting a haircut, the building itself is incentive enough to visit.

i Free; wheelchair accessible

CAINS BREWERY VILLAGE

Stanhope St.; www.breweryvillage.com; store hours vary

A once-abandoned brewery received a new life once this mini-village sprang to life. Not your "typical" village (read: not situated in the countryside with roses climbing up the walls of cottages), Cain's is a collection of vintage and antique stores, food stalls, and, of course, bars. Make sure to check out **Red Brick Hangar,** another market filled with more than 50 local shops that offers wares like band t-shirts, hipster meal-prep services, random trinkets, and artsy photo prints. And if you're feeling spending money on a new tattoo to honor your time in Liverpool, they offer that too—walk-ins accepted. (Just don't accidentally do this while drunk, so you don't regret it the morning after.) Grab a beer at **Peaky Blinders,** a 1920s-inspired pub and walk around the **Baltic Market.** Then, head to **Ghetto Golf** (questionable name, much?) for a neon mini-golf game like no other.

i Prices vary; limited wheelchair accessibility

LANDMARKS

MENDIPS

251 Menlove Ave.; 151 427 7231; www.thenationaltrust.org.uk/beatles; visible 24hr

Imagine the room where John Lennon wrote his first songs—and then imagine the kitchen, dining room, and rehearsal room. From the outside, you can view the building's façade and a commemorative plaque. But to get the full experience, tickets are available via the National Trust, and they include both John Lennon and Paul McCartney's childhood homes, as well as the original windows (yeah, we know that's what you came for) and multiple stories about their childhoods. View the houses the way they were in the 50s—it's like entering a photograph. But no matter how much you love the Beatles, the tour guides ask that you do not steal things from the houses (for real, people do that) and just Let It Be. Okay, we'll show ourselves out now.

i Admission £24; online advance bookings preferred; no wheelchair accessibility

PENNY LANE

Penny Ln.; store hours vary

A barbershop still exists on Penny Lane, one of many shops to capitalize on the Beatles' famous song. Penny Lane Wine Bar, Penny Lane Surgery, Penny Lane Hotel: you get the picture. And if you're looking for a picture of the sign, check out the corner of Penny Lane and Elm Street, or walk down the lane to get to the Penny Lane Development Trust for a colorful Beatles mural and the classic sign. The 86, 80, and 75 buses all take you to nearby stop **Plattsville Road,** but to be honest, there isn't all that much to see on Penny Lane (other than the sign). It's just another pretty brick street. Definitely stroll along, listening to the song, pretending you're with your mates Paul and John. Also, we're sorry that we said Penny Lane so many times in this review; those two words probably appear more often here than in the actual song.

i Prices vary; wheelchair accessible

MUSEUMS

THE BEATLES STORY

Britannia Vaults; 151 709 196; www.beatlesstory.com; open peak days 9am-7pm; open super peak days 9am-8pm; check website for details

In case you couldn't already tell from the thousands of references to the Fab 4 all over the city, the Beatles originated in Liverpool. You can check out their stories at this museum. Inside, after a slightly hefty admission fee, you can follow their trajectory, passing through detailed replicas of significant locations like **Casbah Coffee Club, The Cavern Club, Nems Record Shop,** and their recording studios. Step into the set of the music video for Sgt. Pepper's Lonely Hearts Club Band and explore the **Yellow Submarine.** The audio guide helps lead you through the museum, and even if you're not a Beatles fan (unclear why you're in Liverpool then but ok, sure), you'll learn about the Beatles, their rise to fame, and their eventual separation.

i Admission £16.95, £12.50 reduced; last entry 1hr before closing; wheelchair accessible

MERSEYSIDE MARITIME MUSEUM

Albert Dock; 151 478 4499; www.liverpoolmuseums.org.uk/maritime/index.aspx; open daily 10am-5pm

Liverpool was known as one of the world's most vibrant ports, and you can learn about its history here. Containing an exhibit on the Titanic and one on the Lusitania, as well as exhibits on Liverpool's maritime successes, the museum approaches boats and the sea from all angles. Be sure to check out the downstairs exhibit "Seized!" to hear of some ridiculous smuggling attempts and pretend to catch a drug dealing boat via simulation. The **International Museum of Slavery** is located on the third floor, where guests can read about England's role in the slave trade and the tragedies that accompanied it.

i Free; wheelchair accessible

WALKER ART GALLERY

William Brown St.; 151 478 4199; www.liverpoolmuseums.org.uk/walker; open daily 10am-5pm

A crash course in art history from the fourteenth century through today awaits you inside the doors of the Walker Art Gallery. You don't need to be an art expert; if you follow the rooms from one through 15, you'll see the chronological shift in art trends, grouped by room. Pretty easy to get, if you ask us. So start with a room of filled with multiple renditions of Madonna and Child, and end up in their current exhibition of modern art. If paintings confused you and you don't get what the fuss is all about when you look at Renaissance art, you can also visit the sculpture gallery. And if you've ever seen a picture of Henry VIII, it's likely the same one that's replicated in the gallery (coat and hat for photo op included).

i Free; audio guide £2.50; wheelchair accessible

FOOD

MOWGLI ($)

69 Bold St.; 151 708 9356; www.mowglistreetfood.com; open M-W noon-9:30pm, Th-Sa noon-10:30pm, Su noon-9:30pm

Higher-end Indian street food sounds like an oxymoron, but Mowgli provides high-quality small plates of traditional dishes you likely haven't had before if you're used to your regular Indian restaurant fare. Mowgli meshes zen and club vibes, creating a dimly-lit, trendy space with birdcage decorations overhead, complete with wood seats and tables. Dishes come out as soon as they're ready. If you're only going to get one thing, make it the chaat bombs—aka crispy bread filled with chickpeas, spices, and yogurt.

i Plates from £4; vegan and vegetarian options available; wheelchair accessible

THE BAGELRY ($)

42 Nelson St.; 151 306 5723; www.thebagelryliverpool.com; open Tu-F 9am-5pm, Sa-Su 9:30am-4:30pm

Europe really has good bread covered: we may not be in France enjoying a perfectly-baked baguette, but even British bread is *good*. Unfortunately, that baking skill doesn't always translate to bagels—which is where The Bagelry comes in. Serving 10 styles on eight different bagels (jalapeño cheddar stole our hearts) and novel cream cheese flavors like maple-pecan or spring onion, this sit-down restaurant kicks bagels up a notch. They even come with a fork and knife (which you can ignore). If you're on a tight budget, grab a "daygel" aka yesterday's bagel for half price. Nothing like a lump of carbs to start your day, amiright? Especially when it's served warm and heaped with toppings.

i Bagels from £4, drinks from £2.40; vegan and vegetarian options available; wheelchair accessible

DEATH ROW DINER

32 Hope St.; 151 345 6160; www.deathrowdiveanddiner.com; open M-F 5pm-11:30pm, Sa-Su noon-11:30pm

It could be called Death Row because of the dozens of animals this place likely goes through in a day. (Yikes.) Or maybe it's because every fried meat-loaded meal brings you closer to a heart attack. Morbid, we know. But where else can you get a fried chicken bacon burger called "I dream of Jesus?" You know what you're getting here. Lucky for carnivores, less so for vegans, you can add pastrami fries or chorizo waffles to any meal. Meaty, meaty heaven. Oh yeah, the burgers come stabbed with a lollipop, too. The restaurant's neon wall signs display slightly confusing phrases, and long wood tables are bathed in red light. We'd say it's pretty much the perfect atmosphere to gorge yourself on meat. Here, you'll forget about the concept of vegetables.

i Burgers from £9; no wheelchair accessibility

LOVE THY NEIGHBOR

108 Bold St.; 151 352 2618; www.love-thy-neighbour.co.uk; open M-Sa 8am-11pm, Su 9am-11pm

A café with pink walls, pink neon lights, succulents, and vegan food: yeah, it's your Instagram feed reincarnated. Sounds pretty typical. (Millennials and their avocado toast these days, smh.) Except at night—and all day, we don't judge—they serve killer gin and tonics in bowls, decorated with flower garnishes, because, of course. This is the place to brunch. Let's face it, the beer and chips diet of a Brit doesn't do the best thing for your waistline. Luckily, you can get a hearty açaí bowl or some spiced falafel to fill you up. (With actual nutrients!)

i Entrées from £6, drinks from £8; gluten-free, vegan, and vegetarian options available; wheelchair accessible

NIGHTLIFE

CAVERN CLUB

10 Mathew St.; 151 236 9091; www.cavernclub.org; open M-W 10am-midnight, Th 10am-1:30am, F 10am-2pm, Sa 10am-2am, Su 10am-midnight

Stepping down the three flights of stairs to the Cavern Club is like entering a time machine, especially when the resident Beatles Tribute band is playing. (Is everything in Liverpool Beatles-themed? Yeah, mostly.) But if you look around at the older crowd, the faces of the couples in their 70s reflect the impact of long-lasting Beatlemania. The space itself feels a little like a bunker—you are way underground afterall.

i No cover M-W, Th free until 7pm, then £4; F-Sa free until noon, £2.50 until 8pm, £5 until midnight; Su free until noon, £2.50 until 8pm, £4 until midnight; beer from £4, spirits from £3; wheelchair accessible

BAA BAR

43-45 Fleet St.; 151 708 8673; www.baabar.co.uk; open M-Th 8pm-4am, F-Sa 6pm-4am, Su 8pm-4am

This classic, cheap-drink, student club doesn't disappoint. Sickly-sweet shots are available in scores of flavors, including classics like Birthday Cake and Squashed Frog. Don't ask, just try them for yourself. The bass thumps to the latest pop and hip-hop music, and there are two floors with lots of room to dance. (And dance they do.) If you look around, you'll spot students in groups pop-lock-and-dropping it (or whatever kids these days do). Just embrace the cheap drinks and the young atmosphere to party until 4am, any day of the year except Christmas.

i No cover, drinks from £2; BGLTQ+ friendly; limited wheelchair accessibility; PIN and contactless cards only

THE PHILHARMONIC

36 Hope St.; 151 707 2837; www.nicholsonspubs.co.uk/restaurants/northwest/thephilharmonicdiningroomsliverpool; open M-Sa 11am-midnight, Su 11am-11pm

Paul McCartney once said that the worst part about being famous was not being able to go for a pint at the Philharmonic. Luckily for you, you can! Steeped in history, wandering around inside this pub is akin to exploring a lavish museum. The men's restrooms (really) are works of art in themselves. Local students don't really hang here, since drinks aren't the cheapest, but the opulent atmosphere makes a classy pint (or two) worth it before a night out. Be sure to explore the multiple rooms and shimmering chandeliers, and you might even recognize a face or two in the portraits along the walls.

i No cover, beer from £3, spirits from £3; limited wheelchair accessibility

THE RED DOOR

21-23 Berry St.; 151 709 7040; www.reddoor.co.uk; open M-W 7pm-2am, Th 7pm-4am, F 5pm-4am, Sa 2pm-4am, Su 5pm-1am

Cheap shots and beer can only take you so far, especially if you're craving an expertly-crafted cocktail and ready to splurge. Considering a similar cocktail easily runs you £15 in London, let's call this place an expensive steal. Earlier on weekend nights, live music blasts from the speakers (and when we say blasts, we mean it), until around 10pm when a DJ comes to transform the bar into a club. Everything about the place feels high end but not snooty—brick walls and a giant red door (hence the name) always remind you where you are, while tall seats let you perch at a table as you sip your perfectly-balanced, steel-tin encased fruity drink. Plus, you'll notice being really hot is an employee requirement—everyone who works here is gorgeous. The Red Door is happily located near many of the other bars in the **Ropewalks,** so come for an early evening cocktail, go get drunk on cheaper liquor elsewhere, and come back to dance til 4am.

i No cover, cocktails from £8; BGLTQ+ friendly; limited wheelchair accessibility; live music Th-Sa, discounts if you register online

LONDON

Coverage by **Lucy Golub**

Red telephone booths and double decker buses. Beefeater guards and camera-happy tourists positioned in front of Buckingham Palace. Harry Potter inspiration and the West End. London is a city like no other, with more claims to fame than we can count. From the rich and glitzy Mayfair to the rock 'n roll punk grunge of Camden to the industrial and corporate City of London and hipster on-the-rise Hackney, London's essence can't quite be categorized. The city is booming and living, breathing and evolving—and changing every season. Overwhelming in both size and scale, London can be daunting. Boroughs spread for miles from the center. Yet the city has its quirks that make it feel familiar, like the way people align so expertly on the right side of a Tube escalator, or the chants that fill the streets after an English player scores during a football match. It's puzzling how a modern metropolis feels both so old and so new, when museums hold prehistoric artifacts and contemporary masterpieces just doors away. Between theaters are countless pubs and restaurants, many of which challenge the notion that British food isn't fine dining. And the city is home to a plethora of green spaces, perfect for when you feel overwhelmed by the hustle and bustle of a city that never stops moving.

ORIENTATION

London has well-defined neighborhoods (officially called Boroughs) and is also split into zones on the Underground that circumvent the center of the city. The zip codes are an easy indication of which section of the city your target location is in. **Zone 1,** also known as "central London," includes key tourist points like **Westminster,** home to the **Parliament, Westminster Abbey, the London Eye.** Also in central London are upscale **Chelsea & Kensington** and **Mayfair.** Towards the west and in **Zone 2** you'll find **Notting Hill** and **Portobello Road,** a charming market on the weekends, and a pastel-tinged residential area. Northwest of Zone 2 brings you to grungry and hip **Camden** (and of course, **Camden Market**) and **Hampstead Heath.** To the east of the city center, trendy **Shoreditch** lies on the border of Zone 1 and 2. Further east is **Hackney,** eclectic and quickly filling with hipsters. Between Shoreditch and the center you'll also find the **London Bridge** and the **Tower of London.** Finally, the **Thames River** cuts through the center of the city, and south of the river **Southwark, Shakespeare's Globe,** and **Borough Market.**

ESSENTIALS

GETTING THERE

London is serviced by multiple airports. Most US flights arrive to Heathrow International Airport, and from there you can take the Piccadilly Line into the city center. There's also a more expensive express train. From Gatwick Airport, the easiest route to central London is the Gatwick Express, which runs every 15min. and only takes 30min. to get to Victoria Station. EasyBus also runs an airport transfer service. Multiple routes run from Stansted Airport to the city center as well, like National Express buses that can cost as little as £5 when booked online in advance. Stansted Express trains are quicker to the city center, but they cost a little more. From Luton Airport, buses and trains run to the city as well. From other locations in the UK trains arrive at multiple train stations in London, particularly King's Cross and Victoria. International trains often arrive at St. Pancras.

GETTING AROUND

London's public transportation system is one of the largest and most organized, and is still one of most overwhelming. But don't panic! Public transport is split into the Underground (the Tube), buses, and, if you're going a little further than the center of the city, the Overground. Stations have charts and maps for you to double-check if you're heading in the right direction. If you're going to be using the Tube and bus a lot, you'll want to buy an Oyster card. It's a £5 investment, but it drastically reduces the fares you pay. Or, if you have a contactless credit card, you can use that and avoiding the fee. Bus fares are a flat £1.50, whereas tickets on the Tube depend on which zones you're visiting. You'll likely only need an Oyster card for Zones 1 and 2, because that's where most tourist attractions are. If you pay as you go for an Oyster, you can go to any zone. Make sure you don't lose the card on your ride, as you'll need to tap in and out. The Tube doesn't run 24hr, but most buses do on weekends. If you're out late, you'll likely take the night bus, although Transport for London has expanded the Night Tube to include 24hr service with some stop changes on the weekends.

PRACTICAL INFORMATION

Tourist Offices: There are a few London Tourist Information Centres around the city. One is City of London Information Centre (St. Paul's Churchyard; 020 7332 1456; www.visitlondon.com; open M-Sa 9:30am-5:30pm, Su 10am-4pm).

Banks/ATMs/Currency Exchange: You should have no trouble finding ATMs, banks, and currency exchanges. It's usually better to withdraw pounds than to exchange due to fees. Try HSBC (60 Victoria St.; 0345 740 4404; www.hsbc.co.uk; open M 8am-6pm, Tu 9:30am-6pm, W 8am-6pm, Th 8am-7pm, F 8am-6pm).

Post Offices: Post offices are readily available.

- Camden High Street (112-114 Camden High St.; 0345 722 3344; open M-F 9am-6pm, Sa 9am-5:30pm).
- Great Portland Street Branch (54-56 Great Portland St.; 0845 722 3344; open M 9am-6pm, Tu 9:30am-6pm, W-F 9am-6pm, Sa 9am-12:30pm).

Public Restrooms: Many stores like Asda and Sainsbury's are open all day and have restrooms, and there are also some official public restrooms throughout the city. Some Tube stations also have toilets. There's one in the City of London (Monument St.; www.visitlondon.com/traveller-information/essential-information/toilets-in-london; open 24hr; 50p charge).

Internet: Most cafés, pubs, and restaurants have Wi-Fi. You can also find public Wi-Fi on the street thanks to the new modernized phone booths. Pret à Manger and Starbucks usually have Wi-Fi as well.

BGLTQ+ Resources: There's a BGLTQ+ Tourist Information Centre in Soho, where lots of gay nightlife is located (25 Frith St.; www.gaytouristoffice.co.uk). In June, London decks out in rainbow for Pride.

EMERGENCY INFORMATION

Emergency Number: 999.

Police: Police stations are common and police are often visible in crowded tourist areas. A central station is Charing Cross Police Station (Agar St.; 101 for non-emergency; www.met.police.uk; open daily 24hr).

US Embassy: US Embassy (33 Nine Elms Ln.; 020 7499 9000; www.uk.usembassy.gov; open M-F 8am-5:30pm).

Rape Crisis Center: Rape & Sexual Abuse Support Centre and South London Rape Crisis provides support to women and girls who are victims of sexual assault. Their helpline is 0808 802 9999 (http://www.rasasc.org.uk; helpline available daily noon-2:30pm and 7pm-9:30pm).

Hospitals: London has multiple hospitals in many different areas. Here are two that have emergency care.

- Chelsea and Westminster Hospital (369 Fulham Rd.; 020 8746 8000; www.chelwest.nhs.uk; open daily 24hr).
- St. Thomas' Hospital (Westminster Bridge Rd.; 020 7188 7188; open daily 24hr).

Pharmacies: Pharmacies can also be found on almost every street. Each of the following has multiple locations throughout the city.

- Boots (11 Bridge St.; 020 7930 4571; www.boots.com; open M-F 8am-7pm, Sa 9am-5:30pm, Su 10am-4pm).
- Lloyds Pharmacy (158a Cromwell Rd.; 0207 244 8638; www.lloydspharmacy.com; open M-F 7am-11pm, Sa 7am-10pm, Su 11am-5pm).

SIGHTS

CULTURE

CAMDEN MARKET

Camden Lock; www.camdenmarket.com; market open daily 10am-late; KERB open M-Th 11am-6pm, F-Su 11am-7pm

We love Camden Market, especially for the food. As in, we came here for lunch three days in a row (sorry not sorry). Food should be a multi-course experience. As in, eat a full meal from a food stand and proceed to eat another full meal from a neighboring food stand. #YOLO, right? But the market has more than just endless rows of different cuisines (ranging from fried cheese to lamb burgers). It's split into multiple sections, but know that the tourist-trap stalls of useless souvenirs and graphic tees assaulting your senses when you step off the Tube at **Camden Town** station are not the proper Camden Market. To find the actual market, you'll want to take the Tube to **Chalk Farm** and head to the Stables Market (literally, old horse stables) for vintage clothes galore, leather wares, tons of jewelry, glow in the dark mini golf, and of course, on the other side, the food stalls at **KERB Camden.**

i Establishment prices vary

BARBICAN CENTRE

Silk St.; 020 7638 8891; www.barbican.org.uk; open M-Sa 10am-8pm, Su 11am-8pm

If you're searching for a different kind of night out (a different kind of culture than beer, perhaps), then boy have we got a lucky find for you: the Barbican Centre. Here, you'll find a true center for the arts encased in giant concrete buildings. They've got a movie theater, they've got an art gallery,

they've got Shakespeare plays and dance performances. They've even got the **Symphony,** so get ready for a classy night on the town.

Free; show and exhibit ticket prices vary, Young Barbican tickets for £5; wheelchair accessible

BOROUGH MARKET

8 Southwark St.; 020 7407 1002; www.boroughmarket.org.uk; open M-Th 10am-5pm, F 10am-6pm, Sa 8am-5pm

You get a sample! And you get a sample! And you get a sample! Samples for everyone! Borough Market specializes in produce, cheese, meat, and condiments, in addition to the stalls cooking up fresh lunch. As you wander around the market, artisan mustards on display will call your name, begging to be tasted. Each cheese stall offers multiple types of samples, and (of course) you've got to try them all to determine your favorite. Olive oil? Why yes, of course we're interested in trying that truffle olive oil with this fresh bread next to it. And sure, the cheddar cheese, mmm delicious, I'll have to think about it, though. Oh, it costs £30? Nevermind, thank you for your time. You can likely nab enough samples to equal a small meal, but good luck resisting buying a chunk of cheese (we couldn't).

Free, stall prices vary; limited wheelchair accessibility; limited market M-Tu

BOXPARK SHOREDITCH

2-10 Bethnal Green Rd.; www.boxpark.uk; fashion available M-W 11am-7pm, Th 11am-8pm, F-Sa 11am-7pm, Su noon-6pm; food and drink available M-Sa 8am-11pm, Su 10am-10pm

What's that long line of people on a Saturday night in Shoreditch? A new trendy bar? Some hipster restaurant hybrid pop-up? All of the above! Trendy food stalls are jammed together in shipping containers so you can try novel desserts at **Dum Dums Donutterie** or street fries from **Poptata.** Downstairs, different stores sell wares ranging from soft t-shirts and artsy cards to skincare (shoutout to **Deciem**).

Prices vary; limited wheelchair accessibility

BRICK LANE

Brick Ln.; www.visitbricklane.org; store hours vary

Isn't it funny how just one street can have so many restaurants that have been voted the "best curry in London?" Strange. Urban legend says that all the restaurants on Brick Lane are connected by one underground kitchen. While we think that's not true, it can be a little confusing when a restaurant owner calling out wine deals in front of a storefront leads you into a different restaurant. But embrace it and you might get some free appetizers. Once grungy, now hip and fully vibrant, Brick Lane serves up Indian food that ranges from the stuff of legends to airplane food. A walk along the street, experiencing the smell and sounds of the area provides an insight to the changing landscape—vegan cafés can be found next door to decades-old curryhouses. Street art aficionados, keep your eyes peeled, as some phenomenal **murals** coat the walls of Brick Lane itself and most of the side streets.

Establishment prices vary; wheelchair accessible

LIBERTY LONDON

Regent St.; 020 7734 1234; www.libertylondon.com; open M-Sa 10am-9pm, Su noon-6pm

Founded in 1875, Liberty stands out from most of the **West End's** buildings with its white walls and half-timber facade. Inside, the luxury goods and clothing store could basically be called a museum. Fancy designer dresses decorated with ruffles and tulle hang on racks surrounding the open center. Upstairs, you can sample colognes and touch vibrant fabrics that super wealthy Brits buy for their arts and crafts. Or downstairs, you can sample cosmetics with unpronounceable ingredients promising a plethora of anti-aging properties. We certainly couldn't afford anything inside, but we still enjoyed browsing through the racks, imagining uses for a fluffy hot pink coat.

Item prices vary; wheelchair accessible

CAMBRIDGE

Pint-sized and picturesque, Cambridge has its history is built into its very walls. Biking through the city, you can imagine yourself as one of the bespectacled and backpack-bearing University students studying science and literature. After all, the University of Cambridge has produced some of the world's most influential minds, like Isaac Newton and Charles Darwin. Theoretically, without the University, gravity might not exist (thanks, Isaac). Of course, the colleges look more like gothic cathedrals than typical university buildings. Walk around King's College to visit the cathedral or stop by Trinity College's green pastures. People lounge in parks and libraries, on the green spaces, amid massive shelves of books. Theater and art can be found just around the corner. The Cam River flows through the city as if it were taken out of a painting, bridges spanning the punting patrons. Like its well-known rival Oxford, Cambridge offers old-timey beauty and charm in its quaint streets, well-worth a weekend wander.

The train station is slightly outside of the city center, and it's an easy walk or bus ride. In the center are **King's College,** the tourist center, many chain and local restaurants, and many of the University buildings. **The University of Cambridge** is split up into multiple different colleges, which are spread out around the city. **The Fitzwilliam Museum** is southwest of the center. The city is split by a river (classic) called the **Cam River.** You can walk along the river, but if you're looking for punting in particular, your best bets are to travel southwest to **Mill Pond** or northwest to **Quayside.**

GETTING THERE

Multiple routes run between London and Cambridge. Additionally, you can take a train or bus from London Stansted Airport. Though they're less convenient National Express coach services between Heathrow or Gatwick Airports and Cambridge are still accessible. National Rail trains run between Liverpool Street or King's Cross and Cambridge. You can book in advance for a better fare; the trip is about 60-90min. There are also buses from London Victoria Station to Cambridge whose routes end at Drummer Street.

GETTING AROUND

Many of Cambridge's tourist attractions surround the University, which is located in the city center. Almost everything is easy to reach by foot, but students and visitors alike rely on bicycles. You can rent one at City Cycle Hire at 61 Newnham Road. You can also take the bus, but be aware that multiple different services run throughout the city. Some offer all-day tickets for as little as £3, but your best bet would be to purchase an all-day multi-bus ticket from the bus driver for £8 daily or £33 weekly.

Swing by...

KING'S COLLEGE CHAPEL

King's Parade; www.kings.cam.ac.uk; 01223 331212; during College terms open M-F 9:30am-3:30pm, Sa 9:30am-3:15pm, Su 1:15pm-2:30pm; otherwise open M-Su 9:30am-4:30pm

Cambridge is old and Cambridge is beautiful. Yet reigning supreme for peak grandeur is King's College. Over a century of work resulted in the stunning gothic architecture inside King's College Chapel. The ceilings alone are intricate enough to cause a crick in your neck while admiring their beauty. Don't worry, it's totally worth it. At night, choirs perform **Evensong,** a service that even non-religious people can embrace (plus it's free). When the chapel isn't in service, entering is essentially joining a tourist parade—you can walk through the nave and end up near the transepts that contain information about the chapel. Fun fact: Oliver Cromwell used to parade his troops inside on rainy days.

i Admission £10, £6 reduced; tours £6, £4 reduced, run daily 11am, noon, 2pm, 3pm; last entry 1hr before closing; wheelchair accessible

Check out...

FITZWILLIAM MUSEUM

Trumpington St.; 01223 332900; www.fitzmuseum.cam.ac.uk; open Tu-Sa 10am-5pm, Su noon-5pm

Step inside this museum to get lost in rooms of armor, Ancient Egyptian artifacts, and shelf upon shelf of British pottery. But, for real, you might actually get lost: we were stuck wandering through sarcophagi for quite a few minutes in search for the exit. The museum holds similar wares to the **Ashmolean Museum** in Oxford, meaning you can easily spend a few hours here and still not see everything. We'd recommend sticking to just a few rooms—the Gayer Anderson room and some of the **Matisse** and **Picasso** paintings found upstairs. Of course, you absolutely can't miss the suits full of armor.

i Admission €10, €8 reduced; last entry 5pm; no wheelchair accessibility

Grab a bite at...

AROMI

1 Bene't St; 0122 330 0117; www.aromi.co.uk; open M-Th 9am-7pm, F-Sa 9am-10pm

Every college town needs pizza, and Aromi doesn't disappoint. Your best bet is to take the food to go, since the space isn't huge and seating is limited. No matter where you park yourself to consume your meal, the slices will blow your mind. They're huge, befitting a starving college student who needs fuel as they prepare to write papers due at midnight. They use fresh ingredients and carry staples such as margherita pizzas, focaccia, and even a cheesy basil creation that will make your mouth water. You might not be a student, but you're a starving tourist on a budget—if you come here, you'll should blend right in.

i Pizza from £5; vegetarian options available; limited wheelchair accessibility

Don't miss...

RIVER CAM

Runs along the city; www.visitcambridge.org/things-to-do/punting-bus-and-bike-tours; river open 24hr, company punting hours vary

Poring over old manuscripts in the library, sipping on coffee in a hundreds-of-year-old coffee places, strolling through the colleges of the University—all traditional options for a city steeped in history. But if you're looking for something a touch more athletic and aquatic, the River Cam holds another option: **punting.** Yes, England is known for its football, but this type of punting entails paddling down the moss-green river on what looks like a flat canoe. The concept is simple; one person stands on the boat and paddles while the others sit, eat, and drink. Floating along the river, you might just be able to convince yourself you're a student living in the 1600s. (Maybe that's just the champagne talking.) For the less athletic, you can take a chauffeur-led tour, or simply watch the people below from a vantage point like the famous **Bridge of Sighs.**

i Prices vary; no wheelchair accessibility

LLOYD'S OF KEW

9 Mortlake Rd.; 020 8948 2556; www.lloydsofkewbooks.co.uk; open Tu-Sa 10am-5pm

There's something magical about bookstores. Especially ones where the books spill from the shelves onto piles on the floor and the titles can't be found in an average Barnes and Noble. Lloyd's offers vintage and antiquarian books, and call themselves an emporium of "literary delights for the discerning bibliophile." With free coffee available while you browse, it'd be easy to get lost in the bookstore forever, wandering among ceiling-high shelves, all while avoiding the piles on the floor. They specialize in botanical and horticultural books, which makes sense considering the **Botanic Gardens** are only a few minutes' walk away. So pick up a book before heading to the park.

i Book prices vary; limited wheelchair accessibility; free coffee available

NEAL'S YARD

Between Shorts Gardens and Monmouth St.; area open 24hr, establishment hours vary

Plants, fairy lights, and colorful walls encircle this tiny alley in **Covent Garden.** Although increasingly crowded with more tourists every year (and we're not exactly helping) Neal's Yard feels like a secret garden inside a busy city. Although it's compact, there's a plethora of culinary options at your fingertips. We recommend **Wild Food Café,** a vegan restaurant that could convert any meat eater (at least for a meal) or **Home Slice,** which has some amazing pizza (and long waits). **Neal's Yard Dairy** is also a moo-st (lolz) for any cheese fan. The yard looks like it's taken from a village a few hundred years ago (if you were to remove all the cell phones), and it's a gem.

i Establishment hours vary; wheelchair accessible

NOTTING HILL AND PORTOBELLO ROAD

Notting Hill Gate station; www.portobelloroad.co.uk/the-market; open 24hr, market open M-W 9am-6pm, Th 9am-1pm, F 9am-7pm (antique stalls), Sa 9am-7pm (main day)

Notting Hill, of the movie fame, draws flocks of tourists to **Portobello Road Market** and the picture-perfect white houses with pastel doors. The market offers antiques and jewelry, as well as food and fashion on Saturday. But the gems of Notting Hill can be uncovered in the side streets, not just on the main road. Light pink houses covered in flowers meet pure white streets and long façades on Victorian townhouses—Instagram everything to your heart's desire. We recommend starting at **Ladbroke Grove Station** and heading to **Portobello Road,** but you can veer down side mews if you see something that interests you. If you happen to visit in August, you'll see Notting Hill come alive with **Carnival,** a giant street party that celebrates Caribbean culture.

i Establishment prices vary

SHAKESPEARE'S GLOBE THEATRE

21 New Globe Walk; 020 7902 1400; www.shakespearesglobe.com; exhibition open 9am-5pm

William Shakespeare once wrote "be not afraid of greatness." History nerds, bibliophiles, and regular lay-people alike: come step foot into the Globe to experience Shakespeare's greatness. Stop by for a show, or just take a tour of one of the most influential theatres of all time. Although what stands on the **South Bank** today is just a mere replica, not the real thing (rip), the exhibit tells the story of theater in Shakespeare's time. It demonstrates his legacy, like the phrases he coined (which include "skim milk"). To truly taste the history, tickets can be purchased for performances that entitle you to one standing-room only ticket, just like the peasants of yesteryear.

i Show ticket prices vary, cheapest from £5; tours £13.50, students £11; tours M 9:30am-5pm, Tu-Sa 9:30am-12:30pm, Su 9:30am-11:30pm; wheelchair accessible

LANDMARKS

ST. PAUL'S CATHEDRAL

St. Paul's Churchyard; www.stpauls.co.uk; open M-Sa 8:30am-4:30pm, galleries open 9:30am

No big deal. It's only 528 steps to the top of St. Paul's dome, our personal favorite view of the entire city. Huffing and puffing up stairs that feel more like ladders, you'll see the entire city sprawling before your eyes. The walk up lets you embrace **Christopher Wren's** masterpiece of a building. Yes, the Cathedral costs you (call it penance?), but if you don't want to pay, come for **Evensong,** the evening prayer service. Some lucky visitors will be chosen to bask in daily Evensong from inside the nave. The angelic choir voices echo from the walls of the church as the sunbeams reflect off the glinting mosaics on the ceiling. If a religious service ever felt transcendent, even for someone not religious, it's here, in St. Paul's. Don't worry if the enormity of this testament to faith gives you an existential crisis; it happens to the best of us.

i Admission £18, £16 reduced, free entry for worship only; last entry 4pm; wheelchair accessible (except towers); last entry to gallery 4:15pm

BIG BEN

Intersection of Parliament St. and Great George St.

Sure, you can walk around, but Big Ben will be closed until 2021 due to conservation efforts. This means that even the regular chimings at noon will halt, and this cease in sound will last for the longest time in the tower's history. Fun fact: the tower was renamed Elizabeth Tower after Elizabeth II. The more you know!

i Free; wheelchair accessible

BUCKINGHAM PALACE

Westminster; 3031237300; www.royalcollection.org.uk; State Rooms open July 21-Aug 31 9:30am-7pm, Sept 1-Sept 30 9:30am-6pm; Royal Mews open Feb 1-Mar 25 10am-4pm, Mar 26-Nov 3 10am-5pm, Nov 4-30 10am-4pm

The land of the tea and the home of the Queen, Buckingham Palace is popular with tourists who want to witness the iconic changing of the guard. But we're gonna be real with you: the Changing of the Guard just isn't that exciting after the first couple of minutes. It consists of jostling for space with hundreds of other people to watch guards switch lines in perfect unison. But of course, you gotta do it once. And it is pretty funny to watch kids' trying to get the Beefeaters to crack a smile by the palace. Don't expect to see the Queen, as she doesn't, in fact, invite every tourist in for tea. If you are however desperate to get inside, go online to book an expensive tour to see the **throne room** and other state rooms.

i Admission £24, £22 reduced; last entry 45min. before closing; wheelchair accessible

BRITISH LIBRARY

96 Euston Rd.; 0330 333 1144; www.bl.uk; open M-Th 9:30am-8pm, F 9:30am-6pm, Sa 9:30am-5pm, Su 11am-5pm

The library contains more than 150 million items, including 200 literary gems available to view for free in the Sir John Ritblat Gallery of treasures. England's own **William Shakespeare's folios** are on display inside the dark room, alongside Beatles memorabilia and the **Magna Carta.** Marxists, there's a shelf for you too, covered in original manuscripts and writings. A copy of **Beowulf?** Check. **The Gutenberg Bible?** Check. Original **Mozart** sheet music? Triple check. The library also contains other exhibits that charge and a multitude of places to sit and reflect on the history you've just seen. Head to the website to book your tour.

i Free, some exhibits charge; wheelchair accessible

DR. JOHNSON'S HOUSE

17 Gough Sq.; 0207 353 3745; www.drjohnsonshouse.org; open Oct-Apr M-Sa 11am-5pm, May-Sept M-Sa 11am-5:30pm

You've never heard of Dr. Johnson? That's a shame, because he literally wrote the dictionary. Some of the architecture inside makes you do a double take, like the sliding doors on the second floor, but you'll only need an hour or so here. The very thorough description cards scattered on the tables offer insight into Samuel Johnson's life, friends, and shenanigans. Go find out the reason why there are bars above the front door.

i Admission £7, students £6; no wheelchair accessibility

JEWEL TOWER

Abingdon St.; 0370 333 1181; www.english-heritage.org.uk/visit/places/jewel-tower; open Nov 1-Mar 31 daily 10am-4pm, Apr 1-Sept 30 10am-6pm, Oct 1-31 10am-5pm

Right by **Westminster Abbey** and the **Houses of Parliament,** the Jewel Tower generally has a way shorter line and a way cheaper entrance fee. This makes sense when you figure out the tower used to host King Edward III's royal treasure. Key phrase: used to. Today, the tower is one of the only remaining parts of **Westminster Castle,** and the building is super old. There's not that much to see upstairs, but you can learn about the "Stuff in the Old Jewel House" like the history of weights and measures and old records from the **House of Lords.**

i Admission £5.40, £4.90 reduced; last entry 30min. before closing; no wheelchair accessibility

HOUSES OF PARLIAMENT

Parliament Sq.; www.parliament.uk/visiting; visits available Sa and during recesses

The British government is confusing. So there's the House of Lords, but also regular Lords who aren't involved in the government. Then, the House of Commons are common people—except they're in the Parliament to help make laws. But, additionally, the Prime Minister's opinion matters for legislation. There's a lot going on. Luckily, the overly-informative guided tour (or more reasonable self-guided audio tour) can help you figure out what exactly is going on in these lavishly decorated government buildings. Imagine going to work in a building that looks like the child of a church and a palace, and that's the appearance of the inside. Book in advance and come for the tour, usually only available on Saturdays, and perhaps you'll leave with a better understanding.

i Tour £28, students £23; audio tours £20.50, students £18 (discounts for booking in advance); last entry 4:30pm; wheelchair accessible

KENSINGTON PALACE

Kensington Gardens; 8444827788; www.hrp.org.uk/kensington-palace; open daily 10am-6pm

Home to the Duke and Duchess of Cambridge (that's William and Kate) as well as the Duke and Duchess of Sussex (Harry and Meghan), Kensington Palace is more than just a place to spot your favorite royal couples. With all of the history and drama surrounding the crown, the palace tells the history of the crown but could just as easily be recounting an episode of The Crown, if that show were real. We'd totally watch it. On the tour, you can see the luxurious rooms of royalty, where they wine and dine guests and have important royal meetings. If **Buckingham Palace** is just too crowded but you want to enter a royal building, Kensington's a very solid choice.

i Admission £19.50; last entry Mar 1-Oct 31 5pm, Nov 1-Feb 28 3pm; wheelchair accessible

MARBLE ARCH

Northeast Hyde Park; open daily 24hr

We can admit it's not a very creative name for the giant marble arch perched at the corner of Hyde Park. The arch was designed to be the entrance to **Buckingham Palace** but was later deemed too small. If it draws to mind a similar arch in old Paris, that's no coincidence—part of the inspiration came from the **Arc du Triomphe.** You won't need to spend too long embracing the beauty of the arch, but clearly it's an important landmark because it has its own Tube station. Nearby are **Speaker's Corner** in **Hyde Park,** where legendary orators and random people with opinions spill their guts, as well as the **Tyburn Gallows,** a once-popular place of execution.

i Free; wheelchair accessible

MILLENNIUM BRIDGE

Thames Embankment; open daily 24hr

Since London has a river running through the middle, there are many bridges connecting the two sides. But not all bridges are created equal, and this footbridge stands above (well, literally next to, but hypothetically above) the rest. One of the best views of London comes from the top of **St. Paul's Cathedral,** and one of the best views of St. Paul's can be seen from Millennium Bridge. Walk over the **Thames River** at night to see the lit-up dome, or in the afternoon, it's an easy walk from the **Tate Modern** to St. Paul's. The bridge also appears in *Harry Potter and the Half Blood Prince,* but luckily it's still standing.

i Free; wheelchair accessible

OXFORD STREET

Oxford St.; www.oxfordstreet.co.uk; street open daily 24hr, store hours vary

Shopping on Oxford Street while surrounded by tourists with arms full of shopping bags is practically a London rite of passage. While neighboring **Regent Street** houses luxury retail stores like Chanel and Louis Vuitton, Oxford Street likely holds a more affordable alternative. The term "high street fashion" was practically invented here! For those out of the loop, high street fashion refers to clothes you can buy on a high street (main street) of a city or town, and with a plethora of options including Zara, Topshop, Primark, and H&M, you'll have no lack of choice for retail options.

i Store prices vary; wheelchair accessible

PICCADILLY CIRCUS

London W1J 9HP; open daily 24hr

Not your typical circus with acrobats and clowns, Piccadilly Circus is a bustling roundabout in the center of London. People come from all over the world to hustle through, desperate to get out of the crowds of neon-vest-clad school children, flashing ads, and people who don't know how to cross a street. Take a moment to perch by the metal statue at the center of the circus. Watch the cars zoom by or honk, depending on the traffic. While it's not London's most quiet place to sit and hang, the Circus is the city's heartbeat. Undeniably alive, and most beautiful at night when the streets quiet down. The Victorian buildings and red buses could be taken from a postcard.

i Free; wheelchair accessible

TOWER BRIDGE

Tower Bridge Rd.; www.towerbridge.org.uk; open Apr-Sept daily 10am-5:30pm, Oct-Mar daily 9:30am-5pm

We hate to burst your bubble but the **London Bridge** of " falling down" fame is not this bridge. An exhibit inside explains the bridge's history, and visitors can witness the **Engine Room,** where the magic of bridge-raising happens—it still opens today for large ships. Thrill-seekers can get a ticket to walk on the glass floor rising 137 feet above the **Thames.** Oh bridges, how you thrill

us. For a cheaper option, simply walk over it from the **Tower of London,** its namesake.

i Admission £9.80, £6.80 reduced; last entry Apr-Sept 5:30pm, Oct-Mar 5pm; wheelchair accessible

TOWER OF LONDON

Tower of London; 020 3166 6000; www.hrp.org.uk/tower-of-london; open M 10am-5:30pm, Tu-Sa 9am-5:30pm, Su 10am-5:30pm

Multiple towers comprise the fortress that is the Tower of London. As visitors wait in long lines to enter the castle, they might just spot one of the ravens that is kept in the tower out of superstition. It's said if the ravens leave, "the kingdom will fall." Spooky. The crowds make it hard to grasp the weight and significance of the buildings, but this is the site of long-past tortures, imprisonments, and killings. The most recent execution occured in 1941, which makes history feel a lot closer. While the history of prisoners are gory and slightly horrifying, other parts of the tower like the **Crown Jewels** glimmer with royal history.

i Admission £22.70; guided tours about every 1.5hr; last entry 5pm; wheelchair accessible

TRAFALGAR SQUARE

Trafalgar Sq.; open daily 24hr

Lions and tourists and stairs, oh my! Home to fine art museums and chalk art creators, Trafalgar Square receives thousands of tourists every day. Whether you're seeking the **National Gallery** or a floating Yoda street performer, you'll find it. (Although, sometimes, the pavement art competes with the masterpieces inside the museum.) Make sure to snap a selfie with the big bronze lions flanking **Nelson's Column** and the turquoise fountain nearby. Trafalgar Square is a real pedestrian plaza, home to marches and protests and different public events. You'll likely end up here without even trying.

i Free; wheelchair accessible

WESTMINSTER ABBEY

20 Deans Yd.; 020 722 5152; www.westminster-abbey.org; open M-F 9:30am-3:30pm (late nights W 4:30pm-6pm), Sa 9am-3pm (May-Aug), Sa 9am-1pm (Sept-Apr)

Wow. Wow to the lines snaking around the building from before the first entry time, wow to the ticket price, and finally, wow to the truly breathtaking inside of the buildings, making the wait and the price worth it. The soaring ceilings, intricate carvings, and famous tombs result in crowds that sometimes feel like a concert mosh pit. But you won't notice the jostling when exploring the Gothic Architecture where the majority of Britain's monarchs took the throne. And as of this year, the **Diamond Jubilee Galleries** are finally opened, if the audio tour wasn't enough. These galleries look down on the Abbey from above, offering spectacular views of the **Palace of Westminster** from the **Weston Tower.**

i Admission £22 (£20 online), £17 reduced; tours Apr-Sept M-F 10am, 10:30am, 11am, 2pm, 2:30pm, Sa 10am, 10:30am, 11am; tours Oct-Mar M-F 10:30am, 11am, 2pm, 2:30pm, Sa 10:30am, 11am; all tours £5; limited wheelchair accessibility

MUSEUMS

BRITISH MUSEUM

Great Russell St.; 020 7323 8181; www.britishmuseum.org; open M-Th 10am-5:30pm, F 10am-8:30pm, Sa-Su 10am-5:30pm

This museum has the freaking **Rosetta Stone.** Not the language-learning program, but its namesake that enabled historians to decode hieroglyphics. Pretty sick. The criss-crossed glass ceiling and circular stairs could be works of art themselves. Though there's controversy over the Brits' laying claim to the carvings from the Parthenon, the sculptures reveal centuries of craftsmanship that still stun today. Since there's so much to see, you should focus in on key sections via free guided tour. Our only other suggestion is the **Africa Gallery,** filled with thousands of years of artifacts from countries in Africa. Highlights including the moving **Tree of Life** statue made of weapons from Mozambique, a demonstration of art's ability to make a statement.

i Free; multiple tours throughout the week, updated information available online; wheelchair accessible

MUSEUM OF LONDON

150 London Wall; 020 7001 9844; www.museumoflondon.org.uk; open daily 10am-6pm

Oh, another museum about England, you may think to yourself, stepping inside the high-ceilinged building. But wait! It's a museum about the history of London itself. Artifacts, movies, and interactive displays tell the story of the city that became one of the greatest in the world. You won't get to see everything in one visit, but particularly fascinating are the history from 1850-1940 and the Victorian Walk, a recreation of a street from the mid nineteenth century. A little more gruesome but equally important in the city's history are the stories of the Great Fires (of 1666 and 1834) and the history of the plague. Your head will be spinning with names, dates, and a larger appreciation for the city by the time you leave.

i Free; wheelchair accessible

CABINET WAR ROOMS

Clive Steps, King Charles St.; 020 7416 5000; www.iwm.org.uk/events/cabinet-war-rooms; open daily July-Aug 9:30am-7pm, Sept-June 9:30am-6pm

Come, step into the bunker. Dark and dreary, kind of creepy, and maybe a few hours' wait if you don't book online, the Cabinet War Rooms delve deep into the history of **Winston Churchill's** leadership during World War II. You'll learn about spies and traitors, and see the cramped living quarters of those fighting to win the war. Inside, a mini-museum devoted to Churchill himself follows his life, his political rise, fall, and rise again. It's hard to believe, but they somehow built the bunker and cased it in concrete without anyone above-ground becoming suspicious. And that's just the tip of the iceberg. Just wait until you reach the map room with push pins for every target of a potential bomb.

i Admission £21 (£18.90 online), £16.80 reduced (£15.10 online); last entry July-Aug 5:45pm, Sept-June 5pm; wheelchair accessible

DESIGN MUSEUM

224-238 Kensington High St.; 020 3862 5900; www.designmuseum.org; open daily 10am-6pm

Often when we think of Europe, we think of old stone buildings, castles, and ivy. The Design Museum is the exact opposite. Full of contemporary design and art, from an exhibit on graphics and politics to immersive displays on the "home of the future," this museum emphasizes the here and now. As design shifts through practical and aesthetic changes, you might end up wondering what some of the objects even do. While we can't guarantee the function of the shiny blob-looking thing that's supposedly a light, we can promise that the museum will leave you thinking about how much design impacts everything in your life. From white sneakers to iPhone speakers, the temporary and permanent exhibits connect design to fashion, architecture, engineering, and education.

i Exhibition prices vary, generally from £12; last entry 5pm; wheelchair accessible

IMPERIAL WAR MUSEUM

Lambeth Rd.; www.iwm.org.uk/visits/iwm-london; open daily 10am-6pm

Tea, crumpets, and war: three of the things on which England was built, basically. So it's only fitting that the Brits have (multiple) massive museums dedicated to war, both informational and memorial. In the museum, you can learn about World War I and World War II's causes and impacts on the city today. Don't miss the **Holocaust Exhibition,** a heart-wrenching but informative exploration of the Holocaust and different countries' roles. The museum doesn't boast about winning wars; rather, it examines how different people were affected and how the country moved forward. A visit to this museum might leave you shaken by the devastation that war can cause, but you'll definitely be more informed.

i Free; wheelchair accessible

MUSEUM OF BRANDS, PACKAGING, AND ADVERTISING

111-117 Lancaster Rd.; 0207 243 9611; www.museumofbrands.com; open M-Sa 10am-6pm, Su 11am-5pm

Step inside folks, for a time-machine-esque endless hallway of trinkets and toys. The museum presents time capsules from the 1800s to today, starting with vintage tins for tobacco and soaps and ending with laundry detergent and sugary cereal. It's like an antique shop combined with a grocery store and deli. Anything that has a cabinet for One Direction (and, okay, the Beatles) has our vote. The museum presents an almost sociological study about cultural norms like the role of women and children throughout the years. Particularly interesting are the magazines that only begin to promote slimming down and toning up in the 70s, around the same time when packaged food made an appearance. While the main gallery isn't interactive, some exhibits in other rooms let you create your own brands. We made some liquid Let's Go hand soap—fruity with bursting bubbles, and, of course, all-natural ingredients.

i Admission £9, £7 reduced; wheelchair accessible

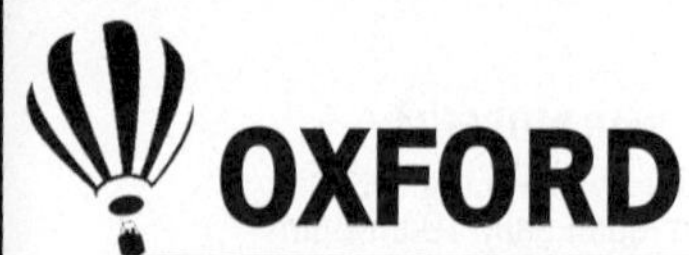

OXFORD

Famed for its university and famous graduates (scores of Prime Ministers and five kings, to name just a few), Oxford's petite and picturesque city calls out to visitors looking to explore centuries past. Bibliophiles and retrophiles alike will find solace in the stone-lined streets and majestic buildings, famous libraries like the Bodleian Library, and centuries-old structures like the Bridge of Sighs. Of course, while the history and academia compel thousands of tourists to Oxford's streets every year, the small city brims with its own life and culture, especially when the students are in session. So step inside the charming city and explore the magnificent architecture of the spired buildings. Stumble upon one of the many colleges and explore the legacy of students past, sometimes controversial political figures like Bill Clinton or Theresa May or imagine you're gallivanting with literary legends like Lewis Carroll (Alice and Wonderland), CS Lewis (The Chronicles of Narnia), and JRR Tolkien (Lord of the Rings). By the end of your stay, you'll likely wish you were studying here, if only to wake up and see the sunlight hit the buildings that look like magic.The city center is quite compact, and has access to the nearby train station, which is west of the city. **George Street** is one of the main avenues; found close by is **Broad Street,** where you'll find **Bodleian Library.** The Tourist Office is on the same street. Don't miss pastel-toned **Holywell Street** nearby. To the south is **High Street,** where you'll find lots of shopping. The University's 38 colleges are scattered throughout the city. Notably, **Christ Church College** is in the south. To the north you'll find the **Ashmolean Museum** and **Pitt Rivers Museum.** The **Cherwell River** runs along the east side.

GETTING THERE

Oxford is an easy train or bus away from London. Trains from Victoria Station and King's Cross are available about every 20min. Book in advance for cheaper fares. The X90 bus stops at Marylebone Rd, Marble Arch, and Victoria. The X90 is slightly cheaper. Fares run at £18 for a return fare for adults and £14 for 16-26 year olds, and the trip is about 100min. long.

GETTING AROUND

Oxford's city center is so tiny that it's almost impossible to get lost. There are also buses that take you everywhere you need to go, with fares ranging from £1.10 to £4.20 for an all-day pass. Return fares are usually around £3, so if you're taking multiple bus trips, your best bet is to invest in an all-day pass. Make sure you don't lose the receipt!

Swing by...

BODLEIAN LIBRARY

Broad St.; 01865 277162; www.bodleian.ox.ac.uk; open M-Sa 9am-5pm, Su 11am-5pm

We'll cut to the chase: to see most of the inside of this masterpiece of a library, you'll have to be a student or researcher. Or cough up extra cash for an extended guided tour. For free, you can, however, see the exterior of buildings in the seventeenth-century quadrangle, and entering the divinity school only costs a hefty £1. Fun fact: the divinity school made an appearance in *Harry Potter and the Sorcerer's Stone* as Hogwarts' infirmary. Another must-see comes in the form of a rotund and robust building: **the Radcliffe Camera.** The gated building near the main library appears in many Oxford postcards.

i *Standard 60min. guided tour £8, extended 90min. tour £14, mini 30min. tour £6, audio tour £2.50, self-guided tour of divinity school £1; limited wheelchair accessibility*

Check out...

ASHMOLEAN MUSEUM

Beaumont St.; 01865 278000; www.ashmolean.org; open Tu-Su 10am-5pm, last F of every month 10am-8pm

Much more traditional than the **Pitt Rivers Museum,** the Ashmolean Museum is still a clown car of a museum. And by that we mean when you think you've seen everything, you'll uncover yet another floor full of seemingly endless exhibits and artifacts. Once you've accepted that you won't see it all, check out our top recommendations: begin with the mummy of Meresamun and learn about Ancient Egypt. Another must-see is the Powhatan Mantle. England's oldest public museum holds half a million years of art and history, so yeah, it's a little overwhelming. If you're a plan-in-advance type of person, make sure to book a visit to the Western Print Room (it's free) to see Michaelangelo's and Raphael's sketches. No big deal.

i *Free; wheelchair accessible*

Grab a bite at...

COVERED MARKET ($$)

Accessible via Market St., High St., or the Golden Cross in Cornmarket St.; www.oxford-coveredmarket.co.uk; open M-Sa 8am-5pm, Su 10am-4pm

What's a city without a market? At first, it seems the only vendors sell slightly tacky Oxford-branded tourist apparel. Head deeper (past the clothing stores) and you'll find a solid selection of places to eat. This is no Camden Market, but a smattering of food stands at the ready to greet visitors. In the mood for something healthy? We recommend **Alpha Bar,** which changes its salad and sandwich options daily. And then, of course, stop at **Ben's Cookies** for a chunky and melty cookie for dessert. Head to the butcher and the **Oxford Cheese Company** to buy picnic foods if you want to go punting on the river.

i *Prices vary*

or at...

TURF TAVERN

4-5 Bath Pl.; 01865 243235; www.greeneking-pubs.co.uk/pubs/oxfordshire/turf-tavern; open daily 11am-11pm

Tucked between two alleys, Turf Tavern is one of Oxford's hidden secrets. And we mean really hidden—we had to obsessively follow our phone's GPS function to find it. But we did that so you don't have to. Walk down **New College Lane,** right across from the **Bodleian Library** and under the **Bridge of Sighs.** On your left, there's a teeny alley called **St. Helen's Passage** that looks like its too small to fit anyone. Follow it, and you'll end up at the pub. Inside, you won't find the world's cheapest drinks, but people mostly come for the history. It used to be a prime location for cockfighting until a fire shut that business down. Fun fact: While some of the *Harry Potter* movies were filmed, cast and crew would camp out in the pub on their breaks.

i *Drinks from £6, entrées from £10; limited wheelchair accessibility*

NATIONAL GALLERY

Trafalgar Sq.; 020 7747 2885; www.nationalgallery.org.uk; open daily 10am-6pm

Showcasing some of Britain and the world's greatest hits, the National Gallery is an album of winners. Room after room, the paintings begin to blur. You might find yourself lost in the rooms of masterpieces in a brain fog. "Is this Da Vinci or Monet?" you think to yourself. Oh you poor lost soul, you'll find both here! Of course, no art museum is complete without (probably) hundreds of paintings of Jesus and Mary, some beheaded soldiers, and mythical creatures. If you get all arted out after only a few rooms, we'd suggest the Impressionist rooms. But if you're looking for directions to **Water Lilies** or **Sunflowers**—good luck, Charlie.

i Free; wheelchair accessible

NATIONAL PORTRAIT GALLERY

St. Martin's Pl.; 020 7306 0055; www.npg.org.uk; open M-Th 10am-6pm, F 10am-9pm, Sa-Sun 10am-6pm

Walking through room after room of paintings of people could definitely be boring. And it is, usually. All those paintings of old kings start to blur together until you're standing in the middle of a gallery yelling "NO MORE I CAN'T TAKE IT!" But luckily, the gallery also holds portraiture in other mediums and some faces that you'll recognize. The contemporary portraits provide a breath of fresh air from the typical portrait styles of earlier centuries. The gallery might best be known for its annual BP Portrait Competition, a summer exhibit showcasing the winners and recognized artists for one of the most important portrait competitions in the world (apparently, there are many). Anyone over 18 can enter a painting for consideration, but the 48 on display in the gallery every summer are breathtaking in scope, talent, and detail that can be appreciated by everyone.

i Free, temporary exhibits charge; wheelchair accessible

SERPENTINE GALLERY

West Carriage Dr.; 020 7402 6075; www.serpentinegalleries.org; open daily 10am-6pm

Strolling through **Kensington Gardens** in need of a restroom, you may wander into this melted building resembling a frisbee. The art can be a little too contemporary for our taste, but the building offers a welcome reprieve from inevitable London rain and an exhibit that changes every summer. The gallery is intimate, as in you can walk around the whole thing in three minutes.

i Free; wheelchair accessible

SHERLOCK HOLMES MUSEUM

221b Baker St.; 020 7224 36888; www.sherlock-holmes.co.uk; open daily 9:30am-6pm

Elementary, my dear *Let's Go* reader, this museum is only worth your time if you're a well-established fan of Sir Arthur Conan Doyle's famed detective. In which case, you'll fit right in with the people sporting with Sherlock caps and "221B" tattoos. Be warned: The wait will be long and tickets to enter the actual house where Sherlock and Watson lived and worked will be expensive. Most of the visit is self-guided up steep steps with little information. At the end of the day, you're in a fake house of a fictional character, so maybe we can suspend our disbelief and be spooked by the human like mannequins climbing out of the ceilings. Or not.

i Free; multiple tours throughout the week, wheelchair accessible

TATE BRITAIN

Millbank; 020 7887 8888; www.tate.org.uk; open daily 10am-6pm

The more mature and refined older sister of the **Tate Modern,** Tate Britain contains room upon room of many of England's most prominent artists, including **Henry Moore** and **Francis Bacon.** Tate Britain also holds some contemporary pieces, but the spectacle comes from the half-millennium of British art. Stepping into the building, you instantly know there's something special here. The circular staircases, massive marble, and stone Duveen Galleries play host to different visiting exhibits that emphasize the impeccable architecture.

i Free; guided tours 11am, noon, 2pm, 3pm; wheelchair accessible

TATE MODERN

Bankside; www.tate.org.uk/visit/tate-modern; open daily 10am-6pm

Three seconds into a virtual-reality-inverted-color-anime simulation, we figured out two things: first, we know nothing about modern art, and second, modern art is pretty freaking weird sometimes. But exploring the industrial brick rectangle that makes up the lobby of one of the two buildings, we realized that part of the experience is watching those art snobs take perfectly imperfect photos in the shadow of the windows and realizing everyone's faking it just a little bit. The museum's collection spans from "classic" modern art of the twentieth century like **Andy Warhol** through to avant garde video splicing and 3D art. Most of it will leave you wondering what it all means.

i Free, temporary exhibits charge; guided tours 11am, 11:30am, noon, 2pm, 2:30pm, 3pm, 3:30pm; wheelchair accessible

VICTORIA AND ALBERT MUSEUM

Cromwell Rd.; 020 7942 2000; www.vam.ac.uk; open M-Th 10am-5:45pm, F 10am-10pm, Sa-Su 10am-5:45pm

Where to begin with this massive museum? The V&A, the self-proclaimed world's leading museum of art and design, does not disappoint. We're often hesitant to pay extra for an exhibit, (it's budget travel after all), but the V&A's temporary exhibits absolutely give you bang for your buck. The museum combines ancient statues and tombstones with modern British design and some unexplainable art. If your feet and neck get tired of looking, take a breather in the stunning red courtyard, but beware of the babies playing in the fountain.

i Free, temporary exhibits ticket varies; free tours 10:30am, 12:30pm, 1:30pm, 3:30pm; wheelchair accessible

OUTDOORS

HAMPSTEAD HEATH

Hampstead Heath; 020 8340 5260; www.cityoflondon.gov.uk/things-to-do/green-spaces/hampstead-heath; open daily 24hr

Less than five miles from the center of the city (and easily accessible via the Northern line to Hampstead) lies an enormous park. City life isn't for everyone, and if you find yourself needing a breather, go for a long walk through fields of grass and meadows, hopefully following the butterflies and not the snakes. Deeper inside the park, **Parliament Hill** offers a skyline view of London. On a nice day, the park serves as London's version of a beach, with a big pond that's surprisingly pleasant to bathe in.

i Free; limited wheelchair accessibility

KENSINGTON GARDENS AND HYDE PARK

Kensington Gardens; www.royalparks.org.uk/parks/kensington-gardens; www.royalparks.org.uk/parks/hyde-park; Kensington Gardens open daily 6am-9:15pm; Hyde Park open daily 5am-midnight

It makes sense that the backyard of **Kensington Palace** is filled with flowers, fountains, hedges, and delicately designed nature. Inside the gardens, the **Orangery** provides charming afternoon tea inside a greenhouse for the orange trees. Close to **Oxford Street,** the gardens' tranquility instantly calms frantic tourists. For another culture hit on the way, stop by the **Serpentine Galleries.** Nearby you'll find the Gardens' larger neighbor, **Hyde Park,** which provides enormous green space in the center of the city. Swans in the **Serpentine River** might look glamorous, but watch out, some say they bite. Every

Sunday morning, **Speakers' Corner** hosts citizens who want to make their opinions known. It's like *Hamilton* except totally not.

i Kensington Gardens free; Hyde Park admission £16, £14 reduced; wheelchair accessible

KEW GARDENS

Accessible via District line; 020 8332 5655; www.kew.org/kew-gardens; open daily 10am-7pm

A train runs through the garden, taking visitors all around the enormous **Botanical Gardens.** They recommend three to fours hours inside, and as soon as you enter it's easy to see why. Any garden that needs its own train clearly has a ton to see. The **Temperate House** reopened after an enormous renovation to become a botanists' dream. Step inside the **Palm House** tropical rainforest to feel transported south of the equator. Instead of a basic picture of banana leaf wallpaper, you can snap a selfie with real banana leaves! The garden contains over 30,000 different types of plants.

i Admission £16, £14 reduced; last entry 6pm; wheelchair accessible

REGENT'S PARK

Regent's Park; 0300 061 2300; www.royalparks.org.uk/parks/the-regents-park; open daily 5am-9:30pm

On one side, well manicured hedges and sculptures could be taken from a postcard of a pristine park. The other half of the park has lots of dogs. Small dogs, big dogs, fluffy dogs, barking dogs. You get the picture. Laughing children glide on scooters and throw tantrums about wanting ice cream. Check out the **London Zoo** because it has giraffes, and you can even pay to feed them. If dogs or giraffes don't do it for you, nearby **Primrose Hill** has one of the best London skyline views, and it's a gorgeous place to watch the sunset. At night, you'll find young people hanging around, often with beer. Cheers to open container laws.

i Free; wheelchair accessible

ST. JAMES PARK

St. James Park; 0300 061 2350; www.royalparks.org.uk/parks/st-jamess-park; open daily 5am-midnight

A few minutes from sights like **Westminster Abbey** and the **Churchill War Rooms,** St. James Park contains a large lake that reflects the three surrounding palaces. It's perfect for a stroll or a picnic (or a nap). For budding ornithologists—bird scientists—more than fifteen species of waterfowl live in the lake. Be sure to note the pelicans. We heard one of them made a cameo in *Finding Nemo*. Just kidding, but their story is almost as cool. Pelicans have been around in the park since 1664, a gift from the Russian ambassador. These days, they're fed once a day so they don't snag the fish from the **London Zoo** as snacks. Feisty.

i Free; wheelchair accessible

FOOD

SNACKISTAN AT PERSEPOLIS ($)

28-30 Peckham High St.; 020 7639 8007; www.foratasteofpersia.co.uk; open daily 11am-8:45pm

London's best restaurant (in our humble opinion) hides at the back of a Persian market. Situated in **Peckham,** an area once considered unsafe but now undergoing the early touches of gentrification, Snackistan is kind of hard to get to. But the best things in life are worth fighting for, and certainly whoever first said that was talking about the bus situation you'll encounter on the way to this restaurant. The menu itself is full of jokes and dotty one-offs, adding to the quirky confusion. We do have to agree with the menu: a sundae that has nuts and fruit in it is a health food. The tapestries and carpets along the walls and floor set the scene: you're in Persia now, eating what just might be the best meal of your life. Grilled halloumi, meze platters, harissa eggs, and delectable daily specials can all be found here.

i Entrées from £4; gluten-free, vegan, and vegetarian options available; limited wheelchair accessibility; card minimum £10

THE CHEESE BAR ($)

Unit 93/94 Camden Stables, Chalk Farm Rd.; www.thecheesebar.com; open M-Th noon-10pm, F noon-1pm, Sa 11am-10pm, Su noon-8pm

The Beatles once crooned, cheese is all you need. Well, maybe that wasn't the lyric exactly, but the meaning is the same. Dairy dreamers can get their fix at this all-cheese based restaurant. The menu contains mouth-watering mac and cheese, raclette, cheese fondue, cheeseburgers, and even some cheese sweets like cheesecake and goat-cheese-and-honey ice cream. Some entrées veer on the expensive side for casual dining, but most are reasonable (London's best grilled cheese for around £6). So get ready to spend a little cheddar…on a lot of cheddar.

i Entrées from £7; vegetarian options available; limited wheelchair accessibility; last seating 30min. before closing

BEN'S COOKIES ($)

35-36 Great Marlborough St.; 020 7734 8846; www.benscookies.com; open M-Sa 10am-8pm, Su 11am-7pm

Ben's Cookies are famous for their giant chunks of toppings instead of the more traditional chips. You'll find stands everywhere: in the Tube, in markets, and of course, in bigger shops on the street. They price cookies by weight, which is a little weird, but as soon as one of the melty ooey-gooey cookies dissolves in your mouth, you won't care about paying the extra 20 pence for a chunkier cookie. If just one cookie won't satisfy your sweet tooth, why not be a little wild and indulge in the cookie monster: a cookie with gelato. C is for Cookie, and B is for Ben's. That's good enough for us!

i Cookies from £1.60; vegetarian options available; wheelchair accessible

BREAKFAST CLUB ($)

12-16 Artillery Ln.; 020 7078 9633; www.thebreakfastclubcafes.com; open M-W 7:30am-11pm, Th-F 7:30am-midnight, Su 8am-10:30pm

Boasting walls decorated with egg-yolk yellow paint and neon "Sex, Drugs, and Bacon Rolls" signs, the restaurant's interior is quirky and a little bizarre. But the Bacon, Egg, and Cheese and Salted Caramel Banoffee Pancakes are enough to draw crowds even without the cute décor. Because the store has multiple locations around the city, you're bound to stumble upon one, but if you end up nearby, we'd recommend the **Spitalfields** location, for it's not-so-secret speakeasy. Step through a refrigerator after telling the hostess you're "here to see the mayor," and you'll end up downstairs at a hidden bar called **The Mayor of Scaredy Cat Town.**

i Entrées from £5.50; vegan and vegetarian options available; wheelchair accessibility

CHURCHILL ARMS ($$)

119 Kensington Church St.; 020 7727 4242; open M-W 11am-11pm, Th-Sa 11am-midnight, Su noon-10:30pm

One of London's most beautiful pubs, the Churchill Arms stands on a street in **Notting Hill,** a tall, proud, and stately building covered in flowers and flags. Take a deep breath, step inside, and inhale the scent of pad thai. Yes, this Winston Churchill memorabilia-loaded pub serves Thai food. In summer, the back conservatory is a little steamy, both because of the hot food and the sun shining through the windows. But if you can come around Christmas, the outside of the pub shines with lights and Christmas trees, a sight to behold. You won't find many locals, but you will find mouthwatering pad thai, which is sometimes even better!

i Entrées from £9; vegetarian options available; limited wheelchair accessibility

GAIL'S BAKERY ($)

128 Wardour St.; 020 7287 1324; www.gailsbread.co.uk; open M-Th 7:30am-7pm, F 7:30am-8pm, Sa-Su 8:30am-8pm

Freshly-baked breads and pastries line the stone counters at this soothing and artisanal bakery. With breakfast served until 3:30pm, Gail's wants to make sure everyone gets a taste of their baker's breakfast. Some locations serve lunch—mostly healthy options with salads and vegetables. Not only nutritious but also philanthropic, they partner with multiple charities to help homeless people and those facing hunger. So you can feel great about those scrambled eggs and toast you devoured inside this shop boasting a cornucopia of pastries. There are also multiple locations scattered throughout the city; check online for details.

Breakfast from £4; gluten-free, vegan, and vegetarian options available; wheelchair accessible

GRANGER AND CO KING'S CROSS ($)

7 Pancras Sq.; 020 3058 2567; www.grangerandco.com/kings-cross; open M-Sa 7am-11pm, Su 8am-10:30pm

We'll cut to the chase. This restaurant's hotcakes (that's British for pancake, ya silly goose) are mindblowing. We tried the ricotta banana hotcakes, which came with a jug of maple syrup to pour to our heart's content. And honeycomb butter. Fluffy and thick, their hotcakes are substantial. We couldn't even finish the plate, which, for a hungry traveler, is a rarity. Though not listed on the menu, hotcakes sometimes come with a strawberry version, not just banana. The natural light coming in through the windows only adds to the aspirational ambience. But for real, hotcakes. Stop reading this and go eat them.

Entrées from £7; gluten-free, vegan, and vegetarian options available; limited wheelchair accessibility

HOME SLICE ($)

13 Neal's Yard; 020 3151 7488; www.homeslicepizza.co.uk; open daily noon-11pm

For some incomprehensible reason, pizza by the slice is a rarity in London. That might be for the best, because none can come close to Home Slice's giant slices. This pizza is like an ideal date: hot and cheesy, yet balanced with other fun and funky ingredients, and big enough to cover the entire table with deliciousness. Okay, maybe that's taking the analogy a bit far. On a nice night, you'd better order to go and sit on one of the benches in **Neal's Yard,** rather than wait for your perfect pie. No starters and no desserts—they cut to the chase.

Pizza slices £4, whole pizzas £20; vegetarian options available; limited wheelchair accessibility

KEU BANH MI DELI ($)

332 Old St.; 020 7739 1164; open M-W 9:30am-9:30pm, Th-Sa 9:30am-10pm

This café serves "big portions of banh mi—a Vietnamese baguette sandwich—for less than a fiver.. Score! Found in **Shoreditch,** it has the obligatory hipster element—in this case, boxy glass lamps hanging from the ceiling. At lunchtime, the restaurant fills up quickly, so we'd suggest takeaway. (Unless you want to fight your way to the window seats to observe the almost uniformly trendy Shoreditch residents.) Other than banh mi, they serve curries and other rice dishes.

Entrées from £6.50; vegetarian options available; limited wheelchair accessibility

MAC FACTORY ($)

152-156 North Gower St.; www.themacfactory.co.uk; open M-F 11am-8pm

Ooey gooey cheesy deliciousness awaits inside this small store. Customers choose from six varieties of mac including the classic Nostalgic (mature cheddar and mozzarella), or more fun and funky options like Hey Mac-Arena (beet chili, tortilla crisps, sour cream, jalepeño). This is not your average box of Kraft: crispy breadcrumbs and perfectly firm noodles make every bite an enlightening experience. The stand at **Camden Market** sometimes has quite a line, but the brick-and-mortar shop in **Euston Square** is big enough to satisfy all your cheesiest cravings.

Entrées from £6; vegetarian options available; wheelchair accessible

NEW JOMUNA ($$)

74 Wilton Rd.; 078287509; www.thenew-jomuna.com; open daily noon-3pm and 6pm-midnight

People know **Brick Lane** as a hub for Indian food, but they'd be missing this **Pimlico** gem. The menu seems to go on for days. But be careful when you order, because those appetizers they push on you at the beginning will most certainly be tacked onto the bill at the end. Regardless, the immense variety of dishes on the menu means even the pickiest Indian food fan is bound to find a meal. The restaurant shines with their flavorful vegetarian meals. The nice hot towel after the meal adds just a touch of luxury that perhaps the fake chandeliers and neon ceiling decor might not have conveyed.

Entrées from £8.25; vegan and vegetarian options available; limited wheelchair accessibility

PILAU ($)

22 Noel St.; 079 5457 6380; www.pilau-restaurant.co.uk; open M-Tu noon-8pm, W-Sa noon-9pm, Su noon-4pm

Think Chipotle—but Indian food and very high quality. Pilau delivers quick and delicious plates, perfect for lunch. Their target customers are people on their lunch break, but who's to say a starving sightseeing won't want to wolf down a bowl of their butter chicken with a side of Naan balls? And if you want to do your good deed for the day: for every meal you buy at Pilau, one gets donated through Akshaya Patra to those in need in India.

Medium plates from £5, entrées from £6; gluten-free and vegetarian options available

PIZZA UNION ($)

25 Sandy's Row; 020 8128 1300; www.pizzaunion.com; open daily 11am-late

An entire margherita wood-fired pizza for only £3.50. What's the catch? There isn't one. Unless you count communal tables, but we're always down for some new friends. They don't accept reservations so expect a line out the door at peak hours. Since the pizzas are made in three minutes flat, it should move quickly. The neon sign inside blares PIZZA BAR - ALL DAY - SUPERFAST, and that's what you get. No fancy frills: just delicious 12-inch pizza, quick and easy. The most expensive meal on the menu is only £6.50—about half the price of nearby **Pizza East's** similar meal.

Pizzas from £3.50; gluten-free, vegan, and vegetarian options available; limited wheelchair accessibility

NIGHTLIFE

QUEEN OF HOXTON

1 Curtain Rd., Shoreditch; 0207 422 0958; www.queenofhoxton.com; open M-W 4pm-midnight, Th 4pm-2am, F-Sa noon-2am, Su noon-midnight

A four-seasons-themed rooftop bar: what more could you ask for? How

about a two-story club with an upstairs game room, murals on the walls, and a basement bar with a bangin' bass system. Or a film club, drag bingo, and hip hop karaoke. With a plethora of bars in **Shoreditch** it can be hard to choose, but Queen of Hoxton's the queen of clubs. Come as you are. You never won't have a good night boogie-ing on down or stopping for an afternoon cocktail. Be warned, though: it can get hot, sweaty and very loud, but aren't the best things in life?

Weekdays no cover, weekend cover varies; BGLTQ+ friendly; limited wheelchair accessibility

THE DRAYTON ARMS

153 Old Brompton St..; 020 7835 2301; www.thedraytonarmssw5.co.uk; open M 11am-11pm, Tu-W 11am-11:30pm, Th-F 11am-midnight, Sa 10am-midnight, Su 10am-11pm

If a speakeasy is a bar hidden behind something else, then what do we call a theatre hidden behind a bar? A watcheasy? Nah, we call it the Drayton Arms. The theatre's no secret, though, and is home to multiple monthly shows, including previews for shows heading to the **Edinburgh Fringe Festival.** It's a small black-box theatre, so there are no bad seats. When ticket prices on the West End get as high as the triple digits, a nice play for a tenner can be the remedy for a theatre-seeking tourist on a budget. Plus, the pub downstairs serves burgers almost too pretty to eat, along with other very high-quality modern British food. Your dinner will likely end up costing you more than the show.

ℹ Entrées from £12, drinks from £5; limited wheelchair accessibility in theater

HEAVEN

17 Villiers St.; 020 7930 2020; www.heavennightclub-london.com; hours vary by gig, usually open until 4am

As we stood at the center of the bouncing stage, surrounded by intoxicated revelers screaming and jumping to the seminal classic "Since U Been Gone," we felt half at home and half sure we'd be instantly trampled. Sweating and singing, the crowd at Heaven embraces their policy of embracing everyone. The bouncers have been known to pick out those who've had a few too many pints to drink, so be careful when you get here. Upstairs, the hip-hop rooms hold even more shirtless men and some classic R&B jams. Downstairs, the cheesy pop palace blares divas from Lady Gaga to Carly Rae Jepsen, and stage dance floor space comes at a premium. Heaven is run by the same people as **G-A-Y** in **Soho** and hosts different events and concerts like drag and theme nights. Here, you can dance and not feel judged by anyone in the room.

ℹ Cover £5 before 1am, £8 after 1am, often free with guest list online or student card; BGLTQ+ friendly; no wheelchair accessibility

RED LION

48 Parliament St.; 020 7930 5826; www.redlionwestminster.co.uk; open M-Tu 8am-11pm, W 9:30am-11pm, Th-F 8am-11pm, Sa 8am-9pm, Su 9am-9pm

Ah, the smell of beer. But not like, stale-frat-house-with-sticky-floors type of beer. No, the beer smell from this pub is pure class from the tap. In this old and well-maintained pub, you'll feel like a real true grownup sipping a pint after a long day's work. Or however British professionals feel. With no TVs or music, people rely on conversation to entertain them. (The horror!) Upstairs, the dining rooms invite hungry people in, but we'd recommend sticking to the downstairs bar by the window.!

ℹ Drinks from £4; limited wheelchair accessibility

THE SOCIAL

5 Little Portland St.; 0207 636 4992; www.thesocial.com; open M-W 3pm-midnight, Th 3pm-1am, F 12:30pm-1am, Sa 6pm-1am

Clubbing in London can go one of two ways: dressed up, your heels or button-downs ready for a big night out in **Mayfair,** or the beer-laden sticky floors of clubs in **Camden.** The Social blurs the lines between them. Since the venue is owned by a record label, there's a heavy emphasis on music here. Most nights you'll find a live gig down by the basement bar. With names like MGMT, Adele, and Vampire Weekend having graced the stage here, there's someone worth seeing to appeal to everyone. You're not getting the see-and-be-seen crowd, nor are you getting aggressive musicheads who don't want to meet people. The kind of people who come here are, well, social.

ℹ Ticket prices vary; BGLTQ+ friendly; limited wheelchair accessibility

TRAPEZE

89 Great Eastern St.; 020 7739 6747; www.trapezebar.co.uk; open Tu-Th 4pm-2:30am, F-Sa 4pm-3:30am

"Welcome, locals and travelers, to the greatest show on earth!" is what we imagine the bartenders at Trapeze saying to us (with their eyes) as they make cocktails that are basically works of art. This circus-themed bar has real trapezes hanging from the ceiling (usually unused) and a nightclub open on the weekends. But even during the week, the bar becomes a dance floor and DJs keep the party going until 3am. Free fresh popcorn fuels your thirst for another drink while you're dancing your butt off. Yes, cocktails are pricey, but that's the price you pay for free beer pong tables, and circus tent-themed boots. Embrace the experience (or just pregame) for a night to remember.

ℹ Beer from £5, cocktails from £9; BGLTQ+ friendly; limited wheelchair accessibility

YE OLDE CHESHIRE CHEESE

145 Fleet St., City of London; 2073536170; open M-Sa 11am-11pm

At almost 500 years old, this pub is just a little older than that leftover pizza you said you were going to throw out yesterday. In fact, according to the expert bartender, the cellars downstairs where people dine are from the 1300s. Legend says **Samuel Johnson** and **Charles Dickens** frequented this pub, and it probably still looks exactly how it did then. There's no music and no TV—just an old clock that doesn't work. The pub draws visitors with history, but keeps them there with reasonably-priced drinks and a historic atmosphere. And Polly, the taxidermied parrot above the bar, makes for a story too.

i Beer from £4, entrées from £11; BGLTQ+ friendly; no wheelchair accessibility

MANCHESTER

Coverage by **Lucy Golub**

The bee symbolizes Manchester—hardworking, industrious, and buzzing around from one thing to the next. You'll find it emblazoned on walls, logos, and even the trash cans on the street. And it fits. Manchester used to be known as Cottonopolis, the textile hub of the world. Today, it's known for music and art (ever heard of a little band called Oasis?), vintage shopping and street murals, its football team, and countless bars and clubs. Manchester is well on its way to London-level trendiness, but hasn't lost its character in its quest to make it to the big leagues. It's not just a mini-London, but rather an evolving creative hub full of history, working its way into the shells of industry that used to occur there. And though they say Brits might not be known as the friendliest people out there, Mancunians might just prove you wrong.

ORIENTATION

Manchester's neighborhoods are distinct but so small you'll be in the next without even realizing. In the center of the city you'll find the **Central Retail District** and **Civic Quarters.** To the east lies **Piccadilly Station,** where the tourist center and trains are located. The city's trendy **Northern Quarter,** home to vintage stores, coffee shops, and lots of nightlife can be found north of the station. West of Piccadilly Station are the **Gay Village** and **Chinatown,** more nightlife hubs. West and slightly south of the center, you'll find **Spinningfields,** home to the **Museum of Science and Industry** and the **People's History Museum,** as well as more restaurants and nightlife. Much further west are **Trafford,** home to **Old Trafford,** the football stadium, and **Media City,** where many TV programs are produced.

ESSENTIALS

GETTING THERE

Flying into Manchester Airport is easy, and trains run every 10min. from the airport to Piccadilly Station. Trains run to Piccadilly Station and Victoria Station from all over England. From there, a bus or tram take you around the city.

GETTING AROUND

Manchester is compact enough that most places are near enough to walk. If you're looking for public transportation, the metro shuttle bus offers multiple routes that can be viewed online at www.tfgm.com. Additionally, the tram has fewer routes but takes you to the areas you'll likely be going. There are taxis, but they are rather expensive. Public transportation runs late enough into the night to be serviceable at most hours.

PRACTICAL INFORMATION

Tourist Offices: The Manchester Tourist Information Centre (1 Piccadilly Gardens, Portland St.; 0871 222 8223; www.visitmanchester.com; open M-Sa 9:30am-5pm, Su 10:30am-4:30pm).

Banks/ATMs/Currency Exchange: Banks and ATMs are prevalent. One is Barclays Bank (88-86 Market St.; 345 734 6345; open M-Tu 9:30am-5:30pm, W 10am-4:30pm, Th-Sa 9:30am-5:30pm, Su 11am-3pm).

Post Offices: Piccadilly Plaza (F4, Londis Store, Portland St.; 161 237 1229; open M-F 10am-6pm, Sa 10am-4pm, Su 11am-3pm)

Public Restrooms: Town Hall Extension Public Toilet (Lloyd St.).

Internet: Most cafés, restaurants, and museums have Wi-Fi.

BGLTQ+ Resources: The Proud Trust provides BGLTQ+ resources and support (49-51 Sidney St.; 7813 981338; www.theproudtrust.org).

EMERGENCY INFORMATION

Emergency Number: 999.

Police: Greater Manchester Police Headquarters (Northampton Rd.; non-emergency 101; www.gmp.police.uk).

Rape Crisis Center: The Manchester Rape Crisis Centre (60 Nelson St.; 0161 660 3347; www.manchesterraoecrisis.co.uk; phoneline available daily 9am-5:30pm).

Hospitals:

- Manchester Royal Infirmary (Oxford Rd.; 161 624 0420; open daily 24hr).
- North Manchester General Hospital (Delaunays Rd.; 161 624 0420; open daily 24hr).

Pharmacies: You'll have no trouble finding pharmacies.

- Boots (32 Market St.; 161 832 6533; boots.co.uk; open M-Sa 8am-8pm, Su 11am-5pm).
- Everest Pharmacy (80 Stockport Rd.; 161 273 4629; www.everestpharmacy.co.uk/; open M-F 9am-7pm, Sa 9am-3pm).

SIGHTS

CULTURE

ROYAL EXCHANGE THEATRE

St. Ann's Sq.; 161 833 9833; www.royalexchange.co.uk; open M-Sa 9:30am-7:30pm, Su 11am-5pm

The architecture of the suspended central theater in the middle of giant colorful marble pillars is a spectacle in itself. Yet on top of the breathtaking enormity of the space itself, the Royal Exchange Theatre hosts shows in their two-performance spaces almost every day. The center theater is the largest theater in the round in the country, and it resembles a Mars rover mixed with a robotic flower. You'll have to see it yourself to understand. The theatre offers different student and early-bird discounts, so you'll be able to watch some classic British theater as well as newer modern shows.

i Free; show prices vary, tickets from £10; wheelchair accessible

AFFLECK'S

52 Church St.; 161 839 0718; www.afflecks.com; open M-F 10:30am-6pm, Sa 10am-6pm, Su 11am-5pm

Don't be surprised when you run into goths sporting neon hair and giant boots buckled up to their knees. Affleck's contains 60 independent stores spread out over four floors, so you can take your pick of vintage denim, floral dresses, American candy, and classic punk rock record shops. And of course, lots of jewelry for obscure body piercings. All we're saying is that if you're looking for a very bedazzled wedding dress and leather gloves while shopping for bath products in the shape of cupcakes and classic Levi Mom Jeans, you've found your place. Come and browse the costumes and the characters of the people you'll meet here.

i Prices vary; wheelchair accessible

MANCHESTER ART GALLERY

Mosley St.; 161 235 8888; manchesterartgallery.org; open M-W 10am-5pm, Th 10am-9pm, F-Su 10am-5pm

Oh, art galleries. You're so cultured and highbrow. That's what we think of when we hear "art gallery," but if you're burned out and have no desire to stare at old paintings of dead people, then you're in luck, because this gallery holds way more than just the typical landscapes and portraits. Some of the best pieces of the gallery come from the re-done caption addendums from the gallery's first feminist takeover. So while you're reading a snooty art historian's interpretations of the juxtaposition of light and dark in the paintings of pre-Raphaelite artists (whose works are beautiful, we'll admit), you can also read a nice little paragraph roasting the men who refused to acknowledge female competency. Snaps. The gallery also hosts contemporary exhibits upstairs, often using multimedia to express political messages. Be sure to check out the mindfulness exhibit. It's as if the art gallery had a rebellious teenage kid—the two different vibes you'll get from the gallery might not match, but they create a full experience (imagine the vibes of Banksy amid seventeenth-century paintings).

i Free; tours available Th, F, Sa, Su; wheelchair accessible

LANDMARKS

JOHN RYLANDS LIBRARY

150 Deansgate; 0161 306 0555; www.library.manchester.ac.uk/rylands; open M-Sa 10am-5pm, Su noon-5pm

The reading room of this library puts basically every American library to shame. Neo-Gothic architecture meets centuries-old books in an old but warmly lit banquet-hall-esque library. If you have any reading to get done, you might not want to do it here, because the room's details will keep your eyes focused on everything but your book. And yet it is an ideal place to work—hushed and somber except for the occasional echo of a step, a camera click, or the brush of pages turning. Make sure you look up (they provide mirrors to avoid sore necks—nice.) and look at the lights, which are indicative of John Rylands claim to fortune: cotton. The books they have on display are not-quite page-turners but are historically important—as in, really old.

i Free; wheelchair accessible

ALAN TURING MEMORIAL

Sackville Park; open 24hr

Ah, Alan Turing: genius, inventor, world-changer. Yet too few know his story, which was made into the 2014 Oscar-nominated film *The Imitation Game*. We'll break it down quickly: Turing basically invented the first computer and assisted the Allies in World War II. But Turing was gay, and when he revealed his identity during an investigation, he ended up losing his job. At the time, being gay was a crime, and his admission led to brutal physical punishment and his eventual death by suicide. Honor his legacy and learn more about his life at this statue in a small park. There he sits in casual clothes, an apple in his palm.

i Free; wheelchair accessible

MANCHESTER CATHEDRAL

Victoria St.; 0161 833 2220; www.manchestercathedral.org; open M 8:30am-5pm, Tu-Th 8:30am-6:30pm, F 8:30am-5pm, Sa-Su 8:30am-6:30pm

When tragedy struck Manchester in the summer of 2017, the city responded with a mural emphasizing the love and connections between people of all backgrounds. This mural was painted on one of the walls of the Cathedral, broadcasting a message of peace. Unlike others you might encounter on your travels, this church feels like a place people actually visit for worship, making it more than just a beautiful testament to the past. Especially intricate are the details on the center quire, which has looked basically the same since 1509. With only a £1 photo permit paid to a sometimes hard-to-find individual welcoming you into the cathedral, the structure is yours to explore and wander as you remember the city's resilience.

i Free; photography permit £1; wheelchair accessible

MUSEUMS

MUSEUM OF SCIENCE AND INDUSTRY

Liverpool Rd.; 0161 832 2244; www.msimanchester.org.uk; open M-Sa 10am-5pm

Manchester used to be called Cottonopolis—the world's hub for

textile production. Today, that claim to fame has dimmed, but the Museum of Science and Industry clings onto its past life as an industrial city. Watch an engine demonstration, and learn about how cotton was spun. And when you get bored of that (it happens to the best of us), head upstairs to the interactive "Experiment!" gallery with 25 hands-on exhibits that feel like games. You can play a Dance Dance Revolution-style game to learn how about recycling, or pedal a bicycle to see your skeleton move. Though you might be playing some of these games with six year-olds, no one's judging.

i Free except for some exhibits; wheelchair accessible

PEOPLE'S HISTORY MUSEUM (SPINNINGFIELDS)

Left Bank; 0161 838 9190; www.phm.org.uk; open daily 10am-5pm

Do you hear the people sing? Singing the song of angry men. Well, kind of. This museum focuses on England's fights for equality for different groups of people—hint: usually the groups are not white French men. But the museum condenses hundreds of years of movements into three floors, and reminds you that there have always been ideas worth fighting for. While the panels, artifacts, and stories may overwhelm you with information, we left feeling angry at the injustice others have experienced, yet empowered and hopeful for progress. The first floor focuses on pre-1945 and the second follows movements from 1945 to the present day. You might just find your next passionate protest here or learn about a movement whose achievements you took for granted.

i Free; wheelchair accessible

NATIONAL FOOTBALL MUSEUM

Urbis Building, Cathedral Gardens; 0161 605 8200; www.nationalfootballmuseum.com; open daily 10am-5pm

Manchester's name instantly brings to mind the soccer team—excuse us, football team—**Manchester United.** Here, at the self-proclaimed best football museum in the world, you can learn all about it. The first floor showcases some fine memorabilia like jerseys and footballs. And if you turn around you'll find some jerseys and footballs. And, in the next room are some more jerseys and footballs accompanied by videos. You get the picture. But upstairs you'll find interactive games you can (pay to) play, like shooting goals. For football fans, this place is surely a must-see. For those less sporty, the exhibits upstairs have some cool photography, and you can learn a fun fact or two to impress your more athletic friends.

i Free; visitor guide package £6, tours £3.50; guided tour part of package M-F 10:30am, 12:30pm, 2:30pm, Sa-Su 11am, 3pm; wheelchair accessible

FOOD

COMPTOIR LIBANAIS ($$)

18-19 The Ave.; 0161 672 3999; www.comptoirlibanais.com/locations/manchester; open M-Th 10am-11pm, F-Sa 10am-midnight, Su 10am-10pm

If we could eat every meal here, we would—and we'd probably never get sick of the Za'atar. Despite being one branch of a larger chain, Comptoir Libanais' offerings taste like perfectly thought-out Lebanese home cooking. The menu includes tons of options for meat eaters and vegetarians alike, and the mini shop inside the restaurant even sells some ingredients so you can cook your own version of the dishes! Unfortunately, we're not good at cooking, but that's why we leave it to the pros here. The food alone would be draw enough, but the decor and ambiance inside is another reason to visit—pastel tiles and mosaics cover the floors and the walls, while colorful chairs and lamps add pops of color that transport you across the world while enjoying some hummus or a cocktail.

i Entrées from £9; vegan and vegetarian options available; wheelchair accessible

COMMON ($)

39-41 Edge St.; 161 832 9245; www.aplacecalledcommon.co.uk; open daily 10am-late

We get it. Common called themselves common because they're just another random brunch place. Except they're totally not. Part hipster-vaguely-American café, part bar, part social club, Common has got it all. Signing up to be a free member online gives you BOGO burgers and different monthly rewards. Or you could stop in and check out their Not Mac 'n cheese (hint: there's corn) or Korean fried chicken. Sandwiches are cheapest weekdays before 5pm, but, if you come later, you might arrive in time for a trivia night or pub quiz. It's hard to capture the vibe, but think wood stools and staff with beards and cool hair welcoming you to the giant restaurant with what might be sheets hanging from the ceiling.

i Entrées from £5; gluten-free, vegan, and vegetarian options available

FIG & SPARROW ($)

20 Oldham St.; 0161 228 1843; www.figandsparrow.co.uk; open M-F 8am-7pm, Sa 9am-7pm, Su 10am-7pm

Half café, half design store (think £20 glasses), Fig & Sparrow is where a hipster goes to get a ~hipster drink~ after a day of thrift shopping or kombucha-brewing. But when you're craving avocado toast, there's no place like a hipster café. Breakfast and people-watching all day—what more could you want? And believe us, the people who eat here are worth watching. We saw some of the most bizarre and mismatched clothing that still somehow looked super cool on these young and beautiful couples strolled into the cafe. Maybe drinking the ridiculously priced $4 (but oh so so good) latte can give us those superpowers, too.

i Entrées from £6, coffee from £4; gluten-free, vegan, and vegetarian options available

NIGHTLIFE

NIGHT & DAY CAFE

26 Oldham St.; 0161 236 1822; www.nightnday.org; open M-Th 10am-2am, F-Sa 10am-4am, Su 9am-10:30pm

People flock to Manchester for the music. And Mancunians flock to Night & Day for the authentic up-and-comers, hazy fog, and obscure band posters. Many now-famous bands and artists performed here in their early days, and, if you're looking to discover some new music, there's often free gigs of relatively unknown or on-the-rise artists. If you're looking to see someone big, we recommend booking in advance. Oh yeah, and not only do they play rock and roll, EDM, and "umm what?" concerts, but they serve breakfast in the morning. Get the name now?

i Cover varies by concert, pints from £4.50, entrées from £8; BGLTQ+ friendly; wheelchair accessible

THE LIAR'S CLUB

19a Back Bridge St.; 0161 834 5111; www.theliarsclub.co.uk; open M-Sa 5pm-4am, Su 5pm-3am

England isn't known for its gorgeous Caribbean weather and beaches. But hey, we can dream. And at The Liar's Club, we can have our dreams come true. If you're craving a tropical drink or a reprieve from the rain, step on down into this tiki-themed paradise. Yes, it's underground, but that adds to the sense that maybe, just maybe, you might be on a beach.Their cocktails are strong and fruity—just the way we like them—and are two for £10 during happy hour. The Liar's Club is one of the only bars open until 4am every night, and if you get hungry, you can pop upstairs to **Crazy Pedro's Part Time Pizza Bar** and get one of their specials of the month (think creations like hot dog pizza).

i No cover, drinks from £8; BGLTQ+ friendly; no wheelchair accessibility

THE WASHHOUSE

19 Shudehill; 0161 839 5287; www.the-washhouse.co.uk; open M-Th 5pm-1am, F 5pm-3am, Sa noon-3am, Su 3pm-11pm

Behind a wall-height tumble dryer lies a hidden speakeasy, luxurious leather booths, mood lighting, and pricey cocktails to boot. The menu veers toward the bold, offering varieties including spicy chili peppers, Coco Pops cereal, and every spirit you can name. Call ahead (phone lines open at noon) to book your washing machine for the night, because they tend to be strict on reservations. Even if you're armed with the address, you'd still probably walk by the nondescript laundromat a few times. They know how to hide this secret. But once you find it, pick up the phone and press the button. You might feel silly and you might feel sneaky—we've been there, but it's a bar experience like no other.

i No cover, cocktails from £10; wheelchair accessible; reservation required

YORK

Coverage by **Lucy Golub**

Are you always reminiscing about "the good old days?" If the modern era doesn't quite cut it for you, York—where the past feels more real than ever—is calling your name. New York is lame. Pull up to the original. The effect of its buildings and cobblestoned streets give York an air of having been ripped from a storybook—albeit an old, regal European storybook. Castle walls surround the medieval city, whose history goes back centuries. From the chocolate trade to railroads to the monarchy, York's past is buried in its stones and dispersed through the air. The spires of York Minster, a church built over 250 years, can be seen from all over the city, reminding you of the passion, labor, and love it took to grow the metropolis. Literature aficionados will fall for Shakespeare's references—Richard III was the Duke of York, after all. The city's charm comes from well-preserved old streets, narrow lanes, timber-framed buildings, and plethora of churches. Yet despite the well-preserved setting, new life grows in York, with museums, nightlife, and arts all around. The present exists in the buildings of the past, calling out to tourists and locals to come see and come explore.

ORIENTATION

In the center of the city lies **York Minster,** the giant cathedral visible from all around the tiny city. Basically everything you'll want to see is in the same general area. The **River Ouse** runs through the center of the city, and multiple bridges connect the two sides. On the south side of the river are **York Station, the National Railway Museum,** and **Micklegate.** The north side holds most of the attractions. Slightly south of the Minster are **the Shambles,** and nearby is much of York's nightlife and restaurant scenes, although some bigger clubs lie on the south side of the river. Slightly east are **Clifford Tower** and **York Castle Museum.** The **Castle Walls** run along the outside of the city center, encircling the quaint town inside.

ESSENTIALS

GETTING THERE

Getting to York via train is a breeze; you'll end up at York Railway station, only about 15min. from the city center. The most convenient airports are Manchester Airport and Leeds/Bradford, and there are trains to take you directly into York from each one. The TransPennie Express will bring you from Manchester, Liverpool, or Newcastle.

GETTING AROUND

York's center is truly tiny. You could basically walk anywhere in less than 15min. from York Minster. There also are buses, and you can access timetables online. You can use a smartcard or pay cash on board (exact change preferred). All day passes are also available for £4.50. Many bus lines don't run 24hr, so be sure to check the return times if you're taking a trip somewhere outside of the city.

PRACTICAL INFORMATION

Tourist Offices: Here is the main tourist office: (1 Museum St.; 019 0455 0099; www.visityork.org; open M-Sa 9am-4pm, Su 10am-4pm).

Banks/ATMs/Currency Exchange: You'll be able to find a bank or ATM easily in the main town center. One is TSB Bank (25 Parliament St.; 019 0462 6887; www.tsb.co.uk/branch-locator/york-parliament-street; open M-F 9am-5pm, Sa 9am-4pm).

Post Offices: York Post Office (22 Lendal St.; 084 5722 3344; open M 9am-5:30pm, Tu 9:30am-5pm, W-F 9am-5:30pm, Sa 9am-4pm).

Public Restrooms: Public Toilets Union Terrace (Clarence St.; open 24hr)

Internet: There is public Wi-Fi in many of the tourist attractions as well as most main streets.

BGLTQ+ Resources: The York LGBT forum ensures the rights and interests of LGBT people in the Yorkshire county and offers support and resources (15 Priory St.; 07731852533; www.yorklgbtforum.org.uk).

EMERGENCY INFORMATION

Emergency Number: 999.

Police: Acomb Police Station (Acomb Rd.; non-emergency number 101; open M 10am-noon, Tu 2pm-4pm, W-Th 6pm-8pm, F 2pm-4pm, Sa 10am-noon).

Rape Crisis Center: Bridge House is a Sexual Assault Referral Centre that provides services for victims of sexual assault (48 Bridge Rd., Bishopthorpe; 033 0223 0362; www.bridgehousesarc.org; phone available daily 9am-5pm).

Hospitals: Below is a convenient hospital.

- York Hospital (Wigginton Rd.; 019 0463 1313; open daily 24hr).

Pharmacies: There are many pharmacies in the city centre.

- Boots (43 Coney St.; 01904 653657; open M-Sa 8:30am-6pm, Su 11am-5pm).

SIGHTS

CULTURE

THE SHAMBLES

Shambles; 019 0455 0099; neighborhood open daily 24hr, store hours vary, market hours 9am-5pm

The most picturesque piece of a picturesque city, The Shambles' narrow paths and low-hanging timber-fronted buildings look like they're taken from a postcard. Three *Harry Potter* stores, and (potentially) counting, join old-fashioned fudge shops and confectionaries and card-and-trinket stores galore. But the history of the streets holds a more grim story—the alleys used to be full of butchers with windows full of hanging animals, blood and guts included. Today, the street's appearance is much more pristine. At the market, locals shop for produce while tourists stock up on York-themed souvenirs, jewelry, and intricately decorated photo frames. Your best bet for an unobstructed view of the street would be to go in the evening, once the shops and the markets have closed.

i Store prices vary; wheelchair accessible

THE ORIGINAL GHOST WALK OF YORK

The King's Arms Pub, Ouse Bridge; www.theoriginalghostwalkofyork.co.uk

We generally steer clear of ghost tours, which are usually just sneaky tourist traps, and not just because we're afraid of being haunted. This ghost tour proved us wrong. Theatrically telling stories while wearing an old-fashioned suit, our guide regaled us with stories of York's ancient haunters. The tour begins with the most beautiful ghost of York, a dark-haired woman clad in a wedding dress who stood outside of the **Church of All Saints,** and finishes near the **Minster** after a story about a field of soldiers. We won't spoil all the fun, but the tour is worth the five quid. It's not scary per se, but the captivating stories teach you more about York's hidden history without the usual gimmicks and scare-tactics of a typical tour.

i Admission £5, £4 reduced; tours daily 8pm; limited wheelchair accessibility

SPARK:YORK

17-21 Piccadilly; www.sparkyork.org; open Su-Th 8am-10:30pm, F-Sa 8am-11pm; food available at noon

People don't often associate centuries-old York with up-and-coming trends. But if you're tired of the gorgeous old buildings that sometimes look like a movie set, Spark brings you back to reality. Here, you'll find the city's young and hip sipping on craft beers and picking at Thai food. Old shipping containers host shops that range from crafts to vintage clothes to food and drink. It's like a mini Camden Market but in the old streets of York. Colorful murals decorate the walls of the outdoor market's ground floor, and up the stairs you can get a drink and sit on a patio, all while quietly people watching.

i Store prices vary; limited wheelchair accessibility

LANDMARKS

CLIFFORD TOWER

Tower St.; 019 0464 6940; www.english-heritage.org.uk/visit/places/cliffords-tower-york; open daily 10am-6pm

What remains of **York Castle** today is mostly ruins, but Clifford's Tower stands tall above York. The tower itself has been around in one form or another for nearly 1000 years and was the site of the 1190 Massacre of the Jews, a horrific piece of oft-forgotten history. On a lighter note, the views from the tower are amazing, especially towards the **Minster.** Although the ticket fee is a little hefty for just a climb up some stairs, the tower marks an excellent starting point for the beginning of your days in York—you really can see everything from this "roofless ruin."

i Admission £5.40, £4.90 reduced; last entry 15min. before closing; no wheelchair accessibility

YORK MINSTER

Deangate; 019 0455 7200; www.yorkminster.org; open M-Sa 9am-4:30pm, Su 12:45pm-3pm

Breathtaking in size and scope, York Minster is one of the most impressive cathedrals in the world, and the largest in Northern Europe. Light filters through the surrounding stained glass windows, illuminating the detailed carvings and intricacies in a rainbow of colorful rays. The organ's light notes and heavy undertones originate from the center of the cathedral, the highest of the notes twinkling and echoing to even the uppermost windows. Every stone is packed with history; the cathedral was built in 637, after all. The underbelly of the church contains an exhibit on its history, but if you're pressed for time we'd suggest buying a ticket to climb the tower for birds eye views of York down below. Even without the extras, the grandeur of the internal and external architecture draw hundreds of thousands of visitors each year.

i Admission £11, in advance £10, students £9; wheelchair accessible

YORK CASTLE WALLS

13 sections throughout the city; www.yorkwalls.org.uk; open 8am-sunset

A little over two miles long, the York Castle Walls are the oldest medieval walls in Europe. The walk itself is narrow, and you'll have to "excuse me" and elbow your way around tourists taking selfies with enormous DSLR cameras if you go at a crowded time. But where else can you walk around the fortress of an entire city? If you don't have time to walk the whole thing (understandable, there's pints to be drank), we recommend climbing up on **Goodramgate** to follow the walk that views **York Minster** and some large mansions behind it. You'll get a taste of the royal life from the time when the walls were built. If the weather is nice, a sunset walk and golden-hour light make for stunning photos.

i Free; no wheelchair accessibility

MUSEUMS

YORK CHOCOLATE STORY

King's Sq.; 019 0452 7765; www.yorkschocolatestory.com; open daily 10am-5pm

This museum traces York's chocolate-making history and its role as one of the world's chocolate capitals. Yes, the guided tour provides you with chocolate samples so you can snack the whole way, as well as information about the founding families, some chocolate samples, demonstrations of chocolate making, and even more chocolate samples. Did we mention there are chocolate samples? There's a different kind for every taste, ranging from sweet milk to cacao nibs. Yeah, there's lots of chocolate here. Learn about the Rowntrees, the Terrys, and the Cravens, and why the air in York sometimes smells like chocolate. Well-practiced tour guides engage their audience, creating a tour that's both informative and fun (and delicious). If that's not enough, you get to make and decorate your own chocolate lollipop at the end of the tour. Sweet!

i Admission £12.50, £11.50 reduced; tours every 15min.; last tour 4pm; wheelchair accessible

YORK ART GALLERY

Exhibition Sq.; 019 0468 7687; www.yorkartgallery.org.uk; open daily 10am-5pm

A recent redevelopment in this old city, York Art Gallery reopened its doors in the summer of 2015, with an eye for timeliness and attention to pertinent world events and how they relate to art. You'll find temporary topical exhibits throughout the entire gallery. During our visit, the highlight was an exhibition called "The Sea is the Limit," focusing on art surrounding refugees. Upstairs, what might as well be millions of ceramics sit on shelves in the Center of Ceramics. In an area that focuses on the past, it's refreshing to wander through galleries containing new art, ranging from unclear representations in contemporary art to photography.

i Admission £7.50, £3.75 reduced; wheelchair accessible

FOOD

BREW AND BROWNIE ($)

5 Museum St.; 019 0464 7420; www.brewandbrownie.co.uk; open M-Sa 9am-5pm, Su 9:30am-5pm

Here's a pro tip that has been tripping us up for weeks—when Brits say pancakes they mean crêpes! Luckily, you can get your American pancake fix here, served with streaky bacon and blueberries, Nutella and bananas, or salted caramel. Count us in. And it's served until late afternoon: what more could you ask for from brunch? (Other than sandwiches, avocado toast, and eggs, which they also serve.) Top-notch quality, central location, and adorable decorations. If you're looking for more of a coffee shop vibe, we'd also suggest the delectable sourdough toasties from their sister store, **Brew and Brownie Bake Shop.**

i Entrées from £4.50; vegan and vegetarian options available; wheelchair accessible

LUCKY DAYS CAFE ($$)

1 Church St.; 019 0473 3992; open daily 9am-5pm

Almost too quaint to be real, the light green walls and wood tables remind us of our non-existent British grandmothers' homes. With three locations spread around the city, the café advertises itself as not the cheapest, but as definitely the best. We'd have to agree. We've tried our fair share of scones, and its famous mature cheddar scone takes the cake. Or takes their classic blueberry and orange zest scone, should we say? Mains come with multiple sides to fill you up, and every detail has been meticulously planned out. If York itself were a restaurant, it would be Lucky Days Café—old, incredibly cute, maybe a little touristy, but ultimately worth it for the quality.

i Entrées from £8; gluten-free, vegan, and vegetarian options available; limited wheelchair accessibility

GREEK STREET FOOD SOUVLAKI ($)

Silver St.; 074 7825 8971; open Tu-F noon-4pm, Sa noon-5pm, Su noon-4pm

Gyros aren't hard to find in Europe—if you were walking down the street, by the time you figured out how to spell "souvlaki," you'd probably find one. But would you find a cheap, massive, freshly cooked, and delicious gyro or chicken souvlaki next to an equally delicious donut stand? We think not. So head over to **The Shambles Market** to pick up your meal. Follow your nose, because you can smell the slow-cooked meat from quite a few stands away. Then wash down the hearty Greek food with some freshly fried donuts from **The Donut Kitchen.** It might not be the healthiest meal of your trip, but it's good for your soul.

i Gyro and souvlaki from £5; vegetarian options available; wheelchair accessible

HUMPIT ($)

12A Church St.; 019 0462 0066; www.humpit-hummus.com; open M-Sa 11am-8pm, Su noon-8pm

The restaurant owners either didn't think about the name, or they really knew what they were doing. Where do you get a fresh pita stuffed with healthy vegetables? Humpit. A quick and healthy lunch? Humpit. Homemade hummus? Humpit. And if you see a person you really like? We'll leave that answer to you. The restaurant is a classic fast-casual place with a counter where you order and generic tables at which to devour your meal. It's basically a vegan mediterranean Chipotle. What they lack in atmosphere (think Chipotle), they make up for in flavor and portion size.

i Entrées from £4.50; gluten-free, vegan, and vegetarian options available; wheelchair accessible

NIGHTLIFE

FOSSGATE SOCIAL

25 Fossgate; 019 0462 8692; www.thefossgatesocial.com; open M-Th 9am-midnight, F-Sa 9am-12:30am, Su 10am-midnight

An all-day coffee shop turns into a bar at night. But when the bottles come out, the venue still retains the cosiness and comfort it has during the day. Upstairs you'll find a casual room with couches and small tables. It's homey inside, and the dim lights and cramped seating somehow help conversation flow (and help your drink of choice as well). Head to the garden out back and mingle with York's young and artsy. Also, we're not kidding when we say the brownies they sell here (all day and night!) are the best we've ever had.

i Cocktails from £6, pints from £4; limited wheelchair accessibility

THE GOLDEN FLEECE

16 Pavement; 01 9046 20491; www.goldenfleecepubyork.co.uk; open daily 10am-midnight

If you're looking for spirits, the Golden Fleece has got you covered, both in the ghoul and alcohol senses. York's (self-proclaimed) most haunted bar might just send chills down your spine. Was that a ghost moving in the corner of your eye or just the skeleton perched at the bar sipping a cocktail? #spooky. If your chair starts to slide, don't panic. It's probably not a ghost, just the slanted floors and the narrow doors dating back to the 1503 birth of this bar. We suggest avoiding the tourists and seeing if you can find a local—we met a man who's been coming to the Golden Fleece for 40 years.

i Pints from £3.60; BGLTQ+ friendly; limited wheelchair accessibility; dog friendly

THE PUNCHBOWL

5-9 Blossom St.; 019 0466 6740; www.jdwetherspoon.com/pubs/all-pubs/england/north-yorkshire/the-punch-bowl-york; open M-Th 8am-midnight, F-Sa 8am-1am, Su 8am-midnight

The Punchbowl is consistently cheap and consistently open. What more could you ask from a bar? You know what you're going to get: ages ranging from just-out-of-high-school lads looking for a cheap pint to full grey-haired groups snacking on fish and chips. The Punchbowl is an excellent option for some classic pub-grub, and they offer multiple meal deals and specials. Wetherspoons overtook the previous pub that used to be there since 1770 so you're basically on a historical tour of the city by drinking here.

i Entrées from £5, pints from £1.99; wheelchair accessible

GREAT BRITAIN ESSENTIALS

VISAS

Britain is not a signatory to the Schengen Agreement, which means it is not a member of the freedom of movement zone that covers most of continental Europe. EU citizens do not need a visa to visit Britain, and citizens of Australia, Canada, New Zealand, the

Citizens of the United States and many of other non-EU countries do not need a visa for stays of up to six months. Those staying longer than six months may apply for a longer-term visa; consult an embassy or consulate for more information. Because Britain is not a part of the Schengen zone, time spent here does not count toward the 90-day limit on travel within that area. Entering to work or study for longer than six months will require a visa. You can learn more at www.ukvisas.gov.uk. Although there is a lot of uncertainty surrounding the recent Brexit, this appears to only affect EU citizens living in the UK and not those who are just visiting.

MONEY

Tipping and Bargaining: Restaurant servers are paid at least the minimum wage, so tipping is slightly different. If you receive table service, the tip might already be included in your bill; this will appear as a service charge. If there is no service charge, you should tip around 10%. You do not need to tip if you order at the counter, or in bars or pubs. If you are staying in a nice hotel (read: not a hostel), you should tip porters £1-2, and tipping the housekeeper is up to your discretion. For taxi drivers, it is customary to round up to the nearest pound, but you don't need to tip. Bargaining is not common in the UK and should probably not be attempted.

Taxes: The UK has a 20% value added tax (VAT), a sales tax applied to everything but food, books, and children's clothing. The tax is included on the amount indicated on the price tag, and all prices stated in *Let's Go* include VAT. Upon exiting Britain, non-EU citizens can reclaim VAT (minus an administrative fee) through the Retail Export Scheme, although the process can only be applied to goods you take out of the country.

HEALTH AND SAFETY

Drugs and Alcohol: The British pint is 20oz. as compared to the 16oz. U.S. pint. The legal age at which you can buy alcohol in the UK is 18; carry around identification in case you are asked for it. Those aged 16 and older can drink beer or wine in a restaurant if they are accompanied by an adult and the adult makes the purchase. The use, possession, and sale of hard drugs is illegal and can carry a penalty of up to seven years in prison for possession alone.
Do not test this. Penalties for cannabis are less severe, but police can issue a warning or on the spot fine of £90 if you're found with it. Smoking is banned in enclosed public spaces, including pubs and restaurants.

Local Laws and Police: There are two types of police offers in the UK: regular officers with full police powers and police community support officers (PCSOs), who have limited police power and focus on community and safety. The emergency number is 999, and the non-emergency number is 101. Learn more at www.police.uk.

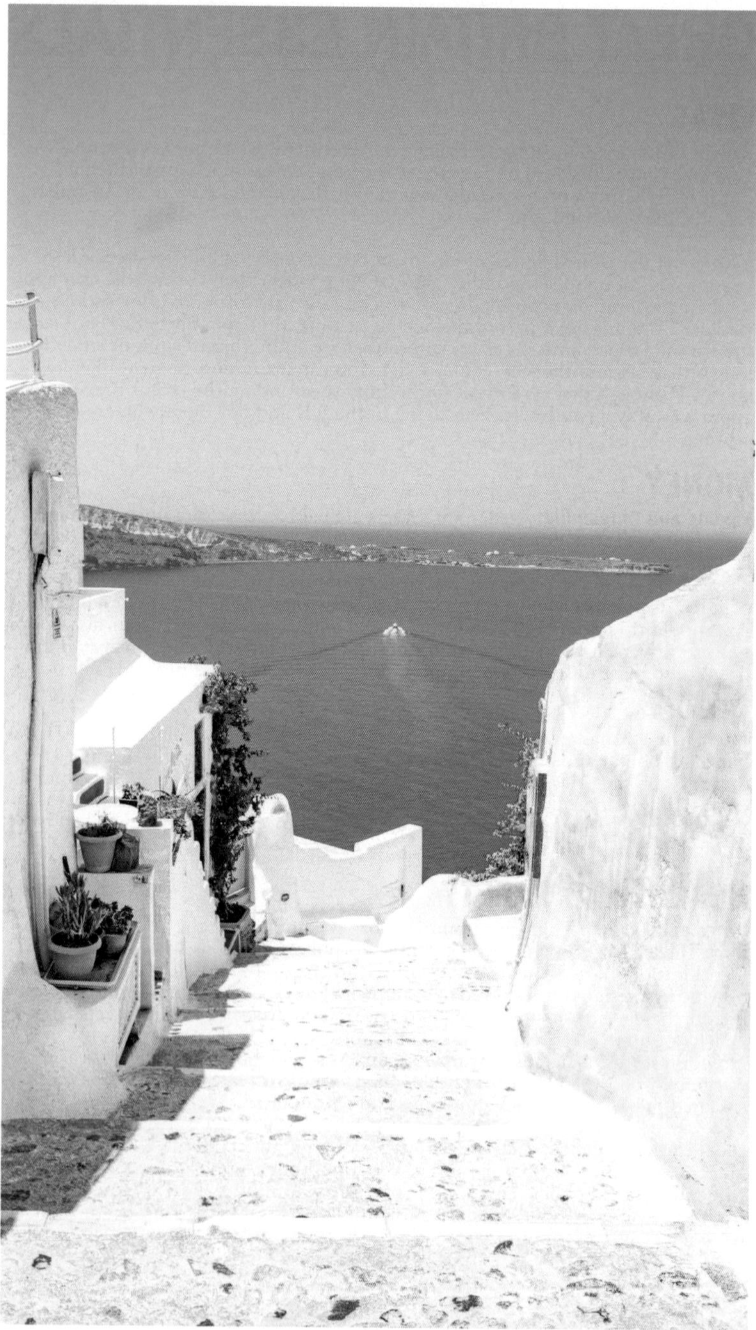

GREECE

Composed of the Aegean blue, an ancient language, and a home with a story (or five), Greece is a country with so much history it almost doesn't know what to do with itself. Their myths are the original soap operas, featuring the flawed and fabulous Greek gods and goddesses. Their musings are the foundations of everything we know about Western civilization. Their olives decorate our martini glasses. Their vices are our vices.

Once a conglomerate of city-states and different empires ruling over the country at various points in history, no two Greek landmarks are alike. Athens shines as the sprawling capital, mixing honking taxicabs and graffitied walls with the commanding sites of the Parthenon and Acropolis. To the north lies Thessaloniki—a seamless blend of modern living and ancient history. Southwest of Athens lies the Peloponnese, a peninsula of mythical legends and mountainous villages. Ferries will bring you to the Cyclades Islands, characterized by powerful winds, rocky islands, white stuccoed churches, and sunsets that will make your heart ache.

No matter what is happening in the country, the Greeks think deeply, care intensely, and party so hard they give validity to the connotations of Greek life. A proud flag always waves fearlessly through their slice of the Mediterranean. Greece is *ouzo,* souvlaki, and mounds of pita. It's endless skies, lapping waves, and miles upon miles of sand. It's soaring Mt. Olympus, acres of olive groves, and a beach that is never too far away. It's a home as long as you're up for an adventure (or five).

ATHENS

Coverage by **Margaret Canady**

As the Greek myths will tell you, Poseidon, god of the oceans, and Athena, god of wisdom, were vying for patronage over the then-unnamed city. Poseidon offered the citizens saltwater, and Athena the first olive tree. In another instance of "girls rule boys drool," the people chose the olive tree and Athena (I mean, come on Poseidon, the city is literally right next to the sea, and regifting is so last millenia), and 3400-plus years later we still have the modern metropolis of Athens. The city, of course, immediately conjures up images of antiquity. Plato and Aristotle walked the streets of ancient Athens, creating some of the modern society's philosophical foundations, all while eating olives. The Acropolis is known as the birthplace of Western civilization and democracy and the Parthenon stands regal over the city. But not everything is ruins of marble. Athens is a car-honking, expletive-loving, graffiti-filled city. Stray cats intermix with a vibrant nightlife where the clubs don't open until midnight and any one of the nine bars in one neighborhood is destined to become a favorite. By day, fulfill your inner history buff—soaking in the thousands of years of art, history, and knowledge. By night, grab a cocktail (or five), hit a rooftop bar (or three), and enjoy urban Athens life.

ORIENTATION

The **Mediterranean Sea** borders Athens to the west, while three mountain ranges circle the cities on its other sides. The city is about a 30min. metro ride away from the **Port of Piraeus**—one of the busiest passenger ports in Europe. The pulse of Athens can be found in two squares of the city center: **Syntagma Square** and, west a few blocks, **Monastiraki Square.** To the south of Monastiraki is the **Acropolis,** which stands on the top of a hill and can be seen from most places in the city center. At the base of Acropolis lies **Plaka**—a picturesque historical neighborhood with flora covered walkways and plenty of shops and restaurants. To the west of Monastiraki is **Gazi,** a neighborhood with a high concentration of cool bars and late night clubs. To the north of Monastiraki is **Psiri,** a neighborhood restaurants and bars with live music such as rembetika, or Greek blues. Farther north will take you totake you to the oldest square in the city: Omonia Square, which doubles as a central metro stop. To the north of the historical city center is **Metaxourgeio,** a neighborhood with a strong sense of community and fewer tourists.

ESSENTIALS

GETTING THERE

If flying, you'll arrive at Athens International Airport (Eleftherios Venizelos). From there, you can take the metro or express bus downtown. The ride will take about 45min. to 1hr and cost €5 or €6, respectively. A taxi to the city center will cost €38 (set price during the day) and will take about 25min. If arriving by port, you'll most likely land at Piraeus Port. You can take the green line from Piraeus Port Station to get to downtown.

GETTING AROUND

Most of the sites and landmarks you'll want to see are all within walking distance, as are the major hostels. The city is serviced by three metro lines and an elaborate bus system. The metro has stations in most major destinations and neighborhoods and runs M-Th and Su 5:30am to 12:30am, and F-Sa until 2:30am; check online for bus schedules. Tickets range from €1.40 for a 1.5hr ticket to €9 for a five-day unlimited ticket.

PRACTICAL INFORMATION

Tourist Offices: Athens Tourism Information (Dionysiou Areopagitou 18; www.visitgreece.gr; open M-F 9am-7pm, Sa-Su 10am-4pm).

Banks/ATMs/Currency Exchange: ATMs can be found throughout the city, especially in tourist-heavy areas. We were particularly fond of this currency exchange place with no fees: Argo Exchange S.A. (Agiou Konstantinou 6; 2105 236636; www.argo-exchange.gr; open M-Sa 8am-9pm, Su 9am-5pm).

Post Offices: Omonia Square Post Office (Koumoundourou 29; 2105 248551; www.athensconventionbureau.gren/node/4240; open M-F 8am-5pm, Sa 8am-2pm).

Public Restrooms: There are public restrooms in the underground station beneath Omonia and Syntagma Squares. Otherwise, you'll need to stop in a restaurant or café.

Internet: Most cafés and restaurants have Wi-Fi. There are internet cafés located around the city, check online for details (www.athensinfoguide.com/geninternet.htm).

BGLTQ+ Resources: Some resources can be found online (www.athensinfoguide.com/gay.htm).

EMERGENCY INFORMATION

Emergency Number: 112.

Police: Dial 100 for emergencies. Athens Municipal Police (Agiou Konstantinou 14; 2105 210606; www.cityofathens.gr).

US Embassy: US Embassy Athens (Leof. Vasilissis Sofias 91; 2107 212951; gr.usembassy.gov).

Rape Crisis Center: WomenSOS (support number: 15900; administrative number: 2131 511113; www.womensos.gr; support number open daily 24hr)

Hospitals: Dial 166 for an ambulance.

- Laik⊠ General Hospital of Athens (Agiou Thoma 17; 2132 060800; www.laiko.gr; open daily 24hr).
- Alexandra General Hospital (Lourou, Athina 115 28; 2103 381100; www.hosp-alexandra.gr; open daily 24hr).

Pharmacies: Pharmacies are located throughout the city; look for the green plus sign. Here are two:

- Pharmacy (near Monastiraki) (Ermou 74; 2103 239616; open M-Sa 8am-11pm).
- Acropolis Pharmacy (Dionysiou Areopagitou 10; 2152 151610; www.acropolispharmacy.gr; open M-F 8am-4pm, Sa-Su 9am-2pm).

SIGHTS

CULTURE

THISION OPEN AIR CINEMA

Apostolou Pavlou 7; 2103 420864; cine-thisio.gr; open last week of Apr-late Oct

Plush red seats, buttery popcorn, a good movie, and...a view of the **Parthenon?** Located at the base of the **Acropolis,** Thision Open Air Cinemas is one of the best open-air movie theaters on the planet. Where else can you watch international movies (English captions provided) underneath the stars, with a more than 2000-year-old monument casually just chilling in the background? The vibes are amazing, needless to say, and the ticket prices are super reasonable.

i Tickets M-W €6, Th-Su €8; tickets only available at cinema before movie, arrive 30min. early to reserve tickets; wheelchair accessible

CHANGING OF THE GUARD AT THE TOMB OF THE UNKNOWN SOLDIER

Syntagma Sq., in front of the Parliament Building

The Changing of the Guard definitely exceeds expectations, even though our only expectations were that they would switch places. The 15-minute choreographed performance consisted of perfectly-synchronized leg extensions that demanded as much core strength and stamina as a professional ballet dancer. Somehow, the two guards reamined in sync, even when facing opposite directions, and never once fell or cracked a smile. To top it off, they wore formal traditional Greek uniforms (which, frankly, makes us wonder how they fought in those dresses). The guards stand guard 24 hours a day at the Tomb of the Unknown Soldier, a

cenotaph dedicated to Greeks killed during war.

Free; wheelchair accessible; changing of the guards every 30min., full unit procession Su 11am

MONASTIRAKI FLEA MARKET

Monastiraki Sq., Ifestou 2; 6946 086114; open daily 8am-6pm

Monastiraki Flea Market isn't exactly a flea market all the time, but it's still pretty cool. Down the narrow street labeled "Athens' Flea Market," you'll find shop after shop of souvenirs and shoes. Adjacent to the fenced **Agora** is where local artists and vendors set up their carts daily to sell handmade jewelry and crafts. Early on Sundays, the surrounding streets are filled with antique sellers.

Free; limited wheelchair accessibility

MAKING GREEK FOOD AT THE GREEK KITCHEN

Athinas 36; 6978 464701;www.greekkitchenathens.com; open M-Sa 9am-7pm

For all you amateur chefs out there (and for those of you who ambitiously say you're going to learn how to cook but only bother to make ramen), come here to learn how to make traditional Greek food at the Greek Kitchen. Located four minutes north of **Monastiraki Square,** you'll be guided through four traditional dishes, including dolmades and tzatziki. Teach a man to fish, they say, but also give him all of the ingredients, a kitchen, professional chefs, and free bread and wine, and you'll be eating well today (and possibly for a lifetime).

Cooking class from €38; no fees if traveling alone; vegetarian class available; limited wheelchair accessibility

LANDMARKS

ACROPOLIS

Acropolis Hill; 2103 214172; open daily 8am-8pm

The Acropolis needs little to no introduction. A universal symbol and iconic monument, it's one of the most prized gifts Ancient Greece left behind, including some of the things founded there: democracy, philosophy, theatre, freedom of expression and speech. Created to celebrate their win over other city-states, the Acropolis, which consists of the **Parthenon,** the **Erechtheion**, the **Propylaia,** and the **temple of Athene Nike,** was completed in 438 BCE. The Parthenon has been used as a church, a mosque, and a bomb storage—which led to its partial demolition in 1687. Just about 2500 years later, after a series of restorations, the acropolis stills stands, imbued with the power and wisdom of the goddess for whom it was erected (Athena), overlooking the city that built it.

Admission €20, €10 reduced; last entry 30min. before closing; wheelchair accessible; special ticket package (admission €30, students €15) provides entry to many major sites, including Acropolis

ANCIENT AGORA AND THE TEMPLE OF HEPHAESTUS

Adrianou 24; 2103 210185; open daily 8am-8pm

Ancient Agora used to be the hub of ancient Athens, where city dwellers gathered to buy and sell goods, meet up with friends, and talk smack about Helena from down the block. Located northwest of the **Acropolis,** we can imagine toga-clad aristocrats walking down the mountain for a gyro in the Agora. Today, visitors can walk through the remnants of the agora to take in the sights for themselves. Make sure to check out the **Temple of Hephaestus,** the best preserved Doric peripteral temple of the ancient greek world. The Temple was made for the god of metalworking and fire, which is pretty lit if you ask us.

i Admission €8, €4 reduced; last entry 7:45pm; wheelchair accessible

LYKAVITTOS HILL

www.lycabettushill.com

The tallest point in Athens is this "mountain," which, at only 910 feet tall, is arguably just a hill trying to act all tall and tough. Still, it's taller than the **Parthenon** and smack dab in the middle of the city, so climbing to the top is well worth the 20 minutes of panting and sweating. The trail zigzags up the south side of the mountain, and with each zig the view gets better and better. At the top you'll find a bell tower, small church, and panoramic views. It's the perfect place to watch the sunset and share a beer or Coke. We found out after the hike that there's a cable car that conveniently takes you up and down the hill, but we can't guarantee amazing calves with that option, so take your pick.

i Free; cable car round-trip €7, runs every 30min; wheelchair accessible by cable car.

SYNTAGMA SQUARE

Pl. Sintagmatos; 2103 254708; open daily 9am-11pm

At the hub of Athens life lies Syntagma Square. Along with peanut vendors and buskers, here (or across the street) you'll find the **Greek Parliament Building, National Garden,** and the **Tomb of the Unknown Soldier.** Syntagma Square has a rich history. A military uprising here in 1843 forced the king to grant the first constitution of Greece. From 2010 to 2012, mass protests were held in the square in reaction to the government debt crisis. When Greeks are not fighting the government, they're also here catching a bus or train at the Syntagma metro station.

i Free; wheelchair accessible

MUSEUMS

ACROPOLIS MUSEUM

Dionysiou Areopagitou 15; 2109 000900; www.theacropolismuseum.gren; open Apr 1-Oct 31 M 8am-4pm, Tu-Th 8am-8pm, F 8am-10pm, Sa-Su 8am-8pm; open Nov 1-Mar 31 M-Th 9am-5pm, F 9am-10pm, Sa-Su 9am-8pm

Here's a sign you need to go to the Acropolis Museum: you accidentally keep saying "metropolis" or "apocalypse" instead of Acropolis. The museum, at the base of **Acropolis Hill,** is both informative and attractive. Informative, as it's geared towards those who flocked to Greece to take in Ancient Greek history. Attractive, since it opened in 2009, complete with modern gray shades, wall-to-wall windows that look out at (and, on the 3rd floor, imitate) the **Parthenon,** and translucent floors complement the old art and marble its there to uphold. It's also features well-preserved artifacts from the old Athena temple, such as friezes (marble sculptures) that adorned the Parthenon. We recommend going to the museum before hiking up the Acropolis so you actually know what you're looking at up there.

i Admission €5, students €3; audio guides €3; last entry 30min. before closing; wheelchair accessible

BENAKI MUSEUM

Koumpari 1; 2103 671000; open W 10am-6pm, Th 10am-midnight, F 10am-6pm, Sa 10am-midnight, Su 10am-4pm

A man with a ridiculously nice white mustache by the name of Antonis Benakis donated his private collection to Greece, known today as the Benaki Museum. The museum has a broad range of artistic goodies with something for everyone: from Byzantine icons to Greek busts and sculpture, and from gold wreaths to wooden dolls, you'll have a blast looking through the three levels of art the Benakis' stashed away over the years.

i Admission €9, students €7; wheelchair accessible; Wi-Fi

MUSEUM OF CYCLADIC ART

Neofitou Douka 4; 2107 228321; cycladic.gren; open M 10am-5pm, W 10am-5pm, Th 10am-8pm, F-Sa 10am-5pm, Su 11am-5pm

The Museum of Cycladic Art writes that the its exhibits explore and appreciate the timelessness of the human figure and how it manifests itself in different ways through time. And it certainly succeeds, curating an informational and interesting display of both ancient and contemporary exhibits revolving around human experience and body. Cycladic refers to the islands and inlets that are found in the central and south Aegean Sea (not, as we originally thought, referring to cyclones or cyclops). The floors are divided by historic era, and the museum's informational plaques walk you through each one's significant features. Don't miss their contemporary art exhibit, which is weird but pleasant change after staring at ancient art.

i Admission to permanent collection €3.50, permanent and visiting exhibit €7; last entry 15min. before close; wheelchair accessible

NATIONAL ARCHAEOLOGICAL MUSEUM OF ATHENS

28is Oktovriou 44; 2132 144800; www.namuseum.gr; open Apr 1-Oct 31 M 1pm-8pm, Tu-Su 8am-8pm

It's hard to imagine what the world was like 20 years ago, let alone 2000. The National Archaeological Museum doesn't just give visitors a glimpse into the past—it'll hand you binoculars and floor-to-ceiling windows. Their collection of artifacts is huge and old (very old), with skeletons dating back 450 BCE, ceramic pots from the fourteenth century BCE, and sculptures of naked Greeks from any century in between. It's easy to lose a couple of hours wandering through the museum, and all the old stuff can start blending together. If this happens, try thinking about the people behind the artifacts: the child from 2500 years ago who played with those wooden dolls, the women who wore Byzantine jewelry 1500 years ago. Just picture your iPhone 7+ displayed in a museum in 1000 years from now.

i Admission €10; galleries cleared 20min. before closing; wheelchair accessible

OUTDOORS

NATIONAL GARDEN

Amalias 1; 2107 215019; open daily sunrise-sunset

Take some time out of your Athens agenda to visit the National Garden, a public park across the street from **Syntagma Square.** One hundred and fifty four square meters hold an oasis of lush trees and shrubbery, curved white gravel pathways, and plenty of benches and ivy covered walkways. A couple of wrong (or right) turns will take you to the small petting zoo with billy goats and ostriches, or maybe to some random marble pillars. It's a great spot to escape the ceaseless cycle of buses and taxis.

i Free; wheelchair accessible

FOOD

AISCHYLOU GRILL HOUSE PSIRI ($)

14-16 Aischylou St., Psyri Sq.; 21 032 441178; grillhouse-psiri.gren

Hunger, heat, thirst, air: these are the four elements that are sure to hit you at least once on a hot summer's day in Athens, so you want (no, need) something cheap, tasty, and filling. Aischylou Grill House Psiri is a mouthful, pun intended. Located at the fork between street 1 and street 2, you'll be first attracted to the restaurant's ivy canopy that extends across the street, creating (blessed) shaded outdoor seating. Next, you'll check out the menu, where everything is less than €10. Finally, your food will come, and it will surely be a mouthful—they don't skimp on the meat platters or the pita sandwiches, and you'll more than likely be taking leftovers home for post lunch, pre dinner munchies.

i Everything under €10; wheelchair accessible

ATLANTIKOS ($)

Avliton 7; 2130 330850; open daily 1pm-1am

If you hadn't read this, you'd probably would have walked by Atlantikos a hundred times. Tucked in a side alley off the main street in the **Monastiraki** neighborhood, none of the hosts try to sell you their food, and for the most part this seafood restaurant sees only locals. Just locals, and hopefully now you, because Atlantikos serves some of the best seafood in Monastiraki, if not Athens. Both their fried and grilled portions are large, filling, and fresh—watch the chefs cook up your grilled tuna from the open kitchen. The best part? Entrées range from €6-8, so you have money left over for *ouzo*.

i Seafood entrées from €6; wheelchair accessible

ARCADIA ($$$)

Makrigianni 27; 2109 238124; www.greek-taverna.gr; open daily 8am-1am

After a hot and sweaty climb to the **Acropolis,** (or an equally interesting but less sweaty trip to the **Acropolis Museum**) Arcadia is the perfect place to get pampered with some really good food. The restaurant, named after a town in Greece symbolizing "simplicity, beauty, and peace," hosts a bustling business, probably because of their prime location and appealing off-white aesthetic. The antique-style *moussaka* (€16.50) is a bit expensive but very big, and will change your world: baked lamb cocooned in roasted eggplant and yogurt sauce? Yes please.

i Salads from €7.50, appetizers from €9, entrées from €10.80; wheelchair accessible

CAFÉ "111" ($)

Ermou 111; 2103 237967; ermou111.blogspot.com/; open M-Sa 8am-5am, Su 8am-midnight

With Café 111's wooden décor and random hanging objects (read: suspended bicycle from ceiling), we kinda got grimy shipwreck vibes. This café serves primarily appetizers and drinks, and a fair amount of locals stop here in the afternoon before going elsewhere for dinner. Considering it stays open until 5am, though, we're curious to know what it's like post-dinner or post-midnight, and if do the people who work there ever get any sleep. (We hope so?)

i Most drinks and appetizers under €10; wheelchair accessible

LOTTE CAFÉ-BISTROT ($)

Tsami Karatasou 2; 2114 078639; open M-Sa 10am-2am, Su 10am-midnight

By day, Lotte is a hip coffee shop, with good R&B music, studious college students, and delicious coffee options. By night, it's a slinking, sexy bar option. The music slows, the sun sets, and beautiful people drink ouzo and cocktails. Sit inside at the antique window seats, or outside next to their small garden and random lamp and couch décor. The café has a friendly staff, a versatile atmosphere that honestly just breathes "I'm cooler than you," and free Wi-Fi.

i Coffee from €2, snacks from €2.50; wheelchair accessible

MANI MANI ($$$)

Falirou 10; 2109 218180; manimani.com.gr; open M-Sa 2pm-11pm, Su 1pm-11pm

If you've been saving up for a special dinner, or you're trying to impress that cute person from your hostel, grab your credit card and head to Mani Mani. The moderately upscale restaurant takes traditional Greek food and gives it a modern twist, using fresh ingredients and creativity to amaze your palette. They serve some of the best olives we've

ever had, and the lamb was simply to die for. Your wallet will moan in pain, but your stomach will be in heaven.
i Starters from €7, salads from €8, entrées from €12; no wheelchair accessibility

QUICK PITTA ($)

Mitropoleos 78; 2103 249285

With a name like "Quick Pitta," this restaurant offers you a simple expectation. The corner restaurant offers both dine-in and speedy takeaway service (thanks to the friendly and attractive waiters), and, most importantly, cheap and delicious pita wraps. You can choose from a variety of meat options. Though we're not sure if it's the best pita in Athens, it's certainly better than anything we might've picked up in the US.
i Pita sandwiches from €2.10, entrées from €7.50; wheelchair accessible

YOGOLICIOUS ($)

Adrianou 48; 2103 237394; www.yogolicious.global/; open M-Th 10am-midnight, F-Sa 10am-1am, Su 10am-midnight

Frozen yogurt shops may have gone out of style a couple years ago, but that doesn't mean you shouldn't try Greek frozen yogurt. Made with Greek yogurt, this is the perfect sweet treat on a hot summer afternoon, and you don't have to feel guilty eating it—one sign read "1.5% fat = 50% calories = Greek yogurt," which is foolproof logic in our book. We got ours at Yogolicious in **Monastiraki Square,** where it's self-service. This means we probably cancelled out all the health due to all the extra toppings we added.
i Frozen yogurt €2 per 100g; wheelchair accessible

NIGHTLIFE

DOS GARDENIAS

Navarchou Apostoli 17; 2103 235349; open daily 5pm-3am

Día de los muertos came early (and to the wrong country). Dos gardenias is a great Latin-themed bar that always seems to attract a full house. Their cocktails are reasonably priced, and they serve high quality alcohol—we're talking glass bottles, people. After a couple of beers, you might pick up their decorative maracas and starting to merengue in your seat. The only downside is that there's no dance floor to show off your Latin dance moves, but don't be afraid to move to the street.
i Beer from €4, cocktails from €6; wheelchair accessible

SIX D.O.G.S

Avramiotou 6-8; 2103 210510; sixdogs.gr; open M-Th 10am-3am, F-Sa 10am-7am, Su 10am-3am

We tried very hard to understand the meaning behind the name and aesthetics of six d.o.g.s, but gave up after our complementary shot (maybe that was their plan all along). The perfect place to start the night, this place has a cool corner bar, two floors of outdoor seating, and a young and energetic ambience. Grab one of their beers on tap or (recommended) one of their specialty cocktails, creative concoctions that conjure images of tree fairy nymphs and other mythical creatures. You'll be ready to hit the party scene, yet also tempted to just spend the night under the multicolored string lit green canopy; on Friday and Saturday they're open until 7am (!).
i Cocktails from €9, beer and wine from €5; wheelchair accessible

A FOR ATHENS 360 COCKTAIL BAR

Ifestou 2; 2103 210006; www.three-sixty.gr; open M-F 9am-3pm, Sa-Su 9am-4am

360 Cocktail Bar has its own special elevator and colored LED lights on the floor and walls. It might be a little extra, but when you arrive at this rooftop bar, you really won't mind. The view of the **Acropolis** and the rest of Athens speaks for itself, and you'll definitely want seats with a view, so make a reservation. The drinks aren't as expensive as they seem. Locals and visitors alike crowd here, all of them relaxed, ready to enjoy some drinks, some friends, and the city.
i Cocktails from €9, entrées from €12; wheelchair accessible; reservations recommended

CANTINA SOCIAL

Leokoriou 6; 2103 251668; open daily 24hr

Cantina Social is one of the most lowkey places we've ever been to. This hole-in-the-wall bar is sandwiched between two chained-up shops, and to enter you have to go through a dark corridor that looks absolutely nothing like an actual bar. After a few moments, the dark corridor opens up to a pleasant courtyard, where locals drink and smoke under string lights and potted plants. The bar is self-service indoors, and everyone is very laid back. The bartender spent 25% of her time making whiskey sours and mojitos, and 75% being DJ. Cantina Social lets you get away from the hub of some of the main bars and streets, and provides long conversations and good drinks.

i Beer from €4, spirits and cocktails from €6; wheelchair accessible

CORINTH

Coverage by **Margaret Canady**

The name "Corinthians" may ring a bell to you, especially if you're familiar with the New Testament. Located on the Isthmus of Corinth, the city is the gateway of the Peloponnese. For this reason, it was an important trading city in Ancient Greece, and was, at one point, the center of early Christianity. Today, modern Corinth is a sleepy little city, and the inhabitants spend their days drinking coffee and lying on the beach. The preserved archaeological sites of Ancient Corinth and Acrocorinth are located on the outskirts of the town, and are worth a visit if you're passing through.

ORIENTATION

Corinth is located on the isthmus that connects **mainland Greece** with the **Peloponnese,** and can be found right on the **Gulf of Corinth.** The city is located about 48 miles west of Athens. New Corinth is relatively small, and most of the city center (which is found near the Gulf) follows a grid pattern. Many of the restaurants, cafés, and shops are on or near the streets of **Damaskinou, Eth. Antistaseos, and Apostolou Pavlou.** Residential neighborhoods are found farther away from the city center and on the hills surrounding the city. **Ancient Corinth** and **Acrocorinth** are found about seven kilometers southwest of the modern city.

ESSENTIALS

GETTING THERE

The easiest way to get to Corinth is via bus. Buses run hourly between Athens and Corinth; they take about 1hr and cost around €8. Main bus lines from all areas of the Peloponnese peninsula also run through Corinth. Corinth is served by the Isthmus KTEL Bus Station, which is about 15min. away from the actual city. A bus from the Isthmus bus station to Corinth runs on the hour and costs €1.20, and a taxi costs about €10.

GETTING AROUND

Getting around Corinth is very easy, and most things in town are about a 10min. walk away. To get to the coastal cities that are adjacent to Corinth, local buses run hourly. To get to Ancient Corinth from Corinth, a local bus station in town runs hourly until 2:30pm (except Su) and costs €1.80 one way; a taxi costs about €10.

PRACTICAL INFORMATION

Tourist Offices: Visit www.visitgreece.gren/destinations/korinthos for more city information.

Banks/ATMs/Currency Exchange: There are several banks and ATMs near the city center, one of which is National Bank (Pilarinou 42-50; 2741 078043; www.nbg.gr; open M-Th 8am-2:30pm, F 8am-2pm).

Post Offices: Corinth Post Office (35 Adimantos St.; 274102 4122)
Public Restrooms: There are no public restrooms, but most cafés and restaurants have restrooms available with purchase.
Internet: Most cafés and restaurants have Wi-Fi.

EMERGENCY INFORMATION

Emergency Number: 112.
Police: Corinth Police Station (2741 077250 or 2741 077263; call 100 in a police emergency).
US Embassy: The closest US Embassy is located in Athens (Leof. Vasilissis Sofias 91; 2107 212951; gr.usembassy.gov).
Rape Crisis Center: WomenSOS (support number: 15900; administrative number: 2131 511113; www.womensos.gr; support number open daily 24hr).
Hospitals: Below is the main hospital in Corinth.

- Corinth General Hospital (Athinon 53; 2741 361400; www.hospkorinthos.gr; open daily 24hr).

Pharmacies: There are several pharmacies in the city center; look for the green cross.

- Giannou Konstantinos M (Papandreou Georgious 45; 2741 076210).

SIGHTS

CULTURE

CORINTH CANAL

Korinth Bridge; open daily 24hr

Near the **Isthmus Bus Station** and about a 15-minute drive from Corinth lies the Corinth Canal, a spectacular structure that evokes both vertigo and the desire to pull out a camera. The canal—finished in 1893—was first proposed in the first century CE; in other words, the "eh…we'll do it tomorrow" mantra lasted for over 18 centuries. The canal really is stunning, though, and its steep rock walls stretch four miles in length and almost 150 feet high. You can stand on the pedestrian bridge and watch small boats pass through, as well as thrill (or death) seekers, who flock to the canal to voluntarily plunge into the abyss held to life only by some rope. Yes, bungee jumping is available and extremely popular on the canal, but we'll let you sign the death consent form yourself.

i Free crossing; wheelchair accessible

LOUTRAKI THERMAL SPA

G. Lekkas St. 24, Loutraki; 2744 062186; www.loutrakispa.gr; open M-F 11am-7pm, Sa-Su 10am-9pm

One beach-residing town over from Corinth lies the city of **Loutraki,** along with the popular Loutraki Thermal Spa. Apparently even the Ancient Greeks were concerned with pore size and supple skin: the thermal baths of Loutraki have been around for nearly 3000 years. And, there's a reason they've lasted so long. Today, with modern facilities and 5000 square meters of pools, saunas, steam rooms, and massage rooms, you too can dip your toe in the fountain of youth (or your entire body, depending on your desire).

i Services from €10; limited wheelchair accessibility; visit with Spa Doctor required for entrance; visit the website to see if you're qualified to enter pools

LANDMARKS

ANCIENT CORINTH

Ancient Corinth; 2741 031207; open daily Nov 1-Mar 31 8am-3pm, Oct 1-15 8am-7pm, Oct 16-31 8am-6pm; summer open daily 8am-8pm

As any person with siblings will know, information is power—the more dirt you have on them, the more they'll bend to your will. Ancient Corinth was kind of like Ancient Greece's middle child. Its prime location between the mainland and the **Peloponnese** made it an ideal trading city, and all the top names wanted control over the city. Today, the remnants of Ancient Corinth can be found a few kilometers southwest of modern day Corinth. Main features include the **Temple of Apollo** and the two main roads of the city that welcomed trade and transportation. Buses run between Corinth and Ancient Corinth (€1.80 one way) every day except Sunday. Just make sure to go early—buses stop at about 2:30pm, and taxis will cost you about €10.

Admission €8, €4 reduced; wheelchair accessible

ACROCORINTH

Acrocorinth; 2741 031266; open daily 8am-3pm

While Acropolis in Athens gets all of the fame and glory, an acropolis is actually a common landmark in Ancient Greece; the word describes a settlement built upon elevated ground. Acrocorinth is Ancient Corinth's acropolis and was used as a fortress and defense system. What's left isn't much—just a bunch of medieval ruins on the top of a hill—but the view of the area is pretty awesome. Just like there's no elevator to success, there's no bus to the top of the hill, so you have three options: drive (if you have a car), hike (if you have strong calves and an hour to spare), or wait for some nice Greek people to offer you a ride.

Free; no wheelchair accessibility

MUSEUMS

ARCHAEOLOGICAL MUSEUM OF ANCIENT CORINTH

Ancient Corinth; 2741 031207; www.corinth-museum.gren; open daily 8am-7pm

The Archaeological Museum can be found in a building on Ancient Corinth's premises, and the first thing you'll notice when you step foot inside is how freaking amazing the air-conditioning is. As your sweat dries and your body returns to a comfortable internal temperature, the next thing you'll notice is that the museum is actually a big little place, filled with many remnants of graves and artifacts from the archaeological site right outside. Tiny vases, utensils, and coins stand among tombs and even a few conserved graves, bones and all. There's interesting information on the walls about Ancient Corinth and archeology in general, including a section about grave robbers and antiquity smugglers.

Admission €8, €4 reduced (included with Ancient Corinth tickets); wheelchair accessible

FOOD

KANDAYLOS ($)

Pilarinou 64; 2741 074848; open M-Sa 11am-1am

When your food comes out on a plate that's twice the size of your face, you know it's gonna be good. Kandaylos serves some of the best traditional Greek food in Corinth, and we can't decide what we liked best the freshly prepared chicken souvlakis, the sheer amount of food you get per serving (this is no artisanal restaurant with small portions; that dinner plate was completely full), or the cheap prices. You'll be wanting to come back for more, but honestly you might have enough leftovers for at least another meal.

Souvlaki and gyro platters mostly under €8, salads and burgers €4; gluten-free and vegetarian options available; wheelchair accessible; Wi-Fi

SABOR BY LEFTERIS ($$)

Agiou Spiridonos 1; 2741 072202; sabor-by-lefteris.business.site/; open daily 8pm-1am

About a 10-minute walk from the **Korinthos Bus Station** lies Sabor, a hidden gem overlooking the city of Corinth. It's fine dining—that is, compared to the souvlaki and gyro fast food places in town—with a view of the sun setting over the gulf that will make your heart sing and your cameras click. Because Corinth isn't a big city, you're not paying the typical fine dining cost. The stomachable prices only make the exceptional Greek- and Italian-inspired cuisine go down even easier.

i Entrées from €10, appetizers from €4; no wheelchair accessibility

PASTEL

Kolokotroni St; 2741 081803; open M-Sa 9am-1am, Su 9am-midnight

The hub of city life in Corinth orbits around the streets between the city center and the coast, where a multitude of cafés and restaurants lines the streets. Corinth's inhabitants spend hours in the early morning and the evenings sitting with friends, talking, smoking, and drinking coffee or cocktails. Pastel was one of our favorite cafés in Corinth, with its quality coffee, comfortable indoor and outdoor seating, and friendly waitresses with really good makeup skills.

i Coffee from €2, cocktails from €8, beer from €3; wheelchair accessible; Wi-Fi

NIGHTLIFE

DOLCE E AMARO

Periandrou 2; 2741 025500; dolceeamaro.gr; open daily 8am-2am

If you're looking to get completely hammered on a Friday night, Dolce E Amaro is not for you. Part café, part restaurant, and primarily a wine bar, Dolce E Amaro serves you upscale looks and a classy affair, all at super reasonable prices for wine by the glass. They'll bring you an iPad with an extensive wine list that displays each wine, where's it from, and what's it's supposed to taste like (oak, chocolate, etc). Each glass is served with tapas, and you'll feel quite fancy as you swirl, smell, and sip.

i Wine from €4; wheelchair accessible

ARTICHOKE

Pilarinou 68; 2741 084233; www.facebook.com/Artichoke.Corinth/; open daily 8am-3am

You're not going to find anyone over the age of 25 at Artichoke. The alternative bar is a popular spot for the young people of Corinth, and it's pretty easy to understand why: the aesthetic is very I'm-cool-and-at-a-bar (i.e. lowlights, lush couches, rock star décor), they serve cheap drinks, and live bands play on the weekends. A little immature, but definitely a fun and solid choice for a night out on the town.

i Beer and wine from €2.50, cocktails from €7; no wheelchair accessibility

KALAMATA

Coverage by **Margaret Canady**

There are two main types of olives that most people remember off the top of their heads: the black ones and the green ones. Kalamata's claim to fame, then, is the black Kalamata olive, grown exclusively in the Kalamata region and exported around the world. Despite the fact that it's a household name, the city itself doesn't see much traveler love, and many pass through quickly to get to the rest of Messinia and the Mani Peninsula. If you give the city a chance though, you'll be pleasantly surprised by the amount of young people in Kalamata spending their days sipping frappe in one of the many cool cafés and spending their nights in the popular bars on the beach. For the culturally inclined, check out the diverse collection of museums in the Historic Center, the annual internationally recognized summer dance festival, and unbeatable shopping finds—including silk scarves and, of course, olive products.

ORIENTATION

Kalamata is located on the **Peloponnese** with a coast on the Mediterranean Sea. It's the second-most populous city in the Peloponnese, as well as the capital of the region of Messenia. At the north end of the city is the **KTEL bus station.** If you cross the **Nedontas Potamos River** and head south of the station you'll find the **Historic Center** or **Old City of Kalamata**—home to many museums and landmarks. Head further south to reach the modern city, characterized by a grid-like neighborhood structure with three main streets running north to south: **Akrita, Faron,** and **Aristomenous.** The north end of Aristomenous is a pedestrian only walkway that leads into **Central Square**—the area where many cafés and restaurants are situated. Continue south and you'll eventually reach the Kalamata coast, which is lined with restaurants, youthful nightlife, and several kilometers of beaches.

ESSENTIALS

GETTING THERE

The city is served by Kalamata International Airport, a small airport that is most active in the summer and sees flights from Thessaloniki and Athens. A taxi from the airport to Kalamata is about €22, and there is also a local bus to the city. KTEL Messinia bus station has buses to and from many cities in Greece, including Athens (€25, approx 3hr), Thessaloniki, (€71, approx 11hr), and closer cities, such as Tripoli, Pyrgos, and Sparta. Check the website (www.ktelmessinias.gr/) for updated bus schedules. If driving, the city can be accessed from Athens and Corinth via the Moreas highway.

GETTING AROUND

Kalamata is a relatively small city, and you can easily walk to most places you need to get to. Everything is about a 10-20min. walk from Central Square. Many people in Kalamata also bike, and this could be ideal if you're staying in the north end of the city (where the only hostel is located) and want to get to the beach; a bike path runs down the center of town. Bike rentals cost around €7 per day. Additionally, there are four local bus lines that leave from the KTEL Messinia bus station. The most useful one is Bus 1, which has hourly departures and goes through the center of the city before heading east along the coast down to the edge of town. Tickets are €1.30 and can be bought on the bus.

PRACTICAL INFORMATION

Tourist Offices: Tourist Information Office (Agion Apostolon Square; 2721 090413; open M-Sa 9am-6pm).

Banks/ATMs/Currency Exchange: Banks and ATMs can be found down and around Aristomenous St. A popular ATM is Piraeus Bank (Polychronous 1 & Aristomenous 43 B; 2721 067000; www.piraeusbank.gr/el/idiwtes; open M-Th 8am-2:30pm, F 8am-2pm).

Post Offices: Hellenic Post Office Elta (Analipseos; 2721 022151; open M-F 7:30am-2:30pm).

Public Restrooms: No public restrooms, but most restaurants and cafés have a restroom you can use with purchase.

Internet: The city offers Wi-Fi in the city center.

BGLTQ+ Resources: Check out www.iglta.org/europe/greece and www.travelbyinterest.com/destination/1087/gay/guide for BGLTQ+ businesses and resources in Greece.

EMERGENCY INFORMATION

Emergency Number: 112.

Police: Police Department of Kalamata (Iroon Polytechniou 24100; 2721 044653).

US Embassy: The closest US Embassy is located in Athens (Leof. Vasilissis Sofias 91; 21 0721 2951; gr.usembassy.gov).

Rape Crisis Center: WomenSOS (support number: 15900; administrative number: 213 1511113; www.womensos.gr; support number open daily 24hr).

Hospitals: Prefecture General Hospital of Kalamata (Antikalamos 241 00; 2721 046000; www.nosokomeiokalamatas.gr/index.php; open daily 24hr).

Pharmacies: There are several pharmacies in the city center; look for the green cross.

- Systegasmena Farmakeia Elissavet Alexidou (Aristomenous 47; 2721 022223; open M-F 8am-3pm and 5:30pm-9:30pm, Sa 8am-2:30pm).

SIGHTS

CULTURE

KALAMATA DANCE FESTIVAL

Athinos 99; 2721 360700; kalamata-dancefestival.gr/index.php/en ; mid-July, annually

Kalamata has gained international attention for its annual dance festival, and we think you should go. The festival has been around for over 20 years, and is held in several venues throughout the city, including the city's **International Dance Center** and the amphitheatre in the medieval **Kalamata Castle.** The festival attracts both Greek and international dance companies, with a large focus on contemporary and modern dance performances; there are also workshops and masterclasses available to the public. Even if you don't know the difference between a posse and a ponche, the festival is designed to be accessible to anyone and everyone who's interested, so make sure to check it out when you're in town.

i Performance tickets from €12; limited wheelchair accessibility; see website for lineup

CENTRAL SQUARE

Central Sq., on Aristomenous; open daily 24hr

Life in Kalamata centers around, go figure, Central Square. At 13,500 square meters, the square is a marble paved rectangle (plot twist), lined with restaurants, cafés, and trees. While it can be pretty barren during the heat of the day, as the sun sets the square hums with life: children running and playing in the fountain at the south end of the square, teenagers showing off their bike tricks, moms with strollers, couples strolling. At Central Square, you're only a few minutes away from everything else in town.

i Free admission; wheelchair accessible

LANDMARKS

HISTORIC CENTER AND THE CHURCH OF YPAPANTI

Historic Center, Kalamata; 2721 022602

At the base of **Kalamata Castle** and just north of the modern city lies the Historic Center of Kalamata. There's a certain charm to this area; the streets, some strung with flags and lights, weave into one another, and you'll find a variety of cafés, local handmade stores, and small bakeries (we recommend **Chrysanthi's Bakery** with enthusiasm). At the north of the Historic Center you'll find the Church of Ypapanti, a Byzantine-style Greek Orthodox church lushly decorated with twilight blue walls and not one, not two, but nine low-hanging chandeliers.

i Free; wheelchair accessible

KALAMATA'S CASTLE

Spartis 28; 2721 083086; open Tu-Su 8am-8pm

Before you enter, an informational plaque will offer you a brief description of the thirteenth-century edifice. On this plaque, the castle is described by some ancient military man as "weak," which is, quite frankly, hilarious (but also kind of a good prime for what to expect). It's a rather small building, with a couple of floors for you to walk around. The top of the castle is flat and shaded with pine trees, providing a good escape from the heat, and offers a lovely view of the city down to the sea, as well as mountainous landscape behind Kalamata. Despite being weak af, the castle has been controlled by no less than the Byzantines, Franks, Slavs, Albanians, Venetians, and Turks.

i Admission €2, €1 reduced; limited wheelchair accessibility

MUSEUMS

ARCHAEOLOGICAL MUSEUM OF MESSENIA

Agiou Ioannou 3; 2721 083485; archmusmes.culture.gr; open M 1:30pm-8pm, Tu-Su 8am-8pm

How old is too old to make use of a museum's activity rooms? Kalamata's Archaeological Museum is kid- and adult-friendly, with a main path that weaves through the museum like the Pamissus River, and four smaller roads that represent the four provinces of the **Messenia Area.** The artifacts are interesting and well-preserved, and include jewelry and figurines from tombs and other archeological excavations. And if you think the museum's activity rooms have no age limit, you can join the third-graders in the museum's large, interactive activities room.

i Admission €3, reduced €2; wheelchair accessible; free English guides available

OUTDOORS

KALAMATA BEACH

Navarinou St.; open daily 24hr

Two kilometers south of the city lies Kalamata's beach, which is long enough to feel uncrowded and popular enough to have something for everyone. The beach is bordered by clear blue water, and dotted with restaurants, cafés, and tiki bars offering great drinks and free umbrella or beach chair use. There are also beach volleyball courts and floating inflatable play areas for kids. At night, the beach becomes a popular place for young people to hang out and grab drinks.

i Free admission; beach umbrellas and chairs available with purchase at a bar/restaurant; wheelchair accessible

FOOD

BLOSSOM OWL / COFFEE SHOP / ROASTERY ($)

Valaoritou 7; 2721 060008; open M-Sa 8am-midnight, Su 9am-midnight

Maybe it was the eight hours we spent here writing, the option of cold brew and chemex coffee, the really good Wi-Fi, or some great combination of the three, but Blossom Owl was one of our favorite spots in Kalamata. A surprisingly hip place that gives off hipster-moves-to-gentrified-Brooklyn vibes, the coffee shop has two buildings and outdoor seating that connects the two. Blossom Owl is consistently full of young people, who often spend hours talking and slowly sipping frappe, as is the tradition in Kalamata. The coffee is exceptional, as are the breakfast options and the homemade sweet shop and its waffle, pancake, and pastry offerings. The items are listed in English, but the descriptions aren't, which is the perfect blend of expectation and surprise.

i Coffee from €1.80, waffles from €2.50, food from €4.40; wheelchair accessible; Wi-Fi

KARDAMO ($)

Sidirodromikou Stathmou 21; 2721 098091; kardamo.gr/?lang=en; open daily 1pm-1am

Kardamo is casually elegant—like a supermodel spotted in a grocery store. The restaurant puts a modern and personal twist on traditional Greek food, such as a beef liver meze in oregano and olive oil, or their handmade pasta dish with smoked pancetta. Their salads are not neglected, either, and the lettuce kinda tastes like the it was given a really good massage with olive oil. You're greeted with a welcome appetizer of toasted bread drenched in olive oil and olives, and the best part is that here, elegant and modern doesn't mean expensive: 99% of the menu is less than €10.

i Entrées €7-10; vegetarian options available; wheelchair accessible

TA ROLLA ($)

Spartis 53; 2721 026218; www.ta-rolla.gr; open M-F 8am-10pm, Sa 8am-7pm

If you were Greek and coming home for dinner, we imagine it would taste something like Ta Rolla. The family-owned restaurant on the northwest corner of the Historic Center has been around since 1924, and it's a popular lunch spot with the locals. For lunch, choose from a variety of traditional Greek meats and vegetables; the okra raguet and moussaka are to die for.

i Entrées under €7-10; vegetarian options available

NIGHTLIFE

TRICKY BAR

Navarinou 161; 2721 110437; open daily 9am-3am

Every beach town has its own version of the tiki bar, and Kalamata is no different. But unlike a lot of places, Tricky Bar's drinks match its thatched roof and Polynesian masks. They have an incredible selection of spirits—the best from Central America—and their exotic cocktails use fresh juice (which makes all the difference). The vibe isn't crazy party—come here for a relaxed and tropical feeling.

i Cocktails from €8, spirits from €7, juice and smoothies from €3; wheelchair accessible

LE JARDIN

Navarinou 202; 2721 098928; kalamatain.gr/new/le-jardin; open daily 9am-3am

Le Jardin is the PG-13 version of *The Secret Garden*. Le Jardin is a popular bar that gets its name from its lush tropical garden. Grab a cocktail and sit underneath a large tree decorated with glowing glass ornaments, or have fun with the hookah on their comfortable lounge chairs. Lush plants attract mosquitoes, but the bar also has beach access during the day, so you can switch between tropical paradise and...tropical paradise.

i Cocktails from €8, wine from €4.50, entrées from €6.50; wheelchair accessible; free parking lot

MYKONOS

Coverage by **Margaret Canady**

The island of Mykonos really has some Dr. Jekyll and Mr. Hyde themes going on. On the surface, there's classic "Mykonos," which is the stereotypical image of Greek island paradise: picturesque white-walled and blue-trimmed buildings, floral canopies, stunning seaside beaches. Tourists of all ages (and A-listers) can be found enjoying the island that—during high season—is sunny, windy, and always bustling. A couple vials of magic potion later (read: your choice of alcoholic libations), and the island's twin sister "MYKONOSSSSS" emerges. The underbelly of the island (literally—the best parties happen at the south end of the island) is home to a never-ending stream of college students, beat drops, and alcohol. The party lasts well into the morning, turns into a darty, and then transforms into a pregame for the night to come. Regardless of your alcoholic or party preferences, you're sure to find a good time in the party hub of the Aegean Sea.

ORIENTATION

Mykonos is part of the **Cyclades Islands** on the Aegean Sea. The island is relatively small, and most of the action of the island occurs on the west and southwest sides. **Mykonos Town** is located right in the middle of the island's west coast. Here, you'll find the majority of the hotels, landmarks, and restaurants—the perfect backdrop for your next Instagram post. To the north of the town is the **New Port of Mykonos**—located in **Tourlos**—where all ferries arrive. The airport is to the east of the town. On the south end of the island are **Paraga, Paradise,** and **Super Paradise Beach.** Here are the hostels and camping accommodations (read: the only cheap places to stay on the island), as well as the majority of young nightlife. Outside of these areas, the island consists of rocky terrain, less-populated beaches, and farmland.

ESSENTIALS

GETTING THERE

The island is served by Mykonos Airport (JMK). Buses between the airport and Mykonos Town run four times a day and cost €1.60, or you can grab a taxi for €29 at any time. Most people reached Mykonos by ferry. All ferries arrive at the Old Port in Tourlos. Many hotels and hostels offer free transport from the port. Otherwise, you can take a sea taxi between the Old Port and Mykonos Town for €2 (10min.), and land taxis are available 24/7.

GETTING AROUND

Mykonos Town is extremely walkable; it takes about 10min. to walk from one edge of town to the other. The island itself is not as easily walkable, and public buses provide hourly transport between Mykonos Town (Fabrika Square) and other popular destinations, such as Paraga Beach, Paradise Beach, and Elia. (The bus ride, is in itself, an adventure—the narrow, steep streets that curve through Mykonos were meant for donkeys, not tour buses, and you'll find yourself both in fear and in awe as the driver, with one hand on the wheel and the other lighting a cigarette, makes the unmakeable turns with grace). Tickets are €1.80 and can be purchased on the bus or at the ticket kiosk. Public buses stop around midnight, and make sure to check the schedule so you don't have to splurge for a taxi. ATVs, cars, and motorbikes are available to rent, but most companies require an international driver's license and have age restrictions.

PRACTICAL INFORMATION

Tourist Offices: There's no physical tourist information center on the island, but information can be found at www.visitgreece.gr/en/greek_islands/mykonos. There are several private tourist agencies in Mykonos Town that offer services and information, such as Mykonos Tours & Travel (Mykonos Hora; 2289 079376; www.mykonos-web.com; open daily 9am-9pm).

Banks/ATMs/Currency Exchange: There are several ATMs throughout Mykonos Town, and there's one at both the Paraga and Paradise Beach accommodations. Here's a bank in the city center: National Bank of Greece (Axioti 6; 2289 077011; www.nbg.gr/; open M-Th 8am-2:30pm, F 8am-2pm).

Post Offices: Post Office of Mykonos (Paralia Cyclades; 8011 138000; open M-F 7:30am-2:30pm).

Public Restrooms: There are public restrooms located at the Old and New Port.

Internet: Most cafés and restaurants have Wi-Fi.

BGLTQ+ Resources: Mykonos is often ranked one of the top gay-friendly tourist destinations in the world. Check out nomadicboys.com/gay-mykonos-guide/ for more information.

EMERGENCY INFORMATION

Emergency Number: 112.

Police: Dial 100 in emergencies. Police Department of Mykonos is located by the airport (22890 22716).

US Embassy: The closest US Embassy is located in Athens (Leof. Vasilissis

Sofias 91; 21 0721 2951; gr.usembassy.gov).

Rape Crisis Center: WomenSOS (support number: 15900; administrative number: 213 1511113; www.womensos.gr; support number open daily 24hr).

Hospitals: Both of the following are private medical centers.

- Mykonian Hygeia (Agiou Ioanni-Agiou Stefanou; 2289 024211; www.mykonos-health.com; open daily 24hr).
- SEA Medical Health Clinic (Aggelika, Ornos 846 00; 2289 027350; www.seamedical.gr; open daily 24hr).

Pharmacies: Pharma Mykonos (Drafaki Mykonou, on the way to the airport; 2289 023900; www.pharmamykonos.gr/en; open M-Sa 9am-11pm, Su 11am-10:30pm).

SIGHTS

CULTURE

CYCLADIC WINDMILLS OF MYKONOS

Kato Mili; 2289 360100; mykonos.gr/en; open daily 24hr

Before Mykonos was known for its picturesque scenery and less-picturesque party scene, the island's main source of income came from its iconic windmills. Built in the sixteenth century, the windmills were used to process wheat, channeling the rocky island's fierce winds for good. Seven of the remaining 16 windmills of Mykonos are on a hill in **Mykonos Town** overlooking the sea. The windmills in town are an iconic landmark, perfect for pictures and as a physical reference point for everything else in town.

i Free; wheelchair accessible; museum entrance at leftmost windmill

RARITY GALLERY

Kalogera 20-22; 2289 025761; www.raritygallery.com; open daily 10am-midnight

A slew of contemporary art galleries adorn **Mykonos Town,** in the hopes that its rich tourists will come in and purchase something for a pretty penny. The best one we saw was Rarity Gallery, with thrilling and carefully curated pieces that challenge today's art scene. You'll spend several minutes staring at hyperrealistic sculptures of a security guard and Carole Feuerman's ladies in swimsuits, 100 percent expecting them to blink or breathe.

i Free, artwork available for purchase; wheelchair accessible

LANDMARKS

CHURCH OF PANAGIA PARAPORTIANI

Kastro neighborhood, Mykonos Town; mykonos.gr/en/the-island/ekklisies-monastiria

Of the 400-plus churches in Mykonos, the Church of Panagia Paraportiani is definitely the most photographed. A five-minute walk from the **Cycladic Windmills,** the fifteenth-century church consists of not one, but five churches built on top or next to one another, giving the edifice a look that resembles blotches of whipped cream. There's a rock stairway that leads to a small lookout between the sea and the church, but the plethora of used condoms makes it less than ideal, unless you're into that symbolic (and other) kind of stuff.

i Free; limited wheelchair accessibility

LITTLE VENICE

Between Kastro and Scarpa neighborhoods, Mykonos Town; mykonos.gr/en/the-island/axiotheata

There aren't any canals, gondolas, or bridges that remind us of Venice in Mykonos, but this neighborhood is still named as such. Buildings with colorful windows and wooden balconies are suspended above the sea, making for an ideal background to watch the sunset. Additionally, along the narrow streets behind the seafront you can find a nice variety of artisan jewelry shops, tourist trinkets, and beachy fashion, as well as chic (read: expensive) cafés and restaurants. In this sense, it is a bit like Venice: a tourist-driven neighborhood with crowds and shops looking for some cold hard euros.

i Free; wheelchair accessible

MUSEUMS

MYKONOS FOLKLORE MUSEUM

Kastro neighborhood, Mykonos Town; 2289 022591; mykonos.gr/en/the-island/mousia; open M-Sa 10:30am-2pm and 5:30pm-8:30pm

Mykonos Folklore Museum looks less like an organized museum and more like an antique collector's side gig. The house, possibly one of the oldest Byzantine era building on the islands, is a structure with an eclectic hodge podge of antiques and artifacts. Downstairs, wooden boats and weapons from the nineteenth century are parked like cars in a garage. It's a cute treasure hunt of goodies, and seems to fit the vibe of Mykonos better than a regular museum.

i Free, small donation requested; limited wheelchair accessibility

LENA'S HOUSE FOLK MUSEUM

Enoplon Dinameon; 2289 022390; mykonos.gr/en/the-island/mousia; open M-Sa 6:30pm-9:30pm, Su 7:30-9:30pm

Part of the Folklore Museum, Lena's House does the museum night shift in **Mykonos Town.** The house, a conserved nineteenth-century style building, captures a moment older than anyone who visits. A living room and two bedrooms host old furnishings, reconstructed attire for Mykonos women in the early 1700s, decorated plates, and artwork. It's hard to believe that streets now lined with tourist shops and artisan fashion stores used to hold houses like these, and it's a gentle reminder that things used to be different (read: less commercial).

i Free, suggested minimum donation €2; wheelchair accessible

OUTDOORS

TRIP TO DELOS

Delos Island, ferry access at seashore of Mykonos Town (Gyalos); 2289 022218; mykonos.gr/en/dilos; departures M 10am and 5pm, Tu-Su 9am, 10am, 11:30am, 5pm

Before Apollo rode his sun chariot across the sky or Artemis stood guardian over the hunt, they were born on the island of Delos. A 30-minute ferry ride from Mykonos takes you to this ancient rocky island, an archaeological treasure in the middle of the Aegean Sea. Delos consists completely of ruins from its peak in the ninth century BCE. In Ancient Greece, the city was considered one of the most sacred cities in Greece, and you can walk through the remnants of what's left of the city: the **Minoan fountain,** the **Doric Temple of the Delians,** and the **Terrace of the Lions.** Give yourself extra time to climb to the top of the mountain—the birthplace of Apollo—for a panorama view of the remnants of a dead city.

i Round-trip transportation €20; island admission €12, students €6; island tours from €10; limited wheelchair accessibility

FOOD

GIORA'S MEDIEVAL WOODEN BAKERY ($)

Agiou Efthimiou; 2289 027784

Giora's Bakery doesn't look that old. To get to this restaurant—tucked away in one of the winding streets of **Mykonos Town**—descend into a white-walled cave heaven and be met immediately with the comfortable smell of coffee and sweets. Pastries are displayed on a table, and served on delicate glass plates, and they are delicious. Honey balls burst with sweet, sweet delight and powdery almond bites are so scrumptious The prices are perfect, and—sorry, this bakery has been here since 1420?

i Baked goods from €1.50, coffee from €3; cash only; no wheelchair accessibility; vegetarian options available

CAPTAIN'S—FOOD FOR SHARING ($$)

Mykonos Waterfront; 2289 023283; www.captainsmykonos.gr; open daily 7am-1am

On the old dock in **Mykonos Town,** there are a slew of expensive restaurants on the seaside, all offering good food, Wi-Fi, AC, a free car, etc. One of our favorites was Captain's Food for Sharing, which has the same prices as other places but with shareable portions. The captain's salad (€10) is the perfect fresh selection for a hot summer day. They also have a wide selection of local beer, including a brew of the week which is a special homemade

concoction made by the owner's brother.

Appetizers from €6, seafood entrées from €11; vegan and vegetarian options available; Wi-Fi; wheelchair accessible

JIMMY'S GYROS ($)

Lakka, Mykonos Town; open daily noon-2am

While waiting for your food at Jimmy's, your eyes will wander to the décor: literally hundreds of pictures of a balding middle-aged man smiling and giving a thumbs up, posing with customer after smiling customer. Jimmy's might not be the definition of classy, but it's a quick place that serves hot food and (comparatively speaking) cheap prices. Most people get the chicken or pork gyro (€5), but there are also burgers (€5), mixed plates (€12), and more. If you're luckier, Jimmy himself might walk in to check on business, twisting rosaries and smiling at customers. If you're lucky, you might just make it on the wall, right next to a Greek 2013 calendar of topless women.

Gyros from €5, entrées from €6; cash only; wheelchair accessible

JOANNA'S NIKOS PLACE TAVERNA ($$)

Megali Ammos; 2289 024251; open daily noon-11pm

Restaurants with a seaview are usually major $$$$ moves, but Joanna's Nikos Place Taverna has managed to maintain reasonable prices on its oceanfront haven. Serving traditional Greek cuisine, the taverna has a slew of homemade platters that must've been cooked by Joanna herself. One note of warning: like mom's cooking, it sometimes can be a crapshoot, so make sure to stick with the seafood or the waitress' recs.

Pasta from €7.50, meat and seafood entrées from €10; vegetarian options available; no wheelchair accessibility; dinner reservations highly recommended

TASOS TAVERNA ($$)

Paraga Beach; 2289 023002; open daily 10am-11pm

There probably isn't a reason to leave Paraga Beach Hostel. But, if you find yourself fed up with the shoddy Wi-Fi and drunk hostel-mates, head to Tasos Taverna, conveniently located two minutes down the beach. The restaurant serves seafood (duh) at fine prices, and there's beach chairs and umbrellas if you want to go for a quick dip between appetizers and entrées.

Appetizers from €5, entrées from €10; vegetarian options available; limited wheelchair accessibility

NIGHTLIFE

CAPRICE BAR

Little Venice, Mykonos Town; 2289 023541; capriceofmykonos.com; open daily 6:30pm-5am

There are way too many bars in **Mykonos Town** that have good music and plenty of space to dance, but everyone acts too cool to get out there and throw it around. Almost all hope was lost until we stumbled upon Caprice Bar, where almost every single person was dancing, drinks in hand. The crowd overflows onto the narrow street that looks into the sea. The crowd is slightly older than the likes of Paradise Beach, so the purpose of Caprice Bar is not to get laid, but simply to have a good time. Besides, their decorations consist solely of huge sunflowers and bowls of tropical fruit—what's not to love? (Except, maybe, the high prices.)

No cover, cocktails from €13, beers from €10; BGLTQ+ friendly; limited wheelchair accessibility

PARADISE BEACH

Guapaloca (6973 016311; guapalocamykonos.com; open daily 10am-4am); Tropicana (2289 023582; tropicanamykonos.com; open daily 9am-1:30am)

Paradise Beach is the unspoken holy grail for the best party scene on the island, if not all of Greece. Young 20-somethings from all corners of the globe travel to the island to drink a shit-ton of alcohol, get on one of the numerous dance club platforms, gyrate their bodies, and scream MYKONOSSSSS into the great Aegean Sea. Technically, there are two clubs, Guapaloca and Tropicana, which have different vibes, but partiers will find a hype DJ and hyper fellow partiers at either location. Paradise Beach is what you expected college to be like, and for a few nights on the island you too can ascend to Paradise.

i No cover, cocktails from €11; BGLTQ+ friendly; limited wheelchair accessibility

SCANDINAVIAN BAR-DISCO-CLUB

Georgouli, Mykonos Town; 2289 022669; www.skandinavianbar.com; open daily 8am-6pm

Not sure what the name Scandinavian is supposed to imply. Maybe a bar so cool its temperature resembles that in Scandinavia? Regardless, this bar and club mix—located in **Mykonos Town**—is a comparable alternative to Paradise Beach. You've got your young people, loud party music, dimmed lights, and ample space both inside and outside to dance. This bar-disco-club-nightlife (as it insists on being called all four) is really trying to be your wingman, too, with drink names like "buttery nipple" and "sperm." Subtle. The only thing missing is the Scandinavians.

i Shots from €5, cocktails from €11, no cover; BGLTQ+ friendly; wheelchair accessible

SANTORINI

Coverage by **Margaret Canady**

In the Miss Universe Pageant of World Geography, Miss Santorini is undoubtedly a top contestant. Take one step onto the island and you might feel as celestial as the ground you stand on; sensational steep cliffs line the crescent shaped caldera, and anywhere you find yourself on the island's inner precipice gives you views you've only dreamed of. The caldera is dotted with white stuccoed villages that look out into the sparkling Aegean Sea hundreds of feet below, and the sunsets stun even the most experienced of travelers. Besides this, there are multicolored beaches to be visited, ancient archaeological sites to be discovered, and exciting nightlife to be had. Santorini is a choose-your-own-adventure type of island, and the best news is there's no wrong choice (as long as you don't miss sunset).

ORIENTATION

Santorini, officially known along with its neighboring islets as **Thira,** is part of the **Cyclades islands** in the Aegean Sea. Though circle-shaped before a volcanic eruption 3600 years ago, the island is now shaped like a croissant, with crescent (or caldera) side facing west. Many of the major points are located on the caldera. The **port of Thira** is located in the middle of the crescent. Midway between the port and the northernmost point of the crescent is the cliff hugging town of **Fira,** the capital and main city in Santorini. Here you'll find a majority of the hostels, tourists, and nightlife. The northernmost point of the crescent is **Oia** with its famous sunset views. **Akrotiri** is found at the bottom of the crescent. On the opposite side of the island is the airport (center), **Ancient Thera** (south of the airport), and the black beaches of **Perissa.** Smack dab in the center is the mountain and village of **Pyrgos,** an often-overlooked mountain with stunning views of its own.

ESSENTIALS

GETTING THERE

Santorini is served by Santorini International Airport. Buses run between the airport and Fira approximately every 90min. between 7am-10pm. Tickets can be bought on board for €1.80. Most people arrive at Santorini via ferry, which dock at the port of Thira. Public buses run from the port to Fira approximately every hour and can be purchased for €1.80 on the bus. Private transport can be arranged to any location and will cost around €15-20, depending on the location, and will be approximately €20 cheaper than a taxi.

GETTING AROUND

The main towns of Santorini are connected by an extensive bus system with reliable time tables. Tickets can be bought on the bus and range from €1.80-€2.50, depending on the location. Buses run approximately between the hours of 7am-10pm daily. Check ktel-santorini.gr/ktel/index.php/en/ for exact time schedules, and call 228 6025404 or visit the main bus terminal in Fira for questions. Otherwise, renting an ATV, car, or motorbike is highly recommended for exploring the island. Motorbikes can only be rented if you have a motorcycle license. Additionally, many rental services have an age minimum for car rentals (23), or require Americans to hold an international driver's license to rent vehicles. There are several services in Fira that do not require an international license, you may just have to look around. ATVs cost €30-35 for 24hr.

PRACTICAL INFORMATION

Tourist Offices: Info is available at www.santorini.gr/?lang=en. Additionally, there are a variety of private tour companies that can arrange tours or provide information, such as Santo-line (Myrtidiotissa 3 Kamari; 2286 032518; santo-line.com/; open daily 9:30am-10pm).

Banks/ATMs/Currency Exchange: There are many ATMs located on the island, especially in the more tourist-heavy hubs of Fira and Oia. The National Bank of Greece is located in Fira (Dekigala 303; 2286 021051; www.nbg.gr/; open M-Th 8am-2:30pm, F 8am-2pm).

Post Offices: Post Office Elta (Dekigala, Thira; open M-F 7:30am-2:30pm).

Public Restrooms: Some restaurants and cafés offer restroom access with purchase.

Internet: Almost all restaurants and cafés offer Wi-Fi.

BGLTQ+ Resources: Check out www.iglta.org/europe/greece/ and www.travelbyinterest.com/destination/1087/gay/guide for BGLTQ+ businesses and hotels in Greece.

EMERGENCY INFORMATION

Emergency Number: 112.

Police: You can call the Department of Thira (Fira, 84700; 22860 22649) or Oia (22860 71954).

US Embassy: The closest US Embassy is located in Athens (Leof. Vasilissis Sofias 91; 21 0721 2951; gr.usembassy.gov).

Rape Crisis Center: WomenSOS (support number: 15900; administrative number: 213 1511113; www.womensos.gr; support number open daily 24hr).

Hospitals: Santorini Hospital (Karterados 84700; 2286 035300; www.santorini-hospital.gr; open daily 24hr).

Pharmacies:

- Pharmacy Zacharopoulos Fira (Fira, across from the taxi stand; 2286 023444; open M-Sa 8am-10pm).
- Pharmacy Oia (Oia 847 02; 2286 071464; open M-F 8am-11pm, Sa 8:30am-10:30pm, Su 9am-10:30pm).

SIGHTS

CULTURE

SANTO WINERY

Pirgos 84701; 2286 022596; www.santowines.gr/en; open daily 9am-11pm

The majority of Santorini's residents is involved in one of two fields: tourism or wine-making. Santo Winery is a celebration of the latter by appealing to the former, and they sure do a damn good job. Part wine tour and part wine-tasting, you can appreciate both the process of making wine and the final product. The wine tasting occurs on an outdoor terrace (with clear glass barriers) and lies smack dab in the center of the caldera—the view of the sea and the island is simply stunning. You'll be sipping wine in style, and the prices for wine flights certainly reflect that (from €31 per person). Hack the system by only getting a glass or two—you can pay as little as €2.50. The waiters might look at you funny, but you'll be too busy taking in the view and that crazy-good wine they just served you.

i Wine tastings from €2.50, full flights from €31, wine tours sans wine €11; 25min. tours multiple times daily; wheelchair accessible

ATLANTIS BOOKSTORE

Nomikos Street; 2286 072346; atlantisbooks.org; open daily 10am-midnight

Once upon a time, a couple of chaps from the UK visited Santorini and, after discovering the island's lack of bookstores, decided to move here and open one. Atlantis Bookstore is a whimsical wonderland for every bookworm visiting Santorini, and you can easily spend an hour in the small and usually crowded traditional cave edifice housing the bookstore. There are books in at least five languages, and each section has a wide but carefully selected collection of books, as well as recommendations written on index cards for each section. There's a surprisingly large collection of rarities and first edition books, too, like a first-edition *Great Gatsby* or English translation of Plato, which are hefty purchases that can reach €5000. The rooftop terrace has seats to read your new purchase, and you can also watch the sunset up here.

i Books from €12; cash preferred; no wheelchair accessibility

LANDMARKS

AKROTIRI

Thera 847 00; 2286 081939; open summer M-W 8am-8pm, Th 8am-3pm, F-Su 8am-8pm; open winter Tu-Su 8am-3pm

We're not going to tell you what to believe, but Akrotiri might lowkey be the lost city of Atlantis. Akrotiri, located on the southwest corner of the island, was a successful port and trading city until the seventeenth century BCE. The city was abandoned, probably due to severe earthquakes. Following its evacuation, the infamous volcanic eruption occurred in 1613, creating the island's caldera and covering and preserving Akrotiri in a thick volcanic ash. Excavations of the city still occur today, and visitors can explore the carefully preserved city, including multi-layered buildings and a drainage system. Plato wrote about Atlantis, and it's speculated that his inspiration might have been Akrotiri, if not the lost center of the island.

i Admission €12, €6 reduced; archaeological special package admission €14, reduced €7; wheelchair accessible

ANCIENT THERA

Ancient Thera Road, on Mt. Mesa Vouno; 2286 023217; open Tu-Su 8am-3pm

Long after the dust settled at Akrotiri, a new city prospered on the island. Founded in the ninth century BCE, Ancient Thera, sitting atop steep **Mt. Mesa Vouno** on the southeast coast of the island, gained importance in Roman and Byzantine eras. Today, you can walk through the ruins of the old agora and stoa, and the mountain offers panoramic views of the sea. There are a couple of options to get to the top: it takes about an hour to hike up from either side of the mountain (the **Perissa** side is an unpaved footpath, the **Kamari** side is a paved road); you can grab a bus to the top that leaves hourly, or you can drive up, which is kind of an experience in itself. The road zigzags at a steep angle, and with its staggering cliffside views without railings, it's not called the "Kamari serpentines" for nothing, and has been listed as one of the most dangerous roads in the world. We prefer the term "epic" as opposed to "dangerous," though.

i Admission €4, €2 reduced; cash only; last entrance 2:30pm; no wheelchair accessibility; round-trip buses to summit €10, hourly 9am-2pm

WATCH THE SUNSET AT OIA

Oia

Watching the sunset at Oia has been listed on many a bucket list on travel websites, and it really is a must-see while on the island. It will be exceptionally overcrowded, and we advise you to either come early (a couple of hours, honestly) to grab a spot on the white stucco cliffs, or you'll be watching the sun set behind some guy's head rather than actually see the horizon. There are less crowded places, too, such as a grassy overlook behind a parking lot, or leading down to **Amoudi Bay.** The explosion of oranges and golds and pinks as the sun descends is unlike any we've seen before. Some dad will ultimately start clapping, as if the sun is setting just for you and your hundred new Santorini friends.

i Free; limited wheelchair accessibility

MUSEUMS

FOLKLORE MUSEUM

Kontochori; 2286 022792; www.santorinis-folkmuseum.com/en; open daily 10am-5pm

Folklore museums tend to be redundant, given their characteristic quality of looking eerily similar to your grandma's old attic. Santorini's, however, is the best one we've ever visited, and it 100 percent has to do with the private tour that's included with the ticket. You're led through the eight-part museum, and each part is explained in full: the cave home dating to 1861 and furniture owned by a family of nine; an original carpenter and shoemaker workshop and tools; a winery and underground cave showing evidence of the volcanic eruption from 36 centuries ago. You also learn a lot about the island, like how it didn't have electricity until the 1950s (!!) and the tradition of capturing and releasing songbirds that exists to this day. It's the best €5 you'll spend here, and it's the perfect predecessor to any of the other museums or sites you'll visit.

i Admission €5, private tour included; limited wheelchair accessibility

MUSEUM OF PREHISTORIC THERA

Downtown Fira; 2286 022217; www.santonet.gr/museums/prehistoric_museum.htm; open Tu-Su 8:30am-3pm

This small museum in the heart of **Fira** offers a glimpse at artifacts and life from the Neolithic era to the Late Cycladic Period. There are clay cooking pots, really incredible frescoes from excavations of **Akrotiri,** and—nipple vases? Not kidding, these ewers (yes, this is a word: it's a jug with a large mouth) from the seventeenth century BCE have nipples on them. It's a little bit boring, as museums can be, but really cool to connect the artifacts to the locations they came from, such as Akrotiri or **Ancient Thera.**

i Admission €6, €3 reduced; cash only; wheelchair accessible

OUTDOORS

CLIMB SKAROS ROCK

Skaros Rock, Imerovigli; open daily 24hr

On this week's episode of Xtreme Sports, climb the majestic Skaros Rock. Located off of **Imerovigli,** this rock used to be home to one of the most important castles on the island, and was inhabited during medieval times because the rock and fortress offered protection from pirates. Not much of the fortress is left, but you can understand how it provided shelter when you ascend: rising high above the sea, the edges are steep and impossible to climb. To climb the rock, pass through the neighborhood of Imerovigli (feeling only slightly jealous of the tanning tourists in exorbitantly-priced hotels). Most of the climb is horizontal with an upward slope, but the final ascent onto the platform of the rock requires a vertical climb that looks

scarier than it actually is. (They don't call it "Skaros" for nothing, amirite?)
i Free; no wheelchair accessibility

RENT AN ATV

Check online for rental locations

There's no efficient way to discover Santorini by bicycle or on foot, and while the bus system is lovely, your time on the island is FLEETING, and you are an independent being who shall not be confined to the BUS SCHEDULE. Hence, your best option is renting an ATV for a couple of days. They comfortably hold two, so if you're traveling with a buddy you can split the price; they're fast, and they're, like, really, really fun. The streets in Santorini are relatively wide and smooth, but of course, always practice caution on turns and in traffic. Many places require you to have an international driver's license, but ask around; there are several in Fira that will rent to you without one.
i From €35/day; many places require a deposit that they refund upon bike return

PERISSA BLACK BEACHES

Perissa Beach; open daily 24hr

No island is complete without a trip to the beach, and Perissa Black Beach offers a relaxed spot to spend a day soaking up the sun and swimming. The beach is black from eroded volcanic molten rock, and pairs nicely with the blue sea and other visual wonders of Santorini. The water is deep—four steps in and you'll be underwater—but very refreshing, and a plethora of restaurants line the beach and offer free umbrellas and chairs with a meal.
i Free; wheelchair accessible; beach chairs and umbrellas available with beach restaurant purchase

FOOD

BRUSCO ($$)

Epar. Od. Pirgou Kallistis; 2286 030944; open daily 9am-12:30am

The mountain and village of **Pyrgos** is often overlooked by visitors to Santorini, though it definitely shouldn't be. The quaint town lies at the highest point of the island, and offers

panoramic views smack dab in the center of Santorini—perfect for sunset and strolling. While there, stop into Brusco, a café with cute seating and cuter food. Their breakfast platter offers seven small servings of food plated in tiny compartments on a wooden plate. The coffee is exceptional, and the outdoor seating is pleasant.
i Breakfast platter from €10, sandwiches from €2.50

FISH TAVERN FRATZESKOS ($$$)

Perissa Beach, closer to Mt. Mesa Vouno; 2286 083488; open daily noon-11:30pm

One of the best restaurants on **Perissa Beach** is Fish Tavern Fratzeskos, a seafood tavern popular with Santorini locals. The tavern is family run, and the seafood is caught fresh daily. A lot of the menu is designed for large families (you can only buy the fresh fish by the kilo, ranging from €35 to €80), but there are plenty of other options that cost less and are single portions. Our favorite was the orzo pasta with seafood (€17), a pasta similar in size and texture to rice. It easily served two people and the seafood was so *clap* damn *clap* good *clap.*
i Appetizers from €4, pasta from €6, fish from €35/kg; wheelchair accessible; beach access and seating

OIA VINEYART ($$)

Sidearas, Oia; 2286 072046; oiavineyart.gr/homepage-en; open daily noon-midnight

We'll look past Vineyart's relatively cheesy name given that it was the best restaurant experience we had in Santorini. Tucked away from the main strip in **Oia,** the restaurant sees few tourists and gives off a very relaxed vibe, with its upstairs outdoor patio strung with lights and filled with honeysuckle. Vineyart offers 130 wines (aka literally every single wine that is produced on the island), while the staff is extremely well-versed in the subtle differences of each bottle and which local cheeses, meats, or smoked salmon will best match your wine of choice. Besides the superb food and wine, Vineyart also sells local art, and oh! Suddenly the name makes a little more sense. A must if you're in Oia, and a great way to experience local culture.

i Cold cuts from €5, cheese from €4, entrées from €12, wine from €6; vegetarian options available; limited wheelchair accessibility

TAVERNA SIMOS ($)

25is Martiou; 2286 023815; www.tavernasimos.gr; open daily noon-midnight

Authentic menu plus shaded rooftop garden plus reasonable prices equals happy eater. Taverna Simos is just a hair north of the main streets of **Fira,** close enough to get to on foot but far enough to be a quiet escape from the crowds. They have a wide selection of food, including a delicious eggplant paste appetizer that goes great with the free bread, the meat dishes from their charcoal grill, and their seafood fillets. The roof garden also has a fabulous view of the sea.

i Entreés from €8, appetizers from €3.70; limited wheelchair accessibility

POSIDONIA GREEK TAVERN ($$)

Imerovigli; 2286 023998; posidonia-santorini.gr/en/; open daily noon-10:30pm

Things we ask ourselves as we fall asleep at night: did Poseidon eat seafood? Seems like it would be problematic. Regardless, his name evokes the sea and its fishies, and the restaurant Posidonia was all up in that. Serving fresh seafood, you'll for sure find something fishy to love. The restaurant is located in **Imerovigli,** but behind all of the restaurants that have a view, which makes it more affordable and less crowded.

i Grilled dishes from €10.50, pasta from €9, appetizers from €5.20

SVORONOS BAKERY ($)

25is Martiou; 2286 023446; open daily 24hr

Svoronos Bakery is in a prime location. A strip of clubs exist right in the heart of **Fira,** and late at night you'll catch drunk partiers stumbling out into the street, and their only desire in that instant is food, cheap food, and they have a choice: McDonald's or Svoronos Bakery? We choose Svoronos: open all day every day, the bakery has a wide assortment of cream-filled pastries and croissants, as well as savory pies, sandwiches, and cheap coffee. Does it taste like a 24-hour bakery? Absolutely. But it's perfect for drunk you at 2am, hungover you at 11am, and hangry you at 3pm—besides, who wants to go to McDonald's when they're in Greece, anyway?

i Pastries from €1.50, coffee from €2; cash only; vegetarian options available; wheelchair accessible

NIGHTLIFE

KIRA THIRA JAZZ BAR

Fira; 2286 022770; open W-Su 9pm-3am

Bars are a dime a dozen in Santorini, but Kira Thira Jazz Bar stands out like a saxophone solo in an improv jazz band (yes, that was a jazz joke). An upright bass is suspended above the bar, and a mannequin sits in the bar in a corner with hundreds of CDs and records, as if listening intently to the music playing over the speakers. The best part of Kira Thira, besides the drinks—which are exceptional because of the quality of liquor—might be the bartender. He's worked here for 22 years, and his energy is electric: he dances to the music and engages in conversation with everyone at the bar almost simultaneously. He's old-fashioned, and therefore not a fan of the new age fancy-schmancy cocktails,

so don't expect a triple beach mojito with four different syrups. Turn off your phone, grab a classic drink, and enjoy some good energy and good music.
Drinks from €8

CASABLANCA SOUL BAR AND CLUB

Ypapantis 12, Fira Downtown; 2286 027188; www.casablancasoul.com; open daily 8:45pm-5:30am

When a bar has a DJ, a live musician, and a drummer, you're almost guaranteed a good time (unless they're all playing different songs, in which case we suggest you find another bar). Casablanca practically oozes with coolness: an upstairs outdoors bar is complete with white lounge chairs, a large dance space, funky soul music, and, of course, all the people. It's like every attractive person on the island was given a special invitation to Casablanca, and they're ready to party. Come dressed to the nines and get ready for a noir night.
Cocktails from €12, wine from €5; cash preferred; no wheelchair accessibility; reservations reccomended

MOMIX

Marinatou 14, Caldera Fira; 6936 177783; www.momixbar.com/momix-santorini; open daily 5pm-4am

MoMix was created by the boys in your high school chemistry class who really, really liked lab day and played around with chemicals haphazardly until something exciting happened. MoMix—short for "molecular mixology"—is chemistry class for grown-ups, and the chemicals are (obviously) alcohol. The menu, shaped like a cube that lights up each time you flip it, has descriptions such as spherification, foaming, intense carbonation, and mouth tricks, just to name a few. There are cocktail bubbles that burst in your mouth, vials and shots of alcoholic concoctions, and "solids," too, such as a crême brûlée that they cook right in front of you. It's as visually entertaining as it is delicious, and come prepared to get some quality Snapchat story content.
Cocktails from €9, macaron vodka shots from €3; wheelchair accessible

THESSALONIKI

Coverage by **Margaret Canady**

Throughout history, the city of Thessaloniki has always came in second place—the second biggest city in modern Greece, the second biggest city of the Byzantine Empire, and the same fate under the Ottoman Empire. No harm, no foul though, because the phrase 'second is the best' exists for a reason. Thessaloniki is an incredibly easy city to love. A laid-back attitude exists no matter where you turn, from the winding streets of the old neighborhoods in Ano Poli all the way down to the city's expansive sea front. It's a big city with a beach mentality, and the city pulses with a multicultural vibrancy that can be found in the cuisine, architecture, and people. Thessaloniki manages to integrate its history into its modern bustle in such a seamless way that you might overlook a 1700 year old monument without blinking an eye. You won't want to, though—there's no rush here.

ORIENTATION

Thessaloniki is located on the northwest corner of the **Aegean Sea** on the **Thermaic Gulf,** and has a popular waterfront that traces the shore. The city center along the shore is in a grid layout, rebuilt after the Great Fire of 1917. Some main streets that run parallel with the shore and cut through the city center include the shop-heavy **Egnatia, Tsimiski,** and **Agiou Dimitriou.** The city center is bounded by the nightlife neighborhood **Ladadika** on one end and the famous **White Tower** on the other; **Aristotelous Square** lies in the middle. Up the hills past the modern grid lies the old neighborhood of **Ano Poli,** conserved Ottoman architecture untouched by the fire.

ESSENTIALS

GETTING THERE

The city is served by Thessaloniki "Makedonia" International Airport and is linked to the other airport of Greece, as well as international cities. From the airport, bus lines X1, 78, or 78N will take you to the city center for €2. Buses and coaches to Thessaloniki arrive and depart from at Macedonia Intercity Bus Station, and connect the city to many cities in Greece and in surrounding countries.

GETTING AROUND

It's relatively easy to get around on foot, especially in the grid neighborhoods closer to the sea (not included in the easy description is the sweat inducing climb up to Ano Poli), and most things are a 20min. walk or less. Thessaloniki is served by a host of public bus lines running from 5am-midnight and cost €1-2 depending on the time and distance. Tickets can be bought on the bus or at the central bus station, but make sure to bring exact change unless you feel like tipping the ticket machine. For more information, visit www.ktelmacedonia.gr or call 059 5533.

PRACTICAL INFORMATION

Tourist Offices: Information centers are located at the airport and Aristotelous Square.

- Tourist Information Office (Aristotelous Sq.; 2310 229070; thessaloniki.travel/en/useful-information/addresses-phone-numbers/information-centers; open daily 9am-9pm).

Banks/ATMs/Currency Exchange: Banks and ATMs are located throughout the city; you'll be able to find one with no problem due to the city's size.

- HSBC Bank (Tsimiski 8; 21 0696 0000; www.hsbc.gr/1/2/gr; open M-F 8am-2:30pm).

Post Offices: Greece is served by ELTA. An ELTA Post Office can be found at Vasileos Irakleiou 38 (231 027 7434; open M-F 7:30am-8:30pm, Sa 7:30am-2:30pm, Su 9am-1:30pm).

Public Restrooms: Restaurants and cafés usually have restrooms available for use.

Internet: The city offers Wi-Fi hotspots in major squares and popular areas.

BGLTQ+ Resources: Thessaloniki offers a welcoming, gay-friendly atmosphere. Thessaloniki has been holding gay pride festivals since 2011, and the Panorama Gay Film Festival since 1996.

EMERGENCY INFORMATION

Emergency Number: 112.

Police: Dial 100 in an emergency.

- Downtown Police Station (Aristotelous 18; 2310 253341; www.astynomia.gr).

US Embassy: There is a US Consulate located in Thessaloniki (43 Tsimiski, 7th Floor; 2310 242905; gr.usembassy.gov). The closest US Embassy is located in Athens (Leof. Vasilissis Sofias 91; 2107 212951; gr.usembassy.gov).

Rape Crisis Center: WomenSOS (support number: 15900; administrative number: 213 1511113; www.womensos.gr; support number open daily 24hr).

Hospitals: Dial 166 for an ambulance.

- Ippokrateio General Hospital of Thessaloniki (Konstantinoupoleos 49; 231 089 2000; www.ippokratio.gr; open daily 24hr).
- General Hospital "St. Demetrios"(Elenis Zografou 2; 231 332 2100; www.oagiosdimitrios.gr; open daily 24hr).

Pharmacies:

- Deligiorgis Pharmacy (Agias Sofias 23; 231 026 0163; www.deligiorgispharmacy.gr; open M-F 8:30am-8:30pm, Sa 8:30am-5pm).
- Pharmacy128 (Agiou Dimitriou 128; 2311 117000; www.pharmacy128.gr; open M-Sa 8am-11:55pm).

SIGHTS

CULTURE

ANO POLI

Ano Poli

Things that don't get easier with time: goodbyes, stagefright, and climbing up the steep hills of Ano Poli. You can distract yourself with the winding roads and pastel-colored surroundings, but at the end of the day it's still a sweaty feat to be conquered. And sure, you could take the bus, but then what would you complain about? It's worth it though: the neighborhood has maintained its Ottoman and Turkish influences, seemingly untouched by a twentieth-century fire. Notable landmarks in the neighborhood include **Vlatadon Monastery** and **Trigonou Tower,** which offer the best views of the city, the walls of the Ottoman fortress **Yenti Koule,** and the hostel **Little Big House,** which might as well be a landmark in our humble opinion.

i Free; limited wheelchair accessibility

ARISTOTELOUS SQUARE AND ATHONOS MARKET

Aristotelous Sq.; market open Tu-Su early mornings and afternoons

At the centrally-located, lamp- and rose-bush-lined Aristotelous Square, families, walkers, and elderly people sit at cafés and take in the sea-front location. In the surrounding streets of the square you'll find the popular central market. In the wee hours of the morning, chefs come to grab the best pick of seafood (there's nothing like the smell of raw fish to really get your blood pumping at 7am). Fish markets rub shoulders with the meat markets, which rub shoulders with fresh fruit stands and small shops. If you're not entirely keen on picking up some anchovies to bring back to the hostel, you can buy olive oil, fresh flowers, and cheap clothes, too.

i Market prices vary; wheelchair accessible

ROMAN FORUM

Olimpou 75; 2310 221260; www.inthessaloniki.com/el/romaiko-forum-arxaia-agora; open daily 8am-3pm

One of the things Thessaloniki does very well is integrating old stuff with new stuff. A good example is the **Roman Forum (Ancient Agora)** that lives smack dab in the middle of a popular restaurant and café neighborhood. The Forum features your typical Ancient Greek remains, including two pools and a theater that once sat 400 people. Underneath, there's a museum that gives a thorough history of the city and the site. An interesting tidbit: the square was occupied by the Germans during World War II and was used as a concentration site for prisoners. The best pictures of the large forum can be taken for free, and the admission price is primarily if you want to go to the museum.

i Admission €4, €2 reduced; wheelchair accessible

LANDMARKS

CHURCH OF AGIA SOPHIA

Agias Sofia; 2310 270253; www.agiasofia.info; open M 1pm-7:30pm, Tu-Su 8am-7:30pm, siesta breaks possible

Greek Orthodox churches have a flair for the dramatic, but we're not mad about it. The Church of Agia Sophia (not the Istanbul one) in Thessaloniki is a prime example, featuring intricate wall decorations, shimmering gold mosaics, and a huge low hanging chandelier made of, we kid you not, golden fowl. The church was a once a basilica, then a church, then a mosque, and then went back to being church in 1912.

This church of a place for worship than a tourist destination, so cover those shoulders and bring your respect.

i Free; wheelchair accessible; appropriate clothing required

ROTUNDA AND ARCH OF GALERIUS

Egnatia 144; 2313 310400; open Tu-F 8am-6:45pm, Sa-Su 9am-3:45pm

The Rotunda of Thessaloniki will spin your head right round as you gaze up at its large dome and rectangular reccesses. While it's gone through some serious wear and tear since 300 CE, there are still remnants of the mosaics and murals left on the concrete walls. Originally created as either a temple for ancient cult worship or as a royal mausoleum (not sure how those two can be confused, but whatever), the rotunda was converted to a Christian church, then to a mosque, and then again to a church (they really need to make up their minds). You might be tempted to lie on the floor to get as much of the dome in your photo as possible, but we recommend you don't from our personal, dirty experience.

i Admission €2, €1 reduced; cash recommended; wheelchair accessible

THE WHITE TOWER

Thessaloniki 546 21; 2310 267832; www.lpth.gr; open Tu-Su 8:30am-3pm

The White Tower, in all its off-white, six-story tall glory, stands as the symbol of Thessaloniki at the city's waterfront. It's a highly photographed monument, and you're basically obligated to visit and photograph it while in the city. The tower, with its swirling steps to the top, short ceilings, and teeny-tiny doors, was once a prison and mass-execution site during Ottoman rule. Today, the tower hosts a museum, and each floor representing a different aspect of Thessaloniki's history. All the info boards in the tower are in Greek, so be sure to get the audio guide (although a word of warning: it might be hard to concentrate on the information because the man sounds like he needs three days of rest and a healthy amount of Nyquil).

i Admission €3, €2 reduced; audio guides available; no wheelchair accessibility

MUSEUMS

JEWISH MUSEUM

Agiou Mina 13; 2310 250406; www.jmth.gr; open M-Tu 10am-3pm, W 10am-3pm and 5pm-8pm, Th-F 10am-3pm, Su 10am-2pm

Thessaloniki was once known as the "Mother of Israel," and Jewish history is virtually inseparable from the history of the city. The city became a safe haven for Jewish refugees from Spain, Portugal, Sicily, Italy, and North Africa, and by the late nineteenth century half of Thessaloniki's population was Jewish—nearly 70,000 people. In 1917, the Great Fire of Thessaloniki occurred, and most of the Jewish neighborhood was destroyed, leaving 53,737 Jews homeless. On July 11, 1941, Axis Powers occupied the city; about 50,000 Jews lived here during this point. By the end of World War II, 99% of the city's Jewish population was lost in the Holocaust. This museum and Holocaust memorial is an incredibly sobering and critically important museum to visit, and we highly recommend that you do make the time to do so.

i Admission €5, student free; wheelchair accessible; photography prohibited

THE MUSEUM OF BYZANTINE CULTURE

Leof. Stratou 2; 2313 306400; mbp.gr/en/home; open daily 8am-8pm

Byzantine is a word that's casually thrown around to describe various cultural things in Greece, particularly Thessaloniki. Yes, the church is from the Byzantine era. Mhm, Byzantine architecture in this neighborhood! I was eating some Byzantine food the other day—oops, make sure you know what you're talking about. Luckily, the Museum of Byzantine Culture is here to answer your questions. This era was a continuation of the Eastern Roman Empire, and starts when Constantinople assumed control (from 330-1453 CE, approximately). The museum is well-curated and features huge rooms with thematic elements and helpful information that gives what the art you're looking at some context and meaning.

i Admission €8, €4 reduced; wheelchair accessible

MUSEUM OF PHOTOGRAPHY

Port of Thessaloniki, Warehouse A; 2310 566716; www.thmphoto.gr; open Tu-Th 11am-7pm, F 11am-10pm, Sa-Su 11am-7pm

Contemporary art gallery in a warehouse? Perfect: all we need are our black turtlenecks, hipster glasses, and Mason jars filled with artisanally roasted coffee. Thessaloniki's Museum of Photography is Greece's only government-funded museum dedicated solely to photography, and with their rotating exhibits featuring a majority of Greek photographers, it's definitely worth a visit. There's a large collection of thoughtfully-curated photographs, so it's well worth a measly €1.

i Admission €2, €1 reduced; wheelchair accessible

ARCHAEOLOGICAL MUSEUM OF THESSALONIKI

Manoli Andronikou 6; 2313 310201; www.amth.gr; open daily 8am-8pm

Before Ancient Greece there was Ancient Ancient Greece, and the Archaeological Museum of Thessaloniki sheds light onto the prehistoric human settlement of the area. You'll find everything from the Paleolithic to the Neolithic Age, as well as Macedonian and Hellenistic artifacts. This translates to spears, gold blossomed myrtle wreaths, a bunch of stuff from tombs, and a third century CE female skeleton with hair. Gnarly.

i Admission €8, €4 reduced; wheelchair accessible

FOOD

ERGON AGORA ($$)

P. Mela 42; 2310 288008; www.ergonfoods.com/restaurants/thessaloniki; open daily 9am-midnight

A quick glance into Ergon Agora and you might think that it's just a cute coffee-to-go type of shop. Then you'll see a long hallway, walk through said hallway, and find yourself in a large room with a sit-down restaurant and specialty grocery store (!). Ergon Agora is the hippest of the hip, with its chic industrial vibes, hipster indie music playlists, and a wealth of homemade brunch and lunch options. Get gooey cream pies and a cappuccino, or specialty eggs with smoked ham, or even go browse the artisan pastas and wines and specialty meat and fish section. Whatever you do, you can't go wrong, and you'll feel as cool as a cucumber doing it.

i Brunch €7, lunch entrées from €4.50, coffee and pastries under €5; vegetarian options available; limited wheelchair accessibility

GARBANZO FALAFEL ($)

Agnostou Stratiotou 6; 2313 075892; open daily 1pm-midnight

Light on the wallet and heavy on the flavor is the name of the game for the street food at Garbanzo Falafel. Located next door to the **Roman Agora,** the shop serves delicious falafel sandwiches and plates at unbelievable prices. All you have to do is choose your sauce and customize your flavors and toppings at the self-service salad bar. Take a seat at their window bar and try not to drop the lettuce and jalapeños you added to the falafel.

i Entrées €3-€5; vegan and vegetarian options available; wheelchair accessible; Wi-Fi

TAVERNA TO IGGLIS ($)

Irodotou 32; 2113 115555; open daily 1pm-12:30am

A neighborhood favorite tucked quietly away in **Ano Poli,** To Igglis is a local tavern with some of the best Greek food in town. Their daily specials are cheap, their meats well-seasoned, and their outdoor seating bustling with high spirits of the human and alcoholic forms. When in season, you must try the tomato salad: fresh tomatoes are diced and tossed with feta, olive oil and basil…Our mouths are watering just thinking about it.

i Specials from €4, entrées from €6.50; vegan and vegetarian options available; wheelchair accessible

CAFÉ AITHRIO ($)

Dim. Tzachila 7; 2310 245981; www.caféaithriothessaloniki.gr; open M-Sa 10am-2am, Su 10am-midnight

If you're bold and decide to climb from the city center to **Ano Poli,** you'll be huffing and puffing all the way up, and you deserve a cold drink once you get there. Café Aithrio—located right next to the Ottoman fortress **Yedi Kule**—is the perfect place to catch your breath, and somehow all of its green and white tables manage to fit perfectly under the shade of the large leafy tree nearby. The inside is elaborately decorated, Turkish lamps and all, and if you look touristy enough the waiter will offer you one of Thessaloniki's free guides to the city.

i Drinks from €3, light snacks from €3; wheelchair accessible

MASSALIA ($$)

Manousagiannaki 6; 2314 003714; open daily 1pm-midnight

If you find yourself starving, dehydrated, and dying just a little in the middle of a hot Thessaloniki day, Massalia is a good refuge. Every item on the menu has pictures, so in your starved state you can haphazardly point to something that looks good that will, in fact, taste good. Prices are reasonable, the main flavor variety comes from the type of meat you choose, and for €1 you get bread with olive oil and fish roe, as well as a light dessert at the end of the meal.

i Entrées from €8; vegetarian options available; wheelchair accessible

ROOTS VEGETARIAN & VEGAN PLACE ($$)

Mpalanou 4; 2310 268063; www.facebook.com/roots.vegan; open daily 10am-2am

After spending any amount of time in Greece, you'll soon realize that most Greek dishes get their variety from the meat; this makes it a bit harder for the visiting leaf-lovers and vegetarians. Luckily, rOOTS (capitalization intentional but not understood) does a solid job of concocting creative vegan and vegetarian options for Thessaloniki. They have a monthly rotating kitchen, the menu is changed biannually, and on certain days they'll offer themed menus, such as their recent Thai food takeover. Veggies are fresh, and you can feel healthy and clean for at least one meal in Greece.

i Entrées from €7.50, coffee and iced tea from €3; vegan and vegetarian options available; wheelchair accessible

NIGHTLIFE

THE HOPPY PUB

Nikiforou Foka 6; 2310 269203; open Tu-Sa 5:30pm-1:30am, Su 5pm-1:30am

This hoppy-go-lucky pub will put a hop in your step. Hopportunity awaits you as soon as you sit down, and hop dog, do they have an great selection of artisanal beers! The beers have hop notch labels and IPAs, and even if you don't like beer, the 300ml on tap are cheap enough to try—and you might even end up liking it. This is the perfect place for a bar hop, or a hoppy ending to your night out on the town.

i Beer on tap and bottles from €3.50; wheelchair accessible

THE BLUE CUP

Salaminos 8; 2310 900666; thebluecup.gr; open M-Th 8:30am-3am, F-Sa 8:30am-5am, Su 10am-3am

We like a man good who's with his hands—and the bartender at The Blue Cup knows how to make a damn good cocktail. Known first for its artisanal coffee, this cool-kid coffee joint turns into a cooler-kid cocktail bar as the sun sets. There's a set menu, but if you don't see something you like, the bartender will concoct something for your liking.

The drinks flow well into the night, especially on the weekends, and you'll be hard-pressed to find outdoor seating. Maybe this is the alcohol talking, but the attractiveness of every waiter and bartender at Blue Cup starts at model status and only goes up from there.
i Cocktails from €8.50; wheelchair accessible

LA DOZE

Vilara 1; 2310 532986; open daily 7pm-5am

The vibe of La Doze can be kinda hard to read: graffiti and stickers? Lone sad disco ball? A lit up palm tree? Eventually, we decided on urban house. This low-key bar is apparently most lit in the winter time, when the empty dance floors fills with shuffling youth. The bar is well-known for its honestly excessive amounts of spirits: they serve 200 whiskeys, and some 120 rums and tequilas. How? Why? Not sure which tequila our cocktail had, but it was pretty good nonetheless.
i Spirits and cocktails from €6; wheelchair accessible

GREECE ESSENTIALS

MONEY

Currency: Few are keen to acknowledge that Greece is saddled in debt. This has led to much controversy over Greece's status in the eurozone. The country still uses the euro as of August 2018, but be sure to check the news before you go.

Taxes: Currently, the value-added tax (VAT) in Greece is 24%, with a 13% excise tax on tobacco, fuel, and alcohol.

SAFETY AND HEALTH

Local Laws and Police: Many parts of Greece, especially Athens and the popular vacation islands, are accustomed to tourists, but make no mistake— illegal behavior will not be taken lightly. Don't drink and drive or behave indecently, as these actions could result in fines or imprisonment. Purchase of pirated goods (CDs, DVDs) can result in heavy fines, as does stealing rock or material from ancient sites. Though Greece decriminalized homosexuality in 1951, it is still frowned upon socially in some areas of the country. In urban areas and some islands, especially Mykonos, attitudes towards the BGLTQ+ community have changed rapidly, and gay and lesbian hotels, bars, and clubs have a larger presence.

Drugs and Alcohol: Attitudes towards alcohol are fairly blasé in Greece, and most visitors can obtain it easily. Drugs are a different story. Conviction for possession, use, or trafficking of drugs, including marijuana, can result in heavy fines or imprisonment. Authorities are particularly vigilant near the Turkish and Albanian borders.

Demonstrations and Political Gatherings: Strikes and demonstrations occur frequently in Greece, especially during the ever-deepening debt crisis. Most demonstrations are peaceful but a few have escalated into more dangerous protests. If a demonstration or tense political situation does occur during your trip, it is advisable to avoid the area of the city where it is taking place and or headfor the islands, where things are typically more peaceful.

HUNGARY

Hungary really loves itself—and we can't blame it. From bragging about the beauties of their Parliament Building to flouting the tall-tale that Hungarians invented everything from hand-washing to Iron Man, the locals are as secure in their national greatness as Americans on the Fourth of July. At first pass, all of this hooplah seems like self-indulgence. But as the days pass, you'll see yourself falling under the Hungarian spell and begin to understand the confidence with which the locals carry themselves.

After all, the Hungarians are descendants of the 1100-year-old nomadic-warrior Magyar tribe. They have withstood invasions and occupations from every corner of the world, from the Mongols, to the Turks, to the Nazis and the Red Army. Their cities and towns have been destroyed countless times. Every monument that's risen against their sky has fallen to ruin—only to be rebuilt. Hungary's heart beats to the sound of revival and rejuvenation. The ever-expanding present of Budapest's technological and economic boom combines with the city's history and becomes characteristic for all of Hungary.

It's no coincidence that the Rubik's cube was created by a Hungarian. The idea of a patchwork, puzzled existence is foundational to the nation's character. As the present and past swirl together, so do the variables which collided to form Hungary's modern cultural powerhouse. Arabic-style synagogues stand kilometers away from Turkish thermal baths, themselves just kilometers away from the most stunning neoclassical Christian basilica in the world. While the traveler tires of twisting and turning the Hungarian Rubik's Cube only growing more and more overwhelmed, the locals know better. They twist and turn all day, and eventually, the colors match up. Who knows? Perhaps solving Hungary's Rubik's Cube really is something worth boasting about.

BUDAPEST

Coverage by **Luke Williams**

Budapest is a city that breathes. As the sun rises and tourists and locals alike flood its near two-millennia old streets, you can feel its quiet inhale. Then, the breath pauses—midday, the afternoon, a brief siesta. And finally, a long exhale: the city practically explodes with life in all its variety. Chinese heritage festivals crop up in an instant in the city's center, college-graduated 20-somethings scour District VII in search of the best party in town, the locals retreat to the northern, southern, and eastern outskirts, fleeing the impending ignition. By day, Budapest's history and global prominence are sovereign—the dress code is business casual and its mission is noble. The night is blurry, punctuated by millions of discarded cigarette butts, smells without origin, and the collective heat and sweat of thousands. Budapest is a city that feels lived in, but it's also a city of undeniable life. The lounging, relaxing, fugue state of the day gives way to the unruly night, and the cycle continues, accompanied by a song only Budapest can score: the symphony of 2000 years of history met with a stubborn, thrilling, utterly eccentric present.

ORIENTATION

The **Danube River** splits Budapest into two distinct halves: **Buda** on the west side and **Pest** on the east. Buda is mostly residential, so you'll be spending the majority of your time trekking Pest's city streets. For most hostels, home is the **Inner City**, the area surrounding **Erzsébet Square**—Budapest's makeshift center, easily identifiable by the massive summertime ferris wheel. Whether you're heading east to party, west to the **Chain Bridge**, or northeast to shopping district **Andrassy út.**, knowing where you are in relation to Erzsébet Square is an infallible method to become familiar with Budapest quickly. The second tool in your arsenal is knowing where you are in relation to the Danube River—the main chunk of Pest you're interested in is bounded by the **Central Market Hall** to the south and the **Hungarian Parliament Building** to the north, two landmarks that are hard to miss. So, knowing where you are along the river's north-south axis that runs between these two buildings will be your saving grace when you're confused and trying to get back to your hostel.

ESSENTIALS

GETTING THERE

Getting to Budapest is easy by plane, train, or bus. Planes fly into Budapest Ferenc Liszt International Airport, from which most city destinations can be reached by public transportation. Routes change frequently depending on destination, so check ahead. Taxis from the airport are also readily available and easily accessible to English speakers. They give a price estimate before the ride and take cash or card, but it's always a good idea to have some cash on hand. Finally, the airport offers shuttle services to the city center through miniBUD (www.minibud.hu), which can be booked in advance.

GETTING AROUND

There are few cities as easily and as pleasantly walkable as Budapest, even when navigating between the Buda and Pest sides of the city. If walking isn't for you, public transportation in the city is fairly efficient, though a bit confusing. Each new ride requires a single ticket to be purchased onsite. Transfers between metro lines are free, but all other transfers (e.g., between bus and metro) are not. However, Budapest's taxis are also plentiful and never far away. Pro tip: Download the Bolt app on your phone—it's practically Uber for taxis, since Uber doesn't work in Hungary. Rides rarely cost more than 3000 HUF and using the app will help you avoid scams.

PRACTICAL INFORMATION

Tourist Offices: Budapestinfo is the city's official tourist office, with information available online at www.budapestinfo.hu. Tourinform is another reputable travel site that provides useful information. Here is a centrally located office: Tourinform (Sütő u. 2, 1052; 1 438 8080; www.tourinform.hu; open daily 8am-8pm).

Banks/ATMs/Currency Exchange: ATMs are available throughout Budapest. Many show the exchange rate and withdrawal equivalency in U.S. dollars before concluding transactions. Currency exchange booths are also widely available in the Inner City, while banks are common in the northern part of the city. Here is a centrally located ATM: Euronet ATM (Erzsébet tér, 1051; 1 224 4666; www.euronet.hu; open daily 24hr).

Post Offices: Post Offices in Budapest are run by Magyar Post. Here is a convenient location: Budapest 5 Posta (Bajcsy-Zsilinszky út 16, 1051; 1 317 2510; www.posta.hu; M-F 8am-8pm).

Public Restrooms: Public restrooms are common in public areas like Erzsébet Square, usually free of charge (Erzsébet tér, 1051; open daily 24hr).

Internet: Some major squares and tourist attractions provide free public Wi-Fi.

BGLTQ+ Resources: www.budapestgaycity.net provides updates on BGLTQ+ friendly businesses in the city and is a hub for information on BGLTQ+ activities and events.

EMERGENCY INFORMATION

Emergency Number: 112.

Police: Police in Budapest can generally be trusted and they have established a reliable presence throughout the city (Szinyei Merse u. 4, 1063; 1 461 8141;www.police.hu; open daily 24hr).

US Embassy: The U.S. Embassy is located at Liberty Square (Szabadság tér; 1 475 4400; hungary.usembassy.gov; open M-F 8am-5pm).

Rape Crisis Center: Rape Crisis Network Europe has a Hungary specific hotline to provide immediate support through Budapest-based Women for Women Together Against Violence (NANE) (00 36 1 267 4900; nane.hu; M-Tu, Th-F 6pm-10pm).

Hospitals: The majority of medical centers in Budapest have English-speaking staff. The US embassy keeps a list of English-speaking doctors as well.

- Heim Pál Gyermekkórház (Üllői út 86, 1089; 1 459 9100; www.heim-palkorhaz.hu; open daily 24hr).
- Downtown Medical Center Kft (Ferenciek tere 7, 1053; 30 870 7427; www.belvarosiorvosicentrum.hu; M-F 8am-8pm).

Pharmacies: Pharmacies are marked with a green "+" sign.

- Delí Pharmacy (Alkotás út 1b; 1 225 0602; open daily 24hr).

SIGHTS

CULTURE

SZENT ISTVAN BAZILIKA (ST. STEPHEN'S BASILICA)

Szent István tér 1, 1051; 1 311 0839; www.bazilika.biz; open M-Sa 9am-5pm; organ concerts M 5pm

We're going to be honest with you, there was no sight in Budapest which affected us more than St. Stephen's Basilica. The 150-year-old neoclassical wonder makes the rest of the city feel irredeemably ordinary, so much so that we'd suggest making St. Stephen's one of your last stops. And perhaps if you're big ol' softies like us, you'll avoid the area around the church like the plague, patiently readying yourself to approach it the way it's meant to be approached: a slow walk down **Zrínyi út** starting at the **Danube,** inviting one of humanity's masterworks to loom larger and larger before you—until, finally, you enter its chambers and words lose their meaning.

i Church 200HUF; panorama and museum 1000 HUF, reduced 800 HUF; organ concerts 3,500 HUF, reduced 3,000 HUF; wheelchair accessible

DOHÁNY ST. SYNAGOGUE

Dohány út. 2, 1074; 533 5696; www.great-synagogue.hu; hours vary, check website

A **UNESCO World Heritage Site,** the second largest synagogue in the world, and one of the world's few synagogues with an organ, Donhány St. Synagogue should not be missed. Completed in 1859 and designated the center of the Budapest ghetto in 1944, the synagogue occupies a coveted spot in Budapesti history too often forgotten. The building itself is stunning—designed by a Jewish architect determined to forge a Jewish style through reviving eastern architectural techniques. Furthermore, the synagogue houses the **Garden of Remembrance**—a memorial collection of mass graves and perhaps the single most moving monument to Budapest's Jewish dead.

i Admission 4500 HUF; wheelchair accessible

SZABADSÁG TÉR (LIBERTY SQUARE)

Szabadság tér, 1054; 70 219 5674; open daily 24hr

Liberty Square is, well, liberating. Not only does it inaugurate your entrance into northern Pest—the affluent, tourist-free, golden-grand-piano-beautiful-Castillo-oooh part of Budapest—but it also is the best place near the **Inner City** to just kick back and relax among the company of some of Budapest's most stunning statues, landscapes, and memorials. Fans of Wes Anderson will be delighted to know an actual "**Grand Budapest Hotel**" calls the Square home, and for you fans of more *ahem* adventurous endeavors, fear not: Liberty Square hosts the Budapest Beer Festival every June and is just minutes away from the **Hungarian Parliament Building**. Of course, the square carries its fair share of controversy too. Recent years have seen protesters gather to contest the Square's central fountain, commemorating the Soviet army's "liberation" of Hungary. In any case, we're sure the statue of Ronald Reagan in the northwest corner will make all of those high tempers just trickle down.

i Free; wheelchair accessible

LANDMARKS

CENTRAL MARKET HALL

Vámház krt. 1-3, 1093; 1 366 3300; www.budapestmarkethall.com; open M 6am-5pm, Tu-F 6am-6pm, Sa 6am-3pm

The Central Market Hall is southern **Pest's** claim to fame. The lifelong passion project of the first mayor of Budapest, the city's largest investment at the time, and probably the single best thing to happen in 1897, the Central Market Hall seems like the unholy lovechild of the world's biggest farmer's market and your local mall's food court. And as with anything unholy, it's downright irresistible. A stand selling Hungarian liquor, paprika, and duck liver all together as soon as you walk in? Check. A butcher shop adjacent to a bakery and another liquor shop? That's how we like our butcher shops. A second story replete with the kitschiest tourist shops you can find and a sprawling traditional Hungarian food court? You bet your brand new scooter. Basically, just imagine that instead of writing "We Didn't Start the Fire," Billy Joel just channeled his synesthetic associative abilities into stocking a grand, absurd shopping center.

i Free; wheelchair accessible

ERZSÉBET TÉR (ERZSÉBET SQUARE)

Erzsébet tér; www.erzsebetter.hu; open daily 24hr

Erzsébet Square is the polar opposite of **Liberty Square**—this is the raucous city center, the big kahuna of Budapest's parks, the grand poobah of the Saturday night hoorah. We're not usually ones to get mathematical, but let's break down the arithmetic: Erzsébet Square has one soccer-field-sized wading pool, two basketball courts, three green spaces, two restaurants, one shopping strip and one skatepark. To cap everything off, during the summer the square's central fountain—a classical rendering of **The Danube River**, personified—is overshadowed by the ferris wheel **"The Budapest Eye."** So bring your buddies, Bud Lites, bathing suits, and blankets, because the sun never sets on Erzsébet Square's empire.

i Free; wheelchair accessible

SZÉCHENYI THERMAL BATH

Állatkerti krt. 9-11, 1146; 1 363 3210; szechenyispabaths.com; open daily 6am-10pm

We here at Let's Go know you're wondering how to pronounce "Széchenyi," so here's the official phonetics straight from the locals: "gi-ant-hot-tub-cas-tle." Got it? So what if the whole place smells like eggs? That's because this hot tub water is au naturel, man—and, come on, we both know everyone who comes to Budapest has to visit this place so they can feel like they've visited Gatsby's mansion at

least once in their lives. Oh, and don't forget the other part of the Gatsby fantasy: Széchenyi puts its 100 year old hot-spring-sourced 15 indoor hot tubs, three outdoor tubs, and 10 indoor saunas to good use every Saturday night, old sport. It's called a "Sparty," and it's a very much appreciated change from Széchenyi's regular programming, a.k.a., weekday grandma water yoga and Chucky Cheese hour.

i Admission (locker included) 5800 HUF, weekends 6000 HUF; last entry 9pm; wheelchair accessible

MUSEUMS

EPRESKERT GARDEN

Bajza út. 41, 1062; open June-Aug, M-F 9am-5pm

In the 1880s the best and brightest of Budapest decided they needed an artist's' garden in the northeast of the city, and thus Epreskert became workshop and gallery to Budapesti sculptors who would later gained global fame. And as fame infamously does, the artists were corrupted: they left the garden and their early work behind, subject to the whims of the elements and ambitious Budapesti burglars. Today, Epreskert comprises the campus for one of Budapest's many universities and the plus one policy can be a little skittish. However, if you're especially kind to the guard out front, guests are allowed in during the summer months to gawk and gape at the closest thing to Medusa's haunt you're ever likely to find. Just remember, what happens in Epreskert Garden, stays in Epreskert Garden.

i Free; wheelchair accessible

KUNSTHALLE BUDAPEST

Dózsa György út 37, 1146; 1 460 7000; www.mucsarnok.hu; open Tu-W, F-Su 10am-6pm, Th 12pm-8pm

City Park's Heroes' Square contains both the **Budapest Museum of Fine Arts** and The Kunsthalle Budapest—literally meaning "Art Gallery Budapest"—facing each other in a most bohemian standoff. Choices, choices. Clearly, we recommend visiting the latter: it's basically Budapest's definitive contemporary art gallery. The themed exhibits rotate annually and always feature some of the city's up-and-coming artists from a wide variety of fields. In 2019, Hungarian architects and their work composed l*e plat principal* (main course). Count on the chillest, hippest, most granola experience you'll have in a Budapest museum—beanbags and hammocks abound throughout the exhibits. The focus is always immersion, so don't be surprised if you find yourself operating a 3D printer or using a miter saw to cut wood for park bench to-be.

i Permanent exhibitions 2200 HUF, all exhibitions 2500 HUF; wheelchair accessible

MAGYAR NEMZETI GALÉRIA (HUNGARIAN NATIONAL GALLERY)

Szent György tér 2; 20 439 7325; en.mng.hu; open Tu-Su 10am-6pm

Besides being housed in the famous and downright breathtaking **Buda Castle,** the Hungarian National Gallery offers plenty to see for the ambitious art-lover. With three floors covering a few distinct artistic periods—from Hungarian art circa 1600-1800 to modern post-structuralist sculptures—the HNG has serious BDE. And when it comes to learning your rudimentary Hungarian history and finally understanding where all the Budapesti street names you can't pronounce come from, there's no place more helpful than the HNG. Better yet, the Hungarian president's palace is literally right next to the nation's foremost art gallery; can we get a standing ovation for Hungary's impeccable ordering of priorities? But seriously, we challenge you to compete in a staring contest with the presidential guard just outside the museum. We're sure you'll win.

i Permanent exhibitions 2800 HUF, all exhibitions 3000 HUF; last entry 5pm; wheelchair accessible

OUTDOORS

GELLÉRT-HEGY (GELLERT HILL)

Paths begin on the Buda side of Szabadság and Erzsébet Bridges; open daily 24hr

Dig out your magical ball of yarn from the bottom of your sock drawer and prepare for the natural labyrinth that is **Gellert Hill.** The longest climbing paths start on the Buda side of the **Szabadság Bridge,** just beside the **Gellert Thermal Bath.** Your 30-60 minute ascent up Buda's second most prominent hill is the nature-lover's delight and the athletic release necessary for all competitive travelers. We promise you won't get lost—all paths lead to the monument-turned-outdoor-mall **Citadella** at the top of the hill—but we can't promise anything about the path you take. Here's some of the greatest hits we've encountered: the **Gellert Hill Cave,** a Catholic church carved into the hill's side; British frat bros convinced that local vendors don't sell lemonade but actually "lemon with aids"; and admirably courageous senior citizens who've put our climbing skills to shame. For those of you feeling ambitious: we recommend walking down the hill and continuing on to ascend **Castle Hill** the same day.

i Free; wheelchair accessible

SZÉCHENYI BRIDGE (CHAIN BRIDGE)

Széchenyi Lánchíd, 1051; open daily 24hr

The Chain Bridge has found itself time and time again at the center of Hungary's cultural consciousness. Finished in 1849, the bridge inaugurated Budapest's first major industrial and economic boom. Commonly compared to the Brooklyn Bridge or Golden Gate, the bridge is also a work of art, embellished with craftsmanship at every inch. One of the best walks in Budapest is to travel from **Erzsébet Square** to **Castle Hill** via the Chain Bridge. Walk through history, past the ancient lion statues guarding the bridge on either side, and over the powerful rush of the not-to-be underestimated **Danube**. And if you're really feeling up for a challenge, walking all three of Budapest's major bridges in one day is an extremely organic way to learn the city and catch some of the most memorable views.

i Free; wheelchair accessible

VÁROSLIGET (CITY PARK)

Kós Károly stny., 1146; www.varosliget.info; open daily 24hr

If **Erzsébet Square** is the grand poobah, then City Park is Budapest's undeniable big cheese. The sprawling, nearly 250 year old park is classic incongruent Budapesti: home to castles, ponds, museums, restaurants, the **Széchenyi Bath,** the **Budapest zoo,** green space galore, and massive monument **Heroes' Square.** We'd recommend spending a good chunk of your day exploring all of the park's nooks and crannies—a little secret we've divined is that the father north you go in the park, the less touristy it gets. As you leave the pretzel stands and high-falutin' restaurants behind, you become a genuine explorer of a place where there's always another surprise, be it a hill in the middle of nowhere, locals walking their dogs, locals sunbathing with their dogs, or the occasional locals sunbathing nude with their dogs. The park is also undergoing renovation until 2021, and new points of interest are opening nearly every season, from the **Patton Park biodome** to the **Second National Gallery.**

i Free; wheelchair accessible

FOOD

KISÜZEM ($)

Kis Diófa u. 2, 1077; 1 781 6705; open Su-W 12pm-2am, Th-Sa 12pm-3am

Sometimes it seems like each of the great European cities has their famous literary cafés: Rome's Caffé Greco inspired Mary and Percy Shelley and La Rotonde in Paris regularly hosted everyone from Hemingway to

Fitzgerald. We submit to you, aspiring traveler, Kisüzem as Budapest's up-and-coming literary café. This place is purebred local—speaking English will garner some squinted eyebrows. But hopefully the locals lounging on the café's windowsills and invading the street curbs in front of Kisüzem will convince you it's worth the weird looks. Sunday nights are silent movie and jazz band night. A rainbow papier-machê zombie head watches over the coffee, beer, and liquor bar. Vines thrust their way out of cracks in the industrial brick wall, past rotating local art that hangs at slanted angles. The lights are barely strong enough to reveal the 40 or so patrons of Kisüzem, eating the most crunchy Hungarian fare around, from pork knuckles to "zombie toast," pig-brains on bread. This is as bohemian as Budapest gets, as eclectic as the city comes.

i Entrées from 1090 HUF, beer from 300 HUF; vegetarian options available; wheelchair accessible

ALFÖLDI VENDÉGLŐ ($)

Kecskeméti út. 4, 1053; 1 952 1351; open daily 11am-11pm

One of the first questions any Budapest local will ask you is "Do you like our goulash?" Goulash is the definitive Hungarian dish—along with fried cheese and duck liver. And no place has better goulash than Alföldi Vendéglo. Situated in the midst of a lively young Budapesti college square, Alföldi Vendéglo is one of the few restaurants in the **Inner City** that regularly draws equal crowds of locals and tourists alike. So sit down, order that goulash, and experience Alölfi's gastronomic wonderland of traditional Hungarian food that's so cheap it will make you seriously question eating anywhere else.

i Entrées from 1490 HUF, beer from 490 HUF; wheelchair accessible

CAFÉ GERBEAUD ($$$)

Vörösmarty tér 7-8, 1051; 1 429 9000; www.gerbeaud.hu; open M-Sa 9am-9pmLook, we know Budapest has like a thousand churches and hundreds of synagogues, but if you ask us, the real holy site of the city is Café Gerbeaud 130-year-old halls—the oldest café halls in Budapest, in fact. We spent more time than we are proud to admit itching for more Hungarian White Esterházy cake and Gerbeaud coffee. Yeah, yeah, Gerbeaud has great breakfast, lunch, and dinner as well. But honestly, why not just do cake for all three? Seems easier to us. Housed in a grand old building practically carved from marble, gold, and a rainbow array of macaroons, this is the Island of the Lotus Eaters, Hansel and Gretel's candy house, Persephone's pomegranate. Order at your own risk. (But, like seriously, order).

i Entrées from 2690 HUF, coffee from 1350 HUF, dessert from 2250; vegetarian options available; wheelchair accessible

KERTEM ($)

Olof Palme stny. 2, 1146; 70 202 7484; www.kertemfesztival.hu; open daily 11am-4am

Nestled in the unexplored southeast corner of the **City Park** and just 15 minutes away from the **Széchenyi Bath**, Kertem is like the reward at the end of a long day you never knew you needed. Arriving to you in local-infused technicolor—various pieces of red, orange, green, and yellow furniture and decor mesh together under the Park's trees to form the largest, most inviting beer garden and grill we've seen in Budapest. If the locals' word can be trusted, you should order the Balkan Burger without hesitation. Almost every one of the 80+ tables had one of these greasy monstrosities on full display. And if the heat of the day is getting to you, Kertem comes equipped with a massive beer and liquor menu…just not in English. So get ready to pull out those translators and perform a mumble session well worth its challenge.

i Entrées from 1500 HUF, beer from 530HUF; vegetarian options available; wheelchair accessible

PRÍMA PÉK ($)

Central location Nádor út. 14, 1051, but locations throughout Pest side; 30 301 2821; open M-Sa 7am-7pm, but hours vary by location

When you come to central Europe, there are only two food items you can't avoid: beer and bread. And while Príma Pék makes the bold choice not to sell beer at its small chain Budapesti bakery, it sure knows how to bring the hot buns. With one location in almost every major area, Príma Pék primes itself to present you with quick, convenient breakfast options. From the Hungarian equivalent of the cinnamon roll to the classic chocolate croissant, this bakery only serves the upper crust. And unlike most crumby Budapesti bakeries, Pék goes against the grain. It's a local establishment through and through, usually without any other English speakers but yourself. But no worries—when they see that kneady look in your eyes, don't break down and rye. Príma Pék is here for you. It knows you deserve butter.

i Baked goods from 200 HUF; vegetarian options available; wheelchair accessible

RAMENKA ($)

Kazinczy u. 9, 1075; 1 792 1193; www.ramenka.hu; open M-Sa 12pm-10pm, Su 12pm-8pm

For those of you hopeless 'ramentics' who really just need someone from home to send noods your way, worry no more—Budapest's surprisingly sizable Chinese and Vietnamese populations have you covered. While the city is actually filled to the brim with pho spots and asian buffets, Ramenka occupies the uncontested top Ramen spot in the city. Sporting six different kinds of ramen, from basic pork belly to vegan, and a solid selection of local craft beers that are distantly asian themed, e.g. "Tokyo Lemonade," Ramenka has truly made miso happy. Moreover,

Ramenka really has that whole aesthetic thing down, planted right in the middle of the party district the most instagrammable Japanese-imitation hole-in-the-wall imaginable. Whether you're a Kyoto native or just really need somebody to shoyu the world, Ramenka will leave an impression that never gyoza-way.

i Ramen from 1790 HUF, beer from 490 HUF; vegetarian and vegan options available; limited wheelchair accessibility

ROSENSTEIN VENDÉGLŐ ($$)

Mosonyi u. 3, 1087; 1 333 3492; www.rosenstein.hu; open M-Sa 12pm-11pm

Budapest cuisine comes in roughly three distinct flavors: traditional Hungarian, traditional Jewish Hungarian, and tourists' choice. While the third option certainly gets a lot of lip service and the first gets all the hip travelers' business, Hungary's Jewish entrées are all too often overlooked. Fortunately for you, Rosenstein Vendéglő is collectively recognized as Budapest's best Jewish fare—complete with everything from rooster testicles to veal cheek to lung soup, the options are endless for the fearless foodie. Of course, the restaurant also has plenty of tame offerings centering around poultry and seafood with an inexplicable penchant for foie gras. The setting is homey, the restaurant family-owned, and the menu is in Hungarian, Hebrew, and English, in that order—a combination that crafts one of the most home-brewed dining experiences Budapest has to offer.

i Entrées from 2400 HUF, beer from 600HUF; vegetarian and vegan options available; reservations recommended

NIGHTLIFE

DOBOZ

Klauzál u. 10, 1072; 20 449 4801; www.doboz.co.hu; open M-Tu 5pm-2am, W-Th 5pm-5am, F-Sa 5pm-6am, Su 5pm-12am

Hey, so, we know we just met, but we uh…We got you a present. So, yeah, um…Doboz means "box," and um, well, we got you a party in a box. But not just any party, a really great party, we promise. It has, like, two big rooms and uncanny self-awareness. One room has no roof, it's just open air with a tree in the middle so you know that

air be crisp. And there's even this steel King Kong sculpture hanging off the tree, watching over all that wholesome conversation. Healthy portions of local art make this party happy. Then there's this other room all about dancing. If you can't make up your mind about what kind of night you want, this is really the best quaint little party we could've given you. Wrapped in a bow and everything, this is a really nice box.
i Cover 1500 HUF, beer from 550 HUF; cash only; BGLTQ+ friendly; wheelchair accessible

INSTANT/FOGASHAZ

Akácfa u. 49-51, 1073; 1 783 8820; www.fogashaz.hu; open daily 4pm-6am

Welcome to Instant, Budapest's clubbiest ruin bar of them all! Ready yourself to dance the night away under the influence of neon pixelated cloud statues hanging overhead and some of the best DJ'ing in town. Wait… we apologize. There's been a mistake. Welcome to Fogashaz, Budapest's only ruin bar with two pizza shops in-house to facilitate all those good conversations you're generating. Wait…oh damn, really? Instant and Fogashaz combined to form the biggest club in Budapest? We're a mega-club now? What? That's like, over ten bars, man! Three floors! Three different vibes! Oh yeah, there's Robot too, your friendly neighborhood classic 80s rock and heavy metal dance club. We forget about Robot…it's kinda niche. (Suffice to say it, Instant/Fogashaz is having an identity crisis. But hey, we're not complaining).
i No cover, beer from 800 HUF; cash only; BGLTQ+ friendly; main floor is wheelchair accessible

SZIMPLA

Kazinczy u. 14, 1075; 20 261 8669; www.szimpla.hu; open daily 12pm-4am

Szimpla rejects all attempts at description in favor of pure, unfiltered experience, baby. We're not sure if it was the giant green kangaroo statue as soon as you walk in, the room full of old TVs playing neverending LSD hallucination tunnels, or the telephone booth with an animatronic alien head that growls at you as you walk by that first convinced us Szimpla is more modern art museum than serious club. You won't find anybody dancing, but what you will find is one of the most radical settings in town to spend your night. Szimpla comes prepared with two floors, seven bars, a wine bar, and a hookah bar. Of course, there's also the fact that Szimpla started the whole ruin bar trend that set Budapest ablaze way back in 2002, so it's, like, kind of a big deal.
i No cover, beer from 600 HUF; cash only; BGLTQ+ friendly; main floor is wheelchair accessible

PONTOON

Id. Antall József rkp. 10, 1052; 30 652 2732; www.pontoonbudapest.com; open daily 12pm-4am

Trust us, as soon as you see the **Danube** a little voice in your head is going to whisper "I want to hang my feet over that thing." Unfortunately, Budapest blocks direct access to the Danube along most of its coast, so that little voice is sorely uninformed. However, Pontoon is a bar that defies the rest of Budapest: Sitting just to the side of the **Chain Bridge** on the **Pest** side, Pontoon is literally on the coast. While there is a small dance floor, three bars, and a two story structure reminiscent of a boat, the best times at Pontoon are had by the river, legs hanging, river breeze blowing in the night. This is the perfect conversational hangout spot with the option for some light dancing—you can count on a live DJ every night. Better yet, Pontoon is one nightlife spot relatively unknown by tourists, so enjoy the local company in one of the most enchanting nightscapes the city offers.
i No cover, beers from 650 HUF; main floor is wheelchair accessible

GYŐR

Coverage by **Luke Williams**

Győr is best described in allegory, and no allegory for Győr is more fitting than the gelato shop. That's right, Győr is Hungary's city-sized gelato shop. Upon arriving, you'll immediately be taken by the seemingly endless variety of flavors, all brought to you in brash baroque architecture: you have yellow caramel-flavored buildings, mint chocolate green, cotton-candy pink, and classic vanilla white. Once you've settled in and chosen your flavor, you get to devour the gelato in a state of mindless bliss—just the same way you take in Győr. The city might as well be a shrunken-down slowed-down Budapest. It's seated on the coast of three rivers, defined by short stout ancient buildings, and fosters an abiding feeling of calm; life just moves slower in Győr. And Győr understands its identity as the soul-searching settle-down spot to or from Budapest, it's engineered to pamper you at every turn. Restaurants and bistros crowd every corner, gelato shops and statues from a forgotten age reveal themselves to be Győr's most prolific product, and the extensive river walk paths offer the perfect break from fast-paced, goal-oriented traveling. And as you finish your gelato, you realize that little moment of self-indulgence was the best five minute break you've had all day—just as Győr is the most colorful, art-filled, food-stuffed two day break from itineraries and long nights you'll have in a while.

ORIENTATION

Nestled in the northwest corner of Hungary, Győr came to prominence as a major steamboat port in the nineteenth century, as major Hungarian rivers **Rába River** and **Mosoni-Duna River** intersect here. The city also lies perfectly between **Budapest**, **Bratislava**, and **Vienna**, making it the perfect spot to spend a few days devoted to R&R between larger cities. The central part of Győr is the **Old Town.** Most of your time in Győr will probably be spent here, and usually close to the center, defined by **Széchenyi Square** sporting Győr's tallest towers as part of the **Benedictine Church**. South of Széchenyi Square the other major points of reference are **The Boatman Fountain**, which marks southern Old Town down **Baross Gábor út.**, and **Chapter Hill,** the northwest corner of Old Town. Besides Old Town, downtown Győr has two other distinct sections: **Western Győr** and **Northern Győr.** Northern Győr is accessible via the **Kossuth Bridge** from riverfront **Dunakapu Square** just north of Széchenyi Square. Western Győr lies to the west of Chapter Hill, and you need only cross the **Rába Bridge** over **Radó Island** to get there.

ESSENTIALS

GETTING THERE

By train or by bus, Győr is easily reachable from Budapest, Bratislava, and Vienna. The Győr train station is the southernmost landmark in the downtown area, located just south of the massive town hall building. Bus stations are located throughout the town, with the central station adjacent to the train station. If you plan on traveling by taxi from the train station or using one at any point during your time in Győr, the "Bolt" app is your best bet.

GETTING AROUND

The easiest way to travel Győr is undoubtedly on foot—it only takes an hour or so to walk the circumference of the entire downtown area. Beyond the city center, walking is generally still the easiest form of transportation for able bodied individuals. Otherwise, the "Bolt" app is always a good choice to coordinate taxis, and buses sometimes stop just west of The Boatman Fountain to facilitate travel to the train station and to areas farther from the city's center.

PRACTICAL INFORMATION

Tourist Offices: There is a very helpful Tourinform office in the heart of Old Town. (Baross Gábor u. 21; 9 633 6817; open M-F 9am-6pm, Sa 9am-4pm, Su 9am-2pm).

Banks/ATMs/Currency Exchange: While there may not be ATMs on every corner, they are available and many business accept credit cards. The information for a central ATM: Euronet ATM (Király út. 20; 1 224 4666; open daily 24hr).

Post Offices: There are multiple post offices in Győr, but the post office closest to the city center is near the National Theater of Győr (Bajcsy-Zsilinszky u. 46; 9 654 7600; open M-F 8am-6pm).

Public Restrooms: Győr doesn't have many public restrooms, but there are two in close proximity to one another in Dunakapu Square. (Dunakapu tér; open daily 24hr).

Internet: Most accomodations in the area as well as most restaurants and cafés offer free Wi-Fi.

BGLTQ+ Resources: While Győr does not have any official BGLTQ+ resources in the city, the Háttér Society runs a support hotline for all of Hungary out of Budapest (Balzac u. 8-10; 1 329 3380; www.en.hatter.hu; open daily 6pm-11pm).

EMERGENCY INFORMATION

Emergency Number: 112.

Police: Police in Hungary are safe to call, but they are allowed to ask for paperwork and identification, so make sure to carry your passport with you. There are no police stations in the Old Town, but there is one just across the river in western Győr (Köztelek utca 4-6; 96 520 083).

US Embassy: Győr is almost equidistant between Budapest, Vienna, and Bratislava, each of which have U.S. embassies. U.S. Embassy Budapest (Szabadság tér 12; 1 475 4400; hungary.usembassy.gov; open M-F 8am-5pm).

Rape Crisis Center: Rape Crisis Network Europe has a Hungary specific hotline to provide immediate support through Budapest-based Women for Women Together Against Violence (NANE) (00 36 1 267 4900; nane.hu; M-Tu, Th-F 6pm-10pm).

Hospitals: Győr's primary hospital is located substantially southeast of the downtown area, but there is general care center located south of the train station. Both hospitals are listed below respectively.

- Petz Aladár Megyei Oktató Kórhaz (Vasvári Pál u. 2-4; 9 650 7900; www.petz.gyor.hu; open M-Sa 9am-8pm).
- Medicover Győr (Hunyadi u. 14; 1 465 3100; medicover.hu; open M 7am-7pm, Tu noon-6pm, W-Th 7am-6pm).

Pharmacies: There are many pharmacies in Győr, but the most central one is run by the Benedictine church in Széchenyi Square.

- Széchenyi Patika (Széchenyi tér 8; 96 550 348; open M-F 7:40am-4pm).
- Benue Pharmacy (Baross Gábor út 4; 96 517 527; open M-F 8am-6pm, Sa 8am-1pm).

SIGHTS

CULTURE

ÁRKÁD GYŐR

Budai út 1, 9027; 96 555 000; www.arkadgyor.hu; open M-F 8am-9pm, Sa 7am-9pm, Su 8am-7pm

Enter the dimension of imagination: welcome to shopping mall Árkád Győr, welcome to the twilight zone. While KFC and Burger King remain untouched in this topsy-turvy parallel universe, nothing else will ever be the same. But that's not necessarily a bad thing—now, you can have Hungarian beer and mall-quality Asian food together. You can visit Hungary's take on Best Buy and Barnes & Noble, waddling along with wienerschnitzel and walnut gelato. Or you can hunker down like Steve Irwin and pull out your binoculars, because this is the wild local's favorite watering hole. And being Győr's largest—and we'd argue, most popular—building, Árkád comes fully equipped with unforgettable stores like… Oh, god. Oh no. That's a Hungarian Crocs store. What is this? Let me out! Let me out!

i Free; wheelchair accessible

NATIONAL THEATER OF GYŐR

Czuczor Gergely u. 7, 9022; 96 520 600; www.gyoriszinhaz.hu; open during showtimes

Győr doesn't have much in the way of large buildings. So in the 1970's when Hungary's littlest city decided it was going to build itself a National Theater for the history books, the architectural-theme was basically a no-brainer. "Let's build a ski slope out of concrete!" they shouted in triumph, cause anything else just would've been too easy. Flash forward 50-odd years and Győr's resident brutalist ski-slope styled building is home to some of the country's most classically-inspired English and Hungarian theater and dance productions to-date—from an "Anna Karenina" ballet to Hungarian history dramas. Do yourself a favor and check their website before arriving to see if there's anything on while you're here—we promise that you'll give their shows two out of two double black diamonds.

i Show prices vary; wheelchair accessible

LANDMARKS

THE BOATMAN FOUNTAIN

Baross Gábor u.; open daily 24hr

In case you've ever wanted to row, row, row your boat, gently down the city street's stream, here's your inspiration. The Boatman Fountain sprouts from the center of one of Györ's major streets, depicting a naked young man in a questionably seaworthy raft pitched at an equally questionable angle on stormy seas—brought to life by low-pressure fountains that are usually home to thirsty sparrows. And in typical Hungarian fashion, incongruency is key: surrounding this beautiful statue is a traveling book store, the National Theater of Győr, and what most certainly has to be one of the world's largest McDonalds. We're not sure if it's the idyllic artsy setting or the allure of McNuggets, but on nice days musicians crowd the fountain like Woodstock, filling the air with every tune from "Lucy In the Sky With Diamonds" to the *Game of Thrones* theme song.

i Free; wheelchair accessible

KÁLÓCZY SQUARE

Kálóczy tér.; open daily 24hr

While Kálóczy Square is adjacent to a public tennis court—offering some very entertaining spectating opportunities—and a few restaurants, this is Győr at its most relaxing. Basically, if the city handed over complete control of one of its major public areas to a freshly vowed-to-silence nun, it would be Kálóczy Square. Comprised of three circular parks and accentuated by a WWI monument, perfectly manicured flower gardens, grimacing old people, and bold public romances, Kálóczy Square will inevitably be the zen center of your eurotrip. Besides assisting you in your journey to Nirvana, Kálóczy Square is also the gateway to northern Győr—an oft-forgotten section of the city sporting beaches, parks, restaurants, and universities galore.

i Free; wheelchair accessible

SZÉCHENYI SQUARE

Széchenyi tér; open daily 24hr

In Györ, there is only one truth: all roads lead to Széchenyi Square. Okay, so maybe that's not like, factually true, but it certainly feels true. This is the beating heart of the small city, made vivid by overeager toddlers jumping in and out of the in-ground water fountains at the center of the wide-open all-white-stone square. Don your sunglasses and casually take in Györ's trademark sights: from the towering **Column of St. Mary** watching over the water fountain cherubs to **St. Ignatius of Loyola Church's** imposing rusted copper towers. The gelato stands here multiply like rabbits, hiding the rest of the real food, of which there is plenty in the square. Before you leave the area, be sure to head north on Jedlik Ányos u. toward the Ark of the Covenant Statue and brand-spanking new riverside **Dunakapu Square**—the second most popular hangout in Györ.

i Free; square wheelchair accessible, church limited wheelchair accessibility

MUSEUMS

KOVÁCS MARGIT PERMANENT EXHIBITION

Apáca u. 1, 9022; 9 632 6739; open Tu-Su 10am-6pm

Chances are you have no idea who famous twentieth-century Jewish-Hungarian sculptor/ceramist Margit Kovács is. But after a visit to the Győr native's permanent exhibition in her hometown, you'll likely become quite the fifth-quarter fan. The exhibition roughly tracks Kovács' career from 1940-1980, and you get a front row seat observing her evolution as an artist. While the beauty of Kovács' ceramic masterpieces is unquestionable, what begins with relatively unaffecting sculptures of soldiers and statesmen culminates in touching, overwhelmingly personal sculptures of women: from the artist's mother's dying face, to the Virgin Mary desperately clinging to her doomed son, to a terracotta colored mother-to-be staring blankly in the distance. This museum's masterful organization and ultra-effective display struck us as essential viewing during your stay in Győr.

i Admission 700 HUF, students 350 HUF; no wheelchair accessibility

BORSOS HOUSE

Apor Vilmos püspök tere 2, 9021; 96 316 329; open Tu-Su 10am-6pm

This museum poses one very powerful question: why was ancient Hungarian male artist Miklos Borsos obsessively sculpting nude female statue after nude female statue in the 1960's? From rooms full of sculptures of women's heads, to rooms of women's busts, to rooms of full-bodied marble women, Borsos' psychology is definitely something worth making another museum about. Of course, we'd be failing our duty if we didn't mention how beautiful these sculptures are—there's a reason Borsos' house in Győr is now the site of one of the city's foremost museums. Yet, our visit really just had us wishing we took that Psych 101 class so that we could better understand the mystery man behind this magnificent work. And if

sculptures of naked ladies doesn't do it for you, Borsos also painted plenty of really sad looking old men.

i Admission 700 HUF, reduced 350 HUF; first floor wheelchair accessible

OUTDOORS

RÁBA RIVER AND RADÓ ISLAND

Walkways on the Rába River coast at the center of the city

If you got a postcard from Győr and it didn't show the Rába River coast, did you really go to Győr? The walk is made up of extensive pathways that run across almost all of downtown Győr's coastline, and together, these pathways are the single best way to get to know the city while soaking in all of its natural splendor. We recommend you start at Dunakapu Square and go southwest from Kossuth Bridge toward Radó Island. When you reach Jedlick Anyos Bridge, stop and smell the roses to the northwest—turns out you're actually smelling beaches, sand volleyball, and sunbathing. Lucky you.

i Free; limited wheelchair accessible

FOOD

MANDALA TEAHAZ (MANDALA TEAHOUSE) ($)

Sarkantyú köz 7, 9021; 96 950 824; M-Th 10am-10pm, F-Sa 10am-11pm, Sunday 2pm-9pm

In case you accidentally slept through the 1960s, don't worry. In the most unpredictable, quirkiest coincidence

of history that must be proof of some higher truth we're not paid enough to interpret, Mandala Teahouse is perfectly preserving the spirit of the sixties in Győr. Untie your tie and walk into Thailand, baby. We've got Buddha heads. We've got Ganesha heads. We've got Chinese dragons, bean bags, incense, hookah, baklava, sandwiches, and tea—so long as you fight the power. And you better be ready to par-tea, because Mandala's tea menu is so large we can guarantee you will discover a new favorite blend: Mandala actually has house-specific blends like THC-Free Cannabis tea that we're sure the rest of the capitalist pigs just aren't ready for.
i Tea from 780 HUF, entrées from 480 HUF; vegetarian options available; wheelchair accessible

A FŰSZERES ($)

Baross Gábor út 28, 9021; 30 942 9763; open M-W 7am-7pm, Th-F 7am-8pm, Sa 8am-8pm, Su 8am-6pm

A Füszeres may not be American, but it still comes equipped with plenty of stereotypes. A Fűszeres' morning meals bank on your fervent nationalism, from The American Breakfast, to The French Breakfast, to The Hungarian Peasant Breakfast. And while its undoing of all that brainwashing your college professors worked tirelessly to perfect is regrettable, the breakfast plates make up for their unfortunate associations with remarkable grace. A Fűszeres was the Hungarian breakfast we had been waiting for—from eggs and bacon, to ham, french toast, waffles, coffee and OJ—it brings you right back home with the perfect Hungarian twist. Pro tip: all the locals go for some variation on the French Toast.
i Entrées from 890 HUF; breakfast until 11:30am; vegetarian and vegan options available; wheelchair accessible

LA MARÉDA RESTAURANT ($$$)

Apáca u. 4, 9022; 96 510 980; website; open M-Sa 8am-10pm, Su 8am-midnight

La Maréda isn't one of those stuffy upscale restaurants that desperately wants to be Parisian and will only serve you if you arrive in your freshly-pleated tuxedo—no, La Maréda is exactly one of those restaurants, but the staff treats you like family even if you arrive in a sweaty t-shirt and carry a faint smell around with you like an old friend. Forget all your silly, misguided notions about southern hospitality being limited to the south, because we're convinced La Maréda earned its spot at the top of Győr's culinary scene both by the prowess of their American/Hunagarian chow and their above-and-beyond service. And much like your ex, you can't miss La Maréda; it's right off of Széchenyi Square and in between some of Győr's best bars. So, whether you're sporting your Sunday best or brushing off your birthday suit, La Maréda will most definitely feel like home.
i Entrées from 2200 HUF, wine from 690 HUF; vegetarian, vegan, and gluten-free options available; wheelchair accessible

NIGHTLIFE

LIMA PUB & CAFÉ

Arany János u. 13, 9021; 20 380 1806; open Tu-Th 4pm-11pm, F-Sa 3pm-2am, Su 3pm-8pm

Lima Pub caters to two primary interests: booze and boardgames. This is an artsy-fartsy millennial beer-den: a projector shines beer-related memes on the wall that change to the music's beat. Hungarian grunge and alternative blasts overhead as groups of friends get competitive playing everything from Risk to Munchkin. Posters for jazz concerts past, colorful abstract art, and books adorn the walls of this large-for-Győr indoor pub. And the beer—this is the beer nut's native setting. While cocktails, wine, and nachos do make a small showing, Lima's focus is undoubtedly on its brews. Featuring a frequently-rotating draft list of five to seven local beers and over 100 bottled Hungarian and Budapesti beers, a visit to Lima is an essential pilgrimage for any worshipper of the pale, sour, and stout god.
i Entrées from 950 HUF, beer from 800 HUF; wheelchair accessible

KIS BOHÉM

Jedlik Ányos u. 17, 9022; 30 361 3223; open M-Th 9am-midnight, F-Sa 9am-2am, Su 2pm-midnight

"Kis Bohém" means "little Bohemian," and honestly this is just false advertising. What Kis Bohém lacks in size, it makes up for in heart. This is good old-fashioned English pub, seemingly carved from a giant block of wood by a master artist and decorated with beer paraphernalia ranging from empty beer mugs through the ages to vintage beer ads reading, "Drink triple. See double. Act single." And while the place we just described may sound more like "Stodgy Old Man" than "Little Bohemian," the pub earns its name and then some—it's been taken over in recent years by social-media savvy young people who have worked tirelessly to infuse the vintage setting with young energy, organizing dance nights, themed dress up nights, and even hanging all the liquor on the bar from hooks upside down so that the drinks can flow just as fast as gravity.

i Beer from 380 HUF; wheelchair accessible

HUNGARY ESSENTIALS

MONEY

Tipping: Tipping is not common in Hungarian restaurants, as it is almost always included in the final price of your meal at around 10-15%. The menu will state the exact percent amount at each restaurant, listed as "service fee." Tipping for other services, like bartending or taxi-driving, is not always expected but is highly appreciated. For bartenders, rounding your payment to the next 100-forint denomination is perfect, and for other services 10% is a good go-to tipping amount.

Taxes: Most goods in Hungary are subject to a value added tax (VAT) of 27%, included in the purchase price of goods. The 27% VAT is a standard rate, though it fluctuates based on the goods bought, so you should ask the retailer for exact rates. Non-EU visitors taking these goods home unused can apply for a VAT refund for goods totalling more than 55,000 HUF at one retailer. To apply for this refund, ask the store for a VAT refund form, sometimes called a tax-free form, and carry your passport with you as retailers may ask to see it. Present the refund form and be prepared to show the unused goods you are exporting at the customs office at your point of departure from the EU, regardless of country. Once your paperwork has been approved by customs, present it at a Tax-Free Shopping Office, also at the point of departure, to claim the refund. Refunds must be claimed within 90 days of the original purchase.

SAFETY AND HEALTH

Local Laws and Police: Police in Hungary can generally be relied upon if you need help, but always have your passport with you, as they are entitled to ask for your documentation.

Tobacco, Drugs, and Alcohol: The drinking and smoking age in Hungary is 18. There is a zero tolerance policy on drinking in public, which is illegal in Hungary. Furthermore, if you are found driving with a BAC of even 0.001%, you could be in serious trouble. Tobacco is tightly regulated in Hungary. Only official tobacco shops are licensed to sell any tobacco products at all, though these shops are plentiful and easy to find. They are marked by signs with the number "18" inside a circle and labeled "Nemzeti Dohánybolt." The signs are brown with red and green. Persons under the age of 18 are not allowed to enter the stores.

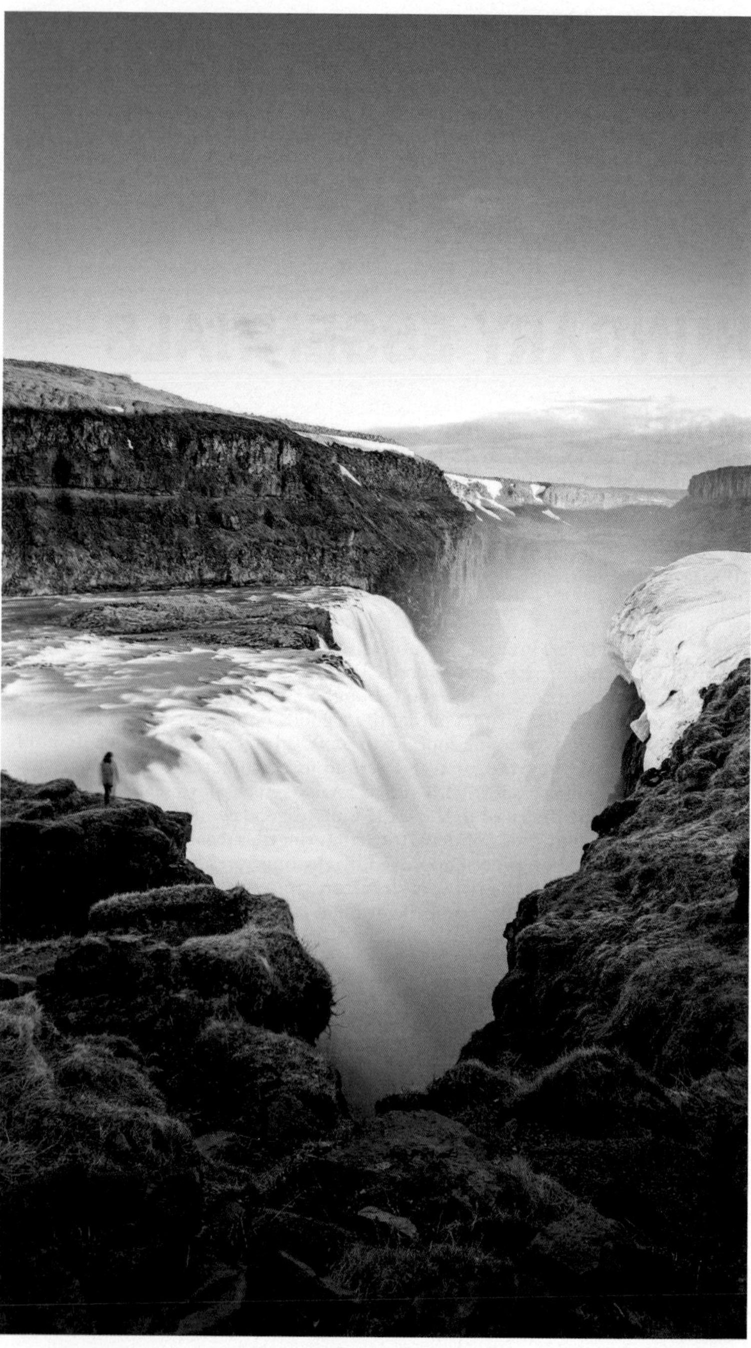

ICELAND

Iceland is HOT with tourists right now. Maybe it's volcanic, or maybe it's Maybelline. The hype is high, and for good reason: Iceland's magnificent natural features are beautiful beyond your wildest dreams. From geothermal hot springs to frozen waterfalls, deep volcano craters to towering glacial peaks, black-sand beaches to staggering rocky cliffs, the landscape holds awe-inspiring mystery at every turn.

For every untouched mountain trail, there's a waterfall teeming with tourist crowds; for every lake in the far-off wilderness, there's a visitor center parking lot brimming with buses; for every hidden valley, there are selfie-stick-wielding tourist groups ready to pounce. Overpriced excursions and commercialized tour packages will bombard you with advertisements from every which way, and the paved streets of Reykjavík will only take you so far.

To experience Iceland's purest beauty, you'll have to do some digging. It's up to you to seek out the raw majesty this country has to offer, and to enjoy it in a way that preserves its wild state. Create your own adventure, and you'll see things no bus tours reach. Trek beyond the crowds, and you'll traverse breathtaking peaks and valleys that few other travellers have discovered. Explore away from the beaten path, and you'll uncover trails through rugged landscapes with scenery that leaves you speechless.

REYKJAVÍK

Coverage by **Marissa Saenger**

After Norse vikings first settled Reykjavík in 874, not many voluntarily made treks out to Iceland in the following centuries however recently there's been an increase in visitors. Unless you're a quirky traveler, Reykjavík will likely be your first impression of Iceland—but don't let it fool you. The coastline views and historic sites are really just the beginning: beyond Reykjavík's city streets await majestic mountains, powerful glaciers, and ethereal volcanic landscapes. Most other travelers will start by asking what you've done elsewhere, as the most popular day-tours and treks take you out to more geographically interesting parts of the country. But, while Reykjavík makes a good starting point for adventures around Iceland, it's worth getting to know a bit better before you hurry up to leave. You'll feel the Norse magic pumping through the city as you walk by Reykjavík's streets, buzzing cafés and bars, well-kept parks or public gardens, and historic landmarks.

ORIENTATION

Reykjavík sits on Iceland's western coast, with the sea to its north and the main bus station **(BSÍ Terminal)** in the center by **Hljómskálagarður Park.** The **Old Harbor** juts out from the northwest corner, and provides a base for many boat and whale watching tours. **Hallgrimskirkja**—the city's towering concrete church—overlooks the main shopping and dining/nightlife streets of **Laugavegur** and **Hverfisgata,** which run roughly east-to-west. **Hlemmur Square,** in the city's eastern half, is another transport hub, with buses running to multiple attractions around and outside of Reykjavík. Public walking and cycling paths border the city, connecting botanical gardens on the eastern edge to a geothermal beach on the southern coast, and wrapping around the northern coast past **Harpa** and **Sólfar.**

ESSENTIALS

GETTING THERE

All international flights will arrive at Keflavík International Airport (KEF). From there, you can take a Flybus airport shuttle to Reykjavík's BSÍ Bus Terminal (about a 45 min. trip; book ahead online at www.re.is/flybus; one-way ticket 3499 kr). The buses have free Wi-Fi, and it's a good idea to map the route from BSÍ to your accommodation as you ride. Walking from there is usually feasible; otherwise you can take another bus from there to get closer to your final destination.

GETTING AROUND

Reykjavík's central areas are easy to traverse on foot, though certain sights or museums might take a bit longer to reach if you're traveling from opposite ends of the city. Bicycle rental is available at some hostels and tourist offices, or from icelandbike.com/bicyclerental_Reykjavík.html and borgarhjol.is/english (prices vary). Public transportation (called Strætó) is available by bus, and the Reykjavík City Card (visitReykjavík.is/city-card/front) includes 24, 48, or 72hr unlimited passes for public bus transport along with other city access benefits. Taxi service is also available year-round through Hreyfill (www.hreyfill.is) and BSR (www.taxiReykjavík.is), though rides tend to be expensive compared to public transport or walking/cycling.

PRACTICAL INFORMATION

Tourist Office: What's On tourist information and booking center (Laugavegur 5, 101 Reykjavík; 551 3600; whatson.is; open Apr-May 8:30am-8pm, 8:30am-10pm Jun-Mar).

Banks/ATMs/Currency Exchange: For currency exchange: Landsbankinn (Austurstræti 11, 101 Reykjavík; 410 4000; landsbankinn.is; open M-F 9am-4pm, service center open M-F 9am-5pm).

Post Offices: Pósturinn/Iceland Post (Stórhöfða 29, 110 Reykjavík; 580 1000; www.postur.is/en; open M-F 9am-5pm).

Public restrooms are available throughout the city and usually involve a payment of 200 kr.

Internet: Wi-Fi access is widely available in most cafés, hotels, bookstores, and bars throughout the city. BSI bus stations and buses also offer complimentary Wi-Fi.

BGLTQ+ Resources: Reykjavík is often listed as one of the most BGLTQ+ friendly cities in the world. Resources can be found at Pink Iceland (101, Hverfisgata 39, Reykjavík; 562 1919; pinkiceland.is/iceland-tips--advice; open Tu-F 9am-5pm).

EMERGENCY INFORMATION

Emergency Number: 112.

Police: Lögreglan (Hverfisgata 113, 105 Reykjavík; 444 1000; logreglan.is; open 8:15am-4pm).

US Embassy: Sendiráð Bandaríkjanna (Laufásvegur 21, 101 Reykjavík; 595 2200; is.usembassy.gov; open M-F 8:30am-5:30pm).

Rape Crisis Center: Accident and Emergency Department, Landspítali University Hospital (Hringbraut 101, 101 Reykjavík; 543 1000; www.landspitali.is/; open daily 24hr).

Hospitals: National Hospital & Emergency Room Fossvogur Landspítali Fossvogi (Áland 6, Reykjavík; 543 1000; landspitali.is; open daily 24hr).

Pharmacies: Pharmacies in Iceland are called Apótek, and are usually open on weekdays and Saturdays during regular hours. Lyfja is the largest chain in Iceland. Commonplace medications like pain relievers, cold/flu/allergy, and eye drops are available over-the-counter. It's a good idea to pack all of your medications with you, as prices can be much higher in Iceland.

- Lyfja Pharmacy: Austurstræti 19, 101 Reykjavík; 552 4045; lyfja.is; open M-F 9am-6pm, Sa 11am-4pm.
- ÍslandsApótek: Laugavegur 46, 101 Reykjavík; 414 4646; islandsapotek.business.site; open M-F 9am-7pm, Sa-Su noon-4pm.

SIGHTS

CULTURE

HALLGRIMSKIRKJA

Hallgrímstorg 101, 101 Reykjavík; 510 1000; hallgrimskirkja.is; open daily Jun-Sept 9am-9pm (tower closes 8:30pm), open daily Oct-Apr 9am-5pm (tower closes 4:30pm); tower closed for Sunday mass from 10:30am-12:15pm.

Visible from almost everywhere in the city, Hallgrimskirkja's 74.5-meter tower reigns powerfully over Reykjavík as one of its most visited and photographed sites. Not to be confused with **Reykjavík Cathedral,** this Lutheran parish is still an active place of worship and the site of several musical performances during the biannual summertime Festival of the Sacred Arts. Inspired by basalt columns from cooling lava, Architect Guðjón Samuelsson designed the concrete structure to honor Iceland's otherworldly landscapes and rugged natural forces. Inside, Iceland's largest pipe organ occupies the entire wall opposite the altar, weighing in at 25 tonnes with 5,275 pipes (some as tall as 10m). If you're lucky, organists or church choirs may be rehearsing while you visit, providing free background music for your wanderings. For a fee, you can take the elevator to a viewing platform high up on the tower; enjoy vast panoramic views of Reykjavík and its surroundings, and perhaps even a glimpse of snow-capped **Snæfellsjökull** in the distance.

i Free entry into church; tower entry adult 1000 kr, child 100 kr; wheelchair accessible.

FISCHER

Fischersund 3, 101 Reykjavík; www.fischersund.com; open M-Sa noon-6pm

Part museum, part wellness boutique, and part experimental artistic venture, Fischer effortlessly draws curious passersby into its inviting open doors. Soothing celestial music and mystical Icelandic herb concoctions create an immersive sensory experience like no other. Four siblings and their father constructed and designed the entire store, with interactive aspects stimulating all of the senses. Visitors are encouraged to breathe in mineral scents, taste healing tea blends, and view entrancing video exhibits embedded in the architecture. Naturopathic remedies for common ailments are explained beneath displays of ancient antidotes—bile from a three-year-old bull is good for back pain, they say. But if that makes you squeamish, don't worry at all: keeping eel skin on your back for nine or eleven days will also do the trick. Handmade soaps, lotions, and essential oil blends are available for purchase, with detailed images describing their scents; it's all presented so artfully that even "dirty leather and animalistic musk" sounds appealing.

i Free entry; product prices vary.

HARPA

Austurbakki 2, 101 Reykjavík; 528 5050; harpa.is; open daily 8am-midnight

Maybe you haven't seen any glaciers or lagoons just yet, but you're yearning for something blue and shiny; Harpa's got your back. Danish architect Ólafur Eliasson designed the concert hall's geometric glass exterior to reflect (literally) and compliment Iceland's dramatic natural features. From the outside, Harpa glimmers with dark blue hues and reflections of the surrounding sea and city. Inside, the prismatic ceiling and glass windows create a different view from every angle. For free, you can walk around multiple floors and admire the outer architecture, but concert halls and other features are blocked off by cheeky signs ("wanna see what we're Haydn?") to tease you into paying for a worthwhile guided tour. The Iceland Symphony Orchestra, Icelandic Opera, and other venerable groups perform here on a regular basis. But, if you don't feel classy enough to attend, there are plenty of more casual shows, like the one-man comedy "How to become Icelandic in 60 minutes," for rag-tag travelers just trying to fit in.

i Free admission, show prices vary; paid guided tours offered every hour M-F from 10am-5pm in summer (June1-August 25); guided tour tickets ISK 1750 for adult, guided tour tickets adult kr 1750, reduced kr 1500, free under 16; wheelchair accessible.

LANDMARKS

PERLAN

Varmahlíð 1, 105 Reykjavík; 562 0200; perlan.is; open daily 9am-10pm

Majestically perched atop the highest hill in Reykjavík, Perlan is impressive both inside and out. For a quick visit, you can admire its impressive dome-shaped glass exterior and surrounding statues, as well as some enjoyable nature trails through the woods up and the hillside. Several exhibits showcase the many awe-inspiring natural wonders of Iceland, including a virtual planetarium experience of the northern lights. If you're adventuring beyond Reykjavík soon, it's a great way to get acquainted with the experiences and features that await you; if not, it's your best bet for experiencing the wonders of Iceland without even leaving the city.

i Ticket prices vary; Áróra showtimes every hour on the hour; last entry 9pm; wheelchair accessible.

SÓLFAR (SUN VOYAGER)

Rekagrandi 14, 101 Reykjavík; 822 2950; sunvoyager.is; open daily 24hr

Ahoy, what's this? You've already seen viking folklore all over the city, but this sculpture is different. Not a viking ship as many may assume, Sólfar honors the sun and commemorates dreams and possibility in journeys to come. A forceful presence on Reykjavík's scenic seaside walking/cycling path, the Sun Voyager aims outward with impressive purpose. Gleaming against striking mountains and an expansive ocean backdrop, Sólfar provides excellent opportunities for wanna-be photographers to show off their high-brow skills. The platform it occupies is accessible from the walking path, and you're almost guaranteed to share your viewing experience with other tourists. But don't worry, it's mesmerizing under any circumstances—especially at sunrise or sunset.

i Free; wheelchair accessible.

STATUE OF INGÓLFUR ARNARSON

Arnarhóll, 101 Reykjavík; open daily 24hr

As you pass by the statue of Ingólfur Arnarson on Arnarhóll, be sure to thank him for founding Reykjavík in 874. One of the first permanent Norse settlers of Iceland, Ingólfur is the reason you're here. Yeah, you're welcome. The name Reykjavík means "smoke cove"—a name chosen for the steam rising from the hot springs throughout the terrain. Next to Ingólfur, a dragon's head decorates his high-seat pillar. The god Odin also hangs out here with his two ravens, an eight-legged horse, and the Worm of Midgard—but don't be intimidated! We're sure Ingólfur was a totally chill guy. The location at the top of a grassy hill in the middle of the city makes for great views of the **Harpa,** the harbor, and seaside nearby, as well as the mountains in the distance.

i Free, open daily 24hr

MUSEUMS

WHALES OF ICELAND

Fiskislóð 23-25, 101 Reykjavík; 571 0077; whalesoficeland.is; open daily 10am-5pm

Dying to see majestic ocean mammals up close, but don't quite have the cash for a whale-watching boat excursion? The Whales of Iceland exhibit by **Reykjavík Harbour** welcomes aspiring marine biologists of all backgrounds and budgets with 23 impressively detailed life-size whale and dolphin renditions. Walk among gentle giants through a dark blue ocean-themed exhibit, complete with the alluring sounds of their underwater calls. A brief audio tour introduces you to each individual species in fascinating detail, but you can also take it at your own pace with interactive touch-screens and video lessons. A feature on humpback migration shares the journeys of real whales the museum's researchers have tagged and a coming-soon underwater immersive experiences promises even more excitement up-close.

i Adult 2900 kr; child 7-15 years 1500 kr, under 7 free; audio guide included; live guided tour daily 1:30pm (included); wheelchair accessible

OUTDOORS

GRASAGARDUR BOTANICAL GARDEN

Hverfisgata 105, 101 Reykjavík; 411 8650; grasagardur.is; open daily 10am-10pm

Iceland may not first come to mind as teeming with plant life, but its vibrant botanical gardens will be the first to prove otherwise. Spread across eight different sections, the living open-air museum boasts 5,000 collections of native and exotic botanical species. A walk or jog through the picturesque garden takes you through various exhibits, featuring rose gardens, mountain herbs, hot spring flora, and northern-belt woods. The vegetation is part of what makes Iceland's landscapes so sensational, and is definitely worth seeing in Grasagardur's artful arrangements. In summer, when most of the flowers are in bloom, the gardens and cafe are especially inviting. Stop by Café Flora for an inventive lunch or snack featuring organic ingredients grown right next to your table—it doesn't get more local than that!

i Free; free 30min. guided tours every Friday 12:40pm June-Aug

SUNDHÖLL REYKJAVÍKUR (REYKJAVÍK SWIMMING POOL)

Barónsstígur 45a, 101 Reykjavík; 411 5350; Reykjavík.is/stadir/sundholl-Reykjavíkur; open M-F 6:30am-10pm, Sa-Su 8am-10pm

When in Reykjavík, do as Icelanders do and go to the swimming pool. A year-round staple in Icelanders' recreation, geothermally heated swimming facilities can be found in nearly every town and city. The centrally located Sundhöll Reykjavíkur greets bathers of all ages with impeccably clean spa-like facilities, including indoor and outdoor lap-swimming pools, various hot and cold tubs, children's pools, and steam rooms. A single entry fee grants you access to everything, including locker use, hot showers, and exercise equipment. It's easy to spend hours getting pruny in rooftop hot pots, decompressing in saunas, and resetting in cold tubs in between. On a clear summer day, join the locals in savoring those precious UV rays late into the evening.

i Admission 1000 kr, child 160 kr; towel rental 600 kr, swimsuit rental 900 kr; wheelchair accessible; must shower with soap before putting on swimsuit to enter pool

SECRET LAGOON

Hvammsvegur, 845 Flúðir; 555 3351; secretlagoon.is; open daily 10am-10pm

Natural hot springs are a must-see in Iceland, but not everyone's wallet can handle **Blue Lagoon** prices. Secret Lagoon is a close second at less than half the cost, and its top-secret location wards off the massive crowds you've been battling at other well-known sights. We'll admit the lagoon isn't entirely a secret—with such a good reputation, it inevitably draws visitors—but you'll still feel sneakily pampered in its peaceful steaming waters. Hidden in the small, quiet town of **Flúðir,** Secret Lagoon feels like your very own giant backyard hot tub. An immense supply of foam pool noodles makes it both tempting and feasible to build yourself a floating lounge chair for maximum relaxation. We say, go for it.

i Adult 3000 kr; senior (67+) and disabled 2200kr; children under 14 free; towel rental 700kr; swimsuit rental 700 kr; last entry 50min before closing; free parking.

CITY WALKING/CYCLING PATHS

Throughout Reykjavík; 411-1111; Reykjavík.is/en/cycle-paths; open daily 24hr

Reykjavík boasts an expansive network of paved walking and cycling trails that go all around and throughout the most scenic parts of the city. The paths wind along the coastline, through wooded parks and flowering fields, and connect all corners of Reykjavík. Pedestrians, runners, and cyclists alike can enjoy the well-kept paths as they traverse the city in their preferred mode of transport or recreation. In some parts, even more trails branch off the path; an impressive 75,866 km of mapped routes provide endless variety in how you can make your around different parts of the city. With a designated path for walkers and runners next to next to another path for cyclists, everyone can cruise at their own pace and enjoy Reykjavík's sights safely.

i Free; bicycle rental prices vary

FOOD

NOODLE STATION ($)

Laugavegur 103, 101 Reykjavík, Iceland; 551 3198; noodlestation.is; open M-F 11am-10pm, Sa-Su noon-10pm

On a chilly, wet Icelandic evening (or any other time, really), a hot soup from Noodle Station will warm your soul from the inside out. The menu keeps things simple with just beef, chicken, and vegetable noodle bowls. Nothing fancy, but they do it well. Flavorful toppings, generous portion sizes, and quick waiters make this place ideal for the weary traveler to fuel up for adventures ahead. Loud and messy noodle-slurping is encouraged here and, while you're at it, you can peruse upcoming events posted on the walls. Conveniently located by Hlemmur Square bus station, it's a great spot to fill up before or after an epic excursion.

i Noodle soup from 960 kr; vegan and vegetarian options available

REYKJAVÍK ROASTERS ($$)

Kárastígur 1, 101 Reykjavík; 517 5535; Reykjavíkroasters.is; open M-Sa 8am-5:30pm, Su 8am-5pm

At Reykjavík Roasters, ambience is everything. That, of course, and great coffee. High-quality brews are made to enjoy slowly here: sip to the sound of your own relaxing record selection on the vintage turntable, with cheerful clinks of café-ware animating the background. Windows surrounding the seating area let sunshine stream in naturally, making the light and earthy color scheme look all the more inviting. Antique furniture, vibrant plants, and coffee-themed decor give the open seating area a homey feel, while the nook behind the counter offers a cozy couch for intimate moments of caffeination. Pastries, kombucha-on-tap, and artisanal chocolates are also great options for getting yourself a classy treat. Understandably popular yet slightly off the beaten path, the café exudes local energy in a low-key setting.

i Coffee from 490 kr, espresso from 450 kr, individual pastries from 480 kr; vegetarian, vegan, and gluten-free options available; BYO cup/mug discount 80 kr; Wi-Fi

BÆJARINS BEZTU PYLSUR ($)

Tryggvagata 1, 101 Reykjavík; 511 1566; bbp.is; open Su-Th 10am-1am, F-Sa 10am-4:30am

Lots of places around Reykjavík will try to convince you they serve the best hot dogs, but this place is the real deal. For cheaper than a coffee, you can crush one of these bad boys and all its yummy fixings: fried onion, honey mustard, mayo, and ketchup. This tiny, retro hot dog hut by Reykjavík's old harbor barely fits its three employees, but serves up wieners with enormous personality from morning 'til late-night munchies. Possibly the only place in Reykjavík that can satiate you for under 500 kr, Bæjarins Beztu Pylsur is absolutely worth a visit (or two, or three) while you're in town.

i Hot dog 470 kr, soda 260 kr; wheelchair accessible

BRAUÐ & CO ($$)

Frakkastígur 16, 101 Reykjavík; 456 7777; braudogco.is; open daily 6am-6pm

If you're lucky enough to snag a seat, Brauð & Co is the perfect place to bask in aromas of freshly-baked breads and pastries (and hopefully mask the stench of your long-unwashed adventure gear). Make sure you look your best, though, as you may end up in the photographs of several tourists stopping to capture vibrant rainbow graffiti-style decor on the café's distinctive outer walls. Tourists and locals alike file in and out at a busy pace, and if the place's only two seats are taken, likely so will you. But first, like everyone else, you'll probably spend a few extra moments ogling and salivating over fresh sourdough rising, pretzels folding, and cinnamon buns rolling just behind the counter.

i Coffee 390 kr, pastries from 390 kr; vegan and vegetarian options available

EMILIE AND THE COOL KIDS ($$)

Hverfisgata 98, 101 Reykjavík; 571 5887; emiliescookies.com; open M-F 8am-5pm, Sa-Su 9am-5pm

Nobody cares how popular you were in high school; all this place wants is to be your friend. Don't believe us? That's okay, we were nerds once too. Try a heavenly home-baked treat from Emilie's bakery and take a minute to process the fact that you are now, in fact, one of the cool kids. Delectable pastries, fresh sandwiches, and soothing hot drinks bring joy to all at affordable (for Iceland) prices in this cheery little café. Nothing beats the hot nutella and milk (790 kr) with a warm-from-the-oven cookie to make you feel at home.

i Espresso 390 kr, bagels 690 kr, sandwiches from 1090 kr; vegan and vegetarian options available; wheelchair accessible

NIGHTLIFE

DRINX, SÆMUNDUR Í SPARIFÖTUNUM

Kex Hostel, Skúlagata 28, 101 Reykjavík; 561 6060; www.kexhostel.is/saemundur-gastro-pub; open 11:30am-11pm

With its stylish interior and hip nightly vibe, the gastro pub at Kex Hostel has become a favorite drink spot amongst locals and travelers regardless of where they may be staying themselves. The casual environment includes bar space, outdoor tables, and cozy couches with books and games, making it an easy place to make new friends as a solo traveler. Young bohemian spirits tend to flock here for happy hour, though the crowd ranges from families with young children to older wanderlusters who are far wiser than you. Most end up staying awhile, enjoying quality conversation and company.

i No cover; happy hour 5-7pm (beer 650 kr, wine 650 kr); BGLTQ+ friendly; Wi-Fi; vegetarian, vegan, and gluten-free options available

PRIKIÐ KAFFIHÚS

Bankastræti 12, 101 Reykjavík; 517 1743; prikid.is; open M-Th 8am-1am, F 8am-1:30am, Sa 11am-4:30am, Su 11am-midnight

Reykjavík's oldest coffee house and a homey restaurant-pub, Prikið wears many hats. Most importantly for your Saturday night, it transforms into a hip-hop dance club on the weekends (and even serves a 'Hangover Killer' breakfast plate the next morning—seriously, what can't this place do?). It's quite popular among young and hipster-y locals, with two floors and an outdoor garden for dancing, eating, drinking, and being merry. Somewhere between happy hour and sunset (we can't keep track either), the vintage saloon-style bar downstairs whips out its disco ball and becomes a hopping dancefloor with frequent live DJ sets.

i No cover; happy hour 4pm-8pm; beer from 690 kr, wine from 1000kr, snacks from 690kr, burgers from 1990 kr; vegan and vegetarian options available

BRYGGJAN BRUGGHÚS

Grandagarður 8, 101 Reykjavík, Iceland; 456 4040; www.bryggjanbrugghus.is/; open daily 11am-11pm

Right on the coast in Reykjavík's Old Harbor, Bryggjan Brugghús is the first independent microbrewery in Iceland and the place to indulge your Icelandic beer fantasy. A generous four hours of happy hour (3-7pm) give you ample time to swirl, sniff, and sample Icelandic pale ales like the connoisseur you've always wanted to be. In addition to stouts and lagers, the bistro serves meals and snacks featuring beer-based sauces and seasonings. The perfect start to a classy evening, a two-hour 'Cheers to Reykjavík' tasting session (8990 kr) walks you through the long menu of specialty beers, serving each brew tapas-style with its ideal pairing of Icelandic delicacy. The bar is lively most afternoons and hosts live jazz performances every Sunday night.

i No cover; drinks from 1100 kr; happy hour daily 3-7pm; brewery tour (3-beer tasting flight included) 3490 kr; vegetarian, vegan, and gluten-free options available; wheelchair accessible

KÍKÍ QUEER BAR

Laugavegur 22, 101 Reykjavík; 571 0194; kiki.is; open W-Th, Su 8pm-1am, F-Sa 8pm-4:30am

Famously the queerest bar in Reykjavík, Kíkí has certainly earned its rainbow stripes. Bumping DJs, unbeatable happy hour specials, and regular drag parties draw in people of all identities to dance the night away. On two different floors of the bar/club, you can make new friends and enjoy colorful disco lights as you sing along with the upbeat tunes we all know and love. The energy picks up later in the night, especially on weekends; in summer months when nights are short, dance parties can easily go from sunset til sunrise. Reykjavík is well-known for its BGLTQ+ pride and progressivism, so it's no surprise that Kíkí Queer Bar delivers.

i No cover; beer from 1000 kr; happy hour 9pm-1am Th-Tu (500 kr beer/shots); BGLTQ+ friendly

RING ROAD

Coverage by **Marissa Saenger**

"Hringvegur." "Þjóðvegur." "Route 1." Each of these names refers to the 1332 kilometer asphalt road encircling Iceland best known as the Ring Road.

Though its popularity grows each year, driving the Ring Road remains your best bet for experiencing as much of Iceland's raw beauty as you can—and at your own pace. A bus tour won't drive to the most untouched trails and rugged areas of Iceland, nor let you hike for hours just to take it all in. Behind the wheel, you'll feel completely free to bypass the crowds, take less-traveled detours, and linger in the places that you find the most exciting. Build your own itinerary to fully experience all of Iceland's wonders in the ways you find most rewarding. Whether it's hiking, swimming, diving, fishing, museum-hopping, photographing, or simply admiring, the trip makes Iceland yours to explore.

However, The Ring Road is not always a walk in the park. Some moments you find yourself surrounded by busloads of tourists, and others you long for company on the trails. Accommodations, gas, and food prices often exceed even the best-planned budgets.

The road and its gauntlet of single-lane bridges will inevitably wear you down. But if you want to have the adventure of a lifetime, the struggle is unquestionably worth it. Ethereal Icelandic scenery invites you to have the time of your life at every corner, never failing to awe and shock you with its beauty. There's no better place and no better way to experience Iceland. Here's how to do it.

BEFORE YOU GO

Renting a Car: It can be intimidating to navigate the hundreds of different rental companies and options, so here's a basic breakdown that can guide your search.

- First and foremost, you must be at least 18 years old and have a valid drivers' license in order to rent a car in Iceland. Some places charge extra if you are under 21 while others require a valid passport at pick-up; every company will have different policies, so be sure to read up on them before arranging your rental. You need a credit card for payment. Make sure you have enough available credit to make the full payment before you go to pick up the car (debit cards will not be accepted).
- Several different companies offer car rental with car pick-up typically at the KEF airport. Booking a few months ahead is generally good practice: availability becomes more and more limited with a general increase in demand from the Ring Road's increasing popularity, especially as high tourist season (June-Aug) approaches.
- Most vehicles in Iceland are manual transmission, so there might be limited selection if you're looking for automatic. Automatic transmission vehicles also tend to be more expensive to rent, so you could save a lot of money by learning to drive manual before you go.

Driving in Iceland: Most of Route 1 is a paved, undivided highway with one lane in each direction. In busier sections near Reykjavík or larger towns, more lanes pop up to reduce congestion. When driving the Ring Road, every traveler must follow a few basic rules:

- Stick to the speed limit of 90 km/hr, the universal Ring Road speed limit. Watch for lower speed limits in certain sections such as tunnels, sharp turns, and gravel roads, where cars usually coast at 80 km/hr. Police officers station themselves all over the road to crack down on this rule, and for good reason: high winds in Iceland can sweep even the largest of vehicles right off the road if they're exceeding this speed. It might be tempting to race through empty strips of sweet, smooth, straight highway, but please stay under the speed limit.

- Only pull off the road at designated stopping points. The views and photo ops are amazing everywhere; you won't miss out if you wait until the next pull-off point. Driving off-road is a serious offense, can devastate surrounding ecosystems, and endanger yourself and other drivers.
- Headlights must be on, and all passengers' seat belts must be fastened, at all times.

In addition to these rules, keep an eye out for single-lane bridges and tunnels: you must yield to drivers coming the opposite way by pulling off into to the designated waiting area before the bridge/tunnel. Some tunnels have a toll that you must pay online within three hours after passing through; be sure to check at the nearest gas station, campground, or hostel to make sure you get this done before the toll amount rises.

Navigation: The Ring Road encircles the entire country; you could follow it the whole way around and never get lost, but many attractions and accommodation sites will require you to go onto other roads. You could use international data to navigate, or add a GPS to your car rental, but both options are expensive and may not be worth it. A good strategy is to use Wi-Fi at your hostel/campground or a café to map your route for the day on Google Maps, and save all the locations you want to hit along the way. You can then download the area between your start and endpoints to use it for offline navigation once you're on the road. Most major sights are labeled by name in Google Maps, and for anything else you can use lat/long coordinates or a Google Maps plus code to find its location.

Accommodations: Hostels are likely the most budget-friendly accommodation option, unless you are planning to camp. Each plan has its pros and cons: camping can give you a lot more flexibility to end your day wherever you want, potentially leaving space for more adventure if you don't have to drive to a set point and sleep somewhere pre-booked. Staying in hostels also requires much more planning and booking in advance, as availability becomes limited during high season when everyone and their cousin is traveling around Iceland. On short notice, it's much easier to find a campsite with space to spend a night than a hostel with any open beds. Before deciding to totally rough it, do some basic calculations to figure out whether camping gear purchase or rental and campervan rental (plus required campsite fees per night stay) actually turn out more economical compared to hostelling, which eliminates the need for a lot of additional gear.

Food: Eating out in Iceland is expensive, andand you won't have a ton of choices when it comes to restaurants outside of Reykjavík. Limited options make it difficult to manage food allergies and dietary restrictions. Stock up on groceries before you hit the road and plan on cooking in either hostel or guesthouse kitchens or on bringing a camping stove. If you're really hardcore, you could even bring a whole trips' supply of meal replacement powder or dehydrated food for pretty cheap...but we won't judge you for splurging on PB&J.

Trip Length: Driving the Ring Road is possible in five days, but only if you want to spend (even more) hours a day in the car, driving past beautiful sights you wish you could stop at. A week is more reasonable, allowing you to pull over and take photos when you want to, throw in a spontaneous extra stop or hike, and retain some semblance of sanity.

What to Bring: Even if you're traveling in summer, pack for all seasons. Seriously, the weather changes drastically from day to day or from hour to hour in most of Iceland, with the average day involving some chilly wind, rain, and clouds. You must bring a rain jacket, along with thermal layers and a warm sleeping bag and tent if you're planning to camp. Sturdy shoes for hiking, a reusable water bottle, camera or phone, and a swimsuit for bathing in hot springs/ geothermal swimming pools will serve you well otherwise. An eye mask might also come in handy, since the summer months stay very bright, even at night.

Bring a friend! A solo trip of the Ring Road can be incredibly rewarding. It can also drive you insane. Going with a friend allows you to split up the driving, have some much-needed human contact during the loneliest times, and split the cost of the car, tent, campsite, and so on more effectively. Plus, Icelandic radio is great (if spotty in places), and you wouldn't want to have to sing along by yourself!

Trip Length A full Ring Road trip can take as little as five days, but to make the most of your trip, we recommend at least a full week. If you're hoping to do some major treks or day-tours, you may want to plan on spending even longer. Honestly, you could spend months on the Ring Road and still not cover everything. The amount of time you want to take depends on your schedule and budget constraints, as car rental costs increase per day of use. Lengthening your trip allows you to spend less time driving and more time exploring each day; there are endless things to do and see, and few people regret making the time for spontaneous once-in-a-lifetime adventures.

Iceland can be divided very roughly into six regions, one of which won't be covered here (the **Westfjords** are sparsely populated, tracked with rough roads, and seldom traveled). Here are the five regions of Iceland you should hit on your trip:

THE GOLDEN CIRCLE

The Golden Circle is, you guessed it, a circle. Starting from Reykjavík, it winds through West Iceland's landscape, hitting several of Iceland's most famous natural and historical landmarks before returning to the capital or continuing to other regions of the country. It's a logical first day for a Ring Road trip, but it can also be booked as a day trip through any of Reykjavík's tour agencies. The waterfalls and geysers are breathtaking, but be prepared to battle crowds all day.

SIGHTS

SKÓGAFOSS

Gönguleið um Fimmvörðuháls, Skógar; www.fi.is/en/hiking-trails/fimmvorduhals; open daily 24hr

One of several major waterfalls along the south coast, Skógafoss first seems like another quick photo stop to check off of your list. But if you plan for it, there's much more to do here than just photograph the massive waterfall dumping millions of gallons of glacial water from an impressive 60 meters above (yawn). A man-made staircase leads to a viewing platform at the top of the falls, from which a hiking trail continues up the mountain. The trail follows the Skógá river, where several smaller waterfalls cascade beside you and incredible views of the glacier Eyjafjallajökull can be seen. Visitors who prepare properly can hike to a bridge 7.5km away, or even further into Þórsmörk Valley, 24.3km from Skógar via the Fimmvörðuháls trek. Trail maps can be found online to guide your hike. If you plan on a long excursion, be sure to use www.safetravel.is as a safety resource and register your hike.

i Free; restrooms 200 kr; directly off of Route 1 to the left, 155km southeast of Reykjavík

ÞINGVELLIR NATIONAL PARK

Þingvallavegur; 482 2660; www.thingvellir.is/en; visitor center open daily 9am-6pm

A classic first stop along the Golden Circle, Þingvellir National Park sets the stage well for your trip with an exciting combined dose of Icelandic history and nature. In the early years of settlement, Iceland established its parliament, Alþing, at this site. From 930 CE on, Þingvellir remained the official annual meeting place for nationwide legal proceedings. In addition to its unique history, the **UNESCO World Heritage Site** also boasts distinctive geological features including a contentintal rift between the North American and Eurasian tectonic plates. No big deal. Walking trails within the park take you through a gorge at the plates' edges, as well as lava fields, waterfalls, and cliffs. In one part of Lake Þingvallavatn, called **Silfra,** tourists can gear up in thick drysuits to snorkel through the crystal-clear glacial waters directly above the rift.

i Free; parking 750 kr; indoor exhibition 1000 kr, 500 kr students; free tours M-F 10am-3pm; wheelchair accessible

HAUKADALUR

8M7X+3P Bláskógabyggð; www.geysircenter.com; open daily 24hr

This is it, the famous stop on the Golden Circle where Iceland's acclaimed Geysir blasts enormous plumes of spray up to 70 meters high, giving all other geysers a serious run for their—wait, what? It's inactive? Better cancel the trip. Actually, there's another geyser called Strokkur, just a few meters from Geysir, that now draws visitors for its similarly impressive eruptions of scalding-hot water. When you visit, you can still see the water pit where Geyser had its glory days, and admire powerful water plumes shooting up from now-famous Strokkur every ten minutes or so. Even between eruptions, Strokkur's curiously bright-blue water pit has a life of its own: it rolls, steams, and gurgles in a mesmerizing continuum, ballooning up into a half-dome bubble for a fleeting magical moment before each burst. Though camera-ready tourist crowds tend not to stray far from this one feature, it's worth checking out the rest of the Haukadalur: crystallized sulfur deposits, bubbling fumaroles, and small steaming rivers punctuate its landscape, and a hiking trail up a small nearby hill leads you away from tourists toward a nice viewpoint of the surrounding area.

i Free admission; stay straight onto Route 365 after passing the northern side of Lake Þingvallvatn, then in 15km, stay straight through the roundabout onto Route 37 then continue following the road straight when it becomes Route 35

KERIÐ CRATER

24R7+P9 Klausturholar; open daily 24hr

A remarkable natural feature often overlooked by Golden Circle tours, the collapsed volcano crater Kerið holds vivid aquamarine water that gets its curiously bright hue from minerals in the (relatively) fresh volcanic rock. Once a cone-shaped volcano, Kerið emptied its magma chamber when it last erupted roughly three thousand years ago, causing the rock to collapse inward and form its curious shape. The resulting caldera features dramatic shades of deep red rock from oxidized iron, which starkly contrasts the radiant blue water it surrounds and the lush green mosses covering its walls. A walking trail encircles the entire crater's upper perimeter (about 300m around), with additional paths down the steep inner edges to view the water up-close.

i Admission 400 kr; free parking; from Haukadalur, follow Route 35 southwest for 47km until the road becomes Biskupstun-gnabraut

SOUTH COAST

The term "South Coast" most commonly refers to the region between Reykjavík and the southern city of **Vík.** This heavily traveled section of the Ring Road includes waterfalls, rock formations, and several of Iceland's famous sand beaches. Like the Golden Circle, tours of the south coast from Reykjavík are popular.

SIGHTS

REYNISFJARA BEACH

CX35+64 Vik; open daily 24hr

Reynisfjara: beach trip, but make it edgy. Frigid waters aside, the striking black sand and protruding lava formations at Reynisfjara certainly put a refreshing spin on your typical day at the beach. Expect more than just a tourist gimmick: the sand particles come from eroded volcanic rock—mostly basalt, which is black or dark gray in color. **Mount Reynisfjall** borders the water, with its naturally-formed caves in the cliffside that you can enter directly from the beach. Inside the caves and along the mountain, basalt columns formed from fracture patterns in rapidly cooled lava give the beach a supernatural and geometric appearance. From the parking lot, the beach extends for a while; a walk along the water is a great opportunity to escape the crowds and take in the beautiful views, with the sea on one side and glaciers on the other.

i *Free; from Route 1, turn right onto 215 and follow to the parking lot at the end*

SÓLHEIMAR ECO-VILLAGE

Solheimavegur, 801 Selfoss; 480 4483; solheimar.is; visitor center open M-F 9am-5pm

If you have any interest in sustainable living, Sólheimar Eco-Village is a worthwhile addition to your **Golden Circle** itinerary. Icelandic environmentalist Sesselja Hreindís Sigmundsdóttir founded Sólheimar in 1930, and today the thriving international community upholds her visions of sustainability, inclusion, health, and artistic expression. With its diversified local economy and organic farming practices, the community self-sufficiently sets an inspiring example for life in harmony with nature. In the visitor center at **Sesseljuhús,** educational exhibits detail the community's inner workings and yield insight as to how it functions within the context of society as a whole. A central café and artisan shop also welcome visitors to sample organically-produced foods and view authentic handcrafted goods. Sólheimar's commitment to environmental consciousness serves as an important reminder that we can all do our part to protect the natural ecosystems that sustain and connect us.

Free; tours and educational workshops available if booked in advance by phone; guesthouse open year-round; wheelchair accessible

EAST ICELAND

If you've made it this far, congratulations! Welcome to the solitude, the untamed wilderness, and the stunning beauty that is East Iceland. You've made it where even Reykjavík's endless tour buses can't reach. Just you, the sheep, and the road. And the road is glorious out here. It winds by the massive glacier **Vatnajökull,** past ethereal glacier lagoons, and through the majestic **East Fjords.** The drive is long and lonely, but you won't want to miss a mile.

SIGHTS

VATNAJÖKULL NATIONAL PARK, SKAFTAFELL REGION

228M+J8 Skaftafell; 470 8300; vatnajokulsthjodgardur.is; open daily 24hr; Skaftafell Visitor Center open daily 9am-6pm

Home to Europe's largest ice cap, Vatnajökull National Park covers a hefty chunk of southeast Iceland and extends inward from near the coastline to almost the middle of the country. Most easily accessible from Route 1, the Skaftafell area of the park offers a large campground and well-equipped visitor center that has everything the outdoorsy traveler could ever need to experience Iceland's awe-inspiring nature. Hiking routes of all types and levels start from the visitor center, ranging from casual walks to multi-hour treks through the entire Skaftafell park area (though some routes only open in summer, due to risks from snow and ice). A popular walking loop just a few kilometers long leads to Svartifoss Waterfall, where surrounding columnar basalt formations create a hypnotising sight. Tour companies based in Skaftafell offer various guided glacier excursions and ice cave tours—the most extreme venture going 2,109m above sea level to Hvannadalshnúkur, Iceland's highest point.

Vatnajökull National Park; tour leaves from Skaftafell

VIKING VILLAGE FILM SET

9CP77267+6V, Höfn; open daily 24hr

When you pass through this cluster of abandoned grass-top huts within a primitive wooden fence, it might feel like you've gone straight to the viking age. How did a village like this even make it into the twenty-first century? Seriously, that architecture is sooo 784 CE. As cool as real viking ruins would look, this is actually just a movie set that's never been used. The movie didn't end up filming, but the entire set remains and features incredible detail. To supplement your visit, the surrounding **Stokksnes** area offers incredible views of **Vestrahorn Mountain's** jagged peaks, uncongested black sand beaches, a rustic café, seal viewing areas, and hiking trails. While striking scenery makes the area popular for photography, you're unlikely to see crowds as it's fairly remote. Ambitious and well-prepared hikers can attempt the 18km all-terrain trail (marked blue on the hiking map at the café), which follows the coast and loops around **Vestrahorn,** with a very steep and rocky section going straight up the mountainside.

i Parking fee 900kr per person (includes access to Viking village film set, beaches, seal viewing, hiking trails, and café)

OTHER SIGHTS IN EAST ICELAND

The drive through the East Fjords is one of the most beautiful sections of the Ring Road, winding up the coast with sheer cliffs on one side and the vast ocean on the other. It's also the emptiest. The gravel roads are well-maintained, but use caution. Finding a place to spend the night out here can be tricky, so be creative. Your best bet is to look in the area around Alistair—the largest town in the region.

NORTHERN ICELAND

From Egilsstaðir, Route 1 turns west and away from the coast. You'll head up into the gorgeous highlands of Iceland's northeastern interior, before descending into the touristy Mývatn area.

SIGHTS

MÝVATN NATURE BATHS

Jarðbaðshólar, 660 Mývatn; 464 4411; myvatnnaturebaths.is; open daily May-Sept 9am-midnight, Oct-Apr noon-10pm, closed January 1st

With the abundant supply of geothermal energy in the Lake Mývatn area, visiting heating pools is a no-brainer. Though the Mývatn Nature Baths consist of man-made lagoons, the warmth of the water comes straight from the center of the earth—well, sort of—and with desolate landscapes surrounding all sides, you'll feel like somewhat of a space pioneer. You know, lounging in your luxurious space-station hot tub in the middle of an uninhabited planet that you just discovered on your heroic intergalactic mission. No? Too nerdy? Okay fine. Well, at least enjoy your sauna and in-pool bar drinks if you're not going to be imaginative with us. And we hope you like sulphur, because you'll be smelling it the entire time. But maybe the next time you catch a whiff of rancid eggs, your memory will travel right back to this soothing spa-like environment—always look on the bright side, right?

i Admission May-Sept 5000 kr, Oct-Apr 4500 kr; student, disabled, and seniors May-Sept 3300 kr; Oct-Apr 3000 kr; swimsuit and towel rental 850 kr; last entry 30min before closing; wheelchair accessible

OTHER SIGHTS IN NORTHERN ICELAND

The volcanic lake Mývatn was formed in the aftermath of an eruption, so it's no surprise that the surrounding landscape is rich in volcanic landforms like **Dimmuborgir**—a lava field with especially strange spires of rock—and the Skútustaðir pseudocraters, a field of craters formed not directly by volcanic eruptions, but by steam. Route 1 stays on the north side of the lake, while Route 848 loops around to the south before rejoining the main road. Akureyri, the first real city since Reykjavík, is a good spot to spend a night or two to recharge.

AKUREYRI

Akureyri's population of just under 20,000 people makes the city a thriving metropolis by Iceland's standards—the country's second-largest, in fact. It certainly doesn't have the attractions and landmarks of a major city, but it is an excellent spot to take a day to rest, resupply, and generally reconnect with civilization. There's a Bónus where you can restock on all your favorite Icelandic groceries at a reasonable (for Iceland, at least) price, and Akureyri Backpackers is an excellent hostel with a restaurant and bar that serve as a hub for the whole town. Akureyri is the main tourist hub outside of Reykjavík, and some of the most popular offerings include whale watching and horseback riding.

SIGHTS

AKUREYRI ART MUSEUM

Kaupvangsstræti 8-12, Akureyri; 461 2610; listak.is; open May-Sept daily 10am-5pm, Oct-Apr daily noon-5pm

...it would be a shame to miss its art museum. Innovative exhibits range from the history of street art in Akureyri to an interactive plant communication platform, with plenty of contemporary works in between.

Combined audio and visual exhibits captivate the senses from all angles, turning your aimless museum meander into a fully immersive experience. Museum curators meticulously and intentionally plan out every detail, down to how the arrangement of works in each room plays against sunlight that streams through patterned window panes. A theme of human connection with nature permeates the museum's collections, with various works provoking existential questions as to how such connections grow and wane.

i Admission 1500 kr; student, child, senior, disabled free; guided tours Th 4pm; wheelchair accessible

MT. SÚLUR (AKUREYRI)

JR66+CG Eyjafjarðarsveit; visitakureyri.is/en/things-to-do/attractions/mountain-sulur-; open daily 24hr

Besides Reykjavík, Akureyri is the most urban place you'll encounter along the Ring Road. The adventurous pioneer you've become, it's only fair that there might be some nature withdrawals once you're cast back into society. Fear not, intrepid explorer, for right before the city entrance rests Mt. Súlur and its glorious 1,213m peak. Just minutes from Akureyri, sturdy wooden posts mark the trail up to Mt. Súlur (a refreshing luxury compared to some not-so-clearly-marked hiking routes in the more remote areas of Iceland). A moderately steep trail, it takes about three hours to hit the summit. There, you can sign your name and read messages from other climbers in a summit logbook stored in a metal box. From atop Súlur, panoramic views of the snow-capped mountain ranges surrounding **Eyjafjörður** are sure to take your breath away, if the hike hasn't already. A second peak can be reached by traversing a narrow ridgeline from the first, if you're aching for more of a thrill. Depending on the season, your descent time might be significantly reduced by snow-patches that you can butt-slide down for nearly the whole way (not the most elegant way down, but pretty fun).

i Free; free parking at trailhead; from Akureyri, follow Súlurvegur up to the end, where there is a parking area and a trail map

AKUREYRARKIRKJA

við Eyrarlandsveg 600, Akureyri; 462 7700; akureyrarkirkja.is; summer M-Th 10am-7pm, F 10am-4pm

Icelandic churches seem to have a thing for cement—we're not sure why, but hey, it works. The **Hallgrimskirkja** equivalent of the North, Akureyri's prominent Lutheran church towers high above the city at the top of 116 steps. As a central landmark, it offers clear views of the surrounding city and its port on Eyjafjörður channel. Built in 1940, the church now houses an impressive 3200-pipe organ and a ship suspended from the ceiling. The ship commemorates a Nordic tradition and safeguards those at sea (which we hope includes tourists on whale-watching tours). Designed by **Guðjón Samúelsson**—one of Iceland's most influential architects—the church blends naturalism and modernism with its pyramid-like renderings of lava-formed basalt columns on either side of the main entrance.

i Free admission; wheelchair accessible

SNÆFELLSNES PENINSULA

From Akureyri, it's a bit of a drive to the Snæfellsnes PeninsulaPeninsula—the final stop on the Ring Road. Route 1 cuts inland a bit, only navigating one or two fjords before reaching Snæfellsnes. This area is sometimes called "Iceland in miniature" by various tour agencies, because it features many of Iceland's main attractions—waterfalls, volcanoes, beaches, and glaciers.

SIGHTS

ARNARSTAPI-HELLNAR WALK

Q98G+9X Arnarstapi; open daily 24hr

If you're looking for an easy, scenic hike by Snæfellsjökull, this is it. A 6km (3km each way) walk between the small towns of Arnarstapi and Hellnar takes you along stunning seaside cliffs with unusual features from lava formations and erosion. Pay close attention to **Gatklettur** among these features, an iconic naturally formed stone archway that looks like a portal to the vast blue ocean beyond. Basalt columns, cliff caves, and rock pillars line the shore, surrounded by the crystal-clear ocean and plenty of seagulls. Look out onto killer views of the glacier Snæfellsjökull, as well as majestic snow-capped mountains on the distant shore and plenty of bird poop on the rock cliffs right in front of you—hey, nobody's perfect. There's a café in Hellnar and a fish and chip stand in Arnarstapi, both ideal for a snack break halfway through the out-and-back walk.

i Free

KIRKJUFELL

WMGV+V4 Grundarfjörður; open daily 24hr

There it is: the curiously pointy free-standing mountain featured in almost every photo or website on tourism Iceland. Now what? Well, climb it, of course! If walking the loop around Kirkjufell's base doesn't satisfy your thirst for adrenaline, then boy, oh boy, are you in for a treat: the haul to the summit is short (about 1.5 hours), sweet, and calls for lots of all-fours scrambling up steep and rocky headwalls. Enjoy an exciting—and a bit reckless—ascent while you brave vertical rope climbs, high wind speeds, and precarious drop-offs that might induce palpitations, or at least a few heart-rate spikes for those brave enough to look down. The trail stays clear, but if you reach a point that looks unsafe to continue, it's best to turn around: other climbers have probably hit these same dead-ends and found a different way up. After the last of three rope scrambles, the 463m-high ridgeline across Kirkjufell's peak offers spectacular views in all directions; just hang on tight your camera so it doesn't get blown away while you take those glorious summit selfies!

i Free; free parking at Kirkjufellsfoss parking lot

GRETTISLAUG (GRETTIRS POOL)

V7J7+JP Hvammur; 453 6506; open daily 24hr

What better way to relax and recenter than soaking in a natural hot spring? This isn't just another geothermally-heated manmade pool: Grettislaug is the real deal, and has the saga history to prove it. According to legend, Grettir was an ancient Icelandic outlaw and giant who swam 7.5 frigid kilometers from the island of Drangey, only reviving himself from hypothermia by the warmth of this very spring. Named after the giant, Grettislaug stands out for its remote location on the coast of northern Iceland, just a stone's throw away from the ocean. Two separate pools, each a slightly different temperature, sit at the edge of a small peninsula; both offer excellent views of **Mt. Tindastóll** and **Drangey Island.** Rugged surroundings, local clientele, and an abundance of natural algae in the waters lend the bathing experience an unforgettably raw Icelandic feel.

i Admission 1000k; free parking; at the end of Route 75 from Aurkeryi, turn left onto Þverárfjallsvegur, take a right turn onto 748, and follow 748 North until the end

OTHER SIGHTS ON THE SNÆFELLSNES PENINSULA

Snæfellsnes has countless attractions beyond those listed here, including **Snæfellsjökull National Park,** where you can book a snowmobile or lava cave tour, the **Lóndrangar rock pillars,** and **Skarðsvík Beach,** a rare white sand beach. The Harbour Hostel, located in the town of Stykkishólmur on the northern coast of the peninsula, is an excellent place to stop for the night or to use as a base for an extra day of exploring.

ICELAND ESSENTIALS

VISAS

Iceland is part of the Schengen Area, which means US, Canadian, Australian, and British citizens may enter without a visa for stays of up to 90 days. Your passport must be valid through at least three months following your planned departure from the Schengen Area.

MONEY

Iceland's currency is the Icelandic króna, abbreviated as ISK officially and as kr locally. It's also sometimes called the Icelandic crown. Since Iceland is an island, it has to import most of its goods; as a result, prices tend to be high. Exchange rates have varied from year to year, with the dollar regaining strength relative to the ISK most recently, but Iceland is expensive regardless, so it's best to budget generously.

Tipping: Tipping in Iceland is not expected. Nearly all prices in stores and restaurants already include gratuity and service charges, so adding a tip is unnecessary. However, it is not rude to tip if you wish to show extra thanks; most will accept appreciatively.

Taxes: The standard VAT in Iceland is 24% (our sincerest apologies to your wallet). For many relevant services including accommodations, food, alcohol, books, condoms, tour operators, and travel agents, the rate is reduced to 11%. Goods and services exempt from VAT include libraries, museum entry, public transport, healthcare, postal services, bank services, and parking. Prices always include their applicable taxes, so the advertised price is the total you pay.

HEALTH AND SAFETY

Drugs and Alcohol: Iceland's legal minimum drinking age is 20. Outside of bars and restaurants, alcohol is only available for purchase at government owned stores called Vínbúðin (besides the 2.25% ABV beer available at grocery stores). Most Vínbúðin locations are only open until 6pm, and do not open at all on Sundays.

Duty-free alcohol purchase is available at Keflavík International Airport upon your arrival, though maximum allowances limit the amount individuals can purchase. Alcohol is taxed heavily and prices tend to be high all over Iceland, so stocking up (within your allowance) at the airport may save you some precious cash. Just be ready to share with (or swat away) the wide-eyed hostel bunkmates who want in on some of your haul.

Drinking in public is generally socially acceptable, provided you clean up your own cans and bottles and do nothing to disturb or offend others. That means no rogue a capella performances of "Despacito" until you're back home (or at least in another country). Driving intoxicated is a serious crime in Iceland: a zero-tolerance policy means drivers can be penalized with a BAC as low as 0.05%. If you're driving the Ring Road, make sure you're completely done driving for the day before opting for a drink.

Weather and Climate: Though moderated by nearby ocean currents, Iceland's subarctic climate is generally cold. The warmest summer days typically approach mid-sixties Fahrenheit, while average winter temperatures sit around freezing or just below (depending on the region). Especially in the highlands and mountainous areas, weather can change rapidly, with high winds, heavy precipitation, and temperature shifts happening often. In summer, sunrise and sunset happen just a few hours apart, but for about two weeks of the year it stays light out for 24 hours a day. In winter, the Northern Lights are visible most nights, but daylight hours dwindle to as low as four per day.

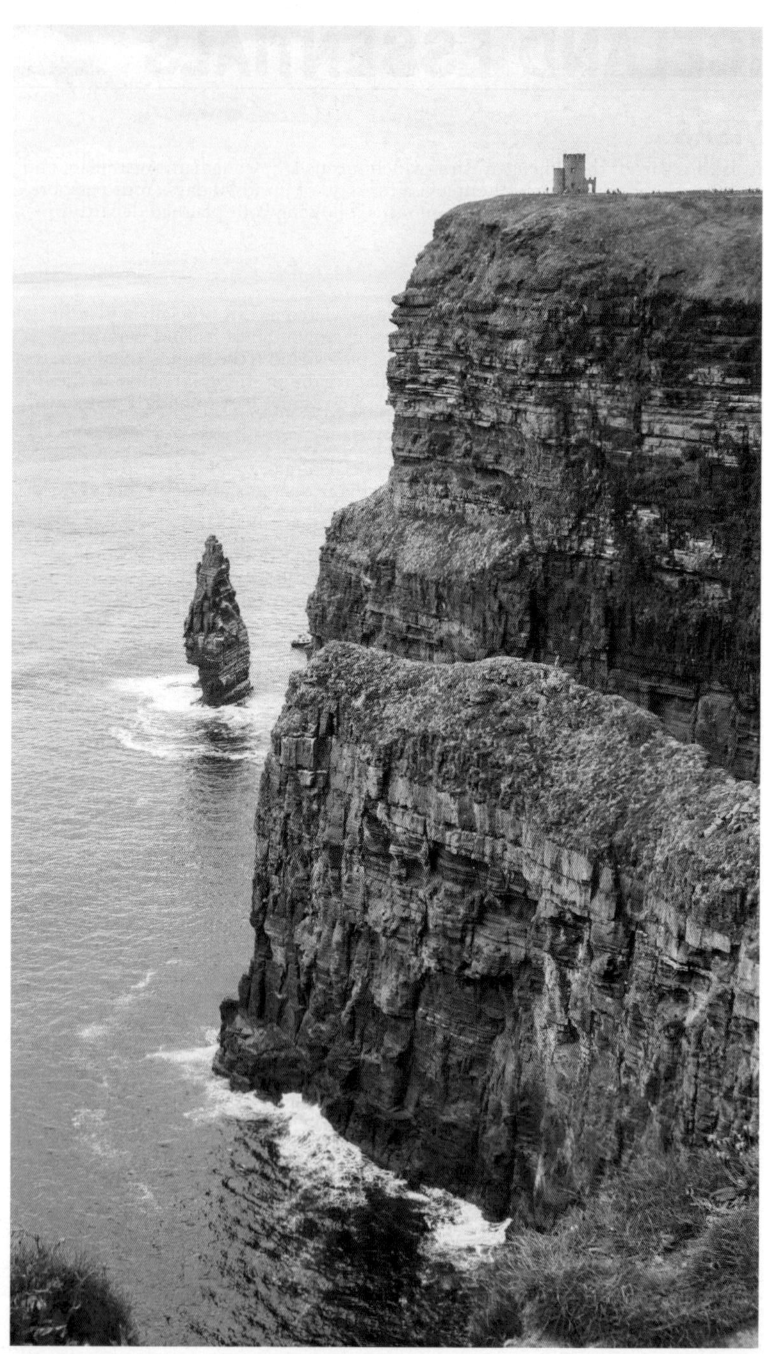

IRELAND

Ireland's hills hold thousands of years of history—yet the country only gained independence in 1922. Most people know the classic images of lush emerald landscapes—and while those hills and mountains are part of Ireland's heart—there is much more to dive into. Rolling green countryside, craggy cliffs, and rocky hikes make up the nation's scenic landscapes, perfect for backpackers and nature lovers. The cities, far from being outdone by the natural world, are filled with books and music, melting pots of cultures once suppressed and now released.

Of course, one can't talk about Ireland without mentioning the beer and whiskey that flow through its veins. (Is it a coincidence that both Guinness and Ireland use the harp as their symbol? We think not.) The Guinness, Jameson, and Teeling factories draw in those pining for a pint (or a shot), and the Cliffs of Moher and Connemara call out to those who would rather spend their life outdoors. Though today Ireland is mostly English-speaking, the people's Gaelic roots and traditions still shape the country's culture. (While you're here, try and learn a little Gaelic, if you can.) Ireland is more than its famed potatoes and Irish coffee: it is an island with spirit, a land of stories and tradition, a place where lore reigns true. The history still writes itself today, a merging of religion, arts, and good spirits, all splashed across the canvas of the country.

DUBLIN

Coverage by **Lucy Golub**

A mix of a modern big city and a quaint historical town, Dublin has everything you could ask for. The city still bears the scars of the country's fight for independence in 1919, so history buffs can find lots of places to see, stories to hear, and museums to explore. The city is the queen of literature, and you'll find many odes to great writers of the age in the names of streets, pubs, and museums. (And, of course, emblazoned on every tacky postcard in a tourist shop.) But this city doesn't live in the past. Today, it thrives, as shown by its new restaurants, bars, museums, arts, and nightlife. You won't run out of things to do, especially if you leave the tourist-filled central part and actually interact with locals. But embrace the live music, the old streets filled with new stores, and the Guinness. You're in Ireland's capital now.

ORIENTATION

Dublin is cut in half by the **River Liffey.** Today, the south side is considered more upscale, although this was not the case in the 1700s. The southern half includes tourist areas like **Temple Bar, Grafton Street, St. Stephen's Green,** and beyond that, **Portobello.** East of Temple Bar, you'll find the students that surround **Trinity College.** The north also has lots to see like the **Garden of Remembrance** and the **Spire** and **O'Connell Street.** The sides of the river connect at many bridges, the most famous of which is called the **Ha'penny Bridge.**

ESSENTIALS

GETTING THERE

Dublin Airport is about 40min. from the city center via public transportation, and there are easy buses taking you right there. Take the Airlink (signs will direct you) to be dropped off at many of the key tourist areas. Tickets cost €7 one-way and €12 round-trip. Buses from other places in Ireland or Northern Ireland also have stops along the River Liffey, and the Irish Rail is another option.

GETTING AROUND

Dublin is very walkable, but if that's not an option for you, the city uses a bus system called Dublin Bus. The Transport for Ireland app can also be useful. Fares are €2-3. The tram system called Luas offers some mobility within the city as well, with Zone 1 tickets costing €2.10. Unlimited day tickets are also available for €7.20. They're supposedly working on an underground subway, as well. Until then, walking, buses and Luas it is!

PRACTICAL INFORMATION

Tourist Offices: Dublin Visitor Center (17 O'Connell St.; 01 898 0700; www.dublinvisitorcentre.ie; open M-F 9am-5pm, Sa 9am-6pm, Su 9am-4pm).

Banks/ATMs/Currency Exchange: Banks and ATMs are all over and easy to find. Here's one: Ulster Bank (33 College Green; 01 702 5400; open M-Tu 9:30am-4:30pm, W 10am-4:30pm, Th-F 10am-4:30pm).

Post Offices: This post office has a special place in Dublin's history but can also send mail (O'Connell St.; 01 705 7000; www.anpost.ie; open M-Sa 8:30am-6pm).

Internet: Most restaurants and cafés have Wi-Fi, as do most stores.

BGLTQ+ Resources: Outhouse is a BGLTQ+ community center (105 Capel St.; 01 873 4999; www.outhouse.ie; open M-F 10am-6pm).

EMERGENCY INFORMATION

Emergency Number: 999 or 112.

Police: Kevin Street Station (Kevin St. Upper; 01 666 9400; www.garda.ie; open daily 24hr).
US Embassy: US Embassy (42 Elgin Rd.; 01 668 8777; www.ie.usembassy.gov; open M-F 9am-5pm).
Rape Crisis Center: The national 24hr helpline can be reached at 1800 77 8888.

- Dublin Rape Crisis Center (70 Leeson St. Lower; 01 661 4911; www.drcc.ie; open M-F 8am-7pm, Sa 9am-4pm).

Hospitals:

- Beaumont Hospital (Beaumont Rd., Beaumont; 01 809 3000; open daily 24hr).
- St. James Hospital (James's St.; 01 410 3000; open daily 24hr).

Pharmacies:

- Hickeys Pharmacy (55 O'Connell St.; 1873 0427; open M-F 8am-10pm, Sa-Su 9am-10pm).

SIGHTS

CULTURE

GUINNESS STOREHOUSE

St. James's Gate; 1 408 4800; www.guinness-storehouse.com; open daily July-Aug 9am-8pm; Sept-June 9:30am-7pm

If you weren't already a Guinness expert from nights at the pub, here's your chance to become a professional. At the heart of the world's largest pint shaped building lies everything you've ever wanted to know about Guinness—and more. Smell the barley roasting; feel the water; see the bubbles. This tour is as close to being inside a beer bottle as you can get. For the full experience, learn how to pour your perfect pint and the best way to drink the beer (yes, this is a thing), samples included (hint: the Guinness-stache is a must). The skybar offers 360-degree views of the whole city, so even if you're not a beer drinker, it's worth it.

i Admission €20, students €18; prices lower if you book in advance; last entry 1hr before closing; wheelchair accessible; free drink with ticket

THE ABBEY THEATRE

26/27 Abbey St. Lower; 1878 7222; www.abbeytheater.ie

The outside of this theater doesn't reveal its special place in Irish literary history, but, in fact, an exhibit at **The Writer's Museum** is devoted to this theater, founded in 1904 by **W.B. Yeats** and **Lady Gregory.** Controversy surrounds the opening of the theater: some works' were banned for supposedly illicit content. Scandalous. Today, the theater sits in a city filled with other performance halls, and they perform a mix of classic Irish plays and new works. But the venue still seeks to bring theater to Ireland, and you should let it by going to see a show. We weren't allowed in, likely because rehearsals were happening, but read up on the history before you see a show to get the full experience.

i Early bird tickets from €10, regular tickets from €25, reduced from €16; wheelchair accessible

GEORGE'S ARCADE

George's St.; ww.georgesstreetarcade.ie; open M-W 9am-6:30pm, Th-Sa 9am-7pm, Su noon-6pm

No city would be complete without a market selling vintage clothes, records, and...artisanal dried fruit? We weren't expecting this, but it's a market, so you're bound to find strange things that you never knew existed (but now desperately need). George's Arcade checks the above boxes and more. Grab a snack and stroll through the covered market, gawking at Irish tourist t-shirts and Italian food stalls. Many of the stalls are closed on Sundays, so your best bet is to avoid peak lunch hours during the week and stop by in the afternoon. Nearby, boutiques like **Om Diva** sit along **Drury Street.** Window-shopping is likely the move here, as these stores tend to be expensive. Some of the vintage shops in the arcade have an occasional steal though, so browse through denim jackets to your heart's content.

i Prices vary, wheelchair accessible

NATIONAL LIBRARY

2/3 Kildare St.; 1 603 2300; www.nli.ie; open M-W 9:30am-7:45pm, Th-F 9:30am-4:45pm, Sa 9:30am-12:45pm

Picture enormous rooms of books and irritable people who shush you when you talk. That could only mean one thing: you're at a library. Home to the largest collection of Irish works in the world, Ireland's National Library stores the literary treasures of many a lifetime. Too bad you can't get past the front desk of the reading room unless you're a registered researcher—which is sad, because the room itself is painted a bright turquoise. You can, however, go in and look, explore the **Yeats** exhibit downstairs, or, if you have any Irish ancestry, you can stop by the family genealogy room to explore your roots. Lockers are available to store bags and coats (which they strictly enforce, so don't try to sneak anything in).

i Free; limited wheelchair accessibility; free lockers

TEMPLE BAR

47/49 Temple Bar; open 24hr

Step into the **Temple Bar** and prepare your ears. Live music rings out in this noisy bar at all hours of the day, and you'll hear more international accents than Irish ones. Temple Bar doesn't draw too many Dublin locals, and is more of a tourist watering hole, but that doesn't mean that you shouldn't at least drop in. Once you tire of the statue-filled beer bar, head out to the rest of the area. Whether you're on a pub crawl or just walking around, explore the nearby pubs and clubs, many of them complete with flowers in the windows and even more live music. You'll always have somewhere to go, and if you get lost, just follow the music (and the tourists).

i Prices vary; limited wheelchair accessibility

LANDMARKS

DUBLIN CASTLE

Dame St.; 1 645 8813; www.dublincastle.ie; open M-Sa 9:45am-4:45pm, Su noon-4:45pm

We'll rip off the bandaid—you won't find princes or princesses in this castle, but you will find gorgeous apartments and the inauguration chambers for each of Ireland's presidents. Basically all of Ireland's history of governance has taken place in this building. You could take a guided tour, but we recommend exploring on your own with the help of the pamphlet they give you. And if you happen to overhear bits of the person leading the guided tour… well… you can't help what your ears hear. Make sure you look up! The intricately decorated ceilings await. While here, you'll also get to see a throne in the middle of a city. While visiting, stop by the **Chester Beatty** library.

i Admission €7, €6 reduced; guided tours €10, €8 reduced; tours roughly every hour; last entry 30min. before closing; wheelchair accessible

CHRISTCHURCH CATHEDRAL

Christchurch Pl.; 1 677 8099; www.christchurchcathedral.ie; open Jan-Feb M-Sa 9:30am-5pm, Su 12:30pm-2:30pm; Mar M-Sa 9:30am-6pm, Su 12:30pm-2:30pm and 4:30-6pm; Apr-Sept M-Sa 9:30am-7pm, Su 12:30pm-2:30pm and 4:30pm-7pm; Oct M-Sa 9:30am-6pm, Su 12:30pm-2pm and 4:30pm-6pm; Nov-Dec M-Sa 9:30am-5pm, Su 12:30pm-2:30pm

At first, Christchurch Cathedral seems like just another church. And then you walk in and realize it is just another church. Except it's a church with hidden features that make it worth exploring despite the price tag. It might not be as impressive as some of the larger European churches at first glance, but you'll have to walk around to fully appreciate the gilded portraits and the history. The cathedral has stood in Dublin for over 1000 years, and its nooks and crannies contain books and small paintings that can be easily overlooked by rushed tourists in a hurry to see the next thing on their must-see list. If you can, take one of the guided tours so you get to explore the crypt (featuring lots of gold plates and some mummified animals). You might as well check out the **Dublinia** next door, where they sell combined tickets.

i Self-guided tour €7, €5.50 reduced; guided tours €11, €9.50 reduced; cash only; tours M-F 11am, 12:10pm, 2pm, 3pm, 4pm; tours Sa 2pm, 3pm, 4pm for €4; last entry 45min. before closing; wheelchair accessibility

GARDEN OF REMEMBRANCE

Parnell Sq. East; 1 821 3021; open daily 8:30am-6pm

Mosaics of rusted weaponry line the bottom of this cross-shaped pool, an ode to a tradition symbolizing the end of battle. This pool acts as a centerpiece for this tranquil garden in the middle of the city. Grassy elevated areas surround the recessed pool in the Garden of Remembrance, an area built to honor those who lost their lives in the 700-year fight for freedom. As this fight ended so recently that Ireland still bears the wounds of battle. Stop by to pause and to reflect, and be sure to check out the statue at the top of the cross depicting the myth of the Children of Lir. When the Queen of England visited Ireland, the first British monarch to do so, she commemorated the men and women who had fought against her own people.

i Free admission; wheelchair accessible

THE SPIRE

O'Connell St.; open daily 24hr

Lost? Look up. If you see a 120-meter (that's almost 400 feet) giant silver shiny needle, congrats! You've found the spire. Built in 2003 after the demolition of Nelson's monument, the spire makes a point (hahaha, get it?) about Ireland's transformation. You can't do anything except look at the big, pointy stick, but it's a pretty cool landmark to get a view of, especially at night. You can even see it from some points across the **River Liffey.** Fitting, as some locals call this baby the "Stiffy on the Liffey." Most likely, your Dublin explorations will bring you past the Spire, but if not, make it a point (gotcha again!) to see it.

i Free; limited wheelchair accessibility

TRINITY COLLEGE

College Green; 1 896 1000; www.tcd.ie; open M-Sa 8:30am-5pm, Su 9:30am-5pm

Elizabeth I—a former Queen of England—founded Trinity college in 1592. Almost 500 years later, the college still holds some of the world's brightest minds. You can walk around on the green and sit, but to go inside, you'll have to take a pricey guided tour. If you do this, you'll get to hear from a living, breathing student, not just an old British man on a radio. It'll also be weird if you're a student yourself—kinda like getting a college tour a few years too late. Probably more compelling, the tour lets you see the **Book of Kells,** an ancient book containing the four Gospels. Time it right and you can check out the cricket team practicing on the field. It's like it's a real school or something! But definitely go inside—otherwise it just feels like a park.

i Free, guided tour and Book of Kells €14, €13 reduced; tours daily every 20min. from 9am-4pm; wheelchair accessible

MUSEUMS

EPIC

CHQ Custom House Quay; 1 906 0861; www.epicchq.com; open daily 10am-6:45pm

If you only have time for one museum during your trip, then this is the one to visit. Once the friendly staffer hands you your "passport," you're free to explore the world of the museum and collect a stamp in each room. If you've ever wanted to learn about the influence of Irish emigrants in every single aspect of your daily life, then you've come to the right place. Irish emigrants developed vaccines, starred in Broadway shows, championed athletic events, and, of course, contributed to drinking culture everywhere. Integrating interactive displays that feel like toys with important messages about Irish culture, EPIC's museum experience is truly epic

i Admission €14, €12 reduced; last entry 5pm; wheelchair accessible

DUBLINIA

St. Michaels Hill; 1 679 4611; www.dublinia.ie; open daily Mar-Sept 10am-6:30pm, Oct-Feb 10am-5:30pm

Ever wanted to know that the Vikings used moss as toilet paper? Neither did we. But you can learn that, and more, at this interactive museum. The first floor teaches visitors about the Vikings, and you can even dress up like a Viking wearing chainmail. Upstairs, you can explore medieval Irish life through lifelike mannequins with leprosy and a scale model of Dublin in 1500. The third floor contains an archaeology lab where you can practice carbon dating. Then head on up to the tower with a view of Dublin. This museum has a little bit of everything, but don't let that deter you. Yeah, this museum's pretty weird, but it's kind of like popping a pimple: there's a lot of gross stuff going on here, and yet, you'll still want to keep going.

i Admission €9.50, €8.50 reduced; last entry 1hr before closing; wheelchair accessible except the tower

NATIONAL GALLERY

Merrion Sq. West; 1 661 5133; www.nationalgallery.ie; open M-W 9:15am-5:30pm, Th 9:15am-8:30pm, F-Sa 9:15am-5:30pm, Su 11am-5:30pm

Almost 700 paintings dating from the fourteenth century to the present fill this museum. Sounds like a lot of art. Which it is, but the layout makes it manageable and even fun to walk through. The building reopened in 2017 after years of refurbishment, and the result is a spacious gallery with lots of light, making it relaxing to explore. Highlights include the Irish Stained Glass exhibit and some of the greats on the third floor like **Rembrandt, Vermeer,** and **Caravaggio.** Since it's around the corner from the **National Museum,** you might as well pop in and leave just a touch more cultured.

i Free; wheelchair accessible

NATIONAL MUSEUM OF IRELAND (NATURAL HISTORY MUSEUM)

Merrion St. Upper; 1 677 744; www.museum.ie/Natural-History; open T-Sa 10am-5pm, Su 2pm-5pm

Taxidermy enthusiasts rejoice! Here you can find two very stuffed (get it?) floors of stuffed animals. Upstairs holds the animals native to Ireland. (Hint: there are a lot of birds and deer.) As you walk through different species of baboons interspersed with opossum babies and other rodents whose names we definitely can't pronounce, you'll marvel at the world's biodiversity and wonder how many species the earth actually has. This museum has occasionally been called the Dead Zoo. (You can imagine why.) Although the specific Dublin connection isn't all that clear, stepping foot inside feels like entering a very climate-confused jungle. Just go with it.

i Free entry; limited wheelchair accessibility

DUBLIN WRITERS MUSEUM

18 Parnell Sq.; 1 872 2077; www.writersmuseum.com; open M-Sa 9:45am-4:45pm, Su 11am-4:30pm

A literary fanatic's heaven, Dublin Writers Museum boasts the history of Ireland's most prolific writers, with artifacts from their lives and panels describing their accomplishment. You're better off coming to this museum if you've already got some interest in literature or poetry—the exhibits aren't particularly interactive as much as they are informative. But hey, when in Dublin, a **UNESCO city of literature,** start cultivating your appreciation for literary greats like **James Joyce, George Bernard Shaw,** and **W.B. Yeats.** Plus, there's a little garden and some grand decorated rooms filled with—you guessed it—books.

i Admission €7.50, €6.30 reduced; last entry 4:15pm; no wheelchair accessibility; free audio guide with entry

OUTDOORS

ST. STEPHENS GREEN

St. Stephen's Green; 1 475 7816; www.ststephensgreenpark.ie; open M-Sa 8am-sunset

Dublin's a busy city—cars honk, people yell, pedestrians go places. But step into this green oasis for a moment's rest, and walk along the outer circle to get a moment of peace—here, the faint murmurs of moving cars get washed out by chirping birds and laughing kids. This park was central to parts of **The Rising,** which you can learn more about by walking around and seeing the statues. Or, you can just look at the statues as you go on a nice long romantic walk. In summer, people picnic in the park until the cops shoo them out at night (Ireland has pretty lax open container laws).

i Free; wheelchair accessible

FOOD

LEO BURDOCK ($)

4 Crown Alley; 1 611 1999; www.leoburdock.com; open M noon-8pm, Tu-W noon-11pm, Th noon-midnight, F-Sa noon-3am, Su noon-midnight

If the sign listing the 100+ celebrities who have dined at the iconic fish and chips shop is any indication, Leo Burdock's is basically a rite of passage. The menu lists only a few options—fish, chips, chicken, and burgers. Fishing and beach gear cover the walls in the back, somehow both touristy and traditional. Burdock's knows they're the best, so they make sure you can read all about their accolades. The price might seem steep until an entire steaming, freshly fried fish and a box of french fries appear before your eyes. And on weekend nights, when the drunchies come calling, Burdocks has your back until 3am.

i Entrées from €7; limited wheelchair accessibility

CORNUCOPIA ($$)

19-20 Wicklow St.; 1 677 7583; www.cornucopia.ie; open M-Sa 8:30am-10pm, Su noon-10pm

Your parents always told you to eat more vegetables. At this charming and quaint restaurant, you can eat your vegetables while feeling like you're at Grandma's kitchen table. Soft floral patterns and light colors provide a super homey atmosphere that can be hard to find while traveling. No Wi-Fi and shared tables complete the farmhouse grandparent and hipster convergence vibe. Vegetarians and vegans: you're in luck. We especially recommend coming for breakfast, because here, the classic Irish breakfast has gotten a makeover. (Veggie sausage anyone?) And meat eaters, you're gonna be alright. The food is so hearty you won't even notice your lack of animal flesh.

i Breakfast from €6, lunch from €9, dinner from €13; gluten-free, vegan, and vegetarian options available; limited wheelchair accessibility

GOOSE ON THE LOOSE ($)

2 Kevin St. Lower; 86 152 9140; open M-F 8:30am-5pm, Sa-Su 9am-5pm

Step inside and come face to face with a goose in goggles, hanging from the ceiling, standing between you and a kitchen that perfectly mastered the art of crêpe-making. Locals frequent this all-day breakfast joint, so you know this place is onto something. Close to **St. Stephen's Green,** you can start your day with a hefty (and not crazily priced) omelette—or a Nutella and ice cream crêpe (if we're being honest) then head over to the park for a nice walk. We've just planned the perfect date. You're welcome.

i Entrées from €4; gluten-free and vegetarian options available; limited wheelchair accessibility;

NOLITA ($$)

64 South Great George St.; 01 478 1590; www.nolita.ie; open M-Th noon-11:30pm, F-Sa noon-2:30am, Su noon-11:00pm

If you're seeking something hip and trendy (Would hip and trendy people use those words? We're not sure.) look no further than NoLIta. This New York-inspired restaurant and bar will make you feel like you're on *Gossip Girl.* Except in Dublin, not the Upper East Side. Anyway, the cocktails are amazing. And if you don't see something you like, ask away—the bartenders know their way around the liquor cabinet. Later at night on the weekends when they stop serving food, the place gets a lot clubbier. The pasta portions are shockingly huge for a nice place, so leave room for the cheesy goodness. Upstairs you can chill in charming-yet-cool garden and discuss how elegant you are now.

i Entrées from €14, cocktails from €11, drinks from €5.50; cash only; limited wheelchair accessibility

POG ($$)

32 Bachelors Walk; 1 878 3255; www.ifancypog.ie; open M-F 8am-5pm, Sa 9am-5pm, Su 10am-5pm

Crowded and bright, Pog's all-day brunch creates healthier versions of your favorite breakfast foods with a vegan focus. And everything is perfectly plated—in fact, the whole restaurant is adorable. The millennial pink plates contrast Insta-perfectly with the floor's turquoise tiles. Their vegan fruit plate draws eyes and cameras from the restaurant-goers. Don't worry about other people judging you: you gotta do what you gotta do for that #fire pic. If you've got a bit of a sweet tooth, the protein pancakes come with your choice of toppings ranging from Nutella to berries to white chocolate chips. The description on the menu doesn't include how awesome the design-your-own pancakes are, so you're gonna have to trust us. Or stick with the green eggs (no ham) and call it a day.

i Entrées from €9, smoothies from €5; vegan and vegetarian options available; limited wheelchair accessibility; sharing tables 40min. max during peak hours

NIGHTLIFE

P.MAC'S

30 Stephen St. Lower; 1 405 3653; open M-Th noon-midnight, F-Sa noon-1am, Su noon-11:30am

The place is on fire—both literally and figuratively. Here, you'll find red candles dripping wax all over the tables (be careful not to leave the candelabras too close to the walls…trust us). Metaphorically, P'Macs combines weird decorations, board games, vaguely metal music, and a killer selection of craft beers to become the kind of place where last call actually makes you sad. They serve a grapefruit beer (one of many varieties) and have an arcade game on the way to the bathroom. It's hard to categorize the vibe, but it's not your typical stuffy pub full of old men drinking Guinness. Instead, you might find a hotel guest snacking away at the bar, mingling with a group of musicians, and pondering the beer choices. It's eclectic in the best way possible.

i No cover, draughts from €7; BGLTQ+ friendly; wheelchair accessible

DICEY'S GARDEN CLUB

21-25 Harcourt St.; 1 478 4841; www.russellcourthotel.ie/diceys-garden; open M-Sa 4:30pm-2am

Want to hit the dance floor to club remixes of your favorite 40 songs (read: the top 40 hits)? Oh, do we have just the place for you. Dicey's ridiculous drink specials that change daily and (tbh) killer pop tunes make it a fun place to dance and get rowdy. You likely won't meet your future spouse here, but you can still meet people if you dance in the courtyard or order food from the grill. One thing to note: the bouncers really don't play. But as long as you don't show up smashed (that's what Tuesday's €1.50 pints and jagerbombs are for) and don't try and bring your drink into the bathroom, you should be all set. Some people report being able to get around the age limit. (Whether you want to try for yourself is up to you.)

i Cover €10, daily drink specials from €2, cocktails from €8; limited wheelchair accessibility; Su-Th age 20+ only, Sa age 21+ only

37 DAWSON STREET

37 Dawson St.; 1 902 2908; www.37dawsonstreet.ie; open M noon-11:30pm, T-Su noon-3am

When you walk in to the whiskey bar, you will immediately come face-to-face with a life-size sparkly zebra. Seems legit. Random but luxurious decorations adorn the walls and seating areas, including enormous anatomical posters, neon lights (#trendy), and lamps shaped like dogs. It somehow all blends together to feel like a cool-kids-only club—except their age limit is usually 23 and up. So it's a cool-twentieskids-only club? On some weekends, the back lounge opens up for only the most elite, but if you can sweet talk your way in, you'll find an intimate, dark space where every detail has been thought through, and though it's hard to explain why, the pieces just fit.

i Pints from €6; cash only; BGLTQ+ friendly; wheelchair accessible; age 23+ some nights

THE HAIRY LEMON

41-42 Stephen St. Lower; 1 671 8949; www.thehairylemon.ie; open M-Th 11:30am-11:30pm, F-Sa 11:30am-1:30am, Su noon-11pm

There's no shortage of pubs to choose from in this city—if you threw a Guinness can at a random wall, you'd likely hit one (but don't do that). There's a reason The Hairy Lemon is filled with locals and packed tables, and it's not the appetizing name. For one, the Teelings whiskey taster lets you sample all your favorite whiskeys, if you can even tell the difference. The outdoor garden and smoking area also draw people to the bar. Mostly, the real attraction is the relaxed atmosphere where you can watch the game, have a meal, and sip on a pint in a true Irish pub.

i Drinks from €6; no wheelchair accessibility; live music Sunday nights

GALWAY

Coverage by **Lucy Golub**

People sometimes call Galway the graveyard of ambition, a moniker locals hold near and dear. The true meaning of the phrase isn't as morbid as you think it is, though. It actually means that people intend to come for a little while, but often end up staying. Rain or shine, Galway sucks you in and holds you captive. There's not much to do or that much to see, but, for some reason, visiting makes you want to stay forever. Only those who commit themselves to exploring this enchanting town the way those who live there do can understand why everyone seems so freaking happy. After a few nights at the pub with live music singing "Piano Man" with a group of strangers and a day "sparching" like the locals by the Spanish arch, you'll slowly fall in love with Galway. You might not notice it happen. But just wait. Soon when you look at the colorful facades of the very short Long Walk, you'll feel your heart swell just a touch and you'll know that Galway part of you now.

ORIENTATION

The River Corrib splits the city. On the east of the river, you'll find the **Latin Quarter, Eyre Square,** and most of the tourist accommodations. To the West, the aptly-named **West End** calls your name with its low-key restaurants and pubs. Along the river, a lovely walk takes you to the **Galway Cathedral,** past the university. If you ever get lost, just find **Galway Bay** to lead you back to the **Spanish Arch,** the beginning of **The Latin Quarter** and site of the **Galway City Museum.** The entire city is within reach of the river, though, because it's all so small.

ESSENTIALS

GETTING THERE

You can fly into nearby Shannon Airport or Knock Airport, but Dublin Airport is also an option. From each airport, take an easy bus transfer via Bus Eireann (from Shannon or Knock) or goBus or citylink (Dublin). You can pay on board, but the best fares come from booking early. Buses run at least once an hour and often every 30min. Galway Coach Station is a few steps from the center of the city.

GETTING AROUND

Galway is a walkable city. The center is made up of a few easy-to-navigate streets. Otherwise, a bus service called Bus Eireann runs between Eyre Square and Salthill and other areas of Galway. Fares are between €2 and €3 depending on distance, and all day tickets can be purchased for €4.70.

PRACTICAL INFORMATION

Tourist Offices: The Galway Tourist Office (Forster St.; 09 153 7700; www.galwaytourism.ie; open M-Sa 9am-5pm)

Banks/ATMs/Currency Exchange: Here is a conveniently located bank: AIB ATM (18 Eyre Sq.; open 24hr).

Post Offices: An Post (3 Eglington St.; 09 153 4727; www.anpost.ie; open M-Sa 9am-5:30pm).

Public Restrooms: Here is a conveniently located restroom: (Eyre Sq.; open 24hr).

Internet: Most restaurants and cafes have Wi-Fi. Banks and other public spaces have available Wi-Fi networks that are easy to find.

BGLTQ+ Resources: Teach Solais LGBT+ Resource Center (Victoria Pl.; www.amachlgbt.com; open W 6pm-9pm, Sat 2pm-4pm); helpline at 1890 929 539.

EMERGENCY INFORMATION

Emergency Number: 999.
Police: Galway Garda Station (Mill St.; 09 153 8000; www.garda.ie).
Rape Crisis Center: Galway Rape Crisis Center (Forster Ct.; 09 156 4800; www.galwayrcc.org); helpline available 80 035 5355 (call M-F 10am-1pm).
Hospitals:

- University Hospital (Newcastle Rd; 091 524 222; open daily 24hr).

Pharmacies: Galway doesn't have any 24hr pharmacies.

- University Late Night Pharmacy (1-2 University Halls; 09 152 0115; open M-F 9am-9pm, Sat 9am-6:30pm, Su noon-6pm).
- Walsh's Pharmacy (Corrib Shopping Centre; 09 156 1605; open M-W 9am-6pm Th-F 9am-8pm, Sat 9am-6pm, Sun 11am-6pm).

SIGHTS

CULTURE

LATIN QUARTER

www.thelatinquarter.ie; neighborhood open daily 24hr; store hours vary

So we'll just get this out of the way: the Latin Quarter isn't Latin. It is, however, adorable. Old-fashioned pubs crop up between coffee shops, claddagh jewelers, tourist trap-y souvenir shops, and upscale boutiques. You won't find too many locals spending time with the musicians playing guitar in the street singing "Galway Girl" or Irish dancing. But at night, the area comes alive when throngs of people descend on the area to pub-hop in search of the best live music. Yes, it's super touristy, but if you embrace it you'll enjoy it.

i Establishent prices vary

ATHENRY ANTIQUES

Sheehan House, Church St.; 086 600 8886; www.athentryantiques.ie; open T-Sa 10am-6pm

Yeah, we know, antiques can be boring. But this store's not. Come in to explore old rugs, vaguely creepy dolls, and memorabilia from World War I, including postcards sent bearing the SS seal. The woman who runs the shop has been there for 12 years, and her stories alone are reason enough to enter the store. The old photos and antique lighters in the back room, however, are relics of another time. When you step across the store's threshold, the smell of old books snakes up your nostrils and transports you to the past. Embrace it.

i Prices vary

CHARLIE BYRNE'S BOOKSHOP

Cornstone Mall, Middle St.; 9 156 1766; www.charliebyrne.com; open M-Sa 9am-6pm, Su noon-6pm

Entering this massive bookshop could go one of two ways: you might feel enlightened by the thousands of books surrounding you, including Irish greats like **George Bernard Shaw** and **W. B. Yeats**. Or you might feel like you're barely literate as you browse through Irish history sections detailing events and historical figures you probably haven't heard of. Either way, it's easy to get lost in the stacks of books, some of them even spilling off shelves and tables. If you're not sure what you want to read, check out the recommendation section towards the front. You might just leave with your new favorite novel.

i Book prices vary

LANDMARKS

SPANISH ARCH

2 The Long Walk; open daily 24hr

This arch is the last remaining part of a medieval wall, built in 1270, that once circled around the city. It's neither big nor tall, but it reminds you of Galway's history—torn down and suppressed yet still standing. The Spanish Arch label, according to the locals, also extends to the nearby grassy areas along the **River Corrib,** and gets truncated to "Sparch." Sparching is a local tradition dating back hundreds of years which entails drinking (non-alcoholic beverages, of course) on the grass on a nice day. So, clearly, the Spanish Arch holds history both old and new.

i Free; wheelchair accessible

EYRE SQUARE

Eyre Sq.; open daily 24hr

The official name for the park is **Kennedy Park** due to JFK's visit to Galway in 1963. That was 50 years ago but okay, sure. Next to the park, a large rusty sculpture that supposedly looks like the Galway Hooker (a fishing boat, obviously), stands along your way to the **Latin Quarter.** In summer, you can't miss the bubble man, who dips ropes in soap to make giant bubbles that pop around the flags representing the 14 Galway Tribes, the families who contributed to the city's beginnings. Even when the weather is cooler people still congregate at this central point to walk their dogs, grab a pint at a bar, or just pass through.

i Free; limited wheelchair accessibility

GALWAY CATHEDRAL

River Corrib West Bank; www.galwaycathedral.ie; open daily 8:30am-6:30pm

This cathedral's marble floors and enormous walls forming the shape of a cross around a central marble pew almost make you forget that this church was built in the 60s. And by the 60s, we mean the 1960s, not the 1560s. In case you forget what time period you're in, the circular mosaic portrait of former president **John F. Kennedy** on the wall in the side chapel, next to a larger-than-life mosaic of Jesus' resurrection, will remind you. While the church isn't old, it is a beautiful work of architecture, and as music wafts from the speakers mounted on the walls, you can explore the wall panels explaining the church's history.

i Free; wheelchair accessible; services held weekdays 9am, 11am, 6pm and Sun 9am, 10am, 11am, 12:30pm, 6pm

MUSEUMS

GALWAY CITY MUSEUM

Spanish Parade; 9 153 2460; www.galwaycitymuseum.ie; open T-Sa 10am-5pm; open Easter Sunday to Sept Su noon-5pm

Picture this: you're hanging out by the **Spanish Arch** and it starts to rain. You could go back home and get in bed, or you could pop into this free museum to learn about the history of Galway, Scottish fishing, the Galway Hooker, and marine biology. It's a slightly odd combination, you got us there, but you might as well peruse the museum's three floors. Some artifacts of note include those lying in the glass cabinets at the center of each room. The panels along the wall explain oft-forgotten history like the **Irish Civil War.** For a history junkie, you'll find lots of things to explore. For someone looking for a game, check out the interactive submarine simulation upstairs. Thank us later.

i Free; wheelchair accessible

FOOD

THE PIE MAKER ($)

10 Cross St. Upper; 9 151 3151; www.thepiemaker.ie; open daily 11:30am-10pm

Apple pie? Yum. Banoffee Pie? Yesss. Slow braised beef and eight degree stout pie? Yes—trust us on this one. This shop sells one type of food: Pies. And they're fantastic. Savory pies can be ordered with either classic mash and mushy peas, or (for the health conscious) a salad. But if you're eating at a pie place, we're not really sure that you're in the right place for a healthy meal. Regardless, the flaky crust and flavorful combination of ingredients make this classic Irish food a must-visit. The restaurant is tiny, surrounding you with the smell of freshly baked pies while random mirrors and candelabras emphasize just how quirky the store is.

i Sweet pies from €5, savory pies from €13; vegan and vegetarian options; wheelchair accessible

DELA ($)

51 Lower Dominick St.; 9 144 9252; www.dela.ie; open M-Th 11:30am-3pm and 6pm-10pm, F-Sa 10am-3pm and 6pm-10pm, Su 10am-4pm and 6pm-10pm

On every wood table in this airy and plant-decorated restaurant, there's a pamphlet advertising their **polytunnel,** aka a huge plastic tube in which the owners grow all their produce. So you know that this restaurant's food is super fresh. It also tastes delicious, and with extensive brunch hours, you can't come to Galway and not brunch here. The hashtag written on every chalkboard is #notallbrunchesarecreatedequal and we'd have to agree, because this meal was one of the best. The Butterscotch pancakes are to die for, as is the adorable farm-house type aesthetic.

i Entrées from €9; vegan and vegetarian options available; wheelchair accessible

THE DOUGH BROS ($)

1 Middle St.; 087 176 1662; open M noon-9pm, Tu-Sat noon-10pm, Sun noon-9pm

The Dough Bros started out as a food truck, and the counter at the back of the restaurant makes sure you don't forget it. A floral arch adorns the door, and a long line of hungry people greets you on the inside. This pizza is absolutely worth the wait if you want something like the Hail Caesar pizza. Cheaper than Domino's (for real) and freshly wood-fired, their pizza begs to be devoured. You can watch the dough being mixed in the machine in the open-air kitchen, in case you want to torture yourself while you starve waiting for your pizza. The expert technique of the cooks is something to admire, too.

i Pizza from €6; gluten-free, vegan, and vegetarian options available; wheelchair accessible

TUCO'S TAQUERIA ($)

6 Abbeygate St. Upper; 09 156 3925; www.tuco.ie; open daily noon-10pm

When people think of Irish cuisine, Mexican food usually doesn't come to mind. Tuco's Taqueria might change the game. They use Irish-style meats like pork and sirloin steak in their concoctions. We'd recommend Tuco's as a casual dinner between the first and second pub visits of the evening...and you can get a beer at Tuco's too. So, if you really can't go a few days without a burrito, Tucos has your answer. They also serve "boxes," which are like a typical burrito bowl—but artsier. We don't judge. There's more seating upstairs in this tiny taco joint.

i Entrées from €6.95; vegetarian options available; wheelchair accessible

NIGHTLIFE

O'CONNELL'S

8 Eyre Sq.; 9 156 3634; www.oconnellsbar-galway.com; open M-Th 10:30am-11:30pm, F-Sa 10:30am-12:30am, Su 12:30pm-11pm

Imagine a fancy pub combined with an outdoor beer garden that looks like its own small street full of other mini-pubs, and another bar outside open on the weekends. Add a pizza truck run by the owners of **The Dough Boys,** walls of whiskey and gin options, and nooks and crannies filled with glass displays of vintage toothpaste containers, cereal boxes, mice poison, and an old phone booth. Then you'll have begun to touch upon the treasure chest that is O'Connell's. With rooms connected by passageways, this bar is worth a visit just to take it all in. Add a classic whiskey ginger, get a little tipsy, and it might just feel like a magica cave of gold.

i Spirits from €6; BGLTQ+ friendly; limited wheelchair accessibility

THE QUAYS

11 Quay St.; 9 156 8347; open M-Sat 10:30am-2:30am, Su noon-midnight

The Quays (pronounced KEYS) is the giant pub you'll end up at at the end of the night, singing along to the live band from one of the three bars inside. They've got a restaurant as well, but we'd recommend coming after dinner for the drinks and atmosphere. In between pints, take a look around—and not just at the rowdy Irish football fans yelling at each other. The stone walls, stained glass and instruments on the wall give off a medieval vibe that doesn't seem like it would work with the glowing dance floor and alternative covers of "Hey Jude," but hey, it does.

i Beer from €5, spirit mixers from €7; BGLTQ+ friendly; limited wheelchair accessibility

ROISIN DUBH

9 Dominick St.; 9 158 6540; www.roisin-dubh.net; open M-Su 5pm-2am depending on concert

It feels like it takes years to walk to this venue, but it's really only a 10-minute walk from the center of the **Latin Quarter.** Named after a centuries-old Irish song, it's only fitting that the bar hosts concerts almost nightly, as well as a silent disco on Tuesdays and stand up comedy. When the weather's nice, the rooftop patio offers a reprieve from the noise, even though it's still super packed, ensuring you won't escape the people. The gigs range from up-and-coming bands to more obscure artists like Ed Sheeran. Maybe you've heard of him?

i Concert ticket prices vary, open mic nights free, silent disco €5; limited wheelchair accessibility

IRELAND ESSENTIALS

VISAS

Citizens of Australia, Canada, New Zealand, and the US do not need visas to visit the Republic of Ireland for up to three months. Note that the Republic of Ireland is not a signatory of the Schengen Agreement, which means it is not part of the freedom of movement zone that covers most of the EU. Accordingly, non-EU citizens can visit Ireland without eating into the 90-day limit on travel in the Schengen area, but will be subject to border controls on entry.

Citizens from the aforementioned countries do not need visas for long-term study or work in the Republic of Ireland, although they must have proof that they are enrolled in a course or proof of employment, apply for permission to stay, and register with immigration authorities upon arrival. For more information on this, consult www.inis.gov.ie.

MONEY

Tipping: Ireland does not have a strong tipping culture. In sit-down restaurants, there may be a service charge already figured into the bill. If not, you can tip 10-15 percent. In bars, tipping is not expected and even looked down upon. Tipping taxi drivers is also not expected, although it's standard to round up to the nearest euro. Hairdressers are generally tipped 10 percent.

Taxes: The Republic of Ireland had a standard 23 percent value added tax (VAT), although some good are subject to a lower rate of 13 percent. Northern Ireland shares the United Kingdom's 20 percent VAT. The prices in *Let's Go* include VAT unless otherwise noted.

SAFETY AND HEALTH

Drugs and Alcohol: Ireland is a land famed for its beer and pub culture, so it's not surprising that alcohol is a common presence in the county. The legal drinking age is 18 in both the Republic of Ireland and Northern Ireland, and this is more strictly enforced in urban areas. Both regions regulate the possession of recreational drugs, with penalties ranging from a warning to lengthy prison sentences. In the Republic, possession of cannabis can result in a quite hefty fine, and repeated offenses can result in imprisonment. Check the Great Britain chapter for more detailed information on drug laws in Northern Ireland.

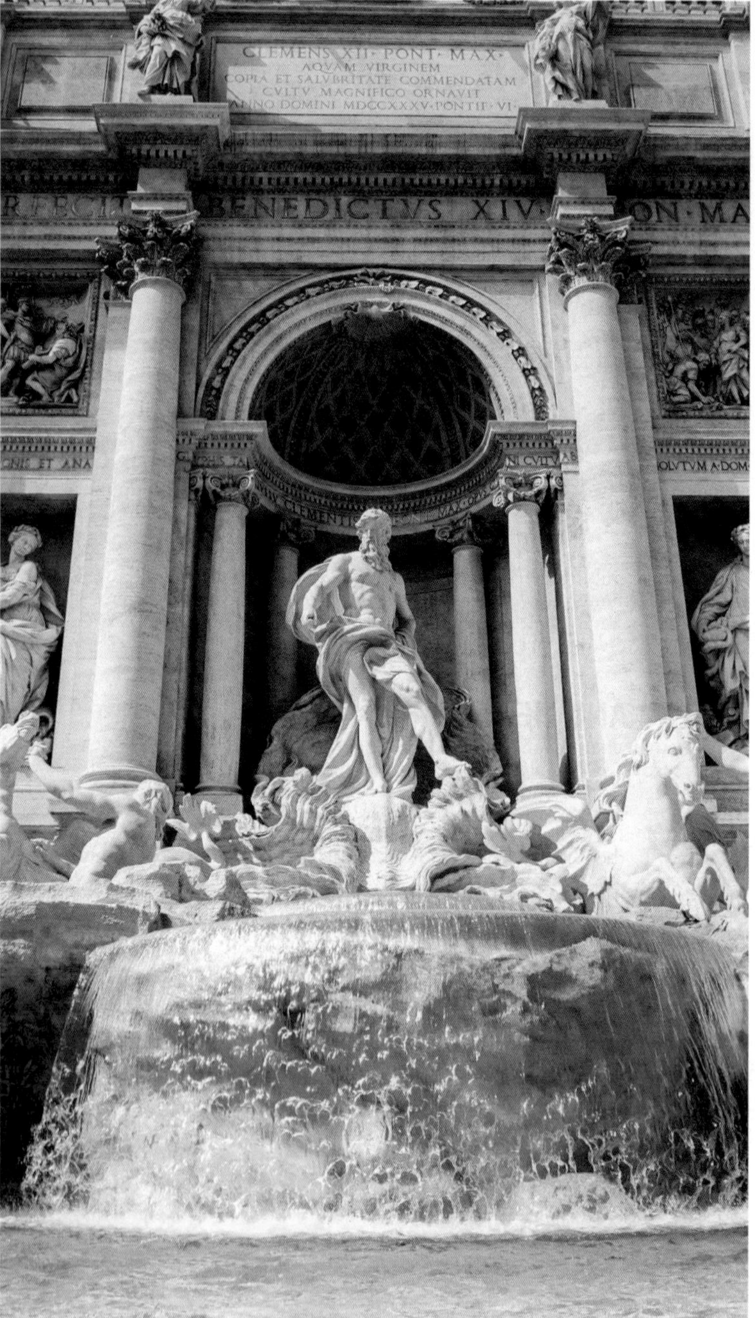
CLEMENS XII · PONT · MAX ·
AQVAM VIRGINEM
COPIA ET SALVBRITATE COMMENDATAM
CVLTV MAGNIFICO ORNAVIT
ANNO DOMINI MDCCXXXV · PONTIF · VI ·
BENEDICTVS XIV ·

ITALY

If in pursuit of some *Eat Pray Love* soul-searching, you will almost always find yourself in Italy. Anything describing the good life can be found in this Mediterranean boot, including some really good boots. Good art? Check. From Michelangelo to Raphael and da Vinci, Dante to Puccini and Vivaldi, the greatest feats of artistic, architectural, and intellectual creation have come from Italy. Good food? Check. Pasta and pizza are staples around the globe, and amazing wine comes out of every Italian region.

In Italy, man's creation, God's creation, and some mix of the two awe and inspire like no other. The sun kisses the beaches of the south and the lush rolling hillsides of Tuscany. Pastel-colored houses stand majestically on the cliffs of Cinque Terre, canals weave through the islands of Venice, and every city has a cathedral or two with soaring arches aiming for the heavens. Italy, of course, is not just one big tourist destination, although sometimes it can seem that way. Real people inhabit this paradise, and the more time you spend here, the more you can point out some special qualities.

To be Italian means almost intrinsically to be a gastronome: an appreciator of good food and ever better wine. Most importantly, to be Italian means to have a deep rooted passion for a few specific things, be it their work, their family, or their football team. This riveting passion pulses through Italy, fueling the fire that has shaped the land of pasta and spritz that we know and treasure today.

CINQUE TERRE

Coverage by **Margaret Canady**

So you've made it to Cinque Terre—we'd personally like to welcome you to paradise. Cinque Terre (pronounced cheen-kway tehr-ray) is a cluster of five villages with some strikingly beautiful commonalities. The villages were built on the precipice of the Ligurian Sea, the homes and terraces sculpted out of the jagged coastline. The houses are pastel-hued; something about the burst of color paired with the fact that their creation seems impossible on this steep terrain leaves visitors stupefied and reaching for their cameras. And boy, are there a lot of cameras. While Cinque Terre sees about 2.4 million visitors a year, only about 4000 people live in all five cities combined. It has become an international tourist destination, and it can be overwhelming, especially during the summer season. This, of course, should not derail you from the villages, but rather should inspire you to give back to the city and invest in it. For the best views and least people, take the time to hike anywhere uphill—the crowds disappear within minutes. When you go into a restaurant or shop, strike up a conversation with the shop owner, and ask them to tell you about their village. We promise you'll love the city a little bit more if you do.

ORIENTATION

Cinque Terre is a 15-kilometer stretch of five villages located on the **Ligurian Sea.** The villages, from north to south, are as follows: **Monterosso, Vernazza, Corniglia, Manarola,** and **Riomaggiore.** Each village is small, with only one or two main roads and several side streets that are easy to navigate.

ESSENTIALS

GETTING THERE

The closest airport is Pisa International Airport, located about 87km south of the villages. The best way to access Cinque Terre is by train. You first have to take a train to either La Spezia Centrale or Levanto. With these two stations as endpoints, the Cinque Terre Express runs between the five villages. Cars are not allowed in most areas of the villages. Paid parking lots are available in La Spezia and Levanto. Both La Spezia and Levanto can be reached by highways A12.

GETTING AROUND

The train is the most convenient way of getting between cities and only takes about 3-5min. between each village. Trains runs very frequently and are reliable, averaging about 2 per hour both ways. One-way tickets cost €4 each. Visitors can also hike between the cities. There are several trails, some of which run along the coast, and some which run up behind the villages. It can take anywhere from 1-3hr to hike between cities. The sole means of traveling within a city is by walking. There are inner city shuttles that can transport passengers up and down the steep mountains. The villages offer day passes, which give you unlimited access to the trains, hiking trails, shuttles, restrooms, and station Wi-Fi. See the tourist center for more details.

PRACTICAL INFORMATION

Tourist Offices: There is a tourist office in every village. Here are two:

- Riomaggiore Tourist Information Office (P. Rio Finale, 26; 01 87 92 06 33; www.parconazionale5terre.it; open daily 8am-7:30pm)
- Monterosso Tourist Information Office (Monterosso Train Station; 01 87 81 70 59; www.parconazionale-5terre.it; open daily 8am-7:30pm)

Banks/ATMs/Currency Exchange: There are ATMs in every village. Avoid the mobile ATMs near the train station since they have higher bank fees.

Post Offices: There is a post office in each village. Here are two:

- Riomaggiore Post Office (V. Pecunia, 7; 01 87 92 01 21; www.poste.it; open M-F 8:15am-1:45pm, Sa 8:15am-12:45pm)
- Manarola Post Office (V. Discovolo, 216; 01 87 92 01 98; www.poste.it; open M-F 8:15am-1:45pm, Sa 8:15am-12:45pm)

Public Restrooms: There are public bathrooms at each of the train stations, they cost €1 or are free with the purchase of a Cinque Terre pass.
Internet: There is Wi-Fi at each of the train stations, but can only be accessed with the purchase of a Cinque Terre pass. Many restaurants have Wi-Fi.
BGLTQ+ Resources: The closest physical resource is located in Pisa at Pinkriot Arcigay Pisa (V. Enrico Fermi, 7; 05 02 32 78; pinkriot.arcigaypisa.it; open Th 6-10pm).

EMERGENCY INFORMATION

Emergency Number: 112
Police: 113. The phone number for Monterosso Town Hall Police is 0187 817525.
US Embassy: The nearest US consulate is located in Florence (Lungarno Vespucci 38; 0 55 26 69 51; it.usembassy.gov/embassy-consulates/florence). The nearest US embassy is located in Rome (V. Vittorio Veneto 121; 3 90 64 67 41; it.usembassy.gov/embassy-consulates/rome).
Rape Crisis Center: Telefono Rosa, based in Rome, provides support and resources at telefonorosa.it as well as a help line at 06 37 51 82 82.
Hospitals:

- Sestri Levante Hospital: (V. Terzi Arnaldo, 37, Sestri Levante; 01 85 48 81; www.comune.sestri-levante.ge.it/polo-ospedaliero-di-sestri-levante; open daily 24hr).

Pharmacies: There is a pharmacy located in each village. Here is one in Monterosso: (Via Fegina, 42; 01 87 81 83 91; open daily 9am-7pm).

SIGHTS

CULTURE

IL PRESEPE DI MANAROLA (THE NATIVITY SCENE OF MANAROLA)

Collina delle Tre Croci, Manarola; cinqueterre.a-turist.com/presepe; 34 73 36 91 87; open early Dec-late Jan daily

When we visited Cinque Terre in the summer, every night we would gaze up at a single house on the **Manarola** mountainside that featured a Nativity scene, the white neon shining bright in the darkness. Christmas in summer, we thought. Exciting! Now, if you can, imagine dozens of nativity scenes lighting up the night sky. Every winter, almost every house on the iconic Manarola skyline features a nativity scene of their own to celebrate the holiday season. Baby Jesuses, angels, and Marys seem to float in the darkness. Santa Claus must have an easy job finding Manarola.

i Free; wheelchair accessible

SAGRA DEI LIMONI (MONTEROSSO LEMON FESTIVAL)

Monterosso; 34 77 70 37 18; www.cinqueterre.eu.com/en/monterosso; usually the 3rd weekend of May (lemon season dependent)

When life gives you lemons, make an endless supply of lemon desserts and call it Sagra dei Limoni. Every year **Monterosso** holds Cinque Terre's Lemon Festival, a weekend-long celebration in May that celebrates the village's famous fruit. If you make it here on this weekend, be prepared to be engulfed in a sea of yellow and to indulge in as much citrus dessert as your heart desires. Locals create desserts such as lemon cake, lemon cream pie, lemon marmalade, and limoncino. Pucker up!

i Free admission, product prices vary; limited wheelchair accessibility

LANDMARKS

CASTELLO DORIA

V. San Francesco, Vernazza; 01 87 81 25 46; www.tellaroitaly.com/castello_doria_vernazza.html; open daily 10am-9pm

Remember when you were seven and your treehouse was a fortress, and your backyard your kingdom? Castello

Doria is like a real-life fortress amid the kingdom of your dreams. The oldest edifice in Cinque Terre and originally part of a castle from the twelfth century, the tower offers arguably some of the best views in the entire area. You get a panoramic view of the ocean touching the horizon, an aerial view of the city of **Vernazza,** and glimpses of **Monterosso** and **Corniglia** among the mountains.

i Admission €1.50; cash only; last entry 8:45pm; no wheelchair accessibility

VERNAZZA

2km south of Monterosso al Mare

Continuing with our analogy, Vernazza is the homecoming queen at Cinque Terre High. Vernazza is the only village with a **natural port,** and many argue that it is the most picturesque of the villages. The main roads are wide so it feels less crowded than some of the other villages, and the **hiking trails** and **Castello Doria** offer fantastic views of the city.

i Wheelchair accessible

CONVENTO DEI CAPPUCCINI E CHIESA DI SAN FRANCESCO (CHURCH OF SAN FRANCESCO AND CAPUCHIN FRIARS MONASTERY)

Salita San Cristoforo, Monterosso; 01 87 81 75 31; www.conventomonterosso.it

A quick climb out of **Monterosso** and suddenly you're transported to a serene world of trails, trees, and the sacred world of the Capuchin Friars. The church and monastery overlook **Monterosso Bay** and offer an unparalleled view. If you're lucky, you'll be able to hear the Gregorian chants echo through the valley. Past the monastery, you can find Monterosso cemetery decorated with fresh flowers and lit candles. It's an experience like no other.

i Free; no wheelchair accessibility

CORNIGLIA

1km south of Vernazza

Corniglia is the forgotten middle child of Cinque Terre. Located smack dab in the middle of the other five villages, it is sadly overlooked by many. Corniglia is the smallest village and is not located on the coast, so when you exit the train station there is an 382-step ascent into the village. Because Corniglia scares away a lot of visitors, it is less hectic and cheaper than its flatter neighbors.

i Limited wheelchair accessibility

MANAROLA

1km south of Corniglia

Manarola is like your rich aunt who has an impeccable sense of fashion and lives in a perfectly-decorated apartment. We might be biased because our hostel was in Manarola, but we think the village offers the best views in Cinque Terre. The **Manarola Overlook** gives you a perfect and unobstructed view of the city at any time of the day, and during sunset you can see the sun pass behind the mountains, perfectly framed by the sea. The city is very clean and empties out as soon as the sun sets.

i Limited wheelchair accessibility

MONTEROSSO AL MARE

Northern-most of the five villages

When we asked the tourist information center about museums, they looked at us incredulously and replied, "There are no museums in Cinque Terre." One simply does not go to Cinque Terre to spend time indoors, let alone in a museum. Monterosso is the quarterback of the football team. The largest of the villages, Monterosso has the most restaurants, hotels, and shops for visitors, as well as the most beaches. The village is probably the most walkable, too, with smooth paved roads that are more horizontal than vertical. It's ideal for families and people who want to pay for beach chairs.

i Wheelchair accessible

RIOMAGGIORE

0.5km south of Manarola

Last but not least, there's Riomaggiore, the little kid next door who kind of reminds you of the Tasmanian Devil. The village is always bustling, with a constant stream of people coming in from docked cruise ships and the train station (it's the first stop after La Spezia). It's easy to lose the crowd, though: climb through the smaller streets to reach better viewpoints and significantly fewer people. Some daredevils like to climb on the rock jetty that runs parallel to the city and offers a great view, but we're not entirely sure if that's legal.

Limited wheelchair accessibility

SANTUARIO NOSTRA SIGNORA DI SOVIORE (SANCTUARY OF OUR LADY OF SOVIORE)

Localita Soviore, Monterosso; 01 87 81 73 85; www.santuariodisoviore.it

This listing comes with a word of warning: getting to the sanctuary from Cinque Terre is no walk on the beach. The hike from Monterosso to the oldest sanctuary in Cinque Terre is about an hour long, completely uphill, and consists almost entirely of narrow paths and uneven stone. When you get there, prepare to be amazed. You'll be met by an unobstructed view of the entire valley that cradles Monterosso. Unforuntely, when we made the trek up, it was a rainy Saturday morning and fog obstructed our view, but we were greeted by choral singing coming from the sanctuary for Sunday mass.

Free; wheelchair accessible if driving up the mountain; respectable clothing required in the sanctuary; café located on hilltop

OUTDOORS

HIKING CINQUE TERRE: THE BLUE PATH

0 10 16 89 01 11; www.cinqueterre.it/en/content/il-sentiero-azzurro-n2;

For centuries, this path was the only road between the villages. Today it is most popular of the hiking trails, and the Blue Path is a very manageable journey, the large majority of which is relatively horizontal. The path offers stunning views of the coastline and glimpses of the villages as you walk closer. You'll walk through vineyards and wildflowers, and it's not one of those boring hikes—your eyes, ears, and nose will be taking in the fresh mountain air, the gorgeous ocean views, and the sweet smell of wildflowers. We recommend going early in the day to beat the heat and the other hikers. Check with the tourist office to see if any sections of the trail are closed due to safety or repair.

Admission €7.50 a day or included in Cinque Terre pass; no wheelchair accessibility

HIKING CINQUE TERRE: SENTIERO DEL CRINALE (THE HIGH PATH)

010 16 89 01 11; www.cinqueterre.it/en/content/sentiero-del-crinale-n%C2%B0-1

High above the cities lies the High Path, the hiking path for #hardcore hikers and backpackers. Now, we're not saying you can't or shouldn't hike this path, but if you think your weekly hour-long yoga class has prepared you for this hike, you're wrong. The path is meant for advanced hikers, and has narrower and steeper sections. It's also over 40 kilometers and the walking time is something between 10-12 hours. If you conquer the path, though, you can look down (literally) upon all the weaklings taking the easy Blue Path.

Free; no wheelchair accessibility; check tourist center for information about safety and hazards

FOOD

LA CANTINA DELLO ZIO BRAMANTE

V. Renato Birolli, 110, Manarola; 01 87 92 04 42; open M-W 10am-1am, F-Su 10am-1am

Not everything has to be fancy-schmancy to be a restaurant in Cinque Terre. La Cantina dello Zio Bramante is a late night place to grab a drink and some food, and its chill vibes welcome any and all. They have a live musician most evenings, and when we went,

the guy had an affinity for playing the harmonica, which is always a plus in our book. They have some fun and cheap bruschetta options, and as you eat you'll be rubbing elbows with the people next to ya, so you might as well strike up a conversation.

i Entrées from €7, bruschetta from €4; limited wheelchair accessibility

IL PESCATO CUCINATO ($)

V. Colombo 199, Riomaggiore; 33 92 62 48 15; website; open daily 11:30am-7:30pm

Eating seafood in Cinque Terre is a definite must, but you don't have to break the bank to experience local cuisine. Il Pescato Cucinato is a takeaway shop in **Riomaggiore** that serves fried fish, calamari, and fried veggies in convenient cones, which are deceptively large but miraculously inexpensive. The takeaway option allows you to eat fried anchovies with one hand, take a picture of the cone with the other, and attempt to walk around without running into anyone. We never figured out how to fit the tartar sauce on the rest of the cone, unfortunately.

i Small seafood cone from €6, large from €8; wheelchair accessible; benches available outside

LUNCHBOX ($)

V. Roma 34, Vernazza; 33 89 08 28 41; open M-Th, Sa-Su 7am-9pm

LunchBox knows exactly what the people want and what they arguably need: perceived free choice and the perfect amount of guidelines. It's a delicious option for takeaway lunch or dinner, with a wide variety of paninis and freshly-made juices available. They give you the option to create your own juices and sandwiches—you can add anything and everything, but 95% of people end up choosing from the suggested menu. Sometimes indecisiveness can be a delicious thing.

i Juices from €4, paninis from €4.50; gluten-free, vegan, and vegetarian options available; limited wheelchair accessibility; Wi-Fi

AGRICULTURAL COOPERATIVE SOCIETY 5 TERRE

All villages, locations vary; 01 87 92 04 35; www.cantinacinqueterre.com/en; open M-Sa 8am-7pm, Su 9am-12:30pm and 2:30-7pm

Many of the sit-down restaurants in Cinque Terre are somewhat expensive and catered towards tourists who are just looking to make it rain. We, of course, are always ballin' on a budget, and the best way to save money is to go to the good ol' grocery store. You'll find a co-op in every village, and they offer a variety of snacks, dry pastas, cheap wines, and cheese/meats that you can take home.

i Prices vary; vegan and vegetarian options available; limited wheelchair accessibility

IL GIGANTE BEACH BAR ($)

V. Fegina, 138, Monterosso; 33 83 39 60 36; open daily 8:30am-7:30pm

Il Gigante could charge twice as much as they currently do and probably still get the same amount of business, but lucky for us, they don't. Located right on the beach, they offer a variety of sandwiches for the hungry beachgoer. I got a salmon and avocado sandwich for only €4.50. Salmon and avocado? At any American restaurant, that would cost at least $14 and your first-born child.

i Sandwiches from €4.50; gluten-free and vegetarian options available; wheelchair accessible

PIZZERIA LA CAMBUSA DI ZAMPOLLI MATIA ALFIO

V. Renato Birolli, 114, Manarola; 01 87 92 10 29; open M-F 7:30am-1pm and 5-8pm, Sa-Su 7:30am-8:00pm

By now you've probably noticed a trend: we reccomend a lot of takeaway places, partly because we didn't want to pay for the high prices of sit down restaurants geared towards tourists, but partly because we also wanted to indulge in the view for as much of our time as possible. Pizzeria La Cambusa Di Zampolli offers up fat slices of focaccia with a variety of toppings, heated up and ready to take away.

i Takeaway €4; cash only; no wheelchair accessibility

NIGHTLIFE

BLUE MARLIN BAR AND CAFÉ

V. Roma, 61, Vernazza; 01 87 81 22 07; open M-Tu 7:30am-midnight, Th-Su 7:30am-midnight

The first thing the bartender asked us when we said hello was "What was the name of Michael J. Fox in *Back to the Future*?" Our frantic response, "Um, Marty McFly?" We wondered if this was some sort of secret Italian game show or something. "Ahhhh, yes!" he exclaimed, and went to tell his coworker in the back. It was a weird encounter, but we ended up staying since Blue Marlin is a low-key bar that attracts people of all ages. Its open patio and easy access to the train station makes it popular by location for passersby and regulars alike. They also do takeaway, so we took our drink to watch the sunset in **Vernazza.** They make a damn good margarita, too.

i Cocktails from €6, focaccia from €8; BGLTQ+ friendly; wheelchair accessible

IL PORTICCIOLO

V. Renato Birolli, 96, Manarola; 01 87 92 00 83; www.ilporticciolo5terre.it; open M-Tu noon-10pm, Th-Su noon-10pm

Every time we walked by, we heard live music and young people laughing and talking over drinks and tapas. When we finally went in, the bartender warmly greeted us and offered us tapas and drinks immediately. Il Porticciolo puts a good amount of effort into its décor, and the effort definitely pays off: exposed rock and walls the color of white sand mix with slow-fading colorful lights. Pretty awesome prices match the aesthetic. FOMO, you've been replaced with €5 cocktails.

i Cocktails from €5, beer and wine from €3.50; wheelchair accessible

FLORENCE

Coverage by **Margaret Canady**

Stendhal Syndrome was named after a French author who visited Florence and promptly went into an ecstatic frenzy, overwhelmed at the city's sheer existence. While his heart palpitations may have actually been sunstroke, we can't help but agree: Florence is undeniably breathtaking. Nearly a third of the world's art treasures reside in this ageless city, and Florence has been called home by some of the most influential minds and artists of human history. Da Vinci, Michelangelo, Brunelleschi, Dante, Raphael, and countless others once walked the same streets you'll find yourself wandering down. There's something simply indescribable about the magic of the city: the way the sun sets perfectly on the Arno, the terracotta buildings fill the gaps between churches, and even the clouds. (They're just prettier here.) Florence is no well-kept secret, of course, and it's safe to assume thousands of people daily (especially in the summer) try to grasp a little bit of Florentine magic as well. If you can dodge and weave through the tour groups, Florence can become your city, too—you just won't get a disorder named after you.

ORIENTATION

Florence is the capital of the region of Tuscany. The city is built on the **Arno River,** with most of the city's landmarks and population found north of the river. **Piazza del Duomo** is the most central square and home to the impressive **Cattedrale di Santa Maria del Fiore.** Northeast of the Piazza is **Mercato Centrale, Basilica di Santa Maria Novella,** and **Santa Maria Novella Train Station.** To the north of the Piazza by several blocks is **Galleria dell'Accademia,** and further north are many of the city's hostels. South of the the Piazza lies remnants of the **Roman grid system,** as well as landmarks such as **Piazza della Signoria, Galleria degli Uffizi,** and finally the Arno. **Over the Ponte Vecchio** and across the river lie the expansive **Boboli Gardens.** East of the gardens is the popular lookout point **Piazzale Michelangelo.**

ESSENTIALS

GETTING THERE

It is relatively easy to get to Florence because of its large size. Florence is served by two airports: Vespucci Airport, the international airport of Florence, and the Pisa International Airport, which is larger but farther away. There are shuttles that run from the airports to Florence's Santa Maria Novella Train Station (Pisa €14, 70min.; Florence €6, 20min.). The city is also a central stop on the Italian train system; a train from Rome is only an 1.5hr away and 2hr from Venice. The train station is centrally located with the city. If arriving by car, highway A1 runs north-south in Italy and has four exits into Florence.

GETTING AROUND

Walking is the suggested mode of transportation in Florence. Most of the things you'll be seeing and doing in the city are usually under a 30min. walk away, but if you're trying to get from one corner of the city to the other, it will take you about 1hr. Bikes are available around the city for rent from Florence By Bike. The city center is a Limited Traffic Access Zone, and cars cannot pass unless they have a permit. Part of Florence's public transportation system is called "Le City Line de Firenze," a series of 4 bus lines that run around the city center. Single-ride 90min. tickets are €1.20, 4 tickets are €4.70; make sure to validate your tickets on board. In late 2018, three new tramway lines will open, linking the airport, the hospital and the central railway station, and main tourist attractions.

PRACTICAL INFORMATION

Tourist Offices: There are four tourist offices. One is by the train station (P. Della Stazione, 4; 0 55 21 22 45; www.firenzeturismo.it/en; open M-Sa 9am-7pm, Su 9am-2pm) and one near P. del Duomo (P. S. Giovanni, 1; 0 55 28 84 96; www.firenzeturismo.it/en; open M-Sa 9am-7pm, Su 9am-2pm).

Banks/ATMs/Currency Exchange: There are ATMs found on many street corners. We were particularly fond of a currency exchange that has no extra fees: Change Exchange Marco Alunno (V. della Ninna, 9; 0 55 21 76 11; open M-Sa 8:15am-7pm, Su 8:15am-6:30pm).

Post Offices: Poste Italiane (V. Pellicceria 3; 05 52 73 64 81).

Public Restrooms: Public restrooms can be found throughout the city near landmarks. They cost €1. The Duomo location is Piazza San Giovanni, 7.

Internet: Almost all cafés have Wi-Fi. The city also offers Wi-Fi in many popular plazas.

BGLTQ+ Resources: Azione Gay e Lesbica (V. Pisana, 32; 37 13 76 17 38; www.azionegayelesbica.it).

EMERGENCY INFORMATION

Emergency Number: 112

Police: Emergency police number 113. Here is a police station: Commissariato di Polizia S. Giovanni (V. Pietrapiana, 50r; 0 55 20 39 11; open M-F 8am-2pm).

US Embassy: Florence houses the US consulate (Lungarno Vespucci 38; 39 05 52 66 951; it.usembassy.gov/embassy-consulates/florence). The nearest US embassy is located in Rome (V. Vittorio Veneto 121; 39 06 46741; it.usembassy.gov/embassy-consulates/rome).

Rape Crisis Center: RAINN; 20 25 01 44 44.

Hospitals: For an ambulance or in case of a medical emergency, dial 118.

- Hospital of Santa Maria Nuova (P. Santa Maria Nuova, 1; 05 56 93 81; www.asf.toscana.it; open daily 24hr).

Pharmacies: There are many pharmacies located throughout the city. Look for the green plus sign. Here are two:

- Farmaceutica di Santa Maria Novella (V. della Scala, 16; 0 55 21 62 76; http://www.smnovella.com; open daily 9am-8pm).
- All'Insegna del Moro Pharmacy (P. di San Giovanni, 20r; 0 55 21 13 43; www.farmaciadelmoro.com/en; open daily 8am-midnight).

SIGHTS

CULTURE

MERCATO CENTRALE (CENTRAL MARKET)

P. del Mercato Centrale, V. dell'Ariento; 05 52 39 97 98; www.mercatocentrale.it; open daily 8am-midnight

Finally, we've found a place to buy your I Love Italia shirts, organic mushrooms, and artisanal pizza all at one quick convenient stop. If you couldn't tell by the name, Mercato Centrale is the **largest market in Florence,** but unfortunately only seems to attract tourists. Outside, the building's perimeter is surrounded by stand after stand of leather goods, which means you'll get an incredible sense of déjà-vu if you walk around long enough. On the first floor of the industrial-esque building are produce stands and meat or seafood vendors, as well as take-away food shops. Upstairs kinda reminded us of Whole Foods: chefs at artisanal restaurants serve their creations, and there's a large seating area for eating. It's a great place to buy a quick trinket and sandwich.

i Free; wheelchair accessible; Wi-Fi

PONTE VECCHIO

Ponte Vecchio; open daily 24hr

No postcard of the **Arno River** would be complete without the Ponte Vecchio smack-dab in the middle. The oldest bridge in Florence has always been a hub for merchants, and today is no different: you'll find an odd combination of cheap souvenir vendors and high-end jewelry stores here. A decent number of tourists take their picture with the iconic three arches found at the middle of the bridge, which is nice and all, but you want to see the bridge in your photos, right? The best place to snap your shot is from the next bridge over, right of the Ponte Vecchio.

i Free crossing; wheelchair accessible; establishment hours vary

CHIANTI WINE TOUR

www.chianti.com/wine/chianti-winetasting.html; tours daily

Every region in Italy produces its own wine, and it's simply a necessity to try the local variety (which, undoubtedly, locals will say is the best in Italy). The region of Florence and Siena produce *chianti,* a fruity red wine that, of course, gets better with age. *Chianti* is available at every restaurant, but the best way to develop your wine palate is to go on a wine tour, which are not as expensive as one may expect. Done right, you can taste the wine of local producers, and get a glimpse of some incredible views too. It's definitely not the least grimy activity you'll ever do (the Tuscan roads were made for horses, not tour buses), but sometimes it pays to be a tourist.

i Guided tours from €49; wheelchair accessible; tour company prices vary

MERCATO SANT'AMBROGIO

P. Lorenzo Ghiberti; 05 52 34 39 50; www.mercatosantambrogio.it; open M-Sa 7am-2pm

If **Mercato Centrale** is six notches too high for your tastes or you're sick of seeing the same five leather purses, Mercato Sant'Ambrogio will more likely suit your fancy. The market is tucked away in the **Santa Croce** neighborhood, and the language of the signs, like the people who visit, are Italian. Next door is **Mercatino delle Pulci,** an antique market that has "Italian grandma" written all over it. The tourists haven't found it yet, so try to keep this gem a secret, yeah?

i Stand prices vary; wheelchair accessible

TEATRO DEL SALE

V. dei Macci, 111 r; 05 52 00 14 92; www.teatrodelsale.com; open Tu-Sa 11am-3pm and 7:30pm-11pm, Su 11am-3pm

A members-only club for wining, dining, and watching performances sounds like the type of party we normal folk usually aren't invited to, but Teatro del Sale is different. An annual membership is welcome to anyone for only €7, and while the dinners are a tad expensive (€35), you're being treated to unlimited food prepared daily by Florentine chef Fabio Picchi (co-owner and creator of the theater with his wife Maria Cassi), as well as nightly performances.

Membership €7, dinner from €35, lunch from €15; wheelchair accessible

LANDMARKS

BASILICA DI SAN LORENZO

P. di San Lorenzo, 9; www.operamediceal aurenziana.org/en/home-2; open Mar 1-Oct 31 M-Sa 10am-5:30pm, Su 1:30pm-5:30pm; open Nov 1-Feb 28 M-Sa 10am-5:30pm

If you're reading this, here's a fun fact about churches: Renaissance architecture was designed with man at the center of importance: he used reason, math, and geometry to design churches and show off his intelligence. Basilica di San Lorenzo is an incredible example of this fun fact. The Medicis were members (and donors, *and* leaders) of the church, and all of the leading characters in the Medici family are buried here. Another fun fact: underneath the church lies a secret room where Michelangelo went into hiding for a couple of months and sketched on the walls of the room. You'll have to take our word for it; you can't go into the room, unfortunately (we tried, but apparently our status as "Best Travel Guide in the Universe" isn't sufficient).

Admission €6, with library €8.50

BASILICA DI SANTA TRINITA

P. di Santa Trinita; 0 55 21 69 12; www.diocesifirenze.it; open daily 7am-noon and 4pm-7pm

Nestled between outposts of Valentino and Dior quietly lies Basilica di Santa Trinita, a 900 year-old church. Repent for your shopping sins by stepping a foot in and taking a quick breather. Built in the Gothic style, the church features a large number of frescoes (most of which are faded, unfortunately), and offers access to its crypt. Basilica di Santa Trinita is quiet and free, in cost and from shoe temptations.

Free; wheelchair accessible

PIAZZALE MICHELANGELO

Piazzale Michelangelo; open daily 24hr

To get to Piazzale Michelangelo, you have to cross the **Arno,** head uphill, walk up some steps, stop for breath, walk up some more steps, and then you're there. (Note: "some steps" is actually, like, a lot of steps.) You can thank us for the Charley horse and the incredible view when you get to the top. From there, you'll see the entire city of Florence, and there is perhaps no better place to watch the sunset. Maybe it's the view, or maybe it's the Spanish guitar playing softly in the background, but the lookout makes us want to pull our lovers close. Make sure you and your lover head up there early, though—it can be hard to get a spot on the edge to see the sunset.

Free; wheelchair accessible with bus

BASILICA SAN MINIATO AL MONTE

V. delle Porte Sante, 34; 05 52 34 27 31; www.sanminiatoalmonte.it; open M-Sa 9:30am-1pm and 3pm-7pm or 7:30pm, Su 8:15am-7pm or 7:30pm

Sometimes, at the right place at the right time, the spirit of religion graces the presence of these dead churches; one lively one makes up for 50 boring churches. Basilica San Miniato al Monte is a special one, and one of our personal favorites in Florence. Next to door to **Piazzale Michelangelo,** the church will get you panting (or praying) as you hike up the steps, but it's so worth it. Sitting on the side of a hill overlooking the city and the Arno, a stunning church face will greet you. Although you can technically talk while inside, we recommend suppressing the urge for speech in favor of taking in the church's majesty. The basilica celebrated its 1000th birthday in 2018, which means it's basically still in its infancy.

i Free; limited wheelchair accessibility

PIAZZA DEL DUOMO

P. del Duomo; 05 52 30 28 85; www.museumflorence.com; open daily 24hr

Let's not judge a city by its church, but if we did that for Florence, we wouldn't be disappointed. Piazza del Duomo is the hub of the city, the center of the historic district, and the main attraction for literally everyone in the world, it seems. At least three monuments find their home in the Piazza, each one complementary to the others. **Cathedral Santa Maria del Fiore,** the third-largest church in the world, reigns large with its intricate facade, topped by Brunelleschi's octagonal Dome. Next to the Cathedral are the **Baptistry of San Giovanni** and **Giotto's Bell Tower.** All three are clad in swirls of olive green and pastel pink, which (somehow) go together.

i Piazza free; cathedral, baptistry and bell tower package ticket €18; limited wheelchair accessibility; reservations required to climb the Dome; monument hours vary

SANTA MARIA NOVELLA

P. di Santa Maria Novella, 18; 0 55 21 92 57; www.smn.it/en; open M-Th 9am-7pm, F 11am-7pm, Sa 9am-6:30pm, Su noon-6:30pm

Here's another fun fact about churches: the back of your neck starts getting pretty strong if you look up at enough arches and ceilings. Santa Maria Novella has everything you'd expect from a church: high arches striped with black-and-white stone, important works of Renaissance art, a really big cross with our main man Jesus. This church features a stunning rose-gold altar, and the facade is simple but elegant. The church sits in a wide plaza that has surprisingly few people, but a lot of good shops and restaurants nearby to explore.

i Admission €7.50; last entry 45min. before closing; wheelchair accessible

MUSEUMS

GALLERIA DELL'ACCADEMIA

V. Ricasoli, 58/60; 05 52 38 86 09; www.galleriaaccademiafirenze.beniculturali.it; open Tu-Su 8:15am-6:50pm

Ok, we know we said there's a lot of must-sees in Florence, but this one is a serious must. The museum is home to Michelangelo's *David,* and no picture can do the sculpture justice. It's hard to look away from the 17ft giant-slayer, who stands with his weight in his right hip and a #beastmode pose. You can walk completely around *David,* and make sure to take some time to soak up every little detail, from the bulging veins in his hands to his knee muscles and his incredibly ripped physique. We thought V-lines were a myth, but holy Old Testament, *David* is ripped. Besides the bod, the museum is actually pretty small and you'll breeze through it. Take some time to look at the Michelangelo's unfinished sculptures that lead to *David;* they provide an insight into the process of the artist's mind and technique

i Admission €8, advance tickets €12; audio guide €6; last entrance 6:40pm; wheelchair accessible; reservations highly recommended

LE GALLERIE DEGLI UFFIZI (UFFIZI GALLERY)

Piazzale degli Uffizi, 6; 05 52 38 85; www.uffizi.it/en/the-uffizi; open Tu-Su 8:15am-6:50pm

Brush up on your art history at one of best museums in Italy. The Uffizi Gallery used to be the Medici's private gallery (we know, who would've guessed it?), and now is the most popular museum in Florence, if not Italy. Two levels of long U-shaped hallways are filled with full-figure statues and busts, and the long views and checkered floor are beautiful enough to be worth the visit. Attached to the hallways are rooms chock-full of magnificent works from magnificent men (food for thought, name a Renaissance woman who isn't nude). **Botticelli's *Birth of Venus*** and **da Vinci's *The Baptism of Christ*** and ***Adoration of the Magi*** are fan favorites. Make sure to spend a couple of hours here in order to get the full experience, and make sure not to miss anything.

High season admission €20, low season €12; high season advance ticket €24, low season €16; last entry 6:35pm; wheelchair accessible; reservation recommended; free entrance on first Su of every month

MUSEO FERRAGAMO (SALVATORE FERRAGAMO MUSEUM)

Palazzo Spini Feroni, P. di Santa Trinita, 5/R; 05 53 56 28 46; https://www.ferragamo.com/museo/it/ita; open daily 10am-7:30pm

If shoes are your best friends, then you'll find new friends here at Museo Ferragamo. Found underneath the original headquarters of international shoe designer **Salvatore Ferragamo,** the museum celebrates his work and other avenues of Italian fashion. Ferragamo lived in California for more than 15 years, and was sought after by the glamour actors and actresses of the 1920s for the perfect shoe. After strolling through his original shoe designs and a rotating exhibit, you'll exit through the gift shop—or in this case, a high end retail store that will attempt to sell you shoes more expensive than your trip to Europe.

Admission €2; free admission first Su of every month

PALAZZO STROZZI

P. degli Strozzi; 05 52 64 51 55; www.palazzostrozzi.org; courtyard open daily 8am-11pm

In a shocking turn of events, it turns out there is a museum in Florence that isn't Renaissance art- or Jesus-related, and that museum is Palazzo Strozzi. Run by an independent foundation of public and private donors, this Renaissance palace is home to a rotating schedule of temporary contemporary art exhibits. Recent works include Italian modern art that paralleled the divided nation in the twentieth century, as well as an interactive experiment testing the hypothesis if plants feel emotion. Hint: it involves you, a two-story slide, and a plant.

Admission price varies based on exhibition; wheelchair accessible

MUSEO NAZIONALE DEL BARGELLO (BARGELLO MUSEUM)

V. del Proconsolo 4; 05 52 38 86 06; www.bargellomusei.beniculturali.it; open daily 8:15am-5pm (closed 2nd and 4th Su, 1st, 3rd, and 5th M)

Often, the sheer amount of old stuff in Florence and Italy can numb you to how cool everything actually is, to the point where you can't help but wonder why this museum is also important. Bargello Museum reads that way too, especially because it isn't as frequently-visited as some of its Florentine counterparts. The history of this Medieval palace is interesting, though: meetings attended by Dante of the Council of One Hundred occurred here, and at one point it was a prison with executions held in the striking courtyard. The museums holds a variety of Renaissance bronzes, enamels, and ceramics, and a couple of Michelangelo's works are here too. It's a gentle warm-up for bigger museums to come.

Admission €8, €6 reduced; audio guides €6; last entrance 4:20pm; wheelchair accessible

OUTDOORS

BOBOLI GARDENS

P. Pitti, 1; 05 52 29 87 32; www.uffizi.it/en/boboli-garden; open daily Nov-Feb 8:15am-4:30pm, Mar 8:15am-5:30pm (6:30pm after daylight savings), Apr-May 8:15am-6:30pm, June-Aug 8:15am-6:50pm, Sept-Oct 8:15am-6:30pm

Across the river, you'll find the Medicis' private gardens, and, like everything else owned by the family, the question is never "go big or go home," it's "go big because the entire city is your home." The gardens are 111 acres of curated beauty. Your wanderings may take you by the lemon gardens, through greenery and rolling hills, past a host of sculptures, and to the **Fountain of Neptune.** The hike up the hill is worth it for a view of **Pitti Palace** and the city. We can only imagine a couple of the Medicis lounging in their garden, surveying the city they literally owned and built.

Admission €10; last entry 1hr before closing; limited wheelchair accessibility (enter from Pitti Square or Porta Romana Square); free ticket on the first Su of each month

BARDINI GARDEN

Costa S. Giorgio, 2; 055 20 06 62 33; www.villabardini.it; open daily Nov-Feb 8:15am-4:30pm, Mar 8:15am-5:30pm, Apr-May 8:15am-6:30pm, June-Aug 8:15am-7:30pm, Sept-Oct 8:15am-6:30pm

Adjacent to the **Boboli Gardens** is the Bardini Garden, which may arguably have the best views of the city—even better than **Piazzale del Michelangelo.** Somehow, the majority of tourists haven't caught wind of this garden, and its smaller size makes it a perfect escape from the bustling streets. The garden is found along a steep hill, but the trail is very relaxed. The outlook, with its sweeping views of the city, also has a restaurant and café, so you can soak up the silence and beauty for a little bit. Make sure to walk down the vine- and flower-covered archway: it's simply perfect.

i Admission €10, €5 reduced, admission included with Boboli Garden ticket; last entry 1hr before closing; limited wheelchair accessibility; closed first and last M of each month

FOOD

ALL'ANTICO VINAIO ($)

V. dei Neri, 74/R; 05 52 38 27 23; www.allanticovinaio.com/en; open Su-F 10:30am-10pm

All'Antico Vinaio has our vote for best panini in Florence, and is a contestant for the best in Italy. They don't skimp on any ingredient that makes up their eight-item menu. For a summer special, they cut a third of a loaf of thick, soft bread, sliced half a ripe tomat and an entire mozzarella ball, sploped on a generous handful of basil leaves, and topped it off with several thick slices of ham. The bad news is that this is no hidden gem, and on any given summer day you'll find all three (!) of their locations have a line at least 30 minutes long. Go for and early lunch or a late dinner if you don't want anything to do with lines that require you to stand in the sun.

i Paninis from €5; cash only; wheelchair accessible

ANTICA TRIPPERIA NERBONE (DA NERBONE) ($)

Mercato Centrale, 1st floor; 0 55 21 99 49; open M-Sa 8am-2pm

Cows have four stomachs, and da Nerbone makes sure no stomachs are forgotten. The traditional market stand has been serving Florence and **Mercato Centrale** since 1872, and it doesn't look like much has changed since then. The menu is in Italian, but basically the options are a variation on how many ways they can cook different parts and types of meat. Their most popular dish is *panini con bollito,* a boiled-beef sandwich dunked in the meat's juices. Da Nerbone's peak hours are during lunch, and the line can get pretty long, but do it for the beef.

i Sandwiches from €4, pastas from €6; cash only; wheelchair accessible

OSTERIA PASTELLA ($$$)

V. della Scala, 17/r; 05 52 67 02 40; www.osteriapastella.it; open daily noon-2:30pm and 7pm-10:30pm

You don't know what you're missing until you've watched pasta be made before your very eyes, only to have it land on your plate within seconds. Osteria Pastella, along with its handmade pasta and fancy interpretations of Italian classics, provides a type of entertainment to its hungry customers and passerby. A chef in the window kneads dough and cuts slices of pasta to order, and if you order the pasta flambé, the pasta is prepared and flamed on a Grana Padano wheel right at your table. The difference in taste is astounding, and it was hard for me to eat other pasta dishes again.

i Pasta from €14, entrées from €18; reservations recommended; vegan and vegetarian options available; wheelchair accessible

CERNACCHINO ($)

V. della Condotta 38R; 0 55 29 41 19; open M-Sa 9:30am-7:30pm

Cernacchino was one of the only places in Italy we visited that used mustard on their paninis, and for that (and more) we are ever so grateful. The restaurant is small but cozy, and if you decide to sit at one of their tables, you'll be rubbing elbows with locals and travelers alike. The choose-your-pasta plates are nothing to write home about, but they make a mean panini—large slices of crunchy bread, thick slabs of meat, and a wide selection at a low cost make it the perfect pit stop for lunch.

i Paninis from €5, entrées from €6; wheelchair accessible

DIM SUM ($$)

V. dei Neri, 37/r; 0 55 28 43 31; www.dimsumrestaurant.it; open T-Su noon-3pm and 7pm-11pm

If your body spontaneously shut down at the mere thought of another pasta or pizza dish, perhaps it's time for a change. No need to leave Italy, though; check out Dim Sum, which, if you can believe it, serves classic Chinese cuisine along with other Asian dishes. The dim is made fresh for sum (we know, sorry) delicious dining, and, with the restaurant's free unlimited green tea, hot oil, and soy sauce, your palate will be invigorated and your body hopefully ready for more pasta, round #324.

i Dim sum from €4 (3pcs), noodles from €8, stir-fry from €10; vegetarian options available; wheelchair accessible

FOODY FARM ($)

Corso dei Tintori, 10/R; 0 55 24 23 27; www.foodyfarm.it/en; open daily 11am-2pm

Farmhouse chic décor plus organic and locally produced food? No, this isn't a new Brooklyn pop-up shop, but Foody Farm in Florence, a farm-to-table restaurant with fantastically fair fares. The restaurant works with about 10 farms in Tuscany to bring you fresh, local ingredients, and it really makes the difference. Their menu boasts food from the "pasture, barnyard, farmyard, garden, and granary," and it can be hard to know what to choose. Luckily, there are half portions, which is perfect for trying different things, sharing with friends, and being kind to your wallet.

i Entrées from €6; vegetarian options available; wheelchair accessible

VIVOLI ($)

V. dell'Isola delle Stinche, 7r; 0 55 29 23 34; ivoli.it/en/home-2; open Tu-Sa 7:30am-midnight, Su 9am-midnight

If we could marry a business, we would get hitched to Vivoli's. Boasting the title of the **oldest gelateria in Florence,** it quite possibly might also be the best. Each batch of gelato is made fresh daily in the "laboratory" next door, and flavors alternate depending on which fruit and ingredients are available. There are no cones, but the portions are large for what you get. The gelato is thick, not overwhelmingly sweet, and absolutely perfect. Try rice gelato with pistachio or *nocciola,* and we promise that you too will hear wedding bells.

i Gelato from €2; cash only; dairy-free options available; wheelchair accessible

NIGHTLIFE

KING GRIZZLY PUB

P. de Cimatori, 5; 32 87 75 63 21; open daily noon-2am

King Grizzly Pub screams toxic masculinity. I mean, come on, the name is King Grizzly, wooden kegs are used as décor, and beer is the unanimously-chosen drink of choice. Walking in, we were expecting to be unimpressed, or even judged, but were pleasantly surprised. The bartenders are welcoming, and the weekend DJ plays good music. At one point, all the guys at the bar started dancing, and since the pub is located on a bustling piazza corner, passerby would often come in and out to dance or watch from the sidelines. You can't help but relax and smile here, and the casual atmosphere makes it welcome for anyone. So, come in, it's just boys being people.

i Drinks from €4; wheelchair accessible

MAYDAY CLUB

V. Dante Alighieri, 16; 05 52 38 12 90; www.maydayclub.it/english.html; open Tu-W 7pm-2am, Th 8pm-2am, F-Sa 7pm-2am

Perusal of Mayday's website is quite the read, seemingly coming straight out a script for a romantic novel. But at this luxury bar, your long-lost lover is not a pirate or an Italian man on a horse, but an artisanal cocktail, concocted from ingredients and liqueurs you've probably never even of heard of. The bartenders are called alchemists with a passion for "chemistry, botany, perfumery, and food science," and after all this hype, our (high) expectations were properly met. The drinks are strong but complex, which is more than we can say for a lot of ex-lovers, so maybe Mayday is our true love.

i Cocktails from €8; cash only; wheelchair accessible

THE FIDDLER'S ELBOW

P. di Santa Maria Novella, 7R; 0 55 21 50 56; www.thefiddlerselbow.com/fiddlers_florence/florence_eng/welcome.htm; open daily 11am-2am

A local Florentine described The Fiddler's Elbow as a place for expats and American transplants, so we had to check it out. It opened in 1990 and is now known as the first Irish pub in Florence, so it's exactly what you would expect: lots of Guinness, Irish accents, and a mix of chatting groups. The outdoor seating has a great view of **Santa Maria Novella,** and it's a good place to go with a group of people.

i Food from €4, drinks from €3.50; limited wheelchair accessibility

RED GARTER

V. de' Benci, 33/r; 05 52 48 09 09; www.redgarter1962.com; open M-Sa 4pm-4am, Su 11:30am-4pm

Take a college party and replace the red solo cups with real glasses and you've got yourself Red Garter. They boast that they're Italy's oldest American bar, which basically translates to getting American teens drunk in Italy since 1962. A raised stage features karaoke and a bunch of drunk sorority girls definitely not singing the right lyrics. There's also a restaurant adjacent to the bar where you can sit and watch American football or real football. Overall, if you're in the mood to get a little sloshy, the Red Garter is the place to do it. They'll call you a taxi when you're ready to go home, be it 10pm or 3:59am, and the nice security guards outside will help you in it. (Some may call them escorts, but tomato, tomahto.)

i Cocktails from €8; wheelchair accessible

SE•STO ON ARNO ROOFTOP BAR

P. Ognissanti, 3 (6th floor of The Westin Excelsior); 05 52 71 51; www.sestoonarno.com; open daily noon-2am

When you open *Let's Go's* imaginary wallet, the only thing you're gonna find in it is a couple of euros and maybe a moth, so reviewing SE•STO is something out of the ordinary. But this rooftop bar is something spectacular, and it combines our two favorite things: great drinks and incredible views. From the luxury of this hotel bar/restaurant (read: plush sofa couches, waiters in white suits, chandelier lighting), you get an unbeatable view of the entire city of Florence, and you can watch the sun set over the Tuscan mountains. As the color and light changes the city and landscape, sunsets will seem to be made from pure magic—or maybe that's just the artisan cocktail talking. Drinks are going to cost you a pretty penny, but it's one of those experiences you can't forgo.

i Drinks from €15, minimum €25 per person between 7pm-9pm; wheelchair accessible; walk-in only for bar, dinner reservations required

MILAN

Coverage by **Joseph Winters**

If you accidentally packed those green velvet Prada sandals with the hand-embellished sequins instead of the calf leather Bottega Veneta ones with the intrecciato borders that you meant to grab, you'll probably be able to buy a new pair once you get to Milan. Industry, particularly fashion, lives side-by-side with history here, and the dynamic duo will permeate every part of your touristic experience. Go about your day, casually sightseeing your way from the grandeur of the fourteenth century Duomo to other marvels of the Renaissance, like Da Vinci's *The Last Supper.* At any point, look up and *voilà*—chances are, you'll be face-to-face with another ultra-fancy boutique. Just be sure to save some money for the real cultural experiences: a night of *aperitivos* (appetizers and tapas), creative cocktails, and the hottest beats in one of Milan's famous nightclubs.

ORIENTATION

Milan is roughly circular; it spreads outwards from the center, where most of the historic sites are located, like the **Duomo, Galleria Vittorio Emanuele II,** and **Teatro alla Scala.** Beyond those, there are many broad *piazzas* (plazas), each bringing a defining characteristic to their neighborhood. The most popular neighborhoods are **Brera, Centrale, Isola,** and **Navigli.** Isola is renowned for alternative culture, Navigli for nightlife, and Brera for high-end shopping. To get the full Milanese experience, we'd recommend spending at least a day in the historic **Duomo and Castello district,** then picking out a couple areas to really delve into for the remainder of your stay.

ESSENTIALS

GETTING THERE

Milan has two international airports: Malpensa Airport (MXP) and Linate Airport (LIN). The former carries more flights from areas outside of Europe while the latter mostly handles domestic and international flights within Europe. You can also take the train into Milan, docking at Milano Centrale. The station receives trains from both MXP and LIN every 20-30min. and from cities such as Florence, Geneva, Paris, Nice, and Rome. It also has connections to Milan's metro system. Bus operators such as Ouibus also serve Milan, docking at the Autostradale Viaggi Lampugnano Coach Station.

GETTING AROUND

The metro will be your ever-faithful best friend in Milan. Tickets are €1.50 per ride within the urban city limits (you probably won't do much outside in the "hinterlands"—as the information sign calls it—anyway), but the best deals are either a 24hr or 48hr ticket, for €4.50 and €8.25, respectively. There's also a carnet of 10 tickets (€13.80), or a nighttime ticket for unlimited use between 8pm and the end of that day's service (€3). You can buy any of these ticket options inside the metro, but the carnets cannot be purchased self-serve. Pick those up at the ticket office. The metro consists of the M1 (red), M2 (green), M3 (yellow), and M5 (purple). There are easy-to-read signs at every station and in every metro car, so navigation should not be a hassle.

PRACTICAL INFORMATION

Tourist Offices: Galleria Vittorio Emanuele II (P. della Scala; 0 28 84 55 55; www.turismo.milanoit; open M-F 9am-7pm, Sa 9am-6pm, Su 10am-6pm)

Banks/ATMs/Currency Exchange: There are ATMs throughout the city, so you should have no problem finding one. Here's the address of HSBC in Milan (V. Mike Bongiorno, 13; 0 27 24 37 41).

Post Offices: Poste Italiane (Milano Centrale, P. Duca d'Aosta; 02 67 07 21 50; open M-F 8:20am-7:05pm, Sa 8:20am-12:35pm).

Internet: There are Wi-Fi hotspots in public squares throughout Milan.
BGLTQ+ Resources: Centro di Iniziativa Gay—ArchiGay Milano (V. Bezzeca 3; 0 25 41 22 25; www.arcigaymilano.org).

EMERGENCY INFORMATION

Emergency Number: 112
Police: 112 for *carabinieri* or 113 for local police.

- Police headquarters (V. Fatebenefratelli, 11; 0 26 22 61; www.questure.poliziadistato.it/milano).

US Embassy: The nearest US Embassy is located in Rome (V. Vittotio Veneto 121; 06 46741). There is a US consulate in Milan (V. Principe Amedeo, 2/10; 02 290351).
Rape Crisis Center: RAINN (800 646 4673) and National Coalition Against Domestic Violence (303 839 1852).
Hospitals:

- Ospedale Niguarda Ca'Granda (P. dell'Ospedale Maggiore, 3; 02 64441; open daily 24hr).

Pharmacies:

- Della Cittadella (Corso di Porta Ticinese, 50; 02 832 1584; open M-Sa 7am-1am, Su 8pm-midnight).

SIGHTS

CULTURE

FIERA DI SINIGAGLIA FLEA MARKET

Ripa di Porta Ticinese; open Sa 8am-3pm

When the Milanese aren't perusing the **Vittorio Emanuele Mall** for a new pair of diamond-studded, crocodile skin stilettos (that's a thing, right?), you might find them doing normal people things, like haggling over a head of cabbage at a street market. It really can't get more authentic than the market on the edges of the **Parco Baravalle.** There are killer deals on veggies, fruits, cheeses, fish, and even some prepared street food delicacies like *arancini di riso*. Pro-tip: swing by at 4pm when the vendors are almost done packing up—lots of the fresh stuff can't be resold, so often times you can pick up food on the cheap.

i Stand prices vary; wheelchair accessible

NAVIGLI

Navigli District; open daily 24hr

Canals? In Milan? They aren't the canals of Venice, but Milan has its own set of boutique and restaurant-lined waterways in the Navigli District, south of the **Duomo.** Home to not one but three universities, students and tourists flock to the area after sunset for some cocktails and *aperitivos*. Pros include quality seafood, beautiful sunsets, and flea markets on the weekends. Cons include having to discern which places are the tourist traps and which are the local joints. The best advice: use your instincts; if a place is serving "Tradishonal Milan Cuisine," chances are it might not be as "tradishonal" as they'd have you believe.

i Store prices vary; wheelchair accessible

PORTA VENEZIA

Porta Venezia; open daily 24hr

Navigli is generally the first place people think of when it comes to Milanese nightlife and culture, but Porta Venezia, on the opposite side of town, offers a different genre of entertainment. Unlike Navigli, which caters to larger hordes of unknowing tourists, you won't find as many Americanized places like "Pizzeria Manhattan" in Porta Venezia. Instead, look for tons of hipster cafés, ethnic restaurants, clubs, and a thriving BGLTQ+ nightlife scene. There's also an interesting park full of science-y attractions, like the **Museum of Natural History** and a **Planetarium,** which offers pretty much the only way to see the stars in Milan due to urban light pollution.

i Store prices vary; wheelchair accessible

LANDMARKS

THE DUOMO

P. del Duomo; 2 72 02 26 56; www.duomomilano.it/en; church open daily 8am-7pm, museum open daily 10am-6pm

It's not like you're going to miss it, since it's pretty much the center of the whole city and reaches a gargantuan height of 158 meters, but the Duomo—the fifth largest cathedral in the world—is non-negotiable as far as tourist destinations go. It took nearly 600 years to build and has since attracted thousands of tourists on the daily, including Mark Twain and Ernest Hemingway (yes, celebrities can be tourists, too). The interior is breathtaking, but for the real deal, clamber onto the rooftop terraces for a panoramic view of Milan. Pro tip: there's little information to be found, so we advise that you buy an audio guide, tour the museum, or research its architectural style to give the Duomo historical context. Or, you know, there's also Wikipedia.

i Admission to church, terrace, and museum €12, combo ticket with terrace access €16; tours every 90min.; wheelchair accessible

THE LAST SUPPER

P. Santa Maria della Grazie, 2; 2 92 80 03 60; www.cenacovinciano.net; open Tu-Su 8:15am-7pm, closed Jan 1, May 1, Dec 25

For some reason, no one ever tells you that *The Last Supper* isn't some painting hanging on a curator's wall, but rather an enormous, **15-foot-high fresco** that completely covers one side of a Dominican monastery. **Da Vinci** used an avant-garde technique called "dry" painting in order to make changes as he went, but it actually ended up making the fresco really hard to preserve. Way to go, Leo. To get in, you'll have to book tickets online way in advance, or hope someone canceled their reservation. Best to play it safe: your trip to Milan pretty much won't count if you skip *The Last Supper.*

i Admission €25 plus €2 booking tax, EU citizens €5 plus €2 booking tax, under 25 free plus €2 booking tax, guided tours daily every 15min. €3.50; last entry 6:45pm; wheelchair accessible

GALLERIA VITTORIO EMANUELE II

P. del Duomo; open daily 24hr

Instead of exhausting your brain through intense study of Renaissance painting or Gothic architecture, invest time into the history behind the world's oldest malls: the Galleria Vittorio Emanuele II. Crash course: the building, completed in 1877, was named after the first king and its architecture makes it a must-see. Stroll through two massive glass-paned hallways that meet in the centrally-located glass dome. Once you've snapped a few photos, there's plenty of perusing to do in—you guessed it—high fashion stores. That isn't to say there aren't some trinket shops and cheap eats sprinkled here and there. Fun fact: There was a McDonald's until 2012, until it was booted out by Prada.

i Store prices vary; wheelchair accessible

L.O.V.E.

P. degli Affari; open daily 24hr

L.O.V.E. might seem an inappropriate name for a statue of a hand flipping the bird, but, in this case, it stands for **Libertà, Odio, Vendetta,** and **Eternità** (Freedom, Hate, Vengeance, and Eternity). It was provocatively added to Piazza Degli Affari, the center of the Italian stock exchange, in 2010. Ever since, hordes of tourists with Gucci handbags bursting with designer clothes and sunglasses have stopped by to snap a picture of this anti-capitalist symbol. The piazza itself is actually relatively quiet—L.O.V.E. will never reach **Duomo** status as a tourist destination—but it offers a worthwhile change of scenery from the more commercial *piazzas* that surround it.

i Free; wheelchair accessible

MUSEUMS

CASTELLO SFORZESCO MUSEO

P. Castello; 2 88 46 37 00; www.milanocastello.it/en; open Tu-Su 9am-5:30pm

Castello Sforzesco Museo is an. . .eclectic mix of Italian art. Seriously, one second you'll be appreciating **Michelangelo's *Pietà Rondanini,*** and the next you'll be admiring a decorative set of silverware from the 1980s. There's the **Museum of Ancient Art, the Museum of Musical Instruments, an Egyptian Museum,** and so on. The best strategy is to select just a few areas, and explore them thoroughly, rather than try to hopelessly sprint through the entire museum to see everything in one shot (we found out the hard way). Don't miss the **da Vinci** museum, though—unfortunately, you won't see THE *Last Supper,* but there's an entire room full of replicas, some nearly as old as the original. You'll turn corner after corner, thinking, "this has got to be the last *Last Supper.*" It won't be.

Admission €5, €3 reduced; last entry 5pm; wheelchair accessible

MUSEO DI STORIA NATURALE DI MILANO

Corso Venezia, 55; 2 88 46 33 37; open Tu-Su 9am-5:30pm

Many, many years ago, before its conquest by the Romans in 222 BCE, and before being captured by the Celts in 400 BCE, and right around the years 1000 to 4.5 billion years BDG (before Dolce and Gabbana), Milan had a pretty rich natural history. The Museo di Storia Naturale di Milano showcases it expertly with an impressive density of dioramas featuring animals and skeletons by region of origin. They even have an entire section devoted to the wildlife of Italy—something often forgotten by the average city-going tourist. Granted, sometimes, the taxidermists were a little too ambitious in planning some of the dioramas; keep your eyes peeled for a particularly wonderful display of two marmosets in the midst of a fierce battle. *Nota Bene:* most of the exhibits are labeled only in Italian.

Admission €3, €1.50 reduced; last entry 5pm; wheelchair accessible

MUSEO TEATRO ALLA SCALA

Largo Ghiringhelli 1, P. Scala; 2 88 79 74 73; www.teatroallascala.org; open daily 9am-5:30pm

Step into the shoes of the Milanese elite (like Armani or Prada) at the Museo Teatro alla Scala and look onto the stage, home to some of Italy's most renowned performing artists, from a third-story box. Imagine it's 1776 and you're settling down for a nearly endless showcase of supersonic arias and unintelligible cantatas. Thankfully, you can snap yourself out of that fantasy by checking out the museum's musical artifacts—of particular note is a copy of **Verdi's *Requiem Mass*** and **Franz Liszt's** piano, gifted to him by Steinway and Sons themselves in 1883.

Admission adult €7, €5 reduced, free under 12 and disabled; audio guide €7; wheelchair accessible

OUTDOORS

LAKE COMO

Como, Italy; open daily 24hr

A mere hour-long train ride away from **Porta Garibaldi** or **Cadorna Station** (€4.80), Como is a playground for the uber-rich. Prices are sky-high for everything, the streets are pristine, and the typical tourist carries a different pair of sunglasses for every hour of the day. If you make the trek to Como, do a quick walk-through of the streets, checking out some historical sites (like its own Duomo—much smaller than Milan's), and soak in some beautiful views of the water. You can take a ferry ride to one of the smaller villages further north. **Bellagio,** the "Crotch of Lake Como" (because Lake Como is shaped like a pair of pants) is very popular, but it's a whole notch (or three) more touristy than Como.

Train from Garibaldi or Cadorna Station €4.80, speed ferry to Bellagio €14.80, regular ferry €10, bus round-trip to Bellagio €3.60; wheelchair accessible

PARCO SEMPIONE

V. Wolfango; open daily 6:30am-8:30pm

Just behind the grandiose **Castello Sforzesco** is Parco Sempione, Milan's largest urban park, home to lots of hidden gems like the **Arco della Pace** (Arch of Peace), an Arc-de-Triomphe-style tribute to Napoleon Bonaparte's victories; the **Arena Civica** (Civic Arena), a sports and music venue built in the early 1800s; the **Acquario Civico** (Civic Aquarium); the **Torre Branca,** a tower you can ride an elevator to the top of for €4, and the **Palazzo dell'Arte,** home of the International Exhibition of Decorative Arts. If none of that piques your interest, it's always nice to sprawl out in the grass and soak up the Milanese sun while locals walk their dogs through the park.

Free; wheelchair accessible

FOOD

FLOWER BURGER ($$)

V. Vittorio Veneto 10; 2 39 62 83 81; www.flowerburger.it; open daily 12:30pm-3:30pm and 7pm-11pm

"Don't be a fool, nutrition is cool!" reads a sign on the wall at Flower Burger. Even though you may have come to Milan for the hunks of breaded meat fried in butter that they call alla Milanesa, it's not like that's what the Milanese eat at every lunchtime; if they did, they wouldn't fit into those teeny cars. At Flower Burger, however, the Milanese have struck a mouthwatering balance between health and flavor; the six burgers served are all vegan, cooked on black, yellow, or pink buns and slathered with delicious homemade "cheese" or "mayo" concoctions, spicy salsas, and—of course—topped with a hearty dose of veggies. There's no Wi-Fi, but that's okay because you'll be too busy devouring your burger to check Facebook anyway.

i Burgers from €6.50, 10% lunch discount; wheelchair accessible

IL MASSIMO DEL GELATO ($)

V. Lodovico Castelvetro, 18; 23 49 49 43; www.ilmassimodelgelato.it; open Tu-Su noon-midnight

With a gelateria on literally every street corner, it can be hard to separate the *fantastico* from the average. Try to restrain yourself from the allure of the first one you spot and seek out Il Massimo del Gelato—the difference in quality is well worth the wait. Self-described as having been "created to conquer the eyes," Il Massimo offers "voluptuous" flavors like 100% dark chocolate, Aztec (chocolate with chili pepper), and classics such as pistachio and gianduja (hazelnut). A surprising favorite: the *limono,* which might just be more lemon-y than sucking on an actual slice of fresh lemon. There are a couple different locations—the original one in the northwest part of Milan has the most flavors, but there's a smaller store right by the **Duomo.**

i Scoops from €2; card minimum €10; vegetarian options available; wheelchair accessible

PAVÉ ($$)

V. Felice Casati, 21; 2 94 39 22 59; www.pavemilano.com; open Tu-F 8am-8pm, Sa-Su 8:30pm-7pm

"Sex, love, and *panettone*" are apparently the ingredients to a life of bliss, according to one of the many typographic posters adorning the walls of this hipster coffee joint. The *panettone* doesn't disappoint, and it's certainly served with a lot of love (but you'll need to look elsewhere to complete the happiness trio). Expect deliciously rich shots of espresso brewed with "traditional values" and "raw materials value." Bad translations aside, it's worth coming for the funky vibes and free Wi-Fi. You might even meet a fellow traveler at their communal table. Serendipitous meetings are encouraged, as Pavé's menu reads "By the way, you should know your greatest love was a stranger once." Maybe that bite of *panettone* really could lead to love, which could lead to... Well, you get the idea.

i Entrées from €6, pastries €5, coffee from €1, wine €20; vegetarian options available; wheelchair accessible

PIZZA AM ($$)

Corso di Porta Romana, 83; 25 11 05 79; www.pizzaam.it; open Tu-F noon-3pm and 7pm-11:30, Sa noon-3:30pm and 7pm-11:30pm, Su 7pm-11:30pm

The Italians know they're famous for pizza, and you'll get the feeling everyone is trying to jump on the pizzeria bandwagon whether it makes sense or not. Use your discerning eye and say no to "Kebab Pizzeria" or similar jack-of-all-trades places like "Pizzeria Restaurante Café Internet!"; there are better places out there, we promise. Pizza AM, with its bright colors, creepy marionettes, and world flags galore, boasts a mere six—but highly sought-after—flavors. In the evenings, hungry patrons form lines that extend down the street. Waiting may not be so bad, though, as the owner appeases hungry soon-to-be customers by offering them free beers and much-needed *aperitivos.*

i Slices from €6; vegetarian options available; wheelchair accessible

NIGHTLIFE

FRIDA

V. Pollaiuolo, 3; 2 68 02 60; www.fridaisloa.it; open M-F 10am-3pm and 6pm-8pm, Sa 6pm-2am, Su noon-1am

Just north of the ultra-polished shopping mall at **Piazza Gae Aulenti** is a grungier student hangout called Isola, where chain stores and clean-cut sidewalks are replaced with hole-in-the-wall bars and urban patches of greenery. Here, you'll find Frida, a café/bar/nightclub/shop hybrid with a lovely patio area surrounded by vine-covered walls and geometric graphic art. Frida boasts an ability to cater to all palates, so whether you're looking for a simple Mai Tai or more creative creations like the "Puppa Puppa" with vodka, peach juice, and passion fruit, this is the place to be.

i Small plates from €5, beer from €5, wine from €7, cocktails €7, gin, rum, or whiskey €9; wheelchair accessible

VINILE

V. Alessandro Tadino 17; 02 36 51 42 33; www.vinilemilano.com; open Tu-Su 6:30pm-2am

Ideal wine night partners: Chewbacca, Prince, and Pikachu. Where can you find them? Vinile—a wine bar for those with oddly specific tastes. Beyond wine, enjoy beer or "Mixing Desk Specials," as well as a Jazz Menu replete with Soul Salads, Rock Snacks, and Funky Sandwiches named after rock and pop legends like Beyoncé. If you're already dizzy from an overdose of eclectic-ness and groovy live music, try to avert your eyes from the disco ball that dimly illuminates the bar. Side note: pretty much every piece of Vinile's décor is for sale, so the fun doesn't ever have to end. If you buy the life-sized R2-D2 replica, our editorial staff would love a photo as proof.

i Wine from €5, beer from €5, cocktails from €7, wine from €5, beer from €5, cocktails from €7, entrées from €7; vegetarian options available; wheelchair accessible

PISA

Coverage by **Margaret Canady**

If you think that the Leaning Tower of Pisa is the only thing Pisa has to offer, you're not looking hard enough. There's no question about whether to visit Piazza dei Miracoli—if there was, the answer would be yes. A UNESCO World Heritage site, the Piazza is home to the Tower, the Baptistery, Camposanto, and the Cathedral, and swarms of tourists visiting the plaza's architectural mistake(s)—there's multiple. But if the only pic in your camera roll from Pisa is the tower, then you're doing the city a disservice. In reality, Pisa is and always has been a college town. The University of Pisa was established in 1343, and includes notable alumni such as five Popes, three Nobel Laureates, and, oh yeah, Galileo Galilei. Today, the students who make Pisa their home fill the streets with laughter and conversation, making the Arno River and the *piazzas* surrounding it their stomping ground. The city is youthful, vibrant, and has lots to offer to young travelers.

ORIENTATION

Pisa developed around the **Arno River**, which runs east-west through the city. **Pisa Stazione Centrale,** the central train station, sits on the south end of the city. **Corso Italia** is the main road that runs north-south through the city, and, if you cross the Arno, this road turns into **Borgo Stretto.** Corso Italia and Borgo Stretto take you through the main *piazzas* of the city, including (from south to north) **Piazza Vittorio Emanuele II, Piazza S. Garibaldi, and Piazza dei Cavalieri. Piazza dei Miracoli** and the famous **Leaning Tower of Pisa** are located on the northwest end of Pisa.

ESSENTIALS

GETTING THERE

Pisa is home to Pisa Galileo Galilei Airport, the international and main airport of Tuscany. There is a Pisa Shuttle (called the "People Mover"—fun fact) between the airport and the train station one-way for €2.70. The airport is 2.5km away from the train station. If arriving by train, you'll most likely enter the city from Pisa Centrale, the main train station. Trains arrive from Florence, Lucca, and Rome. There is also a train station closer to the Tower (Pisa S. Rossore), but not all trains stop here. There is a bus from Florence to Pisa's Piazza Sant'Antonio, but this is generally more expensive than the train and comes less frequently.

GETTING AROUND

Pisa is extremely walkable. From the train station, Piazza dei Miracoli is about a 20min. walk north. The most direct path to the Piazza is to go north on Corso Italia (which turns into Borgo Stretto after crossing the Arno), a left on Via dei Mille, and a right on Via Santa Maria. This will also take you through the most popular and main *piazzas* of Pisa. LAM Rossa buses also run a loop of the city every 20min. or so, and have stops at the city's major destinations (train station, airport, the Tower, etc.) Tickets are €1/hr and can be bought at the train station or at most tabaccherie.

PRACTICAL INFORMATION

Tourist Offices: The Pisa tourist offices provide free maps, luggage service, and other accommodations.

- Train Station Office: (P. Vittorio Emanuele II, 16; 05 04 22 91; www.pisaunicaterra.it; open daily 10am-1pm and 2pm-4pm).
- Piazza dei Miracoli, in front of Leaning Tower: (P. Duomo, 7; 0 50 55 01 00; www.turismo.pisa.it/en/infopoint; open daily Mar 1-Nov 12 9:30am-5:30pm, Nov 13-Feb 28 9am-5pm).

Banks/ATMs/Currency Exchange: There are many ATMs located around the city. Banks can be found on the main road of Corso Italia/Borgo Stretto. One of them is Cassa di Risparmio di Lucca Pisa Livorno (P. Donati, 12A; 0 50 58 10 58; www.bancobpmspa.com/index.php; open M-F 8:20am-1:20pm and 2:30pm-4pm).

Post Offices: There are several Poste Italianes around the city. Here is one open later than most: Poste Italiane (P. Vittorio Emanuele II, 8; 05 05 19 41 14; www.poste.it; open M-Sa 8:20am-7:05pm).

Public Restrooms: A public restroom is available at Piazza dei Miracoli, near the ticket office (P. dei Miracoli; 0 50 55 01 00; www.turismo.pisa.it/en/infopoint).

Internet: Pisa offers 37 Wi-Fi hotspots around the city. Look for the signs labeled "Wi-Fi", with the second "i" replaced with the Leaning Tower. Clever, we know.

BGLTQ+ Resources: Pinkriot Arcigay Pisa (V. Enrico Fermi, 7; 05 02 32 78; pinkriot.arcigaypisa.it; open Th 6pm-10pm).

EMERGENCY INFORMATION

Emergency Number: 112

Police: Police Headquarters (Via Mario Lalli, 3; 0 50 58 35 11; questure.poliziadistato.it/pisa).

US Embassy: The nearest US consulate is located in Florence (Lungarno Vespucci 38; 0 55 26 69 51; it.usembassy.gov/embassy-consulates/florence) and the nearest US embassy is located in Rome (V. Vittorio Veneto

121; 3 90 64 67 41; it.usembassy.gov/embassy-consulates/rome).

Rape Crisis Center: RAINN (20 25 01 44 44).

Hospitals: Santa Chiara Hospital has two branches, the first located near P. dei Miracoli, the other in the east suburbs of Pisa.

- Ospedale Santa Chiara - P. dei Miracoli: (V. Roma, 67; 0 50 99 21 11; www.ao-pisa.toscana.it).
- Stabilimento di Cisanello - east suburbs: (V. Paradisa, 2; 0 50 99 21 11; www.ao-pisa.toscana.it).

Pharmacies: There are many pharmacies in Pisa. Here is one open 24hr: Farmacia Comunale Pisa Spa (Via Niccolini, 6/a; 0 50 55 47 87; www.farmaciecomunalipisa.it; open daily 24hr).

SIGHTS

CULTURE

CORSO ITALIA

Corso Italia; store hours vary

At eye level, Corso Italia is just another street of stores, featuring the likes of Sephora, H&M, Zara, and Gamestop (we don't understand why these keep popping up, seriously—it's 2019). But when you look up, you are reminded that the stores are hosted in century-old works of stop-in-your-tracks stunning architecture. Corso Italia is a wide street lined with both Pisa's past and present, and, as you leave the train station and walk up the street towards the city's landmarks, passing street entertainers blowing bubbles and busking, you'll get the sense that Pisa is young at heart.

i Prices vary; wheelchair accessible

TUTTOMONDO BY KEITH HARING (THE MURAL OF KEITH HARING)

V. Riccardo Zandonai; www.comune.pisa.it/english/doc/the_mural_of_keith_haring.htm; open daily 24hr

Before Banksy, there was **Keith Haring.** Haring was an American pop and graffiti artist who, one day, met a University of Pisa student on the streets of NYC and was inspired to create a work in Pisa. In 1989 he created Tuttomondo on the south wall of the **Church of Sant'Antonio Abate.** The mural is huge, and, at 180 meters, features 30 colorful people dancing in synchronous harmony. Haring was inspired by Pisa's subdued colors adorning the city's historic buildings, and made the mural about peace and harmony. It's a beautiful work and not too far from the train station. *Tuttomondo* was also Haring's last public work; he died a few months later of AIDS.

i Free; wheelchair accessible; mural located on the church on the northwest corner of P. Vittorio Emanuele II

LANDMARKS

LEANING TOWER OF PISA

P. del Duomo; 0 0 83 50 11; www.opapisa.it/en; open Tu-Su 10am-6pm

Maybe *that's* why italics font is called italics—the font is *leaning*! Dad jokes aside, the Leaning Tower of Pisa is, get this, *really* leaning, and despite how many representations you've seen of the tower, it's pretty epic to see in real life. The marble bell tower was continuing to tilt at about 1 milimeter a year until restoration in the early 2000s prevented its seemingly-inevitable horizontal demise. Today, it leans at about a four-degree angle, but experts say it will start tilting again in the twenty-third century. So, it's kinda like when your mom yelled at you to stop slouching—and it worked when you were younger—but then you go to college and forget all your manners and end up spending 24 hours a day slouched over a computer. Unfortunately, your slouch isn't a tourist destination. You can also walk up the tower, but make sure to reserve your tickets early, because only a certain number of people can enter each day.

i Admission €18; no wheelchair accessibility; last entrance 30min. before closing; children under 8 not allowed to climb; hours change depending on season

PIAZZA DEI MIRACOLI

P. del Duomo; www.opapisa.it; open daily 24hr; Baptistery, Camposanto, and Sinopie Museum open daily 8am-8pm

Piazza dei Miracoli is known as the field of miracles, and we decided to unpack this idea whilst exploring. For one, the Catholic Church deemed the Piazza sacred, making it the home of four religious monuments: **the Cathedral,** the Baptistry, the Camposanto, and the Campanile. In 1987, the square was declared a UNESCO World Heritage Site, surrounded by pristine green grass. The Tower, of course, can be found in the Piazza, too. The really miraculous part of the Piazza, however, has to be the sheer amount of tourists that make their way there every day. Almost perfectly in sync, every day thousands of people try to channel Michael Jackson's thriller dance in the Piazza as they attempt to take that infamous picture with the Leaning Tower of Pisa. All they need is music and some rhythmic coordination.

i Free; wheelchair accessible

MUSEUMS

PISA CATHEDRAL

P. del Duomo; 0 50 83 50 11; www.opapisa.it/en; open daily 10am-8pm

The Pisa Cathedral stands in the middle of the **Piazza dei Miracoli** (no, unlike the tower, it doesn't tilt) and acts as though it knows that it's an objectively better monument than that attention-seeking Tower. The Catedral is, like all Italian churches, grandiose, elaborate, and beautiful. Black and white stripes line the outside and inside of the cathedral, mimicking a candy cane. The perimeter of the inside of the church has large, detailed murals depicting stories of Jesus and friends, and the golden ceiling glimmers. The Cathedral is simply waiting for gravity (or God) to strike down the Tower so it can finally have the spotlight.

i Free; wheelchair accessible; arrive 10min. before designated time on ticket; must have shoulders covered and respectable clothing to enter; hours change depending on season

CAMPOSANTO MONUMENTALE (MONUMENTAL CEMETERY)

P. del Duomo, 17; 0 50 83 50 11; www.opapisa.it; open daily 8am-8pm

Legend has it that bodies buried in Camposanto Monumentale will rot in only 24 hours due to the sacred soil upon which the cemetery was built. Not sure if this is something we want to find out first-hand, so we'll take their word for it. The building is shaped like a rectangle, complete with wide arches and an inner courtyard; the marble floor below your feet is actually composed of tombs. Some of the tombstones creaked when we walked on them, which was slightly alarming and made us envision Italian versions of the zombie apocalypse. Then we remembered that the bodies are, in theory, rotten, and not zombie-ready. The cemetery also has three chapels, one of which holds important Catholic relics.

i Admission €5; admission to Baptistery, Camposanto, and Sinopie Museum €8; wheelchair accessible; hours change depending on season

OUTDOORS

ORTO BOTANICO (BOTANIC GARDEN)

V. Luca Ghini, 13; 05 02 21 13 10; www.sma.unipi.it/orto-e-museo-botanico; open daily 8:30am-8pm

The one downside of **Piazza dei Miracoli** is that there are no trees to block out the sun's rays, and it's pretty hard to pose with **the Tower** if you're burning up in the sunlight. Luckily, Orto Botanico is only two minutes away, and their speciality is shade. Stroll through graveled pathways lined by bamboo and magnolia trees, take your nose for a trip down the herbal garden, and traverse the globe in the savannah and tropical greenhouses. We spent a good 10 minutes trying to coerce tiny bugs into the Venus flytrap cage, but to no avail.

i Admission €4, €2 reduced; last entry 1hr before closing; wheelchair accessible

FOOD

IL GELATO DI TOTO ($)

Borgo Stretto, 15; 34 80 82 26 36; www.ilgelatoditoto.it; open M-Th 11am-7pm, F-Su 11am-midnight

After an overeating lunch fiasco, gelato sounds like the last thing we possibly would have wanted to add to our bellies. But in our book, gelato is definitely an essential—all the way up there with ATMs and pharmacies. Il Gelato di Toto was recommended to us by our hostel receptionist, and a few hours of digestion later, we made our way to the small shop on the main road of **Borgo Stretto.** This gelateria promotes the use of all-natural ingredients and gelato made in-house, and we could taste the difference. There were real blackberries and meringue in the gelato, and the limoncello's cream was tart and fresh. The shop also likes to get creative, so look out for fun flavours on a rotating menu.

i Gelato from €2.20; non-dairy options available; limited wheelchair accessibility

PIZZERIA RUSTICANELLA ($)

V. S. Martino, 93; 02 87 16 57 11; open M-Tu 10am-11pm, Th-Su 10am-11pm

While in Tuscany, an essential local food to try is *cecina,* a baked chickpea pancake sliced like a pizza. Pizzeria Rusticanella serves some of the best *cecina*, and with salt, pepper, and lemon, it's the perfect option to take away or eat in their outdoor seating. For some odd reason, we also decided to get a pizza with buffalo cheese (€8) and an eggplant focaccia sandwich (€7), so while our taste buds were in ecstasy, our pants were not. Nevertheless, Pizzeria Rusticanella was a delicious late lunch, and there might have been a repeat sesh if had we not eaten too much.

i Pizza from €5, calzones from €7; vegetarian options available; wheelchair accessible

RISTORANTE AL MADINA DI HAKIM BASSAM ($)

V. S. Martino, 41/45; 05 02 04 09; www.ristorantealmadina.it; open Tu-Sa 11:30am-3pm and 7pm-11:30pm, Su 7-11:30pm

Perhaps Middle Eastern food is better in Italy because it's geographically closer to the Middle East, or, (more likely) Al Madina is straight up an exceptional Middle Eastern restaurant. The menu is broken up into three parts: takeaway, vegan/vegetarian, and meat, but everything you order will be large and cheap. The appetizer plate (€7) features homemade hummus, falafel, eggplant muhammara, and pita bread. We felt pretty fancy sitting among Persian rugs and Arabic decor.

i Take-away from €4.50, entrées from €7; vegan and vegetarian options available; wheelchair accessible

LA GHIOTTERIA ($)

Vicolo delle Donzelle, 9/11; 34 84 06 47 25; open daily noon-3:30pm and 7pm-midnight

La Ghiotteria is the master of generous portions, specifically for their seafood pasta. For €8, you can get a spaghetti dish with fresh crab, mussels, and clams—splitting the entrée will leave you with a full stomach and full wallet (or relatively full; we're on a budget, people). The restaurant is located in an alleyway corner and doesn't look like much from the outside, but the inside has us feeling warm and cozy. Or maybe that was from the wine (€2 for 250ml).

i Entrées from €8; wheelchair accessible

NIGHTLIFE

BAZEEL ($)

Lungarno Antonio Pacinotti, 1; 05 07 91 70 96; www.bazeel.it; open M-W noon-3am, Th-Sa noon-4am, Su noon-3am

On a Friday or Saturday night, students from Pisa and abroad congregate to Bazeel for a good time. The venue has really great outdoor seating on **Piazza Garibaldi,** and with its location right on the **Arno River,** it's the perfect place for a cold drink on a warm night. Their cocktail menu is extensive (over 60 choices), and as the night progresses you'll be joined by throngs of students smoking cigarettes and walking arm in arm down the river. There's a live DJ on the weekends, so we dare you to turn he Piazza into a dance party.

i Cocktails from €6; wheelchair accessible

ROME

Coverage by **Adrian Horton**

You know the legacy of Rome well, though you may not realize it. It's there when you check the date, or celebrate a birthday in October. It's there when you add "etc." to the end of a text instead of continuing ad nauseam, or take a sip from a public drinking fountain. And it's there when you see a fish fry during Lent, or say "when in Rome…" before doing something ill-advised. Rome looms heavily in the global imagination, and for good reason. The Eternal City—officially founded in 753 BCE but likely settled earlier—forms the bedrock of our concept of Western civilization. Rome's 2770-year-old résumé puts most other cities to shame, and includes casual stints as the seat of one of the largest and most powerful empires the world has ever seen, patron saint of Baroque art, headquarters of one of the world's most popular religions, and now the destination for lovers of *la dolce vita* everywhere.

And those are just a few of the highlights. Rome has led more lives than there are enemies of Julius Caesar, and has enchanted visitors for centuries to study, eat, admire, pray, and wander in its well-trod streets. Today, modern Rome attracts millions of tourists every year, which results in the formation of daunting crowds—they're particularly dense near the big monuments, especially during the sweltering summers. Even if you can't handle the lines, though, Rome still charms with an extensive offering of museums, churches, excavation sights, galleries, and sorry, pasta repurposed remains. Oh, and the food—cafés, pasta restaurants, pizza joints, trellis-covered trattorias, and gelato stops galore. Go ahead and enjoy that third scoop, because if there's one place that understands indulgence, it's Rome. Take a deep breath and take in the sunset as it lights up the ochres, burnt oranges, and pinks of the city—you don't have to be an arts and culture buff to appreciate that.

ORIENTATION

Rome has been planned, built, re-planned, rebuilt, and revitalized continuously for over 2770 years, so it's no wonder that old and new meld together throughout the city. While other major cities possess a grid layout or distinct districts, in Rome many of the neighborhoods flow together in a mix of marble, terracotta, tight streets, and churches. Though it's hard to get too disoriented, it can be difficult to discern where one neighborhood ends and another one begins, especially in the old-city area between **Termini Station** and **the Tiber.** To complicate matters, the official districts of Rome *(riones)*, first delineated by Augustus and revised every couple centuries thereafter, don't correspond perfectly to common names for different sections of town. Technically, Rome has twenty-two *riones,* each with their own coat of arms. Knowing them makes for impressive trivia but, as a tourist, you're better off remembering the unofficial, colloquial terms for different areas, which usually refer to famous landmarks nearby or their geographic locations.

If Rome were the four-quadrant graph from sixth grade math, the **Foro Romano** (Roman Forum) would mark the origin point, which is fitting, since the Foro Romano was the heart of the ancient city. The area surrounding the Forum, known colloquially as the **Ancient City,** contains, unsurprisingly, the headliners of Imperial Rome: the **Capitoline Hill** and its world-class museum on the Forum's western edge, the **Palatine Hill** and its former palaces to the south, the Circus Maximus behind the Palatine, and the **Colosseum** to the east. Directly west of the Ancient City is the old historic center of Rome, known as **Centro Storico,** around which the Tiber River bends westward like an elbow. Centro Storico is Rome at its most classic and picturesque—cobblestone streets, buildings that glow in evening sunlight, apartment buildings and *ristorantes* that bump up against Baroque fountains and Medieval churches. This area, about fourteen square kilometers in total, breaks down further into neighborhoods focused on certain monuments: to the northwest, **Navona,** near the elliptical Piazza Navona and the **Pantheon;** to the south, the narrow streets and squares of **Campo de' Fiori;** to the southeast, the old **Jewish Ghetto;** and to the north, the luxury shops and crowds of **Spagna**. Heading west across the Tiber on the **Vittorio Emanuele II bridge,** you reach the walled **Vatican City,** which is technically its own country (with its own post office!). To the north of the Vatican sprawls **Prati,** known for its cheaper accommodations and restaurants. To the south rests **Trastevere,** the former working-class neighborhood that is now a top tourist destination due to the area's quaint restaurants, centuries-old buildings, and ivy-lined streets.

Starting again from the Forum and heading south along the east bank of the Tiber, you reach the **Aventine Hill,** sight of beautiful sweeping views of the city, expensive homes, and not much to eat. Further south lies the neighborhood of **Testaccio,** known for its energy and collection of fine restaurants. Just north of the Forum lies **Monti,** a combination of the Esquiline, Quirinale, and Virinale hills that buzzes with hip cafés, popular aperitivo bars, and boutique shops. Continuing north from Monti is the **Borghese area,** near the Borghese gardens and several notable churches. **Termini Station,** Rome's main transportation hub, resides northeast of Monti and the Ancient City. Most of the city's hostels surround **Termini** and its nearby streets, as do cheap tourist shops, international chain restaurants, and mini-markets. The area in and around Termini marks a gritty break from the other districts of Rome (and is a frequent complaint of unprepared tourists). The streets heading northeast from Termini go toward the blocks with the most popular hostels. Heading southeast, you reach **San Lorenzo,** home to Rome's **Sapienza University,** bars with attitude, and affordable housing. The list of areas may sound daunting, but don't worry—you will develop confidence in your navigational skills as your trip goes on. Rome was designed to be explored by foot (or Vespa, but that requires technique we cannot assume you possess), so strap on those €15 gladiator sandals and get walking. You're bound to find a Baroque *piazza,* narrow street, or enticing café that moves you.

ESSENTIALS

GETTING THERE

From Leonardo da Vinci Airport/ Fiumicino (FCO): Known commonly as Fiumicino, Rome's main airport resides on the coast, 19mi. southwest of the city. The Leonardo Express train runs between the airport and track 25 at Termini, Rome's main train station; the ride takes 30min. and costs €11. Another train, the FM1, stops in Trastevere.

From Ciampino Airport (CIA): Rome's other airport lies 9mi. south of the city center and mainly draws budget airlines. There are no direct train links from Ciampino to the city, but express buses leave every 30min. or so and run directly to Termini. Tickets cost €4.90 and can be purchased at the information desk to the right as you're walking out of the terminal. The ride takes approximately 50min., depending on traffic.

By rail: State-owned Trenitalia operates trains out of Termini, Tiburtina, Ostiense, and Trastevere stations. Termini is open 4:30am-1:30am and its bus stop at Piazza del Cinquecento connects with most bus lines in the city. For those arriving in the wee morning hours, the night bus #175 runs from Tiburtina and Ostiense to Termini.

GETTING AROUND

Rome is a relatively compact city, and the best way to explore its cluster of monuments, churches, and narrow streets is by foot. There are various options for public transportation, however, all operated through ATAC. One ticket costs €1.50 and is valid for 75min. on any combination of vehicles.

By metro: Though not comprehensive for the entire city, the most efficient way to travel to the most popular sights in Rome is by metro. Rome has two metro lines that intersect at Termini Station. Line A, the "tourist line," runs from Battistini to Anagnina and passes through Piazza di Spagna, the Trevi Fountain, and the Vatican Museums (Ottaviano). Line B runs from Laurentina to Rebibbia, and passes through the Colosseum, Ostiense station, and the Testaccio District. Stations are indicated by the red letter "M" on a pole. Tickets can be purchased inside; a single ride costs €1.50 (valid for 60min.) and a day-pass costs €7 (€18 for a 3-day pass and €24 for a week). The metro operates 5:30am-11:30pm and is open until 1:30am on Sa night.

By bus: Buses cover more of Rome than the metro, but are less straightforward to use. ATAC operates city buses 5:30am-midnight, plus a network of night buses *(notturno)*. Check routes and schedules at www.atac.roma.it (on the site, look for the Italian flag in the upper right corner to change the language to English). Tickets, valid for 75min., cost €1.50 and can be purchased at *tabaccherie,* kiosks, and storefronts but NOT on the bus itself. Enter from the rear of the bus, immediately validate your ticket in the yellow machine, and proceed towards the middle.

By tram: The trams, also operated by ATAC, make more frequent stops than buses and can be useful getting to and from Trastevere. As on the buses, tickets cost €1.50 and must be purchased ahead of time (consider buying several to have on you, in case a ticket station is hard to find in a pinch). Useful lines include: #3 (Trastevere, Aventine, Piazza San Giovanni, Borghese Gallery), #8 (Trastevere to Largo Argentina), #9 (Piazza Venezia, Trastevere), and #19 (Ottaviano, Villa Borghese, San Lorenzo).

By taxi: Taxis should be reserved for emergencies or pressing situations. It is technically against the law to hail cabs on the street, but they may still stop if you flag them down. They also wait at stands and can be reached by phone (+39 066645, 063570, 064994, 065551, 064157). Only enter cabs with the marking "Servizio Pubblico" next to the license plate. Be sure to ask for your receipt *(ricevuta)* to confirm the price.

By bike: ATAC operates bike-sharing. Purchase a rechargeable card from any ATAC station in the city. The initial charge is €5, with a €0.50 charge for every additional 30min. Bikes can be parked at stations around the city. Alternatively, companies such as Bici & Baci (+39 01683230567, www.bicibaci.com) loan bikes and mopeds and have stations by the major metro stops (Colosseo, Repubblica, Spagna).

By scooter: The honking, buzzing Vespa is ubiquitous in Rome, as are the daring yet helmeted people who ride them. You can join in on the chaos by renting a two-wheeler, provided you show a valid driver's license and can handle the stress of Rainbow Road on MarioKart. Rates vary by the company, but start at around €30 for 4-8hr.

PRACTICAL INFORMATION

Tourist Offices: Comune di Roma is Rome's official source for tourist information. Green PIT information booths, located near most major sights, have English-speaking staff and sell bus and metro maps and the Roma pass (V. Giovanni Giolitti 34; www.turismoroma.it; open daily 8am-8:30pm).

Post Offices: Poste Italiane are located throughout the city (8 00 16 00 00; www.poste.it), but the main office is located at Piazza San Silvestro 19 (06 69 73 72 16; open M-F 8:20am-7pm, Sa 8:20am-12:35pm).

Luggage Storage: Termini Luggage Deposit (Termini Station, below Track 24 in the Ala Termini wing; 0 64 74 47 77; www.romatermini.com; open daily 6am-11pm; bags max 22kg; max 5 days; 5hr €6, €0.90/hr for hrs 6-12, €0.40/hr thereafter).

EMERGENCY INFORMATION

Emergency Number: 112, 118 (medical emergencies).

Police:

- Police Headquarters (V. di San Vitale 15; 0 64 68 61).
- Carabinieri have offices at V. Mentana 6 (near Termini; 06 44 74 19 00) and at P. Venezia 6 (0667582800).
- City police (P. del Collegio Romano 3; 06468).

Hospitals:

- Policlinico Umberto I. (Vle. del Policlinico 155; 0 64 99 71; www.policlinicoumberto1.it; open 24hr; emergency treatment free).
- International Medical Center (V. Firenze 47; 064882371, 06 08 62 44 11 11; www.imc84.com; call ahead for appointments).

Pharmacies: The following pharmacies are open 24hr.

- Farmacia Internazionale (P. Barberini 49; 0 64 87 11 95).
- Farmacia Risogimento (P. del Risorgimento 44; 06 39 73 81 66).

SIGHTS

CULTURE

BASILICA SAN CLEMENTE

V. Labicana 95; 67 74 00 21; www.basilicasanclemente.com; open M-Sa 9am-12:30pm and 3pm-6pm, Su 12:30pm-6pm

Ancient Rome consisted of thousands of buildings and palaces—a thriving city that Jupiter didn't just zap off the earth when he fell out of favor. Today's Vespa traffic drives on top of medieval ruins, which in turn rest on the streets and homes of the ancient city, buried some twenty to thirty feet underground. Basilica San Clemente takes a knife to this lasagna of history, if you will, revealing three distinct eras of Rome's past. The current basilica was built in the twelfth century, and contains typical Renaissance decorations. One floor down lies the original fourth-century church, with its ghosts of eighth-century frescoes. Another staircase leads down to the first century CE, with the remains of Roman homes, alleys, and spring water faucets. If you thought the ancient city surrounded the Colosseum, think again—it's snaking beneath you.

i Free entrance to the basilica; tickets for the excavation site €10, €5 reduced; last entry M-Sa 12:15pm and 5:30pm, Su 5:30pm; limited wheelchair accessibility

BASILICA SANTA MARIA DELLA VITTORIA

V. 20 Settembre 17; 6 42 74 06 71; open M-Sa 8:30am-noon and 3:30pm-6pm, Su 3:30pm-6pm

Between the **Borghese Gardens** and the front of **Termini Station,** the Basilica Santa Maria della Vittoria showcases Bernini at his most whimsical. The church, considerably smaller than Santa Maria Maggiore or St. Peter's, was designed to resemble a theater, with dozens of flying naked babies and marble likenesses of the wealthy Cornaro family. Bernini's playfulness rises throughout the church—literally, the ceiling, which transitions seamlessly from wood pediment to fresco painting, appears to float away in a haze of pink clouds. Closer to earth, the front of Santa Maria della Vittoria holds the masterful *Ecstasy of St. Theresa,* Bernini's depiction of female pleasure disguised as religious symbolism.

i Free; wheelchair accessible

SISTINE CHAPEL

Musei Vaticani, Vatican City; 6 69 88 46 76; www.museivaticani.va; open M-Sa 9am-6pm

The Sistine Chapel is basically the sixteenth-century Olympics of Renaissance painting—you win just by being included, though the gold medal goes, of course, to Michelangelo's ceiling frescoes, whose technical virtuosity overshadows the other masterful works from **Pinturicchio, Perugino, Botticelli,** and **Ghirlandaio.** Begun in 1508, Michelangelo's defiance of gravity was intended to grace Pope Julius II's private chapel, but the Tuscan artist's stupidly impressive achievement has since gone viral—it's estimated that the Sistine Chapel's paintings are viewed by over 15000 people per day. And a majority of those visitors do not follow the no talking rule (or no photos, for that matter). But no matter how packed the room or how weak people's attempts

to hide their selfies, the Sistine Chapel will command your attention, and also leave you baffled by Michelangelo's ability to endure neck cramps.

i Access to the Sistine Chapel comes with a ticket to the Vatican Museums; adults €16, €8 reduced; first entry 9am; ticket office closes at 4pm; wheelchair accessible; proper dress (covered shoulders, clothes to the knees) is required for the Vatican, though they may let skirts slightly above the knee pass; no photos or talking allowed, or you will be reprimanded

ST. PETER'S BASILICA

P. San Pietro, Vatican City; 6 69 88 23 50; www.vaticanstate.va; open daily Apr-Sept 7am-7pm, Oct-Mar 7am-6pm

As one of the most important examples of Renaissance architecture and one of the most visited pilgrimage sites in the world, St. Peter's Basilica needs no help fighting for attention. Built over the legendary tomb of the Christian martyr whose name it bears, it's the culmination of the Church's power and patronage in the sixteenth and seventeenth centuries. The basilica is the final-exam group project of the biggest names in Baroque art—**Michelangelo, Bernini, Maderno, Bramante,** and whoever laid the incomprehensible amount of precious marble everywhere. It also exemplifies Rome's commitment to recycling: some of St. Peter's marble comes from the Colosseum, while Bernini's stunning *baldacchino* (altar piece) was cast using 927 tons of metal removed from the Pantheon roof. Words fail to describe the staggering impression of St. Peter's interior, just as human eyes fail to process the sheer amount of wealth and beauty within it. Most days, you will need to wait a crazy amount of time to witness the excess of St. Peter's, though your chances are better if you arrive before 9am or after 5pm.

i Free, but up to 3-4 hr wait; wheelchair accessible; covered shoulders, clothes to the knees required for entry; audio guides available (reserve at 0669883229); the dome can be climbed daily 8am-6pm—entrance is at the porch of the Basilica

ALTARE DELLA PATRIA

Piazza Venezia; 6 69 99 41; open daily 9am-5:30pm

This monstrosity of white marble (many Romans refer to it derisively as "the wedding cake" or "the typewriter") is also known as the Monumento Vittorio Emanuele II or "Vittoriano." It was constructed in the late nineteenth century as a testament to, you guessed it, King Victor Emmanuel II, who was elevated from King of Sardinia to the first ruler of a unified Italy. More broadly, the bombastic monument was erected to symbolize the aspirations of the nascent Italian state, which was riding the waves of intense nationalism that swept across Europe in the late nineteenth century. Regardless of your aesthetic judgment of the building, Vittoriano offers quality views from the top and a chance to see Italy's version of the Tomb of the Unknown Soldier. Inside the monument and to the right is the more reserved **Museo di Risorgimento,** which traces the history behind Italy's unification.

i Adults €7.50, under 18 €3.50; wheelchair accessible

PALAZZO VENEZIA

V. del Plebescito 118; 6 69 99 43 88; www.museopalazzovenezia.beniculturali.it; open Tu-Su 8:30am-7:30pm

It takes the eyes a second to adjust to the Palazzo Venezia. Hard corners? No marble? No columns? Where are we? Venice? Well, close. The Palazzo Venezia was indeed gifted to the Venetians in 1564 by Pope Pius IV (gotta keep those relations tight), hence its Medieval style that looks nothing like any of its neighbors. Located just north of the

Capitoline Hill, the Palazzo Venezia has stood as a symbol of power for over 700 years. Mussolini adopted the palace as his headquarters and office; you can still see the balcony where he delivered most of his speeches, including his Declaration of the Italian Empire on May 9, 1936. Today, the balcony appears unadorned, as Rome downplays its fascist past. The focus is instead placed on the Palazzo Venezia museum, which houses frescoes, pottery, and sculpture from the early Christian years to the Renaissance.

i Adults €14, €7 reduced; ticket also valid for the Museo Nazionale di Castel Sant'Angelo; balcony free, on the right side of the palace if you're facing with your back to the Altare della Patria; last entry 6:30pm; wheelchair accessible

PORTA PORTESE

Piazza di Porta Portese; open Su 6am-2pm

Porta Portese provides a break from all of the lavish tourist attractions found throughout Rome. This outdoor market, open only on Sunday mornings, specializes in the cheap, eclectic, and unpolished—things with value in the eye of the beholder. Here, you can find antiques, knick-knacks, cards, figurines, souvenirs as cheap as €1, and racks on racks of clothing to replace the smelly, wrinkled shirts lumped in the bottom of your pack. Located along the Tiber to the south of the city center, Porta Portese lacks the glamour of Rome's monuments, but it attracts a mixed crowd of locals and visitors and will reveal aspects of the city that the Vatican will not.

i Stand prices; limited wheelchair accessibility

VILLA FARNESINA

V. della Lungara 230; 6 68 02 72 68; www.villafarnesina.it; open M-Sa 9am-2pm

When you're a rich banker from Siena, how do you make your presence known in Rome? Build a lavish summer villa and borrow the pope's favorite fresco painter **(Raphael),** of course. Agostino Chigi completed his mansion at the peak of Renaissance style in 1511, complete with floor-to-ceiling frescoes, the typical marble showcases, and airy porticoes. Chigi further cemented his status as the Gatsby of Rome by throwing extravagant parties, during which he allegedly encouraged guests to toss their silver into the Tiber (which he then fished out with a net). These indulgences didn't work out so well for Chigi, as the home was sold to the Farnese family by the end of the sixteenth century. But it works out great for you, old sport, as you can stroll through the still outlandishly-decorated halls and light-toned *loggios* like the Leonardo DiCaprio film extra you long to be.

i Admission €6; last entry 2pm

LANDMARKS

FONTANA DEI QUATTRO FIUMI (AND PIAZZA NAVONA)

P. Navona; open daily 24hr

Like your best night-out stories, the Fontana dei Quattro Fiumi (Fountain of the Four Rivers) is all drama and excess. Designed by **Bernini** for Pope Innocent X, the fountain features a skyscraping Egyptian obelisk atop a pyramid of rocks, cascading water, one roaring lion, and four nude river gods. Bernini designed the fountain as a celebration of four continents, with each god representing the Ganges, the Nile, the Danube, and the Rio de la Plata. Apparently North America was not important enough in 1651 to warrant a shout-out, but judging by the number of English menus on the surrounding Piazza Navona, people today have taken note of America. Ochre-colored apartments, purplish shutters, and flowering window boxes ring the elliptically shaped Piazza Navona, making it one of the more picturesque *piazzas* in the city and a rewarding stop on any walking tour of Rome.

i Free; wheelchair accessible

THE COLOSSEUM

Piazza del Colosseo 1; open daily 8:30am-7:30pm

The Colosseum has over two thousand years of experience at keeping people entertained. It held naval battles, featured wild beasts, and absorbed the blood of thousands of gladiators. It contained 80,000 people and then spit them out in less time than it takes you to get dressed in the morning.

It inspired your favorite sports team arena and one historically inaccurate but highly quotable Russell Crowe movie. And now it hosts upward of 9000 visitors a day, making it Rome's top tourist attraction. To visit the Colosseum, you can book a tour or skip-the-line pass from one of the numerous companies operating in or around it. Or, muster more patience than Emperor Joaquin Phoenix in *Gladiator* and brave the line. The games are long gone, but the Colosseum still captivates.

i Tickets €12, valid for 2 consecutive days at Roman Forum and Palatine Hill; limited wheelchair accessibility; last entry 1hr before sunset; tickets at Forum or Palatine Hill

THE PANTHEON

P. della Rotunda; open daily 9am-7:30pm

The Romans may have had the most powerful empire of their time, but it can be difficult to see the architectural genius through so much crumbling marble. And then there's the Pantheon, one of the best-preserved symbols of the Eternal City (thank you, very rich popes), here to remind you that the Romans really were ahead of their time. The optical illusion of the ceiling—a series of square pediments in concentric circles surrounding the oculus (opening)—will make your head spin (don't worry, there's free seating). The Pantheon's lavishly marbled ground-floor, consecrated today as a Catholic sacred space, also offers its fair share of treasures: **Rafael** is buried here (specifically, creepily exhumed, confirmed dead, and reburied), as well as national hero **King Vittorio Emanuele II.**

i Free; last entry 7pm; wheelchair accessible; entry may be restricted depending on crowd size

THE ROMAN FORUM

V. della Salara Vecchia; open daily 8:30am-7:15pm

On a surface level, the Forum appears to be a series of marble things at various stages of decay. Once the Times Square of Ancient Rome, the Forum has persevered through more than nine lives, including "stage for Cicero," "public looting ground," "Catholic Church reclamation area," "demolition zone for Mussolini," and now "the largest outdoor museum in the world." A visit to the Forum begins with the **Arch of Titus**—notable for its clear depiction of the sack of Jerusalem in the first century CE—and weaves through the remains of temples, *basilicas* (public buildings), the **House of the Vestal Virgins,** and marketplaces. As most of what we see today forms only the corners, slices, or skeletons of the original buildings, a visit to the Forum requires some imagination to fully appreciate its significance. But as the epicenter of Ancient Rome's power and the heart of the old city, the Forum is a must-see in Rome.

i Tickets €12, valid for 2 consecutive days at the Colosseum and Palatine Hill; last entry 7pm; wheelchair accessible

PIAZZA DI SPAGNA

P. di Spagna; open daily 24hr

Despite its butterfly shape, the **Spanish Steps** is a monument of circular reasoning. Why see the Spanish Steps? Because they're famous and important, you say. Why are they famous and important? Because… they're the Spanish Steps? Yes, it's a set of steps (a very manageable 135 of them) leading from Bernini's least impressive fountain below to a church of moderate importance above. In the past, the Spanish Steps served a logistical purpose—connecting the Spanish Embassy with the church—and as a functioned as a symbol of the Bourbon family's wealth (the guys who also funded Versailles). Today, the money is housed in the luxury shops lining the Piazza di Spagna, while the steps have become a hub for the Senate and for people-watching. By Roman ordinance, you can't each lunch here, but you can take a standing five on the smooth marble steps.

i Free; piazza is wheelchair accessible

THE ARCH OF CONSTANTINE

V. di San Gregorio; open daily 24hr

When you've consolidated power, drowned your rival in the Tiber, and paraded his head through the streets of Rome, what's the natural next step? Build a gigantic arch with no practical use, of course. Technically gifted by the (mostly defunct, at this point) Senate of Rome to the emperor Constantine I, Rome's largest triumphal arch still stands beside the Colosseum as a reminder of what would happen if Ancient Rome wanted your money. Though completed in 315 CE, the arch contains details from earlier works also dedicated to the military booty seized by emperors such as Hadrian and Trajan. See Constantine's Arch if you're interested in 3D friezes and the spoils of war; skip it if the coolest thing about an arch to you is walking through it (as this one is fenced off).

i Free; wheelchair accessible

THE CAPITOLINE HILL

P. del Campidoglio; open daily 24hr

Simultaneously the smallest of Rome's seven hills and its most sacred, the Capitoline Hill has upgraded over the years from the city's mint and political center to the home of two massive naked men and their horses (statues, of course). The pair boldly welcomes you to the Piazza di Campidoglio, designed by **Michelangelo** in the fifteenth century and the entrance to the **Capitoline Museums,** the world's oldest public collection of ancient art. The Capitoline today testifies to the egos of past Roman and Italian leaders—an impressive bronze statue of **Marcus Aurelius** dominates the piazza, though it is dwarfed by the neo-Baroque monument to **Vittorio Emanuele II** behind it. You can climb this "wedding cake" building for a heightened view, or look onto the Forum for free from the back end.

i Free; limited wheelchair accessibility

THE PALATINE HILL

Palatine Hill; open daily 8am-7:30pm

Once upon a time, a she-wolf rescued abandoned twin babies—Romulus and Remus—on the Palatine Hill, and nursed them in a cave. One of them (Romulus) went on to found the city of Rome, then killed Remus out of… let's call it brotherly love. Whether or not you believe the founding legend of Rome, it's fact that the Palatine Hill has been inhabited since at least 1000 BCE, and that people likely pulled a Romulus to live there in the years since. During its heyday as the Beverly Hills of Rome in the Republican and Imperial eras, the Palatine Hill was populated with the who's who of the city and adorned with mansions for the emperor and his family (hence, the word "palace"). Visitors today can use their combined Colosseum-Forum-Palatine ticket to visit the **Palace of Domitian,** the remains of **Augustus's house,** and the **beautiful frescoes** in his wife's villa.

i Tickets €12, valid for 2 consecutive days at the Colosseum and Roman Forum; last entry 1hr before sunset; wheelchair accessible; entrance on V. San Gregorio, as well as through the Roman Forum

THE TREVI FOUNTAIN

P. di Trevi; open daily 24hr

You know you need to see the Trevi Fountain, but you're not sure why until you're there—it is impressive. It is massive. It commands the square. It is Baroque architecture at its finest, in that it's beautiful and knows it and will beat you over the head with it (not that you'll mind). By day, the Trevi Fountain, completed in 1762 as a celebration of Agrippa's ancient aqueducts, is a spectacle of excess—money (popes again!), marble, symbolism, people, selfies. By night or dawn, however, the smaller details of Nicola Salvi's artistic triumph trickle through—the precise definition of Poseidon's horses, the strategic pour of water over the rocks, the still edges of the pool, and of course the sound of running water filling the square. Close your eyes, toss a coin, and wish for fifty first dates with Fontana di Trevi. You'll meet a different fountain each time.

i Free; wheelchair accessible

THEATER OF MARCELLUS

V. del Teatro di Marcello; www.tempietto.it; open daily 24hr

Rome displays a constant contradiction between past and present, and few buildings in the Eternal City demonstrate this odd symbiosis better than the Theater of Marcellus. Inaugurated by **Augustus** in 12 BCE, the Theater of Marcellus has been confusing tourists ever since with its passing likeness to the Colosseum. To be fair, it is a large entertainment venue—older and better preserved than the Colosseum, at that—but it is semi-circular whereas the Colosseum is

360 degrees, and your taxi driver will know the difference. Over the years, the structure has served as an apartment building, fortress, quarry, inspiration to Christopher Wren, and glory project for Mussolini. Today, the Theater of Marcellus straddles the gaps between public and private, ancient and modern; the bottom half of the structure—restored in recent years—hosts live musical performances in the summer (check online for schedules), while the top half is composed of privately owned and occupied apartments. Thus, you have two options to access the theater: see a show outside its walls, or somehow befriend the person who reportedly shelled out $10 million last year to live there.

i Free; wheelchair accessible

MUSEUMS

BORGHESE GALLERY

Piazzale Scipione Borghese 5; 68 41 39 79; www.galleriaborghese.it; open Tu-Su 9am-7pm

The Borghese Gallery, located at the northeastern end of the **Borghese Gardens,** imparts a few inescapable lessons, including that money makes the seventeenth-century art world go 'round, Caravaggio was the original master of shade, and Bernini knew a thing or two about rippling muscles (and marble, too). Housed in Scipione Borghese's former party villa (because you're nobody until you have a papal party villa on the edge of town), the private collection is now a must-see museum for Baroque art, with notable works from **Caravaggio, Bernini, Titian, Rubens,** and other titans of excessive detail. Finding a time to visit can get tricky; technically, ticket reservations must be made online for two-hour visiting slots, but they can also be purchased onsite if there are any left-over (though don't expect the staff to be pleased about this). The Borghese Gallery is worth the hassle, though, for a chance to witness what Google Images still can't capture: the virtuosity of Baroque A-listers.

i Adults €15 (including €2 reservation fee), €8.50 reduced (EU students only); though you can try your luck with buying tickets at will call, visiting the Borghese Gallery requires a ticket reservation, which can be bought online or by phone (+39 06 32810); the Gallery admits 360 ticket holders every 2hr starting at 9am, and all guests are required to leave the Gallery after their 2hr tour is up; first entry 9am, ticket office closes at 6:30pm; wheelchair accessible

CAPITOLINE MUSEUMS

P. Campodoglio; www.museicapitolini.org; open daily 9:30am-7:30pm

As you have probably figured out by now, Imperial Rome was not subtle about its accomplishments (see: Colosseum, Trajan's Column, every marble frieze of military takeover). As the house of some of the greatest hits of Roman art, the Capitoline Museum puts on a show of size. Visitors are welcomed by the massive feet of Constantine, whose marble toe is the size of your head (because big feet, well...you know). The museum winds through the large (bronze she-wolf of Rome, exquisite statue of Venus), the huge (remains of Greek bronzes, entrancing bust of Brutus), and the downright colossal (bronze of Marcus Aurelius on a horse, Constantine's head). The classic **marble statues** and **bronze casts** steal the show, but you can get your dose of Renaissance and Caravaggio in the Capitoline's picture gallery and rooms furnished by, you guessed it, the popes.

i Tickets €15, video guides €6; last entry 1hr before closing; wheelchair accessible, call 0667102071 for directions and assistance

PALAZZO MASSIMO (MUSEUM OF ROME)

Largo di Villa Peretti 1; 6 39 96 77 00; www.archeoroma.beniculturali.it; open Tu-Su 9am-7:45pm

Today, Ancient Rome is often summed up by its monuments, mighty ruins, and impressive concrete. But there would be no Colosseum, Forum, or aqueducts without the many ordinary people who worked, wined, dined, shopped, and lived in the city, a fact showcased in the exceptional Palazzo Massimo, a segment of the Museum of Rome next to the entrance of **Termini Station.** A visit to the Palazzo Massimo conjures the recognizably human ghosts of Ancient Rome: take in the colors of the restored full-room fresco from the **Villa of LiV,** then see how busts depict the change of style over time (beards only became a thing because of Hadrian, for example). Don't miss the outstanding **"Boxer at Rest" bronze,** marked with cuts and bruises from an exhausting fight.

Admission €7, free for visitors under 18; ticket valid at all National Roman Museum sites (Baths of Diocletian, Palazzo Altemps, and Balbi Crypt), ticket office closes 1hr before closing; tickets can be booked at www.coopculture.it; wheelchair accessible

MUSEO DELL'ARA PACIS

Lungotevere in Augusta; en.arapacis.it; open daily 9:30am-7:30pm

While most celebratory arches in Rome are all about the "booty booty booty booty rockin' everywhere" (the spoils of war, that is), the Ara Pacis marks a change of pace. Literally translated to "Altar of Peace," the Ara Pacis was commissioned by Augustus in 13 BCE to commemorate an era of uncharacteristic peace and prosperity for Rome. With its scenes of bounty, fertility, and the Imperial family, the Ara Pacis also worked to visually establish a new civic religion for the recently imperialized Roman state (because if you're Augustus, it's not enough to be military conqueror and emperor—you must be father of the people, as well). Restored and now displayed in the Museo dell'Ara Pacis next to the Tiber, the Ara Pacis demonstrates that it was possible for Rome to produce exquisite sculptures without crushing another state first (actually, that's a lie, Augustus was fresh off a campaign in Gaul. But it's the thought that counts?).

Admission €10.50; last entry 1hr before closing; wheelchair accessible

THE BATHS OF DIOCLETIAN

V. Enrico de Nicola 79; www.archeoroma.benicultuali.it; open Tu-Su 9am-7:30pm

Across the street from Termini Station, the remains of Diocletian's baths remind you that public nudity was all the rage back in Ancient Rome, at least in the bathhouse. Today, this mega-complex of personal hygiene, part of the National Roman Museum, houses an exhibit on the written communication of Rome (not that engaging), a room on inscriptions from the Roman republic (somewhat engaging), and **Michelangelo's Cloister,** a garden lined with sculptures of various quality. The baths themselves are difficult to find within the museum—you have to go left from the bookstore, not out the back door of the Cloister that locks behind you and won't let you back in.

Admission €7, free for under 18; ticket valid for 3 consecutive days at all National Roman Museum sites (Palazzo Altemps, Palazzo Massimo, and Balbi Crypt); last entry 1hr. before closing; wheelchair accessible

THE VATICAN MUSEUMS

V.le Vaticano; 6 69 88 46 76; www.museivaticani.va; open M-Sa 9am-6pm, last Su of every month 9am-2pm

A visit to the Vatican demands preparation. You can reserve tickets to skip the line, bring an umbrella to weather the heat, and wear proper shoes to endure the nearly seven kilometers of exhibits. But for all your thinking ahead, nothing can deflect the overwhelming power of the Vatican's opulence. The Vatican has zero chill when it comes to wealth, with over 70000 works of art (20,000 on display)—including some of the most recognizable pieces in the world—and an exorbitant amount of rare marble. The human mind cannot comprehend the sheer amount of detail, talent, luxury, and, of course, power housed in the Vatican. But you can give yourself a few hours to try. Follow the crowd through the **Pinacoteca,** down the intricately tiled and painted hallways and past the map collection. Take in what you can. This is the one of the most extensive and significant collections of art in the world, and even a sliver of it will impress.

Adults €16, booked ahead €20, €8 reduced (students, religious seminaries, disabled persons), booked ahead €12, free last Su of the month; tickets include entrance to Sistine Chapel, and are only valid for the date and time issued; book online to avoid waiting in line for 2-3hr; tours begin every 30min. starting at 9am; last entry 4pm; wheelchair accessible

OUTDOORS

AVENTINE HILL

V. di Santa Sabina; open daily Apr-Sept 7am-9pm, Oct-Mar 7am-6pm

According to legend, **Romulus'** settlement on the Palatine defeated **Remus'** camp on the Aventine for the founding of Rome, but the Aventine has since recouped its losses in the form of views of the city and sun-kissed gardens. A 10-to 15-minute hike from the path along the Tiber, the Aventine features the **Giardino degli Aranci** (Orange Garden), which smells of pine and flower blossoms and offers one of the best sunset perches in the city. From the balcony at the edge of the park, just past the evergreen trees and peaceful fountains, you can see sun-drenched Rome stretch before you, from the Altare della Patria on the right, to the **Vatican** beyond, to **Trastevere** on the left. You may also see some serious PDA, a few selfie sticks, and perhaps a guitar player welcoming the evening with an acoustic rendition of U2's "One."

i Free; wheelchair accessible

GIANICOLO HILL

Open daily 24hr

Gianicolo Hill is to the seven hills of Rome what Lake Champlain is to the Great Lakes—too far away to ever be included, but with enough perks to make a claim. Across the Tiber from the actual hills of Rome (which, really, is not far away at all), Gianicolo is the second-tallest hill in the city, and arguably its greatest vantage point for views of the ancient center, if you can find a spot to look between the trees. Though outside the limits of the Imperial city, Gianicolo has since been embraced by Rome, as signified by its Baroque fountain (the **Fontana dell'Acqua Paola)** and its church. Getting to the top of Gianicolo requires some focus, but if you can manage the roadblocks, confusing street signs, and allure of bar patios, the piazza provides a worthwhile peek at the pink-tan city sprawled across the Tiber.

i Free; wheelchair accessible

VILLA BORGHESE GARDENS

Open daily 24hr

The Villa Borghese Garden is not a destination, but a place to wander. The Garden's maze of gravel paths, less official dirt paths, steps, and occasional roads were designed to get you lost, but that's not at your expense. First designated by Cardinal Scipione Borghese in 1605, and thus the oldest public park in Rome, the Villa Borghese Garden has since filled in with towering trees, overgrown grasses, villas, too many fountains to keep straight, and of course the **Borghese Gallery.** Casual wanderers will also stumble upon some of the lesser known yet still intriguing sights, such as a group of high school kids up to no good, several elderly ladies yelling colorful Italian at their dogs, and a couple of brave joggers attempting to work off the day's pasta lunch.

i Free; wheelchair accessible; entrances include: Porta Pinciana, V. Belle Arte, V. Mercadante, and V. Pinciana

FOOD

BARNUM CAFÉ ($)

V. Del Pellegrino 87; 64 76 04 83; open M-Sa 9am-2am

Open for the better part of the day, Barnum Café shapeshifts from trendy breakfast spot to studious work café to popular aperitivo bar over the course of your waking hours. Like its eponymous circus entertainer, Barnum has many acts, but it always remains a full-time creative space and frequent hangout for Rome's freelancers, alternative types, and internationally-minded crowd. Situated in the heart of the rose-tinted **Centro Storico neighborhood,** Barnum specializes in artful salads, cocktail creations, and actually cold iced coffee (served in a martini glass, no less). Go for a snack, go for a spritz and a bruschetta, or go for an hour of focused laptop time—regardless, you'll feel cooler for doing so.

i Daily specials from €6, coffee from €1.50, juices €4, desserts €5, cocktails from €7; vegan and vegetarian options available; wheelchair accessible

BISCOTTIFICIO ARTIGIANO INNOCENTI ($)

V. della Luce 21; 65 80 39 26; open M-Sa 8am-8pm, Su 9:30am-2pm, closed Aug

Though its exterior beckons to no one, the one-room interior projects all the signs of serious bakery business: a huge oven, baskets of cookies in the window, a large scale to accurately weigh your haul of cookies, and store plaques plastered on top of American political campaign signs from the 1970s. The vintage look isn't a show: the bakery has been operated by the same family for over 50 years, and is subject to the usual non-corporate whims (such as closing the whole month of August for vacation). Innocenti delivers on a wide range of baked goods, but specializes in traditional Italian nut cookies, such as hazelnut bites (*brutti ma buoni*) or almond wedges (some with chocolate). Running about €2 for six or so, you can afford to try a few (or 20).

i Biscuits and cookies by weight (about 6 cookies per €2); vegetarian options available; wheelchair accessible

BONCI PIZZARIUM ($$)

V. della Meloria 43; 63 97 45 16; www.bonci.it; open M-Sa 11am-10pm, Su 11am-4pm and 6pm-10pm

Sure, the Vatican contains the wealth of a country a hundred times its size, but the real treasure might be just outside its walls. We're talking about Bonci Pizzarium, arguably the best take-away pizza in Rome. Founded by famed pizza connoisseur Gabriele Bonci, the Pizzarium seems more like a pizza art museum than a fast food joint, as the crusts are loaded with Willy Wonka-style portions of toppings—mounds of mozzarella, piles of sautéed veggies, and even heaps of seared tuna. (Haven't you heard? Margherita was *so* last season). A word of warning: some gourmet slices (yes, that tuna one) can run several euro more per slice, so check the labels before you accidentally end up with a €15 takeaway pizza bill.

i Pizza from €4 per slice, from €7 per slice for gourmet varieties; vegetarian options available; wheelchair accessible; take-away only; small counter space provided

GELATERIA DELLA PALMA ($)

V. Della Maddalena 19-23; 6 68 80 67 52; www.dellapalma.it; open daily 8:30am-12:30am

Gelateria Della Palma's rainbow palm tree logo doesn't scream "GOOD GELATO," but don't be fooled by the neon: this shop takes gelato as seriously as the color spectrum. Della Palma, on the corner of the Pantheon plaza, specializes in the wacky and wonderful, with over 150 flavors ranging from Kiwi Strawberry to Kit Kat to Sesame and Honey. Yes, it's swimming with people all taking too much time to make a flavor decision, but the quality of gelato and heaping portions render the hassle irrelevant. Plus, there are numerous soy or rice milk and yogurt options for those challenged by dairy and full fat. If you're going to ball out on gelato in Rome (and you should), this is center court.

i Gelato from €2.30; wheelchair accessible

PIANOSTRADA ($$)

V. della Zoccolette 22; 6 89 57 22 96; open Tu-Su 1pm-4pm and 7pm-11:30pm

Recently relocated from Trastevere to a quiet corner of **Monti,** Pianostrada puts a fresh spin on familiar Italian staples. Their menu presents a tour de force of re-energized dishes, from refined street food (i.e., fried everything), to stir-fried veggies with pine nuts and raisins, to the best damn focaccia in Rome. The old trattoria provides inspiration for Pianostrada's pizzas, focaccias, and

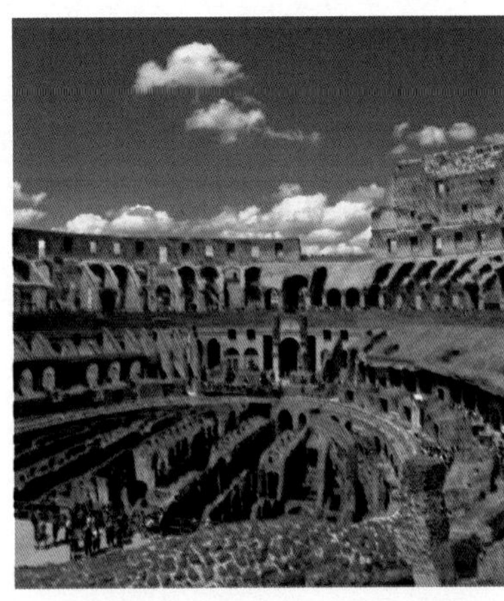

small plates, but their salads, fried dishes, and flavor combinations defy classification. *Ristorante,* this is not. And though it occupies the tail end of the student budget spectrum, Pianostrada's daring take on Italian cuisine, sprightly interior, and spacious back patio justify the cost.

i Primi from €12, secondi from €12, sides from €8, wine from €6 per glass; vegan and vegetarian options available; wheelchair accessible

FORNO CAMPO DE' FIORI ($)

Vicolo del Gallo 14; 6 68 80 66 62; www.fornocampodefiori.com; open M-Sa 7:30am-8pm

There are numerous *fornos* (bakeries) throughout Rome, which can make it difficult to choose one that doesn't hand you a bag of dried-out cookies or surprisingly charge you €4 for a couple biscotti. And then there's Il Forno Campo de' Fiori, which catches your gaze with its bright sign, yet soothes you with sweet, sweet sugar (specifically, a hefty bag of lemon cookies and biscotti for under €2). Il Forno Campo de' Fiori can also tempt you with savory treats, as its paninis, *piadinas,* and various other combos of sliced things and bread are delicious, filling, and mercifully cheap. No seating for this meal; you can pace yourself to all the nearby monuments one chocolate-dipped almond biscuit at a time.

i Biscuits and cookies by weight, sandwiches from €3; vegan and vegetarian options available; wheelchair accessible

LA CARBONARA ($$)

V. Panisperna 214; 64 82 51 76; www.lacarbonara.it; open M-Sa 12:30pm-2:30pm and 7pm-11pm

La Carbonara strikes a hard pose against the games of tourism, starting with a "No TripAdvisor" sign on the door. It's a bold play for a dining scene that runs on reputation and recommendations, but judging by the walls filled with notes and signatures of satisfied patrons, La Carbonara has earned enormous confidence. This no-frills *trattoria* on one of Monti's wider streets keeps its memories close—a case of used wine corks over here, a framed moon chart from a decade ago over there—and its pasta secrets closer. TripAdvisor or no, the reviews are in: the *cacio e pepe* under this framed record and shelf of wine bottles earns five stars (or, perhaps more appreciated, a sincere *grazie* to the waiter).

i Primi from €6, secondi from €8; vegetarian options available; wheelchair accessible

QUE TE PONGO? ($)

V. Della Dogana Vecchia 13; 6 68 80 30 29; open M-Sa 9am-8pm

"Que te pongo? What would you like?" A small, understated "salmoneria" around the corner from the Pantheon asks you. Hmm...a sandwich, you think, one that is not 80% bread and has some flavor and enough protein to fuel these 16,000-step days. "We've got you," the smile from behind the counter seems to say, and the menu confirms it. There are no slim prosciutto pieces here. Specializing in fish of the smoked, pickled, or marinated variety, Que Te Pongo? delivers in taste and quantity where other sandwich shops skate by on a baguette. Their extensive list of sandwich options—combinations of fish, vegetables, and homemade sauce—sell for the respectable price of €5-6 and can also be converted into a salad (€7.50-9). There's minimal seating, so opt for takeaway between monument stops. We hope the lunch sticks with you longer than the smell of salmon on your breath.

i Sandwiches from €5, salads from €7.50, platters from €10; wheelchair accessible

NIGHTLIFE

BAR DEL FICO

P. Del Fico 34/35; 6 68 86 13 73; www.bardelfico.com; open daily 7:30am-2am

To be in Rome is to blend living and leisure, and the city's nightlife generally holds to that mantra. Rome's scene is not the work hard, play hard of many American colleges, or the all-night raging of European club cities. In Rome, it's smooth, easy, and continuous—good food, soothing drinks, fun company, and establishments that shift from café to restaurant to bar throughout the day. Bar del Fico represents the best of these multitasking hangouts, with a consistent crowd of young professionals from morning espresso, to early evening spritzes, to late night cocktails. Taking up half a square in **Centro Storico,** Bar del Fico's packed wrap-around patio sets the tone for nights out in the surrounding restaurants and bars: not rowdy, but definitely not quiet, with plenty of drinks and fresh food to go around.

i Beer from €4, cocktails €8, food from €6; wheelchair accessible; serves Su brunch

BLACKMARKET

V. Panisperna 101; 33 98 22 75 41; www.blackmarketartgallery.it; open daily 7:30pm-2am

BlackMarket is Rome's angsty art school student who matured into a retro hipster with some business sense. Behind a heavy door and curtain on one of **Monti's** busier streets, this combo bar and art gallery keeps things dark—shaded lamps, mahogany-polished furniture, and the pitch black of late nights. It's too moody, from the outside, for some tourists, but its creative cocktail menu has stirred enough buzz to draw both visitors and some locals. A little edgier than your standard wine bar and a little more rebellious than your classy patio cocktail, BlackMarket marks the second or third stop on a night out, when you're ready to upgrade from a small café table to a swanky velvet couch (cocktail glass delicately in hand, of course).

i Beer from €4, cocktails €10; limited wheelchair accessibility

FRENI E FRIZIONI

V. del Politeama 4-6; 6 45 49 74 99; www.freniefrizioni.com; open daily 6:30pm-2am

If you're walking along the Tiber outside **Trastevere** on any given summer night, you'll inevitably be stopped by the sight of a square full of people, mostly mid-20s, lounging outside a restaurant. People drape over the stone walls and down the steps. A man breaks out some John Lennon on his guitar. Plates and wine glasses dot the tables. "I have to be a part of this,"you say, without thinking. Welcome to Freni e Frizioni, Trastevere's go-to spot for aperitivos, drinks, and blending into the scene. There's beer, wine, and croquettes aplenty, but Freni e Frizioni sets a new standard with its cocktails—please see the print-out menu of their creative creations, disguised as album covers. You know what's far cooler than being a Green Day fan in middle school? Sipping a Green Day cocktail on a piazza in Rome while watching the sun brighten every reddish paint job in Trastevere.

i Beer €6, long drinks €7 (decrease by €1 after 10pm), cocktails from €8; aperitivo (7pm-10pm): wheelchair accessible; casual, hip attire

CUL DE SAC

P. di Pasquino 73; 6 68 80 10 94; www.enotecaculdesac.com; open daily noon-4pm and 6pm-12:30am

If you thought "go big or go home" was confined to America, then you haven't seen Cul de Sac's wine selection. Some wine bars offer a booklet; Cul de Sac ups the ante to encyclopedia. The phone book-thick wine list here ranges from Italian, of course, to American and French, and manifests in an extensive collection of bottles lining the walls of Cul de Sac's narrow interior. Come for cured meat and cheese aperitivos, stay for an education in the global expanse of wine and the indulgent ambiance of an Italian evening.

i No cover, wine glasses from €4, cured meat and cheese from €7, primi from €8, secondi from €7; wheelchair accessible

EX DOGANA

Vle. dello Scalo S. Lorenzo 10; 33 43 84 91 85; www.exdogana.com; open Tu-W noon-10pm, Th-F noon-1am, Sa 10am-1am, Su 10am-10pm

It takes effort to prove that Ex Dogana is not too cool for you. The former 1920s train depot in **San Lorenzo** is more complex than nightclub, which requires navigation. It's a mostly local, university-student hangout, which requires either understanding Italian or accepting you're the only one who doesn't. It's located southeast of the **Termini** hostel neighborhood, which means you'll be trekking a good twenty minutes through Rome's less picturesque streets to get there. And the venue hosts primarily live music events, which requires knowing what is going on and when (and not knowing any lyrics). If you think you can hang, then check the lineup of acts online and hit up the electronic dance floor, outdoor lounge area, and themed parties. Congratulate yourself on infiltrating one of Rome's edgiest, most energetic, and unapologetically coolest night spots, though it's probably still too cool for you.

i Free, depending on event; some areas charge €12 for entrance; wheelchair accessible; check online for upcoming concerts or music festivals

THE YELLOW BAR

V. Palestro 40; 6 49 38 26 82; www.the-yellow.com; open daily 24hr

Rows of beer on tap, plastic-cupped cocktails spilling onto the dance floor, and not a word of Italian in earshot—what's the difference between the Yellow Bar and the old familiar college one? Not much, especially that rough tequila shot you just got roped into taking with the new hostel bunk mates. But when the mostly international crowd is as new to Rome as you are and eager to make friends, trying to find the hot underground local spot suddenly seems like a far less important priority. The Yellow is travel partying at its freewheeling and familiar finest (or worst, depending on your comfort level with sweaty and PDA-packed dance floors). A raucous hours-long trap for some, a night-starter for others, the Yellow will induct you into the traveler's scene one way or another.

i No cover, beer €5, cocktails €7; wheelchair accessible; DJ starts around 12:30am; serves coffee and breakfast

SAN GIMIGNANO

Coverage by **Margaret Canady**

San Gimignano has been called the Manhattan of the Medieval, and it's hard to believe that something so antiquated can still thrive in the modern world. The small town, built in the third century, is known for its numerous towers and preserved wall. Situated atop a hill, it looks out over a land of vineyards. We half-expected to see knights on white horses galloping down the cobblestoned streets to save a damsel in distress stuck in Torre Grossa, the tallest tower in the city. But this is 2019, and things have changed—including gender norms and the city's culture. The town is actually a hub for cutting-edge contemporary art and artists, and you'll find several galleries with one-of-a-kind modern art. A day trip to San Gimignano is definitely worth the effort, and it's light-years better than anything Medieval Times Dinner Theater can give you.

ORIENTATION

San Gimignano's shape resembles a rose with only a stub of a stem left over. Most travelers enter from the south of the city (the stem), where you can find **Piazzale Martiri Montemaggio** and the main entrance, **Porta San Giovanni.** The city's main street, **Via San Giovanni**, runs north from the entrance, and if you follow it you'll reach the heart of the city, at which point lies **Piazza della Cisterna** and **Piazza Duomo.** The main entrance leaving Piazza Duomo is **Via San Matteo**, which curves north-west and take you to the north entrance of the city, **Porta San Matteo. Via delle Romite** is a street north of and runs parallel with Via San Matteo and leads to **Piazza Sant'Agostino**. A medieval wall surrounds the entire city.

ESSENTIALS

GETTING THERE

The closest airports are in Pisa (Pisa International Airport) and Florence (Aeroporto di Firenze). The easiest way reach San Gimignano is by car. If arriving from Florence or Siena, you'll take SS2 to Poggibonsi. From here, go along SS68 east and follow the signs to San Gimignano. There are parking lots available on the edge of the city (€2/hr or €20/day). Train lines from Florence and Rome stop at a train station called Poggibonsi. From here, there is a bus that takes you directly to San Gimignano. Tickets for the bus are €2.50 one way and can be bought at the Poggibonsi train station tobacconist.

GETTING AROUND

Cars are forbidden in San Gimignano, so once you park or get off the bus, you'll be walking through the walled city. This is the best way to experience the city, and because there are virtually only two main roads, you (almost certainly) won't get lost. There is also an electric shuttle bus between Porta San Giovanni, Piazza della Cisterna, and Porta San Matteo. The bus is €1 and tickets can be bought at the Tourist Information office or at the tobacconist's.

PRACTICAL INFORMATION

Tourist Offices: Associazione Pro Loco San Gimignano (P. del Duomo, 1; 05 77 94 00 08; www.sangimignano.com/en; open daily 10am-1pm and 3pm-7pm).

Banks/ATMs/Currency Exchange: There are several ATMs located around the city. Here is a bank: Banca Cambiano 1884 S.p.A. (V. S. Giovanni, 3; 05 77 94 22 35; www.bancacambiano.it; open M-F 8:30am-1:30pm).

Post Offices: There is one post office in the city (P. delle Erbe; 05 77 90 77 35; open M-F 8:20am-1:35pm, Sa 8:20am-1:35pm).

Public Restrooms: There are several restrooms located around the city, which cost €0.50 to use. Grab a map from the tourist office for specific details.

Internet: There is Wi-Fi in the three squares of the old town center. Many cafés also have Wi-Fi.

BGLTQ+ Resources: The closest physical resource is located in Pisa at Pinkriot Arcigay (V. Enrico Fermi, 7; 05 02 32 78; pinkriot.arcigaypisa.it; open Th 6-10pm).

EMERGENCY INFORMATION

Emergency Number: 112.

Police: Police Headquarters (Via Mario Lalli, 3; 0 50 58 35 11; questure.poliziadistato.it/pisa).

US Embassy: The nearest US consulate is located in Florence (Lungarno Vespucci 38; 39 055 266 951; it.usembassy.gov/embassy-consulates/florence). The nearest US embassy is located in Rome (V. Vittorio Veneto 121; 0 64 67 41; it.usembassy.gov/embassy-consulates/rome).

Rape Crisis Center: RAINN (80 06 56 46 73).

Hospitals: The closest hospital is located in Poggibonsi.

- Hospital Campostaggia (Loc. Campostaggia; 05 77 99 41; open daily 24hr).

Pharmacies: Here are two pharmacies:

- Municipal Pharmacy (P. della Cisterna, 8; 05 77 99 03 69; open daily 9am-1pm and 4pm-8pm).
- Borsini Pharmacy (V. San Matteo, 17; 05 77 94 03 97; open daily 9am-1pm and 4pm-8pm).

SIGHTS

CULTURE

GALLERIA CONTINUA

V. del Castello, 11; www.galleriacontinua.com; open daily 10am-1pm and 2pm-7pm

If you showed someone Galleria Continua out of context, they would probably assume it was a contemporary art gallery in the heart of New York, San Francisco, or some other city with a big arts scene. Instead, Galleria Continua is pushing the boundaries of modern art in a small, secluded Medieval town. It doesn't make any sense, and yet it works perfectly. The Gallery opened in 1990 in a former cinema, and has woven its way into the folds of the city since. The constantly-rotating exhibits activate the energy of the ancient city, which inspires the art and artists who find themselves here.

i Free; limited wheelchair accessibility

SAN GIMIGNANO 1300

V. Costarella, 3; 32 74 39 51 65; www.sangimignano1300.com; open daily 10am-5pm

Current obsession: those Facebook videos featuring miniature scenes and dollhouse cooking. So, imagine our excitement when we stumbled upon San Gimignano 1300, a free museum that features a miniature version of the

city as it was in 1300. The mini-city, conceived and executed by brothers Michelangelo and Raffaello Rubino (not the famous guys, these are just some dudes from our lifetime), is made entirely from ceramics. The re-creation is meticulously designed, the details of windows and roofs inspiring joy. We enjoyed it more than we care to admit.
i Free; wheelchair accessible

LANDMARKS

PIAZZA DEL DUOMO AND PIAZZA DELLA CISTERNA

P. del Duomo and P. della Cisterna; 05 77 94 00 08; www.sangimignano.com/en; open daily 24hr

The connecting Piazzas del Duomo and della Cisterna are the center of San Gimignano, where you'll find the most hustle and bustle in the city. If coming from the south, you'll first enter through the grandiose archway **Arco dei Becci** into Piazza della Cisterna. Although the plaza was originally used as a market and festival stage, today restaurants and gelaterias line the street, and people sit on the steps of the octagonal well that resides in its center. Walking straight through the Piazza, you'll immediately enter Piazza del Duomo, which is slightly smaller but equally grandiose. This Piazza holds a lot of the main landmarks, including the **Church of Collegiate, Torre Grossa,** and the **Twin Towers.** Long story short, in the thirteenth century, two competing families built two sets of towers to assert their dominance in the city. Just a hunch, but we think it must've been the men who decided this was a good idea. Comparing tower length is such a boy thing.
i Free; wheelchair accessible

TORRE GROSSA

V. di Sant'Andrea, 121; 05 83 97 70 48; www.sangimignano.com/en; open daily Apr 1-Sept 30 10am-7:30pm; Oct 1-Mar 31 11am-5:30pm

In our pursuit of good views, we've climbed more than the average person's fair share of towers. Torre Grossa is a pretty standard one, and on a scale of 1 to "I can't feel my thighs," the climb lands at a 2.5. As you walk up the wide metal staircase, a projection in the center of the bell tower entitled "Medieval Vertigo" provides a historic overview of the tower, which felt a little off putting in the 700 year old edifice. The price is a little steep, too—if we're paying €9, we want to sweat like we would in an extreme Soulcycle class. The views from the top, however, are truly breathtaking. It's only when you're at the top that you realize how secluded the town is from the rest of the world. Surrounded by green vineyards, lush farmlands, and the **Apuan Alps,** there's not much to give away the fact that it's 2019 and not 1619 (other than the parking lot on the outskirts of town).
i Admission €9; last entry 30min. before closing

MUSEUMS

DUOMO DI SAN GIMIGNANO (COLLEGIATE CHURCH OF SAN GIMIGNANO)

P. del Duomo, 2; 05 77 94 03 16; www.duomosangimignano.it; open Apr 1-Oct 31 M-F 10am-7:30pm, Sa 10am-5:30pm, Su 12:30pm-7:30pm; Nov 1-Mar 31 M-Sa 10am-5pm, Su 12:30pm-5pm

If this is the sixth (or 18th) Italian church you've seen on your trip thus far, you should know the drill by now: frescoes and murals, high ceilings and stained glass—and, of course, disdain for your blasphemously exposed shoulders, for shame! The Collegiate Church, located smack dab in the middle of **Piazza del Duomo,** fits nicely into this stereotype, but that doesn't take away from the awe we feel upon stepping into a place of worship. Along the walls, frescoes tell the stories of Creation, Heaven, and Hell; on one panel, the church offers detailed descriptions of Hell's punishment for each of the seven cardinal sins. (We hope exposed shoulders wasn't one of them.) The church also holds the sarcophagus of Saint Fina, the Patron Saint of San Gimignano. Saint Fina died at 15, and when she passed, the wooden board upon which she lay is said to have burst in blooms of violet.

i Admission €4, €2 reduced; wheelchair accessible; covered shoulders and respectable clothing to enter; free audio guide

PALAZZO COMUNALE

P. Duomo, 2; 05 77 28 63 00; www.sangimignano.com/en;open daily Apr 1-Sept 30 10am-7:30pm, Oct 1-Mar 31 11am-5:30pm

Before checking out the Palazzo Comunale, give the site's Wikipedia page a brief skim (for that matter, do this before going to literally any monument anywhere, and you'll feel much more informed and #cultured). Attached to **Torre Grossa,** the Palazzo Comunale consists of two parts: the outside courtyard and stepped gallery with stone arches, and the indoor civic museum and gallery. The civic authority used to address the crowd from this stepped gallery, and inside, would discuss important business stuff in the council chamber. Today, you can view some old Italian art, and that's about it.

i Admission €9, included with ticket to Torre Grossa; not wheelchair accessible

OUTDOORS

LA ROCCA DI MONTESTAFFOLI

V. della Rocca, 13; 05 77 94 00 08; www.sangimignano.com/en/san-gimignano/guide-to-the-town/rocca-di-montestaffoli.asp; open daily 24hr

For the perfect picnic or a stroll during sunset, head over to La Rocca di Montestaffoli. Flora and greenery overrun the ruins of the town's fourteenth-century fortress, and there's usually a musician and/or painter there to entertain and enjoy the view. In the corner there's a fortress tower, and a short walk gives you a sweeping view of the vineyard valleys around the town. Look out for the picture-perfect doorway to the right of the tower: surrounded by lush purple flowers, the doorway will give you a view out and over the city.

i Free; limited wheelchair accessibility

FOOD

GELATERIA DONDOLÍ ($)

P. Della Cisterna, 4; 05 77 94 22 44; www.gelateriadondoli.com; open daily 8am-11:30pm

Gelateria Dondolí has been crowned the **world's best gelato** several years in a row. So, of course, in pursuit of the truth, we had to try it. To avoid a line, go early or late in the day; we went around 12:30pm and the wait was short. There's an overwhelming number of flavors: you can stick with the classics (pistachio, chocolate, ya know) or try some of their specialities (eggnog, grapefruit, etc). After grabbing your gelato, take a seat at the octagonal well in the Piazza or walk around the city. What's our verdict, you ask? Well, it was some pretty damn good gelato. We're basically experts now.

i Gelato from €2.50; non-dairy options available; wheelchair accessible

DAL BERTELLI ($)

V. Capassi, 30; 34 83 18 19 07; open M-Th 11am-7pm, F-Su 11am-midnight

This panini shop gets straight to the point: you're hungry, and they have food. There are literally three things on the menu: a panini with one type of meat, a panini with another type of meat, and a panini with meat and cheese. Mr. Bertelli, the passionate and jolly owner whose family has owned the shop for two generations, spoke only in Italian. Not sure what their secret is, but the sandwich was insane. No condiments, nothing fancy, yet the smoked cheese and cured meat on fresh bread still made our day. As we munched contentedly, the Bertelli patriarch looked on fondly from the framed picture on the wall.

i Paninis from €4; wheelchair accessible

LOCANDA SANT'AGOSTINO ($$$)

P. S. Agostino, 15; 05 77 94 31 41; open daily 11am-11pm

Locanda Sant'Agostino knew they needed to stand out amongst the Italian restaurants that speckle San Gimignano's streets. Sometime along their more than 22-year timeline, they decorated the restaurant with colorful chairs and plateware, lined the walls with row after row of hand-drawn framed rose pictures, hung dry herbs and flowers from the ceiling, and decorated the tables with rose-printed tablecloths. The eclectic décor shines like a rainbow-speckled candle as the sun sets, and fills the courtyard it's in with warmth and cheer. The restaurant is off the beaten path and a bit up a hill, giving you a brief respite from the crowds. Dishes are made individually, and this place is definitely a sit-down, slow-down type of restaurant, but if you're looking for a delicious and hearty meal, this is the place for you. Make sure to try the wild boar, a Tuscany specialty.

i Appetizers from €9, pasta from €13, other entrées from €15; vegetarian options available; wheelchair accessible

SIENA

Coverage by **Margaret Canady**

A walled city situated in the heart of Tuscany, Siena is known for its Medieval architecture and ancient brick buildings. It's easy to spend several hours wandering through the *contrade,* or neighborhoods, stopping to admire the Piazza del Campo, the Duomo, and other landmarks. This isn't some sleepy little town, though. It bursts with sensation—as you take in the Medieval sights, you'll be greeted with the town's chatter, now a combination of locals and visitors. The University of Siena resides here, and its student body comprises nearly half of the town's population. Siena is also a popular destination for students studying abroad, which means even more opportunities to make friends with young strangers—both Italian and not.

ORIENTATION

Siena is built on three hills and the central part of the city is contained within the city walls. The northernmost entrance is **Porta Camollia,** and just outside of this entrance is the train station. From here, **Via di Camollia** (which turns into **Via dei Montanini,** which turns into **Via Banchi di Sopra**) winds southeast into the city center. The city is centered around **Piazza del Campo,** and main streets **Banchi di Sotto** (curves east), **Via di Cittá**, and **Via Giovanni Dupre** (curves southwest) extend from the Piazza. A few blocks to the west is **Piazza del Duomo.** South of here, along Via di Cittá, is the botanical garden. East of Piazza del Campo is the **University of Siena.**

ESSENTIALS

GETTING THERE

The nearest airports to Siena include Pisa National Airport and the Florence Airport. The Siena train station is a stop on the Empoli-Chiusi train line and the end point on the Siena-Grosseto line. Note that the train station is located at the bottom of a steep hill, and getting into town or to accommodations located outside the city walls is best achieved by getting on a bus or hailing a taxi. A bus runs from Florence to Siena (€7.80 one-way), and a bus runs from Rome (€11 one-way) hourly. Finally, if arriving to Siena by car, there are several highways that lead into the city from each direction, including SS73 (west to east) and Raccordo Autostradale Firenze from Firenze. There are several parking garages available on the outskirts of the city and at the train station, and metered street parking is available.

GETTING AROUND

The historic center of Siena is best enjoyed on foot; in fact, traffic is limited and cars need a permit to enter the city. To get into the city, it is best to take the bus. The buses (operated by TIEMME) run frequently from the outskirts of the city and from the train station, and each bus stop has a schedule and automated timetable. The bus stops for the city center are Piazza del Sale or Piazza Gramsci, and bus tickets cost €1.20 one-way. Tickets can be bought on the bus or at most tabaccherie.

PRACTICAL INFORMATION

Tourist Offices: There are two main tourist offices in Siena: one in P. del Campo, and one in P. del Duomo. Here's the information for the former: Siena Info Point (Il Campo, 69; 05 77 28 23 84; www.sienainfopoint.com/; open daily 10am-2pm and 3pm-7pm).

Banks/ATMs/Currency Exchange: There are many ATMs in the city center. Here is a bank: Monte dei Paschi (V. Banchi di Sopra, 84; 05 77 29 41 11; www.mps.it/; open M-F 8:30am-10pm, Sa 9am-5pm).

Post Offices: There are several post offices around the city center. Poste Italiane is one (V. di Città, 142; 0 57 74 64 71; www.poste.it; open M-F 8:20am-1:35pm, Sa 8:20am-12:35pm).

Public Restrooms: There are a few public restrooms available around the city. Here is one near Il Campo: (V. di Beccheria 1; www.comune.siena.it/).

Internet: Many cafés and restaurants offer Wi-Fi.

BGLTQ+ Resources: Movimento Pansessuale Arcigay Siena (V. di Città, 101; www.movimentopansessuale.it/; 393 100 9004; contact from M-F 4pm-8pm).

EMERGENCY INFORMATION

Emergency Number: 112.

Police: Corpo di Polizia Provinciale di Siena (V. delle Sperandie, 47; 05 77 24 14 00; www.provincia.siena.it/index.php/Aree-tematiche/Polizia-provinciale/Contatti2).

US Embassy: The nearest US consulate is located in Florence (Lungarno Vespucci 38; 39 055 266 951; it.usembassy.gov/embassy-consulates/florence/). The nearest US embassy is located in Rome (V. Vittorio Veneto 121; 0 64 67 41; it.usembassy.gov/embassy-consulates/rome).

Rape Crisis Center: RAINN (20 25 01 44 44).

Hospitals: Primo Lotto (Siena Hospital) (Vle. Mario Bracci, 16; 05 77 58 63 04; www.ao-siena.toscana.it; open daily 24hr).

Pharmacies: There are several pharmacies located throughout the city. Here are two:

- Antica Farmacia Quattro Cantoni S.N.C. (V. S. Pietro, 4; 05 77 28 00 36; www.farmaciaquattrocantoni.it; open M-F 9am-7:30pm).
- Antica Farmacia del Campo (Il Campo, 26; 05 77 28 02 34; open M-Sa 9am-7:30pm).

SIGHTS

CULTURE

PALIO DI SIENA

P. del Campo; 33 86 99 80 10; www.ilpalio.org; yearly July 2 and Aug 16

In the land of extreme sports, Palio di Siena falls at the top of the list. *Il Palio,* a biannual horse race that takes place in the Piazza del Campo, is the most anticipated and celebrated event in Siena. Ten horses (ridden bareback by 10 jockeys) represent the 17 *contrade,* or neighborhoods, of Siena. Leading up to the race (which only last 90 nail biting and dangerous seconds) is a four-day series of trials, as well as a large and extravagant parade called **Corteo Storico.** Horse races have been going on since the sixth century in Siena, so neighborhood pride (and rivalries) run deep. Come early, grab some beers and snacks, and pick your favorite neighborhood. Try to not ruffle the feathers of the 16 other *contrade,* lest you be trampled by horse or by people.

i Free; limited wheelchair accessibility; arrive early to secure top seating, paid seating available

PIAZZA DEL CAMPO

P. del Campo; 5 77 29 21 11; www.enjoysiena.it/en/attrattore/Piazza-del-Campo; open daily 24hr

We appreciate Siena's creativity with Piazza del Campo. Most *piazzas* you'll find in Italy are straight and rectangular (*piazza* translates to square, you square), but Piazza del Campo breaks the mold and is fan-shaped, with regal red brick that slopes downward towards the radial center. At the base of the *piazza* is **Palazzo Pubblico,** the original location of the city's government, and radiating from the center are nine lines of limestone that represent the nine government officials that presided over Siena at its peak. Once a marketplace, today the Piazza is still the hub of city life, hosting the biannual **Palio di Siena,** a steady influx of tourists, and young people lounging on the sloped terrain.

i Free; wheelchair accessible

LANDMARKS

DUOMO DI SIENA (SIENA CATHEDRAL)

P. del Duomo, 8; 05 77 28 63 00; operaduomo.siena.it/en; open daily M-Sa 10:30am-7pm, Su 1:30pm-6pm

A trip to Siena (and every other Italian city) wouldn't be complete without a trip to the Duomo. The cathedral, built during the thirteenth century, is packed with elaborate patterns, reminding us of an indecisive interior designer who just couldn't settle on one theme. White and greenish-black candy cane stripes of marble decorate the outside walls and inner columns. Inside, you'll also find mosaic floors, religious busts on the upper perimeter, a marble altar, and a hexagonal dome adorned with gold stars. Make sure to check out the **Piccolomini Library** while inside; it would be a shame to miss it.

i Admission from €5; last entry 30min. before closing; wheelchair accessible; multimedia guides available from €6; tours available from €18

PALAZZO PUBBLICO

P. del Campo, 1; 05 77 29 21 11; open daily 10am-6pm

Palazzo Pubblico screams government, but make it fashion. Construction for this palace started in 1297 and was built to serve as a gathering space for the Republic of Siena's government. Not just any bland government office building, the Palazzo Pubblico, located right in the center of **Piazza del Campo,** is home to **Torre del Mangia,** the tallest tower in Siena, Medieval architecture, as well as the **Museo Civico** and incredible frescoes. Fun fact: in Siena's glory days, the Council of Nine consisted of nine elected officials from Siena's middle class. It was this council that directed the creation of the Palazzo, and it made us think critically about how wonderful things could be if the government actually represented the people.

i Free; admission to museum and tower sold separately; limited wheelchair accessibility; ticket office in main courtyard

MUSEUMS

MUSEO CIVICO (CIVIC MUSEUM)

P. dell Campo, 1; 05 77 29 22 32; www.comune.siena.it/La-Citta/Cultura/Strutture-Museali/Museo-Civico; open daily Mar 16-Oct 31 10am-7pm, Nov 1-Mar 15 10am-6pm

Proposition: if all work offices were painted with frescoes, fewer people would hate their job. Today, Museo Civico hosts a series of frescoed rooms in **Palazzo Pubblico,** the city hall where government officials met and worked (and still do today). The frescos were commissioned by the governing body rather than religious figures, an extremely unusual act during the thirteenth and fourteenth centuries. Many of the frescoes depict secular scenes, including the most famous, ***Allegories of Good and Bad Government,*** a three-walled masterpiece indicating that good government yields happy people and green hills, while bad government leads to sad people and brown hills.

i Admission €9, €8 students; wheelchair accessible; last tickets sold 45min. before closing

OUTDOORS

CLIMBING TORRE DEL MANGIA

P. del Campo, 1; 05 77 29 23 42; open daily Mar 1-Oct 15 10am-7pm, Oct 16-Feb 28 10am-4pm

The rolling streets of hilly Siena are an exercise in themselves, but if you're still not getting enough steps for your FitBit daily minimum, then either lower your expectations or climb Torre del Mangia. With every good Tuscan city comes a good Tuscan tower, and the 400 steps of Siena's don't disappoint. It's a little pricey (€10), but the view is worth it—Torre del Mangia is located smack dab in the middle of the city, so you get a picture perfect view of the fan shaped **Piazza del Campo** below, terracotta rooftops, and the rolling green Tuscan landscape.

i Admission €10; no wheelchair accessibility; last tickets sold 45min. before closing

FOOD

OSTERIA IL GRATTACIELO ($$)

V. Pontani, 8; 33 46 31 14 58; www.osteriailgrattacielo.it; open daily 11:30am-3pm and 7pm-10pm

The best restaurants, we hypothesize, are the ones found on little side streets that you wouldn't find unless you were actually looking for them. Here, lunch and dinner specials are written outside on a small black chalkboard and change daily, which means they're using fresh ingredients prepare their meals. Even though there were only two options, we still couldn't decide, so our waiter brought us smaller portions of each one. Both were delicious—local salami and cheese paired with sweet melon for one, baby gnocchi with pesto for the other—and were so big that we couldn't finish them, leaving us to wonder what an actual regular-sized portion looks like. Darn—looks like we'll have to return to answer that question.

i Entrées from €8; cash only; wheelchair accessible

LA VECCHIA LATTERIA ($)

V. S. Pietro, 10; 347 474 6448; open daily noon-11:30pm

Imagine this: it's 4pm and the sun has decided you're its main target for the afternoon. As sweat oozes out of every pore on your body, you spot a gelato cornershop, and you're about to shell out €6 for a small cup of gelato when suddenly the budget-guide angels start whacking you in back of the head with a freshly-minted travel guide. Don't stop in just any gelateria! The best to be found in Siena is La Vecchia Latteria. Located on a side street near the **Duomo,** it can be hard to spot, which is why we did the hard work for you. Sit back, relax, and enjoy cheap gelato.

i Gelato from €2; cash only; wheelchair accessible

ANTICA TAGLIERE ($)

V. Giovanni Duprè, 24; 05 77 28 29 93; open daily 11am-10pm

It can be hard to find restaurants in Italy that are open all day, so we were thankful to stumble upon Antica Tagliere one afternoon. They specialize in paninis—specifically cheap paninis—which are the perfect light snack or an even lighter dinner. The meditation-esque music didn't really seem to fit the rustic Italian patterns and ceramic piggy decor, but we weren't complaining. Any restaurant that lets us use their Wi-Fi and remain seated for two hours out of the hot sun is a win in our book.

i Paninis from €4, entrées from €6; cash only; wheelchair accessible; Wi-Fi

LA TAVERNA DEL CAPITANO ($$)

V. del Capitano, 6/8; 347 474 6448; open daily noon-11:30pm

The host at La Taverna del Capitano wore a shirt that depicted a series of images: no Wi-Fi, no bar, no restrooms. "Only food," my waiter told me with a grin. The "no jokes, no gimmicks" restaurant prides itself in preparing and serving only the finest Sienese meats available. One of the dishes, a Siena-style *Osso Bucco*, a cross-cut veal shank, is soaked in some rosemary-olive oil-spice concoction for five hours before being cooked and served. If that doesn't get your mouth watering, then you're probably vegetarian and shouldn't be eating here in the first place.

i Appetizers from €7.50, entrées from €8, meat from €14; no restrooms; wheelchair accessible

NIGHTLIFE

PIAZZA DEL CAMPO

P. del Campo; 5 77 29 21 11; open daily 24hr

At night, Piazza del Campo transforms from a sun-scorched tourist attraction to a relaxed hangout spot. Groups of young people sit on the sloped grounds of the *piazza,* drinking beer and snacking, unwinding and conversing, watching the sun sink below the horizon as the buildings change color in the fading light. Be it your last destination of the day or simply a pregame for bigger and better things, the Piazza is a hub of energy, and in the summer the weather is perfect for lounging. It's also a great place to meet people, especially if you're traveling alone—many of the young groups are also travelers looking for a good time.

i Free; wheelchair accessible

BAR IL PATIO

Il Campo, 47; 05 77 28 20 55; open daily 10am-10pm

If lounging on pavement that sees the soles of hundreds of feet every day isn't quite for you, Bar Il Patio might be more up your alley. Its prime location in Piazza del Campo makes it a popular watering hole for locals and tourists, and the bar, with its expansive outdoor seating, is open every day of the week. The prices are a little high, but you're paying for the view, good cocktails, and the peace of mind that comes from knowing your bum isn't sitting on the ground.

i Cocktails from €8, beer and wine from €5, appetizers from €7.50; BGLTQ+ friendly; wheelchair accessible

VENICE

Coverage by **Joseph Winters**

Within minutes, you'll realize why it's the romantic capital of the world. Couples abound, cuddling on guided gondola tours, sipping glasses of wine at canalside *trattorias,* or hugging tight while taking a *vaporetto* ride across the lagoon. And you? Well, your backpack will have to be company enough.

The romanticism of Venice is evidently present in the minds of those who visit: with 20 million visitors each year, Venice is one of the most popular tourist destinations in Italy (and the world—Venice is even considering instituting a tourist cap to limit the number of annual visitors), making many of the city's squares feel alarmingly like mosh pits rather than the far-flung getaways they were designed to be. In fact, the city was established by Romans for the very purpose of being inaccessible and inconvenient: they were fleeing from Barbarians (specifically, the Huns), and, upon reaching the area that would become Venice, they decided to start building on top of a seemingly-uninhabitable lagoon. By pressing wooden posts into the marshy wetland, they created the foundation of what would become one of the most powerful cities of the Middle Ages.

Thankfully for you, you're not in danger of an Attila attack, but you may still need to flee from other tourists. Strolling through St. Mark's Square is a must—the Palazzo Ducale, the Royal Palace, and the Campanile are unquestionably the city's most awe-inspiring landmarks—but you'll need to do a bit more digging to discover what it is that makes Venice so special. Put your map away and roam, far away from the crowds. You may find it in the twisting alleys of Cannaregio, on the nearly-uninhabited island of Tronchetto, or on a lagoon-side park near the Arsenale.

ORIENTATION

You (and everyone else) will enter Venice from either the **Ferrovia** (the train station) or **Piazzale Roma** (the bus stop) in the part of Venice called **Santa Croce.** From there, there are signs clearly marking the route to the two major hubs of the city: **Per Rialto** ("to Rialto") and **Per San Marco** ("to San Marco"). Follow these, or just let yourself be carried by the river of tourists flowing towards these tourist-dense destinations. The **Rialto Bridge** neighborhood is called **San Polo,** and the **St. Mark's Square** area is, believe it or not, **San Marco.** Venice wraps itself around the Grand Canal, which serves to connect all its major islands.

To the south of these areas is **Dorsoduro,** where you'll find the **Gallerie dell'Accademia** and the Peggy Guggenheim Collection, as well as some lovely lagoon-side restaurants facing the island of **Giudecca.** This is a good spot to get away from tourists (except for those staying in Giudecca's famous five-star resort). To the northwest is **Cannaregio,** the historic Jewish Ghetto (the first official ghetto, actually); this is your best bet for what little nightlife can be found in Venice, as well as local restaurants and *cicchetti* (the Venetian equivalent of bar food). On the northeasternmost reaches of the island you'll find **Castello,** home to the Biennale's world-renowned art pavilions, the Byzantine shipyard, cheaper accommodations, and cheap eats (and a much sparser tourist density).

There are three main island destinations for Venice's tourists: **Lido, Murano,** and **Burano.** Lido, to the east, has a small airport and is known for good beaches (the island is really just a massive sandbar). Murano, a ten-minute vaporetto ride from **Fondamente Nove,** is the island most famous for its glass production: all of Venice's glass-blowing factories were moved here in 1295 to prevent the spread of fires throughout the rest of Venice. Burano is a bit more far-flung and is known for lace-making and brightly-colored pastel houses.

ESSENTIALS

GETTING THERE

If you're flying into Marco Polo airport, you have a few options. Taxis take around 15min. (Radiotaxi Venezia, 041 936222, €35) to get to Piazzale Roma. There are also two bus services. ATVO buses are more expensive, leaving the airport every half hour (5:20am-12:20am daily, €15), whereas ACTV buses (the public buses, Line 5) go for €8,and there is an option to get an extended ticket that will let you use the public transportation system in Venice for an extended period of time. If you're coming in by train, you'll get off at the Santa Maria Lucia station (not Venezia Mestre), which is just steps away from the Venetian canals.

GETTING AROUND

Maps will be your best friend in Venice: the city of canals was obviously not designed for intuitive navigation. Just try to look up every now and again to appreciate the cityscape. It is highly recommended that you spend at least some time exploring Venice by foot—it's the best way to escape the most touristy areas. Another option is to take a water taxi. Apparently, there are 159 kinds of watercraft that paddle the canals of Venice, all operated by ACTV (the biggest public transportation provider).

PRACTICAL INFORMATION

Tourist Offices: Tourist offices are just about as plentiful as tourists, so you should have no trouble finding one regardless of which island you happen to be on. Check www.turismovenezia.it for more information. Stazione Ferroviaria (Santa Lucia, 30121, open daily 8am-6:30pm); Piazzale Roma Tourist Office(Piazzale Roma Garage ASM, 30135, open daily 9:30am-3:30pm); San Marco Tourist Office (71/f, San Marco, open daily 9am-3:30pm).

Banks/ATMs/Currency Exchange: Venice wants you to spend your money. A lot of it. It shouldn't be too hard to find a bank, ATM, or currency exchange center. Here's one:

- BNL Venice (Rio Terà Antonio Foscarini, 877/D; 06 00 60; M-F 8:35am-1:35pm and 2:45pm-4:55pm).

Post Offices: Look for Poste Italiane throughout the islands (bright yellow and blue signage).

- Poste Italiane Dorsoduro (Dorsoduro, 1507; 041 520 32 18; open M-F 8:20am-1:35pm, Sa 8:20am-12:35pm).
- Poste Italiane San Marco (Merceria S. Salvador, 5016, 30124; 04 12 40 41 49; open M-F 8:20am-7:05pm, Sa 8:20am-12:35pm).

Internet: There is a Wi-Fi network called VeniceConnected that works throughout the five main neighborhoods of Venice. You can purchase a special code for 24hr (€5), 72hr (€15), or a week (€20) at www.veneziaunica.it. A 24hr pass is also included with the Rolling Venice three-day public transportation package (students 26 and under €29).

Wheelchair Accessibility: Venice's streets are especially narrow and its many canals require climbing flights of occasionally steep stairs. This is an important note for travelers who require a wheelchair, as they will need assistance navigating around Venice's islands.

EMERGENCY INFORMATION

Emergency Number: 113.

Police: As in other Italian cities, there are both the local police and the Carabinieri. Either can help in case of an emergency.

- Carabinieri Piazzale Roma (Piazzale Roma; 04 15 23 53 33).
- State Police, Santa Croce (Sestiere di Santa Croce, 500, 30135; 04 12 71 55 86; open M-F 8am-10pm, Sa 8am-2pm).

U.S. Embassy: There is no US consular embassy in Venice; the nearest ones are in Milan (V. Principe Amedeo, 2/10, 20121 Milan; 02 29 03 51) and Florence (Lungarno Vespucci, 50123 Florence 38; 0 55 26 69 51).

Hospitals: Venice has two good options for hospitals, one of which is open for 24hr emergency care. Your next best bet is the hospital in Mestre, a bus ride away from Piazzale Roma or a train ride away from Santa Lucia station.

- Ospedale SS. Giovanni e Paolo (Castello 6777; 04 15 29 41 11, open M-F 3pm-4pm and 7pm-8pm, Su 10am-11:30am and 3pm-7pm).
- Ospedale San Raffaele Arcangelo (Fatebenefratelli)(Dell'orto,30100, Campo Madonna, 3458, Venice; 0 41 78 31 11; open daily 24hr).

Pharmacies: There aren't any 24hr pharmacies in Venice, but there are a few that are open 9am-7pm daily. For pharmacies open on Su, check the updated roster compiled at www.farmacistivenezia.it.

- Baldisserotto al Basilico-Castello (04 15 22 41 09.

SIGHTS

CULTURE

JEWISH GHETTO

Cannaregio; open daily 24hr

In the year 1516, the Venetian Doge forced the city's Jewish population to move the northwesternmost corner of the island, in the area today known as **Cannaregio.** The result: the world's first official ghetto (the word "ghetto" comes from *geto* from the Venetian dialect), closed off from the rest of the city. Today, it's just another Venice neighborhood (Napoleon incorporated it in 1797), but the area still retains certain characteristics that differentiate it from the rest of Venice. Apart from the five synagogues and the annual conference on Hebrew Studies, the area boasts some of the best food and nightlife in Venice. Look for the classic Venetian *cicchetti* and wine (at a reasonable price, too), but keep an eye out for the international flair in its streets.

i Free; prices vary by establishment; wheelchair accessible

MURANO

Murano Island; open daily 24hr

If Venice had a suburbia, this might be it. But instead of cookie-cutter picket fences, they have glass-blowing furnaces (which is way cooler). Due to Venice's unlucky history with fires (that's what you get when you combine tightly-packed wooden buildings with glass factories), in 1295, the city decided to move all of its glass-blowing production to the island of Murano. Today, Murano is world-famous for the glass it produces; just walk through the town and you'll see *fornace* after *fornace* (furnace), as well as an entire museum devoted to the art of glass. Murano is also a little more real than the mainland; here, you can escape the tourist traps and walk through real neighborhoods, cemeteries, and parks where real Venetians play pick-up soccer games.

i Free; vaporetto from Fte. Nove roundtrip €15; wheelchair accessible

TEATRO LA FENICE

Campo San Fantin, 1965; 41 78 65 11; www.festfenice.com/en; open daily 9:30am-6pm

The name "The Phoenix" is both appropriate and ironic—yes, the sumptuous theater rose from the ashes of devastating fire (1774) to live again, but fire also ravaged the theater in 1836, and yet another fire completely destroyed the theater in 1996. Since then, it has been rebuilt (all over again) to look exactly as the previous one did—solid gold-lined parapets and all. Thanks to this painstaking restoration, the history of the theater has been largely preserved, and you can now walk through the grand foyer, the reception areas, and even the theater itself. Musicians like **Rossini, Stravinsky,** and **Verdi** have all written works specifically for La Fenice, and it is still a world-renowned opera house.

i Admission €10, €7 reduced; free audio guide; book "Walk to the Theater" tour in advance via phone or email (visite@festfenice.com); wheelchair accessible

LANDMARKS

BASILICA DI SAN MARCO

San Marco, 328; 4 12 70 83 11; www.basilicasanmarco.it/?lang=en; open M-Sa 9:45am-5pm, Su 2pm-5pm

When they say San Marco, they're talking about none other than Saint Mark. He's kind of important to the Christian religion, as he casually helped write the Christian Bible. His bones were brought from Alexandria (stolen?) in 828, and they helped put Venice on the map, giving the city power and prestige. Since then, the Byzantine-style building has experienced influence from the ages it has lived through, from the height of the Gothic era's popularity to the emergence of Renaissance painting, making the basilica one of the most complex and magnificent in all of Italy. It's free to admire the interior, but make sure to bring some extra money in with you if you want to see the **museum,** the **loggia,** and the **Pala d'Oro** (which contains the relics).

i Free; St. Mark's Treasure €3, €1.50 reduced; Pala d'Oro €2, €1 reduced; Museo, Cavalli, and Loggia €5, €2.50 reduced; wheelchair accessible

PALAZZO DUCALE

S. Marco, 1; 4 12 71 59 11; www.palazzoducale.visitmuve.it; open daily 8:30am-7pm

The history of the Palazzo Ducale alone makes it a must-visit Venetian landmark and museum. First built in the tenth century, its primarily Gothic architecture shows hints of Renaissance and Napoleonic influence. It had a specific room for every body of the Venetian government, which you can walk through yourself on the museum's pre-planned itinerary. The most impressive is the **Chamber of the Great Council:** a 53m by 25m room fit to hold 2000 noblemen. It's one of the biggest rooms in all of Europe, and it's home to the longest canvas painting in the world, **Jacopo Tintoretto's** *Paradiso.* From there, cross the **Bridge of Sighs** and enter the Medieval prison, which feels like finding yourself onstage during a production of *The Merchant of Venice.*

i Admission €20, €13 reduced; last entry 6pm; wheelchair accessible; tours must be booked in advance online for €20, English tour at 11:45am, "Secret Itineraries" tour at 9:55am, 10:45am, 11:35am

BASILICA DEI FRARI

San Polo, 3072; 4 12 72 86 11; www.basilicadeifrari.it

If you haven't gotten sick of basilicas yet, the Basilica dei Frari in the **San Polo** district is one of the city's most impressive. It even has its own **campanile** (not as high as the St. Mark one, though). Since the façade is done in the Gothic style, it might seem a little plain from the outside, but once you enter you'll be able to see the stunning gilded choir stalls. Singers, along with the basilica's multiple organs, occasionally fill the church with ghostly Italian *chorales* (they don't take song requests, so don't bother asking). Also, **Titian**—one of Venice's most famous Renaissance painters—is buried here, which means you can check out his artwork and his monument.

i Admission €3, €1.50 reduced; 5:30pm; wheelchair accessible; book tours in advance via email at basilica@basilicadeifrari.it

RIALTO BRIDGE

Sestiere San Polo; open daily 24hr

Chances are, you'll cross the Rialto Bridge at some point during your stay in Venice. It's one of four bridges that crosses the **Grand Canal,** connecting the **San Marco** neighborhood to the **San Polo** neighborhood. It's also one of Venice's most popular landmarks—so get ready to wade through a sea of other tourists. The current stone structure was built in 1588, but there were other previous iterations of a bridge, including a floating bridge (1181) and a wooden one (1255). Take note of the ultra-expensive diamond and jewelry shops along either side. Fun fact: these kinds of shops aren't there only to take advantage of the hundreds flush tourists that clamber over the bridge; rather, the high rent for their coveted location helps pay for the bridge's maintenance.

i Free; limited wheelchair accessibility

MUSEUMS

GALLERIE DELL'ACCADEMIA

Campo della Carità, 1050; 4 15 22 22 47; www.gallerieaccademia.it; open M 8:15am-2pm, Tu-Su 8:15am-7:15pm

This is classic museum material: pre-nineteenth century artwork, airy rooms, full of roaming bespectacled fine art students with sketchbooks in hand. Housed in one of the ancient **Scuole Grandi** ("big schools"—founded in 1260) of Venice, the Accademia is an important center for art restoration and preservation. If you aren't sick of them yet, take some time to stroll through the triptychs of the Virgin Mary, a giant *Last Supper* that was deemed heresy by the Church, and works by **Bellini, Tintoretto,** and **Titian.** Or, you know, you can just book it for Da Vinci's *Vitruvian Man* and call it quits; no one's judging you.

i Admission €12, €6 reduced; last entry 45min. before closing; wheelchair accessible

LA BIENNALE DI VENEZIA

A Campiello Tana, 2169/F; 4 15 21 87 11; www.labiennale.org/en/biennale/index.html; open Tu-Su 10am-6pm, F-Sa 10am-8pm

Every two years, La Biennale di Venezia coordinates a monumental showcase of the world's best modern art and design. In between art years, the association organizes a similarly groundbreaking collection of modern architecture. From May to the end of November, the Biennale takes over nearly the entire northeastern corner of Venice in the **Arsenale** and the **Giardini.** Walking through all the exhibits is a hike in itself; wear a comfy pair of shoes because you'll be doing a lot of shuffling. It might be good idea to wear the froofiest getup you packed; lots of inconvenient lace and ridiculous sunglasses will help you blend in with the other locals. No guarantees that it'll help you understand the artistic significance of a video showing a man slicing an apple with a MacBook Air, though.

i 48hr ticket €30, €22 reduced; 24hr ticket €25, €15 reduced; last entry 15min. before closing; wheelchair accessible

MUSEO CORRER

Piazza San Marco, 52; 4 12 40 52 11; www.correr.visitmuve.it; open daily 10am-7pm

It doesn't mean "to run" (that's *correre*), but you might need to run if you plan on getting through the Museo Correr's massive collection of Venetian art and historical artifacts in a timely manner. Housed in the palatial building that encircles **San Marco Square,** a walking tour will take you through the gluttonously posh life of the Venetian elite, from the cream-colored marmorino of the Emperor's bathroom to the **"Dining Room for Weekday Lunches."** There's also a picture gallery that highlights the emergence of international Gothicism in Venice, as well as some really intriguing Venetian artifacts, like an early form of high-heeled shoe that did have a functional purpose: to keep women's feet clean as they strolled the muddy streets of Venice.

i Admission €20, €13 reduced; last entry 6pm; wheelchair accessible

PEGGY GUGGENHEIM COLLECTION

Dorsoduro, 701-704; 4 12 40 54 11; www.guggenheim-venice.it; open daily 10am-6pm

The Guggenheim Collection is one of those museums that makes you question what exactly defines art. Is a blank canvas art? Does *Curved Black Line's* curved black line count? What about *The Way West,* which is literally "uncarved wooden blocks"? Either way, the museum is one of Venice's most popular tourist attractions. The building used to be Peggy Guggenheim's house, so it has a sort of quaint, homey feel. That is, if you consider a mini-mansion on the banks of the Grand Canal to be quaint. Whether you go to ponder the avant-garde art (or should we say "art"?) or to say you saw works by **Picasso, Jackson Pollock,** and **Joan Miró,** the Collection is definitely an unmissable Venetian attraction.

i Admission €15, €9 reduced; 90min. tours for €75 booked in advance via email at prenotazioni@guggenheim-venice.it; last entry 5:30pm; wheelchair accessible

OUTDOORS

GIARDINI DELLA BIENNALE

Sestiere Castello; 4 15 21 87 11; open Tu-Sa 10am-6pm

If you stick to the **San Polo** and **San Marco districts,** you might think all of Venice is devoid of trees. But the northeastern Giardini della Biennale (Gardens of the Biennale) more than make up for chlorophyll-deprived city center. First set up during **Napoleon's** reign, the gardens have been a key part of the Biennale di Venezia's biannual international art exhibition since 1895. Inside the ticketed area are 29 pavilions, each devoted to groundbreaking artwork from a single country. But the gardens' reach extends far beyond the international pavilions; there are public spaces where you'll find people sprawled out on the grass, walking their dogs, or tossing frisbees.

i 48hr ticket €30, students under 26 €22; 24hr ticket €25, students under 26 €15; tours must be booked in advance via email at booking@labiennale.org; wheelchair accessible

FOOD

ACQUA E MAIS ($)

Campiello dei Meloni, 1411-1412, San Polo; 4 12 96 05 30; www.acquaemais.com; open daily 9:30am-8pm

Despite the "Pizza Kebab" places at seemingly every street corner, there actually is a more traditional Venetian street food. Called *scartosso,* it's named for the paper cone that the dish is served in. At Acqua e Mais (literally "Water and Corn"), they fill the *scartosso* with polenta and heap crispy veggies, cod, or black cuttlefish on top—your choice. There's also a cold bar with mixed seafood salad or the no-frills but classic *baccalà,* which is just salted fish whipped with oil to form a pasty cream (it sounds grosser than it is). Perfect for a speedy (and cheap) lunch.

i Cones of polenta with toppings from €3.50, polenta and wine €10; gluten-free, vegan, and vegetarian options available; wheelchair accessible

CANTINE DEL VINO GIÀ SCHIAVI ($)

Dorsoduro, 992, Fondamenta Nani; 4 15 23 00 34; www.cantinaschiavi.com; open 8:30am-8:30pm

Whether you're feeling pecking or penniless on your Venetian adventure, Cantine del Vina già Schiavi (literally "Wine Cellars Already Slaves") is worth a visit. They are legendary for serving dozens of kinds of Venice's famous *cicchetti* (basically mini bruschettas) on the daily, all of which are painstakingly prepared by a little old lady with a penchant for salty cheeses and buttery purees. On any given day, you might find flavors like pumpkin-ricotta-parmesan, tuna-tartare-cocoa, or dried cod cream with garlic and parsley. At €1.20 a pop, a nice-sized plate of these *cicchetti* won't break the bank. Plus, you can take your plate outside and eat on the banks of the canal, just to the side of a high bridge.

i Cicchetti €1.20, sandwiches from €3.50; vegetarian options available; wheelchair accessible

LE SPIGHE ($)

Castello Via Garibaldi, 1341; 4 15 23 81 73; open M-Sa 10:30am-2:30pm and 5:30pm-7:30pm

Although you probably couldn't call her cooking "traditional," Doriana Pressotto's organic-vegetarian-fair trade dishes come with a hefty serving of traditional Italian attitude, completely free of charge. "This system, this is brainwashing us!" she'll exclaim, pointing dramatically to the grocery store across the street while loading your plate with her own, more virtuous vittles. To Pressotto, it's all about the *ennergia* of the food, which is why she's been serving wholesome, affordable, and delicious meals in the vegetable-starved **Castello** area since 2008. Every morning, she prepares around eight different dishes and serves them deli-style until the end of the evening. You can also take your meal to go and have a picnic in the park next door.

i Small plates from €6, medium plates from €8, large plates from €10; gluten-free, vegan, and vegetarian options available; wheelchair accessible

GELATERIA ALASKA ($)

Santa Croce, 1159; 41 71 52 11; open daily 11am-7pm

Finally, a gelato place serving more than just a cup of ice cream. At Gelateria Alaska, gelato comes with a smile (imagine that!) and a story (sometimes a very long one). Mr. Pistacchi, the owner of this 26-year-old creamery, is passionate about quality. All of his flavors are made with seasonal ingredients collected from the Venetian street markets; for example, when he finds apricots, apricot gelato appears on the menu. He doesn't use any artificial ingredients, either (so don't expect green pistachio gelato).

i Scoops from €2.50; vegan and vegetarian options available; wheelchair accessible

NIGHTLIFE

AL TIMON

Cannaregio, 2754; 4 15 24 60 66; open daily 6pm-1am

Don't be alarmed if the bartender gives you a *bacio* or two when you walk into this **Cannaregio** area establishment; kisses on the cheek are the Italian equivalent of the handshake. They happen all the time at Al Timon, because the staff seems to know everyone who walks in. Customers line up for a heaping plate of *cicchetti* (€1 each, and you can choose up to ten per group—which works out great if you're solo or coming with a single friend) and a glass of wine, and then migrate outside to sit on Al Timon's two boats. The soulful Italian jazz, wooden barrels, and melting Venetian sun make for quite a romantic atmosphere.

i No cover, cicchetti €1 (max of 10 per group), wine by the glass from €3

BACARO JAZZ

San Marco, 5546; 4 15 28 52 49; www.bacarojazz.com; open M-Th noon-2am, F-Sa midnight-3am, Su noon-2am

In a city where nightlife is sparse, Bacaro Jazz fills the late-night void with a bizarre mix of classy cocktails and autographed bras. Lots and lots of bras. For 13 years, this cocktail bar-restaurant-jazz club has encouraged visitors to leave behind signed bras as souvenirs, which are then hung from the ceiling in tightly-packed rows. Not all the bras are deemed suitable to go up, though. "These aren't even all of them," the bartender explains. It's anyone's guess where the unhung bras go. As for the food and drink, Bacaro Jazz is more of a bar than a restaurant, serving lots of cocktail-seeking Americans classic and signature drinks for a fair price.

i No cover, pastas and soups (primi piatti) from €12, cocktails from €4

ITALY ESSENTIALS

MONEY

Banks and ATMs: To use a debit or credit card to withdraw money from a bancomat (ATM), you must have a four-digit PIN. If your PIN is longer than four digits, ask your bank whether you can use the first four or if they'll issue a new one. If you intend to use just a credit card while in Italy, call your carrier before your departure to request a PIN. The use of ATM cards is widespread in Italy. The two major international money networks are MasterCard/Maestro/Cirrus and Visa/PLUS. Most ATMs charge a transaction fee, but some Italian banks waive the withdrawal surcharge.

Tipping: In Italy, a 5% tip is customary, particularly in restaurants. Italian waiters won't cry if you don't leave a tip; just be ready to ignore the pangs of your conscience later on. Taxi drivers expect tips as well, but luckily for oenophiles, it is unusual to tip in bars.

Bargaining: Bargaining is appropriate in markets and other informal settings, though in regular shops it is inappropriate. Hotels will often offer lower prices to people looking for a room that night, so you will often be able to find a bed cheaper than what is officially quoted.

SAFETY AND HEALTH

Local Laws and Police: In Italy, you will encounter two types of boys in blue: the polizia (113) and the carabinieri (112). The polizia are a civil force under the command of the Ministry of the Interior, whereas the carabinieri fall under the auspices of the Ministry of Defense and are considered a military force. Both, however, generally serve the same purpose: to maintain security and order in the country. In the case of an attack or robbery, both will respond to inquiries or requests for help.

Drugs and Alcohol: The legal drinking age in Italy is 16. Remember to drink responsibly and to never drink and drive. Doing so is illegal and can result in a prison sentence, not to mention early death. The legal BAC for driving in Italy is under 0.05%, significantly under the US limit of 0.08%.

Travelers with Disabilities: Travelers in wheelchairs should be aware that getting around in Italy will sometimes be extremely difficult. This country predates the wheelchair—sometimes it seems even the wheel—by several centuries and thus poses unique challenges to disabled travelers. Accessible Italy (378 941 111; www.accessibleitaly.com) offers advice to tourists of limited mobility heading to Italy, with tips on subjects ranging from finding accessible accommodations to wheelchair rentals.

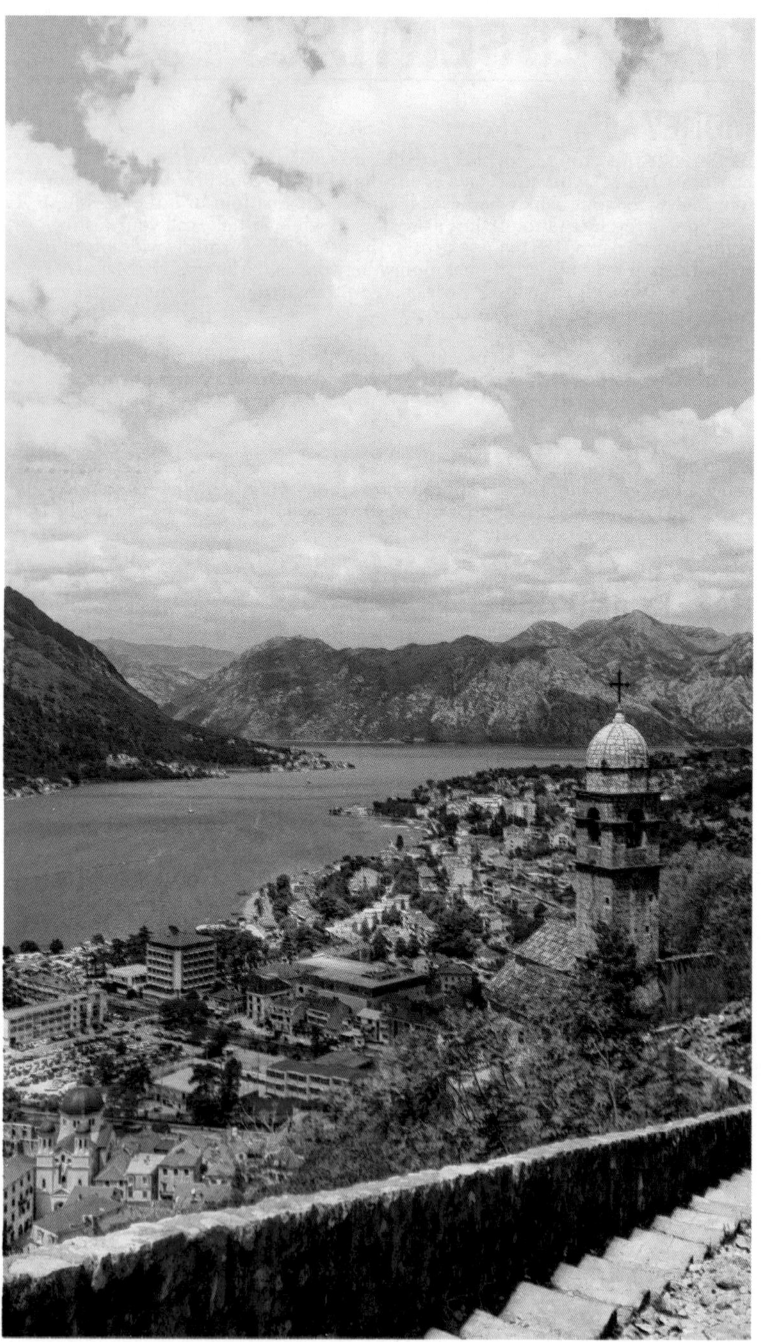

MONTENEGRO

Unless you're a Russian tourist, a Balkan local, or a genuine travel hipster, you probably haven't heard a lot about Montenegro. We won't hold it against you; Montenegro's fairly new to the whole being-a-country-scene, having emerged as an independent nation in 2006. Since breaking off from Serbia, however, Montenegro has been making up for lost time. Basically every "Under the Radar Countries You Need to Visit Right Now!" list that's been published over the last decade has included Montenegro high on their rankings. Every somewhat snobby, somewhat impressive travel guru you've met in the hostel common room has casually slipped in their recent trip to Montenegro ("yes, I backpacked through Budva, have you heard of it?") Every travel blog, travel app, and travel guidebook is rushing to cover Europe's newest hotspot (see, we can be self aware!).

So what's all the buzz about? Montenegro is a miniscule gem of a nation that combines everything we love about the Balkans (cheap prices, free-flowing *rakija,* and mouthwatering *cevapi* sausages) and everything we love about the Mediterranean coast (bright blue waters, delightfully sunny beaches, and delectable seafood platters). Do you prefer your trips to be rambunctious, wild, and generally sleepless? Time to buy a one-way ticket to Budva, a must-see pilgrimage spot for anyone who likes bars, beaches, and Balkan techno. Are you more into charming, historical Old Towns, bright blue bays, and lazy river cruises? Kotor is calling your name. Or are you just trying to relax, recalibrate, and roam through some ruins? We'd like to formally introduce you to Bar, a hidden gem of a coastal town that still hasn't been hit by the tourist wave. Montenegro has something to offer just about every traveler, between its coiling coastlines, majestic mountains, and bustling beaches. Take a deep breath, because you're going to be starting just about everything sentence with "Well, when I was in Montenegro…" from here on out.

BUDVA

Coverage by **Lydia Tahraoui**

Budva is the answer to all the questions you didn't even know you had. Where do you go for the wildest nights and the earliest mornings in all of Montenegro? Budva. What city can lay claim to Europe's most beautiful beach (by 1935 standards, at least)? Budva. A theoretical person is looking to theoretically swim in the nude, so where should they head? Budva, Budva, Budva (just stick to the eastern shore of Jaz Beach, because that's not going to fly citywide). Known as the Miami of Montenegro, Budva is the wild child in a nation filled with generally chill, laid back cities. It's known for beaches, for bars, and for Balkan techno that blasts on until the wee hours of the morn. But don't think Budva's just another pretty face; look past the nightclubs and the beaches to explore the city's ancient Greek past, its charming medieval Old Town, and its many local legends—if you can get past that raging hangover well enough to do so, of course.

ORIENTATION

Budva sits right on the **Adriatic Coast** in southerwestern Montenegro. The **Old Town,** which is referred to as Stari Grad in Montenegrin, lies at the heart of the city. Most of Budva's main landmarks can be found in and around the partially walled Old Town, including the **Citadela Fortress** and **The Holy Trinity Church.** Just west of the Old Town is Budva's most popular swimming spot, **Mogren Beach.** To the immediate south of Budva is **Sveti Nikola Island,** a buzzing tourist hotspot known for lots of flora, lots of fauna, and lots of wild deer. To the east of Budva is **Bečići**, a slightly calmer suburb that boasts a beautiful, award-winning beach (okay, said award was won in 1935, but it totally still counts).

ESSENTIALS

GETTING THERE

The easiest way to get to Budva is either by plane or by bus. If you're arriving to Montenegro by air, you'll land at either Tivat or Podgorica airports. Both airports are pretty close to Budva, and are connected by bus lines. The bus ride from Tivat takes about 50min., and the ride from Podgorica clocks out at around 1.5hr. If you're traveling by land, you can grab a bus to Budva from most major regional cities, including Kotor, Dubrovnik, and Mostar. The bus station is located to the north of the Old Town, and from there you can either take a 20min. ride into town or hitch a five minute cab ride.

GETTING AROUND

Budva is a very walkable city, as most of the major tourist spots are located in close proximity to one another. Some of the night clubs are located well outside of the city center, so you may want to catch a cab on nights out. Just be warned that taxi drivers love to play hike-up-the-price-for-the-unsuspecting-tourist, so ensure the meter is turned on as soon as you climb into the cab.

PRACTICAL INFORMATION

Tourist Offices: Budva Tourist Office (Njegoševa 28; 033 452 750; budva.travel; open Jun-Aug M-Sa 9am-9pm, Su 3pm-9pm, Sep-May M-Sa 8am-8pm).

Banks/ATMs/Currency Exchange: There are a bunch of banks and ATMs around Budva, but most are located just outside the Old Town. Here's one: Prva Banka CG Budva (5 Mediteranska; 033 403 936; open M-F 8am-4pm).

Post Offices: Here's a post office not far from the city center: Pošta (Mediteranska ulica br. 8; 033 452 401; open M-Sa 7am-8pm).

Public Restrooms: Some major tourist spots have an adjoining bathroom. Otherwise, try ducking into a café or restaurant.

Internet: Almost all cafés and restaurants in Budva offer free Wi-Fi.

BGLTQ+ Resources: The closest BGLTQ+ resource center is located in Montenegro's capital, Podgorica. It's called LGBT Forum Progres (Ul. marta 27, 020 674 761, lgbtprogres.me).

EMERGENCY INFORMATION

Emergency Number: 112.
Police: There's a police station in the bus terminal. It's located at Popa Jola Zeca bb. If you're faced with an emergency, call 122 for emergency police attention.
US Embassy: The US Embassy is based in Montenegro's capital, Podgorica. You can reach out to them for assistance while you're in Montenegro: (Dzona Dzeksona 2; 020 410 500; me.usembassy.gov).
Rape Crisis Center: There's a hotline based in Podgorica that you can reach out to. Here's their info: SOS Hotline for Women and Children Victims of Violence Niksic (068 024 086; sosnk.org; open 24hr).
Hospitals: Budva Health Center provides both routine care and emergency services. The emergency clinic is open 24hr:

- Budva Health Center (Popa Jola Zeca; 033 453 501; dzbudva.com).

Pharmacies: Here's a pharmacy just outside the Old Town:

- Apoteka Popović (Vojvođanska; open M-Sa 7am-10pm, Su 8am-10pm).

SIGHTS

CULTURE

OLD TOWN

Stari Grad, open 24hr

We assume that you pulled up to a town known affectionately as the Miami of Montenegro for that wild, mind-blowing, out of control history. Okay, it's true that Budva is better known as the most riotous party hub this side of the Adriatic, but one stroll through the Old Town is enough to prove that Budva isn't just a good time. It's got substance, too. The walled Old Town is Budva's historical center, built on the edge of the peninsula and overlooking the shimmering blue sea. It consists of winding cobbled alleyways, Roman ruins, ornate churches, and your token hip, touristy cafés. It's a good place to get lost in for an evening, both in that charming I-could-stroll-around-this-quirky-medieval-town-for-hours kind of way and in the very real shit-I-can't-figure-out-these-alleyways-wait-where-am-I-again? kind of way. Get you an Old Town that can do both.

i Free, wheelchair accessible

JAZ BEACH

Jaz Beach; open 24hr

A trip to Jaz Beach can be just as jazzy as you want to make it. It's located about three miles from **Old Town** and stretches out for over a mile, which means you've got a whole lot of sandy beach to work with. As we've hinted towards, some stretches are jazzier, if you will, than others; head towards the eastern portion of the beach if you're down to shed your swimsuit, because that is the designated nudist section. If nudity isn't your thing, don't worry: our unclothed friends have only claimed about a quarter mile of the beach, and the other three-fourths are basically your standard, swimsuited fare. For those looking to do more than just lounge, there are plenty of waterborne activities available for your enjoyment, including jet skiing and paddle boating.

i Free; wheelchair accessible

MOGREN BEACH

Mogren bb; open 24hr

Mogren is Budva's most popular beach. That's probably because people get here, see that finally—finally!—they've found a Balkan beach with sand instead of pebbles, and decide to never leave. Fair play. Obviously, the sandy shore is a big selling point, but Mogren also boasts warm blue waters and gorgeous coastal views. As if that weren't enough, Mogren's location is nothing short of ideal. It lies just outside of **Old Town,** and you can get here in under ten minutes. Pro tip: Mogren is divided into two beaches, intuitively dubbed **Mogren I** and **Mogren II.** Mogren II is much less crowded, much less noisy, and just generally better than Mogren I. Just keep going past the rocky tunnel until you hit the second half of the beach.

i Free; €20 sunbed rental; limited wheelchair accessibility

LANDMARKS

CITADELA FORTRESS

Stari Grad, open May-Oct daily 9am-midnight, Sep-Apr daily 9am-5pm

This Citadel has ancient origins—allegedly. Allegedly, the Citadel sits at the site of the former Greek acropolis, but the structure you see standing before you in present day Budva was built under the Austro-Hungarians in 1936. Back in those days, it housed troops, but it now plays the more glamorous role of hosting the hordes of tourists that descend upon Budva annually. What's drawing the masses? We think it has something to do with the stunning seaside views the citadel has to offer. This is arguably the best vantage point for snapping those envy-inducing panoramas that cover the coast, the sea, and the city. The Citadel complex also includes a restaurant, a cozy library, and the city museum.

i Admission €3.50; no wheelchair accessibility

THE HOLY TRINITY CHURCH

Stari Grad open Jun-Sep daily 8am-10pm, Oct-May 8am-noon and 4pm-7pm

First things first, major kudos to the architects of The Holy Trinity Church for choosing this color scheme. It's bold, it's innovative, and it's perfectly picturesque. This Orthodox church may be small, but it packs a punch with its vibrant shades and intricate, ornate interiors. After the Venetians fell at the end of the eighteenth century, Budva's new Austrian leaders allowed the city's Orthodox population to build a church. The result was the rose-and-honey Holy Trinity Church, which sits near the Citadel towards the edge of the **Old Town.** Inside are beautiful, eye-catching frescoes from Greek iconographers, which depict notable religious figures and scenes.

i Free; limited wheelchair accessibility

STATUA BALLERINA

37 Primorskog bataljona; open daily 24hr

There's a lot of intrigue surrounding this graceful sculpture. She goes by a couple different names: "Gymnast from Budva", "Budva Ballerina," "Dancer from Budva," and "Naked Girl Striking a Pose that Makes Your Hamstrings Hurt Just Looking at Her." Some of these nicknames are more popular than others. Her origin story is also highly variable, but one popular local legend tells the story of a young dancer and sailor in love. The sailor would venture out to sea, and each time he returned, his lover would be dancing for him by the shore. However, one day, the sailor didn't come back (gasp!). His lover kept dancing, kept waiting, but he never made it home. Nonetheless, she stayed faithful, stayed in love, and stayed dancing. Her self-sacrifice was honored with the statue, which sits just outside of the **Old Town** against a stunning backdrop of city and sea.

i Free; wheelchair accessible

MUSEUMS

BUDVA MUSEUM

Petra I Petrovića 11; 033 453 308; open M-F 8am-8pm, Sa-Su 10am-5pm

You might as well learn a little something about those streets you're drunkenly stumbling out into at 5am in the morning. This museum contains answers to all of the questions you didn't know you had about the history of Budva, dating all the way back to the Illyrian, Greek, and Roman days. The collections were first established in 1962, but the museum's curators got a real treat when an earthquake struck in 1979 and uncovered over 4,000 ancient archaeological items. The collections aren't especially thematic, and the descriptions could be more descriptive. Nonetheless, Budva Museum manages to weave together regional historical narratives through exhibits containing artistic, archeological, and ethnographic pieces, so stop by to add a bit of historical context to your drunken Budva nights.

i Admission €2; wheelchair accessible

FOOD

PASTABAR ($)

Petra I Petrovića; 067 540 407; open daily noon-11:30pm

It's hard to improve upon pasta. As far as culinary concepts go, pasta is a pretty solid one to start with. Somehow, though, Pastabar has figured out how to make pasta better. This is not your momma's pasta (unless, like, your momma is a seventh generation Italian chef who is really, really good at making pasta. Then it may indeed be similar to your momma's pasta). You've got your standard flavors (pasta carbonara, pasta bolognese) and your creative spins (gnocchi gorgonzola and walnut, risotto tikka masala with shrimp). It's delicious, it's cheap, and it's located right in the heart of the **Old Town.** Seating is limited, but you can grab a takeaway box and enjoy this pasta on the road.

i Pasta from €4; wheelchair accessible

JADRAN ($$)

Slovenska Obala; 068 033 180; restaurant-jadran.com; open daily 7am-1am

Grab a seat next to the sea at Restaurant Jadran, a joint that draws tourists from all across Budva. It's one of the coast's most popular restaurants, in part thanks to its prime waterfront location. Jadran offers a reasonably priced menu packed with regional seafood staples (although, pro tip: the non-seafood dishes are much cheaper, as a rule. Try the *cevapi:* it's a local favorite and competitively priced). Sure, it's a bit of a tourist trap—you'll spot at least ten travelers for every one local, if that. But sometimes you've just got to buy into the whole tourist shebang, and Jadran is practically one of Budva's biggest attractions at this point.

i Entrees from €6; wheelchair accessible

KUŽINA ($)

Zaobilaznica bb; 033 459 480; open daily 6am-1am

If you've got a craving for anything that can be thrown on a grill, look no further than Kužina. This spot is popular among locals, and if that doesn't tip you off towards the quality, then we don't know what will (maybe a recommendation printed in your guidebook? We're just spitballing here). Kužina isn't the most vegan-slash-vegetarian friendly place, but if you're down for some good, hardy Balkan-style meat then you're in for an actual treat. Think big, smoky, perfectly seasoned lamb chops and expertly rolled, juicy, mouthwatering *cevapi* sausages all complemented by fluffy, fresh breads and generous helpings of veggies and fries. Your plate isn't going to be particularly Instagrammable, but it's going to be really damn tasty, and isn't that, like, the whole point of eating?

i Entrees from €5.50; wheelchair accessible

SAMBRA PIZZERIA ($$$)

Iva Mikovića 10; 033 451 308; open daily 8am-1am

If you came to Montenegro looking for good Italian food—wait, you did? Why? No, it's just kind of weird, because if you want good Italian food, then the Balkans might not have been the best travel destination, but whatever, it doesn't matter, you're in luck: Sambra Pizzeria serves up the best Italian cuisine you'll find in Budva. Creamy sauces? Check. Perfectly crispy crusts? But of course. Oh, and those delightfully smelly cheeses? *Delzioso, bella.* Combine this with a laid back, relaxing atmosphere and genuinely friendly service and you've got a recipe for a leisurely, satisfying meal. Sure, you can probably find cheaper pizzas around town, but will they be this authentically tasty? We doubt it.

i Pizza from €7.50; wheelchair accessible

NIGHTLIFE

TOP HILL

Topliški put; 067 478 888; open Fri-Su 11pm-5am

Whoever named Top Hill is a straightforward kind of person. It's Budva's top club. It's on a hill. That hill is called **Toplis Hill.** Seriously, no metaphors, no figures of speech, and no unclear branding here. This is an open air club that's known for drawing some of the most dedicated partiers this side of the Adriatic. You'll be dancing under the moonlight and, let's face it, under the sunlight, too—you're not leaving anytime soon. Up to 5,000 people can fit under the stars at Top Hill, so the place is consistently packed with locals, frat boys, and European bohemes alike. The club regularly books notable headliners, including some of the Balkans' biggest pop and techno names. Note that your taxi here shouldn't cost more than €7, so don't let any profiteering cab drivers finesse you and make sure the meter is on. Stay woke and Let's Go.

i Standard €5 cover, may increase based on headliners/events; limited wheelchair accessibility

CASPER BAR

Cara Dusana 10; 033 402 290; open daily 10am-2am

Your nights in Budva can go one of two ways. Option 1: you can embark on drunken dance rampage across the floor of a crowded, techno-buzzing night club. Option 2: you can have a composed, slightly tipsy night on the town listening to live music and sipping on cocktails because you are an adult and you are classy. Casper Bar is the ideal setting for the latter type of evening. It's a gorgeous, green-filled outdoor spot with cozy, cushioned seats and live music. Located right in the **Old Town,** Casper Bar boasts a large, shady terrace under a smattering of tall trees, creating a relaxed ambiance that's fundamentally conducive to deep discussions and well-informed intellectual debates. Wait, that's why you came to Budva, right—for all the well-informed debates? If not, don't worry, because this can also be a great pregame spot before you transform your Option 2 night into a good old-fashioned Option 1. Okay, sorry, we'll stop with the jargon now.

i Beer from €2.70, wine from €1.80; wheelchair accessible

KOTOR

Coverage by **Lydia Tahraoui**

There's a good reason why cruise ships everywhere take one look at Kotor and think "hey, this would be a good place to dock for the next week or so." Besides plenty of disembarked cruise passengers—easily identifiable by their matching lanyards and vaguely green pallor, courtesy of lingering seasickness—you'll find live street music, winding stone alleyways, and tons of luxuriously lazy cats lounging about the city. This sunny oasis and Montenegrin gem glistens brightly, and we mean that literally. A passing glance at the bright blue bay that wraps around the city's perimeter instantly confirms Kotor's status as a glimmering Balkan jewel. Kotor is known for its laid back, laissez-faire ambiance, so take your time and explore a city where majestic medieval architecture and full string quartet covers of Despacito coexist in blissful harmony.

ORIENTATION

Kotor is tucked away along the southeastern shore of the **Bay of Kotor**, which—somewhat confusingly—also incorporates nearby towns like **Perast** and **Risin**. The heart of Kotor is unambiguously the **Old Town**, a fairytale-like walled city teeming with restaurants, cafés, and, of course, cats. Kotorians of years past carved the Old Town out of dozens of twisting alleyways, way before grid-based city planning was a thing. Because of this, it's difficult to get a solid grasp on the method to the Old Town's navigational madness, because there quite literally isn't one. Just know that the main entrance into the Old Town is through the **Square**

60 YEARS OF LET'S GO

Sixty years ago, Oliver Koppell came to Harvard as a young man with a big idea: to create a travel guide for those who thought travel was beyond their reach.

The 18-year-old entrepreneur found the perfect partner to launch his plan into action: Harvard Student Agencies (HSA). On the floor of his freshman dorm room, Koppell crafted 25 pages of advertisements, brochures, and tips on touring Europe. With the 1960 European Guide in hand, three planeloads of HSA customers set off for Europe, and since then the travel-guide world was never the same. Since then, HSA and Let's Go have constantly succeeded in realizing the dream of accessible budget travel.

By 1986, almost 500,000 Let's Go books were being produced, hitting the shelves just three months after being researched—light-years ahead of the competition. The young trail-blazers at Let's Go continued to embrace modernity when the 1986 team computerized the entire series. In 1988, as another new title was launched, Let's Go's total readership was up to 1,600,000. The 2011 series saw Let's Go's focus return to Europe, its bread and delicious butter; nearly all of the coverage was rewritten from scratch to ensure the highest quality prose and information.

Today, we've continued to refine and perfect our coverage of Europe—as the cities grow and change, we're adapting right along with it. Let's Go Europe 2020 features 672 pages of comprehensive, up-to-date, honest advice on how to make the most of your European experience, all while retaining the mission that Koppell envisioned: making travel as accessible as possible to everyone.

of the Arms, where the **Tourist Information Center's** kiosk is based. Once you walk through that passageway, you'll find yourself in the heart of the **Piazza of the Arms**, the largest square in the Old Town. From there, explore those charmingly narrow alleys even further. To the north of the Old Town is the **Kamelija Shopping Center**, Montenegro's modest answer to the common shopping mall. To the immediate south of the Old Town, just a 4-minute walk away from the heart of the city, lies the bus station.

ESSENTIALS

GETTING THERE

The easiest way to arrive in Kotor is via bus. Bus lines connect Kotor to most major Montenegrin cities, like Budva or Bar. If you're already in the Balkans, chances are you'll be able to find an international route that'll get you straight to the city. There are international bus lines to Kotor originating in Dubrovnik, Mostar, and Belgrade, among others. If you arrive from outside the Balkans, your best bet is to fly into either the Podgorica or Tivat airports. The Tivat airport is closest to Kotor—and probably clocks in as the most scenic airport in all of Europe, for the record. The Podgorica airport, however, is the country's busiest airhub, which means that you're more likely to find diverse flight options going through Podgorica. Either way, bus stations operate not too far from both airports, so hop onto a bus to Kotor from there.

GETTING AROUND

Kotor itself is small and best navigated by foot. Cars cannot traverse the Old Town, though some golf carts still buzz around here. Renting a bike is also a viable option for navigating your way around the city, but just keep in mind that hoards of people often crowd the alleys, especially during high season. That said, we're going to stick to what we said in the first place: you're going to want to walk this city.

PRACTICAL INFORMATION

Tourist Offices: Kotor Tourist Information Center (Square of the Arms; 032 325 950; open daily 8am-8pm).

Banks/ATMs/Currency Exchange: There are a bunch of ATMs located throughout the Old Town. They're particularly concentrated close to the Piazza of the Arms. You can find a bank at the Kamelija Shopping Center. Here's that info: Societe Generale Banka Montenegro (Trg Mata Petrovića; 032 335 227; open M-F 8am-3pm, Sa 8am-1pm).

Post Offices: There are a couple post offices scattered throughout the city. Here's one close to the Old Town walls: Pošta (Square of the Arms; Jun 15-Sep 15 open daily M-Sa 11am-5pm).

Public Restrooms: There aren't a ton of public restrooms, but you can find some at the Kamelija Shopping Center (Square Mata Petrovića; 032 335 380; open daily 8am-11pm).

Internet: Your best bet for connectivity is to stop by just about any of the cafés or restaurants across Kotor.

BGLTQ+ Resources: The closest BGLTQ+ resource center is located in Montenegro's capital, Podgorica. LGBT Forum Progres (Ul. marta 27, 020 674 761, lgbtprogres.me).

EMERGENCY INFORMATION

Emergency Number: 112.

Police: There's a police station not far from the Old Town:

- Policija (Jadranska magistrala; 032 322 222, emergency number 122).

US Embassy: The US Embassy is based in Montenegro's capital, Podgorica. You can reach out to them for assistance while you're in Montenegro:

- US Embassy Podgorica (Dzona Dzeksona 2; 020 410 500; me.usembassy.gov).

Rape Crisis Center: There's a 24hr hotline based in Podgorica that you can reach out to. Here's their info:

- SOS Hotline for Women and Children Victims of Violence Niksic (068 024 086; sosnk.org; open daily 24hr).

Hospitals: Here's Kotor's main hospital:

- Opšta bolnica Kotor (167 Njegoševa 3; 032 325 602, open 24hr).

PERAST

Perast is basically comprised of one street, total. However, to give credit where credit is due it's a really nice street. In fact, this street looks so nice that it's worth going out of your way to see it. What's so special about this singular street? Well, for starters, as you walk up the concrete path, to your left, you'll find Baroque palaces, Romanesque churches, and the quaintest eateries you've ever seen in all your life. Then, to your immediate right—would you look at that!—there's the glistening blue waters of the Bay of Kotor. Out into the not-so-far distance is Perast's big claim to fame: Our Lady of the Rocks, an artificial island that houses a turquoise-domed church. Perast may be one of the smallest towns on the Bay, with its population of 274 locals (and counting), but hey, since when does size matter?

Like we said, Perast literally has one street, which means it's pretty hard to get lost here. The layout is pretty simple: if you're standing at **Palace Zmajević** and facing away from **Our Lady of the Rocks,** the town flanks out to the south east. Along the coast, you'll find restaurants upon restaurants upon restaurants, in addition to mainland sights like the **St. Nikola Church.**

GETTING THERE

If you're heading to Perast, you're going to want to connect through a bigger Montenegrin city. There aren't a ton of direct lines to Perast, so most travelers stop at Kotor. From Kotor, several bus lines make brief (very brief) stops in Perast. Tickets cost around €3. Just note that the bus may not actually drop you off in city center; in fact, the bus will very likely drop you off in what looks like the middle of a highway. Don't worry, though: glance around at this highway "stop" to find stairs descending down into Perast proper.

GETTING AROUND

You can walk from one end of Perast's street to the other in about five minutes, max. If you're planning on visiting Our Lady of the Rocks (and really, you should be planning on visiting Our Lady of the Rocks), you're going to have to travel by boat. The boat ride to the island and back will cost about €6, roundtrip. It takes about seven minutes each way.

Don't miss...

OUR LADY OF THE ROCKS

Our Lady of the Rocks Island; church open daily 9am-6pm

Sit back, because it's story time. Our Lady of the Rocks is not your average island; it's a completely man-made one. The legend goes like this: way back in the fifteenth century, two fishermen found a picture of the Madonna and Child on a pile of rocks. They brought it back with them, but the next morning, it had disappeared. So they went back to the rocks, and there it was again—right where they found it. They interpreted this as the Madonna's desire to stay at this site for the rest of eternity, and so the fishermen vowed to build a church at this site. But first, they needed some land for the church to stand on. The locals joined the cause and began laying rocks in the bay until an islet emerged. Now, on this spot, stands an ornately decorated Catholic church that features—you guessed it—a stunning icon of the Madonna and Child at its center. The church is decorated in the Baroque style, with intricate religious art lining its ornate walls. Attached to the church is a museum featuring local religious relics. On the second floor of this museum, find an outdoor terrace that offers sweeping views of the Bay of Kotor.

i *Roundtrip boat ride €6, church and museum entrance €2; limited wheelchair accessibility*

Check out...

PALACE ZMAJEVIĆ

Obala kapetana Marka Martinovica bb

If there's a worldwide contest for palaces-per-square-mile, we're pretty sure that Perast would end up on top. This tiny town packs 19 palaces onto one narrow seaside strip, and Palace Zmajević is the most famous of them all. Like most of Perast's palaces, it's small and fairly simple—you know, as far as palaces go. The Zmajevićs hold the title as one of Perast's most important noble families of the seventeenth century. You can see the family's trademark insignia, which features a winged dragon and a star, etched onto the palace's façade. The structure sits perched on a formidable stone, and the architecture itself blends natural rock with Baroque detailing. Once upon a time, the building housed the Zmajevićs' expansive library; today, however, it is in its final days of reconstruction. This means that its opening hours can be variable, but even if you can't make it inside, the exterior is still worth checking out.

i Free; wheelchair accessible

Swing by...

ST. NIKOLA CHURCH

Obala kapetana Marka Martinovica bb; open daily 9am-6pm

It's hard to miss Perast's most formidable mainland church, given that it sits right at the center of the town square. The church was first built in 1616, and about a century later, the town's Catholic leaders embarked on an ambitious renovation project. . .that they never finished. Today, the church remains incomplete: there's the "old" St. Nikola Church and the unfinished "new" St. Nikola Church, both standing at the same site. To be fair, they complement each other pretty well. There's also a treasury filled with religious objects and a bell tower that offers incredible views of the Bay and coast line.

i Bell tower admission €1; limited wheelchair accessibility to church, no wheelchair accessibility to bell tower

Grab a bite at...

ARMONIA ($$$)

Obala kapetana Marka Martinovica; 069 508 555; open daily 8am-1am

So, you know how we keep talking about that one street? Well, as you walk down it, you'll find a bunch of seaside restaurants that look quite similar in their set up: waterfront terraces, vibrantly green, delicately winding foliage, and expansive, seafood-heavy menus. Armonia is one such restaurant, except its waterfront terrace feels especially romantic, its foliage looks especially green, and its seafood dishes taste especially fresh. Keep in mind that the dishes here can get a bit pricey. If you're trying to stick to a budget, try out Armonia's meatless options or pasta specialties, which tend to be less costly than, you know, fresh lobster. For a comprehensively spectacular dining experience, try to snag a seaside table around sunset. Perast sunsets are famously magical, and there's something inherently luxurious about enjoying them from a perfectly decorated terrace while munching on the seafood of your dreams.

i Entrées from €7.80; wheelchair accessible

Pharmacies: The main pharmacy in Kotor is located in the Old Town:

- Apoteka Kotor Stari Grad (Stari Grad; 032 322 216; benuapoteka.me open daily 8am-10pm).

SIGHTS

CULTURE

FORTIFICATIONS

Put do Svetog Ivana; open daily 24hr, ticketed 8am-8pm

"City walls" fails to describe the straight-up-the-face-of-a-mountain fortifications that protected the city of Kotor for centuries. We're not quite sure how horses and soldiers made their way up the steep grades of the mountain, because it's near impossible to walk straight up the switchbacks without using the steps to the side. Should you survive, halfway up the mountain lies a small chapel dedicated to the Virgin Mary. You'll need divine help to hike all the way up to the fortress at the top, where even better views of the surrounding mountains await you. If you want to achieve maximum payoff for all that hard labor, time your trek such that you arrive at sunset. We can basically guarantee that the sight of the city, shrouded in a romantic pink glow, will leave you breathless—that is, if the hike itself hasn't already taken care of that. Just be sure to bring plenty of water; the hike is especially draining in the summer.

i €3 during ticketed hours; free outside of ticketed hours; no wheelchair accessibility

KOTOR FARMER'S MARKET

Stari Grad; open Su-F 7am-2pm, Sa 7am-4pm

For a true Montenegrin culinary experience, look no further than Kotor's Farmer's Market. It doesn't get much more authentic than this. Stroll through stalls upon stalls teeming with fresh, local produce sourced from all regions of Montenegro. The market is strategically divided into two sections, which can basically be described as the section that smells good and the section that smells bad. The former carries rosemary, fruits, vegetables, and fragrant flowers. The latter sells plenty of fish, meat, and cheese, which all mix together to produce the most sensually aggressive of aromas. Smelly or not, the goods here all taste great, and that's what we really care about. If you've got a sweet tooth, be sure to try the local jams. Smuckers could never.

i Free; limited wheelchair accessibility

PIAZZA OF THE ARMS

Piazza of the Arms; open daily 24hr

In a town filled with winding alleyways straight out of a storybook, Piazza of the Arms is the most wide-open space you'll find citywide. It's the **Old Town's** largest square, filled with charming restaurant terraces, live music, and enough gelato shops to satisfy the sweetest of sensibilities. It's one of the busiest spaces in all of Kotor, but that's not saying a lot in a city known for its chilled out vibes. Long story short, head to the Piazza to kick off your time in Kotor. It's a good homebase, in no small part because it's also the ideal spot to procure a plethora of delicious snacks to sustain you throughout the day's exploration.

i Free; wheelchair accessible

LANDMARKS

CHURCH OF OUR LADY OF REMEDY

Church of Our Lady of Remedy, Rd to the Fort of St. Ivan; open daily 24hr

You've got to earn a trip to the Church of Our Lady of Remedy. What's the cost? Well, admission is technically free—that is, once you've paid the price of a 500-step ascent up the steep hills of Kotor to finally reach this stone Catholic church. Built around the fifteenth century to honor the Holy Mother for saving the town from the black plague, it's part of Kotor's Fortifications. Accordingly, Virgin Mother and Catholic iconographies decorate the beautiful church. The church itself takes up little space, but views from its steps are absolutely stunning. It sits right near the halfway point for the Fortifications hike, so this is also a good (and scenic!) mid-trek resting point.

i Free; no wheelchair accessibility

ST. NIKOLA CHURCH

Trg Sv. Nikole, open 8am-8pm

If you're trying to clear your sinuses after breathing in all those fishy smells at the market, then it's time to head to St. Nikola Church. Take a big, luxurious sniff and inhale the magical scents of incense, beeswax, and rosemary. Once you're done smelling the place—because, duh, that's obviously the first thing we all do whilst visiting a church—glance up to see a magical mosaic with shimmering silver pieces. This church truly treats all of the senses, but maybe don't try tasting it. Plenty of international Orthodox influences remind you that St. Nikola is the largest and most important Orthodox church in Kotor. Ornate golden crosses gifted by Russia top the majestic bell towers and a Serbian flag hangs from the second floor of the structure.

i Free; limited wheelchair accessibility

MUSEUMS

CAT MUSEUM

Trg Gospa od Andela; 069 628 536; open M-Sa 10am-8pm, Su 9am-5pm

Before you get too excited, we must tell you that you won't find any collections of live cats in the museum. Putting aside how weird of a museum concept that would be, visitors can walk down literally any alley in the Old Town to meet feline friends. This museum, however, enables cat enthusiasts to discover all of the cat images, posters, and paraphernalia they never knew they wanted to see—basically, it's like someone made a shrine to 2013 internet meme humor. Cats are perhaps the most controversial of critters, and this museum is similarly polarizing. It's pretty small, and if you don't already have a proclivity for the common housecat, you probably won't feel too stimulated by the limited collection. On the flipside, if a fervor for felines defines your personality, then welcome to your slice of heaven. Bonus: your €1 entrance fee goes towards supporting Kotor's feral cat population.

i Admission €1; wheelchair accessible

MARITIME MUSEUM

Trg Bokeljske Mornarice 391, 032 304 720, museummaritimum.com; open Apr 15-July 1 M-F 8am-6pm, Su 9am-1pm; July M-F 8am-11pm, Su 10am-4pm; Sept-Oct 15 M-F 8am-6pm, Su 9am-1pm; Oct 15-Apr 15 M-F 9am-5pm, Su 9am-noon

This ain't Sea World: we're at the Maritime Museum and that's as real as it gets. While T-Pain may not agree with our evaluation of this Kotor Museum, this is the place to go for model ships (or model boats, rather). Peep its old naval uniforms, trade documents from Venetian times, and maps on maps on maps. Many of the written documents seen here would commonly be housed in the archives of other cities; it's neat to look at them up close. For the landlubbers out there, the nineteenth century rooms of a local noble family hold just as many treasurers and secrets.

i Admission €4, €1 reduced; wheelchair accessible

OUTDOORS

BAY OF KOTOR

Bay of Kotor

If you're really with it, you refer to the Bay of Kotor exclusively as Boka. The upgraded lingo earns you some serious pretentiousness points for your local knowledge, because that's how Montenegrins refer to this twisting Adriatic bay. It's been inhabited since way back when, and on its coast lie some of Montenegro's most well-preserved medieval towns, including **Kotor**, **Risan**, and **Perast**. The bay lies between dramatic cliffs and features shimmering straits and colorful coves. Lay out by the concrete shore and enjoy the sparkling site of the Bay's pristine blue waters, or jump right in on the action and discover the Bay via boat. Quarter day bay cruises start at €9, or book full-day, intra-city bay cruises for about €40.

i Free from shore; bay cruises start from €9; wheelchair accessible

FOOD

CUKAR PANCAKE ($)

Dobrota; 067 438 018; open daily 8am-1am

Everything tastes sweeter when it's inexpensive, and Cukar's crepes already taste pretty sweet. Cukar bakes up all of your favorite desserts—bubble waffles, ice cream sundaes, and American pancakes all make an appearance. But what Cukar prepares especially well are paper-thin, delightfully-light sweet and savory crêpes filled with Nutella, fresh fruits, ice cream, or ham, cheese, and prosciutto (note the use of or here; Cukar does not whip up Nutella/ham/cheese abominations, at least to the best of our knowledge). The decor stands out as charmingly eclectic, with multicolored pastel table-and-chair combos and whimsical touches straight out of a Hans Christian Andersen fairytale. The terrace views look particularly scenic, as it sits right on the water and faces the **Old Town**.

i Crepes from €1.30; wheelchair accessible

BOKUN ($)

Stari Grad; 069 290 019; open daily winter 8am-11pm, summer 8am-1am

Many people come here for the live music, the exposed stone walls, and the wine. We come here for the sandwiches. Hold the jazz, please, we want the arugula and prosciutto goodness served on a wooden platter. With reasonable prices, delish breakfast entrées, and plenty of seating both outside and inside the trendy interior, Bokun invites travelers to revel in their Balkan brunch betchiness. The sandwiches themselves not only taste somehow simultaneously crunchy and soft, but they also look Instagram-ready. Make all your followers jealous and add a splash of food from Bokun to your feed.

i Sandwiches from €4.50; wheelchair accessible

GALION ($$$)

Suranj bb; 032 325 054; galion.me; open daily noon-midnight

Yes, this is a five star restaurant. Yes, the menu lists five star prices. Yes, it's tough to justify spending €20.80 on grilled octopus when your daily travel dinner consists of bread-and-salami sandwiches. But listen, it's possible to enjoy an affordable dinner at Galion (word to the wise and budget-conscious: look beyond the fish specialities and check out the chicken dishes). The food tastes rich and fills your plate generously, but what you really pay a premium for is the romantic ambiance and the absolutely mind-boggling views of the shimmering bay. Galion looks right onto the water, and blissfully peaceful live music played on the restaurant's deck compliments this beautiful setting.

i Entrées from €12.90; wheelchair accessible

NIGHTLIFE

LETRIKA ART BAR

Stari Grad 426; 069 077 747; open M-Sa 9am-1am, Su 9am-midnight

Letrika Art Bar brands itself as an indie art café, but we swear we heard them playing some Britney Spears followed by a Backstreet Boys bop, so we have our reservations. We concede that the decor itself looks pretty indie (the sign that marks the stone path towards the bar reads: "This is a private sign. Do not read." Oops). But maybe being mainstream isn't such a bad thing, because Letrika has evolved to become one of Kotor's most popular party spots. Hostel crews from across the city flock to Letrika for its wide open terrace-turned-dance-floor and correspondingly danceable soundtrack.

i Beer from €2.20; wheelchair accessible

LADOVINA KITCHEN & WINE BAR

Njegoševa 209; 063 422 472; ladovina.me; open daily 9am-midnight

With its beautifully decorated, foliage-filled terrace and fairly priced drinks, Ladovina makes you want to bring your latest hostel honey here for a romantic date. For the independent biddies out there, though, Ladovina also provides the ideal setting for a relaxing night out. Don't plan on finding wild parties raging on here; it's more of a chill, classy, let's-discuss-our-deepest-desires-but-also-world-politics-and-fancy-wines kind of place. Plus, in addition to all the alcoholic drinks you could dream of (well, we certainly hope you couldn't hope for more, because that's frankly excessive), Ladovina boasts an expensive menu of tasty dishes to snack on. May we recommend a plate of mussels to go with a glass of sauvignon blanc? See, we can be classy sommeliers, too.

i Beer from €2.60, wine from €3.60, main course meals from €12.50; wheelchair accessible

MONTENEGRO ESSENTIALS

VISAS

Montenegro is not a member of the European Union, but entering the EU is one of the nation's key strategic goals. Citizens of EU nations, Australia, Canada, New Zealand, the US, and many other nations may enter Montenegro without a visa and stay for up to 90 days with a valid passport. Citizens of the EU and the former Yugoslav nations may enter with a valid ID card and stay without a residence permit for up to 30 days.

MONEY

Currency: Montenegro uses the euro as its sole currency. In order to get the most competitive exchange rate, it is generally best to withdraw money directly from an ATM. ATMs and banks are very accessible in most major Montenegrin cities.

Tipping: Tipping isn't necessary in Montenegro, but it is becoming increasingly common. Generally, cab drivers appreciate a 5% tip, and it is courteous to tip waitstaff at restaurants around 10%. No one will get angry if you don't leave a tip, but it is a nice thing to do.

SAFETY AND HEALTH

BGLTQ+ Travel: Homosexuality was decriminalized in 1977, and discrimmination against BGLTQ+ individuals was outlawed in 2010. Nonetheless, Montenegrin culture is not very accepting of homosexuality, and homophobia is not unheard of. BGLTQ+ friendly nightlife spots are difficult to find, even in major Montenegrin cities. Locals may react with hostility towards public displays of affection between same-sex couples, and in general, public expressions of BGLTQ+ identity are not welcomed. Gay activists in Montenegro have been targeted with violence in recent years, and BGLTQ+ travelers are encouraged to exercise some caution.

Drugs and Alcohol: There's technically no legal drinking age, but you have to be 18 to purchase alcohol. Remember to drink responsibly and to never drink and drive. The legal blood alcohol content for driving in Montenegro is under 0.05%, significantly lower than the US limit of 0.08%.

LANGUAGE

The official language of Montenegro is Montenegrin, which is mutually intelligible with Serbian, Croatian, and Bosnian. English is widely spoken and understood throughout Montenegro. Some museums may only have limited English descriptions to accompany exhibits, but beyond this, most signs you'll find throughout are translated into English.

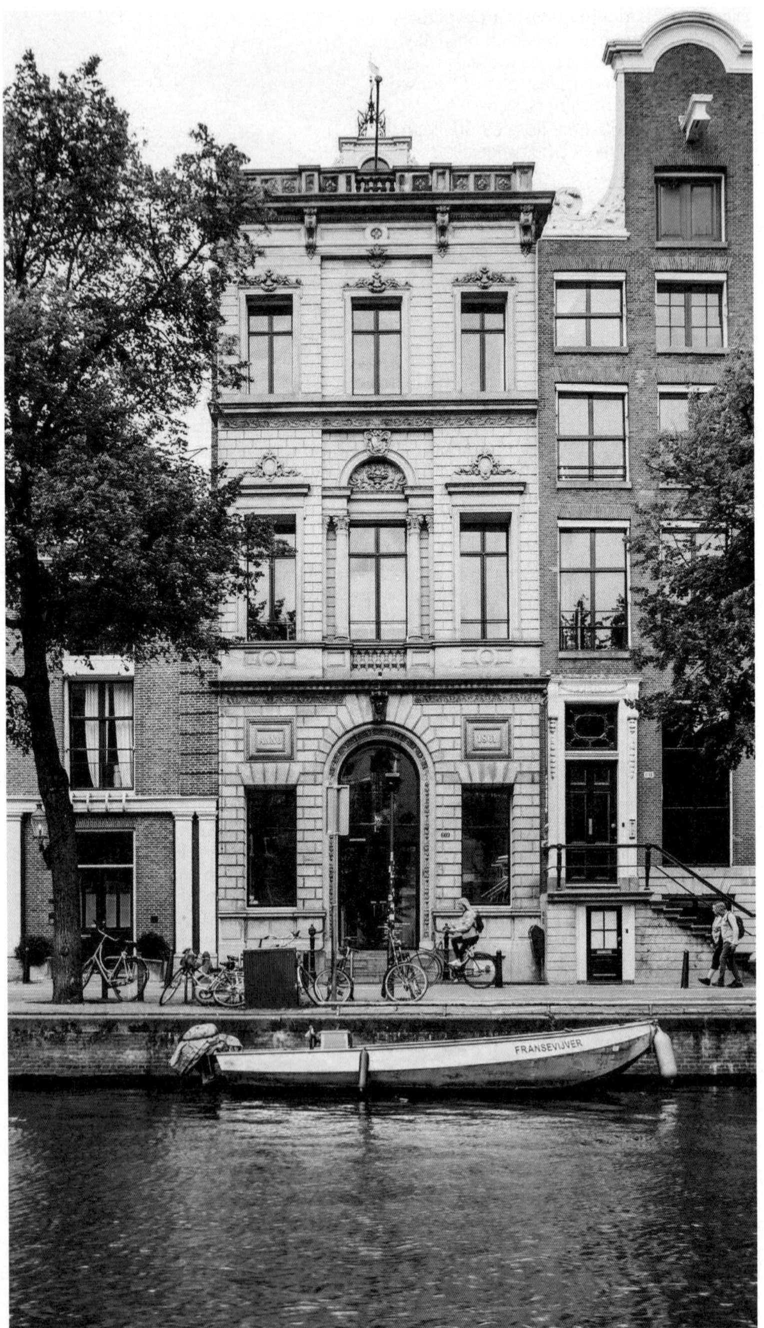
FRANSEVIJVER

THE NETHERLANDS

From its humble beginnings in the dark ages up through today, the growth of the Netherlands' population and cities has centered around the Dutch peoples' ability to master the rivers and ocean that constantly threaten to plunge their country underwater. Today, you can see their mastery of various bodies of water in their canal-lined cities and the countless establishments with some variation of "dam" in their name.

Outside of the world of aquatic engineering, the Dutch have also contributed to global culture. We can thank them for legendary artists like Van Gogh, Rembrandt, and Vermeer, for the Gouda and Beemster cheese varieties, and for Eddie Van Halen. You can enjoy all of these things almost anywhere in the world, but for the real deal...you have to get to the Netherlands and see it for yourself.

Though Amsterdam draws the bulk of tourist traffic for its incredible museums, canals, and anything-goes attitude, both The Hague and Rotterdam are rising to the fore as cultural powerhouses in their own right and round out a trifecta of major cities that can go toe-to-toe with any other major European metropolis. In between the big cities, you'll find pristine towns home to traditional restaurants (serving dishes like *bitterballen* and *kibbeling*), beautiful Medieval architecture, and, frequently, a local university that supplies the vibrant nightlife scenes with a steady stream of hip, party-loving youth. The Netherlands is a student traveler's dream for this reason—the Dutch are masters of making the most of their downtime, and you'll never find yourself in a city or town that lacks at least one good picnic spot and an iconic bar.

AMSTERDAM

Coverage by **Sam Lincoln**

When you say you're going to Amsterdam, a lot of people raise their eyebrows, smile knowingly, and say "oh, Amsterdam, huh?" It's a city known for its tolerance: prostitution is legal, "coffee shops" sell plants more popular than mere coffee beans (marijuana, for those who need it spelled out), and its nightlife can get real wild real quick. With an annual swarm of tourists 16 times larger than its actual population, Amsterdam can be subject to misrepresentation by the weekend-trip frat bros (American or British, take your pick), the borderline adulterous bachelorette parties, and the "I've never done it, but it's Amsterdam!" crowd. Amongst the madness, though, is a city with much more character than you might expect. Highly efficient public transportation and more than 300 miles of dedicated bike paths make exploration easy, while an unmatched enthusiasm for leisure and fun make for round-the-clock entertainment throughout the city. Narrow, katywampus buildings line the iconic canals, some residential but many given over to fantastic local cafés, historic restaurants, and eclectic bars. Throughout the year the city is host to countless festivals, and its legendary art museums draw in the biggest names in painting and sculpture—both historic and contemporary—to join their already formidable permanent collections on display. Amsterdam is perhaps best described by the non-translatable Dutch word gezellig. It's used to describe something that's easy to relax into, that's cozy and fun, and that gives you that nice, warm feeling you get when hanging out with old friends. Come to the Dutch capital and find yourself in the kind of place where, no matter where you come from, you could see yourself living for the rest of your life.

ORIENTATION

Arriving at **Centraal Station**, you'll be on the northern side of the city. A ferry across the harbor (known as the IJ) to the north will bring you to **Amsterdam Noord**, a neighborhood featuring the new **Eye Film Institute** and some cool cafés and restaurants overlooking the harbor. South are some of the more touristy parts of town: the **Red Light District** is a nightlife hotspot and popular among tourists for its debauchery-filled reputation ("red light" comes from the red lights that frame the windows of prostitutes). In the city center, you'll find the **Leidseplein** square, surrounded by a neighborhood full of clubs and restaurants. **Rembrandtplein**, Leidseplein's even more touristy counterpart, is close by. West of the city center are the "nine streets," a hip shopping neighborhood with its fair share of local eateries. Southwest of the center in the **Oud-Zuid** neighborhood is the sprawling **Vondelpark**, the largest park in the city, as well as the **Museumplein** square, around which sit many of the city's most important museums (such as the sprawling **Rijksmuseum**). Just north of the city center, is the **Jordaan** neighborhood which is dotted with tiny canals and beautiful, traditional Dutch architecture. Jordaan is home to a variety of cool local bars and restaurants. South of the city center is **De Pijp**, an increasingly hip neighborhood full of delicious food and stylish young locals hanging out in low-key bars, as well as one of the city's larger markets.

ESSENTIALS

GETTING THERE

Buses, taxis, and trains are all available from Amsterdam's international airport, Schiphol. A train station is located just below the airport and a bus station right outside the arrivals area. Trains run through to Centraal Station, the main station in the city, from which metros, trams, and municipal buses can bring you wherever you need to go (and the city center is just a short walk away). Buses from the airport can deliver you to a number of points throughout the metropolitan area.

GETTING AROUND

Amsterdam has excellent public transport, including buses, trams, ferries, and a metro. All public transportation in Amsterdam can be accessed with an OV-Chipkaart or temporary travel card, which can be purchased at vending machines in the main stations. A variety of options are available, from personalized rechargeable chip cards to single-use or 24hr tickets. You can also consider purchasing the "I amsterdam" city card which provides free entry to many top attractions, a canal cruise, and free public transport. It can be purchased for 24hr, 48hr, 72hr, and 96hr durations on www.iamsterdam.com. Bikes are also a popular way to get around the city—more than a third of Amsterdammers commute to work by bike, and rental shops are all over the city.

PRACTICAL INFORMATION

Tourist Office: Amsterdam has two official tourist offices, but we recommend using the I amsterdam Visitor Centre and website. I amsterdam Visitor Centre Stationsplein: (Stationsplein 1; www.iamsterdam.com/en; open daily 9am-6pm).

Bank/ATM/Currency Exchange: Beware of Travelex and other exchange service ATMs, they often charge exorbitant fees. There's a bank and ATM right in the city center, just off the Dam square: Rabobank (Dam 16; 020 777 8899; office open M-F 9am-5pm, Sa 10am-6pm; ATM open daily 24hr).

Post Office: There is a post service point in Centraal Station. PostNL (De Ruijterkade 26B; 88 225 555; open daily 7am-10pm).

Internet: Internet is widely available throughout the city in cafés, most museums, and most accommodations (hostels, hotels, etc). There are also some publicly accessible Wi-Fi hotspots in the city proper.

BGLTQ+ Resources: For a fairly comprehensive list of BGLTQ+ activities and resources in Amsterdam, see www.iamsterdam.com/en/see-and-do/whats-on/lgbt. There you can find information for many of the city's major BGLTQ+ organizations, the largest of which is COC Amsterdam (020 626 3087; www.cocamsterdam.nl/en).

EMERGENCY INFORMATION

Emergency Number: 112.

Police: There are police stations throughout Amsterdam proper; the central police station is at IJ-Tunnel 2 (open daily 8am-10pm). Another centrally located station is at Nieuwezijds Voorburgwal 35, and is open daily 24hr. The non-emergency police line is 0900-8844.

US Embassy: There is a US Consulate General in Amsterdam that supports the US Embassy in the Hague (Museumsplein 19; visits by appointment; if you need to contact the consulate in an emergency call 020 575 5309 or 070 310 2209 outside business hours, or email amsterdamusc@state.gov).

Hospitals:

- OVLG, Spuistraat (Spuistraat 239a; 020 599 41 00; open M 8am-4:30pm, T 8am-7:30pm, W-Th 8am-4:30pm).

Pharmacies: Pharmacies are scattered throughout the city; check any closed pharmacy after hours or on weekends to find the location of an open one. There's a central pharmacy (often called *aphoteek* in Dutch) in the city center.

- BENU Dam Apotheek (Damstraat 2; 020 624 4331; www.benuapotheek.nl/apotheek/benu-dam-apotheek; open M-F 8:30am-5:30pm, Sa 8:30am-5pm; Su noon-5pm)

SIGHTS

CULTURE

DE HALLEN

Hannie Dankbaarpassage; dehallen-amsterdam.nl/en; open M-Th 7am-1am, Fri-Sa 7am-3am, Su 7am-1am

De Hallen is a beautiful brick indoor/outdoor shopping and cultural center with more or less everything you'd ever need to survive in one spot. On one end sits a public library with lots of work space for professionals or students alike, throughout the center the best artisans sell beautiful local art and ornate crafts of all kinds out of chic boutiques (say that ten times fast), and at the heart of it all is a food hall (or should we say... food *hallen*) selling delicious—though not always cheap—meals pulled from dozens of different cuisines around the world. De Hallen is a great local spot to visit whether you're just stopping by to check it out or looking to spend your entire inheritance.

ℹ Prices vary; limited wheelchair accessibility

EYE FILM

IJpromenade 1; 020 589 1400; www.eyefilm.nl/en; box office open M-Th 10am-10pm, F-Sa 10am-11pm, Su 10am-10pm; exhibition open daily 10am-7pm

The Eye Film Institute is an unmistakable sight on the opposite side of the IJ. Like a crash-landed spaceship from a superior alien civilization, its angular white walls jut up right from the waterfront and give an otherwise monotonous, commercial stretch of the city a sleek and sophisticated flare. Inside you'll find a film museum, archive, some fascinating special exhibitions, and the real treat—a top-of-the-line movie theater showing all kinds of flicks. Go during the day to learn about the magic of movies, or head there at night for a classy screening and a drink at their stunning bar.

ℹ Admission €11, €9.50 reduced, exhibits €14, €11.50 reduced; card only; wheelchair accessible

9 STREETS

Wolvenstraat 9; open daily 24hr (most shops close by 6pm)

Amsterdam has no shortage of shopping streets and districts, but those that are closest to the city center can get overcrowded and overwhelming, particularly as tourists flood the city during peak summer months. For a classier, trendier, and far less chaotic shopping experience, consider heading out to the 9 Streets district. Here you'll find multitudes of smaller shops and local boutiques selling chic clothing, jewelry, art, and more. There are also some delicious and reasonably-priced restaurants throughout. For the local shopping experience—and to hop on that hipster fashion train—go to 9 Streets. It might not be the easiest on your wallet...but hey, life is short!

ℹ Prices vary; wheelchair accessibility varies

PAINTER'S PALACE

Heisteeg 8; www.painterspalace.eu; 068 145 0599; open daily noon-6pm

Part art gallery, part art studio, Painter's Palace is a brand new (if not palatial) space dedicated to painting (and drawing). The ground floor sells art from local artists and printmakers, while the second floor (or the first floor, if you're gonna be European about it) has some couches and all the art supplies you need to get started making some masterpieces! You can show up at any point during opening hours, but you're most likely to be joined by other art-inclined folks if you show up at the end of the day and towards the end of the week. What are you waiting for? Roll up your sleeves, grab a paintbrush, and permanently stain the one pair of nice pants you brought with you!

ℹ Drawing is free, art and art supplies for sale for various prices; no wheelchair accessibility

VRIJ PALEIS

Paleisstraat 107; vrijpaleis.nl; opening hours vary

It's not easy to put Vrij Paleis into a box. It's part art gallery, with its walls occasionally covered with the works of artists both local and international. It's also part performance space, nightlife venue, and artist's studio. Any creative discipline you can think of has probably been showcased here at one point or another. Stop by during the day to glance around at cutting edge art from unknown but up-and-coming artists or just to see the wild variety of found objects sitting around on the floor and walls—you'll find lots of old cash registers, stacks of televisions, and even an entire Renault pickup truck. Slide in at night, however, and you might just find a party. You're more likely to see it hip-hip-happenin' on the night of an exhibition opening, but they also host events on a whim.

ℹ Free admission; no wheelchair accessibility

LANDMARKS

BEJINHOF

Bejinhof; 020 622 1918; begijnhofkapelamsterdam.nl/english-information; open daily 9am-5pm

If you want a break from the tourist-filled city center but you don't want to go through the effort of finding a gorgeous leafy parks, then strolling around the Bejinhof might be a good second choice. As a former *Béguinage* (a home for single women who aren't quite nuns) and a great example of a traditional Dutch *hofje* (a courtyard with some sort of special housing surrounding it, typically for the elderly or women), this grassy square is a tranquil change of pace from the cobblestone-covered downtown. It's also home to the oldest surviving house in the city, **Het Houten Huis** (from way back in 1420). A walk through the Bejinhof and the nearby courtyards of the **Amsterdam Museum** is a pleasant way to recharge your travel batteries.

i Free; wheelchair accessible

ROYAL PALACE

Nieuwezijds Voorburgwal 147; 020 522 6161; www.paleisamsterdam.nl/en; open daily 10am-5pm, closed for royal events

While the Hague might be where the royal family lives, Amsterdam is where they go to work. The Royal Palace, sitting right in the center of the city in the famous **Place du Dam**, is where you would go if you were a head of state being received by the king and welcomed to the country. Of course, you're not a head of state and probably won't ever be but you can nonetheless experience a royal welcome by exploring the palace when it opens its gates to plebeian visitors. It's a gorgeous, massive, and marble-lined palace, as you'd expect, with lots of beautiful rooms to explore. Because it's a working palace, there aren't many information panels taped to the walls.

i Admission €10, €9 reduced; wheelchair accessible

MUSEUMS

HUIS MARSEILLE

Keizersgracht 401; 020 531 8989; www.huismarseille.nl/en; open T-Su 11am-6pm

Housed in not one but two of Amsterdam's stately canal homes is the Huis Marseille, the small but immensely impressive museum that is the city's first to be dedicated solely to the art of photography. In addition to an important permanent collection of modern photography, the Huis is also host to a variety of boundary-pushing (read: wacko, high concept, and cool) special exhibitions that change up four or so times per year. Whether you're coming because you love photography or just because you want to explore a beautifully-maintained set of canal houses, Huis Marseille is a wonderful addition to Amsterdam's already thriving art scene.

i Admission €9, €4.50 reduced; no wheelchair accessibility

ANNE FRANK HOUSE

Prinsengracht 263-267; 020 556 7105; www.annefrank.org/en; open Apr 1-May 30 daily from 9am-10pm, open May 30-Sep 1 daily from 8:30am-10pm, open Sep 1-Nov 1 daily from 9am-10pm, open Nov 1-Apr 1 M-F 9am-7pm, Sa 9am-10pm, Su 9am-7pm

The voice of Anne Frank has touched millions of people throughout the world. Her diary, written while hiding in Amsterdam during Nazi occupation is a reminder not to forget the atrocities of the **Holocaust** and the many innocent lives that it destroyed. Even though Anne's life was eventually claimed, her father Otto made sure her diary was published in order to illuminate the horrifying reality of life under Nazi rule. At the Anne Frank House, visitors can see the small annex that concealed the Frank family for two years before their discovery and arrest in 1944. This museum will give you a new perspective on Anne Frank and deliver a powerful message that you won't be able to ignore. Tickets sell out weeks to months in advance, so make sure to book ahead.

i Tickets €10.50; tickets are valid for specific entry time-slots from opening to an hour before closing; 80% of tickets become available two months in advance at noon

(Amsterdam time) and 20% of tickets are released day-of at 9am (Amsterdam time), but you may have to wait in an online queue to purchase; no photography allowed; no wheelchair accessibility

EMBASSY OF THE FREE MIND

Keizersgracht 123; 020 625 8079; embassyofthefreemind.com/en; open W-Sa 10am-5pm

There are a few reasons to go to the Embassy of the Free Mind. As the self-proclaimed first museum dedicated to free thinking, the Embassy has an incredible library of books and artifacts from thousands of philosophers who dared to go against the grain and restructure their belief system. If that somehow doesn't interest you, then go for the architecture—the Embassy sits within the House with the Heads, a large canal mansion formerly owned by a spectacularly wealthy merchant that has been impeccably restored. If you've ever wanted to read through heretical texts while lounging in an armchair in some old rich dude's drawing room with twenty-five foot ceilings (and haven't we all), this is your chance.

i Admission €12.50, €8.50 reduced; guided tour €7.50 (at 10:30am and 2:30pm) and rare book guided tour €17.50 (only booked ahead-of-time); no wheelchair accessibility

MOCO MUSEUM

Honthorststraat 20; 020 370 1997; moco-museum.com; open M-Th 9am-8pm, F-Sa 9am-9pm, Su 9am-8pm

The Moco Museum, set in a stately townhouse in **Museumplein**, has displayed exhibitions from famous—and sometimes near-mythical—artists like **Salvador Dalí** and the anonymous graffiti master **Banksy**. It's a bit ironic that they'd exhibit the latter artist, since his anti-establishment rhetoric and distaste for institutions led him to recently set his own painting to auto-shred after it sold at auction. The Moco museum highlights specific artists for the bulk of the gallery space, with the top floor dedicated to flaunting their impressive permanent collection featuring artists like **Andy Warhol, Keith Haring, Jeff Koons,** and **Jean-Michel Basquiat.**

i Admission €15, €12.50 reduced; audio guide €2.50; card only; book online to skip the line and for €1 off ticket prices; no wheelchair accessibility

VAN GOGH MUSEUM

Museumplein 6; www.vangoghmuseum.nl/en; open June 21-Sep 1 M-Th 9am-7pm, F-Sa 9am-9pm, Su 9am-7pm, Sep 2-Oct 2019 M-Th 9am-6pm, F 9am-9pm, Sa-Su 9am-6pm, Oct 28-Dec 22 M-Th 9am-5pm, F 9am-9pm, Sa-Su 9am-5pm, Dec 23-Dec 31 M-Th 9am-7pm, F-Sa 9am-9pm, Su 9am-7pm

With his bold, colorful artwork, it's hard to imagine **Van Gogh** as a tortured artist plagued by inner turmoil. Not only does this museum display around 200 of his paintings, more than 500 of his drawings, and almost all of his letters (far, far more of his work than is held at any other single location in the world), but it acquaints you with the Dutch painter's life, inspirations, and influences as well. Follow the development of his iconic style from the beginning (when his art was dark, oily, and very traditional), through to his studies in Antwerp and Paris, befriending of fellow art icons, and finally to his explosive self-portraits and burst in productivity the few months before his death.

i Tickets €19, under 18 free; no photography allowed; wheelchair accessible

RIJKSMUSEUM

Museumstraat 1; 020 674 7000; www.rijksmuseum.nl/en; open daily 9am-5pm

This is it, folks. This is the flagship museum of the Netherlands. The Rijksmuseum consistently ranks as one of the greatest art museums in the world, and you would be remiss not to spend some time—realistically, you could blow somewhere between half a day and a week uncovering all it has to offer—exploring the collections. **Rembrandt's** *The Nights Watch* tends to get lauded as the main masterpiece of the museum, but if you're looking to see some incredible art and want to lose the crowd that swarms the main exhibition halls, head up to the third floor and explore the criminally overlooked modern and contemporary art on display there. If you're itching to learn more about art history or the history of the Rijksmuseum, don't miss the incredible (and frequently ignored) four-story library that sits in the corner of the museum.

i Admission €20; wheelchair accessible

STEDELIJK MUSEUM

Museumplein 10; www.stedelijk.nl/en; open M-Th 10am-6pm, F 10am-10pm, Sa-Su 10am-6pm

Another highlight of the **Museumplein,** the Stedelijk Museum is your one-stop-shop for contemporary art in Amsterdam. Built around a core idea of making art as accessible as possible to the public, the Stedelijk has an eclectic permanent collection and electric special exhibition calendar that brings some of the best modern and contemporary art right to you throughout the year. In addition to all that high falutin' art stuff (prepare to be confused, as is often the case with boundary-pushing modern art) there's also a killer in-house bookstore, should you want to head home with some undeniable, tangible proof that you've gotten indescribably classier on this Amsterdam escapade.

i Admission €18.50, €10 reduced; ticket office closes 30 minutes before museum; wheelchair accessible

OUTDOORS

OOSTERPARK

Oosterpark; open daily 24hr

Oost of the city center (which is Dutch for "east of the city center"), this scenic and decently sized park is home to a huge kid-friendly water feature, the occasional festival or outdoor concert, and lots and lots of lounging locals. As idyllic as the parks closer to the city center can be, if you ever find yourself "Oost of Eden" (ha) then grab some food from a nearby supermarket and take a few relaxing hours to picnic on the lawn away from the hustle and bustle of Amsterdam's main drag. During the summer, there are periodic festivals and music shows to keep things entertaining...but on an unrelated note, say "oost" to yourself a couple times and try not to giggle.

i Free; wheelchair accessible

SARPHATIPARK

Sarphatipark; open daily 24hr

Ideal location in an underrated and relentlessly cool neighborhood? Check. Not many tourists? Check. Lots of locals relaxing on the grass even in the middle of the day in the middle of the work week? Check. Does anyone in this city have an actual 9-5 job? Unclear. It's not very big, but Sarphatipark has a beautiful lawn, stately fountain, winding paths, and a scenic pond with plenty of Dutch ducks. What more could you want? As an added bonus: Sarphatipark is right around the corner from the **Albert Cuyp** market. Grab some cheap local food, make it a picnic, and show off that brightly colored pashmina your friends told you not to buy!

i Free; wheelchair accessible

VONDELPARK

Vondelpark; open daily 24hr

Amsterdam's flagship park has everything a park should have—some scenic water features, lots of grass, a few fountains, some cool sculptures...you get the picture. What sets Vondelpark apart (there are, after all, plenty of parks to choose from in this city) is an open air theater offering festivals, concerts, and even stand-up comedy from June through September. Entrance to these shows is happily free, although there's no guarantee they'll be in English. Even if you don't want to go for the music or to catch a play, Vondelpark is a scenic sanctuary of weeping willows and sweeping lawns in the center of the city and a wonderful place to take a deep breath after a long day of museum-hopping.

i Free; wheelchair accessible

FOOD

BAKERS AND ROASTERS ($$)

Eerste Jacob van Campenstraat 54; www.bakersandroasters.com; open daily 8:30am-4pm

New Zealand isn't really known for its breakfast, and Amsterdam isn't really known for its New Zealand restaurants. No longer! Bakers and Roasters is a breakfast spot in the hip and food-filled **de Pijp** neighborhood that offers incredible, sophisticated-but-hearty New Zealand-inspired breakfast dishes but with a Brazilian twist. This is a culinary mélange that comes a little out of left field, but after eating there...well we're just glad someone thought it up. Portions are reasonable, though prices skew towards the higher end—blame the owners, who go out of their way to ensure everything served is local, from the bread to the produce to the delicious, delicious meats.

i Egg dishes from €11.50, pancakes from €7.50 (for a short stack); vegetarian, vegan, and gluten-free options available; no wheelchair accessibility

IL PRIMO ($$)

Reguliersdwarsstraat 13-15; 020 331 9370; ilprimoristorante.nl; open daily 11am-midnight

Il Primo is an Italian restaurant located on the restaurant-packed **Reguliersdwarsstraat,** right by the beating heart of the city center. A few things make Il Primo stand out from the dozens and dozens of dining options located next door. One is the super reasonable prices—you can get pasta or pizza dishes for less than €12—which are less expensive than nearby competition even though Il Primo still feels like a reasonably upscale affair. If you're looking for the full sit-down meal experience without paying typical prices, Il Primo might be the spot for you. Just be prepared to wait; the food can sometimes take a while to come out.

i Pasta from €8, pizza from €7; vegetarian, vegan, and gluten-free options available; no wheelchair accessibility

LIBERTINE CAFÉ ($$)

Wolvenstraat 22; 020 214 9660; www.libertinecafe.amsterdam; open daily 9am-midnight

Sometimes the best dinner is a really, really late lunch. That's the vibe over at Libertine Café, which feels like a lunch spot that just happens to be open later than its competition. Luckily for us, that means delicious dinnertime food at lunch prices—which are notably cheaper than any nearby "restaurant restaurant." With an Italian skew (try their risotto) and an unlikely soft spot for Lagunitas IPAs, Libertine might just be your saving grace if you find yourself stranded in the **Nine Streets** after all the friendly-looking local boutiques lock their doors in your face at 6pm.

i Soup from €6, seasonal risotto from €16, veggie dishes from €5.50; vegetarian, vegan, and gluten-free options available; no wheelchair accessibility

LOMBARDO'S ($)

Nieuwe Spiegelstraat 50; 020 420 5010; www.lombardos.nl; open daily 11am-10pm

No matter what country you're in, at the end of the day, it's tough to beat a really high quality burger. Though of course we associate them with the United States and its high-cholesterol cuisine, you'd be remiss if you don't try a burger in the Netherlands. In part, that's because the Dutch take their meat really seriously—the beef used by the burger artisans at Lombardi's is delicious and reasonably priced in a city where high quality cuts can set you back a few dozen euros (or more). To top things off, Lombardi's has a cozy ambiance (only 10 seats!) and a fun-loving, food-loving staff that's keen on making your burger—even if you like things vegetarian—a highlight of your trip.

i Burgers from €13, veggie burger from €10; vegan and vegetarian options available; no wheelchair accessibility

MONKS COFFEE ROASTERS ($$)

Bilderdijkstraat 46; 062 313 1661; monks-coffee.nl; open T-Su 8am-5pm

Amsterdam may be more famous for its coffeeshops than its cafés, if you catch our drift, but that doesn't mean they don't take their coffee very, very seriously. The penchant for the artisan side of coffee and tea brewing is on full display at Monks Coffee Roasters, a café located just a short walk or tram ride away from the city center in the ever-hip neighborhood of **Amsterdam-West.** Go for a morning pick-me-up, but stay for a long breakfast (their menu, served until the afternoon, includes a "breakfast burger" with a poached egg, hash browns, and a healthy chunk of bacon on top). As an added bonus? Locals frequently bring their dogs in to hang out while they read the paper and sip their matcha lattes.

i Breakfast from €8, breakfast burger €13; limited wheelchair accessibility

THT RESTAURANT ($$)

IJpromenade 2; 020 760 4820; www.tht.nl/en; open daily from 10am-10pm

Picture this: it's early evening, the sun is just beginning to think about setting, and you're perched on the cantilevered terrace of the THT Restaurant. It's right on a side canal just a few steps away from the IJ, with a beautiful view of Amsterdam proper across the water. Ferries leave regularly to get to this part of town, and in addition to great tapas style food (plates are small, order two or three) with an emphasis on Asian fusion, there's also an in house performance space in case you're wanting to see a concert. Right down the road, less than five minutes away, is the pristine **EYE Film Institute**. It's kinda the perfect setup for the old dinner-and-a-movie gig.

i Plates from €6.20; vegetarian, vegan, and gluten-free options available; card only; no wheelchair accessibility

NIGHTLIFE

THE COOLDOWN CAFÉ ("DE KLEINE")

Lange Leidsedwarsstraat 116; open M-Th 10:30pm-4am, F-Sa 10:30pm-5am, Su 10:30pm-4am

Known affectionately to the locals as the "Kleine Cooldown" or just the "Kleine," this place beats any famous, touristy nightclub for a crazy night. With wild bartenders alternating between serving drinks and DJing (which entails flipping between hit songs, Dutch folk songs, and electronic music every thirty or so seconds, and passing out Santa hats regardless of the month), this is where real Amsterdammers go. A true Kleine Cooldown experience means showing up super late on a weekday, dancing like crazy, dousing your clothes with beer, and not leaving until you've ensured the next day (or, more likely, the rest of the day) is ruined. If you're lucky, you'll even wake up in a Santa hat. Free souvenir!

i Free; no wheelchair accessibility

DISCO DOLLY

Handboogstraat 11; discodolly.nl; open M-Th 11pm-4am, F-Sa 11pm-5am, Su 11pm-4am

If you're out on the town late at night and the streets look suspiciously empty, it's probably because everyone has rolled to Disco Dolly. This nightclub is a wildly popular student venue, and its ambitious set of opening hours ensure that throbbing bass is being pumped day-in and day-out all week long.

Though there is occasionally a cover, it usually won't exceed €10 and allows you to dance your pants off all night to thumping techno, 70s disco, top 40 hits from the early 2000s, and everything in between. Claustrophobes beware—Dolly can pull quite the crowd.

i Covers vary from €0-€10; no wheelchair accessibility

DOOR 74

Reguliersdwarsstraat; 063 404 5122; www.door-74.com; open M-Th 8pm-3am, F-Sa 8pm-4am, Su 8pm-3am

It isn't easy to find Door 74, and that's by design. It's a speakeasy modeled after the clandestine establishments that rose to prominence in prohibition-era America and specialized in allowing a choice, discrete set of clientele to consume illegal alcohol without fear of law enforcement breathing down their necks. Obviously, alcohol is legal in Amsterdam, but that doesn't mean it's not a little fun to sip delicious cocktails in a dimly-lit bar hidden behind a set of blacked out windows and an unmarked door. In case you're still having trouble finding the place, we'll give you a hint—it's between Door 72 and Door 76.

i Cocktails from €12.50; no wheelchair accessibility

HOTEL27

Dam 27; 020 218 2180; www.hoteltwenty-seven.com/en/bar; open M-Th 10am-1am, F-Sa 10am-3am, Su 10am-1am

Let's do a little thought experiment! You're Jay Gatsby, you're in Amsterdam, and you need to find a suitable bar. Inevitably, you find yourself in Hotel27. In addition to being one of the nicest hotels in Amsterdam, it's got one of the city's most decadent cocktail bars. To be clear, the drinks here are ludicrously expensive. The service, however, is ludicrously good. You'll be asked about your every desire and served with cocktails that seemingly reach into the darkest depths of your subconscious and pull dreams you didn't even know you had. Whether you're here for one quick drink before a night out or because you took out another mortgage on your house to afford two or three, Hotel27's bar is a lesson in luxury.

i Mini cocktails from €7, cocktails from €14; wheelchair accessible

WATERKANT

Marnixstraat 246; 020 737 1126; www.waterkantamsterdam.nl/en; open M-Th 11am-1am, F-Sa 1am-3am, Su 11am-1am

Waterkant has perfected the recipe for attracting cool young people: start with a beautiful but strange location (it's on prime canalside real estate, but getting here means walking through a gas station and under a parking garage), mix in a bunch of picnic tables, and top it off with plentiful beers. Dutch locals pack this waterfront bar even during the week to hang out, dangle their legs over the canal, and watch the sunset in a hip and friendly atmosphere. As the night wears on, things get increasingly lively. Tourists tend to miss Waterkant, so you won't have to worry about your obnoxious fellow travellers. Instead, unwind with the cool crowd and try some craft IPAs.

i Beers from €2.90, cocktails from €7.50; limited wheelchair accessibility

THE HAGUE

Coverage by **Sam Lincoln**

The Hague is like a gateway drug to the Netherlands. It's got the things that make the Dutch famous—windmills, Rembrandt, and stroopwafels, to name a few—without the non-stop tourist feeding frenzy of Amsterdam or the concrete jungle modernism of Rotterdam. Art fiends will fall in love with the world-class museums found in and around the city center, which show off plenty of world treasures but make the most room for the local heavy-hitters like Vermeer, Mondrian, and Rembrandt. Those seeking crazy European nightlife will find a motley array of pubs, high end cocktail bars, and all-night clubs that fill up with the city's considerable student population toward the end of each week, and those who prefer to be beach bums will appreciate the ample opportunity the Hague provides for lounging around on a pastel colored oceanfront terrace with a piña colada in hand. The city is also something of a legal mecca, with bodies like the International Court for Justice and the International Criminal Court settling disputes between the world's most powerful countries, corporations, and people. Though Amsterdam is technically the capital of the Netherlands, you'll find the country's executive branch, States General, and Supreme Court all housed here—making it the true seat of the Dutch government.

ORIENTATION

The Hague, though not exactly an example of idealistic European grid-aligned urban planning, is relatively easy to break down into a few distinct neighborhoods. The city's **Centraal Station**—that's Central Station in Dutch, in case you needed that translation—actually lies on the east edge of the city proper, with the **Centrum** neighborhood (which is the city center) just to the west. Here you'll find most of the city's famous museums and landmarks as well as the office of the Dutch prime minister and other important government bodies. To the north of the center is the gradually gentrifying and therefore increasingly hip **Zeeheldenkwartier**—lots of good bars here—and then just north of that is the **Zorgliet** neighborhood where you'll find the mansions of various foreign embassies, the peace palace, and some nice parks. Even further north, right along the ocean is the district of **Scheveningen**, where you can live the #beachlife and explore a number of entertainment complexes. To the east of the **Centrum** is the shockingly large forest of the **Haagse Bos** and within it the residence of the royal family, while to the west and south lie mostly residential neighborhoods.

ESSENTIALS

GETTING THERE

The Hague is easily accessible via train from any of the major cities in the Netherlands. It's a little less than an hour-long train ride from Amsterdam's central station to the Hague's central station, and trains leave every 10-15 minutes. Coming from Schiphol Airport (AMS), which is the main international airport for the Netherlands, it's about a thirty minute train ride on an Intercity train right to the central station. From Rotterdam The Hague Airport (RTM), it's a short bus (#53) or taxi ride into Schiedam where you can take an Intercity train into the Hague proper.

GETTING AROUND

The city center of the Hague is easy to navigate on foot, with the majority of the most popular museums, landmarks, and restaurants within walking distance. For off-the-beaten-path finds, exploring the whole city, or getting to the beach, it's easiest to take one of the many trams or busses that criss cross the city proper. You can purchase tickets for 2 hours (€4), a day (€7.10), and three days (€18). The 2 hour and day tickets can be purchased on the bus or tram either from the driver (for busses) or an on-board ticket machine (for trams), and you can get a three day pass from an HTM service point in one of the Hague's main train stations. If you're interested in renting a bike, you can easily rent from numerous services throughout the city (as well as from some hotels and hostels). Make sure to familiarize yourself with local cycling laws and customs!

PRACTICAL INFORMATION

Tourist Office: The Hague Info Store (Spui 68; 070 361 8860; denhaag.com/en; open M noon-6pm, T-F 10am-6pm, Sa 10am-5pm, Su noon-5pm).

Banks/ATMs/Currency Exchange: There are banks and ATMs scattered around the city and they are easy to find especially in the city center.

Post Office: There are a number of post offices in or around the city center, including one just east of the Binnenhof: PostNL Postkantoor (Turfmarkt 18; open M-F 6:30am-6pm, Sa 9am-5pm).

Internet: Wi-Fi is widely available in most cafés, train stations, and museums around the city.

BGLTQ+ Resources: The organization COC ("International Social Club" in English) is dedicated to supporting members of the BGLTQ+ community throughout The Netherlands. They have an office in The Hague (Scheveningseveer 7; 070 365 90 90; www.cochaaglanden.nl/engels; available by phone M, T, Th, and F from 2pm-6pm. The "COC Café" is open for events).

EMERGENCY INFORMATION

Emergency Number: 112.

Police: The non-emergency police number is 09 00 8844.

US Embassy: There is a US Embassy in the Hague (John Adams Park 1; 70 310 2209; nl.usembassy.gov/embassy-consulate/the-hague; visits by appointment, which you can schedule online; for US Citizens in an emergency call 020 575 5309 or 070 310 2209 outside office hours).

Rape Crisis Center: If you are a victim of sexual assault or violence call 0800-0188 (available 24hr) and you will be put in touch with the closest center.

Hospitals: The Hague region has seven general hospitals, all with 24hr emergency rooms. This is the closest to the city center:

- HMC Westeinde (Lijnbaan 32; 088 979 7900; open daily 24hr; always call 112 first in a life-threatening emergency, for urgent but non-life threatening situations call HMC Westeinde).

Pharmacies: As with many other European cities, the pharmacies in The Hague rotate through who has the night shift. You can find information about where an open pharmacy can be found at any given moment posted on the window or door of a closed pharmacy.

- Pharmacy MCH (Lijnbaan 32; 70 388 7674; open M-F 8am-9:30pm, Sa-Su 9:30-9:30pm)

SIGHTS

CULTURE

VAN KLEEF

Lange Beestenmarkt 109; 070 345 22 73; www.vankleefwinkel.eu/en_GB; open T-Sa 10am-6pm

Sure, the Dutch like their beer and wine as much as the rest of us, but make no mistake: their national liquor is ***jenever.*** *Jenever* (or sometimes *genever*) is the juniper-flavored predecessor to gin. It's also not easy to find the real thing; only liquor made in Belgium, the Netherlands, and two regions of France and Germany can be sold as *jenever.* Van Kleef has the distinction of being the last *jenever* and liqueur company still in the Hague—they've been going at it since 1842, and their historic shop and former distillery (it's no longer legal to distill within the city limits because of the dangers of alcohol vapor in an urban area) is a living museum dedicated to this marvelously boozy tradition.

i Tastings from €0.80; only cards with PINs accepted; no wheelchair accessibility

MADURODAM

George Maduroplein 1; 70 41 624 00; www.madurodam.nl/en; open daily Mar 12-Sep 1 9am-8pm, Sep 2-Oct 31 9am-7pm, Nov 1-Dec 20 11am-5pm, Dec 21-23 10am-6pm, Dec 24-25 11am-5pm, Dec 26-30 10am-6pm, Dec 31 11am-5pm

Founded as a memorial for **George Maduro,** a Dutch war hero, this park (and self-proclaimed "happiest war memorial in the world," which doesn't strike us as an honor that would have much competition) arranges all of Holland's most famous landmarks—from ports to palaces and beyond—in miniature. Watch as tiny barges sail through Amsterdam's canals, a cargo van navigates busy traffic by the **Peace Palace**, or as a KSM jet taxis for takeoff at Amsterdam's international airport. Also included are interactive activities about how the Netherlands manages water levels in its lower-than-sea-level towns (YOU control the floodgates! Will this small village make it through the rainy season, or will it be lost to the rushing tide of doom??). They make for an entertaining way to learn about Dutch engineering. As could perhaps be expected, a lot of what you'll find here is geared towards children...but we both know you're going to blow an hour pushing plastic tub toys around a model river.

Day ticket €17.50 online, €19.50 in person; wheelchair accessible

LANDMARKS

BINNENHOF

2513 AA; tour visitor centre phone 070 757 0200; prodemos.nl/english; tour times vary, visitor center open M-Sa 9am-5pm

Forget Amsterdam, the Dutch government hangs out in the Hague. You can see where it all goes down at the Binnehof, a gorgeous brick castle that dominates the city center. You can explore the scenic Medieval squares inside the complex to your heart's delight, or sign up for one of the many tours given by ProDemo (which has offices just next door) and get a chance to look inside at where the wheels of Holland's democracy turn. No matter what, make sure you take the chance to stroll around the Hofvijver—it's the court pond that sits right next door and makes for an impossibly scenic spot to enjoy some golden late-afternoon sunlight or get a beautiful photo.

Tour prices from €9.50; limited wheelchair accessibility

CELESTIAL VAULT

Machiel Vrijenhoeklaan 175; open daily 24hr

American artist **James Turrell** is an artist who works with the most monumental medium available—the earth itself. Up on a hill overlooking a southern stretch of the beach right to the west of the Hague, the Celestial Vault is a 1996 sculpture that Turrell designed to resemble an artificial crater. You enter the crater through the small arched passageway to the west and lie down on the oblong concrete bench in the center, and place your feet awkwardly above your head as depicted in the diagram on the sign right by the entrance. Then, the carefully measured dimensions of the crater and bench warp your perspective so that sky above you appears to curve like a dome around the crater. It's as if the atmosphere begins and ends at the edges of your peripheral vision—kind of like the ceiling of the Hogwarts dining hall but without the broomsticks.

Free; no wheelchair accessibility

THE PEACE PALACE

Carnegieplein 2; www.vredespaleis.nl/?lang=en; Visitors Centre open Apr-July T-Su 10am-5pm, Aug daily 10am-5pm, Sept-Oct T-Su 10a-5pm, Nov-Mar T-Su 10am-4pm

The Peace Palace is world-famous for its majestic architecture and sweeping gardens. In fact, it happens to be the most photographed building in the city. As the home to the **International Court of Justice** and the **Permanent Court of Arbitration,** it's also one of the world's great centers of peaceful conflict resolution. Unfortunately, unless you're suing a world power or have violated international Maritime law, it can be difficult to get in and see the sights firsthand. The visitors center right at the gates to the palace offers a free, 30 or 40 minute introduction to the history and happenings of the various bodies housed within the palace, but if you really want the grand tour you'll have to time your visit right when the place opens up for tours. It's easiest to do this during the summer, but tours are also offered some weekends during the rest of the year.

Admission to Visitors Centre free, palace guided tours €11, garden tours €7.50; tours offered on select summer weeks and some weekends throughout the year (check website for availability); palace guided tours wheelchair accessible, no wheelchair accessibility for garden tours

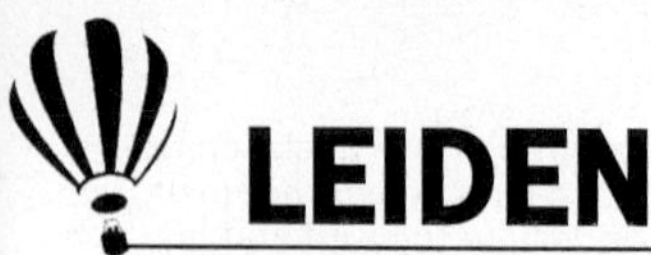

LEIDEN

Leiden feels a little bit too good to be true. It's perched just inland from the coast a few miles north of the Hague, but despite boasting a world-class university and some of the country's most important cultural institutions, the city doesn't feel frenetic. Instead, Leiden is a quiet affair. Beautifully maintained townhouses line its narrow cobblestone streets and houseboats line its lazy canals. You'd have to have some formidable photoshop skills if you wanted to make a city feel more photogenic than Leiden. Despite its immaculate and historic exterior, Leiden is still very much a living and breathing place—it isn't stodgily preserved and the streets aren't painstakingly power washed. It feels precious but not too precious. You've still got that aforementioned university, chock full of students looking to get rowdy on evenings and weekends, and you've still got a beach scene just outside of town that manages to keep things low-key and relaxing despite sitting in plain view of the Hague's casino and nightclub-filled coastal complex. Though it's small enough to explore in a day, the cool-things-worth-checking-out-per-square-foot ratio is quite high and B&B's abound. Who knows? You might just never want to leave.

Leiden can be a difficult city to figure out because of twisting streets and narrow alleys, but it's easy to navigate on foot. There's also a bus system that can get you from one end of the city to another, or from the city center back to the train station, **Leiden Centraal,** which sits just outside the historic part of town. That being said, the walk from the station to the center is beautiful, and well worth it (even if you just do it one way).

GETTING THERE

Leiden is easily accessible by train from any of the Hague's major train stations. It will usually take between 10 and 15min. on an intercity sprinter to get to the Leiden Central Station (Leiden Centraal), and from there it's only a 10-15min. walk before you're in the heart of the city.

It's worth walking around Leiden at least a little bit because there are numerous charming streets and alleys that you won't stumble upon unless you're on foot. Additionally, the city proper is small enough to be fully navigable on foot even if you just want to get from point A to point B. For a quicker commute or to get outside of town—say, to the beach—there is also an extensive bus system that can get you everywhere you need to go.

GETTING AROUND

Check out...

RIJKSMUSEUM VAN OUDHEDEN

Rapenburg 28; 071 516 3163; www.rmo.nl/en; open daily 10am-5pm

Leiden's history may "only" stretch back to 860, but with Leiden University right around the corner, historians and museum curators have been able to pull together an immensely impressive antiquities museum showcasing artifacts from all around the world—including fragments from the Netherlands' past and from the Roman settlements that dotted the region long before. The prominence of the institution (it's the country's official archaeological museum) allows for some phenomenal special exhibitions throughout the year, but their impressive permanent collection is reason enough to while away an afternoon checking out lots of stuff from famous dead people.

i Admission €12.50, students studying related fields can sometimes get in free; wheelchair accessible

Don't miss...

BURCHT VAN LEIDEN

Van der Sterrepad 5; open daily 8am-10pm

Ladies and gentlemen, this is where it all began. The Burcht van Leiden is a circular citadel at the top of a hill (a hill? In the low country? We know, we know) right in the beautiful beating brick heart of central Leiden. It's built at the legendary intersection between the **Oude Rijn** and **Nieuwe Rijn Rivers,** right on the hill where the city was founded years ago—possibly as early as 860. You can climb up to the courtyard of the small fortress to admire the massive old tree growing in the middle, or ascend the wall and treat yourself to a panoramic view of some of Leiden's most majestic architecture.

i Free; no wheelchair accessibility

Swing by...

KATWIJK AAN ZEE

Katwijk Aan Zee; open daily 24hr

Sometimes the only thing better than a popular beach spot is a less popular beach spot. That's exactly what you'll find at this "resort" spot just west of Leiden proper. It's only a few miles up the beach from the Hague's massive beach extravaganza, but it feels like it's a world away. Don't expect much pomp and circumstance—instead, you'll find mellow beach cabins, some bar/restaurants, and a large open stretch of sand. It's close enough to the city that you don't have to make a day out of it, but far enough removed that you won't be distracted by all those damned canals and beautiful historic houses. FYI, summer break (aka beach szn, baby) usually starts in early-mid July for Dutch kids…plan accordingly.

i Free; wheelchair accessibile

Grab a bite at...

LA BOTA

Herensteeg 9-11; 071 514 6340; www.labota.nl/home; open daily 5pm-midnight

La Bota has been a Leiden mainstay for half a century, and it doesn't feel like the interior has changed a bit since. It's a low key, decently cheap (but not totally bargain-basement) place to grab a delicious spot of traditional Dutch dinner after a long day of exploring a traditional Dutch city. As an added bonus, La Both is something of a darling amongst the thriving local student population—expect to be sharing the place with a fair contingent of youngsters looking to unwind from a long day of classes or homework or whatever Dutch students do.

i Daily specials €8; no wheelchair accessibility

MUSEUMS

GEMEENTEMUSEUM

Stadhouderslaan 41; 070 338 1111; www.gemeentemuseum.nl/en; open T-Su 10am-5pm

Because the Gemeentemuseum sits a little bit outside the historic center of town where most of the Hague's prime-time museums are situated, it doesn't necessarily get the spotlight that it deserves. Then again, if it got the spotlight that it deserved you'd be able to see the museum from the **International Space Station.** The museum is a huge array of concrete, brick, and steel—not always architecture that ages well, but it works. Amidst a remarkable permanent collection and ever-gripping, unending array of special exhibitions, you won't want to miss the wing built for the world's largest collection of **Piet Mondrian** paintings (within a larger exhibition for the **de Stijl movement** of which he was a part).

i Admission €16, €12.50 reduced; wheelchair accessible

MAURITSHUIS

Plein 29; 070 302 3456; www.mauritshuis.nl/en; open M 1pm-6pm, T-W 10am-6pm, Th 10am-8pm, F-Su 10am-6pm

Considering its ideal size (not too small to get boring, but not so big you get lost), its position right in the middle of the city, and its beautiful architecture, the Mauritshuis is pretty much the full package. And we haven't even mentioned the art collection—it's rare that every single work of art on display in a museum could genuinely be called a masterpiece, but that's what you'll find. In addition to loads of **Rembrandt** and pieces from older masters like **Peter Paul Rubens,** the Mauritshuis is home to some of **Johannes Vermeer's** ever-elusive paintings. The undisputed highlight is his legendary ***Girl with a Pearl Earring,*** sometimes called the "Mona Lisa of the North" and arguably one of the most famous paintings in the world.

i Admission €15.50, €12.50 reduced; wheelchair accessible

OUTDOORS

SCHEVENINGEN STRAND (SCHEVENINGEN BEACH)

Scheveningen; scheveningen.com/en/beach.php; open daily 24hr

The Hague's massive beach extravaganza can be found in its western district of **Scheveningen.** In addition to some elaborate and touristy trappings (think Ferris wheel, lots of shopping, and a "pleasure pier"), there are also tons of hip restaurants right on the sand and trendy bass-pumping beach clubs dotted up and down the coast. Lest the main drag get crowded on a beautiful day, don't be dismayed—there's more than enough beach to go around (German tourists be damned) and you can find more and more peace and quiet the further north and south you go from the Scheveningen complex. You can also rent a board and compete with beautiful blond surfer locals for some of those sick (just kidding, they're pretty small) northern European waves.

i Free, attraction prices vary; limited wheelchair accessibility, some beach wheelchairs available (call 070 394 2211)

FOOD

IRAWADDY ($)

Spui 202; 070 363 2558; www.irawaddy.nl; open M-Sa noon-9pm

Irawaddy is a rather unassuming restaurant. Frankly, "restaurant" might even be giving it a little bit too much credit. It's really just a tiny corner grocery store specializing in Thai cuisine. At the back is a counter from which you can buy a small and seasonally-rotating selection of Thai dishes. It's basically just takeout, but if you don't want your meal microwaved in Saran wrap then you might want to heat it up on your own. No matter what, you'll be happy you forked over the few euros that you did—this is just about the most authentic, delicious, homemade Thai food you're ever going to have all prepared with love by a woman who triples as a cashier, shelf-stocker, and chef extraordinaire.

i Meals from €8; vegan, vegetarian, and gluten-free options available (but subject to seasonal menu changes); no wheelchair accessibility

BALADI MANOUCHE ($)

Torenstraat 95; 070 444 3877; baladionline.nl; open T-W 9am-6pm, Th-Sa 9am-8pm Su 9am-6pm

Baladi is a tiny little restaurant—there's space for maybe 5 or 6 people to eat inside—specializing in Lebanese *manakish.* In case you're not familiar with *manakish* (we weren't either), it's basically doughy pizza topped with spices, cheese, meat, veggies, or some combination of all of the above. Baladi makes it fresh in a pizza oven right behind the counter, and after ordering you'll have a piping hot pie. It's got hearty food and the servings are generous, but if you're still hungry, you could go back for seconds or thirds and still pay less than you would for a lunch at virtually any other restaurant in the city.

i Manakish from €3.5; vegan and vegetarian options available; no wheelchair accessibility

THE FAT MERMAID ($$-$$$)

Strandweg 19; 070 354 1729; www.thefatmermaid.nl; open M-Th 9am-1am, F-Sa 9am-2am, Su 9am-1am

Scheveningen Strand is overrun with beachfront restaurants selling roughly the same array of expensive fresh seafood and grilled meat. The Fat Mermaid stands out from the fray for a few reasons. One, it's at the end of the busiest stretch of beach spots and set a tad apart from the hubbub. Two, it's relatively affordable, especially if you go for lunch. It also seems like the whole staff are either surfer dudes or surfer dudettes. You'll find locals showing up with a board in hand, grabbing a bite, pulling on a wetsuit, paying their bill, and then running the hundred feet or so between the restaurant and the ocean to spend the rest of the day shredding the gnar.

i Sandwiches from €6; vegan, vegetarian, and gluten-free options available; limited wheelchair accessibility

HAPPY TOSTI ($$)

Korte Poten 5; 070 744 05 44; www.happytosti.nl/den-haag/; open M-F 7:30am-5pm, Sa 9am-6pm, Su 9am-5pm

Happy Tosti is an incessantly upbeat lunch spot. Is there anything more adorable than the words "happy" and "tosti" right next to each other? (*Tostis,* by the way, are just Dutch grilled sandwiches). Some of the seats in the restaurant have been replaced by rope swings hanging from the ceiling, for a little bit of mid-meal entertainment, and their menu revolves around that ultimate comfort food—cheesy grilled sandwiches. As an added bonus, Happy Tosti is committed to offering employment to members of the community whom, because of disabilities visible or invisible, may have trouble finding job opportunities elsewhere. So you can feel good while you eat good!

i Tostis from €4.95, paninis from €6.75, coffee from €2.50; vegan, vegetarian, and gluten-free options available; no wheelchair accessibility

NIGHTLIFE

GRAND CAFÉ VICTORIA

Prins Hendrikplein 10; 70 345 4362; www.grandcafe-victoria.nl; open daily 11am-12am

The Grand Café Victoria is a friendly, upscale bar in **Zeeheldenkwartier,** a neighborhood northwest of the city center that's getting increasingly hipster by the day. Run by a phenomenally friendly guy named Christian who's lived all over the world and only recently settled in the Hague, you're likely to hear more English being spoken here than Dutch on any given evening. Alcoholically, the café's claim to fame is their formidable beer selection. Café Victoria collaborates with a local craft beer shop and offers obscure, delicious drinks produced by some of the best breweries you've never heard of. They also change what's on tap every other night, so you'll never have to worry about having the same beer twice. Thank God!

i Beer from €2.5

BLEYENBERG (THE WAREHOUSE)

Grote Markt 10; 70 800 2120; open F-Sa 11:59pm-5am

Sometimes a cocktail bar just doesn't cut it. Sure, it's nice to relax in a comfortable armchair and sip booze embellished with seasonal accoutrement, but isn't that just a little tame? What if you want to lose yourself and transcend to a higher dimension of mindless dancing? If you find yourself in the Hague craving the kind of bass that can rattle the earth's crust, you should head to Magazijn. From the outside, it doesn't look like much—just a door covered with posters for past gigs. It doesn't look like much from the inside, either, but it's a techno hotspot promising a dark and foggy dance floor and pretty cheap hard alcohol. As a bonus, it sits just a few steps away from the nightlife hub of the **Grote Markt**, so it's not like your options are limited.

i Covers from €10, beer from €2.9, cocktails €9, shots from €2; no wheelchair accessibility

ROTTERDAM

Coverage by **Sam Lincoln**

A thousand years ago, the area that would soon be known as Rotterdam, was first settled. But, things really took off in 1270 when the Dutch built a dam on the river Rotte (get it) so that the city's land—which had been particularly susceptible to floods—could be protected. Rotterdam, well-located on a major distributary of the Rhine River, has grown into a sprawling city with the largest port in Europe and a bustling shipping industry. As one local put it, "we make the money, the Hague counts it, and Amsterdam spends it." Rotterdam is distinct in this triumvirate of iconic Dutch cities not just for its economic prosperity but also for its relentless drive towards modernization. After the city was razed by the German Luftwaffe in World War II, the residents of Rotterdam opted to build a completely new city instead of rebuilding the old one. The downtown has thus become an ever expanding collection of ambitious and eye catching (if not always beautiful) modern architecture, with the city regularly inviting its citizens to help pitch ideas for new and improved spaces and venues. The result is lively nightlife, wacky street art, and cutting-edge cultural institutions all wrapped up in a package that's still largely overlooked by tourists.

ORIENTATION

At the center of Rotterdam is the **Cool** neighborhood, named so because of the main avenue of **Coolsingel** which runs from north to south to **Blaak,** one of the city's main streets. Just southwest of Cool is the **Museumpark,** a complex of many of the city's best museums. Southeast of Cool is the **Stadsdriehoek** neighborhood, which is home to many of the city's most famous buildings—the **Cube Houses** and **Markthal** among them. To the east of Stadsdriehoek lies the swanky **Kralingen** neighborhood, which sits along the **Nieuwe Maas** and just south of **Lake Kralingen.** Just south of Cool and the center of the city sits the neighborhood of **Nieuwe Werk,** an upscale stretch of bars and residences that eventually gives way to a tree-lined stretch of villas right at the entrance of **Het Park.** Across the Nieuwe Mass to the south is the **Kop van Zuid** neighborhood, a new business center connected to downtown by the **Erasmusbrug,** and just north of the **Katendrecht** neighborhood.

ESSENTIALS

GETTING THERE

You can reach Rotterdam by air via Rotterdam the Hague Airport. The E line of Rotterdam's metro runs regularly from the airport to Rotterdam Centraal, the central train station. Central station is also easily accessible from other cities in the Netherlands via numerous InterCity trains. If you're traveling by rail from other European countries, it's also easy to reach Rotterdam—trains from Brussels go directly through Rotterdam Centraal, while trains from Paris, Frankfurt, and Düsseldorf go to Amsterdam (from which you can take an InterCity train straight to Rotterdam).

GETTING AROUND

Thanks to the marvelous public transportation system in the Netherlands, it couldn't be easier to get around Rotterdam. One ticket works for all public transportation within city limits—trams, busses, and the metro. You can buy single tickets for €4, or a day pass for €8. If you're in the Netherlands for a while, you may want to buy an "anonymous OV-chipkaart," which functions as a reusable ticket that you can reload as needed. If you put a minimum of €20 on the card you can also use it to get on InterCity trains. Trains are also cheaper with a card than with a single-use ticket, which you can buy at kiosks in every train station for a mark-up. Make sure to always check in and check out of all transportation with your card—it's how the system calculates your ticket prices.

PRACTICAL INFORMATION

Tourist Offices: There's a small tourist kiosk in Rotterdam Centraal, but the main tourist office is on Coolsingel (Coolsingel 114; 010 790 0185; en.rotterdam.info; open daily 9:30am-6pm).

Banks/ATMs/Currency Exchange: There are banks and ATMs (called *geldautomaats*) located throughout the city, and Rotterdam Centraal has both an ATM and a GWK Travelex currency exchange. GWK Travelex (Stationsplein 19; 010 411 8920; open M-Sa 8am-10pm, Su 9am-10pm).

Post Offices: There are post offices with varying hours located conveniently around the city. Here is a convenient location: PostNL Postkantoor (Botersloot 13-19; 88 225 5555; open M-Sa 7am-10pm, S noon-10pm).

Internet: Free Wi-Fi is widely available in cafés and museums across the city.

BGLTQ+ Resources: For a wealth of information on BGLTQ+ organizations and a BGLTQ+-friendly introduction to the city and its thriving nightlife scene, visit gayrotterdam.nl/en.

EMERGENCY INFORMATION

Emergency: 112.

Police: There is a centrally located police station right next to the town hall (Doelwater 5; 0900 8844; open daily 24hr).

Rape Crisis Center: Rotterdam's Center for Sexual Violence is located within the main location of the GGD Rotterdam-Rijnmond health service, right next to the Leuvehaven metro station (Schiedamsedijk 95; 24hr number 0800 0188; www.centrumseksueelgeweld.nl/csg-en).

Hospital: Rotterdam has several hospitals but Erasmus is one of the most centrally located.

- Erasmus University Medical Center (Emergency: Dr. Molewaterplein 30, 10 704 0145; open daily 24hr. General: Dr. Molewaterplein 40; 10 704 0704).

Pharmacy: Like many other European cities, there will always be a pharmacy (called *apotheek* in Dutch) in Rotterdam open at any time of the day. A closed pharmacy will have a notice in its window that tells you which pharmacy is open during the night and on weekends.

- BENU Erasmus Apotheek (West-Kruiskade 21a; 010 412 9331; open M-F 8:30am-5:30pm).

SIGHTS

CULTURE

HET NIEUWE INSTITUUT (THE NEW INSTITUTE)

Museumpark 25; 010 440 1200; hetnieuweinstituut.nl; open T-W 11am-5pm, Th 11am-9pm, F-Su 11am-5pm

Located right in the artistic heart of the city, the **Museumpark,** the Nieuwe Instituut is a cutting-edge cultural center that's part museum, part archive, and part educational institution. The constantly rotating array of special exhibitions typically focus on architecture and design, but many also address the environmental impact of humanity. You should expect to see some pretty high-concept projects on display that occasionally reach the point of incomprehensibility. As a working institution that preserves a rich history of Dutch design in a city home to some of the Netherlands' most ambitious modern architecture, the Nieuwe Institute should not be overlooked.

i Admission €14, €7 reduced, free Th 5-9pm, wheelchair accessible

MARKTHAL

Ds. Jan Scharpstraat; 298 030 234 6468; markthal.klepierre.nl; open M-Th 10am-8pm, F 10am-9pm, Sa 8am-9am and 10am-8pm, Su noon-6pm

The Markthal (market + hall) was built as a massive indoor space into which Rotterdam's famous outdoor market could move, but the elaborate architecture and prime location brought with it a lofty rent and the outdoor market's stalls stayed put. Instead, a plethora of upscale, trendy food stores moved in, peddling everything from speciality meats to artisanal chocolates and pastries. The locals, who tend to prefer Markthal's less pricey outdoor counterpart, refer to the massive building as "the pencil sharpener" thanks its hollow, cylindrical shape and position opposite a building that looks a lot like a pencil (a few other comparisons have also been made). Nevertheless, the architecture is stunning and it's a great place to have a stroopwafel or some of Rotterdam's delicious cheese.

i Prices vary; hours of individual vendors may vary, wheelchair accessible

ROTTERDAM ZOO

Blijdorplaan 8 or Van Aerssenlaan 49; 0 900 1857; open daily 9am-6pm

It's hard not to love a good zoo. Rotterdam's massive complex is organized according to region of the world, and contains dozens of elaborate and extensive habitats to help their collection of animals—from the typical lions, tigers, and (polar) bears to rarer creatures like tapirs, red pandas, and lowland gorillas—feel right at home. The zoo partners with many breeding programs around the world dedicated to helping some of the earth's most threatened animals escape extinction, and as a result, several endangered or critically endangered species are present throughout the zoo. Located on more than 60 acres of land north of the city center, you could spend a few hours, or a few days, wandering through the various habitats and still not see everything.

i Admission €24.50, €23.50 if purchased online; wheelchair accessible

LANDMARKS

THE CUBE HOUSES

Overblaak 70; 010 414 2285; kubuswoning.nl/en; open daily 10am-6pm

The Cube Houses carry the dubious honor of being Rotterdam's most unusual structures. Designed by the Dutch architect **Piet Blom** as an innovative way to organize living space in an urban environment, the houses sit perched on little concrete "trunks" in the center of the city, just south of **Markthal**. However weird they look from the outside, exploring the interior only gets weirder. Because faces of the cubes are placed on a 45 degree angle to the ground, there are no vertical walls inside and the furniture and appliances all have to be built accordingly. One of the cubes is designated as a "show cube," allowing bewildered visitors to explore a real residence and see how it all fits together.

i Admission €3, €2 reduced; no wheelchair accessibility to Show Cube

HET WITTE HUIS (THE WHITE HOUSE)

Geldersekade 1; 010 414 2142; open daily 3pm-2am

The stately Witte Huis sticks out like a sore thumb on Rotterdam's waterfront skyline. Unlike the glass and steel constructions that have sprung up willy-nilly throughout the past half century, the Witte Huis is the OG Rotterdam skyscraper. In fact, in a testament to Dutch engineering, it's the first high rise built anywhere in Europe. Built in 1898, this beautiful ten-story art nouveau building was somehow spared in the German bombing of Rotterdam, and it remains one of the city's few pre-war icons. Today you can find a café on the ground floor, which is a remarkably beautiful place to grab a coffee or beer in the evening light.

i Free admission; no wheelchair accessibility

MUSEUMS

KUNSTHAL

Westzeedijk 341; 010 440 0300; www.kunsthal.nl/en; open T-Sa 10am-5pm, Su 11am-5pm

The home of Rotterdam's Kunsthal is a dramatic concrete, glass, and steel building designed by the prominent Dutch architect **Rem Koolhaas**. Though plenty of people come just for the architecture, the real treat is the art scattered across seven exhibition spaces. Because the Kunsthal has no permanent collection, it isn't technically a museum. This means it can host constantly changing exhibitions on anything and everything without being tied to a theme, period, or particular set of artists. For the past three summers running, it has also transformed one of its halls into an "All You Can Art" project that invites anyone who happens to visit the Kunsthal to come and create art to be put on display.

i Admission €14, €7 reduced; wheelchair accessible

CHABOT MUSEUM

Museumpark 11; 010 436 3713; www.chabotmuseum.nl/english; open T-F 11am-4:30pm, Sa 11am-5pm, Su noon-5pm

This small, rather unassuming villa in Rotterdam's Museumpark is an underrated modern art gem. Officially dedicated to the Dutch painter and sculptor **Henk Chabot**, the museum houses a rich collection of Expressionist paintings and sculpture. Additionally, it gives wallspace to present-day artistic heirs to the Expressionist tradition, which makes for a cool comparison between old and new takes on similar themes. The small rooms and relative low profile of the villa allows you to get up close and personal with the art. And, because the nearby **Museum Boijmans Van Beuningen** is in the middle of a massive renovation, Chabot acts as a temporary home to work by even more seriously big-ticket artists like **Wassily Kandinsky** and **Piet Mondriaan.**

i Admission €8, €3.60 reduced; no wheelchair accessibility

OUTDOORS

HET PARK

Open daily 24hr

Het Park literally just means "the park" in Dutch. Though the name lacks a certain creativity, it's hard to argue that The Park feels like the definitive outdoor space in the city center. From the wide lawn, you can't see any skyscrapers or steel monoliths casting a shadow on the grass, and there isn't even a view of the river. The only reminder that you're in Rotterdam sits just outside the boundary of the park—the slim tower of the **Euromast**, visible through the trees. In the middle of the park, amid huge old trees and lazy canals, are two stately brick villas—now a swanky restaurant and a wedding venue—that make you feel like you might have accidentally wandered onto the estate grounds of some Dutch aristocrat.

i Free; wheelchair accessible

FOOD

OP HET DAK ($)

Schiekade 189; ophetdak.com; open T-Th 8:30am-5pm, F-Sa 8:30am-8pm, Su 8:30am-5pm

Who doesn't like a rooftop restaurant? It's hard not to. Though big cities have plenty of overpriced venues perched on the top of overpriced real estate with overpriced views of an overpriced neighborhood, Op Het Dak is *not* that kind of spot. Instead, it occupies the top floor and terrace of an otherwise abandoned building that's become a flourishing space for artists and startups to gather, and their food comes straight from a surprisingly large garden that occupies the parts of the roof that aren't otherwise dedicated to the restaurant. There's really no reason why you shouldn't feel good about grabbing a bite at this quirky spot full of young locals who are much cooler than you.

i Breakfast items from €8, all-day plates from €10; vegan, vegetarian, and gluten-free options available; cash only for international cards; no wheelchair accessibility

BREAKFAST IN ROTTERDAM HQ ($)

Stadhoudersweg 96D; www.breakfastinrotterdam.nl; open M-F 8:30am-4:30pm, Sa 9am-4:30pm

This little breakfast joint is improbably located in the back of a small furniture store, and it lacks much obvious signage indicating that it's even there in the first place. Fittingly, every piece of furniture you see in the restaurant is for sale—if you love their breakfast, why not buy the table you ate it on? Started by a couple whose dream was always to have a little food spot of their own, Breakfast in Rotterdam is a delicious and inexpensive place to have a healthy, trendy meal (think avocado toast and açai bowls) and start off your day on the best foot possible. If you're looking for a light but hearty lunch, try their Leg-End ham sandwich with a soft-boiled egg.

i All day breakfast bowls from €6.75, toast from €5.5, sandwiches from €5, coffee from €2; vegan, vegetarian, and gluten-free options available; no wheelchair accessibility

PARQIET ($)

Baden Powelllaan; 06-51001606; www.parqiet.com; open daily 9am-6pm

Everyone likes lounging around in a park with a drink and some hors d'oeuvres, but picnics can be a headache. Why not just cut out the middleman and get your food at the park? That's the beauty of Parqiet, an idyllic eatery in the heart of **Het Park.** They offer a range of breakfast and lunch options, and when the sun shines they'll also set up a bar stand and wood fired pizza oven on the lawn—as well as a small armada of canvas recliners and folding tables—to cater to all who are looking to get some fresh air and great food.

i Breakfast dishes from €4.90, grilled sandwiches from €6.85; vegan, vegetarian, and gluten free options available; limited wheelchair accessibility

NIGHTLIFE

BIRD

Raampoortstraat 24/26/28; bird-rotterdam.nl/en; open T-Th 5:30pm-1am, F-Sa 5:30pm-4am

Bird is nestled underneath Rotterdam's old train station and occupies three of the semi-cylindrical bays that would've been home to decommissioned trains just a few decades ago. Equal parts nightclub, live music venue, and restaurant, Bird's got something for you at all hours of the night. They offer a wide variety of music genres and have a calendar chock-full of live engagements, so check their website and head on over whether you want to dance your pants off to some techno or nod your head knowingly to some smooth jazz. They've also got silent disco nights, in case you want to jam out to your own personal set.

i Beer from €2.90, wine from €5, shots from €2; no wheelchair accessibility

DIZZY

's-Gravendijkwal 127; 010 477 3014; dizzy.nl; open M 3:30pm-11pm, T-Th noon-1am, F-Sa noon-2am

Dizzy is a no-nonsense, unpretentious jazz bar just a little bit west of the city center that boasts a lovely patio in the back and an awesome array of jazz talent. Though the place really shines in the weeks before (and during) Rotterdam's legendary jazz festival, if there's someone performing, then there's really no bad time to come to Dizzy and enjoy a night of classy music and good vibes. Plus, since people who like jazz are cool, Dizzy is a great place to meet a group of people with a higher likelihood of being cool.

i Beer from €3, wine from €4.50; no wheelchair accessibility

THE NETHERLANDS ESSENTIALS

MONEY

Tipping: In the Netherlands, a service charge of 5% is often included in most prices, so there is no need to worry about tipping extra. If you received really good service, it might be nice to round up the bill or leave a small tip, but you are not expected to do so even if there isn't a service charge included. A service charge is sometimes included in taxi fares, but drivers will appreciate if you round up the bill as well. Paying the exact amount, however, is perfectly fine.

Taxes: The marked price of goods in the Netherlands includes a value-added tax, or "VAT." This tax on goods is generally levied at 21%, although it's lower (9%) for food (restaurant-purchased or otherwise) and other miscellaneous goods. Non-EU citizens who are planning on taking goods home unused may be refunded some or all of this tax at the end of their trip. When making purchases, be sure to ask and fill out a VAT form and present it to a tax-free shopping office at the border. You'll also need to get customs officials to stamp your forms.

SAFETY AND HEALTH

Drugs and Alcohol: The Dutch are famously progressive when it comes towards drugs and alcohol, but that doesn't mean anything and everything is necessarily legal. You must be 18 or older to purchase alcoholic beverages of any kind. Drinking in public areas is generally permitted; however cities and towns may have areas in which it is prohibited. In any case, public drunkenness is frowned upon. Soft drugs maybe be purchased legally in coffee shops ("soft drugs" include cannabis and hallucinogenic mushrooms), though possession of more than 5 grams of cannabis is illegal. Minors (under 18) may not purchase or possess soft drugs.

BGLTQ+ Travelers: The Netherlands is accepting of homosexuality and Amsterdam is often thought of as a center for BGLTQ+ tolerance. Homosexuality was decriminalized in 1811, and the first gay bar arrived in 1927. The Netherlands was the first country in the world to legalize same-sex marriage, and the annual Pride parade in Amsterdam draws nearly half a million people to the city. COC Nederland, a Dutch organization founded to support BGLTQ+ people in 1946, is the oldest organization of its kind in the world.

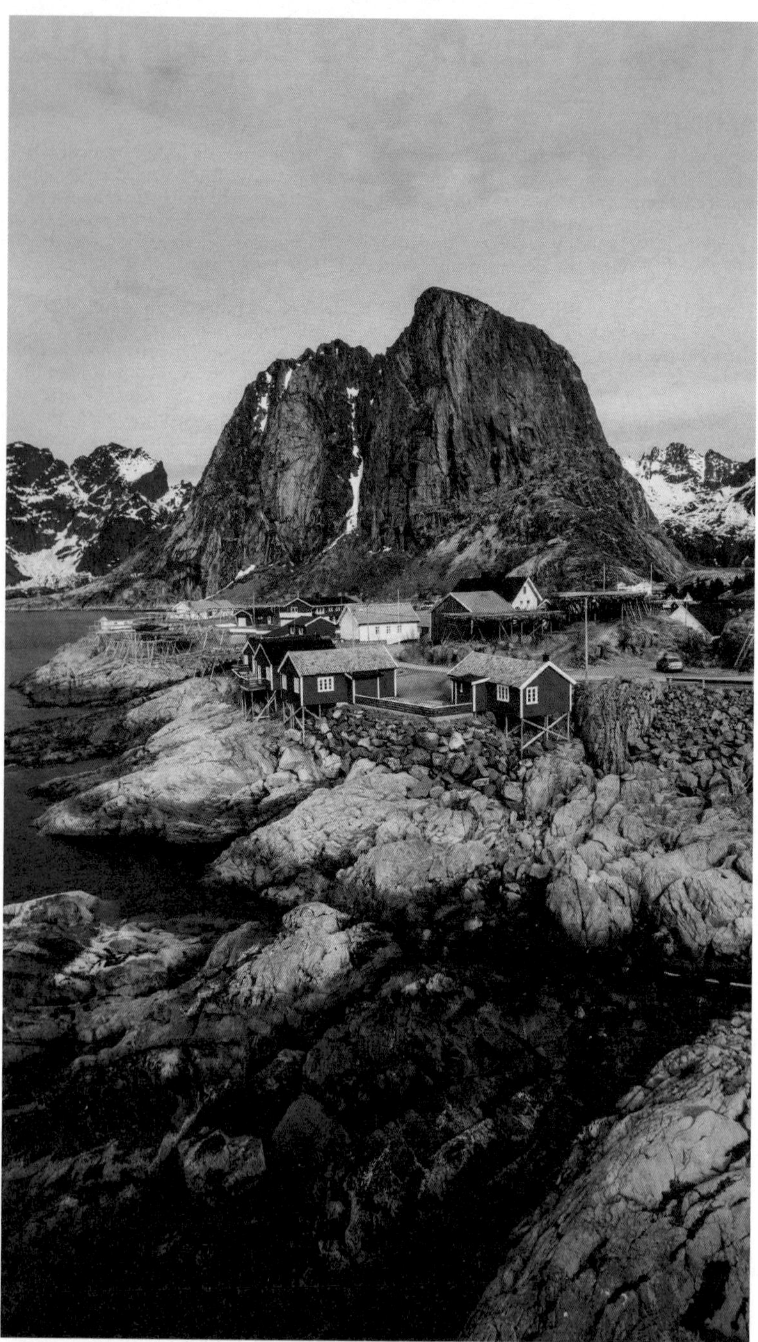

NORWAY

At first glance, Norway seems like another one of those Scandinavian utopias that always lands near the top of those "World's Happiest Countries" rankings. And it's easy to see why when you look at the country's extensive welfare state, featuring universal healthcare and free public universities—not to mention a ridiculously high standard of living. But things are a bit more complicated than that; society in Norway today is far from harmonious. While it's true that the country makes impressive use of renewable energy, especially of hydroelectric power, Norway also has enormous fossil fuel reserves, which are a considerable source of revenue for the government. Though Norwegians are willing to pay the sizable taxes levied by a bureaucracy often labeled as socialist, they are unwilling to buy into the biggest bureaucracy of all: the European Union. While its cities can't quite rival the vibrancy of Stockholm or Copenhagen, Norway boasts national treasures you can't afjord to miss.

Ditch your movie conceptions of Norway. Contrary to public opinion, there's more to this Nordic paradise than vikings, the laboratories of evil scientists, and friendly talking snowmen. Whether you come here for midsummer parties till dawn or some of Europe's best scenery, it's not a surprise that Norway consistently tops the list of the globe's happiest countries. Oslo is where most begin their adventures. This clean, green, capital city machine is chock full of art. Even if you don't spend Munch time in the city, The Scream is a must-see. But let's be real, you can't afjord to to miss out on the nature. Head north to Bergen, and use the city as a base to explore plentiful options for hiking and swimming (and to give your insta a wanderlust boost). With all Norway has to offer, it won't take listening to Kygo to put you on *Cloud Nine,* Norway is *Here for You.*

BERGEN

Coverage by **Eric Chin**

Being a tourist in some cities is too easy, especially in Scandinavia. Credit cards and American dollars are accepted everywhere, menus and museum panels are printed in English, and Segway tours are maddeningly popular. Not in Bergen. Sure, it's a popular tourist destination, especially in the summer. But it's the kind of city where the woman behind the counter at the coffee shop will watch you stare vacantly at the Norwegian menu, prompt you a few times in Norwegian, and then ask, feigning surprise, "Oh, you don't speak Norwegian, do you?" It may seem stiff, but it's honestly a refreshingly authentic experience. Since prices in Bergen are somewhat lower than in Oslo, use the extra cash to experience the surprising sights the small city offers. Take to the high seas to see why Bergen is called "The Gateway to the Fjords," or splurge on some of the freshest seafood (a lot) of money can buy at the Fish Market. If hiking is more your thing, The Seven Mountains, within which Bergen rests, offer trails to suit all abilities, and views to impress anyone.

ORIENTATION

Downtown Bergen is situated around the main square, **Torgallmenningen,** where you'll find expensive stores and chain restaurants. Just north is Bergen Harbor, where the **Fish Market** and **Tourist Information Center** sit on the east end of the harbor. North of the harbor is the historic **Bryggen district** and **Bergenhus Fortress,** which is the sight of **Rosenkrantz Tower** and **Haakon's Hall.** Just east of Torgallmenningen is **Byparken,** a large green with walking trails around a lake. The **KODE art museums** can be found along one side of the park. And to the south is the **University of Bergen.** The area between the square and the university is a hotspot for student nightlife.

ESSENTIALS

GETTING THERE

Bergen Lufthavn, Flesland (BGO) is Bergen's international airport, which receives regular flights from many European cities. From the airport, the easiest way to get to the city center is the Flybussen (www.flybussen.no; NOK 100, NOK 80 reduced) to Bergen bus station (20min.). The train between Oslo and Bergen, a journey of almost 7hr, is famously one of the most scenic rides in Europe (NOK 950, NOK 713 reduced). Trains arrive at Bergen Station.

GETTING AROUND

Bergen is an easily walkable and compact city. Most hostels and guesthouses are also centrally located, so public transportation is often unnecessary. Skyss is Bergen's public transportation system, consisting of buses and a light rail. Single tickets can be bought in advance (NOK 37), on board (NOK 60), or for periods of 24hr (NOK 95), 7 days (NOK 245), or longer. Tickets can be bought at transportation stops. Bergen Taxi (07000; bergentaxi.no) is the largest taxi company in the city. Rates vary wildly, depending on the day of the week and the time of day.

PRACTICAL INFORMATION

Tourist Offices: Bergen Tourist Information Center (Strandkaien 3;55 55 20 00; open daily June-Aug 8:30am-10pm, May and Sept 9am-8pm, Oct-Apr M-Sa 9am-4pm).

Banks/ATMs/Currency Exchange: You can use a credit or debit card almost everywhere in Bergen, but if you need cash, ATMs, known as Minibanks, can be found on the street and in stores like 7-Eleven in the Fish Market area.

Currency Exchange: It's often best to withdraw cash directly from an ATM, but you can change currency at the Bergen Tourist Information Center.

Post Offices: Bergen Sentrum Postkontor (Småstrandgaten 3; 91 23 35 11; open M-F 9am-8pm, Sa 9am-6pm).
Internet: Free Wi-Fi is widely available around Bergen at cafés, bars, and the Tourist Information Center. Internet is also available at the Bergen Public Library (Strømgaten 6; 55 56 85 00; open M-Th 10am-6pm, F 10am-4pm, Sa 10am-3pm).
BGLTQ+ Resources: Bergen Pride (Strandgaten 6; 40 45 65 00; www.bergenpride.no; open M-F 9am-3pm).

EMERGENCY INFORMATION

Emergency Number: 112.
Police: Bergen Sentrum Politistasjon (Allehelgens gate 6; for emergencies call 112, for non-emergencies call 02800)
US Embassy: The nearest US Embassy is in Oslo (Morgedalsvegen 36, 0378; 21 30 85 40).
Hospitals: Haukeland University Hospital (Haukelandsveien 22; for emergencies call 113, for non-emergencies call 05300; open daily 24hr).
Pharmacies: Apoteket Nordstjernen (55 21 83 84; open M-Sa 8am-11pm, Su 1pm-11pm).

SIGHTS

CULTURE

FISH MARKET

Bergen Harbor; hours vary

Never been to an open-air market before? Head over to Bergen's famous Fish Market for a welcoming, if somewhat tame, experience. The atmosphere is busy but relaxed, vendors aren't too pushy, and samples of caviar, reindeer sausage, and a mysterious jam made from cloudberries are plentiful. If you've been saving room in your stomach (and hopefully a large wad of cash) for some of Norway's best fresh fish, you won't be disappointed. Take your pick of salmon, shellfish, and live king crab or lobster, and the vendors will cook it and serve you at a table overlooking the harbor. How's that for farm (er, sea?) to table?

i Stand prices vary; wheelchair accessible

BRYGGEN

Bergen Harbor

Want to feel cultured without having to set foot in a museum? A walk through Bryggen is your best bet. This historic district on the north side of the harbor is immediately recognizable by its traditional red and yellow wooden buildings and the swarms of tourists walking on the street nearby. The buildings were originally used by traders of the **Hanseatic League** as storehouses. Today, they're mostly shops, where modern merchants loosely adhere to the Hanseatic tradition, peddling not stockfish and cereals, but Norwegian flags and Christmas sweaters. It's not immediately apparent from the main street, but you can walk through the front row of buildings and into the alleyways of Bryggen for more interesting and authentic options, like a moose leather shop.

i Shop prices vary; wheelchair accessible

LANDMARKS

HÅKONSHALLEN (HAAKON'S HALL)

Bergenhus; 479 79 577; www.bymuseet.no/en; open daily summer 10am-4pm, winter noon-3pm

Haakon's Hall is the other major building in the **Bergenhus Fortress** complex, and it's perfect if you're tired of poking around the dingy, cobweb-filled rooms of **Rosenkrantz Tower.** Originally a banquet hall constructed in the thirteenth century, the building suffered damage from several major fires (seems to be a recurring theme in Bergen), and has been restored more than once. The dimly-lit rooms are decorated with colorful tapestries, and the cavernous great hall is set with a high table. Today, Haakon's Hall still hosts official dinners and events, for which the dress code includes battle axes and horned helmets (we think).

i Admission NOK 80, NOK 40 reduced; guided tours NOK 20; tours at 10am and 2pm June 24-Aug 15

ROSENKRANTZ TOWER

Bergenhus; 479 79 578; www.bymuseet.no/en; open daily summer 9am-4pm, winter noon-3pm

Rosenkrantz Tower is the most visible piece of **Bergenhus Fortress,** sitting proudly at the entrance to **Bergen Harbor** like a shorter, slightly stubbier, less humanoid Statue of Liberty. The tower was originally a thirteenth-century keep, but has expanded since into its present form. Inside, you can tour the whole building starting with the basement, where the dungeon sits empty, except for an original, thirteenth-century electric dehumidifier. From there, climb through the tower's many rooms: guard rooms, bedrooms, chapel rooms, rooms with cannons, you get the point. Learn about the single battle in which Bergenhus Fortress was involved before stepping out onto the roof and taking in views of Bergen and the harbor.

i Admission NOK 80, NOK 40 reduced, guided tours NOK 20; tours at 10am and 2pm June 24-Aug 15; no wheelchair accessibility

MUSEUMS

KODE 4

Rasmus Meyers allé; 530 09 704; www.kodebergen.no/en; open daily 11am-5pm

Art museums are confusing; they're huge, overwhelming, and it's impossible to see everything. Bergen's art museum, KODE, is different. It's composed of four smaller buildings, KODEs 1, 2, 3, and 4 (not a very creative naming scheme for a bunch of art people), each with different galleries and exhibitions, so check the website to pick the best one for you. Each bite-sized museum is easy to walk through in an hour or two. KODE 4 starts off in classic form: lots of oil paintings of landscapes and church figures. But don't worry, the top floor is devoted to contemporary "art" like a box lined with seal teeth and a giant, plush model of the female reproductive system suspended from the ceiling. Avant-garde?

i Admission NOK 100, NOK 50 reduced; tour times vary, check website for details.; wheelchair accessible

OUTDOORS

MOUNT ULRIKEN

Open daily 24hr

What's that? Oh, you really like hiking, but you're allergic to cable cars? Good news! For true outdoorsy types, it's possible to walk to the base of Mount Ulriken, though it may take over 45 minutes. There are multiple routes to the top of varying difficulty, and, on clear days, the trails will be packed with active types of all sorts. Once you reach the peak, enjoy panoramic views of Bergen or grab a snack at the summit restaurant. If you still haven't broken a sweat, there are more trails from the cable car station, the king of which is a 13-km haul over to the summit of **Mount Fløyen.** This is a challenging hike, so if you want to attempt it, consider using the cable car after all. You deserve it.

i No wheelchair accessibility

FOOD

HORN OF AFRICA ($$)

Strandgaten 212; 954 25 250; www.hornofafrica.no; open T-Th 5pm-10pm, F-Sa 5pm-11pm, Su 5pm-10pm

For almost all of human history, we have eaten with our hands. Why this sudden (in an evolutionary sense) fascination with utensils? Like your My Chemical Romance obsession, it's probably just a phase. Stay ahead of the curve at Horn of Africa, an Ethiopian/Eritrean restaurant that eschews fork and knife in favor of nature's own finely-crafted utensil: your ten fingers. Choose from a selection including sinus-tingling beef tips and buttery chicken wet, and get ready to get down and dirty. The concept of eating with your hands seems pretty self-explanatory, but, just to be sure, the host will demonstrate the nuances of scooping up the spiced meat stews and vegetables with injure, a spongy and slightly sour bread that accompanies all entrées.

i Entrées from NOK 150, combo platters from NOK 215, beer from NOK 60; vegetarian options available; wheelchair accessible

PINGVINEN ($$)

Vaskerelven 14; 556 04 646; www.pingvinen.no

Pingvinen means "penguin" in Norwegian, and that's just about the only animal you won't find on the menu. This gastropub feels like a low-key bar, with ugly wallpaper on one wall and exposed brick on another, but you won't find nachos and wings here. If you can grab a table, ask for an English menu and choose from potato dumplings with mashed swede (a root vegetable, not a jab at Norway's neighbor to the east), wild boar, and even reindeer neck, all prepared to perfection. If you have a bit of extra cash to spend (in the name of cultural immersion, of course), go full-on Norse with a beer from Pingvinen's impressive spread of local brews.

i Entrées from NOK 169, beer from NOK 80; wheelchair accessible

TREKRONEREN ($)

Kong Oscars gate 1; hours vary

Bergen doesn't have much of a street food scene, especially outside the Fish Market. Trekroneren is the one, juicy exception. It's a counter-service sausage stand in the heart of downtown, and an establishment in its own right. Select from over ten varieties, from the familiar bratwurst, to the slightly enigmatic "wild game" sausage. But nothing can top the **reindeer sausage,** topped with mustard, crispy onions, and lingonberry jam. Somehow it works, okay? Just stay away from Rudolph at the Christmas store for a while. It's still a bit of a sore subject for him.

i 150g sausage NOK 60, 250g sausage NOK 90; wheelchair accessible

NIGHTLIFE

GARAGE

Christies gate 14; 553 21 980; www.garage.no; open M-F 3pm-3am, Sa 1pm-3am, Su 5pm-1am

Some of Norway's most famous musical exports are in the rock and metal genres, and Garage is the place to tap into that scene. It feels like one of the first venues you perform at in Guitar Hero—dim lighting, album covers and old setlists plastered on the walls, and an eclectic crowd composed of middle-aged men trying to relive the glory days and college kids hopelessly lost in the wrong decade. Look out for live shows on the weekends, but, even if there's nothing happening on stage, the bar has a great spread.

i No cover, beer and shots from NOK 70; BGLTQ+ friendly; wheelchair accessible

KVARTERET

Olav Kyrres gate 49; 555 89 910; www.kvarteret.no; open M-W 11:30am-10pm, Th-F 11:30am-3:30am, Sa 2pm-3:30am

If you want to find the best local spots and cheapest drinks in any city, it's never a bad idea to follow the local students. In Bergen, they all head to Kvarteret, the city's student culture house. It's run by student volunteers and attracts young people from both near and far. Drinks are reasonably priced in the warehouse-style bar where you'll probably walk into special events like quiz nights, concerts, wine and cheese shindigs, or poetry readings. If you're bold (or bored) enough to go out on a Monday night, swing by Kvarteret's Mikromandag (Micro-Monday) to try local Norwegian microbrews at reduced prices.

i No cover except for special events, drinks from NOK 50; BGLTQ+ friendly

OSLO

Coverage by **Marissa Saenger**

Of the three Scandinavian capitals, Oslo was the last to get its footing as a major metropolis. After a few calamitous fires and devastating bouts of the plague, the city started fresh again in 1624, ultimately evolving into the unique cultural epicenter it is today. Though capital city status bounced around several times between Bergen, Oslo, and Trondheim, Oslo has secured the title for good, and is today Europe's fastest-growing capital. Despite its well-known cosmopolitan significance, the city is down to earth and grounded. Its public buildings, like the Opera House, offer free access and cheap tickets for arts performances. Its museums honor exploration, engineering, and nature, with exhibits on innovation for tackling climate change and accomplishments of Nobel Laureates. The city views itself as a guest in nature, prioritizing conservation of, and easy public access to, the magnificent surrounding forests and mountains. Oslo embodies the Norwegian outdoor philosophy, *friluftsliv,* with a work-life balance culture that views time to in nature as a basic human right for all. Oslo pushes progressive politics forward, celebrating social democracy, labour unions, BGLTQ+ pride, and sustainable development as it works toward becoming one of the world's greenest cities and taking global leadership on climate. Whether you're exploring the city, the Nordmarka trails, the fjord, nearby islands, or museums, you'll find a piece of Oslo that resonates with you and makes you dream of staying longer.

ORIENTATION

Oslo's city center sits right on the **Oslofjord,** the body of water which surrounds piers in front of **Oslo City Hall.** Just to the east, the **Oslo Opera House** is one of the most recognizable buildings in the city due to its sloping glass and marble structure. The main street, **Karl Johans gate,** runs through the busy downtown area, connecting the **Royal Palace** on its western end to **Oslo S** (Oslo Central Station) and the **Tiger Statue** to the east. Along Karl Johans gate are landmarks like the **National Theatre** and Norway's Parliament building, **Stortinget.** A short bus or ferry ride to the western peninsula of **Bygdøy** will take you toward some of Oslo's most famous museums, like **The Fram,** as well as surrounding beaches, forest, and walking or biking trails. The **Akerselva River** runs north from the city center, dividing Oslo's neighborhoods with wealthier residential areas to the west and younger, more diverse areas to the east, like **Grønland,** which houses most of Oslo's nightlife. To the north of the city, the **Nordmarka** forest offers endless hiking, biking, and walking trails as well as swimming lakes, **DNT** cabins, and **Holmenkollbakken,** Norway's famous steel ski jump.

ESSENTIALS

GETTING THERE

Oslo Airport or Gardermoen (Oslo Lufthavn) is Norway's main international airport, about 50km north of the city center. The quickest way to and from the city center is by a 20min. train ride on the Flytoget Airport Express, which leaves from Oslo Sentralstasjon (Oslo S) every 10-20min. Tickets can be booked online at flytoget.no/en (NOK 196 adult, NOK 98 reduced) or purchased at ticket kiosks in the airport and Oslo S. The Flybussen also travels between Oslo Bus terminal (Bussterminalen Grønland) near the city center and Oslo Lufthavn, and is about a 50min. journey (NOK 189 adult, NOK 99 reduced). Trains to other Norwegian cities from Oslo S are operated by NSB (www.nsb.no). SJ operates express trains between Oslo and Stockholm, and buses from Bussterminalen Grønland travel to various destinations around Scandinavia.

GETTING AROUND

Oslo is a very walkable city, but to get to places like Holmenkollen or other destinations outside the city center, it's best to take public transit. Public transport in Oslo is operated by Ruter and consists of trams, ferries, buses, metro, and local trains. A 24hr transit ticket grants you access to all of these services including ferries to nearby islands (excluding Bygdøy), and costs NOK 108. Single ride tickets are NOK 36 and a 7-day ticket costs NOK 285. Before entering a train, ferry, or bus etc, you must validate your ticket by scanning it at a barcode scanner, which are at every station and ticket purchase machine. You can also get free public transit access (and free museum entry) with the Oslo Pass (24hr NOK 595, 48hr NOK 695, 72hr NOK 742). The Oslo city bike sharing program is called Oslo Bysykkel, and a 24hr pass grants you unlimited rides up to 60min. in length for NOK 49. You need to download the Oslo Bysykkel app to access codes to unlock the bicycles.

PRACTICAL INFORMATION

Tourist Offices: Oslo Visitor Center (Jernbanetorget 1; 23 10 62 00; visitoslo.com; Jan-Mar M-Sa 9am-5pm, Su 10am-4pm; Apr M-Sa 9am-6pm, Su 10am-4pm; May-June M-Su 9am; July-Aug M-Sa 8am-7pm, Su 9am-6pm; Sep M-Su 9am-6pm; Oct-Dec M-Sa 9am-5pm, Su 10am-4pm).

Banks/ATMs/Currency Exchange: Avoid exchanging currency at the airport. We've listed a convenient exchange on Oslo's main street. Tavex Currency Exchange (Karl Johans gate 1; 23 89 71 22; tavex.no; open M-F 9am-8pm, Sa 9am-7pm).

Post Offices: Here's a convenient post office: Grønland Post Office (Olafiagangen 5; posten.no; open M-F 9am-5pm, Sa 10am-2pm).

Public Restrooms: Public toilets are available throughout the city. An interactive map is available at pee.place/en/l/Norway showing all facilities.

Internet: Internet is widely available in most cafés, restaurants, and museums, as well as the opera house. In some cases, a code must be sent via SMS for login.

BGLTQ+ Resources: FRI is the national BGLTQ+ organization in Norway (Tollbugata 24; 23 10 39 39; foreningenfri.no; open M-Th 10am-3pm).

EMERGENCY INFORMATION

Emergency Number: 112.

Police: Police in Oslo are generally reliable and responsive.

- Central Police Station (Hammersborggata 12, 0181 Oslo; 22 66 90 50; politiet.no; open M-F 8am-11am, noon-3pm).

US Embassy: The US Embassy is located on the outskirts of Oslo:

- (Morgedalsvegen 36; 21 30 85 40; no.usembassy.gov; open M-F 8am-5pm).

Rape Crisis Center: Dixi is a free and confidential resource center for victims of sexual assault or violence.

- Dixi (Bygdøy allé 1; 22 44 40 50; dixi.no; open M-F 9am-3pm).

Hospitals: Medical centers are generally very reliable in Oslo. We've listed an emergency center.

- Oslo Emergency Ward (Storgata 40; 113 for emergencies only, 11 61 17 for non-emergencies; open daily 24hr).

Pharmacies: Pharmacies are called Apotek in Norway and there are pharmacies all over the city center. We've listed two.

- Vitusapotek Oslo City (Oslo City Stenersgt. 1 E, Plan 2; 23 15 99 50; vitusapotek.no; open M-F 10am-10pm, Sa 10am-8pm).
- Vitusapotek Youngstorget (Youngstorget, Hammersborggata 12; 22 33 35 00; vitusapotek.no; open M-F 9am-7pm, Sa 11am-5pm).

SIGHTS

CULTURE

NOBELS FREDSSENTER (NOBEL PEACE CENTER)

Brynjulf Bulls plass 1; 483 01 000; nobelpeacecenter.org; open daily 10am-6pm

This museum is dedicated to the world's most prestigious and impactful award, the **Nobel Peace Prize.** Poignant exhibitions showcase some of the world's most pressing challenges, as well as individuals and organizations who have bravely stepped up to the plate to tackle them. A walk through Nobel Field exhibit describes every Nobel Peace Prize Laureate since the award's inception until today while the story of **Alfred Nobel,** the inventor of the Nobel Prizes, comes to life in an interactive digital book. After drawing inspiration from the incredible world-changers featured in these exhibits, you can relax in the sustainable café with an eco-friendly coffee or peruse fair-trade handmade goods from all over the world in the shop.

i Admission NOK 120, NOK 80 reduced, under 16 free; English guided tours daily 2pm and 3pm Jun-Aug, Sa-Su 2pm Oct-May; wheelchair accessible

OPERAHUSET OSLO (OSLO OPERA HOUSE)

Kirsten Flagstads Plass 1; 21 42 21 21; operaen.no; box office opening hours M-F 10am-7pm, Sa 11am-6pm, Su noon-6pm

Built to commemorate Norwegian nature and facilitate access to the public, Operahuset sits on the waterfront in a stunning sloped shape formed of granite, marble, and glass. Not only is it possible to walk onto the roof for free, they actually encourage you to do it. The building was designed as a tribute to the Norwegian ideal of access to nature as a human right. Interior design features wooden walls and balconies, showcasing Norwegian nature and history alongside the wide range of arts performances that the ballet and opera hall presents. The lobby and roof are accessible to the public for free at any time day or night making it a beautiful spot to watch the sunset over the city. From atop the roof, observe stunning views of the **Oslo Fjord,** nearby islands,

and the forest surrounding you.

i Free to view on your own or access roof; guided tours NOK 120, NOK 70 reduced; performance ticket prices vary; wheelchair accessible

LANDMARKS

HOLMENKOLLBAKKEN (HOLMENKOLLEN SKI JUMP)

Kongeveien 5; 22 92 32 00; holmenkollen.com; open Oct-Apr 10am-4pm, May-Sep 10am-5pm, June-Aug 9am-8pm

The futuristic ski jump Holmenkollbakken is Norway's most visited tourist attraction, and it's easy to see why. The venue has hosted numerous elite winter sports competitions, including the **1952 Winter Olympics** and **Ski Jumping World Cup.** Here you can admire astounding views over the **Oslo Fjord** and surrounding forest, or go for a whirl in the **Ski Simulator** (NOK 95) which sends you virtually flying down the ski jump at 100 km/hour, or alongside Olympians on alpine slopes. There's also a frisbee golf course, a ski museum featuring equipment used by world-class Olympic athletes, a climate and environment educational exhibition, and an organic pop-up café. Surrounding trails through the **Nordmarka Forest Reserve** extend for hundreds of kilometers, offering endless hiking, nordic skiing, and mountain biking adventures.

i Jump tower and Ski Museum entry NOK 140, NOK 120 reduced, free with Oslo Pass; Ski Simulator NOK 95; limited wheelchair accessibility

AKERSHUS FESTNING (AKERSHUS FORTRESS)

Grev Wedels plass 5; 23 09 39 17; forsvarsbygg.no; open daily 6am-9pm

Akershus Festning is one of Norway's most significant cultural monuments, constructed in the thirteenth century as a military defense fortress. It successfully warded off Swedes and Danes over multiple attempted sieges, and today houses history from the Middle Ages through the present day. Although still an active military area, the fortress grounds are open to the public for free and house many significant sites. Inside the castle, the **Royal Mausoleum** is the resting place of late Norwegian monarchs. Outside, you can explore the various towers, walls, and courtyards with excellent views over the **Oslo Harbor.** At the visitor center, you can sign up for a guided tour or pick up a brochure with detailed information to explore sites around the fortress on your own.

i Free admission to fortress grounds; castle entry NOK 100 adult, NOK 60 reduced; guided tours NOK 100 adult, NOK 80 reduced; guided tours in English 11am, 3pm, 5pm daily; limited wheelchair accessibility

MUSEUMS

NORGES HJEMMEFRONTMUSEUM (NORWAY'S RESISTANCE MUSEUM)

Bygning 21; 23 09 31 38; forsvaretsmuseer.no; open June-Aug M-Sa 10am-5pm, Su 11am-5pm, Sept-Dec 22 M-F 10am-4pm

Norway's Resistance Museum preserves powerful stories of Norwegian resistance against Nazi Germany's occupation of Norway during World War II. Visually captivating exhibits feature dioramas, old news reports, photographs, documents, clothing, and equipment from important events where Norwegians stood up against Nazi Germany. The courage and commitment of those who risked their lives to fight the spread of Nazi ideals in Norway is nothing short of inspiring, though many were imprisoned or exiled as a result of their acts of resistance.The museum's collection of artifacts takes you chronologically through the period of German occupation and brings many of these stories to life, illuminating Norway's critical role in the Allies' ultimate victory.

i Admission NOK 60, NOK 30 reduced; wheelchair accessible

OUTDOORS

SOGNSVANN LAKE

Sognsvann, 0890 Oslo; open daily 24hr

An extensive network of forest trails, called **Nordmarka,** surround Oslo, and Sognsvann Lake is just the beginning. Here, you can swim, fish, picnic, and explore the surrounding trails on foot or by bike. The flat 3.2km walking or running path around the lake is lit up at night and is wheelchair friendly. You could go on forever in the trails through Nordmarka, but Sognsvann is a great place to start or set up base camp. In the summer, it's a popular picnic spot, and a kiosk nearby sells ice cream and snacks. The T-bane takes you right up to a station by the lake, so it's easy to get to but still feels like a magical secret spot in the woods.

i Free; limited wheelchair accessibility (Lake and restrooms are accessible, trail accessibility depends on conditions and trail)

HOVEDØYA

Hovedøya; open daily 24hr

Who knew a place as far north as Norway could have a tropical island feel? Well, in the summer, at least. The island Hovedøya is only eight minutes from the city center by ferry but it's a totally different world. Norwegians are already laid back and on this island, it's a proper summer vacation. Sandy beaches, rocky cliffs, and crystal clear seawater invite you to sunbathe, swim, and enjoy the summer weather in a peaceful and relaxing setting. The island is predominantly a nature reserve, so it's also a wonderful place to explore forested walking trails and lush greenery all around you; if the timing is right, you may even spot some fresh raspberries or blueberries, which are yours to pick. Hovedøya is also famous for its **preserved monastery ruins,** which date as far back as 1147 AD. The island is a great place for hiking, swimming, grilling, picnicking, or hanging out at the open-air café.

i Ferry ticket (round trip) NOK 72, free with Oslo Pass; wheelchair accessible

FOOD

MATHALLEN ($$)

Vulkan 5; 400 01 209; mathallenoslo.no; open daily 10am-6pm

This popular food hall by the **Akerselva River** covers all the culinary bases and then some, with niche specialty vendors and restaurants galore. Food options range from fish and chips to bento boxes, doughnuts to dumplings, salads to burgers, tapas to gelato, and brisket to bread. Champagne bars, microbreweries, and other drink venues also offer quality beverages to compliment your choice of food. Prices

can get steep (you're in Norway, after all), but even on a budget, you still have some solid options, like buffalo wings for NOK 65, pulled chicken sandwich for NOK 95, fried salmon for NOK 89, or salads in the NOK 70-100 range. If you're feeling fancy and want to splurge on artisanal chocolates or extravagant dishes, you'll also have plenty of choices.
i Prices vary; vegetarian, vegan, and gluten-free options available; wheelchair accessible

TUNCO OSLO STREET FOOD ($$)

Torggata 16; tunco.no; open M-Sa 11am-10pm, Su noon-9pm

If you're looking for something a little more classy than fast food but don't want to go totally bankrupt (prices are crazy here, the struggle is real), street food is a great compromise. With tasty woks fusing flavors from all over the world, TUNCO serves some of the best. Not only are their dishes flavorful and healthy, each meal purchase goes toward one meal donated to a child in need. The restaurant was founded by bold backpackers like yourself, whose travels inspired this eatery and its commitment to improving health and sustainability around the world. Feel happy that the noodles in front of you are not only delicious, they also have a positive impact. Find TUNCO inside **Torggata Bad,** which has all kinds of other food stands and bars inside as well as outdoor seating and music, making it a popular hangout for locals.
i Appetizers from NOK 49, bowls NOK 139; limited wheelchair accessibility

ANNE PÅ LANDET–FROGNERPARKEN ($$)

Frognerveien 67; 21 68 70 50; annepålandet.no/frognerparken; open daily 11am-8pm

Not only can you get a sandwich here for under 95 kr (a very rare find in Norway), this café's location makes it especially unique. In the middle of the magnificent **Frogner Park,** you'll have flowers, chirping birds, fountains, beautiful plants, and sculptures all around as you eat and sip coffee. The sunny two-tiered patio borders the free outdoor sculpture park **Vigelandsparken,** whose monolith column of 121 life-size naked human figures towers a phallic, er, fantastic, 14.1m high. **Gustav Vigeland,** a Norwegian sculptor and designer of the Nobel Peace Prize medal, designed all of the park's 212 bronze and granite sculptures, including the popular **Angry Boy,** whom we can all relate to when our hostel-mate's alarm goes off at 5am. The café offers a wonderful vantage point over the park in all directions to compliment its delicious cakes and pastries.
i Desserts from NOK 25, coffee drinks from NOK 34; vegetarian, vegan, and gluten-free options available; wheelchair accessible

NIGHTLIFE

CROWBAR & BRYGGERI

Torggata 32; 21 38 67 57; crowbryggeri.com; open Su-F 3pm-3am, Sa 1pm-3am

Keg stand, anyone? Crowbar does it better: the famed microbrewery serves its home-brewed beers (in a glass, sorry Chad) directly from 1000-liter serving tanks to ensure maximum freshness. Not only does that save you from making a fool of yourself, it's much better beer than you'll get from any party where keg stands are thing. The venue is popular among locals and visitors, a top recommendation for beer aficionados who like niche drinks like Mexican biscotti cake stout. The tap home and guest brews are constantly changing, but always feature creative concoctions, like the 'rose-hipped-hibiscus-dipped flower power sour' or the 'gigantic brain damage' Belgian double. And if you come with a large group or a group-sized appetite, you can order a stout-marinated full suckling pig. The place can have chill vibes or raucous late-night energy, depending on the night and the mood of the crowd.
i Snacks from NOK 36, drinks from NOK 58; limited wheelchair access

PELOTON

Torggata 35; 921 56 181; www.pelotonbar.no; open M-W 8am-11pm, Th 8am-1:30am, F 8am-3:30am, Sa 11am-3:30am, Su noon-11pm

No, this isn't the indoor cycling fitness craze that every yoga mom is currently raving about; this is where bicycle geeks and Tour de France fans come to hang out and drink. Whether you live on

two wheels or have never touched a bike, this laid back pizzeria-bar combo welcomes you for good times and quality refreshments, as well as comfy places to sit and watch the latest tour on big-screen TVs. The decor is decidedly bicycle-themed, with jerseys, helmets, and Giro D'Italia posters adorning the windows and walls. They also have a social cycling club, open to anyone who wishes to join for a bike ride followed by pizza and drinks. On weekends, the bar stays open until nearly sunrise, leaving plenty of time to try a few of their unique drinks, like Velo summer ale, bicicletta spritze, or a corpse reviver cocktail—you know, to replenish your electrolytes after a long, hard bike ride.
i Drinks from NOK 70, pizzas from NOK 125; gluten free, vegan, and vegetarian options available; wheelchair accessible

NORWAY ESSENTIALS

VISAS

Norway is not part of the European Union, but it is part of the Schengen Area, so US citizens can stay in Norway for up to 90 days without a visa.

MONEY

Tipping: Norway's currency is the Norwegian krona, officially abbreviated NOK or kr. Tipping in Norway is not usually expected or required, though if you have received excellent service in a restaurant, it is not uncommon to round the bill to the nearest NOK 10, or leave a tip of 6-10%.

Taxes: Norway's standard VAT rate is an eye-popping 25%, with a few patently Norwegian exceptions like raw fish, which is taxed at only 11.11%. However, tax is included in all advertised prices. Pro-tip: Some souvenir shops in Norway, specifically those with Global Blue or Tax Free Worldwide stickers, will refund the VAT for goods leaving the country with you. The protocol can vary, so ask at the store for instructions to claim your refund.

SAFETY AND HEALTH

BGLTQ+ Travel: Like most of Scandinavia, Norway is very liberal in regard to BGLTQ+ rights. In 1981, Norway became the first country in the world to explicitly ban discrimination in places of employment based on sexual orientation, and that momentum can still be felt today.

Drugs and Alcohol: The legal drinking age is 18 for beverages below 22% ABV and 20 for anything higher. Drinking in public is technically illegal, but it's not uncommon to see beer and wine outside, especially in parks. Grocery stores only sell alcoholic beverages below 4.75% ABV; everything else must be bought from government-owned liquor stores called *Vinmonopolet.* Norway's taxes on alcohol are extremely high.

WEATHER/CLIMATE

As you may have noticed, Norway is pretty far north. Much of the northern region lies within the Arctic Circle, leading to long hours of daylight during the summer and seemingly endless night during the winter, even in southern cities like Bergen and Oslo.

POLAND

Poland has always been history's underdog—but not the Shawshank Redemption kind of underdog, more like the Rocky kind of underdog. The underdog that just keeps getting pounded into the ground, over, and over, and over again, until finally we're five movies, countless black eyes, and 700 years of Prussian/Austrian/German/Russian occupation in and it's high time for a reboot. After being completely decimated by German rule and firebombing in WWII and earning its independence just as the Red Army creeped over the horizon, Poland's 1945 soft-reboot lasted for only a few years before the Soviet's decided to send the "From Russia, with love" letter once again. Communist culture would sweep the Polish streets—figuratively, definitely not literally—for nearly 50 years, and Poland would finally earn its most recent independence in 1990.

And now, á la Creed, Poland has directed a hard-reboot of itself. It's war-torn history and centuries of experience living under a hegemon's heel have allowed it to emerge dignified, but with a long and unforgiving memory. The country comes off at times as exclusively self-interested, dedicated to building and maintaining a culture that endured suppression for all of modern memory. And while Poland doesn't much care if its tourists are #thriving, it's hard not to have a great time anyway. Natural beauty abounds in Poland, from the rivered lowlands to the Tatra Mountains. Polish chefs reacting to decades of communist cuisine consisting exclusively of starch and beets engage in a culinary renaissance, flirting with veganism and going steady with some of the most creative street food we've seen. Poland's art scene is one of the avant-gardiest of Europe and the country's history absolutely seeps into the seams of life in the most spontaneous and sometimes heartbreaking ways. From its affordability, to Krakow's medieval-party-city flavor, to the country's inescapable pride, to Warsaw's Paris of the North, and to the dankest beaches of Gdánsk, Poland may just be the underdog the rest of Europe never saw coming.

GDAŃSK

Coverage by **Luke Williams**

You'd be forgiven for confusing Gdańsk with Disney's Fantasyland—this seaside medieval town features everything from castles, to beaches, to romantic river rafting and sinful amounts of self-indulging. But look again: while peering too closely into Fantasyland yields only disgruntled employees and animatronic artifice, Gdańsk is rich with 1000 years of incredibly complicated history that brings even the most diehard beach bums into its numerous monuments and museums. Most people don't know that Gdańsk was only Polish until the fourteenth century, and until 1945 it was usually a part of Germany called Danzig—with bouts of being Polish or just downright being its own city-state. German by heritage and Polish by geography, Gdańsk has always acted as one of Europe's most powerful port cities—a port city so valuable that it was Poland's refusal to return Gdańsk to Germany after WWI that convinced Hitler to invade Poland—get this—at Gdańsk. And only 40 years after seeing the first shots of WWII, Gdańsk birthed the mega-union "Solidarity" that managed to crucially weaken the Soviet Union's grip throughout Poland. So stop hesitating and hitch a ride on the dankest rollercoaster in town to visit the home of Günter Grass and Arthur Schopenhaur, the Bombay of the Baltic, and the crown jewel of northern Europe.

ORIENTATION

We all have that one sibling who will drive an hour east all the while thinking they're making their merry way west. Well, Gdańsk is a city handcrafted for those poor, navigationally-challenged siblings. Don't worry about spotting the north star, reading wind directions, or telling your left from your right, because downtown Gdańsk is a very compact area: the **Old Town**. Even better, within the Old Town there are only two streets you're really interested in, both running parallel east-west: **Ul. Piwna** and **ul. Dulga**. Housing German relic **The Old Armoury** and city-defining **St. Mary's Basilica,** ul. Piwna is perfect for laying back and taking a break—especially given that most of Gdańsk's best restaurants are densely crowded down this old town road. On the other hand, Dulga offers the essential tourist experience just to the south, complete with the towering Gdańsk **City Hall** and rococo masterpiece **Fontana di Neptune** in the town's spiritual center. Head east down either of these streets and you'll hit the **Vistula River**. A riverside walk north will bring you right to Gdańsk's mascot, the **Zuraw** (Crane), and to many of the higher-end tourist-oriented seafood restaurants. And when you're sick of all the green, red, and white medieval buildings, head northwest by Uber, bus, tram, or train, because a few of Gdańsk's best sites lie just a little bit outside of Old Town, like the **Westerplatte Ruins**, **Brzeźno Beach**, and the **Museum of the Second World War,** to name a few.

ESSENTIALS

GETTING THERE

Trains and buses arrive at Gdańsk Glowny station, a 15min. walk from the center of Old Town. From the station, Bus #111 or Trams #8 or #9 will take you along the western and southern perimeters of the Old Town. Planes arrive at Gdańsk Lech Walesa Airport, 15km (9mi.) west of the Old Town. Trains from the airport travel to Gdańsk Glowny (3.80zł), taking around 30min. A taxi from the airport costs around 60zł.

GETTING AROUND

If you're spending most of your time in and around the Old Town, you should be able to walk to any given destination in less than 15min. But if you choose to explore the tri-city area, then Gdańsk's public transportation system will be more than adequate. The public transport system is comprised of buses and trams, respectively known as the ZTM and ZKM, which serve the tri-city area of Gdańsk, Sopot, and Gydnia. When traveling far within Gdańsk but not as far as Sopot or Gydnia, Uber is generally the fastest way to get to your destination but costs more than much slower public transport option.

PRACTICAL INFORMATION

Tourist Offices: The three main tourist information centers in Gdańsk are located on ul. Długa. One is listed here: (Długi Targ 28/29; 58 301 43 55; www.visitGdańsk.com; open daily summer 9am-7pm, winter 9am-5pm).

Banks/ATMs/Currency Exchange: ATMs can be found all around Old Town. ING Bank branches are located inside Madison Shopping Gallery. Old Town is also full of currency exchange vendors called "kantors." We recommend using ATMs, but if you have to exchange cash, avoid doing so at airports, at vendors marked "change" instead of "kantor," and any vendors that stay open late. A safe option is the Poczta Polska post office that also exchanges money, located a third of the way down ul. Długa (Długa 23/28; 58 301 80 49; www.poczta-polska.pl; open daily 24hr).

Post Offices: A very central post office is located about a third of the way down ul. Długa, one of Old Town's central streets. (Długa 23/28; 58 301 80 49; www.poczta-polska.pl; open daily 24hr).

Public Restrooms: In the Old Town area, public restrooms are available in most cafés and restaurants. A centrally located Costa Coffee with a free public restroom is listed here (Długa 5; 58 719 16 46; www.costacoffee.pl; open daily 7:30am-9pm).

Internet: Most cafés, restaurants, and bars in Gdańsk provide free Wi-Fi.

BGLTQ+ Resources: Although Poland's government doesn't offer many legal rights and protections for the BGLTQ+ community, the people of Gdańsk are generally open-minded and most bars in the city consider themselves "omni-friendly." Poland-wide BGLTQ+ helpline Lambda Warszawa is listed here (22 628 52 22; www.lambdawarszawa.org; open M, W, Th 6pm-10pm, Tu-F 6pm-9pm).

EMERGENCY INFORMATION

Emergency Number: 112; Poland Tourist Emergency Hotline (22 278 77 77 and 608 599 999; open daily 8am-6pm, June-Sept 8am-10pm).

Police: 997; headquarters listed here (ul. Nowe Ogrody 27; 58 321 62 22; open daily 24hr).

US Embassy: The nearest US embassy is in Warsaw (Al. Ujazdowskie 29/31; 22 504 20 00; www.pl.usembassy.gov/pl; open M-F 8:30am-5pm).

Rape Crisis Center: Based in Warsaw, the Feminoteka Foundation provides a helpline for victims of any kind of physical or sexual violence (ul. Mokotowska 29a; 572 670 874; www.feminoteka.pl; open Tu-Th 1pm-7pm).

Hospitals: There are a few hospitals located just west of Old Town.

- Copernicus Podmiot Leczniczy (Nowe Ogrody 1-6; 58 764 01 00; www.copernicus.gda.pl; open daily 24hr).

SIGHTS

CULTURE

GDAŃSK SHAKESPEARE THEATRE

Wojciecha Bogusławskiego 1; 58 351 01 01; www.teatrszekspirowski.pl; tour times vary, check website

300 years before *Hamlet* convinced Sigmund that he did, in fact, love Mommy Freud, traveling English players were busy convincing the people of Gdańsk that William Shakespeare deserved his own Polish theater. And whaddya know? By 1611, Gdańsk had erected the first Elizabethan theater free from England's sweaty underbelly. Alongside boar fights and fencing competitions, Shakespeare productions became an early staple of Gdańsk culture—eventually persuading the townspeople to host Shakespeare-oriented festivities every fall during the **Festival of St. Dominic,** festivities that still occur every September. Unfortunately, WWI destroyed the original theatre but we assure you the

2014 black-bricked Elsinore-inspired reboot is still extremely impressive. Designed by an Italian architect looking to preserve the original stage set-up and to create a "church of theatre" around the stage, the Gdańsk Shakespeare Theatre does inimitable honor to the Sweet Swan of Avon.

i Tours 18zł; wheelchair accessible; tour and show tickets available at theatre or online

FORUM GDAŃSK

Targ Sienny 7; 58 732 61 19; www.forumgdansk.pl; open M-Sa 9am-10pm, Su 9am-9pm

Of all the shopping malls we've been to, Forum Gdańsk is undoubtedly the most pretentious. Taking its name from the Roman "forum"—the center of a Roman city's arts, businesses, and religions—oh wait, we get it now. Welcome to Gdańsk's cultural/religious/economic/artistic center! A surprisingly local hangout, the Forum is a four-story mega mall just enough outside of **Old Town** to keep the pesky tourists away. Inside the mall's doors you'll be bombarded by everything from independent supermarkets to over twenty gelato stands to a movie theater, while a step outside will reveal a massive square serving as a meeting place for food trucks, locals, and street musicians en masse. And don't be afraid to take a hint from the mall's beach-themed halls and splurge a little bit—goods come cheap in Poland, so whether you get your Eurotrash clothing fix from M-House, Medicine, or Mohito, we assure you it won't hurt your wallet anything like Paris would.

i Prices vary; wheelchair accessible

LANDMARKS

ST. MARY'S BASILICA AND NEPTUNE'S FOUNTAIN

Podkramarska 5; 58 301 39 82; www.bazylikamariacka.gdansk.pl; open M-Sa 9am-7pm, Su 11-noon and 1pm-6:30pm

Apparently back in the fourteenth century bricks were all the craze—from brick earrings to brick bread to brick churches. Fortunately, Gdańsk's brick-based-diet produced one of the most remarkable and last remaining brick-gothic European churches: St. Mary's Basilica. The Basilica basically towers over the rest of the city, inviting you to climb (read: crawl) up its tower's 400 stairs and to admire it's all-white interior featuring an absolutely sexy black and gold organ for the ages. And if unsubtle subliminal messaging is your thing, you'll relish in the fact that the pagan monument Neptune's Fountain is placed right next to the Basilica and acts as the de facto center of **Old Town.** While the Basilica insists on silence, legend maintains that when the street musicians play loud enough, the **City Hall** bells ring long enough, and tourists crowd dense enough, Neptune's Fountain flows freely with golden ale.

i Free, panorama 10zł, 5zł reduced; church wheelchair accessible, no accessibility for panorama; last entry for panorama 30min. before closing

WISŁOUJŚCIE FORTRESS

Stara Twierdza 1; 512 418 731; open daily 10am-5:10pm

Guarding the mouth of Gdańsk's port, the Wisłoujście Fortress seems to spring straight out of *Pirates of the Caribbean.* Built on a star-shaped artificial island within another star-shaped artificial island, this 700-year-old walled castle served for 500 years as Gdańsk's lighthouse, only to spend its last 200 years as a military fort and museum. Tours take you through the fortress' impressive barracks, tunnels, and towers, but they're only offered in Polish, so this is really important: tours typically last an hour with the first 30 minutes spent in a skippable Polish-only museum room. The ticket salesperson should give you the option to join the in-progress tour, and as long as it's less than 30 minutes in, you should save yourself some really unneeded frustration with the Polish language and hop in on the middle of the tour for the best experience.

i Tours 15zł, 7zł reduced; last tour 1hr before closing; limited wheelchair accessibility; tours run twice an hour

ZURAW (CRANE)

Szeroka 67/68; 58 301 69 38; www.nmm.pl/zuraw; open daily 10am-4pm

Much like calculus, you'll hear that the Zuraw changed the world, but upon seeing the massive fifteenth-century crane for yourself you'll be left only with questions. But unlike calculus, you shouldn't dismiss this old dinosaur. A quick visit inside Zuraw via its museum will convince you that two pulleys and four human-powered hamster wheels mark this monument as an unmistakable wonder of world engineering. In fact, there's no better place to visit in Gdańsk to get a real appreciation for the sheer age of Gdańsk's merchant marine port—this city has been trading for *centuries,* and unlike your unfortunate Yugi-Oh card trading phase, there's no end in sight for the international power of the city's seaside spectacle.

i Observation free, museum admission 10zł, 6zł reduced; no wheelchair accessibility for museum

MUSEUMS

MUSEUM OF THE SECOND WORLD WAR

Władysława Bartoszewskiego 1; 58 760 09 60; www.muzeum1939.pl; open 10am-6pm Tu-Su

Living up to its name, this museum covers just about every WWII related event from 1914 to 1945, usually through a German, Polish, or Russian perspective. Masterfully merging videos, artifacts, environments, and English info-dumps, this is the model museum experience. Whether you're investigating the contents of a recreated Nazi arms bunker or living through footage of the seige of Leningrad, the MSWW manages to make every moment educational, engaging, and emotional. The museum has impressive collections of Italian, Soviet, and Nazi propaganda and takes advantage of every quiet moment to remind you of the terror implicit in WWII. From the Holocaust to Soviet and German occupation, the MSWW never shies away from displaying war at its most devastating.

i Admission 23zł, 16zł reduced; last entry 1hr before closing; wheelchair accessible

GDAŃSK HISTORICAL MUSEUM

Długa 46; 58 573 31 28; www.muzeumgdansk.pl; open M 10am-1pm, Tu-Sa 10am-6pm, Su 11am-6pm

There's no doubt the Gdańsk City Hall serves as the background in at least 60% of the photos tourists take in Gdańsk. So before you catch yourself hashtagging anything, take some time to explore the inside of good ol' City Hall. Trust us, it won't disappoint. Don't forget, Gdańsk has been basically its own country more than once throughout the last 1000 years, and fittingly, the City Hall feels more like a castle than a normal city hall. The inside keeps so much gold you'll find yourself looking over your shoulder for a dragon or Harry Potter searching for one of those pesky horcruxes. And if you're more of a silver kinda person, don't worry—besides checking out the best the City Hall offers, check out historical exhibits, temporary art exhibits, and a collection of artifacts from Gdańsk's past, like silver 19th century beer tankards complete with religious imagery carved into the side, handle, and lid. So rest easy: turns out you're not the only person who wishes their red solo cups were replaced with silver chalices that have Jesus and his homies carved into their sides.

i Museum 12zł, 5zł reduced, tower 5zł; last entry 45min. before closing; limited wheelchair accessibility

OUTDOORS

THE WALKABLE RUINS OF WESTERPLATTE

Majora Henryka Sucharskiego 70; open daily 24hr

The year is 1939, the month September: Poland's allowed 200 soldiers are stationed on the Westerplatte peninsula, anticipating a German attack. And when 3,500 German soldiers arrive by boat, the Battle of Westerplatte, and WWII, begins. Called by historians the "Polish Thermopylae," the 200 Polish soldiers suffered only 15 casualties and held out for one week before running out of ammunition. And even though the Germans suffered hundreds of casualties before overtaking the Poles, the German commander saluted the enemy soldiers for their bravery before committing them to a prison camp. Visiting the walkable battle ruins is one of the most heartwrenching experiences on European soil. With the waves lapping against the shore, the wind cracking through the woods, and the skeletal concrete ruins jutting against gravity, the ruins of Westerplatte make for an experience you never truly walk away from.

i Free; limited wheelchair accessible

FOOD

KAFËBË ($)

Piwna 64/65; 798 117 532; www.kafebe.pl; open M-F 8am-9pm, Sa-Su 8am-10pm

If you're fragile, maybe stay well away from Kafëbë—it will break all of your expectations. We can't stress this enough, Kafëbë may very well be some of the best food we've had in Europe. Masquerading as a quaint café that goes gleefully unnoticed on a major Gdański street, it's real easy to focus on the other flashier restaurants surrounding Kafëbë. Don't make this mistake. The northern Polish—AKA Kashubian—servers and cooks of Kafëbë treat their job and their food like art, and they will gladly sit down and assist you in ordering from an extensive menu of traditional Kashubian dishes, specializing in cod preparations but also cooking up everything from goose goulash, to chicken frikase and those ubiquitous pierogis. Kafëbë serves traditional Kashubian breakfast all day, homemade cake, and has each of their desserts listed in culinary heritage collections of northern Poland. There is literally nothing not to love about this place, so come on and Kafëbë, bëbë.

i Entreés from 22zł, beer from 10zł; vegetarian, vegan, and gluten-free options available; limited wheelchair accessibility

TAWERNA MESTWIN ($$)

Straganiarska 20; 58 301 78 82; open M 11am-6pm, Tu-Su 11am-10pm

Even though a train ride from Warsaw to Gdańsk is a meager two hours, there exists a massive culinary divide between northern Polish food and central and southern Polish food. While the central and southern regions prefer variations on beets and starch for basically every meal, the north remembers…the sea-faring history of its ancestors—serving radical variations on beets and seafood, boldly leaving starch behind. The locals call this seafood dependency "Kashubian", and the single most traditional place to pick up the Kashubian craze in Gdańsk is undeniably Tawerna Mestwin. Literally in an old northern Polish tavern carved from wood and decorated with every Polish antique imaginable, this homey joint is not only a blast from the 18th century past but a culinary experience for the brave, the wise, and the bold. And if you're feeling especially courageous, let your server order for you—they knows what's good.

i Entreés from 22zł, beer from 7zł; vegetarian and vegan options available; no wheelchair accessibility

BAR TURYSTYCZNY ($)

Szeroka 8/10; 58 301 60 13; www.barturystyczny.pl; open 8am-6pm daily

The Gdańsk restaurant scene is more brutal than *Game of Thrones*—if you last longer than three years, it's a bonafide accomplishment. For this reason, Bar Turystyczny sure does enjoy lauding its 58-year-old-communist-relic status. A holdover from the communist milk bar tradition—imagine your high-school caféteria but staffed only by Polish grandmothers who make it their life's mission to be the best cooks in Poland—Bar Turstyczny both upholds the milk bar tradition of serving the very best authentic Polish food while also defying whatever law states that most milk bars have to be sad, colorless, and kind of dirty. Brought into the twenty-first century with a fresh art-deco makeover, there's no faster and better place to just get down and dirty with grandmother-certified Polish food, from beets to pork chops to cold cucumber soup and potato pancakes, no one walks away from Turystyczny with an empty tummy.

i Entreés from 8zł; vegetarian options available; wheelchair accessible

GVARA ($$)

Chlebnicka 48/51; 795 889 288; www.restauracjagvara.pl; open M-Th 9am-10pm, F-Sa 9am-midnight, Su 9am-10pm

Just like the founders of the infamous Fyre festival, we all have an inner-yearning to see ourselves as the filthy-wealthy foreigner dropped into a seaside setting where the prices are high, the quality of dress and taste higher, and money's no object. Given that Gdańsk hosts an unbelievable number of retired senior citizens with plenty of moola to spare, there's no shortage of high-class dining available. And while the urge to forget about budgets and spend like Jordan Belfort for one night is strong, we found that Gvara is the perfect high-class wine-heavy low(ish)-cost restaurant to indulge your fantasies and taste buds without emptying your wallet. So go ahead, order that half-duck, boar sirloin, or cod with black pudding—Polish food doesn't get preppier than this.

i Entreés from 32zł, beer from 9zł; vegetarian, vegan, and gluten-free options available; wheelchair accessible

NIGHTLIFE

CAFÉ JOZEF K.

Piwna 1/2; 572 161 510; www.jozefk.pl; open M-Th 10am-2am, F-Sa 10am-4am, Su 10am-2am

Taking its name from the central character in Kafka's *The Trial*, this café/bar/dance club takes the literary café idea to a whole new level. Calling itself the "junkyard of imagination," Jozef K's halls, make it all too easy to feel as if you've been metamorphosed into a cockroach and are exploring a lost planet where the walls are made of books, the only light is neon, and every nook and cranny is taken over by the forgotten antiques of Polish past. Student-ridden café by day and Old Bohemia by night, Josef K.'s cocktails taste actually magical—the bartenders treat their creation like performance art and garnish each new concoction with fresh herbs from the bar-side garden. And after one sip from the "Dismissed Suitor" or "Theory of Everything," you'll join the locals hanging off the second floor rafters and jigging to the seductive late-night synths.

i Cocktails from 17zł, beer from 7zł; cash only; wheelchair accessible

PROTOKULTURA AND 100CZNIA

Popiełuszki 5; www.protokultura.pl; open Tu-Th 1pm-midnight, F 1pm-2am, Sa noon-2am, Su noon-midnight

If Gdańsk isn't your first stop in Poland, you probably already know about Poland's understandable obsession with "bar-gardens," our made-up term for collections of bars and restaurants in old parking lots and warehouses. Gdańsk took one look at the bar-garden idea and decided to give the rest of Poland the shaft, opting to do its own thing. Thus, Protokultura and 100cznia were born amidst Gdańsk's shipyards in the form of a Camelot made from three levels of cargo containers. Pizza shops, hummus bars, hookah bars, champagne on draft, local beer hoarders, and classic cocktail creators put up shop inside the cargo containers. Under the rainbow string-light sun the two story Mad Maxian wasteland is surrounded by artificial sandy beaches with plenty of lounge and dancing space, as well as multiple hard-electronic dance floors inside nearby warehouses. Saying that this bar-garden offers something for everyone isn't enough—so let's just call this a once-in-a-lifetime post-apocalyptic promised land and leave the rest to you.

i No cover, beer from 10zł; most areas wheelchair accessible

KRAKÓW

Coverage by **Luke Williams**

Standing atop the carcass of a dead bloodthirsty dragon, King Krakus declared to the tenth century Polish tribes that upon the dragon's cave he would build them a capital city the likes of which the world had never known. And from that moment on, it was like someone tickled Han Solo's nose and caused him to sneeze and his hand to jerk, sending the Millennium Falcon of Cracovian history right into hyperdrive: within 400 years, Kraków would become the most significant central trading hub in Europe. The foremost European medieval Old Town would be constructed along with the Wawel Castle and Renaissance relics in tow. In 200 more years, doctors and scientists would begin teaching at Poland's first university where, with the help of students like Nicolas Copernicus, Kraków would become Poland's intellectual and artistic center. Flashing forward 300 more years lands us at the Nazi reshaping of Kraków, as they restructured the city at their whim and horrifyingly expelled all of Kraków's Jewish population. UNESCO World Heritage Sites, dragon legends, 700-year-old salt mines, the world's oldest shopping mall, and natural splendor fly by as Kraków became witness to the Soviet Union's first attempt at building a "proletariat paradise" and then to being the hometown of the first non-Italian pope in 300 years with Pope John Paul II. And now, Kraków is very much the cultural heart of Poland, vibrant with countless theater venues, a nightlife scene to rival Budapest's, and some of the best Polish cooking we've ever eaten. This is the city of 1,000 faces, where one day may yield a marathon bike ride along the Vistula River and the next day trip to Auschwitz. Kraków's location, history, and artistic background simply give it an unfair advantage that leaves Poland's other major cities just feeling jealous.

ORIENTATION

We hope you're wearing your ruby red slippers because in Kraków there's only one thing you have to remember in order to not get lost: "Follow the yellow brick road!" Okay, so maybe not an actual yellow brick road...more like a grey cobblestone road. Anyways, right in the middle of Kraków is the **Old Town**, and right in the middle of Old Town is the main square **Rynek Główny**, complete with postcard hogs **St. Mary's Basilica** and **Sukiennice (The Cloth Hall)**. Luckily for you, all roads lead back to Rynek Główny—just so long as you know where you are in relation to it. To the south lies local-oriented foodie paradise **Kasimierz**, with its center at Polish fast food and flea market heaven **Plac Nowy** and its high culture located just a bit to the west at **Wawel Castle**. The **Vistula River** runs south of Kazimierz, and crossing the river takes you to **Podgórze**, former home of the **Kraków Jewish Ghetto** and site of **Schindler's Factory**. To the west of Rynek Główny lies the craft-beer and street guitarist infested **Student District** and to the north the more residential **Kleparz District**. And while all these planets operate in a Rynek Główny-centric universe, some of Kraków's greatest hits lie outside the city center. To name a few: Soviet utopia **Nowa Huta** is located two miles east of Old Town, **Wieliczka Salt Mine** eight miles southeast, and the Cracovian nipple-shaped take on the great pyramids **Kopiec Kościuszki** two miles west.

ESSENTIALS

GETTING THERE

Kraków Airport is 15km (9mi.) west of the city, and trains run every 30 min. from 4am-midnight from the airport to Kraków Główny, the main train and bus station, which is a 10-min. walk from Old Town. The journey is 17 min., and tickets (9zł) can be purchased on the platform or onboard. Buses #208 and #252, and night bus #902 (4zł) run from the airport to the city center and take around 40 min. If you're travelling to Kraków by bus or train, you will arrive in Kraków Główny. The bus terminal is on the east side of the station, and you should exit on the west side to walk to Old Town.

GETTING AROUND

Kraków's public transport system consists of buses and trams. Regular service runs from 5am-11pm, with night buses and trams continuing to run, albeit less frequently, afterwards. You can plan your journey using www.jakdojade.pl/Krakow/trasa. Tickets can be purchased at bus and tram stops, and 1hr tickets can be purchased from the driver. Tickets must be validated on board, and you risk being fined by an inspector if you do not validate your ticket. Within the Old Town and the surrounding area, walking is the best way to get around as public transportation doesn't run through the area and isn't necessary for the able-bodied walker. Uber is also a cheap and reliable mode of transportation to any area in the extended city that tends to be more reliable and cost-friendly than taxis.

PRACTICAL INFORMATION

Tourist Offices: InfoKraków is the official city information network run by the city. Information centers are spread throughout Old Town. (Świętego Jana 2; 12 354 27 25; www.infokrakow.pl; open daily 9am-7pm).

Banks/ATMs/Currency Exchange: ATMs are found throughout the city, especially near and in Old Town. In the city, currency exchanges are known as "kantors," some of which give better rates than ATMs. Avoid kantors with English names, such as Western Union and Interchange, and those in tourist areas, such as the Old Town Rynek Glówny. One centrally located Euronet ATM is listed here. (Pijarska 23; 22 519 77 71; www.euronetpolska.pl; open daily 24hr).

Post Offices: The main office is just outside the eastern perimeter of the Old Town. (Westerplatte 20; 12 421 44 89; www.poczta-polska.pl; open M-F 8am-8:30pm, Sa 8am-3pm).

Public Restrooms: There are a few public restrooms near Old Town's Rynek Glówny. One is listed here (Rynek Główny 41; open daily 24hr).

Internet: Most cafés, restaurants, hostels, and fast food restaurants provide free Wi-Fi. Public libraries, identifiable by the phrase "Biblioteki Publicznej," also provide free Wi-Fi.

BGLTQ+ Resources: Though Poland's government doesn't offer many legal rights and protections for the BGLTQ+ community, Krakow is generally considered a BGLTQ+ friendly city. Poland-wide BGLTQ+ helpline Lambda Warszawa is listed here (22 628 52 22; www.lambdawarszawa.org; open M, W, Th 6pm-10pm, Tu-F 6pm-9pm).

EMERGENCY INFORMATION

Emergency Number: 112; Poland Tourist Emergency Hotline (22 278 77 77 and 608 599 999; open daily 8am-6pm, June-Sept 8am-10pm).

Police: Kraków's police headquarters is listed here (Henryka Siemiradzkiego 24; 12 615 26 00; www.krakow.policja.gov.pl; open daily 24hr).

US Embassy: US Consulate General is located east of the Old Town's Rynek Glówny (Stolarska 9; 12 424 51 00; open M-F 8:30am-5pm).

Rape Crisis Center: Based in Warsaw, the Feminoteka Foundation provides a helpline for victims of any kind of physical or sexual violence (ul. Mokotowska 29a; 572 670 874; www.feminoteka.pl; open Tu-Th 1pm-7pm).

Hospitals: The following 24hr hospitals have emergency wards that are obliged to help anyone who arrives regardless of nationality or health insurance status.

- University Hospital of Kraków (Mikołaja Kopernika 36; 12 424 70 00; www.su.krakow.pl; open daily 24hr).
- Health Care Ministry of Internal Affairs and Administration (Kronikarza Galla 25; 12 662 31 50; open daily 24hr).

Pharmacies: Pharmacies are identifiable by the green cross on or protruding from their facade. They are called "aptekas" in Polish.

- DOZ Apteka (Mikołajska 4; 800 110 110; www.doz.pl; open M-F 8am-8pm, Sa 9am-7pm, Su 10am-6pm).
- Mandragora Apteka (Długa 41; 12 422 97 98; www.mandragora.krakow.pl; open M-F 8am-9pm, Sa 8am-3pm).

SIGHTS

CULTURE

CMENTARZ RAKOWICKI (RAKOWICKI CEMETERY)

Rakowicka 26; 12 619 99 00; www.zck-krakow.pl; open M-F 9am-2pm

Yes, you heard us correctly. We are recommending, and better yet, we are thumbpicking, a cemetery. But this isn't just any cemetery. This is the Rakowicki Cemetery—Kraków's 220 year old and largest cemetery that just so happens to be one of the most naturally stunning places you will visit in Europe. Like if the Secret Garden worked a double shift as King Midas' labyrinth, Rackowicki feels almost like a lost forest replete with incredible, high-art level tombstones and crypts that put some of the city's churches to shame. And while the cemetery is open to the public and has become the Cracovian training ground for budding nature photographers in recent years, family and friends of the deceased could very well be present and paying their respects during your visit, so dress respectfully and silently admire the immense beauty and sincerity of one of Kraków's can't-miss sites.

i Free; wheelchair accessible; dress respectfully

NOWA HUTA

Al. Jana Pawła II 232; open daily 24hr

Ever the anti-intellectual twentieth-century version of flat-earthers and climate change deniers, as soon as the Soviets took control of college town Kraków they had one mission: turn the city away from the books and toward rampant industrialism. Ironwork factories and menial labor job offerings cropped up en masse and as small town farmers flooded Kraków's streets, the **Soviet Union** quickly realized the hungry huddled masses would need a place to sleep. Thus began the Soviet's single largest residential project outside of Russia: Kraków's Nowa Huta. A thirty minute Vistula riverside bike ride into the eastern Cracovian suburbs delivers you right to this massive mini-city beginning at **Ronald Reagan Square**. Modeled after the gardens of Versailles, this concrete maze is a monument to socialist realist architecture preserving everything from Soviet-era squares, markets, and movie theaters to abandoned tanks left over from occupation. Just be careful not to catch red fever and start liking how manicured and symmetric this Twilight Zone universe looks; the Soviet's weren't known for throwing the best parties.

i Free; wheelchair accessible; located across from given address, the Cultural Center, beginning at Ronald Reagan Central Square

LANDMARKS

GHETTO WALL FRAGMENT AND GHETTO HEROES SQUARE

Plac Bohaterów Getta 30-001; open daily 24hr

The Nazis weren't interested in destroying Kraków. They wanted to reshape it, to make it the capital of their general government and to create within it the perfect German utopia. And within days of occupation, the

Nazis started viciously sending Kraków's over 20,000 Jews into the southern **Podgórze District**. By 1940, Nazis officially created the Kraków ghetto and inhumanely crammed 20,000 people into an area originally made for under 4,000. As an added part of the oppression the Jewish population of Krakow faced, the Germans forced Jewish men to build a ring of concrete walls that would enclose the ghetto. ghetto. This facilitated the eventual movement of the Jewish population to Auschwitz. Little of the ghetto remains today, but a 12-meter section of the wall still stands in memorial to the unimaginable suffering that occurred within its perimeter.

i *Free; wheelchair accessible*

ST. MARY'S BASILICA

Plac Mariacki 5; 12 422 05 21; www.mariacki.com; open M-Sa 9am-5:30pm, Su 1pm-5:30pm

We're gonna be real with you and say that St. Mary's Basilica is Kraków's gimme destination. The defining landmark of the largest medieval square in Europe and an incredible 700-year-old brick gothic church to boot, St. Mary's basically shouts "VISIT ME" to every tourist that dares take one step into **Old Town**. And while only the biggest of fuddy-duddies would deny the church its wish and not visit one of the most colorful, bombastic, incongruous churches on the continent, for those of you looking for a road-less-traveled church experience we'd recommend visiting separate but equally stunning **St. Anne's Church** or **Saints Peter and Paul Church** both just a short walk away from St. Mary's. That said, St. Mary's does feature Poland's single most important national treasure: a fourteenth-century gothic altarpiece by **Veit Stoss** that holds basically every record a wooden altarpiece can hold. So, don't be afraid to pull out your eenies, meenies, miny's, and moes to make the hard decisions for you.

i *Admission 10zł, 5zł reduced, tower 15zł, 10zł reduced; church is wheelchair accessible*

MUSEUMS

COLLEGIUM MAIUS

Jagiellońska 15; 12 663 13 07; www.maius.uj.edu.pl; open M, W 10am-2:40pm, Tu, Th 10am-5:40pm, F-Sa 10am-2:40pm

For all of you baking soda volcano enthusiasts and Nicolas Cage wannabes, Collegium Maius does double duty as the place where science history nerds go when they die and the repository for all of Poland's national treasures. More formally, Collegium Maius is actually **Jagiellonian Univeristy's** oldest building—which is saying a lot considering the big JU was founded in 1364, is the second oldest university in central Europe, and inspired such students as **Copernicus** and **Pope John Paul II.** Perhaps not for everyone but definitely for all the cool people, tours run through this nerd camp at various times on the daily—highlighting wonders like the first globe made after Columbus' journey that depicts America, busts of **Galileo** and Copernicus, a 700-year-old Polish crown, 400-year-old Turkish minaret, one of **Louis XVI's** favorite clocks from pre "off with his head" **Versaille**, contemporary portraits of **Napoleon Bonaparte**, and a signed photo of Earth sent by Niel Armstrong in 1969.

i *Tour 12zł; tour times vary by day and season, check website; no wheelchair accessibility; tour lasts 45min*

MUSEUM OF CONTEMPORARY ART IN KRAKOW

Lipowa 4; 12 263 40 00; www.mocak.pl; open Tu-Su 11am-7pm

While Kraków has plenty of dusty old art museums that like to brag about a certain single **Da Vinci** painting (cough cough, the National Museum), the **Museum of Contemporary Art** likes to literally mix things up—hosting themed exhibits that change every few months featuring the work of Polish and international avant-garde artists alike. Here lies some of the most meta and mind-blowing short films, sculptures, photography, and paintings displayed in an accessible and extremely well-organized manner. The MOCAK, as locals call it, really focuses on telling a story and bringing modern

AUSCHWITZ

You could travel the world for years and never find another place like Auschwitz, the largest Nazi concentration camp used to systematically murder 1.1 million Jews, Poles, Romas, queer people, and other marginalized ethnic groups. Visiting Auschwitz is enough to convince you that some tragedies are so powerful that they curse the earth they take place on forever. After four years of shipping prisoners in from every corner of Europe and making Auschwitz the world's largest cemetery without any graves, the Soviets liberated the camp in 1944, only to find all but 7,500 sick prisoners already evacuated on one last fatal winter march. Like a gripping abstract painting, walking through Auschwitz is not an outward experience, but an intimately inward one: Auschwitz looks into you just as much as you look into it. If you plan to take the hour and a half bus ride from Kraków's downtown to the visit the horrific nexus of human atrocity, prepare yourself. When people saw former prisoners demand the camps be opened as a museum in 1947, they knew there was plenty to learn from Auschwitz. However, the visit demands solemnity, respect, and strength from all who walk under the iron "Arbeit Macht Frei" sign and through the Gates of Death.

The first thing you need to know is that "Auschwitz" actually denotes three different concentration camps. The museum starts as soon as you see the iron **"Arbeit Macht Frei"** (Work Sets You Free) sign at Auschwitz I—the original 16,000-person camp and the sight of many of the Nazi's most horrific human experiments and executions. **Auschwitz I** is small, but the museum path isn't marked, so we recommend starting at **Block 4** in the northeast corner and moving toward **Block 11** and the **Execution Wall.** Then, move from **Block 18** back north toward the most northwest building, the **Gas Chamber I.** Two miles northwest lies **Auschwitz II-Birkenau,** the infamous home of the **Gates of Death,** the **Death Block,** and the largest gas chamber the Nazis constructed. Auschwitz II—Birkenau is very large, but straightforward to navigate. It's contents will be covered further in its listing. The third camp, **Auschwitz III,** is not open to the public. Finally, a piece of **crucial advice:** If you're planning on visiting Auschwitz without reserving a guide, you **must** arrive at Auschwitz I between 7:30am-9am and your entrance will be free. After 9am, you either must have a ticket (even if reserved online far in advance the wait can be hours long) or be visiting Auschwitz via private tour company, like SeeKraków, Krakville Tours, and KrakówTrip. We recommend either arriving during the 7:30am-9am window or booking a spot on a private tour to avoid the hours-long wait and possibility of not being admitted to the museum. The museum asks that visitors wear thoughtful attire and generally demonstrate the respect that Auschwitz demands.

GETTING THERE

The easiest but most expensive way to forgo the hassle of travel and any line-waiting is to book a private tour and be picked up at your hostel door. However, these generally run from 130-150zł, which means you can save anywhere from 40-60zł by choosing instead to go by bus after 9am. If you arrive at Auschwitz before 9am, you will only pay the round trip bus fare. All told, the most cost-effective way of getting to Auschwitz is via a 1 hour and 30 minute bus ride. Buses from Kraków MDA—adjacent to the main train station Kraków Główny—run almost every ten minutes daily from as early as 7am. Bus #24-29 stop at Auschwitz I with their final destination listed as "Oświęcim main station."

GETTING AROUND

Both Auschwitz I and Auschwitz II-Birkenau are easily walkable and wheelchair accessible. When it comes to transportation from Auschwitz I to Auschwitz II-Birkenau or vice versa, beginning at 10:30am a bus runs between the two sites every 10-20 minutes. Food is also very close to both Auschwitz I and Auschwitz II. The museum café resides in the welcome building at Auschwitz I and the museum caféteria is in the welcome building just east of Auschwitz II—Birkenau. We recommend eating at these options given their convenience, cleanliness, and quality.

Visit...

GAS CHAMBER I

Northwest corner of Auschwitz I; open June, July, and Aug daily 7:30am-8:30pm, open April, May, Sept daily 7:30am-7:30pm, website shows various other hours

After testing the Zyklon B gas in Block 11, the Nazis constructed the first dedicated gas chamber in the northwestern corner of Auschwitz I. A concrete chamber carved into a small hill, SS soldiers proceeded to install hundreds of fake shower heads all over the ceiling, convincing newly arrived prisoners to shed their clothing and belongings and calmly cram into Gas Chamber I. SS soldiers would then pour in Zyklon B from holes in the roof, killing every prisoner in less than 15 minutes. After stripping every corpse of hair, valuable jewelry, and artificial body parts, the SS burned the bodies in the adjacent crematorium. Gas Chamber I became the birthsite of the Nazi's horrific and all too efficient murder factory, inspiring every subsequent gas chamber.

Free with Auschwitz I admission; wheelchair accessible; after 9am only accessible via ticket and guide

AUSCHWITZ I

Ul. Więźniów Oświęcimia 20; 33 844 81 00; visit.auschwitz.org; open June-Aug daily 7:30am-8:30pm, open April, May, Sept daily 7:30am-7:30pm, website shows hours for months not listed above

Auschwitz I is not your everyday museum. Its mission is not only to educate you, but to terrify you, to break you, to leave you speechless and thoughtless and only able to hear the blood pounding through your veins. After walking under the infamous "Arbeit Macht Free" (Work Sets You Free) sign, the museum begins in the northeast corner at Block 4, continuing onto Block 11, then Block 18, and ending at Gas Chamber 1. As you enter former barrack after former barrack, you will be slowly presented with photos and documents, bedrooms and bathrooms, all preparing you for the final onslaught that is seeing the items the Nazis seized from the prisoners before and after murdering them in the gas chambers. Be sure to stop between Blocks 10 and 11 at the Execution Wall and pay your respects—it's one of the few quiet moments of rest during the unimaginably tragic 1.5 hour span of the museum.

Before 9am admission free, after 9am admission 80zł, 70zł reduced; last entry 90min. before closing; reservation recommended; most of museum wheelchair accessible; after 9am only accessible via ticket and guide

AUSCHWITZ II-BIRKENAU

Miejsce Pamięci i Muzeum Auschwitz-Birkenau; 33 844 81 00; visit.auschwitz.org; open June-Aug daily 7:30am-8:30pm, open April, May, Sept daily 7:30am-7:30pm, website shows hours for months not listed above

After the claustrophobic, densely-packed, horrifying experience that is Auschwitz I, stepping into the wide-open outdoors of Auschwitz II-Birkenau somehow feels like an undeserved relief. This is the Nazi's largest concentration camp, constructed entirely by prisoner labor and built to house 100,000 prisoners. The northern side is usually inaccessible to visitors and houses the wooden mixed barracks where men, women, and children lived lives separated by electric fences. The southern side is accessible for walking and houses the brick women's quarters and the open Death Block at the southeast corner—the single worse conditioned block designated specifically for the women condemned to die. To the west you'll find the ruins of the Nazi's largest gas chamber and the modern memorial to the prisoners of Auschwitz. And following the central train tracks in the middle of the camp will lead you directly to the "Gate of Death," the train terminal that has become modern memory's symbol for the unspeakable evil perpetrated at these camps.

Free; last entry 90min. before closing; wheelchair accessible; no guide necessary

art laymen along for the ride, including very helpful historical and contextual plaques next to every piece to explain all of modern art's sometimes egregious cockamamie. And when you're done letting those creative juices flow, take some time to walk around one of Kraków's most affluent residential areas and **Schindler's Factory** both in close proximity to the MOCAK.

i Admission 14zł, reduced 7zł; last entry 1hr before closing; wheelchair accessible

OUTDOORS

ZAKRZÓWEK RESERVOIR

Wyłom 1; park open daily 24hr, swimming daily during daylight hours

Whether it's due to climate change or the effects of 1000-year-old dragon breath, Kraków in the summer gets hot. And as midday rolls around and tourists take frantic shelter in coffee houses, locals know a better place to go: Zakrzówek Reservoir. Housed in the park **Skałki Twardowskiego** located a 15-minute bike ride west of **Old Town,** Zakrzówek Reservoir not only offers great views of the city, but an abandoned rain-filled quarry with crystal clear water and 40-foot tall cliffs to jump off of. Illegal to swim in until just recently, there are two official spots to set up camp on the cliffs that are impossible to miss due to the insane amounts of locals doing everything from tanning to BBQ'ing and swan diving. Besides being one of the best places to get a feel for local life in the city, Zakrzówek's chilly water really is just the refreshing midday adventure every sun-beaten traveler needs.

i Free; park wheelchair accessible

KOPIEC KOŚCIUSZKI (KOŚCIUSZKI MOUND)

Al. Waszyngtona 1; 12 425 11 16; www.kopieckosciuszki.pl; open 9am-sunset

Apparently, whenever a famous Cracovian dies, it's tradition for townspeople from across Poland to carry dirt from all across the country and to pour it onto the gravesite—creating a grassy knoll version of the Great Pyramid of Giza. And not one to be outdone by Egypt, Kraków features six of these massive, round, globe-shaped... Okay, fine. Yes. It's a breast shaped hill. Stop laughing. This is serious. Far and above outsizing the rest of Kraków's buxom monuments, Kopiec Kościuszki brandishes its 200 year-old prominence with glee—sitting atop a mountain that overlooks east Kraków and serves up some of the best views in the city, provided you're well-endowed with enough fitness to make the climb. Upon summiting this shapely hill—dammit, we're done. Just go climb the boob-hill. We promise there are few outdoor attractions in Kraków this titillating.

i Admission 14zł, 10zł reduced; wheelchair accessible by appointment; buy tickets on the southern end of mound's base, enter on the northern end

FOOD

CHIMERA SALAD BAR ($)

Świętej Anny 3; 12 292 12 12; www.chimer.com.pl; open M-Sa 9am-10pm, Su 11am-10pm

Poland does this weird thing where "salad bar" literally means "not a salad bar." Don't go into Chimera expecting your everyday Sweetgreen or Coolgreens—Chimera is really an updated take on the whole communist milk bar concept with a vegetarian and vegan twist. And while Kraków's vegan scene is unlike any other we've seen in Europe, if less concentrated than Warsaw's, Chimera is the uncontested king of the hill. Load up your plate with the most creative and delectable veggie fare in the city, from broccoli tarts and grape leaf mexican spring rolls to salad with mussels and pomegranate crêpes. Once you've assembled your plate's culinary rainbow, take a seat in Kraków's single best area to just chill out and take a break from it all: Chimera is housed in a glass-roofed courtyard overgrown with trees, vines, flowers, and classical paintings that might just convince you you're eating ambrosia in the lost ruins of Shangri-La.

i Entreés from 6zł; primarily vegetarian and vegan options available, gluten-free options available; wheelchair accessible

MR. PANCAKE ($)

Dolnych Młynów 10/1b; 12 278 73 02; www.mrpancake.pl; open M-Th 11am-10pm, F 11am-11pm, Sa 10am-11pm, Su 10am-10pm

Mr. Pancake is a demanding restaurant, urging its patrons to seize their decision making powers and resolve some of life's biggest and most important questions like: "What candy-inspired cocktail am I daydrinking today?" and "Which five of these 60 toppings should butter my breakfast cakes?" What other guides don't tell you is that traveling to Kraków is neither about partying nor history. It's about fearlessly ordering the 1,500 calorie fivestack Original Pornfood pancakes, sporting snickers, pop tarts, kinder, caramel popcorn, and fruit loops to make things more tasteful.

i Pancakes from 11zł, cocktails from 19zł; vegetarian options available; wheelchair accessible

MIĘDZY MIASTOWA ($$)

Dolnych Młynów 10; 577 304 450; www.miastowa.com; open M-F 9am-midnight, Sa-Su 10am-midnight

Look, it may just be the fact that Między Miastowa is located in one of Kraków's most student-friendly nightlife areas or that it calls an old tobacco refinery home, but Między Miastowa is hot. Just a short walk away from one of Kraków's biggest universities, this restaurant is the after-school go-to for college kids who just want great pizza and better beer in a chic, modernist setting after a hard day of classes. From curry and pad thai to sirloins and BBQ ribs to tropical dish preparations, Między Miastowa has a foot in just about every one of the world's culinary waters and it's still managing to swim. Last but not least, Między Miastowa sports a cocktail menu exclusively devoted to downright artistic G&T creations that had us wanting to come back every single night.

i Entreés from 27zł, cocktails from 17zł; vegetarian options available; wheelchair accessible

NIGHTLIFE

KLUB ALTERNATYWY

Mały Rynek 4; 12 422 16 67; open M-Th 6pm-2am, F-Sa 6pm-4am, Su 6pm-2am

It's gonna sound absurd, but Klub Alternatywy earns some serious charm from its being in a multiple-centuries-old cellar and only playing American 80's music on the lowkey old school disco-ball dance floor. If you're livin' on a prayer and just need someone to take a chance on you, this is the perfect club: hidden in a local-haven off of **Rynek Główny** and visited only by local students, this club is welcoming and wild and the perfect place to just let go and dance like a virgin touched for the very first time. And if you find a crazy little thing called love, take a seat in one of the club's numerous lounge areas and consider ordering some traditional Kraków shot cocktails because they're dirt cheap and delicious.

i Beer from 5zł; no wheelchair accessibility

SZOTOTO

Pasaż Bielaka; 536 789 709; open M-Sa 6pm-3am, Su 4pm-midnight

This is a college kid's candy store and the most dangerous pregame you've ever had. Taking Kraków's love for shot cocktails to a new level, Szototo is a shot-only bar with over 70 options on the menu ranging from the glorious hazelnut, coffee, and vodka mix that

is the Monte to the more insane options like the fruity White Walker and fire shot Honey Bunny. And what makes this hidden locals-only joint so dangerous, you ask? The fact that one shot cocktail is no more than two red-blooded American dollars and the bartenders are geniuses trapped by the constraints of the menu who will beg you to let them experiment just. one. more. time. Whether you've already ordered one shot or had five, do yourself a favor and let the bartender have his way. He'll pull from the over 200 bottles of liquers, vodkas, mixers, and garnishes and create a three or four layered technicolor masterpiece right there in your shotglass and his. And after you clink and down his work in one go, he'll probably even give you a discount for letting him indulge himself.

i Individual shots from 6zł, sets of six from 25zł; wheelchair accessible

DOLNYCH MŁYNÓW DISTRICT

Dolnych Młynów 10; most venues open M-W 5pm-2am, Th 8am-3pm, F-Sa 8pm-6am, Su 5pm-10pm

This is Kraków's attempt at a signature Polish staple: the "bar garden," a collection of different bars, clubs, and restaurants all condensed into one small area. Located in the alleys between a series of abandoned and reclaimed factories in the heart of the student district, Dolnych Młynów never slows its roll. If you're feeling a sci-fi themed classic dance club, hit up **Zet Pe Te**. Tired of feeling like a sardine and want to lounge outside and just grab some cheap beers from the outdoor stands? Sounds like a plan. Is **Mr. Pancake** whispering tales of midnight pancakes in your ear? Duh. What about retro-themed **Hala Główna** bar, or mini-dance club and modern bar **Lastriko**, or the three story cocktail-specialist **Mane**? We recommend you go the way of standardizing testing and fill in that "all of the above" bubble to ensure one hell of a night.

i Beer from 5zł; most venues wheelchair accessible

WARSAW

Coverage by **Luke Williams**

Just like your S.O. who broke up with you right before college, Warsaw is unabashedly not interested in you. This city caters to the locals—only in the Old Town will you feel any significant tourist presence at all. Now, you actually have to—God, forbid—ask for an English menu, you have to suffer through infuriating bouts of not being able to eavesdrop, and you are downright forced to experience a city so stubborn you have no choice but to meet it on its own terms. You might ask: what are these terms, Warsaw? To which Warsaw might respond, if it feels like it: don't judge a city by its skyline, my beauty lies inside. Get ready to walk, I don't reveal all my secrets at once. Oh, and forget about NYC, Budapest, and London—all those filthy, dangerous cities. I'm clean as a whistle and by God, if you don't feel warm fuzzies walking around my streets at 2am then something's wrong with you, pal. This is a city for students, for families, for travelers seeking to be confronted with Polish life at its most unadulterated. And hey, that by no means implies it's not also a complete riot of a city. In what other world metropolis could you simultaneously be a city slicker, ski bum, and beach babe all in the middle of May?

ORIENTATION

Warsaw is unfortunately difficult to navigate, especially given its size. For starters, everything is a 30 minute walk away—the city is incredibly spread out. However around strategic hotspots, you can always make camp and orient yourself. First, take note of the **Vistula River**, running north-south and dividing the Warsaw

Downtown from the east bank's residential **Praga** and **South Praga** districts. The west bank of the river brims with stuff to do—the north end is Warsaw's tourist-infested **Old Town**, the south end hides the quiet **Solec District** and massive **Łazienki Park**, and sandwiched in-between is the **Powisle District** (Student District), which houses Warsaw's best coffee shops and finest street food. Moving west from Powisle, you'll arrive upon the monument-laden **Royal Mile**, and moving even farther west brings you to the **Palace of Culture and Science**, announcing your entrance into metropolitan Warsaw. Here, walk north-south down **Marszałkowska Street** for a brisk tour of Warsaw's best shopping and dining, the **Vegan District** just southeast of the PCS, the culinary commons of **Plac Zbawiciela** at the southern end, and the most fashionable hangout in Warsaw along **Chmielna Ul.** just across from the PCS's east side. And if you're like Arya and left wondering what's west of west(eros) Warsaw, the answer is even more downtown—many of the city's best museums are inconveniently located in the **Western Downtown** area we'd wager is responsible for all the sores on our feet.

ESSENTIALS

GETTING THERE

If opting for public transportation from Chopin Airport Terminal A, take the SKM S2 train to the Śródmieście station and the S3 to Warszawa Centralna station (single-trip public transport tickets 4.40zł). From the budget airline-friendly Warsaw-Modlin Airport, take one of the green or yellow shuttles to Modlin Train Station, from which trains run into Warszawa Centralna Station. Some budget airlines from other European countries do, in fact, fly into Chopin Airport instead of Warsaw-Modlin, and that taxis from both of these airports into Warsaw are easily available at the airport and cost no more than 50zł. If you're traveling by train, you'll likely disembark at Centralna as well. A bus journey to Warsaw will drop you off at the main bus station along Aleje Jerozolimskie.

GETTING AROUND

The public transportation system consists of trams, buses, and two metro lines running north-south (blue line M1) and east-west (red line M2). A night bus runs 11pm-5am, and the metro runs from 5am-11pm on weekdays and until 3am on Friday and Saturday. Public transport tickets (single ride 4.40zł) are valid for all three modes of transportation, and can be purchased from green and yellow kiosks or anywhere with a "Bilety" ("Ticket") sign. Unless you're travelling to the outskirts of Warsaw, you'll only need a Zone 1 ticket, which includes the Chopin Airport. 24hr (15zł), 72hr (36zł), and weekend (24zł) tickets are also available. You cannot board the metro without validating your ticket, but you can board the tram or bus without doing so. If a plainclothes police officer catches you without a validated ticket you will be fined 266zł.

PRACTICAL INFORMATION

Tourist Offices: The central tourist information center is Warsaw Tourist Information Center, located in the Old Town (Plac Zamkowy 1/13; 22 635 18 81; www.wcit.waw.pl; open M-F 9am-7pm, Sa-Su 10am-6pm).

Banks/ATMs/Currency Exchange: ATMs are found throughout the city at most banks and by the arrival terminal at the airport. Avoid kantors with English signs and those in more touristy areas. A central Euronet ATM (Ul. Sienna 39; 22 519 77 71; open M-F 7am-7pm, Sa-Su 24hr).

Post Offices: The Polish post office Poczta Polska has a central location in the Palace of Culture and Science (Metro Centrum; 22 620 19 43; www.poczta-polska.pl; open M-F 8am-8pm).

Public Restrooms: Public restrooms aren't extremely common in the downtown area, however they are available in the Palace of Culture and Science's eastern lobby, most cafés, and in some underground street crossings (Stacja Metra Centrum Al.

Jerozolimskie; open daily 6am-10pm).
Internet: Most cafés, restaurants, and fast food restaurants have free public Wi-Fi available. The website wifispc.com/poland/mazowieckie/warsaw provides a map of all the available Wi-Fi hotspots in the city.
BGLTQ+ Resources: Though Poland's government doesn't offer many legal rights and protections for the BGLTQ+ community, Warsaw is generally considered a BGLTQ+ friendly city. Poland-wide BGLTQ+ helpline Lambda Warszawa is listed here. (22 628 52 22; www.lambdawarszawa.org; open M, W, Th 6pm-10pm, Tu-F 6pm-9pm).

EMERGENCY INFORMATION

Emergency Number: 112; Poland Tourist Emergency Hotline (22 278 77 77 and 608 599 999; open daily 8am-6pm, June-Sept 8am-10pm).
Police: Police in Warsaw can generally be trusted and demonstrate a reliable presence throughout the downtown area. The General Police Headquarters of Poland is listed here. (Puławska 148/150; 22 621 02 51; www.policja.pl; open daily 24hr).
US Embassy: The US Embassy in Warsaw is located at the northwest corner of Łazienki Park. (Al. Ujazdowskie 29/31; 22 504 20 00; www.pl.usembassy.gov/pl; open M-F 8:30am-5pm).
Rape Crisis Center: Based in Warsaw, the Feminoteka Foundation provides a helpline for female victims of any kind of physical violence (ul. Mokotowska 29a; 572 670 874; feminoteka.pl; open Tu-Th 1pm-7pm).
Hospitals: Warsaw has a fair number of hospitals sprinkled throughout the city center. Unfortunately, many aren't open on Sunday, and the exceptions are located farther from the downtown area and tend to be smaller, less mainstream medical institutions. Because of this, two non-24hr hospitals are listed below.

- CM Lux Med: Al. Jerozolimskie 65/79; 22 332 28 88; www.luxmed.pl; open M-F 7am-8pm, Sa 8am-4pm.
- Damian Medical Center: Foksal 3/5; 22 566 22 53; www.damian.pl/ul-foksal; open M-F 7:30am-8pm, Sa 8am-3pm.

Pharmacies: Pharmacies are identifiable by the green cross on or protruding from their facade. They are called "aptekas" in Polish.

- Apteka Mirowskwa: Pl. Mirowski 1; 22 620 02 66; open daily 24hr.
- Apteka Farm-Jed: Świętokrzyska 20; 22 827 62 86; www.aptekawaw.pl; open M-F 8am-9pm, Sa 9am-4pm.

SIGHTS

CULTURE

CHOPIN CONCERTS IN ŁAZIENKI PARK

Chopin Statue in Łazienki Park; 22 506 00 24; www.lazienki-krolewskie.pl; summer concerts Su at noon and 4pm

Whether you're an impoverished pianist seeking inspiration from an ancient master or a laymen who's never even tickled the ivories, you'll find something to love on this Sunday's concert at Łazienki Park. If you're fashionable, come equipped with an umbrella, fan, gloves, and glasses to boot, but if you're like the rest of us a nice blanket and hat will do just fine. And hell, in a setting this idyllic—a secret garden in the middle of Warsaw's largest park complete with a pond and statue of the master himself—we'll understand if you make like Ferris Bueller and glaze over at the sight of *A Sunday Afternoon.* But if you're interested in grabbing yourself a good spot in the picture, join the party 20 minutes early.

i Free; wheelchair accessible

KOLO BAZAAR

Obozowa 99; 22 836 23 51; open daily 7am-2pm

Like if SkyMag came to life, if Hoarding: Buried Alive was based out of a parking lot in northwest Warsaw, if Captain Hook's booty was sold from the back of outdated cars for less than 10zł, cash only please—the Kolo Bazaar, eighth Wonder of the World, Island of Misfit Toys, Grand Repository and Material Purgatory brings you the world's rare and forgotten curios. Populated with 70-80 merchants whose livelihood is collecting and selling the material memory of Polish past, this flea market sells everything from first edition printings of *Harry Potter* to golden candlesticks to Polish vintage records. The Bazaar's proximity to **Fort Bema** also makes it perfect for a duel purpose trip from the city center.

i Free; cash only; wheelchair accessible

PRAGA AND SOUTH PRAGA DISTRICTS

East of Vistula River; open daily 24hr

If downtown Warsaw is Polish life unfiltered, then Praga and South Praga are the most plain and simple you can get. Make the journey few tourists ever do and cross a bridge over the Vistula River to visit Warsaw's residential side. To hear the locals tell it, South Praga's **Park Skaryszewski** is something special, probably for its waterside bars, restaurants, and complete lack of tourists. And check out the Soho district just northeast of the park—home to modern art event center **Soho Factory,** the **Neon Museum,** and just generally the grungiest, frou-frouiest section of Warsaw. When you're done discovering your spirit animal, soak in the everyday scenery on a walk north to Praga, punctuated by more strawberry stands and farmers' markets than anyone could count. If by then you're really feeling the local vibes, maybe hop in on a game of soccer with the Polish bros just across from **The Cathedral of St. Mary** and the **Warsaw Zoo.**

i Free; wheelchair accessibility varies; check Soho Factory events at www.soho-facory.pl

LANDMARKS

PALACE OF CULTURE AND SCIENCE

Plac Defilad 1; 22 656 76 00; pkin.pl; observation deck open daily from 10am-8pm

You may not know this, but in 1951 the Soviet Union was just like that weird kid in elementary school who would always "gift" the teacher with all the dead crickets he found during recess. "Feeling cute," the Soviet Union said, "Might invade Poland later." "Uh, thanks, but no thanks," Poland collectively seethed as the Soviet Union "gifted" them Warsaw's central-most building and a communist regime. No biggie. So yeah, the Palace of Culture and Science still stands as the tallest building in all of Poland and still wins the annual award for the most befuddlingly beautiful concrete monstrosity the world has ever seen. It houses educational institutes, tons of museums, over 100 companies, and the observation deck gives a sick view of Warsaw.

i Admission to observation deck 20zł, reduced 15zł; wheelchair accessible

ROYAL CASTLE

Plac Zamkowy 4; 22 35 55 264; www.zamek-krolewski.pl; open Tu-Th 10am-6pm, F 10am-8pm, Sa 10am-6pm, Su 11am-6pm

Neuschwanstein? Neusch-van-stop-it. Edinburgh Castle? Edinboring. Poland prefers the simpler things, and that's why Warsaw's Royal Castle only has one massive ballroom with only 20 crystal chandeliers. Those other castles are just way too showy, aren't they? Besides being the historic seat of Polish kings and their lady-loves, the Royal Castle now houses one of Poland's foremost art collections, straight from the personal royal collection dating back to 1815—perfect for bragging to all your friends who opted for the Louvre that you saw not one, but two Rembrandts, so who's cool now? Along with 85 percent of Warsaw, the castle was tragically burned in WWII and rebuilt after a public funding campaign in 1980. And in the spirit of rebuilding, one of the castles

most dazzling rooms—the Canaletto Room—displays many of the historic paintings of Warsaw used to rebuild the city after its destruction, offering a pretty meta-take on the same-old same-old art museum idea.

Admission 30zł, 20zł reduced; last entry 1hr before closing; wheelchair accessible

MUSEUMS

CSW ZAMEK UJAZDOWSKI

Jazdów 2; 22 628 12 71; www.u-jazdowski.pl; open Tu-W 11am-6pm, Th-F noon-8pm, Sa 10am-7pm, Su 11am-6pm

The CSW is to modern art museums as the Protestant Reformation was to the Christian church—both flip vague, relatively inaccessible institutions on their heads and actively encourage people to get engaged with previously incomprehensible material. The CSW even hands out its own sort-of-Bible, an indispensable guide to the museum's artists, works, and organization that will welcome even the most inexperienced artistic layman into the modern art community's admittedly twisted folds. With three rotating exhibitions housed in one of **Łazienki Park's** castles, the main course is always fresh and always variable—expect art covering anything from the rampant dehumanization of corporate capitalism to a "Touch the Art" exhibit that invites audience participation at every level.

Admission 16zł, 8zł reduced; wheelchair accessible

POLIN MUSEUM OF THE HISTORY OF THE POLISH JEWS

Anielewicza 6; 48 22 47 10 300; www.polin.pl; open M 10am-6pm, W 10am-8pm, F 10am-6pm, Sa-Su 10am-8pm

Don't be afraid to scrutinize the scope of this museum's name. It doesn't actually cover the entire history of the Polish Jews. No, this museum manages to unflinchingly cover the entire history of European Jews. And if that didn't knock your socks off, it does so with inimitable flair—betting all in on the immersion game and completely recreating every environment European Jews encountered in the last 1000 years, from medieval Spain to Industrial Poland to a fifteenth-century arabesque synagogue. But prepare your emotions, because about 40 percent of this massive museum does narrow in and focus on the Polish experience of the Holocaust. Through minimalist presentation and an extremely potent reliance on horrifying anecdotes and primary sources, this museum manages to recreate every grain of terror and ensure that you leave its halls not only wiser, but just a bit more sensitive to one of the greatest tragedies of our time.

Admission 25zł, reduced 15zł; last entry 2hr before closing; wheelchair accessible; plan 2hrs-4hrs for the museum

OUTDOORS

VISTULA RIVER WALKING PATHS

Along Vistula River's west bank between Śląsko-Dąbrowski Bridge and Poniatowski Bridge; open daily 24hr, riverside bars generally open M-Su 11am-midnight, Museum of Modern Art open Tu-F noon-8pm, Sa 11am-8pm, Su 11am-6pm, Copernicus Science Centre open M-F 8am-6pm, Sa-Su 10am-7pm

Following the tradition of every riverside city to come before it, Warsaw just recently completed an expansive series of walking and biking paths, artificial beaches, parks, bars, and restaurants along the **Vistula River's** west bank. And without much hesitation, we'd argue that this riverside delight puts its Budapesti, Chicagoan, and Bostonian peers to shame. Over a mile long, the paths not only offer incredible nightly street food festivals

and on-the-water bars like Plac Zabaw and BarKa, but also offer cultured breaks from the hard work of walking at stops like the **Museum of Modern Art** and the **Copernicus Science Centre**.
i Free, wheelchair accessible

WARSAW UNIVERSITY LIBRARY

Dobra 56/66; 22 552 51 78; www.buw.uw.edu.pl; open M-F 8am-9pm, Sa 9am-9pm, Su 3pm-8pm

Go ahead and leave your classical columned conception of the great libraries behind. Rather than cribbing the ancient Greeks' style, Warsaw University Library opts for a more modern take on the whole "library" thing—leaping right out from the pages of your favorite post-apocalyptic novel, belonging to a world that has left humans behind, where nature has overtaken all of our final memories and monuments. That is to say, the WUL is not just a library. It's a three-tiered overgrown botanic garden spread across the library's courtyard, roof, and observation deck. Explore the creeks, fountains, and vine-covered staircases in this *Alice in Wonderland* meets *The Last of Us* mashup, but don't get too ambitious and try to test out your Polish skills on any of the books inside—unfortunately, a student ID is needed to access the actual library, but you can go check out the stunning main hall.
i Free; limited wheelchair accessibility

FOOD

CAFFE KAFKA ($)

Oboźna 3; 22 826 08 22; www.kawiarnia-kafka.pl; open M-F 9am-10pm, Sa-Su 10am-10pm

On the outside, Caffe Kafka may just look like your everyday coffee shop planted squarely within reach of the local university's caffeine-dependent zombies. But look again: this café is built into the side of a hill with age-old ruins literally at its doorstep. It sports an extensive patio and outdoor lounge area with direct-to-table-or-lounge-chair service. And just like your mom always told you, it's really what's on the inside that counts, which just so happens to be a healthy portion of local art, Polish board games, sofas, tables, and a wall-to-wall bookshelf. Not only is Kafka the comfiest place to take a break in Warsaw, but its food is straight-up killing the traditional Polish game—from classic Polish soups to stellar sweet and savory Polish pancakes.
i Entrées from 12zł, coffee from 6zł; vegetarian options available; wheelchair accessible

EDAMAME VEGAN SUSHI ($)

Wilcza 11; 790 633 122; open Tu-Th noon-9pm, F-Sa noon-10pm, Su noon-8pm

Edamame Vegan Sushi is the nexus of three major movements in the Varsovian food world: the expansion of Polish cuisine into international corners, the influence of Warsaw's Chinese and Vietnamese population on the nation's nosh, and the unstoppable movement toward Universal Varsovian Veganism. As such, Edamame is less of a place at which you can experience mind-bendingly creative sushi filled with everything from tofu to mushrooms to tempeh, but is actually more of a cultural necessity—not to mention they're actually crafting Warsaw's culture by curating a rotating menu of experimental vegan sushi on the daily. It's not uncommon to hear Edamame thrown around casually as the best sushi the city has to offer, and with a literal help from Polish cooks trained in the ways of the quasi-religious roll, we're confident you'll feel the green seaweed, purple rice, and golden tempura love.
i Entrées from 12zł, beer from 15zł; only vegan and gluten-free options available as well; wheelchair accessible

KROWARZYA VEGAN BURGER ($)

Marszałkowska 27/35; 881 777 894; www.krowarzywa.pl; open daily 11am-11pm

"To infinity, and Beyond Burger!," thousands of Varsovian vegans shouted in triumph as they opened Krowarzya Vegan Burger—a quaint little joint specializing in the meat-imitation burger patty the "Beyond Burger." They knew that creating an all-veggie burger paradise that treats flavor combinations like a certified four-year graduated mixologist would be a total win. So for all you cutecumbers who think vegan food is just one giant missed-steak, lettuce direct you to the restaurant that was the veganning of Warsaw's entire vibrant vegan scene. Sit back, relax, and enjoy the lentil things as Krowarzya's smoothies, slaw, and Polish pop wash over your burger-laden belly, digesting what will undoubtedly end up a revolutionary piece of Polish culinary history.

i Burgers from 14.50zł; only vegan options available, all options gluten-free; wheelchair accessible

ZAKLAD MIESNEY WILENSKA 25 ($$)

Wileńska 25; 690 944 944; www.zmw25.pl; open Su-Th 2pm-midnight, F-Sa 2pm-3am

While **Krowarzya** is symphony of veggie-fueled flavor, Zaklad Miesney is a freshly cut still-bleeding masterpiece. Lace up your hiking boots and don your bucket hat because Zaklad is buried deep in the residential **Praga District**. And don't make the mistake of thinking the fun stops with Zaklad's euphoric burgers—their bar and nightlife scene is accented by the most eclectic, bric-á-brac setting we could find. Basically, imagine Banksy opened a restaurant and populated its walls with everything from neon lights to graffiti paintings of cavemen and *Mona Lisa* with a rocket launcher. Then, throw in bloody butcher-ware hanging from the ceiling, high-top seating in the middle of the room, and plenty of lounge space to boot and you've got yourself the spaced out kookoo for cocoa puffs craziness that is Zaklad Mieseney.

i Burgers from 29zł; limited wheelchair accessibility

NIGHTLIFE

PAWILONY NOWY SWIAT (NEW WORLD PAVILION)

Nowy Świat 22-28; 22 826 53 51; www.pawilonynowyswiat.pl; open daily 24hr

Poland is inexplicably obsessed with only three things: dumplings, beets, and collections of bars housed under one roof. Okay, so maybe the third thing isn't too hard to explain—while **Hala Koszyki** brings you a streamlined, bougie beer market, Pawilony Nowy is the hidden local hangout you didn't even know you needed. Rather inconspicuously located on the Royal Mile, just follow the street musicians and you'll arrive at the over 20 bars, 5 restaurants, and a hubba-hubba hookah den that is the old abandoned parking-lot-turned-monument to the confusing Pawilony Nowy. It's plain and simple: if you've ever wanted to be packed in like a sardine in one of the most eclectic settings around, welcome to Pawilony Nowy, where Billy Ray Cyrus, ACDC, and Pawel the drunk street guitarist will score the rhythm of your night with glee.

i Free; limited wheelchair accessibility

PIWPAW BEER HEAVEN

Foksal 16;534 734 945; www.piwpaw.pl; open M-W noon-11pm, Th-Sa noon-midnight, Su noon-11pm

When the owners of PiwPaw Beer Heaven first heard that an American rock band built a city on rock and roll, they took it as a personal challenge to somehow construct an entire two-story bar from discarded bottle caps and neon signs. After accomplishing that unlikely feat, they heard a rumor that some Islamic sects were promising 72 virgins in the afterlife. Not wanting to be outdone, the owners of ol' PiwPaw stocked their bottle cap bar with 79 local-fueled beer taps. Even though PiwPaw is hidden without any kind of sign in the first story of an apartment building near **Ulica Chmielna,** it receives all the local attention it could ever want. When a nearby ice cream store organized its flavors in a rainbow array, PiwPaw's owners accepted the challenge and organized their 79 beer taps on the official Beer Tap Spectrum™, listed as fruity/sweet/sour/pale/lager/IPA/stout just to make sure they hit everybody's taste.

i Beer from 10zł, pizza from 28zł; no wheelchair accessibility; Wi-Fi

POLAND ESSENTIALS

VISAS

Poland is a member of the European, and the Schengen area. Citizens from Australia, Canada, New Zealand, the US, and many other non-EU countries do not require a visa for stays up to 90 days. However, if you plan to spend time in other Schengen countries, note that the 90-day period applies to all Schengen countries.

MONEY

Poland uses the złoty (zł or zł, abbreviated). Currency exchanges are known as "kantors," and those with signs in English, often located in airports or tourists' areas of interests within cities should be avoided. The best are those that advertise "buy" and "sell" rates, which let you calculate exactly how much you will receive. To find out what out-of-network or international fees your credit or debit cards may be subjected to, call your bank. In the case you need to make a withdrawal from your bank account, Polish cities always stock a healthy amount of Euronet ATMs, a reliable ATM service throughout central Europe.

Tipping: In restaurants, tips are not included in the bill, so it's customary to tip 10% or 15% for exceptional service. Be careful with saying "thank you" to your server when they collect the bill, as it means you don't want any change back. In taxis tipping is not expected, but you can tip 10% for good service. Tips of 10% are usually also expected for museum tour guides as well.

SAFETY AND HEALTH

Drugs and Alcohol: The minimum age to purchase alcohol is 18. The legal blood alcohol content (BAC) for driving is under 0.02%, which is significantly lower than the US limit of 0.08%. The possession of any quantity of drugs, including marijuana, can be penalized with up to three-years imprisonment.

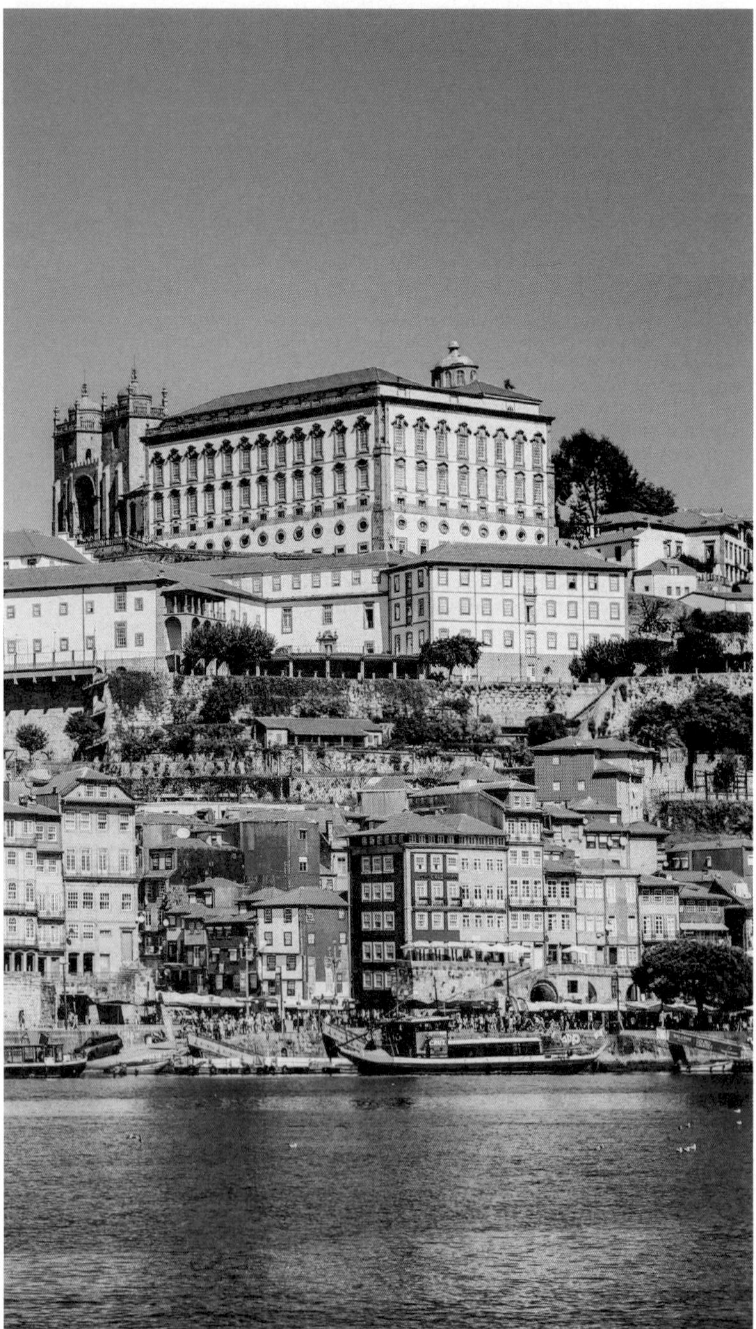

PORTUGAL

Although it's not even half the size of Idaho, Portugal crams thousands of years of rich history—from the Celts to the Romans to the Moors—into its 500-mile sliver of paradise on the westernmost edge of Europe. Medieval cathedrals rub shoulders with Islamic architecture and Roman ruins crumble beneath Neoclassical palaces, all scattered along the country's craggy coastlines and otherworldly forests. Less clogged by tourists than its Spanish neighbor—and really all of Western Europe—Portugal is the unsung hero of the Iberian Peninsula, a budget traveler's dream.

Lisbon and Porto stand out as the country's self-confident cultural capitals, but every region of Portugal has its own special charms. Bask in the somber fado music of the capital, revel in the legendary Lagos nightlife, and soak in the colorful turrets of Sintra's epic hillside palace. Wherever you find yourself in Portugal, the country's saltwater cuisine will be waiting—salt cod, fried eel soup, seafood stew, and the ubiquitous can of sardines will follow you everywhere. Of course, there are other options like Porto's infamous francesinha (a "sandwich" with half a dozen kinds of meat, cheese, and an egg, all drenched in a gravy-like sauce) and Lisbon's high-demand pastéis de nata (mini egg custards). Just remember to wash it all down with a glass of the Douro's silky port wine. With a full belly and happy heart, find yourself a romantic miradouro (viewpoint) and allow yourself to be enveloped by the plucky, glamorous, irresistible heart of Portugal.

CASCAIS

Coverage by **Joseph Winters**

Leave it to the king to spoil a perfectly good secluded summer getaway. In the early nineteenth century, Cascais was a rural fishing village with rugged character, wild and scenic beaches, and lots of local commerce. Then, when King Luís I decided to make the city his summer hideaway, outfitting the village with opulent mansions and luxurious gardens, Portuguese nobility—and later, mere mortals—began flocking to the city in the hopes of finding their own slice of "the king's beach." Cascais remains one of the most popular destinations for Lisbon daytrippers, who descend upon the city to sunbathe, inhale the sea breeze, and slurp up dozens of açaí bowls (we counted at least six açaí joints within a minute of each other). Visitors can spend the day exploring the cozy historic center, sauntering through the peacock-filled Parque de Marechal Carmona and visiting the park's many museums, or biking between far-flung beaches like the Praia do Guincho. The combination of history, fantastic infrastructure, and nature make Cascais an obligatory stop for tourists looking for something a bit more laid-back than the bustle of cosmopolitan Lisbon.

ORIENTATION

From the Cascais train station, it's a short walk southwest towards the beach to arrive in the historic city center. En route to the ocean, you'll pass through the city center, filled with lots of restaurants, souvenir shops, and many an option for accommodations. Along the water is an esplanade that wraps around the coast, all the way west to the scenic **Praia do Guincho** and east towards Lisbon, passing through **Estoril** and beyond (a good walking half-daytrip). West of the city center, just above the esplanade and north of the Cascais marina is the **Bairro dos Museus** (museum district) and the **Parque Marechal Carmona,** Cascais' central green space and home to a handful of small museums, including the Museu das Histórias Paula Rego and the Museu do Mar. The central **Pr. 5 de Outubro** (on the Av. Dom Carlos I) is where the **Cascais Visitor Center** is, as well as several late-night dining and drinking options.

ESSENTIALS

GETTING THERE

If arriving from Lisbon, you have several options: train, car, or bus. The easiest way to get to Cascais is via train. Take the metro green line to Cais do Sodré and from there, switch to the rail network (Comboios de Portugal) towards Cascais (40min., €2.50 on a Viva Viagem card—you'll pay €0.50 if you don't already have one). You'll be deposited at the Cascais train station, just northeast of the city center, and a three-minute walk from the historic city center. You can also drive to Cascais—are convenient if you want to tour the remoter regions of the Sintra-Cascais National Park.

GETTING AROUND

Cascais is easily walkable. The train station, the historic city center, an urban park, and several beaches are all located within 10min. of each other. Some of Cascais' most beautiful beaches, however, are up to 8km from downtown—to reach these, it's best to rent a bike or take public transit—look for the #415 or 405 buses from the Cascais bus station to reach the western Praia do Guincho. For the eastern Praia de Carcavelos, take the train headed towards Lisbon and get off at Carcavelos.

PRACTICAL INFORMATION

Tourist Offices: The Cascais Visitor Center has a shop, a ticket office for some surrounding museums, an auditorium for cultural events and presentations, and an interactive table touchpad with information on what to do in and around the city (Pr. 5 de

Outubro; 91 203 42 14; visitcascais.com; open daily May 1-Sept 30 9am-8pm, Oct 1-Apr 30 9am-6pm).

Banks/ATMs/Currency Exchange: ATMs in Cascais are clustered around the main shopping area and along Avenida D. Carlos I. Look for BPI, Millennium BCP, or the handy-dandy Multibanco sign. Millennium BCP Cascais (R. Sebastião José de Carvalho e Melo 6; 21 112 69 90; millenniumbcp.pt; open M-F 8:30am-3:30pm).

Post Offices: Your trusty CTT stop is a short walk north of the beach in a residential neighborhood. There is a smaller location nearer the train station, as well. CTT main branch (Av. Ultramar 2; 21 482 72 81; ctt.pt; open M-F 9am-6pm).

Public Restrooms: Rejoice! Unlike some Portuguese cities, Cascais is replete with bathroom options. Aside from the toilets you'll find in any of the inexpensive museums in the Bairro dos Museus circuit, you'll find a public WC in the shopping complex at the marina, near the Ponta da Bombeira, and on the western outskirts of the Parque Marechal Carmona.

Internet: Cascais generously offers over a dozen Wi-Fi hotspots throughout the city and on several of its beaches. Look for tall poles reading Cascais Wi-Fi. There's a convenient hotspot outside the Museu do Mar and another in the center of the Parque Marechal Carmona.

BGLTQ+ Resources: The nearest BGLTQ+ resource options are in Lisbon. Try ILGA, the city's oldest NGO fighting for equality without regard to sexual identity (R. dos Fanqueiros, 38; 21 887 39 18; ilga-portugal.pt; open M-F 10am-7pm).

EMERGENCY INFORMATION

Emergency Number: 112

Police: In case of an emergency, call the Portuguese emergency number (112) or get in touch with the local PSP. The police office is in the historic downtown, off the main road leading towards the water. Facing the water, look left while on Alameda dos Combatentes da Grande Guerra.

- Tourist square (Largo Mestre Henrique Anjos; 21 481 40 67; www.psp.pt).

US Embassy: The nearest US Embassy is in Lisbon (Av. das Forças Armadas 133C; 21 727 33 00; pt.usembassy.gov; open M-F 8am-5pm).

Rape Crisis Center: The nearest rape crisis center is in Lisbon, a part of APAV, the Portuguese Association for Victim Support.

- GAV Oeiras (Esquadra de Oeiras da PSP, R. do Espargal 18; 21 454 02 57; apav.pt; open M-F 10am-6pm).

Hospitals: The closest large hospital is CUF Cascais, but a taxi ride to the more popular Hospital de Cascais Dr. José de Almeida might be worth the trouble.

- Hospital de Cascais (Dr. José de Almeida: Estr. Militar, Alcabideche; 21 465 30 00; www.hospitaldecascais.pt; open daily 24hr).
- CUF Hospital Cascais (R. Fernão Lopes 60; 21 114 14 00; www.saudecuf.pt; open daily 24hr).

Pharmacies: There is a 24hr pharmacy just west of the train station on the highway leading to the waterfront. Other than that, the historic city center is home to a number of smaller pharmacies offering daytime services.

- Farmácia Marginal Lda. (Pr. Dr. Francisco Sá Corneiro 1; 21 484 94 40; www.farmaciamarginal.pt; open daily 24hr).
- Farmácia da Misericórdia de Cascais (R. Regimento 19 de Infantaria 67; 21 483 01 41; www.scmc.pt; open M-Sa 9am-7pm).

SIGHTS

CULTURE

CIDADELA ARTS DISTRICT

Av. Dom Carlos I; 21 481 43 00; www.cidadelaartdistrict.com/#cad; establishment hours vary

Part hotel, part ancient military stronghold, and part arts collective, the Cidadela Arts District is a little hard to figure out. As of 2014, the space—found in the courtyard of an ancient citadel—has sought to introduce art into the everyday. Surrounding the courtyard are several galleries, an art magazine's office and first showing room, and even a Portuguese pencil producer. Upstairs, visitors can glimpse the artistic process in one of many open studios. There's also an excellent used bookstore above one of the Arts District's restaurants, which has a surprisingly solid collection of English books in addition their Portuguese collection.

i Prices vary; limited wheelchair accessibility

MERCADO DA VILA (VILLAGE MARKET)

R. Padre Moisés da Silva, 29; 21 482 50 00; www.cascais.pt; open daily 6:30am-midnight; fish and meat market open Tu 8am-2pm, W 6:30am-3pm, Th-F 8am-2pm, Sa 6:30am-3pm, Su 8am-2pm; flowers, fruits, and vegetables market open Tu 8am-4pm, W 6:30am-3pm, Th-F 8am-4pm, Sa 6:30am-3pm, Su 8am-4pm; mercado saloio (traditional market) open W-Sa 6:30am-2pm

This multi-purpose space west of the train station showcases the best of Cascais, from the fishermen's daily catch to fine dining. An enormous covered plaza is flanked by butchers, vegetable farmers, bakeries, and florists, and the adjacent open-air plaza houses a collection of casual restaurants and bars. The diversity of offerings means there's always something going on at the Mercado da Vila, from early morning to late(ish) at night. Check the market schedule for the best days to visit, as well as the monthly theme; in the summer, they've held special markets centered around chocolate, sardines, and even craft beer.

i Prices vary; wheelchair accessible

LANDMARKS

BOCA DO INFERNO (HELL'S MOUTH)

Av. Rei Humberto II de Itália, 642; open daily 24hr

"Hell's Mouth" may be a bit overkill, but this natural rock formation just over a kilometer away from the center of Cascais is an impressive sight. It's an outcropping of an arch carved from rock, formed by eons of waves crashing against the cliff. Summer visitors will see the water gently lapping at the opening, but winter storms unleash a fearsome force through the arch, launching powerful waves high into the air. Thankfully, modern visitors can enjoy the waves from the shelter of a classy restaurant, or at least from high above from a protected walkway. Fun fact: in 1930, a magician named Aleister Crowley faked his death at the Boca do Inferno, only to reappear three weeks later at an magic exhibition in Berlin.

i Free; limited wheelchair accessibility

MUSEU CONDES DE CASTRO GUIMARÃES (CONDES DE CASTRO GUIMARÃES MUSEUM)

Av. Rei Humberto II de Itália, Parque Marechal Carmona; 21 481 53 04; www.cascais.pt; open T-Su 10am-1pm and 2pm-5pm

As if the count couldn't make up his mind on a single style, Castro Guimarães included architectural influences from across the spectrum in his fanciful nineteenth-century mansion: Byzantine domes, Manueline arcades, Italian verandas, Indo-Portuguese cabinets, some Gothic inspiration, and a room painted with shamrocks just for good measure (actually by request from the original Irish owner). Found near the southern edge of the **Parque Marechal Carmona,** the Museu Condes de Castro Guimarães is less a museum and more of an open window into the life of some of the earliest elites to erect lavish vacation homes in Cascais. Be sure to check out the turret room, which holds a host of archaic weaponry, including a very rusty combat sword from the fifteenth century.

i Admission €4, €2 reduced; pre-book tours by phone (groups only); limited wheelchair accessibility; part of the Bairro dos Museus circuit (day pass €13, 3-day pass €19)

MUSEUMS

MUSEU DAS ARTES PAULA REGO (PAULA REGO ART MUSEUM)

Av. da República, 300; 21 482 69 70; casadashistoriaspaularego.com; open Tu-Su 10am-6pm

Housed in a building designed by Pritzker Prize-winning architect **Eduardo Souto de Moura,** this art museum in the heart of Cascais' **Bairro dos Museus** (Neighborhood of Museums) showcases the life's work of **artist Paula Rego.** Born in Lisbon in 1935, Rego has been showered with a multitude of decorations, including honorary doctorate degrees from eight universities like RISD and Oxford, as well as awards from the Queen of

England and the President of Portugal. With a collection of over 500 paintings, etchings, and drawings, the Museu das Artes Paula Rego showcases the artist's passion for Portuguese culture, storytelling, and reinterpreting history through art. The engravings are especially impressive, with three-dimensionality that borders on lifelike.

Admission €5, €2.50 reduced; last entry 5:30pm; limited wheelchair accessibility

MUSEU DO MAR REI D. CARLOS (KING D. CARLOS OCEANIC MUSEUM)

R. Júlio Pereira de Mello; 21 481 59 06; www.cascais.pt; open Tu-F 10am-5pm, Sa-Su 10am-1pm and 2pm-5pm

Long before it was a hip summer residence for Portuguese royalty, Cascais had a history intertwined with the sea. The Museu do Mar digs way back into this background, combining oceanic natural history with firsthand portraits of fishermen who helped build Cascais. Named in honor of D. Carlos I, who was himself an avid fisherman and admirer of the sea, the small museum includes a diverse array of water-themed exhibitions. There's a History of the Ocean room with stuffed seabirds and the 15-foot-long jaw bone of a fin whale, a Seafaring and Navigation collection with scale models of eighteenth-century fishing vessels, and a room dedicated to D. Carlos that features a frightening—but aptly-named—goblinfish.

Admission €3, €1.50 reduced; pre-booked tours only; wheelchair accessible

OUTDOORS

PRAIA DO GUINCHO (GUINCHO BEACH)

Parque Natural Sintra-Cascais; www.cascais.pt; open daily 24hr

Full of thrashing waves, strong winds, and jagged rocks, the Praia do Guincho isn't exactly a tranquil sunbathers' beach. In its heyday, this remote strip of sand was the host of the World Surfing Championships; most of its current visitors come with long hair and wetsuits, their surfboards under one arm, ready to ride some waves, bro. Grab a board for yourself, or enjoy the entertainment as newbies try (unsuccessfully) to find their balance. To get there, we highly recommend biking; there's a single-use bike lane the whole 8km between Cascais and Praia do Guincho, and the views along the way may be even more breathtaking than the beach itself. Sign up online for MobiCascais (€4/day) or try one of the city's rental services (usually €10/day). The #405 or 415 bus from Cascais also makes frequent trips to Praia do Guincho (€1).

Free; no wheelchair accessibility

PARQUE MARECHAL CARMONA (MARECHAL CARMONA PARK)

Av. Rei Humberto II; www.cascais.pt; open daily Nov-Mar 8:30am-5:45pm, open daily Apr-Oct 8:30am-7:45pm

Watch your feet—you'll find roosters and peacocks while wandering through Cascais' central public park. Since the sixteenth century, the grounds currently making up the Parque Marechal Carmona have passed through many wealthy hands, with each owner adding additional flourishes of romanticism to the space. Today, the park has rose gardens, children's play areas, a duck pond, and half a dozen museums (part of the **Bairro dos Museus** network of Cascais museums). If you're lucky, you may get to watch a traditional round of *petanca* or *chinquilho* in an area reserved specifically for these games. On Saturday mornings, the Parque Marechal Carmona hosts an organic farmer's market (8am-2pm).

Free; limited wheelchair accessibility

FOOD

CAFÉ GALERIA HOUSE OF WONDERS ($$)

Largo da Misericordia, 53; 91 170 24 28; open daily 8am-10pm

We usually don't use words like "crave-worthy" or "creative" or even "good" to describe buffet dinners, but Cascais' House of Wonders is all that and more: their spread of vegetable-heavy sides (roasted sweet potato salad, smoky mushroom pilaf, pomegranate baba ghanouj) and seasonal mains (eggplant curry, sweet potato falafel) may make for your best meal in Portugal—for under €15 (€9.75 if you go for lunch). The "Café Galeria" takes has four dining spaces within two adjacent buildings (rooftop terrace, café, buffet room, and an additional sit-down dining room), each decorated with bulk pots of herbs and spices and handwritten messages. "All about sharing and tasting," reads one sign near the buffet. In a country where salad usually means dry lettuce (sometimes with a tomato slice!), House of Wonders is an beacon of hope for foodies everywhere. Pro tip: get yourself a plate of the silky-smooth hummus, served with *chapati,* baked in-house daily.

i Entrées from €9.75 (café) or €14.75 (restaurant); gluten-free, vegan, and vegetarian options available; limited wheelchair accessibility

APEADEIRO ($$)

Av. Vasco da Gama, 252; 21 483 27 31; open Tu-Sa noon-3pm and 7pm-10pm, Su noon-3pm

For quality seafood in Cascais, you'll (ironically) want to stay as far away from the beach as possible—there, you'll find restaurants with breathtaking terraces and menus flawlessly translated into half a dozen languages, but you won't find a lot of authentic Cascais spirit. Only at Apeadeiro, hidden a few blocks from the city center, can you order traditional Portuguese dishes like "typical cod stile" or grab a squid salad with a side of "straw potatoes." From a seat within this life preserver-lined restaurant, guests can watch fresh seafood being grilled right before their eyes, garnished to perfection with parsley, lemon and garlic.

i Entrées from €12; gluten-free and vegetarian options available; wheelchair accessible

NIGHTLIFE

SPICY LOUNGE

R. Marques Leal Pancada, 16A; 91 630 49 83; open daily 10pm-4am

We're not sure what "#1 Warm-Up Bar" means, but the folks at Spicy Lounge can toot their horn as much as they want, because they've undoubtedly got some of Cascais' best late-night partying. From their small space below a pizzeria, Spicy Lounge puts on loud and sweaty dance parties, featuring local artists and DJ sets, while they serve up a flaming hot selection of craft beers and cocktails (some of which are literally on fire). Check their Facebook page to see when they're hosting their Suruba Music night, a monthly jam session, open to all interested artists.

i No cover, drinks from €4; limited wheelchair accessibility

CROW BAR

Trav. da Misericórdia, 1; 21 403 91 64; open Tu-Su 2:30pm-2am

Though nightlife in Cascais is bizarrely dominated by Irish pubs, Crow Bar stolidly holds its ground as a pure metal and rock n' roll bar—no funny business (or shamrocks) allowed. A sign above the bar informs visitors that music requests aren't accepted, "but if you insist, €2 metal, €50 pop, and €100 all the other crap." The menu is similarly intense, including selections like the Valhalla Painkiller (jaeger, fireball, mead) or the Crow Bar Acid Trip (jaeger and pineapple juice), although they may be best known for their comparatively tame espresso martinis. Best plan of action: take whatever the bartender recommends and drink up, no questions asked. And remember to leave a tip; the bartender apparently needs a new tattoo.

i No cover, cocktails from €5; limited wheelchair accessibility

LAGOS

Coverage by **Joseph Winters**

Despite its reputation for raucous nightlife and alluring beaches, Lagos has a lot of important, but easily-overlooked history. Beginning with the Carthaginians, Lagos fell into Roman hands, then to Visigoths, Byzantines, Moors, the Spanish, and finally back to the Portuguese in the 1600s. In its glory days, Lagos was a powerhouse of European trade, though somewhat problematically; the city was home to colonial Europe's very first slave market, found in the downtown Praça do Infante Dom Henrique. The building now houses a museum acknowledging this unfortunate history. In 1755, a massive earthquake and tsunami leveled most of Lagos, so most of what you'll see downtown has been reconstructed since then. But that doesn't make Lagos's architecture any less impressive; there's Baroque architecture, cobblestone streets, and zigzagging alleyways galore.

Perhaps the most exciting part of Lagos lies outside its ancient walls; several of Lagos beaches are world-famous for their crystal waters and natural rock formations. No visit would be complete without taking a walk along the Avenida dos Descobrimentos to the string of beaches starting with the Praia da Batata and culminating in the breathtaking Ponta da Piedade. This sheltered collection of underwater grottos and hidden caves is Lagos's crown jewel, and 40+ tour companies (who, like predatory animals, lie in wait for unwitting tourists as they disembark the regional train) suck in umpteen thousand tourists here annually. Even still, this is required sightseeing—you'll thank yourself when friends at home ask which edition of *National Geographic* your travel photos are from.

ORIENTATION

Walking westward along the beachside **Avenida dos Descobrimentos,** Lagos's largest road, you'll pass the bus terminal and eventually arrive at the **Praça Gil Eanes**. This is the Times Square of Lagos, full of high-end shopping, restaurants, and cafés. From here, sidestreets branch off in every direction, many of which are pedestrian-only, leading to yet more shopping and dining opportunities. A bit further along the Avenida dos Descobrimentos puts you at the **Praça do Infante Dom Henrique**, home to the **Igreja Santa Maria** and the **Mercado de Escravos**, Europe's oldest slave market. Just up the hill from here is Lagos's nightlife neighborhood, roughly along the **Rua Gil Vicente**. Outside the city, continue walking along the Avenida dos Descobrimentos to arrive at Lagos's white sand beaches like the **Praia de Dona Ana** and the **Praia do Camilo.** Eventually the road meets the **Estrada da Ponta da Piedade,** which will lead to—you guessed it—the **Ponta da Piedade,** a group of rock formations along Lagos's coastline—the city's most famous tourist attraction.

ESSENTIALS

GETTING THERE

From the eastern Algarve, trains to Lagos are inexpensive (about €10 from Faro) and reasonably reliable. There are also trains arriving from the north (€24, 5.5hr from Lisbon; €42, 7-8hr from Porto). Surprisingly, fares and travel times by bus from the north are similar, so it really depends on personal preference.

GETTING AROUND

The easiest way to navigate the historic city of Lagos is by foot, although you'll see some bikes wobbling along the uneven streets. If needed, bikes can be rented from many sports shops downtown (try COAST Supply Co. on the R. Cândido dos Reis 58), or you can hire a taxi for around €5 to take you to any of the handful of beaches up to the Ponta da Piedade.

PRACTICAL INFORMATION

Tourist Offices: Praça Gil Eanes (Antigos Paços do Concelho); 28 276 30 31; www.visitalgarve.pt/en).

Banks/ATMs/Currency Exchange: Banks are plentiful in Lagos, and you'd have to try pretty hard to avoid running into an ATM. Here's a convenient location: (Av. dos Descobrimentos 39; 28 277 09 40; bancobpi.pt/particulares; open M-F 8:30am-3pm).

Post Offices: Look for the red and white of CTT in Lagos' cultural center, surrounded by patches of greenery and public fountains. CTT (R. da Porta de Portugal 25; 28 277 02 51; ctt.pt; open M-F 9am-6pm).

Public Restrooms: In Lagos? A pipe dream. Your best bet is to give in and buy an Americano somewhere. Almost all cafés and restaurants offer free restrooms for customers.

Internet: There is no public Wi-Fi available in Lagos, but almost all cafés, restaurants, and hostels have their own private networks you can use after buying something.

EMERGENCY INFORMATION

Emergency Number: 112

Police: We've listed two police station locations.

- PSP (Sítio da Horta do Trigo; 28 278 02 40; www.psp.pt).
- GNR (Largo Convento da Glória; 28 277 00 10; gnr.pt).

Hospitals: The Hospital Distrital de Lagos takes up some prime waterfront property at the south end of historic downtown.

- Hospital S.Gonçalo (Av. Dom Sebastião 129; 80 022 44 24; www.hsglagos.pt; open daily 24hr).
- Hospital Distrital de Lagos (R. do Castelo dos Governadores 14; 28 277 01 00; sns.gov.pt; open daily 24hr).

Pharmacies: Check for pharmacies near the Praça Gil Eanes, as well as along the R. Candido dos Reis. Here are a couple 24hr options:

- Farmácia Ribeiro Lopes (R. Garrett 22; 28 276 28 30; farmaciabarral.com/farmacia-ribeiro-lopes; open M-Sa 8:30am-midnight, Su 9am-7pm).

SIGHTS

CULTURE

LAGOS FARMERS MARKET

R. Mercado de Levante 9; open Apr-Oct W 6pm-10pm, Sa 7am-1pm

If you want to see a bit of the real Lagos, head to the Saturday morning market, located in a large warehouse next to the Lagos bus station. Here, farmers and artisans congregate for a few hectic hours of browsing, sampling, and bargaining—it's a foodie's paradise. Among the avocados, mangos, lettuce, onions, and other typical fare, you'll find Algarvian specialties like *nêsperas* (plum-like fruits called "loquats" in English), live snails, roasted figs, fava beans, and much more. Starting in summer 2018, there's a second weekly market on Wednesday evenings, highlighting small producers and specialty farmers. Many vendors are certified *biológico* (organic), and several local vendors showcase products like homemade Echinacea extracts or—our favorite—*kombuchá artesanal.*

i Prices vary; wheelchair accessible

MAR D'ESTÓRIAS (SEA OF STORIES)

R. Silva Lopes 30; 28 279 21 65; www.mardestorias.com; open M-Sa 10am-midnight

"Buy local, buy Portuguese!" reads a sign at the entrance to this three-story treasure trove of Portuguese culture. Instead of the ubiquitous dog tags (unquestionably the worst souvenir known to man), this shop is all about highlighting Portuguese craftspeople. The first and second floors stock handmade soaps, ceramics, baskets, towels, artwork, photography—all made by homegrown artists. We're talking goat milk soap neatly packaged in a sardine tin, small-batch and locally-roasted chocolate bars (also in sardine tins), and gorgeous marble coasters (often depicting sardine tins). On the rooftop terrace, Mar d'Estórias highlights Portuguese food in much the same way; we reccomedn the fresh mollusks *Bulhão Pato* style.

i Restaurant petiscos from €7, entrées from €12; limited wheelchair accessibility

LANDMARKS

FORTE DA PONTA DA BANDEIRA (FORT OF THE TIP OF THE FLAG)

Cais da Solaria; cm-lagos.pt; open Tu-Su 10am-12:30pm and 2pm-5:30pm

In its prime, the Forte da Ponta da Bandeira was one of the most advanced military forts in the Algarve. Along with the Porta da Vila and Governor's Castle bulwarks, it protected the quay of Lagos from invasion. To enter, you'll use a drawbridge to cross a small moat. Inside is the chapel of Santa Bárbara, coated with tiles from the 1600s. While you visit, be sure to climb onto the roof for a great view of the **Praia da Batata (Beach of the Potato)** to the west and views of Lagos to the east. Pro tip: Forte da Ponta da Bandeira is part of the trio of museums including the **Museu Municipal** and the **Forte da Ponta da Bandeira**—buy a ticket for all three for €6.

i Admission €2, €1 reduced; wheelchair accessible

IGREJA DE SANTA MARIA (CHURCH OF SANTA MARIA)

Pr. Infante D. Henrique; 28 276 27 23; paroquiasdelagos.pt; summer, open daily 9am-7pm, mass M-Sa 7pm, Su 11:30am

Compared to the gold-plated, marble-coated, diamond-studded churches you're probably familiar with, the Igreja de Santa Maria is more austere. Its plain white walls, unremarkable benches (instead of pews), and the modern announcement board at the entrance make it easy to forget that this church was founded in 1498 (although renovated post-earthquake of 1755). This church offers a view into the life of a Lagos resident beyond the gelato, seafood, and souvenir shop. Be sure to note the modern art behind the altar—the bright pinks and yellows patterns are almost psychedelic.

i Free; wheelchair accessible

MUSEUMS

MERCADO DE ESCRAVOS (SLAVE MARKET)

R. da Graça e Praça Infante D. Henrique; cm-lagos.pt; 28 277 17 24; open Tu-Su 10am-12:30pm and 2pm-5:30pm

Portugal's problematic slave history goes back to the fifteenth century, when slaves from West Africa were first brought to the country for household maintenance and heavy labor. When Brazil was discovered, the Portuguese slave trade boomed, and as many as five million Africans were uprooted and sent to the New World. The Mercado de Escravos is an attempt to engage with this history. Housed on two floors in the central **Praça Infante D. Henrique,** it's a museum with virtual recreations of slave-era Lagos, as well as historical artifacts documenting the creation of Lagos and its early dependence on slavery.

i Admission €3; limited wheelchair accessibility

MUSEU MUNICIPAL DR. JOSÉ FORMOSINHO (MUNICIPAL MUSEUM OF DR. JOSÉ FORMOSINHO)

R. General Alberto Silveira; cm-lagos.pt; 28 276 23 01; open Tu-Su 10am-12:30pm and 2pm-5:30pm

This is Lagos's only "traditional" museum, and there's not much of a unifying theme; it's full of sacred art, paintings, archeology, minerals, and more. It was founded in 1932 by Dr.

Jose Formosinho as part of an effort to raise awareness about Lagos's rich history. Perhaps the most exciting part of the museum is the baroque period **Igreja de Santo Antonio (Church of St. Anthony),** located at the museum's entrance. First built in 1707, it boasts lots of gold, wood carvings, and paintings depicting several strange legends about Santo Antonio, including one in which he reattached a devotee's severed foot (after all but telling him that his foot deserved to be cut off).

i Admission €3, €1.50 reduced; no photography allowed

OUTDOORS

PONTA DA PIEDADE (MERCY POINT)

Ponta da Piedade

If you're in your Lagos hostel, chances are you've already been offered several dozen tour packages for the legendary Ponta da Piedade, an area just west of downtown Lagos made up of sandstone rock formations, hidden caverns, and ocean-carved tunnels. In fact, there are over 40 companies offering kayak trips and boat rides to the grottos. Taking a kayak or stand-up paddleboard tour is highly recommended, especially if they include add-ons like snorkeling—most tours will leave from central Lagos (buy tickets in advance from a tour company downtown for €15-30). If you're more comfortable on land, it's well worth walking to the Ponta de Piedade—it's less than a three kilometer trek, and will take you along beachside cliffs (there's a trail, don't worry) that offer panoramic views of the ocean before you.

i Ponta da Piedade free, from €15 for kayak/boat tours; no wheelchair accessibility

PRAIA DE DONA ANA (DONA ANA BEACH)

Praia de Dona Ana

The Praia de Dona Ana is one of the most spacious beaches in Lagos, although it's still sheltered enough to feel cozy. At least, you'll probably feel somewhat cozy (or maybe claustrophobic) while vying for an unclaimed patch of sand on this popular beach. Even with the stiff competition, the Praia de Dona Ana's majestic rock formations, vibrant waters, and silky white sand are worth the 2.5-kilometer trek along the **Avenida dos Descobrimentos.** Once you lay out your beach towel, snorkel, sunbathe, and swim to your heart's content—you can even pick up a refresco or two at the beach bar (or climb up the stairs for something more filling).

i Free; no wheelchair accessibility

FOOD

CAFÉ GOLDIG ($)

R. Infante de Sagres; open Tu-Sa 9am-4pm

Perched above most of historic downtown Lagos, this tiny café is ideal for a mid morning snack, or pick-me-up espresso. Written in cursive on their awning is the message, "Thank you for being mindful," and it's clear that Café Goldig is also mindful in their food prep. As though transplanted straight from some Californian ecovillage, this café offers homemade and whole grain breads, fresh squeezed juices, vegan pastries, and daily lunch specials like zucchini lasagna or beetroot curry. If you're on the go, they can serve any dish as takeaway, too.

i Entrées from €5; gluten-free, vegan, and vegetarian options available; wheelchair accessible

DOIS IRMÃOS (TWO BROTHERS) ($$)

Tr. do Mar 2; 28 218 11 00; open daily 11am-midnight

Given its prime location on the **Praça do Infante Dom Henrique,** right on the water, Dois Irmãos isn't exactly what you'd call a "hidden" gem. But it's certainly a gem, and it's a stellar option if you want to try some of the Algarve's most famous dishes. Offering a long list of broiled, grilled, roasted, and however-else-prepared seafood, an obvious standout is the *Cataplana.* Named after the huge copper bowl it's prepared in, Dois Irmãos's version involves *amêijoas,* and a lot of them. (Best to split this dish with a friend, if you can.) For dessert, the "egg yolk strings with almonds and mint gelato" isn't a bad translation—they actually tease the yolks into thin strings and boil them in sugar syrup. Alongside the ice cream, it makes for quite the sugar rush.

i Entrées from €10; some gluten-free options; wheelchair accessible

O ESCONDIDINHO ($$)

R. do Cemitério 49; 28 276 03 86; open M-Sa noon-3pm and 7pm-10pm, Su noon-3pm

Tucked away atop a hill, next to the Lagos cemetery, and in front of the GNR (police), O Escondidinho (The Little Hidden One in English) is quite aptly named. Once you find it, this seafood joint has a pleasingly no-frills atmosphere, with outdoor seating on blue picnic tables in what looks like a converted driveway. There's quality fish throughout Lagos, but the stuff served at O Escondidinho is simply of a higher caliber. Order grilled squid, sole, mullet, swordfish, cod, all prepared by the boisterous family running the place. If you can't make up your mind—try the special mix grill for two (€35). Plus, due to its hidden location, you may not have to share the space with quite so many hungry tourists.

i Entrées from €8.50 or by kg; some gluten-free options; wheelchair accessible

NIGHTLIFE

THREE MONKEYS

R. Lançarote de Freitas 26; 28 276 29 95; www.3monkeys.me.uk; open daily 1pm-2am

There are few better places in Lagos for monkeying around than at this popular bar just off the main square. Besides drinks like the Espresso Martini (Kahlua, vodka, espresso, coffee beans) or the Grenade Depthcharger (jager, tequila, and an entire Red Bull), Three Monkeys is known for their beer bongs. The staff takes count of everyone who completes this "booze Olympics" challenge, along with their nationality. If you stop by, help lead the US to victory! If you want to keep your wits about you, you can definitely take it easy and enjoy the international tunes. Or—if you're a Swedish female—they cordially invite you to partake in some wholesome "naked dwarf wrestling." On second thought, you might want to be drunk for that one.

i No cover, cocktails from €4.50, shots from €3; wheelchair accessible

MELLOW LOCO

R. do Ferrador 9; 91 345 86 27; open daily 9pm-2am

"Sometimes we're mellow, sometimes we're loco," shrugs the bartender at Mellow Loco. He points to some long-haired surfer bros, whose eyes are glued to a soccer game playing on the bar's flat screen TVs—very mellow, he explains. Later at night, however, you'd better believe this place turns into one of Lagos's most notorious party scenes. After knocking back a couple classic cocktails, you're likely to see partygoers pole dancing, jumping half-naked on the tables, or taking not-quite-PG selfies with the bar's cheesy photo booth. Just try not to end up looking like the Mellow Loco mascot by the end of the night (it's a disheveled goose with a smoke in one hand, a beer in the other, and both eyes x'ed out).

i No cover, cocktails from €4; wheelchair accessible

LISBON

Coverage by **Joseph Winters**

Not quite undiscovered, but still nowhere near as overrun as many other European capitals (no thank you, Paris), Lisbon is a historical, culinary, and cultural Shangri-La. With a history touched by the Romans, Moors, and several centuries of devout Catholicism (ultimately leading to a Portuguese Inquisition, yikes), the city boasts a mélange of traditions unlike any other city on the continent. It's got Medieval castles, massive cathedrals, retro trams and *elevadores,* and enough street art to make the whole city feel like one giant, urban museum. Walk through narrow cobblestoned streets following the scent of ultra-fresh *bacalhau* (cod) or *pastéis de nata* (egg pastries), or simply admiring the myriad Baroque, Gothic, and Islamic influences on the city's makeup.

ORIENTATION

Lisbon hugs the northern shore of the **Tagus River** (*Tejo* in Portuguese), and its most spacious square—**Praça do Comércio**—offers a grand view of the water. To the east are the maze-like streets of historical **Alfama, Mouraria,** and the impressive **Castelo São Jorge.** For a more modern experience, high-end shopping and gourmet eateries are located in the popular neighborhoods of **Baixa** and **Chiado**, just northwest of the Praça do Comércio. For nightlife and cheap eats, Lisboners flock to **Barrio Alto** (which includes the trendy and BGLTQ-friendly **Principe Real)** or **Cais do Sodré** (west along the water from the Praça do Comércio), though **Intendente** (northeast of Baixa) has recently gained popularity among hipster-types. Going north, you'll travel along the luxurious **Avenida da Liberdade,** which starts in **Rossio Square** and goes to the **Marquês de Pombal** before branching off east and west. **Belém,** home to top-notch *pastéis de nata* (custard pastries), museums, and historical buildings, is a quick train or bus ride west of downtown—you'll pass through up-and-coming **Alcântara** to get there.

ESSENTIALS

GETTING THERE

By plane: Flights land in Lisbon at the Aeroporto de Madrid, just a couple of miles north of downtown. To get into the city, the easiest option is by metro. Take the green line to Alameda, and then change for Rossio, Baixa, or wherever your final destination is. You can also take an AeroBus—either Line 1 to Martim Moniz, Praça do Comércio, Cais do Sodré, Rossio, Restauradores, Av. da Liberdade, Marquês de Pombal and Saldanha; or Line 2 to Saldanha, Marquês de Pombal and Sete Rios. Line 1 runs from 7:30am-11pm and Line 2 operates between 7:45am and 10:45pm. The third option is taxi (from Departures) or Uber (from Terminal 1), but be forewarned of this method's high price tag.

By bus: The main bus terminal Sete Rios is just under 3mi. northwest of the city center, near a zoo. If you're coming from southern Portugal, this will likely be your stop. From here, the metro is your best bet for getting into town.

By train: Trains in Portugal are relatively reliable and more spacious than a typical bus. Options for entry include Gare do Oriente (if arriving from the north), Sete Rios, Entrecampos (between Gare do Oriente and Sete Rios), and Santa Apolónia (usually if you're arriving from the north).

By boat: There is a boat option called the Transtejo, which offers transport from Cacilhas, Montijo, and Seixal (to Terminal Fluvial Cais do Sodré); from Barreiro (to Terminal Fluvial Terreiro do Paço); and from Trafaria and Porto Brandão (to Estação Fluvial de Belém).

GETTING AROUND

Walking is the best way to familiarize yourself with Lisbon's snakelike alleyways and panoramic *miradouros.* It's about 1.5mi. between the northwestern

Praça do Marquês de Pombal and the riverfront **Praça do Comercio,** and 1mi. between easterly **Alfama** and the western **Pink Street.** Most inner Lisbon sightseeing lies within this area, which is easily walkable if you've got strong quads. Although biking is next to impossible in some of the city's older neighborhoods, Lisbon has a bike sharing program called Gira with 60 stations around the city. At only €2 a day, it's a good deal if you can plan your daily adventures around the docking stations. The metro is the easiest transit option in Lisbon, and stations are marked with a big letter M. Pro tip: if you're planning on investing in a Lisboa Card (tourist card for reduced fare at museums and other sightseeing), you'll get free use of the metro, bus, and tram lines.

PRACTICAL INFORMATION

Tourist Offices: Lisbon runs a tourist information program called Ask Me Lisboa, with local offices scattered throughout the city, including one in the Lisbon airport. Look for the italic lowercase i, often in purple. Ask Me Lisboa, Lisboa Story Center (Praça do Comércio, 78-81; 91 408 13 66; www.visitlisboa.com; open daily 10am-10pm).

Banks/ATMs/Currency Exchange: There are plenty of banks and ATMs throughout Lisbon. As a general rule, you should never have to walk more than a couple blocks before seeing a blue and white Multibanco sign. Deutsche Bank: Av. António Augusto de Aguiar 23 E/F; 21 780 34 00; db.com/portugal; open M-F 8:30am-3pm

Post Offices: CTT, the national postal service, has an office in every Lisbon neighborhood. Estação dos Correios de Graça/Penha De França (Av. Gen. Roçadas 7A; 21 812 5160; www.ctt.pt; open M-F 9am-6pm).

Public Restrooms: Savvy Lisbon travelers can find restrooms in most of the city's neighborhoods—check grocery stores, tourist offices, and larger parks. If all else fails, plan your restroom use around your museum visits; they have cleaner bathrooms, anyway.

Internet: There is no city-wide Wi-Fi network in Lisbon, but you can buy nearly complete coverage from third-party Wi-Fi hotspot providers if you need consistent connectivity (from MEO: €10/day or €25/week; from NOS: €4/day or €24.90/30 days). Otherwise, look for free Internet access at any tourist office or nearly any shopping center.

BGLTQ+ Resources: ILGA Portugal is a Portuguese BGLTQ+ advocacy organization with headquarters in Lisbon. They offer education services, support for families and individuals, and help organize politically for BGLTQ causes (ILGA Portugal: R. dos Fanqueiros, 40-1100-231 218 873 918; www.ilga-portugal.pt; open W-Sa 7pm-11pm).

EMERGENCY INFORMATION

Emergency Number: 112.

Lisbon Police: The PSP (city police) or GNR (national police) have your back in case you find yourself in trouble.

- PSP (Av. de Moscavide 88, Edifício da PSP; 21 765 42 42; www.psp.pt).
- GNR (Avenida do Mar e das Comunidades Madeirenses 13; 29 121 44 60; gnr.pt).

US Embassy: There is a US Embassy in Lisbon (Av. das Forças Armadas 133C; 21 727 33 00; pt.usembassy.gov/embassy-consulate/lisbon; open M-F 8am-5pm).

Rape Crisis Center: APAV, Victim Support Portugal (Rua José Estêvão, 135 A, Level 1; 21 358 79 00; apav.pt; open M-F 10am-1pm and 2pm-5:30pm).

- Associação de Mulheres contra a Violência–AMCV (R. João Villaret 9; 21 380 21 60; amcv.org.pt; open M-F 10am-6pm).

Hospitals: Lisbon has several 24hr hospitals. Try these for emergency services:

- Hospital de Santa Maria (Av. Prof. Egas Moniz; 21 780 50 00; chln.pt; open daily 24hr).
- Hospital da Luz Lisboa (Av. Lusíada 100; 21 710 44 00; open daily 24hr).

Pharmacies: For all your ointment, salve, and emollient needs, check the streets of Baixa, Chiado, or any populated city square.

- Farmácia Cruz de Malta Lda. (R. Jardim do Tabaco 92-94-96; 21 886 61 26; open M-F 8:45am-7:30pm, Sa 9am-6pm).

SIGHTS

CULTURE

A VIDA PORTUGUESA (THE PORTUGUESE LIFE)

R. Anchieta 11; 21 346 50 73; avidaportuguesa.com; open M-Sa 10am-8pm, Su 11am-8pm

Step through A Vida Portuguesa's front doors and step back in time—nearly everything sold is charmingly vintage, from the handmade notebooks to the retro MiniBasketball kids toys (a bestseller, believe it or not). If you've been discouraged by the abundance of indistinguishable trinket shops in **Baixa** and **Chiado,** the "genuine and touching products of Portuguese origin and design" make for excellent souvenirs. There's a little bit of everything: porcelain swallows (the store's logo), pre-shave oils, artisanal *marmeladas,* infused chocolates, sardine tins, *azulejo* tiles, ceramics. Check out the original store in Chiado, or visit their newer spaces in **Intendente** and in the **Mercado da Ribeira.** (There's also one in **Porto,** if you're traveling out of town.)

i Prices vary; wheelchair accessible

JARDIM BOTÂNICO DE LISBOA (LISBON BOTANICAL GARDEN)

R. da Escola Politécnica 54; 21 392 18 00; museus.ulisboa.pt; open Tu-F 9am-5pm, Sa-Su 9am-8pm

Just steps away from trendy **Principe Real** is the Lisbon Botanical Garden, where you'll find yourself surrounded not by coffee shops and sardine-themed knick knacks, but by silk floss trees and European yews. Designed in the mid-nineteenth century as a scientific garden for the local university, a walk along the steep garden path takes visitors past an impressive collection of plants from around the world, including many in danger of extinction due to habitat loss. Check out the garden's chrysophyllum tree—only a handful are left in the wild, and this one has only once ever produced a single fruit with fertile seeds. Also notable is the Azorean dragon tree, whose red resin (called Dragon's Blood) has been used for everything from wood varnish to magic rituals, and was even featured in Hercules' eleventh labor.

i Garden admission €3, €1.50 reduced; combined ticket (with Museu Nacional de História Natural e da Ciência), €6, €3.50 reduced; Su free until 2pm; last entry 30min. before closing; wheelchair accessible

LX FACTORY

R. Rodrigues de Faria 103; 21 314 33 99; lxfactory.com/en; open daily 6am-4am; individual shop hours vary

In a neighborhood that was once Lisbon's main manufacturing hub, you'll now find one of the city's trendiest boutiques, cafés, and startups. It's like a mini **Chiado,** only more hipster. Flanking a single cobblestoned street just perpendicular to the highway are vegan shoe stores, modular lighting showrooms, thin crust pizzerias, and *so* much street art. Fledgling entrepreneurs have offices above many of the shops, Among the most original spaces is a warehouse turned bookstore-art gallery-café-bar (so you can educate, culture, caffeinate, and intoxicate yourself without crossing the street).

i Prices vary; wheelchair accessible

TIMEOUT MARKET

Av. 24 de Julho 49; 21 395 12 74; timeoutmarket.com/lisboa/en/; open Su-W 10am-midnight, Th-Sa 10am-2am

Thanks to TimeOut Market, you no longer need to trek around all of Lisbon to feast on its finest culinary offerings; in this converted warehouse space you'll find no fewer than 24 restaurants, eight bars, and a dozen retail shops, all of which were handpicked by a panel of independent food experts. In one corner, there's a seafood smorgasbord, from high-end sushi to traditional grilled cod. Another section offers meaty pork bellies and pricey cuts of steak. An entire wall of the market is devoted to *cozinhas de chef* (chef's kitchens), each highlighting a different culinary superstar of Portugal. Of course, if you're in the mood for a cup of soup and a *pastel de nata,* TimeOut's perfect for that, too. Fair warning: you may need to fight for an empty seat in the food court-style communal tables.

i Prices vary; wheelchair accessible

LANDMARKS

CASTELO DE SÃO JORGE (CASTLE OF ST. GEORGE)

Castelo de S. Jorge; 21 880 06 20; castelodesaojorge.pt; open daily 9am-9pm

The Castelo de São Jorge, Lisbon's most popular attraction, is obligatory. Part of a Medieval citadel, the Castelo's history goes deep—all the way back to the Iron Age (seventh to third century BCE). It wasn't until the Moorish occupation in the eleventh century that the area began to reach castle-sized proportions. Past a former elite residential area with unparalleled panoramic views of downtown Lisbon and through huge stone archways, you'll finally enter the castle. Here, you can climb onto the walls and walk the castle's perimeter, oohing and aahing at the #views. The attached archeological site is also fantastic, showing you the layers of the Castelo's history—from excavated Iron Age construction to the ruins of Islamic houses that stood here in the years before Portuguese rule. There's also a museum—it's best to carve out an entire half-day, or at least two solid hours, to explore.

i Admission €8.50, €5 reduced; Câmara Oscura tour 10am-5pm, Núcleo Arqueológico tours 10:30am-5:30pm (both free, first come first served); last entry 8:30pm; limited wheelchair accessibility

ELEVADOR DE SANTA JUSTA (SANTA JUSTA LIFT)

R. do Ouro; 21 350 01 15; www.carris.pt/en/elevators; open daily Mar-Oct 7am-11pm, Nov-Feb 7am-9pm

Since 1902, the Elevador de Santa Justa has been helping Lisboners and weary tourists navigate the steep climb between lower **Baixa** and the **Largo do Carmo.** With wrought iron and wood and Gothic flourishes, it's one of the city's more artful forms of public transport. Today, the elevator ride is less about utility and more about #views, as it deposits riders at a delightful miradouro overlooking the **Praça Dom Pedro IV,** as well as all of Baixa. There's usually a long line of sweaty tourists at the entrance to the elevator, so if you want the viewpoint without the wait, you can reach it (for free!) from the Largo do Carmo via sky bridge (look for the Bellalisa Elevador restaurant).

i Admission €5.15 (includes upper viewpoint access), upper viewpoint only €1.50; no wheelchair accessibility; included with Lisboa Card or day-pass to public transport (purchased within metro for €6.15)

MOSTEIRO DOS JERÓNIMOS (JERÓNIMOS MONASTERY)

Pr. do Império; open Oct-May Tu-Su 10am-5:30pm, June-Sept 10am-6:30pm

It took 100 years to build this behemoth of a monastery, with its gluttonous Manueline and Plateresque frills and flourishes. Commissioned by King Manuel I and funded by Portuguese voyages abroad, you'll find rich history at this monastery, where historical pictograms tell tales of the country's global explorations. Boasting sky-high ceilings and breathtaking stained glass, the Mosteiro dos Jerónimos is a showstopper, for sure. Admission to the church is free, but it's well worth the cash to visit the expansive cloister.

i Cloister admission €10, church entry free; wheelchair accessible; last entry 30 min. before closing

ROSSIO (PRAÇA DOM PEDRO IV) (PEDRO IV SQUARE)

Pr. Dom Pedro IV; open daily 24hr

Since the Middle Ages, Rossio has been one of Lisbon's top cultural spaces. Teeming with tourists and locals alike, visitors meet under the imposing gaze of Dom Pedro IV, perched on a 75-foot column in the middle of the square. Although the square officially bears his name **(Praça Dom Pedro IV),** it remains fondly known as Rossio Square to locals and tourists alike. Meet here for a coffee break in the surrounding cafés or snag some knicknacks in a streetside *loja.*

i Free; wheelchair accessible

MUSEUMS

MUSEU CALOUSTE GULBENKIAN (CALOUSTE GULBENKIAN MUSEUM)

Av. de Berna 45A; 21 782 34 61; gulbenkian.pt; open M 10am-6pm, W-Su 10am-6pm

Though it's a trek from downtown, the Museu Calouste Gulbenkian houses one of Lisbon's best collections of art. Reflecting Gulbenkian's desire to collect artwork representative of all genres, the ***coleção do fundador*** (collection of the founder) takes visitors chronologically through time, starting with Ancient Egyptian statuettes, leading you to Persian tapestries, Greco-Roman sculptures, and ends with a fabulous collection of nineteenth-century European art. Outside the museum is a sprawling park filled with ducks, turtles, and a tranquil interpretive garden where you can digest the hundreds of years of history you just traveled through. On the opposite side of the park is the ***coleção moderna*** (modern collection), home to Portuguese sculptures, paper-based art, and—of course—a healthy number of monochromatic paintings that could forgivably be mistaken for an elementary school art project.

i All-inclusive admission €12.50, founder's collection €10, exhibitions €5, under 29 50% off, free Su after 2pm; tours Su and M 10am; last entry 5:30pm; wheelchair accessible

MUSEU COLEÇÃO BERARDO (BERARDO COLLECTION MUSEUM)

Pr. do Império; 21 361 28 78; museuberardo.pt; open daily 10am-7pm

Boasting works by **Picasso, Miró,** and **Warhol,** the Coleção Berardo is Lisbon's powerhouse modern art museum. Wrap yourself in a fancy scarf and don your biggest sunglasses and head towards **Belém** to take in Portugal's most-visited museum alongside other fashion-forward art fiends. The permanent exhibition starts at the beginning of the twentieth century with the abstract geometric shapes of Dadaism. Then there's Cubism, Surrealism, Informalism, kinetic art, décollage, nouveaux-réalisme—you get the idea. It's envelope-pushing and avant-garde in all the usual ways, whether that means a canvas with a single brush stroke on it or a slurry of seemingly random paint splatters. Once you get all the way through twenty-first-century American pop art, you can chill in the museum's lovely olive garden (not the restaurant, but an actual garden with olive trees).

i Admission €5, €2.50 reduced; audio guide €5; last entry 6:30pm; wheelchair accessible; free on Sa, 30% off with Lisboa Card

MUSEU NACIONAL DE ARTE ANTIGUA (NATIONAL MUSEUM OF ANCIENT ART) ($)

R. das Janelas Verdes; 21 391 28 00; museudearteantiga.pt; open Tu-Su 10am-6pm

The first thing to know about the NMAA is that you'll never have time to truly appreciate everything. The Portuguese Painting and Sculpture room has enough history to last you a week, and that's just one floor. Other attractions include the room of Portuguese Discoveries, which features artwork "borrowed" from Portugal during its conquests abroad. Just make sure you check out the Panels of St. Vincent, a 1450 mural considered to be the greatest achievement of pre-modern Portuguese art; the Belém Monstrance, an ostentatious piece of religious metal work commissioned by King Manuel I and made of gold procured from Vasco da Gama's second voyage to India; and paintings by **Raphael** and **Dürer.** On a less academic note, there's also a room full of explicit art (read: nudes), which you may also want to explore.

i Admission €6, €3 reduced; wheelchair accessible

OUTDOORS

PARKS OF LISBON

Hours typically dawn-dusk

Although Lisbon isn't renowned for its access to the outdoors, there are still a few city parks where you can get your daily dose of chlorophyll. The **Jardim da Estrela,** in the shadow of the basilica that shares its name, is a good option northwest of the city center. It sits on a hill overlooking the São Bento neighborhood, and it's a hotspot for families looking to entertain their young'uns at the duck pond. If you're visiting the **Calouste Gulbenkian Museum,** be sure to bask in the **Gulbenkian Gardens,** which features local and international sculptures, a turtle pond, and an interpretive garden. Just above the **Marquês de Pombal Square** (at the northernmost point of the **Av. da Liberdade**) is the enormous **Parque Eduardo VII,** consisting of a central manicured area filled with clean-cut hedges and neatly-paved walkways, with more natural, tree-covered paths on the hills to either side. Farther from downtown is the **Parque das Nações,** connecting the **Lisbon Oceanarium** to the end of a waterfront walking and biking path (and a fun cable car for €3.95). This narrow patch of greenery takes you through public art installations, with the Tagus River on one side and warehouse-like shops and restaurants on the other. If none of these options are green enough for you, try the hillside **Parque Florestal de Monsanto:** 25 acres of eucalyptus forest broken up by the occasional garden, centered around an environmental interpretation center. You can get there by heading west from the city center. (Buses are the best option—take the #711 from Rossio, leaving every 15min.)

i Free; variable wheelchair accessibility

FOOD

CAFÉ DE SÃO BENTO ($$)

R. de São Bento 212; 21 395 29 11; en.cafesaobento.com; open M-F 12:30pm-2:30pm and 7pm-2am, Sa-Su 7pm-2am

Even when it opened in 1982, Café de São Bento was aiming for a throwback vibe. With its overwhelmingly red décor—from the walls to the tablecloths to the plush chairs—retro photography, and impeccably-dressed waiters, it's as if this steakhouse never left the 50s. The concise menu consists of a handful of steak preparations, from Portuguese style to São Bento style to just plain grilled or in a sandwich. Always serving filet mignon, Café de São Bento was recently declared the best steak in Lisbon by TimeOut magazine, and they even have their own coveted space in the waterfront **TimeOut Market.**

i Appetizers from €8.90, entrées from €16; one vegetarian option, gluten-free options available; no wheelchair accessibility

CANTINHO DO AVILLEZ ($$)

R. Nova da Trindade 18; 21 199 23 69; cantinhodoavillez.pt; open M-F 12:30pm-3pm and 7pm-midnight, Sa-Su 12:30pm-midnight

If you follow Portuguese language cooking shows (who doesn't?), the name José Avillez probably elicits a familiar smile. He hosted the popular cooking show *Improbalicious,* in which he taught viewers how to prepare featured ingredients in unexpected ways. He has since become a gastronomical rockstar across Portugal, from his handful of cookbooks to over a dozen eateries in Lisbon. This particular Cantinho location is where it all began, and visitors can now eat in the studio where his famous cooking show was once filmed. Try a variety of multicultural dishes, from Moroccan tagine to a MX-LX (Mexico-Lisbon) steak sandwich, or stick with traditional Lisbon dishes like octopus salad. Watch as the chefs prepare your meal in the retro-style TV kitchen, and maybe—just maybe—you'll catch a glimpse of the chef himself.

i Petiscos from €6, entrées from €16; reservations recommended; vegan and gluten-free options; no wheelchair accessibility

FOOD TEMPLE ($)

Beco do Jasmim 18; 21 887 43 97; www.thefoodtemple.com; open W-Su 7:30pm-midnight

The steak- and seafood-heavy cuisine of Lisbon is hardly ideal for the intrepid vegetarian—you can only order so many side salads and bread and olive

plates before horrific boredom sets in. Thankfully, Alice Ming has you covered—her tiny Food Temple in Mouraria is 100% plant-based, satiating, and budget-friendly. There's an ever-changing daily menu of a soup, three *petiscos*, an entrée, and desserts. Sample dishes include fried "cod" sandwiches (made with jackfruit and seaweed for that fishy flavor), seitan and couscous salad with sweet potato, cabbage slaw, raw cheesecake—you never know what Ming will whip up on any given day. One thing's for sure: it could be one of your best meals in Lisbon, whether you're a meat-eater or a die-hard vegan. Inside seating is limited (although it's highly recommended, due to a cozy open kitchen), but they have some seating on the steep staircase just outside.

i Petiscos from €2.50, entrées from €10; Portuguese credit cards or cash only; vegan, gluten-free options available; no wheelchair accessibility; reservations recommended

LOJA DAS CONSERVAS (PRESERVES SHOP) ($)

R. do Arsenal 130; 91 118 12 10; open M-Sa 10am-8pm, Su noon-8pm

The Loja das Conservas is the official retailer representing 19 factories of tinned fish production in Portugal—there isn't a square inch of wall space that isn't covered by a different brand of sardine, mackerel, or tuna. Whether you want them marinated in olive oil, with spices, with pickles, in tomato paste, in water, with skin, boneless, or some combination of these attributes—this shop probably has it. There's also an industrial-sized pedal seamer, which you can use to seal your own tin (€1.50, or lock a souvenir keychain inside of it for €12). For a taste of the fish on offer, visit the next-door restaurant. Newly-opened in 2018, it features fish in sandwiches, as petiscos, or mashed into pâté. Chef's recommendation: try the tuna with Portuguese curry sauce.

i Restaurant petiscos from €2, tinned fish from €2; one vegetarian option available; wheelchair accessible

MANTEIGARIA ($)

R. do Loreto 2; 21 347 14 92; open daily 8am-midnight

When it comes to *pastéis de nata,* the custard-filled tarts ubiquitous at any Lisbon bakery, supermarket, or café, two institutions rule the foodscape. A certain pastel shop in **Belém** has an army of devotees, but some would say Manteigaria, a relative newcomer to the nata game, makes the superior pastries. Come see for yourself at their tiny shop in **Chiado,** where there's standing space only, but a kitchen open enough for you to see each step of the the pastéis production process. Watch bakers roll the dough, stuff it into mini muffin tins, and pop them into long and shallow ovens, where the eggy innards of each cup begin to bubble and char.

i Pastéis from €1, coffee from €0.70; vegetarian options; no wheelchair accessibility

PÃO PÃO QUEIJO QUEIJO ($)

R. de Belém 126; 21 362 63 69; paopaoqueijoqueijo.com; open M-Sa 10am-midnight, Su 10am-8pm

This petit eatery near Starbucks (and the notorious **Pastéis de Belém**) might not be much of a looker, but that's not really the point. With a menu of over 50 kinds of baguette sandwiches (€3.75), around 30 salads (€3.95), and over a dozen pitas (also €3.95), Pão Pão Queijo Queijo is the budget backpacker's dream come true: cheap, tasty, and filling—a glorious trifecta. They're famous for their falafel, which some claim is the best in Lisbon. Go here to fill up on delicious Mediterranean food before joining the long line for a pastel de nata next door.

i Entrées from €3.75, combos from €6.95; gluten-free, vegan, and vegetarian options available; wheelchair accessible

TAPISCO ($$)

R. Dom Pedro V 81; 21 342 06 81; tapisco.pt; open daily noon-midnight

If you were deterred by the €100 price tag at Henrique Sá Pessoa's Michelin-starred restaurant, **Alma,** Tapisco is one of the chef's more budget-friendly option for mere mortals. The restaurant's name is a word play between Spanish tapas and Portuguese petiscos, and Tapisco accordingly offers small plates featuring flavors from across the Iberian Peninsula. Octopus salad: check. Patatas bravas: check. La Bomba de Lisboa ranks as one of their most popular dishes: meatballs stuffed with mashed potatoes and fried in panko bread crumbs. Reservations are highly recommended for lunch, as it can get quite busy. If you end up waiting in line, they'll offer you a complimentary glass of vermouth, so maybe queuing up isn't such a horrible fate after all.

i Entrées from €7, drinks from €10; gluten-free and vegetarian options available; no wheelchair accessibility; lunch reservations only

NIGHTLIFE

CASA INDEPENDENTE

Largo do Intendente Pina Manique 45; 21 887 28 42; casaindependente.com; open Tu-Th 5pm-midnight, F-Sa 5pm-2am

With no sign or information marking the front door, it's easy to walk straight past this unassuming cocktail bar and nightclub. But they want it that way—it's part of Casa Independente's image as one of the city's premier underground hangouts, showcasing an eclectic mix of indie music artists from punk rock to electric to the Fanána of their resident band, Fogo Fogo. Inside the building, there are small rooms full of antique furniture, a streetside grand room with a makeshift stage, and a grape-covered patio where visitors can tuck into tepiscos and cocktails—or dance. A true Lisbon institution—try to make it to a weekend concert, when they open up the rooftop terrace, bringing the party into the open air and overlooking all of Intendente.

i Concerts from €6, cocktails from €4.50, tapiscos from €4; cash only under €10; no wheelchair accessibility; resident band Fogo Fogo plays last Su every month

CINCO LOUNGE

R. Ruben A. Leitão 17-A; 21 342 40 33; www.cincolounge.com; open daily 9pm-2am

With its ultra-low lighting (where's my cocktail?), beyond-retro atmosphere (is it 1920?), and smoking-allowed policy (*hacking cough*), Cinco Lounge is about as authentic as it gets. Nestled in a quiet corner of the **Principe Real** neighborhood, this hazy haven harkens back to a time before the neighborhood's gentrification, when Portuguese businessmen could douse their stress in smoke, gin, and raspy conversation (forbidden topics include politics, religion, and—of course—*futebol*). Kick back in the lounge's plush, low-lying chairs and enjoy a classic cocktail or a long list of signature creations. Check out Cinco's famous Finder's Keepers cocktail; served in homemade cans with the recipe written on the back, they even have a can-sealing machine behind the bar counter that will seal your bebida right before your eyes.

i No cover, cocktails from €7.50; no wheelchair accessibility

DAMAS

R. da Voz do Operário 60; 96 496 44 16; open Tu 1pm-2am, W 6pm-2am, F 6pm-4am, Su 1pm-4am, Su 6pm-midnight

Lisbon's bohemian hotspot for alt music and counterculture. Damas is a restaurant by day, nightclub by night, and is a local favorite in historic **Alfama.** The "kamikaze kitchen" (as the chef calls it) churns out daily specials (local and mostly seasonal, of course) until nightfall, when students flood the tiny space for their daily dose of counterculture. Featuring a diverse array of genres from indie to congo to impressionistic folklore, there's always something going on at Damas. As an added bonus, free concerts mean you'll have plenty of money to spend on the cocktail menu.

i No cover, free concerts, cocktails from €8; cash only; no wheelchair accessibility

PORTO

Coverage by **Joseph Winters**

"Porto" or "Oporto"? The Portuguese call it "o Porto" (literally "the port"), so that's the root of all this lost-in-translation "Oporto" business. Rest assured that this northern Portuguese city—definitely called Porto—boasts history, opulence, and a healthy dose of grit that differentiates it from the country's larger capital city. Between baroque cathedrals, neoclassical palaces, and Romanesque ruins, Porto's history is inescapable. Records go as far back as the Celts who settled here near 300 BCE, and Roman influences are still visible in the catacombs and crypts of the city's oldest churches. In fact, the Latin name Portus Cale is the etymological root of the modern name Portugal. Today, the city's energy courses through its vertical streets and ancient alleys, along the River Douro, and into its striking array of glittering architecture, both old and new. Meander through Porto long enough and you'll run into an eclectic mix of UNESCO Heritage Sites, traditional corner stores, and newfangled coffee shops. As for food, expect no-frills dining and plenty of street foods like fried bacalhau (cod), presunto (sliced ham), and the gut-busting francesinha sandwich (four meats plus cheese and a fried egg smothered in gravy-like sauce). The only rule: finish each meal with a glass of the city's famous port wine, produced just steps across the river in the world-renowned cellars of Gaia.

ORIENTATION

In the center of Porto are the cosmopolitan neighborhoods of **Aliados** and **Bolhão.** Here, artisanal boutiques coexist alongside big-name fashion brands, traditional lojas and the city's sprawling municipal market. It's also home to the local university. Just down the hill is Ribeira, stretching from the fabulous **São Bento airport** to the **Douro River.** In between, there's all manner of taverns, wine tastings, and traditional Portuguese food—it's the lifeblood of touristic Porto. Directly across the river (cross the **Ponte Dom Luís I**) is **Vila Nova de Gaia.** It's actually another city, but the single street along the waterfront is constantly saturated by Porto tourists looking for tours (and tastes) at the dozens of wine cellars hugging the river. A few steps west is **Miragia.** Near the water is a formerly Jewish neighborhood that's a little calmer than its easterly neighbors, and up the hill along the **Rua da Cedofeita** is some of Porto's best nightlife. Even further west are Porto's residential areas in the neighborhoods of **Massarelos** and **Boavista,** although there's more to see than just apartment buildings here. Besides the stunning **Casa da Música, Jardim do Palácio de Cristal** humanizes Porto, reminding visitors that the city is about more than just old churches and UNESCO monuments. Keep going and you'll eventually reach **Serralves**—Porto's incredible center for contemporary arts. Porto's westernmost neighborhood is called **Foz do Douro,** along the mouth of the **Douro River.** Recommended only for travelers spending a handful of days in the city, Foz do Douro is laid-back, quiet, and greener than the inner city.

ESSENTIALS

GETTING THERE

Flights arrive from Lisbon and other major European cities northwest of Porto in the Francisco de Sá Carneiro Airport. From here, take the metro's purple line to the city center (€2, 45min.). Public buses run between the city center and the airport, as well, between 5:30am and 11:30pm (€2). Taxis can cost €25 for a ride that—depending on traffic—might take up to an hour. Buses from Lisbon (€19, 3.5hr) may arrive in one of several locations, but the most common is the Campo 24 de Agosto station, just east of the city center. Regional, urban, and interregional trains all arrive in the gorgeous São Bento train station, which is just about as central as you can get—your accommodations likely won't be a long walk from here.

GETTING AROUND

Porto is a relatively small city; going from one end to the other on foot shouldn't take longer than an hour. Porto is far from Europe's most bike-friendly city, but many fearless travelers attempt to navigate the city's windy, uneven cobblestoned streets on two wheels. General tip: If you plan on being a heavy user (of the public transportation system), the €7 24hr pass might be an economical pick. It's good for subways and buses, but not trams. The Porto metro is small but useful for getting around town in a jiffy.

PRACTICAL INFORMATION

Tourist Offices: Porto has many "fake" tourist offices that are really just tour companies trying to snare you into some day-tour of the city for more money than it's worth. Look for the bluish-purple signs, but the words "Official Tourism Office" are also a dead giveaway. City center (Aliados) (R. Clube dos Fenianos 25; 30 050 19 20; www.visitporto.travel; May-Oct open daily 9am-8pm, Aug open daily 9am-9pm, Nov-Apr open daily 9am-7pm).

Banks/ATMs/Currency Exchange: There are banks abound in Porto, with options including Novo Banco, Santander, Millennium Bcp, Banco BPI, and more. Santander Totta (Pr. da Batalha 120; 22 339 45 40; santandertotta.pt; open M-F 8:30am-3pm).

Post Offices: The main CTT office in Porto is in Aliados, at the heart of the city center. Facing the big building up the hill, it's on the right. There's also an office at Batalha, just east of the São Bento train station. CTT Aliados (Praça General Humberto Delgado; 70 726 26 26; ct.pt; open M-F 8:30am-9pm, Sa 9am-6pm).

Public Restrooms: Good luck finding public restrooms in Porto. For desperate times, duck into the nearest mall, grocery store, or major bus or train station.

Internet: Amazingly, all public buses in Porto offer free Wi-Fi access; it only costs a €1.95 ride. Plus, if you happen to be in the city center (near Aliados), there's decent public Wi-Fi coverage. For students attending universities registered with eduroam, you can also log on to connect to Porto University's network when you're nearby (it's near Livraria Lello).

BGLTQ+ Resources: There is no BGLTQ+ resource center in Porto, but the national ILGA network is active in the city and can be contacted for support. Their main office is in Lisbon (R. dos Fanqueiros, 38; 21 887 39 18; ilga-portugal.pt; open M-F 10am-7pm).

EMERGENCY INFORMATION

Emergency Number: 112

Police: The local police (PSP) are your best bet if you find yourself in trouble. They're located in Aliados, to the left when facing up the hill. The GNR (national police) are a bit east of the city center. GNR (R. do Carmo; 22 339 96 00; www.gnr.pt).

US Embassy: The nearest US Embassy is in Lisbon (Av. das Forças Armadas 133C; 21 727 3300; pt.usembassy.gov; open M-F 8am-5pm).

Rape Crisis Center: The nearest rape crisis center is in Lisbon, a part of APAV, the Portuguese Association for Victim Support.

- GAV Oeiras (Esquadra de Oeiras da PSP, R. do Espargal 18; 21 454 02 57; apav.pt; open M-F 10am-6pm).

Hospitals: A centrally-located option is the Hospital Geral de Santo António, just east of the University of Porto. Another option is the more westerly CUF hospital (part of a private chain).

- Hospital Geral de Santo António (Largo do Prof. Abel Salazar; 22 207 75 00; chporto.pt; open daily 24hr).
- CUF Porto Hospital (Estrada da Circunvalação 14341; 22 003 9000; saudecuf.pt; open daily 24hr).

Pharmacies: There aren't a lot of 24hr pharmacies in Porto, but many have decent hours, and a few are even open on Saturday. Check Via Santa Catarina or Rua dos Passos Manuel.

- Farmácia dos Clérigos (R. dos Clérigos 36; 22 339 23 70; www.farmaciadosclerigos.pt; open M-F 9am-7:30pm, Sa 9am-1pm).
- Farmácia Sá da Bandeira (R. de Sá da Bandeira 236/54; 22 207 40 40; www.sadabandeira.com; open M-Sa 8:30am-7:30pm).

SIGHTS

CULTURE

LIVRARIA LELLO (LELLO BOOKSTORE)

R. das Carmelitas 144; 22 200 20 37; www.livrarialello.pt; bookstore open M-F 10am-7:30pm, Sa-Su 10am-7pm; check-in open M-F 9:45am-7:30pm, Sa-Su 9:45am-7pm

More than a bookstore, the Livraria Lello is an architectural masterpiece in the heart of Porto, just next to the local university. The façade combines Gothic elements with Art Nouveau, and the interior's tiled ceiling and majestic central staircase introduce a little Art Deco. What really draws in the crowds, though, is the fact that JK Rowling was a frequent visitor from 1991-1993 while she was teaching English in Porto. The building is said to have inspired the author while she worked on the manuscript that would become *Harry Potter and the Sorcerer's Stone.* Visitors can experience the magic by buying a €5 ticket ("Checking In") down the street, but the ticket is redeemable in the bookstore for €5 off a book of your choice.

i Admission €5; Wi-Fi; limited wheelchair accessibility; tickets available down the street at the "Check-In" or online

MERCADO DO BOLHÃO (BOLHÃO MARKET)

R. Formosa; 22 332 60 24; open M-F 7am-5pm, Sa 7am-1pm

Surrounded by H&Ms and Intimissimis, the Mercado do Bolhão is downtown Porto's down-to-earth oasis of Portuguese culture. Dating back to the mid-nineteenth century, the perimeter of the market is lined with butchers, bakers, fishermen, and more, while the inner circle is devoted to long rows of flower shops and greengrocers, whose vibrant products spill out onto narrow walkways. Veteran shop owners beckon visitors towards them, saying "escolhe, escolhe!" ("choose something!"). No frills—just fresh, quality food.

i Prices vary; limited wheelchair accessibility

PALÁCIO DA BOLSA (PALACE OF THE STOCK EXCHANGE)

R. Ferreira Borges; 22 339 90 13; www.palaciodabolsa.com; open daily Nov-Mar 9am-1pm and 2pm-5:30pm, Apr-Oct 9am-6:30pm

Formerly the seat of the Porto stock exchange, the Palácio da Bolsa is currently home to the city's Commerce Association and is a powerhouse of Portuguese culture. Each room includes details that were meticulously handcrafted exclusively by Portuguese artists, like the sumptuous granite detailing (which took 40 years to complete), or an elaborate wooden table that took one artist three years to design with nothing more than a pocket knife. The big stunner is undoubtedly the magnificent Arab room, slathered in 20kg of gold leaf and covered in Arabic scrawl from the Quran. This room is still used today to receive foreign leaders and even royalty. Tours are mandatory, and help contextualize the palace's role in Porto's history.

i Admission €9, €5.50 reduced; mandatory guided tours every 45min.; last entry 45min. before close; wheelchair accessibly

LANDMARKS

TORRE DOS CLÉRIGOS (CLÉRIGOS TOWER)

R. de São Filipe de Nery; 22 014 54 89; torredosclerigos.pt; open daily 9am-7pm

Even though it's only 75.6 meters tall, the baroque Torre dos Clérigos soars above the rest of the Porto cityscape. It was designed by Nicolau Nasoni in the mid-1700s as part of the Clérigos Church, quickly emerging as one of the main symbols of the city. Visitors can tour the museum's collection of sacred art, admire the church's neoclassical, rococo, and baroque interior from one of several unique vantage points, and culminate in climbing the 240 steps to the top of the tower. A narrow wraparound walkway offers incredible views but little elbow room; claustrophobes beware of having to squish your way around the tower's perimeter (do it for the selfie!).

i Admission €5, €2.50 reduced; guided tour (pre-booked only) of museum, church, and tower €6.50; limited wheelchair accessibility

IGREJA DE SÃO FRANCISCO (SAN FRANCISCO CHURCH)

Pr. Infante Dom Henrique; 22 200 64 93; ordemsaofrancisco.pt; open daily Jul-Sept 9am-8pm, Mar-Jun 9am-7pm, Nov-Feb 9am-5:30pm

Nowhere in Porto is the gluttony of the Baroque more apparent than in this glittering hulk of a church, doused in almost 100kg of gold leaf and littered with sacred art. Dedicated in the fourteenth century to Saint Assisi, it started as your average Gothic cathedral, with a dingy interior and doom-and-gloom façade. But things really started to get out of hand in the eighteenth century, when Portuguese wood carvers began adding gilt woodwork to nearly every square inch of the interior—to this day, the church remains one of the country's most impressive structures. Be sure to check out the polychrome altarpiece known as the Jesse Tree, João Baptista Chapel, and the sculpture-lined catacombs, where prominent Porto natives were once buried.

i Admission €6, €5 reduced; no wheelchair accessibility

PONTE DOM LUÍS I (DOM LUÍS I BRIDGE)

PTE Luiz I; open 24hr

Although Gustave Eiffel (yes, that Eiffel) would have loved to include the Ponte Dom Luís I in his architectural portfolio, his Douro-spanning bridge proposal was tragically rejected by the city of Porto in favor of the current double-decked metal design, put forward by a Belgian architecture society. At its construction in 1881, the 564-foot-long Ponte Dom Luís I was the longest arched bridge in the world. The bottom (for cars and pedestrians) connects the Porto riverbank to the wine cellars of **Gaia,** but the top deck offers much better views. Reserved for pedestrians and public transport, panos and selfies are highly recommended; it's one of the most photogenic spots in Porto.

i Free; wheelchair accessible; transport between the upper and lower decks available

MUSEUMS

MUSEU DE SERRALVES (SERRALVES MUSEUM)

R. Dom João de Castro 210; 80 820 05 43; serralves.pt; open Apr-Sept M-F 10am-7pm, Sa-Su 10am-8pm; Oct-Mar M-F 10am-6pm, Sa-Su 10am-7pm

Running, yelling, lava lamps, Barbies performing sexual acts—the Serralves Museum knows no bounds when it comes to breaking artistic conventions. Despite being far from the city center, this cultural institution has become a destination in its own right, gracing Porto with some of the city's finest contemporary art since 1999. Open your mind and wander through Serralves' ever-changing temporary exhibitions, commissions, and displays, and don't forget to visit to the connected park. It's divided into gorgeous glades, groves, and gardens, lined with hedges, and centered around a romantic duck pond.

i Admission €10, €5 reduced; English tours at 4pm first Sa each month; limited wheelchair accessibility

MUSEU DA MISERICÓRDIA DO PORTO (MISERICÓRDIA DO PORTO MUSEUM)

R. das Flores 15; 22 090 69 60; mipo.pt; open daily Apr 1-Sept 30 10am-6:30pm, Oct 1-Mar 31 open daily 10am-5:30pm

Combining art, history, and architecture, the **Museu da Miséricordia do Porto,** is one of the city's most famous museums. The museum tour begins with a history of the Miséricordia, a charitable organization that has—since 1499—worked for the rights of Porto's underrepresented population by founding hospitals, sanitariums, and schools. The museum also has a stellar collection of sacred art from the sixteenth-eighteenth centuries, but the visit's highlight is undoubtedly the epic church, designed by the Italian architect **Nicolau Nasoni** (who also designed the nearby **Torre dos Clérigos).** Filled with blue and white azulejos and a golden neoclassical altarpiece, it contrasts starkly with the Gothic gloom of many Portuguese cathedrals.

i Admission €5, €2.50 reduced; tours by pre-booking only (scheduled online); last entry 30min; limited wheelchair accessibility

OUTDOORS

JARDINS DO PALÁCIO DE CRISTAL (CRYSTAL PALACE GARDENS)

R. de Dom Manuel II 282; 22 209 70 00; cm-porto.pt; open daily Oct-Mar 8am-7pm, Apr-Sept 8am-9pm

Watch out for peacocks, swans, and roosters as you promenade through the elegant Jardins do Palácio de Cristal. Designed in the mid-nineteenth century by Berliner Emil David, the park's romantic charm is apparent in its shady groves, diverse flower beds, and an ivy-covered chalet that now houses a romantic museum. From the main entrance, meander beneath olive trees, palms and magnolias, on through Sycamore Avenue and arrive at a stunning collection of tiered gardens, each cascading farther downhill towards the **River Douro.** The park is also home to a major branch of Porto's municipal library and an enormous domed sports complex, making it a popular destination for Porto locals.

i Free; limited wheelchair accessibility

FOOD

DATERRA ($)

R. de Mouzinho da Silveira 249; 22 319 92 57; daterra.pt; open Su-Th noon-11pm, F-Sa noon-11:30pm

In stark contrast to the meat and cheese-heavy cuisine of Porto is DaTerra, offering a buffet of fresh and tasty vegan dishes. It's not just salad, either; DaTerra likes playing with traditional Portuguese recipes, veganizing the *francesinha,* de-meating *pica-pau,* and serving up animal-free *alheira* (bread sausage). At under €10, it's a steal, considering you can go back as many times as you want for extra helpings, although it's worth saving room for a the dairy-free *pastéis de nata* (not included in the buffet price). For the super-frugal, takeaway options start at €4.50 and you'd be surprised how much food you can cram into one of those paper boxes.

i Lunch buffet from €7.50, dinner buffet from €9.95; gluten-free, vegan, and vegetarian options available; wheelchair accessible

A PÉROLA DO BOLHÃO ($)

R. Formosa 279; 22 200 40 09; open M-F 9am-7:30pm, Sa 9am-1pm

There are many shops like A Pérola do Bolhão along the streets surrounding the **Mercado do Bolhão,** but few can boast a history as old or a selection as large. The building's intricate façade is a nod to Porto's art nouveau obsession, and the interior walls are coated with azulejos depicting Portugal's Age of Discoveries. Much of these blue tiles are covered by A Pérola's legendary selection of tinned fish, dried fruit, nuts, and candies. In display cases at the windows and in front of the counters are dozens of Portuguese cheeses and processed meats like *ovelheira* (dried pig ears) and regional blood sausage. Mix and match for the ultimate picnic basket and walk to **Aliados** or the **Jardim de S. Lázaro** for an excellent Portuguese snack al fresco.

i Prices vary; gluten-free, vegan, and vegetarian options available; wheelchair accessible

BRICK CLÉRIGOS ($$)

R. Campo dos Mártires da Pátria 103; 22 323 47 35; open W-F noon-4pm and 8pm-2am, Sa 1pm-4pm and 8pm-2am, Su noon-6pm

Old Portugal meets newfangled hipster at this Insta-worthy petiscos restaurant in the shadow of the **Torre dos Clérigos.** Air plants, pressed leaves, artisanal woodwork—the décor (and menu) conspires to provide an updated vibe to Portuguese food. Options include charcuterie platters, a variety of "toasties" (like pineapple and brie), or the popular pork cheek sandwich with garlic mayo and fresh fruits. In accordance with the restaurant's philosophy of friendship and interaction, guests at Brick Clérigos sit at a large communal table, rubbing shoulders with their neighbors and passing the salt to complete strangers. It's like a family meal, only without the family dynamics.

i Petiscos from €8; gluten-free, vegan, and vegetarian options available; no wheelchair accessibility

NIGHTLIFE

ESPAÇO 77

Trav. de Cedofeita 22; 22 321 88 93; open M-F 11am-4am, Sa 6pm-4am

Entering Espaço 77 is like entering a sacred shrine—to Super Bock. With wall-to-wall lockers bearing the beer company's logo and another wall with framed bottles of the Portuguese booze, Espaço 77 has made a name for itself by selling €0.50 bottles of Mini Super Bock. In 2017 alone, sales climbed to 582,000, a number that has grown yearly since their founding in 2010. Also popular is the €2.50 Mini Super Bock plus bifana (beef sandwich) combo, which can be enjoyed between intermittent €1.50 shots (quite the splurge). Sometimes, quantity really is better than quality; for budget travelers and penny-pinching college students, Espaço 77 is an inexpensive godsend.

i Mini Super Bock from €0.50, other beers from €1; no wheelchair accessibility

MAUS HÁBITOS ($)

R. de Passos Manuel 178; 93 720 29 18; www.maushabitos.com; open Tu noon-midnight, W-Th noon-2am, F-Sa noon-4am, Su noon-5pm

Branding themselves as an *espaço de intervenção cultural* (space of cultural intervention), Maus Hábitos's avant-garde art exhibitions, inexpensive concerts, and edgy DJ sets make it one of the city's premier nightlife destinations. It's on the fourth floor of an apartment on the popular **Via Santa Catarina,** but it's discreet enough to still feel somewhat underground. Go for zany parties that last into the early morning like the Groove Ball or Monster Jinx, or go a bit earlier to appreciate political artwork in the space's rotating gallery. Even better, scout things out beforehand at their daytime restaurant, **Vícios de Mesa,** where Instagram-ready dishes of the day like Madonna pizza or avo toast are only €5.50.

i No cover, tickets from €4, cocktails from €7; limited wheelchair accessibility

PORTUGAL ESSENTIALS

VISAS

Portugal is a member of the EU and therefore you do not need a visa if you are staying under 90 days. Your passport must be valid six months beyond the intended date of departure.

MONEY

Taxes and Tipping; A 13% tax (known as value added tax) is included on all restaurants and accommodations in Portugal. As for tipping, it is not customary to tip in Portugal. If a Portuguese restaurant deems you a tourist they may expect more from you than from a local but remember it is not necessary.

SAFETY AND HEALTH

Police: Guarda Nacional Republicana (GNR) covers 98% of Portuguese territory, especially in urban areas. GNR are military personnel. Policía de Segurança Pública (PSP) is a civilian police force based in more populated areas. Not all officers speak English.

Drugs and Alcohol: Using or possessing drugs is illegal in Portugal, but, in 2001, the charge was changed from criminal to administrative, meaning more community service and less (usually no) jail time. The legal drinking age in Portugal is 18.

Crime: Portugal is a safe country but tourists must stay vigilant for petty crimes such as pickpocketing. Safeguard your belongings and especially your passport.

SLOVENIA

If countries were people, Slovenia would be the sexy new kid that's shrouded in mystery. There's something deliciously seductive about how under the radar Slovenia remains (and yes, we mean Slovenia, not Slovakia—don't get it twisted). Once you peel back those layers of mystery, though, be prepared to fall head over heels in love. As one of the successor states to the former Socialist Federal Republic of Yugoslavia, Slovenia has only been around in its current iteration since 1991, but it's been naturally stunning for millennia. Slovenia's storied history is peppered with legendary tales; according to local lore Jason, of Jason and the Argonauts fame, was the famous founder of Ljubljana. It is the ideal representation of Central European charm, bringing together Italian, Austrian, and Balkan influences to create a delectably captivating cultural mix reflected in the nation's cuisine, music, and architecture. Explore the emerging Slovenian street art scene and dip deeper into its Yugoslav history (because we know you didn't learn about this in school).

Slovenia's big claim to fame, however, are its unimaginably pristine naturescapes. With its bright turquoise lakes, jaw-dropping lush hiking trails, and majestic mountain ranges, this tiny country packs quite the punch. From the rushing green rivers of Ljubljana to the impossibly picturesque waters of Lake Bled to the quaintly picturesque coast of Piran, Slovenia is every nature lover's dream.Lace up your hiking boots, pull out your favorite flannel, and drench yourself in some bug spray: it's time to get up close and personal with Europe's most scenic secret gem.

LJUBLJANA

Coverage by **Lydia Tahraoui**

You'll need a good five days to figure out how to pronounce Ljubljana, but only a good five minutes to fall in love with it. Ljubljana has been a hot commodity since its early days: Around 50 BC, the Romans built a military encampment there and, in the 9th century, the Franks took over. Nearly four centuries later, the Bohemians conquered the city briefly before long-term rule passed to the Hapsburg Empire (yikes). Maybe those early conquerors saw what we see: a beautiful, tranquil riverside city that brings together stunning natural views with a laid-back approach to life. No wonder they all wanted a piece.

Today, Ljubljana is one of Europe's most charming capital cities. It's known for being green: it's got green rivers, green parks, and green trees as far as the eye can see. In the summer, the city's many squares spring to life as tourists and locals come together to enjoy cold drinks on the tranquil banks of the Ljubljana River. There's plenty of history here, and you'll stumble upon the city's myths and legends at the top of Ljubljana Castle, inside its museums, and while strolling along cobblestone streets flanked by colorful architecture. Oh, and by the way: it's pronounced lyoo-bley-ah-nuh.

ORIENTATION

The center of the world is **Prešeren Square**. Okay, fine, maybe that was a little hyperbolic. But we'll stand behind the claim that the center of Ljubljana is **Prešeren**. We can prove it. Most of the spots you're dying to see are located in the city center, which is organized in a circular-ish formation. **Prešeren Square** is at the heart of this circle and is bifurcated by the **Ljubljana River,** which runs through the city. You'll find tons of restaurants, cafés, and bars alongside the river. The Square is also home to **Triple Bridge,** or **Tromostovje,** which connect old Ljubljana to the modern city. Head eastwards for historical Ljubljana, and westwards for modern digs. Most of the major tourist hotspots are located within a 30 minute walk of **Prešeren.** Case in point: **Ljubljana Castle** lies right to the east, and **Tivoli Park** right to the west.

ESSENTIALS

GETTING THERE

Don't fly into Ljubljana. No, seriously. If you're the type to catch flights, not feelings, make an exception. Slovenia's main airport, Ljubljana Jože Pučnik Airport is located 26 kilometers outside the city center (read: pretty far away) and there's a limited range of flights coming in. You're better off grabbing a train or bus—it's better, faster, cheaper, smarter. The bus is probably the most cost effective option. The Ljubljana Bus Station is about a 5min. walk from the city center. The Bus Station is also located right by the Railway Station. That's what we call convenience. Train tickets are slightly more expensive, but this is a faster option for you speed demons out there. Ljubljana is well connected to most European cities through both bus and train lines.

GETTING AROUND

Lace up your sneakers, because you'll want to walk this city. The city center is closed off to cars and motorcycles, meaning that you're going to be relying on your feet. There's no need to panic, though. Ljubljana is delightfully compact. Just about everything is concentrated in the city center, and you can get from one end to the other in 50 minutes on foot, easy. If you're not crazy about leisurely strolls, you can rent a bike from the Tourist Information Center.

PRACTICAL INFORMATION

Tourist Offices: Ljubljana Tourist Information Centre (Adamič-Lundrovo nabrežje 2 1000; 01 306 12 15; visitljubljana.com; open daily, 8am-9pm Jun 1 to Sep 30, 8am-7pm 1 Oct to 31 May).

Banks/ATMs/Currency Exchange: There are tons of banks and ATMs across the city. They're particularly concentrated near Preseren Square. Here's one:

- Bankomat UniCredit (01 080 88 00, Wolfova ulica 1, unicreditbank.si, open 24hr).

Post Offices: There are several post offices. Here's one for reference:

- Pošta Slovenije (01 243 16 00, Čopova ulica 11, open M-F 8am-7pm, Sa 8am-12pm).

Public Restrooms: Most major tourist spots have an adjoining bathroom. Here's one right next to Triple Bridge/ Tromostovje:

- Public Toilet Triple Bridge/Tromostovje (open 7am-12am).

Internet: The city operates the WiFree Ljubljana network, which visitors can use in the city center for up to 60 minutes a day. Most cafés and restaurants offer free Wi-Fi.

BGLTQ+ Resources: Legebrita (Trubarjeva 76a, 01 430 51 44, www.legebitra.si, open Tu 12:00-16:00, Thu 12:00-18:00).

EMERGENCY INFORMATION

Emergency Number: 113.

Police: If it's an emergency, call 113. If not, here's a station near the city center:

- Ljubljana Center Police Station (Trdinova ulica 10, 01 475 06 00, policija.si).

US Embassy: Embassy of the United States (Prešernova 31; 01 200 55 00; si.usembassy.gov; appointment only).

Rape Crisis Center: Association SOS (01 080 11 55; drustvo-sos.si; helpline open M-F 12pm-10 pm, Sa-Su 6pm-10pm).

Hospitals:

- University Medical Centre Ljubljana (Zaloška 2, 01 522 50 50, open 24hr).

Pharmacies:

- Ljubljana Central Pharmacy (Prešernov trg 5; 01 230 61 00; open M-F 7:30am-7:30pm, Sa 8am-3pm).

SIGHTS

CULTURE

METELKOVA MESTO

Metelkova ulica 10; metelkovamesto.org; open daily 24hr

If you've got a pair of Doc Martens stuffed into your travel backpack, now is the time to break them out. Metelkova Mesto is described in many ways. The city calls it an alternative cultural center. Its website calls it an autonomous social center. We call it the most indie alt scene this side of the Adriatic. It consists of former military barracks turned activist space, graffiti haven, and urban squat, and houses plenty of NGOs, edgy bars, urban art, and Slovene skateboarders. Take a nice long walk around and acquaint yourself with the edgier side of Ljubljana.

i Ljubljanski grad (Ljubljana Castle)

LJUBLJANSKI GRAD (LJUBLJANA CASTLE)

Grajska planota 1; 01 306 42 93; ljubljanskigrad.si; open daily 9am-9pm

Get ready to feel like Slovene royalty—well, at least for the next hour or so. Ljubljana Castle sits proud and mighty on top of the aptly named Castle Hill. Once you make the scenic trek up to the hill, you'll be privy to breathtaking views of **Old Ljubljana.** You'll also be standing at the base of medieval fortress. It doesn't get much better than that. Even if you don't want to splurge for tickets, you can still enjoy incredible views from Castle Hill for the cheap, cheap price of free. Ljubljana Castle is also home to a jazz club and a restaurant. Food, views, and jazz—wait, why do we have to leave?

i Student €9; 10% discount for online purchases; guided and audio tours available

BLED

Prepare to feel like you've just walked onto the set of a Disney movie, because Bled serves up some serious fairy tale vibes. Medieval castle with breathtaking lake views? Of course. Tiny island complete with an ancient-temple-turned-Baroque-church? You know it. Mystical wishing bell said to grant your deepest desires? Okay, listen, we weren't playing when we said fairy tale. Bled is lovely little resort town at the foothills of the Julian Alps, and the town's big claim to fame is Lake Bled. Trust us, you've never come across a lake this vibrant. Get your cameras ready, because no filters are needed here. Bled also has you covered in terms of gorgeous hiking trails, picturesque viewpoints, and breathtaking natural wonders. There are only a couple places where you can live out your outdoor adventure dreams while simultaneously feeling like a Disney protagonist. Bled's one of them.

Situate yourself using the Bled bus station, which is right in the heart of the town. There's tons of restaurants, cafes, hostels, and shops in this area. Swimming isn't allowed on this side of the lake, since this is town proper, thank you very much. If you start heading westwards, you'll arrive at Camping Bled after a 25 minute walk. The camping area is right next to the boating docks and beach, where you can swim, raft, and kayak away to your heart's content. One of the town's most popular hiking trails is right in this area, and it leads to Mala Osojnica, the hottest spot for sweeping views of the lake. Once you start to leave the lakeshores, there's plenty of outdoor adventure to be had. Vintgar Gorge is about an hour's walk north of Lake Bled and Lake Bohinj is a 40 minute drive to the southwest.

GETTING THERE

It's no secret that the easiest way to travel Slovenia is by car. Bled isn't an exception to this rule. It's a 40 minute drive from Ljubljana to Bled, and makes for an easy trip on the A2/E61 highway. If you don't have a car, your best bet is the bus. There's a bus leaving from Ljubljana to Bled several times an hour, and the trip takes about an hour and fifteen minutes. The Bled bus station is based right in the heart of the town, so the trip from the station to your accommodations should be a pretty quick one.

GETTING AROUND

If you're planning on sticking near Lake Bled, just walk. The town center is fairly small, and though there's a bit of up-and-down hill action, most places are easily accessible by foot. Here's the catch, though: lots of travelers like to use Bled as a homebase while exploring nearby spots like Lake Bohinj, Savica Waterfall, or the Soča River Valley. These natural wonders are up to two hours away from Bled, and that's if you're driving. If you're taking the bus, trip times can double. The easiest way to visit nearby spots is—you guessed it—by driving there. If that's not doable, though, you can stop by the Bled bus station and hop on some public transport.

Don't miss...

MALA OSOJNICA

Ljubljanska cesta 8

We have a theory: 75 percent of travellers who visit Bled decide to do so because they saw one specific picture. You know the one: it's the birds eye view shot that captures the tourmaline waters of the lake, the leafy majesty of the island, and the regal mountains in one breathtaking, intensely Insta-worthy photo. Well, 99 percent of those shots were taken from this spot: the Mala Osojnica viewpoint. You'll get here by hiking up a trail located right next to the Camping Bled grounds. It's about a 20 minute

climb from the start of the trail, and parts of it get pretty steep. Still, the views you get are beyond rewarding. There's a bit of a clamor at the top for the best angles, so just be patient as you prepare to get your pictures.
i Free; no wheelchair accessibility

Check out...

BLED CASTLE

Grajska cesta; www.blejski-grad.si/en/about-bled-castle; Jan-Mar daily 8am-6pm; Apr-June daily 8am-8pm, July-Aug daily 8am-9pm, Sept-Oct daily 8am-8pm, Nov-Dec daily 8am-6pm

This is the grandaddy of Slovenian castles. The earliest mentions of Bled Castle date all the way back to 1011, which means the castle has been around for a hot sec. It's the nation's oldest castle, and still one of the most popular tourist spots in Slovenia. It sits at the top of a 130 meter cliff, so it's got a great vantage point of Lake Bled and the surrounding mountain ranges. Like any self-respecting medieval castle, Bled Castle is complete with multiple towers, courtyards, and a drawbridge. Because it's been around for so long, the castle's been subject to a wide variety of architectural impulses. Some parts are Romanesque, other parts are Gothic, but all parts feel like they could've housed Rapunzel way back in the day. The castle has stepped into the modern era with the establishment of a restaurant, a museum, and a wine cellar, just for good measure.

i Admission €11, student €7, children 14 and under €5; no wheelchair accessibility

Swing by...

BLED ISLAND

Bled Island 4260 Bled; bled.si, open daily 24hr

Listen, we don't want to get cheesy, but Bled Island is one of those places that seems almost too beautiful to be real. Most people get their first glimpse of it from a distance, where they see a foliage-covered, tear-shaped island right in the middle of turquoise waters against a backdrop of regal mountain ranges. Okay, wow. It's the kind of view that takes your breath away. Once you've regained use of your lungs, though, we recommend getting to see the island up close. The most common method is to rent a boat and row over which takes around an hour. You'll soon understand why Bled Island is the setting for many of Slovenian's most beloved legends. It's too stunning to not be mythologized.

i Boat rental €15; no wheelchair accessibility

Grab a bite at...

PIZZERIA RUSTIKA ($)

Riklijeva cesta 13; 04 576 89 00; pizzeria-rustika.si; open daily 12pm-11pm

Everyone goes to Pizzeria Rustika for their first dinner in Bled. In all honesty, it's a rite of passage. Here's why: Pizzeria Rustika serves up drool-worthy pizzas that could comfortably serve up to four small children on a quaint little outdoor terrace right near Bled Castle. The service is quick and the prices are decent. You can expect a pretty big pie from this place, so be ready to pack leftovers for your hike tomorrow. Plus, it's a great spot to mingle with other travelers.

i Pizzas from €9; no wheelchair accessibilty

NEBOTIČNIK (SKYSCRAPER)

Štefanova ulica 1; 04 023 30 78; nebot-icnik.si; night club and café open Su to W 9pm-1am, Th to Sa 9pm-3am, restaurant open M to Sa 12pm-11pm

It's a bar! It's a lounge! It's a café! It's a...skyscraper? Ljubljana's Skyscraper is all this and more. It offers some of the best panoramic views of the city from a 231 meter high vantage point. Modeled after your good-old fashioned American high rise, Nebotičnik is thirteen stories tall. The floors you care about are eleven, twelve, and thirteen—featuring a café, a bar, and an observation deck, respectively. Grab a latte or a glass of wine, and cozy up against sweeping views of Slovenia's capital city.

i Free

LANDMARKS

PREŠERNOV TRG (PREŠEREN SQUARE)

Prešernov trg 1

We love a good town square, and Prešeren is a great one. It's named for Slovene poet France Prešeren. There's something charmingly poetic about his namesake square. It's organized in a circular design and sits right in the heart of city center. Here you'll find colorful buildings, regal statues, and plenty of ice cream. In the summer, you'll hear the intoxicating lilt of live music most evenings. The Square sits right by the **Ljubljana River**, making for gorgeous backdrops and a laid-back atmosphere. Even better, you won't miss it because you'll be walking through it to get to almost anywhere else in Ljubljana. Sit back, eat a snack, and read some poetry. It's what France Prešeren would've wanted.

i Free; book tours from the Tourist Information Center, located to the immediate left of the Prešeren Monument

TROMOSTOVJE (TRIPLE BRIDGE)

Stritarjeva ulica

What's better than one bridge? Three bridges! That's right, folks. You get three bridges for the price of nothing with Tromostovje, a group of three stone arch bridges that connect historical Ljubljana with the modern city. Sitting pretty on top of the Ljubljana River, Tromostovje offers tranquil waterfront views framed by hanging, leafy vines and brightly colored flowers. Long story short: you're going to want to pose here for your next Instagram post.

i Free; wheelchair accessible

ZMAJSKI MOST (DRAGON BRIDGE)

Resljeva cesta 2

Legend has it that Jason, of Jason and the Argonauts fame, founded Ljubljana. For those of you who need a refresher on Greek mythology, Jason was the guy who stole the Golden Fleece. Local lore claims that after the heist, Jason and his Argonauts fled up the Danube River, eventually arriving in Ljubljana. In Ljubljana, Jason and the Argonauts casually stumbled upon a fearsome dragon. With the help of his wife Medea (she's the one who killed all her children, by the way), Jason slayed the beast. After the dragon's death, Ljubjlana became safe to settle in and was transformed into the thriving riverfront city we know and love today. The dragon is still one of Ljubljana's most recognizable symbols, and if you take one look at Dragon Bridge, you'll see what we mean. This arch bridge is adorned with four iconic dragon statues, which pay homage to the city's mythological origins.

i Free; wheelchair accessible

MUSEUMS

NARODNA GALERIJA (THE NATIONAL GALLERY OF SLOVENIA)

Prešernova cesta 24; 01 241 54 18; ng-slo.si; open Tu-W 10am-6pm, Thu 10am-8pm, F-Su 10am-6pm

If you make it to one museum in Ljubljana, this is the one. The National Gallery houses Slovenia's largest collection of fine art and features hundreds of works from Slovenian and European artists. The museum also hosts a rotating series of temporary exhibitions that shed light on art, politics, and creative expression in Slovenia and beyond. The displays provide plenty of info on Eastern European art history, so you'll walk away ready to impress your friends with delightfully specific fun facts about the Slovenian Impressionist movement (1890-1920).

i €5 reduced; guided tours available

MUZEJ SODOBNE UMETNOSTI METELKOVA (MUSEUM OF CONTEMPORARY ART METELKOVA)

Maistrova ulica 3; 01 241 68 25; mg-lj.si; open M-Sa 10am-6pm

We can't guarantee you'll understand every piece at the Museum of Contemporary Art, but we will say that you'll walk out with a pretty solid understanding of Balkan art from the 1960s to the present. Not surprisingly, a lot of the pieces you'll see here are deeply political. In the past century alone, Slovenia's been part the Kingdom of Yugoslavia, been annexed as part of both Nazi Germany and Fascist Italy, joined socialist Federal Yugoslavia, emerged as a major player in the Non-Aligned Movement, and become the independent, democratic Republic of Slovenia after a Ten Day War. The Museum of Contemporary Art does a solid job of tracing how art has been in dialogue with, reacted to, and informed these political developments. Plus, the museum's got some pretty trippy performance art pieces that you're unlikely to forget soon—even if you'd like to.

i Students €2.50; guided tours available, schedule at least five business days in advance

OUTDOORS

MESTNI PARK TIVOLI (TIVOLI PARK)

Večna pot 1000

If you're itching for an escape from the cityscape (haha), look no further. Tivoli Park is a green oasis right in the heart of Ljubljana. It's Ljubljana's oldest and largest park, established in 1813 and covering five square kilometers. There's landscaped pathways, perfectly groomed flower beds, and expansive hiking trails that stretch up and down the city's modest hills. As if that weren't

enough, there's also a tranquil fish pond and a greenhouse on these grounds. It's a diverse and expansive park, to say the absolute least. You could get lost in this park for hours (it's so big that we almost did). A quick tip: You should probably wear your workout shoes, if only to fit in with the dozens of Slovenes who come here for their daily exercise.

i Free; wheelchair accessible

PARK ŠPICA

Gruberjevo nabrežje 20

The Ljubljana River stretches across the city, but perhaps the best river views are found at Park Špica. Just ten minutes outside of the historical center, Park Špica is right on the water. This used to be Ljubljana's main beach, and today, it's been transformed into landscaped river embankment. Take a seat inches away from the riverbank and find yourself surrounded by plenty of foliage and sweeping vines. Several riverboats pass by every hour, and the nearby café has plenty of alcoholic and non-alcoholic beverages to sip on.

i Free; wheelchair accessible

ROŽNIK

Cankarjev Vrh 1

The question of whether the climb up Rožnik Hill counts as a hike is a contentious one. Haters will say that the 391 meter trek is too short and too easy to fit the definition. To this, we say: enough with the hiking

snobbery. There's a nature-filled trail and a breathtaking view at the top, so it counts. Once you reach the "summit," you'll be rewarded with the sight of an adorable pink church that's been around since the sixteenth century. Ljubljana sunsets are consistently remarkable, but we think there's something uniquely special about a Rožnik sunset. Maybe it's the sense of accomplishment you feel after any good hike—hey, it counts!
i Free

FOOD

SARAJEVO 84

Nazorjeva ulica 12; 01 425 71 06; open M-Sa 11am-12am, Su 11am-10pm

If you ask ten locals for a restaurant recommendation in Ljubljana, we're pretty sure that at least seven of them will mention Sarajevo 84. We might not have the scientific data needed to backup this hypothesis, but we remain confident. This is one of the most high profile joints in the city, and it's not hard to see why. There's an expansive menu of Balkan dishes at super fair prices and an array of upbeat Balkan music to listen to while you eat them. Portions are big and the service is quick. Adding to the ambiance, there's also a quirky collection of memorabilia dedicated to the restaurant's namesake—the 1984 Olympics held in Sarajevo, Bosnia.
i Lunch entreés from €4.30; no wheelchair accessibility

ORGANIC GARDEN

Ciril-Metodov trg 11; 08 205 40 50; organic-garden.eu; open daily 10am-9pm

In Slovenia's slow transformation into a bona fide vegan haven, Organic Garden stands as a testament to the fervor of this hippy metamorphosis. The menu features a solid selection of three trademark vegan burgers and a fish option. Pick from other health food selections too, including wraps, smoothies, and cappuccinos prepared with your selection of artisanal milk (almond or oat or rice?). The portions will satisfy you and the food is photogenic—not to mention deliciously prepared with flavorful sauces and condiments. Plus, like any self-respecting vegan restaurant, the space emits eco-chic vibes and accents its walls with pops of green.
i Burgers from €6.90; limited outdoor seating; no wheelchair accessibility

VIGO ICE CREAM

Mačkova ulica 2; 08 205 64 20; vigo-ice-cream.com; open daily 9am-10pm

There are few combinations more satisfying a warm evening, a riverfront view, and a cone of ice cream. Vigo Ice Cream's got you covered on the latter front. Located right in Preseren Square, Vigo offers a solid selection of bougie flavors for a pretty reasonable price. You can build your own sweet treat by adding toppings, toppings, and more toppings—we're talking rich chocolate, cheesecake bites, globs of Nutella, and beyond.
i Two scoops and a cone from €3.60; limited wheelchair accessibility

NIGHTLIFE

SAX PUB

Eipprova ulica 7; 05 180 44 50; saxhostell-jubljana.com; open M-F 9am-1am, Sat 10am-1am, Sun 10am-1am

It's tough to find a Ljubljana night spot that's consistently populated, but Sax Pub is one such unicorn. Attached to a hostel, the pub brings together a diverse crowd of travelers, students, and Ljubljana locals. What's the draw? We think it has something to do with the cheap drinks, the laid back atmosphere, and the great playlist that spans an impressive range of genres and decades. We tried some of the best cider we've ever had in our so-far short, college-aged lives at this hostel.
i Beer from €2; no wheelchair accessibility

CIRKUS KLUB

Trg mladinskih delovnih brigad 7; 04 177 77 47; cirkusklub.si; open W-Sa 11pm-5am

Ljubljana is known for being a laid back, lowkey city, but that doesn't mean you can't party here. Cirkus is the premier choice for locals and travelers alike, and boasts a wide open dance floor that's always reverberating from a diverse range of dancey hits. The DJ blasts everything from that retro 80s anthem to your most recent top 40 fave. For a taste of local culture, take a listen to the slew of popular Slovenian DJs that Cirkus hosts and make sure to check the website to see what's going on. Ljubljana's main party nights are Wednesdays, Fridays, and Saturdays, so plan accordingly.

i Cover from €8; no wheelchair accessibility

KAVARNA TROMOSTOVJE

Prešernov trg 1; 07 039 98 05; open daily 8am-1am

There are plenty of bars and lounges up and down Ljubljana River, but this one's got live music. Prepare to be serenaded by local singers with a remarkably diverse repertoire—we're talking musical covers of everything from Ed Sheeran ballads to the Shrek soundtrack. Somehow, Smash Mouth sounds even better on a warm summer evening next to a glistening river, cold drink in hand. The bar also doubles as a café and restaurant, so if alcoholic drinks aren't your thing, you've still got a diverse menu to select from.

i No cover; wheelchair accessible

PIRAN

Coverage by **Lydia Tahraoui**

Slovenia's only got a couple of miles of coast, but we'll be damned if the Slovenian coast isn't a testament to the general rule that size doesn't matter. It's all about how you use what you've got, and that limited coastland is certainly put to excellent use. Case in point: let us introduce Piran—a glistening seaside city right on the Adriatic. Nestled between Italy to the north and Croatia to the south, Piran has a multinational, multicultural history. Once upon a time, Piran was part of Venice, and that Venetian influence certainly shines through today. All it takes is one good look at the city's brightly colored architecture, or one good bite of a pasta and seafood plate, to see what we mean. Unlike Venice, however, Piran is known for being a chilled-out paradise. Maybe it's the gentle coastal breeze, or maybe it's the lulling sounds of lapping waves. Either way, Piran is definitely in the running for the title of Slovenia's Most Peaceful Seaside Escape.

ORIENTATION

Buckle up folks, we're taking you around Piran. The best place to start is **Tartini Square**, because it's right at the center of the city. You'll find tons of shops, cafés, and restaurants that encircle a wide open, pedestrian-only platform. Find the fishing docks right to the south of Tartini. If you head north of the square, you'll hit two tourist hotspots that are (conveniently!) right next to each other: **St. George's Parish Church** and **St. George's Clock Tower.** If you continue southeast from there, you'll make it to the **Walls of Piran**. West of Tartini is the **Riviera**, where you'll find plenty of bars and eateries—not to mention great views of the Adriatic. If you're looking for more of a party atmosphere, southeast of Piran is the town of Portorož, which is known to be somewhat livelier—and drunker.

ESSENTIALS

GETTING THERE

It takes an 1hr and 20min to drive from Ljubljana to Piran, so if you've got a car, head southwest down the A1 highway. If not, the easiest way to get to Piran is by connecting through Ljubljana. There are several buses that leave from the Ljubljana station to Piran each day, but they tend to take off in the earlier hours. To be safe, try to get to the Ljubljana station before 2pm. Your other option is the train, which runs throughout the day. Book a ticket to Koper, another southern town that isn't too far from Piran. From the Koper train station, catch a bus to Piran. You'll arrive after a scenic 40min. drive.

GETTING AROUND

Piran feels small and is pedestrian friendly. If you're planning on sticking to Piran city limits during your trip, walking is the most efficient way to get around. Lots of people tend to visit Portorož in the same go, and you can also totally walk here. It's about a 40 minute walk, or a 10 minute drive for those of you with a car. There's also a bus that regularly leaves from Piran bus station and stops in Portorož—a trip takes no more than 20 minutes.

PRACTICAL INFORMATION

Tourist Offices: Turistično informacijski center Piran (Tartinijev trg 2, 05 673 44 40; open daily 9am-noon, 12:30pm-5pm).

Banks/ATMs/Currency Exchange: Here's a bank right in Tartini Square:

- Banka Intesa Sanpaolo (Tartinijev trg 1; 05 674 33 80; open M-F 8:30am-4:30pm).

Post Offices: Poštna poslovalnica (Cankarjevo nabrežje 5; 03 071 87 86; open M-F 9am-6pm, Sa 9am-noon).

Public Restrooms: There's a public restroom right across from the bus station with a €1 entry fee.

Internet: Most restaurants, cafés, and hostels offer free Wi-Fi.

BGLTQ+ Resources: Unfortunately, there are no designated BGLTQ+ resource centers in Piran. If you're looking for assistance or info reach out to Legebrita in nearby Ljubljana (Trubarjeva 76a, 01 430 51 44, www.legebitra.si, open Tu noon-4pm, Thu noon-6pm).

EMERGENCY INFORMATION

Emergency Number: 112.

Police: If there's an emergency, call 113. If not, here's a nearby station in Portorož:

- Policijska postaja (Liminjanska cesta 116, 05 617 16 00, portoroz.si).

US Embassy: There isn't a US Embassy office in Piran, but the one in Ljubljana isn't too far and can be of assistance to Americans traveling throughout Slovenia.

- US Embassy: Embassy of the United States (Prešernova 31; 01 200 55 00; si.usembassy.gov; appointment only).

Rape Crisis Center: The closest rape crisis center is based in Ljubljana, but their hotline can be accessed from Bled. Here's their info:

- Association SOS (01 080 11 55; drustvo-sos.si; helpline open M-F noon-10pm, Sa-Su 6pm-10pm).

Hospitals: There isn't a hospital in Piran, but here's a tourist clinic located in the next town over:

- Tourist Clinic Lucija (Zdravstveni dom Piran Cesta solinarjev 1, Lucija, 6320 Portorož, 05 677 33 20).

Pharmacies: All pharmacies are marked with a green cross sign. Here's one near Tartini Square:

- Pharmacy Piran (Tartinijev trg 4, 05 673 01 50, open M-F 7:30am-7pm, Sa 7:30am-1pm).

SIGHTS

CULTURE

WALLS OF PIRAN

Ulica IX. korpusa, wallsofpiran.com, open daily 8am-dusk

It's a truth universally acknowledged that any medieval city in need of protection must be in want of fortified walls. Piran is no exception. As the city expanded, Piran's leaders started to think hey, some security is probably a good idea. So like the savvy, tenth century rulers they were, they decided that their best bet would be some good old-fashioned walls. Yeah, try passing through these babies, potential invaders! The Walls of Piran have been preserved, maintained, and restored over the years. Today, they're not doing a lot of work by way of protection, but they do offer sweeping views of the seaside city and ideal angles for pics.

i Admission €2, students €1.50

TARTINI SQUARE

Tartinijev Trg

It'd be hard to take a trip to Piran and not pass through Tartini Square—it's Piran's largest, most central, and most picturesque square. All superlatives aside, Tartini is a charming gathering place for tourists and locals alike. Named in honor of violinist **Giuseppe Tartini,** this square keeps a statue of good ol' Giuseppe himself in the center of the square since 1896. A quick glance around the square reveals some obvious Venetian influence here: peep Tartini's multicolored, pastel buildings alongside its winding Gothic alleyways. There's also plenty of outdoor cafés and seafood restaurants.

i Free; wheelchair accessible

LANDMARKS

ST. GEORGE'S CLOCK TOWER

Primož Trubar 18a, open daily 10am-8pm

St. George's is a tall, dark, and handsome clock tower, feeling young at 400 years old and standing tall at 150 feet. The tower perches on one of Piran's many hills and is one of the highest points in the city. Like a lot of Piran's landmarks, the clock tower is a testament to Piran's Venetian past. It's been likened to St. Mark's Campanile in Venice, except smaller, quainter, and much more climbable. A winding and narrow staircase makes the trek up slow, since only one person can go up or down at a time, but a refreshing breeze will reward your efforts. The tower was built way back in 1608, and it's now one of the most multinational vantage points you'll find in Slovenia. Case in point: you can catch a peak of Slovenia (obvi), Croatia, and Italy from the top of the tower. Capturing three countries in one panoramic pic? Not bad, St. George's Clock Tower, not bad.

i Admission €2

ST. GEORGE'S PARISH CHURCH

Primož Trubar 18a, open daily 7am-10pm

Right next door to St. George's Clock Tower is St. George's Parish Church. Who would've guessed, right? The church has been around for a hot minute. It was first built in the twelfth century, expanded in the fourteenth century, and then got a total Renaissance makeover in the seventeenth century. It's now got frescoes to boot. The church is dedicated in honor of—how'd you know?!—St. George, who is said to have saved Piran from a raging storm back in the day. You can check out the lovely church interior, along with a modest museum that holds around 20 religious artifacts. If you don't feel like paying an entrance fee, you can see some of the interior through the doorway and get that taste of Venetian religiosity.

i Admission €1.50

MUSEUMS

SERGEJ MAŠERA PIRAN MARITIME MUSEUM

Cankarjevo nabrežje 3, 05 671 00 40; pomorskimuzej.si/en, open Tu-Su 9am-noon, 5pm-9pm

This classical-palace-turned-museum holds some pretty insights into Piran's local history. It was first established in 1954, and in 1967 was renamed after **Sergej Mašera,** a Slovene-sailor-turned-local-hero who tragically died in World War II. The museum focuses on Slovenia, the sea, ships, and stories. There's an archeological exhibit that's filled with ancient maritime artifacts and there's a collection entirely dedicated to the craft of salt-making.

Local legends are woven through all these different exhibits, and you'll walk away knowing just a little more about the history of the Slovenian coast.

i Student €2.50

OUTDOORS

SLOVENE RIVIERA

Slovene Riviera, open daily 24hr

Time to drag along your travel bae! If you don't have one, your most swoon worthy Spotify playlist will do just fine. The Slovene Riviera feels like it was made especially for long, romantic seaside strolls. The Riviera runs up and down Piran's coast, and there's plenty of wide open walkways right on the water. There's less sand than you expected, and more concrete than you bargained for. It's not what you might imagine when you think "coastal quaint," but there's a gentle breeze and crashing waves, which means we're satisfied. On the Piran side, there are gorgeous views of the Adriatic and tons of seaside eateries. Start heading towards Portorož to hit some more beachy areas, which provide the perfect tanning surface for weary and pale travelers.

i Free

FOOD

FRITOLIN PRI CANTINI ($)

Prvomajski trg 10; 04 187 38 72; open daily 11am-10pm

Talk about bang for your buck. Frintolin pri Cantini is a tiny, hole-in-the-wall seafood spot that combines ultra-cheap prices with out of this world quality. It's the student traveler's dream: a self-service joint with outdoor seating and a pretty expansive menu of seafood dishes, including fried fish, cooked fish, stirred fish, battered fish. The plates are absolutely mouthwatering—perfectly crisp, fresh out of Piran's rocky shores, and seasoned just the way seafaring Slovenians have always scarfed down meals. With Fritolin pri Cantini, you're getting what you paid for and then much, much more.

i Plates from €5.20

TRI VDOVE ($$)

Prešernovo nabrežje 4; 05 673 02 90; restaurant-3vdove.si; open daily 11am-12am

When in Piran, do as the Piranos do: Eat seafood. The city's got tons of restaurants that offer a plethora of variations of classic fish dishes, and Tri Vdove is one of our favorites. Not only is the food relatively inexpensive, but the restaurant sits so close to the Riviera that you can practically stick your toes in the water while you chow down. Well, not actually, but turn to your right, and hey, would you look at that, there's the Adriatic Sea. Our favorite thing about Tri Vdove is how welcoming and attentive the wait staff are. The owner and waiters are constantly popping by to make sure you're satisfied, and given how good the food is, there's a high chance you will be.

i Plates from €7

NIGHTLIFE

CLUB ALAYA

Obala 22, 6320 Portorož; 04 161 21 69; open M-Th 10am-1am, F-Sa 10am-3am, Su 10am-midnight

Club Alaya has the beach aesthetic down pat. Fake palm trees? Check. Outdoor cabanas? Check. Beachy bungalows? Don't you know it. Located in nearby Portorož, Club Alaya is a relaxing lounge in the day and transforms into an electronic, dance-y club at night. What stays constant, though, is an expansive drink menu and super friendly bartenders. For a price, you can go all in with the beach experience and get your cocktail served in fresh fruit. It doesn't get much more tropical than a cocktail in a carved-out pineapple. Club Alaya is pretty quiet during the week, but on the weekends, its the beach club of choice for tons of tourists and locals alike. There are regular themed events, ranging from secret discos to dock parties, so check out the club's Facebook page for the latest info.

i Cocktails from €7.50, draught beers from €2.20

CAFINHO PIRAN

Prvomajski trg 3; 04 055 44 10; open daily 7am-3am

Cafinho Piran is one of the few late night spots in Piran, and for that we are grateful. This is a truly well-rounded establishment. There's great craft beer and genuinely delicious seafood plates to snack on. This is the place you'd go to for a chilled out night cap; Cafinho Piran is a great way to end your night on a full stomach, while ensuring that you will wake up hangover free. The staff are extremely outgoing and talkative, so go ahead and strike up a conversation at the bar.

i Beer from €2.70

SLOVENIA ESSENTIALS

VISAS

Slovenia is a member of the EU and the Schengen Area. Citizens from Australia, Canada, New Zealand, the US, and many other non-EU countries do not require a visa for stays up to 90 days.

MONEY

Currency: Slovenia is a member of the Eurozone, and accordingly uses the euro.

Tipping: Tips are not expected in Slovenia, but they are appreciated. As a rule of thumb, it's courteous to round up on any bills. At restaurants, you may wish to tip around 10% for good service.

SAFETY AND HEALTH

BGLTQ+ Travel: Homosexuality was decriminalized in 1976, and today discrimmination against BGLTQ+ individuals is banned by law. BGLTQ+ organizations in Slovenia have been active in combating homophobia, and these organizations maintain a strong presence in Ljubljana. Ljubljana is recognized as being especially gay friendly, but strong BGLTQ+ presence is less established outside of the capital.

Drugs and Alcohol: The legal drinking age in Slovenia is 18. The legal blood alcohol content for driving in Slovenia is under 0.05%, significantly lower than the US limit of 0.08%. The possession of illicit substances for personal use in small quantities is not a criminal act. It is considered to be a misdemeanor, and is punishable by fines range from €42-€210 or up to 5 days in jail.

LANGUAGE

The official language of Slovenia is Slovene, a South Slavic language that shares some similarities with Serbo-Croatian. However, English is widely understood and spoken in Slovenia, especially in major tourist destinations.

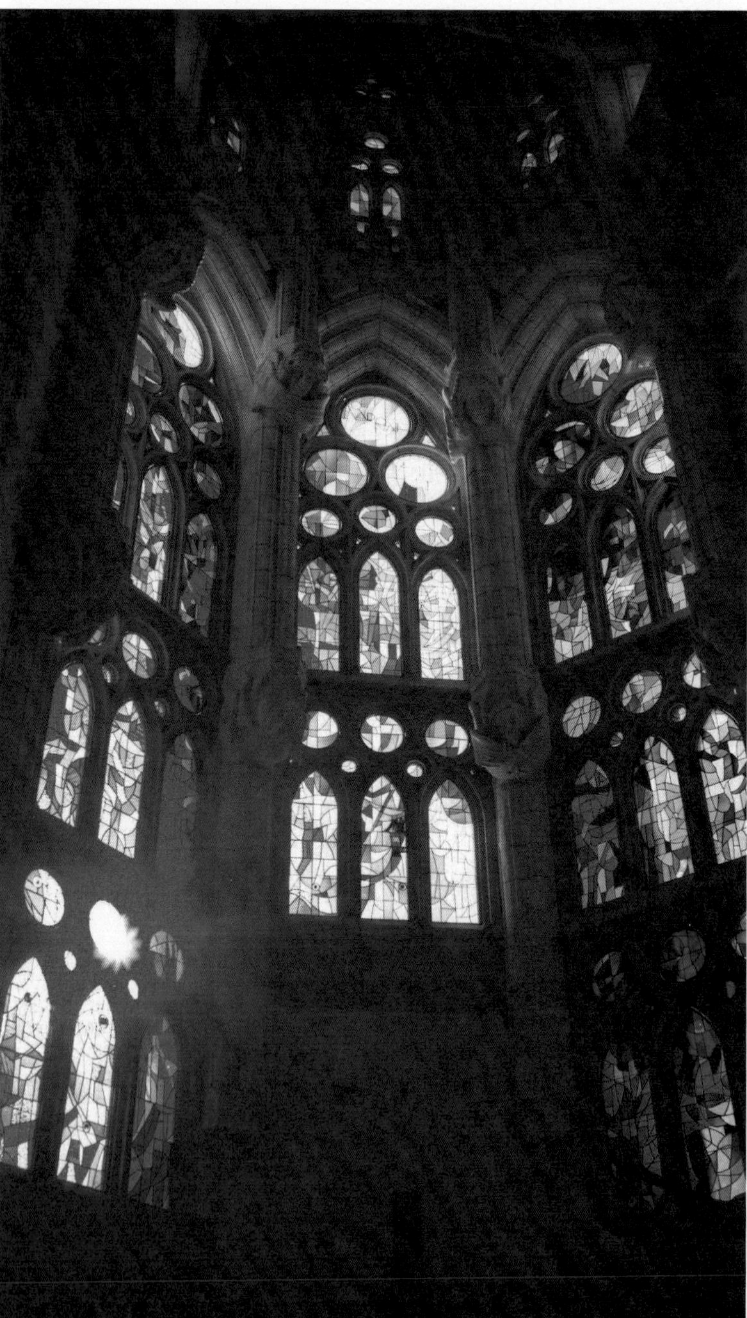

SPAIN

Tapas or pintxos? What about *pinchos? ¿Algo para picar?* Whatever you call Spain's favorite snack, the country's culture is as rich and varied as its gastronomy. From the brooding forests of the northeast to the sun-soaked Mediterranean coast, each region—and every city—offers a different flavor of Spain. And we're talking more than just *patatas bravas* and silky gazpacho; throughout its multi-millennial history, Spain has become a world-class potpourri of art, architecture, and culture.

Boasting everything from metropolises like Madrid and Barcelona to hamlets dotting the Basque country, there are few nations on earth with such a diversity of delights. Run-ins with superstars like Goya, Picasso, and Dalí are daily occurrences. Moorish mosques, Gothic cathedrals, and Baroque palaces are routine sightseeing material. There's so much to do, to photograph, to eat: you'll almost certainly need that midday siesta if you plan on wading through everything the country has to offer.

Whether you find yourself in sun-drenched Valencia or fiercely independent Bilbao, the Spain that welcomes you will do so loudly and proudly, most likely with an icy glass of sangria (or three). You couldn't resist if you tried—under the fuzzy spell of this spiced (and spiked) lemonade, savor the pull of Spain's mesmerizing embrace. In a blur, you'll be sipping your last drink, polishing off your last tapa, and crawling back from your final *fiesta*. Flights home from this dazzling country will always come far too soon.

BARCELONA

Coverage by **Austin Eder**

Known for its beaches, its *fútbol,* and its groundbreaking architecture, Barcelona is one of the most lively and vibrant places on Earth. Walking down its streets is drowning in a sea of color. Dining at its restaurants is being showered with the scents of seafood and sangria. Dancing at its clubs is to being pummeled into the earth with the deafening pulses of techno. But Barcelona, for all its beauty, is not without strife. Its role as Catalonia's capital has forced it into a pivotal position regarding the future of Spain. The country suffered a brief democratic crisis shortly after the Referendum of 2017—its leaders, confronted with an unfavorable outcome, dissolved parliament and called a snap election. Paradoxically, however, the country's future is clearer now than it was a year ago. Secession is a long way off, at least according to experts. So, what does this mean for you, eager backpacker? Well, the issue of Catalan independence aside, Barcelona is already laced with past remnants of political, social, and economic turmoil. Prior to becoming a tourist hotspot, Castell de Montjuïc served as a prison and torture facility. Until a few decades ago, the Bunkers of Carmel—a romantic viewpoint and local student hangout—functioned as a storage facility for weapons. Despite facing some grueling challenges, Barcelona's citizens have proven to be extremely resilient. They've turned their frustrations into art, and now for every reminder of the city's turbulent past, there exists a beacon of a brighter future. Luckily for you, those beacons are open to the public and waiting to explored.

ORIENTATION

Barcelona is a sprawling metropolis with several different neighborhoods. From south to north along the coast lie **Montjuïc,** a hilly district that contains a castle, a botanical garden, a stadium, Barcelona's Plaza de España, and several different museums; **Poble-Sec,** a primarily residential neighborhood famed for its cheap restaurants and bars (check out **Carrer de Blai,** home to Barcelona's infamous €1 tapas); and **El Raval,** a grunge-chic area filled with cutting-edge exhibitions, bohemian bars, and street art. The **Gothic Quarter** is home to **La Rambla** and **Barcelona Cathedral**—two of the city's busiest attractions; south you'll find **Barceloneta,** a beachside neighborhood known for its clubs and cocktail bars, and to the east lies **La Ribera,** previously Barcelona's red-light district. Even further east is **El Poblenou,** which houses Barcelona's tech offices and design showrooms. Inland of these neighborhoods lie **Eixample** and **Gràcia,** which together constitute the majority of the city. **Plaça de Catalunya** serves as the city's de facto center. Important thoroughfares include **La Rambla, Passeig de Gràcia, Passeig de Colom,** and **Avinguda Diagonal,** which splices the city in half. Barcelona's metropolitan center lies south of Avinguda Diagonal and north of **Avinguda del Parallel.**

ESSENTIALS

GETTING THERE

Aeroport del Prat de Llobregat (El Prat Airport) harbors both domestic and international flights. From the airport, you can reach Barcelona's city center via bus, train, or taxi. The Aérobus is an express bus that connects both the international and domestic terminal to Plaça de Catalunya. It departs every 5min. and takes approximately 35min. (one way €5.90, round-trip €10.20). City buses take slightly longer, but cost less (one way €2.15, round trip €4.50). Alternatively, you can take the metro from the airport to Estació Sants, Passeig de Gràcia, or El Clot. The ride lasts 40min. and costs €4.50. Trains to Estació Barcelona-Sants (domestic and international) and Estació de

França (regional) depart from Terminal 1 of El Prat Airport. RENFE trains connect to Bilbao, Madrid, Seville, and Valencia. Barcelona's main bus station is called Estació d'Autobuses Barcelona Nord, and located close to the Arc de Triomf. Buses also depart from Estació Barcelona-Sants and El Prat Airport. Spain's main bus provider is ALSA. Taxis from the airport to the city center cost roughly €35.

GETTING AROUND

The fastest way to get around Barcelona is by metro. A single ride costs €2.15, while a T-10 Zone 1 ticket (10 rides) costs €9.90. Transfers on the Barcelona Metro are free and tickets are compatible with trams, trains, and buses as well. Metro lines are marked by an L before the line number and tram lines are marked with a T. Metros, trams, and trains run from 5am-midnight Su-Th, from 5am-2am on Friday, and 24hr on Saturday. Barcelona's buses travel to more remote places than the metro. The NitBus picks up the slack while the metro is closed, while BarriBuses (max 10 people) traverse the narrow streets of Barcelona's outer districts.

PRACTICAL INFORMATION

Tourist Offices: Plaça de Catalunya (Pl. de Catalunya; 932 853 834; barcelonaturisme.com; open daily 8:30am-9pm)

Banks/ATMs/Currency Exchange: ATMs abound in Barcelona and can be found on every other block in Eixample and Ciutat Vella. Passeig de Gràcia contains a high concentration of banks, including Deutsche Bank Filiale (Passeig de Gràcia, 112; 934 04 21 02; open M-F 8:30am-2pm).

Post Offices: Here's one in the Gothic Quarter (Plaça d'Antonio López; 934 86 83 02; correos.es; open M-F 8:30am-9:30pm, Sa 8:30am-2pm).

Internet: Free Wi-Fi is available at over 500 locations in Barcelona, including museums, parks, and beaches. Wi-Fi zones are marked by a blue "Barcelona Wi-Fi" sign. You can connect for free after accepting the terms and conditions through your browser.

Public Restrooms: Public toilets are few and far between in Barcelona, except near city beaches. Large shopping centres (or the El Corte Inglés department store) are an option, but restaurants are probably your best bet.

BGLTQ+ Resources: Gay Barcelona (gaybarcelona.com) provides up-to-date tips for finding BGLTQ+ friendly restaurants and bars. Casal Lambda is a Spanish non-profit that offers community spaces for socializing, a center for information and documentation, as well as counseling (Av. del Marquès de l'Argentera, 22; 933 19 55 50; open M-Sa 5pm-9pm).

EMERGENCY INFORMATION

Emergency Number: 112.

Police: Police stations are dispersed throughout the city. This one is located on La Rambla (Carrer la Rambla, 43; 932 56 24 30).

US Embassy: Barcelona's US Consulate is located at Passeig de la Reina Elisenda de Montcada, 23 (932 80 22 27; open M-F 9am-1pm).

Rape Crisis Center: The Center for Assistance to Victims of Sexual Assault (CAVA) is located in Madrid, but can provide assistance to persons based in Barcelona (Carrer Alcalá, 124, Suite 1ºA; Madrid; 915 74 01 10).

Hospitals: Hospital Clínic de Barcelona is highly rated and open 24hr (Carrer de Villarroel, 170; 932 27 54 00).

Pharmacies: There are pharmacies located throughout Ciutat Vella and Eixample. Farmacia Clapés is open 24hr and located in the Gothic Quarter (Carrer la Rambla, 98; 933 01 28 43).

SIGHTS

CULTURE

BASILICA DE SANTA MARIA DEL MAR

Plaça de Santa Maria, 1; 933 10 23 90; santamariadelmarbarcelona.org/home/; open M-Sa 1pm-5pm, Su 2pm-5pm

Located in the metaphorical shadow of **Catedral de Barcelona,** Basilica de Santa Maria del Mar is not as grand in stature as its sister, but reigns supreme in experience. Built from the ground up by local townspeople during the early fourteenth century, it only took 54 years to build—take that, **Sagrada Familia!** Like the great buildings of the Roman Empire, this Basilica was constructed ad quadratum, meaning all of its features are based on the geometry of squares. Its side aisles are half the span of the central one and its columns are perfectly octagonal, lending the space an airiness typically absent from buildings this old. Sadly, the interiors aren't as impressively decorated as they used to be, due to a fire in 1936 that burned for 11 days straight. Still, the Basilica's most iconic architectural elements—the rose window and intricate reliefs—remain intact.

i Admission €10, €8 reduced; rooftop tour €8, reduced €6.50; no wheelchair accessibility

GOTHIC QUARTER

North of La Rambla, west of Barceloneta, south of Via Laietana, east of Plaça de Catalunya; establishment hours vary

Soot-covered palms sway in the warm Mediterranean air, intermittently shading the tables that pepper **Plaça Reial.** Welcome to Barcelona's Gothic Quarter, the *barrio* immediately northeast of **La Rambla.** It's here that you'll find some of the city's oldest monuments, and here that you'll catch a glimpse of a past life in Spain. Originally the center of a Roman settlement, then the region's Jewish quarter, and later a sombre lower-class neighborhood, the Gothic Quarter underwent a massive restoration project at the turn of the twentieth century. Today you'll find a hodgepodge of architectural styles, ranging from Medieval to Gothic to Flamboyant to Modernisme. Points of interest include the **Roman Walls,** which skirt Plaça Ramón Berenguer and date to the fourth century CE; the **Columbus Monument,** located at the intersection of Passeig de Colom and La Rambla; the **Catedral de Barcelona;** and of course, **La Rambla,** a tree-covered boulevard that doubles as a pedestrian mall.

i Free; limited wheelchair accessibility

VILLA DE GRÀCIA

Northwest of Avinguda Diagonal, northeast of Via Augusta, southeast of Parc Güell, and southwest of Carrer de Sardenya; establishment hours vary

Not to be confused with **Passeig de Gràcia,** a store-lined, intricately-paved boulevard that connects **Ciutat Vella** to **Eixample,** the district of Gràcia feels removed from the rest of the city, despite the fact that it's only a few metro stops away. It is the atmospheric antithesis of Barcelona's **Gothic Quarter**—calm and cozy, not hectic and overbearing. Tourists are in the minority among the artists and young professionals who live here. At night, Gràcia's sloping streets come alive with patio restaurants serving traditional Catalan *pintxos.* Craft breweries, ethnic eateries, and galleries abound in this vibrant and diverse enclave of Catalan life—its intimate, close-packed streets and predominately low-rise, Mediterranean buildings lending it a distinct, bohemian feel. We recommend taking a stroll down the lively **Carrer de Verdi** and turning right on **Carrer de Ros de Olano.** Eventually you'll arrive at **Plaça Del Sol,** where groups of students gather nightly to sit on the ground, drink, and be merry.

i Free; limited wheelchair accessibility

PALAU DE LA MÚSICA CATALANA

Carrer Palau de la Música, 4-6; 932 95 72 00; palaumusica.cat/en; tours daily 10am-6pm every 30min.

Though Antoni Gaudí gets most of the credit for making this city what it is today, he's not the only Spanish architect who left a lasting impression on Barcelona's skyline. **Lluís Domènech i Montaner,** designer of the Palau de la Música Catalana and **Hospital de la Santa Creui i Sant Pau,** hit a few home runs during his lifetime as well. Deemed a **UNESCO World Heritage Site,** this stunning concert hall is a masterpiece of Catalan modernist architecture. You can gawk at its intricate brick and mosaic exterior for free, but getting past the stone busts and glass columns will cost you a pretty penny (the interior is accessible via guided tour only). We'd typically dissuade you from emptying your pockets to listen to a half-there docent mumble for an hour, but in this case—take the tour. Get ready for an explosion of color and light unlike any you've seen before.

i Admission €20, €11 reduced; guided tours in English, Spanish, French, and Catalan; English tours every hour 9am-6pm; wheelchair accessible with advance notice

MERCAT DE LA BOQUERIA

La Rambla, 91; 933 18 25 84; boqueria.barcelona; open M-Sa 8am-8pm

Oooh, baby, have we got a treat for you! Located at the end of **La Rambla,** lies El Mercat de Sant Josep de la Boqueria. This covered market has roots that stretch back to 1217, making it one of the oldest permanent exchanges in Europe. It wasn't until 1840 that La Boqueria started making a name for itself. The dazzling display of nuts, spices, fruits, vegetables, meat, cheese, and fish behind its stained-glass façade will make your head spin and your stomach rumble. Apparently the market's name derives from the word *boc,* meaning "goat" in Catalan—the most popular meat sold when La Boqueria first opened. Over the centuries, it has expanded from just meat to include fish, produce, and finally today, fully-fledged restaurants.

i Free; food prices vary; limited wheelchair accessibility

MERCAT FIRA DE BELLCAIRE ELS ENCANTS

Carrer de los Castillejos, 158; 932 46 30 30; open M, W, F-Sa 9am-8pm

Mercat Fira de Bellcaire Els Encants, or simply "Els Encants Vells," is a hoarder's daydream and a neat-freak's worst nightmare. Welcoming a whopping 100,000 new visitors each week, it's Barcelona's largest flea market, and the ideal venue to do some serious discount damage. The stalls line one side of a continuously-spiraling ramp that looks like it continues forever. The real draw is the market's pit, covered in everything from rare books to used clothing to overstock furniture to antiquities to vinyls to toiletries to car parts to—shall we go on? Finding treasures here involves a combination of crawling, tip-toeing, and leapfrogging over items that—in the United States—would otherwise reside comfortably on shelves. The vendors here are more open to bartering than any others in Barcelona, so slap on a smile, load up on cash (but not too much; pickpockets are everywhere), and get to talkin'!

i Item prices vary; auctions M, W, and F at 8am; limited wheelchair accessibility

LANDMARKS

CASA BATLLÓ

Passeig de Gràcia, 43; 932 16 03 06; casabatllo.es; open daily 9am-9pm

A dominant silhouette on the **Passeig de Gràcia** and one of the most emblematic works by **Antoni Gaudí,** Casa Batlló was constructed between 1904 and 1906 for one of Barcelona's preeminent families. True to the architect's style, this house has almost no right angles or straight lines, and is outfitted with walls that undulate like waves. It is an ode to the marine world, complete with decorative elements that shimmer like fish scales and turquoise stained glass windows that look like bubbles. Nicknamed the "House of Yawns" because of its gaping iron balconies, its exterior is plastered with lime mortar and sprinkled with fragments of ceramic and colored glass—a technique called *trencadís.* Inside, a wooden stairwell resembling a twisted spine leads guests to the **Noble Floor,** offering a panoramic view of the

treetops and street below. Notice how the windows get smaller and darker as you make your way upstairs. This was a conscious and ingenious design choice made by Gaudí to ensure that the home glows a consistent shade of blue throughout.

i Admission €24.50, €21.50 reduced; VR guide included; last entrance 8pm; limited wheelchair accessibility

CASTELL DE MONTJUÏC

Ctra. de Montjuïc, 66; 932 56 44 45; ajuntament.barcelona.cat/castelldemontjuic/ca; open daily Apr-Oct 10am-8pm, Nov-Mar 10am-6pm

Perched on the western face of Montjuïc, this palatial fortress dates back to the late seventeenth century, making it one of the oldest compounds in Barcelona. Its grounds are very *Alice in Wonderland,* which is surprising considering this place was used as a political prison for three centuries. Despite its tragic history, it is now one of Barcelona's top attractions because of its sweeping views of the sea and city. It's particularly beautiful in the early morning, before the hordes of tourists arrive and the attractions further west **(Jardí Botànic de Barcelona, Estadi Olímpic Lluís Companys, Fundació Joan Miró)** open their gates. You can get to the castle on foot, by taking the escalators near **Palau Nacional,** by riding the bus from **Plaza de España,** or by taking the funicular from Paral·lel station. Our favorite? The **Port Cable Car,** which connects Barceloneta to Montjuïc via air (€11 one way, €16.5 round trip).

i Admission €5, €3 reduced; free every first Su and other Su after 3pm; last entry 7:30pm (Nov-Mar 5:30pm); no wheelchair accessibility

CATEDRAL DE BARCELONA

Pl. de la Seu; 933 428 262; catedralbcn.org; open M-F 12:30pm-7:45pm, Sa 12:30pm-5:30pm, Su 2pm-5:30pm

Located in the heart of the **Gothic Quarter,** the Catedral de la Santa Cruz y Santa Eulalia de Barcelona—or simply the Barcelona Cathedral—keeps watch over the city day and night. At both the front and back entrances, docents stand guard like bouncers. No, you won't have to recite a secret password to get in, but you will have to drop €7 and cover your shoulders with a shawl (free). During the afternoon, stained glass windows infuse the light with jewel-toned specks. One of the only choirs in Spain you can actually walk through, it's an impressive example of craftsmanship—each papal chair crowned with its own wooden spire. A dimly-lit crypt separates the aisle from the altar, and is flanked by multiple small chapels. Before departing through the southern courtyard, be sure to checkout its rooftop viewing platform, accessible via an elevator left of the nave.

i Admission €7; free rooftop access; last entry 30min. before closing; no shorts, no tank tops; wheelchair accessible entrance on Carrer del Bisbe

LA SAGRADA FAMILIA

Carrer de Mallorca, 401; 932 08 04 14; sagradafamilia.org/en/; open daily Apr-Sept 9am-8pm, Oct-May 9am-6pm, Dec 25-Jan 6 9am-2pm

Antoni Gaudí's life-long project, La Sagrada Familia was only 25% done when the architect died in 1926. By the time construction ceases in 2026, it will have taken longer to build than the Egyptian Pyramids. Why is it taking so long, you ask? The short answer: none of the interior surfaces are flat. Still left to build are 10 towers—six of which are larger than the existing ones, and one of which will reach a whopping 566 feet, making the edifice the largest religious building in Europe. As you move from north to south around its exterior, the stone reliefs emulate the story of the birth, life, and death of Jesus Christ. Inside, the transept depicts a parallel journey: that of the evolution of architecture from Medieval times to present. Particularly fascinating is the southern doorway, which is more "modern" than the world's most impressive skyscrapers. Massive white columns come alive each evening when the sun bursts through the stained glass windows. Whether you're in town for two weeks or two hours, it should be at the top of your priority list.

i Admission €15, with audio guide €22, with guided tour €24, with rooftop visit €29; reserve online at least a week in advance;

last entry 30min. before closing; last elevator to Nativity Facade tower 15min. before close; last elevator to Passion Facade tower 15min. before closing; wheelchair accessible

PALAU GÜELL

Carrer Nou de la Rambla, 3-5; 934 72 57 75; alauguell.cat; open Apr-Oct Tu-Su 10am-8pm, Nov-Mar 10am-5:30pm

Gaudí left footprints all over the city, even in **El Raval,** which—until recently—qualified as a Spanish slum. One of his earliest works, Palau Güell lacks the whimsy of Casa Battló and La Sagrada Familia, but this urban palace is sophisticatedly understated; composed of stained wood, black limestone, and gilded iron. Hollow, echoey halls connect stately salons to dark living quarters—each of which is more impressive than the next. That said, the highlight of Palau Güell is undoubtedly the Central Hall. Here, it's clear just how much of an impact Islamic architecture had on Gaudí's development as an artist. The oculus that rises above this multi-purposed room is riddled with holes. During the day, those holes flood the Central Hall with light, and as time passes, they mimic the night sky.

i Admission €12, reduced €9; free every first Su; audio guide included; last entry 1hr before closing; no wheelchair accessibility

ARC DE TRIOMF

Passeig de Lluís Companys; open daily 24hr

Located at the northern end of the promenade of the Passeig de Lluís Companys, the Arc de Triomf is an icon. Unlike its counterpart in Paris, you can walk right up to it without the fear of getting hit by a speeding bus on your way there. Designed in the **Neo-Mudéjar** style, its original purpose was to serve as the main access gate for the **1888 Barcelona World Fair.** Since then, millions of people have passed through it and continued down the palm-tree lined boulevard that extends east from its base. A frieze bearing the Catalan phrase *"Barcelona rep les nacions"* ("Barcelona welcomes all nations") glows above its archway. We interpret this as Barcelona saying, "We love tourists." So, the next time a local food vendor glares at you for saying, "I quiero esto sandwich," let the Arc de Triomf bring you some piece of mind.

i Free; wheelchair accessible

CASA MILÀ

Passeig de Gràcia, 92; 902 20 21 38; lapedrera.com; open M-Su 9am-8:30pm and 9pm-11pm

Casa Milà—popularly known as **La Pedrera**—was Gaudí's last civil work before he dedicated all of his time to **La Sagrada Familia.** Originally a private residence, it's now a **UNESCO World Heritage Site,** cultural center (did someone say jazz?), and home to a few lucky (read: very wealthy) families. Above several multi-million-dollar apartments lies **L'Espai Gaudí,** a mini-museum that contains small-scale models of the architect's most famous buildings and provides visitors with valuable insights into his life and creative process. The guided tour also includes a journey through Casa Milà's grand foyer and one of the apartments. In all honesty, though, the real magic of the building lives in its self-supporting, corrugated facade. Its undulating stones and iron balconies resemble a stone quarry, and together constitute a textbook example of Catalan modernism.

i Admission €22, €16.50 reduced; day and night tour €41; audio guide included; last entry 30min. before closing; limited wheelchair accessibility

HOSPITAL DE LA SANTA CREU I SANT PAU

Carrer de Sant Quintí, 89; 932 91 90 00; open Nov-Mar M-Sa 9:30am-4:30pm, Su 9:30am-2:30pm; Apr-Oct M-Sa 9:30am-6:30pm, Su 9:30am-4:30pm

Just a short walk from **La Sagrada Familia,** this impressive Catalan modernisme complex houses several buildings—expansions of the original compound—that date to 1901. Its founding was 500 years earlier, when six medieval hospitals merged. Today, it's a tourist attraction and "knowledge center," where thinkers congregate to "tackle the challenges of twenty-first-century society." So, why the sudden shift of purpose? Perhaps the majestic façade, tiled domes, frescoe-covered

ceilings, and white marble floors weren't being adequately appreciated by the ill. Ironically, it welcomes more visitors now than it did as a hospital.

Admission €14; with audio guide €17; with guided tour €18; combined with Palau de la Música €25; free entry every first Su; guided tour in English daily 10:30am; wheelchair accessible

FONT MÀGICA DE MONTJUÏC

Plaça de Carles Buïgas, 1; open daily 24hr; shows Th-Sa Nov-Mar 8pm, Apr-Oct 9pm

Spectacular displays of light, color, music, and water acrobatics are what you're in for at the Font Màgica de Montjuïc. Located in front of the **Palau National** on the previous site of **The Four Columns,** this fountain was designed by **Carles Buïgas** in advance of the **1929 Barcelona International Exposition.** The 3,000 person-strong construction process lasted just over a year. Despite being ravaged in the **Spanish Civil War,** it is as glorious today as it was nearly a century ago. For an hour each night, this bubbling cauldron of color captures the attention of thousands of pairs of eyes. Set to classical music playing from surround-sound speakers, these mesmerizing shows elicit oohs and ahhs with every crescendo.

Free; limited wheelchair accessibility

MUSEUMS

FUNDACIÓ JOAN MIRÓ

Parc de Montjuïc; 934 43 94 70; mirobcn.org/en/; open Tu-Sa 10am-8pm except Th 10am-9pm, Su 10am-3pm

Carved into the side of **Montjuïc,** Fundació Joan Miró contains the single greatest collection of works produced by **Joan Miró.** It was designed by one of the artist's closest friends, **Josep Lluis Sert,** and looks a heck of a lot like a stack of white Legos. It's one of the most renowned artistic venues in the world, acclaimed for its airy interior and organic flow. Inside, you'll find the same curves and jagged edges of the foundation's roofline—embodied by the colorful subjects of Miró's paintings and sculptures. The museum also showcases a variety of pieces by other contemporary artists, including long-time legends like **Calder, Duchamp, Oldenburg,** and **Legern,** while the affiliated **Espai 13** focuses on this decade's emerging artists. The complex is expansive and jam-packed, so we recommend purchasing an audio guide and later relaxing in the shady garden to let the information sink in.

Combined €12, reduced €7; temporary exhibition €7, reduced €5; Espai 13 €2.50; sculpture garden free; audio guide €5; Articket BCN €30; last entry 30min. before closing; wheelchair accessible

MUSEU NACIONAL D'ART DE CATALUNYA (MNAC)

Palau Nacional, Parc de Montjuïc; 93 622 03 60; museunacional.cat; open May-Sept Tu-Sa 10am-8pm, Su 10am-3pm; Oct-Apr Tu-Sa 10am-6pm, Su 10am-3pm

Perched on the slopes of Montjuïc, the **Palau Nacional** stands grandly over **Plaza de España.** The grounds, which include a cascading waterfall, never-ending flights of steps, and manicured garden, are worth a visit in and of themselves. Inside this Italian-style behemoth lies an outstanding collection of Romanesque church paintings and frescoes, as well as Catalan art from the late nineteenth and early twentieth centuries (read: a lot of modernisme and noucentisme; upstairs). MNAC also houses several niche pieces, such as Gaudí's handcrafted furniture and

Picasso's cubist work. Palau Nacional's **Oval Hall** (typically closed to the public) is considered one of Europe's best venues to host large-scale events due to its magnificent classical architecture.

i Admission €12, reduced €8.40; temporary exhibition €4/€6; rooftop access €2; audio guide €4; limited wheelchair accessibility

FUNDACIÓ ANTONI TÀPIES

Carrer d'Aragó,, 255; 934 870 315; fundaciotapies.org; open Tu-Th 10am-7pm, F 10am-9pm, Sa 10am-7pm, Su 10am-3pm

Located in the heart of **Eixample,** Fundació Antoni Tàpies is a cultural center and museum dedicated primarily to showcasing the works of **Antoni Tàpies** (shocker!). If you don't know who he is, here's your chance: the guy's a modern art hot-shot known for his whacky 3D paintings, which incorporate waste paper, mud, sticks, and rags. Over time, his focus shifted from painting to furniture-making. The center houses several of these later works, in addition to abstract structures featuring several moving parts. The museum's permanent and temporary exhibitions are displayed in a Modernist building that dates back to 1882. It was the first structure in Eixample to integrate industrial typology and technology, combining exposed brick and iron to create stunning decorative landscapes. Today, the Fundació is distinguishable by its tall row of Art Nouveau rose windows and the massive wire cloud on its roof. Titled **Núvol i Cadira,** it was installed there by Tàpies himself.

i Admission €7, reduced €5.60; last entrance 15 min before closing; wheelchair accessible

MUSEU D'ART CONTEMPORANI (MACBA)

Plaça dels Àngels, 1; 93 481 33 68; macba.cat; open M, W-F 11am-7:30pm, Sa 10am-8pm, Su 10am-3pm; library open M-Th 10am-7pm by appt only

Time to shove a stick up your ass and put in an order for a triple, soy, no foam, vegan latte—we're going to the contemporary art museum! Nah man, we're just messing with you. If you can put up with being frowned at by spectacle-wearing docents, it's an hour or two well-spent. Located on the same plaza as the **Centre de Cultura Contemporània (CCCB)** and **Església de Santa María de Montalegre,** MACBA has quickly risen to the top of Barcelona's museum scene since opening in 1995. Its stark minimalist interior is a far cry from the ribbed vaults and catenary arches that characterize the architecture of the city's major landmarks, making for a welcome change of pace and venue. Now a key player in the modern art world, MACBA harbors some amazing temporary exhibitions (calendar available online). While they vary in medium, explicitness, and immersiveness, it's safe to assume that they all critique contemporary culture.

i Combined €10, reduced €8; temporary exhibition €6, reduced €4.50; free first Su of month; guided tours in English M 6pm; wheelchair accessible

MUSEU PICASSO

Carrer Montcada, 15-23; 932 56 30 00; museupicasso.bcn.cat; open M 10am-5pm, Tu-Su 9am-8:30pm

Barcelona's Picasso Museum is one of the best in the world for two reasons. First, it's free to students. Second, it's located in a restored Medieval building that's so beautiful you'll be tempted to plop down on its central staircase and spend the afternoon staring at its courtyard. Picasso spent part of his youth in Barcelona, which was then undergoing a period of industrial growth. Museu Picasso displays a carefully-curated collection of works produced during his formative years, as well as highlights from his **Blue Period** and the preparatory sketches for Las Meninas, his 58-painting tribute to **Diego Velázquez.** The collection is organized temporally, so you can track Picasso's progression from a technical master to artistic rule-breaker. No assortment of paintings and sketches could better encapsulate the genius' iconic quote: "Learn the rules like a pro, so you can break them like an artist."

Museu Picasso hosts over a million visitors each year, so it's best to arrive first thing in the morning.

i Combined €14, permanent collection €11, temporary exhibitions €6.50, students free; free first Su of every month 9am-7pm, free every other Su after 3pm; free guided tours; last entry 30 min before closing; wheelchair accessible

OUTDOORS

BUNKERS OF CARMEL

Carrer de Marià Labèrnia; 932 56 21 22; bunkers.cat/en/; open daily 24hr

The Bunkers of Carmel keep watch over the city from the top of **Turó de la Rovira,** a 262-meter-tall hill northeast of **Park Güell.** Contrary to its name, there are no bunkers below or around this world-renowned viewing platform. Instead, you'll find a network of abandoned military constructions connected by shantytowns. Now, the only thing preventing the Bunkers from being completely overrun by tourists is its distance from the city center. Once you make it, you'll be greeted with one of the most welcome sights on Earth: the Barcelona skyline. Groups of local twenty-somethings pepper the grounds, armed with picnic blankets, wine, baguettes, and cigarettes. Every night, the sky morphs from pink to purple to periwinkle blue and eventually indigo. On clear nights, the sparkling city below reflects the starry sky above.

i Free; no wheelchair accessibility

PARK GÜELL

Enter on Carrer d'Olot, Carretera del Carmel, nº 23 or Passatge de Sant Josep de la Muntanya; www.parkguell.cat; open daily May-Aug 8am-9:30pm, Sept-Oct, Mar-Apr 8am-8:30pm, Jan-Dec 8:30am-6:30pm

UNESCO World Heritage Site and life-size Candyland, Park Güell was designed in 1910 by architectural mastermind **Antoni Gaudí.** Despite the fact that it looks like it was designed to be photographed, this botanical will knock your socks off when you visit it in person. Park Güell's main entrance looks directly upon **La Escalinata del Dragón.** A masterpiece of mosaic and feat of engineering, it consists of two twin staircases flanked by checkered ceramic walls and split by **El Drac,** a colorful stone and glass salamander that shimmers in the Spanish sunlight. Behind the stairway, the columns of **Nature Square** sprout from the earth like great basalt beams. Take a few minutes to wander through **The Hypostyle Room,** a stunning mosaic colonnade. From the iconic benches above it, you can see all the way to the Mediterranean—past the spires of the two gingerbread-house-esque pavilions that together comprise **The Porter's Lodge.** Other highlights include **The Laundry Room Portico, The Austria Gardens, The Gaudí House Museum,** and the three organic **viaducts** that snake up Turó de Tres Creus. Pro tip: if you enter before 8am, the park's entirely yours to explore, take pictures in, and log roll around—for free!

i Admission €7.50; free before 8am; limited wheelchair accessibility

SANT SEBASTIÀ

Platja de Sant Sebastià; open daily 24hr

With 300 days of sunshine per year, it's no wonder beach-going is one of Barcelona's highest-rated daytime activities. The city's three-mile stretch of golden coastline bustles day and night, with new chiringuitos (beach bars) popping up each summer. San Sebastià is located near the end of the pedestrian promenade that parallels **Passeig de Joan de Borbó.** Still, it's quieter than its northern neighbor, **Playa de Sant Miguel.** Here, waves float over the tanned bodies and colorful towels that checker this piece of nature's carpet. The typical sounds of cars are drowned out by laughter and repeated volleyball spikes. Unfortunately, "secluded" beaches are few and far between in this region. If you're up for the trip, check out the beach's twin in **Sitges,** located 30 minutes south of Barcelona by train. Known as the "Spanish Saint-Tropez," Sitges' white sand beaches, turquoise water, and picturesque downtown are a welcome reprieve from the tourist frenzy of **La Barceloneta.**.

i Free; limited wheelchair accessibility; guard belongings at all times; nudity condoned

PARC DE LA CIUTADELLA

Passeig de Picasso, 21; 638 23 71 15; open daily 9am-9pm

New York has Central Park, Barcelona has Parc de la Ciutadella. A popular destination for picnicking, sunbathing, jogging, and drug deali—wait, what? Yes, you read that correctly. You'll encounter just as many young parents playing catch with their kids as you will red-eyed college students strumming on ukuleles. A n y w a y s, a popular destination for picnicking, sunbathing, jogging, and drug dealing, the park was Barcelona's first green space. Since opening to the public in the mid-nineteenth century, it has expanded to include the **Barcelona Zoo,** the **Parliament of Catalonia,** the **Museum of Natural Science,** the **Als Voluntaris Catalans,** and multiple modern sculptures. The **Cascada**—located on northern corner of the park opposite to the lake and rumored to be one of Antoni Gaudí's favorite fountains—is particularly beautiful, as are the manicured, flowering walkways near the **Umbracle.**

i Free; limited wheelchair accessibility

FOOD

EL PACHUCO ($)

Carrer de Sant Pau, 110; 931 79 68 05; open Su-Th 1:30pm-1:30am, F-Sa 1:30pm-3am

Take it from us: El Pachuco is the real deal. Though its Mexican tapas aren't what we would call "traditional," they hit the nail on the head when it comes to flavor. The tacos are juicy, the margaritas are generous, but the nachos—piled high with freshly-made toppings and big enough to share—are where El Pachuco really shines. It's a small establishment with a capacity of 30 people, tops. You'll know you're in the right place if you see a chalkboard sign that reads, "Keep Calm and Shut the Fuck Up," and a glass door that's perennially propped open by a hoard of hungry locals. Inside, liquor bottles and portraits of the Virgin Mary sit side by side on a wall of shelves, and parties of patrons huddle around wooden tables. El Pachuco has a strict no reservations and no credit card policy, so arrive an hour before standard meal times, cash in hand, if you want to score a table.

i Nachos €11.80, 2 quesadillas €7.20, 5 tacos €8.80, beer from €3.20; cash preferred; vegetarian options available; no wheelchair accessibility

GASTEREA ($)

Carrer de Verdi, 39; 932 37 23 43; open Th-Tu 7pm-1am

Gasterea's still got it. When we first recommended this place back in 2004, it was on the verge of its big break. Now, 15 years later, we can resolutely say that Gasterea serves the best pinchos in all of Barcelona. What initially drew us to this tiny bar was its comically low pricing. And though they've increased over the years due to an explosion in popularity, it remains one of the most inexpensive places to chow down on this side of town. Located on a bustling street in the otherwise quiet, residential neighborhood of **Gràcia,** Gasterea bursts at the seams at night. The hot pinchos—like the large plates—are made to order. If you're having trouble deciding where to start, just ask a bartender for some help. Multilingual and way more knowledgeable than we are, they'll be able to guide you in the right direction. Once you've gotten the ball rolling, feel free to gleefully swan-dive into the sea of fatty cheeses, cured meats, buttery fish, and smooth glazes that compose Gasterea's menu.

i All pinchos €1.90, casseroles €4.50, wine from €2.25, tap beer from €2.25; cash only; vegetarian options available; no wheelchair accessibility

MAOZ VEGETARIAN ($)

Carrer de Ferran, 13; 678 60 49 46; maozusa.com; open Su-Th 11am-1am, F-Sa 11am-2am

While we wouldn't recommend doing so out of respect for the restaurant, you could theoretically eat here for an entire day for less than €5. Located in Barcelona's **Gothic Quarter,** this vegetarian fast food chain is a one-stop shop for all things falafel. In addition to salads and hand-cut fries (highly recommended), they serve up delectable falafel sandwiches that you can continue to refill from the second you step inside until closing. That is, as long as you haven't already scarfed down the warm, whole wheat pita holding yours together. Maoz's toppings are served buffet-style, and vary from deep fried cauliflower to grilled eggplant to marinated chickpeas to diced veggies. Seating is limited to about a dozen stools. If you're in for the long haul, you may have to wait a while before scoring a seat in the bright green interior—a small price to pay for a boat load of food.

i Pita sandwich €4.20, salads from €4.20, fries €2.20, drinks from €1.40; vegetarian options available; no wheelchair accessibility

NABUCCO TIRAMISU ($)

Plaça de la Vila de Gràcia, 8; 932 17 61 01; nabuccotiramisu.com; open M-F 8:30am-9:30pm, Sa-Su 9am-9:30pm

On the hunt for a strong cup of joe? Check out Nabucco Tiramisu, a favorite among young local professionals. Nabucco's espresso is the drink equivalent of getting doused by ice water—a single shot is potent enough to power you through the rest of your day. A floor-to-ceiling mural composed of individual portraits stretches from Nabucco's enticing pastry case all the way back to the café's far end. Opposite the mural stands a wall of white bricks, upon which hang a single hat hook and photo of a man in a top hat. Chipped tables, metal chairs, and lamps set the tone for intimate conversation and quiet work. Hours seem to fly by here, especially if you fill them by alternating between typing and chowing down on one of Nabucco's refreshing fruit tarts, dense cakes, or specialty tiramisu. If you're craving something a little heavier, Nabucco also offers a variety of salads, pizzas, and sandwiches that are equally mouthwatering.

i Drinks from €1, pastries from €3, pizza slice €3, salads and sandwiches from €6; vegetarian options available; wheelchair accessible

BO DE B ($)

Carrer de la Fusteria, 1; 936 67 49 45; open M-Th noon-11:30pm, F-Sa noon-midnight, Su noon-7:30pm

Bookended by the **Catedral de Barcelona** and **L'Aquàrium,** Bo de B serves up scrumptious Mediterranean sandwiches, salads, platters, and plates for a fraction of what they'd cost on **Plaça Nova.** Though his menu is Greek in theme and in flavor, Bo de B's hands-on owner rejects the construct of nationality, frequently code-switching to make sure his guests feel welcome. Particularly noteworthy is the Chicken Tzatziki, served with roasted peppers, spiced potatoes, sun-dried tomatoes, chunks of feta cheese, and yogurt sauce. Unfortunately, plates and platters are only available inside, and considering this hole-in-the-wall joint has a capacity of 15, there's a good chance you'll have to wait a while before sinking your teeth into the most tender chicken in Barcelona. If you're in a hurry, we recommend ordering something para llevar, and heading west to nearby **Plaça de l'Ictineo,** a park and open-air sculpture garden that offers great views of the port.

i Salads from €7, hamburgers from €7; cash only; vegetarian options available; no wheelchair accessibility

CHÖK—THE CHOCOLATE KITCHEN ($$)

Carrer d'Astúries, 93; 933 487 616; chokbarcelona.com/en/; open daily 9am-10pm

You'll feel like a kid in a candy shop in Chök—it'd be hard not to, considering it's a literal candy shop. Of Chök's many locations, our favorite is in **Gràcia,** on the northeast corner of Plaça de la Virreina. Here, rows upon rows of chocolate-covered doughnuts, cronuts, cookies, truffles, beautiful little cakes, and other handcrafted delicacies fill sleek, dazzling displays. Our favorite? Chök's signature **cronuts.** These fluffy pastries are equal parts crispy, airy, and chewy, and coated in a thick chocolate shell. Atop this shell lies an impeccably-piped dollop of cream, as well as a sprinkling of sugar toppings. If you're not already bouncing off the walls, wash

it all down with a lemonade slushy or other sweet drink, available for purchase at select locations, including this one.
i Truffles €0.50, pastries from €1.50, cronuts €3.95; vegetarian options available; limited wheelchair accessibility

FEDERAL CAFÉ ($$)

Passatge de la Pau, 11; 932 80 81 71; federalcafe.es/barcelona-gotic/; open M-Th 9am-11pm, F-Sa 9am-11:30pm, Su 9am-5:30pm

Situated in the **Gothic Quarter,** Federal Café's **Passatge de la Pau** location looks more like a warehouse than a restaurant. Inside, shiny concrete floors reflect the light let in by a wall of east-facing windows, and carved drywall slabs double as art fixtures. Speaking of art, Federal Café's breakfast dishes could pass as miniature landscapes. Whole avocados—sliced thin, fanned out, and served with almost every savory dish—resemble the vibrant green terraces of Machu Picchu. Particularly memorable was the build-your-own breakfast plate, which includes your choice of eggs, bacon, sausage, toast, roasted tomatoes, grilled asparagus, sauteed mushrooms, or Halloumi cheese.
i Breakfast dishes from €7; toast and pastries from €2; vegan and vegetarian options available; wheelchair accessible

KYOKA II ($)

Carrer de Sicília, 93; 931 58 19 36; open daily 11:30am-4pm and 8pm-midnight

A favorite among local students for its low prices and big portions, here you'll be treated to miso soup, an appetizer, rice or noodles, an assortment of various types of sushi, nigiri, and maki, a drink, and a dessert—for just €9.95! The décor here is minimal and infuriatingly cliché, but when you're pinching pennies, the color of your table really won't matter. During lunch time, it's packed with friend groups and young couples—all of whom are eager to pinch their chopsticks around tightly-packed circles of seaweed, tuna, avocado, and cucumber.
i Menú del día €9.95, all-you-can-eat lunch buffet M-F €12.95; vegetarian options available; no wheelchair accessibility

NIGHTLIFE

LE JOURNAL

Carrer de Francisco Giner, 36; 933 68 41 37; open Su-Th 6pm-2am, F-Sa 6m-3am

Wickedly strong mojitos are the name of the game here. This quirky cocktail bar is a fantastic place to start an evening, and an equally good place to end it. Its location near **Passeig de Gràcia** makes it a prime launch pad no matter where you're headed, but for most, it's the first stop on a long trek towards the **Gothic Quarter,** home to Barcelona's most popular clubs and infamous underground piano bars. Inside, a small wooden bar gives way to a larger, sunken room. Le Journal's laid-back ambiance qualifies it as an ideal venue to tell stories, not necessarily to make them. As the evening unfolds, the bar's patrons steadily decrease in age. By midnight, Le Journal is stuffed to its wicker brim with young professionals and artistic types looking for an efficient way to kick off an evening of clubbing.
i Cocktails from €6, smoothies from €4.50; no wheelchair accessibility

MARULA CAFÉ

Carrer dels Escudellers, 49; 933 18 76 90; open W-Th 11pm-5am, F-Sa 11:30pm-6am, Su 11pm-5am

Known for its alternative music scene and live performances, this is the place to go if the thought of bouncing around aimlessly to house music makes you squeamish. Behind several layers of red velvet curtains lies a fully-stocked bar, a dance floor, and an elevated stage, upon which local performers congregate to demonstrate their chops each evening; genres can range from funk to R&B to classic jazz in a single night. The clientele here verges on hipster—you'll see more flannel shirts and band tees than shimmery cocktail dresses and bicep-hugging button-ups. Coincidentally, this clandestine bar hosts fewer creeps than your standard nightclub, making it easy to kick back and actually enjoy the show. Still, we urge you to exercise caution; the area around **La Rambla** is notoriously sketchy at night and is best traversed in groups.
i Cover from €10, shots €4; limited wheelchair accessibility

OPIUM

Passeig Marítim, 34; 932 25 91 00; opiumbarcelona.com; open Su-W noon-5am, Th-Sa noon-6am

Famed as one of the best clubs in the world, Opium's lineups are up there. Its massive capacity, sleek decor, scantily-clad waitresses, and killer sound system attract DJs and artists from around the world, including **David Guetta, Bob Sinclar, Martin Solveig, Armin Van Buuren,** and **Jason Derulo.** This upscale bar-club combo offers stunning views of **Playa de la Barceloneta** and the Mediterranean Sea, making it popular among one-stoppers who roll up at sunset and party until the wee hours of the morning. Inside, mirrors reflect the multi colored spotlights that continually search Opium's crowded dance floor, and tall window panes bear sweat stains left by Brian, the underprepared, overeager frat bro who drunkenly mistook them for exits. If you're only in Barcelona for a night, we encourage you to give Opium a try (not the drug, ya dingo): this club never fails to deliver.

i Cover €20; ticket prices spike for big names; casual cocktail attire; limited wheelchair accessibility

JAMBOREE DANCE CLUB

Plaça Reial, 17; 933 04 12 10; masimas.com/jamboree; open daily 8pm-5am (schedule varies depending on performances)

For the uninitiated tourist, this premier dance club is a soft introduction to the hard-core clubbing promised to them by a Ibiza-frequenting older sibling. But, for those in-the-know, its a convenient place to let your guard down and dance the night away with your closest friends. The regular crowd is easy on the eyes, its concerts easy on the ears, and its drinks easy on the liver. A hike down a steep staircase leads you into the main room, which consists of a steamy brick cave below Barcelona's **Gothic Quarter.** Here, the music veers towards the mainstream, which—while frustrating to the die-hard Jazz fans out there—makes for some great communal moments. Upstairs, the music varies from indie rock to alternative—just depends on the night. Concerts typically take place at 8pm and 10pm (check online for specifications), after which Jamboree transforms into a fully-fledged club.

i Cover from €10, free if organized through hostel; drinks from €5; casual attire; no wheelchair accessibility

SALA APOLO

Carrer Nou de la Rambla, 113; 933 01 00 90; www.sala-apolo.com/en; open Su-Th midnight-5am, F-Sa 12:30am-6am

If an evening of reckless abandon is what you seek, look no further. This 75-year-old concert hall is one of the most visited in Europe, and the unequivocal center of nightlife in Barcelona. Its main floor features an aged, curtain-framed stage that—miraculously—keeps a very active mosh pit away from the on-call DJ. The club's original wood floors still bear the scuffs left by cinephiles who frequented this place decades ago. In addition to a single disco ball, gilded chandeliers hang luxuriously from the 50-foot ceiling. Outside of the pit, the bar and large lounge blur together, spinning in a medley of smoke and dim green light. Here, a refreshingly diverse crowd of angsty teens bobs slowly to the rhythm of reggae, and everyone over the age of 30 stands out like a sore thumb. Music ranges from hip hop to techno to Latin, varying by night.

i Cover from €13, drinks from €7; casual attire

RAZZMATAZZ

Carrer dels Almogàvers, 122; 933 20 82 00; salarazzmatazz.com/en/; open W-F 12:30am-5am, F-Sa 1am-6am

Located in a warehouse not unlike an abandoned airplane hangar, Razzmatazz is a club unlike any other. It has not one, not two, but five rooms, separated by genre and—consequently—by patronage. Every room is outfitted with a bangin' audio system, and each floor remains packed from opening until closing without fail. Hip hop, R&B, Top 40, reaggetón, electro, techno, soul, and funk make regular appearances on the playlists of resident and visiting DJs, but the club has dedicated nights for more unconventional genres like French rap and acid house. We recommend saving some of your energy for the morning. Between the non-stop dancing and having no place to sit (unless you want to drop some serious dough for a VIP table), you'll be too exhausted to make it back to the metro, which conveniently opens as Razzmatazz shuts down. Queues stretch around the block by 11:30pm, so its worth arriving early and getting to know your neighbors while waiting in line.

i Ticket and drink €13 if purchased ahead; up to €32 at door; drinks €7; casual attire; no wheelchair accessibility

GRANADA

Coverage by **Austin Eder**

Famed for the iconic Alhambra, an elaborate palatial fortification located atop a foothill of the Sierra Nevada Mountain Range, Granada's riches extend far beyond this one landmark. With history that dates back thousands of years, it's seen a lot (including three conquests, first by Romans, then by the Umayyad dynasty, and finally by Catholic monarchs!). Now, this city is more deliciously complex than any other in the south of Spain. Evidence of cultural exchange between Eastern and Western societies is apparent in everything from the cross-hatched beams that line several ceilings in the Nasrid Palaces—a quintessentially Moorish structure—to flamenco, the performance art whose origins trace back to the Gypsy caves of Sacromonte. Get lost in the winding maze of streets that is the Albaicín, Granada's Arabic quarter, and travel back in time to the Renaissance with a visit to the Capilla Real, under which rest Granada's final conquerors, Queen Isabella of Castile and King Ferdinand of Aragon. Here, daytime activities abound, such as admiring the graffiti art of El Niño de las Pinturas while strolling through el Realejo, or lounging on a hammock on a hostel rooftop. "Granada," meaning "pomegranate," is a unified whole larger than the sum of many sweet parts. Here, we've united some of the sweetest.

ORIENTATION

Tucked in a crook of the Sierra Nevada Mountain Range, Granada rests at the confluence of four rivers: the **Darro,** the **Genil,** the **Monachil,** and the **Beiro.** Its bus and train stations lie three kilometers northwest of the **Catedral de Granada,** which acts as the de facto city center. If you envisioned Granada as a letter "C," **la Alhambra**—the city's largest attraction—would fall in its center. Starting from the top of the C and curving around clockwise lie **Sacromonte,** Granada's cave community on the northern bank of the Río Darro; **el Albaicín,** its mountainous Arabic quarter; **Centro,** its modern, urban center; and **Realejo,** its graffiti-covered Jewish quarter. **Calle Gran Vía de Colón** runs diagonally (northwest-southeast) through the city center, splitting the Albaicín and el Centro, and intersects with **Calle Reyes Católicos** at **Plaza Isabel la Catolica. Plaza Nueva,** located near the gate of the Alhambra just north of the Catedral, is one of Granada's most famous gastronomic centers. As you move south, Granada grows increasingly more residential and industrial.

ESSENTIALS

GETTING THERE

The bus station is located at Carretera de Jaén (958 18 50 10). AISA buses (958 18 54 80; alsa.es) run throughout Andalucía and connect to the Madrid and Valencia-Barcelona lines. Transportes Rober runs regular services between the station and the city center. To get to the city center from the bus station, take bus SNI and get off at the Catedral stop. The main train station (958 27 12 72) is located at Av. de los Andaluces. RENFE trains run to and from Barcelona, Seville, and several smaller cities. Aeropuerto Federico García Lorca is located about 15km outside of the city and services domestic and international budget airlines. A taxi will take you to the city center (€25) or directly to the Alhambra (€28). You can book a taxi in advance through Radio Taxi (963 70 33 33), but all major stations typically have queues. The bus company Autocares José González offers a direct service between the airport and the city center (€3; 958 39 01 64; autocaresjosegonzalez.com; every hour daily 5:20am-8pm).

GETTING AROUND

Transportes Rober runs almost 40 bus lines around the city as well as smaller direct buses to the Alhambra, the Albaicín, and Sacromonte (€1.20 per ride, €5 for 7 rides; 900 71 09 00; transportesrober.com). The tourist lines are #30, 31, 32, and 34. The circular lines (#11, 13, and 23) make full loops around the city. Rober also runs a special Feria line (€1.40) When most lines stop running at 11:30pm, the Búho lines pick up the slack (€1.30; #111 and 121; daily midnight-5:15am).

PRACTICAL INFORMATION

Tourist Offices: Granada's main tourist office is located at el Ayuntamiento, or the City Hall (Pl. del Carmen; 958 248 280; granadatur.com; open M-Sa 9am-8pm, Su 9am-2pm).

Banks/ATMs/Currency Exchange: Most ATMs are located in Granada's urban center, or the flat part of the city, specifically along Calle Gran Vía de Colón. Interchange is a money-exchange office that services for all major credit cards, including American Express (C. Reyes Católicos, 31; 958 22 45 12; open M-Sa 9am-10pm, Su 11am-3pm and 4pm-9pm).

Post Offices: Puerta Real (Puerta Real, 2, at the intersection of C. Reyes Católicos and Acera del Darro; 902 19 71 97; open M-F 8:30am-8:30pm, Sa 9:30am-2pm). Granada's postal code is 18005.

Public Restrooms: As far as free restrooms go, you're out of luck in Granada. Most establishments that have an entrance fee come equipped with clean restrooms, however.

Internet: Free public Wi-Fi is available at fast food chains and most cafés surrounding major monuments. Don't be afraid to ask waiters and waitresses for passwords: *¿Tiene Wi-Fi gratis?* Otherwise, Biblioteca de Andalucía has desktop computers that you can use for free for up to 1hr (C. Prof. Sainz Cantero, 6; 958 02 69 00; open M-F 9am-2pm). Idolos and Fans offers photocopying, fax, scanning, and Wi-Fi services (Camino de Ronda, 80; 958 52 14 96; open daily 10am-midnight).

BGLTQ+ Resources: Andalucía Diversidad offers information, social services, counseling, legal advice, and other resources to municipalities (C. Victoria, 8; 951 00 38 14; info@andalucialgbt.org).

EMERGENCY INFORMATION

Emergency Number: 112.

Police: The local police HQ is located at C. Huerta del Rasillo (958 20 68 78; open daily 9am-2pm). For major issues, head to the Granada Police Station (Pl. de los Campos (Realejo); 958 808 800; open daily 9am-2pm).

US Embassy: The nearest US Consulate is in Málaga (Av. Juan Gómez Juanito, 8; 952 47 48 91; open M-F 10am-2pm). Spain's US Embassy is located in Madrid (C. de Serrano, 75; 91 587 2200; es.usembassy.gov).

Rape Crisis Center: Call Granada Police Station at 958 808 800.

Hospitals: We've listed the main hospital below.

- Hospital Universitario Vírgen de las Nieves (Av. de las Fuerzas Armadas, 2; 958 02 00 00; open daily 24hr).

Pharmacies: There are few 24hr pharmacies near the intersection of C. Reyes Católicos and Acera del Darro, including:

- Farmácia Martín Valverde (C. Reyes Católicos, 5; 958 26 26 64).

SIGHTS

CULTURE

EL ALBAICÍN

Neighborhood open year-round

Though the Alhambra may draw you to Granada, the Albaicín might make you want to stay—it tends to have that effect on backpackers, who squat in this barrio's homey hostels for weeks, sometimes months longer than they initially anticipated. We recommend setting your map aside and following your feet through this web of winding cobblestone streets, crumbling stone walls, and vine-covered carmens (stucco-covered, open floor plan houses). Today, highlights of this **UNESCO World Heritage Site** include the **Mirador de San Nicolás; Puerta de Elvira,** an eleventh-century Moorish arch that originally served as one of the gates in the city walls; **Calle Elvira,** center of Granada's modern Moorish quarter and home to dozens of merchandise and souvenir shops; **el Mirador de la Placeta Álamo del Marqués,** a private viewpoint that offers the best westward-facing views of the city (open to the public daily 10am-8pm); and **Plaza Larga,** which transforms into a produce market most weekday mornings.

i Free; no wheelchair accessibility

LANDMARKS

CATEDRAL DE GRANADA (GRANADA CATHEDRAL)

C. Gran Vía de Colón, 5; 958 22 29 59; catedraldegranada.com; open M-Sa 10am-6:30pm, Su 3pm-6pm

The Cathedral of Granada was the first major undertaking of Ferdinand and Isabella after conquering the Nasrid Dynasty in 1492, and is the architectural equivalent of flipping the bird. A symbol of power and affluence, it boasts soaring Corinthian columns, a disorienting checkered floor, imposing Baroque organs, numerous chapels outfitted with **Renaissance, Gothic,** and **Rococo detailing,** and a boat-load of religious art and idolatry. If its white stucco walls haven't already drawn your

eyes upward, take a gander at the ceiling and let your focus drift to the back of the nave. As far as stained glass, frescoes, and gilded reliefs go, it's truly one of the most impressive in Europe, rivaling that of the Sainte-Chapelle de Paris and St. Peter's Basilica in Rome. If you're crunched for time, we recommend listening to tracks on the audioguide 1, 4, 6, and 9 for an overview of the history of the cathedral's surroundings.

i Admission €5, €3.50 reduced; wheelchair accessible

LA ALHAMBRA

C. Real de la Alhambra; 958 02 79 71; alhambradegranada.org; open Tu-Sa 9am-6pm, Su 9am-3:30pm

The Alhambra is kind of like Disneyland in that it is truly one of the most magical places on Earth, even though after spending four hours traipsing around this 142,000-square-meter wonderland, you'll begin seriously contemplating log-rolling down the hillside to escape the sun, hour-long lines between attractions, and screams of hungry children. (Read: pack a lunch, or you'll find yourself internally screaming as you savor every last crumb of the €3 bag of potato chips you purchased to avoid starvation.) To clarify, "Alhambra" refers to the entire collection of palaces, gardens, patios, baths, fortresses, and museums that sit atop a hill at the edge of the

Sierra Nevada Mountain Range, not just a singular structure. Among the highlights of this royal city are the **Alcazaba**, a fourteenth-century Moorish fortress that offers a unique peek into Medieval military culture; the **Torre de la Vela,** one of four towers that flank the Alcazaba and the best viewpoint in all of Granada; the **Museo des Bellas Artes,** located in the **Palacio Carlos V,** a magnificent Renaissance building; the **Medina**, a plaza rimmed by public baths, ovens, workshops, and homes; the **Generalife Palace,** a royal mountain getaway, so to speak; and last, but certainly not least, the **Nasrid Palaces**—the permanent residence of Nasrid sultans and Catholic monarchs.

i Admission tickets (€7) include access to the Gardens, Alcazaba, and Nasrid Palaces; tickets available online, at Coral de Carbon, or at any La Caixa Bank ATM in Granada (€15.40); many parts of the Alhambra including the Plaza de los Aljibes can be accessed for free; advance tickets recommended; arrive at 5:30am if trying to buy a ticket day-of; 30min. tours meet at Nasrid Palaces; audio guides €6; limited wheelchair accessibility

MUSEUMS

CAPILLA REAL GRANADA (GRANADA ROYAL CHAPEL)

C. Oficios; 958 22 78 48; capillarealgranada.com; open Mar-Aug M-Sa 10:15am-1:30pm and 4pm-7:30pm, Su 11am-1:30pm and 2:30pm-6:30pm; Sep-Feb M-Sa 10:15am-1:30pm and 3:30pm-6:30pm

The Gothic counterpart to the **Catedral de Granada,** the Capilla Real Granada is one of the city's biggest draws and the official resting place of Queen Isabella of Castile and King Ferdinand of Aragon. The duo commissioned the construction of this chapel for just that purpose in 1504, but it wasn't completed until 1517—a year after Ferdinand kicked the proverbial bucket and thirteen after Isabella kicked hers. Upon entering, you'll be taken aback by the shrine's grandeur. An ornamented wrought-iron gate separates the aisle from the marble mausoleums above the crypt. At the back of the chapel, a gilded altarpiece stretches from floor to ceiling, and Renaissance paintings adorn the walls on either side. An adjacent room has since been converted to a small museum that houses some of Isabella's most prized possessions, including her crown and scepter.

i Admission €5, €3.50 reduced; audio guides included; wheelchair accessible

MUSEO CUEVAS DEL SACROMONTE (SACRAMONTE CAVES)

Barranco de los Negros; 958 21 51 20; sacromontegranada.com; open daily Mar 15-Oct 14 10am-8pm, Oct 15-Mar 14 10am-6pm

A scenic 30-minute walk is all that separates the Museo Cuevas del Sacromonte from the hustle and bustle of **Plaza Nueva,** yet it feels like an entirely different world. Set in a canyon amidst dry brush, cacti, and native wildlife, this open-air museum offers a refreshing take on the history of the region and its original inhabitants: Roma refugees who were expelled at the turn of the fifteenth century. Via a self-led tour through a series of refurbished caves, Museo Cuevas del Sacromonte zooms in on the domestic life of eighteenth- and nineteenth-century Gypsies. Duck and weave from one room to another as you learn about what daily life was like for members of this outcast community and about the Roma origins of Andalusia's iconic dance, flamenco. Museo Cuevas del Sacromonte is truly a treasure trove of information—information that's frequently overlooked by the city's more mainstream museums.

i Admission €5; no wheelchair accessibility

OUTDOORS

MIRADOR DE SAN NICOLÁS

C. Mirador de San Nicolás; open daily 24hr

The final destination of nearly every city walking tour, Mirador de San Nicolás is located in the heart of the **Albaicín** and is Granada's second-most popular attraction. Daily, tourists congregate here to snap a picture of the **Alhambra**—now eye-level—and the snow-capped Sierra Nevadas that loom behind it. This cobblestone square is especially busy around 9pm, when street performers and local artisans flood its tree-canopied center and the hilltop fortress is spotlighted by horizontal beams of sunlight. Though striking at sunset, we recommended paying the **Mirador** a visit at sunrise. If you arrive early enough, you'll have the place to yourself, save the locals that shuffle along Callejón Atarazana carrying heaping bags of groceries. Take a seat on the plaza's low, southern-facing wall—worn smooth by literal centuries of sweaty bottoms—and watch the sun ascend behind eight centuries of history.

i Free; no wheelchair accessibility

HIKING IN THE SIERRA NEVADAS

South of Granada

Not only does Granada's location at the base of the Sierra Nevada Mountain Range contribute to the city's characterization as one of the most stunning urban landscapes on Earth, it also affords some killer hiking options. If you're feeling the need to get in some additional vertical, strap on your most supportive sneakers and take Bus #138 to **Monachil.** Though only 20 minutes from the city center, this European hiking hub feels as remote on its edges as it does in the park center. The trails that depart from Monachil will take you through dry, open plains as well as lush forests, and eventually connect to a small waterfall, where you can strip off, jump in, and cool down.

i Bus €1.50; guided hostel tours from €10; bus runs hourly in both directions; no wheelchair accessibility

FOOD

BAR ÁVILA ($)

C. Verónica de la Virgen, 16; 685 42 49 06; open M-F 9am-midnight, Sa 9am-5pm

If you're on the hunt for tasty tapas, set your scope on Bar Ávila. This dive is a local favorite, frequented primarily by working couples and grandfatherly-types. In traditional Granadan fashion, every drink is served with a tapa. What's unique about Bar Ávila, however, is that you get to choose which one. The *carne en salsa* is dependably delicious and pairs wonderfully with a caña of Cerveza Alhambra, the city's local draft. As far as larger plates go, Bar Ávila's *calamares fritos* strikes a perfect balance between salty, spicy, and sour. Enjoy your meal at the dark granite counter or at a table around back—either way, you're sure to leave this bar's napkin-littered interior full and satisfied.

i Caña y tapa €2; vegetarian options available; no wheelchair accessibility

CAFÉ - BAR REINA MONICA ($$)

C. Panaderos, 20; 633 21 71 18; open daily noon-midnight

The five words you've been longing to hear ever since you left the States: all-you-can-eat buffet. Cheap food in the Albaicín is hard to come by, so we were shocked when we encountered a sign around the corner from the Mirador de San Nicolás that advertised a drink, bottomless tapas, and a dessert for just €10. With over 30 varieties of tapas, scrumptious paellas, roasted vegetables, and traditional tostadas, Café-Bar Reina Monica is the place to try out menu items you've been hesitant to sample out elsewhere. If you don't like something, go back for something else—here, doing so won't send you into the red. Speaking of red, the stuffed tomatoes are an all-around win, as are the vibrant checked tablecloths that pop below the blue flower pots that dangle from this restaurant's façade.

i Buffet from €10, bocadillos from €3; vegan and vegetarian options available; limited wheelchair accessibility; Wi-Fi

RESTAURANTE HICURI ART VEGAN ($$)

Pl. de los Girones, 4; 858 98 74 73; restaurantehicuriartvegan.com; open M-Sa noon-11pm

Perhaps the most common stereotype about veganism is that it perpetuates a lifestyle of deprivation. Restaurante Hicuri Art Vegan turns this stereotype on its head, serving up heaping plates of micronutrient-dense comfort food such as burgers, stir-fry, smoothies, tiramisu, and cheesecake. As for the other stereotypes, however, it leans into full-throttle. The restaurant's Birkenstock-wearing, Kombucha-sipping (wait, did we just describe the entire population of California?) customers look as if they could—at any moment—spring from their wooden chairs, join hands, and sing Kumbaya. Similarly, the splattering of blossoming plants and floor-to-ceiling murals of children climbing trees under the contemplative gaze of a personified Mother Earth scream peace-loving hippie.

i Menú del día from €13.80, starters from €5, burgers from €7.50, smoothies from €4; caters to all dietary constraints; no wheelchair accessibility

TAKEME SUSHI ($$$)

C. Príncipe, 4; 958 22 20 79; takemesushi.com; open daily 12:30pm-4:30pm and 8pm-midnight

Located in **Centro-Sagrario,** this tastefully-decorated, hole-in-the-wall sushi joint caters primarily to graduate students. Its hefty prices are enough to scare off undergraduates (and us, at first), but if you're looking for a quick fix, Takeme should be your first pick. We recommend skipping the sashimi and instead opting for a combo platter (€14), which often consists of maki, a few pieces of buttery nigiri, and a traditional side dish (for details, check out the chalkboard on the wall right of the register). The product quality is shockingly high for an itty-bitty restaurant in an itty-bitty city in the middle of a country known for everything besides raw fish—a statement supported by Takeme's overflowing dining room.

i Nigiri from €3.50, maki from €6; vegan and vegetarian options available; no wheelchair accessibility; Wi-Fi

NIGHTLIFE

BOHEMIA JAZZ CAFÉ

Pl. de los Lobos, 11; bohemiajazzcafe.negocio.site; open daily 3pm-2:45am

Arguably the coolest bar in Granada, there's enough eye fodder on Bohemia's walls, booze in Bohemia's cocktails, and soul in Bohemia's playlist to keep you occupied for hours. By day, it's an intimate hangout for artistic types and elderly locals, who sip on coffee concoctions topped with towers of whipped cream. By night, its curious ambiance is magnified by the low and rhythmic pulse of live jazz music. Here, wooden tables are surrounded by hundreds of photographs, frilly lamp shades, art deco posters, abstract art, and vintage knick-knacks.

i Coffee from €2.50, sundaes from €4.50, cocktails from €6; no wheelchair accessibility

EL BAR DE ERIC

C. Escuelas, 8; 958 27 63 01; open daily 9am-2am

Owned by Eric Jiménez—lead drummer of Los Planetas—this rock-and-roll-themed bar in the center of Granada is decked out in funky black-and-white wallpaper and a smattering of photo art, posters, and tickets. Here, you can get a taste of trendy fusion food during the afternoon and of Granada's local music scene at night—once the clock strikes 10pm, this welcoming restaurant transforms into a poppin' venue for up-and-comers, attracting young people from across the city.

i Wine from €2.80, coffee from €1.30, raciones from €6; vegan and vegetarian options available; wheelchair accessible

BOOM BOOM ROOM

C. Cárcel Baja, 10; 608 66 66 10; boomboomroom.es; open Su-Th 3pm-6am, F-Sa 3pm-7am

Upon entering Boom Boom Room at 11pm on a Thursday, we thought we'd stepped into the foyer of an abandoned cruise ship. Turns out that in its previous life, this high-end discotec was a cinema, hence the grand entryway, towering ceilings, and split-level set up. According to its website, BBR is committed to being Granada's number-one nightlife destination for the city's millennial population, and boy, does it deliver. Enter and you'll find yourself surrounded by overly-groomed men donning white button-ups that pucker around their biceps and ladies wearing flashy dresses that echo the flashes of the multi-colored strobe lights dangling from the ceiling. On paper, BBR opens at 3pm; in reality, it opens at midnight. Arrive at 2am on a Friday for prime partying.

i Cover €10, drinks from €5; check Facebook page for drink promos; wheelchair accessible; cocktail attire

IBIZA

Coverage by **Austin Eder**

Though acclaimed for its nightlife, the White Isle—named for its abundance of white buildings —offers a ton of daytime activities. Whether you want to fill your time cooking like a lobster on a sandy beach or hiking Sa Talaiassa to work off a hangover, Ibiza has a little something for everyone. But who are we kidding? If you're reading this, odds are you're interested in one thing and one thing only: partying. Cut to Ibiza Town ("Eivissa"), the island's largest city. Here, time is seldom acknowledged, shots are sold in pairs, and the low rumble of bass plays deafeningly. Ibiza's true colors shine brightest against the pitch-black backdrop of the early morning, when the island's clubs flood with music lovers eager to experience the type of debauchery seen only in films. Inside, anonymity reigns supreme—each flash of a strobe light another chance to reinvent oneself, each crowd another opportunity to succumb to one's senses. It'd be hard to run out of things to do on this well-endowed island, which boasts some of the world's most picturesque coves, rustic villages, imposing fortresses, and wildest locals. Sounds amazing, right? Well, for the most part, it is. But (and there's always a but), Let's Go would recommend that female travelers visit Ibiza as part of a group. Although Facebook groups and internet forums geared towards solo travel abound, they're not actively monitored and are—or were, when we last checked—filled with men looking for "female companions" to escort them on their island getaways. So, unless you're wanting to get a taste of the sugar-baby-slash-potential-murder-victim lifestyle, try to befriend your hostel roommates. Otherwise, it's time to mentally and physically prepare yourself for evenings of unwanted solicitations by drunken dude groups, which seem to keep on comin' no matter what you wear, where you are, or what time of night it is.

ORIENTATION

Ibiza is a Spanish island located approximately 185 kilometers southeast of **València.** At just 25 kilometers wide and 45 kilometers long, it's one of the smallest Balearic Islands. **Ibiza Town** ("Eivissa"), located on the southeast corner of the island, is Ibiza's largest city, followed by **San Antonio** (located on the western seaboard) and **Santa Eulària des Riu** (located on the eastern seaboard, north of Ibiza Town). Important thoroughfares to keep in mind while navigating Ibiza Town include **Avinguda de Santa Eulària des Riu,** which runs north-south and connects the **Port d'Eivissa** to **Dalt Vila,** Ibiza's historic walled town; and Avenida d'Isidor Macabich, which runs east-west through Ibiza Town's urban center and contains one of the city's most popular bus stops. Avenida de Sant Jordi leads southwest to **Playa d'en Bossa,** home to some of Ibiza's hottest clubs. Even further south lies **Aeroport d'Eivissa,** the island's primary airport. Avinguda C-731 connects Ibiza Town to San Antonio. On the west side of the island, north-south **Avinguda del Doctor Fleming** and east-west **Passeig de la Mar** together skirt the **Port de Sant Antoni. Carrer de Madrid** cuts straight north from San Antonio's Baleària terminal into the center of the city. Ibiza's most frequented nightclubs are located in and around Ibiza Town, but San Antonio attracts a consistent crowd of young adults due to its slightly lower prices.

ESSENTIALS

GETTING THERE

There are two ways to get to Ibiza: by plane and by ferry. Flights out of Barcelona and Valencia are considerably cheaper than ferries if you book several weeks in advance. Aeroport d'Eivissa is located 6km south of Ibiza Town, and accepts major airlines as well as budget ones including Ryanair, Spanair, Iberia,

Air Europa, and Vueling. To get to Eivissa from the airport, take Bus #10 (€3.50; payable on board) to Avinguda d'Espanya. Buses depart from the airport every 30min. and the average travel time is 20min. Alternatively, taxis to the city center cost €20 and take about 15min. Overnight ferries run between Barcelona/Valencia and Ibiza daily, and are timed to arrive at daybreak. When purchasing your ferry ticket, remain cognizant of the destination name. Both Port d'Eivissa and Port de Sant Antoni, located in Ibiza Town and San Antonio respectively, harbor Baleària and Trasmediterránea ferries. Choose the port closest to your hotel or hostel, as traversing the island can be costly. The Baleària and Trasmediterránea terminals of the Port d'Eivissa are located about 1km east of Eivissa proper. Bus #10 swings by Delta Discos (Av. España 7), the stop closest to the terminals, every 30min. and will take you to the city center.

GETTING AROUND

Despite being so small, Ibiza is difficult to navigate, especially if you're not willing or able to shell out a hefty chunk of cash for private transportation. All of Ibiza's cities can be crossed on foot in under 1hr. Travel between cities and to more remote clubs, coves, and villages is either cumbersome or costly. Most buses are operated by Alsa. Unfortunately, Ibiza's most scenic coves and quaint villages are inaccessible via public transportation. Bus #10 runs between the airport and the port, crossing through Ibiza Town, while bus #30 connects Ibiza Town to the San Antonio Bus Terminal (C. Londres, 7; 971 34 01 11). It departs every hour on the hour and the journey lasts approximately 50min. (€2; payable on board). Buses operate from 7am until midnight. After dark, services are taken over by the "Discobus," which shuttles around club-hoppers until 6am (€3.50; payable on board). If you find yourself in a transportation bind, taxis often loiter outside of clubs just after closing. During the summer months, expect to wait in a long line unless you try waving one down yourself.

PRACTICAL INFORMATION

Tourist Offices: Tourist offices are located at the airport, as well as the ferry terminals in Eivissa and San Antonio. Ibiza Town (Paseo de Vara de Rey, 1; 971301900; ibiza.travel; open M-Sa 9am-8pm, Su 9am-2pm)

Banks/ATMs/Currency Exchange: ATMs are dispersed throughout both Ibiza Town and San Antonio. IIbiza Town: CiaxaBank (Carrer d'Antoni Palau, 8; 971 80 98 00; caixabank.es; open M-F 8:15am-2pm).

Post Offices: Ibiza's main post office is located at Av. d'Isidor Macabich, 67 (902 19 71 97; correos.es; open M-F 8:30am-8:30pm, Sa 9:30am-1pm).

Public Restrooms: Public restrooms are few and far between in Ibiza Town (try the one located on Avinguda Santa Eulária des Riu near the Estación Maritima), and nonexistent in San Antonio. Most establishments that have an entrance fee—museums, clubs, or restaurants from which you purchase food or drink—come equipped with clean restrooms.

Water: Bottled water only, folks. In 2015, Ibiza's Ministry of Health deemed tap water "unfit for human consumption." Odds are a glass or two won't kill ya, but drink too much of it and you may end up with a hole in your stomach.

Internet: Free Wi-Fi is available at most restaurants and cafés, but seldom at or around monuments. Still, it never hurts to ask: *¿Tiene Wi-Fi gratis?*

BGLTQ+ Resources: Ibiza is a major BGLTQ+ summer destination with plenty of gay bars, festivals, and club nights including the long running La Troya party at Space and legendary woman-only weekend at Velvet Ibiza. More information about navigating the island can be found online at ellgeebe.com and iglta.org.

EMERGENCY INFORMATION

Emergency Number: 112.

Police: Ibiza's police headquarters is located in Eivissa, although local branches are dispersed throughout the island.

- Ibiza Town (Comisaría de Policía; Avinguda de la Pau; 971 39 88 83)

- San Antonio (Policia Local; Av. Portmany, 17; 971 34 08 30)

US Embassy: The Palma de Mallorca Consular Agency covers all four Balearic Islands (including Ibiza) and is open on an appointment basis only (Carrer de Porto Pi, 8; 971 40 37 07; pmagency@state.gov).

Rape Crisis Center: In the event of an emergency, call 112 and contact the US Consulate. Though based in Palma, the officers can provide assistance filing reports with the police and seeking medical treatment.

Hospitals: Hospital Can Misses, located in Ibiza Town, is open daily 24hr (Carrer de Corona; 971 39 70 00). In the event of an emergency, call 112.

Pharmacies: Farmacia Escudero Rouppas, located northeast of Ibiza Town, is open daily 24hr (Calle Atzaro, 8; 971 39 48 82).

SIGHTS

CULTURE

DALT VILA

North of Ibiza Town

Designated as a **UNESCO World Heritage** site in 1999, Dalt Vila is the best-preserved coastal fortress on the Mediterranean and a magnificent example of Renaissance military architecture. To make the most of your visit, we recommend beginning at the **Portal de Ses Taules,** Dalt Vila's main gate, and continuing in a rough semicircle towards **Portal Nou,** located on the west side of the city. Continue up the steep cobbled ramp and you'll find yourself at the start of a truly magical journey, surrounded by white-washed residences, artisanal shops, climbing vines, flowering trees, and sweeping city-wide views. It's impossible to get lost here—continue walking upwards and you'll eventually make it to the **Catedral de Eivissa,** visible from almost anywhere in Ibiza Town. Significant alleyways, plazas, portals, and buildings are marked with signs in Spanish, English, and French.

i *Free; limited wheelchair accessibility*

CATEDRAL DE EIVISSA

Pl. de la Catedral; Ibiza Town; 971 39 92 32; open Tu-Su 10am-2pm and 5pm-8pm

At the tippy top of Dalt Vila sits the Catedral de Eivissa, the most iconic silhouette on the Ibiza skyline. Despite looking so massive from the **Portal de Ses Taules,** it's teeny up close. Yet considering it's served only the residents of Dalt Vila's for the last six centuries, it's never really faced a capacity problem. The Catedral de Eivissa underwent a series of major refurbishments during the eighteenth century, and to say that the windows don't match the drapes would be an understatement. Its heavy flying buttresses and rectangular clock tower stand in stark contrast to the barrel ceilings and Baroque altarpiece inside.

i *Free; limited wheelchair accessibility*

LANDMARKS

CALA BASSA

Cala Bassa; Sant Josep de sa Talaia; open daily 8am-midnight

As tempting as the shoreline along Avinguda del Doctor Fleming may be, do yourself a favor hold out for Cala Bassa, one of the most scenic coves on Ibiza's western coast. Located only 11 kilometers southwest of San Antonio, Cala Bossa seems worlds away from the contained frenzy of the city's day clubs. Here, families, couples, and solo travelers lounge along a horseshoe of golden sand, and yachters bob atop the turquoise water of the **Cap de Sa Serra.** Cala Bassa has exploded in popularity since the opening of the **Cala Bassa Beach Club,** a resort and restaurant planted 100 meters away amidst a forest of gnarled Sabina trees. While its presence here may prevent you from finding a plot of free sand after 1pm, it also means you'll have access to clean restrooms, cool drinks, and hearty—albeit overpriced—food during your stay.

i *Free, drinks from €3; limited wheelchair accessibility*

EL ARENAL

Ibiza Town (Eivissa)

El Arenal is a quirky, beachy neighborhood wedged between **Dalt Vila** and the **Port d'Eivissa.** It's here that you'll find Ibiza Town's trendiest boutiques, freshest markets, and fanciest restaurants. Pastel pink, yellow, and orange buildings are sprinkled with bright blue and green shutters, and linked together by canopies of dark pink bougainvillea. Points of interest include the **Estatua Vara de Rey,** a tribute to an Ibizan General who died in the 1898 Battle of El Caney, fought between Spain and the U.S. over Cuba; **Carrer Lluís Tur i Palau,** the restaurant-lined street that hugs the port; **Placa de sa Riba,** a palm-covered plateau that looks northeast along the coast; and **Mercado Viejo,** an outdoor marketplace located at the base of the **Portal de Ses Taules.**

i *Free; wheelchair accessible*

SUNSET IN SAN ANTONIO

Caló el Moro; San Antonio; arrive 30min. before sunset

Regardless of where you decide to watch it, experiencing a sunset on Ibiza's western coast—like exploring the streets of **Dalt Vila**—is absolutely non-negotiable. The sunset here is world-famous, and for a good reason. Every night around 9pm, the horizon is set ablaze with a profuse red glow. The waves settle, the sails calm, and the water begins to twinkle. The light cast by the receding sun is so powerful that virtually everything separating you from it—the passersby, the catamarans, the buoys, **Illa Sa Conillera**—is reduced to a stark silhouette. Our favorite place to watch the sunset? **Caló des Moro,** located on the northern fringes of San Antonio.

i *Free; wheelchair accessible*

OUTDOORS

BOAT PARTIES

Playa d'en Bossa Pier; Ibiza Town; 628 94 48 09; oceanbeat.es/en/; boarding begins at 1pm, meet at Forever Bar (Camino 1002, 16) at 12:30pm for breakfast and ticket verification

Did you even go to Ibiza if you didn't go to a boat party? Despite the obvious risks they pose (read: sea sickness and claustrophobia), they're a critical component of a trip to Ibiza, especially if you've classified yourself as a "Dartier." Parties range in quality and price, and typically the two go hand-in-hand. You can generally expect that the more you spend, the more fun you'll have. We found that the parties offered by **Oceanbeat** are the best bang for your buck. If you book online, €80 will buy you a champagne breakfast, four hours aboard a decked-out catamaran, free drinks the entire time you're on the water, a burlesque show, a six-hour after party at Bora Bora (Playa D'en Bossa; 971 30 19 06; open daily 9am-6am), and three free entrances to some of Ibiza's wildest nightclubs. Considering entrance alone to the likes of **Privilege, Sankeys, SWAG, and Es Paradis** run between €35 and €75 a pop, the **Oceanbeat Ibiza Boat Party** is—in our opinion—worth its price tag. (Be sure to check Oceanbeat's website for details regarding your trip prior to departure, as venues and times are subject to change.)

i *€80 per head, VIP pass €200; no refunds; no wheelchair accessibility; beach attire recommended*

OCEAN BEACH IBIZA

Carrer des Molí, 12-14; San Antonio; 971 80 32 60; oceanbeachibiza.com; open daily noon-10pm (W noon-9pm)

All of the fun of a boat party, less of the claustrophobia. Ocean Beach Ibiza, located just south of San Antonio, is an all-day affair like no other. This hotel-club combo runs opposite to its nocturnal counterparts in Ibiza Town, offering tourists the chance to remain plastered for as close to 24 hours as humanly possible. The party gets going daily at around 2pm, and is a feast for the eyes and spirit. Bikini-clad waitresses weave between white daybeds and yellow umbrellas carrying bottles of Dom Pérignon, and people congregate around Ocean Beach's 600-square-meter pool sipping on overpriced drinks. While the floaties and decor may differ day by day, Ocean Beach's mission always remains the same: to put on a hell of a show. When we visited, we were showered in champagne (last Friday of every month)—turns out the smell is hard to get rid of. If the thought of spending a day elbowing through a sea of oiled bodies to get a better view of the headliner doesn't appeal to you, check out **Pearl,** Ocean Beach's rooftop bar, for some of San Antonio's best craft cocktails (€8).

i *Entrance cost varies based on time of week and year; reserve tickets online at least 2 weeks in advance (€15 electronically + €20 at door); single lounger €70; two gin cocktails €10, individual cocktails from €8; Wi-Fi; limited wheelchair accessibility*

SA COVA - WINE TASTING IN SANT MATEU D'ALBARCA

Diseminado Aubarca, 4; Sant Mateu d'Albarca; 971 18 70 46; open weekdays 10:30am-6pm, Sa 11am-2pm

As far as day drinking goes, it doesn't get much better than a private vineyard tour and wine tasting in **Sant Mateu,** a tiny town located about 20 kilometers north of Ibiza Town. **Sa Cova,** Ibiza's first for-profit winery, is open to visitors on a year-round basis. Tasting tours cost €17 and include four glasses of wine and tapas—a steal in Balearic terms. Though the appeal and intrigue of Ibiza's **Playa d'en Bossa** is unquestionable, the island's true beauty lies in its quiet, secluded villages. Spend an afternoon exploring Sant Mateu's cobblestone streets, bougainvillea-covered buildings, and long rows of grapevines. Neither you nor your palate will be disappointed. (Sa Cova Winery is accessible by taxi and by bus.

i *€17 per head; tours must be arranged in advance; have cash on hand; no wheelchair accessibility*

FOOD

S'ESCALINATA EIVISSA ($$)

Carrer Portal Nou, 10; Ibiza Town; 653 37 13 56; sescalinata.es/ibiza/; open daily 10:30am-2:30am

Certainly the coolest restaurant in **D'Alt Vila** and a strong contender for the coolest restaurant in Ibiza Town, S'Escalinata Eivissa is an indoor-outdoor establishment where patrons dine on leather bean bag chairs under the shadows cast by D'Alt Vila's iconic white buildings. Considering its stellar ambiance, S'Escalinata Eivissa's offerings are surprisingly cheap. Food ranges from Mediterranean classics like seasoned hummus and pita bread to heartier dishes like burgers and warm wraps, and is sure to appease carnivores and herbivores alike. So kick your feet up on a refurbished produce-box-turned-coffee-table, breathe in the aroma of citrus, and get lost in the twists and turns of the succulents that line the small, sloping plaza around you. We recommend arriving just before sunset to secure a seat and ordering a glass of sangria (€5) or pint of beer (€5).

i *Bocadillos from €7.50, tapas from €7, salads from €11, breakfast from €3.50; vegetarian options available; no wheelchair accessibility; Wi-Fi*

CAN GOURMET ($)

Carrer de Guillem de Montgrí, 20; Ibiza Town; 635 26 66 66; can-gourmet.com/ibiza/; open M, W-Su 9:30am-10pm

Ibiza is famous for being a monetary black hole. Euros go flying in and never come out. It's difficult to find a meal for under €10, let alone a big ass sandwich—Can Gourmet's specialty. This iconic establishment is a sub shop through and through, serving up delectable and satisfying bocadillos for an eye-popping €6—cheaper than any cocktail you can find on this God-(un)forsaken island. Colorful potted plants and sombrero hats hang from the second floor balcony down to the pavement. Streetside, the "ham-mobile"—a bright green convertible truck stuffed with pig butts—displays the day's offerings, which vary slightly depending on what produce the owner decided to pick up that morning.

Seating room in Can Gourmet's tiny interior is limited. We recommend ordering a bocadillo and bottle of craft beer para llevar and heading northeast to the port, which is just two blocks away. If you're overwhelmed by the number of tapas on Can Gourmet's menu, just ask for one of each of the restaurant's three most popular dishes.

i Sandwiches from €6; vegetarian options available; limited wheelchair accessibility

PASSION CAFÉ - PLAYA D'EN BOSSA ($$$)

Ctra. de Platja d'en Bossa (Edificio Bossamar); Ibiza Town; 971 30 51 30; passion-ibiza.com; open daily 9am-midnight

Rolling off a long night at **Hï** and looking for a way to kill your hangover? Head to Passion Café for a menu that ranges from vegetable-packed smoothies to greasy chicken burgers, it's got a little something for everyone. Passion Café is the trendiest health food spot on Ibiza, and has become so popular in recent years that it now has seven different locations and a cult-like following. Particularly delicious are the watermelon and feta salad and full breakfast, which includes a half an avocado, scrumptious scrambled eggs, lox, grilled Halloumi cheese, and crunchy sourdough toast.

i Smoothie bowl from €10.50, full breakfast from €14; vegetarian options available; wheelchair accessibility varies

RESTAURANTE GOLDEN BUDDHA ($$)

Carrer de Santa Rosalia, 35; San Antonio; 971 34 56 33; goldenbuddhaibiza.com; open daily 10am-3:30am

Food's good; view's better. Restaurante Golden Buddha is the ultimate place to watch the sunset in Ibiza. Its menu boasts a wide array of breakfast, lunch, and dinner options that range from the types of dishes you'd find in a standard New York bistro to traditional Thai curry. What really sets Golden Buddha apart from the rest of the bars on the waterfront is its massive elevated patio, which is furnished with dozens of tables, low couches, and four-post gazebos designed for day-long lounging. Sailboats and catamarans float across an island-dotted harbor, and passerby stroll casually along **Passeig de Ponent.** If you're looking for something a little more upbeat, check out **Café del Mar,** a live music venue and neighborhood favorite located a couple blocks south. To secure a front-row seat at either of these establishments, arrive at least an hour before sunset.

i Salads from €9.50, burgers from €12.90, desserts from €4.50, beer from €3; vegetarian options available; limited wheelchair accessibility

NIGHTLIFE

AMNESIA

Ctra. Ibiza a San Antonio, Km 5; San Rafael; 971 19 80 41; amnesia.es; open M-Sa midnight-6am

Conveniently located in the middle of fucking nowhere, Amnesia is—regrettably—an absolutely essential clubbing experience. Although the bumpy, 40-minute bus ride will test your patience, it will all feel worth it when you step foot inside Amnesia's packed interior. This 5,000-person capacity club is split into two sections, each with its own decor and lineups. The **Club Room**—a cavernous, stone-lined pit overflowing with raging, overly-perfumed twenty-somethings—is transformed daily. The **Terrace,** famous for its sunrise sessions, is guarded by the club's infamous ice canons and covered by a greenhouse-esque trellis. People naturally migrate here as the night drones on, eager to catch a glimpse of the light peeking through the windows above. Contrary to what its name suggests, every night at Amnesia is unforgettable—a fact attributable to its extremely diverse program. Sets vary from techno to house to bass to Latin, so make sure to check online before purchasing your ticket. Pro tip: drinks cost more upstairs than down.

i Cover from €35, water €9, cocktails from €15; no dress code

USHUAÏA

Platja d'en Bossa, 10; Ibiza Town; 971 39 67 10; theushuaiaexperience.com; open daily 4pm-midnight

An immediate hit upon opening in 2011, Ushuaïa (pronounced ooh-sh-why-ah) blows the competition out of the water as far as stage production goes. A go-to location for a #darty, this luxury hotel complex shuts down promptly at midnight. Consequently, Ushuaïa's open-air floor is a hotbed for "final-nighters," people who need to be sober enough to make their 7am ferry but want to squeeze every last ounce of enjoyment out of the island beforehand. The result? Some of the most incredible communal moments in the history of clubbing. This open-air venue is arguably the most enjoyable place on the island to experience a lineup. Of course, it helps that those lineups are headlined by artists like **David Guetta** and **Martin Garrix.** Against the backdrop of a setting sun, Ushuaïa's massive stage explodes in lights, fire, and confetti at all the right moments, keeping the audience in constant ecstasy. If the poolside debauchery proves to be too much for you, check out Ushuaïa Tower's rooftop lounge, which offers stunning views of the club and island below.

i Cover from €40; beach attire recommended

EDEN

Calle Salvador Espriu; San Antonio; edenibiza.com; open daily midnight-6am

Eden's proximity to long-time competitor **Es Paradis** has kept both venues on their toes since the early 90s. As a result, they're frequently stepping up their game, and now boast reputations for being two of the best clubs on the island. But, of the two, Eden's got the (five-inch-heeled) leg up. It boasts the island's best sound system and a beautiful, garden-themed interior, making it a favorite among die-hard house fans and DJs alike. A night at Eden is truly a religious experience, but not in the biblical sense. On the spectrum of holiness, where grandma's snowflake-embroidered tracksuit lies on one end and stripper's ruffled thong lies on another, Eden skews heavily towards the latter. Sets take place in the double-decker main room, which is so chock-full of lights, speakers, and people that you'll inevitably find yourself disoriented, no matter your degree of inebriation. Our advice? Give in to the chaos. Let the chest-shattering pulses of bass knock you to your knees—where

you'll inevitably find yourself begging for mercy from your hangover the next morning.

i Cover from €25; casual cocktail attire; check calendar before purchasing tickets

PACHA

Avinguda d'Agost, 8; Ibiza Town; 971 31 36 00; pachaibiza.com; open daily 11pm-6am

Stomping ground of Europe's rich and famous, Pacha is held dearly in the hearts of locals and considered a must-visit for tourists making their clubbing rounds. With over 45 years of party-planning under its belt, Pacha boasts one of the biggest talent rosters on Ibiza. Take your pick from the cream of the electronic music crop—with headliners like **David Guetta, Calvin Harris, Martin Solveig, Sven Väth,** and **Alesso** splattered across the calendar, there's no way to go wrong. That said, Pacha's known for two parties in particular: **Flower Power** and **F*** Me I'm Famous.** If you score tickets to either of those shows, you're golden. As its name suggests, Flower Power is a blast to the past on a scale so large it makes your bell bottoms look small. Expect soul, pop, funk, and other hits from the last four decades, set to the backdrop of exquisite and immersive handmade decorations. On other nights, Pacha's white, black, and red interior speaks for itself, brought to the life by the people within it.

i Cover from €40, €20 more at door; mixed drinks from €18, beer from €12; cocktail attire recommended; parties often fill up weeks in advance

MADRID

Coverage by **Joseph Winters**

Unlike other European cities, Madrid's identity can't be distilled into a single colossal monument. Instead, the spirit of Madrid is dispersed in the splendor of the smaller things: a Medieval alley here, a neoclassical palace there, all mishmashed into the city's more modern lilt. As the third-largest city in the European Union, visitors can expect a lot from Madrid—from architecture to gastronomy to nightlife, it delivers. For centuries, Spain has churned out world-class artists, and much of their work eventually finds its way back to the capital city. Madrid's so-called Golden Triangle of Art—the Museo del Prado, Centro de Arte Reina Sofía, and Museo Thyssen-Bornemisza—house thousands of works by Spanish legends like Goya, Picasso, Dalí, and Miró, as well as Flemish and Italian icons of the art world. And then there's the food. *Tapas* may be a worldwide phenomenon at this point, but there's no better place to *tapear* (literally "to go eat tapas") than Madrid. As the culinary crossroads of Spain, Madrid isn't limited by regional cuisine; visitors can find traditional flavors of Valencian *paella* or Madrileñan blood sausage in age-old taverns, right next to LA-esque health bars serving up cold-pressed juices. It's the late-night *churros con chocolate,* however, that capture our hearts every time. And they're only part of Madrid's nightlife situation—the city is notorious for insomnia. Once the sun sets and the temperature drops to a reasonable level, the streets flood with bar-hoppers and party-goers, everyone scouting out that next glass of sangria. The wildest tourists inevitably find their way into Madrid's epic *teatros*: massive theaters-turned-concert venues, where world-class musicians and deejays flood the city's soundscape, impervious to the brightening skies of early morning.

ORIENTATION

Downtown Madrid is roughly circular. Most of the city's action is bounded to the west by **Palacio Real** and its **Campo del Moro,** and to east by the **Parque del Buen Retiro** and the **Paseo del Prado,** an enormous thoroughfare that's home to the city's Golden Triangle of museums (**Museo del Prado, Museo Nacional Centro de Arte Reina Sofía,** and the **Museo Thyssen-Bornemisza).** The aptly-named **"Centro"** of Madrid is in—you guessed it—the center of the city, made of the commercial streets between the **Plaza Mayor** and the **Puerta del Sol** (known as **"Sol"**). East of the Centro is **Huertas** (the name of its main street), also called **Barrio de las Letras** (Neighborhood of the Letters). Central but relatively quiet, it's famous for having been home to writers like Lope de Vega and Cervantes. To the northeast, after crossing the ultra-highway known as the **Gran Vía,** visitors are welcomed into **Chueca,** Madrid's well-known BGLTQ+-friendly neighborhood. But perhaps "friendly" is an understatement; this neighborhood, with its gay bars and homoerotic fashion stores, is radically accepting. Even without its gay identity, Chueca is popular for its trendy cafés and shopping, as well as for its nightlife. The other half of northern Madrid (northwest) is **Malasaña,** the Bohemian arts district, where you'll find an extraordinary concentration of concept stores, art supply shops, and Insta-ready dining options. If you keep going west, the **Plaza de España** and **Templo de Debod** are worth knowing about. South of Centro, the three neighborhoods of interest—from west to east—are **La Latina, Embajadores,** and **Lavapiés.** All three are less commercial than the northern half of Madrid, and everything from shopping to sleeping to tapas-ing is less expensive here. La Latina is known for traditional Spanish vibes and a killer flea market called **El Rastro** (every Sunday morning), and Lavapiés is particularly multicultural. Finally, in the southeasternmost corner of the city is the **Atocha Train Station.**

ESSENTIALS

GETTING THERE

By plane: Flights to Madrid arrive in the bustling Madrid-Barajas airport some 10mi. outside the city center. There are four terminals: most international flights will arrive in terminals 1-3, while flights operated by Iberia usually land in terminal 4. Each terminal offers connection to downtown via the metro's Line 8. It operates from 6:05am-1:30am, takes around 45min., and costs €4.50, not including the €2.50 one-time cost of a refillable refillable Tarjeta Multi public transport card. Taxis are also available from Barajas, but are much more expensive. (€30, 30min.)

By bus: There are two main bus stations in Madrid. The Intercambiador de Avenida de América is slightly north of downtown and is also a metro stop with connections to lines 6, 7, and 8. The more southerly station is called Estación Sur de Autobuses, also with a metro station—this one's called Méndez Álvaro and it connects to Line 6.

By train: Renfe is the national train operator, and trains arrive in Madrid from throughout the Iberian Peninsula, with many connections through France. The network is highly convenient, but it's the AVE trains that take the cake for incredible service. AVE tickets are more expensive than regular trains, but they can cut travel time by more than half, depending on the journey.

GETTING AROUND

By foot: As with any city, the best way to dive into local culture is to walk. Everywhere. In all seriousness, it's worth thinking twice before taking the metro everywhere; Madrid is highly walkable, and it's the unexpected gems between points A and B that you're likely to remember most. To get from the northernmost edge of Malasaña to the border of Lavapies is only a mile: child's play for a weathered traveler like you.

By bus: To take advantage of the bus and metro networks, travelers will need to pick up a Tarjeta Multi card at any metro station. It costs €2.50 and remains valid for 10 years—you refill it every time you need take another ride. Madrid's 200-line bus system (Empresa Municipal de Transporte, or EMT) shuttles through the city M-F 6am-11:30pm and Sa-Su 7am-11pm, with most buses passing a stop at least every 15min.

By metro: With more than 300 stations, Madrid's metro network is the second largest in Europe, and using it is highly intuitive. There are a dozen numbered lines crisscrossing the city from 6am-1:30am, and trains arrive at most stations every two minutes during rush hours. Line 8 routes through Nuevos Ministerios to the airport. Load up your Tarjeta Multi with ten trips (€12.20) or pay as you go (starting at €1.50/trip).

By train: Trains within the city? You betcha. Cercanías trains run between the northern Nuevos Ministerios and the southern Atocha train station (and beyond). They're not too expensive and can be useful if you want a direct route with fewer stops than a metro journey.

By bike: There's a bike share program called BiciMAD offering over 1500 bikes at 120 stations around town. Each time you check out a bike, the session lasts two hours.

PRACTICAL INFORMATION

Tourist Offices: The main tourist office is in Pl. Mayor, but there are a number of booths in Madrid's other main squares, including Sol. Look for the orange italic "i". They'll weigh you down with plenty of free maps, museum guides, event information, etc. Plaza Mayor (Pl. Mayor 27; 91 578 78 10; www.esmadrid.com; open daily 9:30am-9:30pm).

Banks/ATMs/Currency Exchange: There are ATMs throughout the city, and plenty of banks along the east-west Gran Vía, as well as a bit further south in the area between Callao and Sol. Deutsche Bank (Centro) (C. de Toledo 33; 913 64 20 24; www.db.com/spain; open M-Th 8:30am-4:30pm, F 8:30am-2:15pm).

Post Offices: Correos is the national mail carrier, and they have a couple offices along the Gran Vía, one between Sol and Callao, and several more throughout the city center, including offices in Malasaña and northern Chueca. Correos (Puerta del Sol) (C. de Preciados 3; 902 19 71 97; www.correos.es; open M-Sa 10am-10pm, Su 11am-9pm).

Public Restrooms: When nature calls, use a little ingenuity to find relief without paying for it. There are public restrooms in the city's many cultural centers and museums, many of which can be accessed without a ticket. Otherwise, El Corte Inglés, Spain's favorite department store, has locations throughout the city offering free public restrooms.

Internet: There is no official Wi-Fi network of Madrid, but between the city's countless restaurants, shopping malls, and cafés offering free Internet access, you should have no trouble finding a way to get online.

BGLTQ+ Resources: The Federation of Lesbian, Gay, Trans and Bisexual people (FELGTB in Spanish) offers a directory of BGLTQ+-related events, information, and has a hotline for victims of discrimination (C. Infantas 40, Madrid; 913 604 605; www.felgtb.org; M-Th 8am-8pm, F 8am-3:30pm).

EMERGENCY INFORMATION

Emergency Number: 112.

Police: Madrid's police regularly occupy the city's most crowded spaces like Callao, Sol, and just outside some of the classier hotels of Gran Vía. You can find their offices near the Paseo del Prado, but there are other locations on Gran Vía and in Malasaña and Chueca. In case of an emergency, dial 112 for quick police support.

- National Police (Centro) (C. de Leganitos 19; 915 48 79 85; www.policia.es).
- Municipal Police (Huertas) (C. de las Huertas 76-78; 913 22 10 21; www.policia.es).

US Embassy: There is a US Embassy in Madrid (C. de Serrano 75; 915 872 200; es.usembassy.gov; open M-F 8am-2pm).

Hospitals: Madrid has several large hospitals east of Parque del Retiro, as well as some options to the north in the Chamartín neighborhood and beyond. In an emergency, dial 112 to be taken to the best location for your needs.

- Gregorio Marañón Hospital (C. del Dr. Esquerdo 46; 915 86 80 00; www.madrid.org; open daily 24hr).
- Hospital Vithas Nuestra Señora de América (C. de Arturo Soria 103-107; 902 29 82 99; www.vithas.es; open daily 24hr).

Pharmacies: Pharmacies and herbolarias are a dime a dozen in Madrid. Pretty much any major Madrid thoroughfare has a pharmacy on every few blocks. Here are two 24hr options:

- Farmacia Central 24 Horas (Paseo de Santa María de la Cabeza 64; 914 73 06 72; open daily 24hr).
- Farmacia Trébol Retiro (Av. de Menéndez Pelayo 45; 914 09 57 59; www.grupo.famaciastrebol.com; open daily 24hr).

SIGHTS

CULTURE

MERCADO EL RASTRO (EL RASTRO FLEA MARKET)

C. Ribera de Curtidores and surrounding streets; open Su 9am-3pm

Although it's officially capped out at 3500 vendors, El Rastro, Madrid's historic flea market, seems to go on forever, an endless sprawl of vintage stamps, Tibetan singing bowls, secondhand clothing, and who even knows what else. Founded over 400 years ago, El Rastro (the trail) refers to the tanneries that used to cover the area, and the trail of blood that followed animal carcasses as they were hauled here from the slaughterhouse. Things are a bit less gruesome today: explore themed streets specializing in used books and painting supplies, pick up some low-cost souvenirs for your family back home, and allow yourself to meander up and down the hill.

i Prices vary; wheelchair accessible

CHUECA

Chueca; neighborhood open daily 24hr

They mean it when they say Chueca is the BGLTQ+ epicenter of Madrid. Heck, it's the gayest place in Spain—if you're there during orgullo week (Madrid's gay pride celebration, usually at the beginning of July), the neighborhood takes on an almost aggressive BGLTQ+ vibe. Rainbows are everywhere; you can eat them (in gluten-free bakeries and cafés), wear them (as silken ponchos or risqué booty shorts), and photograph the heck out of them (flags, banners, and posters line every street). There's also a proliferation of erotic shops, if that's your thing. After dark, the neighborhood takes on a grittier feel, with hordes of locals and tourists bar-hopping well into the early morning, whether at Michelin-starred tapa joints or somewhat-sketchy "100% Gay" bar/sauna "experiences."

i Prices vary; wheelchair accessible

CINE DORÉ

C. Santa Isabel 3; 913 69 32 25; mecd.gob.es; box office open Tu-Su 4:15pm-15min. after the beginning of the last film (usually 10pm), café open Tu-Su 5pm-12:15am, bookstore open Tu-Su 5:30pm-10pm

Unlike your typical neighborhood movie theater, you won't find Avengers, Hollywood rom coms, or Adam Sandler anywhere near the Cine Doré. Founded in 1922, this national Spanish theater specializes in avant-garde experimental films—think BGLTQ+ features, black and white Westerns, and silent movies from the national archives. There are three theaters, one of which is a recreation of the original, antique auditorium. Be sure to check if the outdoor rooftop cinema (with its own bar!) is open; it doesn't get much better than Spanish sangria and a show en plein air. Even if you don't end up watching anything, the building itself is worth checking out; it features a neoclassical facade and a vibrant art nouveau interior with a café and bookstore, covered head to toe with playful blue and white tiles.

i Tickets €2.50, €2 reduced; limited wheelchair accessibility

EL TEATRO REAL (THE ROYAL THEATER)

Pl. de Isabel II; 91 516 06 00; www.teatro-real.com; open for tours daily 10:30am-4:30pm

Posh tourists looking for a place to flash their fanciest getup should look no further than Madrid's Royal Theater. "El Real," as it is commonly known, was originally completed in 1850 under the auspices of Queen Isabella I, who dreamed of a theater to rival the rest of the continent's lavish opera houses. She certainly got it—the Teatro Real was one of Europe's premier performance venues for some 75 years before it closed in 1925 for safety reasons. Thankfully, it was nothing a few million euros couldn't fix (€100 million, actually)—and it again serves as the epicenter of Madrid's fine performing arts. Catch a concert by the **Spanish National Orchestra,** performances by the **National Ballet,** and of course the throaty warble of a good **Puccini, Verdi,** or **Händel** opera. Curious visitors can also tour the building (alone or with a guide), exploring the building's wraparound rotonda, which grants access to the stage's 28 boxes, including the royal boxes and state rooms. The whole place is strung with artwork from the **Museo del Prado** and the **National Heritage** art collections.

i Self-guided tour €7, €6 reduced; General Tour (€8, students €6) daily at 10am, 11am, noon, 1pm; Technical Tour (€16, €14 reduced) daily at 10am; Artistic Tour (€12, €10 reduced) daily at 9:30am; Night Tour (€30) after performances; last entry 3:30pm; limited wheelchair accessibility; combined ticket with Palacio Real €15

MATADERO MADRID

Pl. de Legazpi 8; 915 17 73 09; www.mataderomadrid.org; open Tu-F 4pm-9pm, Sa-Su 11am-9pm

What was once a disused slaughterhouse has gained new life as Matadero Madrid, a contemporary arts center just south of the city center. The complex is owned by the Madrid City Council, which uses the complex to host a constantly-rotating array of artists from across the artistic spectrum. Matadero's spaces include **Cineteca,** devoted exclusively to documentary films; the **Avant Garden,** featuring environmental exhibitions; and a graphic and interior design-focused **Central de Diseño.** Programming changes frequently, but past events have included poetry festivals, Muslim graphic novel expositions, circus performances, etc. Whatever the specifics, Matadero guarantees a place to "create, reflect, learn, and enjoy." The best part: they're proud to offer almost all of its spaces and events free of charge.

i Free; limited wheelchair accessibility; event information and tickets available online or at box office

MERCADO DE SAN ANTÓN (SAN ANTÓN MARKET)

C. Augusto Figueroa 24; 913 30 07 30; www.mercadosananton.com; open M-Sa 10am-10pm, Su 10am-midnight

Though they call themselves a "traditional market," we have trouble imagining Japanese takeout and a solar energy collector in Madrid's fifteenth-century food bazaars. Not that the upgrades are unappreciated; Mercado de San Antón's panoply of international tapas and artisanal nom noms makes it a delicious addition to the **Chueca** district. Built from the ground up in 2002, the interior is just as gorgeous as the rest of this trendy neighborhood, and the food is, too. Look for French macarons, *foie gras pintxos*, freshly-picked peaches, homemade sushi—it's a gourmet wonderland in there. The ground floor does to-go offerings and market staples (like fruits and veggies), while the second floor has ample seating with a view of the central courtyard. For stunning views outside the Mercado, head to the top floor, where there's a lovely terrace with its own chic restaurant.

i Eat-in prices vary; Wi-Fi; wheelchair accessible

PLAZA DE TOROS DE LAS VENTAS

C. de Alcalá 237; plaza tours: 687 73 90 32, bullfights: 913 56 22 00; plaza tours: www.lasventastour.com; bullfights: www.las-ventas.com; open daily 10am-5:30pm

Seating as many as 25,000 spectators, Madrid's Las Ventas bullring is by far the largest in Spain, outdone only by one in Mexico City and another in Venezuela. It was designed in the decadent Mudéjar (Moorish) style by José Espeliú, with ornate arched windows, patterned ceramics every which way, and an imposing front door known colloquially as the "Gate of Glory." For aspiring toreros (bullfighters), exiting victorious through these doors is the ultimate goal. To see the plaza for yourself, the best way is to attend a fight—watching the sumptuously-clad bullfighters wrangle the bulls into submission is quite the hair-raising experience. Tickets—which can be purchased online or at the gates—come at a variety of price points depending mostly on whether you sit in the sol o sombra (sun or shade). Otherwise, you can go on an audio-guided tour of the plaza during closing times, which gets you access to the ring itself, but also to normally off-limits places like the royal box or the **Puerta de Cuadrillas,** where the torero solemnly waits before entering the ring.

i Plaza tours €14.90, €11.90 reduced, bullfights admission from €4.90-74.90 (depending on seats); guided tours must be pre-purchased (www.lasventastour.com); tours at 9:30am, 11:30am, and 3pm, duration 90min.; last entry at 5:30pm; limited wheelchair accessibility

LANDMARKS

TEMPLO DE DEBOD (TEMPLE OF DEBOD)

C. Ferraz 1; 913 66 74 15; templodedebod.memoriademadrid.es.com; open Apr-Sept Tu-F 10am-2pm and 6pm-8pm, Sa-Su 10am-2pm; Oct-Mar Tu-F 9:45am-1:45pm and 4:15pm-6:15pm, Sa-Su 10am-2pm

Bet you weren't expecting to find an Egyptian temple in the heart of downtown Madrid, were you? Construction started in 2200 BCE under the auspices of King Adijalamani and completed over several centuries before being abandoned some 8000 years later. 1800 years later, Egypt decided to build a dam that would flood the temple, and they decided to donate the building to Madrid as a thank you to Spanish archeologists who had helped with its preservation. To this end, it was disassembled brick by brick, and the whole thing was painstakingly shipped to the Spanish capital, where it now rests atop a grassy hill next to **Plaza de España.**

i Free; last entry 15min. before close; limited wheelchair accessibility; max visit duration 30min.

ANDÉN 0: ESTACIÓN MUSEO CHAMBERÍ (PLATFORM 0: CHAMBERÍ STATION MUSEUM)

Pl. de Chamberí; 902 44 44 03; www.metromadrid.es; open Th 10am-1pm, F 11am-7pm, Sa-Su 11am-3pm

Andén 0 offers a glimpse into Madrid's recent history; built in 1919, it was the city's first metro stop, connecting the neighborhood of **Chamberí** to **Bilbao** and **Iglesia** stations. It was designed by Antonio Palacios, inspired by the Parisian design and filled with blue and white cobalt tilework. During the Spanish Civil War, its underground tunnels were converted into warehouses and refugees—protection from air bombings. When the Madrid metro expanded in the 1960s, it had outgrown Chamberí and the station was retired for forty years, but a restoration project completed in 2008 saw it reopen to the public. Visitors are greeted with a short film about the station and can then descend the original metro steps to the main platform, which is decorated with tile advertisements for cafés of the 1920s and old-fashioned gadgets.

i Free; guided tours every hour; last entry 30min. before close; wheelchair accessible

BASILICA SAN FRANCISCO EL GRANDE (BASILICA OF SAN FRANCISCO EL GRANDE)

C. San Buenaventura 1; 913 65 38 00; www.esmadrid.com; open July-Aug Tu-Su 10:30am-1pm and 5pm-7pm, Sept-June Tu-Sa 10:30am-1pm and 4pm-6:30pm

Just down the street from the show-stopping **Royal Palace** and **Royal Theater** is yet another possession of the Spanish crown: the grandiose Royal Basilica. Featuring the largest dome in Spain, it was built in the eighteenth century by Francesco Sabatini, based on a design by Francisco Cabezas. The basilica's décor is just as magnificent as the architecture; hardly a square inch is free from gold, silver, or the brush strokes of Spanish masters. **Goya** is the main highlight—look for his work in the **Chapel of San Bernardino.** Admission to the basilica is free during morning mass, but to see the museum you'll need to attend a guided tour (Spanish only); ask the staff when the next one will begin.

i Admission €5, €3 reduced; last entry 30min. before close; limited wheelchair accessibility; admission free Sep-June Sa 10:30am-12:30pm, July-Aug Sa 5pm-7pm

ESTADIO SANTIAGO BERNABÉU (SANTIAGO BERNABÉU STADIUM)

Av. de Concha Espina 1; 913 98 43 00; www.realmadrid.com; open M-Sa 10am-7pm, Su 10:30am-6:30pm

The uninitiated may be put off by the chintziness of the Bernabéu tour, but a stadium pilgrimage is non-negotiable for anyone with even a passing interest in the world of soccer. Bernabéu Stadium, built in 1947 and boasting a seating capacity of 80,000 spectators, is one of the world's most famous fútbol locales and home to the city's beloved Real Madrid team. The stadium has hosted a number of important matches through the years, most notably the 1982 FIFA World Cup (Italy won). Tours are a bit pricey, but they grant you access to otherwise off-limits places like the royal box, the players' dressing room, and the press room. The chintz comes in when you "make your dream come true" by having a photo of yourself taken against a green screen, onto which they project your favorite Real Madrid player.

i Tours €25; audio guide €5; limited wheelchair accessibility; tours on game day only offer limited access to facilities starting 5hr before the match

PALACIO REAL (ROYAL PALACE)

C. Bailén; 914 54 97 00; www.patrimonionacional.es; open daily Oct-Mar 10am-6pm, Apr-Sep 10am-8pm

Although its 3,400 rooms are only a fourth of the original floor plans, we'll let it slide; King Felipe V's extravagant palace is one of Madrid's most stunning pieces of architecture. It was built to replace the Moorish Alcázar (castle), which occupied the site until it burned down in 1734. Even though it's called the Royal Palace, the royal family doesn't actually live there anymore; they live in the less-decadent **Palacio de la Zarzuela** outside the city center, reserving the Royal Palace for state events and ceremonies. Be on the lookout for the palace's collection of five **Stradivarius** violins, which are still used in occasional performances. Once you're done ogling the velvet-covered throne room and the silken Salón de Gasparini, head outside to the sweeping **Plaza de la Armería** to check out the royal pharmacy and armory (a strange combo, but why not?).

i Admission €10, €5 reduced; guided tours €4, audio guide €3; last entry 1hr before close; wheelchair accessible; free admission 2hr before close

CENTROCENTRO PALACIO DE CIBELES AND PLAZA CIBELES

Pl. de Cibeles 1; 914 80 00 08; www.centrocentro.org; open Tu-Su 10am-8pm, observation deck open Tu-Su 10:30am-1:30pm and 4pm-7pm

A headquarters so central, they had to name it CentroCentro—the breathtaking, Neoclassical Palace of Cibeles used to serve a surprisingly mundane function: as the "Communications Cathedral," it was the headquarters of the National Postal Service. Ever since 2007, however, it's served as seat of the Madrid City Council, and currently hosts a plethora of cultural events, workshops, exhibitions, conferences, and even live performances. There's a bookshop, a café, tourist information, two restaurants, wide-open lounge areas—quite the multi-purpose cultural center. The eighth floor even has an observation deck with sweeping views of the city. Head here for a bit of R&R, a bite to eat, or a bombardment of tourist pamphlets and information packets. It's just up the street from the **Museo del Prado** on Madrid's largest boulevard.

i Free, observation deck admission €2; Wi-Fi; wheelchair accessible; free admission to the observation deck first W every month

PLAZA MAYOR

Pl. Mayor; www.madrid.es; open daily 24hr

Originally designed in 1617 in the Herrerian style by Juan Gómez de Mora, Plaza Mayor has been the epicenter of Madrid for some 400 years, although this urban confluence was an important meeting point long before then. Bullfights, weddings, the beatification of San Isidro Labrador—Madrid's patron saint—all occurred here, along with the more sinister autos de fe, hangings and burnings at the stake during the Spanish Inquisition. Today, it's a lively tourist hub lined with coffee shops, souvenirs, and Madrid's main tourist office. Be sure to check out the 237 wrought-iron balconies protruding from the surrounding buildings, as well as the gorgeous frescoes on the façade of the **Real Casa de la Panadería,** a royal bakery from the 1590s that was responsible for setting a city-wide price on fresh bread so the poor could afford it. The square burned to the ground in 1790 and was reconstructed by Juan de Villanueva.

i Free; wheelchair accessible

MUSEUMS

MUSEO CENTRO DE ARTE REINA SOFÍA

C. Santa Isabel 52; 917 74 10 00; www.museoreinasofia.es; open M 10am-9pm, W-Sa 10am-9pm, Su 10am-7pm

Full of odd angles, geometric shapes, and paint splats, it isn't hard to guess the Museo Reina Sofía's genre. Spread over four floors, the collection is an ode to twentieth-century artwork, taking visitors on a fantastical tour from surrealism to movements like "situationist utopian urbanism." The most exciting part, however, is the second floor's cubism display. Beginning with the foundations of the movement at the beginning of the twentieth century, the museum has a superb collection of **Miró, Gris, Braque,** and more, all of which is a dramatic buildup to the most famous painting in the whole city: **Picasso's** Guernica. Painted for the Spanish State in 1937, this enormous cubist masterpiece—roughly 11 by 26 feet—condemns the bombing of the Basque town of Guernica by a Spanish rebel group. Since its debut at the Paris International Art Exhibition, it has become a world-famous symbol against oppression, violence, and war. Lining the Guernica room is ample documentation of the creative process, provided in large part by Picasso's partner at the time. If you can tear your eyes away from the museum's showstopper, look for more works by big-name Spanish masters like **Dalí, Barradas, Masson,** and **Gargallo.** The collection is arranged by theme rather than artist, so you never know whose artwork may be around the corner.

i Admission €10 at box office, €8 online, students under 25 free; audio guides €4.50, €3.50 reduced, guided tours by request; last entry 30min. before close; wheelchair accessible; Wi-Fi; admission free M 7pm-9pm, W-Sa 7pm-9pm, Su 1:30pm-7pm

MUSEO DEL PRADO

C. Ruiz de Alarcón 23; 913 30 28 00; www.museodelprado.es; open M-Sa 10am-8pm, Su 10am-7pm

A Madrid visit sans Prado is basically a felony—it's the Louvre of Spain. Its collection of Spanish art is without a doubt the best in the world, and its colossal collection of 7,500 paintings, 4,800 prints, and 1000 sculptures from the twelfth to the twentieth century (of which some 1,300 works are on display) makes it one of the greatest museums in the world. Enter from the imposing **Plaza de Murillo** into a grand foyer and traverse through centuries of European masterpieces, with a particular emphasis on Spanish painters like **El Greco, Murillo, Velázaquez,** and—perhaps the museum's best-represented artist—**Goya.** Spread throughout the Palacio de Villanueva's three grand stories, visitors can also admire works by **Bosch, Botticelli, Raphael, Rembrandt,** and a deluge of other big-name painters and sculptors. Even the least art-savvy will appreciate Goya's Saturn Devouring His Son, a famous self-portrait by **Dürer,** and Bosch's spellbinding Garden of Earthly Delights. Take your time but be realistic; a whole week wouldn't be enough to cover everything—plan to spend a minimum of two hours roving through this spectacular collection.

i Admission €15, students under 25 free; permanent collection audio guides €4, each temporary exhibition €3.50, combined €6; last entry 30min. before close; wheelchair accessible; free admission to permanent collection and 50% off temporary exhibitions M-Sa 6pm-8pm, Su 5pm-7pm; no photos allowed

MUSEO DE HISTORIA DE MADRID (MUSEUM OF HISTORY OF MADRID)

C. Fuencarral 78; 917 01 18 63; www.madrid.es/museodehistoria; collection open Tu-Su 10am-8pm, gardens and chapel open Tu-Su 10am-3pm

Housed in a **Baroque hospice** from the seventeenth century, this museum's collection chronicles Madrid's history entire history as the capital of Spain. Tours start in 1561, when Felipe II named Madrid the capital of a vast empire that stretched from Italy to the Netherlands. Moving into the eighteenth century, the next floor covers the Bourbon Dynasty, an emerging "enlightened" elite, and the beautification of the city by Charles III. A final section presents Madrid's industrialization and emergence as a modern world capital. Throughout the collection are enormous wall maps illustrating the city's growth, as well as a number of paintings you'll recognize from your own jaunts through Madrid. At the end of the visit is an impressive 1:814 scale model of the city as it looked at the end of King Ferdinand VIII's reign. A quality history lesson, to be sure, but the best part is that admission is always free.

i Free; free tours from noon-5pm must be booked 48hr in advance; wheelchair accessible; no tours July-September

MUSEO LÁZARO GALDIANO

C. Serrano 122; 91 561 60 84; www.museodelazarogaldiano.es; open Tu-Sa 10am-4:30pm, Su 10am-3pm

Some people collect stamps or marbles, but that was clearly too blasé for the illustrious Lázaro Galdiano, who would much rather collect masterpieces of European art. Thanks to his expensive hobby and his end-of-life donation to the Spanish State, mere mortals can now visit his astounding collection, housed in the five stories of his opulent estate a few blocks north of the **Parque del Retiro.** Starting with the ground floor, visitors can gawk at the Galdiano's fabulous collection of Italian, German, Flemish, Dutch, French, and—of course—Spanish paintings, which covers a period of nearly 2500 years, from the fourth century BCE to the first half of the twentieth century. Frescoes by **Villamil,** landscapes by **Bosch,** portraits by **El Greco**—it's hard to believe this stuff was sitting somewhere as mundane as a living room for so long. The highlight of the collection lies in the **Goya** room: two small but exquisite pieces titled The Witches and The Witches' Sabbath. The entire top floor (called "The Cabinet") showcases most of the 13,000 other artifacts the collector amassed during his lifetime, from ivories to silverware to terracotta figurines.

i Admission €6, €3 reduced; guided tours by appointment only €8; limited wheelchair accessibility; admission free Tu-Sa 3:30pm-4:30pm, Su 2pm-3pm, first F every month 5pm-9pm

MUSEO NACIONAL THYSSEN BORNEMISZA

Paseo del Prado 8; 917 91 13 70; www.museothyssen.org; open Tu-Su 10am-7pm

What it lacks in size, it makes up for in quality; this hard-to-pronounce museum hosts a formidable concentration of big-name artists, from **Gauguin** to **Picasso** to **Miró.** Founded in 1992 from the private stockpile of a single German-Hungarian art collector, the **Thyssen-Bornemisza** collection moved to Madrid mostly by circumstance, along with some gentle nudging from the baron's Spanish wife, Carmen Cervera (she was Miss Spain in 1961). The collection doubled a year after opening when the Spanish government added 775 pieces of art and grew even more when Cervera loaned her own hoard of 429 works. The result: a magnificent traipse through artistic history from triptychs of the thirteenth century all the way to the early twentieth century. The visit is an entourage of **Van Gogh, Renoir, Kandinsky, Rembrandt, Dalí.** It's like the red carpet but with dead painters. As part of the Paseo del Prado's Golden Triangle of Art (which also includes the Prado and Reina Sofía), a visit is all but obligatory for any Madrid tourist.

i Admission €12, €8 reduced; audio guide €5, multimedia guide €6; last entry 1hr before close; wheelchair accessible; free admission to permanent collection M noon-4pm

MUSEO DEL ROMANTICISMO

C. de San Mateo 13; 914 48 10 45; www.mecd.gob.es; open Nov-Apr Tu-Sa 9:30am-6:30pm, Su 10am-3pm; May-Oct Tu-Sa 9:30am-8:30pm, Su 10am-3pm

With its plush Isabelline furniture, exotic costumbrista paintings, and no fewer than fifteen mini grand pianos, this museum conveys the Romantic message loud and clear. It's housed in the former palace of the Marquis of Matallana, built in 1776 and inaugurated as a museum in 1924. A tour of the building passes through a number of thematic rooms, all meticulously arranged to recall Romantic themes. There are decked-out antechambers, anterooms, great halls, luxurious dining rooms—all of which offer insight into nineteenth-century Romantic life. Be sure to appreciate the museum's impressive collection of artwork, including a large **Goya** painting in the chapel and a not-so-serious "Satire of the Romantic Lover's Suicide," which reveals a self-deprecating side to this schmaltzy, sentimentalist movement.

i Admission €3, students under 25 free; audio guides €2; wheelchair accessible; free admission Sa 2pm-close

MUSEO SOROLLA

Paseo del General Martínez Campos 37; 913 10 15 84; www.museosorolla.es; open Tu-Sa 9:30am-8pm, Su 10am-3pm

The Sorolla Museum offers far more than a peek into the artist's life—Sorolla lived here from 1911 to his death in 1923, filling the house with his own sketches, landscapes, portraits, and "color notes" (just for fun). Every inch of the mansion breathes Sorolla; besides the 1,294 paintings scattered throughout the interior, the estate itself was built from the ground up to his liking, based on sketches Sorolla had drawn for the architect Enrique María de Repullés y Vargas. Today, the house is stunningly preserved. Visits pass through a grand foyer with Valencian windows, an Andalusian courtyard with blue and white tilework, and Sorolla's cavernous study, where many of his most famous works were produced. You'll end up not in the gift shop, but in the gardens, which are filled with miniature hedges, fountains, and more gorgeous floral tilework.

i Admission €3, students under 25 free; audio guides €2.5, guided tour Tu-F 5pm €3; limited wheelchair accessibility; free admission on Sa, Su from 2pm-8pm

REAL ACADEMIA DE BELLAS ARTES DE SAN FERNANDO

C. Alcalá 13; 915 24 10 34; www.realacademiabellasartessanfernando.com; open Tu-Su 10am-3pm (closed Aug)

At various times in its history, this building has been a lavish residence, a royal art academy, one of Europe's first printmaking workshops, and now a fine arts museum and gallery. Despite being smack dab in the center of Madrid, it doesn't get nearly as many visitors as its bigger siblings on the Paseo del Prado, but its history as an art institute is rife with interesting Spanish culture. **Goya** himself was once a director of the academy, and there's an entire room dedicated to thirteen of his paintings, as well as his paint palette, made of dark walnut and framed in gilded laurel leaves. Separate from the art gallery is the **Calcografía Nacional** (free admission), where visitors can see selections from the 30,000-strong collection of engraved prints, including a massive collection completed by Goya in the early 1800s.

i Admission €8, students under 25 free; guided tours Tu, Th, F at 11am; last entry 15min. before close; wheelchair accessible; free entry to Calcografía Nacional, free entry to permanent collection on W

OUTDOORS

PARQUE DEL BUEN RETIRO

Pl. de la Independencia 7; www.esmadrid.com; open daily Apr-Sep 6am-midnight, Oct-Mar 6am-10pm

Aptly named "Park of the Pleasant Retreat," Madrid's most popular green space is the city's answer to its sticky, sweltering, let's-just-spend-the-day-inside-where-there's-air-conditioning midsummer days. But not even the best department store's AC can match the reinvigorating qualities of El Retiro's shaded walkways, rose gardens, and the great **Estanque Grande,** a huge man-made pool where visitors can splash around in their own rented rafts and kayaks. Boasting more than 300 acres and over 15,000 trees, Parque del Retiro was designed in the 1630s by the likes of Cosimo Lotti (the man behind Florence's famous Boboli Gardens) to be a royalty-only stomping ground and performance center. Today, El Retiro is completely free and open to the public—after a few expansions and a bit of touching up, the park has become a symbol of Madrid, complete with an expansive rose garden, a "Forest of Remembrance," and endless walkways between its many monuments, fountains, and sculptures. It's worth checking out the three museums/exhibition centers in the park, too (they're all free): **Palacio de Velázquez, Casa de Vacas,** and the **Palacio de Cristal.**

i Free; limited wheelchair accessibility

CAMPO DEL MORO

Paseo Virgen del Puerto; 914 54 88 00; www.esmadrid.com; open daily Oct-Mar 10am-6pm, Apr-Sept 10am-8pm

Lying humbly in the imposing shadow of the **Royal Palace,** the Moorish Gardens got their name when a twelfth-century troop of Muslims parked

themselves here before launching an (unsuccessful) attack against Christian forces. More recently, the gardens were a stomping ground for Spanish royalty and their esteemed visitors, finally being converted into an open-access public park in the mid-twentieth century. The grand, exquisitely-manicured central Pradera was designed with Versailles in mind—although they don't quite match those gardens' extravagance, there's something special in the serenity of these gardens, hidden from the swarm of tourists amassing at the Royal Palace's façade. Shaded walking paths cover the perimeter of the gardens, passing through quiet glens, flocks of peacocks, and a duck pond.

i Free; park empties 30min. before close; limited wheelchair accessibility

REAL JARDÍN BOTÁNICO (ROYAL BOTANICAL GARDEN)

Paseo del Arte; 914 20 80 17; www.rjb.csic.es; open daily Nov-Feb 10am-6pm, Mar 10am-7pm, Apr 10am-8pm, May-Aug 10am-9pm, Sept 10am-8pm, Oct 10am-7pm

Parque del Retiro not lush enough for you? Next door, Madrid's Royal Botanical Gardens have some 90,000 plants and over 1,500 trees; more than enough chlorophyll for all your herbivorous needs. Founded in 1755, the gardens found their current home near the **Museo del Prado** in 1781 under the direction of Charles III. Madrid's architectural all-stars **Sabatini** and **Villanueva** are behind the gardens' design, roughly dividing the gentle hillside into four sections: the Terrace of Plots, of Botanical Schools, the romantic Flower Plan, and a Laurel Terrace. A self-guided tour meanders past rhododendron collections, Californian sequoias, Japanese ornamentals, and more. There's a small museum-bookstore-café at the top of the hill, adorned with Mexican palms, a reflective pond, and a statue of **Linnaeus,** the esteemed Swedish naturalist.

i Admission €4, €2 reduced; guided tours by appointment only at 10am, noon, 4pm; last entry 30min. before close; wheelchair accessible; admission free Tu after 5pm

FOOD

SALA DE DESPIECE ($$)

C. de Ponzano 11; 917 52 61 06; www.saladedespiece.com; open M-Th 1pm-5pm and 7:30pm-12:30am, F 1pm-4:30pm and 7:30pm-1:30am, Sa 12:30pm-5:30pm and 7:30pm-1:30am, Su 12:30pm-5:30pm and 7:30pm-12:30am

Entering the Sala de Despiece is like stumbling into a typical **Chamberí** butcher shop. Everything is spotlessly white, from the waiters' aprons to the shiny wall tiles; a decorative austerity inspired by the local butcheries and fish markets. Unlike a typical restaurant, guests don't sit at tables, but on bar stools facing the butcher himself, where they can watch their food as it is sliced, tenderized, or julienned into an array of delicious final products. Since ingredients are the number one priority, the menu changes frequently but is presented as a product list, handwritten in blue, with different categories for product name, origin, preparation, and portion size. Anything meaty is bound to be fantastic, but their signature Rolex (pork belly and foie gras with truffles) is to die for.

i Entrées from €9; gluten-free and vegetarian options available; no wheelchair accessibility; no reservations except for Mesa de Despiece (next door 12-seat restaurant, minimum tasting menu €35)

CASA DANI ($)

Mercado de la Paz, C. Ayala 28; 915 75 59 25; www.casadani.es; open M-F 7am-7:30pm, Sa 7am-4:30pm

Tortillas españolas (Spanish tortillas) are a cross between a quiche, omelet, hash browns, and a tortilla. Potato-loaded and ham and cheese-studded, they're basically a miracle of Iberian cuisine, and Casa Dani has a special knack for preparing them. This sprawling restaurant is technically part of the **La Paz Market** north of the **Parque del Retiro,** but La Paz's other offerings feel like a sideshow to Casa Dani; the restaurant takes up around half of the place, with a fancy sit-down restaurant, a bar, a takeaway booth with its own food court-style seating area, and another sit-down restaurant (the outdoor terrace) just outside the market's entrance. Swarms of locals and tourists alike queue up around lunchtime for Spanish classics—if you're not going for the Spanish tortilla, try the marinated snails, *torreznos* (thinly-sliced bacon), or *salmorejo* (bread and tomato purée).

i *Entrées from €9, menu of the day €11; cash only; gluten-free, vegan, and vegetarian options available; wheelchair accessible*

CASA JULIO ($)

C. de la Madera 37; 915 22 72 74; open M-Sa 1pm-3:30pm and 6:30pm-11:30pm

Founded by—you guessed it—Julio, this tiny restaurant in **Malasaña** is now owned by his fourth-generation descendants, who faithfully continue their forefathers' mission to craft the best *croqueta*s in Madrid. For the uninitiated, croquetas are fried dough balls stuffed with savory meats, cheeses, herbs, and veggies, and they're dangerously addictive. Since frying the first ones in 1921, Casa Julio has garnered quite the cult of followers, from celebrities to the humble, hungry tourist. Tradition mandates that you try a simple jamón-stuffed croqueta, but the most popular flavor involves a lip-smacking spinach and mushroom situation. Thankfully, you don't have to decide on just one; they come in groups of six (€6) or twelve if you're famished (€12). There are only five tables plus bar seating, so count on a wait if you're coming at peak mealtimes.

i *Croquetas €7 for 6, tapas from €6; gluten-free and vegetarian options available; wheelchair accessible*

CASA SALVADOR ($$)

C. Barbieri 12; 915 21 45 24; www.casasalvadormadrid.com; open M 1:30pm-4pm, Tu-Th 1:30pm-4pm and 8:30pm-11pm, F-Sa 1:30pm-4pm and 8:30pm-11:30pm

Anthony Bourdain loved this place when he visited in 2010, although Ernest Hemingway had already granted Casa Salvador the golden seal of approval a few decades prior. Naturally, it's a required visit if you find yourself in the **Chueca** neighborhood. Unlike the hipster restaurants surrounding it, Casa Salvador harkens back to the good old days when Chueca was filled not with matcha lattes, but with bullfighting all-stars. Beginning in the 1940s, toredores could stop here for some pre-fight chopped veal, cod fritters, monkfish, and the house specialty: oxtail stew. Not exactly a light lunch, but maybe all that offal is the real secret to successful bullfighting. Regardless, guests can also appreciate the bullfighting legacy through the restaurant's impressive collection of drawings, photography, and sculpture devoted to the sport. Either that or a mouthful of tripe, you decide.

i *Entrées from €12, menu of the day €25; gluten-free and vegetarian options available; wheelchair accessible*

CASA TONI ($)

C. de la Cruz 14; 915 32 25 80; open daily noon-4pm and 7pm-midnight

Despite its central location in prime tourist trap territory, Casa Toni's cuisine is anything but watered-down for the finicky tourist's palate. Adventurous eaters will appreciate a simple, traditional menu with offerings like *zarajos* (braided lamb intestines) and *orejas a la plancha* (grilled pig ears). The whole menu, listed on a tall blackboard outside the restaurant, is an ode to scrap meat, featuring a wide range of animal odds and ends. Sautéed kidneys, lamb neck glands in sweet bread, blood sausage—this place isn't for the faint of heart, although they do have some more familiar offerings like garlicky mushrooms or fried eggplant. For the optimal experience, grab a pal and order a few dishes in typical tapas style.

i Tapas from €3.50, entrées from €7; gluten-free and vegetarian options available; no wheelchair accessibility

CHOCOLATERÍA SAN GINÉS ($)

Pasadizo San Ginés 5; 913 65 65 46; www.chocolateriasangines.com; open daily 24hr

Pharmacies, sure. Hospitals, of course. But a 24hr chocolate shop? At any time of the day (since 1890!), Chocolatería San Ginés is prepared to deliver its famous churros-and-chocolate combo. And by chocolate, we mean of hot cocoa variety—only the drink they serve at San Ginés is nothing like your run-of-the-mill Swiss Miss packet. Thick, dark, and highly potent, it's like a melted chocolate bar in a cup. (Perfect for churro dipping.) Although it's popular at all hours, things pick up around 4am as weary party-goers wind down at the chocolatería's iconic dark green booths. Best hangover cure? Maybe not, but good luck resisting the wafting scent of molten chocolate as you stumble out of the next-door **Joy Eslava** nightclub.

i Chocolate €2, with six churros €4; gluten-free, vegan, and vegetarian options available; limited wheelchair accessibility

CHUKA RAMEN ($$)

C. Echegaray 9; 640 65 13 46; www.chukaramenbar.com; open Tu 8:30pm-11:30pm, W-Sa 1:30pm-3:30pm and 8:30pm-11:30pm

It might take some planning to get into this elusive ramen bar hidden among the taverns of **Huertas**—their hours are limited and the place fills up fast—but a single slurp of their shoyu ramen is worth the fuss. Carefully crafted following the Hokkaidō tradition and filled with assari-style smoked fish, seafood, pork, chicken, mushrooms, and seaweed, the umami elixir is like a portal to the Orient. The rest of the menu—a fusion of Chinese and Japanese offerings—features a similarly meticulous attention to details, whether in the form of steam buns, gyozas, or seasonal dishes like whole roasted cauliflower and Iberian pork barbecued à la Cantonese. It'll cost you a few extra euros, but come on, this isn't Panda Express.

i Ramen from €15; gluten-free and vegetarian options available; wheelchair accessible; reservations recommended

LA PECERA ($)

C. Velarde 2; 918 26 74 45; www.wearelapecera.com; open Tu-Su 2:30pm-10:30pm

Sure, Madrid's got plenty of helado (ice cream). But a simple scoop on a sugar cone would be way too vanilla (pun intended) for an heladería straddling Madrid's two trendiest neighborhoods, **Malasaña** and **Chueca.** At La Pecera, ice cream is served Japanese-style, from a soft waffle "cone" shaped like a fish with its mouth wide open (called a *taiyaki).* The process is simple: choose vanilla or chocolate for your doughy taiyaki, pick a soft-serve flavor (options include matcha and salted caramel), and top it with powdered butter cookies, caramelized almonds, or chocolate syrup. They don't technically list step 4 (snap a photo for the Insta), but the temptation is irresistible. Despite being a relatively young Madrid establishment, La Pecera has become so popular that a sign outside the door has to tell visitors which street to spill onto; there's always a snaking queue of hipsters at this hole-in-the-wall, especially just after dinnertime.

i Taiyaki €3.50, with toppings €4.50; vegetarian options available; no wheelchair accessibility

LA TASQUERÍA ($$)

Duque de Sesto 48; 914 51 11 00; www.latasqueria.com; open M-Sa 1:30pm-4pm and 8:30pm-11pm, Su 1:30pm-4pm

The name of this classy but affordable restaurant is a combination between *tasca* (tavern) and *casquería* (a place serving offal). Yes, offal. Chef Javi Estévez—who was once a contestant on Top Chef—is crazy about the stuff, offering a menu stuffed with all manner of brains, tongue, gizzards, tripe, tails, and more. Somehow, Estévez manages to elevate these unspeakable "scrap" meats to lofty, mouth-watering heights, serving them in a chic eatery you'd never expect from such taboo cuisine. It takes an adventurous spirit, but if there's ever a reliable place to open your mid to offal, this is it; all the dishes are masterfully executed. Try some duck heart with raspberries, gizzards with lettuce and anchovies, or test your limits with the famous suckling pig head, adorned with a side of tripe and pig snout.

i Entrées from €10, tasting menu €39; gluten-free options available; no wheelchair accessibility

PANADERÍA PANIC ($)

C. Conde Duque 13; 910 86 22 01; open M-F 9:30am-9pm, Sa 9:30am-3pm

The malty aroma of yeast pours from this boutique bakery like a beacon, beckoning sourdough lovers from across Madrid to the northwestern corner of **Malasaña.** There are plenty of other bakeries in the city offering daily-baked breads, but Panadería Panic stands above the rest; it started out as the pet project of a Javier Marca, former art director at a Madrid magazine, when in 2013 he finally opened the doors at Panic, offering a small selection of ciabattas, baguettes, and other artisanal loaves. Everything is sourdough, all the grains are organic, and the only ingredients used in his bread are flour, water, and salt; few ingredients equal big flavor, according to Marca. His customers agree—locals frequently clear out the shelves well before closing hours, toting baskets with loaves of 100% rye, spelt, and oat flour.

i Bread from €3.80/kg; cash only; gluten-free, vegan, and vegetarian options available; wheelchair accessible

PEZ TORTILLA ($)

C. Pez 36; 643 91 99 84; www.peztortilla.com; open M-W 6pm-2am, Th noon-2am, F-Sa noon-2:30am, Su noon-2am

Four amigos, a passion for beer, and a hankering for the cheese-filled comfort of a good tortilla, and you've got the perfect recipe for Pez Tortilla, a trendy eatery in the **Malasaña** neighborhood. At any given time, there are some thirty or so beers available (tap or in cans), including quirky foreign ones like Extra Horny, Hopulent IPA, and Northern Monk Heathen, as well as their own house brew. Obviously, you'll want to pair your pint with a tortilla—the fifteen-strong menu of flavors changes weekly, but a couple stalwart options like brie with truffles and jamón—their most popular tortilla—are always on offer. Of course, there's always the purist clásico with caramelized onion: a divinely cheesy experience that borders on religious.

i Tortilla pincho from €3, croquetas 2 for €2; vegetarian options available; limited wheelchair accessibility

RAYÉN VEGANO ($)

C. Lope de Vega 7; phone 675 38 20 72; www.rayenvegan.com; open M 1pm-4:30pm, W-F 1pm-4:30pm, Sa-Su 11am-4:30pm

Looking for lovingly-sourced, colorful, plant-based cuisine in the heart of meaty Madrid? Fittingly, you'll find it in the **Huertas** (gardens) district, in Rayén's adorably picnic-esque space. Founded by chefs Noemi (Kundalini yogi and astrologist) and Paulo (church organist who loves cats), Rayén has been dishing up organic and local veggies since 2013, based on a philosophy involving oneness with the world, compassion for all living things, and as much matcha as possible. Their creative menu features a handful of seasonal offerings, from polenta pizzas to marinated tempeh dishes. The best move, however, is to order a daily special: either a combo menu (two dishes) or a salad. "Salad" is a bit of an understatement, though, as the dish description is usually the length of a novelette; it takes a minute or so for the waiter to read through an epic ingredients list that includes six or seven raw and cooked veggies, a handful of grains and pulses, three dressings and marinades, crispy toppings, and—of course—an avocado. Served with your weight in bread and homemade hummus.

i Entrées from €10.90, menu of the day €12.90; gluten-free, vegan, and vegetarian options available; wheelchair accessible; menu of the day only available weekdays, kitchen closes 3:30pm

SUPERCHULO ($$)

C. de Manuela Malasaña 11; 910 23 27 06; www.superchulomadrid.com; open Su-Th 1pm-12:30am, F-Sa 1pm-2:30am

"Count colors, not calories" is the slogan of this on-trend **Malasaña** eatery, although we suspect they're also counting Insta likes—everything from the garden hanging from the ceiling to the veggie-filled earthenware bowls is drop-dead gorgeous. For tourists missing LA-style bistros where eating out is a chic fashion statement, this is your Madrid sanctuary. The menu is full of "rainbow food" and littered with hashtags, like a #pornfood section that includes guacamole bao stuffed with tempeh and peanuts, #sorrynotsorry nachos with four homemade sauces, and Flower Power pizza with creamed potato and edible flowers. And instead of salads, they offer—of course—Buddha bowls, all customizable with social media darlings like sweet potatoes, falafel, and the ubiquitous half avocado.

i Entrées from €10.50, menu of the day €11.90; gluten-free, vegan, and vegetarian options available; wheelchair accessible

NIGHTLIFE

SALMON GURU

C. Echegaray 21; 910 00 61 85; www.salmonguru.es; open Tu-Th 5pm-2am, F-Sa 5pm-2:30am, Su 5pm-2am

Those unfamiliar with the gastro-bartending world may not know about Diego Cabrera, but he's quite the mixology hotshot. Not only has he won recognition for being the country's best barman (2011 from the Spanish magazine "The Best of Gastronomy"), his first bar Le Cabrera was named best in the country in an international bartenders' convention. Salmon Guru is his latest pet project, and it's quickly become a shining star of the **Huertas** neighborhood. Choose from a small handful of featured creations—think spicy concoctions like Chipotle Chillón, with seven mysteries mescal and fiery chipotle syrup. They don't serve cocktails in fishbowls or anything like that, but you can order some actual fish if you're feeling peckish. The food menu also offers chicken chupa-chupas (like lollipops, but with poultry), mini burgers with foie gras, and other mischievous mashups.

i No cover, cocktails from €11; no wheelchair accessibility

CAFÉ CENTRAL

Pl. del Ángel 10; 913 69 41 43; cafecentralmadrid.com; open daily 11:30am-2:30am

For hep cats lookin' to get down with the world's best finger zingers, Café Central is undoubtedly Madrid's best jazz pad, you dig? In all seriousness, this small café near **Plaza Mayor** is known as the premier jazz venue in Spain. With nightly concerts since 1988, they've accumulated some 13000 performances, hosting big names from Wynton Marsalis to George Adams. The experience is unexpectedly intimate—a tiny stage sits mere feet away from the nearest diners, and there's only space for an audience of a few extra chairs. Reservations, which can be made over the phone or at the café starting at 6pm (concerts are at 9pm), are highly recommended.

i Events from €12, entrées from €7, cocktails from €7; limited wheelchair accessibility; MasterCard not accepted; reservations highly recommended

FABRIK

Av. de la Industria 82; 902 93 03 22; grupo-kapital.com/fabrik; open Sa 11pm-6am, sometimes Su

Madrid has a thing for big nightlife venues, but Fabrik, a world-renowned party colossus, is on a whole different level. It's considered one of Europe's highest-quality nightlife locales, and for good reason. Apart from the converted warehouse's three-tiered stage and four dance areas, the outdoor terrace features sixteen bars and its own river. Yes, a river. Party-goers can expect big sound, lots of lasers, and freezing nitrogen fog machines to fill the club with smoke; they really don't hold back. Hosting a variety of the world's most famous DJs, many of Fabrik's parties are themed—think "Mega Panic Water Party" or "Peace and Love" Fabrik. Sometimes they grant free entry to the first arrivals (up to 1000 people) who come in costume, so be sure to check the website before your pilgrimage.

i Cover €18 (1 drink included); no wheelchair accessibility; opening hours sometimes begin early in the afternoon, check website for event-specific information; to get there, take the metro to Fuenlabrada, followed by the 496 or 497 bus

TEATRO BARCELÓ

C. Barceló 11; 914 47 01 28; www.teatro-barcelo.com; open Th-Sa 11:55pm-6am

Roughly straddling the middle of two of Madrid's swankiest neighborhoods—**Chueca** and **Malasaña**—Teatro Barceló is a sleek, stylish nightclub with an impressive history as one of Madrid's premier meeting points for artists, politicians, and activists. The building went up in the 1930s but really blossomed in the 80s, the epicenter of the post-Franco countercultural movement called the Movida Madrileña. In 1980, Mayor Tierno Galvan, who was a major supporter of the movement, was inaugurated at the Barceló, and ever since then the building has been a revolving door for high-profile international personalities. **Andy Warhol, Prince, the Rolling Stones**—they've all made pilgrimages to Teatro Barceló. The space is a shiny, gleaming, and glassy complex—nothing like some of Madrid's ancient theaters-turned-concert venues. Each concert or "session" pulses with lively energy, whether it's a light show on "Pure Saturday" or a "MYércoles" Wednesday disco. Be sure to dress nicely and buy your tickets ahead of time (mobile tickets can be shown to the bouncer)

i Cover from €20, drinks from €10 (1 drink) or €18 (2 drinks); no wheelchair accessibility; prices typically increase later in the night; check website for daily details and entry to the guest list; drinks prices differ for men and women; cocktail attire recommended

TEATRO JOY ESLAVA

C. del Arenal 11; 913 66 54 39; www.joy-eslava.com; open Su-Th midnight-5:30am, F-Su midnight-6am

Illuminating the backstreets of **Plaza Mayor** every single night since 1981, Joy Eslava is a legendary nightclub of Madrid. Housed in a grandiose half-acre theater with space for a thousand people on four stories, Joy Eslava emanates hip hop, reggaeton, pop, and more with a formidable 40,000-watt blast of sound. There's a weekly events list, each night with its own theme from "We Love Mondays" dance celebrations to "aggressive concept parties" on Sundays. Regular programming is punctuated (and often preceded) by special events from international celebrities like Julio Iglesias or Vance Joy. Even after some 13,000 performances, Joy Eslava manages to make each night memorable in its own way—and that's accounting for the inevitable booze-induced fog you're bound to experience.

i Cover (with 2 drinks) €16, events from €12; limited wheelchair accessibility; 18+

TEATRO KAPITAL

C. Atocha 125; 914 20 29 06; open W midnight-close, Th midnight-5:30am, F-Sa midnight-6am,

Housed in an alluring theater-turned-nightclub with seven floors, Teatro Kapital is by far central Madrid's largest club—the indubitable Goliath of the city's nightlife. Everything is centered around the building's main stage, which is your typical rager room/dance floor.

What makes the place special are the themed rooms around the theater's perimeter—check out karaoke studios, a rooftop terrace, a Latin room called the "Mojito and Cuba Libre Area," and a Kissing Room with its own cocktail bar. There's something for nearly every mood—if you can get in. Apart from ID verifying your age (18+ only), plan on dressing to impress a bouncer at the entrance. Think elegant: your nicest shirt, dressier shoes (ditch the Tevas), and consider combing your hair, for goodness' sake. Arriving early (before 1am) also boosts your chances of getting in the door.

i Cover before 1:30am €17 with QR code discount (includes 2 drinks), after 1:30am Th €16 (1 drink), F €18 (1 drink), Sa €19 (1 drink), without QR code discount €25 (1 drink); no wheelchair accessibility; QR code available at www.discomadrid.com

PALMA

Coverage by **Austin Eder**

Jokingly referred to as the seventeenth German state, Mallorca is the largest of the four Balearic islands and a popular vacation destination for what seems like all Europeans, minus Spaniards. Walking around, you'll hear more German than Spanish, and if not for the quintessentially Spanish architecture, dry landscape, and turquoise water, it'd be difficult to differentiate Mallorca from a vibrant landlocked city in central Europe. Palma, the island's capital city, dates back to about 100 BCE. Here, homeless individuals and European moguls walk the same streets—share the same benches—without ever acknowledging one another. Palma is a city of striking contrasts. To explore its plazas, beaches, monuments, and restaurants is just as much a reawakening of the moral conscience as it is a reawakening of the senses.

ORIENTATION

Palma is located about 250 kilometers east of **Valencia,** on the southeastern tip of Mallorca. Ferries arrive at **Portopí,** a small neighborhood located on the southwestern corner of the **Puerto de Palma.** Just north of Portopí is the **Castell de Bellver**—a hilltop fortress that offers 360-degree views of Mallorca. **Avinguada de Gabriel Roca** begins at the Baleària terminal and traces the circumference of the port, connecting the waterfront barrios of **El Terreno, Son Armadams, Santa Catalina,** and **La Lonja** to the city center. The city center consists of the area corralled by Avinguda de Gabriel Roca to the south, **Avinguda de Gabriel Alomar** to the east, **Avenida de Alemanya** to the north, and the **Torrent de Sa Riera** to the west. Most museums and major landmarks are located in **La Seu,** the region just north of the **Parc de la Mar. Avenida d'Antoni Maura** is located just west of the Royal Palace and runs north-south, connecting the port to **Plaça de la Reina.** Two important pedestrian thoroughfares include **Carrer del Conquistador** and **Carrer de Colom,** the latter of which leads directly to **Plaça Major. Sindicat,** east of Plaça Major, is quieter and more residential than its western counterparts. Here you'll find many of Palma's bed-and-breakfast-style accommodations, as well as its most authentic restaurants.

ESSENTIALS

GETTING THERE

Palma is accessible by plane and by ferry. Palma de Mallorca Airport, located 8km east of the city center, services domestic and international flights. Bus #1 runs in a loop between the airport, the city center, and the port, departing every 15min. (€5; 971 214 444). Hours of operation depend on the time of year as well as whether you are traveling to or from the airport (Nov-Apr to city daily 6am-1:15am, Nov-Apr to airport daily 5:15am-1am; May-Oct to city daily 6am-1:45am, May-Oct to airport 5:15am-2am). Bus #21 connects the airport with S'Arenal, the beachside neighborhood south of the city. Taxis from the airport to the city center cost €25 and take about 20min. Baleària and Trasmediterranea ferries arrive at the Puerto de Palma de Mallorca, located 5km southwest of the city center. From the port, you can take Bus #1 or a taxi (€20; queued outside of the Baleària and Trasmediterránea terminals) to the city center.

GETTING AROUND

Palma is very well-connected as far as public transportation goes. Bus #2 runs in a loop connecting the city center with Santa Catalina and Balanguera. Buses are operated by EMT, which offers a helpful interactive map online at emtpalma.cat/en/lines-timetables. Taxis can sometimes be hard to track down, especially at obscure hours. If you have an early flight or ferry, it may be wise to make arrangements for within-city transportation beforehand (971 72 80 81). A single metro line runs between Plaça d'Espanya to the Universidad de las Islas Baleares (€1.60 per trip). Renting a bike or scooter (highly recommended!) will allow you to access coves, beaches, and towns that are otherwise inaccessible via public transportation.

PRACTICAL INFORMATION

Tourist Offices: Informació Turística de Mallorca (Plaça de la Reina, 2; 971 17 39 90; infomallorca.net; open M-Sa 8:30am-8pm)

Banks/ATMs/Currency Exchange: ATMs are dispersed about every fifth block within the bounds of Avinguda de Gabriel Alomar. Several banks are located on Passeig del Born, including BBVA, CaixaBank, and Santander.

Post Offices: Palma's main post office is located at C. Jaime III, 15, near El Corte Inglés (971 72 31 09; correos.es; open M-Sa 9:30am-9:30pm). Palma's postal code is 07001.

Public Restrooms: Public restrooms are few and far between in Palma. Most establishments that have an entrance fee come equipped with clean restrooms.

Internet: Free Wi-Fi is available near major monuments such as the Catedral de Santa Maria and Lonja de Mallorca. Some cafés offer access to Wi-Fi with the purchase of a drink. Don't be afraid to ask waiters and waitresses for passwords: ¿Tiene Wi-Fi gratis?

BGLTQ+ Resources: In Mallorca, Palma is the natural epicenter of a thriving gay culture. The island's umbrella organization for LGBT resources is called Ben Amics (benamics.com). A complete map of certified BGTLQ+ friendly accommodations can be found online at guia.universogay.com/palmademallorca or mallorcagaymap.com.

EMERGENCY INFORMATION

Emergency Number: 112.

Police: Comisaría De Distrito Centro (C. Ruiz De Alda, 8; 971 22 55 24).

US Embassy: Embajada de los Estados Unidos de América (Carrer de Porto Pi, 8; 971 40 37 07; pmagency@state.gov; appointment only).

Rape Crisis Center: In the event of an emergency, call 112 and later contact the US Consulate. They can provide assistance filing a report with the police and seeking medical treatment.

Hospitals: Below are two convenient 24hr locations.

- Hospital General de Mallorca is located about 900m north of La Seu (Plaça de l'Hospital, 3; 971 21 21 46; open daily 24hr).
- Hospital Psiquiàtric de Palma de Mallorca is also an option, located 2km north of the city center (Camí de Jesús, 40; 971 21 23 00; open daily 24hr).

Pharmacies: Pharmacies, like ATMs, abound in Palma.

- Farmacia Balanguera is located between the two hospitals listed above (Carrer de la Balanguera, 15; 971 45 87 88; open daily 24hr).

SIGHTS

CULTURE

PLAÇA MAJOR

Plaça Major; 971 71 94 07; plaza open daily 24hr, establishment hours vary

Day or night, this picturesque plaza buzzes with activity. It is the cultural heart of Mallorca's capital city, known for its craft market and assortment of cafés, bars, and artisanal shops. Here, yellow buildings with bright green shutters encase a large rectangle of grey pavers, atop which pigeons peck and children scamper. The area just southwest of Plaça Major—**Palma's Old Town**—is filled with tall Eclectic buildings, Art Nouveau window casings, overpriced gelaterias, 100-year-old candy stores, upscale clothing boutiques, and the pearl factories for which Mallorca is famous. We recommend starting from **S'hort del Rei** and heading north along **Carrer del Conquistador,** then branching left on **Carrer de Sant Domingo.** From there, follow your feet down the narrow, sloping streets ahead.

i Free; limited wheelchair accessibility

SANTA CATALINA

North of Carrer de Sant Magí, east of Carrer de Joan Crespí; establishment hours vary

Ah, the wonders of gentrification. Located just inland of the **Puerto de Palma,** this hilly neighborhood is now home to some of Palma's tastiest restaurants, edgiest art galleries, trendiest boutique shops, and costliest real estate. Just ten years ago, however, such was not the case. According to some locals we spoke with during our time in Mallorca, Santa Catalina is still trying to escape its reputation as a shabby enclave for squatters, drug dealers, and misfits. Remnants of its previous identity are scattered about in the form of uncleared heaps of litter, vacant ground-floor apartments, and facades ornamented with impassioned anti-tourist messages. Don't come by yourself after dark, but Santa Catalina is one of the only areas in Palma that has yet to be fully overtaken by the tourism industry.

i Free; limited wheelchair accessibility

LANDMARKS

CATEDRAL DE SANTA MARIA DE PALMA

Plaça de la Seu; 902 02 24 45; catedraldemallorca.org; open Apr-May M-F 10am-5:15pm, Jun-Sep M-F 10am-6:15pm, Oct M-F 10am-5:15pm, Nov-Mar M-F 10am-3:15pm, all Sa 10am-2:15pm

If you weren't knocked on your ass by the short urban hike up to La Seu (or by the €7 entrance fee), you will be once you step foot into this quintessentially Gothic cathedral. There's so much stained glass, it's like a disco ball was taken apart and repurposed. While many of the cathedral's original features—the massive flying buttresses, the ornamented stone facades, the rose windows and stained glass that lines the central aisle, the soaring 44-meter nave—remain intact, several cosmetic changes were undertaken during this time, including moving the choir closer to the altar. Odds are if you arrive at opening or just before closing, you'll have the entire place to yourself.

i Combined admission to cathedral and Museo Diocesà €7; wheelchair accessible

LONJA DE MALLORCA

Plaça de la Llotja, 5; 672 23 35 55; open Tu-Su 10:30am-1:30pm and 5:30pm-11pm

With soaring ribbed vaults and spiraling stone columns that resemble palm trees, this civil building was designed during the fifteenth century, and long served as a center of mercantile activity during Spain's Golden Age. As the centuries passed and trade declined, however, the building's function changed according to need. Today, it stands empty—a single, expansive room that's free for you to explore, to touch, and to lounge about. The area immediately surrounding this Gothic monument is known as **La Lonja,** a vibrant after-dark destination for locals and tourists alike.

i Free; wheelchair accessible

MUSEUMS

ES BALUARD

Plaça de la Porta de Santa Catalina, 10; 71 90 82 00; esbaluard.org; open Tu-Su 10am-8pm

Located within the walls of the **Sant Pere,** a sixteenth-century building on Palma's bay, this art museum lays special emphasis on the artistic currents of the second half of the twentieth century. The permanent collection consists of works made exclusively by Balearic artists, or artists somehow related to this stunning Spanish archipelago, and covers the entire spectrum of contemporary expression: painting, sculpture, drawing, photography, video—you name it! Even if you're not of the artistic persuasion, this complex of contrasts is worth a visit for the grounds alone. Kick back and sip on a glass of sangria at Es Baluard's small restaurant, or head towards the southern wall for a spectacular view of La Seu and the Puerto de Palma.

i Admission €6, reduced €4.50, grounds free; wheelchair accessible

MUSEO DE MALLORCA

Carrer de la Portella, 5; 971 17 78 38; open Tu-F 10am-6pm, Sa-Su 11am-2pm

Situated in a refurbished seventeenth-century palace at the intersection of **Carrer de la Portella** and **Carrer de Can Pont i Vic,** the Museo de Mallorca boasts an exhaustive collection of Balearic decorative arts. Its contents range from Roman pediments to Moorish ceramics to Catholic art, which collectively provide visitors with a comprehensive overview of Mallorca's history, as well as some unique insights into the values of its inhabitants over the last two millennia. Although generally fascinating, the Museo de Mallorca is not for everyone, as it lacks English descriptions. If you have a hard time getting excited about unlabeled pieces of stone, we recommend skipping this museum and heading to the nearby **Baños Árabes,** the only existing ruins of the Arab city of Medina Mayurqa.

i Admission €2.40, reduced €1.20; locker deposit €2; limited wheelchair accessibility

OUTDOORS

CALA COMTESSA

Carrer de les Nanses; open daily 24hr

As enticing as **Playa de Can Pere Antoni**—the beach closest to Palma's historic center—might be, do yourself a favor and head nine kilometers southwest to Cala Comtessa. Here, a small stretch of spotless, yellow sand is bookended by shallow tide pools, and offers a spectacular view of **Illa de Sa Caleta,** a tiny uninhabitable island located some 200 meters offshore. A stretch of warm, turquoise water connects the two—the beach and the island—and is so clear you can see your reflection in it. If amenities—snacks, restrooms, and rentable loungers—are what you're looking for, we recommend heading to the neighboring **Playa de Illetes,** located 400 meters northeast via Passeig Illetes.

i Free; limited wheelchair accessibility

S'HORT DEL REI

Av. d'Antoni Maura, 18; open daily 24hr

This manicured garden located at the base of the Royal Palace of La Almudaina serves as a welcome reprieve from both the heat of the unrelenting Spanish sun and anear-endless tourist frenzy occuring on the Plaça de la Reina. Here, the air is 10 degrees cooler and 10 decibels quieter, stirred only by the occasional squawk of a seagull flying overhead or gust of Mediterranean wind floating inland. Take a seat on a wooden bench or low stone planter and gaze at the water archways that criss-cross before you. Bearing many a fallen flower petal and many a glob of melted gelato, the S'hort del Rei is as much a place for people-watching as plant-watching. Continue south towards the **Parc de la Mar,** a seafront plaza with a man-made lake, and you'll encounter the **Arco de la Drassana,** a tenth-century arch that spans a picturesque swan-filled pond.

i Free; no wheelchair accessibility

FOOD

EL PERRITO ($$)

Carrer d'Anníbal, 20; 971 68 85 69; open M-F 8am-8pm, Sa 8am-4:30pm

Located in the up-and-coming neighborhood of **Santa Catalina,** El Perrito serves up scrumptious brunch options from dawn until dusk. Take a seat outside at one of four marble tables or inside in El Perrito's canine-themed salon and choose from a variety of morning classics such as eggs benedict with crispy serrano ham, bagel with cured salmon, avocado, and cream cheese, or fruit salad with nuts, yogurt, chia, and muesli. Because this kitchy hangout is one of the most affordable breakfast options in Palma, it attracts a lot of other young travelers. Especially around lunch-time, you'll find the dark grey, succulent-filled interior overflowing with locals (and their pets). Arrive before 11am to score a table.

i Breakfast items from €2; vegetarian options available; limited wheelchair accessibility

LA CUADRA DEL MAÑO ($$$)

Carrer del Miracle, 8; 636 04 07 40; open Tu 7pm-midnight, W-Sa 7pm-12:30am, Su 1pm-5:30pm

Even though it's located in Palma's most tourist-dense area, La Cuadra del Maño is the antithesis of a tourist trap. Its small, rustic interior is decked out with dark wooden beams, long rectangular tables, and an assortment of knickknacks so obscure it'd leave an antiques auctioneer scratching his head. Here, everyone knows everyone; bartenders slap patrons on their backs upon entering, the owner and grill master kisses guests on their cheeks upon taking each of their orders. The menu is a vegetarian's worst nightmare, consisting of only four items: steak, steak, steak, and more steak. Each piece comes from a different part of the cow, and is served with two heaping sides of perfectly-seasoned potatoes and corn. If you're looking for a place to splurge, this is the place to do it.

i Entrées from €15; reservation recommended for parties larger than 2; limited wheelchair accessibility

YOU BUY WE COOK ($$)

Mercado del Olivar, Plaça de l'Olivar, 4; 691 35 10 35; eltenedor.es; open Tu-Th 11:30am-4pm, F-Sa 11:30am-4:30pm

Located on the second floor of the **Mercado del Olivar,** You Buy We Cook will prepare anything—and we're talking anything—you purchase downstairs for a flat rate of €3.50. Craving freshly-grilled salmon? Ready in two minutes. Need some help shelling oysters? A waiter will crack 'em open at your table. Just found out your hostel doesn't have an oven after impulse-buying a chicken? They can whole-roast it for you. Although its décor is nothing special, this was undoubtedly one of the coolest gastronomic experiences we've ever encountered. The market is so close you can smell the citrus, aged cheese, and cured ham from your cloth-covered table. Here, the cost of your meal will ultimately come down to how well you barter for it.

i Flat cooking fee €3.50, wine from €2.50; cash only; vegetarian options available; no wheelchair accessibility

NIGHTLIFE

LAB COCKTAIL BAR

Carrer de Sant Magí, 22; 649 54 78 16; barlabacademy.com; open Su-Th 7pm-2:30am, F-Sa 7pm-3am

As its name suggests, LAB's specialty is craft cocktails, but it also offers a variety of bottled wines, expensive champagnes, and beers on tap. Cocktails range from the classics to unique creations with names like "Take Off Your Cool" and "Fuckin' Around," and are accompanied by handy graphs that pit alcohol content against sweetness, bitterness, and acidity. We recommend the "Hootie Hoo," which consists of Bacardi rum shaken with fresh lime juice and sweetened with sugar. To give you a sense of how potent these concoctions truly are, ours was served in a studded iron teapot that you must pour out carefully into a shot glass, limiting consumption to one small gulp at a time.

i Cocktails from €9, wine from €4; no wheelchair accessibility

BLUE JAZZ CLUB

Paseo Mallorca, 6, 8th floor; 971 72 72 40; bluejazz.es/carta; open M-W 5pm-midnight, Th 5pm-1am, F-Sa 11am-2am, Su 11am-midnight

You! Yes, you! Time to take a shower and coif that hair because visiting this rooftop club involves passing as a guest at a five star hotel. Located eight stories above **Hotel Saratoga's** spotless, shimmery lobby lies Blue Jazz Club, a lounge and live music venue that offers spectacular views of the **Puerto de Palma** and **Catedral de Santa Maria.** Here, a sea of white and black leather chairs gives way to a square blue bar, which in turn opens up to a small scenic patio. You'll also find a rooftop pool, sleek tan loungers, and a few thatch umbrellas. We recommend heading straight to the rooftop at 9pm to watch the sunset behind the **Bellver Castle,** then going downstairs for some long-lasting cocktails and soulful tunes. Because of the venue and the clientele, Blue Jazz Club attracts some pretty stellar headliners, especially during the summer months. Concerts take place every Thursday, Friday, and Saturday at 10pm, 11pm, and 11pm, respectively, and occasionally on Mondays at 9pm.

i Cocktails from €9, beer from €3, wine from €4, soda from €2.50; limited wheelchair accessibility

SEVILLE

Coverage by **Austin Eder**

Seville is one of Europe's most significant cultural hubs, and evidence of its turbulent past can be found in everything from its buildings to its food to its dance. Walking down the broad Avenida de Constitutión, you'll find yourself awestruck by the city's architectural brilliance and you will question how such opulence could be created without the aid of the technological luxuries we enjoy today. A stroll down the narrow streets of Santa Cruz will transport you to an entirely different era—even here, in the quarter with the darkest history, the city's riches are reflected in the delicate marble and iron window casings that cling to pastel walls. You'll notice that Seville truly comes to life just before nightfall, when its shaded alleyways are illuminated by the sinking Mediterranean sun and rooftop mosaics begin to glisten. Getting lost in Casco Antiguo is as crucial a component of a trip to Seville as is a visit to the magnificent Plaza de España or towering Catedral de Sevilla. Don't be afraid to set down your map and get walking—in the event you really do get lost, we'll be here to guide you back.

ORIENTATION

Seville's city center spans both the eastern and western banks of the **Guadalquivir,** with the bulk of tourist activity occurring in **Casco Antiguo** on the western side. Here, you'll find the city's major landmarks, museums, and nightlife. **Santa Cruz** extends roughly from the southernmost tip of Parque de María Luisa to a few blocks north of the Catedral. Northwest of Santa Cruz lies **El Arenal,** which contains **Plaza de Toros** and some upscale options for nightlife. Northeast of Santa Cruz lies **San Bartolomé,** a less picture-perfect, arguably more authentic version of its southern neighbor. Immediately north of Santa Cruz is **Alfalfa,** a popular nightlife destination among students and young professionals (and coincidentally, where you'll find most of the city's hostels). West of Alfalfa is **Museo,** home to—you guessed it—a boat load of museums, and further north still lie **Feria** and **Macarena.** Across the river lies **Triana,** Santa Cruz's eastern counterpart, and **Los Robles,** a vibrant residential neighborhood.

ESSENTIALS

GETTING THERE

Aeropuerto de Sevilla is located 10km from Seville and taxis or pre-arranged cars will drive you to Casco Antiguo—the city center—for a flat rate that hovers around €30. Alternatively, buses to Plaza de Armas, the city's main bus station, depart from the airport from 5:20am to 12:50am daily and take approximately 35min. You can buy your ticket on board for €4 (€6 returning). Aeropuerto de Sevilla is the main airport serving Andalucía, and is a base for budget airlines such as TAP Portugal, Ryanair, and Vueling. The airport connects to dozens of destinations in Europe and Northern Africa, but can only be accessed by connecting flight from North America. Seville Santa Justa is the city's main train station, and provides trains to stations throughout Spain. You can book train and bus tickets online or at each respective station.

GETTING AROUND

Seville is a fairly well-connected city with integrated metro, bus, and tram systems, but you can traverse the city center on foot from north to south in under an hour. Most buses depart from Puerta de Jerez (south of Casco Antiguo) or Plaza Ponce de Leon (east of Casco Antiguo), and operate daily from 6am to 11:30pm (night buses run from midnight to 2am and depart from the Prado). Seville Metro (tickets from €1.30) consists of one line with 22 stops that runs 18km throughout the greater metropolitan area. MetroCentro, Seville's tram network, travels south from Plaza Nueva, the centre of the city, and has four stops, covering a total distance of 1.4km (€1.20, purchased at stations).

PRACTICAL INFORMATION

Tourist Offices: Tourist offices are dispersed throughout the city. Seville's main tourist office is called Oficina Sevilla Centro (Pl. de San Francisco, 19; 955 471 232; open M-F 9am-7:30pm, Sa-Su 10am-2pm)

Banks/ATMs/Currency Exchange: Like pharmacies, you can find ATMs sprinkled throughout the city. Make sure you have enough cash on you to cover the cost of transportation into the city before departing, as taxis only take cash.

Post Offices: Some hostels will hold packages for you, but don't count on it. To send mail, visit Correos, the city's main post office (Av. de la Constitución, 32; 902 19 71 97; correos.es; open M-F 8:30am-8:30pm, Sa 9:30am-1pm).

Public Restrooms: As far as free restrooms go, you're out of luck in Seville. In total, there are two, both located near Plaza de España. Most establishments that have an entrance fee come equipped with clean restrooms.

Internet: Free public Wi-Fi is available at Starbucks, McDonald's, and most cafés surrounding major monuments such as the Catedral de Sevilla and Alcázar de Sevilla. Don't be afraid to ask waiters and waitresses for passwords: ¿Tiene Wi-Fi gratis?

BGLTQ+ Resources: Seville lacks specific, in-person resources; however, more information about navigating Spain's BGLTQ+ culture can be found online at gayiberia.com and gayinspain.com.

EMERGENCY INFORMATION

Emergency Number: 112.

Police: Officers are stationed near most attractions and actively monitor for petty crime and protests during the day. The headquarters closest to Casco Antiguo is located in Triana on Calle Betis, a popular street for nightlife (C. Betis, 40; 954 28 95 06).

US Embassy: Seville's US Consulate is located at Pl. Nueva, 8 (954 218 751; open M-F 10am-1pm by appointment, email sevillecons@state.gov).

Rape Crisis Center: The Assistance Center for Victims of Sexual Assault (CAVAS) offers free services to individuals who have suffered some type of sexual aggression, including emergency accompaniment to hospitals, legal help, and psychological support (+34 91 574 01 10; +34 91 574 32 64; rcne.com/contact/countries/spain/).

Hospitals: The following are open 24hr.

In the event of a medical emergency, call 112.

- Hospital Victoria Eugenia of Spanish Red Cross (Ronda de Capuchinos, 11; 954 35 14 00; hospitalveugenia.com)
- Hospital San Juan de Dios (Av. Eduardo Dato, 42; 954 93 93 00; sjd.es/Seville/?q=hospital-san-juan-de-dios-Seville)

Pharmacies: Pharmacies are prolific in Seville. Farmacia Republica Argentina is open 24hr, located in Triana, a 20-minute walk from Casco Antiguo (Av. de la República Argentina, 10; 954 27 66 87).

SIGHTS

CULTURE

SANTA CRUZ Y SAN BARTOLOMÉ

Pl. de Santa Cruz; establishment hours vary

Taking a winding stroll through the colorful neighborhood of Santa Cruz will likely be the highlight of your sightseeing experience in Seville—it certainly was for us. Previously the city's **Jewish Quarter,** Santa Cruz is corralled by **Jardines de Murillo** to the south and **Alfalfa** to the north, and consists of blocks upon blocks of tightly-spaced residences, restaurants, and flamenco theaters. We recommend departing from **Plaza de Santa Cruz**—home to a manicured garden and several small ceramic shops—at around 6pm and heading northwest.

i Free; limited wheelchair accessibility

CASA DE PILATOS

Pl. de Pilatos, 1; 954 22 52 98; fundacionmedinaceli.org/monumentos/pilatos/; open daily 9am-7pm

Constructed at the turn of the sixteenth century, the Casa de Pilatos is the most important residence in Seville behind the **Alcázar**. It was commissioned by Pedro Enríquez de Quiñones, Adelantado Mayor of Andalucía at the time, and features one of the largest azulejo—or Spanish painted, tin-glazed tilework—collections in the world. The house and gardens, a mixture of Italian Renaissance and Spanish Mudéjar styles, are impeccably preserved and, in many respects, more impressive than any other compound in the region, Alcázar included. Dark gilded rooms are interspersed with bright open courtyards, and Greco-Roman statues, artifacts, and imagery are littered throughout. Purchase your tickets online or in person—a worthwhile splurge despite the hefty entrance fee.

i Admission €8 for ground floor, €10 for entire grounds; free for children under 10 and EU residents on M from 3pm-7pm; audio guide included; limited wheelchair accessibility

PALACIO DE LA CONDESA DE LEBRIJA

C. Cuna, 8; 954 22 78 02; palaciodelebrija.com; open M-F 10:30am-7:30pm, Sa 10am-2pm and 4pm-6pm, Su 10am-2pm

The Palacio de la Condesa de Lebrija, or the Palace of the Countess of Lebrija, possesses the same grandeur and opulence as the **Alcázar**, just on a smaller scale—almost as if someone shrunk it by 50%, then copied and pasted it between a tapas bar and flower shop on **Calle Cuna**, a popular destination for discount-clothing shopping. Today the palace houses an impressive, intimate, and interactive exhibit of Grecian, Roman, and Moorish art. Gawk at the impressive carvings that adorn the marble columns around the central courtyard, swerve between the massive Chinese and

Persian pots that obscure its long tiled walkways, and and tiptoe around the millennium-old mosaics that pave the ground floor—all so close you could practically touch them.

i Ground floor admission €6, entire grounds €9; limited wheelchair accessibility

IGLESIA DEL SALVADOR

Pl. del Salvador, 3; 954 21 16 79; catedraldeSeville.es/iglesia-de-el-salvador/; open Sep-June M-Sa 11am-6pm, Su 3pm-7:30pm; July-Aug M-Sa 10:30am-5:30pm, Su 3pm-7:30pm

Seville's got no shortage of churches. If you're struggling to decide which to visit, take our word and cut straight to Iglesia del Salvador, where you're sure to get your fill of religious idolatry and baroque architecture. From the outside, this thirteenth-century behemoth could pass for a secular building. Its brick façade blends seamlessly with the terracotta-colored paint of the clothing manufacturing plant next door, and if not for its large rose window and tiled dome, you might mistake it for an upscale hotel. As you walk from the back to the front of the church, details grow more ornate: corinthian columns give way to finely-carved, hand-painted abutments; white stucco ceilings transition into graphic frescoes; and eye-level shrines bloom into three-dimensional altarpieces that seemingly stretch into the heavens.

i Admission €4, joint ticket to Iglesia del Salvador y Catedral de Seville €9; limited wheelchair accessibility

MERCADO DE TRIANA

C. San Jorge, 6; open M-F 9am-early afternoon, Sa 10am-early afternoon, Su noon-5pm

Mercado de Triana is one of two markets open daily in Seville, the other being **Mercado Lonja del Barranco,** which is located on the east side of the **Guadalquivir.** Upon entering, you'll be bombarded with the scents of fresh seafood, cheese, herbs, wine, and cured meats. Wind through this dimly-lit, humid maze, tasting as you go. Unlike Mercado Lonja del Barranco, the goods are not astronomically-priced; like Mercado Lonja del Barranco, you can watch as booth owners prepare your meal directly in front of you. Beyond produce, this market includes several stalls of hand-thrown ceramic cookware. If you're looking to explore handmade crafts further, exit through the doors on the north side of the complex, which are carved into the walls of an ancient castle, and make a right on **Calle Jon de la Inquisición.** On summer Sundays from 9am-2pm, the cobblestone street on the banks of the Guadalquivir transforms into "**Paseo des Artes,**" where local artists congregate to showcase beautiful jewelry, woodwork, and leatherwork. **Centro Cerámica Triana,** located at Calle Callao 16, is also worth a visit.

i Prices vary; limited wheelchair accessibility; best time to visit is around noon Th-Sa

LANDMARKS

CATEDRAL DE SEVILLA (Y LA GIRALDA)

Av. de la Constitución; catedraldeSeville.es; Cathedral open M 11am-3:30pm, T-Sa 11am-5pm, Su 2:30pm-6pm; Giralda open Sep-June M 11am-3:30pm, T-Sa 11am-5pm, Su 2:30pm-6pm, July-Aug M 9:30am-3:30pm, Tu-Sa 9:30am-4pm, Su 2:30pm-6pm

Completed in the sixteenth century, Seville Cathedral is the world's third largest church behind Catedral Basílica Santuário Nacional de Nossa Senhora Aparecida in Brazil and St. Peter's Basilica in Rome. It is truly the Redwood Forest of religious structures—upon walking inside, you'll feel dwarfed by its massive corinthian columns and soaring 140-foot ceiling, which is decorated with intricate stone decals and complemented by gilded altarpieces. Oh, also, the remains of **Christopher Columbus** are housed here, which is pretty cool. The Giralda, or bell tower, stretches 343 feet into the air and can be ascended free of charge. To avoid an hour-long queue, purchase your ticket to the Cathedral at the **Iglesia del Salvado**r (combined entrance €8).

i Admission €9, €4; reduced with audioguide €12, students €7; purchase in advance online or in person; wheelchair accessible

PLAZA DE ESPAÑA

Av. de Isabel la Católica; open daily 24hrs

Upon stepping foot in the square, you'll feel as if you've been transported to a different era—a different world even. Soaring towers flank both ends of the semicircular complex, serving as visual counterpoints to the **Vicente Traver** fountain and primary entryway that stands behind it. Separating the paved plaza from the buildings that surround it is a shallow moat, upon which ducks paddle and rowboats (€6 per half hour) glide. The building's tiled alcoves, decorated in the **Art Deco** style, bring life and color to the Plaza de España, and are great places to put your feet up after exploring the surrounding **Parque de María Luisa.** Although much of the compound is occupied by the Spanish government, you can explore the marvelous interior by climbing the grand staircase on the southern rim.

i Free; limited wheelchair accessibility

ALCÁZAR DE SEVILLE

Patio de Banderas; 954 50 23 24; AlcázarSeville.org; open daily 9:30am-5pm

The Alcázar is, without a doubt, Seville's biggest tourist attraction, and consists of a maze of tiled courtyards, soaring archways, and lush gardens. Built on the remains of an Abbasid Muslim residential fortress for Peter of Castile, the compound has been deemed by experts "the preeminent example" of Mudéjar architecture on the Iberian peninsula. The Alcázar's age can be seen in its slight imperfections—here an archway is a bit off center, there a window tilts slightly to the left. It was designated a **UNESCO World Heritage Site** in 1987, and remains Europe's oldest palace still in use (the royal family lives upstairs!).

i Admission €9.5, €2 reduced, free under 16; book tickets online at least a day in advance; limited wheelchair accessibility

PLAZA DE TOROS (MAESTRANZA)

Paseo de Cristóbal Colón, 12; 954 22 45 77; realmaestranza.com; open daily 9.30am-7 pm, except on bullfighting days until 3pm

This magnificent yellow and white stadium, still in use today, was constructed in 1761 and holds up to 12,000 spectators each Sunday between April and September. It is considered one of the world's most challenging environments for matadors not only because of its lofty history, but also because of the viewing public, which is considered one of the most unforgiving in all of bullfighting fandom. Each chaperoned tour begins with a trek through a succinct historical exhibit that traces bullfighting's evolution from a horseback sport to the performance art that it is today, as well as a trip through the holding pens on the ground floor.

i Admission €8, €5 reduced; free M 3pm-7pm; audio guides included; limited wheelchair accessibility

MUSEUMS

CENTRO ANDALUZ DE ARTE CONTEMPORÁNEO (CAAC)

Av. Américo Vespucio, 2; 955 03 70 70; caac.es; open Tu-Sa 11am-9pm, Su 10am-3:30pm

Located on the west side of the Guadalquivir north of Triana, Centro Andaluz de Arte Contemporáneo one of the city's furthest attractions. Don't let CAAC's distance deter you: housed in a refurbished monastery, CAAC's permanent collection pays special attention to the history of contemporary Andalusian creativity in the context of the international artistic environment through media including (but not limited to) painting, sculpture, photography, and video. The museum includes a small restaurant and bar, which hosts local performance artists most weekend afternoons.

i Admission €1.80 for temporary exhibitions, €3 for entire museum; free Tu-F 7pm-9pm, all day Sa; limited wheelchair accessibility; advisable not to walk alone from Casco Antiguo

MUSEO DEL BAILE FLAMENCO

C. Manuel Rojas Marcos, 3; 954 34 03 11; museodelbaileflamenco.com; open daily 10am-7pm

Museo del Baile Flamenco is a one-stop-shop for all things flamenco, offering a digestible take on the history, practice, and allure of this unique dance form. It is a performance venue, museum, and gallery all in one, and upon entering, you'll be handed a card with summaries of the contents of each room, making it easy to prioritize what you'd like to see. We recommend visiting the museum, attending a performance, then meandering through the gallery (in that order). Shows begin at 5pm, 7pm, 9:45pm, and 10:15pm daily; arrive at least 15 minutes early to snag a seat in the front row and experience the athleticism and grace first-hand.

i Admission €10, €8 reduced; show tickets €20, students €14; combined €24, students €18; limited wheelchair accessibility

MUSEO DE BELLAS ARTES

Pl. del Museo, 9; 955 54 29 31; juntadeandalucia.es/cultura/museos/MBASE/?lng=es; open Tu-Sa 9am-8pm, Su 9am-3pm

The Museo de Bellas Artes is Seville's premier art museum, housing millions of dollars of paintings, sculptures, and furniture from the fifteenth through early twentieth centuries (think lots of winged babies) in a cathedral that dates back to 1594. High ceilings, ornate frescoes, and white marble staircases characterize the interior of this building—in and of itself a piece of art. There's enough here to keep visitors engaged and entertained for days, but for the less artistically-inclined, the entire museum can be covered in just under two hours.

i Admission €1.50; wheelchair accessible

OUTDOORS

PARQUE DE MARÍA LUISA

Paseo de las Delicias; 955 47 32 32; open daily 8am-10pm

New York has Central Park, Seville has Parque de María Luisa. Though this expansive, lush plot of greenery, fountains, paved boulevards, tiled courtyards, monuments, and exedras has existed since the seventeenth century, it wasn't until 1911, under the skilled eye of landscape architect **Jean-Claude Nicolas Forestier** (who also designed the gardens of Champ-de-Mars in Paris), that it assumed its present shape. This botanical garden's main complexes include the **Plaza de España, Costurero de la Reina,** and the **Plaza America,** all of which deserve a visit both for their design and their contents.

i Free; bikes available to rent near the Plaza de España; limited wheelchair accessibility

JARDINES DE MURILLO

Av. de Menéndez Pelayo; open daily 7am-midnight

The Jardines de Murillo were overhauled at the same time as **Parque de María Luisa** as a part of an initiative to improve transportation within and around the **Santa Cruz** neighborhood. This highly-manicured, quiet park consists of a network of dirt pathways, palm trees, low shrubbery, and ceramic courtyards, with most activity centering around five roundabouts. Though located parallel to **Avenida de Menéndez Pelayo,** one of the city's busiest streets, Jardines de Murillo feels like a little slice of paradise, secluded from the tourist frenzy occurring just on the other side of **the Alcázar's** exterior walls.

i Free; limited wheelchair accessibility

METROPOL PARASOL (LAS SETAS)

Pl. de la Encarnación; open M-F 10am-11pm, Sa-Su 10am-11:30pm

See Seville from a different perspective and ascend the Metropol Parasol, a massive wooden sculpture (at 490 by 230 feet, it claims to be the largest freestanding wood structure in the world!) whose latticed frame shades the bustling **Plaza de Encarnación.** The base of the structure houses a small, upscale market, as well as several restaurants and a popular underground exhibit that showcases **Roman ruins and artifacts** excavated on-site. As much of the **Antiquarum** can be viewed through the floor-to-ceiling glass panes that encase it, we recommend strolling right by to the elevator. Sunset is by far the most popular time to visit, but get there a little earlier to avoid waiting in line. Apart from **the Giralda**, the Metropol Parasol offers the best 360-degree view of Seville.

i Lift to top €3, admission to Antiquarum €2.10, cocktails from €5; limited wheelchair accessibility

FOOD

LA BRUNILDA TAPAS ($)

Calle Galeria, 5; 954 22 04 81; labrunildatapas.com; open Tu-Sa 1pm-4pm and 8:30pm-11:30pm, Su 1pm-4pm; closed Aug

Hands-down the best (affordable) tapas in Seville. La Brunilda has a reputation— there was already a line when we arrived at 1pm on a Sunday. Upon entering, you'll be greeted by an attentive waitstaff, a cavernous but updated interior, and a small but thoughtfully-curated menu of omnivorous starters and large plates such as Risoto de Idiazábal y setas. We particularly enjoyed the cod fritters with pear aioli, a dense fish patty fried crisp to the touch and served with a light, semi-sweet glob of cream. Arrive a half hour before opening to ensure that you score a table.

i Starters from €3.20, meats from €4.50, wine €2.60; vegetarian options available; limited wheelchair accessibility

LA CACHERRERÍA ($)

C. Carlos Cañal, 14; 954 21 21 66; open M-Th 8:30am-10pm, F 8:30am-midnight, Sa 9am-3am, Su 10am-10pm

With nothing but a couple of tables and a sun-worn awning outside of its narrow front door, La Cacherrería is easy to miss. But walk right past it and you'll be missing out on one (or three) of the best mojitos of your life, not to mention some stellar food and an unparalleled dining experience. La Cacherrería's interior can best be described as witches'-den-meets-junkyard-chic-meets-grandpa's-last-garage-sale. Among other things, globes, bull horns, evil eyes, cuckoo clocks, accordions, Nepali flags, and a couple of miniature phonographs hang from its jet-black ceiling, and hundreds of pennies are stacked perilously on the bricks that compose its northern wall. Serving up scrumptious bagel sandwiches, fresh wraps, and large parfaits, La Cacherrería is the closest you'll get—food wise, at least—to an American brunch. Seating is limited, so if you're hoping to sit as you slurp down your drink, swing by between 4 and 7pm.

i Bagels, wraps, salads, and toasts from €4.50; smoothies, milkshakes, and parfaits from €2.50; Cruzcampo on tap €1, wine from €2.50, cocktails from €3; vegetarian options available; no wheelchair accessibility

ALMAZEN CAFÉ ($)

C. San Esteban, 15; 955 35 97 64; open Tu-W 9am-8pm, Th Sa 9am-11pm, Su 9am-2pm

Almazen is a jewel of a café, located in the hip, artistic neighborhood of **San Bartolomé.** Ample seating, free Wi-Fi, an easily-navigable menu, and a bilingual staff make dining here easy. Almazen Café is particularly popular for its homemade breakfast, which includes decadent parfaits, fruit tartlets, and a variety of cakes and coffees. Highlights from the afternoon menu include Chorizo Criollo and Empanadas Porteñas—rich, meaty dishes that pair wonderfully with a glass of red wine, craft beer, or blended iced tea. Enjoy your meal inside surrounded by original artwork or outside on a covered patio;

either way, you'll leave full, happy, and ready to take on the day.
i Tapas from €3; drinks from €1; vegan and vegetarian options available; Wi-Fi; limited wheelchair accessibility

CRÉEME HELADO ($)

Pl. del Museo, 2; 954 91 08 32; creeme.es; open Su-Th noon-9pm, F-Sa noon-midnight

Créeme was, without a doubt, the best helado we had in Seville, and, according to local experts, is a top contender for best helado in all of Spain. Churned slowly and crafted solely with all-natural ingredients, this ice cream has a rich, buttery texture that lingers. Flavors range from classics like vanilla and caramel to more unique varieties such as chocolate and fig, pine nut, and mixed berry, and every scoop is served with a complementary dollop of sweet cream. Take a cone *para llevar* (to go) or enjoy a cup in Créeme's wood-paneled, modern interior.
i Ice cream from €3; gluten-free and vegan options; wheelchair accessible

NIGHTLIFE

LA CARBONERÍA

C. Levíes, 8; 954 21 44 60; open daily 7am-2am

Every evening at 9:30pm and midnight, something akin to magic happens at La Carbonería. The locals lounging on the tree-covered garden patio extinguish their cigarettes, the lights inside begin to dim, and the cacophony of multilingual chatter, clinking glasses, and creaking of wooden benches begins to quiet down. The flamenco performance is one of the most authentic in the city, and lasts between 30 minutes and a full hour. The bar itself is tucked away in one of the quietest parts of the city, between **Santa Cruz** and **San Bartolomé**, so don't fret if you find yourself walking in what may seem like the wrong direction. You'll know you've made it when you spot the small black lettering on its doorway—"La Carbonería," lit by the soft glow of the lights that line the courtyard.
i Mojitos €5, liter of sangria €9, cocktails €6; food from €11; free flamenco shows daily; wheelchair accessible

LA BICICLETERIA

Feria 36; 608 73 48 06; open daily between 10pm-midnight, closes whenever the party dies down

Knock slow, knock hard. Entrance is not guaranteed to all at this clandestine bar, but you'll increase your chances of getting if you approach its graffitied door confidently and speaking the language (or are attached to the hips of people who do). A visit to La Bicicleteria will reveal a side of Seville very few tourists get to experience. Inside, a small sunken room pulses with the smooth sounds of jazz, reggae, and old rock and smoke twirls in the yellow cones of light cast by lamps that hang low to the ground. The décor, like the clientele, is bohemian and non-conformist, and on a good night, itfeels more like an attending intimate house party than anything else.
i No wheelchair accessibility; weekdays are as popular as weekends; preferable not to attend or walk home alone

BODEGA SANTA CRUZ

Calle Rodrigo Caro, 1A; 954 21 16 94; open M-Sa 8am-midnight, Su 8:30am-midnight

A bustling bar located steps from the **Catedral**, Bodega Santa Cruz—or Las Columnas as locals call it—is steeped in character and authenticity. Don't let the boisterous crowd outside of its tall double doors frighten you off; if you manage to squeeze through to Bodega Santa Cruz's long mahogany bar, you'll be rewarded with cheap beer and tasty tapas, all served within a matter of seconds. On weekend evenings, flamenco musicians gather on the front porch for free performances.
i Tapas from €2, cheap beer on tap; cash only; limited vegetarian options available

SPAIN ESSENTIALS

VISAS

Spain is a member of the European Union and is part of the Schengen Area, so US citizens can stay in Sweden for up to 90 days without a visa.

MONEY

Tipping and Bargaining: Native Spaniards rarely tip more than their spare change, even at expensive restaurants. Don't feel like you have to tip, as the servers' pay is almost never based on tips. Bargaining is common and necessary in open-air and street markets. Do not barter in malls or established shops.

Taxes: Spain has a 10% value added tax (IVA) on all means and accommodations. The prices listed in Let's Go include IVA. Retail goods bear a much higher 21% IVA, although the listed prices generally include this tax. Non-EU citizens who have stayed in the EU fewer than 180 days can claim back the tax paid on purchases at the airport.

SAFETY AND HEALTH

Drugs and Alcohol: Recreational drugs are illegal in Spain, and police take these laws seriously. the legal drinking age is 16 in Asturias and 18 elsewhere. In Asturias, it is still illegal for stores to sell alcohol to those under the age of 18.

Local Laws and Police: There are several types of police in Spain. The policía local wear blue or black uniforms, deal more with local issues, and report to the mayor or town hall in each municipality. The guardia civil wear olive-green uniforms and are responsible for issues more relevant to travelers: customs, crowd control, and national security. Catalonia also has its own police force, the Mossos d'Esquadra. Officers generally wear blue and occasionally sport berets. This police force is often used for crowd control and to deal with riots.

SWEDEN

"Hej hej!" This is the typical greeting in Sweden—pronounced 'hey hey!' in a cheerful singsong tone—and it basically only gets more charming from there. Though the Scandinavian powerhouse sits at the forefront of innovation and modernization, Sweden's culture is laid-back enough that *fika,* or a coffee and pastry break, is a quintessential part of nearly every Swede's lifestyle. (It's all about that work-life balance.) When you think of Sweden, your mind probably jumps to ABBA, IKEA, and meatballs—and maybe even that goofy muppet character: the gibberish-speaking Swedish chef. While you're not wrong about their Swedish origins (besides the muppet guy), there's a whole lot more to Sweden than its furniture exports. The country boasts some of the largest and most culturally diverse cities in Scandinavia, as well as one of the most progressive and open-minded cultures in the world.

Not one to fall behind in any sort of category, Sweden also features some of the most vast and well-preserved natural landscapes in all of the Nordic countries, ranging from forest to glacier to tundra. Whether you're island-hopping among the many archipelagos along its coastline or admiring modern art in a cutting-edge gallery, studying the history of the viking ages or tomorrow's technological innovation, or indulging in traditional meatballs, you'll find something about Sweden that speaks to you.

MALMÖ

Coverage by **Marissa Saenger**

Sweden and Denmark have a complicated relationship. Though not officially known, it's widely believed that the two countries have gone to war with each other more times than any other two countries in the world. Right across Øresund from Denmark's capital, Copenhagen, Malmö has stuck in the middle of every aggressive bump the whole way through. The city changed hands frequently between the two nations, but ultimately joined the Swedish Empire for good in the winter of 1658. Securing Malmö's place on Swedish maps, the Swedish army pulled the ultimate sneak-attack on Denmark by crossing the frozen Øresund into Copenhagen. An important commercial center throughout the Industrial Revolution, Malmö's rapid cosmopolitan development can still be seen in its culture today. Constantly growing and modernizing, the city acts as an epicenter of cultural diversity and innovation. The Malmö experience ranges from ancient Gothic architecture to fresh contemporary art, quaint cobblestone old-town squares to energetic modern neighborhoods and forested city parks to sandy public beaches.

ORIENTATION

Malmö is fairly small compared to other major cities, but has distinct areas, each with its own character. **Gamla Staden** (Old Town) is the main central area, where you'll find **Malmö Centralstation** as well as most of the city's cultural and historical landmarks, like **Malmöhus Castle, Lilla Torg,** and **Malmö City Library.** North of Gamla Staden, **Västra Hamnen** is the exclusive residential neighborhood with claims to fame as the first carbon-neutral district in Europe, and home to the tallest building in Scandinavia, **Turning Torso**. West of the city center, **Ribersborg** stretches along the city's coastline with beaches and open grass areas. South of Gamla Staden, Malmö becomes more residential, but no less interesting to explore. **Pildammsparken** and **Folkets Park** provide ample recreational offerings, along with live shows and pop-up bars. Surrounding Folkets Park, the international neighborhood **Möllevången** has more falafel restaurants than you could ever hope to count, and serves as a cultural hub of the city through theater, dance, and art.

ESSENTIALS

GETTING THERE

Malmö Airport (MMX), sometimes called by its old name, Sturup, is a small airport located about 30km east of the city center in the **Svedala Municipality**. It connects to a number of cities in Europe, and services regular bus transfers to and from the city center; book your ticket at www.flygbussarna.se. From there, drive about 40min. to reach the city. Depending on where you're coming from, it may be cheaper to fly into Copenhagen Airport (CPH), which connects to many more cities within and around Europe, and take a 35min. train into Malmö. Trains arrive at Malmö Central Station (Malmö C) in Gamla Staden.

GETTING AROUND

Thanks to its relatively small size, Malmö is an easily walkable city—though, if you plan to cover every corner, your best option is a bicycle. The city's extensive bicycle infrastructure includes paths between the roads and sidewalks designated specifically for bikes (more people bike here than drive). Malmö by Bike is the city's official public bikeshare system, which maintains several pick-up and return stations all throughout the city. Buses are the main public transportation within the city, and you can buy a Jojo card at Malmö C for discounted single-fare, 24hr, or 72hr bus and train passes.

PRACTICAL INFORMATION

Tourist Offices: Malmö has no official tourist offices, but 'InfoPoints' throughout the city offer tourist information. Staff at each InfoPoint can answer your questions or provide maps, guides, and brochures to help you explore. TravelShop (Carlsgatan 4 A, 211 20 Malmö; 0 403 07 016; malmocity.se/en/turistinformation; open daily 10am-5pm).
Banks/ATMs/Currency Exchange: ATMs are available throughout the city. There are also several places to exchange currency; if you're arriving at Central Station, the most convenient option is Forex Bank (Malmö centralstation, Lokgatan 1, 211 20 Malmö; 1 021 11 664; forex.se; open M-F 7am-8pm, Sa-Su 10am-6pm).
Post Offices: Malmö has several post offices and mailboxes. Full postal service is available at Postombud på ICA Maxi Västra Hamnen (Masttorget 12, 211 77 Malmö; 7 713 33 310; postnord.se; open daily 8am-10pm).
Public Restrooms: Free public restrooms are called "Toalett" and are available in most parks and outside of public buildings. More information on public restrooms is available at malmo.se.
Internet: Free Wi-Fi is available in public buildings like libraries, as well as most cafés, restaurants, hotel lobbies, and bars.
BGLTQ+ Resources: RFSL is the Swedish Federation for BGLTQ+ rights (Stora Nygatan 18, 211 37 Malmö; 8 501 62 900; rfsl.se).

EMERGENCY INFORMATION

Emergency Number: 112.
Police: Malmö Drottninggatan (Drottninggatan 18, Malmö; 114 14; polisen.se; open M-Th 8am-7pm, F 8am-3pm, Sa 8am-2pm).
US Embassy: There is no US Embassy in Malmö. The closest one is in Copenhagen (Dag Hammarskjölds Allé 24; 33 41 71 00; telephone open M-F 8:30-noon, appointments M-Th 9am-noon). However, for passport-related issues, you can go to Migrationsverket Nationellt Immigration Service Center (Agnesfridsvägen 111; 7 712 35 235; migrationsverket.se; open M-F 9am-3pm).
Rape Crisis Center: Find one at Gynekologimottagning akut Malmö. Their website links directly to their phone number, find it here: (plan 2, 214 66 Malmö; 7 716 41 463; vard.skane.se; open daily 24hr).
Hospitals: In Skåne, there are university hospitals, emergency hospitals, and local hospitals, each with different care and specialized service offerings.

- Akutavdelning Malmö (Emergency Ward Malmö): (Carl-Bertil Laurells gata 9, 214 28 Malmö; 0 403 36 650; vard.skane.se; open daily 24hr).
- Skåne University Hospital, SUS, Malmö: (Inga Marie Nilssons gata 47, 214 21 Malmö; 0 403 38 050; vard.skane.se).

Pharmacies: Pharmacies are called "apoteket," and are available throughout the city.

- Apotek Hjärtat: (Södra Förstadsgatan 30, 211 43 Malmö; 7 714 05 405; apotekhjartat.se; open M-F 9:30am-6pm, Sa 10am-4pm).

SIGHTS

CULTURE

RIBERSBORGS KALLBADHUS

Limhamnsvägen, Brygga 1; 0 402 60 366; ribersborgskallbadhus.se; open M-F 9am-9pm, Sa-Su 9am-6pm

What could be more freeing than a naked dip in the ocean? Bathing suits aren't a thing here, which means you'll *really* be out in the open at this open-air bathing facility. At the end of a long pier off Ribersborg beach, enclosed swimming areas are gender-separated and well out of sight from the beach. So besides all the other people chilling au naturale in your respective section, you have total privacy to skinny-dip and sauna in the buff. If you're brave enough to enter the open water beyond the pier, you'll probably no longer be completely out of view—and neither will the swimmers from the opposite section. But don't let this alarm you; it's not a big deal. Try booking a massage to round out your Swedish spa experience.

i Admission SEK 70; massage from SEK 320

SANKT PETRI KYRKA (ST. PETER'S CHURCH)

Göran Olsgatan 4; 0 402 79 043; svenska-kyrkanmalmo.se; open daily 10am-6pm

Built in the 14th century, St. Peter's Church is the oldest building in Malmö. But don't let its age fool you: this gargantuan gothic structure is one tough cookie, with the history to prove it. Every time something knocked it down, this church got right back up again: it collapsed twice in the 1400s and suffered major damages from a famous act of iconoclasm in the Danish Reformation. Subsequent renovations and reconstructions have more or less torn it down completely, but no amount of whitewashing or structural dismantling could keep it from dominating the spiritual scene for long. Today, the building's 98-meter-tall bell tower signifies its prominence over **Stortorget Square,** and its late medieval frescoes contrast starkly with its bright interior. Along with regular worship, the church sometimes hosts public music events, though its primary function to many Swedes is free coffee service in the winter.

i Free; wheelchair accessible

MALMÖ STADSBIBLIOTEK (MALMÖ CITY LIBRARY)

Kung Oscars väg 11; 04 066 08 500; malmo.se; open M-Th 10am-7pm, F 10am-6pm, Sa-Su 11am-5pm

Part Renaissance castle, part stylish glass cube, Malmö City Library looks more like a royal palace than a public institution. The building sits beside a canal overlooking **King's Park,** and makes for a great sightseeing stop or a browse through its bookshelves. A cylindrical entrance connects the castle with the newer Calendar of Light, which shines brightly with natural sunlight through glass walls on all sides. Inside both parts, you can peruse books, encyclopedia volumes, music, magazines, newspapers, and more, or snag a cozy study spot to work on your latest project. With offerings for all interests and ages, the library draws patrons from near and far. If you're a particularly needy intellectual, free Wi-Fi and an attached café, along with lovely views of the city, provide the essentials to inspire in your scholarly ventures.

i Free; wheelchair accessible

LANDMARKS

HARBOR SCULPTURES

Posthusplatsen

Other than falafel joints and bicycles, there are few things you'll see more of in Malmö than sculptures. They're spread all over the city, but if you want to cut down walking time and enjoy public art in one place, head over to the **Western Harbor.** From Malmö Central Station, walk or bike the harbor and see sculptures of all shapes and sizes decorating the bustling city streets. From elegant historic monuments to abstract modern designs, the art pieces feature work like the non-violence sculpture of a knotted gun and the relics of maritime history. Throughout the harbor, peep the architectural design, as well as plenty of lively places to enjoy a meal or drink.

i Free; wheelchair accessible

KARL X GUSTAV STATUE

Stortorget; open daily 24hr

The Karl X Gustav statue dominates **Stortorget** with the powerful presence of this former Swedish king. When closely analyzing the statue's orientation, notice that this horse's backside faces toward Copenhagen; this gesture is very intentional, blowing an emblematic

fart in the Danes' general direction. Sweden and Denmark's now-friendly rivalry goes way back to the good old days when this guy was king, so he's probably giggling in his grave right now at the prospect of farting on Denmark. Proudly facing the rest of Sweden, King Karl's statue directly overlooks the brilliant work of architecture that is **Malmö City Hall.**

i Free; wheelchair accessible

LILLA TORG

Lilla Torg; open daily 24hr

Lilla Torg ("Little Square") lives up to its name literally, but flouts an impressively big personality and a big-time reputation. The busy square in **Malmö's Old Town** boasts restaurants, cafés, bars, and shops that keep people coming day and night. The old architecture and cobblestone roads lend the area its classic charm, but the energy stays high thanks to popular eateries with continuous good vibes. Though there's a lot more to see in Malmö, you could easily spend an entire day or more simply soaking up the sunshine and sharing quality conversation over coffee, drinks, or people-watching in the streets of Lilla Torg.

i Prices vary; wheelchair accessible

MUSEUMS

MALMÖ CHOKLAD MUSEET (MALMÖ CHOCOLATE MUSEUM)

Möllevångsgatan 36B; 0 404 59 505; malmochokladfabrik.se; open M-F 10am-6pm, Sa 10am-3pm

There's an old saying about how chocolate is the cure to all ailments, and at Malmö Chokladfabrik, they take wellness very seriously. The museum exhibit in the factory provides detailed insight on how cacao beans are grown, harvested, dried, fermented, cleaned, conched, mixed, and moulded into the glorious concoction we call chocolate today. This careful set of processes is called bean-to-bar production, and it's a few steps up in quality from your average Hershey kiss. Malmö Chokladfabrik is the only bean-to-bar producer in Sweden, which they say makes all the difference in their chocolate's exceptional aphrodisiac and anti-inflammatory properties. Enter the museum for free on your own, but to get the full experience, sign up for a guided tour and enjoy generous tasting opportunities throughout.

i Free entry to museum; guided tours T-F 2pm, Sa 11am and 1pm SEK 100, SEK 80 reduced; chocolate tastings (book in advance) SEK 350; no wheelchair accessibility

MALMÖ MUSEUM

Malmöhusvägen 6; 0 403 44 400; malmo.se; open daily 10am-5pm

Inside Scandinavia's oldest standing Renaissance castle, Malmöhus, you'll find museum exhibits that have almost nothing to do with the castle. An aquarium, natural history section, modern art showcase, and various temporary exhibits take you all the way back to the Big Bang and up through today, with plenty of kid-oriented interactive stations along the way. If you think you might be missing something, you're not; this is indeed the Malmö Museum, in all its eclectic glory. A moat surrounds the castle, which also used to be a prison and served as a temporary residence for concentration camp survivors that the Swedes secretly rescued during World War II. Suffice to say there's a lot going on here and that's basically been the case since 1434.

i Admission SEK 40, SEK 20 reduced, under 19 free; wheelchair accessible

OUTDOORS

PILDAMMSPARKEN

Pildammsparken; open daily 24hr

Pildammsparken is your best bet for getting your nature fix in the city. Its forested walking paths and covert grassy knolls make perfect hideaways for settling down with a book or a picnic. A trail around the lake takes you past vibrant rose gardens, a castle-like old water tower, elegant sculptures, and an open outdoor gym complete with pull-up bars and crossfit ropes. Next to the lake, there's an esteemed Michelin-star restaurant, Bloom in the Park—your budget is probably better suited to a picnic, but for the view and quality of food, it might be well worth a splurge. Sporty locals tend to gather here for group workouts in the evenings, and pick-up soccer or volleyball games frequently break out on the open grassy spaces. An outdoor amphitheater in the park hosts free summer concerts, if you're looking for quality entertainment that doesn't break the bank.

i Free; limited wheelchair accessibility

RIBERSBORGSSTRANDEN

Open daily 24hr

Who needs a Mediterranean beach vacation when the glorious **Øresund** is right at your doorstep? Okay, so it's not *quite* the same... but hey, a beach is a beach—and many consider this one to be one of Sweden's best. Ribersborgsstranden stretches for about three kilometers along Malmö's western coast, with soft sand and green space for the lazy summer beach day you've been dreaming about since you arrived in Scandinavia. Whether you spend your time sunbathing, picnicking, or pier-jumping, here you can catch a refreshing break from Malmö's bustling city streets. In the evenings, groups gather for barbecues and salsa parties, or to enjoy salty sea air while watching the sunset. A bit more primal than **Ribersborg Kallbadhus,** there's a designated beach area for nude bathing—though it doesn't have quite the same spa-like offerings for skinny-dippers as its upscale peer on the pier.

i Free; wheelchair accessible

FOOD

LILLA KAFFEROSTERIET ($$)

Baltzarsgatan 24, 21; 0 404 82 000; lillakafferosteriet.se; open M-F 8am-6pm, Sa-Su 10am-6pm

Coffee breaks, called *fika,* are an integral daily Swedish ritual—and there's no better place in Malmö to *fika* than here. Contrary to its name ("little coffee roastery"), Lilla Kafferosteriet is actually quite large. Multiple rooms span three levels of seating, and an outdoor patio provides ample space to sprawl. With copious seating, it's easy to stay a while; and that's exactly what people do. Without Wi-Fi, guests surrender digital distraction to converse and relax. It's the kind of place you sit down and talk or read for hours, leaving stress behind as you enter the door. The rustic interior feels intimate and relaxed, with fresh coffee aromas wafting gloriously throughout. Equally as memorable as its charming atmosphere, Lilla Kafferosteriet's coffee is cream of the crop: sourced, roasted and brewed with the utmost attention to quality, it's excellent on its own or with a delectable home-baked dessert.

i Espresso SEK 26, pastries and desserts from SEK 28; gluten-free, vegan, and vegetarian options available; limited wheelchair accessibility

SALTIMPORTEN CANTEEN ($$)

Grimsbygatan 24; 7 065 18 426; saltimporten.com; open M-F noon-2pm

Saltimporten Canteen is one of Malmö's best-kept secrets. Okay, it's not totally a secret—locals flock here daily to be first in line for lunch—but its out-of-the-way location in a warehouse-type building makes it feel like you discovered a hidden haven for culinary delight. If you're willing to make the trek through an industrial part of the West Harbor, cash in your reward in the form of an excellent meal. Each day, the chefs make a single dish for lunch, and with just one dish to focus on, they make it fantastic. Only open weekdays from noon until 2pm, the renowned eatery draws crowds from all over each day. Due to its high reputation, seating is usually packed, so it's best to get there early and beat the crowds. But if you happen to get there at a busier time, there's plenty of space to sit outside, and we can assure you the food is well worth the wait.

i Lunch SEK 110; gluten-free, vegan, and vegetarian options available; wheelchair accessible

MALMÖ SALUHALL ($$)

Gibraltargatan 6; 4 062 67 730; malmosaluhall.se; open M-Th 10am-7pm, F 10am-9pm, Sa 10am-5pm, Su 11am-4pm

Even the pickiest eaters will find food they love at Malmö Saluhall. Sort of an upscale version of a cafeteria, the food hall packs fancy meats and cheeses, freshly-caught fish, gourmet chocolates and ice cream, handmade salads and pastries, sizzling brick-oven pizzas, and specialty drinks under one roof. Each restaurant and vendor specializes in what they sell, so whatever your choice, you will get the best of the best. Even if you don't try everything (though it's tempting), just walking around all

of the different displays counters is a culinary adventure in itself. Spend some time sniffing out all the different options before settling on a favorite (or two or three) to enjoy in whatever section of open-air seating you please.
i Prices vary; gluten-free, vegan, and vegetarian options available; Wi-Fi; wheelchair accessible

NIGHTLIFE

BASTARD

Mäster Johansgatan 11; 0 401 21 318; bastardrestaurant.se; open Tu-Th 5pm-midnight, F-Sa 5pm-1am

Maybe you thought the drink menu looked good, or maybe you just wanted to make a dad joke along the lines of "what did you just call me?" at the bar. No matter what brings you to Bastard, though, you're likely to have a great night. The modern European gastropub serves distinctive food and cocktails with a playfully edgy flare, but if you can't afford the fancy stuff, the beer list tastes just fine. Drinks range from local Bastard lager to wine from all over the world, with plenty of clever (read: hilariously profane) cocktail names thrown into the mix. The menu features tasty charcuterie plates, oven-fired pizza, and sumptuous seasonal desserts. Popular not only for its creative drinks and dishes, Bastard boasts a boisterous social atmosphere that lights up its outdoor garden on a nightly basis.
i Drinks from SEK 75; gluten-free, vegan, and vegetarian options available; wheelchair accessible

MALMÖ BREWING CO. & TAPROOM ($$)

Bergsgatan 33; 7 339 21 966; malmobrewing.com; open Su-Th 4pm-midnight, F 4pm-3am, Sa noon-3am, Su 4pm-midnight

Malmö doesn't quite specialize in the big-city club scene you'd find in Berlin, but it does brew a thriving craft beer scene like you'd find in your dad's wildest dreams. The pioneers of this craft beer movement, Malmö Brewing Co. & Taproom, proudly pour over 40 home and guest brews at the bar on any given night. Along with signature beers, they serve local mead on tap as well as red, white, and even orange wines. Also like in your dad's wildest dreams, this place *seriously* commits to its barbecue. An American-style menu boasts full slabs of baby back ribs, brewmasters' brisket, and classic burger specials, either as individual dinners or shared group platters. It's a popular hangout on any given evening, getting especially packed on weekends when the steady stream of rock music blares late into the night.
i Drinks from SEK 75; BGLTQ+ friendly; Wi-Fi; no wheelchair access

STOCKHOLM

Coverage by **Marissa Saenger**

Congratulations, you've made it to Stockholm: the biggest, baddest, and brightest city in all of Scandinavia. The city offers travelers a handful and a (meatball) mouthful: history buffs can wander magnificent palaces, cathedrals, museums, and cobbled old-town city streets; artists can appreciate contemporary work from photography to music and dance; foodies can taste all kinds of artisanal creations, from coffee to meatballs and microbrew craft beer; and outdoor adventurers can travel to nearby nature reserves and islands to frolic through beautiful forests. Stockholm's hostels, cafés, and bars overflow with energetic travelers and thoughtful locals with all kinds of backgrounds and stories. Whether you're here for a long, Stockholm-syndrome-inducing visit, or just a short stop on your Europe adventure, the Stockholm experience is yours to create.

ORIENTATION

Stockholm spans multiple islands and districts. The **Norrmalm District** surrounds **Stockholm Central** with popular shopping streets, like **Drottninggatan.** To the west, **Kungsholmen Island** is a growing residential area home to **Stockholm City**

Hall. **Östermalm,** to the east, is Stockholm's most extravagant neighborhood—chock-full of high-end brand name retail stores and expensively-dressed (and wealthy AF) people. Directly south of Norrmalm sits the island **Gamla Stan—** Stockholm's classic Old Town—where you'll find the **Royal Palace** and several historic landmarks, as well as hordes of tourists crowding cobbled streets and overpriced cafés, souvenir shops, and restaurants. **Djurgården** is an island south of Östermalm, with many notable museums like the **Vasa Museum,** as well as the theme park **Gröna Lund** and the **Rosendals Trädgård** garden**.** Directly south of Gamla Stan, the trendy district **Södermalm** has hipster hangouts galore, like **Fotografiska,** bohemian cafés, and organic vegan restaurants.

ESSENTIALS

GETTING THERE

Stockholm's main airport is Stockholm Arlanda, which is about 40km north of the city center and serves major airports in Europe, Asia, and North America. The easiest way to get to the city center from here is an approximately 20min. ride via the Stockholm-Arlanda express (arlandaexpress.com). If you arrive by train, you'll get off at Stockholm Centralstation (Stockholm C). The SJ operates trains to and from destinations around Sweden. From Stockholm C, walk or take public transit to your accommodation, depending on its location.

GETTING AROUND

Public transportation in Stockholm includes buses, a metro system called Tunnelbana, trams, and ferries that go to the islands around the city. Purchase tickets on the SL app or at ticket kiosks in major stations, as well as at Pressbyrån convenience stores. You must purchase tickets ahead of time, as you cannot buy them on the buses, trams, or trains. For short trips, buy single-journey tickets for each trip; but, if you plan on using public transportation more than once or twice, it makes the most sense to purchase a travel card for SEK 20. If you want to bicycle around, rent your wheels from a rental agency or bicycle shop.

PRACTICAL INFORMATION

Tourist Offices: Stockholm Visitor Center (Kulturhuset, Sergels Torg 5; 08 508 285 08; visitstockholm.com; open M-F 9am-6pm, Sa 9am-4pm, Su 10am-4pm).

Banks/ATMs/Currency Exchange: Most places in Stockholm are now cash-free, so you likely won't need to withdraw currency. But if you do want some for things like tipping tour guides or buying fruit from outdoor markets, you can exchange at Ria Money Transfer & Currency Exchange in Norrmalm (Mäster Samuelsgatan 46; 08 679 75 09; riafinancial.com; open M-F 8:30am-8pm, Sa 11am-5pm, Su 11am-4pm).

Post Offices: Sweden's postal service is called PostNord, and it has few brick-and-mortar locations. You can drop off mail in streetside mailboxes, or go to private mail centers like Mail Boxes Etc. (Birger Jarlsgatan 39, 111 45 Stockholm; 08 454 31 91; mailboxesetc.se; open daily M-F 8am-7am, open Jun 20 8am-5pm, closed Jun 21).

Public Restrooms: Stockholm has public toilets available throughout the city. A map of all facilities is available at swedentips.se/public-toilets-stockholm.

Internet: The Stockholm Visitor Center, Central Station, and Arlanda Airport all have free Wi-Fi. Internet is also available in many shops, cafés, and museums for free.

BGLTQ+ Resources: RFSL is the Swedish Federation for BGLTQ+ rights (Saltmätargatan 20; 08 501 629 00; rfsl.se; open M 1pm-3pm, W 1pm-4pm, F 10am-noon).

EMERGENCY INFORMATION

Emergency Number: 112. For non-emergency 24-hour medical advice, call 1177.

Police: The police number for non-emergency incidents is 11 414. Norrmalm's Police Station is located at (Kungsholmsgatan 43; 07 711 414 00; polisen.se; open M-F 8am-8pm, Sa-Su 10am-6pm).

US Embassy: There is a US Embassy in Stockholm (Dag Hammarskjölds väg 31; 08 783 53 00; se.usembassy.gov; open M-F 8am-4:30pm).

Rape Crisis Center: Södersjukhuset, one of Stockholm's main hospitals, has a 24hr telephone hotline and an emergency clinic for rape victims (Sjukhusbacken 10, floor 3; 08 616 46 70; sodersjukhuset.se; open daily 24hr).

Hospitals: Sweden medical facilities deliver relatively high-standard of care and are consistently reliable.

- Södersjukhuset SÖS (Sjukhusbacken 10; 08 616 10 00; sodersjukhuset.se; open daily 24hr).

Pharmacies: Pharmacies are called "apotek" and are widely available around Stockholm. There is a 24hr pharmacy across the street from Stockholm Centralstation.

- Apoteket C W Scheele (Klarabergsgatan 64; 07 714 504 50; apoteket.se; open daily 24hr).

SIGHTS

CULTURE

ROSENDALS TRÄDGÅRD

Rosendalsvägen 38, 115 21 Stockholm; 08 545 812 70; rosendalstradgard.se; open daily Apr-Oct 11am-5pm, Oct-Dec and Feb-Mar 11am-4pm

Though not far from bustling tourist hotspots like the **Vasa Museum** and **Gröna Lund**, Rosendals Trädgård is a peaceful sanctuary for off-the-beaten-path explorers. A rose garden, orchard, vineyard, and greenhouse hide furtively within a forested park; follow the nature trails toward the park's western side to find the garden's main attractions. A biodynamic greenhouse café serves organic lunches and desserts made with ingredients straight from the gardens and an on-site artisanal bakery. Help yourself to delicious cakes and pastries, top them with fresh organic whipped cream, and enjoy your treats among vibran to enjoy in the fresh air. If you feel inspired to start growing things yourself, the nursery sells seeds and gardening equipment. Rosendals Trädgård also staffs a boutique, which sells homemade goods like fresh jams, breads, and spice blends. The nearby castle, **Rosendals Slott**, once served as the royal family's get-away spot; tour its interior on guided tours or wander its gardens on your own.

i Free; shops and café are cash free; gluten-free, vegan, and vegetarian options available; limited wheelchair accessibility (flat dirt and gravel paths)

DROTTNINGHOLM PALACE

178 02 Drottningholm; 0 840 26 280; kungahuset.se; open daily Jul-Sept 10am-5pm, Oct-Dec 10am-4pm

If you have time for the trip to Drottningholm, there's a lot you can do and see. Now the Swedish King and Queen's permanent residence, the palace houses brilliant artwork and lavish interior design. It's all the magnificence and beauty of Versailles, but with friendly Swedish security guards watching your every move instead of grumpy French ones. Regular guided tours of the palace interior can help you keep straight which **King Gustaf** was which, though regardless of whether you master any history, it's a spectacular sight. If you don't feel like paying to dodge tourist crowds inside, the palace gardens are enormous and free to the public. For a fee, visit the **Chinese Royal Pavillion**, which has a beautiful pagoda and gallery that helped Drottingholm become a **UNESCO World Heritage Site** in 1991. To make the most of your visit, set aside a few hours to explore the various gardens and pack your own lunch to avoid overpaying at the café.

i Palace admission SEK 140, SEK 70 reduced, combined admission (palace, theater, and pavilion) SEK 190, SEK 170 reduced; limited wheelchair accessibility

RIDDARHOLMSKYRKAN (RIDDARHOLM CHURCH)

Kungliga slottet; 0 840 26 100; kungligaslotten.se; open daily Jul-Sept 10am-5pm, Oct-Nov 10am-4pm

Riddarholm Church is Stockholm's oldest preserved building, founded in 1270 as a Franciscan monastery. The first book ever printed in Sweden came off the press right here in 1483. The church also served as a burial site for Swedish royalty until 1950, meaning several Swedish monarchs rest here in extravagant sarcophagi. Today, deceased monarchs go to the **Royal Cemetery** instead, but the church remains a commemorative site within the Royal Court's jurisdiction. It's spectacular from the outside alone, but inside there's much more to explore. Remarkably elaborate burial monuments fill tombs within the church, including those of medieval kings and more than a handful of Gustavs. On the inner walls, Seraphim shields honor late knights from the **Royal Order of the Seraphim,** Sweden's highest order of chivalry. Summer concerts (included with entry) feature Gregorian and classical music.

i Admission SEK 50, SEK 25 reduced, disabled free; wheelchair accessible through separate entrance

STOCKHOLMS STADSHUS (STOCKHOLM CITY HALL)

Hantverkargatan 1; 08 508 29 000; stockholm.se; open daily 8:30am-4pm; access by guided tour only

In Stockholm City Hall, you can walk the same steps as Nobel Prize-winning guests of honor and see where representatives gather for political debate. Because it's an active place of governance, the City Hall only admits visitors on guided tours (unless you're there to get married in a three-minute civil wedding ceremony, which anyone can do). These 45-minute tours grant you exclusive access to the famous **Blue Hall,** where the **Nobel Prize Banquet** proceedings take place, as well as the golden mosaic ballroom where celebrations and dancing follow. You'll also go through the historic **Stockholm City Council** meeting room, though if that's not enough time for you to take it all in, meetings are open for public attendance and streamed online for free.

i Apr-Oct admission SEK 120, SEK 100 reduced; Nov-Mar admission SEK 90, SEK 70 reduced; tower closed Nov-Mar; daily English tours Jun 7-Aug 26 every half hour 9am-4pm, Sept-May noon and 2pm; wheelchair accessible

LANDMARKS

MONTELIUSVÄGEN

Monteliusvägen; visitstockholm.com; open daily 24hr

To get the best views of Stockholm for free, head up to Monteliusvägen and take a short walk along the scenic cliffside path. The flat and easily walkable trail follows the Northern shore of **Södermalm,** with gorgeous views over the water from high up on a cliff. From here, the view includes most historic buildings in Stockholm, for a dramatic panorama rich with cultural significance. Parks and benches line the other side of the path, so you can easily stop to smell the roses or sit down and take in the view. It's a great spot to visit any time of day, but sunsets over the skyline look especially fantastic.

i Free; limited wheelchair accessibility

STOCKHOLM PALACE

107 70 Stockholm; 08 402 61 30; kungahuset.se; open daily 9am-5pm

Stockholm Palace is your one-stop shop for nearly all things Swedish royalty in the heart of the city. For free, wander the palace's inner courtyard and enter the dazzling **Royal Chapel,** complete with gold and marble decor. Within the palace, several museums and exhibits offer a more up-close look at the monarchs. In the **Royal Apartments,** browse through lavish state rooms, banquet halls, galleries, ballrooms, and guest apartments. **Gustav III's Museum of Antiquities** holds a stone collection of magnificent sculptures, and the **Treasury** holds regalia like crowns and swords of state. In the **Royal Armoury,** memorabilia like weapons and clothing are preserved from important moments in history. Every day, the ceremonial changing of the guard is open for the public to watch. **The Royal Swedish Army Band** sometimes accompanies the ceremony with ABBA hits, though unfortunately, the guards don't have a special dance routine for that.

i Free admission to the inner courtyard and Royal Chapel; combination access tickets SEK 180, SEK 90 reduced; limited wheelchair accessibility

RIKSDAGSHUSET (PARLIAMENT HOUSE)

Riksgatan 1; 08 786 40 00; riksdagen.se; Jun 24-Aug 16 M-F noon, 1pm, 2pm, and 3pm, Sept-June Sa-Su 1:30pm

The Swedish Parliament, Riksdagshuset, is where legislators call the shots. The **Riksdag** (Parliament) comprises 349 proportionally elected representatives, and is the supreme decision-making body of all of Sweden. Inside, they're usually doing important stuff, like, you know, governing and all that, so tourists only enter through guided tours or public hearings in Swedish. You must show up early for a security check, as each tour is limited to 28 people; you'll feel really important if you do make the cut, but try not to piss off the armed security guard following your tour group around. Inside, peep a look at the architecturally distinctive chambers and committee meeting rooms in both the new and old parts of the building. Tours are limited to weekends outside of the summer holiday season, but in the spirit of transparency, the Parliament opens all debates and votes to public attendance for free.

i Free; open only for guided tours and public hearings; wheelchair accessible

MUSEUMS

FOTOGRAFISKA (PHOTOGRAPHY MUSEUM)

Stadsgårdshamnen 22; 08 509 00 500; fotografiska.com; open Su-W 9am-11pm, Th-Sa 9am-1am

If you thought you had any photography talent, you'll think again after a visit here. The museum holds astonishing photo exhibits that makes your travel pictures look totally amateur—but hey, it's cute that you've tried. Exhibits rotate every few months and the museum often hosts artists of current exhibitions to present to visitors about their work. Content tends to be relevant and fresh, often pertaining to current events or timely political issues. From bone-chilling images of wartime suffering to lighthearted scenes of everyday life, the themes and styles cover a great deal of ground. The museum offers various levels of photography courses, so that you too can aspire toward the caliber of its works. The trendy café-bar upstairs offers beautiful views of the city skyline, and attracts local artists and hipster crowds with its live music performances during weekend evenings.

i Admission SEK 165, SEK 135 reduced, children under 12 free; wheelchair accessible

SJÖHISTORISKA (MARITIME MUSEUM)

Djurgårdsbrunnsvägen 24; 08 519 54 900; sjohistoriska.se; open Tu-Su 10am-5pm

The Maritime Museum carries a comprehensive collection of historic nautical paraphernalia, including navigation instruments, weapons, figureheads, art work, and intricate models of all types of vessels. Magnificently preserved relics from **King Gustav III's** headquarters ship Amphion decorate the museum's inner entrance, and it only gets better from there. Marvel at the ingenuity of the engineering behind each vessel's creation and admire artifacts from iconic voyagers, submarines, and wartime naval fleets. Stories of both the ships and their seafaring travelers come to life in the museum's various exhibits where you can see and read about what life was like on board for captains, passengers, and mercenaries alike. Special exhibits on sea rescue and shipping trade round out the museum's offerings.

i Free; wheelchair accessible

VASA MUSEUM

Galärvarvsvägen 14, 115 21 Stockholm; 08 519 548 00; vasamuseet.se; open daily 8:30am-6pm

Though it's usually one of the most tourist-crowded places in all of Stockholm, the Vasa Museum is the one thing everyone who visits must see. "Have you seen the Vasa?" locals ask you instantaneously open learning that you're a visitor, and who are you to let them down? Once you go inside,

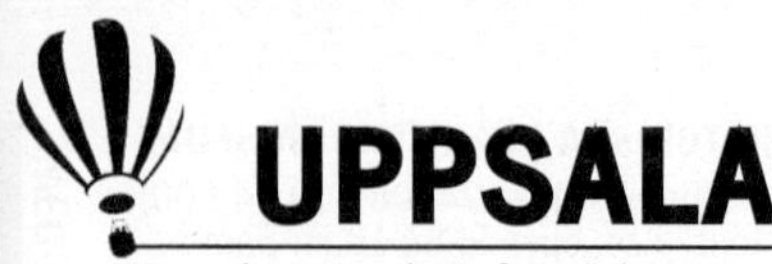

UPPSALA

Uppsala is Sweden's fourth largest city, but it doesn't get nearly as much tourist attention as its history suggests that it deserves. Among its notable historical sites, Uppsala Cathedral is the ecclesiastical center of all of Sweden and Scandinavia's largest church. Uppsala University, the oldest center of higher education in all of northern Europe, is the driving force of the city. Its palpable energy courses through the many university-run museums and gardens, and you may be surprised to learn that several foundational scientific discoveries were made here. Uppsala, the original college town (the university was founded in 1477), offers many student-friendly prices and discounts in most places throughout the city, and with 40,000 students enrolled in the university, lots of young people can be found roaming the streets. The atmosphere is relaxed compared to larger and busier cities and with significantly fewer tourists, it's a nice quiet break from the bustling streets of Stockholm.

Uppsala is a compact city. The **Centrum district** contains **Uppsala Central Station,** shopping and restaurants, and the **Linnaeus Museum** and gardens. Just west of Centrum, across the **Fyris River,** the district **Fjärdingen** is home to **Uppsala Cathedral, Gustavianum, Uppsala Castle,** the **Botanical Garden,** and **Uppsala University.**

GETTING THERE

Uppsala is an easy 45min. direct train ride from Stockholm Central. Trains between Stockholm and Uppsala run frequently throughout the day and are operated mostly by SJ. Purchase round-trip tickets online (sj.com) or at Stockholm C and Uppsala Central Station (Uppsala C) for around SEK 100 (ticket prices vary depending on the time of day).

GETTING AROUND

Given its compact layout, Uppsala is very easily walkable. A bus system called Stadstrafiken connects major points around the city center; buy tickets at machines near major bus stops for SEK 35.

Don't miss...

GUSTAVIANUM

Akademigatan 3; 018 471 75 71; gustavianum.uu.se; open Tu-Su 10am-4pm

Inside Gustavianum—the museum of Uppsala University—explore relics from the University's past, from art work, books, maps, and scripts to old scientific instruments like galvanometers, spectrometers and telescopes that constituted cutting-edge advances back in their day. Some of science's great innovators and world-shakers studied at Uppsala University and developed many of the methods, instruments, and formulas we use in science today. The museum also houses a Mediterranean and Nile Valley exhibit with hieroglyphic engravings, mummy cases, pots, and other artifacts from the Nubian period in Egypt. A viking age exhibit showcases relics that archaeologists found in a viking boat grave, including horse remains, household items, dog collars and weapons—you know, the essentials for the afterlife.

i Admission SEK 50, SEK 40 reduced, under 19 free; guided tours in English included with entry 1pm daily; wheelchair accessible

Check out...

UPPSALA CATHEDRAL

Domkyrkoplan; 018-430 35 00; uppsaladomkyrka.se; open daily 8am-6pm, closed for major services

Uppsala Cathedral isn't a regular church; it's a cool church. And by cool, we mean it's the world's largest Evangelical Lutheran Church, with 20 side chapels and ornate burial monuments for big-shot kings like Gustav Vasa. As the seat of the legendary Archbishop of Uppsala, it's also the most important church in all of Sweden. If you don't believe us, just look at its soaring Baroque towers and extravagant Neo-Gothic interior. Intricate fresco paintings and stained-glass windows surround gold-plated shrines, precious treasury items, enormous organ pipes, and a dazzling silver and crystal crucifix at the high altar. The church suffered serious damage from a fire in 1702 and has been reinvented through multiple restorations and extensions since its consecration in 1435. You can even take a guided tour around this bad boy, it's so damn big and full of history—if you want to learn more about the church's architectural timeline and cultural significance, then it's definitely worth your time.

i Free; wheelchair accessible

Swing by...

BOTANISKA TRÄDGÅRDEN (BOTANICAL GARDEN)

Villavägen 6-8; 018 471 28 38; botan.uu.se; open daily May-Sept 7am-9pm, Oct-Apr 7am-7pm

The Botanical Garden is just one of Uppsala University's three major gardens, the other two being the Linnaeus Garden and Linnaeus' Hammarby (a museum area with a park, garden, and other buildings. The Linnaeus Garden is Sweden's oldest botanical garden, and cares exclusively for plants that the famous botanist Carl Linnaeus grew himself. Here, learn about Linnaeus's sexual system (for plant classification, don't be cheeky) and floral clock for plant development. At the overall garden site, exhibits include vibrant flowers, medicinal wonder-plants, a tropical greenhouse with rainforest species, and an orangery with figs, oranges, olive trees, Linnaean laurel trees and more. In the summer, Café Victoria serves coffee, ice cream, and other goodies on site.

i Free, tropical greenhouse entry SEK 50; limited wheelchair accessibility

Grab a bite at...

BASTARD BURGERS ($$)

Dragarbrunnsgatan 43A; 092 06 99 99; bastardburgers.se; open M-Th 11am-8pm, F 11am-9pm, Sa noon-9pm, Su noon-7pm

Bastard Burger takes your classic student fast-food hangout to a whole new level, with punk rock themed decorations and inventive twists on greasy grill favorites. Bite into a juicy burger (meat or vegan) dressed up in flavorful combinations like 'The Los Angeles' with caramelized onions, jalapeño, and honey dressing, or 'The Umami-Truffled London' with housemade truffle mayo, pickled red onion, pepper jack cheese, and cheddar. For every burger combo and side, there's a mouthwatering vegan version on their climate-friendly menu, so you can get all of the meat-sweats and drool-worthy flavor for a much smaller carbon footprint. To go with your burger, try one of their tasty vegan shakes, "Animal-Style" fries with smoked tofu and bastard dressing, or a "Little Bastard" beer to wash it all down.

i Burgers from SEK 109; gluten-free, vegan, and vegetarian options available; wheelchair accessible you'll see what all the hype is about. A seventeenth-century warship, Vasa, sank on its maiden voyage just outside Stockholm harbor in 1628, and it wasn't until 333 years later that a monumental feat of engineering succeeded in removing it from the site of the wreck. Teams of engineers, chemists, and archaeologists managed to preserve and reconstruct nearly the entirety of the ship, so that it now commands center stage in the world-famous museum. Aside from its inability to float, the Vasa was a brilliant vessel—think elaborate warships from *Pirates of the Carribbean,* but real. No less impressive than the vessel itself, the efforts by which historians lifted and restored it are remarkable stories of ingenuity. The museum allows you to read and watch videos about this process, as well as the history of the ship and those aboard.

i Admission SEK 150; free audio guide download available; wheelchair accessible

OUTDOORS

HELLASGÅRDEN

Hellasgarden, Nacka; 08 716 39 61; hellasgarden.se; open M-F 10am-9pm (sauna hot 10:30am-8:30pm), Sa-Su 10am-6pm (sauna hot until 5pm)

Hellasgården is your natural haven just outside Stockholm, where you can walk beautiful nature trails, swim in a pristine lake, warm up in an indoor sauna before and after your swim, and pick berries and mushrooms in the surrounding forest. There's also a raw vegan health food café, an outdoor gym, and yoga, because if you're coming all the way out here to enjoy time in nature, you're probably the type of person who would be into those things. The setting feels perfect for a summer day outdoors, where you can go paddle boarding or kayaking on the water. It's easily reachable from the city easily on public transport, or with a lovely bike ride through the surrounding nature reserve.

i Admission SEK 70, towel rental SEK 35, locker rental SEK 20; indoor facilities wheelchair accessible

HAGAPARKEN

Hagaparken; 08 402 60 00; visithaga.se; open daily 24hr, butterfly house open 10am-5pm

Hagaparken is not your average city park; it's part of the **Royal National City Park,** where the **Crown Princess of Sweden** and **Prince Daniel, Duke of Västergötland,** live in their summer palace. Despite its royal status, the entire park is open for the public to enjoy. You could spend a full day exploring expansive trail networks, boating docks, historic buildings, greenhouses, gardens, and even royal burial grounds within the enormous park. There's ample open grassy space for picnics, pick-up spikeball games, or relaxing with friends, as well as public bathing areas for a refreshing summer swim. Inside the **Värdshuset Koppartälten** (copper tent), you can enjoy fresh, locally-sourced meals and snacks. A tropical rainforest inside the **Butterfly House** keeps over 1,000 butterflies, and a coral reef inside **Haga Ocean Aquarium** keeps multiple species of shark. Various cultural landmarks, like a **Turkish Kiosk** and **Chinese Pavilion,** add architectural variety and interesting history to the park's long list of attractions.

i Free; limited wheelchair accessibility (uneven surface within Butterfly House and Haga Ocean aquarium houses)

STOCKHOLM ADVENTURES

Kungsbro strand 2; 08 33 60 01; stockholmadventures.com; open daily 9am-6pm, dock hours vary; closed for midsommar and Christmas

With the abrupt disappearance of Stockholm's city bikeshare system, you may flounder for a quick way to get around. Stockholm Adventures has got your back, with bicycle, kayak, and other rental options for reasonable prices. Stockholm Adventures rents out equipment you can use to explore on your own, and they also have all kinds of guided tours for adventurous travelers to try out. Choose from wildlife safaris through the forests around Stockholm, paddle boarding or sailing in the archipelago, and tours that you can do with a guide or by yourself. In the winter, they rent out snowshoes and ice skates, so no matter the weather or time of year, there's always a fun way to explore.

i Bicycle rental SEK 190/3hrs; kayak rental SEK 250/2hrs; no wheelchair accessibility; guided and self-guided tour prices vary

FOOD

GREASY SPOON ($$)

Tjärhovsgatan 19; greasyspoon.se; open M-F 8am-4pm, Sa-Su 9am-4pm

This hole-in-the-wall brunch spot in **Sodermalm** is anything but greasy, though it is refreshingly unpretentious and cozy as can be. The menu features all your favorite English breakfast classics, with some innovative extras thrown into the mix. Wash down your fluffy-as-ever bacon scotch pancakes with a boozy brunch classic like the espresso martini; or, go the "my body is a temple" route with a healthy chia pudding dish and cleansing beetroot latte. Weekday breakfast deals from 8am-11am cut menu prices down for early birds, but with food so good, it's worth a visit any time of the week. Go all in for a filling brunch of decadent french toasts and smoked salmon rosti or enjoy a lighter snack like avocado toast. From bottomless coffee to bloody marys to Fucking Hell lager, there's a drink to match any mood and any meal.

i Espresso SEK 30, light dishes from SEK 49, meals from SEK 115; vegetarian, vegan, and gluten-free options available; limited wheelchair accessibility

HERMANS

Fjällgatan 23B; 08 643 94 80; open daily 11am-10pm

At Hermans, the views over **Stockholm Harbor** look almost as good as the all-you-can-eat hot food and salad bar buffet. This progressive eatery in **Södermalm** blasts the motto "give peas a chance," and puts their cooking where their mouth is with healthy local and organic dishes. It offers all the variety and flavor of any high-quality buffet, but it's so healthy you can enjoy it without guilt or sluggishness from stuffing your face. The spread ranges from innovative salads to hearty pastas, tasty vegetable dishes to flavorful hummus varieties, and more types of legumes than you knew existed. The buffet also includes homemade sauces and dressings, home-baked artisan breads, coffee, and a wide selection of tea. The seating offers a fabulous viewpoint over Stockholm's harbor and skyline, which you can enjoy on a flowery outdoor patio on a sunny day, or indoors from cozy window seating.

i Lunch buffet SEK 140 11am-3pm; dinner buffet SEK 220, SEK 200 reduced 3pm-9pm; weekend buffet SEK 265, SEK 200 reduced, 11am-9pm; desserts from SEK 28; gluten-free, vegan, and vegetarian options available;

KALF & HANSEN ($)

Mariatorget 2, 118 49 Stockholm; 08 551 531 51; kalfochhansen.se; open M-F 11am-9pm, Sa 11am-8pm, Su 11am-5pm

For delicious authentic Nordic fare without typical Nordic prices, head to Kalf & Hansen's contemporary fast-food café in **Södermalm.** The 100 percent organic menu features hearty wraps, sandwiches, salads, and hot dishes made from local and fair-trade ingredients; against all odds, the high-quality food is somehow cheaper than almost anywhere else in the city. They put a modern twist on traditional Nordic classics, offering tasty vegan substitutions for any meaty dish (don't worry carnivores, you can still fill your plate with ethically-raised meat). The restaurant itself is just as progressive as its environmentally-conscious menu, with 100 percent renewable electricity and organic or repurposed materials used in all of its decor. Smoothies, fresh juices, desserts, and beers also come at refreshingly low prices, making Kalf & Hansen the perfect place for a guilt-free indulgence in the flavors of Scandinavia.

i Coffee SEK 20, beer SEK 35, hot meals from SEK 65; gluten-free, vegan, and vegetarian options available; limited wheelchair accessibility

JOHAN & NYSTRÖM ($$)

Swedenborgsgatan 7; 08 530 224 40; johanochnystrom.se; open M-F 7am-9pm, Sa-Su 8am-9pm

Any café in **Södermalm** likely fits the bill for hipster haven, but at Johan & Nyström even the most artsy bohemians would feel mainstream. Maybe it's the kombucha and raw vegan desserts, or maybe it's the hand-selected organic direct trade coffee whose tasting notes came from subtle changes in soil alkalinity at high-altitude cultivation conditions in Peru. Whatever it is, they're on the cutting edge of contemporary café craftsmanship, and it's definitely working. Even the seating areas have a stylish aesthetic, with artwork and plants covering teal-hued walls and decorative pillows lining cozy nooks. If you're dying to learn how to recreate that heavenly capp-oat-ccino (cappuccino with oat milk, because you know, eco-friendly hippie vegan stuff), you can take a course on barista basics and become a coffee connoisseur yourself.

i Espresso SEK 32; gluten-free, vegan, and vegetarian options available; wheelchair accessible locations in Odengatan and Norrlandsgatan

NIGHTLIFE

BREWDOG

Ringvägen 149B; 08 30 72 17; brewdog.com; open M 4pm-11pm, Tu-Th 4pm-midnight, F-Sa 2pm-1am, Su 2pm-11pm,

Another hipster craft beer bar, but this one's all about dogs. In a place that revolves around man's best friend (whether you're thinking of dogs or beers, you're right), it only makes sense that the atmosphere feels incredibly friendly. Whether you're here with your pup, on your own, or with friends, you'll likely meet some cool people here. Brewdog's inventive line of microbrews showcases experimental flavors and blends, like chocolate orange stouts, tangerine IPAs, and goose with pink himalayan salt and coriander. Treat your pooch to an all-beef patty and alcohol-free beer for doggy date night, or otherwise share tasty snacks like fried cauliflower or chicken wings with friends. The unpretentious venue draws young and fun-loving crowds for board games, good times, and quality beer.

i Beers from SEK 69; vegan and vegetarian options available; limited wheelchair accessibility (ramps to enter building, but steps in restrooms)

AIFUR

Västerlånggatan 68b; 08 20 10 55; aifur.se; open Su-Th 5pm-11pm, F-Sa 5pm-midnight

Aifur Krog & Bar transports its guests completely back to the Viking Age with rugged decorations, viking-age drinks, and a rustic candlelit interior. From the bar, you can watch as viking-dressed staff welcome each guest with a cowhorn, a bellowing announcement, and boisterous applause from the entire restaurant. Live music most nights features a lute or recorder, and singing from pantaloon-clad musicians. The drink menu reflects Stockholm's alcoholic past, with full pages of different beers, wines, and meads. Drinks come in creatively-shaped glasses and chalaces and are a fairly generous size for their price. If you want to eat in the restaurant, make a reservation, although anyone is welcome at the bar. It may be a bit of a tourist gimmick, but it's actually a really fun experience. And hey, the drinks come pretty cheap for Stockholm, so we're definitely not complaining.

i Drinks from SEK 58; limited wheelchair accessibility (no access in restaurant-area or restroom, bar area accessible)

NOMAD

Upplandsgatan 2; 08 20 20 42; nomad.bar; open Su-Th 5pm-11pm, F-Sa 5pm-1am

Nomad serves traditional Swedish delicacies by day, and lights up the party in its lively outdoor courtyard by night. Young people flock here on a nightly basis for the cheap drinks, a hip and energetic atmosphere, and frequent live music performances. You never really know what to expect on any given day, as performances range from folk to EDM, and clientele from traveling millennials to hardcore older locals. On weeknights, it's a great spot to lounge on comfortable outdoor couches with a drink, and on weekends the courtyard turns into an uproarious party space where anything goes. And, its location right next to a popular hostel makes it a great spot to meet other young travelers.

i Drinks from SEK 30; limited wheelchair accessibility

SWEDEN ESSENTIALS

VISAS

Sweden is a member of the European Union and is part of the Schengen Area, so U.S. citizens can stay in Sweden for up to 90 days without a visa.

MONEY

Sweden's currency is the Swedish krona, officially abbreviated SEK and locally used interchangeably with kr.

Cash: Most establishments in Sweden are transitioning to be entirely cash-free, and in many cases only cards are accepted. However, you can still withdraw cash at ATMs or exchange currency at banks or exchanges.

Tipping: Tipping in Sweden is neither expected nor required; a gratuity is often included in the service charge at restaurants. If there is no service included, or if you wish to show thanks for excellent service, feel free to tip 5-10% or round your bill to the nearest SEK 10.

Taxes: Sweden's value-added tax (VAT) is 25%, and is included in all posted prices. Purchases from some stores in Sweden are eligible for a VAT refund upon departure, provided you save the receipts and obtain required documentation at the time of purchase.

SAFETY AND HEALTH

BGLTQ+ Travel: Like the rest of Scandinavia, Sweden is very progressive when it comes to BGLTQ+ rights. Hostels, restaurants, and nightlife establishments are very friendly towards the BGLTQ+ community, and many Swedish cities have dedicated BGLTQ+ nightlife venues.

Drugs and Alcohol: For beverages under 2.25% ABV, there is no purchasing age minimum, however some stores set their own age requirements. Alcohol with ABV above 2.25% is strictly regulated, and can only be purchased in bars, restaurants, and designated government stores called systembolaget. The purchasing age is 20, and opening hours for Systembolaget tend to be limited to weekdays until about 6pm. At bars and restaurants, alcohol consumption must stay within the premises.

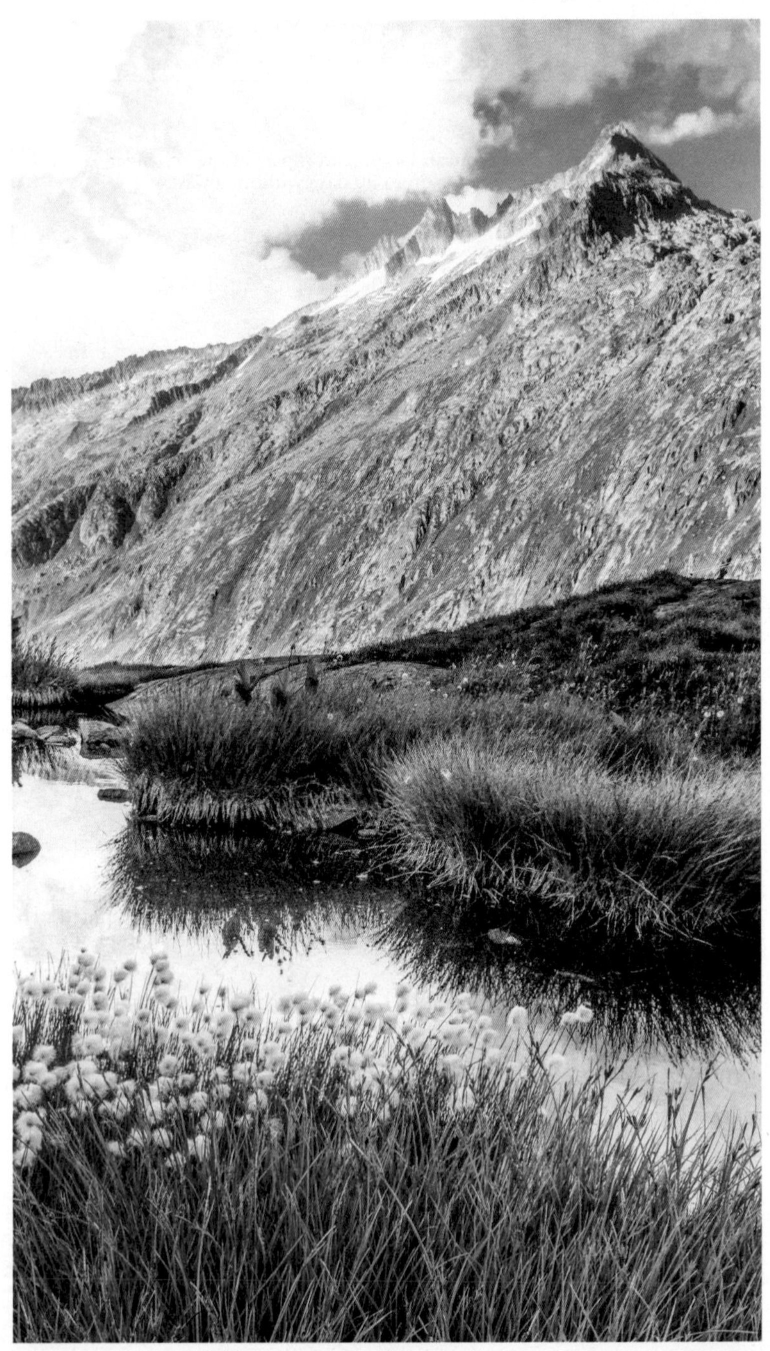

SWITZERLAND

Switzerland feels too good to be true. As a landlocked island nestled in between the perennial world powers of France, Italy, and Germany, it seems a miracle that the country has escaped conquest and pillage for hundreds of years. With some exploration, questions begin to arise. Where is the dirt? Where is the crime? How did you fit such immense mountains in such a small country? Why is everyone standing for this harboring of foreign tax-evasion? Against all odds, the society seems to march along with the efficiency of a Swiss watch. People speaking German, French, Italian, and Romansch all coexist merrily, shepherds thrive amongst peaks that look sharp enough to spear their sheep, and rivers that flow through crowded cities are sparkling clean.

After spending some time in Switzerland, you may find that some of this perfect image is too good to be true. As it turns out, the nation of alpine hospitality and the Red Cross have a troublesome history of nativism. The omnipresent wealth and miraculous neutrality has been maintained through centuries of harboring ill-begotten wealth. Those rosy-cheeked alpine shepherds and their herds are mostly munching on crisp agricultural subsidies. And Lord is it expensive.

Yet, you may realize as well, that for a lowly backpacker in Switzerland, that carefully constructed image of Swiss perfection holds up pretty well for a few weeks. Those cities of ill-begotten wealth are so friendly. We could frolic in those squeaky clean rivers and lakes all year long. And, the Alps. Sweet glory, the Alps! Rugged peaks in the center of Europe, ancient farmhouses next to alternative nightlife, glacier traverses with a cheese stand on each end! These mountains are our paradise. Is it too good to be true? A little. But the image sure is fun.

GENEVA

Coverage by **Will Rhatigan**

Strolling along the Rhone, past Geneva's row of bank headquarters and cocktail lounges that require either an arm or leg for entry, you'd think this city could only be fun for the "poor-people-should-just work-harder" crowd. But if your hardest efforts have thus far failed to bring you gold-plated wine glasses, don't reach for the scalpel just yet. Beyond its glittering financial institutions and appointment-only storefronts selling watches that cost more than your house, Geneva's natural beauty and rich history offer amazement and exploration even for those of us without a limb to spare.

Perched on the tip of Lac Léman (Lake Geneva), where the long alpine lake turns into the Rhone and begins its journey down to the Mediterranean Sea, Geneva is where many other movements have started as well and remains the point of origin for major international decisions. Transformed into a near-Protestant theocracy by Jean Calvin in the 16th Century, Geneva led the religious movement that birthed many moral justifications for modern capitalism. Yet, as the home of many international humanitarian organizations, the city is at the heart of both most major world problems and their potential solutions at once. But if you're not worried about any of that hullabaloo, Lac Léman must be one of the most beautiful stretches of water in the world. The surrounding mountains promise perhaps the best hiking from an urban area anywhere, and a thriving cultural scene turns out to hold a lot more than just bank deals and spreadsheets.

ORIENTATION

Despite its enormous international influence, Geneva is a shockingly small place, with rolling vineyards and cow pasture only two miles from its city center. The city sits at the westernmost tip of Switzerland, at the point where **Lac Léman** flows into the long **Rhone River,** with suburbs extending on all sides into neighboring France. The Rhone splits the neighborhoods into **Rive Droite**, the Northern side, and **Rive Gauche**, the Southern side. In the Rive Droite you'll find **Gare Cornavin** (the main train station), the headquarters of most of the international organizations, and the airport. The lakeside **Paquis District** is filled with upscale hotels and international restaurants, while **Les Grottes** sits behind the station and holds some of the hipper restaurants and younger crowds of the city. **Old Town,** with the picturesque **Place du Bourg-de-Four** at its center, perches on a steep hill on the Rive Gauche, while the lakeside strip on this side of the river boasts the gorgeous **Jardin d'Anglais** and a long strip of parks culminating next to the **Jet d'Eau.** The best hiking nearby lies across the border with France to the South (only 3 miles away!), while the hometown lake can provide the rest of the outdoor activity you'll need plus a few weeks extra.

ESSENTIALS

GETTING THERE

Geneva holds the second largest international airport in Switzerland after Zurich. The airport is located 4km from the city center and is easily accessible via public transportation. Upon arrival at the airport, you can pick up a free transit pass from a machine at baggage claim that is valid for 80 minutes within the greater Geneva area. Almost all international trains come into Gare Cornavin (Cornavin Station), which also serves as the central point at which all local train and bus lines converge. From both the airport and Gare Cornavin, the train and bus lines can carry you almost anywhere within the greater Geneva area.

GETTING AROUND

Geneva is a small city that can be easily crossed on foot or by bike. Rent a bike from the Genève Roule shops located all around the city for 4 hours of free riding with a 20CHF deposit. Geneva has also has an efficient public transportation system that is particularly useful if you want to reach the nearby suburbs and rural areas. A mixture of buses and on-road trams reach most points in the city, the schedules of which can be found by downloading the Transports Publics Genevois App (TPG). If staying in a hotel, hostel, or campsite, you can pick up a free Geneva Transport Card at the reception desk that will be valid for the length of your stay. If not, tickets are available for purchase at automated machines located at every stop. A one hour-use ticket cost 3CHF.

PRACTICAL INFORMATION

Tourist Offices: Geneva Tourist Information Office (18 Rue du Mont-Blanc; 022 909 70 00; open M-W 9am-6pm, Th 10am-6pm, F-S 9am-6pm, Su 10am-4pm).

Banks/ATMs/Currency Exchange: Famous for finance, Geneva has banks all over the city. The most common ATMS are run by La Poste Banque. A convenient one: 18 Rue du Mont-Blanc (right next to the tourist office).

Post Offices: Post offices are located all around the city, but again the most convenient is next to the tourist offices (18 Rue du Mont-Blanc; 0848 888 888; open M-F 7:30am-6pm, Sa 9am-4pm).

Public Restrooms: Geneva has public restrooms sparsely scattered around the city, most of which are much cleaner than those in neighboring France. Otherwise, most cafés won't be too troublesome about letting you use theirs.

Internet: The city of Geneva boasts more than 78 spots with free public wifi. You can get a map with the tourist information office with all the locations.

BGLTQ+ Resources: The main BLGTQ+ helpline in Switzerland is 0800 133 133.

EMERGENCY INFORMATION

Emergency Number: General: 112; Police: 117; fire department: 144; Swiss helicopter rescue service: 1414.

Police: Cantonal Police Station Paquis (6 Rue de Berne; 022 427 81 11).

US Embassy: Consular Agency in Geneva (7 Rue Versonnex; 22 840 51 60; ch.usembassy.gov/embassy/locations-in-switzerland/consular-agency-geneva/; open M 8:30am-11am, 1:30pm-4:30 pm, Wednesday 1:30am-11am, 1:30pm-4:30pm; Th 10am-1pm, services by appointment only).

Rape Crisis Center: Switzerland Violsecours (3 Pl. des Charmilles; 022 345 20 20; www.rcne.com/contact/countries/switzerland).

Hospitals:

- Geneva University Hospital (4 Rue Gabrielle-Perret-Gentille; 022 372 33 11; open daily 24hr).

Pharmacies:

- Pharmacie Amavita Gare Cornavin (Gare Cornavin; 058 878 10 00; open M-Sa 7am-11pm, Su 9am-11pm).
- Pharmacie Populaire Cité (3 Rue de la Confédération; 022 318 69 01; open M-F 8am-7pm, Sa 9am-6pm).

SIGHTS

CULTURE

MARCHÉ DES GROTTES

Place des Grottes, open Th 2pm-8:30pm

Promenading along the Rhone with Geneva's suit-clad businessmen and lanyard-sporting international diplomats, it might appear as if everyone in this city is suspended in perfect propriety by a plank taped to their spines. Walk up the hill of **Les Grottes** on a Thursday afternoon, however, and find a scene as laid back and relaxed as your favorite Portland hippy commune. Food trucks and roadside stands sell local meat, wine, and cheese while young locals crowd the square and set down picnic blankets on the concrete to enjoy wooden platters of charcuterie. It's hard to wade through the tightly packed picnics to actually get a taste of the food, but whether or not you make it, you'll discover that Geneva has more energetic markets than those that deal in capital and commodities.

i Stand prices vary; arrive early to secure picnic space; wheelchair accessible

PLACE DU BOURG-DE-FOUR

Place du Bourg-de-Four; open daily 24hr

Once home to a Roman forum and the number one cattle trading scene in Geneva, the Place du Bourg-de-Four is now a lively plaza full of tables in the center of **Old Town.** Once you make it up the steep cobblestone streets below the hilltop square, revitalize yourself for the rest of the day by enjoying an espresso or wind down with a glass of wine on the wide patio of one of the various cafés and relax in the shadows cast by looming eighteenth-century buildings.

i Restaurant prices vary; limited wheelchair accessibility

SHEDRUB CHOEKHOR LING MONASTÈRE ET CENTRE BOUDDHISTES (BUDDHIST MONASTERY)

7660 Route des 3 Lacs, Monnetier-Mornex, France; 045 094 28 52; sanghasaleve.wixsite.com; open W-Su 10am-noon, 2pm-6pm

The journey to this tranquil monastery is a process that has been repeated since time immemorial. You start on the valley floor, ignorant and unwise. Casting your eyes to the heavens, a bright light pierces your vision. Teetering on the edge of a mountain far above is a shrine, a temple. You know that your ignorance can be banished at this sanctuary. For many long years you climb the mountain, straining all your muscles against the punishing rock. Finally, you reach the top, and find a peaceful shrine overlooking the valley below, and a small gift shop. Searching for answers, you look down to whence you came, and realize the wisdom was in you along. Perched on top of **Le Salève** mountain, this Buddhist temple, inaugurated by the Dalaï Lama himself, is a haven of peace and natural beauty.

i Free; no wheelchair accessibility

LANDMARKS

CATHÉDRALE ST. PIERRE

24 Place du Bourg-de-Four; 022 311 75 75; www.cathedrale-geneve.ch; open June 1-Sept 30 M-F 9:30am-6:30pm, Sa 9:30am-5pm, Su noon-6:30pm; Oct 1-May 31 M-Sa 10am-5:30pm, Su noon-5:30pm

The site of **Jean Calvin's** revolutionary sermons, St. Pierre's Cathedral—a **European Heritage Sight**—sits in the heart of Geneva's old city. The building's ornate façades contrast sharply with its simple Protestant interior, a physical testament to the city's diverse and often contradictory cultural composition. Two towers jut from the roof of the church: the south-facing one hold five bells, while the northern one boasts a stunning panoramic view of the city and of the **Jet d'Eau** in the distance.

i Church admission free; entrance to tower 5 CHF; limited wheelchair accessibility.

JET D'EAU (GENEVA WATER FOUNTAIN)

Quai Gustave-Ador; open daily Nov 16-Mar 5 10am-4pm; Mar 6-April 30 M-Th 10am-sunset, F-Su 10am-10:30pm; daily May 1-Sept 10 9am-11:15pm; Sept 11-Oct 29 M-Th 10am-sunset, F-Su 10am-10:30pm

The Jet d'Eau is a really large water fountain. That might not sound that exciting, but in a city with no major skyscrapers, a jet of water shooting one-hundred and forty meters into the air is pretty awe-inspiring. Originally built to control the excess pressure from a hydroelectric plant, the jet became so popular with the citizens of Geneva that they institutionalized it as a symbol of the city's progress. A long dock reaches out to the fountain itself that you can walk on if you're willing to take the risk of a sudden change in wind soaking you with water falling one-hundred forty meters from the sky. The Empire State's great really, but we'll take this skyscraper over any one made of steel.

i Free

MUSEUMS

MUSÉE INTERNATIONAL DE LA CROIX-ROUGE ET DU CROISSANT-ROUGE (INTERNATIONAL MUSEUM OF THE RED CROSS AND RED CRESCENT)

17 Avenue de la Paix; 022 748 95 11; www.redcrossmuseum.ch; open daily 10am to 6pm Apr-Oct, 10am-5pm Nov to Mar

Sitting just below the headquarters of the world's most prominent humanitarian group, the Museum of the Red Cross and the Red Crescent presents the organization's work in a series of expertly-crafted, harrowing exhibits that force us to confront the most pressing moral issues of our time. Divided into the group's three fields of work—defending human dignity, restoring family ties, and reducing natural risks—the museum places you face to face with the challenges of care providers and the suffering of those affected by wars and natural disasters. An automatically operated audio-guide accompanies you around the museum, confronting you with the voices of survivors as you look upon art constructed in concentration camps and wade through chains to see the complete records of World War I prisoners of war. This museum may emotionally harrow you, but you won't leave it without a greater appreciation of the human rights battles that must constantly be fought and a respect for those fighting them.

i Admission 15 CHF, reduced 7 CHF; wheelchair accessible

MUSÉUM D'HISTOIRE NATURELLE GENÈVE (GENEVA MUSEUM OF NATURAL HISTORY)

1 Route de Malagnou; 022 418 63 00; open Tu-Su 10am-5pm

Lions, tigers, and bears, oh my! The Geneva Museum of Natural History is the dream of every seven-year-old in the world who wants to be a zoologist when they grow up. Housing an enormous collection of taxidermied animals, from Kiwis to Armadillos to this mouse thing that has legs like a rabbit, the museum instills a deep sense of amazement in the marvelous range of creatures that exist in this world we live in. The exhibits don't neglect our role in the wacky diorama of wildlife either, dedicating a large archaeological exhibition to the development of the human species from Australopithecus to the present day. Clearly understanding your place in the family of life on earth relative to every other species, it's hard to leave without feeling a sense of immense gratitude that you weren't born a horned toad.

i Admission free; special exhibitions 6CHF; wheelchair accessible

OUTDOORS

LE SALÈVE

Route du Téléphérique, Étrembières, France; 33 4 50 39 86 86

Alright, let's be honest, you didn't come to Geneva for the banking. Framing every photo of the **Lac Léman** shoreline in alpine splendor, this massive ridge of cliffs is what separates Geneva from the hundreds of other drab lakeside metropolises (think Cleveland) and makes it maybe the most naturally gorgeous city in the world. On the top of the row of cliffs is a tranquil green meadow full of cows softly swinging their bells back and forth, from which you can see stunning views of the city, the lake, and the **French Alps.** The mountain is also a popular take-off spot for paragliders, who you can watch jumping off the cliffs and soaring through the air. Just three miles South of Geneva in neighboring France, the mountain is a moderate two hour hike to the top. Other options include biking up a road on the backside, or, if you're not feeling the outdoor part of the mountains, taking the **Téléphérique** (Cable Car) to an overlook.

i Téléphérique free with Transport Card

LE PETIT SALÈVE

Château d'Etrembières, 135 Chemin du Chalet, Etrembières, France

Craving some time in the mountains and want to escape the crowds of the city? With no road, and no cable car to the top, the slightly smaller Petit Salève has all the mountaintop beauty and gorgeous views of the **Salève** itself, but without the hundreds of people being dropped off on the summit every hour. Hike up a series of narrow trails, starting from a picturesque alpine farm at the **Château d'Etrembières.** Although the twists and turns can be a

bit confusing, follow this rule and you'll be at the summit in no time: go up.
i Free; 40 minutes by public transport outside of Geneva

FOOD

PIZZERIA DAGLI AMICI ($)

16 Rue Maunoir; 022 736 30 70; pizzeriadagliamici.ch; open M-Th 11am-2:30pm, 6pm-11pm, F 11am-2:30pm, 6pm-midnight, Sa 6pm-midnight, Su 6pm-11pm

When trying to find a place to eat at Geneva, it feels like every one of the stylish, lively restaurants with outdoor dining requires the sacrifice of at least a second-born child for entry. Somehow Dagli Amici bucked this trend. We don't know why anyone goes anywhere else. Offering a huge list of pizzas with ingredients like tuna, capers, and gruyère for only 10CHF, Dagli Amici might have the hottest deal in the city, period (we've been charged 12CHF for a single Kebab). But Dagli Amici isn't your crusty neighborhood pizza joint. The unbelievably delicious pizzas are served alongside an extensive beer and wine list, in an elegantly designed building with a beautiful outdoor veranda. Keep that second kid for now, folks.
i Pizzas from 10 CHF; take-out available

ANGOLETTA ($)

16 Place du Bourg-de-Four; 022 310 57 14; open daily 7am-midnight

Nestled in the heart of **Old Town** at **Place du Bourg-de-Four**, Angoletta is the ideal spot to relax and chat away a summer afternoon while you watch people lazily meander through the ancient square. With tables set up on a wide outdoor patio alongside several other cafés, Angoletta invites you to spend a few hours while you sip an espresso, down a beer, or just munch on any one of their wonderfully cheap (relatively) paninis and sandwiches.
i Paninis from 6.70 CHF, beers from 4.30 CHF, cocktails from 15 CHF

RED SEA SPÉCIALITÉES ÉRYTHRÉENNES (ERITREAN SPECIALITIES) ($$)

4 Rue de Montbrillant 022 740 44 66; open M-Sa 11am-11pm

You'll often see crowds of people in suits marching confidently through the streets of Geneva sporting name tag lanyards. Who are these people, you ask? Why are they always wearing name tags? They are international diplomats, we answer. Why they insist on wearing their name tags at all times, we do not know. Moral of the story: Geneva is an extremely international city. With that, luckily for you, comes food from every corner of the globe. At Red Sea, that corner is Eritrea, and we're so glad it's in Geneva. Served on top of injira, soft Eritrean crepes, the food is rich and flavorful, comprising a variety of stews and spicy vegetable medleys. On Tuesday, Wednesday, Friday, and Saturday nights, stop in for a sumptuous buffet that will leave your chest so puffed out that you'll be strutting down the street like one of Geneva's diplomats yourself.
i Main courses from 16 CHF, buffet from 21 CHF; vegetarian and vegan options available

PARFUMS DE BEYROUTH ($)

18 Rue de Berne; 022 731 66 58; open M-Th 11am-2am, F-Sa 11am-6am, Su 11am-2am

It's late. You're drunk. You're hungry. Despair sets in. But wait. What light? Green tree lights up the starry night? Smells of meat and smells of spice? Oh kebab, light of my life! In a city that seems to hibernate after 9pm, Parfums de Beyrouth is an oasis of sweet, sweet kebab and falafel in the midst of a desert of empty swiss supermarkets. Cut scene. It's noon. You're taking your fiancé's mother out to lunch. You sit at a sunlit outdoor table while the finest hummus and tabouli in Geneva warms her up to the prospect of you marrying her daughter. Whatever your level of virtuosity for the occasion, Parfums de Beyrouth has you covered.
i Shawarma and Kebab from 8 CHF, Falafel from 7 CHF

NIGHTLIFE

BARBERSHOP

14 Blvd. Georges-Favon; 022 320 71 92; open M-W 11:30am-midnight, Th 11:30am-1am, F 11:30am-2am, Sa 6:30pm-2am

This bar is decorated with objects you'd find in any classic American frat house: empty liquor bottles, inflatables object, posters, and action figures line the walls. If you're in luck, you'll encounter the kind server with a luscious beard who'll share his stories with you. An obvious favorite among students, Barbershop is the place to go if you're looking to meet locals and try some out-of-the-box cocktail concoctions.

i Beer from 5 CHF, cocktails from 13 CHF; wheelchair accessible

LES VOLONTAIRES

26 Rue de la Coulouvrenière; 41 22 321 44 28; open W-Th 5pm-midnight, F 5pm-2am, Sa 6pm-2am

Sometimes, after tiptoeing through the sparkling clean streets of a Swiss city all day, you just want to throw your head back and scream along with the Bee Gees. With a chill, wood-paneled space that often hosts live bands, Les Voluntaires is the perfect spot to relax and suck in some sweet, sweet American music that makes a mockery of the Geneva's former two-century ban on dancing. If you're lucky they'll open up the mic and you'll be able to hop on and belt out one more verse to expunge the last of your sinful musical energy.

i No cover; beers from 5 CHF

TONY'S COCKTAIL LOUNGE

10 Quai de la Poste; 022 310 11 33; open M 7am-2:30pm, Tu-Th 7am-2am, F-Sa 7am-4am

Every night is a new party at Tony's, where one day you might find bumping hip hop, the next couples twirling around to salsa, and the next a zumba session. Whatever gets people on the dance floor is what gets played at Tony's, and they rarely seem to fail. While you can grab some classic pub fare earlier in the day, Tony's is a place to dance, or at the very least watch people who actually know how to dance spin your crush in elegant circles around the dancefloor. Empty tables in the back are for when you want to rest your tired feet and politely decline the barkeep when she tries to get you to dance with the locals.

i No cover; cocktails from 13 CHF

GIMMELWALD

Coverage by **Will Rhatigan**

"You're going to Gimmelwald? You probably mean 'Grindelwald?'"
"No, Gim-mel-wald."
"Are you sure?"

This is the default conversation you will have with most Swiss people, who will be convinced that you really want to visit the huge resort town named after Dumbledore's childhood-friend-turned-arch-nemesis. Stand your ground and tell them that it is, without a doubt, Gimmelwald that you seek. This is a small village, and when we say small, we mean that livestock outnumber locals. Together with the neighboring village of **Mürren,** Gimmelwald is one of the last traffic-free towns in Switzerland and floats a mile off the ground at the pristine base of the Bernese Alps.

Cached in this final secluded corner of the alps, Gimmelwald safeguards miles and miles of remote hiking trails and countless adventures from paragliding to mountain biking to rock climbing. The village is protected by its remote location that keeps the hordes of tourists in the valley below away, but also guarantees that only the most determined backpackers find their way to the mountain paradise. Cars are banned in Mürren and Gimmelwald, so travelers are left with the options of hiking nearly 2,000 feet up, or taking a 6CHF cable car (one-way!). If you ever make it though, you'd be among a select few with access to hundreds of square miles of unspoiled alpine landscape, with only jagged glaciated peaks and unruly mountain cattle to constrain your freedom.

ORIENTATION

Gimmelwald and Mürren sit in the middle of the **UNESCO Berner Oberland World Natural Heritage Area**, comprising a region of outstanding natural beauty centered around the towering **Eiger, Jungfrau,** and **Mönch** mountains. This area is almost exclusively accessed through **Interlaken**, a popular resort town that sits at the base of the alps. The small villages, located on the eastern side of the long **Lauterbrunnen** valley, opposite the major mountains, atop a menacing row of cliffs. Gimmelwald is comprised of a single winding street, where a few hostels and hotels, farmhouses, and self-serve meat-and-cheese stands welcome adventurous customers. Mürren is a village nearly 1,000 feet higher on the mountain, accessible only on foot or cable car, that holds several restaurants, hotels, and outdoor stores along its single main street. From both of these small towns, an enormous network of hiking trails and other outdoor activities can be accessed in mere footsteps. For any other needs, travel to the small town at the bottom of the valley, **Stechelberg**, then take a short bus ride to **Lauterbrunnen**, where a slightly more diverse range of stores pop up. We're not sure what you expected, but Gimmelwald is definitely not Manhattan!

ESSENTIALS

GETTING THERE

Getting to Gimmelwald is a worthy trek. The Bernese Oberland region is accessed almost exclusively from Interlaken, the closet substantial city. Many cities around Switzerland and in neighboring countries connect directly to Interlaken by train. From the main Interlaken station, Interlaken Ost, take a 20 minute regional train ride to Lauterbrunnen. From here, take a bi-hourly village bus to Stechelberg-Schilthorn, where you can either begin an hour-long hike up to Gimmelwald, or catch a cable car for 6CHF. Mürren is either an additional 6CHF cable car away, or 45 minutes more uphill on foot. Neither village is accessible by car, bus, or any other conventional mode of transportation.

GETTING AROUND

The easiest (and most fun, we argue) way to get around the Lauterbrunnen Valley is on foot. Trails from Gimmelwald take you to Mürren in 45 minutes, Stechelberg in an hour, and Lauterbrunnen in about 2 hours. If you're in a rush, cable car is the most efficient means of transportation, bringing you down into the valley within 5 minutes for 6CHF. Within each village, your two feet are all you ever need, with each main street stretching for no more than a half mile. Since public transportation can be quite expensive within Switzerland, you may want to consider a few discounts such as the half-fare card, which grants you half-price on all public transportation, or several other expensive deals that allow unlimited use of transit. If you plan to mostly hike in the Gimmelwald area, however, we recommend that you pay each fare individually and try to travel on foot as much as possible.

PRACTICAL INFORMATION

Tourist Offices: Lauterbrunnen Tourismus (460 Stutzli, Lauterbrunnen; 033 856 85 68; open daily 8:30am-noon, 2pm-6:30pm).

Banks/ATMs/Currency Exchange: As a very small village, Gimmelwald has no banks of its own. For a nearby bank, take the cable car down to Lauterbrunnen, where there are a few small banks. A convenient one: Raiffeisenbank Lauterbrunnen (Im Raiffeisenhaus; 033 828 82 88; open M-F 8am-11am, 2pm-5pm).

Post Offices: Again, it is necessary to travel down to Lauterbrunnen for a post office. The easiest is Post CH AG Filiale (469A Bei der Zuben; 084 888 88 88; open M-F 9am-11:30 am, 2pm-5:30pm, Sa 9a,-11:30am).

Public Restrooms: The friendly hostel employees are often happy to let you use their restrooms if you ask. Otherwise, you are conveniently situated in the world's largest bathroom (just make sure to use proper wilderness protocol).

Internet: Wi-Fi is available at most of the lodging options in Gimmelwald. Otherwise, a trip down to

Lauterbrunnen or up to Murren will be necessary, where several cafés offer free Wi-Fi. The cable car stations at both Murren and Schilthornbahn offer free Wi-Fi as well.

BGLTQ+ Resources: The main BLGTQ+ helpline in Switzerland is 080 013 31 33.

EMERGENCY INFORMATION

Emergency Number: General: 112; Police: 117; Fire Department: 144; Swiss Helicopter Rescue Service: 1414.

Police: Polizeiwache Lauterbrunnen (469 Stutzli, Lauterbrunnen; 41 31 638 86 40).

Rape Crisis Center: Espace de Soutien et de Prévention-Abus Sexuels (2 Av. de Rumine, Lausanne ; 084 851 50 00; www.espas.info; open by appointment).

Hospitals: There are no hospitals in Gimmelwald itself. The closest doctor is in Lauterbrunnen and the closest hospital is in Interlaken.

- Doctor: Arztpraxis Caramed (3822 Lauterbrunnen; 033 856 26 26; open by appointment).
- Hospital: Spital Interlaken (77 Weissenaustrasse, 3800 Unterseen; 033 826 26 26; open daily 24hr).

Pharmacies: The closest pharmacies are in Wengen and Interlaken.

- Wengen Apothek (2823 Wengiboden; 033 855 12 46; open M-Tu 9am-5pm, Th-F 9am-5pm, Sa 9am-4pm).
- Apothek H. Busse (Hauptstrasse 9, Unterseen; 033 822 80 40; apothekebusse.ch; open M-F 7:30am-12:15pm, 1:15pm-6:30pm, Sa 7:30am-4pm).

SIGHTS

CULTURE

GIMMELWALD SAUSAGE AND CHEESE STANDS

Gimmelwald main street; open daily 24hr (some variation by shop)

There tend to be two reigning conceptions of medieval life: the first includes cottages, sheep, families gathering around campfires to praise the lord, and absolutely no bubonic plague whatsoever. The second, more realistic version conjures images of people dying from pestilence, torturing each other, and getting burnt on the stake 24 hours a day. Yet, somehow, Gimmelwald keeps the idyllic vision alive. In the tiny mountain village, the farmers chat along the street, cows wander innocently, and everyone seems to trust each other. If you need any more convincing of this medieval idyll, check on the meat and cheese stores all along Gimmelwald's main street. At every other farmhouse you'll see signs for "alpkäse" (alpine cheese) pointing around the corner. Follow the signs, and you'll usually end up in someone's small barn, with a fridge full of cheese and a jar to place your payment. No cashier, no hours, no security. Simply pay for your rich alpine cheese like an honest Swiss farmer and go. Just don't be the one to break the idyll!

i Free; cheese prices vary; wheelchair accessibility varies by stand

ROTSTOCKHÜTTE

Boganggenalp, elevation 2039m; 33 855 24 64; www.rotstockhuette.ch; hours vary by season, open daily for breakfast, lunch, and dinner

Sitting at the center of a gorgeous ring of snow-capped mountains, Rotstockhütte is the Lauterbrunnen Valley's most quintessentially Swiss alpine hut. After a long hike through winding forest paths and wide-open meadows full of lumbering cattle, Rottstockhütte appears just at the point where the base of the snow-capped peaks comes into vision. Built out of rough stone and accessible only by a simple footpath, the hut itself only contributes to the illusion of nineteenth-century pastoral bliss that the landscape conveys from Gimmelwald upwards. Hikers can stay the night, but a quick stop in to grab some specialities for lunch and take in the welcoming atmosphere is enough to experience high alpine culture for an afternoon.

i Sandwiches from 8 CHF, beer from 4CHF; overnight stay 70 CHF; no wheelchair accessibility

SCHWARZ MÖNCH

Hotel Pension Gimmelwald; 033 855 17 30; open daily noon-10pm

Along with cheese, melted cheese, and meat accompanied by cheese, Switzerland is famous for rich, dark beer. You might expect the best to be found in a hip urban microbrewery, but for an art as homegrown as traditional brewing, you can't do better than one of the quaintest villages in the Alps. Brewed and served exclusively at the bar of the log-cabin **Hotel Pension** in Gimmelwald, Schwarz Mönch, ranks number one in the world for Dark Swiss Beer. Enjoy a pint of the famous brew on the wide open deck of the hotel's restaurant. With nothing below you but cows, small wooden houses, and the famous Schwarzmönch mountain that the beer was named after, you'll feel like one of the Swiss monks who invented the dark beer hundreds of years ago on another isolated hillside.

i 25cl from 4.50CHF; limited wheelchair accessibility

LANDMARKS

TRÜMMELBACHFÄLLE

Trümmelbachfälle, Lauterbrunnen; 33 855 32 32; www.truemmelbachfaelle.ch; open daily 9am-5pm

Feel tiny and powerless at this **Unesco World Natural Heritage Site** as 20,000 liters (per second) of melted glacier come crashing down in front of you. The Trümellbach Falls are a set of ten, mostly subterranean waterfalls that exclusively drain the snowmelt and glaciers of the **Eiger, Mönch,** and **Jungfrau** mountains. The trails and tunnels that meander through the mountains provide astounding views of the cascading water. Not down for hiking but still up for the views? Take the elevator to the sixth floor and walk down.

i Adults 11CHF; limited wheelchair accessibility

BRINDLI

Accessible from Mürren; open daily 24hr

This is quite simply the most astounding viewpoint we have ever encountered. On an unassuming ridge stretching down from **Birg** to **Mürren,** the Brindli reaches suddenly upward, forming a tiny pinnacle surrounded by sky. To get there, you briefly leave the main trail from Mürren to **Rotstockhütte** and ascend a short, steep trail. The trail flattens out on a knife-edge ridge, where you clutch a cable on one side as you hop from rock to rock. Finally, ascend a bit more to an isolated bench with a perfect three-hundred and sixty degree panorama of your surroundings. You'll see the **Eiger, Jungfrau,** and **Monch** on one side, the **Schiltorn** on the other, and cows with log cabins everywhere in between. Oh my, Switzerland! You're too much.

i Free; no wheelchair accessibility

OUTDOORS

KLETTERSTEIG MÜRREN-GIMMELWALD (VIA FERRATA)

Intersport Stäger Sport Chalet Enzian, 3825 Mürren; 033 855 23 55; open daily 9am-6pm

Does dangling above a 3,000 foot abyss with only a wobbly giant staple supporting your weight appeal to you? No? Ok, say you were secured to a metal cable with a harness so you'd only slide 10 feet down the rock face if you fell? Maybe? Great, that's all we need. A German translation of the more commonly known Italian term "via ferrata," the Klettersteig Mürren-Gimmelwald falls somewhere between a hike and a rock climb, with a narrow, exposed trail traversing the edge of the Lauterbrunnen Valley cliffs, and a continuous metal cable that you clip into for safety. While most of the trail is pretty mellow as via ferratas go, there are a few spots, like the row of metal staples drilled directly into the cliffside—feel nerve-wracking no matter how confident you are on the rocks. The three-cable bridges over waterfalls and the one-hundred-meter-long narrow suspension bridge over a chasm give hikers little goosebumps, too.

i Free; equipment rentals 25CHF from Stäger Sport; no wheelchair accessibility

GIMMELWALD-ROTSTOCK-HÜTTE-MÜRREN HIKE

Gimmelwald cable-car station; open daily 24hr

If you want to get out for a big day of exploration in the mountains from Gimmelwald, this is your classic route. Just don't take it lightly—at over 12 miles and over 5,000 feet of elevation gain, the Gimmelwald-Rotstockhütte-Mürren loop represents a hard-fought battle between human and mountain. From Gimmelwald, follow signs for **Im Tal** until you reach a junction. Continue straight, climb through well-trafficked cow pastures, and follow signs for **Rotstockhütte**. Rise out of the pastures into enormous untouched meadows just as you arrive at the hut, where you can continue to summit the nearby peaks if snow conditions permit, or turn towards **Mürren** to pass a scattering of tiny alpine farmhouses. Heading down towards Mürren, climb the viewpoints of **Wasenegg** and **Schiltalp** along the way for stunning panoramas, before taking the familiar wide footpath down from Mürren to Gimmelwald to finish the loop. After that, if you're still capable of moving, maybe get a drink?

i Free; limited wheelchair accessibility

FOOD

BASE CAFE ($)

Fuhren 460B, Lauterbrunnen; 077 977 11 06; open daily 8am-10pm

Diving 3,000 feet off a cliff can be a bit tough on the stomach. It might make you nauseous, if you're a big softy, but the hike up makes everyone a bit hungry. Refuel at BASE Cafe whether you've spilt your lunch all over an alpine valley or you're just a tad bit knackered after your stroll up to your afternoon BASE jump. Serving as the launch point for BASE jumpers in the **Lauterbrunnen** valley, the comfortable sofas and coffee tables in the cafe allow you to rest and recharge for your next adventure, all while chowing down on relatively cheap sandwiches, pizzas, and burgers to reenergize you Don't let the chill atmosphere fool you though; photos of base jumpers, paragliders, and wingsuit flyers line the wall to remind you that this is only a place for

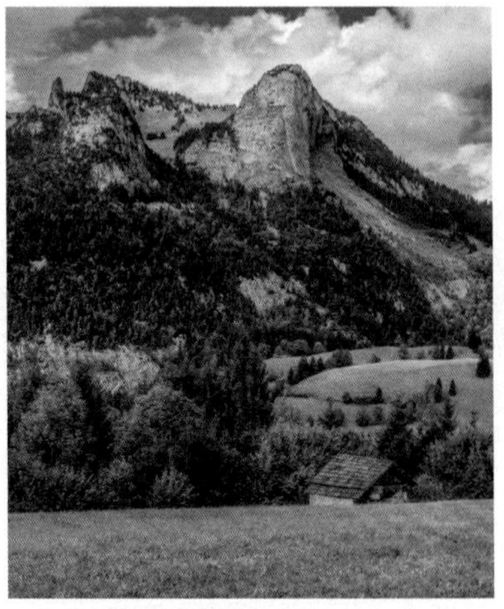

temporary relaxation.

i Sandwiches from 10CHF; cash only; wheelchair accessible

HOTEL SCHÜTZEN ($$)

Auf der Fuhren 439, Lauterbrunnen; 033 855 50 50; open for lunch and dinner, hours vary

Switzerland is a rather innocuous-sounding word. Schweiz (say this loudly, in a deep voice, from the back of your throat), is a hefty, burly, 500-pound noise. You've come to the German part of Switzerland and things are heavy here. If you want to experience, the fullest, thickest part of Swiss culture, come to Hotel Schützen for a meal that leaves you ready to grow a long mustache, hurrumph loudly, and take up the Flugelhorn. On the alpine-facing deck of a log cabin restaurant, grab steaming pots of fondue, sizzling bratwursts, and burgers nearly the size of your head. Only those with the longest mustaches leave the deck without a flugelhorn-playing belly 2 sizes larger.

i Burgers from 19.50 CHF; limited wheelchair accessibility

STEINBOCK HOTEL RESTAURANT-PIZZERIA ($$)

Bahnhofpl. 477B, 3822 Lauterbrunnen; 033 855 12 31; open daily 11:30am-1:45pm, 5:30pm-9pm

In a mountain village where the second largest building is a barn, Steinbock

Hotel is a Colossus—a Colossus in a very swiss-mountaineer sense, of course. The Steinbock is a log cabin to rule all log cabins, towering next to the Launterbrunnen train station to give you a grand welcome to the valley of log cabins. It's probably not the landmark you're here for though; serving up huge variety of pizzas on an outdoor deck directly facing the **Jungfrau** across the valley, the restaurant offers the best literal and figurative taste of the Alps as soon as you arrive. Best of all, every one of the delicious pizzas is only costs 15CHF on Sundays.

i Pizzas from 18CHF; 15CHF on Sundays; wheelchair accessible

THAM CHINESE RESTAURANT ($$)

Rouft 1067A CH-3825, Mürren; 033 855 28 28; www.tham.ch; open daily 11am-9pm

Finishing up a long hike from the base of the valley to Mürren, there is nothing more disappointing than discovering that the Swiss sausages waiting for you at the village's many restaurants require the sacrifice of your two most valuable backpack items for purchase. But fear not, weary traveler. Hidden behind a typical, and adorable, wooden house lies an unassuming alm for all suffering: tender, juicy, fried rice. Tham Chinese Restaurant is a relaxed family owned business that brings reasonably priced cuisine from China and Singapore to the picturesque Mürren hillside. Munch under a classic red-and-white striped umbrella and the sign advertising "snacks and drinks" as you look out over the alps and all the fools eating expensive bratwursts. Hope exists on yonder mountain top!

i Meals from 14.50CHF; limited wheelchair accessibility

NIGHTLIFE

HORNER PUB

Beim Pfrundhaus 417A, Lauterbrunnen; 033 855 16 73; www.hornerpub.ch/en; pub open daily 9am-12:30am, bar/club open F-Sa midnight-2:30am and on busy weeknights

The Lauterbrunnen Valley is a place for adventurers, and adventurers love to drink. This may not be true everywhere, but when the most popular sports are base jumping and paragliding, the adventurers are a thrill-seeking, rowdy bunch, and the drinking routinely gets rowdy too. As literally the only pub in this small mountain town, Horner draws motley crews (extreme sports athletes), life-long travellers, and adventure-seeking local seasonal employees on any night of the week. Exchange war stories at the hefty wooden tables downstairs until midnight, then head up the stairs to the hilarious club, where you and whatever new friends you make can lose your minds thrashing about on the small dance floor to a single disco ball and bumping American pop. It's not a Berlin warehouse, but throw a village full of adrenaline junkies together in a cramped wooden house and it's guaranteed to get wild.

i Pints from 6.50; limited wheelchair accessibility to club

MOUNTAIN HOSTEL BAR

Mountain Hostel Gimmelwald; 033 855 17 04; hours vary

At the iconic hostel in Gimmelwald, where guests from all over the world sleep together on narrow bunks high up in the mountains, the bar always hops with energy and tales from years of travel. On any given night, you're guaranteed to find crowds of backpackers hanging out by the board games indoors, around a fire outside, or just staying close to their beer tabs at the bar. In a town where the second rowdiest thing going on is the spring sheep-shearing, the hostel bar provides the closest thing to a rowdy night out in Gimmelwald. Club lights or not, backpackers who like to stay in remote hostels in the Swiss mountains tend to tell some pretty good stories.

i Beer from 5CHF; limited wheelchair accessibility

LAUSANNE

Coverage by **Will Rhatigan**

Often overlooked in favor of nearby Geneva, "Lausanne-geles," as the young locals call it, is a gorgeous lakeside city that has all the natural beauty of its internationally famous neighbor with an atmosphere that feels five times more alive. Like many impudent younger siblings, Lausanne may not carry the worldwide influence and seriousness of its haughty older brother, but it is without a doubt more fun. Built atop three hills overlooking Lac Léman in Lausanne feels impossible to get from point A to point B without stopping for five minutes at the top of every staircase to marvel at its picturesque views. From the top of the hills, the city stretches out in a sea of ancient red rooftops, all framed by the wide waters of the lake and the towering alps. A mix of fascinating museums, thriving nightclubs, and over 2,000 years of history, stretching back to the Roman empire, lie within its labyrinth of streets. Lausanne, can't you see, sometimes your sites just hypnotize me.

ORIENTATION

Sitting on the Northern shore of **Lac Léman**, Lausanne is in the Western, French-speaking region of Switzerland, across the lake from and slightly West of the **Swiss Alps,** and South of the **Jura** mountains. To avoid the disease of lake-side swamps, the city's wealthy medieval residents built their elegant homes on three steep hills about a mile from the shoreline. These hilltops house **Vieille Ville,** Lausanne's old town, with some buildings dating back to the thirteenth century. The steepness of the streets can make the city particularly difficult to navigate, with streets on one "level" often parallel the rooftops of the "level" below, creating a truly 3-dimensional design. In the space between the hills lies the **Flon** district, a formerly run-down neighborhood that has been freshly renovated and now rocks a Disney-World-like nightlife scene. Along the shoreline stretches the **Ouchy** neighborhood, home to the **Musée Olympique**, several prominent art institutes, and a seemingly endless strip of gorgeous lakeside parks.

ESSENTIALS

GETTING THERE

Since Lausanne has no international airport of its own, most travelers choose to fly into Geneva and take the Swiss Federal Rail System (SBB) into the city. The main train station, Lausanne Gare, connects to all of the other major Swiss cities, with trains running from Geneva to Lausanne every 5 minutes to half an hour from 6am to just past midnight, depending on the day of the week. Purchase tickets at automated booths at the station, or download the SBB mobile app to buy tickets online. Since train tickets tend to be quite expensive, it is best to book super-saver tickets ahead of time online, or look into the generally less expensive, but also less efficient, bus system.

GETTING AROUND

Most of Lausanne's central city, positioned around the three main hills, is easily walkable. Although a bike sharing program is available, the steep slopes and frequent staircases often make walking more efficient. The lakeside Ouchy district lies about a mile from the city center, making the metro and bus system quite useful. Luckily, almost all accommodations offer free transport cards, which allow for unlimited free transit use for a maximum of 15 days within the Lausanne metropolitan area. The two automated metro lines meet at the central Flon station, running north-south and east-west, and are the fastest way to travel long-distances within the city. The bus system is also quite efficient, connecting to points off the main metro axes. If you don't have a transit card, purchase tickets at automated machines in all stations, from 3.60CHF for one hour of unlimited use.

PRACTICAL INFO

Tourist Offices: Tourist Information Center (6 Pl. de la Navigation; 021 613 73 73; high season open daily from 9am-7pm, low season 9am-6pm).

Banks/ATMs/Currency Exchange: Like all of Switzerland, Lausanne has banks everywhere. The most common ATMS are run by UBS or BCV. A convenient one: (1 Place Saint-Francois; 021 215 41 11; open daily 24hr).

Post Offices: Post offices are located all around the city, under the name "La Poste." A convenient one: La Poste (43B Avenue de la Gare; 084 888 88 88; open M-F 8am-8pm, Sa 8am-4pm, Su 4pm-7pm).

Public Restrooms: Lausanne has public restrooms sparsely scattered around the city, most of which are much cleaner than those in neighboring France. Otherwise, most cafés won't be too troublesome about letting you use theirs.

Internet: Wi-Fi is available throughout the main station, but you will need a Swiss cell number to access it. Free Wi-Fi is available at tourist information centers, and in many cafés throughout the city.

BGLTQ+ Resources: The main BLGTQ+ helpline in Switzerland is 080 013 31 33.

EMERGENCY INFORMATION

Emergency Number: General: 112; Police: 117; Fire Department: 144; Swiss helicopter rescue service: 1414.

Police: Lausanne Police Hall (33 Rue St. Martin; 021 315 15 15).

US Embassy: Consular Agency in Geneva (7 Rue Versonnex; 022 840 51 60; ch.usembassy.gov/embassy/locations-in-switzerland/consular-agency-geneva/; open M 8:30am-11am, 1:30pm-4:30 pm, W 1:30am-11am, 1:30pm-4:30pm; Th 10am-1pm, services by appointment only).

Rape Crisis Center: Espace de Soutien et de Prévention-Abus Sexuels (2 Av. de Rumine, 084 851 50 00; www.espas.info; open by appointment).

Hospitals: In the case of emergency, always call 112. Here is a convenient hospital:

- Lausanne University Hospital (46 Rue de Bugnon; 021 314 11 11; open daily 24hr).

Pharmacies: Pharmacies are marked by a green plus-sign hanging outside. Here are two convenient locations:

- Pharmacie SUN Store (1 Batiment CFF Quai; 058 878 55 00; open daily 7am-11pm)
- Pharmacie 24 (3 Avenue de Montchoisi; 021 613 12 24; open daily 8am-midnight).

SIGHTS

CULTURE

LE FLON

Place de l'Europe; flon.ch; open daily 24hr

Once an unsavory site of leather tanneries and a railroad depot, Le Flon neighborhood has exchanged the stenches of rawhide and coal for the sweet smells of sweaty bodies and alcohol. Nestled in a once uninhabited valley between two of Lausanne's wealthy hilltops, Le Flon has gained a reputation as a nasty part of town. Then, the city decided to renovate it into its own personal version of an adult Disneyland. Descend from the elegant nineteenth century neighborhoods on all sides into Le Flon, and find yourself transported one hundred years into a hedonistic future. The valley is now composed of modern buildings, holding bars, huge nightclubs, and fashion boutiques. After a night in one of the famous clubs, it'll be up to you to decide which smells you prefer.

i Free; wheelchair accessible

VIEILLE VILLE (OLD TOWN)

Pl. de la Cathédrale; open daily 24hr

After a few weeks traveling in Europe you might start feeling jaded about cobblestone streets and ancient stone buildings. Lausanne's version will make your amazement feel brand new. The nest of hilltop streets that make up Vieille Ville is jaw-droppingly beautiful. Every turn of a corner makes you stop and say, "Ok, this must be the most gorgeous street I've seen in my life." With shockingly tourist-free cobblestone streets, endless views over the red-roofed town, and ancient attractions like the **Cathédrale de Lausanne** and the **Club le XIIIème Siècle** all hidden away under stone arches, the old town of Lausanne is the most medieval place you could go in the modern world outside of a U.S. House of Representatives debate on abortion rights.

i Free; wheelchair accessible

LANDMARKS

CATHÉDRALE DE LAUSANNE

Pl. de la Cathédrale; 021 316 71 60; www.cathedrale-lausanne.ch; open Oct-Mar daily 9am-5:30pm, Apr-Sept M-Sa 9am-7pm, Su 10am-6pm; prayer service M-F 7:30am; tower visit open M-Sa 9:30am-5:30pm, Su 1pm-5pm

Towering above an endless sea of red roofs on one of the tallest hills in the city, the Cathédrale de Lausanne is the Really Big Church™ worth seeing even if you've been wading through enormous European churches for months. The inside is a physical manifestation of the Protestant reformation that rollicked the city, with enormous arched ceilings that have been stripped of all ornamentation and general fun. The view from the tower, or just the view from the plaza outside, boasts a look over the entire city, **Lac Léman**, and the distant Alps. So even if you've had a lifetime's worth of gothic architecture, trust us, this will make adding yet another church visit to your itinerary worth your time.

i Free; tower admission adult 5CHF, students 3CHF; limited wheelchair accessibility

ÉGLISE SAINT-FRANÇOIS (CHURCH OF ST FRANCIS)

Pl. St. Francois; 021 331 56 38; www.saintf.ch; open Tu-F 10am-noon and 4pm-6:40pm

But wait: there's one more church. No really, this one is different, we swear. You'll find this large Franscican-monastery-(forcibly)-turned-Protestant-church tucked among the chic boutiques of the **Place St. Francois.** Dating back to the thirteenth century, the Church has undergone countless renovations; currently, it lost a bit of holy vigor to host concerts and art exhibitions. Attend one of the **Concerts Saint-François** every Saturday at 5pm to get your weekly taste of tunes with a little holy accent.

i Free; concerts Sa 5pm; no wheelchair accessibility

ESPLANADE DE MONTBENON

3 Allée Ernest-Ansermet; open daily 24hr

If we're really breaking it down, Lausanne's best feature is its wide array of breathtaking views. There's a bit more to it than that, but an ancient city, on hill, on a lake, in the mountains? That's just a recipe for visual success. Amongst the many picturesque vistas, the Esplanade de Montbenon boasts the best in town. A verdant park stretching in front of the **Palais de Justice**, the Esplanade hosts intermittent public markets and music parks. But best of all is its offering of beautiful green lawns, fountains, and shade trees that hang off the edge of an enormous hill at the back of the city, making the park an ideal spot to lay back and take in the beautiful city.

i Free; wheelchair accessible

MUSEUMS

MUSÉE OLYMPIQUE

Quai d'Ouchy 1; 21 621 65 11; www.olympic.org/museum; open daily 9am-6pm

Do YOU have what it takes to be an Olympian? Can you jump higher, run faster, shoot guns, and do ten different kinds of martial arts better than the rest? Are YOU a champion? Unlikely, bucko. After playing the simulation tests of hand-eye coordination, memory, shooting accuracy, and speed at the Olympic Museum, you will very likely have your dreams of glory crushed. Along with the ridiculously fun Wii-Fit-esque sport simulations, the enormous museum houses fascinating exhibits on the ancient Greco-Roman Olympics, the history of the modern games, and the most inspiring stories of the tournament's athletes. Learn about the summer Olympics, in which athletes compete in tasks of strength, agility, concentration, and speed of all kinds, and the winter olympics, in which people try thirteen different kinds of sliding. Located just down **Lac Léman** from the International Olympic Committee's longtime headquarters, the musée also boasts the most gorgeous view out of a museum front door we've ever seen.

Admission18CHF, students 12CHF; wheelchair accessible

MUSÉE DE L'ÉLYSÉE

18 Avenue de l'Élysée; www.elysee.ch; 021 316 99 11; open Tu-Su 11am-6pm

Oh, so you think photography is the art of the future? You think that it makes sense and has clear meanings, unlike all that preposterous contemporary art floating around? Well not today, buddy. If you thought photography made sense, you obviously haven't been to an art museum dedicated entirely to photography. Featuring everything from yellow and black pixelated shots that look eerily similar to when you would zoom in too much on your 2005 cameraphone, to blurry sideways shots of tractors driving over snow, the Musée de l'Élysée will shatter any perception that photography can't confuse the hell out of you.

Free; wheelchair accessible

OUTDOORS

LE CUBLY BELVEDÈRE

45 Avenue des Alpes Montreux; open daily 24hrs

Although this stunning mountain is in Montreux, a beautiful Swiss town twenty minutes up the lake from Lausanne, it's an alpine exploration not to be missed. Starting directly at the Montreux station, exit west and follow the clearly marked hiking signs pointing up (at any fork, it won't matter which path you take). The first section of the hike brings you up staircases and through narrow cobblestone paths between ancient homes in the hillside town itself before diving into the woods. Then you'll pass through charming cow pastures and tiny alpine cottages before coming out to the unbelievable scene of **Lac Léman** in front of the towering Swiss Alps. This 4-hour hike couldn't be more captivatingly Swiss if it tried.

Free; tickets to Montreux 15-25CHF; 3-5 hours total hiking time; no wheelchair accessibility

PARC LOUIS BOURGET

1 Prom. de Vidy; 021 315 57 15; open daily 24hr

Parc Louis Borget is the hottest spot on the endless strip of seemingly identical parks along Lausanne's **Lac Léman** coastline. On a sunny afternoon, you can run for miles along the waterfront with at least one hopping barbecue in your frame of vision at all times. With wide green lawns, twisting forest paths, public beaches, and the omnipresent and always gorgeous alps visible on the other side of the lake, Parc Louis Bourget is a paradise designed to be lounged at and played in for hours on end. Lausanne's residents don't let this gem go underappreciated, consistently giving it the respect it deserves. Spending an afternoon at the huge park with the thousands of other beachgoers feels like a worship service to nature, yet also somehow calm and unclaustrophobic.

Free; wheelchair accessible

FOOD

BULLDOG BAR ET RESTO ($$)

28 Rue du Petit-Chene; 021 320 60 30; open M-Sa 9am-midnight, Su 10am-midnight

When most people hop off the train in Lausanne, they know just two things: the alps are nearby and there are lots of hills to climb. Just a minute's walk up a preposterously steep street from the main train station, Bulldog Bar et Resto fulfills both those expectations right off the bat. Although the restaurant's relatively cheap pizza, burgers, and Swiss specialties won't shock most people, the magnificent rooftop terrace on which their standard pub fare is served certainly will. Sprinkling on a stunning view over **Lake Geneva** and the ancient rooftops of Lausanne over every dish, Bulldog makes its pizzas taste like haute cuisine.

i Pizzas from 16CHF; wheelchair accessible

LA MOSAIQUE ($)

70 Avenue d'Ouchy; 021 601 17 93; open M-F 10:30am-3pm, 5:30pm-10pm, Sa-Su 10:30am-10pm

Mosaique has everything you could want after a really tough day of swimming at the Ouchy beaches and lounging in the shade: large portions, innovative spicy flavors, and energy-refueling helpings of meat. Ok, you might want to take a jog on the beach at some point after but either way, the original mix of Ethiopian and Indian cuisine served at Mosaique will fill you up and still leave you lusting for more. Indulge your most gluttonous side and chow down on their popular wraps surrounded by giraffe sculptures.

i Wraps from 10CHF, take-out available; wheelchair accessible

THE GREEN VAN COMPANY ($)

8 Rue de Port-Franc; 079 945 00 60; www.thegreenvan.ch; open M-Th 11am-11pm, F-Sa 11am-midnight, Su 11am-11pm

Picture this: It's late. You're tired. You're drunk. You've been clubbing in the **Flon** district. Etcetera, etcetera—you know the deal. Oh, you're also a disciple of organic living and an avid locavore? What is to be done? We'll tell you what's to be done, cowboy. Go to the Green Van Company, where you can chow down on all the greasy drunk food you want and maintain your perfect organic conscience. Serving burgers, fries, and salads, with all local and organic ingredients (you can eat those alpine cows!), Green Van Company is perfectly crafted for the needs of drunken environmentalists all over the world.

i Burgers from 8CHF; wheelchair accessible

NIGHTLIFE

CLUB LE XIIIÈME SIÈCLE (13TH CENTURY CLUB)

10 Rue Cité-Devant; 021 312 40 64; M-W 4pm-midnight, Th 4pm-1am; F 4pm-2am; S 6pm-2m, Su 6pm-midnight

After a hearty campaign of slaying heretics and infidels, sometimes you just need a few pints of ale to simmer down your boiling blood. So grab your squire, a few severed heads, perhaps even a damsel in distress or two, and head into Club le XIIIème Siècle to smash beer mugs together with your comrades and recount tales of exploits long past. With doorways dating back to the 1200's, and a bar that's been nearly continuously open ever since, this dimly-lit, low-ceilinged space has so much history packed into its stone walls that you'll end up looking around the corner for a band of brigands carrying torches underneath every narrow archway. Operating as a nightclub until last year, the space got too rowdy for **Vieille Ville's** gentile residents, who forced the place into a more relaxed vibe. That said, clanging pints where knights once dined is an experience not to be missed.

i Beer from 4.50CHF, wine from 6CHF, cocktails from 15CHF; limited wheelchair accessibility

MAD CLUB

23 Rue de Genève; 021 340 69 69; www.madclub.ch; open Th-Su 11pm-5am

AAAHH! AAAAAH! That's pretty much all there is to say on this one. All night, all weekend, MAD club is ambitious in calling itself mad, but, WOW, they are right. It is furious in there. Settled in the heart of the rambunctious **Flon** district, the club minces no words in describing its true purpose: you come here to rage. Hosting enormous parties with titles like Waka Loca, La Tempuratura, and, well, mad reggae, this club loves its many themes, but maintains just one level of energy. Every Sunday is the MAD gay party, where posters showing ridiculously muscular men give you an idea of the vibes to expect inside. Let us repeat, AAAAHHH!

i Parties vary in price, often free; limited wheelchair accessibility; LGBTQ+ friendly

LUCERNE

Coverage by **Will Rhatigan**

Outdoors, culture, history. Those are the three essential boxes that we like to check off for every city we visit. Usually it's a take two, lose one type of situation. Yet somehow, with a population of just over 400,000, Lucerne scores an A+ on all three categories. Sitting on the edge of a long lake on the edge of the Swiss Alps, Lucerne is surrounded by some of the most astounding natural beauty you'll see in Europe. With hardly a suburb to speak of, the city center is just a quick jog away from an over 6,000-foot hike on the towering Pilatus mountain. Once you come down from the mountains and likes to check out what the city itself is actually about, you'll find yourself in a medieval paradise that seems to hop of the pages of The Brothers Grimm. Ancient castle walls encircle the settlement, and 700-year old bridges and guild buildings abound. When you aren't on the lookout for magical beasts, you'll discover that Lucerne is also a thriving cultural hub, with a well-known university, music playing on the streets, and a lakeshore seething with youthful energy every summer night. Did I mention you can float down the roaring River Reuss that rushes through it all? Nice work, Lucerne.

ORIENTATION

An hour train-ride southwest of **Zurich**, Lucerne is smack in the middle of Switzerland, on the Northwestern shore of **Lake Lucerne**, and on the very edge of the **Swiss Alps**. The **River Reuss** slices through it all, dividing the city roughly into the **Alstadt** (old town) on the northern bank, and the **Neustadt** (new town) on the southern bank, although the Alstadt crosses the river a bit. Most of the historical attractions frame the River Reuss near the Altstadt, while the modern Neustadt houses most of the city's many students and trendier culture and restaurants. To the west, the ancient fortification of **Museggmaur** frames the boundary of the central city, while the park-lined shores of Lake Lucerne ring the other side.

ESSENTIALS

GETTING THERE

Since Lucerne has no major airports of its own, most visitors will arrive by train. All long-distance trips arrive at the Hauptbahnhof (main train station) in the city center, where buses connect easily to all other points in the city. The closest international airport is in Zurich, which is roughly a 1hr train ride away. Tickets to Lucerne can be purchased from automated kiosks at the station, or online from the SBB CFF mobile application.

GETTING AROUND

Most of the Albstadt (old city) can be easily explored on foot, and lends itself to very scenic walks-- the distance from the main train station and city center to the historic walls is less than 1km. Restaurants in the Neustadt can be slightly farther away, but are rarely more than a 15min walk from the station. If you wish to travel to some of the more outlying areas of the compact city, regularly running buses are widely available and run regularly, with tickets available from 2.70CHF for a 1hr pass. For longer excursions, the most convenient intercity travel leaves by train from the Hauptbahnhof.

PRACTICAL INFORMATION

Tourist Offices: Tourist Information Luzern (Zentralstrasse 5; 041 227 17 17; open M-F 8:30am-7pm, Sa-Su 9am-5pm).

Banks/ATMs/Currency Exchange: Some of the most common banks in Lucerne are UBS and Raiffeisen. A convenient one: ATM Bankomat Raiffeisen Bank (Haldenstrasse 6; open daily 24hr).

Post Offices: Most offices in the German-speaking part of Switzerland take the name Post CH AG. A convenient one: Post CH AG (Hauptpost, Bahnhofpl. 4; 0848 888 888; open M-F 7:30am-6:30pm, Sa 8am-4pm).

Public Restrooms: Public restrooms are available at many parks and monuments around the city. Note that the toilets in these restrooms often do not have seats, a fact that can be somewhat disconcerting for many North Americans.

Internet: Wi-Fi, "WLAN," is free in the train station and around the city center for one hour. Look for the network "Luzern." Otherwise, many local cafés offer free Wi-Fi.

BGLTQ+ Resources: LGBT+ Helpline of Switzerland (Bern, Montbijoustrasse 73; 0800 133 133; hello@lgbtelpline.ch; www.lgbt-helpline.ch/en); Queer Office hosts weekly meetings every Tuesday at Neubad (hallo@queeroffice.ch; www.queeroffice.ch).

EMERGENCY INFORMATION

Emergency Number: General: 112; Police: 117; fire department: 144; Swiss helicopter rescue service: 1414.

Police: Luzerner Polizei (Kasimir-Pfyffer-Strasse 26; 041 248 81 17)

US Embassy: The closest US Consulate is Consular Agency Zurich (Dufourstrasse 101; 031 357 70 11; open M-F 10am-1pm).

Rape Crisis Center: Lucerne has no dedicated rape crisis center. But RAINN (Rape, Abuse, and Incest National Network) hotline that provides live, secure, anonymous crisis support for victims of sexual violence, their friends, and familiies over RAINN's website (800 656 4673; www.rainn.org, open daily 24hr).

Hospitals:

- Lucerne Cantonal Hospital (Spitalstrasse; 041 205 11 11; open daily 24hr).

Pharmacies: Pharmacies in German are called Apotheken. Two of the most convenient:

- BENU Bahnhof Luzern (RailCity; 041 220 13 13; open M-Sa 6am-10pm, Su 8am-8pm)
- TopPharm Dr. Schmid's Lake Pharmacy (Kapellpl. 10; 041 410 88 80; open M-F 8:30am-6:30pm, Sa 8am-4pm).

SIGHTS

CULTURE

JESUTENKIRCHE (JESUIT CHURCH)

Bahnhofstrasse 11A; 077 489 05 79; open Monday 9:30am-6:30pm, Tu 6:30am-6:30pm, W 9:30am-6:30pm, Th-Su 6:30am-6:30pm

Alright, alright, alright, we know you've seen a lot of churches in Europe. Just hear us out for one more. Through our travels to more ancient churches than God Himself can keep track of, Jesutenkirche is the most beautiful we've ever found. We're not kidding. Far from the threatening gargoyles and imposing gray walls of most gothic monstrosities, Jesutenkirche is a light, joyful celebration of life. With a color scheme of pink and white, the church is reminiscent of a baby shower or rabbits frolicking about in the spring. Carved wooden flowers and angelic murals adorn the ceiling, an ornate pink organ lines the back wall, and a heart is carved above the entranceway. While most medieval churches remind us of religious persecution and executions, this one reminds us of love.

i Free; limited wheelchair accessibility

WOCHENMARKT (WEEKLY MARKET)

Bahnohoffstrasse and and Rathausquai; www.luzerner-wochenmarkt.ch; open Tu 6am-1pm, Sa 6am-1pm

Since an unknown date long ago in the middle ages, farmers, merchants, and craftsmen have gathered on the banks of the river **Reuss** to hawk their wares. What you'll find on a stroll through the lively market today is only a little different than when the tradition first began. Sample alpine cheese, charcuterie made with all manner of animals, and fresh vegetables grown in high mountain gardens. Stretching in a line of quaint stalls between the medieval Kapellbrücke and Spreurbrücke bridges, the market gives little indication that you haven't actually traveled back to the year 1400.

i Stall prices vary; wheelchair accessible

LANDMARKS

MUSEGGMAUR

Museggmauer; 041 410 81 87; www.museggmauer.ch; open daily 8am-7pm

If you're not yet convinced that Lucerne is a modern fairly-tale paradise, climb up any of the nine towers in the city's ancient fortifications for an experience that will force you to question if the existence of cars was just a dream you had last night. Extraordinarily, most of the towers are unattended for most of the day, and visitors can merely walk up the hill towards the ancient city walls and ascend the fortifications whenever they choose. From the top, you can feast your eyes on an incredible panorama of the **River Reuss, Lake Lucerne,** the red roofs of the old city, and the snow-capped **Swiss Alps** in the background. From up there, it can be hard to believe that Lucerne is a major modern city and not the setting of Snow White.

i Free; no wheelchair accessibility

KAPELLBRÜCKE (CHAPEL BRIDGE)

Kapellbrücke; 041 220 16 60; www.luzern.com/en/chapel-bridge, open daily 24hr

The oldest surviving wooden bridge in Europe? Across one of the most gorgeous rivers in Europe? With the most ancient bridge murals in Europe? With a lot of flowers, in Europe? Alright pal, we get it—the scenery surrounding Kapellbrücke is not to be missed. Since its original construction in 1333 as part of Lucerne's fortifications, the bridge has survived countless invasions over its history, only to be nearly destroyed and rebuilt due to a 1993 fire. Spanning 672 feet across the **River Reuss**, in an illogical diagonal design that we assume exists just so that we can see more of its beauty, the iconic bridge is the literal and symbolic heart of Lucerne. At the center, the "Wasserturm" (water tower) reaches high out of river, alternately used as a dungeon, torture chamber, and souvenir shop over the city's history. Just please, visit this bridge.

i Free; wheelchair accessible

MUSEUMS

BOURBAKI PANORAMA

Löwenpl. 11; 041 412 30 30; www.bourbakipanorama.ch; open daily 9am-6pm

This is one really big painting. Since that's not a ton of material for an entire museum, the curators have transformed this one giant 360-degree mural into a full historical exhibit, bringing it to life with voiceovers, sculptural additions, and a movie one floor below exhibiting the history of the mural's events. Completed by **Edouard Castres** in 1881, the massive work of art depicts a defining event in Swiss history, the internment of 87,000 asylum-seeking French soldiers during the 1871 **Franco-Prussian War**. In a background of snowy countryside, masses of soldiers under the command of general **Charles-Denis Bourbaki** can be seen marching wearily over the Swiss frontier, laying their rifles in stacks, and hobbling into Swiss hospitality. It's just one painting, but it's perhaps done more to shape and represent the Swiss national identity than all other works combined. Oh, and don't miss the **Bourbaki Kino/Bar** on the way out.

i Adults 12 CHF, students 10 CHF; limited wheelchair accessibility

THE ROSENGART COLLECTION

Pilatusstrasse 10; 041 220 16 60; www.rosengart.ch/en/welcome; open daily 10am-6pm

Pablo Picasso. Paul Klee. Pierre-Auguste Renoir. What do all of these artists have in common? Tremendous cults of personality surrounding their careers. The **Collection Rosengart** leans further into the shadows of these famous men, simply listing their names in progressively large print based on their reputation on its brochure. The museum itself parallels this hierarchy, devoting a floor and a half to Picasso's work and life, a floor to Paul Klee, then scattering some of the most famous impressionists in between. The collection is a showcase of the most famous art of the twentieth century, and has little more to offer besides the tremendous flex of owning more famous art than you. Take that, peasant!

i 18 CHF adults, 10 CHF students; wheelchair accessible

OUTDOORS

LAKE LUCERNE

Ufschötti Park; www.lakelucerne.ch, open daily 24gr

Like every other Unbelievably Gorgeous Swiss Lakeside City™, Lucerne boasts a crystal clear water-body within steps of its liveliest district. Along with the rest of Switzerland, the water is sparkling clean (something that befuddles those of us familiar with American urban rivers), offering visitors the unique experience to frolick, play, and get generally wet and wild in the harbor of a world-renowned metropolis. While warms days find the parks all along Lucerne's shorefront packed with people bathing in this almost frustratingly perfect sanitation situation, our favorite spot is the **Ufschötti Park** on the South side of the lake, where crowds of students come out to play en masse and a bridge overflows with locals throwing backflips into the water. After a beautiful day on Lake Lucerne, just about everyone's patriotism will collapse into an overpowering yearning for life in an Unbelievably Gorgeous Swiss Lakeside City™.

i Free; wheelchair accessible

PILATUS

Access from Krienz or Alpnachstad; www.pilatus.ch, open daily 24hr

Wherever you are in Lucerne, it's impossible to forget that you're in the **Alps** for more than a few seconds. If you improbably forget amidst the castles and medieval houses for even a second, the shadow of the towering, sharp, stone-capped Pilatus mountain will be sure to remind you around the next corner. Once rumored to be the haunt of Lucerne's fire-breathing Dragons, the mountain retains its majesty of yore, rising thousands of feet above all the neighboring hills and offering a 360-degree view of Lucerne and the Swiss Alps. For the sluggish, the world's steepest cog railway ascends one side, while a cable car climbs the other, all to a luxurious hotel at the summit. But for the best experience of the Pilatus, start hiking at **Alpnachstad** for a shockingly solitary all-day trek through forests, cow pastures, rugged alpine meadows, and threatening boulder fields near the top. At just 20 minutes from the center of Lucerne, the Pilatus might be the most remarkably tranquil urban hike we've ever experienced.

i Free; limited wheelchair accessibility

FOOD

BARBÈS SPÉCIALITÉS MAROCAINES (MOROCCAN SPECIALITIES) ($$)

Winkelreidstrasse 62; 41 210 00 90; www.barbes.ch; open M-Sa 10am-12:30am, Su 4pm-11:30pm

While your octogenarian grandmother may have taught you that fine dining means silver spoons, elbows off the table, and a very particular arrangement of silverware, Barbès discards this formality and serves up a luxurious cuisine that won't make you feel like you're being watched by a swarm of hawkeyed grannies. Specializing in Moroccan cuisine, the casual, brightly decorated restaurant has kefta, tabouli, and falafel mastered to the point that when you finish your 8-dish sharing platter, you'll be begging for a second round. The food is served on wide, beautifully mosaiced platters, and seems to urge you to lay back in your chair like an ancient prince hoping someone will slowly drop grape leaves into your mouth. With a bowl of pitas to be used as utensils served with each meal, there's no room for silver spoons in this opulent eating extravaganza. Take that, Grandma.

i Sandwiches from 12CHF; 8 dish sharing platters from 42CHF; limited wheelchair accessibility

BÄCKEREI KOCH ($)

Kramgasse 1; 041 410 33 24; open M-Sa 6:30am-4pm

Chocolate and bread and pies, oh my! While most Swiss people view only cheese as their national cuisine, sweets, sweet breads, and bready sweets, are indisputably this small country's greatest food gifts to the world. Visiting an ancient alpine village, you can't leave without at least sampling an ancient Swiss bakery. Sitting on the banks of the **River Reuss** in the heart of **Old Town**, Bäckerei Koch is the most quintessential Swiss bakery you can find—it's housed in a medieval building, staffed by friendly old ladies, and home to a heavenly countertop of sumptuous sweet treats. Try any bread for the most pillowy-soft wheat dream you could imagine, unbelievably rich chocolate, or a dessert or egg pie that packs more flavor into each thick square inch that than a juicy can of lard. Leaving, you'll wonder if the Swiss are really so friendly or if they've just plied everyone's affection with sugar.

i Treat prices vary; wheelchair accessiblity

DA ERNESTO ($$$)

Rathausquai 11; 41 410 17 44; www.da-ernesto.ch; open daily 11:30am-11:30pm

With the flower-laden **Kapellbrücke** on one side, brightly colored ancient homes in the background, and the rushing crystal clear waters of the **Reuss** surging between it all, the Lucerne waterfront seems to good to be true. Seriously, Venice could never. Although the outdoor tables lined up on the riverbank all boast prices that may scare you back to your greasy American trickle of a river, the experience of lounging on a cobblestone street while aquamarine water rushes by just under your feet is too damn picturesque to pass up. Da Ernesto is the closest you'll get to an affordable riverside meal. Most of the bougier Italian dishes will send you right back home, but split an (admittedly small) pizza with a friend and your gorgeous surroundings will stuff you up with so much awe that you'll forget you're still hungry.

i Pizzas from 17.50; wheelchair accessible

JEFF'S BURGER ($$)

Hirschmattstrasse 29; 041 210 10 15; www.jeffs-burger.ch; open M-W 11:30am-2pm, 5:30pm-11:30pm, Th 11:30am-2pm, 5:30pm-11pm, F-Sa 11:30am-2pm, 5:30pm-11:30pm

Lucerne offers infinite opportunities to get yourself exhausted to the point of collapse—think **Mt. Pilatus,** swimming the **Reuss**, boating in **Lake Lucerne,** or any other of the tens of alpine peaks nearby. Stumbling back into the city after a long day in the mountains, your heart, soul, and digestive tract will demand nothing more than a fat hamburger shoved down your gullet. Jeff's Burger is quite simply the best exhaustion/starvation quencher in the city. Even as your top priority may be the satiation of bodily desires, these fresh, heaping burgers pack more than just subsistence. Made of all-Swiss Angus beef, the burger will take you back to mountain pastures you had traversed earlier in the day, and either give you a touch of guilt for chowing down on your bovine friends, or fill you with self-righteousness as you remember what a tranquil life your hamburger meat was living in the mountains. Either way, you probably won't care once you get the burger into your starving mouth.

i Burgers from 15; vegetarian options available; limited wheelchair accessibility

NIGHTLIFE

BUVETTE BAR

Inseli Park; open daily 11:30am-midnight, dependent on weather

On hot summer evenings, the entire 20-something population of Lucerne rushes out of their apartments at once, grabs picnic baskets, and fills the riverside parks from end to end with laughter and relaxation. Buvette is just one of many nearly identical outdoor bars that line the Lucerne lakefront and dish out drinks to the lounging crowds. Housed in a green trailer with a sheet metal roof, Buvette serves reasonably priced drinks and spins big band music that always attracts a few elegant couples to twist and swirl in the glow of the dim yellow lights. Even if you aren't up for the most memorable night of your summer romance, sitting on the grass with a bottle of beer and breathing in the laughter and gentle flow of the lake is enough to fill your heart with love for the world at large.

i Beers from 5CHF; wheelchair accessible

KAFFEE KIND

Baselstrasse 27; kaffee-kind.ch; open daily 6pm-2am

Even in a city so overrun with castles, cottages, and covered bridges that you expect all seven of Snow White's dwarves to hop out around any corner, dark, brooding, dwarf-cynical hipsters must find a place to lurk over a fair-trade mug of beer. Despair not, aspiring Bon Iver member; far from Lucerne's dwarfish abodes on the thoroughly modern nightlife hub of

Baselstrasse, Kaffee Kind invites you to cast your elvish naivete away and sneer like a real aloof urban man. With a dark, industrial-chic decor, a creative cocktail menu, and brooding Indie-rock spinning most nights of the week, the bar invites every slam poet, conceptual artist, and anarcho-syndicalist commune member in the city to sit back, ruminate, and prepare material for a coming transgressive punk-rock opera with side illustrations in watercolor.

i Wine from 6.50 CHF, Cocktails from 13CHF; BLGTQ+ friendly; wheelchair accessible

ZÜRICH

Coverage by **Will Rhatigan**

What do you get when you combine the financial prowess of New York and the cultural conservatism of the birthplace of Swiss Protestantism? Zürich. If that sounds like the closest thing you can imagine to hell on earth, you may want to avoid the **Bahnhoffstrasse**, the row of banks, chocolatiers, and watchmakers that runs through the center of the city reminding everyone that the spirit of capitalism began here, in Zürich, five hundred years ago when Ulrich Zwingli inaugurated the Swiss Protestant reformation.

Luckily for those of us who don't strut around wearing starched suits and $10,000 timepieces, Zürich, a city poised at the crossroads of Western Europe, is a product of many more factors than just the two that have been ironed permanently into its reputation. For thousands of years, travellers journeying from Italy to Germany to France have criss-crossed their way through the city on their way out of the Alps, bringing ideas and influences from every corner of the globe to the once sleepy Swiss town. So beyond the austere churches and menacing financial institutions lies a wealth of hidden gems that slid under the watchful gaze of the city's once religious rulers. Every year, daring artists and students bring Zürich further from its pious history, spraying the scrubbed clean walls with graffiti, raging all night in the once industrious warehouses, and generally experiencing joy and love where their stiff-necked forebears once sniffed around. See just how far the youth have come when you make your trip, and, maybe, lend a helping hand and cause a bit of trouble yourself.

ORIENTATION

Zürich is perched on the northwest tip of the long, narrow **Lake Zürich** in the (relatively) flat plain of Central Switzerland. On both sides of the city, long ridges of steep, low mountains hem in the urban area to a narrow stripe, and the Swiss Alps crown the opposing tip of the lake in the background. The city itself is compact, with its tight land area giving the illusion of smallness, which is broken as you realize that no neighborhood goes without its own cultural significance. At the center of the city lies **Old Town,** a picturesque blend of ancient architecture and winding cobblestone streets that seem to have remained unchanged for at least a century. **Old Town** is neatly split in half by the **River Limmat,** with the **East Bank,** nicknamed **"Niederdorf"** or **"Dörfli,"** hiding narrow pedestrian streets jammed full of restaurants, shops, and bars, and the West Bank defined by **Bahnhoffstrasse**, boasting Zürich's financial district, rows of preposterously expensive clothing boutiques, and the most coveted real estate in Switzerland. While many tourists will never travel outside of Old Town, the further out neighborhoods of **Langstrasse**, **Gewerbeschule**, and **Zürich West** boast the youngest residents and most interesting alternative scenes in all of conservative Switzerland. Immediately to the west of Old Town, **Langstrasse** hosts the heart of Zürich's nightlife scene, with bumping clubs and somewhat seedy strip joints that nearly resemble the prudish Swiss' version of a red light district. To the north, **Gewerbeschule** is a hip neighborhood full of international restaurants and cooler-than-you students cruising around on bikes. To the West and across a set of train tracks lies **Zürich West**, a former industrial wasteland that has been reclaimed to become the home of cavernous warehouse clubs and every other alternative use of a warehouse that you can think of.

ESSENTIALS

GETTING THERE

Most travelers to Zürich and all other points in central Switzerland will fly into Flughafen Zürich (Zürich Airport), a major international hub just twenty minutes from the city center. The airport is accessible from almost anywhere, with connections to over 150 destinations. After landing in the airport, a 6.80CHF train will take you to the main station, Zürich Hauptbahnhof, where public transportation connects to most other points in the city.

GETTING AROUND

Zürich is a medium-sized city, with most of its major attractions easily accessible on foot in the **Alstadt** and near Lake Zürich, and several other interesting neighborhoods that are best reached though public transportation. The Zürich Transport Network (ZVV) controls all the transportation in the canton of Zürich and includes tram, bus, boat, and train. The three former options traverse the city and Lake Zürich, and run daily from 5am-12:30am. Tickets can either be purchased for one hour of use from 4.40CHF, or for 24 hours from 8.80CHF. On Friday and Saturday, the night network (Nachtnetze) can carry you back from the club, running from 1am-5am with an additional 5CHF addition to your transit pass. Tickets can be purchased from automated kiosks at all transit stops, or online from the SBB CFF mobile app.

PRACTICAL INFO

Tourist Offices: Zürich Tourist Information (Hauptbahnhof Zürich; 044 215 40 00; open M-Sa 8am-8:30pm, Su 8m-6:30pm).

Banks/ATMs/Currency Exchange: As one of the largest financial centers in Europe, Zürich is filled with banks. Some of the most common are UBS and Raiffeisen. A convenient one: UBS Branch (Bahnhofstrasse 72; 044 237 83 50; open M-F 9am-5pm).

Post Offices: Most offices in the German-speaking part of Switzerland take the name Post CH AG. A convenient one: Post CH AG (Kasernenstrasse 97 Sihlpost; 084 888 88 88; open M-F 6:30am-10:30pm, Sa 6:30am-8pm, Su 10am-10:30pm).

Public Restrooms: Public restrooms are available at many parks and monuments around the city. Note that the toilets in these restrooms often do not have seats, a fact that can be somewhat disconcerting for many North Americans. Additionally, public restrooms are available at many public tram stops, but will require 1CHF for entry.

Internet: A free hour of Wi-Fi is available at all Swiss train stations, but you will need a Swiss phone number to register. The Zürich Airport offers two hours of free Wi-Fi as well. Otherwise, many restaurants and cafés around the city will be happy to share their internet access.

BGLTQ+ Resources: LGBT+ Helpline of Switzerland (Bern, Montbijoustrasse 73; 0800 133 133; hello@lgbtelpline.ch; www.lgbt-helpline.ch/en, open daily 24hr).

EMERGENCY INFORMATION

Emergency Number: General: 112; Police: 117; Fire department: 144; Swiss helicopter rescue service: 1414.

Police: Zürich is a medium-sized city with many police stations. A centrally located one: Kantonspolizei Zürich (Limmatquai 61; 044 247 29 80, open M-F 7am-5:30pm).

US Embassy: Consular Agency Zurich (Dufourstrasse 101; 031 357 70 11; open M-F 10am-1pm).

Rape Crisis Center: Zürich has no dedicated rape crisis center. For immediate assistance, contact the police or the general emergency number.

Hospitals: Here are two centrally located hospitals:

- University Hospital of Zürich

(Rämistrasse 100; 044 255 11 11; open daily 24hr).
- Municipal Hospital Triemli (Birmensdorferstrasse 497; 044 416 11 11; open daily 24hr).

Pharmacies: Pharmacies in German are called apotheken. Here are two of the most convenient:
- Bellevue Apotheke (Theaterstrasse 14; 044 266 62 22; open daily 24hr).
- TopPharm Dr. Schmid's Lake Pharmacy (Kapellpl. 10; 041 410 88 80; open M-F 8:30am-6:30pm, Sa 8am-4pm).

SIGHTS

CULTURE

OLD TOWN

Open daily 24hr

Although most European cities that managed to avoid bombings, invasions, and catastrophic fires for a few hundred years can boast a gorgeous old town, it's rare that the relics of medieval life keep their edge through the centuries. In Zürich, however, the old town is the heart of town, hosting the hottest shopping street on **Bahnhoffstrasse,** the rowdy nightlife and bustling cheap restaurants of **Niederdorfstrasse,** and landmarks like the **Grossmünster** and **Fraumünster** churches that have stood for nearly 800 years. Framing the **River Limmat** on both sides, the attractions of the old town are awash with natural beauty, and stretch all the way to the banks of **Lake Zürich** where the **Alps** can be seen far in the distance. Ususally we wouldn't think that old means cool, but trust us on this one.

i Free; wheelchair accessible

LANGSTRASSE

Bahnohoffstrasse and and Rathausquai; www.luzerner-wochenmarkt.ch; open Tu 6am-1pm, Sa 6am-1pm

Although you might have mostly heard of Zürich's famous banking, watchmaking, and chocolate, the stereotypically staid Swiss city boasts the rowdiest nightlife district for hundreds of miles. Langstrasse, a long avenue with enough clout to lend its name to its whole neighborhood, is the alternative heart of Switzerland,

and will challenge every conception you have left that these flugelhorn-blowin', cow-tippin', money-grabbin' Swiss don't know how to throw down on the weekends. Venture just over the **Sihl** River from **Old Town**, and you'll find every vistage of snobbiness gone, along with the residents' inhibitions. Well-loved bars, underground clubs tucked beneath head shops, and spooky strip clubs approaching a conservative country's version of a red light district await you, full of young locals who are having so much fun that you'll start believing that not everyone in this city works in finance.

i Free; wheelchair accessible

LANDMARKS

GROSSMÜNSTER

Grossmünsterplatz; 044 252 59 49; www.grossmuenster.ch; open daily 10am-6pm, tower 10am-5:30pm

Two stunning church towers with views overlooking an ancient city and the surrounding mountain range—yawn. Typical. Yet, the Grossmünster is no typical church. It was the birthplace of Protestantism in Switzerland when **Ulrich Zwingli** served as parishioner in the sixteenth century. The Protestant transformation can be seen in the church's architecture. The sloping Gothic arches of the original 1220 Catholic Cathedral have been stripped of all their former ornamentation, leaving only lifeless gray walls. As much as the Protestant reformers tried to stamp out all legend and superstition, the church remains steeped in folklore and rumored to be the place where the two patron saints of Zürich, **Felix and Regula**, carried their own severed heads after an execution. If you're up to the

GLARUS VALLEY

With Zurich an international urban hotspot, and most of the Swiss Alps serving as the tourist getaway for the rest of Europe, it's hard to imagine that anywhere in Switzerland is still truly the paradise of cows, shepherds, and mountain meadows reminiscent of fairy tale anthologies. Yet somehow, just an hour and a half south of Zürich, lies one of the few regions left in the Swiss Alps where sheep outnumber tour buses, and not a word is spoken in English. In the few mountain valleys surrounding the quiet town of Glarus, the Old Switzerland lives on. Glarus's historic district was destroyed by a fire and the modern town has nothing much to show off in itself. However, the rural hinterlands framing the city in the shadow of enormous mountains, hide some of the last untrammelled rural bliss in Western Europe.

Glarus is a medium-sized town located at the confluence of two long Alpine valleys. While there is surely plenty to discover in Glarus itself, we focus this mountain exploration on the countryside. After all, you didn't leave **Zürich** to wander around city streets. To the east lies the valley of **Klöntal,** where the gorgeous **Klöntalersee Lake** awaits you, along with tranquil mountain pastures and quiet rural villages. To the south, the larger **Linthal Valley** stretches out, where hikes high into the alps can be accessed from the resort village of Braunwald, located nearly 2,000 feet above the valley floor by cable car. For the ultimate tour of the region, take the bus down to **Linthal Braunwaldbahn,** a cable car to Braunwald, and hike through one of several trails all the way over a mountain path down to Klöntal.

GETTING THERE

From the Zürich main station (Zürich HB), the S25 train to Linthal runs directly to Glarus hourly from 6:43am to 5:43 pm and takes about one hour. Tickets can be purchased from automated kiosks at the station, or online from the SBB CFF mobile application. Other options include taking the RE for Chur to Ziegelbrücke, then transferring to a local train that stops in Glarus, or can carry you directly to Linthal Braunwaldbahn for access to the tourist village of Braunwald.

GETTING AROUND

Upon reaching Glarus, a local bus, the 504, can take you to all points in the Klöntal valley until Klöntal Platz, from which the only way to keep ascending in elevation without a car is on foot. Tickets for this bus are purchased onboard from the conductor, and vary based on the length of your journey up to 7CHF. To reach Braunwald from Glarus, the local S6 train from Linthal departs once every hour. Hopping off the train at Linthal Braunwaldbahn, a cable car can take you directly to Braunwald, or you can save a bit of money by taking the approximately 1.5 hour hike.

Don't miss...

BRAUNWALD TO KLÖNTAL HIKE

Begin from Braunwald

For the most remote, picturesque, and comprehensive experience of the Swiss Alps in a single day, this 15-mile all-day hike is our number one recommendation. Beginning from the cable-car station at Braunwald, follow signs for Gumen to pass through the quiet upper slopes of the local ski resort, where meandering cows will have taken over the trails in the summer. At Gumen, you'll pass the top of the resort, and begin down a narrow trail along the edge of a steep valley, following signs for Bützi. From here,

the trail will leave the lush meadow to switchback through steep boulder fields, traverse several false summits, and eventually, just as you think you're about to begin descending, deposit you on a rugged and bare alpine plateau, covered by vast snowfields that may make following the trail difficult. Continue across this moon-like landscape to Erigismatt, a small hut surrounded by jagged peaks, before climbing the final steep pitch between the Bös Fullen and Pfannestock Mountains to traverse the pass between the two valleys. From this summit, you'll begin a long descent down to Klöntal on a single trail, watching as the snow turns to rock, then scrubby grass, then lush, cow traversed pastures, before dropping through a mile of deciduous woodland and leaving you in the blissfully pastoral village of Klöntal. It's hard to fit all of the landscapes of the Alps into one hike; this is our best try.
Free; no wheelchair accessibility; check snow conditions and weather before attempting

Check out...

KLÖNTALERSEE

Klöntalersee; open daily 24hr

Although you've just come from your fourth gorgeous Swiss Alpine city, we promise you that this is one more lake that you won't want to miss. Whereas most of the famous Swiss lakes are facing the Alps, Klöntalersee is truly in the Alps, with jagged peaks rising directly from its shores 7,000 feet into the sky on all sides. From the middle of the lake, it's hard not to feel the last of your lingering self-importance slip away as the majesty of the earth screams down on you. Even as foreboding mountains rise around it, the lake is easily accessible from Glarus, and has the grassy shores of your summer camp pond with the views of a glacial ice cave. Swim, rent a boat, or just sit on the shore—whatever you do, the mountains will probably freeze you in place.
Free; limited wheelchair accessibility

Swing by...

IM PLÄTZ (IN THE PLACE) ($$)

Klöntal Plätz; 055 640 13 74; open Tu-Su 10am-8pm

As thou collapse on the ground after thine harrowing pilgrimage from Braunwald to Klöntal, the hunger, thirst, desolation, and weakness of spirit that assails you may feel too burdensome to bear. But soft ye, desperate wanderer, for thine hour of truth hast not yet arrived. Cast thine eyes to the heavens, and thou shalt see before thee a shining light of salvation, beckoning thine spirit out of sickness and despair towards hope and jubilation. For thine hunger is to be no more! Sweet glory, a humble wooden tavern awaits you, and inside, the virtuous country folk meet thee with meat of the lamb, flesh of the swine, and fruits of the earth, hearty enough to fortify thy soul for the travels that face thee. Indeed, the spirit of the Lord is in the people of the salt of the earth and the food of the humble, and the traveler shall bow down before the peasant and bless him for furnishing him with vittles for his wanderings, at this place of most dire need, the Klöntal Plätz bus stop.
Entreés from 18.50CHF; limited wheelchair accessibility

task, we recommend taking the 187 narrow stairs up to the top of one of the towers (**Karlstrum**) for a sweeping panorama of Zürich.

Free; tower admission 4CHF adults, 2CHF students; no wheelchair accessibility

OPERNHAUS ZÜRICH (ZÜRICH OPERA HOUSE)

Falkenstrasse 1; 044 268 66 66; neu.schauspielhaus.ch; interior hours and showtimes vary

While you may fancy yourself not too shabby at yodeling after a few days in the Alps, you won't be able to keep progressing your game unless you take a lesson from the professionals. Come on down to the Zürich Opera House for some *fancy* yodeling, also known as "Opera," and pick up all the hot tips for your next vocal mountain adventure. Alright, realistically the tickets might be a little more expensive than a poor yodeler like you would want to spring for, but an exploration of the building is awe-inspiring in itself. As Zürich's one token Giant Neo-Baroque Edifice™, the Opera House is a smorgasbord of columns, carved facades, and valiant angels beckoning you to worship the wealthy opera-goers inside. If pseudo-Roman opulence isn't your thing, you'll be just as happy passing an afternoon on the steps overlooking the sprawling **Sechseläutenplatz** square for some of the most fascinating people-watching in Europe.

Ticket prices vary; wheelchair accessible

MUSEUMS

LANDESMUSEUM ZÜRICH (SWISS NATIONAL MUSEUM)

Museumstrasse 2; 044 218 65 11; www.nationalmuseum.ch/d/zuerich; open Tu-W 10am-5pm, Th 10am-7am, F-Su 1am-5pm

Still confused how the diverse collage of different religions and languages surrounding Zürich ever congealed into a single conservative country? Look no further, young Herodotus; the Swiss National Museum offers enough juicy tidbits on the formation of the Helvetian Confederacy to keep even the most pretentious history buff occupied. The Switzerland-focused museum houses exhibits on the country's modern challenges, the workings of its government, local archaeology, and influential ideas, providing you with enough knowledge to understand the nation's history and enough nuance to offer criticism. For a shorter highlight reel, walk through the chronological history section to finally understand how a nation of ruthless mercenaries and centuries of brutal warfare transformed into the land of cheese, chocolate, and genteel bank fraud.

Adults 10CHF, students 8CHF; wheelchair accessible

FIFA WORLD MUSEUM

Seestrasse 27; 043 388 25 00; www.fifamuseum.com; open Tu-Sa 10am-6pm

Recent corruption scandals have left FIFA branded as fraudulent, political, and strictly money-driven. The sport it purports to represent, however, remains full of grace, athleticism, and passionate fans concerned with simpler things than international money laundering. The FIFA World Museum is nonetheless an unmissable pilgrimage for any avid soccer fan, holding inside the the most famous players' jerseys, the balls from every major international tournament, and the iconic golden World Cup trophy itself. Upstairs, the museum takes a lighter tone, with a variety of soccer simulation games allowing you to test your skills against the best in the world. Taking a swing at FIFA soccer pinball, you can't help feeling like you're seconds from the big trophy yourself. Unfortunately the museum is quite expensive, but come on, you think the guys taking 15 million dollar bribes are going to let you in for free?

Admission 24CHF, students 18CHF; wheelchair accessible

OUTDOORS

ZÜRICH ARBORETUM

Mythenquai 9; 044 201 75 00; about daily 24hr

Mmmm yes, another absolutely stunning lakeside park in an absolutely stunning Swiss city. Yada, yada, we've seen it before. But come on, you came to this country for a reason, and if you can't appreciate an immaculately maintained public park overlooking a crystal clear lake and glistening white mountains a few times, you're probably better off going back home to Cleveland. Just an easy 5-minute walk from the heart of **Old Town,** the arboretum is a natural oasis of rare trees, bushes, and flowers, in the heart of a city that is, admittedly, a clean and beautiful oasis in itself

i Free; wheelchair accessible

FOOD

ÄSS BAR ($)

Winkelreidstrasse 62; 41 210 00 90; www.barbes.ch; open M-Sa 10am-12:30am, Su 4pm-11:30pm

Alright ha, ha, ha, very funny. No, it isn't you uncouth swine! Ok, laugh if you want, but this bakery will have the last laugh when you lay your potty mouth down on the floor begging for another bite. No, Äss Bar is not sex club. The word "äss" plays on the Swiss German term for edible, and connects into the bakery's goal of sustainability. Rather than letting excess pastries go waste, Äss Bar collects yesterday's treats from bakeries all around the city and sells them for half price. In a city of 6CHF baguettes, a day-old cheese pie is a gift from the heavens. Oh, an old pastry doesn't suit your high and mighty self? Hate to break it to you buddy, but thinking you're too good for day-old croissants kinda makes you look like an äss.

i Sandwiches from 12CHF; 8-dish sharing platters from 42CHF; wheelchair accessible

BRASSERIE LOUIS ($)

Niederdorfstrasse 10; 044 250 76 80; open M-W 11:30am-midnight, Th 11:30am-1am, F 11:30am-2am, Sa noon-2am, Su noon-11pm

Elegant servers drifting from table to table, refined duck legs and lapin, and a long list of the finest wines to complement the meal. All staples of traditional Brasserie culture that have made French cuisine world-renowned. But wait. You're in Switzerland, you can't afford that shit. Luckily, Brasserie Louis knows that, and to the right of its elegant indoor dining room it offers Louis take-out, to satisfy us fine-food connoisseurs without jobs in securities trading. Grab a steaming baguette full of fresh-cooked steak, vegetables, or chicken, and sit outside enjoying the ambiance on lively Niederdorfstrasse while dreaming of the day when you finally make it to the inside of the restaurant.

i Sandwiches from 10.50CHF; wheelchair accessible

RACLETTE FACTORY ($$)

Rindermarkt 1; 044 261 04 10; www.raclette-factory.ch/englisch; open daily 11:30am-10pm

Raclette Factory presents itself as a new, sophisticated rendition of an ancient Swiss tradition. When you translate the elegant "raclette" into its English equivalent, "fat blobs of melted cheez," however, the elegance slides off a bit. But screw elegance, a heaping plate of dripping fondue will rock your world. If you can spin this fatty delight as a cultural experience, all the better for your health conscience. Despite its brutishly simple nature, raclette is a delicacy in Switzerland, and tends to carry the usual monstrous prices. Enter Raclette Factory, which can leave you with a cheesy wonderland and enough money left over for your heart surgery.

i Sharing platter from 15CHF; limited wheelchair accessibility

STAZIONE PARADISO ($$)

Wasserwerkstrasse 89A; info@stazioneparadiso.ch; www.stazioneparadiso.ch; open daily 11am-midnight

In a city with a picturesque river and spacious lakefront parks, there seems to be no reason for a gritty riverside hangout under a bridge. But Stazione Paradiso does it all the same, and the young people of Zürich cherish it just as much as they do the grassy shores of Lake Zürich. Housed in an improbably obtained Berlin Railroad Car that brings the rowdier city's vibe with it, Stazione Paradiso serves up drinks and simple Italian food whenever the weather is warm enough. Although the location nearly under a high bridge north of **Gewerbeschule** isn't the most beautiful on the **River Limmat**, locals flock to it on warm summer evenings to eat and drink on the large outdoor patio, and crowd the cement steps down to the river when the tables fill up. Sure, there's plenty of room to picnic on manicured grass elsewhere, but somehow you just feel a little closer to your friends when huddled around a plate of pasta on a gravel riverbank.

i Meals from 14CHF, wine from 7.5 CHF; wheelchair accessible

ZA'ATAR ($)

Brauerstrasse 78; 043 243 80 33; www.zaatar.ch; open M-F 11am-2pm, 5pm-11pm, Sa-Su 5pm-11pm

Generally in Europe, Lebanese food means one of two things: carefully arranged platters of fresh hummus, tabouli, and roasted vegetables to be slowly sampled on a relaxed evening, or greasy kebabs to be desperately shoved down your gullet at 3am. Za'atar offers the best of both worlds, serving delicious *Mezze* tasting platters of local specialities, along with dripping Shawarma sandwiches to quench any drunken hunger. Unlike your typical kebab shop, the cooks at Za'atar will fry up you meat right in front of your eyes, rather than slicing it off a giant skewer of rotating mystery meat, as is the standard.

i Sandwiches from 9.50CHF; wheelchair accessible

NIGHTLIFE

KASHEME

Neugasse 56; 044 272 66 08; kasheme.com; open T-W 5pm-midnight, Th 5pm-2am, Sa-Su 5pm-4am, Su 7pm-midnight

Chill chill chill man. It's all good. No one wants any trouble at Kasheme. It's all about peace and love and respect for your fellow man. This place isn't just a bar. No way, brother; Kasheme is living room, record store, and studio, where they stand for conscious listening to one another, to music, to the world—but also to the universe, Mother Earth, and all its creatures. See, there's no need to be stressed here. You can chill and make connections with your fellow brothers, sisters, and creatures. They've even laid rugs and couches down for you, and have a totally vintage record player in the middle spinning smooth, groovy tracks from all over this planet all night long, baby. Oh yeah, grab a drink and take a journey to planet transcendent relaxation. Absolutely radical, brother; rhodunkously good vibes.

i Beers from 5CHF, cocktails from 17CHF, shots from 5CHF; wheelchair accessible

KON-TIKI COFFEESHOP AND BAR

Niederdorfstrasse 24; 044 251 35 77; kontikibar.ch; open M-Th 11am-midnight, F-Sa 11am-2am, Su 11am-midnight

Since 1955, when Kon-Tiki was founded for any "roughnecks, adventurers, and similarly-minded people" who happened to be drifting through straight-laced Zürich, the tropical-themed coffee shop and bar has been a cult hotspot for the city's art and alternative communities. In the midst of traditional Swiss bars and restaurants on cobbled **Niederdorfstrasse** in Zürich's **Old Town,** Kon-Tiki screams out from the crowd with a bright neon Hawaiian script sign. Inside, giant carved wooden heads stare down at you as you sip coffee until the live bands come on at night. As you mingle with the other adventurers, grab a fresh empanada or one of their, erm, speciality brownies for the ultimate relaxation.

i Beer and shots from 5CHF; cocktails from 15.50CHF; partial wheelchair accessibility

SCHICKERIA

Neufrankengasse 4; 078 729 95 45; schickeria.ch; open M-W 5pm-midnight, Th 5pm-2am, F-Sa 5pm to 4am

Even with a new DJ spinning original tracks six nights a week, Schikeria is a place for chilling. But don't come expecting the lay-on-the-coach-to-Justin-Bieber's-tantalizing-voice type of chilling that you're used to at home. The crew at Schickeria is serious about creating a relaxed vibe, and take that goal to an art form. A small indoor bar with padded seating and a live DJ spinning at all times dishes out the drinks, a wide outdoor veranda brings the shade, wooden barrels with tall plants sprouting out them provide the décor, a food truck parked perpetually on the side keeps the relaxers fed. On a warm summer night, if you're not chilling at Schickeria you're not with it, and if Schickeria's not open, you shouldn't be chilling.

i Beer from 7.5CHF, Cocktails from 15CHF; wheelchair accessible

SWITZERLAND ESSENTIALS

VISAS

Although not a member of the European Union, Switzerland is a part of the free-travel Schengen area, so US citizens can stay in the country for up to 90 days without a Visa.

MONEY

Currency: The currency used in Switzerland is the Swiss Franc (CHF), which is a bit of an anomaly considering that all surrounding nations use the Euro. Acceptance of credit cards is widespread is Switzerland, but travellers to rural areas should withdraw some Swiss Francs from a bank before departing.

Tipping: Do not feel obligated to tip in Switzerland as a federal law replaced tips with an all-inclusive bill in the 1970's. If you feel particularly happy with your service, you can round up the bill to the nearest five or ten francs without being rude. However, servers will not expect this courtesy, so don't worry if you're on a backpackers budget and can't afford to tip at every restaurant.

SAFETY AND HEALTH

Drugs and Alcohol: The legal drinking age in Switzerland is 16 for Beer and Wine, and 18 for Spirits. While you may see many stores selling marijuana, only varieties of the plant with a very low content of THC, the psychoactive ingredient, are legal in Switzerland. Laws for other drugs are less punitive than those found in the US, but all other narcotics are nonetheless illegal.

Electricity: Insistent on uniqueness, Switzerland uses the special type J power outlet, a strange three-pronged design that is only otherwise used in Liechtenstein and Rwanda (why these countries we do not know). In many older buildings, the regular type C plugs used in the European Union will fit into the sockets, but most new construction uses sockets that are sunken in diamond-shaped holes, making the use of any other plugs impossible. Luckily, adaptors can be bought for around 7CHF at most supermarkets in the country. The most reliable store to purchase an adaptor from is Migros, a supermarket chain found all over Switzerland.

INDEX

M

N

O

P

R

S

T

V

W

Y

Z

ACKNOWLEDGMENTS

First, we'd like to thank the Researcher-Writers who are truly the core of *Let's Go*. We could not have produced this guide without you and could not be prouder of all of the hard work and time you all dedicated to *Let's Go* this summer—from researching, writing, to sharing your weirdest experiences with us. Thank you Jessica for your surfing lesson stories and heartwarming FaceTimes; to Luke for your insane determination (ahem, those 40,000+ daily step counts) and braving the mosquito infestation in Gyor; to Lydia for giving us the most extreme FOMO with your sunset pictures and beach-filled adventures; to Marissa for your endless energy and environmentally-conscious travel tips; to Megan for finding the best desserts in Germany and taking on every route with a smile; to Sam for introducing us to the concept of an all-you-can-eat pancake cruise and your uncanny ability to befriend every local you encounter; and to Will for always saying yes to new experiences (like that time you got blessed by the local shaman) and eating enough Swiss cheese for all of us back in Cambridge—and finally to all of last year's Researcher-Writers. We could not have asked for a better team.

Thank you to Emily, Dan, and Dyan at Placepass for supporting us. We are so grateful for the opportunities you have given us, and for a partnership that makes our work possible.

A huge thank you to our Board of Directors. Your constant support and dedication has inspired us to work hard to make *Let's Go* the best it can be. To Nathaniel for always being available to lend Francesca a hand with the bookplan, book design, or simply provide moral support through the many editorial decisions throughout the year. To Nicole, we so appreciate the time you've given to us; your advice has been indispensable. To Michael, aka the InDesign Wizard, your support and willingness to help kept Francesca sane during production. Kristine and Austin, thank you for meticulously scouring the book during proofs. Your attention to detail is unparalleled. A special thanks to Patrick who has been with us every step of the way. We always cherished your long emails about website design, advertising strategies, and so much more. You've been a constant source of support for Jessica as she's navigated the all too unfamiliar world of marketing.

Thank you to our families who have struggled to understand what it is we do on a daily basis yet who checked in and consistently offered their support. Thank you to our friends and blockmates for always being there to provide a respite from the long days at work.

Finally, thank you to everyone at HSA who supported us through the highs and lows of this past year. To James and Dara, who have been with us since the beginning. To Amy and Annelise, for listening to our problems and triumphs as they arose. To Jim, for your advice and thoughtful questions as we worked through typical publishing problems. To the business office, for your invaluable help and experience. And, of course, to all the managers who supported us in any way we could as they worked towards producing the book now in your hands.

PUBLISHING DIRECTOR, Jessica Luo
EDITOR IN CHIEF, Francesca Malatesta
ASSOCIATE EDITOR, Michelle Borbon

PRESIDENT, HARVARD STUDENT AGENCIES, James Swingos
GENERAL MANAGER, HARVARD STUDENT AGENCIES, Jim McKellar

ABOUT US

BY STUDENTS, FOR STUDENTS

Let's Go publishes travel guides written by its team of Researcher-Writers, who are all students at Harvard College. Armed with pens, notebooks, and laptops (hopefully, with chargers), our student researchers travel across Europe on pre-planned itineraries, hopping from city to city to seek out invaluable travel experiences for our readers. Because we are a completely student-run company, we have a unique perspective on how students travel, where they want to go, and what they're looking for when they get there. Whether you want to venture into the crater of Mount Etna, kayak in Lagos, or museum-hop in London, our guides have got you covered. We write for readers on a budget who know that there's more to travel than tour buses.

SIXTY YEARS OF WISDOM

Let's Go has been on the road for 60 years and counting. We started in 1960 with a small, 20-page pamphlet that included travel tips and food, accommodations, and activity recommendations for Europe's major cities. Over the last six decades, however, our Researcher-Writers have written guides covering almost every corner of the planet. Europe? Check. Australia? You betcha. India? Been there, done that. And despite the growth, our witty, candid guides are still researched and written entirely by Harvard students on shoestring budgets who know how to deal with everything from debit card fraud to stolen phones to bad cuttlefish. This year's guide is the third in full-color, and features a content architecture that allows readers to easily pinpoint reviews of sights, restaurants, and food in any given city. And, of course, like all other *Let's Go* guides, the one in your hand still features the same witty and irreverent voice that has been carried by *Let's Go* teams for decades.

THE *LET'S GO* COMMUNITY

More than just a travel guide company, *Let's Go* is a community that reaches from our headquarters in Cambridge, MA all across the globe. Our staff of dedicated student editors, designers, writers, and tech nerds is united by a shared passion for travel and desire to help other travelers get the most out of their experiences. We love it when our readers become part of the *Let's Go* community as well—when you travel, drop us a postcard (67 Mt. Auburn St., Cambridge, MA 02138, USA), send us an email (marketing@letsgo.com), or check us out our website (www.letsgo.com).